THE LIBRARY

OF

LITERARY CRITICISM

OF

ENGLISH AND AMERICAN AUTHORS

VOLUME VI
1855 – 1874

EDITED BY CHARLES WELLS MOULTON
ASSISTED BY A CORPS OF ABLE CONTRIBUTORS

GLOUCESTER, MASS.
PETER SMITH
1959

Copyright 1904
BY
THE MOULTON PUBLISHING COMPANY
Reprinted 1959
BY
PETER SMITH

To

Professor George Saintsbury, M. A.

INTRODUCTION.

For to oratory and poetry, unless of the highest degree of eloquence, little thanks are given: but history, in whatever manner executed, is always entertaining.—PLINY THE YOUNGER, 114 (?) *Letters, tr. Melmoth and Bosanquet, bk.* v., *Letter* vii.

History is like sacred writing, because truth is essential to it; and where there is truth, the Deity himself is present, nevertheless, there are many who think that books may be written and tossed out into the world like fritters.—CERVANTES, 1605, *Don Quixote, tr. Jarvis, pt.* ii, *ch.* iii.

Industrious persons, by an exact and scrupulous diligence and observation, out of monuments, names, words, proverbs, traditions, private records and evidences, fragments of stories, passages of books that concern not story, and the like, do save and recover somewhat from the deluge of time.— BACON, FRANCIS LORD, 1605, *Advancement of Learning, bk.* ii.

In a word, we may gather out of history a policy no less wise than eternal; by the comparison and application of other men's forepassed miseries with our own like errors and ill deservings.—RALEIGH, SIR WALTER, 1614, *A History of the World, Preface, vol.* II, *p.* v.

> I do love these ancient ruins
> We never tread upon them, but we set
> Our foot upon some reverend history.

—WEBSTER, JOHN, 1623, *Dutchesse of Malfy, Act* V, *sc.* 3.

All history that is not contemporary is suspicious: as the books of the Sibyls and Trismegistus, and so many others that have obtained credence in the world, are false, and will be found to be false to the end of time. It is not thus with contemporary authors.—PASCAL, BLAISE, 1669, *Thoughts, tr. Wright, ch.* xv, ii.

There being others, besides the first supposed author, men not unread, nor unlearned in antiquity, who admit that for approved story which the former explode for fiction; and seeing that ofttimes relations heretofore accounted fabulous have been after found to contain in them many footsteps and reliques of something true. . . . I might also produce example, as Diodorus among the Greeks, Livy and others among the Latins, Polydore and Virunnius accounted among our own writers. But I intend not with controversies and quotations to delay or interrupt the smooth course of history; much less to argue and debate long who were the first inhabitants, with what probabilities, what authorities each opinion hath been upheld; but shall endeavor that which hitherto hath been needed most, with plain and lightsome brevity, to relate well and orderly things worth the noting, so as may best instruct and benefit them that read. Which, imploring divine assistance, that it may rebound to his glory, and the good of the British nation, I now begin.—MILTON, JOHN, 1670, *The History of Britain, bk.* i.

The prodigious lies which have been published in this age in matters of fact, with unblushing confidence, even where thousands or multitudes of eye and ear witnesses knew all to be false, doth call men to take heed what history they believe, especially where power and violence affordeth that privilege to the reporter that no man dare answer him, or detect his fraud; or, if they do, their writings are all supprest. As long as men have liberty to examine and contradict one another, one may partly conjecture, by comparing their words, on which side the truth is like to lie. But when great men write history, or flatterers by their appointment, which no man dare contradict, believe it but as you are constrained.—BAXTER, RICHARD, 1691? *Reliquiæ Baxterianæ.*

It is the most agreeable talent of an historian to be able to draw up his armies and fight his battles in proper expressions, to set before our eyes the divisions, cabals, and jealousies of great men, to lead us step by step into the several actions and events of his history. We love to see the subject unfolding itself by just degrees, and breaking upon us insensibly, so that we may be kept in pleasing suspense, and have time given us to raise our expectations, and to side with one of the parties concerned in the relation. I confess this shows more the art than the veracity of the historian; but I am only to speak of him as he is qualified to please the imagination; and in this respect Livy has, perhaps, excelled all who ever went before him or have written since his time. He describes everything in so lively a manner that his whole history is an admirable picture, and touches on such proper circumstances in every story that his reader becomes a kind of spectator, and feels in himself all the variety of passions which are correspondent to the several parts of the relations.—ADDISON, JOSEPH, 1712, *On the Pleasures of Imagination, Spectator, No.* 420.

That the study of history, far from making us wiser, and more useful citizens, as well as better men, may be of no advantage whatsoever; that it may serve to render us mere antiquaries and scholars, or that it may help to make us forward coxcombs, and prating pedants, I have already allowed. But this is not the fault of history: and to convince us that it is not, we need only contrast the true use of history with the use that is made of it by such men as these. We ought always to keep in mind, that history is philosophy teaching by examples how to conduct ourselves in all the situations of private and public life; that therefore we must apply ourselves to it in a philosophical spirit and manner; that we must rise from

particular to general knowledge, and that we must fit ourselves for the society and business of mankind by accustoming our minds to reflect and meditate on the characters we find described, and the course of events we find related there.—ST. JOHN, HENRY (VISCOUNT BOLINGBROKE), 1735, *Letters on the Study and Use of History, p.* 191.

History is only a confused heap of facts. —CHESTERFIELD, LORD, 1750, *Letters to his Son, London, Feb.* 5.

The philosopher has the works of omniscience to examine; and is therefore engaged in disquisitions to which finite intellects are utterly unequal. The poet trusts to his invention, and is not only in danger of those inconsistencies to which every one is exposed by departure from truth, but may be censured as well for deficiencies of matter as for irregularity of disposition or impropriety of ornament. But the happy historian has no other labour than of gathering what tradition pours down before him, or records treasure for his use. . . . Yet, even with these advantages, very few in any age have been able to raise themselves to reputation by writing histories.—JOHNSON, SAMUEL, 1751, *The Rambler, No.* 122.

History, which is, indeed, little more than the register of the crimes, follies, and misfortunes of mankind.—GIBBON, EDWARD, 1776, *History of the Decline and Fall of the Roman Empire.*

Now an historian is a person who assumes a character of great dignity, and addresses himself to a most respectable audience. He undertakes to communicate information, not to his equals only or inferiors, but to the greatest, and most learned men upon earth. He wishes them to listen to him, and to listen with pleasure, to believe his testimony, and treasure up his sayings as lessons of wisdom, to direct them in the conduct of life, and in the government of kingdoms. In so awful a presence, and with views so elevated, what style is it natural for him to assume? A style uniformly serious, and elegant, clear, orderly, and emphatical, set off with modest ornaments to render it pleasing, yet plain and simple, and such as becomes a man whose chief concern it is to know and deliver the truth.— BEATTIE, WILLIAM, 1776–79, *Essays on Poetry and Music, p.* 202.

We do not draw the moral lessons we might from history. On the contrary, without care it may be used to vitiate our minds and destroy our happiness. In history a great volume is moulded for our instruction, drawing the materials of future wisdom from the past errors and infirmities of mankind. It may, in the perversion, serve for a magazine furnishing offensive and defensive weapons for parties in Church and State, and supply the means of keeping alive, or reviving dissensions and animosities, and adding fuel to civil fury. History consists, for the greater part, of the miseries brought upon the world by pride, ambition, avarice, revenge, lust, sedition, hypocrisy, ungoverned zeal, and all the train of disorderly appetites, which shake the public with the same

"troublous storms that toss
The private state, and render life unsweet."

These voices are the *causes* of those storms. Religion, morals, laws, prerogatives, privileges, liberties, rights of men, are the *pretexts*. The pretexts are always found in some specious appearance of a real good.— BURKE, EDMUND, 1790, *Reflections on the Revolution in France.*

As the epic poem and romance may be made to contain the floating materials of all knowledge, their mother, history, may still more easily be made into the firm pulpit of every moral and religious opinion; and every department of morality, moral theology, moral philosophy and casuistry finds its leader in ancient history.— RICHTER, JEAN PAUL FRIEDRICH, 1807, *Levana.*

Past times are to us a book with seven seals. What you call the spirit of the times is at bottom your own spirit, in which the times are mirrored.— GOETHE, JOHANN WOLFGANG, 1808, *Faust.*

What want these outlaws conquerors should have
But History's purchased page to call them great?
A wider space, an ornamented grave?
Their hopes were not less warm, their souls were full as brave.
—BYRON, LORD, 1816, *Childe Harold, Canto* iii, *st.* 48.

Some historians, like Tacitus, Burnet, and the Abbé Raynal, are never satisfied without adding to their detail of events the secret springs and causes that have produced them. But both heroes and statesmen, amid the din of arms, and the hurry of business, are too often necessitated to invert the natural order of things; to fight before they deliberate, and to decide before they consult. A statesman may regulate himself by events; but it is seldom that he can cause events to regulate themselves by him. It often happens, too, both in courts and in cabinets, that there are two things going on together, a main plot and an under plot; and he that understands only *one* of them will, in all probability, be the dupe of both.— COLTON, CHARLES CALEB, 1820–22, *Lacon.*

History, it has been said, is philosophy teaching by examples. Unhappily, what the philosophy gains in soundness and depth the examples generally lose in vividness. A perfect historian must possess an imagination sufficiently powerful to make his narrative affecting and picturesque. Yet he must control it so absolutely as to content himself with the materials which he finds, and to refrain from supplying deficiencies by additions of his own. He must be a profound and ingenious reasoner. Yet he must possess sufficient self-command to abstain from casting his facts in the mold of his hypothesis. Those who can justly estimate these almost insuperable difficulties will not think it strange that every writer should have failed, either in the narrative or in the speculative department of history.—MACAULAY, THOMAS BABINGTON, 1828, *History, Edinburgh Review, Critical and Miscellaneous Essays.*

To study man from the past is to suppose that man is ever the same animal. Those who studied the career of Napoleon had ever a dog-eared analyst to refer to.— DISRAELI, BENJAMIN (EARL OF BEACONSFIELD), 1832, *Contarini Fleming.*

History casts its shadow far into the land of song. — LONGFELLOW, HENRY WADSWORTH, 1835, *Outre-Mer.*

The historian has a noble and great mission; but it is not by making us weep over all that fails; it is not by placing before us, fragment by fragment, detail by detail, the mere material fact, the succession of crises by which this world of the dead with their immediate effects, have passed away;—above all, it is not by dragging forth at every instant, from the midst of this collective and complex world, the single wretched and feeble individual, and setting him in presence of the profound "Mystery of time" before "unfathomable darkness;" to terrify him with the enigma of existence—it is not so that this mission can be fulfilled.—MAZINI, JOSEPH, 1840, *Monthly Chronicle, No. 23.*

History itself is nothing more than legend and romance. — WRIGHT, THOMAS, 1846, *England in the Middle Ages.*

The world's history is a divine poem of which the history of every nation is a canto and of every man a word. Its strains have been pealing along down the centuries, and, though there have been mingled the discords of roaring cannon and dying men, yet to the Christian philosopher and historian —the humble listener—there has been a divine melody running through the song which speaks of hope and halcyon days to

come.—GARFIELD, JAMES ABRAM, 1856, *The Province of History, Williams Quarterly, June.*

All persons, taken one by one, are but elements of a great social organism, to whose laws of providential growth they must be held subordinate. History cannot be resolved into a mere series of biographies; nor can the individual be justly estimated in his insulation, and tried by the mere inner law of his own particular nature. —MARTINEAU, JAMES, 1856, *Personal Influence on Our Present Theology: Newman—Coleridge—Carlyle.*

If they wished to understand history they must try to understand men and women. For History is the history of men and women, and of nothing else. . . . If, therefore, any of you should ask me how to study history I should answer, Take by all means biographies, wheresoever possible autobiographies, and study them. Fill your minds with live human figures. . . . Without doubt History obeys, and always has obeyed, in the long run, certain laws. But those laws assert themselves, and are to be discovered, not in things, but in persons; in the actions of human beings; and just in proportion as we understand human beings, shall we understand the laws which they have obeyed, or which have avenged themselves on their disobedience. This may seem a truism; if it be such, it is one which we cannot too often repeat to ourselves just now, when the rapid progress of science is tempting us to look at human beings rather as things than as persons, and at abstractions (under the name of laws) rather as persons than as things.—KINGSLEY, CHARLES, 1860, *The Limits of Exact Science as Applied to History, p. 4.*

History travels by the high road which has no end, and whose branches knit kingdom with kingdom; but is not the historian sometimes tempted into an *impasse*, whence he must make his way back again, but where, for all that, he may have come upon something that more than paid him for losing his way! I have found it so sometimes when I was meandering about an old Italian town, and stumbled on the tomb of some stock actor in our great tragi-comedy in which I had an interest.—LOWELL, JAMES RUSSELL, 1864, *Letter to Motley, Dec. 28; The Correspondence of John Lothrop Motley, ed. Curtis, vol. II, p. 196.*

One lesson, and only one, history may be said to repeat with distinctness: that the world is built somehow on moral foundations; that, in the long run, it is well with the good; in the long run, it is ill with the wicked. But this is no science; it is no more than the old doctrine taught long ago by the Hebrew prophets. The theories of M. Comte and his disciples advance us, after all, not a step beyond the trodden and familiar ground. If men are not entirely animals, they are at least half animals, and are subject in this aspect of them to the conditions of animals. So far as those parts of man's doings are concerned, which neither have, nor need have, any thing moral about them, so far the laws of him are calculable. There are laws for his digestion, and laws of the means by which his digestive organs are supplied with matter. But pass beyond them, and where are we? In a world where it would be as easy to calculate men's actions by laws like those of positive philosophy as to measure the orbit of Neptune with a foot-rule, or weigh Sirius in a grocer's scale.—FROUDE, JAMES ANTHONY, 1864, *The Science of History, Short Studies on Great Subjects, vol. I, p. 22.*

History may be written in many ways. The best, the only true way, consists in the minute examination of documents and of facts, and in a complete and conscientious exposition of them. The historian forgets himself in the presence of his work, and has no care except for truth. He imposes nothing, he proposes; and although it is impossible that the long sojourn in the midst of doctrines, and of the strife of systems, should have left his thoughts indifferent, he would aim at the appearance of impassiveness, in consequence of the impartiality of his judgment, and the sincerity of his studies.—RIBOT, THÉODULE, 1874, *English Psychology, p. 257.*

Above all things, in our historical investigations let us be exact. Here there is no justification of haste and lack of precision. So far as practicable, let us go to original sources of information. If we are obliged to receive information at secondhand, let us insist on knowing where our informant received his knowledge and his impressions. This process involves, of course, the study or the examination of many books, rather than the reading of a few. But it is the application to systematic research of those methods which alone are fruitful of success in the affairs of business as well as in the affairs of study. For, however broad and however comprehensive our general knowledge, it is, in the last analysis, only the application of our knowledge to minute details that accomplishes results and brings reward. Even in the practical work of our daily life, the chief advantage, perhaps the only advantage, of large general knowledge is the ability it gives the better to command and manage the details of special and minute affairs. . . . There is no atonement for carelessness. If the historical student is unwilling to seek for the truth, even in the remotest recesses of darkness, he will have to be content to see his work lightly esteemed.—ADAMS, CHARLES KENDALL, 1882, *A Manual of Historical Literature, Introduction, p. 30.*

What have we a right to demand of an historian? First, surely, stern veracity which implies not merely knowledge but honesty. An historian stands in a fiduciary position towards his readers, and if he withholds from them important facts like to influence their judgment, he is guilty of fraud, and, when justice is done in this world, will be condemned to refund all the moneys he has made by his false professions, with compound interest. This sort of fraud is unknown to the law, but to nobody else. "Let me know the facts!" may well be the agonized cry of the student who finds himself floating down what Arnold has called "the vast Mississippi of falsehood, History." Secondly, comes a catholic temper and way of looking at things. The historian should be a gentleman, and possess a moral breadth of temperament. There should be no bitter protesting spirit about him. He should remember the world he has taken upon himself to write about is a large place, and that nobody set him up over us. Thirdly, he must be a born story-teller. If he is not this, he has mistaken his vocation. He may be a great philosopher, a useful editor, a profound scholar, and anything else his friends like to call him, except a great historian.— BIRRELL, AUGUSTINE, 1884, *Obiter Dicta. First Series.*

And they call this history. This serving up in spiced dishes of the clean and the unclean, the wholesome and the noxious; this plunging down into the charnel-house of the great graveyard of the past, and stirring up the decaying carcasses of the outcasts and malefactors of the race. No good can come of such work: without plan, without purpose, without breadth of view, and without method; with nothing but a vague desire to amuse, and a morbid craving for novelty. If there is one common purpose running through the whole history of the past, if that history is the story of man's growth in dignity, and power, and goodness, if the gathered knowledge and the gathered conscience of past ages does control us, support us, inspire us, then is this commemorating these parasites and off-scourings of the human race worse than pedantry or folly. It is filling us with an unnatural contempt for the greatness of the past—nay, it is committing towards our spiritual forefathers the same crime which Ham committed against his father Noah. It is a kind of sacrilege to the memory of the great men to whom we owe all we prize, if we waste our lives in poring over the acts of the puny creatures who only encumbered *their* path.—HARRISON, FREDERIC, 1894, *The Use of History, The Meaning of History, p. 9.*

History is not only a science. It is also an art. To be a great historian one must be a great artist. That incommunicable attribute of genius, creative of poetic power, is necessary to any one who would make the past live before us. . . . I suppose that in the present day we are not likely to lose sight of this truth. Our danger rather is to forget that without learning, accuracy, critical power, good sense, candour, no literary gifts, however brilliant, will enable any one to write anything worthy of the name of history. The man who does not possess these endowments is absolutely disqualified for the work of the historian.— LILLY, WILLIAM SAMUEL, 1897, *Essays and Speeches, p. 212.*

The function of history in education is perhaps not yet clearly apparent to all those who teach it. But all those who reflect are agreed to regard it as being principally an instrument of social culture. The study of the societies of the past causes the pupil to understand, by the help of actual instances, what a society is; it familiarises him with the principal social phenomena and the different species of usages, their variety and their resemblances. The study of events and evolutions familiarises him with the idea of the continual transformation which human affairs undergo, it secures him against an unreasoning dread of social changes; it rectifies his notion of progress. All these acquisitions render the pupil fitter for the public life; history thus appears as an indispensable branch of instruction in a democratic society.—LANGLOIS, AND SEIGNOBOS, 1898, *Introduction to the Study of History, ed. Berry, p. 332.*

CONTENTS.

CONTENTS

PAGE.

ENGRAVINGS.

CHARLOTTE BRONTË

After an Original Painting by Alonço Chappel.

MARY RUSSELL MITFORD

Engraving by Thomson. From an Original
Drawing by F. R. Say.

The
Library of Literary Criticism

of

English and American Authors

VOLUME VI

Charlotte Brontë

1816–1855

Born, at Thornton, 21 April 1816. Early life spent at Haworth. At school at Cowan's Bridge, Sept. 1824 to autumn of 1825. At Miss Wooler's school at Roehead, Jan. 1831 to 1832. Returned there as a teacher, 29 July 1835 to spring of 1838. Situation as governess in 1839. At home, 1840. Governess, March to Dec. 1841. To school at Brussels with her sister Emily, Feb. 1842. Returned to Haworth, Nov. 1842. Returned to Brussels school as teacher, Jan. 1843. Returned to Haworth, 2 Jan. 1844. Published poems with her sisters, 1846. "Jane Eyre" published 1847. Visits to London: with Emily, June 1848; Nov. 1849 (when she was made acquainted with Thackeray); 1850; 1851; 1853. Married to Arthur Nicholls, 29 June 1854. Visited Ireland with her husband, and returned with him to Haworth. Died there, 31 March 1855. *Works:* Contrib. to "Poems: by Currer, Ellis and Acton Bell," 1846; "Jane Eyre," 1847; "Shirley," 1849; "Villette," 1853; all under pseudonym of Currer Bell. *Posthumous:* "The Professor: by Currer Bell," 1857; "Emma" (a fragment), Pub. in "Cornhill Magazine," April 1860. She *edited* (under pseud. of "Currer Bell") a new edition of "Wuthering Heights, and Agnes Grey," with selections and prefaces, 1850. *Collected Works* with those of her sisters Anne and Emily (7 vols.), 1872–73. *Life* by Mrs. Gaskell, 4th edn., 1858; by Clement K. Shorter, 1896.—SHARP, R. FARQUHARSON, 1897, *A Dictionary of English Authors, p.* 32.

PERSONAL

I sent a dose of cooling admonition to the poor girl whose flighty letter reached me at Buckland. It was well taken, and she thanked me for it. It seems she is the eldest daughter of a clergyman, has been expensively educated, and is laudably employed as a governess in some private family. About the same time that she wrote to me, her brother wrote to Wordsworth, who was disgusted with the letter, for it contained gross flattery to him, and plenty of abuse of other poets, including me. I think well of the sister from her second letter, and probably she will think kindly of me as long as she lives.
—SOUTHEY, ROBERT, 1837, *To Caroline Bowles, The Correspondence of Robert Southey with Caroline Bowles, p.* 348.

I think the poems of Currer much better than those of Acton and Ellis, and believe his novel is vastly better than those which they have more recently put forth. I know nothing of the writers, but the common rumour is that they are brothers of the weaving order in some Lancashire town. At first it was generally said that Currer was a lady, and Mayfair circumstantialized by making her the *chère amie* of Mr. Thackeray. But your skill in "dress" settles the question of sex. I think, however, some women have assisted in the school scenes of "Jane Eyre," which have a striking air of truthfulness to me— an ignoramus, I allow, on such points.— LOCKHART, JOHN GIBSON, 1848, *Letter to Miss Rigby, Nov.* 13; *Correspondence of Lady Eastlake, ed. Smith, vol.* I., *p.* 222.

Averse to personal publicity, we veiled our names under those of Currer, Acton and Ellis Bell,—the ambiguous choice being dictated by a sort of conscientious scruple at assuming Christian names positively masculine, while we did not like to declare ourselves women, because—without at that time suspecting that our mode of writing and thinking was not what is called "feminine"—we had a vague impression that authoresses are likely to be looked on with prejudice; we had noticed how critics sometimes use for their chastisement the weapon of personality, and for their reward a flattery which is not true praise.— BRONTË, CHARLOTTE, 1850, *Biographical Notice by Currer Bell.*

Lewes was describing Currer Bell to me yesterday as a little, plain, provincial, sickly looking old maid. Yet what passion, what fire in her! Quite as much as in George Sand, only the clothing is less voluptuous.—ELIOT, GEORGE, 1853, *Letter to Sarah Hennell, March 28; George Eliot's Life as related in her Letters and Journals,* ed. Cross, vol. I, p. 221.

Between the appearance of "Shirley" and that of "Villette," she came to me;— in December, 1850. Our intercourse then confirmed my deep impression of her integrity, her noble conscientiousness about her vocation, and her consequent self-reliance in the moral conduct of her life. I saw at the same time tokens of a morbid condition of mind, in one or two directions; —much less than might have been expected, or than would have been seen in almost any one else under circumstances so unfavourable to health of body and mind as those in which she lived; and one fault which I pointed out to her in "Villette" was so clearly traceable to these unwholesome influences that I would fain have been spared a task of criticism which could hardly have been of much use while the circumstances remained unchanged. . . . She might be weak for once; but her permanent temper was one of humility, candour, integrity and conscientiousness. She was not only unspoiled by her sudden and prodigious fame, but obviously unspoilable.—MAR-TINEAU, HARRIET, 1855-77, *Autobiography,* ed. Chapman, vol. II, p. 24.

Since I saw you I have made three charming trips,—to Wales, Devonshire, and Yorkshire. The last was especially interesting, as I visited Haworth and Bolton Priory. The day was dreary in extreme, with gloomy fog half veiling the mysterious hills, which, resting on their folded arms, bowed solemnly as we swept by. Not a breath of wind was stirring; all was still, as if in sleep. As I stood on the doorstep of the parsonage, and gazed into the narrow garden enclosure, which separates the house from the desolate graveyard, with its green mounds and mossy monuments, it seemed to me that the black gnarled shrubbery, and the dank, brown flower-beds, where the wilted stocks hung heavy with the wet, wonderfully symbolized dear Charlotte Brontë's sorrows. And seeing the scene in its hour of desolation, it was easy to fancy the sunbursts and wild breezes from the heathery moorland, and the spotless, snowy moonlights.—CHANNING, W. H., 1857, *To Mrs. Hawthorne, Dec. 29; Nathaniel Hawthorne and his Wife,* ed. Hawthorne, vol. II, p. 167.

Genius as she was, she is beautifully attentive to the smallest practical matters affecting the comforts of others. She is intensely true, and draws from actual life, cost what it may; and in that little remote world of hers—a village, as it seems, of a hundred years back—facts came to light of a frightful, unmitigated force; events accompanied them, burning with a lurid glow and setting their very hearts on fire. She is like her books, and her life explains much in them which needs explanation.— FOX, CAROLINE, 1857, *Memories of Old Friends,* ed. Pym, Journal, July 9, p. 336.

I remember the trembling little frame, the little hand, the great honest eyes. An impetuous honesty seemed to me to characterize the woman. Twice I recollect she took me to task for what she held to be errors in doctrine. Once about Fielding we had a disputation. She spoke her mind out. She jumped too rapidly to conclusions. . . . She formed conclusions that might be wrong, and built up whole theories of character upon them. New to the London world, she entered it with an independent, indomitable spirit of her own; and judged of contemporaries, and especially spied out arrogance or affectation, with extraordinary keenness of vision. She was angry with her favourites if their conduct or conversation fell below her ideal. Often she seemed to me to be judging the London folk prematurely: but perhaps the city is rather angry at being judged. I fancied an austere little Joan of Arc marching in upon us, and rebuking our easy lives, our easy morals. She gave me the impression of being a very pure, and lofty, and high-minded person. A great and holy reverence of right and truth seemed to be with her always. Such, in our brief interview, she appeared to me.—THACKERAY, WILLIAM MAKEPEACE, 1860, *The Last Sketch, Cornhill Magazine, vol.* 1, *p.* 486.

In the sombre web of her existence there shone one thread of silver, all the brighter and more blessed for the contrast—it was the warm, steady, unfailing friendship of her school-fellow "E." [Ellen Nussey]. "Ma bien aimée, ma précieuse E., mon amie chère et chérie," she calls her in one of her earlier letters. "If we had but a cottage and a competency of our own, I do think we might live and love on till death, without being dependent on any third person for happiness." "What am I compared to you?" she exclaims; "I feel my own utter worthlessness when I make the comparison. I am a very coarse, commonplace wretch." But the affection that overflowed in such loving extravagance was no passing sentiment. As life deepened and grew more and more intense—and fuller of pain—for each, the closer became their attachment, the more constantly Charlotte turned for sympathy and support to her faithful companion. . . . In her, indeed, she found all the greater rest and refreshment because of the difference in their natures. Her individuality colors the Caroline Helstone of "Shirley."— GILDER, RICHARD WATSON, 1871, *The Old Cabinet, Scribner's Monthly, vol.* 2, *p.* 100.

The garden is less spacious than it was in Charlotte's time, new classrooms having been added, which cut off something from its length. But the whole place was strangely familiar and pleasant to our eyes. Shut in by surrounding houses, more than one window overlooks its narrow space. Down its length upon one side extends the shaded walk, the "allée défendue," which Charlotte paced alone so many weary hours, when Emily had returned to England. Parallel to this is the row of giant pear-trees—hugh, misshapen, gnarled—that bore no fruit to us but associations vivid as memories. From behind these in the summer twilight the ghost of "Villette" was wont to steal, and buried at the foot of "Methuselah," the oldest, we knew poor

Lucy's love-letters were hidden to-day. A seat here and there, a few scattered shrubs, evergreen, laurel, and yew, scant blossoms, paths damp, green-crusted—that was all. Not a cheerful place at its brightest; not a sunny spot associated in one's mind with summer and girlish voices. —TRAFTON, ADELINE, 1871, *A Visit to Charlotte Brontë's School at Brussels, Scribner's Monthly, vol.* 3, *p.* 188.

By her life, even more than by her labours the author of "Jane Eyre" must always teach us the lessons of courage, self-sacrifice and patient endurance of which our poor humanity stands in such pressing and constant need.—REID, T. WEMYSS, 1876, *Charlotte Brontë, Macmillan's Magazine, vol.* 35, *p.* 18.

Those who would understand Charlotte, even more than those who would understand Emily, should study the difference of tenderness between the touch that drew Shirley Keeldar and the touch that drew Lucy Snowe. This latter figure, as Mr. Wemyss Reid has observed with indisputable accuracy of insight, was doubtless, if never meant to win liking or made to find favor in the general reader's eyes, yet none the less evidently on that account the faithful likeness of Charlotte Brontë, studied from the life, and painted by her own hand with the sharp austere precision of a photograph rather than a portrait. But it is herself with the consolation and support of her genius withdrawn, with the strength of the spiritual arm immeasurably shortened, the cunning of the right hand comparatively cancelled; and this it is that makes the main undertone and ultimate result of the book somewhat mournfuller even than the literal record of her mournful and glorious life.—SWINBURNE, ALGERNON CHARLES, 1877, *A Note on Charlotte Brontë, p.* 81.

Some American tourists had before called to look at the garden, but the family are not pleased by the notoriety with which Miss Brontë has invested it. However, Mademoiselle Héger kindly offered to conduct us over any portion of the establishment we might care to see, and led the way along the corridor, past the classrooms and the *réfectoire* on the right, to the narrow, high-walled garden. We found it smaller than in the time when Miss Brontë loitered here in weariness and solitude. Mademoiselle Héger explained that, while the width remains the same, the erection of the classrooms for the day-pupils has diminished the length by some yards. Tall houses surround and shut it in on either side, making it close and sombre, and the noises of the great city all about it penetrate here only as a far-away murmur. There is a plat of verdant turf in the centre, bordered by scant flowers and damp gravelled walks, along which shrubs of evergreen and laurel are irregularly disposed. A few seats are placed here and there within the shade, where, as in Miss Brontë's time, the *externats* eat the luncheon brought with them to the school; and overlooking it all stand the great old pear-trees, whose gnarled and deformed trunks are relics of the time of the hospital and convent.—WOLFE, THEODORE, 1885, *Scenes of Charlotte Brontë's Life in Brussels, Lippincott's Magazine, vol. 36, p. 545.*

The loving admirers of Charlotte Brontë can never feel much enthusiasm for Mr. Nicholls. Mrs. Gaskell states that he was not attracted by her literary fame, but was rather repelled by it; he appears to have used her up remorselessly, in their short married life, in the routine drudgery of parish work. She did not complain, on the contrary, she seemed more than contented to sacrifice everything for him and his work; but she remarks in one of her letters, "I have less time for thinking." Apparently she had none for writing. Surely the husband of a Charlotte Brontë, just as much as the wife of a Wordsworth or a Tennyson, ought to be attracted by literary fame. To be the life partner of one to whom the most precious of Nature's gifts is confided, and to be unappreciative of it and even repelled by it, shows a littleness of nature and essential meanness of soul. A true wife or husband of one of these gifted beings should rather regard herself or himself as responsible to the world for making the conditions of the daily life of their distinguished partners favourable to the development of their genius. But pearls have before now been cast before swine, and one cannot but regret that Charlotte Brontë was married to a man who did not value her place in literature as he ought. —FAWCETT, MILLICENT GARRETT, 1889, *Some Eminent Women of our Times, p. 109.*

It almost makes one's blood boil to think of that warm, imaginative, hungry and thirsty girlish heart, beating against its bars, under-rated and misunderstood by the sprightly, amiable, but withal undiscerning and self-opinionated man who was its ideal. . . . He is a bright, vain, handsome octogenarian, charming and delighting to charm, eager to talk, and as eager for an audience, as exacting of homage and subservience as in the days when schoolgirls trembled at his glance. Imagine him fifty years ago, and you can hardly go wrong in imaging a very fascinating personage; then recollect that fifty years ago or thereabouts the little Yorkshire nursery-governess took her first flight to Brussels, and there beheld "Paul Emanuel"—*et voilà tout!*—WALFORD, LUCY BETHIA, 1890, *The Home of Charlotte Brontë, Longman's Magazine, vol. 15, pp. 310, 311.*

One of the most notable persons who ever came into our old bow-windowed drawing-room in Young street is a guest never to be forgotten by me, a tiny, delicate, little person, whose small hand nevertheless grasped a mighty lever which set all the literary world of that day vibrating. I can still see the scene plainly!—the hot summer evening, the open windows, the carriage driving to the door as we all sat silent and expectant; my father, who rarely waited, waiting with us; our governess and my sister and I all in a row, and prepared for the great event. We saw the carriage stop and out of it sprang the active, well-knit figure of young Mr. George Smith, who was bringing Miss Brontë to see our father. My father, who had been walking up and down the room, goes out into the hall to meet his guests, and then after a moment's delay the door opens wide, and the two gentlemen come in, leading a tiny, delicate, serious, little lady, pale, with fair, straight hair, and steady eyes. She may be a little over thirty; she is dressed in a little *barége* dress with a pattern of faint green moss. She enters in mittens, in silence, in seriousness; our hearts are beating with wild excitement.—RITCHIE, ANNE ISABELLA THACKERAY, 1891, *My Witches' Caldron, Macmillan's Magazine, vol. 63, p. 251.*

Story-telling, as we shall see, was a hereditary gift in the Brontë family, and Patrick inherited it from his father. Charlotte's friend, Miss Ellen Nussey, has often told me of the marvellous fascination with which the girls would hang on their father's lips as he depicted scene after scene of some tragic story in glowing words and with harrowing details. The breakfast would remain untouched till the story had passed the crisis, and sometimes the narration became so real and vivid and intense, that the listeners begged the vicar to proceed no farther. Sleepless nights succeeded storytelling evenings at the vicarage.—WRIGHT, WILLIAM, 1893, *The Brontës in Ireland*, *p.* 15.

Taken as a whole, the life of Charlotte Brontë was among the saddest in literature. At a miserable school, where she herself was unhappy, she saw her two elder sisters stricken down and carried home to die. In her home was the narrowest poverty. She had, in the years when that was most essential, no mother's care; and perhaps there was a somewhat too rigid disciplinarian in the aunt who took the mother's place. Her second school brought her, indeed, two kind friends; but her shyness made that school-life in itself a prolonged tragedy. Of the two experiences as a private governess I shall have more to say. They were periods of torture to her sensitive nature. The ambition of the three girls to start a school on their own account failed ignominiously. The suppressed vitality of childhood and early womanhood made Charlotte unable to enter with sympathy and toleration into the life of a foreign city, and Brussels was for her a further disaster. Then within two years, just as literary fame was bringing its consolation for the trials of the past, she saw her two beloved sisters taken from her. And, finally, when at last a good man won her love, there were left to her only nine months of happy married life. "I am not going to die. We have been so happy." These words to her husband on her death-bed are not the least piteously sad in her tragic story.—SHORTER, CLEMENT K., 1896, *Charlotte Brontë and Her Circle*, *p.* 21.

I must confess that my first impression of Charlotte Brontë's personal appearance was that it was interesting rather than attractive. She was very small, and had a quaint old-fashioned look. Her head seemed too large for her body. She had fine eyes, but her face was marred by the shape of the mouth and by the complexion. There was but little feminine charm about her; and of this fact she herself was uneasily and perpetually conscious. It may seem strange that the possession of genius did not lift her above the weakness of an excessive anxiety about her personal appearance. But I believe that she would have given all her genius and her fame to have been beautiful. Perhaps few women ever existed more anxious to be pretty than she, or more angrily conscious of the circumstance that she was *not* pretty. . . . Her letters show that she enjoyed the recollection of these visits, and the society at our house; but my mother and sisters found her a somewhat difficult guest, and I am afraid she was never perfectly at her ease with them. Strangers used to say that they were afraid of her. She was very quiet and self-absorbed, and gave the impression that she was always engaged in observing and analyzing the people she met. She was sometimes tempted to confide her analysis to the victim.—SMITH, SIR GEORGE MURRAY, 1901, *In the Early Forties, The Critic, vol.* 38, *pp.* 53, 55.

THE PROFESSOR

Charlotte Brontë wrote "The Professor" long before "George Eliot" took up her pen; and she must at least receive credit for having been in the field as a reformer of fiction before her fellow-labourer was heard of. She was true to the conditions she had laid down for herself in writing "The Professor." Nothing more sober and matter-of-fact than that story is to be found in English literature. And yet, though the landscape one is invited to view is but a vast plain, without even a hillock to give variety to the prospect, it has beauties of its own which commend it to our admiration. . . . Though a sad, monotonous book, has life and hope, and a fair faith in the ultimate blessedness of all sorrowful ones, shining through all its pages; and it closes in a scene of rest and peace.—REID, T. WEMYSS, 1877, *Charlotte Brontë, A Monograph, pp.* 221, 222.

Even the wise and cordial judgment which had discerned the note of power and sincerity perceptible in the crude coarse outlines of "The Professor" may well have been startled and shaken out of all judicial balance and critical reserve at sight of the sudden sunrise which followed so fast on that diffident uncertain dawn.—SWINBURNE, ALGERNON CHARLES, 1877, *A Note on Charlotte Brontë, p.* 46.

It has an interest, particularly as showing the restricted nature of its author's invention, but as a story it is ineffective and unpleasant.—BIRRELL, AUGUSTINE,

1887, *Life of Charlotte Brontë* (*Great Writers*), *p.* 95, *note.*

JANE EYRE
1847

I now send you per rail a MS. entitled, "Jane Eyre," a novel in three volumes, by Currer Bell. I find I cannot prepay the carriage of the parcel, as money for that purpose is not received at the small station-house where it is left. If, when you acknowlege the receipt of the MS. you would have the goodness to mention the amount charged on delivery, I will immediately transmit it in postage stamps. It is better in future to address Mr. Currer Bell, under cover to "Miss Brontë, Haworth, Bradford, Yorkshire," as there is a risk of letters otherwise directed not reaching me at present. To save trouble, I enclose an envelope. — BRONTË, CHARLOTTE, 1847, *Letter to Messrs. Smith and Elder, Aug.* 24.

I have finished the adventures of Miss Jane Eyre, and think her far the cleverest that has written since Austen and Edgeworth were in their prime. Worth fifty Trollopes and Martineaus rolled into one counterpane, with fifty Dickenses and Bulwers to keep them company—but rather a brazen Miss.—LOCKHART, JOHN GIBSON, 1847, *Letter to Mrs. Hope, Dec.* 29; *Life of J. G. Lockhart, ed. Lang, vol.* I, *p.* 310.

We have said that this was a picture of a natural heart. This, to our view, is the great and crying mischief of the book. Jane Eyre is throughout the personification of an unregenerate and undisciplined spirit, the more dangerous to exhibit from that prestige of principle and self-control which is liable to dazzle the eye too much for it to observe the inefficient and unsound foundation on which it rests. It is true Jane does right, and exerts great moral strength, but it is the strength of a mere heathen mind which is a law unto itself. No Christian grace is perceptible upon her. She has inherited in fullest measure the worst sin of our fallen nature— the sin of pride. Jane Eyre is proud, and therefore she is ungrateful too. It pleased God to make her an orphan, friendless, and penniless—yet she thanks nobody, and least of all Him, for the food and raiment, the friends, companions, and instructors of her helpless youth—for the care and education vouchsafed to her till she was capable in mind as fitted in years to provide

for herself. . . . Altogether the autobiography of Jane Eyre is pre-eminently an anti-Christian composition. There is throughout it a murmuring against the comforts of the rich and against the privations of the poor, which, as far as each individual is concerned, is a murmuring against God's appointment—there is a proud and perpetual assertion of the rights of man, for which we find no authority either in God's word or in God's providence —there is that pervading tone of ungodly discontent which is at once the most prominent and the most subtle evil which the law and the pulpit, which all civilized society in fact has at the present day to contend with. We do not hesitate to say that the tone of mind and thought which has overthrown authority and violated every code human and divine abroad, and fostered Chartism and rebellion at home, is the same which has also written Jane Eyre. . . . If we ascribe the book to a woman at all, we have no alternative but to ascribe it to one who has, for some sufficient reason, long forfeited the society of her own sex.—RIGBY, ELIZABETH (LADY EASTLAKE), 1848, *Vanity Fair and Jane Eyre, Quarterly Review, vol.* 84, *pp.* 172, 173, 176.

I have read "Jane Eyre," and shall be glad to know what you admire in it. All self-sacrifice is good, but one would like it to be in a somewhat nobler cause than that of a diabolical law which chains a man soul and body to a putrefying carcass. However, the book *is* interesting; only I wish the characters would talk a little less like the heroes and heroines of police reports.— ELIOT, GEORGE, 1848, *Letter to Charles Bray, June; George Eliot's Life as related in her Letters and Journals, ed. Cross, vol.* I, *p.* 138.

Not many months ago, the New England States were visited by a distressing mental epidemic, passing under the name of the "Jane Eyre fever," which defied all the usual nostrums of the established doctors of criticism. Its effects varied with different constitutions, in some producing a soft ethical sentimentality, which relaxed all the fibres of conscience, and in others exciting a general fever of moral and religious indignation. It was to no purpose that the public were solemnly assured, through the intelligent press, that the malady was not likely to have any permanent effect either on the intellectual or moral constitution. . The book which caused the distemper would probably have been inoffensive, had not some sly manufacturer of mischief hinted that it was a volume which no respectable man should bring into his family circle. Of course, every family soon had a copy of it, and one edition after another found eager purchasers.— WHIPPLE, EDWIN PERCY, 1848, *Novels of the Season, Essays and Reviews, vol.* II, *p.* 355.

We take Currer Bell to be one of the most remarkable of *female* writers; and believe it is now scarcely a secret that Currer Bell is the pseudonyme of a woman. An eminent contemporary, indeed, has employed the sharp vivacity of a female pen to prove "upon irresistible evidence" that "Jane Eyre" *must be* the work of a man! But all that "irresistible evidence" is set aside by the simple fact that Currer Bell *is* a woman. We never, for our own parts, had a moment's doubt on the subject. That Jane herself was drawn by a woman's delicate hand, and that Rochester equally betrayed the sex of the artist, was to our minds so obvious, as absolutely to shut our ears to all the evidence which could be adducted by the erudition even of a *marchande des modes;* and that simply because we know that there were women profoundly ignorant of the mysteries of the toilette, and the terminology of fashion (independent of the obvious solution, that such ignorance might be counterfeited, to mislead), and felt that there was no man who *could so* have delineated a woman—or *would so* have delineated a man. The fair and ingenious critic was misled by her own acuteness in the perception of details; and misled also in some other way, and more uncharitably, in concluding that the *author* of "Jane Eyre" was a heathen educated among heathens—the *fact* being, that the *authoress* is the daughter of a clergyman! This question of authorship, which was somewhat hotly debated a little while ago, helped to keep up the excitement about "Jane Eyre"; but, independently of that title to notoriety, it is certain that, for many years, there had been no work of such power, piquancy, and originality. Its very faults were faults on the side of vigour; and its beauties were all original. The grand secret of its success, however,—

as of all genuine and lasting success,—was its *reality.* From out of the depths of a sorrowing experience, here was a voice speaking to the experience of thousands. The aspects of external nature, too, were painted with equal fidelity,—the long cheerless winter days, chilled with rolling mists occasionally gathering into the strength of rains,—the bright spring mornings,—the clear solemn nights,—were all painted to your *soul* as well as to your eye, by a pencil dipped into a soul's experience for its colours. Faults enough the book has undoubtedly; faults of conception, faults of taste, faults of ignorance, but in spite of all, it remains a book of singular fascination. A more masculine book, in the sense of vigour, was never written. Indeed that vigour often amounts to coarseness,—and is certainly the very antipode to "lady like."—LEWES, GEORGE HENRY, 1850, *Currer Bell's "Shirley," Edinburgh Review, vol.* 91, *p.* 158.

"Jane Eyre" is the real spar—the slow deposit which the heart of genius filters from the daily stream of time and circumstance. "Shirley" is its companion, made to order, fair to look upon, but lacking the internal crystal. Open the earlier work where you will, this crystal sparkles in your eyes; break it up piecemeal, and every fragment glitters. Turn over the first chapter, and pause at hazard. There is no apparent consciousness of wisdom—no parading of truths or setting forth of paradoxes—no dealing in aphorisms, axioms, or generals of any kind. Yet one could preach a sermon from every sentence. —DOBELL, SYDNEY, 1850, *Currer Bell, Life and Letters of Sydney Dobell, ed. Jolly, vol.* I, *p.* 179.

How well I remember the delight, and wonder, and pleasure with which I read "Jane Eyre" sent to me by an author whose name and sex were then alike unknown to me; the strange fascinations of the book; and how with my own work pressing upon me, I could not, having taken the volumes up, lay them down until they were read through!—THACKERAY, WILLIAM MAKEPEACE, 1860, *The Last Sketch, Cornhill Magazine, vol.* 1, *p.* 487.

I have been reading novels—"Jane Eyre," among the rest. It was very pleasant to me for its inexperience. It is a girl's dream of the world not yet known, or only glimpsed from afar. But there is a real power in it, and the descriptions of scenery are the best I know, out of Ruskin. —LOWELL, JAMES RUSSELL, 1867, *To C. E. Norton, July* 8; *Letters of James Russell Lowell, ed. Norton, vol.* I, *p.* 390.

Those who remember that winter of nine-and-twenty years ago know how something like a " Jane Eyre" fever raged among us. The story which had suddenly discovered a glory in uncomeliness, a grandeur in overmastering passion, moulded the fashion of the hour, and "Rochester airs" and " Jane Eyre graces" became the rage. The book, and its fame and influence, travelled beyond the seas with a speed which in those days was marvellous. In sedate New England homes the history of the English governess was read with an avidity which was not surpassed in London itself, and within a few months of the publication of the novel it was famous throughout two continents. No such triumph has been achieved in our time by any other English author; nor can it be said, upon the whole, that many triumphs have been better merited. It happened that this anonymous story, bearing the unmistakable marks of an unpracticed hand, was put before the world at the very moment when another great masterpiece of fiction was just beginning to gain the ear of the English public. But at the moment of publication "Jane Eyre" swept past "Vanity Fair" with a marvellous and impetuous speed which left Thackeray's work in the distant back-ground; and its unknown author in a few weeks gained a wider reputation than that which one of the master minds of the century had been engaged for long years in building up. The reaction from this exaggerated fame, of course set in, and it was sharp and severe.— REID, T. WEMYSS, 1877, *Charlotte Brontë, A Monograph, p.* 8.

The gift of which I would speak is that of a power to make us feel in every nerve, at every step forward which our imagination is compelled to take under the guidance of another's, that thus and not otherwise, but in all things altogether even as we are told and shown, it was and it must have been with the human figures set before us in their action and their suffering; that thus and not otherwise they absolutely must and would have felt and thought and spoken under the proposed conditions. It is something for a writer to have achieved if he has made it worth our fancy's while to consider by the light of imaginative reason whether the creatures of his own fancy would in actual fact and life have done as he has made them or not; it is something, and by comparison it is much. But no definite terms of comparison will suffice to express how much more than this it is to have done what the youngest of capable readers must feel on their first opening "Jane Eyre" that the writer of its very first pages has shown herself competent to do. In almost all other great works of its kind, in almost all the sovereign masterpieces even of Fielding, of Thackeray, of the royal and imperial master, Sir Walter Scott himself—to whose glorious memory I need offer no apology for the attribution of epithets which I cannot but regret to remember that even in their vulgar sense he would not have regarded as other than terms of honour—even in the best and greatest works of these our best and greatest we do not find this one great good quality so innate, so immanent as in hers.— SWINBURNE, ALGERNON CHARLES, 1877, *A Note on Charlotte Brontë, p.* 13.

The story of Charlotte Brontë's life is one of the most fascinating in our language. The English reading world is acquainted with her novels, and many have enjoyed "Jane Eyre" as much perhaps as did a mother of several grown-up daughters who took the book from one of them with a reproof for reading a novel—something she had never done, and who was discovered in the night poring over it. She had opened it to see what it was, and had remained up all night to settle the question for herself.—HOLLOWAY, LAURA C., 1883, *An Hour with Charlotte Brontë, p.* 7.

I hope I shall not be called a Puritan or a Philistine if I say that the morality of Charlotte Brontë's work always strikes me as being radically unhealthy. The ethical quality of the productions of any novelist whose experience of life was so narrow and so painful as hers must be either morbidness or weakness; and it is hard to see how "Jane Eyre" can be considered anything but morbid in spite of its singular power. The objection to its whole conception is that the abnormal is treated as if it were the normal, and the reader is led to make wide ethical generalizations from a series of really exceptional instances. . . . In "Jane Eyre" the furnace of emotion is heated seven times more than it is wont to be heated in the healthy life of every day; the atmosphere is that of a Turkish bath, but there is no welcome douche to brace up the relaxed tissues of feeling.—NOBLE, JAMES ASHCROFT, 1886, *Morality in English Fiction, pp.* 48, 49.

It is easy to understand the great interest and excitement such a tale at once created. Most books are born dead, and it is always a startling moment when you first discover that you are holding an exception in your hands. "Jane Eyre" was a live coal dropped by some unknown hand —from some unknown quarter—amongst the literary coteries and "log-rollers." There was no mistake about it, here was a book at first hand.—BIRRELL, AUGUSTINE, 1887, *Life of Charlotte Brontë* (*Great Writers*), *p.* 100.

Not long after, "Consuelo," in Mr. Shaw's admirable translation, took possession of Young America. The fame of it hardly exists now. But there must be something real in it to account for the hold it took, and the impulse it gave. I can remember that again and again I threw it down to go to work, with a feeling which, if expressed in words, would have been, "Will you waste your time in reading a French novel, when a woman like this can write a book like this?" But when "Jane Eyre" came, nobody threw that down till he had finished it. — HALE, EDWARD EVERETT, 1888, *Books That Have Helped Me, p.* 12.

Miss Brontë's novels are day-dreams and memories rather than stories. In "Jane Eyre" she is dealing with the eternal day-dream of the disinherited; the unfortunate guest at life's banquet. It is a vision that has many shapes: some see it in the form of a buried treasure to make them suddenly wealthy—this was the day-dream of Poe; or of a mine to be discovered, a company to be formed—thus it haunted Balzac. The lodging house servant straight of foundlings dreams, and behold she is a young countess, changed at nurse and kept out of her own. The poor author dreams of a "hit," and (in this novel) Miss Brontë dwelt in fantasy on the love and the adventures that might come to a clever governess, who was not beautiful. . . . "Jane Eyre" is her best story, and far the most secure of life, because it has plenty of good, old-fashioned, foolish, immortal romance.—

LANG, ANDREW, 1889, *Charlotte Brontë, Good Words, vol.* 30, *p.* 239.

In the first place she was known to Mr. Rochester and to Currer Bell herself, as she is known in England to-day, as Jane *Air*, not as Jane *Ire;* and in the second place she is not autobiographical, Mr. Birrell to the contrary, notwithstanding. . . . It is difficult, even in these days of Anna Karenina and of Robert Elsmere, to understand the sensation created by Jane Eyre when she first appeared, over forty years ago. She was read and re-read, discussed and dissected, anatomized and anathematized, on both sides of the Atlantic, as no ideal woman has been treated before or since; and she achieved at once a triumphant notoriety which has never been equalled in simple fiction. . . . She has outlived censure, and she needs no praise. Time has granted her a patent of nobility. To those who remember her in her youth she has lost none of her charms. Those who now meet her for the first time in her matronly maturity will find much to admire in her and very little to reprehend. —HUTTON, LAURENCE, 1890, *The Curiosities of Jane Eyre, The Book Buyer, vol.* 7, *pp.* 500, 501.

To say that we little girls had been given "Jane Eyre" to read scarcely represents the facts of the case; to say that we had taken it out without leave, read bits here and read bits there, been carried away by an undreamed-of and hitherto unimagined whirlwind into things, times, places, all utterly absorbing and at the same time absolutely unintelligible to us, would more accurately describe our states of mind on that summer's evening as we look at Jane Eyre—the great Jane Eyre—the tiny little lady.—RITCHIE, ANNE ISABELLA THACKERAY, 1891, *My Witches' Caldron, Macmillan's Magazine, vol.* 63, *p.* 252.

I do not think that she was exactly what can be called a great genius, or that she would ever have given us anything much better than she did give; and I do not think that with critical reading "Jane Eyre" improves, or even holds its ground very well. It has strength, or at any rate force; it has sufficient originality of manner; it has some direct observation of life within the due limits of art; and it has the piquancy of an unfashionable unconventionality at a very conventional time. These are good things, but they are not necessarily great; and it is to me a very suspicious point that quite the best parts of Charlotte Brontë's work are admittedly something like transcripts of her personal experience.—SAINTSBURY, GEORGE, 1895, *Corrected Impressions, p.* 159.

Of Charlotte's work it is "Jane Eyre" only that can be called a masterpiece. . . . With all its faults,its narrowness of range, its occasional extravagances, "Jane Eyre" will long be remembered as one of the most creative influences of theVictorian literature,one of the most poetic pieces of English romance, and among the most vivid masterpieces in the rare order of literary "Confessions."—HARRISON,FREDERIC,1895,*Studies in Early Victorian Literature, pp.* 151, 162.

In 1847 the world was startled by the publication of a story of modern life named "Jane Eyre," by an anonymous author. Here were a sweep of tragic passion, a broad delineation of elemental hatred and love, a fusion of romantic intrigue with grave and sinister landscape, such as had never been experienced before; to find their parallel it was necessary to go back to the wild drama of Elizabeth.—GOSSE, EDMUND, 1897, *A Short History of Modern English Literature, p.* 354.

"Jane Eyre" is after all but a glorified example of the "one novel" which everybody is said to "have in him." It is not quite certain that Charlotte Brontë had any more novels in her as great, or nearly as great, as "Jane Eyre," at any rate neither "Villette" nor "Shirley" has proved it. But this suspected limitation in her range may not unreasonably be claimed by her admirers as additional testimony to that truth, force, and intensity of this personal and almost autobiographic utterance which has raised it to the rank of a classic.— TRAILL, HENRY DUFF, 1897, *Social England, vol.* VI, *p.* 283.

There never was a plot which pretended to be a plot, of looser texture than that of "Jane Eyre." It abounds with absurdities and inconsistencies. The critics of Charlotte Brontë's time had no difficulty in pointing them out; they lie, indeed, on the surface for all to see. . . . The main secret of the charm that clings to Charlotte Brontë's books is, and will always be, the contact which they give us with her own fresh, indomitable, surprising personality,—surprising, above all. In spite of its conventionalities of scheme,"JaneEyre"has,

in detail, in conversation, in the painting of character, that perpetual magic of the unexpected which overrides a thousand faults, and keeps the mood of the reader happy and alert. The expedients of the plot may irritate or chill the artistic sense; the voice of the story-teller, in its inflections of passion, or feeling, or reverie, charms and holds the ear almost from first to last. The general plan may be commonplace, the ideas even of no great profundity; but the book is original.—WARD, MARY AUGUSTA, 1899, *ed. Jane Eyre, Introduction.*

A study of Charlotte Brontë's novels suggests the judgment that while in all of them there is much that is of high value and interest, there is only one part of one of them that leaves the distinct impression of unmistakable greatness, namely, the relation between Rochester and Jane Eyre. This may seem a small achievement on which to base security of fame, but it is not to be measured by the number of pages in which it is contained. It struck a new note in the history of fiction—a note which has added many grand and subtle harmonies to itself in the works of succeeding writers, and the sweetness and power of which will never die away.—OLIPHANT, JAMES, 1899, *Victorian Novelists, p.* 77.

The characters are creations, and their appearance marks an epoch in literature, marks a distinct and definite era in the history of the novel. Before their appearance we had had personages in fiction. In "Jane Eyre," for the first time in English fiction, the intensity of life-craving which dominates a woman who loves is presented in the pages of the novel; and the voice of the outcry of her longing comes to the world.—STODDARD, FRANCIS HOVEY, 1900, *The Evolution of the English Novel, p.* 63.

The MS. of "Jane Eyre" was read by Mr. Williams in due course. He brought it to me on a Saturday, and said that he would like me to read it. There were no Saturday half-holidays in those days, and, as usual, I did not reach home until late. I had made an appointment with a friend for Sunday morning; I was to meet him about twelve o'clock, at a place some two or three miles from our house and ride with him into the country. After breakfast on Sunday morning I took the MS. of "Jane Eyre" to my little study, and began to read it. The story quickly took me captive. Before twelve o'clock my horse came to the door, but I could not put the book down. I scribbled two or three lines to my friend, saying I was very sorry circumstances had arisen to prevent my meeting him, sent the note off by my groom, and went on reading the MS. Presently the servant came to tell me that luncheon was ready; I asked him to bring me a sandwich and a glass of wine, and still went on with "Jane Eyre." Dinner came; for me the meal was a very hasty one, and before I went to bed that night I had finished reading the manuscript. The next day we wrote to "Currer Bell" accepting the book for publication.—SMITH, SIR GEORGE MURRAY, 1901, *In the Early Forties, The Critic, vol.* 38, *p.* 52.

From the beginning to the ending of her story, Jane Eyre moves a living and consistent soul; from the child we know grow the girl and woman we know, vivid, energetic, passionate, as well as good, conscientious, devoted. It was a figure which might have well astonished and alarmed the little fastidious world of fifty years ago, far more smug and complacent than the larger world of to-day, and far more intolerant of any question of religious or social convention; and it is no wonder that the young author should have been attainted of immorality and infidelity, not to name that blacker crime, impropriety. In fact, it must be allowed that "Jane Eyre" does go rather far in a region where women's imaginations are politely supposed not to wander; and the frank recognition of the rights of love as love, and its claims in Rochester as paramount to those of righteous self-will in St. John, is still a little startling. . . . The whole story, so deeply of nature, is steeped in the supernatural; and just as paradoxically the character of Jane Eyre lacks that final projection from the author which is the supreme effect of art, only because she feels it so intensely that she cannot detach it from herself.—HOWELLS, WILLIAM DEAN, 1901, *Heroines of Fiction, vol.* I, *pp.* 222, 227.

SHIRLEY
1849

I have read "Shirley" lately; it is not equal to "Jane Eyre" in spontaneousness and earnestness. I found it heavy, I confess, though in the mechanical part of the writing—the compositional *savoir faire*—there is an advance.—BROWNING, ELIZABETH BARRETT, 1850, *To Mrs. Jameson,*

April 2; *The Letters of Elizabeth Barrett Browning, ed. Kenyon, vol.* I, *p.* 442.

"Shirley" is a Holiday of the Heart. It is glad, buoyant, sunshiny. The imagination is liberated, and revels in its liberty. It is the pleasant summer-time, and the worker is idling among the hills. The world of toil and suffering lies behind, but ever so far away. True, it must again be encountered, its problems resolved, its sores probed; the hard and obstinate war again waged manfully; but in the meantime the burn foams and sparkles through the glen; there is sunshine among the purple harebells; and the leaves in the birken glade dance merrily in the summer wind.— SKELTON, JOHN (SHIRLEY), 1857, *Charlotte Brontë, Fraser's Magazine, vol.* 55, *p.* 579.

"Shirley" disgusted me at the opening, and I gave up the writer and her books with a notion that she was a person who liked coarseness. How I misjudged her! and how thankful I am that I never put a word of my misconceptions into print, or recorded my misjudgments of one who is a whole heaven above me. — KINGSLEY, CHARLES, 1857, *Letter to Mrs. Gaskell, May* 14.

It is what we should describe as a novel good "all round." It has no weak side; it is the most perfect piece of writing the author has left behind her. There is not the terrible sweep of passion we see in "Jane Eyre"; the roughnesses of life are smoothed down a little, and it seems altogether more humanized and humanizing. —SMITH, GEORGE BARNETT, 1875, *The Brontës, Poets and Novelists, p.* 231.

"Shirley" has, and deserves to have, many friends, and contains passages of great daring and beauty; but, as a whole, it must be pronounced (by me) inferior alike to its predecessor, and its successor. It lacks the splendid unity of "Jane Eyre," the uniqueness of "Villette." It is a series of portraits and exteriors—all good, some superb; but to pursue the metaphor, one walks through a book as through a picture gallery, always ready to go on, but never averse to turn back, since continuity of impression is of necessity impossible.—BIRRELL, AUGUSTINE, 1887, *Life of Charlotte Brontë (Great Writers), p.* 122.

The heroine is Emily Brontë, as she might have been if the great god, Wünsch, who inspires day-dreamers, had given her wealth and health. One might as readily fancy the fortunes of a stormy sea-petrel in a parrot's gilded cage. "Shirley" cannot live with "Jane Eyre."—LANG, ANDREW, 1889, *Charlotte Brontë, Good Words, vol.* 30, *p.* 239.

Her second book, "Shirley" (1848), was less powerful than her first, and much more artificial. It showed perhaps something of the strain the writer put on her mettle, and fully bent on exceeding, if possible, the previous natural and spontaneous effort. But it was also revolutionary to the highest degree, casting aside the discreet veil of the heroine which almost all previous novelists had respected, and representing the maiden on the tip-toe of expectation, no longer modestly awaiting the coming of Prince Charming, but craning her neck out of every window in almost fierce anticipation, and upbraiding heaven and earth, which kept her buried in those solitudes, out of his way.—OLIPHANT, MARGARET O. W., 1892, *The Victorian Age of English Literature, p.* 307.

VILLETTE
1853

I am only just returned to a sense of the real world about me, for I have been reading "Villette," a still more wonderful book than "Jane Eyre." There is something almost preternatural in its power.—ELIOT, GEORGE, 1853, *Letter to Mrs. Bray, Feb.* 15; *George Eliot's Life as related in her Letters and Journals, ed. Cross, vol.* I, *p.* 220.

The most striking book which has been recently published here is "Villette," by the authoress of "Jane Eyre," who, as you know, is a Miss Brontë. The book does not give one the most pleasing notion of the authoress, perhaps, but it is very clever, graphic, vigorous. It is "man's meat," and not the whipped syllabub, which is *all* froth, without any jam at the bottom.—PROCTER, BRYAN WALLER, 1853, *Letter to James T. Fields, Feb.;* "*Barry Cornwall*" *and Some of His Friends, Harper's Magazine, vol.* 52, *p.* 60.

Takes rank at once with "Jane Eyre," displaying the same vigour—the same exhuberant power—the same bold outline—the same dramatic conception—and the same invincible mastery and fusion of elements usually considered repugnant to romance. — CURTIS, GEORGE WILLIAM, 1853, *Villette and Ruth, Putnam's Magazine, vol.* 1, *p.* 535.

Have you all read "Villette"? and do you not admire the book, and own it as one of the great books of the time? I confess that I have seldom been more impressed with the genius of the writer, and seldom less drawn to her personally. She has nerves of such delicate fineness of edge that the least touch turns them, or she has had an exasperating experience. Whether she calls herself Jane Eyre, or Lucy Snowe, it does not matter—it is Miss Brontë. She has the intensity of Byron—of our own Fanny Kemble. She unconsciously infuses herself into her heroine. It is an egotism whose fires are fed by the inferior vitality of others; and how well she conceives others! how she daguerreotypes them!—SEDGWICK, CATHARINE M., 1853, *To Dr. Dewey, April; Life and Letters, ed. Dewey, p.* 349.

One or two of the *dramatis personæ* evoke sentiments of approval on account of their originality, conspicuous amongst them being Mr. Paul Emanuel and Miss de Bassompierre; but on the whole the book is disappointing, for there is no one character whose fortunes we are anxious to follow; and a novel which fails to beget a personal interest must be said to have lost its chief charm.—SMITH, GEORGE BARNETT, 1875, *The Brontës, Poets and Novelists, p.* 236.

Something has already been said of the true character of that marvellous book, in which her own deepest experiences and ripest wisdom are given to the world. Of the manner in which it was written her readers know nothing. Yet this, the best beloved child of her genius, was brought forth with a travail so bitter that more than once she was tempted to lay aside her pen and hush her voice forever. Every sentence was wrung from her as though it had been a drop of blood, and the book was built up by bit and bit, amid paroxysms of positive anguish, occasioned in part by her own physical weakness and suffering, but still more by the torture through which her mind passed as she depicted scene after scene from the darkest chapter in her own life, for the benefit of those for whom she wrote. It is from her letters at this time also we get the best indications of what she was passing through. Few, perhaps, reading these letters would suppose that their writer was at that very time engaged in the production of a great masterpiece, destined to hold its own among the ripest and finest

fruits of English genius. — REID, T.
WEMYSS, 1877, *Charlotte Brontë, A Monograph, p.* 127.

The tale deserves the epithet, wonderful.
All honour to the author who wielded the
magical wand that "evolved" its scenes
and incidents; all credit to the critics who
celebrated the feat "with one burst of acclamation." But the great world does
not care a straw whether a work of fiction
is a miracle of evolution or not, but only
whether the thing evolved is an interesting
novel.—BAYNE, PETER, 1881, *Two Great
Englishwomen, p.* 243.

"Villette" appears to be a thing of
memories rather than of dreams; of bitter
memories, too, and of despairing resigna-
tions. If people do not read it, one can
only say, like the cook in "Ravenshoe,"
that one "does not wonder at it."—LANG,
ANDREW, 1889, *Charlotte Brontë, Good
Words, vol.* 30, *p.* 239.

"Villette" is full of scenes which one can
trace to incidents which occurred during
Miss Brontë's visits to us. The scene at
the theatre at Brussels in that book, and
the description of the actress, were suggested
by Rachel, whom we took her to see
more than once. The scene of the fire
comes from a slight incident to the scenery
at Devonshire House, where Charles Dickens, Mr. Foster, and other men of letters
gave a performance. . . . In "Villette" my mother was the original of "Mrs.
Bretton"; several of her expressions are
given *verbatim.* I myself, as I discovered,
stood for "Dr. John." Charlotte Brontë
admitted this herself to Mrs. Gaskell, to
whom she wrote: "I was kept waiting
longer than usual for Mr. Smith's opinion
of the book, and I was rather uneasy, for I
was afraid he had found me out, and was
offended."—SMITH, SIR GEORGE MURRAY,
1901, *In the Early Forties, The Critic, vol.*
38, *p.* 59.

GENERAL

It seems to us, that the authoress of
"Jane Eyre" combines all the natural and
incidental attributes of the novelist of her
day. In the ecclesiastical tendencies of
her education and habits—in the youthful
ambiguity of her politics—in a certain
old-world air, which hangs about her
pictures, we see her passports into circles
which otherwise she would never reach.
Into them she is carrying, unperceived,
the elements of infallible disruption and

revolution. In the specialties of her religious belief, her own self-grown and glorious
heterodoxies—in the keen satiric faculty
she has shown—in the exuberant and
multiform vigour of her idiosyncrasy—in
her unmistakable hatred of oppression,
and determination to be free—in the onward
tendencies of a genius so indisputably original, and in the reaction of a time
on which, if she lives, she cannot fail to act
strongly, we acknowledge the best pledge
that the passport, already torn, will be one
day scattered to the winds.—DOBELL,
SYDNEY, 1850, *Currer Bell, Life and Letters of Sydney Dobell, ed. Jolly, vol.* I, *p.* 183.

To think of your asking such a question
as "Do I care about Charlotte Brontë"!
As if I did not care everything I am capable
of caring for anything! As if Levi and I
hadn't read her books with rapture, and
hadn't looked forward to the publishing
of Mrs. Gaskell's book about her as one of
the most interesting things that could happen; as if we didn't lament her loss to the
world every year of our lives!—THAXTER,
CELIA, 1857, *To E. C. Hoxie, March* 28;
Letters, ed. A. F. and R. L., p. 8.

The circulation of Charlotte Brontë's
novels has always been large, and grows
larger and larger every year.—HASSARD,
JNO. R. G., 1871, *The New York Mercantile Library, Scribner's Monthly, vol.* 1, *p.*
364.

Charlotte Brontë was all genius and
ignorance. — McCARTHY, JUSTIN, 1872,
*George Eliot and George Lewes, Modern
Leaders, p.* 137.

In proportion to her means of cultivation, is about the most remarkable of recent literary phenomena.—STEPHEN, LES-
LIE, 1874, *Hours in a Library, p.* 221.

One of the greatest among women. . . .
Some portion of a faculty such as this,
some touch of the same god-like and
wonder-working might of imperious moral
quality, some flush of the same divine and
plenary inspiration, there was likewise in
the noble genius and heroic instinct of Charlotte Brontë. Some part of the power
denied to many a writer of more keen and
rare intelligence than even hers we feel "to
the finest fibre of our nature" at the slight,
strong touch of her magnetic hand.—
SWINBURNE, ALGERNON CHARLES, 1877,
A Note on Charlotte Brontë, pp 1, 68.

It is seldom that the critic has so enticing
a bit of work cut out for him as is afforded

by the Brontë literature, and in particular by Charlotte Brontë. The mysterious thing called genius, of which critics ought to feel themselves the humble ministers and hierophants, has not often lent himself so kindly to scientific inquisition. The celestial spark, the immortal germ, can in this instance be traced in its origin, followed in its development, estimated in its fruits.—BAYNE, PETER, 1881, *Two Great Englishwomen*, p. 326.

Say that two foreigners have passed through Staffordshire, leaving us their reports of what they have seen. The first, going by day, will tell us of the hideous blackness of the country, but yet more, no doubt, of that awful, patient struggle of man with fire and darkness, of the grim courage of those unknown lives; and he would see what they toil for, women with little children in their arms; and he would notice the blue sky beyond the smoke, doubly precious for such horrible environment. But the second traveller has journeyed through the night; neither squalor nor ugliness, neither sky nor children, has he seen, only a vast stretch of blackness shot through with flaming fires, or here and there burned to a dull red by heated furnaces; and before these, strange toilers, half naked, scarcely human, and red in the leaping flicker and gleam of the fire. The meaning of their work he could not see, but a fearful and impressive phantasmagoria of flame and blackness and fiery energies at work in the encompassing night. So differently did the black country of this world appear to Charlotte, clear-seeing and compassionate, and to Emily Brontë, a traveller through the shadows.—ROBINSON, A. MARY F., 1883, *Emily Brontë* (*Famous Women*), p. 5.

Turning to the Brontës, does not one feel the very heartbeats of womanhood in those powerful utterances that seem to spring from some central emotional energy?—BLIND, MATHILDE, 1883, *George Eliot* (*Famous Women*), p. 6.

Charlotte Brontë probably never realized what a serious thing it is to be a poet, or even to write poetry. She regarded poetry as a mode of expressing herself always quite open to her whenever she chose to give it the preference over prose. Her verses therefore are articles of manufacture, the poetry of commerce, and must be classed accordingly. They are certainly made of

good materials—sound sense, fortitude, and affection. Occasionally a friendly reader will discern traces of a happier mood, when she ceases to be a manufacturer, and almost becomes a singer.—BIRRELL, AUGUSTINE, 1887, *Life of Charlotte Brontë* (*Great Writers*), p. 89.

The lady who writes has a headache, and feels internally wretched. She is "conducting herself very creditably, considering"; but her dark brow shows how limited is the life she looks out upon, and how a passionate heart eager for love and happiness beats itself against the wires of her little world. When society is better or worse than it is to-day, when governesses no longer exist, these tales will tell people what life looked like to governesses. In them we are always at the governess's point of view. A young lady who is a guest and not a guest, a servant and not a servant, poor and clever among the dull and rich, is watching them, despising them, detesting them, and taking her proud, envious notes of them and their ways. . . . Now here was a modern prophetess, as it were, a fierce Yorkshire Deborah, with clear, forbidding, condemning eyes—here was a heart almost never out of pain. It is cruel and touching, the picture of Miss Brontë studying the reviews of her books, "in hopes of extracting precept and advice from which to profit." There is uncommonly little gold in all the sands of reviews, even when the critic, like Mr. G. H. Lewes, has himself written what he takes for a romance.—LANG, ANDREW, 1889, *Charlotte Brontë, Good Words, vol. 30*, pp. 237, 239.

Not until the greatest of women romancers arose in Charlotte Brontë was passion represented as it could only have been conceived by a woman.—RALEIGH, WALTER, 1894, *The English Novel*, p. 253.

Charlotte Brontë had, in the highest degree, that which Ruskin had called the "pathetic fallacy," the eye which beholds Nature coloured by the light of the inner soul. In this quality she really reaches the level of fine poetry. Her intense sympathy with her native moors and glens is akin to that of Wordsworth. She almost never attempts to describe any scenery with which she is not deeply familiar. But how wonderfully she catches the tone of her own moorland, skies, storm-winds, secluded hall or cottage. . . . Charlotte Brontë

LEIGH HUNT

*Engraving by H. W. Smith. From a
Portrait by J. Hayter.*

SAMUEL ROGERS

*Engraving by H. Robinson. From a Portrait
by Sir Thomas Lawrence.*

is great in clouds, like a prose Shelley. . . . Charlotte Brontë painted not the world, hardly a corner of the world, but the very soul of one proud and loving girl. That is enough; we need ask no more. It was done with consummate power. We feel that we know her life, from ill-used childhood to her proud matronhood; we know her home, her school, her professional duties, her loves and hates, her agonies and her joys, with that intense familiarity and certainty of vision with which our own personal memories are graven on our brain.— HARRISON, FREDERIC, 1895, *Studies in Early Victorian Literature, pp.* 154, 155, 162.

The first of women-writers of every age. —BENSON, ARTHUR CHRISTOPHER, 1895-96, *Essays, p.* 277.

Charlotte Brontë was likewise deficient in humour. This might be safely inferred from her works, where there are hardly any humourous characters or situations; and the inference would be confirmed by her life. Her letters, often excellent for their common sense and their high standard of duty, and sometimes for their dignity, are almost destitute of playfulness. Neither does she seem to have readily recognized humour in others. She admired Thackeray above almost all men of her time, but she was completely puzzled by him when they met. She lectured him on his faults and quaintly adds that his excuses made them worse. The humourist was playing with too serious a mind. Had Miss Brontë been as Irish in nature as she was by blood she would not have made this mistake.— WALKER, HUGH, 1897, *The Age of Tennyson, p.* 105.

The pain of unrequited affection is the feeling she never tires of depicting, and in describing this she has no equal. Her novels may end happily, but not till they have been made the medium of exhibiting the suffering which the master passion brings with it when unaccompanied by hope. Nowhere else are to be found such piercing cries of lonely anguish as may be heard in "Shirley" and "Villette." They are the very *de profundis* of love sunk in the abyss of despair. And their author insists throughout how much greater this suffering must be for women than for men, both because they are doomed to bear in silence, and because they have not the distraction of an active career.—MACKAY, ANGUS M., 1897, *The Brontës: Fact and Fiction, p.* 41.

Her style has none of the sharp falsetto note that might be expected from a woman in a passion; in spite of her fondness for melodramatic incident, Miss Brontë bridles her tongue and speaks with a terseness, a precision of phrase, and a reticence that might well serve as models for such modern masters of sensational fiction as Hall Caine. Charlotte Brontë is in very truth an imaginative artist in prose. She is loyal to the traditions of the best English literature. She has a delicate sense of the worth of words and of the possible beauty of sentences and of the charm of the carefully-wrought paragraph. And this instinct for style is one more reason— and a prepotent one—why her novels are not going to be speedily swept into the dust-bins like the thousand and one novels of the "lady novelists" of to-day,—improvisers all, ready and slovenly reporters of personal anecdote *"femmes qui parlent."*—GATES, LEWIS E., 1900, *Studies and Appreciations, p.* 163.

In one direction Miss Brontë's experience was adequate, namely, in her contact with nature. From her books one comes to know how largely in her life the clouds, the ragged hills, the wide spaces of the Yorkshire moors under sunset or moonlight, made up for the inadequacy of human society and interests. It is true, she has the Gothic trick of setting off her incidents by a sympathetic background; but in a deeper fashion than this she makes nature enter into the warp and woof of her stories through the part which it plays in the most essential elements in them, the inner life of her heroines. — MOODY, WILLIAM VAUGHN, AND LOVETT, ROBERT MORSS, 1902, *A History of English Literature, p.* 375.

Samuel Rogers.

1763–1855

Born at Stoke Newington, 30 July 1763. Educated at schools at Stoke Newington and Hackney. Entered his father's bank about 1775. Contrib. to "Gentleman's Mag.," 1781. Visit to Scotland 1789; to Paris 1802. Gained prominent position as poet; also as collector and patron of fine arts. Visits to Italy, 1815 and 1822. Offered Laureateship, but declined it, 1850. Died, in London, 18 Dec. 1855. Buried in Hornsey Churchyard. Unmarried. *Works*: "An Ode to Superstition" (anon.), 1786; "The Pleasures of Memory" (anon.), 1792; "Epistle to a Friend" (anon.), 1798; "Verses written in Westminster Abbey after the funeral of the Rt. Hon. C. J. Fox" (anon.), [1806]; "The Voyage of Columbus" (anon.), 1810 (priv. ptd., 1808); "Poems," 1812; "Miscellaneous Poems" (with E. C. Knight and others; anon.), 1812; "Jacqueline" (anon.), 1814; "Human Life," 1819; "Italy," pt. i. (anon.), 1822; pt. ii., 1828; revised edn. of the whole, 1830; "Poems" (2 vols.), 1834. *Posthumous*: "Poetical Works," 1856; "Table Talk," ed. by A. Dyce, 1856; "Recollections," ed. by W. Sharpe, 1859 (2nd edn. same year). *Life*: "Early Life," by P. W. Clayden, 1887; "Rogers and his Contemporaries," by P. W. Clayden, 1889.—SHARP, R. FARQUHARSON, 1897, *A Dictionary of English Authors*, p. 240.

PERSONAL

He is a good poet, has a refined taste in all the arts, has a select library of the best editions of the best authors in all languages, has very fine pictures, very fine drawings, and the finest collection of Etruscan vases I ever saw; and moreover, he gives the best dinners to the best company of men of talents and genius I know; the best served, and with the best wines, liqueurs, etc. . . . His books of prints of the greatest engravers from the greatest masters in history, architecture, and antiquities, are of the first class. His house in St. James's Place, looking into the Green Park, is deliciously situated, and furnished with great taste.—BURNEY, CHARLES, 1804, *Diary, May* 1.

Rogers is silent,—and, it is said, severe. When he does talk, he talks well; and, on all subjects of taste, his delicacy of expression is pure as his poetry. If you enter his house—his drawing-room—his library —you of yourself say, this is not the dwelling of a common mind. There is not a gem, a coin, a book, thrown aside on his chimney-piece, his sofa, his table, that does not bespeak an almost fastidious elegance in the possessor. But this very delicacy must be the misery of his existence. Oh the jarrings his disposition must have encountered through life!—BYRON, LORD, 1813, *Journal, Nov.* 22.

I think you very fortunate in having Rogers at Rome. Show me a more kind and friendly man; secondly, one, from good manners, knowledge, fun, taste, and observation, more agreeable; thirdly, a man of more strict political integrity, and of better character in private life. If I were to choose any Englishman in foreign parts whom I should wish to blunder upon, it should be Rogers.—SMYTH, SYDNEY, 1815, *To Lady Holland, Feb.* 1; *Letters, ed. Austin.*

Nose and chin would shame a knocker,
Wrinkles that would puzzle Cocker;
Mouth which marks the envious scorner,
With a scorpion in each corner,
Turning its quick tail to sting you
In the place that most may wring you;
Eyes of lead-like hue and gummy,
Carcass pick'd out from some mummy;
Bowels (but they were forgotten
Save the liver, and that's rotten).
Skin all sallow, flesh all sodden,—
Form the Devil would fright God in.
Is't a corpse stuck up for show,
Galvanized at times to go?
With the Scripture in connexion,
New proof of the resurrection,
Vampire, ghost, or ghoul, what is it?
I would walk ten miles to miss it.
　　—BYRON, LORD, 1818, *Question and Answer.*

At parting, Rogers gave me a gold-mounted pair of glasses, which I will not part with in a hurry. I really like S. R., and have always found him most friendly. —SCOTT, SIR WALTER, 1828, *Journal, May* 25; *Life by Lockhart, ch.* lxxvi.

What a delightful house it is! It looks out on the Green Park just at the most pleasant point. The furniture has been selected with a delicacy of taste quite unique. Its value does not depend on fashion, but must be the same while the fine arts are held in any esteem. In the drawing-room for example, the chimney-pieces are carved by Flaxman into the most beautiful Grecian forms. The book-case is painted by Stothard, in his very best manner, with groups from Chaucer, Shakespeare, and Boccacio. The pictures are not numerous; but every one is excellent. In the dining-room there are also some beautiful paintings. But the three most remarkable objects in that room are, I think, a cast of Pope taken after death by Roubiliac; a noble model in terra-cotta by Michael Angelo, from which he afterwards made one of his finest statues, that of Lorenzo de' Medici; and, lastly a mahogany

table on which stands an antique vase.
—MACAULAY, THOMAS BABINGTON, 1831,
To Hannah M. Macaulay, June 25; *Life
and Letters,* ed. *Trevelyan, ch.* iv.

An elegant, politely malignant old lady
I think.—CARLYLE, THOMAS, 1832, *Journal,
Jan.* 13; *Thomas Carlyle, a History of the
First Forty Years of His Life,* ed. *Froude,
vol.* II, *p.* 187.

I breakfasted with Mr. Rogers tête-â-tête
staying with him from ten till one o'clock.
A very agreeable morning, and I left with
feelings of enhanced respect. There was
very little of that severity of remark for
which he is reproached. Candor and good
sense marked all he said.—ROBINSON,
HENRY CRABB, 1835, *Diary, Nov.* 29;
Diary, Reminiscences and Correspondence,
ed. *Sadler.*

It is a fine thing when a light burns so
clear down into the socket, isn't it? I, who
am not a devout admirer of the "Pleasures
of Memory," do admire this perpetual
youth and untired energy; it is a fine thing
to my mind. Then, there are other noble
characteristics about this Rogers. A common friend said the other day to Mr. Kenyon, "Rogers hates me, I know. He is always
saying bitter speeches in relation to me, and
yesterday he said so and so. *But,*" he continued, "if I were in distress, there is one
man in the world to whom I would go without doubt and without hesitation, at once,
and as to a brother, and *that* man is *Rogers.*"
Not that I would choose to be obliged to a
man who hated me; but it is an illustration
of the fact that if Rogers is bitter in his
words, which we all know he is, he is always
benevolent and generous in his deeds. He
makes an epigram on a man, and gives him
a thousand pounds; and the deed is the
truer expression of his own nature. An uncommon development of character, in any
case.—BROWNING, ELIZABETH BARRETT,
1844, *To Mrs. Martin, Dec.; Letters of
Elizabeth Barrett Browning,* ed. *Kenyon, vol.*
I, *p.* 222.

I met Rhymer near your door, and he
looked so unusually complacent that I
guessed he had been at his old work, endeavouring to make some one dissatisfied.
. . . You must not be disconcerted by
his remarks, for, if I may be allowed to
parody the observation applied to Charles
II., I should say that Rhymer is known
never to have *said* a kind thing, or never to
have *done* an unkind one. He has come to

the assistance of many a man of genius in
those vicissitudes to which individuals of
that class are more than any other liable
when they depend on literature for support.
Towards artists his good word to would-be
patrons, possessed of more gold than taste,
has never been wanting; yet, such is his
peculiarity that, while ready to *serve,* he is
seldom willing to avoid offending, and evidently finds a pleasure in saying disagreeable things. Even his compliments, and
they are few and far between, have something in them which leaves those present in
doubt whether they do not admit of another
and less kind interpretation, although the
individual to whom they are addressed may
not be aware of it. . . . His age and
infirmities screen him from the correction
which his malice so frequently merits; and,
aware of his impunity, he thinks himself
privileged to annoy all those with whom he
comes in contact. But no, not all; for to
the rich and great he is as obsequious as he
is insolent to those who are not in a position
to gratify his *parvenu* taste for grandeur.—
BLESSINGTON, MARGUERITE COUNTESS,
1845, *Strathern.*

Forster called, went with him to Rogers'.
Found the old man very cheerful, thinner
than when I last saw him, but in very good
spirits. He told all his stories "over again."
. . Took leave of dear old Rogers once
more. I think indeed for the last time. I
cannot make out his character. He is surely
good-natured, with philanthropic and religious feelings, but his fondness for saying
a sharp thing shakes one's certainty in
him: his apparent desire too to produce
effect, I think, sometimes awakens doubts
of his sincerity in some minds.—MACREADY,
W. C., 1851, *Diary, May* 4; *Reminiscences,*
ed. *Pollock.*

There is something preternatural in the
cold, clear, marbly paleness that pervades,
and, as it were, penetrates his features to a
depth that seems to preclude all change,
even that of death itself. Yet there is
nothing in the least degree painful or repulsive in the sight, nothing that is suggestive
of death.—PATMORE, PETER GEORGE, 1854,
My Friends and Acquaintance, vol. I, *p.* 160.

It was a curious commentary on his counsel to hear Sydney Smith's account of Mr.
Rogers's method of comparison. The story
is in print, but imperfectly given, and evidently without any consciousness that "the
brooding dove" of Shakespeare is concerned

in it,—"the brooding dove, ere yet her golden couples are disclosed." The conversation took place soon after Rogers had given forth his epigram on Lord Dudley:

"Ward has no heart, they say: but I deny it,
Ward *has* a heart;—and gets his speeches by it."

"Has Rogers written anything lately?" asked somebody; to which another replied, —"No, I believe not. Nothing but a couplet."

"Nothing but a couplet!" exclaimed Sydney Smith. Why, what would you have? When Rogers produces a couplet, he goes to bed:

And the caudle is made:
And the knocker is tied:
And straw is laid down:

And when his friends send to inquire,—'Mr. Rogers is as well as can be expected'."— MARTINEAU, HARRIET, 1855–77, *Autobiography, ed. Chapman, vol.* I, *p.* 324.

The death of the poet Rogers seems almost like the extinction of an institution. The world by his departure has one object the less of interest and reverence. The elegant hospitality which he dispensed for nearly three quarters of a century, and in which Americans had a large share, is brought to an end, and a vacuity is created which no Englishman can supply. . . . Rogers's breakfasts were the pleasantest social meetings that can be conceived of. There you met persons of every variety of intellectual and social distinction, eminent men and attractive women, wits, orators, dramatists, travelers, artists, persons remarkable for their powers of conversation, all of whom found themselves on the easiest terms with their venerable host, whose noon of life was reached in the last century. Even bores, in his society, which discouraged all tediousness, and in the respect which his presence inspired, seemed to lose their usual character, and to fall involuntarily into the lively and graceful flow of conversation of which he gave the example. . . . Mr. Rogers was of low stature, neither slightly nor sturdily proportioned; his face was rather full and broad than otherwise, and his complexion colorless. . . . In conversation, Mr. Rogers was one of the most agreeable and interesting of men; he was remarkable for a certain graceful laconism, a neatness and power of selection in telling a story or expressing a thought, with its accessories, which were the envy of the best talkers of his time. His

articulation was distinct, just deliberate enough to be listened to with pleasure, and during the last ten to twelve years of his life slightly—and but very slightly— marked with the tremulousness of old age. His ordinary manner was kind and paternal; he delighted to relate anecdotes illustrative of the power of the affections, which he did with great feeling. On occasion, however, he could say caustic things; and a few examples of this kind, which were so epigrammatic as to be entertaining in their repetition, have given rise to the mistake that they were frequent in his conversation.— BRYANT, WILLIAM CULLEN, 1855, *Samuel Rogers, Editorial Article, New York Evening Post.*

Holland House has four-and-twenty youthful pages in it now—twelve for my lord and twelve for my lady; and no clergyman coils his leg up under his chair all dinner-time, and begins to uncurve it when the hostess goes. No wheeled chair runs smoothly in, with that beaming face in it; and——'s little cotton pocket-handkerchief helped to make (I believe) this very sheet of paper. A half-sad, half-ludicrous story of Rogers, is all I will sully it with. You know, I dare say, that, for a year or so before his death, he wandered and lost himself, like one of the Children in the Wood, grown up there and grown down again. He had Mrs. Procter and Mrs. Carlyle to breakfast with him one morning—only those two. Both excessively talkative, very quick and clever and bent on entertaining him. When Mrs. Carlyle had flashed and shone before him for about three-quarters of an hour on one subject, he turned his poor old eyes on Mrs. Procter, and, pointing to the brilliant discourser with his poor old finger, said (indignantly), "Who is *she?*" Upon this, Mrs. Procter, cutting in, delivered—(it is her own story)—a neat oration on the life and writings of Carlyle, and enlightened him in her happiest and airiest manner; all of which he heard, staring in the dreariest silence, and then said (indignantly as before), "And who are *you?*"—DICKENS, CHARLES, 1856, *To Washington Irving, July* 5; *Letters, ed. Dickens and Hogarth.*

Rogers was unceasingly at war with the late Lady Davy. One day at dinner she called across the table: "Now, Mr. Rogers, I am sure you are talking about me" (not attacking, as the current version runs). "Lady Davy," was the retort, "I pass my life in defending you."—HAYWARD, ABRAHAM, 1856, *Samuel Rogers, Selected Essays, vol.* I, *p.* 135.

My uncle's conversation could hardly be called brilliant. He seldom aimed at wit, though he enjoyed it in others. He often told anecdotes of his early recollections and of the distinguished persons with whom he had been acquainted. These he told with great neatness and fitness in the choice of words, as may be understood by an examination of the prose notes of his poems. But the valuable part of his conversation was his good sense joined with knowledge of literature and art, and yet more particularly his constant aim at improvement, and the care that he took to lead his friends to what was worth talking about.—SHARPE, SAMUEL, 1859, *Some Particulars of the Life of Samuel Rogers.*

Whatever place may be assigned to Samuel Rogers among poets, he deserves to hold the highest place among men of taste; not merely of taste for this or that, but of general good taste in all things. He was the only man I have ever known (not an artist) who felt the beauties of art like an artist. He was too quiet to exercise the influence he should have maintained among the patrons of art; but, as far as his own patronage extended, it was most useful. He employed, and always spoke his mind in favor of Flaxman, Stothard, and Turner, when they were little appreciated by their countrymen. The proof of his superior judgment to that of any contemporary collector of art or *vertu* is to be found in the fact that there was nothing in his house that was not valuable. — LESLIE, CHARLES ROBERT, 1860, *Autobiographical Recollections, ed. Taylor, p.* 155.

His personal appearance was extraordinary, or rather, his countenance was unique. His skull and facial expression bore so striking a likeness to the skeleton pictures which we sometimes see of Death, that the facetious Sydney Smith (at one of the dressed evening parties . . .) entitled him the "Death-dandy!" And it was told (probably with truth) that the same satirical wag inscribed upon the capital portrait in his breakfast-room, "Painted in his lifetime."—JERDAN, WILLIAM, 1866, *Men I Have Known.*

Spedding (of course) used to deny that R. deserved his ill Reputation: but I never heard any one else deny it. All his little malignities, unless the epigram on Ward be his, are dead along with his little sentimentalities; while Byron's Scourge hangs over his Memory. The only one who, so far as I have seen, has given any idea of his little cavilling style, is Mrs. Trench in her Letters.—FITZGERALD, EDWARD, 1872, *To W. F. Pollock, Nov.* 20; *Letters and Literary Remains, ed. Wright, vol.* II, *p.* 44.

It has been rumored that he was a *sayer* of bitter things. I know that he was a *giver* of good things—a kind and amiable patron, where a patron was wanted; never ostentatious or oppressive, and always a friend in need. He was ready with his counsel; ready with his money. I never put his generosity to the test, but I know enough to testify that it existed, and was often exercised in a delicate manner, and on the slightest hint.—PROCTER, BRYAN WALLER, 1874(?), *Recollections of Men of Letters, ed. Patmore, p.* 150.

Innumerable were the jokes on the *tête morte* of Rogers. Ward, afterwards Lord Dudley, asked him how it was, since he was so well off, he did not set up his hearse; Mackintosh wondered why, when at an election time he could not find accommodation at any hotel in a country town, he did not seek a snug lie down in the churchyard; a French valet, mistaking him for Tom Moore, threw the company into consternation by announcing him as "M. Le Mort"; Scott advised him to try his fortune in medicine in which he would be sure to succeed, if there was any truth in physiognomy, on the strength of his having a perpetual *facies Hippocratica;* Hook, meeting him at Lord Byron's funeral, gave him the friendly caution to keep out of the sight of the undertaker lest that functionary should claim him as one of his old customers; but the story which caps all is that in the *John Bull,* to the effect that when Rogers one night hailed a coach in St. Paul's churchyard, the jarvey cried—"Ho, ho, my man; I'm not going to be had in that way: go back to your grave!"—BATES, WILLIAM, 1874–98, *The Maclise Portrait Gallery of Illustrious Literary Characters, p.* 13.

His head was very fine, and I never could quite understand the satirical sayings about his personal appearance which have crept into the literary gossip of his time. He was by no means the vivacious spectre some of his contemporaries have represented him. His dome of brain was one of the amplest and most perfectly shaped I ever saw, and his countenance was very far from unpleasant. His turn of thought was characteristic, and in the main just, for he loved the best, and was naturally impatient of what was low and mean in conduct and intellect. —FIELDS, JAMES T., 1875, *"Barry Cornwall" and Some of his Friends, Harper's Magazine, vol.* 51, *p.* 793.

My first look at the poet then in his seventy-eighth year, was an agreeable surprise, and a protest in my mind against the malignant injustice which had been done him. As a young man he might have been uncomely if not as ugly as his revilers had painted him, but as an old man there was an intellectual charm in his countenance and a fascination in his manner which more than atoned for any deficiency of personal beauty.—MACKAY, CHARLES, 1877, *Forty Years' Recollections of Life, Literature and Public Affairs, from* 1830 *to* 1870.

When I used to go and sit with Mr. Rogers, I never asked him what I should read to him without his putting into my hands his own poems, which always lay by him on his table.—KEMBLE, FRANCES ANN, 1882, *Records of Later Life, p.* 66.

You could not fancy, when you looked upon him, that you saw a good man. It was a repulsive countenance; to say it was ugly would be to pay it a compliment, and I verily believe it was indicative of a naturally shrivelled heart and contracted soul. . . . With enormous power to do good, how did Rogers use it? If he lent— and it was seldom he did—to a distressed brother of the pen, he required the return of a loan with interest—when it could be had; if he gave, it was grudgingly and with a shrug. He was prudence personified; some one said of him: "I am sure that as a baby he never fell down unless he was pushed, but walked from chair to chair in the drawing-room, steadily and quietly, till he reached a place where the sunbeams fell on the carpet."—HALL, SAMUEL CARTER, 1883, *Retrospect of a Long Life, pp.* 370, 371.

Rogers had now [1804] cut himself entirely free from business. His youngest brother Henry had become the active partner and working head of the banking firm, and there was no occasion for the chief partner to trouble himself with its concerns. His income, though not large, was sufficient for one who had only a bachelor's

establishment to maintain, and who "led the life of satisfied desires." He had no expensive habits beyond those which sprang from a determination to make his house the ideal abode of the man of taste and the man of letters. He had not even the ambition to become the patron of poor authors, though circumstances were continually forcing that duty on him. His wish was to surround himself with what was best, and he chose his friends as he chose his pictures and his furniture,—for their quality in this noblest sense. It soon became known that the charming house in St. James's Place, about which society was talking, was open to all who had claim to be regarded as men of letters, or artists, or wits, or statesmen: though of the latter, it was chiefly the whigs who found themselves at home.— CLAYDEN, P. W., 1887, *The Early Life of Samuel Rogers, p.* 395.

He was willing to take great pains and trouble for his friends, his friends' friends, and even for people who had no claim upon him—whether it were simply providing for their amusement, in obtaining them places in the British Museum, or under the Government (as with Cary, the translator of Dante, and others), or in negotiating with publishers for the publication of their works (as with Wordsworth).—SCHUYLER, EUGENE, 1889–1901, *Samuel Rogers, Italian Influences, p.* 338.

THE PLEASURES OF MEMORY
1792

"The Pleasures of Memory," by Mr. Rogers, is another effort of the modern muses which calls for admiration; the subject is happily chosen, and its polished flow of verse and tender sentiment have justly made it a favorite with the public.—DRAKE, NATHAN, 1798–1820, *Literary Hours, vol.* II, *No.* XXIX, *p.* 118.

It is not uninteresting, even as a matter of speculation, to observe the fortune of a poem which, like the "Pleasures of Memory," appeared at the commencement of this literary revolution, without paying court to the revolutionary tastes, or seeking distinction by resistance to them. . . . No production, so popular, was probably ever so little censured by criticism. It was approved by the critics, as much as read and applauded by the people; and thus seemed to combine the applause of contemporaries with the suffrage of the representatives of Posterity.—MACKINTOSH, SIR

JAMES, 1813, *Rogers's Poems, Edinburgh Review, vol.* 22, *pp.* 38, 39.

He is a very lady-like poet. He is an elegant but feeble writer. He wraps up obvious thoughts in a glittering cover of fine words; it is full of enigmas with no meaning to them; is scrupulously inverted, and scrupulously far-fetched; and his verses are poetry chiefly because no particle, line, or syllable of them reads like prose. . . . You cannot see the thought for ambiguity, of the language, the figure for the finery, the picture for the varnish. The whole is refined and frittered away into an appearance of the most evanescent brilliancy and tremulous imbecility. There is no other fault to be found with the "Pleasures of Memory" than a want of taste and genius.—HAZLITT, WILLIAM, 1818, *Lectures on the English Poets, Lecture* III.

The name of Mr. Rogers will naturally awaken the recollection of the delight experienced from the perusal of his "Pleasures of Memory": thus making this very *reminiscence* illustrative of the propriety of the title of the poem. That poem, conceived with so much delicacy and truth, and executed with so much care and polish, will maintain the reputation which it has acquired. It is a happy union of the sweetness of Goldsmith with the finish of Pope. It has gone through countless editions, and equally charms the young on the coming, and the aged on the parting, year. 'Tis a sort of staple commodity in the market of booksellers.—DIBDIN, THOMAS FROGNALL, 1824, *The Library Companion, p.* 738, *note.*

In the "Pleasures of Memory" we are forcibly reminded of Goldsmith and the "Deserted Village." We feel how deeply the genius of that exquisite writer had affected the mind of Rogers in his youth. There is a striking similarity of style, of imagery, and of subject. . . . Out of the "Pleasures of Memory" sprung the "Pleasures of Hope." The direct imitation of both style, manner, subject and cast of subject, by Campbell, is one of the most striking things in the language; the peculiarities of the style and phraseology only, as was natural by an enthusiastic youth, much exaggerated.—HOWITT, WILLIAM, 1847, *Homes and Haunts of the Most Eminent British Poets, vol.* II.

Although its highest passages are not so high as the finest in "The Pleasures or Hope," it is freer from traces of juvenility,

and, with less of ardent enthusiasm, may be said to be better sustained throughout. Yet it also has its more prominent passages; and these, as it strikes me, are the twilight landscape with which it opens; the introduction to the tale of Derwent Lake; the allusion to the Savoyard Boy leaving the Alps; the apostrophe to the Bee, as illustrative of the powers of memory; the affecting reference to a deceased brother; and the lines on Greenwich Hospital.—MOIR, D. M., 1851–52, *Sketches of the Poetical Literature of the Past Half-Century, p.* 48.

"The Pleasures of Memory" is an excellent specimen of what Wordsworth calls "the *accomplishment* of verse"; and it was well worthy to attract attention and admiration at the time when it appeared; for at that time poetry, with few exceptions, was to be distinguished from prose by versification and little else. "The Pleasures of Memory" is an essay in verse, not wanting in tender sentiment and just reflection, expressed, graceful no doubt, but with a formal and elaborate grace, and in studiously pointed and carefully poised diction, such as the heroic couplet had been trained to assume since the days of Pope.—TAYLOR, SIR HENRY, 1880, *The English Poets, ed. Ward, vol.* IV, *p.* 89.

Rogers's "Pleasures of Memory" was not only better than any other imitation of Akenside, but it was better than Akenside. There was a simpler and truer grace of style, due partly to change of literary fashion; a theme pleasant to every reader; and the ease of a man of taste who could give and take refined pleasure, but "whose sails were never to the tempest given." Samuel Rogers might have become an English author of great mark if, at some time before he was forty years old, his bank had broken.—MORLEY, HENRY, 1881, *Of English Literature in the Reign of Victoria with a Glance at the Past, p.* 117.

The secret of Rogers' poetical reputation, which lasted for many years, is not easy to understand. The utmost that can be said in favour of the "Pleasures of Memory," to which he owed his fame, is that it has somewhat of Goldsmith's sweetness though without his strength, and that the sentiment of the poem claims the reader's sympathy. But if we seek in poetry for high imaginations, for rare fancy, for an exquisitely felicitous use of language, we shall not find them in the smooth lines of

Rogers. — DENNIS, JOHN, 1889, *Samuel Rogers, Leisure Hour, vol.* 38, *p.* 386.

HUMAN LIFE
1819

"I'm told, dear Moore, your lays are sung
  (Can it be true, you lucky man?)
By moonlight, in the Persian tongue,
  Along the streets of Ispahan.
" 'Tis hard; but one reflection cures,
  At once, a jealous poet's smart.
The Persians have translated yours,
  But Lauderdale has mine by heart."

— LUTTRELL HENRY, 1819(?), *Rogers to Moore, on the Hearing that Lord Lauderdale had "Human Life" by heart.*

These are very sweet verses. They do not, indeed, stir the spirit like the strong lines of Byron, nor make our hearts dance within us, like the inspiring strains of Scott; but they come over us with a bewitching softness that, in certain moods, is still more delightful—and soothe the troubled spirits with a refreshing sense of truth, purity, and elegance. They are pensive rather than passionate; and more full of wisdom and tenderness than of high flights of fancy, or overwhelming bursts of emotion—while they are moulded into grace, at least as much by the effect of the moral beauties they disclose, as by the taste and judgment with which they are constructed.—JEFFREY, FRANCIS LORD, 1819–44, *Rogers's Human Life, Contributions to the Edinburgh Review, vol.* III, *p.* 120.

The poem itself is one of the most beautiful things in any language. It is human life from the cradle to the tomb, with all its pleasures, aspirations, trials, and triumphs. . . . Never, either, were the varied scenes of English life more sweetly described.—HOWITT, WILLIAM, 1847, *Homes and Haunts of the Most Eminent British Poets, vol.* II.

ITALY
1822-28

A poem full of moral and descriptive sweetness, and written in the chastened tone of fine taste.—HALLAM, HENRY, 1837–39, *Introduction to the Literature of Europe, pt.* i, *ch.* iii, *par.* 60, *note.*

"Italy," to our mind, is the freshest and finest of all the compositions of its author—the one most unequivocally his own, and the one whose passages most frequently recur to mind, from their peculiar graces of style and language. . . . Whatever portion of the writings of Samuel Rogers may die, this tale cannot.—MOIR, D. M., 1851–52, *Sketches of the Poetical Literature of the Past Half-Century, pp.* 51, 53.

After the passionate melancholy and intense ideality of "Childe Harold," the tone of "Italy" will seem languid and its colors faint, especially to the young; but it wears well to the end. Men who have lived through the Byron age, in their own lives, are a little shy of the poetry which is so strongly associated with past conflicts and spent storms; but the mellow wisdom, the genial sympathy, the graceful pictures, and the perfect taste of Rogers, are not fully appreciated till our shadows have begun to lengthen. It is, indeed, a delightful poem; a work of such perfect art that the art is nowhere seen; with just the right amount of personal feeling; with a warm sense of all that is attractive to a poet and a scholar in Italy, a generous judgment of all that is distasteful to an Englishman and a Protestant, and full of charming pictures which seem to demand those exquisite illustrations of Stothard and Turner with which they are so inseparably united in our minds.—HILLARD GEORGE STILLMAN, 1853, *Six Months in Italy, p.* 551.

Save on this solitary occasion, however, the amiable Muse of Rogers never forgot what was due to her self-respect, and clung close to the manner of Goldsmith, slowly and faintly relaxing the rigour of versification in a blank verse "Italy," but never, in a single graceful line, quite reaching the point of poetry.—GOSSE, EDMUND, 1897, *A Short History of Modern English Literature, p.* 319.

GENERAL

I can visit the justly-admired author of "The Pleasures of Memory," and find myself with a friend, who together with the brightest genius possesses elegance of manners and excellence of heart. He tells me he remembers the day of our first meeting at Mr. Dilly's; I also remember it, and though his modest, unassuming nature held back and shrunk from all appearances of ostentation and display of talents, yet even then I take credit for discovering a promise of good things to come, and suspected him of holding secret commerce with the Muse, before the proof appeared in shape of one of the most beautiful and harmonious poems in our language. I do not say that he has not ornamented the age he lives in, though he were to stop where he is, but I do hope he will not so totally deliver himself over to the arts as to neglect the Muses; and I now publicly call upon Samuel Rogers to answer to his name, and stand forth in the title page of some future work that shall be in substance greater, in dignity of subject more sublime, and in purity of versification not less charming than his poem above mentioned.—CUMBERLAND, RICHARD, 1807, *Memoirs Written by Himself, vol.* II, *p.* 229.

The last Argonaut of Classic English poetry, and the Nestor of our inferior race of living poets.—BYRON, LORD, 1821, *On Bowles's Strictures on Pope.*

I confess that I cannot understand the popularity of his poetry. It is pleasant and flowing enough, less monotonous than most of the imitations of Pope and Goldsmith, and calls up many agreeable images and recollections. But that such men as Lord Granville, Lord Holland, Hobhouse, Lord Byron, and others of high rank in intellect, should place Rogers, as they do, above Southey, Moore, and even Scott himself, is what I cannot conceive. But this comes of being in the highest society in London. What Lady Jane Granville called the Patronage of Fashion can do as much for a middling poet as for a plain girl like Miss Arabella Falconer.—MACAULAY, THOMAS BABINGTON, 1831, *To Hannah M. Macaulay, June* 3; *Life and Letters, ed. Trevelyan, ch.* iv.

One of our greatest poets and finest prose writers; who to this unstable fame adds the more imperishable renown of being one of the most honourable men, and most uncompromising friends of civil and religious liberty, who have appeared in any age.—BROUGHAM, HENRY LORD, 1839-43-55, *Historical Sketches of Statesmen who Flourished in the Time of George III, vol.* I, *p.* 341.

Professional authors are apt either to sneer at a banker or merchant who obtains applause for transient literary offerings, or to attempt to lure him by lying idealities into their own Slough of Despond. There is hardly a hack in Great Britain, who has not, either in penny newspaper or sentimental magazine, directed his popgun of wit against Samuel Rogers, the banker and poet.—WHIPPLE, EDWIN PERCY, 1844, *Poets and Poetry of America, Essays and Reviews, vol.* I, *p.* 38.

Rogers is the poet of home; his charm consists in painting the scenes of infancy—

portraying the endearments of youth; and he is read by all with such pleasure in mature life, because he recalls ideas and revives images which all have known, but which have been almost forgotten though not destroyed by the cares and anxieties of life.— ALISON, SIR ARCHIBALD, 1853, *History of Europe, 1815-52, ch.* v.

Rogers was a poet of *culture.* His workmanship is artistic in a high degree, his diction as clear and polished as art can make it, and his versification everywhere elegant, refined, and graceful. He paints us finely-finished pictures, suffused with soft and mellow light, and exhibits them in carefully carven frames—pictures that awaken gentle sympathy and stimulate quiet thought—pictures that please without moving us. He is often tender in sentiment and wise in reflection; but he lacks force and originality, and is altogether destitute of passion. He never annoys us with the faults of taste and style which disfigure the writings of some greater poets; but, on the other hand, he never thrills our emotions nor fires our imaginations as they do. He manipulates the heroic couplet with skill and grace.—MILES, ALFRED H., 1891, *The Poets and the Poetry of the Century, Crabbe to Coleridge, p.* 127.

Rogers's title to a place among the representatives of the most brilliant age—the drama apart—of English poetry cannot now be challenged, but his rank is lower than that of any of his contemporaries, and his position is due in great measure to two fortunate accidents: the establishment of his reputation before the advent, or at least the recognition, of more potent spirits, and the intimate association of his name with that of greater men. He has, however, one peculiar distinction, that of exemplifying beyond almost any other poet what a moderate poetical endowment can effect when prompted by ardent ambition and guided by refined taste. Among the countless examples of splendid gifts marred or wasted, it is pleasing to find one of mediocrity elevated to something like distinction by fastidious care and severe toil. It must also be allowed that his inspiration was genuine as far as it went, and that it emanated from a store of sweetness and tenderness actually existing in the poet's nature.—GARNETT, RICHARD, 1897, *Dictionary of National Biography, vol.* XLIX, *p.* 14.

Mary Russell Mitford
1787–1855

Born, at Alresford, Hampshire, 16 Dec. 1787. At school in London, 1798–1802. Precocious literary ability. Lived with her parents at Reading, 1802–1820. They removed to Three Mile Cross, near Reading, April 1820; she lived there till 1851. Contrib. "Our Village" to "Lady's Mag." from 1819. Play "Julian" produced at Covent Garden, 15 March 1823; "Foscari," Covent Garden, 4 Nov. 1826; "Rienzi," Drury Lane, 9 Oct. 1828; "Charles I.," Victoria Theatre, July 1834; libretto of opera "Sadak and Kalascade," Lyceum Theatre, 20 April 1835. Contributed to various periodicals. Friendship with Mrs. Browning begun, 1836. Civil List Pension, 1837. Edited "Finden's Tableaux," 1838–41. Removed to Swallowfield, near Reading, 1851. Died there, 10 Jan. 1855. Buried in village churchyard. *Works*: "Miscellaneous Poems," 1810; "Christina," 1811; "Watlington Hill," 1812; "Blanche of Castile," 1812; "Narrative Poems on the Female Character," 1813; "Julian," 1823 (3rd edn. same year); "Our Village," vol. i., 1824; vol. ii., 1826; vol. iii., 1828; vol. iv., 1830; vol. v., 1832 (complete, 1843); "Foscari," 1826; "Dramatic Scenes, Sonnets and other Poems," 1827; "Rienzi," 1828 (4th edn. same year); "Stories of American Life," 1830; "The Sister's Budget" (anon.),1831; "American Stories for Children," 1832; "Charles the First," 1834; "Belford Regis," 1835; "Sadak and Kalascade" [1835]; "Country Stories," 1837; "Works" (Philadelphia), 1841; "Recollections of a Literary Life" (3 vols.), 1852; "Atherton," 1854; "Dramatic Works" (2 vols.), 1854. *Posthumous*: "Life . . . in a selection from her Letters," ed. by A. G. L'Estrange (3 vols.), 1870 [1869]; "Letters . . . Second series," ed. by H. Chorley (2 vols.), 1872. She *edited*: "Stories of American Life," 1830; "Lights and Shadows of American Life," 1832; "Tales for Young People . . . Selected from American Writers," 1835; "Fragments des Œuvres d'A. Dumas," 1846.— SHARP, R. FARQUHARSON, 1897, *A Dictionary of English Authors*, p. 200.

PERSONAL

Our residence is a cottage—no, not a cottage—it does not deserve the name— messuage or tenement, such as a little farmer who had made twelve or fourteen hundred pounds might retire to when he left off business to live on his means. It consists of a series of closets, the largest of which may be about eight feet square, which they call parlors, and kitchens, and pantries; some of them minus a corner, which has been unnaturally filched for a chimney; others deficient in half a side, which has been truncated by the shelving roof. Behind is a garden about the size of a good drawing-room, with an arbor which is a complete sentry-box of privet. On one side a public-house, on the other a village shop, and right opposite a cobbler's stall. Notwithstanding all this, "the cabin," as Bobadil says, "is convenient." It is within reach of my dear old walks; the banks where I find my violets; the meadows full of cowslips; and the woods where the wood-sorrel blows.— MITFORD, MARY RUSSELL, 1820, *Letter to Sir William Elford, April 8; Life of Mary Russell Mitford, ed. L'Estrange, vol. I, ch. xv.*

You must know I have a great horror about hearing about Miss M., for she once wrote me a letter in which she called me a delightful poet, and no less delightful *proser*; which I did not know whether to take for a panegyric, or a satire; so I never answered the letter, which was horribly unpolite; and I have ever since, when I hear her name mentioned, not known whether to feel remorse or satisfaction.—HUNT, LEIGH, 1825, *To Elizabeth Kent, Jan. 4; Correspondence, ed. Hunt, vol. I, p. 235.*

We found Miss Mitford living literally in a cottage, neither *ornée* nor poetical,— except inasmuch as it had a small garden crowded with the richest and most beautiful profusion of flowers,—where she lives with her father, a fresh, stout old man who is in his seventy-fifth year. She herself seemed about fifty, short and fat, with very gray hair perfectly visible under her cap,and nicely arranged in front. She had the simplest and kindest manners, and entertained us for two hours with the most animated conversation and a great variety of anecdote, without any of the pretensions of an author by profession, and without any of the stiffness that generally belongs to single ladies of her age and reputation.—TICKNOR, GEORGE, 1835, *Journal, July 26; Life, Letters and Journals, vol. I, p. 418.*

It is long since I have been so pleased with any one,whether for sweetness of voice,

kindness and cheerfulness of countenance
(with *one* look which reminds me of a look, I
shall meet no more), or high-bred plainness
of manner. I was fascinated.—CHORLEY,
HENRY FOTHERGILL, 1836, *Autobiography,
Memoir and Letters, vol.* I, *p.* 200.

Our coachman (who, after telling him
that we were Americans, had complimented
us on our speaking English, and "very good
English too,") professed an acquaintance of
some twenty years' standing with Miss M.,
and assured us that she was one of the "cleverest women in England," and "the doctor"
(her father) an " 'earty old boy." And
when he reined his horses up at her door,
and she appeared to receive us, he said,
"Now you would not take that little body
there for a great author, would you?" And
certainly we should have taken her for
nothing but a kindly gentlewoman, who
had never gone beyond the narrow sphere
of the most refined social life. . . . Miss M.,
is truly "a little body," and dressed a little
quaintly, and as unlike as possible to the
faces we have seen of her in the magazines
which all have a broad humour bordering
on coarseness. She has a pale-gray, soul-lit
eye, and hair as white as snow; a wintry
sign that has come prematurely upon her,
as like signs come upon us, while the year
is yet fresh and undecayed. Her voice has a
sweet, low tone, and her manner a naturalness, frankness, and affectionateness that
we have been so long familiar with in their
other modes of manifestation, that it would
have been indeed a disappointment not to
have found them. She led us directly
through her house into her garden, a perfect bouquet of flowers. "I must show you
my geraniums while it is light," she said,
"for I love them next to my father."—
SEDGWICK, CATHARINE M., 1839-41, *Letters
from Abroad to Kindred at Home, vol.* I,
p. 46.

> None hath told
> More pleasant tales to young and old.
> Fondest was she of Father Thames,
> But rambled to Hellenic streams;
> Nor even there could any tell
> As Mary Mitford. . . . Verse! go forth
> And breathe o'er gentle breasts her worth,
> Needless the task; but, should she see
> One hearty wish from you and me,
> A moment's pain it may assuage,—
> A rose-leaf on the couch of Age.

—LANDOR, WALTER SAVAGE, 1854, *To
Mary Russell Mitford.*

I must say that personally I did not like
her so well as I liked her works. The charming *bonhommie* of her writings appeared at
first in her conversation and manners; but
there were other things which sadly impaired its charm. It is no part of my business to pass judgment on her views and
mode of life. What concerned me was her
habit of flattery, and the twin habit of disparagement of others. I never knew her
respond to any act or course of conduct
which was morally lofty. She could not believe in it, nor, of course, enjoy it: and she
seldom failed to "see through" it, and delight in her superiority to admiration. She
was a devoted daughter, where the duty
was none of the easiest; and the servants
and neighbors were sincerely attached to
her. The little intercourse I had with her
was spoiled by her habit of flattery.—
MARTINEAU, HARRIET, 1855-77, *Autobiography, ed. Chapman, vol.* I, *p.* 316.

It was a great, warm, outflowing heart,
and the head was worthy of the heart. People have observed that she resembled Coleridge in her granite forehead—something,
too, in the lower part of the face—however
unlike Coleridge in mental characteristics,
in his tendency to abstract speculation, or
indeed his ideality. There might have been
as you suggest, a somewhat different development elsewhere in Berkshire—not
very different, though—souls don't grow
out of the ground. I agree quite with you
that she was stronger and wider in her conversation and letters than in her books.
Oh, I have said so a hundred times. The
heat of human sympathy seemed to bring
out her powerful vitality, rustling all over
with laces and flowers. She seemed to think
and speak stronger holding a hand—not
that she required help or borrowed a word,
but that the human magnetism acted on
her nature, as it does upon men born to
speak. . . . If she loved a person, it was
enough. She made mistakes one couldn't
help smiling at, till one grew serious to
adore her for it. And yet when she read a
book, provided it wasn't written by a
friend, edited by a friend, lent by a friend,
or associated with a friend, her judgment
could be fine and discriminating on most
subjects, especially upon subjects connected with life and society and manners.—
BROWNING, ELIZABETH BARRETT, 1855,
To Mr. Ruskin, Nov. 5; *Letters of Elizabeth Barrett Browning, ed. Kenyon, vol.*
II, *pp.* 216, 217.

It surprised me to hear allusions indicating that Miss Mitford was not the invariably amiable person that her writings would suggest; but the whole drift of what they said tended, nevertheless, towards the idea that she was an excellent and generous person, loved most by those who knew her best.—HAWTHORNE, NATHANIEL, 1856, *English Note-Books, vol.* II, *p.* 19.

I think I should have recognized her anywhere. The short, plump body, the round, cheerful old face, with cheeks still as rosy as a girl's, the kindly blue eye, the broad, placid brow, and bands of silver hair peeping from beneath the quaint frilled cap, seemed to be all the features of the picture which I had previously drawn in my mind. But for a gay touch in the ribbons, and the absence of the book-muslin handkerchief over the bosom, she might have been taken for one of those dear old Quaker ladies, whose presence, in its cheerful serenity, is an atmosphere of contentment and peace. Her voice was sweet, round, and racy, with a delicious archness at times. Sitting in deep arm-chairs, on opposite sides of the warm grate, while the rain lashed the panes and the autumn leaves drifted outside, we passed the afternoon in genial talk.—TAYLOR, BAYARD, 1858, *At Home and Abroad, ch.* XXXV.

Hers was the history of a credulous woman sacrificing herself to an utterly worthless idol—told over again; but with some difference from its usual formula. The heroine, who stakes her all on a love attachment—who braves ill-repute, ill-usage, want, even—for some worthless, showy creature who has first won her heart, then drained her purse, lastly, left her in the mire of disgrace,—is, and ought to be, an object of generous charity; but the woman who perils her delicacy of nature to screen a vicious parent, not being interesting, is confounded in his shame, and meets with less pity than is awarded to a Marion Lescaut, or an Esmeralda. There is no survivor who can be pained by a plain statement of matters as they really stood in the present case.—CHORLEY, G. F., 1870, *Miss Austen and Miss Mitford, Quarterly Review, vol.* 128, *p.* 205.

I can never forget the little figure rolled up in two chairs in the little Swallowfield room, packed around with books up to the ceiling, on to the floor—the little figure with clothes on, of course, but of no recognized or recognizable pattern; and somewhere out of the upper end of the heap, gleaming under a great, deep, globular brow, two such eyes as I never, perhaps, saw in any other Englishwoman—though I believe she must have French blood in her veins to breed such eyes, and such a tongue; for the beautiful speech which came out of that ugly (it was that) face, and the glitter and depth too of the eyes, like live coals—perfectly honest the while, both lips and eyes—these seemed to me attributes of the highest French, or rather Gallic, not of the highest English woman. In any case, she was a triumph of mind over matter, of spirit over flesh.—KINGSLEY, CHARLES, 1875 (?), *Letter to James Payn, Some Literary Recollections by Payn, p.* 64, *note.*

Women have generally represented Dr. Mitford as amiable and pleasant; there was something cheering and hearty in his familiarity. The character is not uncommon; he was one of those good-looking, profligate spendthrifts, who, reckless of consequences, bring misery upon their families and remain dear to their mothers and daughters. . . . Dr. Mitford often did kind actions, which it is unfair to ignore; he seems even to have had some sort of generosity, and the ease with which he parted with his money was one of his most unfortunate weaknesses. But Miss Mitford's appreciation of her father was mostly due to filial devotion. Never was affection more severely tried. She had to see thousands, seventy thousand pounds, passing out of his careless hands until he became dependent upon the small pittance she could earn by arduous literary labor.—L'ESTRANGE, A. G., 1882, *The Friendships of Mary Russell Mitford.*

In her character, she was a matchless specimen of a well-educated Englishwoman, correct in taste and feeling, clever and self-reliant. As a describer of rural life and scenery in their happiest and most genial aspects, she is allowed to have been unrivalled. Although considerably advanced in life, she had the liveliness and winning manners of a child. Some women never seem to grow old, and she was one of them. Her tongue ran on so incessantly concerning the details of village life, that each of my visits might have afforded the material of a popular article. Short in stature, with a tall, gold-headed cane in hand, she invited me to walk with her through the green lanes in the neighbourhood; the trees, wild flowers, and birds, offering objects of garrulous remark at every step.—CHAMBERS, WILLIAM, 1882, *Story of a Long and Busy Life, p.* 75.

On her tenth birthday Dr. Mitford took the child to a lottery-office, and bade her select a ticket. She determined—guided, to all appearance, by one of the unaccountable whims of childhood—that she would have none other than the number 2,224. Some difficulty attended the purchase of the coveted number, but the little lottery patroness had her way at last, and on the day of drawing there fell to the lot of the happy holder of ticket No. 2,224 a prize of £20,000. Alas! the holder of the fortunate ticket was happy only in name. By the time his daughter was a woman, there remained to Dr. Mitford, of all his lottery adventure had brought him, a Wedgwood dinner-service with the family crest!—HALL, SAMUEL CARTER, 1883, *Retrospect of a Long Life, p.* 405, *note.*

There are intelligent persons who make a living out of their fellow-creatures by pretending to read character in hand-writing. What would they make, I wonder, out of this delicate, microscopic writing, looking as if it were done with a stylus, and without blot nor flaw? The paper is all odds and ends, but not a scrap of it but is covered and crossed, the very flaps of the envelopes, and even the outside of them, having their message. The reason of this is that the writer, a lady, had lived in a time when postage was very dear; like Southey, she used to boast that she could send more for her money by post than any one else; and when the necessity no longer existed, the custom remained. How, at her age, her eyes could read what she herself had written used to puzzle me.—PAYN, JAMES, 1884, *Some Literary Recollections, p.* 62.

In the case of Miss Mitford, indeed, it seems quite hopeless to search for even the ghost of a love-story and, although she certainly did devote her life with touching unselfishness to the comfort and support of a very exacting father, it cannot for a moment be urged that, in so doing, she relinquished any distinct desire or prospect of matrimony. Perhaps the exacting qualities of her parent inclined her unconsciously to remain single; for, with all her unsparing devotion, she must, in the course

of sorely-tried years, have grown to regard men very much as Dolly Winthrop regarded them,—"in the light of animals whom it had pleased Heaven to make naturally troublesome."—REPPLIER, AGNES, 1891,*Three Famous Old Maids, Lippincott's Magazine, vol.* 47, *p.* 390.

OUR VILLAGE
1824–32

We have no passion for "breaking a butterfly upon the wheel," and should not notice this little volume, if we were not on the whole pleased with its contents. The sketches of country scenery, in which it abounds, have such a convincing air of locality; the human figures, interspersed among them, are touched in such a laughter-loving, good-humoured spirit of caricature, innocent, and yet often pungent withal, that we scarcely know a more agreeable portfolio of trifles for the amusement of an idle hour. Abundant matter for small criticism, indeed, might be found in the details of the work. . . . We have taken the trouble of making these observations, because Miss Mitford is really capable of better things; and we have no doubt that our hints will not be thrown away on her.—GIFFORD, WILLIAM, 1824, *Our Village, Quarterly Review, vol.* 31, *pp.* 166, 168.

After dinner I read one of Miss Mitford's hawthorny sketches out of "Our Village," which was lying on the table; they always carry one into fresh air and green fields, for which I am grateful to them.—KEMBLE, FRANCES ANN, 1831, *Records of a Girlhood, June* 7, *p.* 416.

During my convalescence, I read a considerable part of Miss Mitford's "Village," perhaps for the third time. Her short sketches, overflowing with life and beauty, refresh me when I am too weak for long stories, and she has often been a cheering friend in my sick room.—CHANNING, WILLIAM ELLERY, 1841, *To Miss Aikin, Dec.* 15; *Correspondence of William Ellery Channing and Lucy Aikin, ed. Le Breton, p.* 410.

It would be a great injustice were we not to devote a few words of admiration to the charming sketches of Miss Mitford, a lady who has described the village life and scenery of England with the grace and delicacy of Goldsmith himself. "Our Village" is one of the most delightful books in the language: it is full of those *home scenes* which form the most exquisite peculiarity, not only of the external nature, but also of the social life of the country. . . . Whether it is the pet greyhound Lily, or the sunburnt, curly, ragged village child, the object glows before us with something of that daylight sunshine which we find in its highest perfection in the rural and familiar images of Shakespeare.—SHAW, THOMAS B., 1847, *Outlines of English Literature, p.* 389.

It is a book that Washington Irving might have been justly proud to claim as his own; nay, it is doubtful whether any work of his exhibits a finer insight into character, more exquisite appreciation of humor, more touching pathos, or a more delicate perception of the beautiful in nature.—CONANT, SAMUEL STILLMAN, 1870, *Mary Russell Mitford, Harper's Magazine, vol.* 40, *p.* 410.

Nearly half a century ago the present writer was taken, at a very early age, to a little tea-party at Chelsea, where all were elderly except herself; and while the seniors, chiefly tired men of letters and their wives, were recreating themselves with a game of whist, there was no happier person than the youngest, who in a sofa corner first made acquaintance with "Our Village." As long as I read, I was enthralled. I knew little, then, of real country life, but I can truly say of Miss Mitford that then and thereafter

She gave me eyes, she gave me ears;

in fact, opened a gate into a path leading to pleasures that have been prolonged throughout my life. Her style became my ideal; it was never over-weighted with allusion or metaphor, but had a freshness peculiar to itself, and to wilding thickets "such as Hobbima or Ruysdael might have painted," full of violets and funguses, ringdoves and squirrels, yet at some unexpected turn bringing one to a crumbling vase or mouldy statue.—MANNING, ANNE, 1870, *Mary Russell Mitford, Macmillan's Magazine, vol.* 21, *p.* 346.

The charming country sketches of "Our Village" rank not far below White's "Selborne" in accuracy, and surpass them in variety and ornament. — SAINTSBURY, GEORGE, 1886, *Specimens of English Prose Style, p.* 331.

One of the most delightful and natural and genially humorous writers in the language. Her sketches of life in "Our Village," of the "Talking Lady," the "Talking

Gentlemen," of poachers, seamstresses, domestic servants, young men and old men of local note, remain, after half a century of imitations, as fresh as if they had been written yesterday. No human being ever had a cheerier or more sympathetic outlook on the world. Her sympathies, with a certain waywardness, turned rather toward characters that the respectable world frowns upon, with lawless, good-hearted characters and coquettish beauties. She liked to show the good side of such beings to the world.—MINTO, WILLIAM, 1894, *The Literature of the Georgian Era, ed. Knight, p.* 289.

When Miss Mitford wrote "Our Village," the reading world recognized a new note, a fresh sympathy, the beginning of a literary epoch. The modern short story was perhaps born to the world straight from Miss Mitford's heart. There never was a kinder or a larger one, and although the largest room of her cottage, as she says, was only eight feet square, it proved to be more than most palaces in its ability to harbor and to nourish human sympathies. — FIELDS, ANNIE, 1900, *Mary Russell Mitford, The Critic, vol.* 37, *p.* 512.

DRAMAS

She says that her play will be quite opposed, in its execution, to "Ion," as unlike it "as a ruined castle overhanging the Rhine, to a Grecian temple." And I do not doubt that it will be full of ability; although my own opinion is that she stands higher as the authoress of "Our Village" than of "Rienzi," and writes prose better than poetry, and transcends rather in Dutch minuteness and higher finishing, than in Italian ideality and passion.—BROWNING, ELIZABETH BARRETT, 1837, *To Mrs. Martin, Jan.* 23; *Letters of Elizabeth Barrett Browning, ed. Kenyon, vol.* I, *p.* 47.

Miss Mitford's early poems prove the absence of an ear for rhythm; and her sense of natural beauty, so eloquent in prose, struggles in vain for expression through the difficulties of rhythm. She succeeds better in dramatic verse, and some of her scenes have much tragic power. Her study of the Greek dramatists, especially Euripides, is often distinctly traceable; and in the address of Claudia to Rienzi, as also in that of Annabel to Julian, we find the very thoughts of Iphigenia pleading with Agamemnon.— BETHUNE, GEORGE WASHINGTON, 1848, *The British Female Poets, p.* 318.

In no other act or attempt of her life did Miss Mitford manifest any of those qualities of mind which are essential to success in this the highest walk of literature. It does not appear that she had any insight into passion, any conception of the depths of human character, or the scope of human experience. Ability of a certain sort there is in her plays, but no depth, and no compass. —MARTINEAU, HARRIET, 1855, *Biographical Sketches, p.* 41.

POETRY

In our cursory examination of this little volume, we have noticed several unpoetical and ungraceful, and not a few ungrammatical lines. It must be apparent, we think, to every one, that Miss Mitford's taste and judgment are not yet matured; that her poems ought to have been kept back much longer, and revised much oftener, before they were submitted to the public; and, above all, that she wanted some friend who, without wounding her feelings, or damping the fire of her genius, would have led her to correcter models of taste, and taught her more cautious habits of composition. That such instruction would not have been thrown away, we judge from many pleasing passages scattered through her little volume, which do no discredit to the amiableness of her mind and the cultivation of her talents. When she attempts to describe the higher passions, as in "Sybille," she fails from want of strength for the flight. But in the description of natural scenery, or the delineation of humbler and calmer feelings she is more successful.—GIFFORD, WILLIAM, 1810, *Mary Russell Mitford's Poems, Quarterly Review, vol.* 4, *p.* 517.

Her first claims on the public were no doubt as a poetess, in her early "Sketches," and in her "Christina, the Maid of the South Seas," a six-canto production of the Sir Walter Scott school, of considerable merit; but she is chiefly to be remembered as the author of "Our Village," so full of truth, and raciness, and fine English life; and for her three tragedies, "Julian," "The Vespers of Palermo," and "Rienzi," the last of which was, I believe, eminently successful in representation. Her latter verses are all able and elegant; but she is deficient in the nameless adaptation of expression to thought accomplished by some indescribable, some inexpressible collocation of the best words in their best places, apparently quite necessary for the success of poetical phrase.

This power, on the contrary, Mary Howitt possesses in perfection; while she is somewhat wanting in the essential matter—the more solid materials—which Miss Mitford seems to have ever at command. The one is mightiest in facts, the other in fancy.— MOIR, D. M., 1851–52, *Sketches of the Poetical Literature of the Past Half-Century.*

LETTERS

I am inclined to think that her correspondence, so full of point in allusions, so full of anecdote and recollections, will be considered among her finest writings. Her criticisms, not always the wisest, were always piquant and readable. She had such a charming humor and her style was so delightful, that her friendly notes had a relish about them quite their own.—FIELDS, JAMES T., 1871, *Yesterdays with Authors, p.* 275.

It was an unusual combination of powers which made this shrewd delineator of rural manners also one of the few women dramatists whose works have succeeded not only in the library, but on the boards. Her plays are no longer acted, her stories no longer read, but she still lives in her letters: strongly prejudiced, excessive in praise of those she loved, but lively, observant, obviously sincere, and deriving a pathetic interest from the life of self-sacrifice and hard work, the sunny side of which they usually chronicle.—MAYER, GERTRUDE TOWNSHEND, 1894, *Women of Letters, vol.* II, *p.* 163.

Her Letters are almost as interesting as "Our Village," and the attractiveness of both springs from the writer's own personality, her enthusiasm for books and friends, her devotion to animals, and her great love for flowers, so prettily recognized by the gardeners, who "were constantly calling plants after her, and sending her one of the first cuttings as presents." That which she loved, moreover, she observed with unerring attention, and described with a light touch and graphic humour, tempered and refined by a generous loving-kindness for humanity, which long trials could not weaken.—JOHNSON, R. BRIMLEY, 1896, *English Prose, ed. Craik, vol.* V, *p.* 301.

GENERAL

North.—"Miss Mitford has not, in my opinion, either the pathos or humor of Washington Irving; but she excels him in vigorous conception of character, and in the truth of her picture of English life and manners. Her writings breathe a sound, pure, and healthy morality, and are pervaded by a genuine rural spirit—the spirit of merry England. Every line bespeaks the lady."—WILSON, JOHN, 1826, *Noctes Ambrosianæ, Nov.*

Her ability was very considerable. Her power of description was unique. She had a charming humor, and her style was delightful. Yet were her stories read with a relish which exceeded even so fair a justification as this—with a relish which the judgment could hardly account for; and this pleasant, compelled enjoyment was no doubt ascribable to the glow of good spirits and kindliness which lighted up and warmed everything that her mind produced. She may be considered as the representative of household cheerfulness in the humbler range of the literature of fiction.—MARTINEAU, HARRIET, 1855, *Biographical Sketches, p.* 37.

The letters of Miss Mitford have no pretension of character of works of art; they are mere medleys, such as one scrawls off in an odd half-hour to an uncritical friend; more, perhaps, because something must be said than because one has anything to say, and rather following one's pen than guiding it. We cannot say, therefore, *materiem superavit opus:* if interesting matter is wanting, the tone will not atone for its absence. To review Miss Mitford's other writings is beyond our present purpose. She

had, we repeat, talent and facility, but no genius; she wrote for bread, chained to her desk all day long. She produced, under these adverse circumstances, dramas which had and deserved a temporary success, and one of which is even yet not dead. She produced, no doubt, a mass of contributions to periodicals, which have perished with the periodicals themselves. The best of her works, as we have said before, is "Our Village," and the next best is "Belford Regis," in which she photographs (for she has not imagination enough to paint anything but portraits) the life of a country town.— SMITH, GOLDWIN, 1870, *Miss Mitford's Letters, The Nation, vol.* 10, *p.* 212.

"Our Village" and "Belford Regis" are as fresh and sweet as the English daisies, whose praises Chaucer sings in "The Flower and the Leaf."—EGAN, MAURICE FRANCIS, 1889, *Lectures on English Literature, p.* 26.

Though "Atherton," her one attempt at the novel proper, contains some charming passages, it is wanting in varied interest, and the progress of the story is too slow. She had not, in fact, enough imagination to construct a plot or create a character. Persons and scenes which were before her, whether in books or in nature, she could describe and even "compose," but more ambitious attempts proved a failure.—JOHNSON, R. BRIMLEY, 1896, *English Prose, ed. Craik, vol.* V, *p.* 301.

Robert Montgomery
1807–1855

Poetaster, was born at Bath in 1807, the natural son of one Gomery, a clown. In 1830 he entered Lincoln College, Oxford; in 1833 took his B.A. with a fourth class; in 1835 was ordained; and, with the exception of four years in Glasgow (1838–42), was minister of Percy Street Chapel, London, until his death on 3d December 1855. Of his thirty-one works in verse and prose, two—"The Omnipresence of the Deity" (1828; 29th ed. 1855) and "Satan" (1830)—are remembered by Macaulay's onslaught in the "Edinburgh Review" for April, 1830.—PATRICK AND GROOME, *eds.* 1897, *Chambers's Biographical Dictionary, p.* 671.

PERSONAL

Did you ever hear much of Robert Montgomery, commonly called Satan Montgomery because the author of "Satan," of the "Omnipresence of the Deity," and of various poems which pass through edition after edition, nobody knows how or *why?* I understand that his pew (he is a clergyman) is sown over with red rosebuds from ladies of the congregation, and that the same fair hands have made and presented to him, in the course of a single season, one

hundred pairs of slippers. Whereupon somebody said to this Reverend Satan, "I never knew before, Mr. Montgomery, that you were a *centipede.*"—BROWNING, ELIZABETH BARRETT, 1845, *To H. S. Boyd, July* 21; *Letters of Elizabeth Barrett Browning, ed. Kenyon, vol.* I, *p.* 265.

I send you a treasure. I do believe it is the autograph of the great Robert Montgomery. Pray let me have it again. I would not lose such a jewel on any account. I have read it, as Mr. Montgomery desires, in the presence of God; and in the presence of God I pronounce it to be incomparable. Glorious news! Robert Montgomery writes to Longman that there is a point at which human patience must give way. Since the resignation and Christian fortitude of a quarter of a century have made no impression on the hard heart and darkened conscience of Mr. Macaulay, an injured poet must appeal to the laws of his country, which will doubtless give him a redress the more signal because he has been so slow to ask for it. I retain you. Consider yourself as fee'd.—MACAULAY, THOMAS BABINGTON, 1853, *To Mr. Ellis, Aug.* 16; *Life and Letters, ed. Trevelyan, ch.* xiii.

Called upon Mr. Robert Montgomery, *preacher and poet,* as he calls himself. He is full of excitement about the value of his own works. He is undoubtedly clever, and a man of sterling genius; but his great and lamentable weakness—his personal vanity —is really painful to witness. It was with much difficulty I could get away from him. The following is a specimen of the way he usually treats his darling subject—the extension of his fame:—"Now, my dear Mr. Blakey, I esteem your writings highly: you and I are far beyond the age. Now, do quote me wherever you can, and do it largely, and in the highest terms of eulogy. Our grand principles are the same; therefore, you can do it better than any one else. Now, mind, '*Robert* Montgomery, preacher and poet, not *James.*' I know I tower far above all my enemies. I have had a Satanic struggle with them for years, but now I am at the top of the tree. Whenever you can get a paragraph into any newspaper or magazine, do remember and give me a lift. You know it is our duty to assist each other." I cannot tell the fiftieth part of what he talked on this subject. But the spectacle was very lamentable, and really humiliating. He filled my pockets full with his works.— BLAKEY, ROBERT, 1853, *Memoirs, ed. Miller, p.* 214.

Beyond his vanity, there was no harm in him; nay, his nature was generous and kindly.—HALL, SAMUEL CARTER, 1883, *Retrospect of a Long Life, p.* 414.

The Rev. Robert Montgomery, the author of "Satan," once consulted me concerning the illustrating of another of his great poems, "Woman." He was a handsome and popular clergyman, full of words, but his poetic gift perhaps fairly to be estimated from some lines in "The Real Devil's Walk," a rather lengthy imitation of Coleridge's. Montgomery meets the Devil in Piccadilly; and they pass without greeting, for

" Montgomery knew nothing of Satan,
Though Satan knew Montgomery. "
—LINTON, WILLIAM JAMES, 1894, *Threescore and Ten Years, p.* 174.

GENERAL

Shepherd.—"The verra deevil himself's got dull in the haum's o' that Rab Montgomery—cauldrifed, as if hell were out o' coals,—a' its blast-furnaces choked up wi' blue silent ashes—and the dammed coorin' and chitterin' in corners, as if fire were frost."—WILSON, JOHN, 1830, *Noctes Ambrosianæ, April.*

His writing bears the same relation to poetry which a Turkey carpet bears to a picture. There are colours in the Turkey carpet, out of which a picture might be made. There are words in Mr. Montgomery's verses, which when disposed in certain orders and combinations, have made, and will again make, good poetry. But, as they now stand, they seem to be put together on principle, in such a manner as to give no image of anything in the "heavens above, or in the earth beneath, or in the waters under the earth."—MACAULAY, THOMAS BABINGTON, 1830, *Mr. Robert Montgomery's Poems, Critical and Miscellaneous Essays.*

Horace instructs us that neither gods nor man endure mediocre poetry, and consequently Mr. Montgomery had no course, but to address his song to the third estate, whose liberal patronage of every thing bad may reasonably be reckoned on. The arch enemy's care for discord must needs be gratified by such verses as we see before us, and as a love of deceit he will be pleased with lines simulating poetry by the capital letter at the head of each,

"Like dead-sea fruits that tempt the eye,
But burn to ashes on the lips."

As Milton may be read in Heaven so this is precisely the book fit for Hades, and though we trust we hate the Enemy as vehemently as all good Christians ought to hate him, yet we own we wish him no worse than a patient perusal of this work to his honour. He will here bathe in a stream of molten lead. Every page is fraught with the weariness that protracts time, and makes a duodecimo a doomsday book.—FONBLANQUE, ALBANY, 1830, *Montgomery's Satan, Westminster Review, vol.* 12, *p.* 356.

I never could get through a volume of Robert's yet.—BARTON, BERNARD, 1832, *To Mr. Fulcher, Oct.* 29; *Memoir, Letters and Poems, ed. his Daughter, p.* 118.

First, however, we shall discharge to Mr. Montgomery that debt which our critical duty imposes upon us. The time, we think, has arrived when Mr. Montgomery may glean from criticism some valuable and impartial suggestions. The sweeping and virulent abuse which was lavished so indiscriminately on his poetry necessarily creates reaction. And every honest and generous mind must feel more willing to praise than to defame one who has been so unfairly assailed. Yet, knowing the natural vanity of a poet, we doubt, while to many we shall seem to overvalue Mr. Montgomery's present performance, whether we shall even satisfy himself of our desire to be just. Be that as it may—as Mr. Montgomery himself says in his Preface, *commenta opinionum delet dies.* We shall proceed at once to quote passages which will prove, we fully trust, to the satisfaction of every candid reader, that our author's powers have been greatly maligned; and that whatever the rank to which as a poet he belongs—he at least possesses many and not inconsiderable attributes of his high calling.—LYTTON, SIR EDWARD GEORGE BULWER, 1832, *Montgomery's Messiah, New Monthly Magazine, vol.* 35, *p.* 147.

Humour may be divided into three classes; the broad, the quiet, and the covert. Broad humour is extravagant, voluble, obtrusive, full of rich farce and loud laughter: —quiet humour is retiring, suggestive, exciting to the imagination, few of words, and its pictures grave in tone:—covert humour, (which also comprises quiet humour), is allegorical, typical, and of cloven tongue—its double sense frequently delighting to present the reverse side of its real meaning, to smile when most serious, to look grave when most facetiously disposed. Of this latter class are the comic poems of the ingenious Robert Montgomery, a humourist whose fine original vein has never been rightly appreciated by his contemporaries. He has been scoffed at by the profane for writing unmeaning nonsense, when that very nonsense had the most disinterested and excellent moral aim; he has passed for a quack, when he nobly made his muse a martyr; he has been laughed at, when he should have been admired; he has

been gravely admired when his secret laughter should have found response in every inside. He has been extensively purchased; but he has not been understood. . . . At some future time, and when his high purpose can no longer be injured by a discovery of its inner wheels and movements, springs and fine escapements—at such a period, he may perhaps vouchsafe a *key* to all his great works; meantime, however, in his defense, because we are unable to bear any longer the spectacle of so total a misconception of a man's virtues and talents in the public mind, we will offer a few elucidatory comments upon two of his larger productions. . . . Here are his own soft yet reproachful, sweet yet terrible words—no German flute was ever more tenderly searching. nor, when based on an ophecleide accompaniment, more confounding.—HORNE, RICHARD HENGIST, 1844, *A New Spirit of the Age.*

Granted that he had very little, if any, of "the vision and the faculty divine"; granted that some of his similes were so impossible as to prove that with him words sometimes stood for real thoughts; yet the manifest gusto with which Macaulay performed his task of flagellation was little to his credit. Let any one read but two pages of the forgotten poems, and he will see that the poor clergyman had done nothing to deserve so tremendous an infliction of the bastinado.—FARRAR, FREDERIC WILLIAM, 1890, *Literary Criticism, The Forum, vol.* 9, *p.* 280.

One may well have thought that Pye had provided enough weak poetry for one publisher, but for Pye and Tupper together one can hardly find apology sufficiently ample. Had Robert Montgomery joined, and made the trio, it would have been the last straw, which neither the reputation of Hatchard or any other mortal publisher could have survived.—HUMPHREYS, ARTHUR L., 1893, *Piccadilly Bookmen: Memorials of the House of Hatchard, p.* 71.

With an unfortunate facility in florid versification Montgomery combined no genuinely poetic gift. Macaulay, in trying to anticipate the office of time, only succeeded in rescuing him from the oblivion to which he was properly destined. His style of preaching is said to have resembled that of his poetical effusions.—SECCOMBE, THOMAS, 1894, *Dictionary of National Biography, vol.* XXXVIII, *p.* 323.

Julius Charles Hare
1795–1855

Born at Valdagno, Italy, Sept. 13, 1795; died at Hurstmonceaux, Sussex, England, Jan. 23, 1855. An English divine and theological writer, archdeacon of Lewes 1840. He held the living of Hurstmonceaux from 1832. Among his works are "Mission of the Comforter" (1846); "The Contest with Rome" (1852); "Vindication of Luther" (1854); conjointly with A. W. Hare, "Guesses at Truth" (1827).—SMITH, BENJAMIN E., ed. 1894–97, *The Century Cyclopedia of Names, p.* 481.

PERSONAL

Hare is a passionate lover of German literature and philosophy. He has the air of a man of talent, and talks well. I was struck with his great liberality. We had so many points of contact and interest that I chatted with him exclusively till past twelve, paying no attention to the music, or the numerous and fashionable company.—ROBINSON, HENRY CRABB, 1825, *Diary, March* 18; *Diary, Reminiscences and Correspondence, ed. Sadler.*

I went to St. Mary's to-day, and heard a weak, elderly man preach upon, "And this is the victory which overcometh the world, even your faith." There was something in the manner eminently impressive, though something like weakness and monotony of voice gradually made it rather less so. The style, too, seemed quite a repetition of Jeremy Taylor, and poetical illustrations were poured in abundantly. Then, again, I was more touched by the evangelical tone of the matter, in defence of simple "justification of faith," than I have been before for some months. Yet my pleasure in listening was slightly disturbed by an occasional doubt as to how far I might really follow him as a guide through the mazes of discussion, and whether the figurative style might not be a sort of elaborate weakness. Great, then, was my delight to hear, when I came away, that it was Julius Hare, one of the "Guessers at Truth," the associate of Thirlwall, the brother of Augustus Hare, and altogether one of the greatest minds and best scholars in our university. Since this I have had a key to the full meaning of what he said on many points, and his whole figure is associated with feelings of reverence.—WILLIAMS, ROWLAND, 1839, *Note Book, Feb.* 3; *Life and Letters, ed. his Wife, vol.* I, *p.* 49.

Archdeacon Hare joined us,—as nervous, dragged-looking a man as in his portrait, but far more genial and approachable than that would lead you to expect. Plenty of pleasant talk but nothing extremely marked.—FOX, CAROLINE, 1847, *Memories of Old Friends, Journal, May* 17, *p.* 236.

Hearty thanks for both your very kind letters. Hare's death is more to us, and I think more to the Church than even we thought it would be. We scarcely knew what his genial spirits and look were to us, or how much there was in his deepest heart which was receiving good and scattering good. His last months were very satisfactory witnesses of the man by the unvarying patience, cheerfulness and thankfulness which he was manifesting, without one false or affected or canting word in the midst of unusual suffering. In his last days he was so utterly wasted and prostrated that he could do no more than show tenderness and affection to all about him.—MAURICE, FREDERICK DENISON, 1855, *Letter to Charles Kingsley, Feb.* 2; *Life, ed. Maurice, vol.* II, *p.* 255.

His duties as Archdeacon were especially congenial to him. With his clergy he felt none of the difficulty of making himself understood which shackled him with his parishioners. He delighted in his church visitations, in which the war against pews, then at its height, called forth all his characteristic vehemence; he found most congenial work in the preparation of his lengthy charges, in which he entered into all the ecclesiastical subjects of the day to a degree which makes them almost an ecclesiastical history of their times.—HARE, AUGUSTUS J. C., 1890, *Dictionary of National Biography, vol.* XXIV, *p.* 371.

Julius Hare, born in 1795, belonged to a family distinguished by a fatal fluency in letter-writing, so that the few facts in his career, the few works produced by him, and his beautiful character and life, so full of every grace of sweetness and courtesy, so irreproachable and graceful, are swamped by the flood of details, both intellectual and external, which a remorseless fidelity has gathered together.—OLIPHANT, MARGARET O. W., 1892, *The Victorian Age of English Literature, p.* 146.

GENERAL

"The Guesses" are well worth reading; nay, buying: very ingenious, with a good deal of pedantry and *onesidedness* (do you know this German word?), which, I believe, chiefly comes from the Trinity Fellow, who was a great pedant.—FITZGERALD, ED-WARD, 1838, *Letters, vol.* I, *p.* 44.

This evening Archdeacon Hare's "Life of John Sterling" arrived. The portrait is very unsatisfactory, the volumes full of exquisite interest, though of a very mixed kind. Julius Hare has, I believe, done his part admirably well, but F. D. Maurice has (by his letters) quite spoiled us for any other handling of such a subject.—FOX, CAROLINE, 1848, *Memories of Old Friends, Journal, Jan.* 25, *p.* 248.

Of all the disciples of Coleridge, Julius Charles Hare may be reckoned the most direct and confessed. . . . With all Hare's noble enthusiasm and captivating spirit of Christian culture, it cannot be said that he is much of a leader of thought himself. He is critical, didactic, philosophic in tone, always cultured. He writes at times with a fine, if desultory, eloquence; and his books, especially the "Guesses at Truth," which he published along with his brother first in

1828, were much read, and felt to be highly stimulating forty years ago. I can never forget my own obligation to some of them; yet it must be confessed that both author and writings are now somewhat dim in the retrospect. They have lived on, and this no doubt mainly because both reflected for the greater part the movement of his time rather than added any new and creative force to it.—TULLOCH, JOHN, 1885, *Movements of Religious Thought in Britain During the Nineteenth Century, pp.* 27, 28.

Though prolonged collegiate life and extreme intellectual refinement prevented his success as a parish priest, Julius Hare was eminently successful as an archdeacon. His annual "Charges" were elaborated with the utmost care, and still form important contributions to the ecclesiastical history of the time. He entered with warmth into every controversy of the time, the Hampden, the Gorham, and the rest, steadily opposing the dogmatic and Romanising tendencies, as he considered them, of the "Oxford Movement," and standing forward as one of the most prominent champions of the "Broad Church" school in its earlier career.—NEVINSON, H. W., 1887, *Celebrities of the Century, ed. Sanders, p.* 540.

Sir William Hamilton
1788–1856

Scottish philosopher, was born March 8, 1788, at Glasgow, where his father and grandfather held the chairs of Anatomy and Botany; in 1816 he made good his claim to the old baronetcy which the Covenanting heir lost in 1688 for refusing the oath of allegiance. After gaining high distinction at Glasgow, he went in 1809 to Balliol College as Snell exhibitioner and graduated in 1810. He was called to the Scottish bar in 1813, but had almost no practice; in 1820 he stood unsuccessfully for the chair of Moral Philosophy in Edinburgh; in 1821 he became a professor of History. In 1829 he published in the *Edinburgh Review* a famous critique of Cousin's doctrine of the Infinite; this and other articles were collected in 1852 as "Discussions in Philosophy and Literature." In 1836 he became a professor of Logic and Metaphysics; and on these subjects he lectured in alternate years till the end of his life, gathering around him enthusiastic disciples. His lectures were published in 1859–61 by Mansel and Veitch; his principal work was his edition of Reid (1846; with notes 1862), defending what he believed to be Reid's sound philosophical doctrine of common sense. Ill-health diminished his power of work; but he edited Dugald Stewart's works in 1854–55, and was generally able with an assistant to perform the duties of his class till his death 6th May, 1856.—PATRICK AND GROOME, *ed.* 1897, *Chambers's Biographical Dictionary, p.* 457.

PERSONAL

John Wilson's triumph is gratifying, and I greatly rejoice in it. His excellent and amiable rival, Sir William Hamilton, is like a fine miniature picture, which cannot be viewed too near, and could bear to be seen through a microscope. He retires most

honourably from a contest which has produced testimonies to his virtues and abilities, a contest which forced them into observation, and has thrown aside the veil of scrupulous modesty that shrouded his fine qualities and great attainments.—GRANT, ANNE, 1820, *To her Daughter, July* 26;

Memoir and Correspondence, ed. Grant, vol.
II, *p.* 245.

Born in Scotland, but educated at Oxford, and afterwards prosecuting his studies on his journeys on the Continent, he has collected a greater store of knowledge than most men I have ever met with, either in Great Britain or elsewhere. His reading is immense, for he has considered no branch of science entirely foreign to his pursuits, and his memory is admirable. He undoubtedly is one of the first classical scholars in Great Britain, and one of the few now living in that country who in Germany would be considered as eminent ones. With a singularly good taste and choice he has studied our own literature, and he is perfectly well acquainted with all that there is best and most solid in it, and, in particular, with our most eminent philosophers. He perhaps is the only Briton who can claim any acquaintance with them at all. After such a description you will conceive that my surprise at meeting with such a gentleman in Scotland was not ill founded. His views are bold, comprehensive, original, like those of a German, yet his judgment clear, and his discourse refined, like that of an Englishman. Every respectable German who arrives in Edinburgh, has a home in his house, and even in intellectual respects he here feels himself at home.—VON SCHEEL, ALBERT, 1827, *Reise in Gross Britannien im Sommer.*

Sir William has the reputation of being one of the most learned men in England; and you cannot be long in his company till you must be convinced that his knowledge of books is extensive and surprising. But I am of opinion that this prodigious stock of acquired information has been obtained at the cost of some important and valuable intellectual qualities. His mind seems to have been unable to digest the load of matter presented to it, and functional derangement has been induced by the influence of repletion.—BLAKEY, ROBERT, 1838, *Memoirs, ed. Miller, p.* 111.

In the year 1814, it was that I became acquainted with Sir William Hamilton. . . . So exquisitely free was Sir William from all ostentation of learning that, unless the accidents of conversation made a natural opening for display, such as it would have been affectation to evade, you might have failed altogether to suspect that an extraordinary scholar was present. On

this first interview with him, I saw nothing to challenge any special attention, beyond an unusual expression of kindness and cordiality in his *abord.* There was also an air of dignity and massy self-dependence diffused over his deportment, too calm and unaffected to leave a doubt that it exhaled spontaneously from his nature, yet too unassuming to mortify the pretensions of others. . . . In general, my conclusion was, that at that time I had rarely seen a person who manifested less of self-esteem, under any of the forms by which ordinarily it reveals itself—whether of pride, or vanity, or full-blown arrogance, or heart-chilling reserve. . . . Here is a man (it will be said by the thoughtful reviewer of his own age), able to have "made the world grow pale" with the enormity of his learned acquisitions, had he been more often confronted with the world, or, when face to face with it, more capable of ostentatious display.—DE QUINCEY, THOMAS, 1852-71, *Sir William Hamilton, Works. ed. Masson, vol.* V, *pp.* 308, 309, 310, 317.

In Memory of
Sir William Hamilton, Baronet,
Professor of Logic and Metaphysics,
In the University of Edinburgh,
Who died 6th May, 1856, Aged 68 Years.
His Aim
Was, by a pure philosophy, to teach
that
Now we see through a glass darkly.
Now we know in part:
His Hope
That in the life to come,
He should see face to face,
And know even as also he is known.
—INSCRIPTION ON TOMB, 1856, *St. John's Chapel, Edinburgh.*

Perhaps it was in 1824 or 1825. I recollect right well the bright affable manners of Sir William, radiant with frank kindliness, honest humanity, and intelligence ready to help; and how completely prepossessing they were. A fine firm figure of middle height; one of the finest cheerfully-serious human faces, of square, solid, and yet rather *aquiline* type; a little marked with small-pox—marked, not deformed, but rather the reverse (like a rock rough-hewn, not spoiled by polishing); and a pair of the beautifullest, kindly-beaming hazel eyes, well open, and every now and then with a lambency of smiling fire in them, which I always remember as if with trust and gratitude. Our conversation did

not amount to much, in those times; mainly about German books, philosophies and
persons, it is like; and my usual place of
abode was in the country then. . . . I did
not witness, much less share in, any of his
swimming or other athletic prowesses. I
have once or twice been on long walks with
him in the Edinburgh environs, oftenest
with some other companion, or perhaps
even two, whom he had found vigorous
and worthy: pleasant walks and abundantly enlivened with speech from Sir William.
He was willing to talk of any humanly-
interesting subject; and threw out sound
observations upon any topic started; if
left to his own choice, he circled and
gravitated, naturally, into subjects that
were his own, and were habitually occupying him;—of which, I can still remember
animal magnetism and the German revival of it, not yet known of in England,
was one that frequently turned up. . . .
He was finely social and human, in these
walks or interviews. Honesty, frankness,
friendly veracity, courageous trust in
humanity and in you, were charmingly
visible. His talk was forcible, copious, discursive, careless rather than otherwise; and,
on abstruse topics, I observed, was apt to
become embroiled and revelly, much less
perspicuous and elucidative than with a
little deliberation he could have made it.—
CARLYLE, THOMAS, 1868, *Letter to Veitch,*
Feb. 19; *Memoir of Sir William Hamilton by John Veitch, pp.* 122, 123, 124.

On questions of philosophy his opinions
uttered in conversation so nearly resembled
those delivered in his lectures and other
works, that I can add but little. . . .
Looking back on these and such indications of interest in matters higher even
than philosophy, and remembering the
respectful and even reverential strain of
every allusion in speech or writing to
Christianity and the Christian Scriptures,
it is with a peculiar pleasure that I think of
so great a mind as having, in the days of
doubt and restless speculation, satisfied
itself with that common Christian belief
with which so many of the loftiest human
intellects have been contented, and as
having proved, with a yet deepened sense,
its value, as I humbly believe, amid the
discipline of affliction and the shadows of
death.—CAIRNS, JOHN, 1869, *Letter to
Veitch, Memoir of Sir William Hamilton
by John Veitch, pp.* 271, 275.

The ground of his nature was simplicity;
—its strength was sustained and nourished
from this root. All through life there was
a singleness of aim, a purity, devotion, and
unworldliness of purpose, and a childlike
freshness of feeling, which accompanied,
guided, and in a great measure constituted
his intellectual greatness. To the vulgar
ambitions of the world he was indifferent
as a child; in his soul he scorned the common artifices and measures of compromise
by which they are frequently sought and
secured. To be a master of thought and
learning, he had an ambition; in this
sphere he naturally and spontaneously
found the outlet for his powers. But this
craving, passionate as it was, never did
harm to the moral nature of the man. The
increase of years, the growth of learning
and fame, took nothing away from the
simplicity of his aim, his devotion to its
pursuit, or his freshness of heart.— VEITCH,
JOHN, 1869, *Memoir of Sir William Hamilton, p.* 372.

Neither his ambition nor his success was
such as to absorb his time in professional
pursuits. His life was mainly that of a
student, and the following years, marked
by little of outward incident, were filled by
researches of all kinds, through which he
daily added to his stores of learning, while
at the same time he was gradually forming
his philosophic system. The outward and
visible traces of these researches remain
in his common-place books, especially in
one which, having been in constant use, is a
valuable record of his studies from this
time onwards to the close of his life. He
did not withdraw himself from society, but
his favorite companions were the books of
his own and of every library within his reach.
Among these he lived in a sort of seclusion,
from which only now and then, when stirred
by some event of the world around, did he
come forth, in vigorous pamphlets, to denounce or protest, or remonstrate, as the
case might be.—HAMILTON, MISS E., 1880,
Encyclopædia Britannica, Ninth ed., vol. XI.

Hamilton was much loved by his pupils,
and to all who came to him for information
he was kind and condescending. His
temper, however, was imperious. He was
impatient of opposition, and being an
ardent reformer, was pretty often opposed;
but he was more frequently engaged in
a quarrel with some public body than
with private individuals. He had all the

waywardness of genius. . . . He was, however, always a strictly honourable, and sometimes even a generous opponent, and he enjoyed the respect and esteem not only of his friends, but of the public up to the last; and if

" He can't be wrong whose life is in the right,"

we have a strong testimony to the correctness of the Hamiltonian theory. . . . His philosophical erudition has probably never been equalled, but it was far too vast to be accurate. It would be difficult to name a philosophical author whose system he had thoroughly mastered, with two exceptions—Aristotle and Reid. If he erred in any respect in his exposition of these writers, it was not from want of acquaintance with their works, but from his desire to assimilate their systems to his own. But even as regards Stewart, I think he cannot always be acquitted of errors of another kind. His great erudition had another ill effect. When about to write on any subject, he consulted so many authors, and made so many extracts, that the work soon extended beyond all reasonable dimensions, and unless compelled by the pressure of necessity (as in the case of his lectures) to give the results to the world, he ultimately became disheartened, and abandoned the effort in despair.—MONCK, W. H. S., 1881, *Sir William Hamilton (English Philosophers), pp.* 11, 12.

Hamilton made a profound impression upon his hearers. His striking appearance, fine head and piercing eye, his dignity, earnestness, and air of authority, combined with the display of wide reading and dialectical ability to produce admiring sympathy. He introduced various plans for effectually catechising his hearers, called upon them for public recapitulations of his teaching, and frequently entertained them in his own house. . . . In private life Hamilton showed a most affectionate nature. He was perfect as a son, brother, husband, and father. His power of concentration enabled him to do much work in the room used by his family. He made friends of his children, encouraged their studies, and joined in their games. Besides his serious studies, he was fond of light literature, and had a fancy for the grotesque, and even the horrible, enjoying fairy tales and Mrs. Radcliffe's romances. He had much mechanical skill and amused himself by binding his books. After his illness

he became rather irritable, and at all periods was an uncompromising, and when his pugnacity was aroused, an unsparing antagonist.—STEPHEN, LESLIE, 1890, *Dictionary of National Biography, vol.* XXIV, *p.* 230.

GENERAL

"Cousin," I pronounce beyond all doubt the most unreadable thing that ever appeared in the *Review.* . . . It is ten times more *mystical* than anything my friend Carlyle ever wrote, and not half so agreeably written. It is nothing to the purpose that he does not agree with the most part of the mysticism, for he affects to understand it and to explain it, and to think it very ingenious and respectable and it is mere gibberish.—JEFFREY, FRANCIS LORD, 1829, *To Macvey Napier, Correspondence of the late Macvey Napier, p.* 68.

In truth, what characterizes Sir W. Hamilton is precisely the Scottish intellect; and he is only attached to the philosophy of Reid and Stewart because their philosophy is the Scottish intellect itself applied to metaphysics. . . . Inferior to Reid in invention and originality, and to Stewart in grace and delicacy, he is perhaps superior to both, and certainly to the latter, by the vigour of his dialectic; I add, and by the extent of his erudition. Sir W. Hamilton knows all systems, ancient and modern, and he examines them by the criticism of the Scottish intellect. His independence is equal to his knowledge. He is, above all, eminent in logic. I would speak to you here as a philosopher by profession. . . . That Sir W. Hamilton has, perhaps, less originality than Reid, Stewart and Brown. Sir W. Hamilton is very superior to Brown, especially as a logician. Were the articles of Sir W. Hamilton collected, we should have a book infinitely more distinguished than the writings—very ingenious, but superficial and diffuse—of Brown. Sir W. Hamilton has not even the very slightest appearance of obscurity. His style is substantial and severe, but of a perfect plainness for every one acquainted with the subject and not incapable of attention. No one is more opposed to, no one is more devoid of, the vagueness and obscurity of the German philosophy in several of its most celebrated authors.—COUSIN, VICTOR, 1836, *Letter to Prof. Pillans, June* 1; *Memoir of Sir William Hamilton by John Veitch, pp.* 189, 190.

He seems to have read every writer, ancient and modern, on logic and metaphysics, and is conversant with every philosophical theory, from the lowest form of materialism to the most abstract development of idealism; and yet his learning is not so remarkable as the thorough manner in which he has digested it, and the perfect command he has of all its stores. Everything that he comprehends, no matter how abstruse, he comprehends with the utmost clearness, and employs with the most consummate skill. He is altogether the best trained reasoner on abstract subjects of his time.—WHIPPLE, EDWIN PERCY, 1845, *British Critics, Essays and Reviews, vol.* II, *p.* 145.

When we advert to the various topics elaborately treated by him, which we cannot so much as enumerate to our readers, and see how slightly we have touched his solid mass of doctrine even at the few points which have attracted us, we are more impressed than ever with profound admiration for his largeness of learning and thoroughness of mind. That the one sometimes tempts to a superfluous display, and the other to an intellectual scorn more merited by his victims than graceful to himself, will be most readily forgiven by those who understand the author and know his writings best. In him the old scholastic spirit seems embodied again; its capacity for work; its vehemence of disputation; its generous intellectual admirations; its fineness of logical apprehension; the want of perspective and proportion in its mental view. Books and thoughts are evidently the population of his world; they form the natural circle of his friendships and his enmities; their reputations touch his sense of equity and honor; their rivalries and delinquencies furnish the needful amusement of a little gossip and scandal. Where the range of knowledge is so vast, this enclosure of the whole intensity of life within the sphere of notional speculation involves no narrowness; but can scarcely fail to impart a warmth of zeal, which others can scarcely believe to be excited by formulas and theories.—MARTINEAU, JAMES, 1853-68, *Essays, Philosophical and Theological, vol.* II, *p.* 290.

Sir William Hamilton has been chiefly known hitherto by a couple of remarkable articles in *The Edinburgh Review*—one on the Philosophy of Cousin, and the other on

the current Theories of Perception. Nothing can exceed the evidence of logical ability in these papers, nor the easy mastery they exhibit over all the erudition pertaining to their respective subjects. Yet we are inclined to think that these admirable qualities have passed with hasty or inconsiderate readers for more than their worth, serving, indeed, popularly to accredit Sir William with a philosophic *prestige* to which, as it appears to us, he is by no means indisputably entitled. — JAMES, HENRY, 1853, *Works of Sir William Hamilton, Putnam's Magazine, vol.* 2, *p.* 470.

Sir William, though metaphysically the most formidable man in Europe, is an humble Christian; though the most learned of men, he is ready to bow before the spirit that informed the mind of Paul.—WIGHT, O. W., 1855, *ed. The Philosophy of Sir William Hamilton, Introduction, p.* xiii.

The Scottish Stagirite, the metaphysician of recent Europe.—MASSON, DAVID, 1859, *British Novelists and Their Styles, p.* 162.

By far the greatest metaphysician who has appeared in the British empire during the present century, is Sir William Hamilton. In his union of powerful thinking with profound and varied erudition, he stands higher, perhaps, than any other man whose name is preserved in the annals of modern speculation.—BOTTA, ANNE C. LYNCH, 1860, *Hand-Book of Universal Literature, p.* 506.

In the examination which I have now concluded of Sir W. Hamilton's philosophical achievements, I have unavoidably laid stress on points of difference from him rather than those of agreement; the reason being, that I differ from almost everything in his philosophy on which he particularly valued himself, or which is specially his own. His merits, which, though I do not rate them so high, I feel and admire as sincerely as his most enthusiastic disciples, are rather diffused through his speculations generally, than concentrated on any particular point. They chiefly consist in his clear and distinct mode of bringing before the reader many of the fundamental questions of metaphysics; some good specimens of psychological analysis on a small scale; and the many detached logical and psychological truths which he has separately seized, and which are scattered through his writings, mostly applied to resolve some special difficulty, and again lost sight of. I can hardly point to anything he has done towards helping the more thorough understanding of the greater mental phenomena, unless it be his theory of Attention (including Abstraction), which seems to me the most perfect we have: but the subject, though a highly important, is a comparatively simple one.—MILL, JOHN STUART, 1865, *An Examination of Sir William Hamilton's Philosophy, vol.* II, *p.* 337.

The Natural Realism of Hamilton is as thoroughly opposed to the Dogmatic Idealism of Berkeley as the former himself believed it to be, and that any attempt to identify them would have produced greater surprise in no one, probably, than in Hamilton himself.—STIRLING, JAMES HUTCHISON, 1866, *Was Sir William Hamilton a Berkeleian? Fortnightly Review, vol.* 6, *p.* 228.

There is no part of the country where his writings have not produced a deep and permanent impression, and where he is not revered as one of the greatest thinkers of our times. He has greatly enlarged the knowledge of multitudes in regard to the reach and importance of the discussions which are recorded in the history of philosophy. He has redeemed the history itself from the contempt and reproach under which it had fallen, as being but a dry catalogue of the disputes of learned triflers and the subtleties of pedantic logomachists. . . . He has, in fact, done more than any and than all of the writers of his time to waken the historic spirit among our philosophers. At the same time he has guided it most wisely and to the most soiid results, teaching it to be critical as well as curious, to be self-reliant as well as reverent. The clearness of his own judgment, the candour of his temper, the sagacity of his interpretations, the vigour and independence of his own critical estimates, as they were constantly exemplified in his treatment of the writers to whom he so often referred, and from whom he so largely quoted, were most salutary to his American readers, who were in danger of being blindly credulous or ignorantly self-reliant—either too contemptuous or too irreverent of the past— either excessively conceited or excessively partisan.—PORTER, NOAH, 1869; *On the Influence of Sir William Hamilton's Writings in America, Memoir of Sir William Hamilton by John Veitch, Appendix, p.* 425.

The greatest British supporter of *a priori* philosophy in this century. . . . From the time of his extraordinary examination at Oxford, his erudition and encyclopedic reading became a subject of wonder and exaggerated rumour. He seems to have had something of the same book-devouring turn as Johnson. . . . Of late years both the extent and the accuracy of Hamilton's scholarship have been questioned, but with all deductions he still remains what he was represented to De Quincey as being— "a monster of erudition."—We do not here attempt any outline of his philosophy; and his philosophical abilities are still matter of dispute.—As regards style, he had, with his prodigious memory, a fine command of language; his command of the language of controversy, especially for the purpose of summarily "putting down" an antagonist, is at least as good as his command of the language of philosophical exposition. In both operations he is masterly. He had a taste for antithesis and pithy compression. He was also notably studious of method, of good arrangement; more, apparently, from a love of mechanical symmetry, than from any lively sympathy with the difficulties of the reader.—MINTO, WILLIAM, 1872-80, *Manual of English Prose Literature, pp.* 526, 528.

As Mill's is a *sweated* mind, often entangled in the sudorific blankets, when wanting to move, and incapable of walking, though a splendid rider—of hobbies—so Sir William Hamilton's was a swollen mind. The good Sir William was the Daniel Lambert of Philosophy. He had the shark's, the ostrich's enormous appetite, with no more power of discrimination than the ostrich or the shark. Quantity was everything, quality nothing. Blending the shark and the ostrich, he could make a decent meal of bricks, empty barrels, copper bolts, and tenpenny nails. He is almost the only learned man that Scotland has had since George Buchanan, and there are no signs that Scotland will ever have a learned man again. But his learning was a pedantic plethora, an apoplectic monstrosity, an asthmatic ventriloquism squeaking and growling through layers and convolutions of fat. It would be difficult to say whether Sir William Hamilton devoured books and systems, or was devoured by them. The result, at all events, was chaotic conglomeration. Little would it

have mattered how many books or systems
Sir William Hamilton had swallowed, if he
had not been tormented by the unhappy
yearning to be a creator of systems himself.
—MACCALL, WILLIAM, 1873, *The New
Materialism.*

He is the most learned of all Scottish
metaphysicians. . . . When he was
alive, he could always be pointed to as redeeming Scotland from the reproach of
being without high scholarship. Oxford
had no man to put on the same level.
Germany had not a profounder scholar, or
one whose judgment in a disputed point
could be so relied on. Nor was his the
scholarship of mere words: he knew the
history of terms, but it was because he was
familiar with the history of opinions. In
reading his account, for example, of the
different meanings which the word "idea"
has had, and of the views taken of sense-
perception, one feels that his learning is
quite equalled by his power of discrimination. No man has ever done more in clearing the literature of philosophy of commonplace mistakes, of thefts and impostures.
He has shown all of us how dangerous it is
to quote without consulting the original, or
to adopt, without examination, the common traditions in philosophy; that those
who borrow at second hand will be found
out; and that those who steal, without
acknowledgment, will, sooner or later, be
detected and exposed. He experiences a
delight in stripping modern authors of their
borrowed feathers, and of pursuing stolen
goods from one literary thief to another,
and giving them back to their original owner.
For years to come, ordinary authors will
seem learned by drawing from his stores.—
McCOSH, JAMES, 1874, *The Scottish Philosophy, pp.* 415, 416.

Hamilton maintained staunchly, and,
as it seems to us, very mistakenly, the doctrine of immediate, direct knowledge of
physical objects in perception. The Scottish school, more especially Hamilton,
while far in advance of the Lockian philosophy, was most unfavorably affected by
it, and was unable to construct a consistent,
complete system. We feel more inclined
to censure than to praise it.— BASCOM,
JOHN, 1874, *Philosophy of English Literature, p.* 315.

Hamilton can scarcely be said to have
left a complete and systematic statement or
demonstration of his philosophical views.

The very multifariousness and minuteness
of his scholarship stood partly in the way of
this. Still, his philosophical attitude was
clearly marked, and his doctrine exerted a
wide influence, in America as well as in
Great Britain. . . . Hamilton, now,
with reference to the substance of his views,
is the child of Reid and Kant. He is superior to Reid in dialectical agility, but far inferior to Kant in the spirit of critical, patient
and systematic thoroughness. . . . The
real source of Hamilton's strength and of
his widely diffused and quickening influence is to be found, as in the case of Kant,
in his practical, urgent recognition of that
dynamic, ideal side of mind and life, which,
as an instrument of literal, theoretical cog-
nition, he was unable to turn to any account. To this should be added the contagion of his dialectical ardor and the example of his immense erudition. His defect
is, that he does not raise philosophy out of
that quagmire of psychology in which
(under Kantian inspiration?) he recognized
that it was sunk. He complained of the
substitution of "superficial psychology"
for "metaphysics," and the complaint
holds good against himself.—MORRIS,
GEORGE S., 1880, *British Thought and
Thinkers, pp.* 285, 294, 300.

I believe that no philosophic writer of
the present century has had the same influence in cultivating metaphysical speculation as Sir William Hamilton, nor perhaps is there any other in whose works so
many important philosophical problems
have been mooted, if not solved. "*Pru-
dens interrogatio,*" says Bacon, "*est dimi-
dium scientiæ*"; and if Hamilton does not
always propound his theories in the form
of interrogations, they are not (even when
erroneous) less valuable as steps towards
a final solution.—MONCK, W. H. S., 1881,
*Sir William Hamilton (English Philos-
ophers), p.* 163.

In moral spirit Hamilton was allied to
Reid, not to Hume, and he followed in the
line of the earlier Scottish thought as represented by Reid; but he carried this up to
far higher issues than had been before
dreamt of. Both Reid and Stewart had
properly returned to psychology—in a word,
to consciousness, as they were forced to do
by the meagre analysis on which Hume had
proceeded. Hamilton thoroughly accepted
their method, that of a scrutiny of consciousness in its fullest integrity; but he

was clearer and more precise in his test
and criteria. And not satisfied with the
somewhat partial and faltering applications of psychological results to metaphysical questions by the earlier thinkers, Hamilton boldly grappled with the highest
questions of philosophy regarding our
knowledge of being, Infinite and Absolute
Reality. Even the manner and style of
dealing with the psychological and logical
questions took new forms in his hands.
He brought the questions nearer to the
methods of the learned, and to the treatment of them in other schools.—VEITCH,
JOHN, 1882, *Hamilton (Philosophical Classics), p.* 25.

Hamiltonianism shows, on the face of it,
a mingling of Kantian and Scottish elements. I do not believe that there is any
real fusion in Hamilton of these elements,
nor need this astonish us, if we consider the
incompatibility of the two doctrines. Any
attempt to ingraft the Agnostic relativity
of the "Critique" upon the Natural Realism of the Scottish philosophy is, I hope to
show, contrary to the genius of the latter.—
SETH, ANDREW, 1885, *Scottish Philosophy, p.* 149.

Hamilton's learning was very great, and
included many obscure subjects. He was
especially familiar with the period of the
revival of learning. But he often used his
knowledge with too little discrimination,
and often cites "authorities" with much
indifference to the context or to their relative importance. The effect produced
upon contemporaries by Hamilton's philosophy was due to his commanding character, as well as his wide reading and great
dialectical power. His influence has declined partly from the fragmentary nature
of his writings, and partly from his peculiar
position as a thinker. A thorough Scot, he
carried on the tradition of the national
philosophy of common sense with much
wider knowledge than his predecessors,
and with logical faculties sharpened by his
Aristotelian studies. His acquaintance
with German philosophy was applied by
him rather to fortify than to modify his
opinions. His inconsistencies, real or
alleged, are probably due chiefly to the attempt to combine divergent systems. He
endeavoured to give more precision to the
fundamental principle of the veracity of
consciousness by setting forth as tests of
our original cognitions their necessity,

simplicity, and so forth.—STEPHEN, LESLIE,
1890, *Dictionary of National Biography,
vol.* XXIV, *p.* 231.

Sir William Hamilton's English is bald
without simplicity, and severe without impressiveness. The "Lectures," it is true,
contain passages of considerable power and
animation when he is making preparations
to clinch his argument with an extract from
the poets. But in common with the rest of his
writings, they are so interwoven with quotations, and these frequently of great length,
that the movement of his prose is arrested
before any impetus has been acquired, and
the curious reader is hurried away from
Hamilton to some one else. It is consequently peculiarly difficult to do justice to
Hamilton's style by means of selections.
Even at its best, however, it is wholly
destitute of the charm which springs from
aptly arranged words and nicely balanced
sentences. Its supreme merit is clearness.
—MILLAR, J. H., 1896, *English Prose, ed.
Craik, vol.* V, *p.* 332.

Hamilton was a man of vast reading,
and though it had been questioned whether
his learning was as exact and profound as
it appeared to be, there can hardly be a
doubt that it was great enough to hamper
the free play of his thought, and that it
explains two of his characteristic faults.
One is the excessive technicality of his
diction. His style, otherwise clear and
good, is overloaded with words specially
coined for the purposes of the logician and
metaphysician. The second fault is his
inability to resist the temptation of calling
a "cloud of witnesses," without making
any serious attempt to weigh their evidence.
Hamilton was a disciple of the Scottish
school of philosophy, and a great part of
his life was devoted to an elucidation of
Reid.—WALKER, HUGH, 1897, *The Age of
Tennyson, p.* 167.

He attained a position in the history of
philosophy of which Scotland might well be
proud. But he spoke to a studious and a
narrow class, and powerful as his influence
was, it never guided the nation's thought,
and never attempted to mould her history.—
—CRAIK, SIR HENRY, 1901, *A Century of
Scottish History, vol.* II, *p.* 227.

The strong personality and immense philosophical erudition of Sir William Hamilton.—UPTON, C. B., 1902, *Life and Letters of James Martineau, ed. Drummond,
vol.* II, *p.* 355.

James Gates Percival

1795–1856

An American poet and geologist; born in Kensington, Connecticut, Sept. 15, 1795. In 1815 he graduated at Yale, at the head of his class. After leaving college he taught school for a time, studied medicine and practiced in Charleston, South Carolina. In 1822, while in the last-named place, he published "Prometheus" and "Clio." In 1824 Dr. Percival was appointed assistant army surgeon and professor of chemistry in the United States Military Academy, but resigned after a few months to become a surgeon in the recruiting service at Boston. At that time he contributed to the *United States Literary Magazine* and published a collection of his poems (2 vols. 1826). In 1827 he removed to New Haven, Connecticut, where he published the third part of his tragedy, "Clio." In 1834 he made a particular study of geology, and in the year following was appointed to make a geological and mineralogical survey of Connecticut, in connection with Prof. Charles U. Shepard. In 1843 he published "Dream of a Day." In 1853 he surveyed the lead region of the American Mining Company in Wisconsin, and in 1854 was appointed geologist of that state. A complete collection of his poems was published in two volumes (1859). He died in Hazel Green, Wisconsin, May 2, 1856.—KELLOGG, DAY OTIS, *ed.*, 1897, *New American Supplement to the Encyclopædia Britannica, vol.* IV, *p.* 2347.

PERSONAL

Yet it must be added that, on the whole, his life was a complete shipwreck. He lived to excite admiration and wonder; yet in poverty, in isolation, in a complete solitude of the heart. He had not, I think, a single vice; his life was pure, just, upright. How then did he fail? The truth seems to be, that he was deficient in that sympathy which binds man to man, and hence, he was an anomaly in the society among which he dwelt—a note out of tune with the great harmony of life around him. He was a grand intellect, a grand imagination, but without a heart. That he was born with a bosom full of all love and all kindness, we can not doubt; but the golden bowl seems to have been broken, almost at the fountain. By the time he was twenty he began to stand aloof from his fellow-man. I think he had been deeply injured—nay ruined—by the reading of Byron's works, at that precise age when his soul was in all the sensitive bloom of spring, and its killing frost of atheism, of misanthropy, of pride, and scorn, fell upon it, and converted it into a scene of desolation. The want of a genial circle of appreciation, of love and friendship, around his early life, left this malign influence to deepen his natural shyness into a positive and habitual self-banishment from his fellow-man. Such the sad interpretation I put upon his career.— GOODRICH, SAMUEL GRISWOLD, 1856, *Recollections of a Lifetime, vol.* II, *p.* 140.

Slender in form, rather above than under the middle height, he had a narrow chest, and a peculiar stoop, which was not in the back, but high up in the shoulders. His head, without being large, was fine. His eyes were of dark hazel, and possessed uncommon expression. His nose, mouth, and chin were symmetrically, if not elegantly formed, and came short of beauty only because of that meagreness which marked his whole person. His complexion, light without redness, inclined to sallow, and suggested a temperament somewhat bilious. His dark brown hair had become thin above the forehead, revealing to advantage the most striking feature of his countenance. Taken all together, his appearance was that of a weak man, of delicate constitution, —an appearance hardly justified by the fact; for he endured fatigue and privation with remarkable staunchness. Percival's face, when he was silent, was full of calm, serious meditation; when speaking, it lighted up with thought, and became noticeably expressive. He commonly talked in a mild, unimpassioned undertone, but just above a whisper, letting his voice sink with rather a pleasing cadence at the completion of each sentence.—SHEPARD, CHARLES U., 1866, *Reminiscences, The Life and Letters of James Gates Percival, ed. Ward, p.* 383.

I have not sought to conceal the peculiarities of Percival, or to tone down every expression which relates to others, though I have not intended to print what would cause pain in any one. To give a plain and true narrative of the poet as he lived and labored has been my only aim and purpose; and I cannot part with a work which has engaged me for nearly a decade of years and which, in the providence of God, I have been spared to complete, without saying that, with all my studies of Percival,—and I believe there is not much more to be known,—the simple reverence for his genius and attainments which I had in boyhood has increased with a riper knowledge of his character.—WARD, JULIUS H., 1866, *Life and Letters of James Gates Percival, Preface, p.* vii.

It is a sad story. The rarest and most varied endowments, the most favorable opportunities, the most devoted friends did not rescue him from the most pitiable poverty, misanthropy and despair. He limited his own renown, disappointed his own expectations, and thwarted his own projects. The suicide which in early life he repeatedly attempted was the epitome of his whole career. He was his own worst enemy. It is hardly too much to say that his life was prolonged self-destruction—not in purpose but in fact. Yet, so far as it appears from the present biography, he had none of the baser vices of mankind. Neither alcohol nor opium beclouded his intellect, he was not lazy nor forgetful, nor dissipated nor unkind. He was keenly sensitive in respect to the good opinions of his fellows, though he detested empty flattery, and shrank like a hermit from that public attention which is the penalty and the plague of distinguished men. He performed the most wearisome literary drudgery for the most meagre rewards, and, though he must be said to have been negligent in the extreme respecting his engagements, he was punctilious in respect of scientific accuracy.—GILMAN, D. G., 1866, *The Life of Percival, The Nation, vol.* 3, *p.* 346.

In character, Percival seems to have been a Coleridge who had some pride of independence, a Coleridge with scruples. . . . What disgusted me first with him was the pretended attempt at suicide. If he had been in earnest, he would have never made himself visible in the orchard in time to be antidoted with coffee. It gives a flavor of insincerity to all the rest that follows.—LOWELL, JAMES RUSSELL, 1866, *To C. E. Norton, Oct.* 25; *Letters, ed. Norton, vol.* I, *p.* 375.

As a philologist Percival was the most remarkable man of his generation. Self-taught, he was conversant with the literature, in the original, of every country of Europe. Many of the dialects he mastered sufficiently to employ in writing poetry. When Ole Bull landed in this country, Percival greeted him with a poem written in Danish. Percival's last printed poem was written in German. Prof. Shepard says that he is known to have written verse in thirteen different languages; he imitated all the Greek and German meters, amusing himself in 1823 with rendering select passages from Homer in English hexameters, with the encouraging approbation of Prof. Kingsley. In the 40's he printed a series of excerpts from the three leading groups of European languages—the Slavonic, the German, the Romanic. Each of these three groups embraces four languages; the Slavonic—Polish, Russian, Servian, Bohemian; the Germanic—German, Low Dutch, Danish, Swedish; the Romanic—Italian, Spanish, Portuguese, French. Material assistance was given by Percival to Dr. Webster in the editorial work connected with the publication of the great dictionary that bears the name of the latter. Percival engaged to correct the proofsheets, but speedily his great scholarship in etymologies and scientific bearing of words caused his work to be greatly amplified. It amounted in fact to correcting and editing of the manuscript.—LEGLER, HENRY E., 1901, *James Gates Percival, An Anecdotal Sketch and a Bibliography, p.* 41.

GENERAL

We should sincerely regret that powers, so fine as Mr. Percival evidently possesses, should want that self-consciousness, which they ought to inspire, or should feel a doubt of that public favour, they so truly deserve: and though he probably does not rely on anything he has yet written, as giving him a fair title to the rank of a classical American poet, yet we feel no hesitation in saying, that he shares with few the gifts, which might make him one.—EVERETT, EDWARD, 1822, *Percival's Poems, North American Review, vol.* 14, *p.* 14.

There is an excessive diffuseness in the style of Mr. Percival. It is not sufficiently compact. It wants pith and point; it lacks the energy which conciseness imparts. Everything is drawn out as far as possible; always flowing and sweet, and therefore sometimes languid and monotonous. His poetry is too much diluted. It consists too much in words, which are music to the ear, but too often send a feeble echo of the sense to the mind. There is also a superabundance of images in proportion to the thoughts. They skip about the magical scene in such numbers, that they stand in the way of one another and of the main design. He is too careless in selection; whatever occurs to him he puts down and lets it remain.— WARE, HENRY, JR., 1826, *Percival's Poem, North American Review, vol. 22, p.* 327.

The poem before us is, in our opinion, not only one of the most successful efforts of its author, but a production of singular beauty and excellence in its kind. It is not properly a didactic poem, for it does not aim at the regular delivery of precepts, and still less does it depend for its interest upon anything like narrative. It is a series of poetical pictures, connected by a common subject, and drawn with that freedom of outline and richness of coloring peculiar to the author.—BRYANT, WILLIAM CULLEN, 1826, *United States Review, March.*

The most prolific and fanciful of our poets. . . . He has all the natural qualities of a great poet, but he lacks the artistic skill, or declines the labour, without which few authors gain immortality. He has a brilliant imagination, remarkable command of language, and an exhaustless fountain of ideas. He writes with a facility but rarely equalled, and when his thoughts are once committed to the page, he shrinks from the labour of revising, correcting, and condensing. . . . He possesses in an eminent degree the creative faculty, and his genius is versatile. He has been an admirer and a student of nature, and he describes the visible world, in its minutest details, with feeling and accuracy. The moral tendency of his writings is generally correct; but in one or two poems there is a strain of misanthropy, and in some of his earliest ones there are imitations of skepticism.—GRISWOLD, RUFUS W., 1842, *The Poets and Poetry of America, pp.* 160, 161.

The poetical celebrity of our author is widely extended. The amount of his writings has scarcely been equalled by any American poet. He is certainly a man of genius, and unites to the vivid imagination of the bard, the observing eye of the minute naturalist. But his fancy is under very little regulation or restraint. His verse, though it flows in a melodious stream, seems without art; in his descriptions, objects of greater and less importance are thrown together without proportion, and, notwithstanding all his beauties, the reader is overwhelmed even to weariness with the multitude of his images. But whatever faults severe criticism may lay to his charge, the public voice has long since proclaimed Dr. Percival a true poet, and has assigned him a place with the few choice spirits who grace the upper walks of our literature.—EVEREST, CHARLES W., 1843, *The Poets of Connecticut, p.* 238.

Perhaps a facile power of expression has tended to limit his poetic fame, by inducing a diffuse, careless, and unindividual method; although choice pieces enough can easily be gleaned from his voluminous writings to constitute a just and rare claim to renown and sympathy.—TUCKERMAN, HENRY THEODORE, 1852, *A Sketch of American Literature.*

However much distinguished Mr. Percival may be for his classical learning, and for his varied attainments in philology and general science, he will be chiefly known to posterity as one of our most eminent poets, for the richness of his fancy, the copiousness and beauty of his language, his lifelike descriptions, his sweet and touching pathos, as well as, at times, his spirited and soul-stirring measures.—CLEVELAND, CHARLES D., 1859, *A Compendium of American Literature, p.* 414.

With a nature singularly unplastic, unsympathetic, and self-involved, he was incapable of receiving into his own mind the ordinary emotions of men and giving them back in music; and with a lofty conception of the object and purposes of poesy, he had neither the resolution nor the power which might have enabled him to realize it. He offers as striking an example as could be found of the poetic temperament unballasted with those less obvious qualities which make the poetic faculty. His verse carries every inch of canvas that diction and sentiment can crowd, but the craft is cranky, and we miss that deep-grasping keel of reason which alone can steady and give direction. His mind drifts, too waterlogged to answer the helm, and in his longer poems, like "Prometheus," half the voyage is spent in trying to make up for a leeway which becomes at last irretrievable. If he had a port in view when he set out, he seems soon to give up all hope of ever reaching it; and wherever we open the logbook, we find him running for nowhere in particular, as the wind happens to lead, or lying-to in the merest gale of verbiage. . . . Percival was only too ready to be invented, and he forthwith produced his bale of verses from a loom capable of turning off a hitherto unheard-of number of yards to the hour, and perfectly adapted to the amplitude of our territory, inasmuch as it was manufactured on the theory of covering the largest surface with the least possible amount of meaning that would hold words together. . . . He spent his life, like others of his class, in proclaiming himself a neglected Columbus, ever ready to start on his voyage when the public would supply the means of building his ships. Meanwhile, to be ready at a moment's warning, he packs his mind pellmell like a carpet-bag, wraps a geologist's hammer in a shirt with a Byron collar, does up Volney's "Ruins" with an odd volume of Wordsworth, and another of Bell's "Anatomy" in a loose sheet of Webster's Dictionary, jams Moore's poems between the leaves of Bopp's Grammar,—and forgets only such small matters as combs and brushes.—LOWELL, JAMES RUSSELL, 1867-71, *Life and Letters of James Gates Percival, My Study Windows,* pp. 178, 186, 190.

Percival's poetry (though more highly esteemed forty years ago) fails to answer the reader's expectations, or to hold the attention beyond half a dozen pages. He undoubtedly had a perception of the beauty of nature, and there are frequent glimpses of this beauty in his poems; but they are fragmentary, scattered hints, rather than completed pictures, and remind us of the "broken crockery" school in the sister art of music. His thoughts, or, rather, his phrases, deflected by the turning corners of rhyme, run away with him, taking a new direction in every verse, and leading into eddies of words that even his friend the lexicographer could not have helped him out of, and that makes the perplexed reader wonder where, when, and how the many-jointed sentence is going to end. Percival had his poetic visions, doubtless, but he forgot that the word poet means *maker,* and he neglected the continuous labor and thought that might have shaped his glowing conceptions into forms of enduring beauty. His name and his works belong to the literary history of the country, but only a few of his simpler poems will remain to justify in some measure his reputation among his contemporaries.—UNDERWOOD, FRANCIS H., 1872, *A Hand-Book of English Literature, American Authors, p.* 165.

Though recognized by friends as a poet of the first (American) class, he never succeeded in interesting the great body of his intelligent countrymen in any but a few of his minor poems. He ranks among the great sorrowing class of neglected geniuses. A man of large though somewhat undigested erudition, knowing many languages and many sciences, he was seemingly ignorant of the art of marrying his knowledge to his imagination. When he wrote in prose, he was full of matter; when he wrote in verse, he was full of glow and aspiration and fancy, but wanting in matter.—WHIPPLE, EDWIN PERCY, 1876-86, *American Literature and Other Papers, ed. Whittier, p.* 85.

His carelessness has consigned him, along with others far less gifted, to oblivion.—PATTEE, FRED LEWIS, 1896, *A History of American Literature, p.* 170.

James Gates Percival was one of those unhappy mortals that never can get the sentimental nonsense shaken out of them by even the roughest contact with the world. He was bound to take a despairing view of everything. No amount of worldly success could persuade him to be cheerful. He was determined to write, and when he found that people read and rather liked his poetry, he vowed that he would write no more. It is needless to add, these oft-repeated vows of silence were broken whenever circumstances seemed to justify. Then because he was not exalted to a pinnacle higher than that occupied by a Byron or a Moore, the reading public was denounced for its sordid taste. . . . In spite of his Byronic tendencies, there is a nervous power in his verse that places him far above the majority of his predecessors. His fancies pour forth in a tumultuous flood that bewilders more than it pleases the reader. But some of his lighter pieces, like "The Coral Grove" show the delicacy of his fancy when not clouded by his constitutional melancholy. His "May" and "Seneca Lake" fully deserve the wide circulation which they enjoy.—ONDERDONK, JAMES L., 1899-1901, *History of American Verse, pp.* 153, 154.

Hugh Miller

1802–1856

Born, at Cromarty, 10 Oct. 1802. At school at Cromarty. Apprenticed to stonemason, 1819–22. Journeyman mason, 1822–34. Contrib. to "Inverness Courier," 1829. Accountant in Commercial Bank, Cromarty, 1834 to Dec. 1839. Married Lydia Falconer Fraser, 7 Jan. 1837. To Edinburgh, Dec. 1839. Editor of "The Witness," Jan. 1840; part proprietor, 1845. Visit to England, 1845. Brain gave way suddenly under severe illness; committed suicide, at Shrub Mount, near Edinburgh, 24 Dec. 1856. Buried in Grange Cemetery. *Works:* "Poems written in the Leisure Hours of a Journeyman Mason" (anon.), 1829; "Letters on the Herring Fishery" (anon.; from "Inverness Courier"), 1829; "Words of Warning to the People of Scotland," 1834 [?]; "Scenes and Legends of the North of Scotland," 1835; "Letter . . . to Lord Brougham," 1839; "Memoir of William Forsyth," 1839; "The Whiggism of the Old School," 1839; "The Old Red Sandstone" (from "The Witness"), 1841; "The Two Parties in the Church of Scotland," 1841; "The Two Mr. Clarks" (anon.), 1843; "Sutherland as it was and is" (anon.), 1843; "The Riots in Ross" (anon.), 1843; "Sutherland and the Sutherlanders" (anon.), 1844; "First Impressions of England, and its People," 1847; "Footprints of the Creator," 1849; "Thoughts on the Educational Question," 1850; "My Schools and Schoolmasters," 1852; "The Fossiliferous Deposits of Scotland," 1854; "Geology versus Astronomy," [1855]; "Strange but True," [1856]. *Posthumous:* "The Testimony of the Rocks," 1857; "The Cruise of the Betsey," ed. by W. S. Symonds, 1858; "Sketch-book of Popular Geology," ed. by his wife, 1859; "The Headship of Christ," 1861; "Essays," ed. by P. Bayne, 1862; "Tales and Sketches," ed. by his wife, 1863; "Edinburgh and its Neighbourhood," ed. by his wife, 1864; "Leading Articles on Various Subjects," ed. by J. Davidson, 1870. He *edited:* "Sermons for Sabbath Evenings," 1848. *Life:* "Life and Letters," by P. Bayne, 1871.—SHARP, R. FARQUHARSON, 1897, *A Dictionary of English Authors, p.* 198.

PERSONAL

Dearest Lydia,—My brain burns, I *must* have *walked;* and a fearful dream arises upon me. I cannot bear the horrible thought. God and Father of the Lord Jesus Christ, have mercy upon me. Dearest Lydia, dear children, farewell. My brain burns as the recollection grows. My dear, dear wife, farewell.—MILLER, HUGH, 1856, *Letter to his Wife, Dec.* 24.

In the last days of 1856, Hugh Miller died, a self-sacrificed martyr to science. At the great work which was to complete his service to his country and mankind he toiled on with indomitable resolution, amid the paroxysms of fearful disease. His powerful brain, wearied with the sustained tension of twenty years, recoiled from its work, and, as it were, groaned and struggled for rest. But that adamantine will knew no flinching. Ever, as the paroxysm passed by, and the soft glow of the old genius spread itself again along the mind, the most intense and unremitted exertion was compelled. The light burned nightly in his chamber, long after the midnight hour, as Hugh Miller continued to write, the body failing, the nerves fluttering, the brain still held to its work only by that indomitable will. He feared madness might dash the pen from his hand before the last line was traced. But the work was finished. On the last day of his life Hugh Miller said it was done. Madness and the grave could not at least deprive him of that. Then, as might have been expected, despite consultation with a physician, the paroxysm returned with redoubled fury; ere it again subsided, Hugh Miller was no more.—BAYNE, PETER, 1857, *Hugh Miller, Essays in Biography and Criticism, First Series, p.* 361.

Hugh Miller has very strikingly worked out this idea in his admirable autobiography, entitled, "My Schools and Schoolmasters." It is extremely interesting, even fascinating, as a book; but it is more than an ordinary book,—it might almost be called an institution. It is the history of the formation of a truly noble and independent character in the humblest condition of life,—the condition in which a large mass of the people of this country are born and brought up; and it teaches all, but especially poor men, what it is in the power of each to accomplish for himself. The life of Hugh Miller is full of lessons of self-help and self-respect, and shows the efficacy of these in working out for a man an honorable competence and a solid reputation.— SMILES, SAMUEL, 1860, *Brief Biographies.*

Who in Edinburgh, old enough to remember him, can forget the figure of that massively-built man, roughly apparelled in gray, or some dusty, reddish-brown, like an ex-stonemason not ashamed of himself, or the sad, resolute look of his sandy-coloured face, the features of which seemed smaller than they were from the quantity of reddish hair that matted his great round head? There was such a prevailing impression of reddishness, and even of stony reddishness, in his approach, that one instinctively thought of his own "Old Red Sandstone." His head might have been taken as a model for that of Gurth in "Ivanhoe," or, with a little alteration, for that of Rob Roy—for whom also he would have been no inapt model for breadth of chest, and personal strength. As a stonemason, he used to lift or roll weights twice as great as an ordinary man could manage. He had a pride in this; and one of his habits, I noticed, was an inquisitiveness as to the physical measurements and capabilities of those with whom he came in contact. "What is your height?" he would say, suddenly facing you, or "What is the girth of your chest?" looking at you sideways; and, if you were not prepared with an exact answer, he seemed surprised.— MASSON, DAVID, 1865, *Dead Men Whom I Have Known, Macmillan's Magazine, vol.* 12, *p.* 83.

He was a man raised up in Divine Providence for the time and the age. His business was to fight,—and, like the war-horse that saith among the trumpets, Ha, ha, and smelleth the battle afar off, fighting was Miller's delight. On the eve of what was to prove a desperate conflict, I have seen him in such a high and happy state of eagerness and excitement, that he seemed to me like some Indian *brave*, painted, plumed, leaping into the arena with a shout of defiance, flashing a tomahawk in his hand, and wearing at his girdle a very fringe of scalps, plucked from the heads of enemies that had fallen beneath his stroke. He was a scientific as well as an ardent controversialist; not bringing forward, far less throwing away, his whole force on the first assault, but keeping up the interest of the controversy, and continuing to pound and crush his opponents by fresh matter in every

succeeding paper. When I used to discuss subjects with him, under the impression perhaps that he had said all he had got to say very powerful and very pertinent to the question, nothing was more common than his remarking, in nautical phrase, "Oh, I have got some shot in the locker yet —ready for use if it is needed!"—GUTHRIE, THOMAS, 1873, *Autobiography and Memoir, ed. his Sons, vol.* II, *p.* 2.

The conversation of Hugh Miller, though agreeable and instructive, was not equal in charm to that of Robert Chambers. The mind of Hugh Miller was so wedded to the study of geology as to leave him but little inclination to diverge into the wider fields of history, philosophy, romance, and poetry, where he might have roamed to his own advantage, and that of the world, had time allowed and preoccupation not prevented. The no-wise related subjects of geology and the politics of the Free Church of Scotland occupied him fully; geology for the love he bore in it, and the Free Church politics for the discussion and dissemination of which he had become dependent for the daily bread of himself and his household.—MACKAY, CHARLES, 1887, *Through the Long Day, vol.* I, *p.* 86.

Miller's features were rugged, but his calm, grey eyes and pleasing smile softened their austerity. His voice was gentle. Not mixing much in general society, he reckoned himself a working man to the end, but he carried himself with much natural stateliness.—MILLER, HUGH, 1894, *Dictionary of National Biography, vol.* XXXVII, *p.* 410.

I count it as one of the privileges of my life to have known Hugh Miller, and as one of its chief losses that he was so suddenly removed when I had hardly realized the full value of his friendship and of his genial enthusiasm. His writings formed my earliest geological text-books, and I shall never cease to look back upon their influence with gratitude. They ought to be far more widely read than they seem now to be. Assuredly no young geologist will find more stimulating chapters than those penned by the author of the "Old Red Sandstone."—GEIKE, SIR ARCHIBALD, 1895, *Letter to Mr. Leask, Hugh Miller by W. Keith Leask (Famous Scots Series), p.* 150.

His funeral was the largest Edinburgh had seen since that of Chalmers, and by his side in the Grange Cemetery he was laid. To the mass of his countrymen abroad he was the greatest of living Scotchmen. His works had given him a European reputation in science, while to those at home the work he accomplished as a tribune of the people had given him a position second only to that of Guthrie.—LEASK, W. KEITH, 1896, *Hugh Miller (Famous Scots Series)*, p. 116.

GENERAL

In Mr. Miller we have to hail the accession to geological writers of a man highly qualified to advance the science. The work is to a beginner worth a thousand didactic treatises.—MURCHISON, SIR RODERICK IMPEY, 1842, *Address before the Royal Geological Society*.

A geological work ["Old Red Sandstone"] has appeared, small in size, unpretending in spirit and manner, its contents the conscientious and accurate narrative of fact, its style the beautiful simplicity of truth, and altogether possessing, for a rational reader, an interest superior to that of a novel.—SMITH, JOHN PYE, 1843, *Scripture and Geology, Third Ed.*

In Mr. Miller's charming little work ["Old Red Sandstone"] will be found a very graphic description of the Old Red fishes. I know not a more fascinating volume on any branch of British geology.—MANTELL, GIDEON ALGERNON, 1844, *The Medals of Creation*.

The works of Hugh Miller have excited the greatest interest, not only among scientific men, but also among general readers. There is in them a freshness of conception, a power of argumentation, a depth of thought, and a purity of feeling, rarely met with in works of such character, which are well calculated to call forth sympathy, and to increase the popularity of a science which has already done so much to expand our views of the plan of creation. The scientific illustrations published by Mr. Miller are most happily combined with considerations of a higher order, rendering both equally acceptable to the thinking reader. But what is in a great degree peculiar to our author is the successful combination of Christian doctrines with pure scientific truth.—AGASSIZ, JEAN LOUIS RODOLPHE, 1850, *ed. Footprints of the Creator, Introduction*.

"The Old Red Sandstone" was the first purely scientific volume published by Mr. Miller; and it placed him at once in the very front rank of geological observers and writers. Not the least attractive portion of this volume is that which introduces us to a knowlege of the author's own history, and tells us how he first became attracted to the study of geology, though without being conscious of what he was doing. . . . Never had fishes so fascinating a historian. Their dry bones wake into life beneath his pen, and scenes of the antediluvian world almost become matters of personal knowledge to us.—CHANDLER, MISS, 1851, *Hugh Miller and Popular Science, North American Review, vol. 73, pp. 451, 454.*

One of the most original writers of this age.—BARNES, ALBERT, 1855, *Essays and Reviews, vol. II, p. 346.*

Hugh Miller stands alone, as far as I am aware, among self-educated men of recent times, first, in the thoroughness of his education, the technically disciplined and ordered thinking to which he attained, secondly, in the absence from his books and letters of all extravagance, histrionism; paradox, of all traces of that furious, teeth-gnashing humor which has been so much in vogue in our century. Great instincts of order and of common sense, inherited from his father, allied him to what was stable in the institutions of his country. Religion, integrity, continence, moderation, obedience,—all those virtues against which the waves of modern anarchism beat wild, saw him fighting behind their bulwark. They are shallow critics who recognize genius only, as Uriel recognized Satan, by the violence of its gestures and the devilishness of its scowl; in healthful times men of genius have neither affected a perverse singularity, nor taken as their dialect an everlasting snarl. THAT HUGH MILLER WAS A MAN OF GENIUS WOULD NEVER HAVE BEEN CALLED IN QUESTION HAD HIS WORKS NOT BEEN SO FREE FROM THE DISTEMPERS OF GENIUS!—BAYNE, PETER, 1871, *The Life and Letters of Hugh Miller, vol. II, p. 497.*

Hugh Miller, the author of "The Old Red Sandstone" and "The Testimony of the Rocks," the devotee and unfortunately the martyr of scientific inquiry, brought a fresh and brilliant literary ability, almost as untutored and spontaneous as that of his immortal countryman, Robert Burns, to bear on the exposition of the studies to which he literally sacrificed his life.—McCARTHY, JUSTIN, 1879, *A History of Our Own Times from the Accession of Queen Victoria to the Berlin Congress, ch.* xxix.

The scientific value of these works is generally acknowledged; their literary merit is hardly less marked. Though his verses were never particularly successful, Hugh Miller was a thorough poet at heart. Metre was not the most suitable vehicle for the expression of his thoughts, and it was not yet the custom to cut up prose into lines of unequal length with capital letters at the beginning and call that poetry. But in his power of picturesque and fervid prose, he may at least claim a high rank among poetical writers.—OLIPHANT, MARGARET O. W., 1892, *The Victorian Age of English Literature, p.* 372.

Hugh Miller will always occupy a peculiar place in the history of geology, and in the ranks of geological literature. He was not in any sense a trained geologist. He lacked the habit of patience and detailed investigation in departments of the science that did not specially interest him, but which were essential as a basis of accurate induction and successful speculation. . . . Hugh Miller's unique position is that of a poetic student of the geological side of Nature, who possessed an unrivalled gift of vividly communicating to others the impressions made on his own mind by the observation of geological fact and by the inference which such observation seemed to warrant. His lively imagination led him to seize more especially on those aspects of the past history of the earth which could be most vividly realized. He loved to collect the plants and the animals of which the remains have been entombed among the rocks, and to re-people with them the scenes in which they lived long ages ago. Each scattered fact was marshalled by his eager fancy into its due place in the mental picture which he drew of such long-vanished lands, lakes, rivers, and seas. His enthusiasm supplied details where facts were wanting, and enabled him to kindle in his readers not a little of the burning interest which he felt himself.—GEIKE, SIR ARCHIBALD, 1895, *Letter to Mr. Leask, Hugh Miller by W. Keith Leask (Famous Scots Series), pp.* 147, 148.

The Witness started with a circulation of six hundred. Its position among the Scottish papers was at once assured, and no greater proof of the personality of the editor and the quality of "the leaders" remains than in the curious fact that, now after half a century, to the great mass of the people his name has been not Miller, nor Mr. Miller, but Hugh Miller. As in the similar case of John Bright the people seized on the fact that here was a writer and speaker sprung from themselves, and his Christian name was as familiar as his surname.—LEASK, W. KEITH, 1896, *Hugh Miller (Famous Scots Series), p.* 99.

But whatever the scientific value of Miller's geological discoveries, and whatever the equipment of exact science which he brought to their elucidation, he had two qualities which make him almost unique as a scientific writer—a wealth of imagination, and a marvellous power of picturesque description, instinct with moral feeling. No writer has treated geological discoveries with more of that artistic skill which is rarely applied to any but the outward and obvious aspects of nature; and no writer can more readily make his descriptions serve as vehicles of moral emotion, and of deep human sympathy. That his art, however natural, was perfect in its kind, is seen in the entire absence of anything that is akin to fine writing or rodomontade. There is no tawdriness of ornament, and its absence gives that force and dignity which must surely prevent Miller's writing, however limited on its scientific side, from being altogether forgotten or neglected.— CRAIK, HENRY, 1896, *English Prose, vol.* v, *p.* 476.

A great deal of Miller's work was done for *The Witness.* He was a most conscientious as well as a most able journalist, and he brought to his occupation a rare literary power. There was an imaginative and poetic strain in his nature which sometimes showed itself in the weaker form of writing, but often gave eloquence to his descriptions and fervour to his argument. This is the living part of him; for it is certainly not their scientific value that causes Hugh Miller's books to be still read. . . . In their geological aspect they merely supply the raw material of science. Miller had not the previous training requisite to give his work the highest value. He knew little or nothing about comparative anatomy, and therefore could not himself deal with the fossils he discovered. In the view of modern experts his scientific value lies in his strong common sense and his keen powers of observation amounting almost to genius. His function is to stimulate others rather than to sway thought by great discoveries.—WALKER, HUGH, 1897, *The Age of Tennyson, pp.* 178, 179.

Douglas William Jerrold

1803–1857

1803, Douglas William Jerrold was born in London on January 3. His father was Samuel Jerrold.—1809, School at Sheerness.—1813, Entered the navy as mid-shipman in December.—1816, Started life in London as a compositor.—1821, His first play, "More Frightened than Hurt," produced at Sadlers Wells.—1824, August, married Mary Swann. —1825, Engaged at a salary to write pieces for the Coburg Theatre when wanted.—1829, "Black-Eyed Susan" and "Thomas à Becket" at the Surrey.—1838, "Men of Character" illustrated by Thackeray.—1839, "Handbook of Swindling."—1840, Edited and partly wrote, "Heads of the People," illustrated by Kenny Meadows.—1841, *Punch* started, with Jerrold as one of the principal contributors ("Mrs. Caudle's Curtain Lectures," "Punch's Letters to His Son," &c.)—1843-4, Edited the *Illuminated Magazine* ("Chronicles of Clovernook," &c.)—1845-8, Edited *Douglas Jerrold's Shilling Magazine* ("St. Giles and St. James"; the "Hedgehog Letters"; "Twiddlethumb Town," &c.).—1846-8, Edited *Douglas Jerrold's Weekly Newspaper* ("Barber's Chair," &c.).—1852,Became editor of *Lloyd's Weekly Newspaper.*—1854, "The Heart of Gold" (the last of upwards of sixty plays), produced at the Princess's.—1857, Died June 8.—JERROLD, WALTER, 1893, *ed. Bon-Mots of Charles Lamb and Douglas Jerrold, Introduction, p.* 11.

PERSONAL

When I behold the false and flatter'd state
  Which all ambition points at, and survey
The hurried pageants of the passing day,
  Where all press on to share a fleeting fate,
Methinks the living triumphs that await
  On hours like thine, might tempt the proud
    to stay.
For on a green and all unworldly way,
  Thy hand hath twined the chaplet of the
    great,
And the first warmth and fragrance of its fame,
  Are stealing on thy soul. The time shall be
When men may find a music in thy name,
  To rouse deep fancies and opinions free;
Affections fervid as the sun's bright flame,
  And sympathies unfathom'd as the sea.
—BLANCHARD, LAYMAN, 1824, *To D. W. J.*

Never did I see a handsomer head on an uglier body. Douglas Jerrold is small, with stooping shoulders; but the head placed upon those shoulders is truly magnificent. He has the head of a Jupiter on the body of a Thersites. A high, broad, cheerful, arched forehead; a very fine mouth; a well-shaped nose; clear, heaven-blue eyes; make the face of Jerrold one of the handsomest.— KALISCH, LUDWIG, 1855, *Cologne Gazette, Aug.* 12; *The Life and Remains of Douglas Jerrold by William Blanchard Jerrold, p.* 307.

My first impression was one of surprise,— not at his remarkable appearance, of which I was aware; — the eyes and mobile countenance, the stoop, and the small figure, reminding one of Coleridge, without being like him,—but at the gentle and thoughtful kindness which set its mark on all he said and did. Somehow, all his good things were so dropped as to fall into my trumpet, without any trouble or ostentation. This was the dreaded and unpopular man who must have been hated (for he *was* hated) as *Punch* and not as Jerrold,—through fear, and not through reason nor feeling. His wit always appeared to me as gentle as it was honest,—as innocent as it was sound. I could say of him as of Sydney Smith, that I never heard him say, in the way of raillery, any thing of others that I should mind his saying of me. I never feared him in the least, nor saw reason why any but knaves or fools should fear him.—MARTINEAU, HARRIET, 1855-77, *Autobiography, ed. Chapman, vol.* II, *p.* 32.

He was a very short man, but with breadth enough, and a back excessively bent,—bowed almost to deformity; very gray hair, and a face and expression of remarkable briskness and intelligence. His profile came out pretty boldly, and his eyes had the prominence that indicates, I believe, volubility of speech, nor did he fail to talk from the instant of his appearance; and in the tone of his voice, and in his glance, and in the whole man, there was something racy,—a flavor of the humorist. His step was that of an aged man, and he put his stick down very decidedly at every footfall; though as he afterwards told me that he was only fifty-two, he need not yet have been infirm. . . . I like Douglas Jerrold very much.—HAWTHORNE, NATHANIEL, 1856, *English Note-Books, vol.* II, *April 5.*

Men who linger wistfully on the memory of that tiny frame; on that eager, radiant face; on those infantine ways, with their wonderfully subtle and elaborate guilelessness; on that ailing constitution and fiery blood; on that joyous, tender, teasing, frolicsome, thoughtful heart; must always think of him, less as the flashing wit and scathing satirist,—than as of some marvellously gifted, noble, and wayward child, the sport of nature and the delight of man. He will be recalled to those who knew and loved him, not by any big and sounding appellation, but by some affectionate and soft diminutive;—not as brilliant Douglas nor magnificent Douglas, but simply and fondly as *dear* Douglas.—DIXON, HEPWORTH, 1858, *Athenæum, Dec. 25.*

A man, too, of whom I will say that, let the judgment on his remaining writings be permanently what it may, and let tongues have spoken of him this or that awry, there breathed not, to my knowledge, within the unwholesome bounds of what is specially London, any one in whose actual person there was more of the pith of energy at its tensest, of that which in a given myriad anywhere distinguishes the one. How like a little Nelson he stood, dashing back his hair, and quivering for the verbal combat! The flash of his wit, in which one quality the island had not his match, was but the manifestation easiest to be observed of a mind compact of sense and information, and of a soul generous and on fire.—MASSON, DAVID, 1859, *British Novelists and Their Styles, p.* 235.

There was nothing cynical nor sour in his heart, as I knew it. In the company of children and young people he was particularly happy, and showed to extraordinary advantage. He never was so gay, so sweet-tempered, so pleasing, and so pleased as then. Among my own children I have observed this many and many a time. When they and I came home from Italy, in 1845, your father went to Brussels to meet us, in company with our friends, Mr. Forster and Mr. Maclise. We all travelled together about Belgium for a little while, and all came home together. He was the delight of the children all the time, and they were his delight. He was in his most brilliant spirits, and I doubt if he were ever more humorous in his life. But the most enduring impression that he left upon us, who are grown up,—and we have all often spoken of it since—was, that Jerrold, in his amiable capacity of being easily pleased, in his freshness, in his good nature, in his cordiality, and in the unrestrained openness of his heart, had quite captivated us. Of his generosity I had a proof within these two or three years, which it saddens me to think of now. There had been an estrangement between us—not on any personal subject, and not involving an angry word—and a good many months had passed without my seeing him in the street, when it fell out that we dined each with his own separate party, in the Stranger's Room of· a club. Our chairs were almost back to back, and I took mine after he was seated and at dinner. I said not a word (I am sorry to remember), and did not look that way. Before we had sat so long, he openly wheeled his chair around, stretched out both his hands in a most engaging manner, and said aloud with a bright and loving face that I can see as I write to you, "For God's sake let us be friends again! A life's not long enough for this."—DICKENS, CHARLES, 1859, *To Blanchard Jerrold, The Life and Remains of Douglas Jerrold, p.* 356.

Douglas Jerrold at home, might generally be found on Sundays surrounded, not by big-wigs who would have been glad to find themselves in his society—not by old, serious professors of all branches of learning—certainly not—but by young men yet unknown to fame. He loved the buoyancy, heartiness, and the boldness of youth. It was his glory to have about him six or seven youngsters, hardly reached their majority, with whom he could talk pleasantly, and to whom he poured out his jokes, grateful for the heartiness of the reception they got from warm blood. It was the main thing about his individuality that he was himself always young. "A man is as old as he feels," he insisted continually; and then casting back the solid flakes of his silvered hair, he would laugh and vow that few men of five-and-twenty were younger than he. His words, when he spoke seriously among his young guests, generally conveyed some generous advice, or some offer of service. Many men date their literary advancement from the study of Douglas Jerrold.—JERROLD, WILLIAM BLANCHARD, 1859, *The Life and Remains of Douglas Jerrold, p.* 286.

Absurd as the bare idea of bitterness must appear in connection with such a nature as his, to those who really knew him, the reason why strangers so often and so ridiculously misunderstood him, is not difficult to discover. That marvellous brightness and quickness of perception which has distinguished him far and wide as the sayer of some of the wittiest, and often some of the wisest things also, in the English language, expressed itself almost with the suddenness of lightning. This absence of all appearance of artifice and preparation, this flash and readiness which made the great charm of his wit, rendered him, at the same time, quite incapable of suppressing a good thing from prudential considerations. It sparkled off his tongue before he was aware of it. It was always a bright surprise to himself; and it never occurred to him that it could be anything but a bright surprise to others. All his so-called bitter things were said with a burst of hearty school-boy laughter, which showed how far he was himself from attaching a serious importance to them. Strangers apparently failed to draw this inference, plain as it was; and often mistook him accordingly. If they had seen him in the society of children; if they had surprised him in the house of any one of his literary brethren who was in difficulty and distress, if they had met him by the bed-side of a sick friend, how simply and how irresistibly the gentle, generous, affectionate nature of the man would then have disclosed itself to the most careless chance acquaintance who ever misunderstood him! Very few men have won the loving regard of so many friends so rapidly, and have kept that regard so enduringly to the last day of their lives, as Douglas Jerrold.—COLLINS, WILLIAM WILKIE, 1863, *My Miscellanies.*

On the occasion of the first performance of Jerrold's comedy of "Time Works Wonders," I had the good fortune to occupy a seat in his private box, and I well remember his feeling of delight, at the close, when he contemplated the success he had achieved. . . . Arrived at the door of the hotel, I could not help repeating the gratification I felt at the author's well-merited triumph,

when Jerrold, turning his eye full upon me, and smacking his chest with his hand, exclaimed, with a degree of exultation which was most natural under the circumstances, "Yes; and here's the little man that's done it!"—HODDER, GEORGE, 1870, *Memories of My Time.*

Douglas Jerrold worked at a desk without a speck upon it, using an inkstand in a marble shell clear of all litter, his little dog at his feet. If a comedy was in progress, he would now and then walk rapidly up and down the room, talking wildly to himself. "If it be *Punch* copy, you shall hear him laugh presently as he hits upon a droll bit." And then, abruptly, the pen would be put down, and the author would pass out into the garden, and pluck a hawthorn leaf, and go nibbling it, and thinking, down the side walks; then "in again, and vehemently to work," unrolling the thought that had come to him along little blue slips of paper, in letters smaller than the type in which they were presently to be set.—JACOX, FRANCIS, 1872, *Aspects of Authorship, p.* 14.

Jerrold would perceive the germ of a retort before you had well begun to form your sentence, and would bring it forth in full blossom the instant you had done speaking. He had a way of looking straight in the face of one to whom he dealt a repartee, and with an expression of eye that seemed to ask appreciation of the point of the thing he was going to say, thus depriving it of personality or ill-nature. It was as if he called upon its object to enjoy it with him, rather than to resent its sharpness. There was a peculiar compression with a sudden curve or lift up of the lip that showed his own sense of the fun of the thing he was uttering, while his glance met his interlocutor's with a firm unflinching roguery and an unfaltering drollery of tone that had none of the sidelong furtive look and irritating tone of usual utterers of mere rough retorts. —CLARKE, CHARLES AND MARY COWDEN, 1876, *Douglas Jerrold and His Letters, Gentleman's Magazine, N. S., vol.* 17, *p.* 500.

His heart was as kindly a one as ever beat in a human bosom; and his hand most liberal, and often far more liberal than his means might have justified. He was once asked by a literary acquaintance, whether he had the courage, to lend him a guinea. "Oh yes," he replied, "I've got the courage; but I haven't got the guinea." He had always the courage to do a kind action; and when he had the guinea, it was always at the command of the suffering and the distressed, especially if the sufferer from pecuniary woe was a brother of the quill, and an honest laborer in the field of literature.—MACKAY, CHARLES, 1877, *Forty Years' Recollections of Life, Literature and Public Affairs from* 1830 *to* 1870.

Jerrold lived to be a prosperous man; but no one ever accused him of generosity or sympathy; his wit, which, unlike that of his associate, often

"Carried a heart-stain away on its blade,"

was ever biting, bitter, and caustic, and careless as distinguishing friend from foe. Many of his brilliant *bon mots* and witticisms are current in literary cliques; but I have rarely heard one repeated that was not calculated to give somebody pain. Long neglect, doubtless, soured his temper, and when reputation and comparative wealth came to him—somewhat late in life, and, I believe, after years of privation— they found him, like the wholesome draught which the thunder-storm has converted into a sour and deleterious drink. Few countenances expressed a character more truthfully than did that of Jerrold; it was highly intellectual, but severe, and exceedingly sarcastic—just that of one whom a prudent man would not covet for a foe, and would hardly expect to hail as a friend.— HALL, SAMUEL CARTER, 1883, *Retrospect of a Long Life*, p. 398.

Jerrold's capacity for study was enormous, and his perseverance indefatigable; night and morning he worked at Latin, French, and Italian, besides getting through a vast amount of reading.—JERROLD, WALTER, 1890, *Chambers' Encyclopædia, vol.* VI, p. 304.

GENERAL

We must make a charge here, too, against our accomplished author, which we have elsewhere made more than once. He is too fond of repartee. He can bear to be told this, for he shares the fault in very illustrious company. Congreve always made wit too much the business, instead of the ornament of his comedies. In Mr. Jerrold's dialogue passages are every now and then peeping out, which seem to have been prepared "cut and dry" for the scene. The speaker has evidently brought them with him; he has not caught them on the scene by the help of some light of dialogue or suggestion of present circumstances. We beg of Mr.

Jerrold to consider this more curiously in his next production, and we beg of him to lose no time in favouring us again.—FORSTER, JOHN, 1834, *The Drama, New Monthly Magazine, vol.* 41, *pt.* II, *p.* 516.

I am truly proud of your remembrance, and have put the "Story of a Feather" on a shelf (not an obscure one) where some other feathers are, which it shall help to show mankind which way the wind blows, long after *we* know where the wind comes from. I am quite delighted to find that you have touched the latter part again, and touched it with such a delicate and tender hand. It is a wise and beautiful book.— DICKENS, CHARLES, 1843, *Letter to Douglas Jerrold, The Life and Remains of Douglas Jerrold, ed. Jerrold, p.* 113.

A little of his writing goes a great way. You stop very often, and do not return to the book for another dose, till next week, or so. The exceptions to this are chiefly in his acted comedies, where there is plentiful admixture of brilliant levity and stinging fun; but in all else he usually reads you a lesson of a very trying kind. Even his writings in "Punch" give you more of the baton, than the beverage "in the eye."— HORNE, RICHARD HENGIST, 1844, *A New Spirit of the Age, p.* 172.

He had a sailor's heart; 'twas thus he drew
The sailor's character with touch so true:
The first that gave our stage its British tar,
Impulsive, strenuous, both in love and war;
With English instinct, using still his blade
Against the strong, the weaker cause to aid.
While Dibdin's song on English decks is sung,
While Nelson's name lives on the sailor's
    tongue,
Still Susan's tenderness and William's *faith*
Shall weave for Jerrold's tomb a lasting *wreath*.
—TAYLOR, TOM, 1857, *Spoken at the Adelphi Theatre, July* 29.

He tried many things, and he produced much; but the root of him was that he was a humorous thinker. He did not write first-rate plays, or first-rate novels, rich as he was in *the elements* of playwright and novelist. He was not an artist. But he had a rare and original eye and soul,—and in a peculiar way he could pour out himself. In short, to be an essayist was the bent of his nature and genius. . . . Inveterately satirical as Jerrold is, he is even "spoonily" tender at the same time, and it lay deep in his character; for this wit *bon vivant*, the merriest and wittiest man of the company, would cry like a child as the night drew on and the talk grew serious. No theory could be more false than that he was a cold-blooded satirist—sharp as steel is sharp, from being hard. The basis of his nature was sensitiveness and impulsiveness. His wit is not of the head only, but of the heart —often sentimental, and constantly *fanciful*: that is, dependent on a quality which imperatively requires a sympathetic nature to give it full play. Take those *Punch* papers which soon helped to make *Punch* famous, and Jerrold himself better known. Take the "Story of a Feather" as a good expression of his more earnest and tender mood. How delicately all the part about the poor actress is worked up! How moral, how stoical the feeling that pervades it! The bitterness is healthy—healthy as bark. —HANNAY, JAMES, 1857, *Douglas Jerrold, Atlantic Monthly, vol.* 1, *pp.* 4, 6.

The obscure player's son has stamped the impress of his genius upon the literature and character of his age and country, with an authentic and royal seal. Like most men who have achieved permanent fame, and won for themselves a definite *status* in the republic of letters, in science, or in art, he had to struggle through long years of toil, poverty, and neglect before he could command a platform high enough to compel the public to listen to him, and acknowledge the supremacy of his intellect.— PHILLIPS, G. S., 1859, *Douglas Jerrold, North American Review, vol.* 89, *p.* 432.

The leading characteristic of Douglas Jerrold's nature was earnestness. He was in earnest in his abhorrence of all things mean and interested; earnest in his noble indignation at wrong and oppression; earnest in the very wit with which he vented his sense of detestation for evil-doing. He was deeply earnest in all serious things; and very much in earnest when dealing with less apparently important matters, which he thought needed the scourge of sarcasm. Any one who could doubt the earnestness of Jerrold should have seen him when a child was the topic; the fire of his eye, the quiver of his lip, bore witness of the truth of the phrase he himself uses in his charming drama of "The Schoolfellows," showing that to him indeed "children are sacred things."—CLARKE, CHARLES AND MARY COWDEN, 1876, *Douglas Jerrold and His Letters, Gentleman's Magazine, N. S. vol.* 17, *p.* 350.

Were *Punch* and Douglas Jerrold the John the Baptists, the forerunners, of the new literature that was one of the chief means to this end? *Punch* from the first, under all its brightness, its bitterness, its pointed irony, its terrible, scorching sarcasm, hid a most tender heart. It took the side of the poor and the oppressed. Its sympathies were with the under dog in the fight. In its columns, unless my memory plays me false (and I am at this moment unable to verify the assumption) brilliant, mocking, tender, satirical, kindly, impetuous Douglas Jerrold published the first distinctively Christmas story.—DORR, JULIA C. R., 1885, *Christmas and its Literature, The Book Buyer, vol.* 2, *p.* 284.

The subtlest wit of the century.—MACKAY, CHARLES, 1887, *Through the Long Day, vol.* I, *p.* 253.

His reputation as a brilliant wit, for which he himself had anything but an affection, has overshadowed his literary fame. His brightly-written essays always repay perusal, but his plays have not held the stage, and his novels are little read.—HAMILTON, J. A., 1892, *Dictionary of National Biography, vol.* XXIX, *p.* 351.

People who speak bitterly speak in most cases from mere excess of feeling. It is much the same with Douglas Jerrold. In his imagination he spares no sarcasm to give effect to his invectives; he strives to the utmost to make each sentence as pointed as possible, nay, as one of his critics remarked, every word seems to have been especially sharpened before being used. He wrote, as Hawthorne says, with an honest and manly purpose; he was thoroughly sincere; he earnestly desired to make the world better, to lighten its suffering, and give a nobler dignity to life. But like Carlyle he lacked the higher qualities of the teacher: gentleness, forbearance, patience. He was too impulsive, too eager, too desirous of enforcing his views with peremptory sternness. An author who sees scarcely anything but the imperfection of human nature and the injustice of the world, who is so severe upon our faults, and who shows so little indulgence for our weakness, seems to take up a position outside the range of our sympathies, and thus alienates himself from his fellow men. There can be no doubt that Douglas Jerrold's writings fail of their full effect from this cause. We feel that we are not so black as we are painted; that the world is not so selfish, so mean, and so cruel as the satirist represents. Douglas Jerrold was never as widely popular as Dickens, but during his lifetime his reputation had spread so far that he had many readers and many ardent admirers. When he died it was felt that there was a public loss. Since then his influence as a writer seems to have passed away year by year.—COPPING, ED-WARD, 1892, *Douglas Jerrold, New Review, vol.* 7, *p.* 364.

A sort of very inferior Hook on the other side of politics, with a dash (also very inferior) of Hood, whose "Mrs. Caudle's Curtain Lectures" and similar things were very popular at and a little before the middle of the century, but whose permanent literary value is of the smallest, if indeed it can be said to exist.—SAINTSBURY,

GEORGE, 1896, *A History of Nineteenth Century Literature, p.* 210.

Another writer very popular in his day, though now gone out like so many more, Douglas Jerrold, asked and obtained an entrance into the Magazine, where he scarcely can have found himself at home. He contributed a few of his characteristic farcical stories, and was vigorously denounced by Warren, who took the trouble to write to the Blackwoods solemnly asserting that his sole motive was of the highest kind, to implore them to put an end to contributions which were impairing the tone of the Magazine and disgusting its readers. I do not suppose this adjuration had any effect; but Jerrold's contributions did not continue very long.—OLIPHANT, MARGARET O. W., 1897, *William Blackwood and His Sons, vol.* II, *p.* 241.

John Wilson Croker

1780–1857

Born, in Galway, 20 Dec. 1780. Educated at schools in Cork and Portarlington. To Trinity Coll., Dublin, Nov. 1796; B. A., 1800. Entered at Lincoln's Inn, 1800. Studied law for two years. Contrib. letters on French Revolution to "The Times"; and assisted in starting "The Cabinet" and "The Picnic." Returned to Dublin, 1802. Called to Irish Bar, 1802. Married Rosamond Pennell, 1806. M. P. for Downpatrick, May 1807 to 1812. Acting Chief Secretary for Ireland, 1808. Assisted in starting "Quarterly Review," Feb. 1809; contrib. frequently to it, 1809–57. LL.B. and LL.D., Dublin 1809. Secretary of the Admiralty, 9 Oct. 1809 to Nov. 1830. F. R. S., 5 July 1810. M.P. for Athlone, 1812–18; for Yarmouth, I. of W., 1819–20; for Bodmin, 1820–26; for Aldeburgh, 1826–27; for Dublin Univ., 1827–30; for Aldeburgh, 1830–32. Appointed Privy Councillor, 16 June 1828. First to make use of term "Conservatives," in "Quarterly Review" for Jan. 1830. Retired from public life, Aug. 1832. Chiefly occupied in literary pursuits till his death. Died, at Hampton, 10 Aug. 1857. Buried at West Moulsey. *Works:* "Theatrical Tears" (anon.), 1804; "Familiar Epistles to Frederick Jones, Esq." (anon.), 1804; "An Intercepted Letter" (anon.), 1804; "Songs of Trafalgar," 1804; "The History of Cutchacutchoo" (anon.), 1805; "The Anazoniad" (anon), 1806; "A Sketch of the State of Ireland" (anon.), 1808; "The Battle of Talavera" (anon.), 1809; "Key to the Orders in Council," 1812; "A Letter on the fittest style . . . for the Wellington Testimonial," 1815; "Monarchy according to the Charter" (anon.), 1816; "Stories for Children from the History of England," 1817; "A Second Letter from the King to his People," 1821; "Two Letters on Scottish Affairs" (under pseud. of Edward Bradwardine Waverley), 1826; "Progressive Geography for Children," 1828; "Military Events of the French Revolution of 1830," 1831; "History of the Guillotine" (from "Quarterly Review"), 1853; "Correspondence with Lord John Russell on . . . Moore's Diary," 1854; "Essays on the Early Period of the French Revolution" (from "Quarterly Review"), 1857. *Posthumous:* "The Croker Papers"; correspondence and diaries, ed. with *life*, by L. J. Jennings (3 vols.), 1884. He *translated:* Chateaubriand's "Monarchy according to the Charter," 1816; "Royal Memoirs of the French Revolution," 1823; and *edited:* "Memoirs of the Embassy of the Marshal de Bassompierre," 1819; Lady Harvey's "Letters," 1821–22; "The Suffolk Papers," 1823; Horace Walpole's "Letters to Lord Hertford," 1824; Countess of Suffolk's "Letters," 1824; Boswell's "Life of Johnson," 1831; "John, Lord Hervey's Memories of the Court of George II," 1848.—SHARP, R. FARQUHARSON, 1897, *A Dictionary of English Authors, p.* 70.

PERSONAL

Your paper is a *very* good one—lively and wise too, as is your wont. It has received an unique compliment. Mr. Croker pronounces it "charming both for the sense and pleasantry." I scarcely think he ever said a word in favour of any other article not his own.—LOCKHART, JOHN GIBSON, 1845, *Letter to Miss Rigby, July* 8; *Memoirs of Lady Eastlake, ed. Smith, vol.* I, *p.* 165.

His best place was his desk at the Admiralty; his best action was in his office; and the most painful part of his life was the latter part, amidst an ignoble social reputation, and the political odium attached to him by Mr. Disraeli's delineation of him in "Coningsby."— MARTINEAU, HARRIET, 1857, *Biographical Sketches, p.* 68.

While Macaulay is thus ascending to the House of Peers, his old enemy and rival Croker has descended to the grave, very noiselessly and almost without observation, for he had been for some time so withdrawn from the world that he was nearly forgotten. He had lived to see all his predictions of ruin and disaster to the country completely falsified. He continued till the last year or two to exhale his bitterness and spite in the columns of the *Quarterly Review*, but at last the editor (who had long been sick of his contributions) contrived to get rid of him. I never lived in any intimacy with him, and seldom met him in society, but he certainly occupied a high place among the second-rate men of his time; he had very considerable talents, great industry, with much information and a retentive memory. He spoke in Parliament with considerable force and in society his long acquaintance with the world and with the public affairs, and his stores of general knowledge made him entertaining, though he was too over-bearing to be agreeable. He was particularly disliked by Macaulay, who never lost an opportunity of venting his antipathy by attacks upon him.—GREVILLE, CHARLES C. F., 1857, *A Journal of the Reign of Queen Victoria from* 1852 *to* 1860, *ed. Reeve, Sept.* 6, *p.* 377.

The immense correspondence of all kinds which he left strips away disguises. If he had been the unjust, selfish, and bad man described by his foes, this correspondence would have told the tale. That his character was not without defects, assuredly he would have been the last to pretend. He sometimes held extreme opinions, and was extreme in his way of advocating them. He was of a combative disposition, ever ready 'for a fray, and seldom happier than when the cry of battle rung in his ears. He was a redoubtable opponent, as his enemies found out to their cost; and a man who struck so hard, and so often, was sure to make many enemies. But any fair-minded reader who dispassionately considers his life and work, with the aid of the materials which are now produced for the formation of a right conclusion, will speedily be convinced that, so far from being wholly "bad," the vehement controversialist had, after all, a kindly heart and a generous nature; and that in everything he undertook he was animated by a lofty sense of duty, which alone could entitle him to respectful recollection. — JENNINGS, LOUIS J., 1884, *ed. The Correspondence and Diaries of the Late John Wilson Croker, vol.* I, *p.* 3.

Notwithstanding his eminent services and his real merit, it is not by these that he is known to the present generation, who are indebted for their ideas of him rather to his enemies than his friends. To most men under fifty he is the Croker only of Boswell's Johnson or the Rigby of Mr. Disraeli's "Coningsby." . . . That Mr. Croker was not the man he has been painted by either of those two redoubtable antagonists, may reasonably be inferred from his relations with the eminent men who were his regular and familiar associates. But that two writers so utterly unlike each other as Macaulay and Disraeli should have agreed only in depreciating Croker, unless there was something in the man corresponding to the picture they have drawn of him, is hardly to be credited.—KEBBEL, T. E., 1884, *John Wilson Croker, The Fortnightly Review, vol.* 42, *p.* 689.

One would fain believe that the correspondent of Scott, the adviser of Peel, and the friend of Wellington was not the base and unscrupulous sycophant whom Mr. Disraeli has painted under the name of Rigby. But to any one who carefully studies Mr. Jennings's own account of the relations between his hero and Lord Hertford, one thing is clear—no impartial critic can ever, as regards the gravest charge against Croker, give a more favorable verdict than "not proven"; and even his modified form of acquital can be gained only by an apologist who frankly admits the moral coarseness or want of delicacy which, perhaps, explains conduct that, in any person endowed with ordinary sense of what is becoming and of good report, would argue the most disgraceful turpitude.— DICEY, A. V., 1885, *John Wilson Croker, The Nation, vol.* 40, *p.* 122.

Councillor Crawley, a character in Lady Morgan's "Florence Macarthy," is a representation of John Wilson Croker. The portrait was so life-like in all its dominant particulars that it afforded as much amusement to his friends as to his foes. It was a revenge for his strictures, in his "Familiar Epistles" (1804), on the Dublin stage.— FREY, ALBERT R., 1888, *Sobriquets and Nicknames, p.* 73.

He was manifestly a man of strict honour, of high principle, of upright life, of great courage, of untiring industry, devoted with singleness of heart to the interests of his country, a loyal friend, and in his domestic relations unexceptionable. Living in the days when party rancour raged, prominent as a speaker in Parliament, and wielding a trenchant and too often personally aggressive pen in the leading organ of the tory party, he came in for the very large share of misrepresentation which always pursues political partisans. His literary tastes were far from catholic in their range, and he made himself obnoxious to the newer school by the dogmatic and narrow spirit and the sarcastic bitterness which are apt to be the sins that more easily beset the self-constituted and anonymous critics of a leading review. Thus to political adversaries he added many an enemy in the field of literature. As he never replied to any attack, however libelous, it became the practice among a certain class of writers to accuse him of heartlessness and malignity.—MARTIN, SIR THEODORE, 1888, *Dictionary of National Biography, vol.* XIII, *p.* 131.

From both sides this very important Personage in his generation has been done to death, or rather has been exhibited in all his cleverness and bitterness and officialism as a man for whom there was no milk of human kindness to spare. It was natural, perhaps, in those days when Whigs and Tories were ever at each other's throats, and even so mild and genial a man as William Blackwood spoke of his opponents as "the cursed Whigs," that Macaulay should cut to pieces in his most incisive way his political antagonist. But that the same individual

should also be assailed in the house of his friends, and set up as an image of scorn in that house for the warning and edification of future generations, was a hard fate. —OLIPHANT, MARGARET O. W., 1897, *William Blackwood and his Sons, vol.* I, *p.* 473.

The life of a writer has been said to be a warfare upon earth, and Croker's experience was largely in support of the proposition. From his first appearance in literature to his last he was the object of unjust and unsparing attack. Political differences largely accounted for this, as did also the fact that he was frequently on the winning side. . . . His judgments on literary and political matters, even after his retirement from parliament and public life, had great influence. As a politician he was always at least consistent, and Irishmen especially should remember that he advocated the Catholic claims nearly a quarter of a century before the passing of the Emancipation Act by a government of which he was a member. He sometimes held extreme views, and supported them with vigour, and occasionally with bitterness. Had he imparted less of a certain arrogance of tone into his speeches, he might have made fewer enemies, and his manners towards strangers or those who did not know him certainly savoured of harshness; but, as was said of Dr. Johnson, there was "nothing of the bear about him except the skin." —SILLARD, P. A., 1898, *John Wilson Croker, The Gentleman's Magazine, vol.* 285, *pp.* 157, 158.

EDITION OF BOSWELL'S JOHNSON
1831

That part of the volumes before us, for which the editor is responsible, is ill-compiled, ill-arranged, ill-expressed, and ill-printed. Nothing in the work had astonished us so much as the ignorance or carelessness of Mr. Croker with respect to facts and dates. Many of his blunders are such as we should be surprised to hear any well-educated gentleman commit, even in conversation. The notes absolutely swarm with misstatements, into which the editor never would have fallen, if he had taken the slightest pains to investigate the truth of his assertions, or if he had even been well acquainted with the very book on which he undertook to comment. . . . Indeed, the decisions of this editor on points of classical learning, though pronounced in a very authoritative tone, are generally such, that if a schoolboy under our care were to utter them, our soul assuredly should not spare for his crying. It is no disgrace to a gentleman, who has been engaged during nearly thirty years in political life, that he has forgotten his Greek and Latin. But he becomes justly ridiculous, if, when no longer able to construe a plain sentence, he affects to sit in judgment on the most delicate questions of style and metre.—MACAULAY, THOMAS BABINGTON, 1831, *Boswell's Life of Johnson, Critical and Miscellaneous Essays.*

There may have been something of the feeling of a party writer on one side towards a party writer on the other side in Macaulay's condemnation of Croker's Boswell for bad scholarship, gross carelessness, bad English, and weak judgment; but the weak book certainly came to pieces in the strong man's hand. Of Croker's imperfect understanding of Johnson himself, Macaulay said little, for his own insight into Johnson's character was much less deep than Carlyle's. An edition of Croker's Boswell was afterwards issued in which all discovered errors were corrected.—MORLEY, HENRY, 1881, *Of English Literature in the Reign of Victoria with a Glance at the Past,* p. 249.

I should be wanting in justice were I not to acknowledge that I owe much to the labors of Mr. Croker. No one can know better than I do his great failings as an editor. His remarks and criticisms far too often deserve the contempt that Macaulay so liberally poured on them. Without being deeply versed in books, he was shallow in himself. Johnson's strong character was never known to him. Its breadth and length, and depth and height were far beyond his measure. With his writings even he shows few signs of being familiar. Boswell's genius, a genius which even to Lord Macaulay was foolishness, was altogether hidden from this dull eye. No one surely but a "blockhead," a "barren rascal," could with scissors and paste-pot have mangled the biography which of all others is the delight and the boast of the English-speaking world. He is careless in small matters, and his blunders are numerous. These I have only noticed in the more important cases, remembering what Johnson somewhere points out, that the triumphs of one critic over another only fatigue and disgust the reader. Yet he has added considerably to our knowledge of Johnson. He knew men who had intimately known both the hero and his biographer, and he gathered much that but for his care would have been lost for ever. He was diligent and successful in his search after Johnson's letters, of so many of which Boswell with all his persevering and pushing diligence had not been able to get a sight. . . . That monstrous medley reached no second edition. In its new form all the worst excrescences had been cleared away, and though what was left was not Boswell, still less was it unchastened Croker. His repentance, however, was not thorough. He never restored the text to its old state; wanton transpositions of passages still remain, and numerous insertions break the narrative.—HILL, GEORGE BIRKBECK, 1887, *ed. Boswell's Life of Johnson, Preface, vol.* I, *pp.* xxiii, xxiv.

The book was in truth a monument of editorial industry and editorial skill, and enriched by a large amount of curious information, of which subsequent editors have not failed to avail themselves.—MARTIN, SIR THEODORE, 1888, *Dictionary of National Biography, vol.* XIII, *p.* 128.

Croker's achievement, consider it how you will, remains the most preposterous in literary history. He could see nothing in the "Life" but a highly entertaining compilation greatly in need of annotation and correction. Accordingly he took up Boswell's text and interlarded it with scraps of his own and other people's; he pegged into it a sophisticated version of the "Tour"; and he overwhelmed his amazing compound with notes and commentaries in which he took occasion to snub, scold, "improve," and insult his author at every turn. What came of it one knows. Macaulay, in the combined interests of Whiggism and good literature, made Boswell's quarrel his own, and the expiation was as bitter as the offense was wanton and scandalous. —HENLEY, WILLIAM ERNEST, 1890, *Views and Reviews, p.* 194.

There is no doubt that he was probably the only man then living who was capable of doing it, for his knowledge of the political and social history of Johnson's time was perhaps second to none, and, besides, he knew the most celebrated survivors of the generation which could remember Johnson and Boswell; and his social position enabled him to prosecute his researches in every direction. The work cost him two years of laborious and painstaking research, and that, undeniable faults apart, he did it well is attested by the fact that his successors have been able to add but little to what he has done.—SILLARD, P. A., 1898, *John Wilson Croker, The Gentleman's Magazine, vol.* 285, *p.* 153.

GENERAL

North.—"They, ["Thoughts on Ireland"] to be sure, were written when he was very young, and the style has the faults of youth, inexperience, and over imitation of Tacitus; but still one may see the pace of the man's mind there; and a very fiery pace it is."— WILSON, JOHN, 1823, *Noctes Ambrosianæ, March.*

John Wilson Croker more than approached the editor in sarcastic sallies and biting wit: he gave early proof of such powers in his poem on the Irish stage; intimated talents active and argumentative in his speeches; and a poetic feeling and spirit approaching Scott in his Peninsular battles. To his pen, many articles full of wormwood are attributed; and also some of the papers on America, which were not received in a tone of thankfulness by the men of the West.—CUNNINGHAM, ALLAN, 1833, *Biographical and Critical History of the Literature of the Last Fifty Years.*

Mr. Croker has often been hardly judged and bitterly criticised. In his long account of his "quarrels *with* authors" I rather think that, upon the whole, he is the loser, and that he has often been made to suffer more punishment than he ever inflicted. He committed one of the most grievous faults in any author—he wrote too much. In his self-assumed office of censor of the politics of England and her empire he appeared too often in his invidious capacity: the recurrence of his reviews was not only too frequent, but his special performances were too diffuse. Readers were tired with the iteration of his acrimony, and the mechanical structure of his style became at last monotonous. He established a rope's-end school of criticism, and was not satisfied without his showing us the ropewalk in which his scourges were woven. He so often flourished his lash, that at last people began to look on him as compelled, like a bedridden fox-hunter, to be obliged to crack his whip for the sake of old habits. Chastising and criticising seemed to him synonymous. He appeared to keep a file of

damaging paragraphs; he was the historian of indiscreet expressions; and he carefully illustrated obscure particulars of mean scandals. . . . Much of his literary character might be traced to his own idiosyncrasy, affected by the prolonged practice of controversy. . . . Mr. Croker was a *Red Indian* in critical literature, and his memory is buried under a pyramid of scalps.— MADDYN, DANIEL OWEN, 1859, *Chiefs of Parties Past and Present, vol.* II, *pp.* 84, 85.

He was not averse to raking for materials in the sinks and sewers of literature, though the thin disguise of rebuke that he pretends gives an unpleasant impression of character. He had much sagacity in discerning what it was probable people would do or say. But Mr. Croker had also many disqualifications. He was not a scholar. His acquaintance with Latin was probably slender, but be that as it may, he had not even the average reading of a scholar. He was an Irishman, and had the inaccurate mind of his countrymen. It was not only that he was liable to mistakes, such, *e. g.*, as confounding the two brothers Warton— who is not liable?—but he had not an accurate habit of literary language. He had no sense of poetry, and no cultivated taste. He knew little or nothing of the history of our language or literature, and did not even know that there was anything to be known. As Secretary to the Admiralty, he had shared the odium of mal-administration or jobbery, which attached to that department. He had augmented it by his violent Tory politics, especially by a tone of virulence which pervaded his conversation, and his articles in the Tory journal. It is to be regretted that Macaulay should have forgotten the dignity and decencies of criticism in his attack upon him (in his review of Madame D'Arblay's "Diary"), yet it is not perhaps going too far to say that Mr. Croker's mind had the stamp which is generally called "low." If any one now could do so, Mr. Croker perhaps could have cleared up the doubtful allusions to persons in Pope's "Satires." Beyond this we could not have expected anything from his editing.—PATTISON, MARK, 1872–89, *Pope and his Editors, Essays,* ed. *Nettleship, vol.* II, *p.* 376.

It is in his connection with the "Quarterly Review," from its foundation in 1809, for over forty years, that his career is interesting. His devotion to the journal was extraordinary; and it is evident from the perusal of his always recognizable articles that his heart was in the business. The extraordinary number of these papers, the ardent, eager style in which they were written, show that he was prompted by each subject to a deliverance; just as a popular speaker in the House of Commons is prompted to a sudden reply. But the angry, hostile, and too often malicious tone of these papers shows that his passion, rather ·than a calm, judicial temper, was what imparted to them their spirit. It is impossible at the same time not to admire the amount of general knowledge acquired in the particular case, and the vigorously malignant fashion in which he exposed follies and contradictions; but, at the same time, there was often vast unfairness shown in straining the sense to make a point.— FITZGERALD, PERCY, 1882, *A Slashing Reviewer, Belgravia, vol.* 47, *p.* 22?.

And what delirious aberration of tasteless caprice can possibly have suggested the admission of a doggerel epithalamium by Croker—of all scribblers on record!—into the very last niche of this radiant and harmonious gallery of song? "You have a very great name of your own"—"But I may be allowed to confess"—here is proper lyric stuff to wind up with! There is a due conformity of cadence and of style in these twenty villainous lines which should have sufficed to exclude them from any collection above the literary level of an old annual— *Gem, Keepsake,* or *Souvenir.* O Sminthian Apollo! what a malodorous mouse to nail up on the hinder door of such a gracious little chapel, under the very nose as it were of the departing choir! Were but this utterably miserable rubbish once duly struck out and swept away, the close of a beautiful volume would be beautiful and appropriate beyond all praise or thanks.—SWINBURNE, ALGERNON CHARLES, 1891–94, *Social Verse, Studies in Prose and Poetry, p.* 108.

His criticisms were too often marked by a peculiar acrimony, which was attributed to personal spite or revenge for satire directed against himself; but we believe this to be a mistake, as Croker appears to have been singularly insensible to adverse criticism. His review of Macaulay's History was undoubtedly an act of vengeance to which he had looked forward, but it must be remembered that Macaulay had treated Croker's edition of Boswell with such an unmerciful flaying as even an eel would cry out against. Macaulay and Croker had many duels in Parliament, in which the brilliant orator, whose arguments often had many weak points for a watchful enemy to seize upon, did not always come off a victor. . . . He was the conscientious and painstaking editor of many valuable papers. —OLIPHANT, MARGARET O. W., 1892, *The Victorian Age of English Literature, p.* 70.

Two ponderous volumes of letters and diary which have been published in these latter years—have good bits in them; but they are rare bits, to be dredged for out from quagmires of rubbish. The papers are interesting, furthermore, as showing how a cleverish man, with considerable gifts of presence and of brain, with his reactionary Toryism dominant, and made a fetich of, can still keep a good digestion and go in a respectable fashion through a long life— backwards, instead of "face to the front." —MITCHELL, DONALD G., 1897, *English Lands Letters and Kings, The Later Georges to Victoria, p.* 279.

Rufus Wilmot Griswold

1815–1857

Editor, born at Benson, Vt., Feb. 15, 1815; spent much of his early life in travel at home and abroad; became a printer, then a Baptist preacher, and afterward a journalist. In 1841 he brought out an anonymous volume of poems and a volume of sermons. He became chief editor of *Graham's Magazine,* Philadelphia, in 1842–43, and of *The International Magazine* of New York in 1850–52. He was author of "Poets and Poetry of America" (Philadelphia, 1842); "Prose Writers of America" (1846); "Washington and the Generals of the Revolution" (2 vols., 1847); "Curiosities of American Literature" (1847); "The Republican Court" (New York, 1854); and other works, and published the first edition of Milton's prose works in America (New York, 2 vols., 1847). He was also engaged as one of the editors of the works of Edgar A. Poe, (New York, 3 vols., 1850). Died in New York city, Aug. 27, 1857.—BEERS, HENRY A., *rev.* 1897, *Johnson's Universal Cyclopædia, vol.* IV, *p.* 45.

PERSONAL

To the reader of our magazine his death is a matter of interest, since it was under his care and direction that it first achieved a high literary tone and rank and acquired authority. To us individually, the loss is that of one of our nearest and dearest friends. . . . Few persons ever possessed warmer, more enthusiastic or more steadily devoted friends; and amid the many trials, changes and darker days to which the life of the purely literary man is so liable, Dr. Griswold never wanted those who proved themselves most truly attached to him. As a friend, no man ever exerted himself more than Dr. Griswold, and it may be said with the utmost truthfulness that of the many literary passages of arms in which he was engaged, a striking proportion were inspired by a chivalrous and almost incredible spirit of devotion to the interests of others. When he thought it possible to aid a friend he would spare no exertion, and would do everything in the most unselfish and noble spirit. The writer has had frequent and personal proof of this, during the course of an intimacy of years, and can testify to the remarkable earnestness with which Dr. Griswold was wont to exert himself in benefiting a friend. Few men ever lived who, to so truly kind a heart, to ease of manner, conversational ability, and genial humor . . . added such varied learning.—LELAND, CHARLES G., 1857, *Graham's Magazine.*

He was a man of rather small figure [1840], a very intelligent face, with the eyes deep-set, good forehead showing an early inclination to the loss of front hair, sharp and trenchant nose, short, full beard and mustache (adopting the European fashion in advance of most other Americans), and a habit of holding down the head a trifle and looking keenly out from beneath the overhanging brows, not a little impressive when he was very much in earnest. . . . That Rufus Wilmot Griswold, the latter part of whose personal life was clouded by a most unfortunate marriage, and whose reputation has been worse pulled to pieces than that of any other man of the century, did great and meritorious services to our growing literature, and assisted in fostering many writers, who, without his encouragement, would hopelessly have laid down the pen, there is no question whatever.—MORFORD, HENRY, 1880, *John Keese, his Intimates; Morford's Magazine, June.*

POETS AND POETRY OF AMERICA
1842

The book should be regarded as *the most important addition which our literature has for many years received.* It fills a void which should have been long ago supplied. It is written with judgment, with dignity and candor. Steering with a dexterity not to be sufficiently admired, between the Scylla of Prejudice on the one hand, and the Charybdis of Conscience on the other, Mr. Griswold in "The Poets and Poetry of America," has entitled himself to the thanks of his countrymen, while showing himself a man of taste, talent, and tact.—POE, EDGAR ALLAN, 1842, *Mr. Griswold and the Poets, Works, ed. Stedman and Woodberry, vol.* VIII, *p.* 157.

Although we deem Mr. Griswold deserving of a little gentle correction for his literary beneficence, we are not insensible to his merits. The work before us must have demanded the labour of years. . . . We think therefore that Mr. Griswold has succeeded as well in his task as the nature of the case admitted; and his patient research and general correctness of taste are worthy of praise; that his difficulties and temptations would have extenuated far graver errors than he has committed, and that his volume well deserves the approbation it has received.—WHIPPLE, EDWIN PERCY, 1844, *Griswold's Poets and Poetry of America, North American Review, vol.* 58, *p.* 3.

In these sketches we find reason to admire the author's impartiality and kindness. We have been unable to find a single instance in which he has suffered any of the usual grounds of prejudice to warp his judgment or to scant his eulogy; and where it has been his duty to refer to obliquities of temper and conduct, he has done so with a singular delicacy and gentleness.—PEABODY, ANDREW P., 1856, *American Poetry, North American Review, vol.* 82, *p.* 236.

That *Hic Jacet* of American mediocrities of the first generation.—WOODBERRY, GEORGE E., 1885, *Edgar Allan Poe (American Men of Letters), p.* 172.

I have just been looking over the headstones in Mr. Griswold's cemetery, entitled "The Poets and Poetry of America." In that venerable receptacle, just completing its half century of existence—for the date of the edition before me is 1842—I find the names of John Greenleaf Whittier and Oliver Wendell Homes next each other, in their due order, as they should be. All around are the names of the dead—too often of forgotten dead.—HOLMES, OLIVER WENDELL, 1891, *To Whittier, Life and Letters of John Greenleaf Whittier, ed. Pickard, vol.* II, *p.* 756.

LIFE OF POE
1850

In September 1850, the third volume of Poe's works when published was found to be prefaced by the anxiously looked-for "Memoir"—the "labour of love" of Rufus Griswold. The secret of the man's disinterested aid was soon manifest; never before had so slanderous a collection of falsehoods and libels—so calumnious a product of envy, hatred, and malice—been offered to the public as this "Memoir" of an illfated child of genius. The distress and indignation of Mrs. Clemm were intense, and she continually, when alluding to Griswold, writes of him as "that villian." . . . Mr. Graham, and many others who had been personally acquainted with Poe, took up cudgels in his defense, but, as Griswold's "Memoir" prefaced the poet's works, and all refutations and objections were published in the ephemeral pages of periodicals, until 1874 this veritable *scandalum magnatum* remained unexpunged.—INGRAM, JOHN H., 1880, *Edgar Allan Poe, His Life, Letters and Opinions, vol.* II, *p.* 242.

The most important of all of Mr. Redfield's publications, however, were the works of Edgar Allan Poe. It was also through Mr. Griswold that he was induced to undertake the publication of Poe's works, now one of the most popular authors of the day. Dr. Griswold had offered the works to nearly all the leading publishers, who declined to undertake the publication. He finally persuaded Mr. Redfield to try the experiment of issuing two volumes first, which were published and had a fair sale—then the third, and finally the fourth, volume were added to complete the works. The sale reached about fifteen hundred sets every year. . . . Mr. Redfield thinks great injustice has been done by certain critics to Rev. Dr. Griswold, in reflecting upon him as Poe's biographer. In a recent letter to me he says: "Griswold never received a cent for his labors. Poe named him as his literary executor shortly before he died, although they had quarreled not long before. Griswold's labor was no joke. Few men would have undertaken it with no hope of

reward. It is fashionable nowadays to throw mud at him. Knowing, as I did, both of the men, and knowing also how assiduously Griswold labored to say everything he could in the biography in Poe's favor, it is very annoying to read these things. The matter of the biography was all read over to me, talked and discussed before printing, and I *know* he did his best to 'set down naught in malice.' He was obliged, as he thought, to state the facts in all cases, and he did state them, favorably as he could to Poe. I *know* he tried to do so. Now he is accused everywhere, by people who know nothing about it, of vilely slandering Poe. I had a better opportunity than any one else to know all about it, and I know he did not."—DERBY, JAMES CEPHAS, 1884, *Fifty Years among Authors, Books and Publishers, pp.* 586, 587.

Poe showed tact in choosing Griswold, and builded better than he knew. He could select no more indefatigable bookwright to bring together his scattered writings, and he counted upon Death's paying all debts. In this Poe was mistaken. For once Griswold wrote as he thought and felt, and his memoir, however spiteful and unchivalrous, was more sincere than many of the sycophantic sketches in the bulky volumes of his "Poets and Poetry." Malice made him eloquent, and an off-hand obituary notice of the poet was the most nervous piece of work that ever came from his pen. It was heartless, and, in some respects, inaccurate. It brought so much wrath upon him that he became vindictive, and followed it up with a memoir, which, as an exhibition of the ignoble nature of its author, scarcely has a parallel. Did this in the end effect Poe's fame injuriously? Far otherwise; it moved a host of writers, beginning with Willis and Graham, to recall his habit of life, and reveal the good side of it. Some have gone as far in eulogy as Griswold went toward the opposite extreme. It seemed a cruel irony of fate that Poe's own biographer should plant thorns upon his grave, but he also planted laurels. He paid an unstinted tribute to the poet's genius, and this was the only concession which Poe himself would care to demand.—STEDMAN, EDMUND CLARENCE, 1885, *Poets of America, p.* 265.

Dr. Griswold was always a little "queer," and I used to scold and reprove him for it. He had got himself into great trouble by his remarks on Edgar A. Poe. Mr. Kimball and others, who knew the Doctor, believed, as I do, that there was no deliberate evil or envy in those remarks. Poe's best friends told severe stories of him in those days—*me ipso teste*—and Griswold, naught extenuating and setting down naught in malice, wrote incautiously more than he should. These are the words of another than I. But when Griswold was attacked, then he became savage. One day I found in his desk, which he had committed to me, a great number of further material collected to Poe's discredit. I burnt it all up at once, and told the Doctor what I had done, and scolded him well into the bargain. . . . It is a pity that I had not always had the Doctor in hand—though I must here again repeat that, as regards Poe, he is, in my opinion, not so much to blame as a score of writers have made out. The tales, which were certainly most authentic, or at least apparently so, during the life of the latter, among his best friends regarding him, were, to say the least, discreditable, albeit that is no excuse whatever for publishing them. —LELAND, CHARLES GODFREY, 1893, *Memoirs, pp.* 201, 202.

No piece of biography in the annals of literature has so unenviable a reputation as that memoir which Dr. Rufus W. Griswold, acting as Poe's literary executor, prefixed to the first complete edition of his works. Its authenticity has been attacked from the time of its appearance, and no words of objurgation have been too harsh to characterize the man who penned it; at the same time very little of its substance has ever been invalidated. . . . Griswold has not lacked other defenders, who were well acquainted with both men. In writing a biography of Poe some years ago, the present writer had occasion to investigate the charges made against Griswold. The result was a conviction that the documents he quoted were genuine, and that the impression he gave of Poe's character and career was just, while his errors were due to Poe's own falsehoods. The question of Griswold's discretion in his memoir is governed by the fact that Poe's defects and troubles were notorious at the time, and could not be concealed; the question of Griswold's motives is more difficult, but is now more easily to be judged. It is also fair to Griswold to add that the characterization he gave is that which has uniformly

prevailed in tradition in the best informed literary circles in this country.—WOODBERRY, GEORGE E., 1894, *Poe in the South, The Century, vol.* 48, *pp.* 572, 573.

GENERAL

This is a book ["Prose Writers of America"] of which any critic in the country might well have been proud, without reference to the mere industry and research manifested in its compilation. These are truly remarkable; but the vigor of comment and force of style are not less so; while more independence and self-reliance are manifested than in any other of the series. There is not a weak paper in the book; and some of the articles are able in all respects.—POE, EDGAR ALLAN, 1842, *Mr. Griswold and the Poets, Works, ed. Stedman and Woodberry, vol.* VIII, *p.* 158.

He has done a useful work, and he has done it well. The book now before us ["Prose Writers of America"] is more than respectable; it is executed ably, and in many parts brilliantly. In some respects it is an extraordinary work; such as few men in America, perhaps, besides its author, could have produced, and he only after years of sedulous investigation, and under many advantages of circumstances or accident. He has long shown himself to be of Cicero's mind: *"Mihi quidem nulli satis eruditio videntur, quibus nostra ignota sunt."* The distribution of the various writers into their classes, and the selection of representatives of each class or type, exhibit much skill. Many passages present fine specimens of acute, original, and just criticism, eloquently delivered. We differ from Mr. Griswold sometimes, but never without feeling that we owe it to the public in all cases to give a reason why we do not assent to the conclusion of so candid and discriminating a judge.—WALLACE, HORACE BINNEY, 1846, *Literary Criticisms and Other Papers.*

But stay, here comes Tityrus Griswold, and leads on,
The flocks whom he first plucks alive, and then feeds on,—
A loud-cackling swarm, in whose feathers warm-drest,
He goes for as perfect a—swan as the rest.
—LOWELL, JAMES RUSSELL, 1848, *A Fable for Critics.*

This elegant volume ["The Republican Court"] was received by acclamation on its first appearance. We are quite certain that the sober second judgment of the public will confirm the first opinion, and in some respects magnify its approbation. . . . Its solid literary merits are yet to be fully appreciated. We do not know where else one-half so much information respecting our early American history can be found. . . . Dr. Griswold has evidently been much favored in the use of private family memorials, and he has worked up his material with much artistic taste in the grouping and great spirit in the narrative. The volume stands amoung our important historical monuments.—OSGOOD, SAMUEL, 1855, *The Republican Court, Christian Examiner, vol. 59, p. 142.*

If any one deserves a place and an honorable mention in these pages, it is Rufus Wilmot Griswold, not only for his learning and literary achievements, which will place him on a level with many of our best authors, but because he has done more than any other man to make American writers known and honored both at home and abroad.— CLEVELAND, CHARLES D., 1859, *A Compendium of American Literature, p. 690.*

Elisha Kent Kane
1820–1857

American explorer, after taking a medical degree at Pennsylvania, where he was born, entered the United States Navy as assistant-surgeon, and was attached to the first American Embassy to China. He next travelled extensively in Asia, Africa, and Eastern Europe, and saw service in the Mexican War of 1848. He was appointed surgeon and naturalist to the first Grinnell Expedition for the recovery of Franklin, projected in 1850, and on his return, in 1852, published a personal narrative of "The United States Grinnell Expedition in Search of Sir John Franklin" (1854). The careful study of the ice formations is the chief scientific merit of the work. Dr. Kane took command of the second Arctic Expedition from New York, fitted out by Mr. Grinnell and Mr. Peabody for the recovery of Franklin, and was only rescued after a three years' absence by a relief party sent out by the United States Government. "The Second Grinnell Expedition" (1856) describes as the result of this expedition the examination of the far northern coast-line, and the probable discovery of an Arctic sea surrounding the pole. —SANDERS, LLOYD C., ed., 1887, *Celebrities of the Century, p. 622.*

PERSONAL

A noble life is in thy care,
  A sacred trust to thee is given;
Bright Island! let thy healing air
  Be to him as the breath of heaven.
The marvel of his daring life—
  The self-forgetting leader bold—
Stirs, like the trumpet's call to strife,
  A million hearts of meaner mould.
Eyes that shall never meet his own
  Look dim with tears across the sea,
Where from the dark and icy zone,
  Sweet Isles of Flowers! he comes to thee.
Fold him in rest, O pitying clime!
  Give back his wasted strength again;
Soothe, with thy endless summer time,
  His winter-wearied heart and brain.
—WHITTIER, ELIZABETH H., 1857, *Dr. Kane in Cuba.*

Let us, then, citizens of Philadelphia, do honor to the memory of the dead—our illustrious dead—in the manner which best becomes him and us; with dignity, with moderation, with decorum, with no exaggerated ostentation, with no effort to make mere ceremonial transcend the limits of actual feeling. Let us show we feel this blow deeply. While other communities may exceed us in display, let Philadelphia—the city of Kane's birth, and education, and manhood, show the deepest and most earnest feeling.—REED, WILLIAM B., 1857, *Remarks at the Obsequies of Elisha Kent Kane.*

He had always been subject to sea-sickness in a very acute and distressing form, manifesting itself in a constant retching without power to obtain relief, and giddiness, which a comparatively slight roughness of the sea—for instance, a four or five knot breeze—invariably brought to him, and which scarcely abated in severity through the longest voyage: it was therefore infinitely worse than the short, violent, and spasmodic form. The occurrence of this malady increased his general debility, but did not prevent his frequent presence and activity on deck. . . . Throughout the entire cruise he seldom fell asleep until late in the morning, and four or five hours was in general his maximum of rest. His sleep, too, was very light. It was scarcely ever necessary to more than utter his name to make him open his eyes; and if it was accidentally mentioned in the cabin, within hearing of his bunk, he would awake immediately.—GOODFELLOW, HENRY, 1857, *Letter, Biography of Elisha Kent Kane by William Elder, p.* 277.

Time was when he should gain his spurs of
    gold!
  From royal hands, who wooed the knightly
    state;
The knell of old formalities is tolled,
  And the world's knights are now self-con-
    secrate.
No grander episode doth chivalry hold
  In all its annals, back to Charlemagne,
  Than that lone vigil of unceasing pain,
Faithfully kept through hunger and through
    cold,
  By the good Christian knight, Elisha Kane!
—O'BRIEN, FITZ-JAMES, 1857, *Kane.*

Dr. Kane was five feet six inches in height. In his best health he weighed about one hundred and thirty-five pounds. He had a fair complexion, with soft brown hair. His eyes were dark gray, with a wild-bird light in them when his intellect and feelings were in genial flow; when they were in the torrent-tide of enraptured action, the light beamed from them like the flashing of scimitars, and in impassioned movement they glared frightfully. . . . In company, when the talk ran glib and everybody would be heard, he was silent, but tense and elastic as a steel spring under pressure. He had a way of looking attentive, docile, and interested as a child's fresh wonder; but no one would mistake the expression for the admiration of inexperience or incapacity; yet it cheated many a talker into self-complaisance that lost him his opportunity of learning something of the man which he wanted to know. This was the thing in his demeanor which people called reserve: the reserve of absorbed attentiveness he had; but there was nothing of strained reticence in his manner. . . . Dr. Kane was a marksman, a brilliant horseman, and a first-rate pedestrian. Foottramps, and the chase without the usual relish for its accompaniments, were a passion with him. Horses and dogs were something more than pets and indulgences to him; but, much as he enjoyed the exercise and excitement of the forest and field, he was tender to the objects and instruments of the chase to an extent that verged on sentimentalism; but there was nothing of this in his composition.—ELDER, WILLIAM,

1857, *Biography of Elisha Kent Kane, pp.* 249, 250, 254.

Of Kane's conduct under the exceptionally prolonged and adverse circumstances attendant on his second Arctic voyage, it is to be said that he displayed the characteristics of a high and noble character. Considerate of his subordinates, assiduous in performing his multifarious duties as a commander, studying ever to alleviate the mental and physical ailments of his crew, and always unsparing of himself whenever exposure to danger, hardships, or privations promised definite results. It is not astonishing that these qualities won and charmed all his associates, equals or subordinates, and that they followed him unhesitatingly into the perils and dangers that Kane's enthusiastic and optimistic nature led him to brave, with the belief that to will was to do. —GREELEY, GEN. ADOLPHUS WASHINGON, 1893, *Explorers and Travellers: Men of Achievement, p.* 270.

The public estimate of Dr. Kane was shown throughout the civilized world in various forms: by the gift of a service of silver from the Queen, by the medals and decorations of learned societies, by resolutions of Congress, and the State legislatures, by countless poetical tributes and eulogies, and at the last by a long funeral triumph from New Orleans to Philadelphia, with the learned, the noble, and the good everywhere mingling in its train. I need not here dwell upon the well-known traits of his character—his magnetic personality, his indomitable energy, his masterful will, his marvellous tact in emergencies, his courage and patience and generosity, his genial humor, his love of science and research, his devotion to the highest interests of humanity, and that religious faith which sustained him in the darkest hours. Such traits did not merely shine before the world, but on a nearer view, where there could be neither applause nor ambition—in unrecorded kindness toward dependents upon whom he lavished his bounty, and protégés whom he sought to refine and elevate. If ever in any such instance his aims may have seemed quixotic in the eyes of the prudent they could have exposed him to the serious misapprehension of none but inferior souls.— SHIELDS, CHARLES W., 1898, *The Arctic Monument Named for Tennyson by Dr. Kane, The Century Magazine, vol.* 56, *p.* 492.

GENERAL

The book is really magnificent. I do not think that I have ever met with one which gives such vivid pictures of Arctic scenery. Nay, I am quite sure that I never did; and indeed, I feel that I owe you more thanks for it, and for your warm-hearted inscription, and your memorial of me in the wilderness, than I could well inclose in as many words; so I will say nothing about it, only beg you to accept that volume of my poems containing the line which (as C. Weld writes) came into your mind when you stood first before the great minaret.—TENNYSON, ALFRED LORD, 1856, *Letter to Dr. Kane, Nov. 12; The Century Magazine, vol.* 56, *p.* 485.

I am reading Dr. Kane's book. Six pages could give all the actual knowledge it contains; but that fearful conflict of men with the most terrible powers of nature, and so bravely sustained, makes the story like tragedy; and I read on and on, the same thing over and over, and don't skip a page.— DEWEY, ORVILLE, 1856, *To his Daughter Mary, Nov.* 24; *Autobiography and Letters, ed. Dewey, p.* 246.

Next to "Dred" we read Dr. Kane's books, the two volumes of the Arctic expedition. Oh, how we did enjoy that! Full of beautiful pictures taken on the spot by Dr. Kane himself, which we looked at together and admired and commented upon and enjoyed as much as they could be enjoyed by anybody. Brave, splendid Dr. Kane! We watch the papers for every bit of news of him which floats to us from that far-off tropical Cuba where he has gone to recover, if he can, from the everlasting chill he got among the icebergs with the thermometer seventy-five degrees below zero!— THAXTER, CELIA, 1857, *To E. C. Hoxie, Jan.* 18; *Letters, ed. A. F. and R. L., p.* 5.

If it were possible, and at the same time comfortable to the purpose and limits of this memoir, to digest the results which are in danger of being overlooked by the general reader, it would be a labor of love to endeavor its accomplishment; but that service must be rendered to the public and to the memory of Dr. Kane as an author and cultivator of physical science under other conditions. I expect, as I hope, that it will be done by a more competent hand. The mass of unedited manuscript left by Dr. Kane will some day be material for a work such as he would have executed, whenever the man shall be found to supply the loss which natural science sustained by his early removal from his own great field of labor. Variously endowed as he was for observing and resolving the phenomena of nature, and skilled as he was, beyond all men equally qualified for collecting the data, in the art of writing for general instruction, the loss to the public in this unfulfilled purpose of writing a book of Arctic science such as would have satisfied himself, is beyond estimate, and, it is to be feared, will never be wholly supplied.— ELDER, WILLIAM, 1857, *Biography of Elisha Kent Kane, p.* 198.

Lastly Dr. Kane performed those extraordinary researches beyond the head of Baffin's Bay which obtained for him our gold medal at the last anniversary, the highest eulogy of our late President, and the unqualified admiration of all geographers. At that time, however, we had not perused those thrilling pages which have since brought to our mind's eye the unparalleled combination of genius with patient endurance and fortitude which enabled this young American to save the lives of his associates. With what simplicity, what fervor, what eloquence, and what truth, he has described the sufferings and perils from which he extricated his icebound crew, is now duly appreciated, and you must all agree with me that in the whole history of literature there never was a work written which more feelingly develops the struggles of humanity under the most intense sufferings, or demonstrates more strikingly how the most appalling difficulties can be overcome by the union of a firm resolve with the never-failing resources of a bright intellect.—MURCHISON, SIR RODERICK IMPEY, 1857, *President's Address before the Royal Geographical Society of London.*

The superiority of mind to body never had a more striking illustration than in the case of Dr. Kane. He triumphed by sheer energy of will. The fiery spirit which might have worn out others quickened and exalted him. In his vivid conceptions and striking language he was essentially a poet —one of those who live thrice the life of common men in quickness and sensibility. So that we may not pronounce his life short or his death untimely. His eager spirit wrung from fate a triumphant experience seldom granted even to fourscore. He achieved fame and success in the eye of the world in a noble sphere of action, and has left a most enduring monument of his exertions in his truthful and eloquent writings. — DUYCKINCK, EVERT A., 1862, *National Portrait Gallery of Eminent Americans, vol.* II, *p.* 297.

Dr. Kane's merits, not merely as a naturalist and a daring explorer, but as a writer, are conspicuous in his works, especially in his account of the second expedition. The narrative of the dangers and sufferings of the party is given with a simplicity and vividness that place the work in the foremost rank of descriptive writings.—HART, JOHN S., 1872, *A Manual of American Literature, p.* 251.

Unquestionably one of the most remarkable men of his age.—LANMAN, CHARLES, 1885, *Haphazard Personalities, p.* 243.

Dr. Kane reached New York, Oct. 11, 1855. He prepared his narrative of the journey for the press, the sales of the book the first year reaching sixty-five thousand copies. He wrote to his friend and publisher, George W. Childs: "The book, poor as it is, has been my coffin."—BOLTON, SARAH KNOWLES, 1893, *Famous Voyagers and Explorers, p.* 303.

He has enriched our literature with two octavo volumes which are not only valuable as scientific records, but as mere narratives will always have the charm of Robinson Crusoe for the young and the old; and though his own Arctic discoveries and theories should be obscured by further explorations, his fame will rest upon his rare illustration of that sentiment of philanthropy which is the chief glory of our nature.— SHIELDS, CHARLES W., 1898, *The Arctic Monument Named for Tennyson by Dr. Kane, The Century Magazine, vol.* 56, *p.* 492.

Robert Owen
1771-1858

Social reformer, born, a saddler's son, at Newtown, Montgomeryshire, 14th May 1771. At ten he was put into a draper's shop at Stamford, and by nineteen had risen to be manager of a cotton-mill. In 1799 he married the daughter of David Dale, the philanthropic owner of the New Lanark cotton-mills, where next year he settled as manager and part-owner. He laboured to teach his workpeople the advantages of thrift, cleanliness, and good order, and established infant education. He began social propagandism in " A New View of Society" (1813), and finally adopted socialism; he lost much of his influence by his utterances on religion. His socialistic theories were put to the test in experimental communities at Orbiston near Bothwell, and later at New Harmony in Indiana, in County Clare, and in Hampshire, but all were unsuccessful. In 1828 his connection with New Lanark ceased; and, his means having been exhausted, the remainder of his days were spent in secularist, socialistic, and spiritualistic propagandism. He died 17th November, 1858.—PATRICK AND GROOME, *eds.* 1897, *Chambers's Biographical Dictionary, p.* 712.

PERSONAL

Mrs. Browning tells me that Robert Owen of Lanark has been converted to a belief in the immortality of the soul by these spirit-rappings. Now, knowing Robert Owen, I think that he would most assuredly have been converted without them, for he, in spite of his crotchets, is a thoroughly kind and honest man, who has no interest in disbelieving a future state.—MITFORD, MARY RUSSELL, 1853, *To Mr. Starkey, June* 2; *The Friendships of Mary Russell Mitford, ed. L'Estrange, ch.* xxv.

He was the same placid happy being into his old age, believing and expecting whatever he wished; always gentlemanly and courteous in his manners; always on the most endearing terms with his children, who loved to make him, as they said, "the very happiest old man in the world"; always a gentle bore in regard to his dogmas and his expectations; always palpably right in his descriptions of human misery; always thinking he had proved a thing when he had asserted it, in the force of his own conviction; and always really meaning something more rational than he had actually expressed. It was said by way of mockery that "he might live in parallelograms, but he argued in circles"; but this is rather too favorable a description of one who did not argue at all, nor know what argument meant.—MARTINEAU, HARRIET, 1858, *Biographical Sketches, p.* 279.

On the whole, Owen's private career was remarkably free from anything like romantic incident. He rose by his own skill and prudence, from a very humble place to that of a wealthy and influential manufacturer. He married young and happily, and frequently expressed his satisfaction in the family which grew up around him. Had he been intent on mere worldly greatness, his shrewdness and capacity for affairs might have made him a millionaire, a member of Parliament, the founder of a family. But the peculiarities of his understanding and of his sympathies, led him into a public course of life, in which he exhibited startling contrasts. His success in all his undertakings as a boy and a young man, his social influence and great popularity in middle life, were in curious opposition to his subsequent failure in all his projects, to the antipathy felt towards him by the world, and to the obscurity of his old age. The manly and well-directed vigour of the first half of his life, were in direct antagonism to the useless activity and hopeless ill-success of the latter half: the unbelief of his nonage and ripe manhood, show strangely by the foolish credulity of his old age. And from first to last there is a remarkable inconsistency, between his vehement denial of moral responsibility, and on the other hand, his kindness of disposition, his regular conduct, his universal benevolence, his contempt of riches and luxury, and his unwearied and munificent support of projects of philanthropy.—SARGANT, WILLIAM LUCAS, 1860, *Robert Owen and his Social Philosophy, Introduction, p.* xxiii.

Mr. Owen was ambitious, and his ambition prompted him to seek what he regarded as the good of his fellow-men. No dishonourable action is recorded of him, and his private life was free from reproach. Yet, however ample the folds of our charity, a candid review of his career, upon his own showing, leaves no room to doubt that "a deceived heart turned him aside,"and that his endowments and rare opportunities of usefulness were made unvailable for any great or permanent results by reason of the obliquity of his moral vision. . . . Deduct from our estimate of his life and character whatever such as think least of him may demand, and there is enough left to give him a place among those who have aimed and striven to benefit their fellow-men. He would have done great good if he had known how. Or add to such an estimate what ever his most ardent admirers may claim for him, and it will not raise him to the sphere of those who, in a humbler way, have actually accomplished much greater things for mankind.—PACKARD, FREDERICK A., 1866, *Life of Robert Owen, p.* 249.

There was no magnetic influence from him, a man of one idea, unpoetic, without a spark of imagination, very wearisome in his singular capacity for reiteration.—LINTON, WILLIAM JAMES, 1894, *Threescore and Ten Years, p.* 156.

Owen may be described as one of those intolerable bores who are the salt of the earth. To the whigs and the political economists he appeared chiefly as a bore. . . . He was essentially a man of one idea; that idea, too, was only partially right, and enforced less by argument than by incessant and monotonous repetition. Yet he will certainly be recognised as one of the most important figures in the social history of the time. His great business capacities enabled him to make an important stand against some of the evils produced by the unprecedented extension of the factory system. He was not in sympathy with any political party. . . . Personally, according to Robert Dale Owen, who no doubt speaks the truth, he was most amiable. His ruling passion was benevolence; he was exceedingly fond of children; spent a fortune to promote the welfare of his race, and had a command of temper which enabled him to conciliate opponents. He had apparently all the obstinacy without the irritability generally attributed to his countrymen. His son says that he was so like Brougham in person that he might have been taken for him, but, with a vanity as great as Brougham's, he had what Brougham unfortunately wanted—the power of making even his vanity subsidiary to his principles. —STEPHEN, LESLIE, 1895, *Dictionary of National Biography, vol.* XLII, *pp.* 451, 452.

GENERAL

It is surely not required of any one who forms an estimate of Robert Owen's system, that all he has written must have been read and must be remembered. It would be as fair, in estimating the capabilities of a practical lawyer, to demand a remembrance of the contents of all the deeds he had drafted throughout a very long professional career. We question the power of human patience to accomplish the task. Owen seems to have even tired some of his own nearest and most devoted friends by his monotonous reiteration—a difficult thing for a social prophet to accomplish, and one that evinces powers of humdrum almost superhuman. Any specimen will do for a type of the whole continuous stream, of which any one passage is as like the rest as one bucketful of water from a burn is like every other. Things that are common enough in one time or place are curious in others; and though the sect have been so liberally treated to their master's eloquence, it is as unknown to the ordinary public who read magazines and reviews as the works of Occam, Erigena, or Balbus.— BURTON, JOHN HILL, 1849, *Socialism in Britain, North British Review, vol.* 12, *p.* 89.

So entire was the suitability, thus far, of the man to his age, that there can be little doubt that if he had been gifted with the power in which he was most deficient— reasoning power—he would have been among the foremost men of his generation. —MARTINEAU, HARRIET, 1858, *Biographical Sketches, p.* 273.

Robert Owen, born in Newtown, North Wales, in 1771, was like my grandfather, a self-made man. His specific plans, as a Social Reformer, proved, on the whole and for the time a failure; and this, for lack of cultivated judgment and critical research, and of accurate knowledge touching what men had thought and done before his time; also because he strangely over-rated the ratio of human progress; but more especially, perhaps, because, until late in life, he ignored the spiritual element in man as the great lever of civilized advancement. Yet with such earnestness, such vigor, such indomitable perseverance, and such devotion and love for his race did he press, throughout half a century, these plans on the public, and so much practical truth was there, mixed with visionary expectation, that his name became known, and the influence of his teachings has been more or less felt, over the civilized world. A failure in gross has been attended by sterling incidental successes; and toward the great idea of co-operation—quite impracticable, for the present at least, in the form he conceived it —there have been, even since his death, very considerable advances made, and generally recognized by earnest men as eminently useful and important.—OWEN, ROBERT DALE, 1874, *Threading My Way, p.* 43.

Owen was thus a visionary, like St. Simon and Fourier; but, unlike them, he had a most beneficent effect on the social progress of his country. His economic doctrines were crude and often absurd; his theory of marriage was, to say the least, peculiar; his socialistic views were Utopian: but he succeeded in proving that a factory could be made to benefit both master and workman; he initiated the reform in the condition of the laboring classes; he laid the firm foundation on which the co-operative movement of our times is erecting its successful edifice. England must thank him, above all, for his success in preventing socialism from consolidating with Chartism —a movement different from the superficially analogous cases on the continent. . . . Owen deprecated all violence, and placed no reliance on the Chartist ideal. He desired reform, but it was voluntary, not compulsory reform. His kind heart and unquenchable confidence taught him to seek a change only through peace, love and education; his socialism was not destructive, but constructive; his activity engendered neither unrest nor disaffection.— SELIGMAN, EDWIN R. A., 1886, *The Christian Socialists, Political Science Quarterly, vol.* 1, *pp.* 216, 217.

Robert Owen died in 1858 at the advanced age of eighty-seven years. He began as a pure philanthropist and ended as a socialist. His belief that man is the product of inherited capacities and external circumstances, early associations and social environment, led him to insist very truly upon careful education of the young, and upon the importance of ethical training generally. In this direction we of to-day owe him much, as we do to all pioneers, and it is as a pioneer that posterity will chiefly regard him.—GIBBINS, H. de B., 1892, *English Social Reformers, p.* 150.

Robert Owen may justly be regarded as the founder of English Socialism, Co-operation, and indirectly of Chartism. . . . The strange chances which raised him from the position of a draper's apprentice to that of a partner in a flourishing firm of Manchester manufacturers, and in 1800 installed him as chief partner at the New Lanark Mills, imprinted on his quietly tenacious nature the belief that external circumstances decided not only a man's career, but also his whole character and conduct. Fortunately for his work-people, this usually noxious creed was transformed by the sunshine of his beneficent nature into a source of life-giving activity and persistent endeavour to mould his "hands" at New Lanark until they should become "fully formed men and women." Spacious dining and lecture halls attested his care for their physical and mental welfare. His sale of provisions to them at nearly cost price, and distribution of the profits of this store, marked him out as the father of Co-operation in our land; and his profit-sharing arrangements gained him the same honour in regard to "industrial partnership."—ROSE, J. HOLLAND, 1897, *The Rise of Democracy, pp.* 41, 42.

The typical representatives of these utopian socialists are St. Simon and Charles Fourier in France, and Robert Owen in England. . . . As I now attempt to make clear to you, through him, the essence of utopian socialism, it is because he is less known, but especially because in my opinion he is the most interesting of the three great utopists. It is he who on the one side most clearly shows to us the genesis of the modern proletarian ideal, and on the other side has been of the greatest influence upon other socialistic theorists. . . . We distinguish two periods in his life. In the first he is what we call an educationalist, a man who interests himself especially in the education of youth and expects through it an essential reformation of human society. The chief work of this epoch is the book "A New View of Society." In the second period he is a socialist; and his most important work is "A Book of the New Moral World."—SOMBART, WERNER, 1898, *Socialism and the Social Movement in the* 19th *Century, tr. Atterbury, p.* 25.

Thomas Hart Benton
1782–1858

Was born near Hillsborough, N. C., and studied for some time at the University of that State, at Chapel Hill, but did not remain to graduate. He removed to Tennessee, and afterwards, in 1813, to Missouri. In the Senate, he was a strong and persistent advocate of a specie currency, acquiring by his efforts the epithet of "Old Bullion." Two other measures with which he was largely identified were the reduction of the price of lands, with a view to promote settlement, and the construction of a railroad to the Pacific. On retiring from the Senate, he devoted himself to literary pursuits, and prepared for publication the important works which have been named. These were "Thirty Years' View,' or a History of the Workings of the American Government for Thirty Years, from 1820 to 1850," 2 vols., 8vo.; "An Examination of the Dred Scott Case," and an "Abridgement of the Debates of Congress from 1789 to 1856," 15 vols., 8vo.—HART, JOHN S., 1872, *A Manual of American Literature, p.* 237.

PERSONAL

Benton is a caricature likeness of Louis Philippe—the same rotundity, the same pear-shaped head, and about the same stature. The physical expression of his face predominates. His lower features are drilled into imperturbable suavity, while the eye, that undrillable tale-teller, twinkles of inward slyness as a burning lamp-wick does of oil. He is a laborious builder-up of himself—acting by syllogistic forecast, never by impulse. He is pompously polite, and never abroad without "Executive" manners. He has made up his mind that oratory, if not a national weakness, is an un-Presidential accomplishment, and he delivers himself in the Senate with a subdued voice, like a judge deciding upon a cause which the other Senators had only argued. He wears an ample blue cloak, and a broad-brimmed hat with a high crown, and lives, moves, and has his being, in a faith in himself which will remove mountains of credulity. Though representing a State two thousand miles off, he resides regularly at Washington, drawing a handsome income from his allowance of mileage, and paying rare and brief visits to his constituency, whose votes he has retained for more than twenty years—an unaccountable exception to the anti-conservative rotation of the country's gifts of office.—WILLIS, NATHANIEL PARKER, 1851, *Calhoun and Benton, Hurry-Graphs.*

Benton was not only a man of tremendous passions, but unrivalled as a hater. Nor did his hatred spend itself entirely upon injustice and meanness. It was largely personal and unreasoning. He was pre-eminently unforgiving.—JULIAN, GEORGE W., 1883, *Political Recollections, p.* 92.

Senator Thomas Hart Benton, of Missouri

(although it has often been stated that the duel was forced upon him), deeply regretted his meeting with Lucas (in which the latter was killed), and some time previous to his death Colonel Benton destroyed all the papers he had in his possession or that he could obtain concerning the affair.—TRUMAN, BEN C., 1884, *The Field of Honor, p.* 479.

He was a faithful friend and a bitter foe; he was vain, proud, utterly fearless, and quite unable to comprehend such emotions as are expressed by the terms despondency and yielding. Without being a great orator or writer, or even an original thinker, he yet possessed marked ability; and his abounding vitality and marvelous memory, his indomitable energy and industry, and his tenacious persistency and personal courage, all combined to give him a position and influence such as few American statesmen have ever held. His character grew steadily to the very last; he made better speeches and was better able to face new problems when past three-score and ten than in his early youth or middle age. He possessed a rich fund of political, legal, and historical learning, and every subject that he ever handled showed the traces of careful and thorough study. He was very courteous, except when provoked; his courage was proof against all fear, and he shrank from no contest, personal or political. He was sometimes narrow-minded, and always wilful and passionate; but he was honest and truthful. At all times and in all places he held every good gift he had completely at the service of the American Federal Union. —ROOSEVELT, THEODORE, 1886, *Thomas Hart Benton (American Statesmen), p.* 364.

Was a large, heavily framed man, with black curly hair and whiskers, prominent features, and a stentorian voice. He wore the high, black-silk neck-stock and the double-breasted frock-coat of his youthful times during his thirty years' career in the Senate, varying with the seasons the materials of which his pantaloons were made, but never the fashion in which they were cut. When in debate, outraging every customary propriety of language, he would rush forward with blind fury upon every obstacle, like the huge, wild buffaloes then ranging the prairies of his adopted State, whose paths he used to subsequently assert, would show the way through the passes of the Rocky Mountains. He was not a popular speaker, and when he took the floor occupants of the galleries invariably began to leave, while many Senators devoted themselves to their correspondence. In private life Colonel Benton was gentleness and domestic affection personified, and a desire to have his children profit by the superior advantages for their education in the District of Columbia kept him from the constituents in Missouri, where a new generation of voters grew up who did not know him and who would not follow his political lead, while he was ignorant of their views on the question of slavery.—POORE, BEN: PERLEY, 1886, *Reminiscences of Sixty Years in the National Metropolis, vol.* I, *p.*66.

Benton was not a great orator, as Webster was, but he was a powerful pleader and an indomitable spirit, and his nature was cast in a heroic mould. Like most of the public speakers of his time, he affected classic allusion and plentifully interlarded his speeches with references to the ancients. He had great fondness for a barbarous phrase of his own invention which he called the "principle *demos krateo.*" This phrase, which he had borrowed from the Greek, he used and misused on every possible occasion in speaking and in writing. Like others of his time, he drew copiously from Greek and Roman history to illustrate his meaning; as we have seen, the Trojan war was made use of by way of illustrating his fight against the salt tax.—BROOKS, NOAH, 1893, *Statesmen, Men of Achievement, p.* 116.

GENERAL

There is certainly no modesty in the book which leads the author to curtail the account of his own exploits; while, on the other hand, few statesmen have ever so generously celebrated the merits of their contemporaries in the same walk. There is a general ease and amenity in its pages, the apparent indication of an unruffled mind.— DUYCKINCK, EVERT A., 1862, *National Portrait Gallery of Eminent Americans, vol.* II, *p.* 198.

A book ["Thirty Years' View"] of the greatest consequence to the student of American history. The author was a shrewd observer, and during all the period of which he wrote he was in the United States Senate. His account is remarkable for its simplicity of style, and for the admirable spirit with which he treats political foes as well as political friends. In no other work can be obtained so good an account of passing political events during those important years which extended from 1820 to 1850.—ADAMS, CHARLES KENDALL, 1882, *A Manual of Historical Literature, p.* 567.

He better knew how to translate the thoughts of great thinkers into a dialect which the multitude could interpret and understand than any other politician of his time. . . . Benton was master of our mother tongue; spoke and wrote it in its purity, power, simplicity, and all men understood "the meaning" and "the bearing." . . . The "Thirty Years' View," a work which he imagined would be immortal, is that whereon he mainly rested his hopes of future fame. The cream of his best speeches is therein collected. In many respects it is a valuable contribution to the political literature of the times, and supplies an important desideratum in our annals. But is it not straining panegyric somewhat to denominate the work history? For ourselves, we cannot concede to it that appellation unless we accept the late General Benning's characterization of history as correct: "History," said he, "is true in general, and false in every particular." "The View" is full of inaccuracies, some of them too gross for pardon. In too many

instances personal feeling gives tinge to statement of fact. The truth is not presented in *white* light, not because the author did not mean to be candid, for his instincts were honest, if not generous, but because it was simply impossible for him to be impartial.—WADDELL, JAMES D., 1882, *Thomas Hart Benton, International Review, vol.* 12, *pp.* 481, 482, 486.

As a writer, Mr. Benton's reputation will rest mainly upon his "Thirty Years' View," and upon his "Abridgment of the Debates of Congress," which he brought down from 1789 to 1850, in sixteen volumes,—an invaluable work, compiled after he had passed the age of seventy-four, and the closing portion dictated in a whisper on his death-bed. . . . To no statesman is this country more indebted than to Benton for the maintenance of correct views upon the true function of government in relation to this question of "soft" money.—FULLER, MELVILLE W., 1887, *"Old Bullion," The Dial, vol.* 8, *pp.* 13, 15.

Benton's style as an orator was easy, full, and strong, showing him well acquainted with his subject and confident of his powers. The "Thirty Years' View" is noted for its excellent arrangement and for a style easy and fluent yet not diffuse.—MANLY, LOUISE, 1895, *Southern Literature, p.* 159.

George Combe
1788–1858

Phrenologist and moral philosopher, was born, a brewer's son, in Edinburgh, October 21, 1788. He became a Writer to the Signet in 1812, and practised till 1837, when he devoted himself to popularising his views on phrenology and education. Through Spurzheim he became a convert to phrenology, and wrote "Essays on Phrenology" (1819) and "Elements of Phrenology (1824, 9th ed. 1862). But his most important production is "The Constitution of Man" (1828; 10th ed. 1893), which was violently opposed as inimical to revealed religion. He numbered amongst his friends Cobden, Robert Chambers, and "George Eliot." He travelled and lectured in the United Kingdom, Germany, and America, and published "Notes on the United States" (1841). Combe married, in 1833, Cecilia (1794–1868), daughter of Mrs. Siddons; he died 14th August 1858. Other works were "Lectures on Popular Education" (1833), "Moral Philosophy" (1840), "Principles of Criminal Legislation" (1854), "The Currency Question" (1855), "The Relation between Science and Religion" (1857). Combe's ideas on popular education were carried out for some years in a secular school which he founded in Edinburgh in 1848, where the sciences were taught, including physiology and phrenology. See "Life" by C. Gibbon (1878), and Combe's views and articles on "Education," collected by Jolly (1879).—PATRICK AND GROOME, *eds.*, 1897, *Chambers's Biographical Dictionary, p.* 236.

PERSONAL

His remarkable self-esteem; his self-consciousness, rendering him very faintly impressionable; his good-nature and real benevolence; his shrewdness and caution; the absence of all keen sensibility, and the presence of a constant sense of justice,—all fitted him to hold any given ground well against unscrupulous and passionate adversaries. No romance of duty dazzled him; no idolatry of the ideal intoxicated him; no sympathy with human passion or devout aspiration put him off his guard. Standing above the perils of gross selfishness and dishonesty, and below those which attend high intellectual and spiritual gifts, he was the man to hold a certain ground, and he held it steadily, cheerfully, and well.—MARTINEAU, HARRIET, 1858, *Biographical Sketches, p.* 142.

George Combe, the English author, encountered a full share of the vicissitudes of genius. He was capable of much theoretical goodness, but was not practical in that respect. He wrote in his old age, "Few men have enjoyed more of the pleasures and brilliance of life than myself"; yet he died in the King's Bench, where he had taken refuge from his creditors, not leaving enough to pay the expenses of his funeral.—BALLOU, MATURIN M., 1886, *Genius in Sunshine and Shadow, p.* 166.

Combe was remarkably even-tempered and mildly persistent; he was thoroughly amiable in all his family relations, and liberal in cases of need, though his formality and love of giving advice exposed him to some ridicule. He was essentially a man of one idea. His want of scientific training predisposed him to accept with implicit confidence the crude solution of enormously complex and delicate problems propounded by the phrenologists, and for the rest of his life he propagated the doctrine with the zeal of a religious missionary.—STEPHEN, LESLIE, 1887, *Dictionary of National Biography, vol.* XI, *p.* 429.

GENERAL

This ["A System of Phrenology"] is a long, sober, argumentative exposition of a very fantastical, and in our humble judgment, most absurd hypothesis. The author, however, is undoubtedly a man of talent as well as industry;—and while many of his remarks indicate no ordinary acuteness, it is impossible not to admire the dexterity with which he has occasionally evaded the weak, and improved the plausible parts of his argument—and the skill and perseverance he has employed in working up his scanty and intractable materials into a semblance of strength and consistency. Phrenology, in his hands, has assumed for the first time, an aspect not absolutely ludicrous;—and, by retrenching many of the ridiculous illustrations and inconsistent assumptions of its inventors, as well as by correcting its terminology, and tempering its extravagance, he has so far succeeded in disguising its inherent absurdity as to afford a decent apology for those who are determined, or at least very willing, to believe. After all, however, that radical absurdity is so glaring, that in spite of his zeal and earnestness, we really have great difficulty in believing the author to be in good faith with us; and suspect that few reflecting readers will be able to get through the work without many starts of impatient surprise, and a general uneasy surmise that it is a mere exercise of intellectual ingenuity or an elaborate experiment upon public credulity.—JEFFREY, FRANCIS LORD, 1826, *Phrenology, Edinburgh Review, vol.* 44, *p.* 253.

A man must be called a conspicuous member of society who writes a book approaching in circulation to the three ubiquitous books in our language—the Bible, "Pilgrim's Progress," and "Robinson Crusoe." George Combe's "Constitution of Man" is declared to rank next to these three in point of circulation. . . . The world owes him much, however disappointed it may be that it does now owe him more.—MARTINEAU, HARRIET, 1858, *Biographical Sketches, pp.* 133, 144.

A man who was well known—almost famous—among the last generation, but of whom little is heard at the present day. Within a short time after his death the sale of "The Constitution of Man" had reached 100,000 copies; now the book is rarely read. Its author was in correspondence with men of learning and rank—even with the royal family—yet his memory cannot shield from ridicule the doctrine of which he was a leading apostle. Finally, he labored long and hard in behalf of reforms which the present generation enjoy with seldom a thought of the obloquy heaped upon their earlier champions. This may seem hard, but it is certainly not unnatural. The impression made upon the world during the lifetime of George Combe was due to his advocacy of opinions contrary to, or in advance of, those of his time, rather than to his possession of unusual bodily or mental powers. In fact, the essential mediocrity of his nature was cheerfully recognized when he said, at the age of forty-four, "No man whose brain does not exceed the average more than mine is of importance to the world."—WILDER, B. G., 1878, *George Combe, The Nation, vol.* 27, *p.* 304.

George Combe has been dead twenty years, and his name is almost forgotten. Many of his teachings, which were bitterly opposed when he uttered them, are quietly accepted. His theories of religion, of education, of the treatment of the insane and criminal classes, are more or less approved, and even the doctrine that mind is a function of the brain, which he was among the first to assert, and for which he was denounced as an infidel, has taken its place among the data of science. But the system of phrenology to which he gave himself with such intense devotion is discredited by science, and, like Mr. Combe himself, is now seldom heard of.—YOUMANS, ELIZA A., 1879, *The "Autobiography" of George Combe, The Popular Science Monthly, vol. 15, p. 109.*

There was no combination or definite party, but many shared in a movement in which George Combe in every way deserves the pre-eminence. He was a man of spotless character and the most sincere enthusiasm, combining an earnest Christian theism with the most hesitating belief in views of man's constitution and responsibility which seem constantly shading off into Materialism. Many of his special dogmas have vanished with the progress of knowledge, especially of that natural knowledge on which his system was based; but there are also important aspects of his teaching, in its bearing on education, which survive, and have entered with enlightening force into our modern educational theories. Not only so, but imperfect as we must judge, both from a philosophical and religious point of view, many of Combe's generalizations, in which he reposed implicit confidence, we feel that there was a healthy element in his speculations. They were as salt in the intellectual and religious atmosphere, and at a time when there was so much to harden and sometimes darken religious feeling, they helped to nourish a broader and freer opinion not without its beneficent bearing on religion. It is, however, in other directions that we must look for the chief influences which at this time affected religious opinion in Scotland.—TULLOCH, JOHN, 1885, *Movement of Religious Thought in Britain During the Nineteenth Century, p. 83.*

His writings were for many years extremely popular with the half-educated, and though his theories have fallen into complete discredit he did something, like his friend Chambers, to excite an interest in science and a belief in the importance of applying scientific method in moral questions. —STEPHEN, LESLIE, 1887, *Dictionary of National Biography, vol. XI, p. 429.*

In common with Horace Mann, he [Dr. Howe] held Mr. Combe to be one of the first intelligences of the age, and esteemed his work on "The Constitution of Man" as one of the greatest of human productions.— HOWE, JULIA WARD, 1899, *Reminiscences, 1819-1899, p. 133.*

Thomas Babington Lord Macaulay
1800–1859

Born, at Rothley Temple, Leicestershire, 25 Oct. 1800. Early education at a day-school at Clapham; at school at Little Shelford, near Cambridge, and afterwards at Aspenden Hall, Herts., 1812–18. Matric. Trin. Coll., Camb., Oct. 1818; English Prize Poem, 1819 and 1821; Craven Scholarship, 1821; B. A. 1822; Fellow of Trin. Coll., Oct. 1824 to 1831; M. A. 1825. Student of Lincoln's Inn; called to Bar, 1826. Contrib. to periodicals from 1823. Commissioner in Bankruptcy, Jan. 1828. M. P. for Calne, Feb. 1830. Commissioner of Board of Control, June 1832. Sec. to Board, Dec. 1832. M. P. for Leeds, Dec. 1832. In India, as Mem. of Supreme Council, 1834–38. M. P. for Edinburgh, 1839; re-elected, 1841 and 1846. Sec. for War, 1839–41. Paymaster-General, 1846–48. Defeated at Edinburgh 1847; withdrew from political life. Lord Rector, Glasgow Univ., Nov. 1849. F. R. S. Nov. 1849. Prof. of Ancient Hist., Royal Acad., 1850. Fellow of University of London, 1850–59. Trustee of British Museum, 1847. Re-elected M. P. for Edinburgh, July 1852. Mem. of Institute of France, 1853. Knight of Prussian Order of Merit, 1853. Hon. D. C. L., Oxford, June 1854. Pres. of Philosophical Inst., Edinburgh, 1854. Member of Academies of Utrecht, Munich, and Turin. Created Baron Macaulay, 10 Sept. 1857. High Steward of Borough of Cambridge, 1857. Died, in London, 28 Dec. 1859. Buried in Westminster Abbey. *Works:* "Pompeii" [1819]; "Evening" [1821]; "Critical and Miscellaneous Essays" (Philadelphia, 5 vols.), 1841–44; "Lays

THOMAS BABINGTON MACAULAY

From a Steel Engraving.

HENRY HALLAM

From an Engraving by Sartain.

of Ancient Rome," 1842; "Critical and Historical Essays" (from Edinburgh Rev.), 1843; "History of England," vols. i, ii, 1849, vols. iii, iv, 1855; vol. v (*posthumous*), ed. by Lady Trevelyan, 1861; "Inaugural Address" [at Glasgow], 1849; "Speeches" (2 vols.), 1853 (edn. "corrected by himself," 1854). *Posthumous:* "Biographies contributed to the Encyclopædia Britannica," 1860; "Miscellaneous Writings," ed. by T. F. Ellis, 1860; vol. v of "History of England" (*see* above), 1861. *Collected Works:* ed. by Lady Trevelyan (8 vols.), 1866. *Life:* By Sir G. O. Trevelyan, 1876.—SHARP, R. FARQUHARSON, 1897, *A Dictionary of English Authors*, p. 178.

PERSONAL

I poke one line into Tom's vile scrawl to say that he goes on in the usual Pindaric style; much desultory reading, much sitting from bower to bower; Spenser, I think, is the favourite poet to-day. As his time is short, and health, I think, the chief object just now, I have not insisted on much system. He read in the sun yesterday and got a little headache. Since "Childe Hugh," a long poem on Hunt's election, really a good parody, has been shown us, I have discovered in the writing-box an Epithalamium of many folio pages on Mr. Sprague's marriage. I do compel him to read two or three scenes of Metastasio every day, and he seems to like it. His talents are very extraordinary and various, and his acquirements wonderful at his age. His temper is good, and his vivacity a great recommendation to me, but this excess of animal spirits makes some certain studies seem a little dry and dull. I will tell you honestly as a true friend, what indeed you know already and mentioned to me, that his superiority of talents makes competitors necessary for him, for that he is a little inclined to under-value those who are not considerable or distinguished in some way or other. I have talked with him gently on the subject, telling him how valuable and worthy people may be who are neither brilliant in talent nor high in situation.—MORE, HANNAH, 1810, *Letter, May; Life and Letters of Zachary Macaulay, ed. Knutsford, p.* 288.

I had a most interesting companion in young Macaulay, one of the most promising of the rising generation I have seen for a long time. . . . He has a good face,—not the delicate features of a man of genius and sensibility, but the strong lines and well-knit limbs of a man sturdy in body and mind. Very eloquent and cheerful. Overflowing with words and not poor in thought. Liberal in opinion, but no radical. He seems a correct as well as a full man. He showed a minute knowledge of subjects not introduced by himself.—ROBINSON, HENRY

CRABB, 1826, *Diary, Nov.* 29; *Diary, Reminiscence and Correspondence, ed. Sadler.*

Dined yesterday with Lord Holland; came very late, and found a vacant place between Sir George Robinson and a common-looking man in black. As soon as I had time to look at my neighbor, I began to speculate (as one usually does) as to who he might be, and as he did not for some time open his lips except to eat, I settled that he was some obscure man of letters or of medicine, perhaps a cholera doctor. . . . Having thus settled my opinion, I went on eating my dinner, when Auckland, who was sitting opposite me, addressed my neighbor, "Mr. Macaulay, will you drink a glass of wine?" I thought I should have dropped off my chair. It was *Macaulay,* the man I had been so long most curious to see and to hear, whose genius and eloquence, astonishing knowledge, and diversified talents have excited my wonder and admiration for such a length of time, and here I had been sitting next to him, hearing him talk, and setting him down for a dull fellow. I felt as if he could have read my thoughts, and the perspiration burst forth from every pore of my face, and yet it was impossible not to be amused at the idea. It was not till Macaulay stood up that I was aware of all the vulgarity and ungainliness of his appearance; not a ray of intellect beams from his countenance; a lump of more ordinary clay never enclosed a powerful mind and lively imagination. He had a cold and a sore thorax, the latter of which occasioned a constant contraction of the muscles of the throat, making him appear as if in momentary danger of a fit. His manner struck me as not pleasing, but it was not assuming, unembarrassed, yet not easy, unpolished, yet not coarse, there was no kind of usurpation of the conversation, no tenacity as to opinion or facts, no assumption of superiority, but the variety and extent of his information were soon apparent, for whatever subject was touched upon he evinced the utmost familiarity with it; quotation, illustration, anecdote, seemed ready in his hands for every topic. --GREVILLE, CHARLES C. F., 1832, *A Journal of the Reigns of King George IV and King William IV, ed. Reeve, Feb.* 6.

An emphatic, hottish, really forcible person, but unhappily without divine idea. — CARLYLE, THOMAS, 1832, *Journal, Jan.* 13; *Thomas Carlyle, A History of the First Forty Years of his Life, ed. Froude, vol.* II, *p.* 187.

His memory is prodigious, surpassing any thing I have ever known, and he pours out its stores with an instructive but dinning prodigality. He passes from the minutest dates of English history or biography to a discussion of the comparative merits of different ancient orators, and gives you whole strophes from the dramatists at will. He can repeat every word of every article he has written, without prompting; but he has neither grace of body, face, nor voice; he is without intonation or variety; and he pours on like Horace's river, while we, poor rustics, foolishly think he will cease; and if you speak, he does not respond to what you say, but, while your last words are yet on your lips, takes up again his wondrous tale. He will not confess ignorance of any thing, though I verily believe that no man would ever have less occasion to make the confession. I have heard him called the most remarkable person of his age; and again the most overrated one. You will see that he has not left upon me an entirely agreeable impression; still I confess his great and magnificent attainments and powers. I wish he had more address in using them, and more deference for others.—SUMNER, CHARLES, 1839, *To George Hillard, Feb.* 16; *Memoir and Letters of Sumner, ed. Pierce, vol.* II, *p.* 65.

Went to Bowood to dinner. . . Macaulay wonderful; never, perhaps, was there combined so much talent with so marvelous a memory. To attempt to record his conversation one must be as wonderfully gifted with memory as himself.—MOORE, THOMAS, 1840, *Diary, Oct.* 21; *Memoirs, Journal and Correspondence, ed. Russell, vol.* VII, *p.* 283.

He is absolutely renowned in society as the greatest bore that ever yet appeared. I have seen people come in from Holland House, breathless and knocked up, and able to say nothing but "Oh dear, oh mercy." What's the matter? being asked.

"Oh, Macaulay." Then every one said, "That accounts for it—you're lucky to be alive," etc.—BROUGHAM, HENRY LORD, 1842, *To Napier, Aug.* 14; *Selections from the Correspondence of Macvey Napier, ed. Napier, p.* 403.

Yes, I take great credit to myself; I always prophesied his greatness from the first moment I saw him, then a very young and unknown man, on the Northern Circuit. There are no limits to his knowledge, on small subjects as well as great; he is like a book in breeches. . . . Yes, I agree, he is certainly more agreeable since his return from India. His enemies might perhaps have said before (though I never did so) that he talked rather too much; but now he has occasional flashes of silence, that make his conversation perfectly delightful. But what is far better and more important than all this, that I believe Macaulay to be incorruptible. You might lay ribbons, stars, garters, wealth, titles before him in vain. He has an honest, genuine love of his country, and the world could not bribe him to neglect her interests. —SMITH, SYDNEY, 1845?-55, *A Memoir of the Rev. Sydney Smith, by Lady Holland.*

In Parliament, he was no more than a most brilliant speaker; and in his speeches there was the same fundamental weakness which pervades his writings,—unsoundness in the presentment of his case. Some one element was sure to be left out, which falsified his statement, and vitiated his conclusions; and there never was perhaps a speaker or writer of eminence, so prone to presentments of cases, who so rarely offered one which was complete and true. My own impression is, and always was, that the cause of the defect is constitutional in Macaulay. The evidence seems to indicate that he wants heart. He appears to be wholly unaware of this deficiency; and the superficial fervour which suns over his disclosures probably deceives himself, as it deceives a good many other people; and he may really believe that he has a heart. To those who do not hold this key to the interpretation of his career, it must be a very mysterious thing that a man of such imposing and real ability, with every circumstance and influence in his favour, should never have achieved any complete success. As a politician, his failure has been signal, notwithstanding his irresistible power as a speaker, and his possession of every possible facility. As a practical legislator, his failure was unsurpassed, when he brought home his Code from India.—MARTINEAU, HARRIET, 1855-77, *Autobiography, ed. Chapman, vol.* I, *p.* 262.

Macaulay is the lion. He has been asked to meet us seven times, so that it has got to be a sort of joke. But he is very agreeable, not in perfectly good health, and not, I imagine, talking so much for effect as he used to, or claiming so large a portion of the table's attention; but well enough to be out a great deal in the evenings, and with fresh spirits.—TICKNOR, GEORGE, 1856, *To W. H. Prescott, July* 17; *Life, Letters and Journals, vol.* II, *p.* 323.

I was too much engaged with these personal talks to attend much to what was going on elsewhere; but all through breakfast I had been more and more impressed by the aspect of one of the guests, sitting next to Milnes. He was a man of large presence,—a portly personage, gray-haired, but scarcely as yet aged; and his face had a remarkable intelligence, not vivid nor sparkling, but conjoined with great quietude,—and if it gleamed or brightened at one time more than another, it was like the sheen over a broad surface of the sea. There was a somewhat careless self-possession, large and broad enough to be called dignity; and the more I looked at him, the more I knew that he was a distinguished person, and wondered who. He might have been a minister of state; only there is not one of them who has any right to such a face and presence. At last,—I do not know how the conviction came,—but I became aware that it was Macaulay, and began to see some slight resemblance to his portraits. But I have never seen any that is not wretchedly unworthy of the original. As soon as I knew him, I began to listen to his conversation, but he did not talk a great deal,—contrary to his usual custom; for I am told he is apt to engross all the talk to himself. Probably he may have been restrained by the presence of Ticknor and Mr. Palfrey, who were among his auditors and interlocutors; and as the conversation seemed to turn much on American subjects, he could not well have assumed to talk them down. I am glad to have seen him,—a face fit for a scholar, a man of the world, a cultivated intelligence. — HAWTHORNE, NATHANIEL, 1856, *English Note-Books, July* 13; *vol.* II, *p.* 103.

I sat next him at your table and tried to enter into conversation with him, telling him that he and Livy were under mutual obligations; and that I doubted whether in his ballads of Rome he was most indebted to Livy or Livy to him. It would not do. Yet it was no small compliment, for there was hardly a genius so exalted as Livy's in all the interval between Æschylus and Dante. But there are some who do not know it, and this was probably the case with Macaulay.—LANDOR, WALTER SAVAGE, 1858, *Letter to Forster, Jan.; Walter Savage Landor, a Biography by John Forster, bk.* vii.

I cannot describe him better than by saying that he was exactly that kind of a face and figure which by no possibility would be selected, out of even a very small number of persons, as those of a remarkable personage. He is of the middle height, neither above nor below it. The outline of his face in profile is rather good. The nose, very slightly aquiline, is well cut, and the expression of the mouth and chin agreeable. His hair is thin and silvery, and he looks a good deal older than many men of his years —for, if I am not mistaken, he is just as old as his century, like Cromwell, Balzac, Charles V., and other notorious individuals. How those two imposters, so far as appearances go, Prescott and Mignet, who are sixty-two, look young enough, in comparison, to be Macaulay's sons. The face, to resume my description, seen in front, is blank, and as it were badly lighted. There is nothing luminous in the eye, nothing impressive in the brow. The forehead is spacious, but it is scooped entirely away in the region where benevolence ought to be, while beyond rise reverence, firmness and self-esteem, like Alps on Alps. The under eye-lids are so swollen as almost to close the eyes, and it would be quite impossible to tell the colour of those orbs, and equally so, from the neutral tint of his hair and face, to say of what complexion he had originally been. . . . His whole manner has the smoothness and polished surface of the man of the world, the politician, and the new peer, spread over the man of letters within. I do not know that I can repeat any of his conversation, for there was nothing to excite very particular attention in its even flow.—MOTLEY, JOHN LOTHROP, 1858, *To his Wife, May* 30; *Correspondence, ed. Curtis, vol.* I, *pp.* 236, 237.

I sympathised with you when I read of Macaulay's death in the *Times*. He was, was he not, your next-door neighbor? I can easily conceive what a loss you must have had in the want of his brilliant conversation. I hardly knew him: met him once, I remember, when Hallam and Guizot were in his company: Hallam was showing Guizot the Houses of Parliament then building, and Macaulay went on like a cataract for an hour or so to those two great men, and, when they had gone, turned to me and said, "Good morning, I am happy to have had the pleasure of making your acquaintance," and strode away. Had I been a piquable man I should have been piqued, but I don't think I was, for the movement after all was amicable. . . . Peace be with him.—TENNYSON, ALFRED LORD, 1860, *To the Duke of Argyll; Alfred Lord Tennyson, a Memoir by his Son, vol.* I, p. 458.

One paper I have read regarding Lord Macaulay says "he had no heart." Why, a man's books may not always speak the truth, but they speak his mind in spite of himself; and it seems to me this man's heart is beating through every page he penned. He is always in a storm of revolt and indignation against wrong, craft, tyranny. How he cheers heroic resistance; how he backs and applauds freedom struggling for its own; how he hates scoundrels ever so victorious and successful; how he recognizes genius, though selfish villains possess it! The critic who says Macaulay had no heart, might say that Johnson had none; and two men more generous, and more loving, and more hating, and more partial, and more noble, do not live in our history. Those who knew Lord Macaulay knew how admirably tender and generous, and affectionate he was. It was not his business to bring his family before the theatre footlights, and call for bouquets from the gallery as he wept over them.— THACKERAY, WILLIAM MAKEPEACE, 1860, *Nil Nisi Bonum, Roundabout Papers.*

One late grave has been opened in the Historical Aisle of the South Transept, to receive the remains of the poet and historian who, perhaps, of all who have trod the floor of the Abbey or lie buried within its precincts, most deeply knew and felt its manifold interests, and most unceasingly commemorated them. Lord Macaulay rests at the foot of the statue of Addison, whose character and genius none had painted as he; carrying with him to his grave the story of the reign of Queen Anne, which none but he could have told.—STANLEY, ARTHUR PENRHYN, 1868, *Historical Memorials of Westminster Abbey, p.* 319.

He was the tyrant of the table, and rarely tolerated any talk but his own. . . . Macaulay sat still only when compelled by sheer force, and then only for a few seconds. A professional talker or a rival he put down in an instant, without the slightest hesitation or compunction, and trampled him into the bargain if he showed any signs of resistance.—PEABODY, CHARLES, 1870, *The Edinburgh Reviewers, Gentleman's Magazine, N. S. vol.* 5, p. 556.

There are some men who gain such *mastery* over their libraries for practical purposes, that it would be a crime to curtail their collections. Such pre-eminently was Lord Macaulay, of whom one might say what Dryden did of Ben Jonson, "He invaded authors like a monarch." Surrounded by his many thousand volumes, he could summon any one to his hands in a moment; and, by a felicity of memory which might well be called instinct, could put his finger almost instantly on the passage sought for. How he used this and his other faculties his works sufficiently tell. No writer had ever his intellectual materials more thoroughly in hand. When his memory failed as to facts it told him at once where to look for them.—HOLLAND, SIR HENRY, 1871, *Recollections of a Past Life, p.* 395.

Thomae Babington Baroni Macaulay
Historico doctrina fide vividis ingenii lumini-
bus praeclaro
Qui primus annales ita scripsit
Ut vera fictis libentius legerentur,
Oratori rebus copioso sententiis presso amini
motibus elato
Qui cum otii studiis unice gauderet
Nunquam reipublicae defuit,
Sive India litteris et legibus emendanda
Sive domi contra licentiam tuenda libertas
vocaret,
Poetae nihil humile spiranti
Viro cui cunctorum veneratio
Minoris fuit quam suorum amor
Huius collegii olim socio
Quod summa dum vixit pietate coluit
Amici maerentes S. S. F. C.
—JEBB, RICHARD CLAVERHOUSE, 1875, *Inscription on Statue, Trinity College.*

He had a massive head, and features of

a powerful and rugged cast, but so constantly lit up by every joyful and ennobling emotion that it mattered little if, when absolutely quiescent, his face was rather homely than handsome. While conversing at table no one thought him otherwise than good-looking: but, when he rose, he was seen to be short and stout in figure. . . . His clothes, though ill put on, were good, and his wardrobe was always enormously overstocked. Later in life he indulged himself in an apparently inexhaustible succession of handsome embroidered waistcoats, which he used to regard with much complacency. He was unhandy to a degree quite unexampled in the experience of all who knew him. When in the open air he wore perfectly new dark kid gloves, into the fingers of which he never succeeded in inserting his own more than half way. . . . Macaulay's extreme sensibility to all which appealed to the sentiment of pity, whether in art or in nature, was nothing short of a positive inconvenience to him. He was so moved by the visible representation of distressing scenes that he went most unwillingly to the theatre, for which, during his Cambridge days, he had entertained a passionate, though passing, fondness. I remember well, how, during the performance of "Masks and Faces," the sorrows of the broken-down author and his starving family in their Grub Street garret entirely destroyed the pleasure which he otherwise would have taken in Mrs. Stirling's admirable acting. And he was hardly less easily affected to tears by that which was sublime and stirring in literature, than by that which was melancholy and pathetic.—TREVELYAN, GEORGE OTTO, 1876, *Life and Letters of Lord Macaulay.*

Lord Macaulay lived a life of no more than sixty years and three months. But it was an extraordinarily full life of sustained exertion—a high table-land without depressions. . . . For a century and more, perhaps no man in this country, with the exception of Mr. Pitt and of Lord Byron, had attained at thirty-two the fame of Macaulay. His parliamentary success and his literary eminence were each of them enough, as they stood at this date, to intoxicate any brain and heart of a meaner order. But to these was added in his case an amount and quality of social attentions such as invariably partake of adulation and

idolatry, and as perhaps the high circles of London never before or since have lavished on a man whose claims lay only in himself, and not in his descent, his rank, or his possessions. . . . Macaulay was singularly free of vices, and not in the sense in which, according to Swift's note on Burnet, William III. held such a freedom; that is to say, "as a man is free of a corporation." One point only we reserve; a certain tinge of occasional vindictiveness. Was he envious? Never. Was he servile? No. Was he insolent? No. Was he prodigal? No. Was he avaricious? No. Was he selfish? No. Was he idle? The question is ridiculous. Was he false? No; but true as steel and transparent as crystal. Was he vain? We hold that he was not. At every point in the ugly list he stands the trial; and though in his history he judges mildly some sins of appetite or passion, there is no sign in his life, or his remembered character, that he was compounding for what he was inclined to.—GLADSTONE, WILLIAM EWART, 1876, *Lord Macaulay, Quarterly Review, vol.* 142, *pp.* 2, 3, 6.

So far as we have to speak of Macaulay as a man, the most extreme panegyric will scarcely reach into exaggeration. As a son, and as a brother, as a politician, or as a man of the world, in every position into which he was thrown by the accidents of life, the great historian of England was in all respects without blame.—FROUDE, JAMES ANTHONY, 1876, *Lord Macaulay, Fraser's Magazine, N. S. vol.* 13, *p.* 676.

He was a boy in spirit all his life long, and yet, when he was a boy, it was one of a queer kind. What would the boys themselves say to a boy who never knew how to skate, or swim, or shoot, or row, or drive, and didn't care enough about his ignorance to try to mend it? a boy who never liked dogs? What would the boys of an older growth say to a boy who was so clumsy that when a barber said he might pay him whatever he usually gave the person who shaved him, he replied, "In that case, I should give you a great gash on each cheek"? a boy who, when he reached the kid-glove age, always wore out-doors perfect new dark gloves, into which he never got his fingers more than half way; who has left on record only one instance in which he knew one tune from another, and who seems never to have been in love in all his life? And yet he was the exact opposite of a little prig. He was the life and soul of his father's big family of boys and girls— Selina, Jane, John, Henry, Fanny, Hannah, Margaret, and Charles. In this circle he was king. . . . Nothing could be more beautiful than Macaulay's love for his sisters Hannah and Margaret, which they repaid with a devotion all the more profound because the brother they loved was a brother to be very proud of. They were the nearest to him of all the children in sympathies, but not in age, being respectively ten and twelve years younger than he. . . . It was one of the good things about Tom Macaulay that he was just as fond of his sisters' society when he was a great and busy man as he was before, and that when his little nephews and nieces began to grow up about him, they never knew that he was any body in particular, except dear Uncle Tom, who was always giving them great treats and taking them to see the shows.—LLOYD, D. D., 1879, *The "Tom" Side of Macaulay, Harper's Magazine, vol. 58, pp.* 605, 606, 607.

Macaulay, says his nephew and historian, dressed badly but not poorly. Such was the uncle, already grown famous, of young Otto Trevelyan. But Tom Macaulay, of 1820-1825, was altogether slovenly. He was an undergraduate of Trinity when a certain don sent him an invitation to dinner. Macaulay, who (at that time) hated society, had already written a letter of refusal, when some comrades burst into his room, and being informed of the correspondence pending, told Macaulay that "he must accept." As the invitation was for that very day, they further decided that Macaulay must be washed, scrubbed for the occasion, for in those days he was excessively negligent of his personal appearance. And the thing was done *vi et armis.* —MURRAY, GRENVILLE, 1881, *Personal Reminiscences, The Swiss Times.*

I used . . . to look in during the course of the day, upon whatever circle might be gathered in the drawing or morning rooms, for a few minutes at a time, and remember, on this occasion of my meeting Macaulay at Bowood, my amazement at finding him always in the same position on the hearth-rug, always talking, always answering everybody's questions about everything, always pouring forth eloquent knowledge; and I used to listen to him till I was breathless with what I thought ought to have been *his* exhaustion. As one approached the room, the loud, even, declamatory sound of his voice made itself heard like the uninterrupted flow of a fountain. He stood there from morning till evening, like a knight in the lists, challenging and accepting the challenge of all comers. There never was such a speech-"power," and as the volume of his voice was full and sonorous, he had immense advantages in sound as well as sense over his adversaries. Sydney Smith's humourous and good-natured rage at his prolific talk was very funny. Rogers's of course, was not good-humored.—KEMBLE, FRANCES ANN, 1882, *Records of Later Life, p.* 281.

I have much pleasure in giving you any information in my power respecting Lord Macaulay. He died in his library at Holly Lodge. For some time before he had been in ill-health from weak heart. His servant, who had left him feeling rather better, found on his return his master fainting in his chair. I was quickly sent for, got him removed to his couch, where he expired in a few moments. None of his family were with him. His sister, Mrs. Trevelyan, arrived soon after his death, accompanied by her son, then a very young man, but now, I believe, the Irish Secretary. At the time of his seizure Lord Macaulay was reading a number of the "Cornhill Magazine," then a new publication; and, as far as my memory serves me, he was reading Thackeray's "Adventures of Philip." Holly Lodge is still standing and is, I believe, unaltered. You will find it on the top of Campden Hill, next the Duke of Argyll's.—JOYCE, DR. THOMAS, 1883, *Letter to Laurence Hutton, Literary Landmarks of London, p.* 203.

In one thing all agree—critics, public, friends, and opponents. Macaulay's was a life of purity, honour, courage, generosity, affection, was manly perseverance, almost without a stain or a defect. His life, it was true, was singularly fortunate, and he had but few trials, and no formidable obstacles. He was bred up in the comfortable egoism of the opulent middle classes; the religion of comfort, *laisser-faire,* and social order was infused into his bones. But, so far as his traditions and temper would permit, his life was as honourable, as unsullied, and as generous, as ever was that of any man who lived in the fierce light that beats upon the famous. We know his nature and his career as well as we know any man's; and we find it on every side wholesome, just, and right.—HARRISON, FREDERIC, 1894, *Studies in Early Victorian Literature, p.* 68.

ORATORY

Tickler.—"An ugly, cross-made, splay-footed, shapeless little dumpling of a fellow, with a featureless face too—except indeed a good expansive forehead—sleek puritanical sandy hair—large glimmering eyes—and a mouth from ear to ear. He has a lisp and a burr, moreover, and speaks thickly and huskily for several minutes before he gets into the swing of his discourse: but after that nothing can be more dazzling than his whole execution. What he says is substantially, of course, mere stuff and nonsense; but it is so well worded, and so volubly and forcibly delivered—there is such an endless string of epigram and antithesis—such a flashing of epithets—such an accumulation of images —and the voice is so trumpetlike and the action so grotesquely emphatic, that you might hear a pin drop in the house. Manners Sutton himself listens. It is so obvious that he has got the main parts at least by heart—but for this I give him the more praise and glory. Altogether, the impression on my mind was very much beyond what I had been prepared for—so much so that I can honestly and sincerely say I felt for his situation most deeply, when Peel was skinning him alive the next evening, and the sweat of agony kept pouring down his well-bronzed cheeks under the merciless infliction."—WILSON, JOHN, 1831, *Noctes Ambrosianæ, August.*

I say, Sir, that I admit the learned gentleman's eloquence, and feel it peculiarly, not only from the admiration it excites, but from the difficulty it imposes upon the humble individual whose fortune it is—*haud passibus æquis*—to follow him. But I am relieved, in some degree, by the reflection that, as from the highest flights men are liable to the heaviest falls, and in the swiftest courses to the most serious disasters, so, I will say, it is the most brilliant eloquence sometimes interrupted by intervals of the greatest obscurity, and the most impassioned declamation defeated by the most fatal contradictions; and I must assert that the speech of the learned gentleman had points of weakness which no imprudence or want of judgment ever surpassed, and carried within itself its own refutation beyond any other speech I almost ever heard. . . . Not satisfied with those vague generalities, which he handled with that brilliant declamation which tickles the ear and amuses the imagination, without satisfying the reason, he unluckily, I think, for the force of his appeal, thought proper to descend to argumentative illustration and historical precedents.—But whence has he drawn his experience? Sir, he drew his weapon from the very armoury to which, if I had been aware of his attack, I should myself have resorted for the means of repelling it.—CROKER, JOHN WILSON, 1831, *Speech in the House of Commons on the Reform Bill, Sept. 22; The Croker Papers, ed. Jennings, vol. II, p.* 130.

His maiden speech electrified the House, and called forth the highest compliments to the speaker from men of all parties. He was careful to preserve the laurels he had thus so easily and suddenly won. He was a man of shrewd mind, and knew that if he spoke often, the probability was, he could not speak so well; and that consequently there could be no more likely means of lowering him from the elevated station to which he had raised himself, than frequently addressing the House. In this he was quite right, for he had no talents for extempore speaking. . . . His personal appearance is prepossessing. In stature he is about the middle size, and well formed. His eyes are of a deep blue, and have a very intelligent expression. His complexion is dark, and his hair of a dark-brown colour. His face is rather inclined to the oval form. His features are small and regular.—GRANT, JAMES, 1835, *Random Recollections of the House of Commons from the Year* 1830 *to the Close of* 1835.

Not thus Macaulay; in that gorgeous mind
Colour and warmth the genial light combined;
Learning but glowed into his large discourse,
To heat its mass, and vivify its force.
The effects he studied by the words were made
More than the art with which the words were said!
Perhaps so great an orator was ne'er
So little of an actor; half the care,
Giv'n to the speaking which he gave the speech,
Had raised his height beyond all living reach:
E'en as it was, a master's power he proved
In the three tests—he taught, he charmed, he moved.
Few compass one; whate'er their fault may be,
Great orators alone achieve the three.
—LYTTON, SIR EDWARD GEORGE BULWER, 1860, *St. Stephen's.*

I cannot read Lord Macaulay's "Speeches" without feeling that they are more than mere brilliant compositions, such as every one will at once allow them to be. They are, I conceive, documents of very great value for that important portion of English history which is included between the latter years of George IV.'s reign, and the commencement of the reign of Queen Victoria.—MAURICE, FREDERICK DENISON, 1860, *Lord Macaulay, Macmillan's Magazine, vol.* i, *p.* 242.

No man ever possessed to a greater degree than Lord Macaulay the real secret of an orator,—the power to enter into, and to arouse at will, the emotions which sway masses of mankind. Rhetorical, in the proper sense of the word, he was not. The distinction is not easy to give exactly; but perhaps we may find it in this, that the strength of the orator lies in power and sincerity; while the rhetorician is an artist only, bent on temporary success, with or without convictions, as the case may be. By the former spirit Macaulay was always actuated; to the latter he was always a stranger. Some wonderful critics have indeed declared that, wanting heart himself, he never reached the hearts of others —that he coloured his characters from the mere love of effective contrasts, heedless of the truth of his portraits. Astonished silence is the only answer to such criticism as this.—LANCASTER, H. H., 1860, *Lord Macaulay's Place in English Literature, North British Review, vol.* 33, *p.* 449.

I never heard Macaulay speak in the House, where, although by no means an orator, he always made a strong impression. He spoke as he wrote—eloquently, in the choicest diction—smooth, easy, graceful, and ever to the purpose; striving to convince rather than persuade, and grudging no toil of preparation to sustain an argument or enforce a truth. His person was in his favor; in form as in mind he was robust, with a remarkably intelligent expression, aided by deep-blue eyes that seemed to sparkle, and a mouth remarkably flexible. His countenance was certainly well calculated to impress on his audience the classical language ever at his command —so faithfully did it mirror the high intelligence of the speaker. Yet he never created enthusiasm, and seemed aiming only to convince.—HALL, SAMUEL CARTER, 1883, *Retrospect of a Long Life, p.* 133.

ESSAYS

"Edinburgh Review" came last night. A smart, vigorous paper by Macaulay on Horace Walpole. Ambitious, too antithetic; the heart of the matter not struck. What will that man become? He has more force and emphasis in him than any other of my British contemporaries (coevals). Wants the root of belief, however. May fail to accomplish much. Let us hope better things.—CARLYLE, THOMAS, 1833, *Journal, Nov.* 1; *Thomas Carlyle, A History of the First Forty Years of his Life, ed. Froude, vol.* II, *p.* 301.

What I have said about Bacon's philosophy is widely at variance with what Dugald Stewart and Mackintosh have said on the same subject. . . . If I am in the wrong, my errors may set the minds of others at work, and may be the means of bringing both them and me to a knowledge of the truth. I never bestowed so much care on anything that I have written. There is not a sentence in the latter half of the article which has not been repeatedly re-cast. I have no expectation that the popularity of the article will bear any proportion to the trouble which I have expended on it. But the trouble has been so great a pleasure to me that I have already been very greatly overpaid.—MACAULAY, THOMAS BABBINGTON, 1836, *To Napier, Nov.* 26; *Selections from the Correspondence of Macvey Napier, ed. Napier, pp.* 180, 181.

The *Bacon* is, as you say, very striking, and no doubt is the work of an extremely clever man. It is so very long that I think you might have cut it in two, there being an obvious division. But (not to trouble you with the superfluous enumeration of its good qualities), it has two grievous defects, —a redundancy, an over-crowding of every one thing that is touched upon, that almost turns one's head; for it is out of one digression into another, and each thought in each is illustrated by twenty different cases and anecdotes, all of which follow from the first without any effort. This is a sad defect in Macaulay, and it really seems to get worse instead of better. I need not say that it is the defect of a very clever person—it is indeed exuberance. But it is a defect also that *old age* is liable to.—BROUGHAM, HENRY LORD, 1837, *To Napier, July* 28; *Selections from the Correspondence of Macvey Napier, ed. Napier, p.* 196.

Macaulay's article is splendid. It would

have killed Playfair, who took me to task for inserting a similar view of Bacon's character (written by Dr. Lee) in the "Edinburgh Encyclopædia." I think the Reviewer has taken an extreme view of Bacon's conduct.—BREWSTER, DAVID, 1837, *To Napier, July 27; Selections from the Correspondence of Macvey Napier, ed. Napier, p.* 149.

We have been much entertained and interested in Macaulay's "Life of Hastings" in the *Edinburgh;* but some of it is too gaudily written, and mean gaudiness, unsuited to the subject—such as the dresses of the people at Westminster Hall; and I think Macaulay's indignation against Gleig for his adulation of Hastings, and his not feeling indignation against his crimes, is sometimes noble, and sometimes mean and vituperative.—EDGEWORTH, MARIA, 1842, *To Mrs. R. Butler, March* 10; *Life and Letters, ed. Hare, vol.* II, *p.* 289.

His critical Essays exhibit a wide variety of knowledge, with a great fertility of illustration, and enough of the salt of pleasantry and sarcasm to flavour, and in some degree disguise, a somewhat declamatory and pretentious dogmatism.—CROKER, JOHN WILSON, 1849, *Mr. Macaulay's History of England, Quarterly Review, vol.* 84, *p.* 549.

Macaulay's style, like other original things, has already produced a school of imitators. Its influence may distinctly be traced, both to the periodical and daily literature of the day. Its great characteristic is the shortness of the sentences, which often equal that of Tacitus himself, and the rapidity with which new and distinct ideas of facts succeed each other in his richly-stored pages. He is the Pope of English prose: he often gives two sentiments or facts in a single line. No preceding writer in prose, in any modern language with which we are acquainted, has carried this art of abbreviation, or rather cramming of ideas to such a length; and to its felicitous use much of the celebrity which he has acquired is to be ascribed. There is no doubt that it is a most powerful engine for the stirring of the mind, and when not repeated too often, or carried too far, has a surprising effect. Its introduction forms an era in our historical composition.—ALISON, SIR ARCHIBALD, 1859, *Macaulay's History of England, Blackwood's Magazine, vol.* 65, *p.* 387.

Of all who wrote in the *Edinburgh Review,* not one contributor stamped his compositions with such inimitable workmanship. The articles were often unequal in power of statement and weight of matter; but they were uniform in brilliancy, and in the resources of a style that could decorate the superficial and hide the sophistical with varied graces, with ingenuity of thought, and variety of allusion, with sparkling fancies, and a sonorous arrangement of words that titillated the ears with luscious cadences.—MADDYN, DANIEL OWEN, 1859, *Chiefs of Parties Past and Present, p.* 120.

His "Essays" make us think of Addison, though at first they rather suggest the amazing difference between the two men and the two periods.—MAURICE, FREDERICK DENISON, 1860, *Lord Macaulay, Macmillan's Magazine, vol.* 1, *p.* 243.

The most remunerative collection of essays ever published in this or any other country.—CURWEN, HENRY, 1873, *A History of Booksellers, p.* 105.

The astonishing success of this celebrated book must be regarded as something of far higher consequence than a mere literary or commercial triumph. It is no insignificant feat to have awakened in hundreds of thousands of minds the taste for letters and the yearning for knowledge; and to have sworn by example that, in the interests of its own fame, genius can never be so well employed as on the careful and earnest treatment of serious themes.—TREVELYAN, GEORGE OTTO, 1876, *Life and Letters of Lord Macaulay.*

His "Essays" are as good as a library; they make an incomparable manual and vademecum for a busy, uneducated man who has curiosity and enlightenment enough to wish to know a little about the great lives and great thoughts, the shining words and many-coloured complexities of action, that have marked the journey of man through the ages. Macaulay had an intimate acquaintance both with the imaginative literature and the history of Greece and Rome, with the literature and the history of modern Italy, of France, and of England. Whatever his special subject, he contrives to pour into it with singular dexterity a stream of rich, graphic, and telling illustrations from all these widely diversified sources.—MORLEY, JOHN, 1876, *Macaulay, Fortnightly Review, vol.* 25, *p.* 499.

With the "Essay on Milton" began

Macaulay's career, and, brilliant as the career was, it had few points more brilliant than its beginning. . . . A style to dazzle, to gain admirers everywhere, to attract imitators in multitude! A style brilliant, metallic, exterior; making strong points, alternating invective with eulogy, wrapping in a robe of rhetoric the thing it represents; not, with the soft play of life, following and rendering the thing's very form and pressure. For, indeed, in rendering things in this fashion, Macaulay's gift did not lie.—ARNOLD, MATTHEW, 1879, *A French Critic on Milton, Mixed Essays*, pp. 237, 238.

Say what we will, Macaulay's "Essays" remain a brilliant and fascinating page in English literature. The world is never persistently mistaken in such cases. Time enough has elapsed, since their publication, to submerge them in oblivion had they not contained a vital spark of genius which criticism is powerless to extinguish. If not wells of original knowledge, they have acted like irrigating rills which convey and distribute the fertilizing waters from the fountain-head. The best would adorn any literature, and even the less successful have a picturesque animation, and convey an impression of power that will not easily be matched.—MORISON, JAMES COTTER, 1883, *Macaulay (English Men of Letters)*, p. 105.

Whatever defects he may have, when that vast work, the history of criticism, is finally written, Macaulay will be sure of a chapter, and a chapter of no small significance.—BRADFORD, GAMALIEL, JR., 1895, ed. *Macaulay's Life of Samuel Johnson*, p. 8.

In prose more vigorous influences were at work. In 1825, Macaulay marked an epoch in criticism by contributing to the *Edinburgh Review* his elaborate article on Milton, the earliest example in English of the modern *ètude*, or monograph in miniature, which has since become so popular a province of letters. When our period closes, Macaulay is a cabinet minister. His career as an essayist was mainly prior to 1840, at which date he had shown himself neither ballad-writer nor historian. In his famous reviews he created a species of literature, partly biographical, partly critical, which had an unrivalled effect in raising the average of cultivation. Countless readers found in the pages of Macaulay's "Essays" their earliest stimulus to independent

thought and the humane study of letters. —GOSSE, EDMUND, 1897, *A Short History of Modern English Literature*, p. 332.

Macaulay's essays are lively and entertaining, but their literary merit has been overestimated. They are really the chips and *débris* of his history, and though there are brilliant passages among them, they are for the most part carelessly written. The best that can be said of some of them is that they are more interesting than the books which Macaulay pretended to review. In others, serious subjects are treated in a wanton and superficial manner. They are rather dangerous reading for young people, or indeed for any who cannot discriminate readily between the true and false in literature. He has a bad habit of cumulative repetition and deals too frequently in sharp antitheses. His style of argument in reply to what he calls Sadler's Refutation is in the most domineering parliamentary vein. We feel less compunction in exposing the errors in Macaulay's writing, for he was always most unmerciful in his criticism of others.—STEARNS, FRANK PRESTON, 1897, *Modern English Prose Writers*, p. 52.

Macaulay had the unusual good fortune to reach at a bound the highest step in the ladder of fame. The critics were disturbed because he did not stop to show them his passports, and they at once began to call him back, but their shrill notes were lost in the torrents of popular acclaim. He made his debut in the *Edinburgh Review* with the famous essay on Milton, and nothing that he produced later quite equalled it. While he is not a great critic, he arouses interest in his subject, which is perhaps more important, especially with young readers, and this is the secret of his continued popularity. The contrasts between Carlyle, De Quincey, and Macaulay are very marked. Carlyle is a great poet, muscular, homely, lurid; De Quincey is a great artist, incisive, subtle, brilliant; Macaulay is a great reporter of affairs, aboundingly picturesque—"a symphony in purple and gold." His art was not evolved, it was cast.—GEORGE, ANDREW J., 1898, *From Chaucer to Arnold, Types of Literary Art*, p. 654.

His want of success was far greater than he knew. It was not merely in the analysis, but in the discovery of genius that he at times failed. The swaggering judgment which he passed on Boswell, in rhetoric as clever as it is swollen, shows that the mind of the man who delighted—and not without good reason delighted—an earlier generation by three volumes of "Critical and Historical Essays," was something worse than uncritical.—HILL, GEORGE BIRKBECK, 1898, *Eighteenth Century Letters, Introduction, p.* xxiv.

As an essayist Macaulay occupies an almost unique position in English literature. He created the historical essay, a form of literature exactly suited to the time in which he lived, a brief, clear, and illuminating introduction to some great era or some dominating personality. It is perfectly true that the more one knows about the era or the personality, the less one cares for Macaulay's introduction; but it is none the less valuable to the beginner for its stimulating quality, its power to awaken the interest in the past and the far away. Macaulay has been well called an almost unsurpassed leader to reading, and his essays have been to hundreds and thousands the door through which they entered into the great world of past politics, history, and literature. Macaulay is seldom a good critic, never an impartial judge; he is always, as in the "Essay on Milton," an advocate pleading his cause. But—and this is the great merit of his work—his causes are almost always right. He is biased indeed, but in favor of liberty, toleration, decency, and good faith.—PARROTT, THOMAS MARC, 1900, *ed. Essays on Milton and Addison by Thomas Babbington Macaulay, Introduction, p.* xix.

POEMS

It is a great merit of these poems that they are free from ambition and exaggeration. Nothing seems overdone; no tawdry piece of finery disfigures the simplicity of the plan that has been chosen. They seemed to have been framed with great artistical skill, with much self-denial and abstinence from anything incongruous, and with a very successful imitation of the effects intended to be represented. Yet here and there images of beauty and expressions of feeling are thrown out that are wholly independent of Rome or the Romans, and that appeal to the widest sensibilities of the human heart. In point of homeliness of thought and language there is often a boldness which none but a man conscious of great powers of writing would have ventured to show.—WILSON, JOHN,

1842, *Lays of Ancient Rome, Blackwood's Magazine, vol.* 52, *p.* 823.

These poems, therefore, are not the worse for being un-Roman in their form; and in their substance they are Roman to a degree which deserves great admiration. . . . We have not been able to detect, in the four poems, one idea or feeling which was not, or might not have been, Roman; while the externals of Roman life, and the feelings characteristic of Rome and of that particular age, are reproduced with great felicity, and without being made unduly predominant over the universal features of human nature and human life. Independently, therefore, of their value as poems, these compositions are a real service rendered to historical literature; and the author has made this service greater by his prefaces, which will do more than the work of a hundred dissertations in rendering that true conception of early Roman history, the irrefragable establishment of which has made Niebuhr illustrious, familiar to the minds of general readers.—MILL, JOHN STUART, 1843, *Macaulay's Lays of Ancient Rome, Westminster Review, vol.* 39, *p.* 106.

You are very right in admiring Macaulay, who has a noble, clear, metallic note in his soul, and makes us ready by it for battle. I very much admire Mr. Macaulay, and could scarcely read his ballads and keep lying down. They seem to draw me up to my feet as the mesmeric powers are said to do.—BROWNING, ELIZABETH BARRETT, 1843, *Letters of Elizabeth Barrett Browning addressed to Richard Hengist Horne, Oct.* 5.

The last publication of Mr. Macaulay—his "Lays of Ancient Rome"—may fairly be called, not an exhumation of decayed materials, but a reproduction of classical vitality. The only thing we might object to, is the style and form of his metres and rhythms, which are not classical, but Gothic, and often remind us of the "Percy Reliques." There is no attempt to imitate the ancient metres. In other respects these lays are Roman to the backbone; and where not so, they are Homeric. The events and subjects of the poems are chosen with an heroic spirit; there is all the hard glitter of steel about the lines!—their music is the neighing of steeds, and the tramp of armed heels, their inspiration was the voice of a trumpet.—HORNE, RICHARD HENGIST, 1844, *A New Spirit of the Age, p.* 219.

The most brilliant and rapid of all contemporary writers, his poetry is an array of
strong thoughts and glittering fancies
bounding along on a rushing stream of feeling. It has almost the appearance of
splendid impromptu composition.—WHIP-
PLE, EDWIN PERCY, 1845, *English Poets of
the Nineteenth Century, Essays and Reviews,
vol.* I, *p.* 340.

The dreamy rhymer's measured snore,
Falls heavy on our ears no more;
And by long strides are left behind
The dear delights of woman-kind,
Who win their battles like their loves,
In satin waistcoats and kid gloves,
And have achieved the crowning work
When they have truss'd and skewer'd a Turk.
Another comes with stouter tread,
And stalks among the statelier dead.
He rushes on, and hails by turns
High-crested Scott, broad-breasted Burns;
And shows the British youth, who ne'er
Will lag behind, what Romans were,
When all the Tuscans and their Lars,
Shouted, and shook the towers of Mars.
—LANDOR, WALTER SAVAGE, 1846, *To
Macaulay, Miscellaneous Poems; Works,
vol.* VIII, *p.* 151.

Mr. Macaulay's "Lays of Ancient Rome"
differed initially from Mr. Lockhart's
Spanish translations in this, that the latter
worked from the native materials, which he
refined and improved; the former simply
from the general scope and spirit of ancient
legends. Taking it for granted, according
to the very probable theory of Niebuhr,
that the semi-fabulous traditions of all
infant nations must have existed primarily
in a metrical form, he re-transferred some of
the portions of early Roman history back
into the shape which might be supposed to
have been their original one ere historicized
by Livy, and this with great consummate
imaginative and artistic ability. He is
entirely of the Homer, the Chaucer, and
Scott school, his poetry being thoroughly
that of action; and sentiment is seldom
more than interjectionally introduced—the
utmost fidelity being thus shown to the
essential characteristics of that species of
composition which he has so triumphantly
illustrated.—MOIR, D. M., 1851-52, *Sketches
of the Poetical Literature of the Past Half-
Century, p.* 300.

That he was imbued with the very soul
of poetry is sufficiently evinced by his
"Battle of Lake Regillus" and his moving
"Legends of Rome."—ALISON, SIR ARCHI-
BALD, 1853, *History of Europe, 1815-52.,ch.* v.

His [Maginn's] "Homeric Ballads" are
vigorous and genuine poems in their own
way; they are not one continual falsetto,
like the pinchbeck "Roman Ballads" of
Lord Macaulay.—ARNOLD, MATTHEW, 1861,
On Translating Homer.

Not even in the palmy days of Scott and
Byron was such an immediate and enormous circulation attained.—CURWEN,
HENRY, 1873, *A History of Booksellers,
p.* 104.

Lord Macaulay's "Lays of Ancient
Rome" was a literary surprise, but its
poetry is the rhythmical outflow of a
vigorous and affluent writer, given to splendor of diction and imagery in his flowing
prose. He spoke once in verse, and unexpectedly. His themes were legendary, and
suited to the author's heroic cast, nor was
Latinism ever more poetical than under his
thoroughly sympathetic handling. I am
aware that the "Lays" are criticised as
being stilted and false to the antique, but to
me they have a charm, and to almost every
healthy young mind are an immediate delight. Where in modern ballad-verse will
you find more ringing stanzas, or more
impetuous movement and action? Occasionally we have a noble epithet or image.
Within his range—little as one who met
him might have surmised it—Macaulay
was a poet, and of the kind which Scott
would have been first to honor. "Horatius"and "Virginius" among the Roman
lays, and that resonant battle-cry of "Ivry"
have become, it would seem, a lasting
portion of English verse.—STEDMAN, ED-
MUND CLARENCE, 1875-87, *Victorian Poets,
p.* 250.

Nobody, least of all Macaulay himself,
has ever put them forward as constituting
a great poem, still his poetical powers, little
as he cultivated them, are not inconsiderable. They are quite enough, when supported by the vivid and accurate knowlege
of the topics he is handling, and fired by his
genuine historical enthusiasm, to create a
poem good of its kind and in its degree; a
poem, moreover, which, unlike many
more ambitious compositions, is alive and
not dead. He has at any rate succeeded in
making Roman heroes and Roman traditions household words at the average English fireside, and it is not everyone who
could have done that.—DOYLE, SIR FRAN-
CIS HASTINGS, 1887, *Reminiscences and
Opinions, p.* 180.

Macaulay was, perhaps, at his best in his four "Lays of Ancient Rome." Whatever else he wrote required some qualities of mind other than those which have made all that he wrote popular. The "Lays of Ancient Rome" called into play just those powers which he had in perfection, and required no more. . . . Macaulay caught the swing of Scott's romance measure, made it a little more rhetorical, without loss—some might say rather with increase of energy,—and brought into play his own power of realizing in his mind all that he told.—MORLEY, HENRY, 1887, *ed. Lays of Ancient Rome, Preface.*

"The Lays" are dated 1842; they have passed through edition after edition; and if Matthew Arnold disliked and contemned them, the general [reader] is wise enough to know them by heart. But a book that is "a catechism to fight" (in Johnson's phrase) would have sinned against itself had it taken no account of them, and I have given "Horatius" in its integrity. . . . As for "The Armada," I have preferred it to "The Battle of Naseby," first, because it is neither vicious nor ugly, and the other is both; and, second, because it is so brilliant an outcome of that capacity for dealing with proper names which Macaulay, whether poet or not, possesses in common with none but certain among the greater poets.— HENLEY, WILLIAM ERNEST, 1891, *ed. Lyra Heroica, p.* 353, *note.*

I believe the critics of the grand style call them "pinchbeck," which I fancy is meant to be scornful—I can only say that they are still ringing in my ears with a note as fresh as they had fifty years back. I have said them over on their own ground; I have proved the truth of every epithet; and now, with the Sicilian deeds of Pyrrhus as my day's work, it is the notes of the "Prophecy of Capys" which come first home to me at the thought of the "Red King" and his bold Epirotes.—FREEMAN, EDWARD A., 1892, *A Review of My Opinions, The Forum, vol.* 13, *p.* 153.

If the boys of England could be polled as to their favourite poet, Sir Walter Scott and Lord Macaulay would doubtless divide the honours, and if the favourite poem were in question, "Horatius" would probably be voted first. . . . Macaulay was a master of prosody and had a thorough command over the instrument of rhyme. His versification is without flaw, though

it is said to lack the spontaneous variety which avoids monotony. It displays a vigour and vividness which command both eye and ear and which is maintained without any sacrifice of form.—MILES, ALFRED H., 1894, *The Poets and the Poetry of the Century, Keats to Lytton, pp.* 276, 281.

It is a gross and vulgar critical error to deem Macaulay's poetical effects vulgar or gross. They are *popular;* they hit exactly that scheme of poetry which the general ear can appreciate and the general brain understand. They are coin for general circulation; but they are not base coin. Hundreds and thousands of immature and 'prentice tastes have been educated to the enjoyment of better things by them; thousands and tens of thousands of tastes, respectable at least, have found in them the kind of poetry which they can like, and beyond which they are not fitted to go. And it would be a very great pity if there were ever wanting critical appreciations, which, while relishing things more exquisite and understanding things more esoteric, can still taste and savour the simple genuine fare of poetry which Macaulay offers.—SAINTS- BURY, GEORGE, 1896, *A History of Nineteenth Century Literature, p.* 227.

The mention of Macaulay reminds me of the charm I found in his "Lays of Ancient Rome," which came out when I was fitting for college. Certain critics, of whom the late Matthew Arnold is perhaps the most noteworthy, tell us that the "Lays" are not poetry; but on that question I am content to be wrong with John Stuart Mill and "Christopher North" and Henry Morley and Edmund Clarence Stedman, if they *are* wrong, rather than to be right with Matthew Arnold, if he *is* right.—ROLFE, WILL- IAM J., 1896, *The Elementary Study of English, p.* 52.

THE HISTORY OF ENGLAND
1849–1855

The mother that bore you had she been yet alive, would scarcely have felt prouder or happier than I do at this outburst of your graver fame. I have long had a sort of parental interest in your glory, and it is now mingled with a feeling of deference to your intellectual superiority which can only consist, I take it, with the character of a female parent.—JEFFREY, FRANCIS LORD, 1848, *Letter to Macaulay, Life and Letters of Lord Macaulay, ed. Trevelyan, ch.* xi.

Finished Macaulay's two volumes. How

admirable they are; full of generous impulse, judicial impartiality, wide research, deep thought, picturesque description, and sustained eloquence! Was history ever better written?—CARLISLE, LORD, 1849, *Journal, Jan.* 6.

The first two volumes of Macaulay's "History" have had a most brilliant success, but I cannot help thinking that the work has meretricious attractions which may pall upon the public taste.   There can be no doubt that, to produce a startling effect, the author does exaggerate very much, if he may be defended from positive misrepresenting.   I rejoice that such good principles as those which he inculcates should be found in such a popular work.—CAMPBELL, JOHN LORD, 1849, *Journal, Jan.* 11; *Life, ed. Mrs. Hardcastle, vol.* II, *p.* 248.

Macaulay's success has been enormous; indeed, such as to convince one his book cannot be worth much—that is, in a high sense, for in a low one his two volumes have got him £10,000.   A young officer said to me, "That is what I call history.   We took five copies at our depot."—MILNES, RICHARD MONCKTON (LORD HOUGHTON), 1849, *To Mrs. MacCarthy, May* 19; *Life, Letters, and Friendships, ed. Reid, vol.* I, *p.* 432.

I have just finished Macaulay's two volumes of the "History of England" with the same feeling that you expressed—regret at coming to the end, and longing for another volume—the most uncommon feeling, I suppose, that readers of two thick octavo volumes of the history of England and of times so well known, or whose story has been so often written, ever experienced. In truth, in the whole course of reading or hearing it read I was sorry to stop and glad to go on.   It bears peculiarly well that severe test of being read aloud; it never wearies the ear by the long resounding line, but keeps the attention alive by the energy shown.   It is the perfection of style so varied, and yet the same in fitness, in propriety, in perspicuity, in grace, in dignity and eloquence, and, whenever naturally called forth in that just indignation which makes the historian as well as the poet.   If Voltaire says true that "the style is the man " what a man must Macaulay be! But the man is in fact as much more than the style, as the matter is more than the manner.   It is astonishing with what ease Macaulay wields, manages, arranges his

vast materials collected far and near, and knows their value and proportions so as to give the utmost strength and force and light and life to the whole, and sustains the whole.   Such new lights are thrown upon historic facts and historic characters that the old appear new, and that which had been dull becomes bright and entertaining and interesting.—EDGEWORTH, MARIA, 1849, *Letter to Dr. Holland, April* 2; *Life of Maria Edgeworth by Zimmern, p.* 299.

He has written some very brilliant essays —very transparent in artifice, and I suspect not over honest in scope and management, but he has written *no history;* and he has, I believe, committed himself ingeniously in two or three points, which, fitly exposed, would confound him a good deal, and check his breeze from El Dorado. Chiefly, his bitter hatred of the Church of England all through is evident; it is, I think, the only very strong feeling in the book; and his depreciation of the station and character of the clergy of Charles II. and James II. to-day is but a symptom. . . .   I doubt if Macaulay's book will go down as a standard edition to our *historical* library, though it must always keep a high place among the specimens of English rhetoric.—LOCKHART, JOHN GIBSON, 1849, *To Mr. Croker, July* 12; *The Croker Papers, ed. Jennings, vol.* III, *pp.* 192, 193.

The sect of Quakers has been in high dudgeon with Macaulay, for what they consider an unjust attack upon Penn in his History.   They demanded an interview, which he at once granted, and they remonstrated with him upon what they considered his aspersions on their fame, particularly as referring to the transaction of the money which was extorted from the girls who went out to meet Monmouth for the use of the maids of honour, and which was carried on by Penn.   The Quakers denied the facts, but Macaulay produced all the official documents on which he had founded his statement, and they were entirely *floored.*   Macaulay offered to print the documents from which he had gathered his facts, but they were in no hurry to accept this proposal, and said they would confer further before they gave their answer.   Macaulay was much amused by this incident, and contrived to please the Quakers by his courtesy.—GREVILLE, HENRY, 1849, *Leaves from His Diary, Feb.* 7, *ed. Enfield, p.* 320.

Mr Macaulay's historical narrative is poisoned with a rancour more violent than even the passions of the time; and the literary qualities of the work, though in some respects very remarkable, are far from redeeming its substantial defects. There is hardly a page—we speak literally, hardly a page—that does not contain something objectionable either in substance or in colour: and the whole of the brilliant and at first captivating narrative is perceived on examination to be impregnated to a really marvelous degree with bad taste, bad feeling, and, we are under the painful necessity of adding—bad faith. These are grave charges: but we make them in sincerity, and we think that we shall be able to prove them; and if, here or hereafter, we should seem to our readers to use harsher terms than good taste might approve, we beg in excuse to plead that it is impossible to fix one's attention on, and to transcribe large portions of a work, without being in some degree infected with its spirit; and Mr. Macaulay's pages, whatever may be their other characteristics, are as copious a repertorium of vituperative eloquence as, we believe, our language can produce, and especially against everything in which he chooses (whether right or wrong) to recognise the shiboleth of Toryism. . . . Mr. Macaulay's Historical Novel. . . . We accuse him of a habitual and really injurious perversion of his authorities. This unfortunate indulgence, in whatever juvenile levity it may have originated, and through whatever steps it may have grown into an unconscious habit, seems to us to pervade the whole work—from Alpha to Omega—from Procopius to Mackintosh—and it is on that very account the more difficult to bring to the distant conception of our readers. Individual instances can be, and shall be, produced; but how can we extract and exhibit the minute particles that colour every thread of the texture?—how extract the impalpable atoms that have fermented the whole brewing? We must do as Dr. Faraday does at the Institution when he exhibits in miniature the larger processes of Nature.—CROKER, JOHN WILSON, 1849, *Mr. Macaulay's History of England, Quarterly Review, vol.* 84, *pp.* 550, 553, 561.

But as he announced a History, the public received as a *bona fide* History the work on which he purposes to build his fame. If it had been announced as a historical romance, it might have been read with almost unmixed delight, though exception might have been taken to his presentment of several characters and facts. He has been abundantly punished, for instance, for his slanderous exhibition of William Penn. But he has fatally manifested his loose and unscrupulous method of narrating, and, in his first edition, gave no clue whatever to his authorities, and no information in regard to dates which he could possibly suppress. Public opinion compelled, in future editions, some appearance of furnishing references to authorities, such as every conscientious historian finds it indispensable to his peace of mind to afford, but it is done by Macaulay in the most ineffectual and baffling way possible, —by clubbing together the mere names of his authorities at the bottom of the page, so that reference is all but impracticable. Where it is made, by painstaking readers, the inaccuracies and misrepresentations of the historian are found to multiply as the work of verification proceeds. In fact, the only way to accept his History is to take it as a brilliant fancypiece,—wanting not only the truth but the repose of history,— but stimulating, and even, to a degree, suggestive.—MARTINEAU, HARRIET, 1855-77, *Autobiography, ed. Chapman, vol.* I, *p.* 263.

The one thing which detracts from the pleasure of reading these volumes is the doubt whether they should have been written. Should not these great powers be reserved for great periods? Is this abounding, picturesque style suited for continuous history? Are small men to be so largely described? Should not admirable delineation be kept for admirable people? We think so,—you do not want Raphael to paint sign-posts, or Palladio to build dirt pies. . . . The life of a great painter is short; even the industry of Macaulay will not complete this history. It is a pity to spend such powers on such events; it would have been better to have some new volumes of essays solely on great men and great things. The diffuseness of the style would have been then in place; we could have borne to hear the smallest *minutiæ* of magnificent epochs. If an inferior hand had executed the connecting links, our notions would have acquired an insensible perspective: the works of the great artist, the best themes would have stood out from the canvas; they are now confused by the equal brilliancy of the adjacent inferiorities.—BAGE-HOT, WALTER, 1856, *Thomas Babbington Macaulay, Works, ed. Morgan, vol. II, p. 98.*

On several subjects I should venture to differ from Mr. Macaulay; but I cannot refrain from expressing my admiration of his unwearied diligence, of the consummate skill with which he has arranged his materials, and of the noble love of liberty which animates his entire work. These are qualities which will long survive the aspersions of his puny detractors,—men who, in point of knowledge and ability, are unworthy to loosen the shoe-latchet of him they foolishly attack.—BUCKLE, HENRY THOMAS, 1857, *History of Civilization in England, vol. I, ch. vii, note.*

My attention was first directed to the subject of the following pages by finding in Lord Macaulay's picture of William Penn a character, so inconsistent with itself, that one would not expect to meet with it until we discover a country inhabited by centaurs, or succeed in catching a living mermaid. I was thus led to examine the authorities on which he relies. A short time served to convince me that the dark stains with which he has disfigured the portrait of Penn were not to be found in the original, but owed their existence solely to the jaundiced eye of the artist.—PAGET, JOHN, 1858, *An Inquiry into the Evidence Relating to the Charges Brought by Lord Macaulay against William Penn, Introduction, p. iii.*

I have only recently read over again the whole of his "History of England" with undiminished pleasure and admiration, though with a confirmed opinion that his style is not the very best, and that he is not the writer whom I should be most desirous to imitate; but what appears to me most admirable and most worthy of imitation in Macaulay is the sound moral constitution of his mind, and his fearless independence of thought, never sacrificing truth to any prejudice, interest, or preconceived opinion whatever. Above all he was no hero worshipper, who felt it incumbent on him to minister to vulgar prejudices or predilections, to exalt the merits and palliate the defects of great reputations, and to consider the commission of great crimes, or the detection of mean and base motives, as

atoned for and neutralized by the possession of shining abilities and the performance of great actions. Macaulay excited much indignation in some quarters by the severity with which he criticised the conduct and character of the Duke of Marlborough, and the Quakers bitterly resented his attacks upon Penn. He was seldom disposed to admit that he had been mistaken or misinformed, and I thought he was to blame in clinging so tenaciously to his severe estimation of Penn's conduct after the vindication of it which was brought forward, and the production of evidence in Penn's favor, which might have satisfied him that he had been in error, and which probably would have done so in any case in which his judgment had been really unbiased. I always regretted, not for the sake of Penn's memory, but for the honour of Macaulay himself, that he would not admit the value and force of the exculpatory evidence, and acknowledge, as he very gracefully might, the probability at least of his having been in error. But the case of the Duke of Marlborough is very different, and reflects the highest honor on his literary integrity and independence.—GREVILLE, CHARLES C. F., 1860, *Journal of the Reign of Queen Victoria from 1852 to 1860, ed. Reeve, Jan. 2, p. 515.*

He does not wear Hallam's spotless ermine, and in reading his pages, we fail to feel that a new Chief Justice has taken his place on the great bench of historians. On matters of detail issue has been joined with him by different critics more or less competent. Lord Macaulay's knowledge of facts was so extraordinary, and so minute, that in any controversy the chances decidedly are that he is correct, and his opponents in the wrong. At the same time a body of adverse criticism exists in reference to the "History," which is entitled to serious consideration. Such writers as the Bishop of Exeter, Mr. Lothbury, Mr. Paget, Mr. Dixon, Mr. Babington, have brought a series of objections against different portions of the "History" in which it is difficult to believe that there is no substratum of reality.—ARNOLD, FREDERICK, 1862, *The Public Life of Lord Macaulay, p. 357.*

His history is like a cavalry charge. Down go horse and man before his rapid and reckless onset. His "rush" is irresistible save by the coolest judgment and the most cultivated intellects. Ranks are broken, guns are spiked, and away sweeps the bold dragoon to arrive at a fresh square.—KEBBEL, THOMAS EDWARD, 1864, *Essays upon History and Politics.*

He never seems to doubt what he narrates, nor to doubt that what he says is the absolute truth. His style, hence, becomes cumbrous and heavy-glittering, it may be, but glittering like cut steel or polished lead; and, if looked at in the writings of some of his imitators, in whose hands the historian's mannerisms and peculiarities are not relieved by sterling qualities, appears both ridiculous and offensive. — FRISWELL, JAMES HAIN, 1869, *Essays on English Writers, p. 30.*

He has brought to this work a new method of great beauty, extreme power. . . . When he is relating the actions of a man or a party, he sees in an instant all the events of his history, and all the maxims of his conduct; he has all the details present; he remembers them every moment, in great numbers. He has forgotten nothing; he runs through them as easily, as completely, as surely, as on the day when he enumerated or wrote them. No one has so well taught or known history. . . . He is not a poet like Michelet; he is not a philosopher like Guizot; but he possesses so well all the oratorical powers, he accumulates and arranges so many facts, he holds them so closely in his hand, he manages them with so much ease and vigour, that he succeeds in recomposing the whole and harmonious woof of history, not losing or separating one thread. The poet reanimates the dead; the philosopher formulates creative laws; the orator knows, expounds, and pleads causes. The poet resuscitates souls, the philosopher composes a system, the orator redisposes chains of arguments; but all three march towards the same end by different routes, and the orator, like his rivals, and by other means than his rivals, reproduces in his work the unity and complexity of life.—TAINE, H. A., 1871, *History of English Literature, tr. Van Laun, vol. II, bk. v, ch. iii, pp. 423, 425, 426.*

The day of their publication, 17th Dec., 1855, will be long remembered in the annals of Paternoster Row. It was presumed that 25,000 copies would be quite sufficient to meet the first public demand; but this enormous pile of books, weighing fifty-six tons, was exhausted the first day, and eleven thousand applicants were still unsatisfied. In New York one house sold 73,000 volumes (three different styles and prices) in ten days, and 25,000 more were immediately issued in Philadelphia—10,000 were stereotyped, printed, and in the hands of publishers within fifty working hours. The aggregate sale ·in England and America, within four weeks of publication, is said to have exceeded 150,000 copies. Macaulay is also stated to have received £16,000 from Mr. Longman for the copyright of the third and fourth volumes.—CURWEN, HENRY, 1873, *A History of Booksellers, p. 106.*

It may be thought that the successful work of that great master in the art of descriptive history would have deterred me from my attempt; but, on the contrary, it acted as an incentive, since it breaks off just at the point where the great difficulties of the new government began, and the new system finally consolidated itself. I should not have been contented with my work had I not (to keep up the simile) attempted the ascent of this last height, from which I might hope to survey the past and the future, the whence and the whither of the history.—VON RANKE, LEOPOLD, 1875, *A History of England, Principally in the Seventeenth Century, vol. VI, p. 144.*

What his violins were to Stradivarius, and his fresco to Leonardo, and his campaigns to Napoleon, that was his "History" to Macaulay. How fully it occupied his thoughts did not appear in his conversation; for he steadily and successfully resisted any inclinations to that most subtle form of selfishness, which often renders the period of literary creation one long penance to all the members of an author's family. But none the less his book was always in his mind; and seldom indeed did he pass a day or turn over a volume without lighting upon a suggestion which could be turned to useful purposes.—TREVELYAN, GEORGE OTTO, 1876, *ed. Life and Letters of Lord Macaulay, ch. xi.*

Its vivid word-painting of characters and great events, and the splendid use in such descriptions of his vast knowledge of details, gave as great an impulse to the literature of history as Gibbon had done in his day, and his "Historical Essays" on the times and statesmen between the Restoration and Pitt are masterpieces of their kind.— BROOKE, STOPFORD A., 1876, *English Literature (Primer), p. 133.*

Certainly history had never before in our country been treated in a style so well calculated to render it at once popular, fascinating, and fashionable. Every chapter glittered with vivid and highly coloured description. On almost every page was found some sentence of glowing eloquence or gleaming antithesis, which at once lent itself to citation and repetition. Not one word of it could have failed to convey its meaning. The whole stood out in an atmosphere clear, bright, and incapable of misty illusion as that of a Swiss lake in summer. He was not a Gibbon, but he wrote with all Gibbon's delight in the picturesqueness of a subject, and Gibbon's resolve to fascinate as well as to instruct his readers. Macaulay's history tries too much to be an historical portrait gallery. The dangers of such a style do not need to be pointed out. They are amply illustrated in Macaulay's sparkling pages. But it is something to know that their splendid qualities are far more conspicuous still than their defects. — McCarthy, Justin, 1879, *A History of Our Own Times from the Accession of Queen Victoria to the Berlin Congress, ch.* xxix.

This is undoubtedly the most brilliant and the most popular history ever written in the English language. Though the work covers a period of only seventeen years, and those not among the most eventful ones in English annals, yet the splendor of the author's style has caused it to be more universally read than any other history in English literature. It shows vast research, extraordinary power in the portraiture of individual character, and a literary skill that is unrivalled.—Adams, Charles Kendall, 1882, *A Manual of Historical Literature, p.* 463.

There is here a wide field of choice. Shall we go back to the art of which Macaulay was so great a master? We could do worse. It must be a great art that can make men lay aside the novel and take up the history, to find there, in very fact, the movement and drama of life. What Macaulay does well he does incomparably. Who else can mass the details as he does, and yet not mar or obscure, but only heighten, the effect of the picture as a whole? Who else can bring so amazing a profusion of knowledge within the strait limits of a simple plan, nowhere encumbered, everywhere free and obvious in its

movement? How sure the strokes, and how bold and vivid the result! Yet when we have laid the book aside, when the charm and the excitement of the telling narrative have worn off, when we have lost step with the swinging gait at which the style goes, when the details have faded from our recollection, and we sit removed and thoughtful, with only the greater outlines of the story sharp upon our minds, a deep misgiving and dissatisfaction take possession of us. We are no longer young, and we are chagrined that we should have been so pleased and taken with the glitter and color and mere life of the picture. . . . Macaulay the artist, with an exquisite gift for telling a story, filling his pages with little vignettes it is impossible to forget, fixing these with an inimitable art upon the surface of a narrative that did not need the ornament they gave it, so strong and large and adequate was it; and Macaulay, the Whig, subtly turning narrative into argument, and making history the vindication of a party. The mighty narrative is a great engine of proof. It is not told for its own sake. It is evidence summed up in order to justify a judgment. We detect the tone of the advocate, and though if we are just we must deem him honest, we cannot deem him safe. The great story-teller is discredited; and, willingly or unwillingly, we reject the guide who takes it upon himself to determine for us what we shall see.—Wilson, Woodrow, 1896, *Mere Literature and Other Essays, pp.* 167, 168.

No historian who has yet written has shown such familiarity with the facts of English history, no matter what the subject in hand may be: the extinction of villenage, the Bloody Assizes, the appearance of the newspaper, the origin of the national debt, or the state of England in 1685. Macaulay is absolutely unrivalled in the art of arranging and combining his facts, and of presenting in a clear and vigorous narrative the spirit of the epoch he treats. Nor should we fail to mention that both Essays and History abound in remarks, general observations, and comment always clear, vigorous, and shrewd, and in the main very just.—McMaster, John Bach, 1897, *Library of the World's Best Literature, ed. Warner, p.* 381.

His chief monument is the "History of England." It is only a fragment, though it is a colossal fragment. . . . It was his aim to make the past a living reality to his readers, and to invest historical facts with all, or more than all, the interest of fiction. His brilliant success was largely due to the artistic use of infinite detail in narrative and in the portrayal of character. But, as he soon found when he began to write, this method required vast space. He cannot fairly be charged with diffuseness in the "History," except, perhaps, in some cases where he develops a general statement with redundant illustration. On the other hand, he often condenses into a few words or sentences the results of wide reading and laborious research. A careful study of almost any chapter will show that, relatively to the mass of particulars which he communicates, his style is, on the whole, compact. But even a greater conciseness of language could not have materially reduced the amount of room which his plan, by its very nature, demanded.—JEBB, SIR RICHARD CLAVERHOUSE, 1900, *Macaulay, a Lecture Delivered at Cambridge on Aug. 10, p. 9.*

The enemies of Macaulay at the present time assail rather his methods than his opinions, and so far they are clearly right for a historian has as much right to his opinions as "a Christian or an ordinary man." They allege in substance that his "History" is a misplaced eulogy of a second-rate Dutchman, that he wrote a style in which the truth could not be told, that he was as much the mouthpiece of a party as counsel in court are the mouthpieces of their clients, that he confounded William Penn, the founder of Pennsylvania, with another person of the same name, and that he said the oaks of Magdalen when he should have said the elms. The last charge is true. . . . The general accusation against Macaulay really resolves itself into this, that he overstated his case and was too much of his own opinion. I do not think it is altogether wise to deny that there is some truth in this charge. The proper answer is that the vehemence of Macaulay's Whiggery and the unqualified manner in which he condemns Marlborough and Penn are incidental defects of a very noble quality, the quality of moral indignation. Macaulay was no arm-chair politician judging of temptations which he had never felt, and of circumstances in which he had never been placed. He sat in the House of Commons, in the Cabinet, in the Council of the Governor-General of India. He knew public life as well as any man of letters ever knew it. But the knowledge did not make him a cynic or a pessimist. He had an almost passionate belief in the progress of society and in the greatness of England.— PAUL, HERBERT, 1901, *Macaulay and his Critics, Men and Letters, pp.* 289, 295.

GENERAL

North.—" The son of the Saint, who seems himself to be something of a reviewer, is insidious as the serpent, but fangless as the slow-worm."—WILSON, JOHN, 1830, *Noctes Ambrosianœ, April.*

I hear that Mr. Macaulay is to be returned. If he speaks half as well as he writes, the House will be in fashion again.— DISRAELI, BENJAMIN (EARL OF BEACONSFIELD), 1831, *The Young Duke.*

Macaulay has obtained the reputation which, although deservedly great, is yet in a remarkable measure undeserved.—POE, EDGAR ALLAN, 1841, *Macaulay's "Essays," Works, ed. Stedman and Woodberry, vol.* VII, *p.* 123.

He delights everyone—high or low, intelligent or ignorant. His spice is of so keen a flavor, that it tickles the coarsest palate. He has the hesitating suffrages of men of taste, and the plaudits of the million. The man who has a common knowledge of the English language, and the scholar who has mastered its refinements, seem equally sensible to the charm of his diction. No matter how unpromising the subject on which he writes may appear to the common eye, in his hands it is made pleasing. Statistics, history, biography, political economy, all suffer a transformation into "something rich and strange." Prosaists are made to love poetry, Tory politicians to sympathize with Hampden and Milton, and novel readers to obtain some idea of Bacon and his philosophy. The wonderful clearness, point and vigor of his style, send his thoughts right into every brain. Indeed, a person who is utterly insensible to the witchery of Macaulay's diction must be either a Yahoo or a beatified intelligence.—WHIPPLE, EDWIN PERCY, 1843, *Macaulay, Essays and Reviews, vol.* I, *p.* 12.

Writes like a man; that is the reason why men of sense and women of spirit are attracted by his style. There is nothing effeminate, cockneyish, dainty, or far-fetched in it; but an essential and pervading

manliness.— TUCKERMAN, HENRY THEO-
DORE, 1849, *Characteristics of Literature,*
p. 187.

The brilliant Macaulay, who expresses
the tone of the English governing classes of
the day, explicitly teaches that *good* means
good to eat, good to wear, material commodity; that the glory of modern philosophy is its direction on "fruit"; to yield
economical inventions; and that its merit
is to avoid ideas and avoid morals. He
thinks it the distinctive merit of the Baco-
nian philosophy in its triumph over the old
Platonic, its disentangling the intellect
from theories of the all-Fair and all-Good,
and pinning it down to the making a better
sick chair and a better wine-whey for an
invalid;—this not ironically, but in good
faith—that "solid advantage," as he calls
it, meaning always sensual benefit, is the
only good.—EMERSON, RALPH WALDO,
1856-84, *English Traits; Works, Riverside
Ed., vol.* v, *p.* 234.

Macaulay seems to me the historian of
sophistication, a man who writes only and
always for "society," and knows as little
of any primitive existence as a New Zea-
lander could know of Mayfair. Everybody
admires him, of course, but nobody believes in him—at least, so far as my experience goes.—OLIPHANT, MARGARET O.
W., 1856, *To Mr. Blackwood, Letters, ed.
Coghill,* p. 163.

Take at hazard any three pages of the
"Essays" or "History," and, glimmering
below the stream of the narrative you, as it
were, you, an average reader, see one, two,
three, a half-score of allusions to other historic facts, characters, literature, poetry,
with which you are acquainted. . . .
Your neighbor, who has *his* reading, and
his little stock of literature stowed away in
his mind, shall detect more points, allusions,
happy touches, indicating not only the prodigious memory and vast learning of this
master, but the wonderful industry, the
honest, humble previous toil of this great
scholar. He reads twenty books to write a
sentence; he travels a hundred miles to
make a line of description.—THACKERAY,
WILLIAM MAKEPEACE, 1860, *Nil Nisi
Bonum, Roundabout Papers.*

His copiousness had nothing tumid,
diffuse, Asiatic; no ornament for the sake
of ornament. As to its clearness, one may
read a sentence of Macaulay twice, to judge
of its full force, never to comprehend its
meaning. His English was pure, both in
idiom and in words, pure to fastidiousness.
. . . Every word must be genuine English, nothing that approached real vulgarity,
nothing that had not the stamp of popular
use, or the authority of sound English
writers, nothing unfamiliar to the common
ear.—MILMAN, HENRY HART, 1860, *The
History of England by Macaulay, Memoir.*

Above all, we thank Macaulay for the
English-heartedness which throbs transparently through his writings, and which
was so marked a characteristic of his life. .
. . With Macaulay the love of country
was a passion. How he kindles at each
stirring or plaintive memory in the annals
he was so glad to record.—PUNSHON, WILL-
IAM MORLEY, 1862, *Macaulay, Exeter Hall
Lectures, vol.* 39, *p.* 508.

He abounds in the stock metaphor, the
stock transition, the stock equipoise, the
stock rhetoric, the stock expedients generally of Addison, Robertson, Goldsmith, etc.
—STIRLING, JAMES HUTCHINSON, 1868,
Jerrold, Tennyson, and Macaulay.

What first strikes us in him is the extreme
solidity of his mind. He proves all that he
says, with astonishing vigour and authority.
We are almost certain never to go astray
in following him. If he cites a witness, he
begins by measuring the veracity and intelligence of the authors quoted, and by correcting the errors they may have committed,
through negligence or partiality. If he
pronounces a judgment, he relies on the
most certain facts, the clearest principles,
the simplest and most logical deductions.
If he develops an argument, he never loses
himself in a digression; he always has his
goal before his eyes; he advances toward
it by the surest and straightest road. If he
rises to general consideration, he mounts
step by step through all the grades of generalization, without omitting one; he feels
the ground every instant, he neither adds
to nor subtracts from facts; he desires
at the cost of every precaution and research, to arrive at the precise truth. . . .
Rarely was eloquence more sweeping than
Macaulay's. He has an oratorical impetus;
all his phrases have a tone, we feel that he
would govern minds, that he is irritated
by resistance, that he fights as he discusses.
In his books the discussion always seizes
and carries away the reader; it advances
evenly, with accumulating force, straightforward, like those great American rivers,

impetuous as a torrent and wide as a sea. This abundance of thought and style, this multitude of explanations, ideas, and facts, this fast aggregate of historical knowledge goes rolling on, urged forward by internal passion, sweeping away objections in its course, and adding to the dash of eloquence the irresistible force of its mass and weight.—TAINE, H. A., 1871, *History of English Literature, tr. Van Laun, vol.* ii, *bk.* v, *ch.* iii, *pp.* 411, 414.

Macaulay's composition is as far from being abstruse as printed matter can well be. One can trace in his writing a constant effort to make himself intelligible to the meanest capacity. He loves to dazzle and to argue, but above everything he is anxious to be understood. His ideal evidently is to turn a subject over on every side, to place it in all lights, and to address himself to every variety of prejudice and preoccupation in his audience. Yet his simplicity is very different from the simplicity of such writers as Goldsmith and Paley. His is far from being a homely style. He does not studiously affect Saxon terms. Without being so scholastic and technical as De Quincey, he is not scrupulous about using words of Latin origin, and admits many terms that Dean Alford would have excluded from "the Queen's English." Besides, although he were an Anglo-Saxon Pharisee in his choice of words, his turns of expression are not simple in the sense of being familiar and easy. His balanced sentences, abrupt transitions, pointed antithesis, and climatic arrangement, elevate him out of the ranks of homely authors, and constitute him, as we have said, preeminently artificial.—MINTO, WILLIAM, 1872-80, *Manual of English Prose Literature, p.* 103.

Macaulay, historiographer in chief to the Whigs, and the great prophet of Whiggery which never had or will have a prophet, vehemently judged that a man who could pass over from the celestial Whigs to the infernal Tories must be a traitor false as Judas, an apostate black as the Devil.—THOMPSON, JAMES, 1876-91, *A Note on Forster's Life of Swift, Essays and Phantasies, p.* 285.

Macaulay, divested of all the exorbitancies of his spirit and his style, would have been a Samson shorn of the locks of his strength. . . . He never wrote an obscure sentence in his life, and this may seem a small merit, until we remember of how few writers we could say the same. . . . Macaulay is like the military king who never suffered himself to be seen, even by the attendants in his bedchamber, until he had had time to put on his uniform and jack-boots. His severity of eye is very wholesome; it makes his writing firm, and firmness is certainly one of the first qualities that good writing must have. But there is such a thing as soft and considerate precision, as well as hard and scolding precision. Those most interesting English critics of the generation slightly anterior to Macaulay,—Hazlett, Lamb, De Quincey, Leigh Hunt,—were fully his equals in precision, and yet they knew how to be clear, acute, and definite without that edginess and inelasticity which is so conspicuous in Macaulay's criticisms, alike in their matter and their form.—MORLEY, JOHN, 1876, *Macaulay, Fortnightly Review, vol.* 25, *pp.* 496, 505, 507.

First of all, Macaulay is a model of style—of style not merely as a kind of literary luxury, but of style in its practical aspect. When I say that he is a model of style, I do not mean that it is wise in any writer to copy Macaulay's style, to try to write something that might be mistaken for Macaulay's writing. So to do is not to follow in the steps of a great writer, but merely to imitate his outward manner. So to do is not the part of a disciple, but the part of an ape. But every one who wishes to write clear and pure English will do well to become, not Macaulay's ape, but Macaulay's disciple. Every writer of English will do well, not only to study Macaulay's writings, but to bear them in his mind, and very often to ask himself, not whether his writing is like Macaulay's writing, but whether his writing is such as Macaulay would have approved. . . . He was a great scholar, a great writer, a great historian, a great man. Those who can most clearly see his real faults are those who know his writings best, and who therefore admire them most. And those who know them best and admire them most will also be the first to mark what can not fairly be called faults, those gaps in the way of looking at things which belong to the man and his time, as other gaps of the same kind doubtless belong to other men and other times. Macaulay is a man who already belongs to a past age; but without such men in past ages, the present age could not have been what they

have helped to make it.—FREEMAN, ED-
WARD A., 1876, *Lord Macaulay, International Review, vol. 3, pp.* 690, 696.

Macaulay never seems to have known
either pain or mortification. He succeeded
in everything which he undertook; and if
there be any lesson which is taught only in
the school of severity, that lesson he never
learnt. A defect of some kind there undoubtedly was in him. We admire, but he
fails deeply to interest. He rarely stirs
our enthusiasm; he never touches our
deepest emotions. In the midst of his brilliancy his writing is commonplace, though it
is commonplace of the very highest kind.—
FROUDE, JAMES ANTHONY, 1876, *Lord Macaulay, Fraser's Magazine, n. s., vol.* 13,
p. 693.

The laboriousness of Macaulay as an
author demands our gratitude; all the
more because his natural speech was in
sentences of set and ordered structure,
well-nigh ready for the press. It is delightful to find, that the most successful
prose-writer of the day was also the most
painstaking. Here is indeed a literary
conscience. . . . For the style of Macaulay, though a fine and a great, is without
doubt a pampering style, and it leaves upon
the palate a disrelish for the homely diet of
mere truth and sense.—GLADSTONE, WILL-
IAM EWART, 1876, *Lord Macaulay, Quarterly Review, vol.* 142, *pp.* 7, 37.

The truth which explains if it does not
harmonize the conflicting opinions about
Macaulay is that his distinctive merits and
defects are merely the obverse and reverse
aspects of one and the same quality. The
association between seeing clearly and seeing narrowly is a well-nigh universal law of
the human mind; and the undeniable narrowness of Macaulay's view was due
neither to willful blindness nor yet to defect of vision, but to the preterhuman
vividness with which he saw whatever he
happened at the moment to be looking at.
Any object, or event, or quality which he
sets himself to contemplate is illuminated
as with an electric light, and, amid the
dazzling brilliance which it rays around, all
sense of shade and gradation is lost. This
is the explanation of that luminous clearness of his color which has been so much
and so justly admired: it is also the explanation of that lack of proportion and relation and that total absence of perspective which have been equally complained

of in his compositions.—JONES, CLARENCE
H., 1880, *Lord Macaulay, His Life and
Writings, p.* 246.

The writer who has done most, without I
suppose intending it, to promote hypocrisy in literature is Macaulay. His "every
schoolboy knows" has frightened thousands into pretending to know authors with
whom they have not even a bowing acquaintance. It is amazing that a man who
had read so much should have written so
contemptuously of those who have read
but little; one would have thought that the
consciousness of superiority would have
forbidden such insolence, or that his reading would have been extensive enough to
teach him at least how little he had read of
what there was to read; since he read some
things—works of imagination and humour,
for example—to such very little purpose,
he might really have bragged a little less.—
PAYN, JAMES, 1881, *Some Private Views,
p.* 47.

I recall no writer who is Macaulay's equal
in this art of covering his larger surfaces
with minute work which is never out of
place. Like the delicate sculpture on the
sandals of Athene in the Parthenon, it detracts nothing from the grandeur of the
statue. Or, to take a more appropriate
figure, it resembles a richly decorated
Gothic porch, in which every stone is curiously carved, and yet does its duty in bearing the weight of the mighty arch as well as
if it were perfectly plain.—MORISON,
JAMES COTTER, 1883, *Macaulay (English
Men of Letters), p.* 47.

It can hardly be said that Macaulay belonged to the very highest order of minds.
I do not think that he did. In no department except the historical did he show pre-
eminent capacity, and even his "History"
is open to the charge of being only a splendid
and ornate panorama. . . . Macaulay
unquestionably *had* genius of a kind: the
genius which moulds the results of immense
industry into a coherent and consistent
whole. This is a fine and a most rare gift;
and we are not wrong when we assert that
its owner must always be, even when not of
the highest order, a man of genius. . . .
He is one of the greatest masters of the
English tongue. The march of his ordered
prose is measured and stately. Still it is
ponderous, compared at least with the unaffected freedom and flexible life of Shakespeare's, or Fielding's, or Charles Lamb's.

But the art with which this defect is concealed is, like every other detail of Lord Macaulay's art, perfect in its way. The style is ponderous,but there is no monotony. Short sentences, which, like the fire of sharpshooters through cannon, break the volume of sound, are introduced at stated intervals into each paragraph. A Junius-like epigram follows the imposing burst of eloquence with which Burke or Brougham might have clenched a great harangue. There is no slovenliness in these finished pages.—SKELTON, JOHN, 1883, *Essays in History and Biography*, *pp.* 279, 280.

Macaulay's style—his much-praised style —is ineffectual for the purpose of telling the truth about anything. It is splendid, but *splendide mendax*, and in Macaulay's case the style was the man. He had enormous knowledge, and a noble spirit; his knowledge enriched his style and his spirit consecrated it to the service of Liberty. We do well to be proud of Macaulay; but we must add that, great as was his knowledge, great also was his ignorance, which was none the less ignorance because it was wilful; noble as was his spirit, the range of subject over which it energized was painfully restricted.—BIRRELL, AUGUSTINE, 1884, *Obiter Dicta, p.* 30.

I fancy Macaulay will descend the stream of time more by virtue of the brilliant point lace of his narrative, than by inherent truth or reliability of sentiment or statement.—MORRISON, A. H., 1886, *The Art Gallery of the English Language, p.* 44.

His "Essays" and his "History" exhibit the most popular style which any English author has ever possessed. Competent critics object to its glaring defects, but have never denied its power.—SAINTSBURY, GEORGE, 1886, *Specimens of English Prose Style, p.* 364.

One of the most remarkable qualities in his style is the copiousness of expression, and the remarkable power of putting the same statement in a large number of different ways. This enormous command of expression corresponded with the extraordinary power of his memory. At the age of eight he could repeat the whole of Scott's poem of "Marmion." He was fond, at this early age, of big words and learned English; and once, when he was asked by a lady if his toothache was better, he replied,

"Madam, the agony is abated!" He knew the whole of Homer and of Milton by heart; and it was said with perfect truth that, if Milton's poetical works could have been lost, Macaulay would have restored every line with complete exactness. Sydney Smith said of him: "There are no limits to his knowledge, on small subjects as on great; he is like a book in breeches." His style has been called "abrupt, pointed, and oratorical." He is fond of the arts of surprise—of antithesis—and of epigram.— MEIKLEJOHN, J. M. D., 1887, *The English Language: Its Grammar, History and Literature, p.* 351.

Since his death and the commitment of his writings to posterity and to criticism, his prose still has a substantial place in English Letters. The one who denies his claim to be ranked among the first examples of English style, must see to it that he be prepared to maintain his difficult position. . . . The prose of Macaulay in respect to its clearness was in every sense true to the claims of the *home language.* There are but few representative writers of English whose style so happily avoids the extreme of pedantry on the one hand, and that of purism, on the other. . . . Macaulay was the Lombard of his age—a master of sentences. What his biographer, Mr. Trevelyan, states, would seem to be confirmed, "that he never allowed a sentence to pass muster until it was as good as he could make it," until every sentence ran as smoothly as running water and every paragraph closed with a telling clause.— HUNT, THEODORE W., 1887, *Representative English Prose and Prose Writers, pp.* 389, 392, 398.

Macaulay is a master of all the figures that lent themselves to effective denunciation—irony, innuendo, epigram, as well as damaging similitudes. . . . The richness of vituperative phraseology, the profusion of the illustrative comparisons, the invention of turns of thought to heighten the effect, are Macaulay's own, and cannot be imitated, although they may be appropriated and reproduced.— BAIN, ALEXANDER, 1888, *English Composition and Rhetoric, pt.* II, *pp.* 247, 248.

He had no time to let his own mind work, and took all his opinions as he found them ready made for him in books, and determined by his temperament. It is curious to compare his letters with those of a man like Carlyle and to see how exclusively Macaulay confines himself to giving the news. He never discusses a subject, though he occasionally announces a view. Neither the profoundly imaginative nor the profoundly speculative nature could bear such a life as his. But his lack of originality made it all the easier for him to produce a great quantity of excellent and valuable work. He had a wonderful memory, unfailing industry, a vivid conception of the past and a unique style; and he was thoroughly interested in his subject. He said the things that the most intelligent people thought, so eloquently and incisively that they began at once to pride themselves on their own cleverness.—SCUDDER, VIDA D., 1889, *ed. Macaulay's Essay on Lord Clive, p. 4.*

The vice of Macaulay's style is its unrelieved facility, its uniform velocity.— WATSON, WILLIAM, 1893, *Excursions in Criticism, p. 110.*

His rhetorical power is manifest in the "Lays of Ancient Rome" as in his speeches, and if they are hardly poetry they are most effective declamation. His essays are equally unapproached in their kind. He ascribes the invention of the genus to Southey, but claims, rightly, to have improved the design. In striking contrast to most periodical literature, they represent the greatest condensation instead of the greatest expansion of knowledge, and the sense of proportion, and consequent power of effective narrative, are as remarkable in his best essays—especially the essays on Clive and Warren Hastings—as the clearness of style and range of knowledge. The first part of the "History" shows the same qualities, though the latter volumes begin to suffer from the impracticable scale.— STEPHEN, LESLIE, 1893, *Dictionary of National Biography, vol.* XXXIV, *p. 417.*

Macaulay is brilliant and emphatic, but we weary at last of his everlasting *staccato* on the trumpet.—HARRISON, FREDERIC, 1894, *Studies in Early Victorian Literature, p. 19.*

The popular impression that Macaulay is the best of paragraphers is probably not far from the truth. The great rhetorician bestowed unlimited pains upon his paragraphs, and no preceding writer began to equal him in conscious appreciation of the importance of that structure. His unity is rhetorical, rather than logical; but as such it is nearly always unimpeachable. The sections that contain real digressions are few indeed. In the matter of proportion by bulk he is nearly always admirable. He knows his principal point, and it is on this that he enlarges. His emphasis-proportion is consciously paragraphic. He reveals very great variability in sentence-length, and drives home his main topic and his main conclusion in simple sentences. When he masses clauses it is to relieve each of emphasis and show the unity of the group as amplifying some previous terse generalization. He shows such deliberate observance of this principle that he forms the first basis for the generalization made in a former chapter: in the best modern paragraphs the distance between periods is inversely as the emphasis of each included proposition. Nevertheless, in this matter of distribution of emphasis, Macaulay is not faultless. It has been the general verdict of critics that he not infrequently over-emphasizes; that he magnifies clauses into sentences.—LEWIS, EDWIN HERBERT, 1894, *The History of the English Paragraph, p. 142.*

His popularity was honestly won by the energy and capacity of his mind, and by an eloquence which, whatever its faults may be, at any rate was able to enliven the weight of his learning. By the resources and the quickness of his memory, by his erudition, and his command of his erudition, by his fluency and studied clearness, he has gained no more than the rank he deserves as an exponent of the matter of history, and as a critic of opinions. No amount of distaste for Whiggery or for common sense can with justice be allowed to detract from Macaulay's fame. . . . The weaknesses of his style were known to himself, but among them he had no cause to reckon the vices of pretence or vanity. He knew the things that he appeared to know, and much more; and his reputation is only a fair tribute paid to him by those who have learned from him. . . . No writer is placed at such a disadvantage as Macaulay, when his worst passages are taken up and criticised minutely. With no writer is criticism so apt to be unjust, simply because it is impossible to represent in detail a genius which was great by the extent of its empire, rather than by any mystery of its inner shrines. To remember particular bits of Macaulay's prose is not always as satisfactory as to remember his heroic ballads. But in the variegated mass of his writings, and in the impression of life and zest in all that he wrote, the particular faults and fallacies may easily and rightly pass out of notice.—KER, W. P., 1896, *English Prose, ed. Craik, vol.* v, *pp.* 410, 417.

Clearness is one of Macaulay's most obvious merits; he never leaves you in doubt as to his meaning. But this clearness is partly due to the fact that he never grapples with difficult problems or deep thoughts for which language offers inadequate expression. He never goes out of his own depth; but neither does he ever take you out of yours; and this, though it has won him many readers, is a doubtful virtue. Sometimes the clearness is gained at the expense of exactness; statements are made too absolutely. His complete mastery over his material is often astonishing, when the amount of that material, the wealth of detail, is considered. In the art of constructing a complex narrative he has few equals. *Animation*, a quality which depends on a good many others; in Macaulay's case on his own interest in his story, on the swing of his sentences, on his pictorial phrases, his contrasts and comparisons, his energy in bestowing praise and blame, above all, on his love of the concrete. His *diffuseness* is a very serious fault, but, as it is not combined with dullness, it attracts many readers who would be bewildered by a quick succession of thoughts. Of the qualities of *strength, pathos*, and *humour*, and again of the *rhythm*, it may be said briefly that Macaulay has them all in the degree in which a good, but not the very greatest, orator has them. Those finer and subtler effects which, though they would be lost in speech, are in place on the printed page, are not to be found in him. —FOWLER, T. H., 1897, *XIX-Century Prose, p.* 57.

Hallam and Wordsworth, Dickens and Thackeray and Carlyle are names not hard to place. Each of these has his evident and peculiar stamp. The same cannot be said of Macaulay. The clue to his genius is not easy to follow. To read his works is to delight the attention and inspire the feelings. But when we are asked to estimate him, we hesitate. In the cause of this hesitation, real difficulty must be added to something of reluctance. . . . His was a mind whose strength was closely allied to its weakness; which was too brilliant to be cautious, and too quick to be profound. His faults therefore lie side by side with his merits. Yet from every repeated appeal to his work, from weighing what is best in it against its acknowledged blots, we return with a conscious right to the assertion that, despite many failings, time will vindicate a great and an immortal name.—MACGREGOR, D. H., 1901, *Lord Macaulay, pp.* 2, 5.

Macaulay's style is clear, highly-coloured, lively, almost passionate; and above all, it is filled with a strong personality. In every line we seem to hear these words:— " I, Thomas Macaulay, a conscientious man of learning, and a friend of liberty, have by my studies arrived at this result; whether the matter, from the point of view of an inhabitant of another world, happened exactly as I related it or not, I do not know; but that is how *I* saw it." The secret of Macaulay's style is antithesis. It occurs so often that one would think his use of it was intentional, but for the frequency which he had recourse to it in his parliamentary speeches which proves that this peculiar style was natural to him. Antithesis is quite suitable to Macaulay's conception of history; absolute historical truth too, is beyond the reach of the greatest human genius; it is only by presenting both sides of the question that a fair average amount of truth can be arrived at. —ENGEL, EDWARD, 1902, *A History of English Literature, rev. Hamley Bent, p.* 467.

Thomas DeQuincey

1785–1859

Born, in Manchester, 15 Aug. 1785. Educated privately at Salford; at Bath Grammar School, 1797 [?]-99; at school at Winkfield, Wilts, 1799–1800. To Manchester Grammar School, winter of 1800. Ran away from latter, July 1802. Lived a roving life in Wales, July to Nov., 1802. To London, Nov. 1802; after great distress there reconciled with family. Matric. Worcester Coll., Oxford, 17 Dec. 1803; left, without degree, 1807. Friendship with Coleridge begun, 1807. Visit to Oxford, and in London 1808. Student of Middle Temple, 1808 [?]. With Wordsworth at Grasmere, Dec. 1808 to Feb. 1809. Settled in cottage at Townend, Westmoreland, Nov. 1809. In Edinburgh with Professor Wilson, winters of 1814–15 and 1815–16. Habitual taking of opium began, 1813. Married Margaret Simpson, winter of 1816. Contrib. to "Blackwood" and "Quarterly Review." Edited "Westmoreland Gazette," 1819–1820. To London, 1821. Through Lamb's introduction, became contributor to "London Magazine," in which the "Confessions of an Opium-Eater" appeared, Oct. to Nov., 1821. Contrib. to "London Magazine," 1821–24; to Knight's "Quarterly Magazine," 1824. In Westmoreland, 1825. Contrib. to "Blackwood," 1826–49. Settled in Edinburgh, 1828; wife and children joined him there, 1830. Contrib. to "Edinburgh Literary Gazette," 1828–30; to "Tait's Magazine," 1834–51. Relapse into opium habit after wife's death in 1837; improvement in 1844. In Glasgow, March 1841 to June 1847. To Edinburgh, 1847. Died there, 8 Dec. 1859. Buried in West Churchyard, Edinburgh. *Works:* "Confessions of an English Opium-Eater" (anon.), 1822; "Klosterheim" (anon.), 1832; "The Logic of Political Economy," 1844; "Selections, grave and gay, from his writings," edited by himself (4 vols.), 1853–60. *Collected Works:* in 20 vols., 1853–55. *Life:* by H. A. Page, 1877; by Prof. Masson, 1881. —SHARP, R. FARQUHARSON, 1897, *A Dictionary of English Authors, p.* 77.

PERSONAL

De Quincey is a singular man, but better informed than any person almost that I ever met at his age.—SOUTHEY, ROBERT, 1810, *To John Rickman, Jan.* 21; *Life and Correspondence of Robert Southey, ed. C. C. Southey, ch.* xxi.

His person is small, his complexion fair, and his air and manner are those of a sickly and enfeebled man. From this circumstance his sensibility, which I have no doubt is genuine, is in danger of being mistaken for effeminateness. At least coarser and more robustly healthful persons may fall into this mistake.—ROBINSON, HENRY CRABB, 1812, *Diary, June* 17; *Diary, Reminiscences and Correspondence, ed. Sadler.*

You make one mistake, indeed two, but I will notice only one. I have had, you say, no doubt many unavoidable reasons for the delay. Now, in fact I have not; scarcely any at all, excepting my own native stupidity, which I greatly regret, but cannot remedy. I move slowly whenever I am uncommonly witty. Nevertheless, if you are more particular about quantity than quality I am perfectly ready to oblige you by changing my style. But articles as droll a3 this I really cannot produce faster; dull reviews, morality, &c. (and some wit, such as some I saw in your December No.), as fast as you please. In fact I have never left my paper, except on Thursday once to see Prof. Wilson—twice during the week to get some breakfast—dinner every day, and to write three letters this morning.—DE QUINCEY, THOMAS, 1821, *Letter to W. Blackwood, Jan.* 6; *William Blackwood and His Sons, ed. Oliphant, vol.* I, *p.* 426.

On Wednesday the 28th, and Thursday, 29th of October, 1821, I passed the evening at Taylor and Hessey's in company with the author of "Confessions of an English Opium-Eater," published in Nos. 21 and 22 of the *London Magazine.* I had formed to myself the idea of a tall, thin, pale, gentlemanly-looking, courtier-like man; but I met a short, sallow-looking person, of a very peculiar cast of countenance, and apparently much an invalid. His demeanour was very gentle, modest, and unassuming; and his conversation fully came up to the idea I had formed of what would be that of the writer of those articles. . . . The Opium-Eater appears to have read a great deal, and to have thought much more. I was astonished at the depth and *reality,* if I may so call it, of his knowledge. He seems to have passed nothing that occurred in the course of his study unreflected on or unremembered. His conversation appeared like the elaboration of a mine of results: and if at any time a general observation of his became matter of question or ulterior disquisition it was found that he had ready his reasons at a moment's notice; so that it was clear that his opinions were the fruits of his own reflections on what had come before him, and had not been taken up from others.—WOODHOUSE, RICHARD, 1821, *Notes of Conversations with Thomas De Quincey, De Quincey and his Friends, ed. Hogg, pp.* 72, 73.

To-day, too, I saw De Quincey: alas, poor Yorick!—CARLYLE, THOMAS, 1828, *To B. W. Procter, Jan.* 17; *Life by Conway, p.* 244.

You will doubtless read the last "Tait's Magazine." It contains the first of a series of articles by DeQuincey on Wordsworth. Poor DeQuincey had a small fortune of eight or nine thousand pounds, which he has lost or spent; and now he lets his pen for hire. You know his articles on Coleridge: Wordsworth's turn has come now. At the close of his article, he alludes to a killing neglect which he once received from the poet, and which embittered his peace. I know the facts, which are not given. De Quincey married some humble country-girl in the neighborhood of Wordsworth; she was of good character, but not of that rank in which W. moved. The family of the latter never made her acquaintance nor showed her any civilities, though living comparatively in the same neighborhood. *"Hinc illæ lacrimæ."* When you now read DeQuincey's lamentations you may thus better understand them.—SUMNER, CHARLES, 1839, *To George S. Hillard, Jan.* 23; *Memoir and Letters of Sumner, ed. Pierce, vol.* II, *p.* 45.

Conceive a little, pale-faced, wo-begone, and attenuated man, with short indescribables, no coat, check shirt, and neckcloth twisted like a wisp of straw, opening the front door of his room in — street, advancing toward you with a hurried movement, and half-recognizing glance; saluting you in low and hesitating tones, asking you to be seated, and after he had taken a seat opposite you, but without looking you in the face, beginning to pour into your willing ear a stream of learning and wisdom as long as you are contented to listen to, or lend him the slightest clue. . . . His head is small, how can it carry all he knows? His brow is singular in shape, but not particularly large or prominent: where has nature expressed his majestic intellect? His eyes—they sparkle not, they shine not, they are lustreless: can that be a squint which glances over from them towards you? No, it is only a slight habit one of them has of occasionally looking in a different direction from the other; there is nothing else particular about them: there is not even the glare which lights up sometimes dull eyes into eloquence; and yet, even at first, the *tout ensemble* strikes you as that of no common man, and you say, ere he has opened his lips: "He is either mad or inspired."— GILFILLAN, GEORGE, 1845, *Literary Portraits, First Series.*

DeQuincey is a small old man of seventy years, with a very handsome face, and a face, too, expressing the highest refinement; a very gentle old man, speaking with the greatest deliberation and softness, and so refined in speech and manners as to make quite indifferent his extremely plain and poor dress. For the old man, summoned by. message on Saturday by Mrs. Crowe to his dinner, had walked on this stormy, muddy Sunday ten miles, from Lass Wade, where his cottage is, and was not yet dry; and though Mrs. Crowe's hospitality is comprehensive and minute, yet she had no pantaloons in her house. Here De Quincey is very serene and happy among just these friends where I found him; for he has suffered in all ways, and lived the life of a wretch for many years, but Samuel Brown and Mrs. C. and one or two more have saved him from himself, and defended him from bailiffs and a certain Fury of a Mrs. Macbold (I think it is), whom he yet shudders to remember, and from opium; and he is now clean, clothed, and in his right mind. . . . He talked of many matters, all easily and well, but chiefly social and literary; and did not venture into any voluminous music. When they first agreed at my request, to invite him to dine, I fancied some figure like the organ of York Minster would appear. In *tête-à-tête*, I am told, he sometimes soars and indulges himself, but not often in company. He invited me to dine with him on the following Saturday at Lass Wade, where he lives with his three daughters, and I accepted.—EMERSON, RALPH WALDO, 1848, *Letter, Feb.* 21; *A Memoir of Ralph Waldo Emerson, ed. Cabot, vol.* II, *p.* 520.

When he came out to receive me at his garden-gate I thought I had never seen anything so small and pale in the shape of a great man, nor a more impressive head on human shoulders. The unmistakable alabaster shine, which I had noticed in other opium-eaters, was on his face, and the restlessness of his body also proclaimed his well-known habit. Next after his personal appearance I was struck with his exquisite courtesy. There was a finish and elegance in his diction also which recalled something of Leigh Hunt's manner, and belonged perhaps to a particular era. I need hardly say that the habits of my host at Lass Wade were very eccentric.—FIELDS, JAMES T., 1852, *Letter, A Second Shelf of Old Books by Mrs. Fields, Scribner's Magazine, vol.* 5, *p.* 467.

Very decisively he realized my plan of moving in a separate world (having no doubt realities of its own); moreover, he neither spoke nor acted in the every-day world like any one else, for which, of course, I greatly honored him. He was then (1814) in the habit of taking opium daily as an article of food, and the drug, though used for years, had scarcely begun to tell on his constitution, by those effects, which, sooner or later, overtake every one of its persevering votaries. . . . His voice was extraordinary; it came as if from dreamland; but it was the most musical and impressive of voices. In convivial life, what then seemed to me the most remarkable trait of DeQuincey's character, was the power he possessed of easily changing the tone of ordinary thought and conversation into that of his own dream-land, till his auditors, with wonder, found themselves moving pleasantly along with him in a sphere of which they might have heard and read perhaps, but which had ever appeared to them inaccessible and far, far away! Seeing that he was always good-natured and social, he could take part, at commencement, in any sort of tattle or twaddle. The talk might be of "beeves," and he could grapple with them, if expected to do so, but his musical cadences were not in keeping with such work, and in a few minutes (not without some strictly logical sequence) he could escape at will from the beeves to butterflies, and thence to the soul's immortality, to Plato, and Kant, and Schelling, and Fichte, to Milton's early years and Shakespeare's sonnets, to Wordsworth and Coleridge, to Homer and Æschylus, to St. Thomas of Aquin, St. Basil, and St. Chrysostom. But he by no means excluded them from real life, according to his own views of that life, but would recount profound mysteries from his own experiences—visions that had come over him in his loneliest walks among the mountains, and passages within his own personal knowledge, illustrating, if not proving, the doctrines of dreams, of warnings, of second sight, and mesmerism. And whatever the subject might be, every one of his sentences (or of his chapters, I might say) was woven into the most perfect logical texture, and uttered in a tone of sustained melody.— GILLIES, ROBERT PEARCE, 1854, *Memoirs of a Literary Veteran.*

Let this strange commentator on individual character meet with more mercy and a wiser interpretation than he was himself capable of. He was not made like other men; and he did not live, think, or feel like them. A singular organization was singularly and fatally deranged in its action before it could show its best quality. Marvellous analytical faculty he had; but it all oozed out in barren words. Charming eloquence he had; but it degenerated into egotistical garrulity, rendered tempting by the gilding of his genius.—MARTINEAU, HARRIET, 1859, *Biographical Sketches, p.* 100.

Malmesbury met us, the future diplomatist, drinking claret and playing whist with Eden and Charles Fox; the brilliant though discursive writer whom we have so recently lost, DeQuincey, was there, entering hall with coat buttoned to the throat, and gown drawn close about him to conceal the rents in his threadbare habiliments.— GREEN, JOHN RICHARD, 1859–1901, *Oxford During the Eighteenth Century, Oxford Studies,* ed. Green and Norgate, p. 242.

His tastes were very simple, though a little troublesome, at least to the servant who prepared his repast. Coffee, boiled rice and milk, and a piece of mutton from the loin, were the materials that invariably formed his diet. The cook, who had an audience with him daily, received her instructions in silent awe, quite overpowered by his manner; for, had he been addressing a duchess, he could scarcely have spoken with more deference. He would couch his request in such terms as these: "Owing to dyspepsia afflicting my system, and the possibility of any additional derangement of the stomach taking place, consequences incalculably distressing would arise, so much indeed as to increase nervous irritation, and prevent me from attending to matters of overwhelming importance, if you do not remember to cut the mutton in a diagonal rather than a longitudinal form." —GORDON, MARY, 1862, *Christopher North, A Memoir of John Wilson, p.* 327.

The next slide of the lantern is to represent a quite peculiar and abnormal case. It introduces a strangely fragile, unsubstantial, and puerile figure, wherein, however, resided one of the most potent and original spirits that ever frequented a tenement of clay. He shall be called, on account of associations that may or may not be found out, Thomas Papaverius. . . . In what mood and shape, shall he be brought forward? Shall it be as first we met at the table of Lucullus, whereto he was seduced by the false pretense that he would there meet with one who entertained novel and anarchical opinions regarding the Golden Ass of Apuleius? No one speaks of waiting dinner for him. He will come and depart at his own sweet will, neither burdened by punctualities nor burdening others by exacting them. The festivities of the afternoon are far on when the commotion is heard in the hall as if some dog or other stray animal had found its way in. The instinct of a friendly guest tells him of his arrival; he opens the door, and fetches in the little stranger. What can it be? A street-boy of some sort? His costume, in fact, is a boy's duffle great-coat, very threadbare, with a hole in it, and buttoned tight to the chin, where it meets the fragments of a particoloured belcher handkerchief; on his feet are list-shoes, covered with snow, for it is a stormy winter-night; and the trousers—some one suggests that they are inner linen garments blackened with writing-ink, but that Papaverius never would have been at the trouble so to disguise them. What can be the theory of such a costume? The simplest thing in the world—it consisted of the fragments of apparel nearest at hand. Had chance thrown to him a court single-breasted coat, with a bishop's apron, a kilt, and top-boots, in these he would have made his entry.—BURTON, JOHN HILL, 1862, *The Book Hunter, ed. White, p. 29.*

His sensitiveness was so extreme, in combination with the almost ultra-courtesy of a gentleman, that he hesitated to trouble a servant with any personal requests without a long prefatory apology. My family were in the country in the summer of 1825, when he was staying at my house in Pall Mall East. A friend or two had met him at dinner, and I had walked part of the way home with one of them. When I returned, I tapped at his chamber-door to bid him good night. He was sitting at the open window, habited as a prize-fighter when he enters the ring. "You will take cold," I exclaimed. "Where is your shirt?" "I have not a shirt—my shirts are unwashed." "But why not tell the servant to send them to the laundress?" "Ah! how could I presume to do that in Mrs. Knight's absence?" —KNIGHT, CHARLES, 1863, *Passages of a Working Life During Half a Century, p. 236.*

He was a pretty little creature, full of wire-drawn ingenuities; bankrupt enthusiasms, bankrupt pride; with the finest silver-toned low voice, and most elaborate gently-winding courtesies and ingenuities in conversation: "What wouldn't one give to have him in a Box, and take him out to talk!" (That was *Her* criticism of him; and it was right good). A bright, ready and melodious talker; but in the end an inconclusive and long-winded. One of the smallest man-figures I ever saw; shaped like a pair of tongs; and hardly above five feet in all: when he sat, you would have taken him, by candle light, for the beautifullest little Child; blue-eyed, blonde-haired, sparkling face,—had there not been a something too, which said, "*Eccovi*, this Child has been in Hell!"—CARLYLE, THOMAS, 1866, *Edward Irving, Reminiscences, ed. Norton, vol. II, p. 152.*

I did not like him.—PROCTER, BRYAN WALLER, 1874(?) *Recollections of Men of Letters, ed. Patmore, p. 211.*

With that noble honesty and candour for which, no less than for intellectual endowments and highest mental cultivation, he was distinguished, and with a child-like simplicity and most captivating kindness, he expressed the feeling—amounting to a deep-seated conviction of what was imperatively demanded—that the physician should be informed, with the most scrupulous fidelity, as to all the habits of his patient. I then learned, as I had been led to believe, that for a long period Mr. De Quincey's indulgence in opium was extremely limited; though the total abandonment of its use he had found to be (and with this conclusion, in a case of confirmed habit, medical men will not be disposed to differ) inconsistent with that enjoyment of that bodily health, but more particularly that state of mental calmness and tranquility, the possession of which he desiderated above all things. . . . How much the substantial power and brilliant fancy of his writings had to do with opium-eating, I do not inquire; but that it helped to keep active and entire, during so many years of bodily feebleness, that large and constant-working brain—that, in a word, it fed it, I have no manner of doubt. And further, that the almost singular immunity Mr. DeQuincey enjoyed from headache, which, in the course of his long life, he never knew—a common source of annoyance, oftentimes of misery, to ordinary-living students—was likely enough due to the opium, I also believe.—BEGBIE, DR. WARBURTON, 1876, *Thomas DeQuincey; His Life and Writings, ed. Japp, vol.* II, *pp.* 296, 297.

Opium cannot communicate to the brain any power or faculty of which it is not already possessed; although (as in DeQuincey's case), by subduing an enemy, which had by its painful assaults on a remote part of the nervous system temporarily paralyzed the central powers of the intellect, it could again restore harmony of action to these powers. It could in no way *create* moral affections, though it might resuscitate them, by removing from them an overpowering load of physical suffering. It could add no iota to the great light of the majestic intellect, although when this might be suffering a temporary eclipse, as was too frequently the case with this great writer, when his gnawing malady pervaded his entire consciousness with torments which dominated the power of thought—it might, under such circumstances, restore that great light, by dissipating the shadow that obscured it.—EATWELL, SURGEON-MAJOR W. C. B., 1877, *A Medical View of Mr. DeQuincey's Case, Thomas DeQuincey; His Life and Writings, ed. Japp, Appendix, vol.* II, *p.* 338.

His other extravagance grew out of the morbid value he set upon his papers and their not being disturbed. He was in the habit of accumulating these till, according to his own description, he was "snowed up," which meant when matters came to such an extremity that there was not a square inch of room on the table to set a cup upon, that there was no possibility of making his bed for the weight of papers gathered there, that there was no chair which could be used for its legitimate purpose, and that the track from the door to the fireplace, which had always to be considered, had been blotted out, even for his own careful treading; then he locked the door upon this impracticable state of things, and turned elsewhere; leaving his landlady, if simple and honest, fearfully impressed with the mysterious sin of meddling with his papers, but, if dishonest, with such a handle for playing upon his morbid anxieties, as was a source of livelihood. At his death there were, I believe, about six places where he had these deposits, it may be imagined at what expense.—SMITH, MRS. BAIRD, 1877, *Thomas DeQuincey; His Life and Writings, ed. Japp, vol.* I, *p.* 363.

The romance of Mignon is hardly more pathetically beautiful than that which passed in this vale at the time. DeQuincey, heart hungry, found in little Kate Wordsworth all that divine beauty and sweetness which Nature was aiming at in her flowers, streamlets, and rosy dawns. To walk these grassy lanes, to watch the growth of her mind, to listen to her lyrical voice—this was his library, his study, his heaven. He had often known what it was to wander all night, cold and nearly starved, along the streets of London, huddling with the wretched of both sexes under any rude shelter from sleet and rain; he had touched, albeit morally unscathed, the very floor of the pit of poverty and every horror; little by little he had toiled upward, and the benediction of his life, the spirit of his dawn after the long, black night, was little Kate, nestling in his heart, interpreting for him the meaning of the world in her unconscious grace and joyousness. At sunset on June 4, 1812, she went to bed in good health; at dawn she was dead. "Never," wrote her unhappy friend—"never from the foundations of those mighty hills was there so fierce a convulsion of grief as mastered my faculties on receiving that heart-shattering news." His visits were no longer to Allan Bank, but to the little grave. Many a night of frantic grief did DeQuincey pass on that grave. Then she rose again for him, and as he walked the fields her form appeared, but always on the opposite side of the field.—CONWAY, MONCURE DANIEL, 1881, *The English Lakes and their Genii, Harper's Magazine, vol.* 62, *p.* 177.

A more gracious and genial personage I never met. Picture to yourself a very diminutive man, carelessly—very carelessly—dressed; a face lined, careworn, and so expressionless that it reminded one of "that chill, changeless brow, where cold Obstruction's apathy appalls the gazing mourner's heart"—a face like death in life. The instant he began to speak, however, it lit up as though by electric light; this came from his marvellous eyes, brighter and more intelligent (though by fits) than I have ever seen in any other mortal. They seemed to me to glow with eloquence. . . . The announcement of luncheon was perhaps for the first time in my young life unwelcome to me. Miss DeQuincey did the honors with gracious hospitality, pleased, I think, to find that her father had so rapt a listener. I was asked what wine I would take, and not caring which it was, I was about to pour myself out a glass from the decanter that stood next to me. "You must not take that," whispered my hostess, "it is not port-wine, as you think." It was in fact laudanum, to which DeQuincey presently helped himself with the greatest *sang-froid*. I regarded him aghast, with much the same feelings as those with which he himself had watched the Malay at Grasmere eat the cake of opium, and with the same harmless result. The liquor seemed to stimulate rather than dull his eloquence. —PAYN, JAMES, 1884, *Some Literary Recollections, pp.* 48, 49.

A man, once seen, never to be forgotten. His appearance has been often described, but generally, I think, with a touch of caricature. He was a very little man (about 5 feet 3 or 4 inches); his countenance the most remarkable for its intellectual attractiveness that I have ever seen. His features, though not regular, were aristocratically fine, and an air of delicate breeding pervaded the face. His forehead was unusually high, square, and compact. At first sight his face appeared boyishly fresh and smooth, with a sort of hectic glow upon it that contrasted remarkably with the evident appearances of age in the grizzled hair and dim-looking eyes. The flush or bloom on the cheek was, I have no doubt, an effect of his constant use of opium; and the apparent smoothness of the face disappeared upon examination. . . Mr. DeQuincey's eyes were dark in colour, the iris large, but with a strange flatness and dimness of aspect, which, however, did not indicate any deficiency of sight. So far as I have observed he saw distant objects tolerably well, and almost to the very end of his life he could read the smallest print without spectacles. . . . No one who ever met DeQuincey could fail to be struck, after even the briefest intercourse, with the extreme sweetness and courtesy of his manners. He had the air of old-fashioned good manners of the highest kind; natural and studied politeness, free from the slightest ostentation or parade; a delicacy, gentleness, and elegance of demeanour that at once conciliated and charmed. . . . In his mode of conversing, as in everything else, his

courtesy of manner was observable. He never monopolized talk, allowed every one to have a fair chance, and listened with respectful patience to the most commonplace remarks from any one present. The fact that anyone was, for the time, a member of the company in which he also happened to be, evidently in his eyes entitled the speaker to all consideration and respect. But he had a just horror of bores, and carefully avoided them.—FINDLAY, JOHN RITCHIE, 1885, *Personal Recollections of Thomas DeQuincey, pp.* 2, 4, 5, 8.

There glided noiselessly into the room, like a shadow, a little weird-looking old man, saffron-colored, with unkempt hair, dirty collar, long snuff-brown coat, feet sliding about in large India-rubber galoches, and extended to me a wee, fleshless hand, more like a bird-claw than "the prehensile organ of man's supremacy." . . . As he closed the book a strange light seemed to glow through his eyes and illuminate his face. He began to talk with a voice that seemed to flow out of the unknown—low, mellifluous, ceaseless, filling one with awe. We listened almost breathless and soon found ourselves sitting on the floor at his feet, looking into his transfigured face like entranced children. On, on, he discoursed, as I have never heard mortal discourse before or since. If one could imagine all the wisdom, sentiment, and learning to be crushed from DeQuincey's many volumes of printed books, and to be poured out, a continuous stream, he might form some conception of that long discourse—how long we knew not. When the monologue ceased I looked at my watch, and found it was three o'clock in the morning.—WRIGHT, O. W., 1888, *A Winding Journey Around the World.*

DeQuincey, with his clever brains and shallow character.—MORLEY, JOHN, 1888–90, *Studies in Literature, p.* 17.

This inclusion of DeQuincey among those who were past and gone was one of the eccentric incidents which surrounded that man of genius. When Mr. Fields inquired for him more particularly he was assured of his death, although "after a search," he writes, "I found him alive and well in a cottage ten miles out of Edinburgh. I inquired for him again in London in 1852, and authors and critics, with very few exceptions, were uncertain where he lived, and one, a man of mark, declared to me that he heard then his name for the first time." It is already too well known for me to dwell upon it here, that the writings of Thomas DeQuincey had never been collected until they were gathered together by Mr. Fields and printed in an edition of twenty-two volumes, published consecutively in Boston. This might well account for his being unknown in England by a busy writer, for "who read an American book" in those days, and these twenty-two volumes might be considered American, inasmuch as DeQuincey had never signed his papers in the English Reviews, which were therefore only discoverable by their style.—FIELDS, ANNE, 1889, *A Second Shelf of Old Books, Scribner's Magazine, vol. 5, p.* 466.

If, ever after this, the reader would still have something more, let him take these lines from Thomson's "Castle of Indolence" with the assurance that all who ever saw DeQuincey in his old age recognize in them the most startlingly accurate description of him, as if by some prophetic anticipation, that could possibly be given in succinct metre:

"He came, the bard, a little Druid wight
Of withered aspect; but his eye was keen,
With sweetness mixed. In russet brown bedight,
As is his sister of the copses green,
He crept along, unpromising of mien.
Gross he who judges so! his soul was fair."

If the name "bard" may be extended to a prose-writer of the bardic class, this description also is exact in almost every point.—MASSON, DAVID, 1889, *ed. The Collected Writings of Thomas DeQuincey, General Preface, vol.* I, *p.* xxvi.

So meagre are the known facts in a life of seventy-four years, during nearly forty years of which DeQuincey, though never popular, was still recognised as a great name in English letters, while during the same period he knew, and was known to, not a few distinguished men. But little as is recorded of the facts of his life, even less is recorded of his character, and for once it is almost impossible to discover that character from his works. The few persons who met him all agree as to his impenetrability,—an impenetrability not in the least due to posing, but apparently natural and fated. DeQuincey was at once egotistic and impersonal, at once delighted to talk and resolutely shunning society. To him, one is tempted to say, reading and

writing did come by nature, and nothing else was natural at all. With books he is always at home. A DeQuincey in a world where there was neither reading nor writing of books, would certainly either have committed suicide or gone mad.—SAINTS-BURY, GEORGE, 1890, *DeQuincey, Essays in English Literature,* 1780–1860, *p.* 314.

From childhood to old age, indeed, De Quincey was a puzzle to all who knew him. In manners he was a courtly gentleman: in appearance, as Miss Mitford writes, he looked like a beggar. With knowledge that seemed boundless, he frequently acted like a child or a fool; always courteous in speech, he could be bitter, inconsiderate, and even malicious, in print; shy and reserved in society, he wrote of himself with a shamelessness that almost reminds us of Rousseau; regardless of money he scattered it among the most worthless of beggars, and was constantly in pecuniary difficulties. DeQuincey had the warmest affection for his wife and children, but he often left them to live, nobody knew how, in solitary lodgings. Throughout the night he would ramble for miles over the country, or write for the press, and the best part of the day was given to slumber, to be followed frequently by nervous suffering, and a wretchedness "not utterable to any human ear." With a mind of amazing versatility, and many a beautiful trait of character, it is impossible to read DeQuincey's life without seeing that it was, in great measure, a wreck, and that this failure was due, as in the case of Coleridge, to opium.—DENNIS, JOHN, 1891, *DeQuincey, Leisure Hour, vol.* 40, *p,* 241.

Another very slovenly fellow was De Quincey, and he was devoted to reading in bed. But DeQuincey was a very vandal when it came to the care and use of books. He never returned volumes he borrowed, and he never hesitated to mutilate a rare book in order to save himself the labor and trouble of writing out a quotation.—FIELD, EUGENE, 1895, *The Love Affairs of a Bibliomaniac, p.* 36.

It was on the 13th of July, 1852, that I saw Mr. DeQuincey for the first time; but the welcome that he gave me at this first meeting was that of an old friend. . . . And now I was seated beside the author himself, a listener to the dulcet tones of that earnest but softly subdued voice, often tremulous with emphasis, and most musical when most melancholy. Gladly and gratefully would I have compounded for listening only. But Mr. DeQuincey was jealous of his rights as a listener too, even where, as in my case, those rights might have been absolutely renounced to our common advantage. Nothing could better manifest the innate courtesy, the even sensitive considerateness of the man, than his conduct in this respect. A master of the art of conversation, this he is on all sides known to have been; but I do not remember to have seen any injustice done to his surpassing attainments as a good listener. He was always for giving away; scrupulously on the watch for any, the slightest, token of interruption, objection, comment, assent, question, or answer, nothing could exceed the tone of unaffected deference with which he gave heed as well as ear to whatever his companion might have to say.—JACOX, FRANCIS, 1895, *Recollections, DeQuincey and his Friends*, ed. Hogg, pp. 219, 220.

From infancy to old age, we find in him this unique combination—love of meditation, and quick reactions which demanded the stimulus of contact with common human nature. There was in him none of the impatience with the ignorant and rude that is so commonly associated with culture, with the love of meditation and of abstract thought. Wherever he goes he has, in a very marked degree, the art of making himself at home. If others cannot sympathize with him in his lofty thoughts and imaginings, he can sympathize with them, in their thought and concerns, and in such a measure that he gains at once their secret and affection. As we follow him through his long life, we find him a kind of center of attraction for persons of the most contrasted natures, temperaments and social positions: his rare courtesy, which was born of his quick sympathies and kindly hospitalities, which delighted in making all with whom he had to do completely at home, has been celebrated by all with whom he came in contact; and by the servants as decidedly as by their masters.—JAPP, ALEXANDER H., 1895, *DeQuincey and His Friends*, ed. Hogg, p. 1.

In old Scottish fashion I have sought to place this "stone upon the cairn" of the man who treated me and counselled me with an utmost paternal tenderness. Above and beyond all questions of intellectual power, of scholarship, or beauty of style,—*what human lesson stands out clear and strong throughout these recollections?* That, surely, *of perfect, unswerving kindness in daily life;* an antique, chivalrous courtesy and gracious consideration for people of every class, whatever their temper, whatever their foibles. If ever man attained unto the fullest measure of that Scripture which ordains—"having compassion one of another, love as brethren, be pitiful, be courteous"—that man was THOMAS DeQUINCEY. —HOGG, JAMES, 1895, *DeQuincey and His Friends, Preface, p. xii.*

Poverty is sometimes a noble and respectable thing, and when the issues have any sort of greatness there is a kind of excitement in the alternate downfalls and successes of the penniless but courageous struggle. But when the strife is for a few pounds, when the milkman's bill is the rock in the way, and shillings and pence the munitions of war, the echo of that dreary and hopeless fighting in the dark has nothing but misery in it. DeQuincey puts forth his privations, his wanderings about from one lodging to another, sometimes waylaid in his bed by a furious creditor, sometimes suffering torture for want of a box of Seidlitz powders, always with elaborate explanation of how in the extraordinary combination of fate it has come to be so, but can never by any calculation of human probabilities be so again—to the publisher who never seems to refuse the necessary dole, but inevitably is sometimes a little impatient and provoked by the perpetual messengers and the dole on the other side of a page or two at a time.—OLIPHANT, MARGARET O. W., 1897, *William Blackwood and His Sons, vol.* I, *p.* 423.

CONFESSIONS OF AN ENGLISH OPIUM-EATER
1821-22

Have you heard anything of a book which every body (meaning every idle Athenian eager for novelty) is now reading? It is called the "Confessions of an English Opium Eater." Many strange things and persons have I encountered in my journey through life, and, among the rest, this same Opium Eater. I spent an idle half day talking with him fourteen years ago in London, when he was a student at Oxford, and met him once since. I directly recognised him through the thin disguise in his book: I am since assured that I have not been mistaken. Ask more about him, if you have any taste remaining for oddities.—GRANT, ANNE, 1823, *To Mrs. Brown, Feb, 13; Memoir and Correspondence, ed. Grant, vol.* II, *p.* 330.

That thrice-double demoniac the æconomical opium-eater.—BEDDOES, THOMAS LOVELL, 1824, *To Thomas Forbes Kelsall, April* 17; *Letters, ed. Gosse, p.* 24.

I send you a bantering "Epistle of an Old Gentleman whose Education is supposed to have been neglected." Of course, it was *suggested* by some letters of your admirable Opium-Eater, the discontinuance of which has caused so much regret to myself in common with most of your readers.—LAMB, CHARLES, 1825, *To the Editor of the London Magazine.*

DeQuincey seems like a man bound on a journey to a certain place, the way to which is straight, but who prefers wandering out of the road, to which he occasionally returns—and immediately deviates off in another direction. It is not difficult to see that a long time must pass before he reaches his journey's end, or that, when he does reach it, the purpose for which he started may be rendered unavailable by the delay. This is the more unpardonable in DeQuincey, who, in the "Confessions of an English Opium-Eater," has produced one of the most charming books in the language, by making it simple in style and natural in expression.—MACKENZIE, R. SHELTON, 1854, *ed. Noctes Ambrosianæ, vol.* I, *p.* 5, *note.*

I wrote, in September, 1821: "We never read anything more deeply interesting than the 'Confessions of an English Opium-Eater.' We can put implicit faith in them. They have all the circumstantial sincerity of Defoe. They are written in a fine flowing style, in which the author is perfectly forgotten." After the publication of two articles on the Pleasures and Pains of Opium, the majority of their readers doubted the reality of these Confessions. The author, in a letter to the editor of the magazine, declared that the narrative contained a faithful statement of his own experience as an Opium-Eater, drawn up with entire simplicity, except in some trifling deviations of dates and suppressions of names which circumstance had rendered it expedient should not be published.— KNIGHT, CHARLES, 1863, *Passages of a Working Life During Half a Century, p.* 185.

Of all these miscellaneous writers Carlyle was the most original, and Thomas De Quincey the greatest writer of English prose. DeQuincey's style has so peculiar a quality that it stands alone. The sentences are built up like passages in a fugue, and there is nothing in English literature which can be compared in involved melody to the prose of the "Confessions of an English Opium-Eater."—BROOKE, STOPFORD A., 1876, *English Literature (Primer), p.* 138.

DeQuincey himself, in descanting on the Dream-faculty, says, "Habitually to dream magnificently, a man must have a constitutional determination to reverie." In that sentence he announces the true law of all literature that comes under the order of pure phantasy. But in his case, in spite of the strength of the dream-element, we cannot proceed far till we discover that his determination to reverie was but the extreme projection of one phase of a phenomenal nature balancing its opposite. He was also shrewd, observant, master of a fine humour that demanded contact with life for its free exercise. From a nice examination of details he was under an inborn necessity to rise to the principle that relates them, linking the disparate together; deeply interested in the most practical and dry of studies—political economy. He was skilled in the exercises of the analytic understanding—a logician exacting and precise—else his dreaming had never gained for him the eminence it has gained. Surely it is calculated to strike the most casual reader on a perusal of that first edition of the "Confessions," that his powers of following up sensational effects and tracing with absolute exactness the most delicately varying shades of experience, and recording them with conscientious precision, were as noticable as were the dreams to which they were served to give effect. No proper ground has been laid for a liberal and sympathetic appreciation of DeQuincey till these points have been clearly apprehended; and assuredly this is one of the cases where, as he himself has well said, "not to sympathise is not to understand."—JAPP, ALEXANDER H., 1877, *Thomas DeQuincey; His Life and Writings, vol.* I, *p.* 1.

The extraordinary autobiography contained in these "Confessions" loses nothing in the telling; the style of DeQuincey is always refined, and his English perfect, while for the more striking qualities of the narrator we would almost say that the pictures of the wanderings of the friendless lad through the pitiless streets and his strange companionship with poor Ann of Oxford Street and her unhappy sisters are almost too powerful. The sensation excited by the "Confessions" was immense. Many critics regarded them as entirely a work of imagination, and, as we have said, it is still doubtful how much of the narrative may be genuine. DeQuincey, however, always asserted it to be so, and the point can never be cleared up now.—OLIPHANT, MARGARET O. W., 1892, *The Victorian Age of English Literature*, p. 58.

While all controlled reasoning was suspended under the incantation of opium, his quick mind, without conscious intent, without prejudice or purpose, assembled such mysterious and wonderful sights and sounds as the naked soul might see and hear in the world of actual experience. For De Quincey's range of action and association was not as narrow as might seem. He had walked the streets of London friendless and starving, saved from death by a dram given by one even more wretched than he, only a few months after he had talked with the king. DeQuincey's latent images are therefore not grotesque, or mediæval, not conditioned by any philosophical theory, not of any Inferno or Paradise. The elements of his visions are the simple elements of all our striking experiences: the faces of the dead, the grieving child, the tired woman, the strange foreign face, the tramp of horses' feet. And opium merely magnified these simple elements, rendered them grand and beautiful without giving them any forced connection or relative meaning. We recognise the traces of our own transfigured experience, but we are relieved from the necessity of accepting it as having an inner meaning. DeQuincey's singular hold on our affection seems, therefore, to be his rare quality of presenting the unusual but typical dream or reverie as a beautiful object of interest, without endeavoring to give it the character of an allegory or a fable.—CARPENTER, GEORGE R., 1897, *Library of the World's Best Literature, ed. Warner, vol.* VIII, p. 4558.

GENERAL

Convince yourself that your work *is* what you call it, as nearly as your honest powers could make it; and the man who censures it either tells you nothing that you did not know before, or tells you lies; both of which

sorts of intelligence you will find it a very simple matter to light your pipe with. There was a luckless wight of an *opium-eater* here, one DeQuincey, for instance, who wrote a very vulgar and brutish Review of "Meister" in the *London Magazine.* I read three pages of it one *sick* day at Birmingham; and said: "Here is a man who writes of things which he does not rightly understand; I see clean over the top of *him*, and his vulgar spite, and his commonplace philosophy; and I will away and have a ride on (Badams') Taffy, and leave *him* to cry in the ears of the simple." So I went out, and had my ride accordingly; and if DeQuincey, poor little fellow, *made* anything of his review, he can put it in his waistcoat pocket, and thank the god Mercurius.—CARLYLE, THOMAS, 1825, *To John A. Carlyle, Jan.* 22; *Early Letters, ed. Norton*, p. 323.

Did you read "Blackwood"? and in that case have you had deep delight in an exquisite paper by the Opium-eater, which my heart trembled through from end to end? What a poet that man is! how he vivifies words, or deepens them, and gives them profound significance.—BROWNING, ELIZABETH BARRETT, 1843, *To Mr. Westwood, Dec.* 31; *Letters, ed. Kenyon, vol.* I, p. 161.

This very clever work ["Logic of Political Economy"] is intended to unravel intricacies and to expose sundry errors in the application of the Ricardian theory of value. It would, however, have been more popular and successful had it been less scholastic. It is right to be logical, but not to be perpetually obtruding logical forms and technicalities on the reader's attention. This sort of affectation is little noticed in a brief essay like the Templars' Dialogues; but in a goodly-sized volume like the present it becomes tiresome and repulsive.—McCULLOCH, JOHN RAMSAY, 1847, *Literature of Political Economy*, p. 20.

Well learned in ancient and modern tongues, he has written a vast quantity, but when his transcendental and unintelligible metaphysics are weeded out, the actual substance of his works will be in a small space. With the German school of philosophy he is well acquainted, and has endeavored, chiefly by translation, to make his countrymen familiar with it. He has written a great deal—chiefly for magazines. Sometimes he is extremely graphic and picturesque, but his great fault is diffuseness, want of concentration, and an inability to discuss a subject without digressions—*apropos* to nothing. His writings have been published in America in a collected form; this has not been done in England, where only a selection could obtain a sale.—MACKENZIE, R. SHELTON, 1854, *ed. Noctes Ambrosianœ, vol.* I, *p.* 362, *note.*

Strip the style off and leave the matter in Mr. DeQuincey's essays, and you would find that it is like taking the sound out of a grove of pines.—KING, THOMAS STARR, 1861, *Books and Reading, Substance and Show and Other Essays, ed. Whipple, p.* 382.

The key-note of preparation, the claim which pre-eminently should be set forth in advance, is this: that DeQuincey was the prince of hierophants, or of pontifical hierarchs, as regards all those profound mysteries which from the beginning have swayed the human heart, sometimes through the light of angelic smiles lifting it upwards to an altitude just beneath the heavens, and sometimes shattering it, with a shock of quaking anguish, down to earth. As it was the function of the hierophant, in the Grecian mysteries, to show the sacred symbols as concrete incarnations of faith, so was it DeQuincey's to reveal in open light the everlasting symbols, universally intelligible when once disclosed, which are folded in the evolutions of dreams and of those meditations which most resemble dreams; and as to the manner of those revelations, no Roman *pontifex maximus,* were it even Cæsar himself, could have rivalled their magisterial pomp.—ALDEN, HENRY M., 1863, *Thomas DeQuincey, Atlantic Monthly, vol.* 12, *p.* 345.

The books that Mr. DeQuincey, first and last, tantalized his admirers by projecting, in divers and diverse lines of authorship—now a great history, now an exhaustive philosophy of the mind, now an elaborate fiction,—were many enough to indicate his nearness of kin to Coleridge and Herder, both of whom he has somewhere termed "men of infinite title-pages"; indeed, he used to mention his hearing Coleridge own that his title-pages alone (titles, that is, of works meditated but unexecuted) would fill a large volume; and of Herder he takes it to be clear that, if his power had been commensurate with his will, all other authors must have been put down, and that many generations would have been unable

to read to the end of his works.—JACOX, FRANCIS, 1872, *Aspects of Authorship, p.* 307.

As a literary critic, his catholicity of spirit and breadth of view were unique among the men of his time. Rarely indeed, if ever, has a mind so calm, unprejudiced, and comprehensive, been applied to the work of criticism. In his own day he was usually numbered among the "Lakers," or partisans of Wordsworth, Coleridge, and Southey. He was so only in the sense of treating these remarkable men with justice. He, better than Jeffrey himself, knew the shortcomings of Wordsworth, condemned his theory of poetic diction, and made fun of absurdities in "The Excursion;" but he felt the shortcomings with calm discrimination, and was not misled by them into undervaluing the striking originality of Wordsworth's genius. He was one of the most devout of the admirers of Shakespeare and as we have seen, entered with passionate rapture into the majestic harmonies of Milton; but he had no part in the common bond of the Lakers—their wholesale contempt for Pope. . . . The melody of DeQuincey's prose is pre-eminently rich and stately. He takes rank with Milton as one of our greatest masters of stately cadence, as well as of sublime composition. If one may trust one's ear for general impression, Milton's melody is sweeter and more varied; but for magnificent effects, at least in prose, the palm must probably be assigned to De Quincey. In some of DeQuincey's grandest passages the language can be compared only to the swell and crash of an orchestra. —MINTO, WILLIAM, 1872–80, *Manual of English Prose Literature, pp.* 47, 71.

His paper entitled "Confessions of an Opium-Eater" is undoubtedly powerful writing; but his "Reminiscences" and "Biographical Essays" stand in a different predicament. These are in my opinion often poor and without merit. I do not know any instance in the writings of an author of note comprehending so much pedantry, pretension and impertinence. They are all divergence. Even in the splenetic parts he cannot adhere to his subject; but must recede to some opinion of his own which has no connection with the matter on hand, or he refers to some classical or German author for the sake of exhibiting his learning, or general knowledge. His style therefore becomes wearisome, inconsequent, and parenthetical to an offensive degree.—PROCTER, BRYAN WALLER, 1874(?), *Recollections of Men of Letters, ed. Patmore, p.* 211.

None, we think, have so dipped their pens in the varied lines of sunshine and gloom, or been able to fix that which is fleeting and transient. . . . DeQuincey lived in a dream-world until dreams became, as it were, the substantial realities of his existence.—DAVEY, SAMUEL, 1876, *Darwin, Carlyle and Dickens.*

If we take the "Confessions of an Opium-Eater" and follow it with, for an example, the essay on Shakespeare, then pursue the fortunes of the Spanish Nun, and wind up with a careful reading of the "Logic of Political Economy," we shall come away with a dazzling impression of DeQuincey's range as a thinker, a student, and a writer. But this impression does not grow proportionately stronger on reviewing the whole bulk of his writings. We gradually lose faith in the comprehensiveness which at first seemed so positive and radical a characteristic. We observe also, that he repeats himself, that he covers large spaces with a very thin integument of thought, or with a sham, apparitional kind of humor, and that his monotony has not the charm of that other monotony belonging to the styles of more creative writers. To acknowledge this is by no means to belittle DeQuincey's claims to our remembrance, but it enables us to define some things concerning him more clearly, perhaps, than they have usually been defined.—LATHROP, GEORGE PARSONS, 1877, *Some Aspects of De Quincey, Atlantic Monthly, vol.* 40, *p.* 569.

To the appreciation of DeQuincey, the reader must bring an imaginative faculty somewhat akin to his own, a certain general culture and large knowledge of books and men and things. Otherwise much of that slight and delicate allusion that gives point and color and charm to his writings will be missed; and on this account the full enjoyment and comprehension of DeQuincey must always remain a luxury of the literary and intellectual. But his skill in narration, his rare pathos, his wide sympathies, the pomp of his dream descriptions, the exquisite playfulness of his lighter dissertations, and his abounding though delicate and subtle humor, commend him to a larger class.—FINDLAY, JOHN RITCHIE, 1878, *Encyclopædia Britannica, vol.* VII.

What would DeQuincey be without his style? Rob him of the dazzling fence of his rhetoric, his word-painting, and rhythm,—strip him of his organ-like fugues, his majestic swells and dying falls,—leave to him only the bare, naked ideas of his essays,—and he will be DeQuincey no longer.—MATHEWS, WILLIAM, 1881, *Literary Style, p.* 10.

The crowning glory of his writings is their style, so full of involved melody, so exact and careful, so rich in magnificent apostrophes, so markedly original, so polished and elaborate. He never forgot that the prose writer, if he wishes to attain excellence, must be as much of an artist as the poet, and fashion his periods and paragraphs with as much care as the poet elaborates his rhymes and cadences. Many passages might be quoted from DeQuincey of which the melody is so striking as to irresistibly attract attention, and make us linger lovingly over them, apart altogether from the matter they contain.—NICOLL, HENRY J., 1882, *Landmarks of English Literature, p.* 364.

Nobody puts better on his canvas an aspect of nature, or gives us in more detailed and faithful circumstance the surroundings of a human scene. He is not so happy with men, because, for one thing, of his habit of detractation, which forbade him from seeing into what Wordsworth prosaically calls "the very heart of the machine"; and finally, perhaps, from his own eccentricities and out-of-the-way thoughts. He wrote many volumes of essays, and criticisms of various kinds, and his best work has found a place among English classics. The delicate wit and irony of the essay upon "Murder as one of the Fine Arts" has moved many a reader to such a laugh, tempered with a thrill of visionary excitement and horror, as is rare among the laughters of literature. It is undue honour to this curious little monster in literature to place him by the side of Lamb; but the connection of both with the greater group of poets supplies an arbitrary link of association.—OLIPHANT, MARGARET O. W., 1882, *Literary History of England, XVIII-XIX Century, vol.* II, *p.* 28.

The master builder of the Eastern type is DeQuincey. . . . He gives us minarets and pinnacles, as well as domes and cupolas, in his terse, clean cut contractions and iterations. He piles thought on thought, not in flats, nor yet altogether in climax, though climax plays its part, too; but in glittering and audacious phrases, which rear their slender shafts up to the very clouds, and look down, star-crowned, from their giddy heights, upon the impassive sphinx, the loathsome crocodile, the oozy mud of the Nile.—MORRISON, A. H., 1886, *The Art Gallery of the English Language, p.* 30.

Some of his sentences are almost as long and as sustained as those of Jeremy Taylor; while, in many passages of reasoning that glows and brightens with strong passion and emotion, he is not inferior to Burke. He possessed an enormous vocabulary—in wealth of words and phrases he surpasses both Macaulay and Carlyle; and he makes a very large—perhaps even an excessive—use of Latin words. He is also very fond of using metaphors, personifications, and other figures of speech. It may be said without exaggeration that, next to Carlyle's, De-Quincey's style is the most stimulating and inspiriting that a young reader can find among modern writers.—MEIKLEJOHN, J. M. D., 1887, *The English Language: Its Grammar, History and Literature, p.* 349.

DeQuincey's infirmities caused many blemishes in his work; many articles are fragmentary; his reading, though wide, was desultory; he is often intolerably long-winded and discursive, and delights too much in logical wire-drawing; his reason is too often the slave of effeminate prejudices, and the humour with which he endeavours to relieve his stately passages is too often forced and strongly wanting in taste. But imperfect as is much of his work, he has left many writings which, in their special variety of excellence, are unrivalled in modern English.—STEPHEN, LESLIE, 1888, *Dictionary of National Biography, vol.* XIV, *p.* 390.

For pure rigmarole, for stories, as Mr. Chadband has it, "of a cock and of a bull, and of a lady and of a half-crown," few things, even in DeQuincey, can exceed, and nothing out of DeQuincey can approach, the passages about the woman he met on the "cop" at Chester, and about the Greek letter that he did not send to the bishop of Bangor, in the preliminary part of the "Confessions." . . . Few English writers have touched so large a number of subjects with such competence both in information and in power of handling. Still

fewer have exhibited such remarkable logical faculty. One main reason why one is sometimes tempted to quarrel with him is that his play of fence is so excellent that one longs to cross swords. For this and for other reasons no writer has a more stimulating effect, or is more likely to lead his readers on to explore and to think for themselves. In none is that incurable curiosity, that infinite variety of desire for knowledge and for argument which age cannot quench, more observable. Few if any have the indefinable quality of freshness in so large a measure. You never quite know, though you may have a shrewd suspicion, what DeQuincey will say on any subject; his gift of sighting and approaching new facets of it is so immense. Whether he was in truth as accomplished a classical scholar as he claimed to be I do not know; he has left few positive documents to tell us. But I should think that he was, for he has all the characteristics of a scholar of the best and rarest kind—the scholar who is exact as to language without failing to comprehend literature, and competent in literature without being slipshod as to language.—SAINTSBURY, GEORGE, 1890, *DeQuincey, Essays in English Literature,* 1780–1860, *pp.* 317, 330.

I don't know DeQuincey well enough to write anything about him. I have not read a line of him these thirty years. I never write about anybody without reading him through so as to get a total impression, and I have not time enough to do that in his case now. The only feeling I find in my memory concerning him is, that he was a kind of inspired *cad*, and an amplification of that with critical rose-water wouldn't answer your purpose.—LOWELL, JAMES RUSSELL, 1890, *To R. W. Gilder, Oct.* 9; *Letters of James Russell Lowell, ed. Norton, vol.* II, *p.* 421.

This at least may be said without fear of controversy: that his position in literature is unique, for he dwells in a land of dreams to which no other English author has access. His phantasies have been called by the absurd name of prose-poetry, which is, and always must be, an impossible form of literature; but in the border-land between poetry and prose DeQuincey reigns supreme.—DENNIS, JOHN, 1891, *DeQuincey, Leisure Hour, vol.* 40, *p.* 244.

Not to know DeQuincey is to be ignorant of some of the most remarkable literary products of the century. . . . For breadth of scope, for power and delicacy of thought, and for beauty and clearness of style, he is surpassed by none of his contemporaries, if, indeed, he is equalled by any one of them. In logic, humor, irony; in subtle power of analysis; in an apparently intuitive skill in adapting language to thought; in richness of illustration; in his unparalleled imagination, DeQuincey stands in the very front rank of authors of all time.—BELFIELD, HENRY H., 1892, *ed. Joan of Arc and Other Selections from De-Quincey, Prefatory Note.*

DeQuincey's talent lay more in a narrative and imaginative writing than in literary criticism. He was too digestive and sensational, too much of a rhetorician, to rank with the greatest critics. His liveliness of fancy and the rapid play of his remarkable information, together with his verbal brilliancy, found their most congenial field in his extraordinary rambling sketches. But his knowledge of literature was so wide and sympathetic, and he had such genuine philosophical insight, that he stands well as a writer on literary topics. His best work in this field is to be found fragmentarily all through those numerous volumes which he composed after his late commencement as an author.—MCLAUGHLIN, EDWARD T., 1893, *ed. Literary Criticism for Students, p. 118.*

DeQuincey is as hard to hold as the Old Man of the Sea. He eludes analysis and baffles description. His great fault as an author is best described, in the decayed language of the equity draughtsman, as multifariousness. His style lacks the charm of economy, and his workmanship the dignity of centralization. A literary spendthrift is, however, a very endurable sinner in these stingy days. . . . DeQuincey's magnificence, the apparent boundlessness of his information, the liberties he takes, relying upon his mastery of language, his sportiveness and freakish fancies, make him the idol of all hobbledehoys of a literary turn.—BIRRELL, AUGUSTINE, 1894, *Essays about Men, Women and Books, pp. 67, 68.*

When we ask ourselves whether DeQuincey's paragraphs are units we find it necessary to limit the word unity more closely than usual. Classical unity, severe, selective, exclusive, he rarely shows. On the other hand his essays were preceded by the most careful analysis, and there is no doubt that he considered each paragraph with regard to unity. We may say of his longer paragraphs that the best show unity in somewhat wide variety, while in all cases he returns consciously, from digressions within the paragraph, to the topic. As a rule his long and numerous digressions proceed by whole paragraphs.—LEWIS, EDWIN HERBERT, 1894, *The History of the English Paragraph, p. 137.*

For range of power, for great diversity of subject, for poetic, philosophic, and logical cast of mind, for depth of feeling, for an *inspiring vitality of thinking,* for periodic and impassioned prose which, running through the whole gamut of expression, is unequalled in English Literature, no more educating author could be selected for advanced students than Thomas DeQuincey.—CORSON, HIRAM, 1894, *The Aims of Literary Study, p. 60.*

Through the door of Wordsworth and Coleridge, DeQuincey entered, and then became one of the main channels by which their influence was diffused and made operative in moulding the thoughts of other men after the image of theirs. . . . DeQuincey, by virtue of his combining great emotional sensibility with great intellectual subtilty, belongs to the order of genius; but he does not belong to the first rank in it. He has genius, but it is not creative; originality and independence, but they are employed in analysing, interpreting, and expounding.—HODGSON, SHADWORTH H., 1895, *On the Genius of DeQuincey, DeQuincey and his Friends, ed. Hogg, p. 321.*

Another author who was a prime favorite with me about this time was DeQuincey, whose books I took out of the State Library, one after another, until I had read them all. We who were young people of that day thought his style something wonderful, and so indeed it was, especially in those passages, abundant everywhere in his work, relating to his own life with an intimacy which was always more rather than less. His rhetoric there, and in certain of his historical studies, had a sort of luminous richness, without losing its colloquial ease. I keenly enjoyed this subtle spirit, and the play of that brilliant intelligence which lighted up so many ways of literature with its lambent glow or its tricksy glimmer, and I had a deep sympathy with certain morbid moods and experiences so like my own, as I was pleased to fancy. 1 have not looked at his "Twelve Cæsars" for twice as many years, but I should be greatly surprised to find it other than one of the greatest historical monographs ever written. His literary criticisms seemed to me not only exquisitely humorous, but perfectly sane and just; and it delighted me to have him personally present, with the warmth of his own temperament in regions of cold abstraction; I am not sure that I should like that so much now. . . . He was a great little creature, and through his intense personality he achieved a sort of impersonality, so that you loved the man, who was forever talking of himself, for his modesty and reticence. He left you feeling intimate with him but by no means familiar; with all his frailties, and with all those freedoms he permitted himself with the lives of his contemporaries, he is to me a figure of delicate dignity, and winning kindness.— HOWELLS, WILLIAM DEAN, 1895, *My Literary Passions, pp.* 175, 176.

It is significant that most estimates of the value of DeQuincey's work concern themselves with his style. He was not a great thinker. Keen as were his powers of analysis, he was not always a logical thinker. Above all, he was not capable of sustained, systematic thinking. His writings are full of beginnings that end nowhere, and of promises that are never performed. His very habit of analysis led to a lack of proportion in his work. Little ideas get as much space as big ones. One is sometimes wearied by the feeling that it is not the thought that he is getting, but the author's power of saying things, irrespective of their worth, in a pleasing and original form.— BAKER, FRANKLIN T., 1896, *ed. Revolt of the Tartars by Thomas DeQuincey, p.* 6.

As a critic his value is perhaps overestimated. On the one hand, he united with Coleridge and Carlyle in introducing English readers to German literature and philosophy. He was also among the first to appreciate the new poetry of Wordsworth and Coleridge, and to contend for its just place in literature. On the other hand, he failed to appreciate French literature, slighted Goethe, scorned Crabbe, preferred Dickens to Thackeray, and ventured to attack the Republic of Plato. . . . De Quincey's value as a critic is not the measure of his excellence. His most popular and interesting works, the works by which he himself set most store, are those pieces of

imaginative reminiscence beginning with the "Confessions of an English Opium-Eater," and proceeding through the "Suspiria de Profundis" (including "Levana," "Savannah-la-Mar," etc.), and the "Autobiographic Sketches," to "The English Mail Coach." Not only did these catch the taste of the time and set a fashion on both sides of the Atlantic, but they also hold a peculiar place in English literature.— BALDWIN, CHARLES SEARS, 1896, *ed. DeQuincey's Revolt of the Tartars, Introduction, p.* xxiv.

His writings are pre-eminently exegetical, lacking in the imperative mood. He analyzes, interprets, or expounds after his subtle, philosophic, though somewhat eccentric and paradoxical manner; taking nothing for granted, probing into everything he touches, and illuminating it by some flash of originality. Though not always a sound thinker, he marshals his arguments with an orderly precision, which is invaluable in a good cause. Exactness, carried to the verge of pedantry, is the conspicuous merit of his style; which is further strengthened by a scrupulous attention to the conditions of effective comparison, and by the explicitness with which his statements and clauses are connected. Even his grammar and punctuation are singularly clear and careful. Beneath this vigorous intellectuality lurks a curiously deliberate and "dæmonic" kind of humour, which largely consists in the sudden introduction of an unexpected point of view, and use of dignified language for the discussion of trivialities, and the application of artistic or professional terms to records of crime and passion. . . . His style is essentially decorative, and he aims consciously at sublimity of thought and diction. He does not shrink from daring appeals to the infinite, and risks bewildering his reader by dizzy flights to the uttermost limits of time and space. He builds up his sentences and his paragraphs with a sensitive ear for the music of words. One phrase seems like the echo of another, and even the impression of distance in sound is cunningly produced. His finest passages are distinguished by the crowded richness of fancy, the greater range and arbitrariness of combination, which are the peculiar attributes of poetry.—JOHNSON, R. BRIMLEY, 1896, *English Prose, ed. Craik, vol.* v, *pp.* 260, 261.

The prose of DeQuincey will always find some admirers attracted by its elaborate involution, its untiring amplitude of description and richness of ornament, which have all the appearances of eloquence except those that are true. We only see how limited and artificial it is when we imagine a prose style formed upon DeQuincey's model, and adapting that model to changing needs. The spuriousness of the coin is soon detected when we attempt to pass it outside the narrow circle which DeQuincey made his own, and where his ingenuity and inventiveness assure him a meed of respect.—CRAIK, HENRY, 1896, *English Prose, Introduction, vol.* v, *p.* 5.

He swayed men; but he rarely taught them, or fed them.—MITCHELL, DONALD G., 1897, *English Lands Letters and Kings, The Later Georges to Victoria, p.* 40.

His manner of writing was at once extremely splendid and extremely precise. He added to literature several branches or provinces which had up to his day scarcely been cultivated in English; among these, impassioned autobiography, distinguished by an exquisite minuteness in the analysis of recollected sensations, is pre-eminent. . . . DeQuincey is sometimes noisy and flatulent, sometimes trivial, sometimes unpardonably discursive. But when he is at his best, the rapidity of his mind, its lucidity, its humour and good sense, the writer's passionate loyalty to letters, and his organ-melody of style command our deep respect. He does not, like the majority of his critical colleagues, approach literature for purposes of research, but to obtain moral effects. DeQuincey, a dreamer of beautiful dreams, disdained an obstinate vassalage to mere matters of fact, but sought with intense concentration of effort after a conscientious and profound psychology of letters.—GOSSE, EDMUND, 1897, *A Short History of Modern English Literature, pp.* 322, 323.

His "prose fantasies" are the most popular parts of his writings. The instructed lover of the best English prose will probably feel that they are a little *too* popular—that they are not so perfect in art as the less known dreams of Boccaccio and Petrarch in Landor's "Imaginary Conversations"— but few would now deny to them an abiding place in English literature.—FOWLER, J.H., 1897, *XIX-Century Prose, p.* 35.

He himself classified his writings under three heads,—autobiographical, critical and imaginative. In all three the matter is of less worth than the style which enshrines it; a style whose one weakness it is to deploy on too slight provocation its inexhaustible phraseological resources, and to recognize no season in which a miracle of expression is out of place.—HERFORD, C. H., 1897, *The Age of Wordsworth, p.* 70.

The interest of DeQuincey is that of an experimenter and pioneer in English prose. He may, in fact, be described as the inventor of that variety of prose—a questionable variety in the hands of many of his successors—which has been named the "poetic": a form in which to attain the ends of vivid description or of impassioned narrative, the restraints which the elder prose-masters deliberately imposed upon themselves in respect both of construction and vocabulary were as deliberately thrown off. In other words, the attempt was for the first time made to arouse emotions as vehement in the mind of a reader through the medium of prose as are or may be excited by the instrumentality of verse. In some of DeQuincey's most famous passages this exaltation of the *emotional* power of prose is overwhelmingly felt.—TRAILL, HENRY DUFF, 1897, *Social England, vol.* VI, *p.* 29.

He represents the reaction from the polish, reserve, and coldness of the eighteenth century to the warmth and glow of the seventeenth century,—the golden period of English prose. His masters are Milton, Jeremy Taylor, Fuller, and Browne, whose eloquence, rich coloring, and elaborate ornamentation he inherits. To these qualities he has added the finish and elegance of the eighteenth century writers, and the freedom, deep feeling, and lofty spiritual tone of our own age. In fineness of texture and in beauty of coloring he is unequalled save by Ruskin, whom he surpasses in form and general pictorial and sound effects. He is sometimes guilty of bad taste or bathos, but when at his best is a supreme master of the "grand style." With an imagination as great as Carlyle's, his style is more chastened, rhythmical, and exquisite, though not showing so much industry or moral earnestness. He has a finer rhetorical and critical faculty than Macaulay, and is more stately and vivacious than Landor. DeQuincey's unique power lies in his imagination, which is extraordinary. In his best passages there is a poetic loftiness, a phantasmagoric charm, and a spectacular gorgeousness which seizes and holds the mind of the reader with its subtile power. Even when we cannot accept the soundness of his conclusions on philosophical questions, or the accuracy of his statements in the historical and biographical essays, we delight in surrendering ourselves to his wonderful fancy. When he has on his magic robes, few can mount so high.—WAUCHOPE, GEORGE ARMSTRONG, 1898, *ed. Confessions of an English Opium-Eater, p. 18.*

It is a cause of pride that Americans were the first to conceive the idea of putting the 150 magazine articles of DeQuincey into permanent form. It is not the only instance of our recognition of the value of the British article before it was praised at home. The sixteen volumes are full of the keenest intellectual perception—exact, penetrative, analytic. They are never dull, because they are lighted up with a playful humor and fun-loving fancy not at all incompatible with passion and pathos.— GEORGE, ANDREW J., 1898, *From Chaucer to Arnold, Types of Literary Art, p.* 651.

A trait of DeQuincey closely allied to his habit of digression, and one which the general reader must always regard as a defect, is his tendency to overload his sentences with irrelevant particulars. He appends relative clause to relative clause in several degrees of subordination, and often adds to such a combination a parenthesis within a parenthesis. Obviously, this excessive qualification is generally due to DeQuincey's sometimes finical desire for exactness. . . . In one respect DeQuincey is far from a model writer, and that is in his ungovernable habit of digressing from his given theme. He not only digresses from his main theme, but he digresses from his first digression, and sometimes even from his third.—CLARK, J. SCOTT, 1898, *A Study of English Prose Writers, pp.* 397, 399.

Two serious charges are to be brought against DeQuincey as a writer,—diffuseness and triviality. He cannot resist the slightest temptation to digress, and even in the most solemn pages of his Confessions, and in the midst of the touching story of Joan of Arc's childhood, he is capable of falling into a queer kind of "rigmarole" made up of pedantry and mirthless jesting. In reading him we are often visited by an uncomfortable sense of dealing with a nature not quite responsible and not quite human. He illustrates both the defects and the virtues of the romantic temper; its virtues in the enkindled splendor of his fancy and the impassioned sweep of his style; its defects in his extravagance, his unevenness, his failure to exercise adequate self-criticism.—MOODY, AND LOVETT, 1902, *A History of English Literature, p.* 304.

Washington Irving
1783–1859

Born, in New York, 3 April 1783. Educated at private schools, 1787–99. In a lawyer's office, 1801–04. Contrib. to "Morning Chronicle," under pseud. of "Jonathan Oldstyle," 1802. Travelled in Europe, 1804–06. Edited "Salmagundi," with his brother, William, and J. K. Paulding, Jan. to Oct., 1807. Partner with his brothers in a mercantile house, 1810–17. Assistant Editor of "Analectic Mag.," 1813–14. In England, 1815–20. Travelled on Continent, 1820–25. Attaché to the U. S. A. Legation at Madrid, 1826–29. Sec. to U. S. A. Legation in London, 1829–32. Medal of Roy. Soc. of Lit., 1830. Hon. LL.D., Oxford, 1831. Returned to New York, 1832; settled at Sunnyside. Contrib. to "Knickerbocker Mag.," 1839–40. U. S. A. Ambassador to Spain, 1842–46. Returned to America, April 1846. Unmarried. Died, at Sunnyside, 28 Nov. 1859. *Works:* "A History of New York" (under pseud. of "Diedrich Knickerbocker") 1809; "The Sketch-Book of Geoffrey Crayon," 1819; "Bracebridge Hall" (by "Geoffrey Crayon," 2 vols.), 1822; "Letters of Jonathan Oldstyle," 1824 (3rd edn. same year); "Tales of a Traveller" by ("Geoffrey Crayon"), 1824; "A History of . . . Cristopher Columbus" (3 vols.), 1828; "A Chronicle of the Conquest of Granada," 1829; "Voyages . . . of the Companions of Columbus," 1831; "The Alhambra" (by "Geoffrey Crayon"), 1832; "Complete Works" (pubd. in Paris), 1834; "Abbotsford and Newstead Abbey" (anon.), 1835; "Tour on the Prairies," 1835; "Legends of the Conquest of Spain" (anon.), 1835; "The Crayon Miscellany" (anon.), 1835; "Astoria" (3 vols.), 1836; "The Adventures of Captain Bonneville," 1837; "Biography and Poetical Remains of M. M. Davidson," 1841;

WILLIAM HICKLING PRESCOTT

From an Engraving by H. W. Smith.

WASHINGTON IRVING

From an Engraving by H. B. Hall. After a Drawing by Wilkie, 1828.

"The Life of Oliver Goldsmith," 1844; "A Book of the Hudson" (edited by "Geoffrey Crayon"), 1849; "The Life of Mahomet," 1850; "The Lives of Mahomet and his Successors," 1850; "Chronicles of Wolfert's Roost," 1855; "Life of Washington," vols. I, II, 1855; vol. III, 1856; vol. IV, 1857; vol. V, 1859; "Wolfert Webber," 1856; "Works" (15 vols.), 1857. *Posthumous:* "Spanish Papers," ed. by P. M. Irving, 1866; "Biographies and Miscellaneous Papers," ed. by P. M. Irving, 1867. He *translated:* Navarette's "Collection de los Viages, etc.," 1825; and *edited:* Campbell's "Poems," 1810; Bonneville's "Rocky Mountains," 1843. *Collected Works:* in 1 vol., 1834; in 27 vols., 1880–83. *Life:* "Life and Letters," by P. M. Irving, 1862–63.—SHARP, R. FARQUHARSON, 1897, *A Dictionary of English Authors, p.* 145.

PERSONAL

Poor Washington is dead three months ago! I almost shed a tear when I heard it: it was a dream of mine that we two should be friends.—CARLYLE, THOMAS, 1823, *To John A. Carlyle, Nov.* 11; *Early Letters, ed. Norton, p.* 294.

He is so sensible, sound, and straightforward in his way of seeing everything, and at the same time so full of hopefulness, so simple, unaffected, true, and good, that it is a privilege to converse with him, for which one is the wiser, the happier and the better.—KEMBLE, FRANCES ANN, 1833, *Letter, April* 10; *Records of a Girlhood, p.* 572.

At Paris I had the happiness to know Washington Irving, whom I found as amiable as he is eminent.—BRYDGES, SIR SAMUEL EGERTON, 1834, *Autobiography, vol.* II, *p.* 169.

There is no man in the world who could have given me the heartfelt pleasure you have, by your kind note of the 13th of last month. There is no living writer, and there are very few among the dead, whose approbation I should feel so proud to earn. And with everything you have written upon my shelves, and in my thoughts, and in my heart of hearts, I may honestly and truly say so. If you could know how earnestly I write this, you would be glad to read it—as I hope you will be, faintly guessing at the warmth of the hand I autobiographically hold out to you over the broad Atlantic. . . . I have been so accustomed to associate you with my pleasantest and happiest thoughts and with my leisure hours, that I rush at once into full confidence with you, and fall, as it were naturally, and by the very laws of gravity, into your open arms.—DICKENS, CHARLES, 1841, *To Irving; Life and Letters of Washington Irving, ed. Irving, vol.* III, *pp.* 164, 165.

The mansion of this prosperous and valiant family, so often celebrated in his writings, is the residence of Washington Irving. It is approached by a sequestered road, which enhances the effect of its natural beauty. A more tranquil and protected abode, nestled in the lap of nature, never captivated a poet's eye. Rising from the bank of the river, which a strip of woodland alone intercepts, it unites every rural charm to the most complete seclusion. From this interesting domain is visible the broad surface of the Tappan Zee; the grounds slope to the water's edge, and are bordered by wooded ravines; a clear brook ripples near, and several neat paths lead to shadowy walks or fine points of river scenery. The house itself is a graceful combination of the English cottage and the Dutch farmhouse. The crow-stepped gables, and tiles in the hall, and the weather cocks, partake of the latter character; while the white walls gleaming through the trees, the smooth and verdant turf, and the mantling vines of ivy and clambering roses, suggest the former.—TUCKERMAN, HENRY THEODORE, 1853-96, *Homes of American Authors, ed. Hubbard, p.* 291.

He was in the habit of rising in the night, between twelve and four o'clock, and reading, or even writing for half an hour or an hour. He did not get, on the average, more than four hours' sleep at night, but often took short naps in the afternoon and evening. This natural, or at least habitual, irregularity of sleep, became aggravated to extreme nervousness and restlessness after an attack of fever and ague in the autumn of 1858. He was still suffering from the effects of this when I saw him. But beneath all these disturbances lay a deeper difficulty, which was distinctly mentioned to me in his physician's letter as "enlargement of the heart," accompanied by "an obstructed circulation." Under these influences, with growing age to weaken the power of resistance, his health gradually declined, until the flame of life, which had been getting paler and feebler, was blown out, as it were, by a single breath: a gentle end of a sweet and lovely life,—such an end as Nature prepares by slow and measured approaches and consummates with swift kindness when she grants the blessing of euthanasia to her favorite children.— HOLMES, OLIVER WENDELL, 1859, *Remarks at a Meeting of the Massachusetts Historical Society, Dec.* 15; *Proceedings, vol.* 4, *p.* 421.

I had the pleasure of meeting Mr. Irving in Spain; and found the author, whom I had loved, repeated in the man,—the same playful humor, the same touches of sentiment, the same poetic atmosphere, and what I admired still more, the entire absence of all literary jealousy, of all that mean avarice of fame, which counts what is given to another as so much taken from one's self,—

> "And rustling, hears in every breeze
> The laurels of Miltiades."

—LONGFELLOW, HENRY WADSWORTH, 1859, *Remarks at a Meeting of the Massachusetts Historical Society, Dec.* 15; *Proceedings, vol.* 4, *p.* 394.

Great and varied as was the genius of Mr. Irving, there was one thing he shrunk with a comical terror from attempting; and that was a *dinner-speech.* A great dinner, however, was to be given to Mr. Dickens in New York, as one had already been given in Boston; and it was evident to all, that no man but Washington Irving could be thought of to preside. With all his dread of making a speech, he was obliged to obey the universal call, and to accept the painful pre-eminence. . . . Under the circumstances,—an invited guest, with no impending speech,—I sat calmly, and watched with interest the imposing scene. I had the honor to be placed next but one to Mr. Irving, and the great pleasure of sharing in his conversation. He had brought the manuscript of his speech, and laid it under his plate. "I shall certainly break down," he repeated over and over again. At last, the moment arrived. Mr. Irving rose, and was received with deafening and long-continued applause, which by no means lessened his apprehension. He began in his pleasant voice; got through two or three sentences pretty easily, but in the next hesitated; and, after one or two attempts to go on, gave it up, with a graceful allusion to the tournament, and the troops of knights all armed and eager for the fray; ended with the toast, "Charles Dickens, the guest of the nation." "There," said he, as he resumed his seat under a repetition of the applause which had saluted his rising,— "there I told you I should break down; and I've done it." There certainly never was made a shorter after-dinner speech: I doubt if there ever was a more successful one. The manuscript seemed to be a dozen or twenty pages long; but the printed speech was not as many lines.—FELTON, CORNELIUS CONWAY, 1859, *Remarks at a Meeting of the Massachusetts Historical Society, Dec.* 15; *Proceedings, vol.* 4, *pp.* 411, 412.

William Irving, the father of the great author, was a native of Scotland—one of a race in which the instinct of veneration is strong—and a Scottish woman was employed as a nurse in his household. It is related that one day while she was walking in the street with her little charge, then five years old, she saw General Washington in a shop, and entering, led up the boy, whom she presented as one to whom his name had been given. The general turned, laid his hand on the child's head, and gave him his smile and his blessing, little thinking that they were bestowed upon his future biographer. The gentle pressure of that hand Irving always remembered, and that blessing, he believed, attended him through life. Who shall say what power that recollection may have had in keeping him true to high and generous aims? . . . From the time that he began the composition of his "Sketch Book," his whole life was the life of an author. His habits of composition were, however, by no means regular. When he was in the vein, the periods would literally stream from his pen; at other times he would scarcely write anything. For two years after the failure of his brothers at Liverpool, he found it almost impossible to write a line. He was throughout life an early riser, and when in the mood, would write all the morning and till late in the day, wholly engrossed with his subject. In the evening he was ready for any cheerful pastime, in which he took part with an animation almost amounting to high spirits. These intervals of excitement and intense labor, sometimes lasting for weeks, were succeeded by languor, and at times by depression of spirits, and for months the pen would lie untouched; even to answer a letter at these times was an irksome task.

—BRYANT, WILLIAM CULLEN, 1860, *Washington Irving, Orations and Addresses, pp.* 98, 149.

I had always too much earnest *respect* for Mr. Irving ever to claim familiar intimacy with him. He was a man who would unconsciously and quietly command deferential regard and consideration; for in all his ways and words there was the atmosphere of true refinement. He was emphatically a gentleman, in the best sense of that word. Never forbidding nor morose, he was at times (indeed always, when quite well) full of genial humour,—sometimes overflowing with fun. . . . Mr. Irving was never a systematic collector of books, and his little library at Sunnyside might have disappointed those who would expect to see there rich shelves of choice editions, and a full array of all the favorite authors among whom such a writer would delight to revel. Some rather antiquated tomes in Spanish,—different sets of Calderon and Cervantes, and of some modern French and German authors,—a presentation-set of Cadell's "Waverley," as well as that more recent and elegant emanation from the classic press of Houghton,—a moderate amount of home-tools for the "Life of Washington," (rare materials were consulted in the town-libraries and at Washington)—and the remainder of his books were evidently a haphazard collection, many coming from the authors, with their respects, and thus sometimes costing the recipient their full (intrinsic) value in writing a letter of acknowledgment. . . . One rather curious characteristic of Mr. Irving was excessive, unaffected modesty and distrust of himself and of his own writings. Considering how many a *débutant* in letters, not yet out of his teens, is so demonstratively self-confident as to the prospective effect of his genius on an expecting and admiring world, it was always remarkable to hear a veteran, whose fame for half a century had been cosmopolitan, expressing the most timid doubts as to his latest compositions, and fearing that they were unequal to their position,—so unwilling, too, to occupy an inch of ground to which any other writer might properly lay claim.—PUTNAM, GEORGE P., 1860, *Recollections of Irving, Atlantic Monthly, vol.* 6, pp. 603, 608, 609.

The first ambassador whom the New World of Letters sent to the Old. He was born almost with the republic; the *pater patriæ* had laid his hand on the child's head. He bore Washington's name: he came amongst us bringing the kindest sympathy, the most artless, smiling good will. His new country (which some people here might be disposed to regard rather superciliously) could send us, as he showed in his own person, a gentleman, who, though himself born in no very high sphere, was most finished, polished, easy, witty, quiet; and, socially, the equal of the most refined Europeans. If Irving's welcome in England was a kind one, was it not also gratefully remembered? If he ate our salt, did he not pay us with a thankful heart? Who can calculate the amount of friendliness and good feeling for our country which this writer's generous and untiring regard for us disseminated in his own? His books are read by millions of his countrymen, whom he has taught to love England, and why to love her. . . . Was Irving not good, and, of his works, was not his life the best part? In his family, gentle, generous, good-humoured, affectionate, self-denying: in society, a delightful example of complete gentlemanhood; quite unspoiled by prosperity; never obsequious to the great (or, worse still, to the base and mean, as some public men are forced to be in his and other countries); eager to acknowledge every contemporary's merit; always kind and affable to the young members of his calling; in his professional bargains and mercantile dealings delicately honest and grateful; one of the most charming masters of our lighter literature; the constant friend to us and our nation; to men of letters doubly dear, not for his wit and genius merely, but as an example of goodness, probity, and pure life.—THACKERAY, WILLIAM MAKEPEACE, 1860, *Nil Nisi Bonum, Roundabout Papers.*

On retiring for the night, at half past ten, his niece Sarah, who always took charge of his medicines, went into his room to place them, as usual, within easy reach. "Well," he exclaimed, "I must arrange my pillows for another weary night!" and then, as if half to himself, "If this could only end!" or "When will this end!" she could not tell which; for, at the instant, he gave a slight exclamation, as if of pain, pressing his hand on his left side, repeated the exclamation and the pressure, caught at the footboard of the bed, and fell backward to the floor. The sound of his fall and the screams of Sarah brought the whole family in an instant to his room. I raised his head in my arms. Every means was resorted to to recall animation, and continued until a physician—Dr. Caruthers, from a distance of two miles—arrived, who pronounced life entirely extinct. He had passed away instantaneously. The end for which he had just been sighing—the end, which to him had no terrors—had come. His departure was sudden; but so he was willing it should be. In the fulness of years, with unclouded intellect, crowned with the warmest affections of his countrymen, and with an assured hope of a happy immortality, he had gone down, according to his own pathetic aspiration, "with all sail set." Who that loved him would have wished to recall him!—IRVING, PIERRE M., 1864, *The Life and Letters of Washington Irving, vol.* IV, *p.* 326.

It was only a quiet old gentleman of six-and-seventy who was buried awhile ago from his home upon the Hudson: yet the village shops were all closed; the streets, the houses, the station, were hung in black; thousands from the city thirty miles away thronged the high-road leading to the little church where prayers were to be said. How shall we explain this? The author is dead, indeed, whose writings were admired by all; but there is something worthier to be said than this:—At the little church lay the body of the man whom all men loved.—MITCHELL, DONALD G., 1864, *Washington Irving, Atlantic Monthly, vol.* 13, *p.* 701.

Washington Irving—the least American of Americans I ever encountered. He was not brilliant in conversation; but good sense, as well as good nature, made him a most agreeable companion.—PLANCHÉ, J. R., 1872, *Recollections and Reflections, vol.* I, *p.* 119.

It is not necessary to dwell upon the small scandal about Irving's un-American feeling. If there was ever a man who loved his country and was proud of it; whose broad, deep, and strong patriotism did not need the saliency of ignorant partisanship, it was Washington Irving. He was like his namesake an American, and with the same pure loyalty and unpartisan candor. —WARNER, CHARLES DUDLEY, 1881, *Washington Irving, p.* 118.

Washington Irving, when I knew him, was past the zenith both of his life and his fame. He was inclined to rest and be thankful, to wear placidly the crown of bays that his intellectual activity had woven for him, in earlier years; and so I found him, as others found him, sleepy in a double sense—physically and mentally. —HALL, SAMUEL CARTER, 1883, *Retrospect of a Long Life, p.* 421.

"Sunnyside" and its neighborhood is already classic soil. As each season recurs uncounted pilgrims visit its delightful precincts. The winding lane, shaded by magnificent elms and chestnuts, through whose foliage the sunlight at intervals finds its way; the tumbling brooklet chasing along grassy slopes, under steep banks and down the rocky ravine; the noble Hudson, sweeping in grandeur past bold promontories and thriving villages, bearing on its bosom the commerce of a thriving country; the quaint little ivy-covered cottage itself, with white walls and antique weathervanes—all these combine to please the taste and to feed the imagination; and, far more than the simple marble slab that marks his last resting place on the slope of Sleepy Hollow, form the enduring monument of the man who introduced American letters and literature to the notice of the world.—HULBERT, HENRY W., 1884, *Magazine of American History, vol.* 12, *p.* 161.

In the evening of life, surrounded by those that were near and dear—with "troops of friends,"—good health—an income derived from his literary labours more than sufficient for the modest wants of his household—with a name honoured wherever our language is spoken, and without a single hostile voice being raised against him, he certainly presented a beautiful picture of a serene and happy old age. The traditionary recollection of his early life is burdened with no stain of any sort, and his whole career was marked by undeviating integrity and purity, insomuch that no scandalous whisper was ever circulated against him. Along with great simplicity of manners, he was characterized by perfect uprightness, and was invariably kind and gracious to all. It was impossible to detect from his conversation that he grounded the slightest title to consideration upon his literary fame.— WILSON, JAMES GRANT, 1885, *Bryant and His Friends, p.* 175.

The stone that marks his grave is a plain slab of white marble on which are engraved his name and date alone, without any memorial inscription. The path that leads to the entrance gate of the plot is so worn by the feet of visitors that a stranger hardly needs to ask his way to the place. I confess I heard not without a secret pleasure that the relic-hunters so chip and hammer the stone that marks Irving's grave as to make its frequent renewal necessary. It did not seem to me a grievous wrong, nor in any true sense a profanation of the grave, but rather a testimony to the lovableness of Irving's character, and an evidence of the wide extent of his fame, that, from filling the circle of the educated and refined among his countrymen, has now come to include that lower stratum of our common humanity which has only instinctive and, so to speak, mechanical ways of expressing its feelings. Who is so insensible to the good opinion of his kind as not to think such a trodden path as this that leads to Irving's grave better than any written line of praise, and the very destruction of his monument, by this reprehensible clipping and chipping, a more enduring testimony to his work than any monument of brass!—COOK, CLARENCE, 1887, *A Glimpse of Washington Irving at Home, The Century, vol. 34, p. 53.*

When he died an old man, a lock to which he himself had always kept the key was found to guard a braid of hair and a beautiful miniature, with a slip of paper marked in his own handwriting, "Matilda Hoffman." No less faithfully had he kept her Bible and Prayer-Book throughout his life. Of the miniature his publisher George P. Putman, told the story of having once had it retouched and remounted for its possessor, forty years after Miss Hoffman's death. "When I returned it to him in a suitable velvet case," said Mr. Putman, "he took it to a quiet corner and looked intently on the face for some minutes, apparently unobserved, his tears falling freely on the glass as he gazed." Who shall say that the cherishing of such a memory as this did not find its direct expression in the gentle chivalry with which he bore himself, as a writer and as a man, towards all women. —HOWE, M. A. DE WOLFE, 1898, *American Bookmen, p. 11.*

One fact about him will perhaps bear emphasis; that with all his gentlenesses he was strong and firm and full of spirit. He was susceptible to advice, yet nobody ever forced him to do a thing that was against his mind or conscience. That he was amiable, congenial, companionable—we do not forget these traits of his; we should remember, too, that he never faced an emergency to which he did not prove himself equal. His personal hold upon his contemporaries was plainly due to the fact that their confidence in him as a man was as perfect as their delight in him as an artist. What he did was, after all, only a little part of what he was.—BOYNTON, HENRY W., 1901, *Washington Irving, p. 116.*

SALMAGUNDI
1807

We have no hesitation in saying at the outset, that we consider the good papers of "Salmagundi," and the greater part of the Knickerbocker, superior to the "Sketch-Book." . . . It ["Salmagundi"] was exceedingly pleasant morning, or after-dinner reading, never taking up too much of a gentleman's time from his business and pleasures, nor so exalted and spiritualized as to seem mystical to his far-seeing vision. . . . Though its wit is sometimes forced, and its serious style sometimes false, upon looking it over we have found it full of entertainment, with an infinite variety of characters and circumstances, and with that amiable, good-natured wit and pathos, which shows that the heart has not grown hard while making merry of the world.—DANA, RICHARD HENRY, 1819, *The Sketch Book, North American Review, vol. 9, pp. 323, 334, 344.*

We all remember the success of "Salmagundi," to which he was a large and distinguished contributor; with what rapidity and to what extent it circulated through America; how familiar it made us with the local pleasantry and the personal humours of New York, and what an abiding influence it has had in that city, by forming a sort of school of wit of a character somewhat marked and peculiar and superior to every thing our country has witnessed, except, perhaps, that of the wits of the Anarchiad in Connecticut.—EVERETT, EDWARD, 1822, *Bracebridge Hall, North American Review, vol. 15, p. 206.*

The production of Paulding, Irving, Verplanck, and perhaps of others, in partnership:—the papers of Paulding are more

sarcastic, ill-natured, acrimonious,—bitter,
—than those of Irving: but quite as able.
Those by Verplanck we do not know; we
have only *heard* of him as one of the
writers.— NEAL, JOHN, 1825, *American
Writers, Blackwood's Magazine, vol.* 17,
p. 61.

The better pieces are written in Mr. Irving's best manner. Take it altogether, it
was certainly a production of extraordinary
merit, and was instantaneously and universally recognised as such by the public. It
wants of course the graver merits of the
modern British collections of Essays; but
for spirit, effect, and actual literary value,
we doubt whether any publication of the
class since "The Spectator," upon which
it is directly modelled, can fairly be put in
competition with it.—EVERETT, ALEX-
ANDER HILL, 1829, *Irving's Life of Columbus, North American Review, vol.* 28, *p.* 116.

The little paper called "Salmagundi,"
written by Washington and William Irving
and James Kirke Paulding, was simply
Addison's great ghost, transferred to New
York and transformed into a censor of
Knickerbocker society. Its Launcelot
Langstaff, William Wizard, and Anthony
Evergreen, its essays on men and things of
the day, and its occasional sharp thrusts of
wit, made their little shivery sensations
in provincial New York, and were duly
and promptly forgotten. — RICHARDSON,
CHARLES F., 1887, *American Literature,*
1607-1885, *vol.* I, *p.* 264.

A HISTORY OF NEW YORK BY DIEDRICH KNICKERBOCKER.

1809

I beg you to accept my best thanks for
the uncommon degree of entertainment
which I have received from the most excellent jocose of New York. I am sensible,
that, as a stranger to American parties
and politics, I must lose much of the concealed satire of the piece; but I must own,
that, looking at the simple and obvious
meaning only, I have never read anything
so closely resembling the style of Dean
Swift as the annals of Diedrich Knickerbocker. I have been employed these few
evenings in reading them aloud to Mrs. S.,
and two ladies who are our guests; and our
sides have been absolutely sore with laughing. I think, too, there are passages which
indicate that the author possesses powers
of a different kind, and has some touches
which remind me much of Sterne.—SCOTT,

SIR WALTER, 1813, *Letter to Carson Brevoort,
April* 23.

It is painful to see a mind as admirable
for exquisite perception of the beautiful, as
it is for its quick sense of the ridiculous,
wasting the richness of its fancy on
an ungrateful theme, and its exuberant
humor in a coarse caricature.—VERPLANCK,
GULIAN C., 1818, *Address before the New
York Historical Society, Dec.* 7.

It has the same faults and same good
qualities in its style, its wit and humour,
and its characters are evidently by the
same hand, as the leading ones in "Salmagundi," though not copies from them. They
are perfectly fresh and original, and suited
to their situations. Too much of the first
part of the first volume is laborious and up-
hill; and there are places, here and there,
in the last part, to which there is the same
objection. Our feelings seldom flag in the
second.—DANA, RICHARD HENRY, 1819,
*The Sketch Book, North American Review,
vol.* 9, *p.* 345.

A work to be compared with anything
of the kind in our language; a book of
unwearying pleasantry, which, instead of
flashing out, as English and American
humour is wont, from time to time, with
long and dull intervals, is kept up with a
true French vivacity from beginning to
end; a book which, if it have a fault, has
only that of being too pleasant, too sustained a tissue of merriment and ridicule.—
EVERETT, EDWARD, 1822, *Bracebridge Hall,
North American Review, vol.* 15, *p.* 206.

Conceived, matured, and brought forth,
in a bold, original temper—unaided—and
alone—by Irving: more entirely the natural
thought, language, humour, and feeling of
the man himself—without imitation or
plagiarism—far more—than either of his
late works: It was written, too, in the
fervour and flush of his popularity, at
home—after he had got a name, such as no
other man had, among his countrymen;
after "Salmagundi" had been read, with
pleasure, all over North America: In it,
however, there is a world of rich allusion—
a vein of sober caricature—the merit of
which is little understood here. . . .
By nine readers out of ten, perhaps,
"Knickerbocker" is read, as a piece of
generous drollery—nothing more. Be it
so. It will wear the better. The design of
Irving himself is not always clear: nor was

he always undeviating, in his course. Truth or fable, fact or falsehood—it was all the same to him, if a bit of material came in his way. In a word, we look upon this volume of "Knickerbocker," though it *is* tiresome, though there *are* some wretched failures in it; a little overdoing of the humorous— and a little confusion of purpose, through- out—as a work, honourable to English literature—manly — bold — and so *alto- gether original*, without being extravagant, as to stand alone, among the labours of men.—NEAL, JOHN, 1825, *American Writers, Blackwood's Magazine, vol. 17, pp. 61, 62.*

At the first appearance of my work, its aim and drift were misapprehended by some of the descendants of the Dutch worthies; and I understand that now and then one may still be found to re- gard it with a captious eye. The far greater part, however, I have reason to flatter myself, receive my good-humoured picturings in the same temper in which they were executed; and when I find, after a lapse of forty years, the haphazard pro- duction of my youth still cherished among them,—when I find its very name become a "household word" and used to give the home stamp to everything recommended for popular acceptation, such as Knicker- bocker societies, Knickerbocker insurance companies, Knickerbocker steamboats, Knickerbocker omnibuses, Knickerbocker bread, and Knickerbocker ice,—and when I find New Yorkers of Dutch descent priding themselves upon being "genuine Knicker- bockers,"—I please myself with the per- suasion that I have struck the right cord; that my dealings with the good old Dutch times, and the customs and usages derived from them, are in harmony with the feel- ings and humors of my townsmen; that I have opened a vein of pleasant associations and quaint characteristics peculiar to my native place, and which its inhabitants will not willingly suffer to pass away; and that, though other histories of New York may appear of higher claims to learned accep- tation, and may take their dignified and appropriate rank in the family library, Knickerbocker's history will still be re- ceived with good-humored indulgence, and be thumbed and chuckled over by the family fireside.— IRVING, WASHINGTON, 1848, *A History of New York, The Author's Apology.*

The most remarkable instance of obtuse- ness to light letters that I ever met with occurred in another region. Goeller, a German editor of Thucydides, in annotat- ing a passage of the Greek historian, de- scribing the violence of the Athenian fac- tions, gives two modern illustrations: one of the Guelf and Ghibelline parties in Italy; the other—he cites Washington Irving and his book very gravely in Latin—the factions of long pipes and short pipes in New York, under the administration of Peter Stuyve- sant. Imagine this erudite and ponderous German poring over Knickerbocker as seriously as over Guicciardini's "History of the Italian Republics."—REED, HENRY, 1850-55, *Lectures on English Literature from Chaucer to Tennyson, p. 343.*

The happy idea of a humorous descrip- tion of his native town, under the old Dutch governors, was no sooner con- ceived than executed with inimitable wit and originality. — TUCKERMAN, HENRY THEODORE, 1852, *A Sketch of American Literature.*

In the class of compositions to which it belongs, I know of nothing happier than this work in our language. It has prob- ably been read as widely, and with as keen a relish, as anything from Mr. Irving's pen. —EVERETT, EDWARD, 1859, *Remarks at a Meeting of the Massachusetts Historical Society, Dec. 15; Proceedings, vol. 4, p. 396.*

Of all mock-heroic works, "Knicker- bocker's History of New York" is the gay- est, the airiest, and the least tiresome.— BRYANT, WILLIAM CULLEN, 1860, *Wash- ington Irving, Orations and Addresses, p. 114.*

The work abounds in humor and droll- ery from beginning to end, and in this respect is excelled by few if any works of a similar character and aim that were ever published. — ADAMS, CHARLES, 1870, *Memoir of Washington Irving, p. 53.*

After some preliminary essays in humor- ous literature his genius arrived at the age of *indiscretion*, and he produced at the age of twenty-six the most deliciously audacious work of humor in our literature, namely, "The History of New York, by Diedrich Knickerbocker." . . . It may be said of Irving that he not only caricatured, but had the courage of his caricatures. The persons whom he covered with ridicule were the ancestors of the leading families of New York, and these families prided themselves on their descent. After the publication of such a book he could hardly enter the "best society" of New York, to which he naturally belonged, without running the risk of being insulted, especially by the elderly women of fashion; but he conquered their prejudices by the same grace and geniality of manner by the same unmistakable tokens that he was an inborn gentleman, through which he afterward won his way into the first society of England, France, Germany, Italy, and Spain.— WHIPPLE, EDWIN PERCY, 1876-86, *American Literature and Other Papers, ed. Whittier, p.* 43.

It tickled the very midriff of the country, from Maine to Georgia, and years afterward the echoes of the thing were still running up and down England and France. It was too funny, some of the good dames of Albany thought; and they were a long time in forgiving the author.—MORSE, JAMES HERBERT, 1883, *Washington Irving, The Critic, vol.* 3, *p.* 137.

A sober and just eulogy of the early settlers of New York would never have been conferred upon them the immortality which they enjoy in the "Knickerbocker," nor embalmed them in such affectionate remembrance as we all hold them in. People are not proud to claim kinship with ancestors who are merely ridiculous, nor would it now be considered an honor to descend from Irving's heroes, if his genius had not thrown about his amusing portraiture of them an atmosphere of fond regard—if we did not see in them certain qualities of human nature that touch our hearts. The humour that depicted them was poetic as well as playful, and they exist for us in that Indian-summer haze of content and comfortable innocence which fortunately hides the faults of all the dear departed out of this life.—WARNER, CHARLES DUDLEY, 1883, *Irving's Humor, The Critic, vol.* 3, *p.* 139.

We need not speak of him at great length, for his strictly historical works were few, and his fame was mainly achieved in other walks of literature. Nor did he have a great influence upon the development of historical writing among us, unless in the way of general influence upon American style. In fact, it is quite possible that no one of his mature and sober pieces of writing had as much real effect on the progress of American historiography as the admirable humorous composition with which he began, as far back as 1809,— the "History of New York" by Diedrich Knickerbocker. Aside from its striking success as a literary production, the book had a great effect in awakening interest in the early or Dutch period of New York history. Descendants rushed with sober indignation to the defense of ancestors at whom the genial humorist poked his fun, and very likely the great amount of work which the state government in the next generation did for the historical illustration of the Dutch period, through the researches of Mr. Brodhead in foreign archives, had this unhistorical little book for one of its principal causes. But, on the other hand, he made it permanently difficult for the American public to take a serious view of those early Dutch days. Oloffe the Dreamer and Walter the Doubter, Abraham with the ten breeches and Stuyvesant with the wooden leg, have become too thoroughly domesticated among us to admit of that.—JAMESON, J. FRANKLIN, 1891, *The History of Historical Writing in America, p.* 97.

THE SKETCH-BOOK
1819

Everywhere in it I find the marks of a mind of the utmost elegance and refinement, a thing as you know that I was not exactly prepared to look for in an American. . . . Each of the essays is entitled to its appropriate praise, and the whole is such as I scarcely know an Englishman that could have written it. The author powerfully conciliates to himself our kindness and affection. But the Essay on Rural Life in England is incomparably the best. It is, I believe, all true; and one wonders, while reading, that nobody ever said this before. There is wonderful sweetness in it.—GODWIN, WILLIAM, 1819, *Letter to James Ogilvie, Sept.* 15; *Life and Letters of Washington Irving, ed. Irving, vol.* I, *p.* 422.

We believe that the public law of literature has entirely exempted periodical publications from the jurisdiction of the ordinary critical tribunals; and we therefore notice the first number of this work without any intention of formal criticism, but simply for the purpose of announcing its appearance, and of congratulating the

American public that one of their choicest favorites has, after a long interval, again resumed his pen. It will be needless to inform any that have read the book, that it is from the pen of Mr. Irving. His rich, and sometimes extravagant humor, his gay and graceful fancy, his peculiar choice and felicity of original expression, as well as the pure and fine moral feeling which imperceptibly pervades every thought and image, without being anywhere ostentatious or dogmatic, betray the author in every page; even without the aid of those minor peculiarities of style, taste, and local allusions, which at once identify the travelled Geoffrey Crayon with the venerable Knickerbocker.—VERPLANCK, GULIAN C., 1819, *Analectic Magazine, July.*

But though it is primarily for its style and composition that we are induced to notice this book, it would be quite unjust to the author not to add, that he deserves very high commendation for its more substantial qualities; and that we have seldom seen a work that gave us a more pleasing impression of the writer's character, or a more favorite one of his judgment and taste. . . . It seemed fair and courteous not to stint a stranger on his first introduction to our pages: but what we have quoted, we are persuaded, will justify all that we have said in its favour. . . . We have found the book in the hands of most of those to whom we have the thought of mentioning it.—JEFFREY, FRANCIS LORD, 1820, *The Sketch Book, Edinburgh Review, vol.* 34, *pp.* 161, 168, 176.

Few recent publications have been so well received in England as "The Sketch-Book." Several of the Waverley novels have passed through fewer editions than this agreeable work, and the journals of the most consequence have paid the highest compliments to its merit. We are nevertheless free to confess that we think "The Sketch-Book" as a whole, inferior to the author's earlier writings.—EVERETT, EDWARD, 1822, *Bracebridge Hall, North American Review, vol.* 15, *p.* 208.

Of the merit of his "Knickerbocker" and New York stories, we cannot pretend to judge. But in his "Sketch-Book" and "Bracebridge Hall" he gives us very good American copies of our British Essayists and Novelists, which may be very well on the other side of the water, or as proofs of the capabilities of the national genius, but

which might be dispensed with here, where we have to boast of the originals. Not only Mr. Irving's language is with great taste and felicity modelled on that of Addison, Goldsmith, Sterne, or Mackenzie; but the thoughts and sentiments are taken at the rebound, and as they are brought forward at the present period, want both freshness and probability. Mr. Irving's writings are literary *anachronisms.* He comes to England for the first [the second] time; and, being on the spot, fancies himself in the midst of those characters and manners which he had read in the Spectator and other approved authors, and which were the only idea he had hitherto formed of the parent-country. Instead of looking round to see what *we are,* he sets to work to describe us as *we were*—at second-hand. —HAZLITT, WILLIAM, 1825, *The Spirit of the Age.*

The "Sketch-Book" is a timid, beautiful work; with some childish pathos in it; some rich, pure, bold poetry: a little squeamish, pulling, lady-like sentimentality: some courageous writing, some wit, and a world of humour, so happy, so natural, so altogether unlike that of any other man, dead or alive, that we would rather have been the writer of it, fifty times over, than of every thing else that he has ever written.—NEAL, JOHN, 1825, *American Writers, Blackwood's Magazine, vol.* 17, *p.* 64.

Every reader has his first book: I mean to say, one book, among all others, which, in early youth, first fascinates his imagination, and at once excites and satisfies the desires of his mind. To me, this first book was the "Sketch-Book" of Washington Irving. I was a school-boy when it was published, and read each succeeding number with ever-increasing wonder and delight,—spellbound by its pleasant humor, its melancholy tenderness, its atmosphere of revery; nay, even by its gray-brown covers, the shaded letters of the titles, and the fair, clear type,—which seemed an outward symbol of the style. How many delightful books the same author has given us, written before and since,—volumes of history and of fiction, most of which illustrate his native land, and some of which illuminate it, and make the Hudson, I will not say as classic, but as romantic as the Rhine! Yet still the charm of the "Sketch-Book" remains unbroken; the old fascination still lingers about it; and whenever I open its pages, I open also that mysterious door which leads back into the haunted chambers of youth.—LONGFELLOW, HENRY WADSWORTH, 1859, *Remarks at a Meeting of the Massachusetts Historical Society, Dec. 15; Proceedings, vol. 4, p. 393.*

The style of the sketches is everywhere his own—pure, chaste, easy, flowing; often elegant, and always appropriate to the theme in hand; rich, yet not extravagant with varied and pertinent imagery—pleasant flowers of speech intermingling themselves with his graceful and facile style, presenting themselves not in gorgeous superabundance as in some artificial garden of beauty, but constantly occurring in a sort of natural order and variety, like the floral adornments that greet us as we glance along some cultivated and beautiful landscape.—ADAMS, CHARLES, 1870, *Memoir of Washington Irving, p. 93.*

Pathos is the great touchstone of humor, and Irving's pathos is always a lamentable failure. Is it not very significant, that he should have made so little of the story of Rip Van Winkle? In his sketch which has won so wide a fame and given a lasting association to the Kaatskills, there is not a suspicion of the immense pathos which the skill of an industrious playwright and the genius of that rare actor, Mr. Jefferson, have since developed from the tale. The Dame Van Winkle that we know now is the creation of Mr. Boucicault; to him it is we owe that vigorous character,—a scold, a tyrant to her husband, but nevertheless full of relentful womanliness, and by the justice of her cause exciting our sympathy almost as much as Rip himself does. . . . Certainly we should, as the case stands, have missed the whole immortal figment, had not Irving given it to us in germ; the fact that our playwright and our master comedian have made it so much greater and more beautiful does not annul that primary service; but, looking at the matter historically, we must admit that Irving's share in the credit is that of the first projector of a scientific improvement, and the latter sort of person always has to forego a great part of his fame in favor of the one who consummates the discovery. I am willing to believe that there was a peculiar advantage in Irving's treatment; namely, that he secured for his story a quicker and more general acceptance than might have been granted to something more profound; but

this does not alter the critical judgment that we have to pass upon it. If Irving had grasped the tragic sphere at all, he would have shone more splendidly in the comic. But the literary part of him, at least, never passed into the shade: it somehow contrived to be always on that side of the earth which was towards the sun.—LATHROP, GEORGE PARSONS, 1876, *A Study of Hawthorne, pp. 304, 305, 306.*

His stories of "Rip Van Winkle" and the "Sleepy Hollow" are among the finest pieces of original fictitious writing that this century has produced.—CHAMBERS, ROBERT, 1876, *Cyclopædia of English Literature, ed. Carruthers.*

One of those strokes of genius ["Rip Van Winkle"] that recreate the world and clothe it with unfading hues of romance; the theme was an old-world echo, transformed by genius into a primal story that will endure as long as the Hudson flows through its mountains to the sea. A great artist can paint a great picture on a small canvas.—WARNER, CHARLES DUDLEY, 1881, *Washington Irving (American Men of Letters), p. 119.*

Every reader of Washington Irving knows the story of Rip Van Winkle's adventure of the Kaatskill Mountains,—that delightful, romantic idyl, in which character, humor, and fancy are so delicately blended. Under the spell of Jefferson's acting we are transported into the past, and made to see, as with bodily eyes, the old-fashioned Dutch civilization as it crept up the borders of the Hudson: the quaint and quiet villages; the stout Hollanders, with their pipes and schnapps; the loves and troubles of an elder generation.—WINTER, WILLIAM, 1881, *The Jeffersons (American Actor Series), p. 201.*

The best example of his powers is the "Sketch-Book," mild, cheerful, fanciful, thoughtful, humourous. "The Wife," "The Pride of the Village," and "The Broken Heart," are gems of sentiment and description. "Rip Van Winkle," and "Sleepy Hollow" are among the finest pieces of fiction to be found in any literature. As we read, we are all drawn to beauty, gentleness, sunshine, elevating seriousness, or chastening sorrow. It is fundamentally the fascination of the *man.* We are captivated by the poetic graces of his fancy and the liquid music of his style; but behind all, under all, pervading all, is the deeper charm of the genial and sensitive soul in sympathy with the human heart.— WELSH, ALFRED H., 1883, *Development of English Literature and Language, vol.* II, *p.* 305.

It is in the "Sketch-Book" that Irving first appeals to us as a torch-bearer in the great procession of English prose-writers. In "Knickerbocker" he had been dancing or skipping in the lightness of his heart to a delicious measure of his own; in "Salmagundi" he had waked up to a sense of literary responsibility, without quite knowing in what direction his new-found sense of style would lead him. In the "Sketch-Book" he is a finished and classic writer, bowing to the great tradition of English prose, and knowing precisely what it is that he would do, and how to do it. . . . If the mark of any modern writer is to be found on the early style of Washington Irving, it appears to me to be rather that of Cobbett than of any other. . . . It has taken its place in literature, and there is hardly a page in it which does not appeal to us with the salutary lesson that "there was a noble way, in former times, of saying things simply, and yet saying them proudly."—GOSSE, EDMUND, 1883, *Irving's "Sketch-Book," The Critic, vol.* 3, *pp.* 140, 141.

The best that ever came from his pen, one of the ten or twelve choicest books produced by an American: "The Sketch-Book."—RICHARDSON, CHARLES F., 1887, *American Literature,* 1607-1885, *vol.* I, *p.* 267.

In ten minutes I had gone to the house and returned to the barn with "The Sketch-Book." I had not read the story since I was a boy. I was disappointed in it; not as a story, of course, but the tale was purely a narrative. The theme was interesting, but not dramatic. The silver Hudson stretches out before you as you read; the quaint red roofs and queer gables of the old Dutch cottages stand out against the mist upon the mountains; but all this is descriptive. The character of Rip does not speak ten lines. What could be done dramatically with so simple a sketch? How could it be turned into an effective play? Three or four bad dramatisations of the story had already been acted, but without marked success. Yates, of London, had given one in which the hero dies; one had been acted by my father, one by Hackett,

and another by Burke. Some of these versions I had remembered when I was a boy, and I should say that Burke's play and the performance were the best; but nothing that I remembered gave me the slightest encouragement that I could get a good play out of any of the existing materials. . . . I got together three old printed versions of the drama and the story itself. The plays were all in two acts. I thought it would be an improvement in the drama to arrange it in three, making the scene with the spectre crew an act by itself. This would separate the poetical from the domestic side of the story. But by far the most important alteration was in the interview with the spirits. In the old versions, they spoke and sang. I remember that the effects of this ghastly dialogue was dreadfully human, so I arranged that no voice but Rip's should be heard. This was entirely my own invention. . . . In the seclusion of the barn, I studied and rehearsed the part; and by the end of the summer, I was prepared to transplant it from the rustic realms of an old farm-house to a cosmopolitan audience, in the city of Washington, where I opened at Carusi's Hall, under the management of John T. Raymond. . . . To be brief, the play was acted with a result that was, to me, both satisfactory and disappointing. I was quite sure that the character was what I had been seeking, and I was equally satisfied that the play was not. The action had neither the body nor the strength to carry the hero; the spiritual quality was there, but the human interest was wanting. This defect was not remedied until five years later, when I met Dion Boucicault, in London. Then, he agreed to rewrite the drama for a consideration agreed upon between us. He never seemed to think much of his labour in this play; but I did, and do still, with good reason. His version was still cast in three acts. Later, I divided the first act into two, making the end of the dance the end of an act, rather than the end of a scene, and enlarged and strengthened it in various ways suggested by my experience. It will thus be seen that the play is by no means the work of one mind, but both as to its narrative and dramatic form, has been often moulded, and by many hands.— JEFFERSON, JOSEPH, 1895, *Rip Van Winkle as played by Joseph Jefferson, Introduction, pp.* xii, xiii, xiv, xv.

BRACEBRIDGE HALL
1822

We have no hesitation in pronouncing "Bracebridge" quite equal to any thing which the present age of English literature has produced in this department. In saying this, we class it in the branch of essay-writing. . . . Besides the episodical tales, he has given us admirable sketches of life and manners, highly curious in themselves, and rendered almost important by the good-natured mock gravity, the ironical reverence, and lively wit, with which they are described. We can scarce express the delight with which we turn to the definite images such work excites, from the vagueness and generality of ordinary story-writing, where personages without prototypes in any society on earth speak a language learned out of books, without a trait of nature, life, or truth.—EVERETT, ED-WARD, 1822, *Bracebridge Hall, North American Review, vol.* 15, *pp.* 209, 223.

We have received so much pleasure from this book, that we think ourselves bound in gratitude, as well as justice, to make a public acknowledgment of it,—and seek to repay, by a little kind notice, the great obligations we shall ever feel to the author. . . . The great charm and peculiarity of this work consists now, as on former occasions, in the singular sweetness of the composition, and the mildness of the sentiments,—sicklied over perhaps a little, now and then, with that cloying heaviness into which unvaried sweetness is too apt to subside. The rhythm and melody of the sentences are certainly excessive: As it not only gives an air of mannerism, from its uniformity, but raises too strong an impression of the labour that must have been bestowed, and the importance which must have been attached to that which is, after all, but a secondary attribute to good writing. It is very ill-natured in us, however, to object to what has given us so much pleasure; for we happen to be very intense and sensitive admirers of those soft harmonies of studied speech in which this author is so apt to indulge himself; and have caught ourselves, oftener than we shall confess, neglecting his excellent matter, to lap ourselves in the liquid music of his periods—and letting ourselves float passively down the mellow falls and windings of his soft-flowing sentences, with a delight not inferior to that which we derive

from fine versification.—JEFFREY, FRANCIS LORD, 1822-44, *Bracebridge Hall, Contributions to the Edinburgh Review, vol.* IV, *pp.* 213, 214.

"Stout Gentleman"—very good; and a pretty fair account of a real occurrence; "Student of Salamanca": beneath contempt: Irving has no idea of genuine romance; or love—or anything else, we believe, that ever seriously troubles the blood of men:—"Rookery"—struck off in a few hours; contrary to what has been said: Irving does not labour as people suppose—he is too indolent—given, too much, we *know*, to revery; "Dolph Heyliger"; "The Haunted House"; "Storm Ship"— all in the fashion of his early time: perhaps—we are greatly inclined so to believe—perhaps the remains of what was meant for "Salmagundi," or "Knickerbocker": —the rest of the two volumes quite unworthy of Irving's reputation.—NEAL, JOHN, 1825, *American Writers, Blackwood's Magazine, vol.* 17, *p.* 66.

In by-gone times, when Irving left that Hall, he left sitting in an old oak chair, in a small parlor of the Boar's Head, a little man with a red nose and an oil-skin hat. When I came away he was sitting there still!—not a man *like* him, but the same man—with the nose of immortal redness and the hat of an undying blaze!— DICKENS, CHARLES, 1842, *Speech at New York Dinner, Feb.* 18; *Speeches and Sayings, p.* 28.

As a genial chronicle of upper-class English life and character, nothing better could be asked for. Irving's mannerism had now become inveterate, but it was a mannerism in which well-balanced sentences, genuine humour, faithful descriptions, and hearty morality always had a place. His refinement of style was sometimes excessive, and his readers never completely lose sight of the rhetorician manipulating the printed words.—RICHARDSON, CHARLES F., 1887, *American Literature, 1607-1885, vol.* I, *p.* 271.

A HISTORY OF CHRISTOPHER COLUMBUS
1828

This is, on the whole, an excellent book; and we venture to anticipate that it will be an enduring one. Neither do we hazard this prediction lightly, or without a full consciousness of all that it implies. . . . For we mean, not merely that the book will be familiarly known and referred to some twenty or thirty years hence, and will pass into solid binding into every considerable collection; but that it will supersede all former works on the same subject, and never be itself superseded.—JEFFREY, FRANCIS LORD, 1828, *Life and Voyages of Columbus, Edinburgh Review, vol. 48, p. 1.*

This is one of those works, which are at the same time the delight of readers and the despair of critics. It is as nearly perfect in its kind, as any work well can be; and there is therefore little or nothing left for the reviewer, but to write at the bottom of every page, as Voltaire said he should be obliged to do if he published a commentary on Racine, *Pulchre! bene! optime!* —EVERETT, ALEXANDER HILL, 1829, *Irving's Life of Columbus, North American Review, vol. 28, p. 103.*

I esteem it the first of American classics, and can never be affected enough to join in the clamour against his crystal flow of purest English.—ALEXANDER, JAMES W., 1829, *Familiar Letters, Feb. 17; ed. Hall, vol. I, p. 122.*

Having access to original and fresh documents relating to the life of Christopher Columbus, he was encouraged and enabled to undertake and execute a great historical work, and on a subject the most rich in details, and the most magnificent in its results, of any that ever employed the pen of the historian. He brought to the task all his great and diversified powers. His materials were selected with judgment, studied with diligence, arranged with skill, exhibited with fidelity, polished with taste and recommended by finished specimens of a graceful, flowing, and dignified composition. The discovery of America was essentially a domestic theme. Though the enterprise was begun in Europe, it was consummated on this side of the Atlantic. The settlement of this New World seems to be a theme peculiarly appropriate to the pen of an American writer, who would naturally feel and appreciate, most deeply and justly, the inestimable value of the discovery, and the mighty consequences of the establishment of great nations on this continent, with their language and institutions, their freedom and religion, their arts and sciences spreading themselves over its surface. The choice was most propitious, and the "History of the Life and Voyages of Columbus" will probably become the standard work on

that subject through all succeeding ages. It equals the most distinguished historical compositions, not only in the dignity of the subject, but in the judgment, skill, spirit, and felicity of its execution.—KENT, JAMES, 1832, *Literature, Commerce and Fine Arts, Memoirs and Letters, ed. Kent, p. 234.*

Since I have been here, I have contrived (by reading a half-hour in the night and a half-hour in the morning) to peruse the whole of Irving's "Life of Columbus," in three volumes. It is quite an interesting work, though I think too much spread out by repetition of the same thoughts and descriptions. It is, in all respects, however, reputable to the literature of our country.— STORY, JOSEPH, 1836, *To William Wetmore Story, Feb. 21; Life and Letters, ed. Story, vol. II, p. 229.*

It is open to the charge of too much rhetorical color here and there, and it is at times too diffuse; but its substantial accuracy is not questioned, and the glow of the narrative springs legitimately from the romance of the theme. Irving understood, what our later historians have fully appreciated, the advantage of vivid individual portraiture in historical narrative. His conception of the character and mission of Columbus is largely outlined, but firmly and most carefully executed, and is one of the noblest in literature.—WARNER, CHARLES DUDLEY, 1881, *Washington Irving (American Men of Letters), p. 155.*

The short time in which it was prepared, not more at any rate than two years, shows that it cannot have been a work of original research carried out absolutely after the modern manner. It was in fact based on the documentary publications of Don Martin Fernandez de Navarrete, though with much use of the libraries of Obadiah Rich, then our consul at Madrid, of Navarrete himself, of the Duke of Veragua, and of the Council of the Indies, and of other libraries at Madrid and Seville. The result was an excellent piece of historical work, as well as a literary production which it would be superfluous to praise.—JAMESON, J. FRANKLIN, 1891, *The History of Historical Writing in America, p. 98.*

THE CONQUEST OF GRANADA
1829

Mr. Irving has seldom selected a subject better suited to his peculiar powers than the conquest of Granada. Indeed, it would hardly have been possible for one of his warm sensibilities to linger so long among the remains of Moorish magnificence with which Spain is covered, without being interested in the fortunes of a people whose memory has almost passed into oblivion, but who once preserved the "sacred flame" when it had become extinct in every corner of Christendom, and whose influence is still visible on the intellectual culture of modern Europe.—PRESCOTT, WILLIAM HICKLING, 1829, *Irving's Conquest of Granada, Biographical and Critical Miscellanies, p.* 109.

One of the most important and one of the most charming of Irving's historical works. —ADAMS, CHARLES KENDALL, 1882, *A Manual of Historical Literature, p.* 403.

It was long after my acquaintance with his work that I came to a due sense of Irving as an artist, and perhaps I have come to feel a full sense of it only now, when I perceive that he worked willingly only when he worked inventively. At last I can do justice to the exquisite conception of his "Conquest of Granada," a study of history which, in unique measure, conveys not only the pathos, but the humor of one of the most splendid and impressive situations in the experience of the race. Very possibly something of the severer truth might have been sacrificed to the effect of the pleasing and touching tale, but I do not understand that this was really done. — HOWELLS, WILLIAM DEAN, 1895, *My Literary Passions, p.* 32.

THE ALHAMBRA
1832

On the whole, we consider the work before us as equal in literary value to any of the others of the same class, with the exception of "The Sketch-Book"; and we should not be surprised if it were read as extensively as even that very popular production. We hope to have it in our power, at no remote period, to announce a continuation of the series, which we are satisfied will bear, in the booksellers' phrase, several more volumes.—EVERETT, EDWARD, 1832, *Irving's Alhambra, North American Review, vol.* 35, *p.* 281.

Go to the Moorish fountains, sparkling full in the moonlight—go among the water-carriers and the village gossips, living still as in days of old—and who has travelled among them before you, and peopled the Alhambra and made eloquent its shadows?

Who wakes there a voice from every hill and in every cavern, and bids legends, which for centuries had slept a dreamless sleep, or watched unwinkingly, start up and pass before you in all their life and glory?— DICKENS, CHARLES, 1842, *Speech at New York Dinner, Feb.* 18; *Speeches and Sayings, p.* 28.

The book abounds in delightful legends, and yet these are all so touched with the author's airy humor that our credulity is never overtaxed; we imbibe all the romantic interest of the place without for a moment losing our hold upon reality. The enchantments of this Moorish paradise become part of our mental possessions without the least shock to our common sense.— WARNER, CHARLES DUDLEY, 1881, *Washington Irving (American Men of Letters), p.* 251.

To speak of Granada is to speak of the Alhambra, but one falters at describing the vastness and the delicacy of that last effort of the Spanish Moor; one falters at treading in Irving's footsteps even in the humblest way, for he made the place and all its memories so thoroughly his own. The hotel beneath the walls bears his name; his "Tales" are sold by importunate venders; the guide shows the rooms in which he slept with an air of mysterious reverence, and wherever one turns one feels the presence of the American writer who, more than any man, has preserved the memory of the Moor.—CHATFIELD-TAYLOR, H. C., 1896, *The Land of the Castanet, p.* 161.

LIFE OF OLIVER GOLDSMITH
1844

Everything combines to make this one of the most fascinating pieces of biography in the English language. Enough is known of the personal history and character of Goldsmith, to tempt us to recur to the subject with fresh interest; but he has not been so bandied about by life-writers and reviewers as to satiate curiosity. The simplicity, and even the weaknesses of his nature, call forth feelings of affection; and the charm of his writings, so unaffected, so naïve, so transparent in their crystal purity of expression, attracts us to more intimate acquaintance with the author. Mr. Irving was in possession of abundant materials to do justice to the subject. He had only to insert his exquisite magnetic needle into the mass, to give a choice and shapely form to all that was valuable in the labors of previous biographers. He has done this in a manner which leaves nothing to be desired.—RIPLEY, GEORGE, 1849, *New York Tribune.*

For my part, I know of nothing like it. I have read no biographical memoir which carries forward the reader so delightfully and with so little tediousness of recital or reflection. I never take it up without being tempted to wish that Irving had written more works of the kind; but this could hardly be; for where could he have found another Goldsmith?—BRYANT, WILLIAM CULLEN, 1860, *Washington Irving, Orations and Address, p.* 140.

It is one of the best biographies in the whole range of English literature, just, full, brilliant. It forms a counterpart to Boswell's "Johnson"; no one whose idea of Goldsmith has been formed by Boswell can afford to neglect Irving's presentation of the Irish poet and novelist. In spirit and style this small book is worthy to stand on the shelf with its author's choicest works.— RICHARDSON, CHARLES F., 1887, *American Literature,* 1607-1885, *vol.* I, *p.* 276.

LIFE OF WASHINGTON
1855-59

Candor, good judgment that knows no bias, the felicity of selections, these are yours in common with the best historians. But, in addition, you have the peculiarity of writing from the heart, enchaining sympathy as well as commanding confidence; the happy magic that makes scenes, events, and personal anecdotes present themselves to you at your bidding, and fall into their natural places and take color and warmth from your own nature. The style, too, is masterly, clear, easy, and graceful; picturesque without mannerism, and ornamented without losing simplicity. Among men of letters, who do well, you must above all take the name of Felix, which so few of the great Roman generals could claim. You do everything rightly, as if by grace; and I am in no fear of offending your modesty, for I think you were elected and foreordained to excel your contemporaries. —BANCROFT, GEORGE, 1855, *To Irving, May* 30; *Life and Letters of Washington Irving, ed. Irving, vol.* IV, *p.* 194.

You have done with Washington just as I thought you would, and, instead of a cold, marble statue of demigod, you have made

him a being of flesh and blood, like ourselves—one with whom we can have sympathy. The general sentiment of the country has been too decidedly expressed for you to doubt for a moment that this is the portrait of him which is to hold a permanent place in the national gallery.— PRESCOTT, WILLIAM HICKLING, 1856, *To Irving, Jan.* 3; *Life and Letters, ed. Irving, vol.* IV, *p.* 204.

I referred to his last and chief work, the "Life of Washington" and asked if he felt on finishing it, any such sensation as Gibbon enjoyed over the last sheet of the "Decline and Fall." He said that the work had engrossed his mind to such a degree that before he was aware, he had written himself into feeble health; that in the midst of his labor he feared he would break down before the end; that when at last the final pages were written, he gave the manuscript to his nephew to conduct it through the press, and threw himself back on his red-cushioned lounge with an indescribable feeling of relief. He explained that the chief fatigue of mind had resulted from care required in the construction and arrangement of materials, and not in the literary composition of the successive chapters.—TILTON, THEODORE, 1859-69, *A Visit to Washington Irving, Sanctum Sanctorum, p.* 10.

I confess, my admiration of this work becomes the greater the more I examine it. In the other writings of Irving are beauties which strike the reader at once. In this I recognize qualities which lie deeper, and which I was not sure of finding — a rare equity of judgment; a large grasp of the subject; a profound philosophy, independent of philosophical forms, and even instinctively rejecting them; the power of reducing an immense crowd of loose materials to clear and orderly arrangement; and forming them into one grand whole, as a skilful commander, from a rabble of raw recruits, forms a disciplined army, animated and moved by a single will.—BRYANT, WILLIAM CULLEN, 1860, *Washington Irving, Orations and Addresses, p.* 145.

Precisely what was wanted Mr. Irving has given: such charming, faithful, truthful pictures of the great hero of our Revolution as should carry knowledge of him, of the battles he fought, of his large, self-denying, unswerving patriotism, of the purity of his life, into every household. No man could have done this work better; nor do we think that any other will ever do it as well.—MITCHELL, DONALD G., 1864, *Washington Irving, Atlantic Monthly, vol.* 13, *p.* 700.

The work was regarded by the author as the most important of his productions, and as, in some sense, the crown of his literary career. It partakes of his well-known characteristics as a writer; and will probably acquire a permanent place in our literature as the standard life of Washington. For the purposes of an historical student, the last two volumes will probably be found the most important. The phases of political life which Irving saw, however, were not always the phases which the student will now desire to see; and, therefore, too high expectations must not be raised. Recourse must constantly be had to other sources of information.—ADAMS, CHARLES KENDALL, 1882, *A Manual of Historical Literature, p.* 581.

Although not a biography of the very highest rank, it is in every way worthy of its position as the standard life of a remarkable man and the crowning work of a brilliant literary career.—PATTEE, FRED LEWIS, 1896, *A History of American Literature, p.* 126.

There are passages in it that for incisiveness of characterization and for finish of form are the equal of anything that he produced in the days when his intellectual vigor was unimpaired; but the reader cannot escape the feeling that the author's grasp of the materials relating to the subject was feeble, and that his heart was not in his work.—MORSE, EDWIN W., 1897, *Library of the World's Best Literature, ed. Warner, vol.* XIV, *p.* 7999.

GENERAL

I know Washington Irving well, and when he was here two or three years ago, he promised to me to contribute regularly. The last time I saw him in London he repeated his promises; but he said, when he looked at our "audaciously original Magazine," he did not think he could give anything that could appear to advantage in it. These, of course, were mere phrases; but I do think he has perhaps been rather overestimated. He is a man of an amiably elegant mind, and what he does do is well conceived and finely polished, but I rather think he is not a person of great originality

or strength.—BLACKWOOD, WILLIAM, 1820, *Letter to Maginn, Oct.* 18; *William Blackwood and His Sons, ed. Oliphant, vol.* I, *p.* 378.

Through all the writings of our distinguished countryman, even in his earlier and sprightlier productions, we meet with occasional sentiments of high and grave import, the genuine growth of ardent feeling which go directly to the heart. Nothing can be more soothing and gratifying to meditative minds than such pensive, chaste, and mellowed reflections, arising from views of autumnal scenery, the ruins of ancient art, and the monuments of departed greatness.—KENT, JAMES, 1832, *Literature, Commerce and the Fine Arts, Memoirs and Letters, ed. Kent, p.* 233.

Mr. Irving has travelled much, has seen many vicissitudes, and has been so thoroughly satiated with fame as to grow slovenly in the performance of his literary tasks. This slovenliness has affected his handwriting. . . . Irving's style is inimitable in its grace and delicacy, yet few of our practised writers are guilty of more frequent inadvertences of language. In what may be termed his mere English, he is surpassed by fifty whom we could name. —POE, EDGAR ALLAN, 1841, *A Chapter on Autography, Works, ed. Stedman and Woodberry, vol.* IX, *pp.* 190, 229.

I don't go up-stairs to bed two nights out of the seven—as a very creditable witness near at hand can testify—I say I do not go to bed two nights out of the seven without taking Washington Irving under my arm; and, when I don't take him, I take his own brother, Oliver Goldsmith.—DICKENS, CHARLES, 1842, *Speech at New York Dinner, Feb.* 18; *Speeches and Sayings, p.* 28.

To a true poet-heart add the fun of Dick Steele,
Throw in all of Addison, *minus* the chill,
With the whole of that partnership's stock and
    good-will,
Mix well, and while stirring, hum o'er, as a spell,
The fine *old* English Gentleman, simmer it well,
Sweeten just to your own private liking, then
    strain,
That only the finest and clearest remain,
Let it stand out of doors till a soul it receives
From the warm lazy sun loitering down through
    green leaves,
And you'll find a choice nature, not wholly
    deserving
A name either English or Yankee,—just Irving.
—LOWELL, JAMES RUSSELL, 1848, *A Fable for Critics.*

Washington Irving, one of the finest of modern humorous writers.—REED, HENRY, 1850-55, *Lectures on English Literature from Chaucer to Tennyson, p. 362.*

Few, very few, can show a long succession of volumes, so pure, so graceful, and so varied as Mr. Irving. To my poor cottage, rich only in printed paper, people often come to borrow books for themselves or their children. Sometimes they make their own selection; sometimes, much against my will, they leave the choice to me; and in either case I know no works that are oftener lent than those that bear the pseudonym of Geoffrey Crayon.—MITFORD, MARY RUSSELL, 1851, *Recollections of a Literary Life, p. 516.*

Grace is an electric light evolved by the action of successive parts of the subject on the mind. It is the source of that fresh and delightful fragrance which always exhales from Irving's writings. . . . The pleasantness which he diffuses over subjects the most barren . . . arises chiefly from the instinctive quietness with which he seizes everything. . . . The art of this system consists in the gentleness and fineness of the rays. . . . Looking only at the style and manner of his works, we find a grace as inherent as that of childhood; a gentle gayety as variable yet as unfailing, as unfatiguing as the breezes of June; an indestructible presence of good taste, simplicity, and ease. . . . What renders the merit more singular in Irving is that, successful and inimitable as the charm is, it is obviously not spontaneous or unconscious.—WALLACE, HORACE BINNEY, 1856, *Literary Criticism.*

His English style, so pure, so delicate, so clear, so rhythmical,—the natural expression of a pure, beautiful, and harmonious soul, exquisitely attuned to all that is lovely, graceful, and noble in nature and life,—embodying a character painted in immortal colors by the genius of Plato; his imagination, so gentle, and so powerful, that brightened everything it touched, as the genial sunshine kindles the landscape into beauty; his ready and delightful wit and humour, that exhilarated us, not with tumultuous laughter, except, perhaps, in those sallies of the sportive genius of his youth. . . . But with a serene gladness of spirit; his pathos, so tender, so true, so full of feeling for every form of sorrow, toned with a sweet, lingering sadness from

the unforgotten sorrow of his early days, —what a combination of attractive qualities, adorning his personal character, and clothing his literary works with an inexpressible charm!—FELTON, CORNELIUS CONWAY, 1859, *Remarks at a Meeting of the Massachusetts Historical Society, Dec. 15; Proceedings, vol. 4, pp. 409, 410.*

> Chaucer I fancied had been dead
>   Some centuries, some four or five;
> By fancy I have been misled
>   Like many: he is yet alive.
> "The Widow's Ordeal" who beside
>   Could thus relate? Yes, there is one,
> He bears beyond the Atlantic wide
>   The glorious name of Washington.

—LANDOR, WALTER SAVAGE, 1863, *A Tale by Washington Irving, Heroic Idyls with Additional Poems, Works, vol. VIII, p. 350.*

The books I have lately been reading are the works of Washington Irving. None of our present writers write such pure English; he reminds me of Addison, but has more genius and a richer invention. Perhaps on the whole he is more like Goldsmith.—LANDOR, WALTER SAVAGE, 1863, *To Mrs. Graves-Sawle, Jan. 19; Letters, ed. Wheeler, p. 228.*

Perhaps, of all American writers, in Washington Irving the polite air of the man of the European world is the most seen; but then, of all American writers, Washington Irving is the one who most sedulously imitated, and most happily caught the spirit of European writers, formed under aristocratic as well as popular influences;—of all American writers he is thus the least American.—LYTTON, EDWARD BULWER LORD, 1863-68, *Caxtoniana, Miscellaneous Prose Works, vol. III, p. 491.*

In his "Knickerbocker" and other works, has given us the very choicest brand, all sparkling and stimulating. But Irving is too refined, sweet, and shy for general appreciation. Besides, Irving is not an American humorist. He is more English than American, more cosmopolitan than either.—COX, S. S., 1875, *American Humor, Harper's Magazine, vol. 50, p. 699.*

Irving might have walked arm-in-arm with Addison, and Addison would have run no risk of being discomposed by a trans-Atlantic twang in his companion's accent. Irving, if he betrays his origin at all, betrays it somewhat in the same way as Longfellow, by his tender, satisfied repose in the venerable, chiefly the venerable in English society and manners, by his quiet delight in the implicit tradition of English civility, the scarcely-felt yet everywhere influential presence of a beautiful and grave Past, and the company of unseen beneficent associations.—DOWDEN, EDWARD, 1878, *Studies in Literature, p. 470.*

His humor is distinguished by its constituent of feeling. It is the genial coloring of his humorous conceptions, not their mechanism, that wins our interest. He hardly ever puns; for the pun is a logical fallacy, and Irving does not play with the forms of thought. His humor seldom becomes wit; for wit is the product of analytic insight, and his mind is neither analytic, nor specially gifted with insight. He often makes us smile, but seldom—especially in his later writings—elicits a broad guffaw; for his conceptions are charged with a feeling softened by culture, and tempered by geniality.—HILL, DAVID J., 1879, *Washington Irving, p. 209.*

Irving's literature, walk round it and measure it by whatever critical instrument you will, is a beneficent literature. The author loved good women and little children and a pure life; he had faith in his fellow-men, a kindly sympathy with the lowest, without any subservience to the highest; he retained a belief in the possibility of chivalrous actions, and did not care to envelop them in a cynical suspicion; he was an author still capable of an enthusiasm. His books are wholesome, full of sweetness and charm, of humor without any sting, of amusement without any stain; and their more solid qualities are marred by neither pedantry nor pretension.— WARNER, CHARLES DUDLEY, 1881, *Washington Irving (American Men of Letters), p. 303.*

No work of his is wanting in powerful passages; but his prevailing characteristics are versatility and grace. He belonged historically to both worlds, and was equally at home in each; he reflected the quiet philosophy of the "Tatler" and "Spectator," adding to it the pathos which dims the eye of the reader over "The Wife," "Widow and Son," the "Broken Heart," and "Pride of the Village." He started the vein of burlesque which has run through his country's literature, but under the restraints of temperance and culture that have unfortunately been discarded. The evenness of his manner leads the minor critics of an age delighting in outrages and

violence, to do scant justice to the range of his always unaffected sympathy, and ever genuine passion.—NICHOL, JOHN, 1882-85, *American Literature, p. 173.*

He is refreshingly deliberate; never in a hurry. Like Byron's "gentleman," he "never perspires." He takes his time, and tells you his story in his own way. The most delightful of gossips, the most ingratiating of "Roundabouts." There is a good deal of the "Guardian," "Tatler," "Spectator" and old coffee-house wit and wisdom about him. But though sometimes gossipy, he is never flimsy, like so many of our modern magazine writers of "padding." He knows how to be solid, to choose his words, to look all around his thoughts, to have thoughts that will bear looking at. His wit is never forced; he is seldom on the broad grin. In him, indeed, are germs of an American humor since run to seed in buffoonery; but he is never outrageous—always within delicate bounds. His fun never goes mad, but is in excellent subordination to his narrative or discourse. His wit always plays about his subject like summer lightning. His laugh, or more often his grave smile, rises naturally, and is never affected; he is never strained or flashing, but often full of a deep and pathetic purpose; and his jokes, when they come, seem woven into the very texture of his style, instead of sticking up outside like a cocked hat! We have seldom the rollicking fun of Dickens, but often a touch of his tenderness. It is the satire of Swift, without his sour coarseness. The grace of Sterne, without his sham sentiment. The delicate flavour of Charles Lamb, without, however, the sly but severe bite of Lamb's satire.—HAWEIS, HUGH REGINALD, 1882, *American Humorists, p. 23.*

The poet and romancer give back more than they borrow from the scenes which lend them their inspiration. What was this broad stream that runs by your walls before it was peopled by the creative touch of your story-teller's imagination? It is no longer Hudson's river,—it is Irving's. The trumpet of Anthony Van Corlear still rings over the wide expanse of the Tappan Zee. The rolling balls of the old nine-pin-players are still heard by the voyager, thundering in the far-off Kaatskills. There is not a brook that tumbles into the river which does not babble the name of Irving, not a wave which does not murmur its remembrance. I walk through thronged thoroughfares, and all at once my fancy carries me back to the days and scenes of Irving's New Amsterdam. The pavement becomes a great turf, a few scattered houses show their gables here and there. One stands apart, more lordly than the rest. What is this sound I hear from the stoop that stretches along its side? It is a strange sound to be heard through all this tumult, but I must be half dreaming. Hark! Abrupt, intermittent, rhythmical, resonant, emphatic; it must be,—it is,— the wooden leg of brave, peppery, pugnacious, irrepressible old Peter Stuyvesant, —Hard Koppig Piet,—the hard-headed, hot-hearted, one-legged but two-fisted Governor of this ancient Manhattan, already a flourishing settlement with burgarmeesters and schepens in place of aldermen and constables. Sagacious old Dutchman, to fix on this tongue of land,—a tongue that laps up the cream of commerce of a continent.—HOLMES, OLIVER WENDELL, 1883, *Irving's Power of Idealization, The Critic, vol. 3, p. 138.*

Scott is not more identified with Scotland than Irving with the Hudson. He has touched it with imperishable charm and he rules the river as well as the city by the divinest right. On a still June morning the loiterer upon the ferry-boat from Staten Island looks with a smile toward the drowsy shore of Communipaw haply to catch a glimpse of the hardy voyagers launching bravely away for Hellgate and the Boiling Pot and the Hen and Chickens. The traveller hastening by rail to Albany strains his eyes beyond the vanishing gable of Sunnyside and, forgetting the political Brom Bones of to-day, listens for the tramp of the Headless Horseman, and looks wistfully for the flying Ichabod and the comely Katrina. As he winds and darts among the Highlands he hears far away the softened blast of Anthony's nose, and, while the clouds gather and the river smooths itself to an oily calm, his ear catches the long roll of the distant game among the Catskill Mountains and he knows that Rip Van Winkle is tasting the ancient Hollands of the mysterious players at whom he gazes. The humane genius, the gentle and kindly fancy of Irving, have thrown upon the city and its neighborhood, upon the winding channels of the river, its meadows, and villages, and

airy uplands, a soft radiance of romance, that glamor familiar in the lands of older civilization but unknown elsewhere upon this Continent; and it is doubtful which has given the stream and valley of the Hudson their most picturesque renown,— the voyage of the discoverer, or the story of the Revolution, or the genius of Irving.— CURTIS, GEORGE WILLIAM, 1883, *Irving's "Knickerbocker," The Critic, vol. 3, p. 140.*

In whatever estimation Mr. Irving may be generally held as an historian, his proper rank is among the first of American historical scholars, however much it may be overshadowed by his brilliant reputation as an essayist who held the mirror up to nature, and showed the times its own form and features. Had he been born fifty years later the world might have gained a novelist; but it may be questioned whether, if it had lost the historian, its loss would not have been greater than its gain.—GAY, SYDNEY HOWARD, 1883, *Irving the Historian, The Critic, vol. 3, p. 142.*

If the Hudson is to us something more than a mere waterway and convenient natural agency for "moving the crops to tide-water"; if the Catskills are something more than a good place for establishing summer hotels, it is to Irving that the fact is due. If there is a touch of poetry, or romance, or human interest, about the background of New York, a mellow suggestion of myth and superstition, a legendary halo that soothes the sight tortured by the flaring, garish noon of our materialism, it is Irving who put it there.—SEDGWICK, A. G., 1883, *Washington Irving, The Nation, vol. 36, p. 292.*

Of all authors, Irving was perfectly suited to the taste of the time, insomuch that the epoch included by the publication of his "Sketch-Book" and of his "Life of Margaret Miller Davidson" might well be called by his name; he was its essence. That his influence was not powerful every one admits; but it was certainly pervasive. In one word, he was systematic; and his sentiment was kept from declining into sentimentality by his playfulness and fine sense of humor, while it was preserved from evaporating in mere revery by benevolence and desire for approbation.— WHITE, GREENOUGH, 1890, *Sketch of the Philosophy of American Literature, p. 55.*

He saw life through the literary atmosphere, and had no theories to ventilate. no reforms to advocate, no specific moral to enforce. His style was individual, lucid and musical. The moral beauty, integrity and generosity of his character shine through his books. The fact of his giving up, in favor of Prescott, the design, cherished for years, of writing the history of the conquest of Mexico—and never allowing Prescott to suspect the extent of his sacrifice is a characteristic trait of a man truly lovable and widely loved. His books do good to all who read them, and are likely to outlast many works of far greater intellectual force and acumen: their union of taste, simplicity and repose gives them a hold upon our inmost and least variable sympathies.—HAWTHORNE, JULIAN, AND LEMMON, LEONARD, 1891, *American Literature, p.* 45.

Irving is in his way a skillful paragrapher. No matter how great the license of his subject, he always gives an impression of unity. He follows the loose order almost exclusively, keeping his statement of details closely within the limits prescribed by his opening sentence. His transitions are faultless, the number of connectives being greater, however, than the placing of words requires. About one-quarter of his sentences are shorter than 15 words, and nearly one-half (41 per cent.) are under 20 words. He adapts the short sentence to the smooth and graceful manner of Addison. He does not, indeed, ever succeed in flashing out a complex thought in a telling and emphatic way; but as a type of the urbane, leisurely, correct manner, he is exemplary. —LEWIS, EDWIN HERBERT, 1894, *The History of the English Paragraph, p.* 135.

No later American writer has surpassed him in charm. Before Irving had discovered the beauty of the Hudson, the river was as lovely as it is to-day, but its legends were little known. He it was who peopled the green nooks of Sleepy Hollow and the rock crags of the Catskills. His genius was not stalwart or rugged, and it did not conquer admiration; it won its way softly, by the aid of sentiment and humor. "Knickerbocker's History," and the "Sketch-Book," and the "Alhambra," are his titles to fame; not the "Columbus" or the "Washington." He had the conscience of the historian and he could color his narrative artistically and give it movement; but others could do this as well as he. But to call into being a civilization, to give

to a legend the substance of truth, to present a fiction, so that it passes for fact and is accepted by the people and gets into common speech—this is a feat very few authors have ever accomplished. Irving did it, and his greatest work is not any one of his books—it is the Knickerbocker legend.— MATTHEWS, BRANDER, 1896, *An Introduction to the Study of American Literature, p.* 54.

Unluckily, something more than extreme amiability, even when combined with the soundest sense, is necessary to the attainment of greatness in literature; and it is a fact that Washington Irving went far to blast the rich promise of his natural parts, and to render his admirable equipment of no avail by his blind and obstinate devotion to an obsolete and exploded convention. He did well to study Addison, Goldsmith, and Sterne with profound attention. He did very ill to imitate them with a fidelity as servile as it is ridiculous. No excellence was too great, no mannerism too trivial for him to mimic. Types of character and tricks of style, modes of thought and turns of phrase, all are appropriated and reproduced with the most painful exactitude. And they suffer sadly in the process. Pleasing and pertinent reflections become chilly and colourless platitudes; while exquisite humour is transformed into a laboured archness. . . . One crowded hour of Sir Walter Scott's careless and often slovenly prose is worth an age of Washington Irving's insipidities; and a single "tow-row" of Mr. Stevenson's thunder is infinitely more alarming than all the storms in which the clouds "roll in volumes over the mountain tops," the rain "begins to patter down in broad and scattered drops," the wind "freshens," the lightning "leaps from cloud to cloud," the peals "are echoed from mountain to mountain," and, in short, all the elements go through their appropriate and stereotyped evolutions with the punctuality, precision, and tameness of clock-work. The bones of the skeleton, to employ a familiar metaphor, are adjusted with the utmost nicety and correctness, but they have lost the potentiality of life. On the other hand, it is to be said, that the close study of such writers as Washington Irving selected for his models could scarce be barren of all good result; that if he never rises to animation he never sinks below a tolerably high standard of elegance; and that he everywhere preserves a spotless purity of idiom.—MILLAR, J. H., 1896, *English Prose, ed. Craik, vol.* V, *pp.* 233, 234.

To Washington Irving belongs the title of the Founder of American Literature.—MORSE, EDWIN W., 1897, *Library of the World's Best Literature, vol.* XIV, *p.* 7991.

When a writer has won the title of the Father of American Literature—a name conventionally given to Washington Irving—it becomes plain that he is very important as a figure in our native development in letters. . . . Viewed in relation to current production in history or to what had already been done, he is seen to have possessed the instinct and habit of the true historian, the modern workman. I mean that he went to the sources and spared neither time nor labor in getting together his materials. Witness the years spent in the libraries and other repositories of Spain, when he was working on his "Columbus" and other main books. The result is that, in spite of the enormous amount of research since expended upon the Italian whose name is associated with our country's discovery, the Irving biography is confessedly a standard one to-day, and this quite aside from its literary merits. . . . His manner of writing as a whole, in its unobtrusive breeding and beauty, is admirable, and may well be put before us as a model of the kind of effect it aims for. It is especially valuable at the present time for its lack of strain, its avoidance of violence or bizarre effects, when our later writers incline to hunt for startling words and queer constructions; anything to excite and seem "original." Irving's style impresses one as a whole, rather than in particulars,—and that is the higher art.—BURTON, RICHARD, 1898, *Literary Likings, pp.* 249, 253, 266.

Irving was no trained scholar. He was far even from the critical habit of the New England historians, and further still from such learning as is now apt to make history something like exact science. It may be doubted whether Irving's Goldsmith or his Washington can be accepted as the Goldsmith or the Washington who once trod the earth; yet his Goldsmith and Washington, and the other personages whom he introduced into their stories, are at least living human beings. His work is perhaps half-way between history and fiction; imaginative history is perhaps the best name for it. As usual, he was preoccupied almost as much with a desire to write charmingly as with a purpose to write truly; but in itself this desire was beautifully true. Throughout, one feels, Irving wrote as well as he could, and he knew how to write better than almost any contemporary Englishman.—WENDELL, BARRETT, 1900, *A Literary History of America, p.* 178.

Irving was not a great original thinker, reformer, or masterful spirit in any field. He founded no definite school, though he has had a most helpful and genial influence on all literature since. He saw much beauty, and makes us see it, especially in the romantic past. Whether he created, or found ready to his hand, the best legendary lore of the Hudson Valley, is a problem still discussed. His effects always seem to be attained with as little effort as Raphael's, but this, surely, is but evidence of perfect balance, sanity, instinctive self-knowledge.— LAWTON, WILLIAM CRANSTON, 1902, *Introduction to the Study of American Literature, p.* 83.

James Henry Leigh Hunt
1784-1859

Born, at Southgate, 19 Oct. 1784. At Christ's Hospital School, 1792-99. Contrib. to "Juvenile Library," 1801; to "European Mag.," 1801; to "Poetical Register," 1801-11; to "The Traveller," 1804-05. Clerk to his brother Stephen, 1803[?]-05. Dramatic critic to "The News" (started by his brother John), 1805. Clerkship in War Office, 1806[?]-08. Edited "The Examiner," 1808-21; frequently contributed afterwards. Married Marianne Kent, 3 July 1809. Edited "The Reflector," 1810. Imprisoned in Surrey gaol, for remarks in "Examiner" on Prince Regent, 3 Feb. 1813 to 3 Feb. 1815. Settled at Hampstead, 1816. Friendship with Shelley and Keats. Edited "The Indicator," Oct. 1819 to March 1821. Edited, and wrote, "The Literary Pocket-Book," 1819-22. Sailed for Italy, 15 Nov. 1821, but driven by storm to land at Dartmouth. Sailed again, May 1822; arrived at Leghorn, June. Contrib. to "New Monthly Mag.,"

1821–50.   Edited "The Liberal" (with Shelley and Byron), 1822–23.   To Genoa with Byron, Sept. 1822.   In Florence, 1823–25.   Edited "The Literary Examiner," 1823. Returned to England, Sept. 1825.   Lived at Highgate, 1825–28.   Edited "The Companion," Jan. to July, 1828.   Contrib. to "The Keepsake," 1828.   Lived at Epsom, 1828–30 [?].   Edited "The Chat of the Week," June to Aug., 1830.   Edited (and wrote) "The Tatler" 4 Sept. 1830 to 13 Feb. 1832.   Lived in Chelsea, 1833–40.   Contrib. to "Tait's Mag.," 1833; to "Monthly Chronicle," Oct. 1838 to Feb. 1839.   Edited "Leigh Hunt's London Journal," 1834 to Dec. 1835; "The Monthly Repository," July 1837 to April 1838.   Contrib. to "Musical World," Jan. to March, 1839.   Lived in Kensington, 1840–53.   Play, "A Legend of Florence," produced at Covent Garden, 7 Feb. 1840. Contrib. to "Westminster Rev.," 1837; To "Edinburgh Review," 1841–44; to "Ainsworth's Mag.," 1845; to "Atlas," 1846; etc.   Crown Pension of £200, Oct. 1847.   Edited "Leigh Hunt's Journal," 1850–51.   Lived in Hammersmith, 1853–59.   Contrib. to "Musical Times," 1853–54; to "Household Words," 1853–54; to "Fraser's Mag.," 1858–59; to "Spectator," Jan. to Aug. 1859.   Died, at Putney, 28 Aug. 1859.   Buried in Kensal Green Cemetery.   *Works:*   "Juvenilia," 1801; "Classic Tales" (5 vols.), 1806–07; "Critical Essays on the Performers of the London Theatres" (from "The News"), 1807; "An Attempt to show the Folly . . . of Methodism" (anon., from "Examiner"), 1809; "Reformist's Reply to the Edinburgh Review," 1810; "The Feast of the Poets" (anon.), 1814; "The Descent of Liberty," 1815; "The Story of Rimini," 1816; "The Round Table" (with Hazlitt, from "Examiner," 2 vols.), 1817; "Foliage," 1818; "Hero and Leander," 1819; "Bacchus and Ariadne," 1819; "Poetical Works," 1819; "The Literary Pocket-Book" (4 vols.), 1819–22; "The Months" (selected from vol. I. of preceding), 1821; "Ultra-Crepidarius," 1823; "Lord Byron and some of his Contemporaries," 1828; "The Companion," 1828; "The Tatler," 1830–32; "Christianism" (anon.; priv. ptd.), 1832 (enlarged edn. called: "The Religion of the Head," 1853); "Poetical Works," 1832; "Sir Ralph Esher," 1832; "The Indicator and the Companion" (2 vols.), 1834; "Captain Sword and Captain Pen," 1835; "The Seer," 1840–41; "The Palfrey," 1842; "One Hundred Romances of Real Life" (from "Leigh Hunt's London Journal"), 1843; "Poetical Works," 1844; "Imagination and Fancy," 1844; "Wit and Humour selected from the English Poets," 1846; "Stories from the Italian Poets" (2 vols.), 1846; "A Saunter through the West-End" (from "Atlas"), 1847; "Men, Women and Books" (2 vols.), 1847; "A Jar of Honey from Mount Hybla," 1848; "The Town" (2 vols.), 1848; "A Book for a Corner," 1849; "Readings for Railways," 1849; "Autobiography" (3 vols.), 1850; (later edns. expanded 1859 and 1860); "Table-Talk," 1851; "The Religion of the Heart," 1853; "The Old Court Suburb," 1855; "Stories in Verse," 1855; "Poetical Works" (Boston, 2 vols.), 1857.   *Posthumous:*   "Poetical Works," ed. by his son, 1860; "Correspondence," 1862; "Tale for a Chimney Corner," 1869; "Day by the Fire," 1870; "Wishing Cap Papers" (from "Examiner"), 1873.   He *translated:* Tasso's "Amyntas," 1820; F. Redi's "Bacchus in Tuscany," 1825; and *edited:* Shelley's "Masque of Anarchy," 1832; Sheridan's Dramatic Works, 1840; The Dramatic Works of Wycherley, Congreve, Vanbrugh and Farquhar, 1840; Chaucer's Poems Modernized (with Horne and others), 1841; T. Hunt's "Foster Brother," 1845; "Finest Scenes" from Beaumont and Fletcher, 1855; "The Book of the Sonnet" (with S. A. Lee, *posthumous*), 1867. *Life:*   "Autobiography," 1850, etc., "Life," by Cosmo Monkhouse, 1893.—SHARP R. FARQUHARSON, 1897, *A Dictionary of English Authors, p.* 142.

PERSONAL

What though, for showing truth to flatter'd
    state,
Kind Hunt was shut in prison, yet has he,
In his immortal spirit, been as free
As the sky-searching lark, and as elate.
Minion of grandeur! think you he did wait?
Think you he nought but prison-walls did see,
Till, so unwilling, thou unturn'dst the key?
Ah, no! far happier, nobler was his fate!
In Spenser's halls he stray'd, and bowers fair,
Culling enchanted flowers; and he flew

With daring Milton through the fields of air:
To regions of his own his genius true
Took happy flights. Who shall his fame impair
When thou art dead, and all thy wretched
    crew?
—KEATS, JOHN, 1815, *Written on the Day that Mr. Leigh Hunt left Prison.*

Leigh Hunt's weather-cock estimation of you I cannot account for, nor is it worth while to attempt.   He first attacks you

when he had never read your works; then a
friend, Barnes, brought him your "Excursion," pointed out your sonnets, and
Leigh Hunt began to find that he really
should have looked through a poet's works
before he came to a conclusion on the
genius displayed in them. . . . When first I
knew Leigh Hunt, he was really a delightful fellow, ardent in virtue, and perceiving
the right thing in everything but religion—
he now finds "no end in wandering mazes
lost," perplexes himself, and pains his
friends. His great error is inordinate personal vanity, and he who pampers it not, is
no longer received with affection. I am
daily getting more estranged from him;
and, indeed, all his old friends are dropping
off.—HAYDON, BENJAMIN ROBERT, 1817,
*To Wordsworth, April 15; Life, Letters and
Table Talk, ed. Stoddard, pp.* 196, 197.

Leigh Hunt is a good man and a good
father—see his Odes to all the Masters
Hunt;—a good husband—see his sonnet to
Mrs. Hunt;—a good friend—see his Epistles
to different people;—and a great coxcomb
and a very vulgar person in everything
about him. But that is not his fault, but
of circumstances.—BYRON, LORD, 1818,
Letter to Mr. Moore, June 1.

Had I known a person more highly endowed than yourself with all that it becomes a man to possess, I had solicited for
this work the ornament of his name. One
more gentle, honorable, innocent and
brave; one of the most exalted toleration
for all who do and think evil, and yet himself more free from evil; one who knows
better how to receive and how to confer a
benefit, though he must ever confer far
more than he can receive; one of simpler,
and, in the highest sense of the word, of
purer life and manners, I never knew.
—SHELLEY, PERCY BYSSHE, 1819, *The
Cenci, Dedication to Leigh Hunt.*

You will see Hunt—one of those happy souls
Which are the salt of the earth, and without
  whom
This world would smell like what it is—a tomb;
Who is, what others seem; his room no doubt
Is still adorned by many a cast from Shout,
With graceful flowers tastefully placed about;
And coronals of bay from ribbons hung,
And brighter wreaths in neat disorder flung,
The gifts of the most learned among some
  dozens
Of female friends, sister-in-law and cousin.
—SHELLEY, PERCY BYSSHE, 1820, *Letter
to Maria Grisborne.*

I have no quarrel with you, nor can I
have. You are one of those people that I
like, do what they will; there are others
that I do not like, do what they may. I
have always spoken well of you to friend or
foe, viz: I have said you were one of the
pleasantest and cleverest persons I ever
knew; but that you teased any one you
had to deal with out of their lives.—HAZ-
LITT, WILLIAM, 1821, *Letters, Four Generations of a Literary Family, vol.* I, *p.* 133.

In spite of "Rimini," I must look upon
its author as a man of taste and a poet. He
is better than so; he is one of the most
cordial-minded men I ever knew, and
matchless as a fireside companion. I mean
not to affront or wound your feelings when
I say that in his more genial moods he has
often reminded me of you. There is the
same air of mild dogmatism—the same condescending to a boyish sportiveness—in
both your conversations. His hand-writing
is so much the same with your own, that I
have opened more than one letter of his,
hoping, nay, not doubting, but it was from
you, and have been disappointed (he will
bear with my saying so) at the discovery of
my error. L. H. is unfortunate in holding
some loose and not very definite speculations (for at times I think he hardly knows
whither his premises would carry him) on
marriage—the tenets, I conceive, of the
"Political Justice" carried a little farther.
For anything I could discover in his practice, they have reference, like those, to
some future possible condition of society,
and not to the present times. But neither
for these obliquities of thinking (upon
which my own conclusions are as distant as
the poles asunder)—not for his political asperities and petulancies, which are wearing
out with the heats and vanities of youth—
did I select him for a friend; but for qualities which fitted him for that relation.—
LAMB, CHARLES, 1823, *The Tombs in the
Abbey, in a Letter to Robert Southey, Esq.*

He is a man of thoroughly London make,
such as you could not find elsewhere, and I
think about the *best* possible to be made of
this sort: an airy, crotchety, most copious
clever talker, with an honest undercurrent
of reason too, but unfortunately not the
deepest, not the most practical—or rather
it is the most *un*practical ever man dealt
in. His hair is grizzled, eyes black-hazel,
complexion of the clearest dusky brown;
a thin glimmer of a smile plays over a face

of cast-iron gravity. He never laughs— can only titter, which I think indicates his worst deficiency. . . . His house excels all you have read of,—a poetical *Tinker-dom*, without parallel even in literature. In his family room, where are a sickly large wife and a whole shoal of well-conditioned wild children, you will find half a dozen old rickety chairs gathered from half a dozen different hucksters, and all seemingly engaged, and just pausing, in a violent hornpipe. On these and around them and over the dusty table and ragged carpet lie all kinds of litter,—books, papers, egg-shells, scissors, and last night when I was there the torn heart of a half-quarter loaf. His own room above stairs, into which alone I strive to enter, he keeps cleaner. It has only two chairs, a bookcase, and a writing-table; yet the noble Hunt receives you in his Tinkerdom in the spirit of a king, apologises for nothing, places you in the best seat, takes a window-sill himself if there is no other, and there folding closer his looseflowing "muslin cloud" of a printed nightgown, in which he always writes, commences the liveliest dialogue on philosophy and the prospects of man (who is to be beyond measure "happy" yet); which again he will courteously terminate the moment you are bound to go: a most interesting, pitiable, lovable man, to be used kindly but with discretion.— CARLYLE, THOMAS, 1834, *To Alexander Carlyle, June* 27; *Thomas Carlyle, A History of the First Forty Years of His Life, ed. Froude, vol.* II, *p.* 354.

He lives far from town,—in Chelsea,—in a humble house, with uncarpeted entry and stairs. He lives more simply, I think, than any person I have visited in England; but he possesses a palace of a mind. He is truly brilliant in conversation, and the little notes of his which I have seen are very striking. He is of about the middle size, with iron-gray hair parted in the middle, and suffered to grow quite long.—SUMNER, CHARLES, 1839, *To George S. Hillard, Jan.* 27; *Memoir and Letters of Sumner, ed. Pierce, vol.* II, *p.* 47.

I felt age coming on me, and difficulties not lessened by failing projects: nor was I able, had I ever been so inclined, to render my faculties profitable "in the market." . . A man only can do what he can do, or as others will let him. Suppose he has a conscience that will not suffer him to reproduce the works of other people, or even to speak what he thinks commonplace enough to have become public property. Suppose his conscience will not allow him to accommodate himself to the opinion of editors and reviewers. Suppose the editors and reviewers themselves will not encourage him to write on the subjects he understands best, perhaps do not understand the subjects themselves; or, at least, play with him, and delay him, and keep him only as a resource when their own circle fails them. Suppose he has had to work his way up through animosities, political and religious, and through such clouds of adversity as, even when they have passed away, leave a chill of misfortune round his repute, and make "prosperity" slow to encourage him. Suppose, in addition to all this, he is in bad health, and of fluctuating as well as peculiar powers; of a temperament easily solaced in mind, and as easily drowsed in body; quick to enjoy every object in creation, every thing in nature and in art, every sight, every sound, every book, picture, and flower, and at the same time really qualified to do nothing, but either to preach the enjoyment of these objects in modes derived from his own particular nature and breeding, or to suffer with mingled cheerfulness and poverty the consequences of advocating some theory on the side of human progress. Great may sometimes be the misery of that man under the necessity of requesting forbearance or undergoing obligation; and terrible will be his doubts, whether some of his friends may not think he had better have had a conscience less nice, or activity less at the mercy of his physique.—HUNT, LEIGH, 1850-60, *Autobiography.*

Leigh Hunt was there, with his cheery face, bright, acute, and full of sensibility; and his thick grizzled hair combed down smooth, and his homely figure;—black handkerchief, grey stockings and stout shoes, while he was full of gratitude to ladies who dress in winter in velvet, and in rich colours; and to old dames in the streets or the country who still wear scarlet cloaks. His conversation was lively, rapid, highly illustrative, and perfectly natural.—MARTINEAU, HARRIET, 1855-77, *Autobiography, ed. Chapman, vol.* I, *p.* 287.

Towards the end of June, 1822, the long-expected family of the Hunts arrived by sea from England. . . . I found him a gentleman and something more; and with a quaint fancy and cultivated mind. He was in high spirits, and disposed to be pleased with others. His anticipated literary projects in conjunction with Byron and Shelley were a source of great pleasure to him—so was the land of beauty and song.— TRELAWNY, EDWARD JOHN, 1858–78, *Records of Shelley, Byron and the Author, p.* 117.

Drove to Hammersmith, where we found Leigh Hunt and his two daughters awaiting us. It was a very tiny cottage, with white curtains and flowers in the window, but his beautiful manner made it a rich abode. The dear old man talked delightfully about his flowers, calling them "gentle household pets."—FIELDS, JAMES T., 1859, *Diary, June* 30; *Biographical Notes and Personal Sketches, p.* 64.

I found Leigh Hunt living in a pleasant little cottage at Hammersmith. . . . On entering the little parlor, used as a "study," a tall figure, dressed in a morning gown, with a large cape, came forward and grasped my hand with a sort of feminine tenderness and enthusiasm. . . . Leigh Hunt is now nearly eighty years of age; and yet his complexion has the fairness and freshness of youth. His hair is as white as the bloom of an almond tree, and as full and glossy as the head of a child. His brow is broad and beautiful, and his eye as gentle and as clear as that of a woman who has never seen a cloudy day. His heart is as merry as a bird's and his look and manner alternately playful and pensive, but without a shadow of sadness.—FULLER, HIRAM, 1859, *Sparks from a Locomotive.*

One characteristic of Leigh Hunt, for which few gave him credit, was his great capacity for work. His writings were the result of immense labor and painstaking, of the most conscientious investigation of facts, where facts were needed; and of a complete devotion of his faculties towards the object to be accomplished. Notwithstanding his great experience, he was never a very rapid writer. He corrected, excised, reconsidered, and elaborated his productions (unless pressed for time), with the most minute attention to details.—OLLIER, EDMUND, (?) 1859, *Spectator, Sept.* 3.

An odd declaration by Dickens that he did not mean Leigh Hunt by Harold Skimpole. Yet he owns that he took the light externals of the character from Leigh Hunt, and surely it is by those light externals that the bulk of mankind will always recognize character. Besides, it is to be observed that the vices of Harold Skimpole are vices to which Leigh Hunt had, to say the least, some little leaning, and which the world generally imputed to him most unsparingly. That he had loose notions of *meum* and *tuum*, that he had no high feeling of independence, that he had no sense of obligation, that he took money wherever he could get it, that he felt no gratitude for it, that he was just as ready to defame a person who had relieved his distress as a person who had refused him relief,—these were things which, as Dickens must have known, were said, truly or falsely, about Leigh Hunt and had made a deep impression on the public mind. Indeed, Leigh Hunt had said himself: "I have some peculiar notions about money. They will be found to involve considerable difference of opinion with the community, particularly in a commercial country. I have not that horror of being under obligation which is thought an essential refinement in money matters." That is Harold Skimpole all over. How then could D. doubt that H. S. would be supposed to be a portrait of L. H.? —MACAULAY, THOMAS BABINGTON, 1859, *Journal, Dec.* 23; *Life and Letters, ed. Trevelyan, ch.* xv.

Four or five years ago, the writer of these lines was much pained by accidentally encountering a printed statement, that Mr. Leigh Hunt was the original of Harold Skimpole in "Bleak House." . . . The fact is this:—Exactly those graces and charms of manner which are remembered in the words we have quoted, were remembered by the author of the work of fiction in question, when he drew the character in question. Above all other things, that "sort of gay and ostentatious wilfulness" in the humoring of a subject, which had many a time delighted him, and impressed him as being unspeakably whimsical and attractive, was the airy quality he wanted for the man he invented. Partly for this reason, and partly (he has since often grieved to think) for the pleasure it afforded him to find that delightful manner reproducing itself under his hand, he yielded to the temptation of too often making the character *speak* like his old friend. He no more thought—God forgive him! that the admired original would ever be charged with the imaginary vices of the fictitious creature, than he has himself ever thought of charging the blood of Desdemona and Othello, on the innocent Academy model who sat for Iago's leg in the picture.—DICKENS, CHARLES, 1859, *Leigh Hunt, All the Year Round, vol.* 2, *p.* 207.

His whole life was one of pecuniary anxiety. His father was a refugee from America, the representative of a Barbados family, whose fortunes had declined; and although Isaac Hunt was a man who could at dangerous junctures put forth resolution and energy, it seems evident that he was inclined to repose on the traditions of his family, and on a vague general hopefulness, rather than active endeavour. Emerging from the Bluecoat School, Leigh Hunt found himself placed in the hereditary condition of an impoverished relative; and the employment sought for him was such as could be found, rather than such as suited either his natural disposition or his training, which had been exclusively scholastic. By the force of accidental circumstances, he became . . . a writer for the periodical press, in itself not a very certain mode of livelihood, and one not calculated to develop regular business habits. In addition to these untoward circumstances, there was a peculiarity of his character—it was no affectation when he declared himself entirely incompetent to deal with the simplest question of arithmetic. The very commonest sum was a bewilderment to him. He learned addition in order that he might be fitted for his place in a public office. It was a born incapacity, similar to that of people who cannot distinguish the notes of music or the colours of the prism. Perpetually reproached with it, very conscious of his mistakes, he took his deficiency to heart, and, with the emphatic turn of his temperament, increased it by exaggerating his own estimate of it. Thus he regarded himself as a sort of idiot in the handling of figures; and he was consequently incapacitated for many subjects which he could handle very well when they were explained to him in another form. A secondary consequence was the habit, acquired very early, of trusting to others.—HUNT, THORNTON, 1862, *Correspondence of Leigh Hunt, vol.* I, *p.* 110.

I have said that he was a beautiful old man. In truth, I never saw a finer countenance, either as to the mould of features or the expression, nor any that showed the play of feeling so perfectly without the slightest theatrical emphasis. It was like a child's face in this respect. At my first glimpse of him, when he met us in the entry, I discerned that he was old, his long hair being white and his wrinkles many; it was an aged visage, in short, such as I had not at all expected to see, in spite of dates, because his books talk to the reader with the tender vivacity of youth. But when he began to speak, and as he grew more earnest in conversation, I ceased to be sensible of his age; sometimes, indeed, its dusky shadow darkened through the gleam which his sprightly thoughts diffused about his face, but then another flash of youth came out of his eyes and made an illumination again. I never witnessed such a wonderfully illusive transformation, before or since; and, to this day, trusting only to my recollection, I should find it difficult to decide which was his genuine and stable predicament,—youth or age. I have met no Englishman whose manners seemed to me so agreeable, soft, rather than polished, wholly unconventional, the natural growth of a kindly and sensitive disposition without any reference to rule, or else obedient to some rule so subtle that the nicest observer could not detect the application of it. His eyes were dark and very fine, and his delightful voice accompanied their visible language like music. . . . He must have suffered keenly in his lifetime, and enjoyed keenly, keeping his emotions so much upon the surface as he seemed to do, and convenient for everybody to play upon. Being of a cheerful temperament, happiness had probably the upperhand. His was a light, mildly joyous nature, gentle, graceful, yet seldom attaining to that deepest grace which results from power.—HAWTHORNE, NATHANIEL, 1863, *Up the Thames, Our Old Home, pp.* 314, 318.

He was held up to shame as an enemy of religion, whereas he was a man from whose heart there came a flowing pity spreading itself over all nature and in every channel in which it was possible to run. I remember a passage in one of his writings in which he says he never passed a church, of however unreformed a faith, without an instinctive wish to go in and worship for the good of mankind. And all this obloquy, all this injustice, all this social cruelty never for one moment soured the disposition or excited a revengeful feeling in the breast of this good man. He had as it were—I have no other phrase for it—a superstition of good. He did not believe in the existence of evil, and when it pressed against him, in the bitterest form against himself, he shut his eyes to it. . . . We know that through all the difficulties of a more than usually hard life he kept to the end a cheerfulness of temper which the most successful might have envied. — MILNES, RICHARD MONCKTON (LORD HOUGHTON), 1869, *An Address.*

To be seated at the same table with Leigh Hunt was, I thought, like seeing Byron and Shelley by reflected light; and I could not but watch, with a curiosity amounting almost to awe, every movement of his face, and every word that fell from his lips. True, I soon discovered that, after all, he was but a mortal man, and that, despite the history of his past career, he talked and acted as a being of ordinary instincts rather than as one who might be supposed to have wings to fly with. Still I was constantly reminded of the indisputable fact that Leigh Hunt was "somebody," and that I was assuredly complimented in being brought into such close companionship with him. I hardly dare venture to describe his personal appearance, further than to say he *looked* the man of that refined intellectual power which had given him his place in the literature of his time; that his complexion seemed strangely to harmonize with his hair (for he wore no whiskers, and moustaches at that time had not found their way to this country), in one uniform tint of iron-gray; and that his shirt-collar ascended from his neck in a *négligé* manner, which might be considered slovenly, but which was picturesquely effective in its loose luxuriance. There was, moreover, a sort of valetudinarian air about him, and he appeared extremely particular as to what he ate and drank, preferring, he said, the mildest form of nutriment, such as he was accustomed to at home—"just the wing of a chicken," and "only a moderate quantity of sherry and water" being especially demanded. . . . At length our host prevailed upon his distinguished visitor himself to "favor us with a tune"—a knowledge of music being known to be one of Mr. Hunt's accomplishments. With this request he most readily complied, and good-humoredly observed, "I will give you a favorite *barcarolle* which I was in the habit of playing to Birron and

Shelley in Italy" (he pronounced the first name as if it were spelt as I have written it —with two rr's and the "i" short). He executed the task with a spirit and delicacy which could hardly have been expected from an amateur who had passed the greater part of his days in the cultivation of literature.—HODDER, GEORGE, 1870, *Memories of My Time.*

I well remember the last time I saw him at Hammersmith, not long before his death in 1859, when, with his delicate, worn, but keenly intellectual face, his large, luminous eyes, his thick shock of wiry gray hair, and a little cape of faded black silk over his shoulders, he looked like an old French Abbé.—FORSTER, JOHN, 1872-74, *Life of Charles Dickens, vol.* III, *p.* 27, *note.*

Hunt was a little above the middle size, thin and lithe. His countenance was very genial and pleasant. His hair was black; his eyes were very dark, but he was short-sighted, and therefore perhaps it was that they had nothing of that fierce glance which black eyes so frequently possess. His mouth was expressive, but protruding; as is sometimes seen in half-caste Americans. . . . Leigh Hunt was always in trouble about money; but he was seldom sad, and never sour. The prospect of poverty did not make much impression on him who never possessed wealth. . . . Hunt had a crotchet or theory about social intercourse (between the sexes), to which he never made any converts. He was at one time too frequently harping on this subject. This used to irritate Hazlitt, who said, "D—— him; it's always coming out like a rash. Why doesn't he write a book about it, and get rid of it." Hunt did not press these opinions upon any one to a pitch of offence. He himself led a very domestic and correct life. And I am bound to say that, during an intimacy of many (forty) years, I never heard him utter an oath, although they were then very common; and I never heard from him an indelicate hint or allusion.—PROCTER, BRYAN WALLER, 1874(?), *Recollections of Men of Letters, ed. Patmore, pp.* 195, 196, 197.

Leigh Hunt's inability to appreciate the comparative value of monies was well known. It was real, not affected. I have seen it myself more than once. For that, his conversation, and his brilliant touch on the piano, was he best known socially. I am a staunch admirer of Dickens, but I cannot waver in my belief that Leigh Hunt was the model of "Horace Skimpole," at least until that lightsome individual began to exhibit his darker shades. The similarity is too marked in more things than can be mentioned here. I know that Dickens denied this, and that there is nothing more to be said; but the very first time I read the very first number of "Bleak House," which describes Skimpole, I said "There is Leigh Hunt!"—GRUNDY, FRANCIS H., 1879, *Pictures of the Past, p.* 165.

As to Leigh Hunt's friendship for Keats, I think the points you mention loom equivocal, but Hunt was a many-laboured and much belaboured man, and as much allowance as may be made on this score is perhaps due to him—no more than that much. His own powers stand high in various ways —poetically higher perhaps than is at present admitted, despite his detestable flutter and airiness for the most part. But assuredly by no means could he have stood so high in the long run, as by a loud and earnest defence of Keats. Perhaps the best excuse for him is the remaining possibility of an idea on his part, that any defence coming from one who had himself so many powerful enemies might seem to Keats rather to damage than improve his position. —ROSSETTI, DANTE GABRIEL, 1880, *Letter, Recollections of Rossetti, ed. Caine, p.* 179.

Leigh Hunt attempted no defence for Keats when the bread was taken out of his mouth, and that Keats felt this neglect and remarked upon it in a letter in which he further cast some doubt upon the purity of Hunt's friendship. Hunt, after Keats's death, said in reference to this: "Had he but given me the hint!" The *hint,* forsooth! Moreover, I can find no sort of allusion in *The Examiner* for 1821, to the death of Keats. I told Rossetti that by the reading of the periodicals of the time, I formed a poor opinion of Hunt. Previously I was willing to believe in his unswerving loyalty to the much greater men who were his friends, but even that poor confidence in him must perforce be shaken when one finds him silent at a moment when Keats most needs his voice, and abusive when Coleridge is a common subject of ridicule. It was all very well for Hunt to glorify himself in the borrowed splendour of Keats's established fame when the poet was twenty years dead, and to make much of his intimacy with Coleridge after the homage of

two generations had been offered him, but I know of no instance (unless in the case of Shelley) in which Hunt stood by his friends in the winter of their lives, and gave them that journalistic support which was, poor man, the only thing he ever had to give, whatever he might take. I have, however, heard Mr. H. A. Bright (one of Hawthorne's intimate friends in England) say that no man here impressed the American romancer as much as Hunt for good qualities, both of heart and head.—CAINE, HALL, 1882, *Recollection of Dante Gabriel Rossetti, p.* 177.

Leigh Hunt's sensitive delicacy was one of his most marked characteristics, and one that peculiarly impressed itself on those who enjoyed personal communion with him. He was delicate as a woman in conduct, in words, in ways of thinking. I have heard him use paraphrase in speaking of things that the generality of men are accustomed to mention plainly, as a matter of course; and though he could—on occasion—use very straightforward terms in treating a poetical subject warmly, or in reprobating a vice sternly, and employ very playful terms when treating a humorous subject wittily, I never heard him utter a coarse or a light word in the many times I have heard him converse with freedom among intimate friends. Airy elegance, sportive fancy, marked his lively talk; levity never.— CLARKE, MARY COWDEN, 1882, *Leigh Hunt, The Century, vol.* 23, *p.* 706.

I did not know Leigh Hunt in his prime; but I knew him well when he lived at Edwardes Square, Kensington. He was then yielding gradually to the universal conqueror. His son tells us, "He was usually seen in a dressing-gown, bending his head over a book or over a desk." Tall and upright still, his hair white and straggling, scattered over a brow of manly intelligence, his eyes retaining much of their old brilliancy combined with gentleness, his conversation still sparkling, though by fits and starts—he gave me the idea of a sturdy ruin that, in donning the moss vest of time, had been recompensed for gradual decay of strength by gaining ever more and more of the picturesque. . . . Testimonies to his nature are abundant. His famous sonnet, "Abou Ben Adhem," may have been inspired by an Eastern apothegm, but it was none the less an outpouring of his own large heart. As for his life it was one of the utmost simplicity and frugality; indeed, he carried the latter virtue to such an extreme that his son, in writing to me, describes his father's diet as consisting often only of bread.—HALL, SAMUEL CARTER, 1883, *Retrospect of a Long Life, p.* 391.

He was an old man with snowy hair. . . . But his eyes were still brilliant, and the fascinating grace of his manner was unimpaired. He was naturally rather tall and of a slender figure, but incessant daily toil at the desk caused him to stoop somewhat, though his son says of him, "he was straight as an arrow and looked slenderer than he really was," but this was in earlier years, before time and toil had left their impress. At the period of our visit, Leigh Hunt had reached his seventy-fifth year. . . . But Leigh Hunt was there, with his elegance and charm, like a prince in hiding. . . . He wore the dignity and sweetness of a man not only independent of worldly ambitions, but one dependent upon unworldly satisfactions. There was no sense of defeat because he was a poor man, nor even of inadequacy, except for lack of time and strength to "entertain strangers." He wore the air of a noble laborer—ceaseless, indefatigable; and when we remember that the wolf was driven from his door through so long a life by his busy pen, a pen unarmed with popular force, he might well feel that the struggle had been an honorable one.—FIELDS, ANNIE, 1888, *A Shelf of Old Books, Scribner's Magazine, vol.* 3, *pp.* 288, 289.

When I first knew Leigh Hunt he was verging on fifty-five, and resided in Edwardes Square, Kensington, the region which furnished him with material for one of the most agreeable of his books, "The Old Court Suburb." From the airy, lightsome cheeriness of so many of his writings, I had expected to find him all briskness and vivacity. On the contrary, as he sat and talked among his books, busts, and engravings, tall, dark-complexioned, with thoughtful brow and expressive hazel eyes, his grayish-black hair flowing down to his shoulders, he gave you the impression of courteous dignity and repose. In a grave, sweet voice, he spoke frankly, but always kindly, of the notable men with whom he had been intimate, and of whom a junior as I was might wish to hear, Shelley and Keats, Hazlitt and Charles Lamb. Of his later and then living contemporaries it was Thackeray about whom he showed most enthusiasm.—ESPINASSE, FRANCIS, 1893, *Literary Recollections and Sketches, p.* 338.

Though Leigh Hunt's character was simple and his gifts distinct, he is not easy to class either as an author or a man. His literary pretensions were well summed up by Charles Lamb in the couplet:—

"Wit, poet, proseman, partyman, translator,
Hunt, thy best title yet is 'Indicator.'"

With a nature filled with poetry, but yet most faulty as a poet; learned beyond the average, but hardly a scholar; full of sweet thoughts, but no thinker; vivacious and sportive to an extraordinary degree, yet falling short of supreme qualities as a humourist, Leigh Hunt scarcely attained to the first rank of writers, except as a sentimentalist, an anthologist, and a gossip, yet he so nearly touched it at so many points, and there is such a special quality in almost everything he wrote, that one hesitates to set him in a duller circle.—MONKHOUSE, COSMO, 1893, *Life of Leigh Hunt* (*Great Writers*), *p.* 238.

Hunt, a man of amiable disposition, good and pure, a Bayard *sans peur* and *sans reproche*, had his conduct little affected by "free" thinking. At worst it left him with a childish carelessness of pecuniary obligations, and also to a considerable disregard of misconstruction. He went on his quiet, pleasurable way, never outraging Mrs. Grundy in his private life, not unconcerned at world-wrongs, speaking honestly but with kindness of all men, and fairly earning his reputation as "the gentlest of the wise." But his family, perhaps spoiled by his easiness, inherited that easiness rather than the chivalrousness, which had kept him free from blame. He had eight children, sons and daughters. Of his daughters, Florimel, the eldest, Mrs. Gliddon, was a handsome woman; Julia, the second daughter, a *petite* and pretty coquette; Jacintha, whom her father used to call "monkey-face," was the good wife of one of my pupils who, forsaking engraving, got his living by literature. Of two of the sons, Percy and Henry, government clerks, I knew but little, nor cared to know more. . . . John Hunt, the eldest son, though a man not without brains, may have had some mental weakness to excuse his conduct. After breakfasting with a friend, he would borrow a book and pledge it at the nearest pawnbroker's; he would try to borrow money in his father's name from his father's friends, on one awkward occasion the father being in the house at which he called; such like tricks were not infrequent. Vincent, the youngest, was a very lovable fellow. . . . A weak repeat of his father, gentle but without moral fibre, he died almost before reaching manhood. Thornton, the second son, I knew best, a man rather below average height, deserving rather than his sister the name of "monkey-face," but bright, clever, and very winning, a man in spite of his physiognomy who had his way with women; far too much so, it was notorious, with the pretty wife of his friend George Henry Lewes, the two men only quarreling over the expense of the double family.—LINTON, WILLIAM JAMES, 1894, *Threescore and Ten Years, pp.* 115, 116, 117.

She [Mrs. Duncan Stewart] saw much of Leigh Hunt, of whom she was wont to say that she believed him to be the only person who, if he saw something yellow in the distance, and was told it was a buttercup, would be disappointed if he found it was only a guinea.—HARE, AUGUSTUS J. C., 1895, *Biographical Sketches, p.* 149.

I remember a visit from another hero of those times. We were walking across Kensington Square early one morning, when we heard some one hurrying after us and calling, "Thackeray, Thackeray!" This was also one of Byron's friends—a bright-eyed, active old man, with long, wavy white hair, and a picturesque cloak flung over one shoulder. I can see him still, as he crossed the corner of the Square and followed us with a light, rapid step. My father, stopping short, turned back to meet him, greeting him kindly, and bringing him home with us to the old brown house at the corner where we were then living. There was a sort of eagerness and vividness of manner about the stranger which was very impressive. You could not help watching him and his cloak, which kept slipping from its place, and which he caught at again and again. We wondered at his romantic, foreign looks, and his gayety and bright, eager way. Afterwards we were told that this was Leigh Hunt. We knew his name very well, for on the drawing-room table, in company with various Ruskins and *Punches,* lay a pretty, shining book called "A Jar of Honey from Mount Hybla," from which, in that dilettante, childish fashion which

is half play, half impatience, and search for something else, we had contrived to extract our own allowance of honey.— RITCHIE, ANNE THACKERAY, 1895, *Chapters from Some Unwritten Memoirs, p.* 60.

Mr. Hunt was striking in appearance— tall, dark, grizzled, bright-eyed, and rather fantastically dressed in a sacerdotal-looking garment. He received us with cordiality tinged with ceremony. . . . Mr. Hunt was most amiable: he discoursed about poetry as exhilaratingly as Ruskin does about art. He spoke of his own writings, and quite unaffectedly. It appeared to give him pleasure to do so. Perhaps if he talked less about them it would have been because he thought the more. He seemed proud of his old age, speaking with a smile of his *soixante et mille ans.* He gave me the impression of being rich in the milk of amiability and optimism. I do not think this was feigned, for I often heard of him as a benevolently minded man. I could hardly realise that this was the Mr Hunt who had written that underbred book about "Byron and his Contemporaries." I suppose age and experience had mellowed him.— LOCKER-LAMPSON, FREDERICK, 1895, *My Confidences, pp.* 337, 338.

There was another respect in which the accomplished essayist suffered injustice. I refer to the report which spread abroad after the appearance of Dickens's "Bleak House," that the creation of Harold Skimpole was borrowed from Hunt. The prevalence of this impression naturally afforded much pain to the individual most concerned, and his feelings were communicated to the author, who came down to Hammersmith in order to tender Hunt his solemn assurance that he had not designed anything of the kind, and that he would do anything in his power to make reparation for the unintentional wrong. Hunt told my informant that Dickens was affected almost to tears; but I never heard of any public or direct disavowal.—HAZLITT, W. CAREW, 1897, *Four Generations of a Literary Family, vol.* I, *p.* 292.

Leigh Hunt was of tall stature, with sallow, not to say yellow complexion. His mouth lacked refinement and firmness, but he had large, expressive eyes. His manner, however, had such fascination that, after he had spoken for five minutes, one forgot how he looked. He wrote the most charming letters, perfectly alike in both form and spirit. I particularly enjoyed the simple, old-fashioned suppers to which he frequently invited me. His daughter played and sang for us, and Leigh Hunt told us the most delightful stories of his Italian travels, and of Shelley and Byron (whom he always called "Birron"). I lived on the north side of the park, and I remember I used to get over the palings to cross Kensington Gardens, and thus shorten the distance home; the palings of those days were easily negotiated by an active young man.— SMITH, SIR GEORGE MURRAY, 1901, *In the Early Forties, The Critic, vol.* 38, *p.* 48.

THE STORY OF RIMINI
1816

Who loves to peer up at the morning sun;
With half-shut eyes and comfortable cheek,
Let him, with his sweet tale, full often seek
For meadows where the little rivers run;
Who loves to linger with that brightest one
Of Heaven—Hesperus—let him lowly speak
These numbers to the night, and starlight
  meek,
Or noon, if that her hunting be begun.
He who knows these delights, and too is prone
To moralize upon a smile or tear,
Will find at once a region of his own,
A bower for his spirit, and will steer
To alleys where the fir-tree drops its cone,
Where robins hop, and fallen leaves are sere.
—KEATS, JOHN, 1816, *On Leigh Hunt's Poem, "The Story of Rimini.*

This poem should be read twice to form a just opinion of its merits; the unusual, and in many places, the awkward versification will be apt to disgust the reader; we found more pleasure in the second perusal than the first. It contains some exquisite expressions of sentiment, and many passages that show an accurate and nice observation of the most delicate emotions of the human heart; the author also discovers a fine perception of harmony, in choosing the seasons and the picturesque circumstances of landscape, to accompany the joyous and painful feelings of the human breast. Many persons have judged that Lord Byron must possess a bad heart, because he delights in painting the bad and violent passions almost exclusively. By the same rule, Mr. Hunt should be presumed to have a most amiable character, since he so frequently describes frankness, openness, cheerfulness, &c. He does this almost to satiety; and there is a repetition of such description that becomes insipid.—TUDOR, W., 1816, *Rimini, North American Review, vol.* 3, *p.* 281.

We will venture to oppose his Third Canto of the "Story of Rimini" for classic elegance and natural feeling to any equal number of lines from Mr. Southey's Epics or from Mr. Moore's Lalla Rookh.—HAZLITT, WILLIAM, 1825, *The Spirit of the Age.*

Is full of delicate and refined fancy; but the diction is often deformed by a peculiar and intolerable coxcombry of language, to which has been given the significant appellation of *cockneyism.* It is a mixture of the *concetti* of second-rate Italian poetry with the smug arcadianism of a London citizen masquerading as a shepherd.—SHAW, THOMAS B., 1847, *Outlines of English Literature, p.* 431.

Except Chaucer himself, no painter of processions has excelled the entrance of Paulo to Ravenna, in the Story of Rimini.— MITFORD, MARY RUSSELL, 1851, *Recollections of a Literary Life, p.* 311

His "Story of Rimini," published in 1816, being, as it was, indisputably the finest inspiration of Italian song that had yet been heard in our modern English literature, had given him a place of his own as distinct as that of any other poetical writer of the day. Whatever may be thought of some peculiarities in his manner of writing, nobody will now be found to dispute either the originality of his genius, or his claim to the title of a true poet.—CRAIK, GEORGE L., 1861, *A Compendious History of English Literature and of the English Language.*

The poem has many pleasing, and some very sweet lines, but by endeavouring to be singular, or to exhibit somewhat of a novelty in his verse, he has introduced expressions and phrases that do not fall harmoniously upon the English ear. I mean they want that natural flow and those verbal combinations which are most pleasing. Some one, I remember, attacked his use of the word "swirl,"—

  "—Swirl into the bay."

If this were the only objection to the structure and language of a poem that contains many fine lines, with what may be called here and there a concetto, it would be indeed hypercritical to notice them. Whoever has seen a vessel with a gentle breeze and strong tide in her favour run into a bay and anchor, will feel how very descriptive of the actual fact the word he thus used.—REDDING, CYRUS, 1867, *Personal Reminiscences of Eminent Men, vol.* II, *p.* 202.

It is conceived in the spirit of Chaucer
and has in it lines worthy of Dryden.—IRE-
LAND, ALEXANDER, 1891, *Dictionary of National Biography, vol.* XXVIII, *p.* 269.

Of his poems, the "Story of Rimini,"
which we should rank among the highest, is
full of charming poetical conceits. . . . But
the whole composition lacks depth; it is
charming upon the surface, but there is
nothing to be found below.—OLIPHANT,
MARGARET O. W., 1892, *The Victorian Age
of English Literature, p.* 98.

He never realised the proper dignity of
poetry, and in discarding monotony, became slipshod. Hard polish was replaced
by limp jerkiness, and the couplet in his
hands grew pert and garrulous. There are
beautiful passages in the poem worthy of
the great reform to be inaugurated, but
they are few and far between. In the matter
of language, again, he could not *maintain* a
high standard. His very simplicity was in
part artificial, and he had a singular taste
for giving ordinary words an original significance which ruined his phrases, though
it never made him obscure. The poem was
considerably revised, but the changes related principally to the final development
of the plot and are not all improvements.
In old age Leigh Hunt referred to "Rimini"
as the work of a "Tyro," but it does not
contain any signs of youth from which he
was afterwards exempt, and reaches as
high a level as any of his longer pieces. It
proves conclusively that he was not, in the
highest sense, a poet.—JOHNSON, REGI-
NALD BRIMLEY, 1896, *Leigh Hunt, p.* 95.

Executed with ever so much of delicacy
—but not a sign or a symbol of the grave
and melancholy tone which should equip,
even to the utmost hem of its descriptive
passages, that tragic story of Dante.—
MITCHELL, DONALD G., 1897, *English Lands
Letters and Kings, The Later Georges to Victoria, p.* 149.

AUTOBIOGRAPHY
1850–60

Heaven bless the reader, and all of us:
and enable us to compare notes some day
in some Elysian corner of intuition, where
we shall be in no need of prefaces and explanations, and only wonder how any of
us could have missed the secret of universal
knowledge and happiness.—HUNT, LEIGH,
1850, *Autobiography of Leigh Hunt, Preface.*

Well, I call this an excellent good book,

by far the best of the autobiographic kind
I remember to have read in the English
language; and, indeed, except it be Boswell's of Johnson, I do not know where we
have such a picture drawn of human life as
in these three volumes.—CARLYLE, THOMAS,
1850, *Letter to Leigh Hunt, Jan.* 17; *Thomas
Carlyle by Conway, p.* 208.

His "Autobiography" is brimming with
expressions of good will to all mankind, and
frank confession of youthful offences. His
philanthropic sentiment was overflowing.
Uncle Toby was his ideal —"divine Uncle
Toby." "He who created Uncle Toby was
the wisest man since the days of Shakespeare." "As long as the character of Toby
Shandy finds an echo in the heart of man,
the heart of man is noble." In point of
style, his model was Addison. In simplicity
and felicitous grace of expression he may be
contrasted with the more robust and careless vigour predominant in the early days
of the *Edinburgh Review* and *Blackwood.*
He particularly excels in the graceful
touches of humorous caricature.—MINTO,
WILLIAM, 1872–80, *A Manual of English
Prose Literature, p.* 541.

One of the most interesting books ever
written is Leigh Hunt's biography of himself,—an autobiography almost unequaled.
It is a book that ought to be read by all
who wish to get authentic information of
Hunt's contemporaries. It abounds in pen
portraits of many writers who have long
ago passed into fame.—FIELDS, JAMES T.,
1885, *Recollections of Leigh Hunt, Some
Noted Princes, Authors, and Statesmen of Our
Time, ed. Parton, p.* 140.

The book is one of the most graceful and
genial chronicles of its kind in our language.
—IRELAND, ALEXANDER, 1891, *Dictionary
of National Biography, vol.* XXVIII, *p.* 272.

It is a fascinatingly interesting work, containing vivid pictures of the literary society
of his time, characteristic vignettes of his
most illustrious contemporaries, besides revealing, by what it omits rather than by
what it says, the singularly fine temper,
delicate sense of humour, generous bearing,
and ultra-conscientiousness of its author.—
ARCHER, THOMAS, 1892, *The Poets and the
Poetry of the Century, Southey to Shelley, ed.
Miles, p.* 306.

A work which no one can read without
loving, or at least liking, the author. He
was a master of the art of portrait-painting,

clear, humorous and sympathetic.—Cornish, F. Warre, 1896, *Leigh Hunt, Temple
Bar*, vol. 108, *p.* 195.

POEMS

His self-delusions are very lamentable—
they have enticed him into a Situation
which I should be less eager after than that
of a galley Slave. . . . There is no greater
Sin after the seven deadly than to flatter
oneself into an idea of being a great Poet.—
Keats, John, 1817, *To Benjamin Robert
Haydon, May* 11; *Letters of John Keats, ed.
Colvin, p.* 15.

One of Hunt's most apparent characteristics is his cheerfulness. His temperament is obviously mercurial. His fondness for the gayer class of Italian writers indicates a sympathy with southern buoyancy not often encountered in English
poetry. His versification is easy and playful; too much so, indeed, for imposing
effect. He seems to have written generally
under the inspiration of high animal spirits.
His sentiment is lively and tender, rather
than serious and impressive. The reviewers
have censured him with rather too much
severity for occasional affectations. With a
few exceptions on this score his "Story of
Rimini" is a charming poem. "The Legend of Florence," written at a later period,
is one of the most original and captivating
of modern plays. Many of his "Epistles"
glow with a genial humour and spirit of
fellowship which betray fine social qualities.
He lives obviously in his affections, and
cultivates literature with refined taste
rather than with lukewarm assiduity.—
Griswold, Rufus Wilmot, 1844, *The
Poets and Poetry of England in the Nineteenth Century, p.* 194.

No living poet has that obvious and overflowing delight in the bare act of composition, of which this poet gives sign. "Composition" is not a word for him—we might
as well use it of a bird—such is the ease
with which it seems to flow! Yet he is an
artist and constructor also, and is known to
work very hard at times before it comes out
so bright, and graceful, and pretending to
have cost no pains at all. He spins golden
lines round and round, as a silk-worm in
its cocoon. . . . His sympathies with men
are wide as the distance between joy and
grief: and while his laughter is audible and
resistless, in pathos and depth of tender
passionateness, he is no less sufficient. The

tragic power of the "Story of Rimini," has
scarcely been exceeded by any English
poet, alive or dead; and his "Legend
of Florence," is full of the "purification
of pity," and the power of the most
Christian-like manhood and sympathy.—
Horne, Richard Hengist, 1844, *A New
Spirit of the Age.*

At the outset of his career, his ambition
was to excel as a bard. His principal success, however, seems chiefly to lay in a certain vein of essay-writing, in which fancy
and familiarity are delightfully combined.
Still he has woven many rhymes that are
not only sweet and cheerful, but possess a
peculiar grace and merit of their own, besides illustrating some capital ideas relating
to poetical diction and influence. They are,
to be sure, deformed by some offences
against the dignity of the muse, in the
shape of affectations and far-fetched conceits.—Tuckerman, Henry Theodore,
1846, *Thoughts on the Poets.*

It is in vain here to attempt to speak of
the poetic merits of Leigh Hunt. A host of
fine compositions comes crowding on our
consciousness. "The Legend of Florence,"
a noble tragedy; "The Palfrey"; "Hero
and Leander"; "The Feast of the Poets";
and "The Violets"; numbers of delightful
translations from the Italian, a literature in
which Leigh Hunt has always reveled; and
above all, "Captain Sword and Captain
Pen." We would recommend every body,
just now that the war spirit is rising among
us, to read that poem, and learn what horrors they are rejoicing over, and what the
Christian spirit of this age demands of us.
But we must praise the lyrics of this volume:
—the pathos of the verses "To T. L. H.,
six years old, during a sickness," and the
playful humor of those "To J. H., four
years old," call on us for notice; and then
the fine blank verse poems, "Our Cottage,"
and "Reflections of a Dead Body," are
equally importunate. If any one does not
know what Leigh Hunt has done for the
people and the age, let him get the pocket
edition of his poems, and he will soon find
himself growing in love with life, with his
fellow-men and himself.—Howitt, William, 1847, *Homes and Haunts of the Most
Eminent British Poets, vol.* ii, *p.* 417.

With acute powers of conception, a
sparkling and lively fancy, and a quaintly
curious felicity of diction, the grand
characteristic of Leigh Hunt's poetry is

word-painting; and in this he is probably without a rival, save in the last and best productions of Keats, who contended, not vainly, with his master on that ground. In this respect, nothing can be more remarkable than some passages in "Rimini," and in his collection entitled "Foliage,"— much of which he has since capriciously cancelled; and he also exercised this peculiar faculty most felicitously in translations from the French and Italian, although, in some instances, he carried it to the amount of grotesqueness or affectation. His heroic couplet has much of the life, strength, and flexibility of Dryden—of whom he often reminds us; and in it he follows glorious John, even to his love for triplets and Alexandrines.—MOIR, D. M., 1851–52, *Sketches of the Poetical Literature of the Past Half-Century, Lecture* v.

Of his poems, besides "The Story of Rimini," his "Palfrey" is a fine, merrily tripping tale most pleasantly told; his "Captain Sword and Captain Pen" is full of power and pathos; of vivid description and terrible scene-painting; of noble sentiment and glorious aspirations; his drama, "A Legend of Florence," was successful on the stage, and is successful in the closet. A better companion for a summer day's ramble than the pocket edition of Leigh Hunt's poems we cannot conceive.—LANGFORD, JOHN ALFRED, 1861, *Prison Books and Their Authors, p.* 329.

He was an inveterate hoper, his face ever toward the sunrise. . . . Few poets have managed to scatter so much sunshine as Leigh Hunt.—CONWAY, MONCURE DANIEL, 1870, *The Leigh Hunt Memorial, Harper's Magazine, vol.* 40, *p.* 256.

Leigh Hunt's distinction as a poet is to be inspired by pleasure which never steals from his senses the freshness of boyhood, and never darkens his heart with the shadow of unsatisfied desire. . . . His poetry was not the poetry of thought and passion—which we have in Shakespeare; nor—to use Leigh Hunt's own words—that of "scholarship and rapt ambition," which we have in Milton. He would have passed his whole life writing eternal new stories in verse, part grave, part gay, of no great length, but "just sufficient," he says, "to vent the pleasure with which I am stung on meeting with some touching adventure, and which haunts me till I can speak of it somehow."— DOWDEN,

EDWARD, 1880, *English Poets, ed. Ward, vol.* IV, *pp.* 340, 341.

No one-sided sentiment of reaction against our so-called Augustan literature disqualified Leigh Hunt from becoming, as he afterwards became, the greatest master since the days of Dryden of that heroic couplet, which had become to most minds indissolubly associated with the prosaic versification of the eighteenth century school.—KENT, ARMINE T., 1881, *Leigh Hunt as a Poet, The Fortnightly Review, vol.* 36, *p.* 226.

Leigh Hunt, like Hazlitt, wrote largely in newspapers, in magazines, and reviews, and collected these writings into volumes which exist and are laid up on dusty shelves where nobody thinks of disturbing them. But Leigh Hunt did what Hazlitt could not do. There came out of his heart at last two exquisite little poems, which, to apply our favourite test, would, if all he ever wrote was swept away by some conflagration, linger in individual memories for generations, and flutter down orally through the mist of years, indestructible and sacred. One of these scraps of verse is the exquisite little fable called "Abou Ben Adhem": the other, Lines addressed "To T. L. H., six years old, during a sickness."—OLIPHANT, MARGARET O. W., 1882, *Literary History of England, XVIII–XIX Century, vol.* II, *p.* 252.

We have need to search long and in many places before finding anything more profoundly expressive of the wonder and awe of the soul of man brought face to face with the mystery of time than Hunt's "Thought on the Nile." As a whole, however, Hunt as a poet may be said to be the apostle of those who perceive nothing poetic that is not petty. There is the reverse of largeness in nearly everything from his pen. There is an affectation of the bird-like in the very movement of his verse. Hunt chirps of hawthorn and lilacs.—CAINE, HALL, 1883, *Cobwebs of Criticism, p.* 148.

Poetry was his first, his last, his most constant love; and if by prose he had to win the meat and the raiment of life it was poetry that to him was life itself. In one respect—and sufficient note has hardly been taken of it—Hunt's place is a singularly high one, for he is among the originators.—NOBLE, JAMES ASHCROFT, 1886, *The Sonnet in England and Other Essays, p.* 130.

Turning to the consideration of his poetry, we can see the same obvious faults in it as in his prose. It is often trivial in subject, always slight in treatment, and pet ideas are sometimes allowed to run to seed. He was too much inclined to use words in unusual connections and with a meaning of his own, though without producing obscurity. It may also perhaps be criticised with less compunction than his prose, because it was his chosen work, written in times of comparative leisure, and by which he hoped to live.—JOHNSON, REGINALD BRIMLEY, 1891, *ed. Essays of Leigh Hunt, Introduction, p.* xxvii.

He wrote no great poems, to be sure; for here, as in his prose, he is earnestly bent on carving little baskets out of cherry-stones—little figures on cherry-stones—dainty hieroglyphics, but always on cherry-stones!—MITCHELL, DONALD G., 1897, *English Lands Letters and Kings, The Later Georges to Victoria, p.* 147.

In my boyhood his poetry had given me much enjoyment, and increased that which I had derived from other poetry. The Greeks had, as he felicitously remarked, "invented the poetry of gladness," and by that portion of it his own had been suggested in part. He had a vivid appreciation of nature as seen from the classical point of view, and his sonnets possess a singular sense of proportion, the finest of them being one entitled "A Thought on the Nile," written, I think, in competition with two composed on the same day by Shelley and Keats.—DEVERE, AUBREY, 1897, *Recollections, p.* 330.

"The Story of Rimini," his longest poem, still delights in its best pages, full as they are of reminders not only of older poets like Spenser, but of Keats, whom Hunt so strongly influenced; and such lines as those to "Jenny," or upon "Abou Ben Adhem," are simply unforgetable.—RHYS, ERNEST, 1897, *Library of the World's Best Literature, ed. Warner, vol.* XIII, *p.* 7794.

Hunt was the first who seriously set himself to tell a tale in Chaucer's manner, to imitate his sprightly familiarity, his genial unconstraint. He only succeeded in showing how rare and difficult a thing that Chaucerian grace of manner is. He is unconstrained enough, but his unconstraint, though not without moments of charm, is apt to recall the slovenly ease of an underbred man. He is at his best in describing scenery; for the human drama and its tragic climax he lacks sinew; the concentrated pathos of Dante dissolves away in his hands into a tender romantic dream. Nor did Hunt attempt to reproduce the dramatic element in the telling, which was Chaucer's final and most brilliant contribution to the Tale.—HERFORD, CHARLES HAROLD, 1902, *English Tales in Verse, Introduction, p.* liii.

GENERAL

He of the rose, the violet, the spring,
The social smile, the chain for Freedom's sake:
And lo!—whose steadfastness would never take
A meaner sound than Raphael's whispering.
—KEATS, JOHN, 1817, *Sonnet Addressed to Haydon.*

I was employed looking over law papers all the forenoon; I then walked in the rain to Clapton, reading by the way the "Indicator." There is a spirit of enjoyment in this little work which gives a charm to it. Leigh Hunt seems the very opposite of Hazlitt. He loves everything, and, excepting that he has a few polemical antipathies, finds everything beautiful.—ROBINSON, HENRY CRABB, 1820, *Diary, Oct.* 29; *Diary, Reminiscences and Correspondence, ed. Sadler.*

A more amiable man in society I know not; nor (when he will allow his senses to prevail over his sectarian principles) a better writer.—BYRON, LORD, 1821, *A Second Letter on Bowles's Strictures on Pope.*

To my taste, the Author of "Rimini" and Editor of the *Examiner* is among the best and least-corrupted of our poetical prose-writers. In his light but well-supported columns we find the raciness, the sharpness, and the sparkling effect of poetry, with little that is extravagant or far-fetched, and no turgidity or pompous pretension. Perhaps there is too much the appearance of relaxation and trifling (as if he had escaped the shackles of rhyme), a caprice, a levity, and a disposition to innovate in words and ideas. Still the genuine master-spirit of the prose-writer is there; the one of lively, sensible conversation; and this may in part arise from the author's being himself an animated talker. Mr. Hunt wants something of the heat and earnestness of the political partisan; but his familiar and miscellaneous papers have all the ease, grace, and point of the best style of Essay-writing. Many of his effusions in the *Indicator* show, that if he had devoted himself exclusively to that mode of writing, he inherits more of the spirit of Steele than any man since his time.—HAZLITT, WILLIAM, 1825, *On the Prose Style of Poets, Table-Talk.*

The most vicious of all styles, the style of Mr. Leigh Hunt and his miserable followers. —KEBLE, JOHN, 1825, *Sacred Poetry, Quarterly Review, vol. 32, p. 216.*

Have you seen that wondrous Life of Byron? Was it not a thousand pities Hunt had borrowed money of the man he was to disinhume and behead in the course of duty afterwards? But for love or money I cannot see Hunt's book, or anything but extracts of it, and so must hold my tongue. Poor Hunt! He has a strain of music in him too, but poverty and vanity have smote too rudely over the strings.—CARLYLE, THOMAS, 1828, *Letters to B. W. Procter, Jan. 17; Thomas Carlyle by Conway, p. 244.*

His prose is gossiping, graceful, and searching, and charms many readers.— CUNNINGHAM, ALLAN, 1833, *Biographical and Critical History of the Literature of the Last Fifty Years.*

We have a kindness for Mr. Leigh Hunt. We form our judgment of him, indeed, only from events of universal notoriety—from his own works, and from the works of other writers, who have generally abused him in the most rancorous manner. But, unless we are greatly mistaken, he is a very clever, a very honest, and a very good-natured man. We can clearly discern, together with many merits, many serious faults, both in his writings and in his conduct. But we really think that there is hardly a man living whose merits have been so grudgingly allowed, and whose faults have been so cruelly expiated. . . . In some respects Mr. Leigh Hunt is excellently qualified for the task which he has undertaken. His style, in spite of its mannerism, nay, partly by reason of his mannerism, is well suited for light, garrulous, desultory *ana*, half critical, half biographical. We do not always agree with his literary judgments; but we find in him what is very rare in our time, the power of justly appreciating and heartily enjoying good things of very different kinds. He can adore Shakespeare and Spenser without denying poetical genius to the author of "Alexander's Feast," or fine observation, rich fancy, and exquisite humour to him who

imagined Will Honeycomb and Sir Roger de Coverley. He has paid particular attention to the history of the English drama from the Age of Elizabeth down to our own time, and has every right to be heard with respect on that subject. — MACAULAY, THOMAS BABINGTON, 1841, *Comic Dramatists of the Restoration, Edinburgh Review; Critical and Miscellaneous Essays.*

Do you know Leigh Hunt's exquisite essays called "The Indicator and Companion," &c., published by Moxon? I hold them at once in delight and reverence.— BROWNING, ELIZABETH BARRETT, 1844, *To Mrs. Martin, Nov. 16; Letters, ed. Kenyon, vol. I, p. 216.*

In religious feeling, however, he has been misrepresented. It is certain that no man was ever more capable of the spirit of reverence; for God gifted him with a loving genius—with a genius to love and bless. He looks full tenderly into the face of every man, and woman, and child, and living creature; and the beautiful exterior world, even when it is in an angry mood, he smooths down softly, as in recognition of his sentiency, with a gentle caressing of the fancy—Chaucer's irrepressible "Ah, benedicite," falling forever from his lips!— HORNE, RICHARD HENGIST, 1844, *A New Spirit of the Age, p. 183.*

One of the pleasantest writers of his time, —easy, colloquial, genial, humane, full of fine fancies and verbal niceties, possessing a loving if not a "learned spirit," with hardly a spice of bitterness in his composition. He is an excellent commentator on the minute beauties of poetry. He has little grasp or acuteness of understanding, and his opinions are valueless where those qualities should be called into play; but he has a natural taste, which detects with nice accuracy what is beautiful, and a power of jaunty expression, which conveys its intuitive decisions directly to other minds.— WHIPPLE, EDWIN PERCY, 1845, *British Critics, Essays and Reviews, vol. II, p. 154.*

I took up Leigh Hunt's book "The Town" with the impression that it would be interesting only to Londoners, and I was surprised, ere I had read many pages, to find myself enchained by his pleasant, graceful, easy style, varied knowledge, just views, and kindly spirit. There is something peculiarly anti-melancholic in Leigh Hunt's writings, and yet they are never boisterous. They resemble sunshine, being at once bright and tranquil.—BRONTË, CHARLOTTE, 1849, *Letter to W. S. Williams, April* 16; *Charlotte Brontë and Her Circle, ed. Shorter, p.* 195.

With every wish to maintain an esteem for Mr. Hunt as a writer—an esteem that dates from my earliest boyhood—I must protest against his painstaking use of my dramatic success—such as it has been—as an illustration of the injustice set down to Mr. Hunt's old brotherhood of journalists; namely, that they would make "a dead set" against any manager who should refuse to risk his treasury on their stage experiments! An odd compliment this, at parting, from the first editor of the *Examiner* to the journalists of 1850. It is a pity in the summing up of his literary life—a life that has been valuable to letters and to liberty—that Mr. Hunt should have sought the cause of his own stage disappointments in the fancied stage tyranny and meanness of others. Pity, that his ink, so very sweet in every other page of his "Autobiography," should suddenly curdle in the page dramatic.— JERROLD, DOUGLAS, 1850, *Mr. Leigh Hunt's Theory of Theatrical Success, The Athenæum.*

His name is associated in our minds with all manner of kindness, love, beauty, and gentleness. He has given us a fresh insight into nature, made the flowers seem gayer, the earth greener, the skies more bright, and all things more full of happiness and blessing. By the magical touch of his pen, he "kissed dead things into life." Age, which dries up the geniality of so many, brought no change to him. To the last he was spoken of as the "gray-haired boy,"— "the old-young poet, with gray hairs on his head, but youth in his eyes,"—and the perusal of his "Autobiography" written in his old age, serves to bring out charmingly the prominent features of his life.—SMILES, SAMUEL, 1860, *Brief Biographies.*

I have been so strangely taken lately with Leigh Hunt's letters. I used to love his writings when I was quite young, and I believe I like best, what he liked best; a green lane to walk in, or a pleasant window looking out upon a sunny, sloping field with trees. L. H., I think, must have loved an old-fashioned garden, with high walls and broad gravel walks, with espaliers and gooseberries, currants and vegetables, *set* within beds of flowers. He is the very soul and pith of pleasantness. Who but he

could have spoken in spring of being "gay and vernal and daffodilean?" There is a poem in that last word. I wonder if, when I grow old, and comfortable, and chatty, I have it in me to be anything of a Christian Leigh Hunt; or would the Christian element resist and decompose the Leigh Huntian?—I think not.—GREENWELL, DORA, 1863, *Letter to Prof. Knight, Aug.* 15; *Memoirs of Dora Greenwell, ed. Dorling, p.* 75.

To pass from Hazlitt to Leigh Hunt is like passing from a rough landscape sketch by Salvator, in which, according to Coleridge, the rocks take vague likeness of the human figure, to a garden scene by Lancret, with a group seated round a fountain engaged in dining off peaches, and listening to a gentle shepherd who is playing a guitar or telling a pleasant story. Leigh Hunt is as constitutionally gay as Hazlitt is constitutionally saturnine.—LYTTON, EDWARD BULWER LORD, 1867-68, *Charles Lamb and Some of His Companions, Miscellaneous Prose Works, vol.* I, *p.* 114.

Few men have effected so much by mere exquisiteness of taste in the absence of high creative power; fewer still, so richly endowed with taste, have so frequently and conspicuously betrayed the want of it. . . . This observation principally refers to his poetry, which, in spite of such vexatious flaws, nevertheless possesses a brightness, animation, artistic symmetry, and metrical harmony which lift the author out of the rank of minor poets, particularly when the influence of his example upon his contemporaries is taken into account. He excelled especially in narrative poetry. . . . As an appreciative critic, whether literary or dramatic, he is hardly equalled; his guidance is as safe as it is genial. The no less important vocation of a censor was uncongenial to his gentle nature, and was rarely essayed by him.—GARNETT, RICHARD, 1881, *Encyclopædia Britannica, Ninth Ed., vol.* XII.

Of all authors indeed, and probably of all readers, Leigh Hunt had the keenest eye for merit and the warmest appreciation of it wherever found. He was actively engaged in politics, yet was never blind to the genius of an adversary; blameless himself in morals, he could admire the wit of Wycherley; and a freethinker in religion, he could see both wisdom and beauty in the divines. Moreover, it is immensely to his credit that this universal knowledge, instead of puffing him up, only moved him to impart it, and that next to the pleasure he took in books was that he derived from teaching others to take pleasure in them. Witness his "Wit and Humour" and his "Imagination and Fancy," to my mind the greatest treasures in the way of handbooks that have ever been offered to students of English literature, and the completest antidotes to pretence in it.—PAYN, JAMES, 1881, *Some Private Views, p.* 48.

As pure-minded a man as ever lived, and a critic whose subtlety of discrimination and whose soundness of judgment, supported as it was on a broad base of truly liberal scholarship, have hardly yet won fitting appreciation.—LOWELL, JAMES RUSSELL, 1883–90, *Fielding, Address on Unveiling the Bust of Fielding, Taunton, Sept.* 4; *Prose Works, Riverside Ed., vol.* VI, *p.* 57.

Hunt's literary position in London exposed him to many assaults of criticism, his natural infirmities as a writer exposed him to many more. Perhaps there are few, if any, faults of which Hunt as a critic was not guilty.—CAINE, HALL, 1883, *Cobwebs of Criticism, p.* 148.

The faculty of over-refining which he deprecated in Coleridge was his own failing. He did not temporize with wrong; yet the ever-abiding spirit of gentleness and charity which was with him seemed to break the force of his scorn. To use a choice and expressive Saxon phrase, Leigh Hunt was not pig-headed. He lacked the victorious brute energy, the "insolence of health," as Hazlitt called it, which admits of no hesitancy, and clears its way straight to its end. His nature was too representative. Every possible bearing which a question might take appealed to him and deterred him. He had, as his son pointed out, a Hamlet-like deliberation, in which are yet elements of the finest wisdom and courage. —GUINEY, LOUISE IMOGEN, 1884, *An English Literary Cousin, Atlantic Monthly, vol.* 54, *p.* 471.

His affections fertilized and blessed the hearts of all his readers. His idolatries were only tendered to what is pure and noble in art. You admire his enthusiasm because it is *wisely* bestowed. For instance, when he has once taught his reader to discriminate what is *true* in poetry, there never can be any further mistake in judgment. He is almost infallible as a guide to the student. . . . He was as personal an essayist

as Montaigne, but never obtrusive nor offensive. He liked to be candid with his readers, and always treated them with open-heartedness and joyous cordiality.— FIELDS, JAMES T., 1885, *Recollections of Leigh Hunt, Some Noted Princes, Authors and Statesmen of Our Time, ed. Parton, pp.* 138, 139.

Of the many charms of Hunt's writings, perhaps the most powerful is the personal accent which brings the writer near to us. It seems strange at first sight that we should feel this with regard to a man whose work was so largely critical, for the traditional view of criticism is that it is something essentially abstract and *un*human— not to say *in*human—but the very thing which makes Leigh Hunt a memorable worker in this field of literature is that in his hands criticism became vascular and alive, a thing of flesh and blood.—NOBLE, JAMES ASHCROFT, 1886, *The Sonnet in England and other Essays, p.* 128.

What appears, now, in the retrospect, all but incomprehensible in this regard, is the circumstance that, at the outset of his career, Leigh Hunt was for several years together in the early part of this century assailed by more than one of the leading organs of public opinion with a scurrility that was often nothing less than ferocious and malignant. It arose clearly from the completest mis-apprehension, by his vilifiers, alike of his writings and of his character. His writings, both prose and verse, remain to this day intact—unaltered and unmodified. Nothing in them having been cancelled or withdrawn, they can speak for themselves. His character, again, such as it was then, continued, in all essentials, identically the same to the very end— ripened, it may be, with the mere lapse of years, but otherwise unchanged.—KENT, CHARLES, 1889, *ed. Leigh Hunt as Poet and Essayist, Biographical Introduction, p.* xi.

If the collector of first editions requires an instance from which to justify the faith which is in him against those who cry out that bibliography is naught, Leigh Hunt is a good example to his hand. This active and often admirable writer, during a busy professional life, issued a long series of works in prose and verse which are of every variety of commonness and scarcity, but which have never been, and probably never will be, reprinted as a whole. Yet not to possess the works of Leigh Hunt is to be ill equipped for the minute study of literary history at the beginning of the century.— GOSSE, EDMUND, 1891, *Gossip in a Library*, p. 285.

Leigh Hunt takes high rank as an essayist and critic. The spirit of his writings is eminently cheerful and humanising. He is perhaps the best teacher in our literature of the contentment which flows from a recognition of every-day joys and blessings. A belief in all that is good and beautiful, and in the ultimate success of every true and honest endeavour, and a tender consideration for mistake and circumstance, are the pervading spirit of all his writings. Cheap and simple enjoyments, true taste leading to true economy, the companionship of books and the pleasures of friendly intercourse, were the constant themes of his pen. He knew much suffering, physical and mental, and experienced many cares and sorrows; but his cheerful courage, imperturbable sweetness of temper, and unfailing love and power of forgiveness never deserted him.—IRELAND, ALEXANDER, 1891, *Dictionary of National Biography*, vol. XXVIII, p. 273.

Charming as his "Story of Rimini" is, long as it will maintain for him a place among the poets of his time, notable as its influence has been on the use of the heroic couplet, it is as a critic that Hunt takes his highest place in the literature of the century. In truth, he was well equipped for the critic's office. He had a keen eye, an open mind, an even judgment, a warm but intrepid heart, and a light, incisive utterance. There were few of his illustrious contemporaries who were not indebted to him for vindication or exposition.—ARCHER, THOMAS, 1892, *The Poets and the Poetry of the Century, Southey to Shelley*, ed. *Miles*, p. 306.

A sort of poetic *Baedeker* ["Imagination and Fancy"] or Tourist's Guide to Parnassus.—WATSON, WILLIAM, 1893, *Excursions in Criticism*, p. 6.

He marked a moment in literature, the transition from the aristocracy to the democracy of letters. He was only a mortal, though he lived with the Immortals; but he has his place near them, and does not deserve to be altogether lost in the crowd. He was a vagabond of literature, a hack of genius. He wrote about everything: politics, economics, Shakespeare, Byron, Italy, scenery, art, the Quattro Poeti, the modern writers, actors, and singers, the drama, the stage. He wrote so rapidly and indiscriminately, turning out his articles as the baker turns out his rolls, that the commonplace of the printer's boy, waiting below for copy, might have been invented for him. Writing was as easy to him as talking —and how he talked, Carlyle and Hazlitt have told us.—CORNISH, F. WARRE, 1896, *Leigh Hunt, Temple Bar*, vol. 108, p. 186.

His strength lies, as he himself suspected, in the brief narrative poems of which "Abou Ben Adhem" is the highest example. Here the impulse is from without, the lines are prompted by the enjoyment of a "tale that is told," and by the desire to express and impart that pleasure. The critical powers guide the creative, and lend them a vigour not their own. His manner at such times is simple and lucid, playful or tender according to circumstances, but always sincere and glowing. His ear, so keen for judgment, directs the rhythm, and makes the verse flowing and easy. His many admirable translations are composed in the same spirit. A loyal enthusiasm for the original prompts him to a rare fidelity in language and style, often achieved with marked success. Could Hunt have *maintained* these qualities of taste and self-control for any considerable period, he might have taken high rank as a poet. . . . He lacks passion, dignity, and restraint, his imagination is almost entirely fanciful; but by the winning charm of his own fresh and cultured personality he attracts and even occasionally subdues.—JOHNSON, REGINALD BRIMLEY, 1896, *Leigh Hunt*, pp. 104, 105.

When Leigh Hunt commenced to write essays, he was plainly under the spell of a past age, and the *Connoisseur* was admittedly his model. Nor did he ever wholly succeed in throwing off the faded garments of the eighteenth century, and there is always present in his style a touch of archaism which makes one rank him with the earlier essayists rather than with his own vigorous contemporaries. In 1812 he was known only as an unusually capable dramatic critic, and it was not till seven years later that he began in the "Indicator" to revive the essay on the lines of Addison and Goldsmith. He cannot, however, be placed in the first rank of English essayists. In all his work there is a lack of virility, and he had no special endowment of pathos or of humour. When it is said that he could write commonplace gracefully, his merits and defects are summarized. His essays bear nowhere the impress of a strong personality, they contain no fresh creations, and they scarcely ever deviate from one level of unemotional calm. Yet he had indubitable skill in writing on familiar subjects, and he wielded a simple style that on rare occasions became even eloquent.—LOBBAN, J. H., 1896, *ed. English Essays, Introduction, p.* liv.

The great mass of his work, though it has qualities which raise it far above ordinary journalism, still has some of the defects of journalism upon it. . . . His criticism is the reverse of methodical; it rarely attempts to grasp and never succeeds in grasping the whole of the subject; it is the last criticism to go to if what one wants is the latitude and longitude of the writer or the book in the great chart of literature. It may almost be said of Hunt's criticism of poetry in the late Laureate's words that "it cannot understand, it loves"; and by virtue of love it frequently detects and reveals peculiarities of the subject which more strictly intelligent treatment has missed. For this irregular, desultory "impressionist" criticism, as well as for his topographical narratives and descriptions, his sketches of manners, his stories and anecdotes, his eighteenth-century essay-writing adjusted to a looser nineteenth-century standard— Leigh Hunt's style is excellently suited. Save now and then when his poetic fit comes on while he is wielding the pen of prose, it cannot be said to be a very dignified or distinguished style; it is even, as has been hinted, sometimes slipshod and out-at-elbows, suggestive of the peculiar and rather slovenly ease and *bonhomie* which characterised its author's whole life and conversation. But at its best it can be almost beautiful; and except when it is at its very worst (which is very seldom) it is always agreeable.—SAINTSBURY, GEORGE, 1896, *English Prose, ed. Craik, vol.* v, *pp.* 248, 249.

An essayist, poet, and translator, full (at his best) of grace and charm in a kind quite of his own, he lacked both the stamina and the piercing imaginative vision which make Hazlitt so great. In temperament he was more akin to Lamb, but he equally lacked Lamb's rarer qualities both as a man and as a writer; and his chief function in literature was to further the ease, vivacity and grace of which, though in a far choicer

kind, Lamb was a master in prose, and Chaucer and Ariosto in verse.—HERFORD, C. H., 1897, *The Age of Wordsworth, p.* 84.

He was never strong enough to make his bitterness respected. Honeyed words became him better. . . . We follow such a writer with no sense of his having addressed our intellectual nature, but rather with a sense of pleasurable regalement to our nostrils by some high wordy perfume.— MITCHELL, DONALD G., 1897, *English Lands Letters and Kings, The Later Georges to Victoria, pp.* 144, 146.

Leigh Hunt had a certain bright chivalry on behalf of whatever assumed to itself the cherished name or the aspect of Liberty; at times he could present a gallant front to her foes. But Hunt's shafts, if occasionally keen, were always light-timbered, and rather annoyed the enemy than achieved their ruin.—DOWDEN, EDWARD, 1897, *The French Revolution and English Literature. p.* 249.

As evil-tongued a critic as could be found. —OLIPHANT, MARGARET O. W., 1897, *William Blackwood and his Sons, vol.* I, *p.* 133.

When we turn to his books, we find in his "Autobiography" perhaps the most complete and individual expression of the man: his charming fancy, his high spirits, wit, gayety, and abiding good-nature. But the same lightness and ease of style, the same kindliness and shrewdness of thought and observation, are to be found in his essays, so often written *currente calamo* for some one of his weekly periodicals. Such are the papers on the "Deaths of Little Children," "The Old Lady," "The Maid-Servant," and "Coaches." His contributions, whether as a poet or as a critic and appreciator of poetry, are, it is said, not read as much as they were ten, twenty years ago; but they make alone a remarkable contribution to nineteenth-century literature.— RHYS, ERNEST, 1897, *Library of the World's Best Literature, ed. Warner, vol.* XIII, *p.* 7793.

Some of his shorter narrative poems, like "Abou Ben Adhem" and "Solomon's Ring," have achieved a transcient immortality, if the phrase may be allowed. He is interesting as a link between the literary group of the early part of the century and that of the second quarter, since he was intimate with Carlyle.— JOHNSON, CHARLES F., 1900, *Outline History of English and American Literature, p.* 351.

Henry Hallam

1777-1859

Born, at Windsor, 9 July 1777. At Eton, 1790–94. Contrib. to "Musæ Etonenses," 1795. Matric. Ch. Ch., Oxford, 20 April 1795; B.A., 1799. F. S. A., 12 March 1801. Student at Inner Temple; called to Bar, 2 July 1802. Commissioner of Records; afterwards Commissioner of Stamps, 1806–26. Married Julia Elton, 1807. Withdrew from legal practice and engaged in historical studies. Vice-Pres. of Soc. of Antiquaries, 1824–59. Royal Medal for historical achievements, 1830. Lived mainly in London. M. A., Oxford, 1832, Hon. D. C. L., 5 July 1848. Founder and Treasurer of Statistical Soc., 1834. Bencher of Inner Temple, 1841. Hon. Prof. of History to Royal Society. Foreign Associate of Institute of France. Hon. LL.D., Harvard Univ., 1848. Died, at Penshurst, Kent, 21 Jan. 1859. *Works:* "A View of the State of Europe during the Middle Ages," 1818 (supplementary vol. of "Notes," 1848); "The Constitutional History of England," 1827; "The Introduction to the Literature of Europe" (4 vols.), 1837–39; "Letters addressed to Lord Ashley, etc.," [1844]. He *edited:* A. H. Hallam's "Remains," 1834.—SHARP, R. FARQUHARSON, 1897, *A Dictionary of English Authors, p.* 122.

PERSONAL

Do you know Hallam? Of course I need not ask you if you have read his "Middle Ages": it is an admirable work, full of research, and does Hallam honour. I know no one capable of having written it, except him; for, admitting that a writer could be found who could bring to the task his knowledge and talents, it would be difficult to find one who united to these his research, patience, and perspicuity of style. The reflections of Hallam are at once just and profound—his language well chosen and impressive. I remember being struck by a passage, where, touching on the Venetians, he writes, "Too blind to avert danger, too cowardly to withstand it, the most ancient government of Europe made not an instant's resistance: the peasants of Unterwald died upon their mountains—the nobles of Venice clung only to their lives." This is the style in which history ought to be written, if it is wished to impress it on the memory.—BYRON, LORD, 1823–32, *A Journal of the Conversations of Lord Byron with the Countess of Blessington.*

I had a long visit this morning from Hallam, whom I never saw before, because he was not in London, either in 1819 or 1835, when I was here. It gratified me very much. He is such a man as I should have desired to find him; a little sensitive and nervous, perhaps, but dignified, quiet, and wishing to please. . . . Mr. Hallam is, I suppose, about sixty years old, gray-headed, hesitates a little in his speech, is lame, and has a shy manner, which makes him blush, frequently, when he expresses as decided an opinion as his temperament constantly leads him to entertain. Except his lameness, he has a fine, dignified person, and talks pleasantly, with that air of kindness which is always so welcome to a stranger.—TICKNOR, GEORGE, 1838, *Journal, March* 24; *Life, Letters and Journals, vol.* II, *pp.* 144, 145.

The historian is a fine-looking, white-haired man of between sixty and seventy. Something in the line of feature reminds one of Cuvier and Goethe, all is so clear and definite. He talks much, but with no pedantry, and enjoys a funny story quite as much as a recondite philological fact. He thinks the English infatuated about German critics, and showing it by their indiscriminate imitation of them, tasteless as he considers them.—FOX, CAROLINE, 1840, *Memories of Old Friends, ed. Pym, Journal, Sept.* 4; *p.* 271.

The great historian is long past the "middle ages" now. He is paralysed in the right leg, the right arm, and slightly in the tongue. His face is large, regularly handsome, ruddy, fresh, and very good-humoured. He received me with great cordiality, and we had half an hour's talk. He begged me to leave my address, and I suppose he means to invite me to something or other. . . . His mind does not seem essentially dimmed, and there is nothing senile in his aspect, crippled as he is. He is a wreck, but he has not sunk his head downwards, as you sometimes see, which is the most melancholy termination to the voyage. His mind seems bright and his spirits seem light.—MOTLEY, JOHN LOTHROP, 1858, *To his Wife, June* 6; *Correspondence, ed. Curtis, vol.* I, *p.* 251.

The reader of his weighty (not heavy) works, impressed with the judicial character of the style both of thought and expression, imagined him a solemn, pale student, and might almost expect to see him in a Judge's wig; whereas, the stranger would find him the most rapid talker in company, quick in his movements, genial in his feelings, earnest in narrative, rather full of dissent from what everybody said, innocently surprised when he found himself agreeing with anybody, and pretty sure to blurt out something awkward before the day was done—but never giving offence, because his talk was always the fresh growth of the topic, and, it may be added, his manners were those of a thoroughbred gentleman. — MARTINEAU, HARRIET, 1859, *Biographical Sketches, p.* 77.

In his general manner rather cold and dry, he would occasionally deliver an energetic opinion, pregnant with good sense and refined taste. I used at first to feel some shrinking from his critical faculty, but no one could be more tolerant or encouraging; and if he made objections it was generally without harshness. He was in the full possession of his high faculties when I first had the opportunity of benefiting, in a small degree, by the quiet exhibition of his varied acquirements. The great sorrow of his life had not then chilled his energy. He lived to recover, outwardly, the loss which gave occasion to the noblest elegiac poetry in our language.— KNIGHT, CHARLES, 1863, *Passages from a Working Life During Half a Century, p.* 310.

I received the most touching letters from Hallam himself, written on the very days of these great losses of his life. His own latter years were clouded by a paralytic seizure, which I mention only from the effect on him, rarely found in such cases, of diffusing a placid gentleness over the sterner qualities of his mind. He still indeed clung to society; but submitted patiently to the altered conditions of his appearance in it. A physician can best estimate the moral rectitude expressed in this gentle acquiescence, supervening on a mind disputative and dogmatical in its natural bent. . . . It is not generally known that he refused a baronetcy, pressed upon him in the most flattering terms by Sir Robert Peel. He came to consult me on the subject, and, although reluctantly,

I acquiesced in the reasons which led him finally to decline it. The statue of Hallam in St. Paul's strikingly portrays his massive intellectual features, and the general aspect of the man.—HOLLAND, SIR HENRY, 1871, *Recollections of Past Life, pp.* 226, 227.

EUROPE DURING THE MIDDLE AGES
1818–1848

An able and interesting performance, connected in a good measure with our earlier history. . . . His work is a sort of an introduction to the earlier histories of the ensuing countries (France, Portugal, Italy, and Germany), and should be read with promptitude and diligence by every one interested in such studies. The notes are full of erudition.—DIBDIN, THOMAS FROGNALL, 1825, *Library Companion.*

All the subjects that have been glanced at in these earlier lectures are there (in Hallam's work on the Middle Ages) thoroughly considered by this author with all the patience of an antiquarian and the spirit and sagacity of a philosopher; the French history; the feudal system; the history of Italy; the history of Spain; the history of Germany; of the Greeks and Saracens; the history of ecclesiastical power; the constitutional history of England; the Anglo-Saxon and the Anglo-Norman; afterwards to the end of the civil wars between the Roses, with a concluding dissertation on the state of society during the Middle Ages. I should have been saved many a moment of fatigue, some almost of despair, if these volumes had appeared before I began my lectures.—SMYTH, WILLIAM, 1828-39, *Lectures on Modern History, Lecture* VIII.

"The State of Europe During the Middle Ages" is full of information for all who desire to be informed of the political and social condition of those kingdoms and states which arose out of the ruins and ashes of the empire of Rome. To show order emerging from confusion, the decisions of law taking the place of those of violence and passion, and a line of defence raised to protect the weak and the peaceable against the strong and tyrannous, was the task which Hallam assigned to himself; and he has accomplished all he undertook.—CUNNINGHAM, ALLAN, 1833, *Critical and Biographical History of the Literature of the Last Fifty Years.*

Notwithstanding the interesting character of the Aragonese constitution, and the amplitude of materials for its history, the subject has been hitherto neglected, as far as I am aware, by continental writers. Robertson and Hallam, more especially the latter, have given such a view of its prominent features to the English reader, as must, I fear, deprive the sketch which I have attempted, in a great degree, of novelty.—PRESCOTT, WILLIAM HICKLING, 1837, *Ferdinand and Isabella, Introduction, note.*

By those students, therefore, who are able to make free use of French and German, Hallam will be not very highly esteemed. Even the best of his chapters, those on "The Constitutional History of England" and "The State of Society in the Middle Ages," have been superseded by the more successful investigations of Stubbs, Guizot, and others. The literary qualities of the work are not such as to attract the general reader, though the author's unfailing impartiality cannot but secure the respect of every thoughtful student.— ADAMS, CHARLES KENDALL, 1882, *A Manual of Historical Literature, p. 153.*

The "History of the Middle Ages" and the "Constitutional History of England" were produced in the early part of his life. The former is perhaps his greatest work, and it is impossible not to admire the large and noble investigation of universal life into which the writer enters, perceiving in every change of living its after development, and tracing from step to step the bursting of successive husks, the opening out of new channels, the gradual rise and growth of the forces with which we are now familiar in their far distant origin, so much unlike, yet so closely connected with the present issues—and at the same time the dyings off, the failures, the unproductive attempts of the past.—OLIPHANT, MARGARET O. W., 1882, *Literary History of England, XVIII–XIX Century, vol. III, p. 244.*

Hallam's works helped materially to lay the foundations of the English historical school, and, in spite of later researches, maintain their position as standard books. The "Middle Ages" was probably the first English history which, without being merely antiquarian, set an example of genuine study from original sources. Hallam's training as a lawyer was of high value

and enabled him, according to competent authorities, to interpret the history of law even better in some cases than later writers of more special knowledge. Without attempting a "philosophy of history," in the more modern sense, he takes broad and sensible views of facts.—STEPHEN, LESLIE, 1890, *Dictionary of National Biography, vol. XXIV, p. 97.*

Since then [1848] much has been added to our knowledge, especially as to the organisation of feudal relations, both in town and country, in the history of the English constitution, and the land-system at home and abroad. But no book has filled the whole space occupied by Hallam with his breadth of view and patient comparative method. At present, perhaps, the most valuable portions of his work are the first four chapters on France, Italy, and Spain, and the concluding chapter on the state of society, much of which, it is true, may now be corrected by later research.—HARRISON, FREDERIC, 1894, *Some Great Books of History, The Meaning of History, p. 105.*

CONSTITUTIONAL HISTORY OF ENGLAND
1827

Mr. Hallam is, on the whole, far better qualified than any other writer of our time for the office which he has undertaken. He has great industry and great acuteness. His knowledge is extensive, various and profound. His mind is equally distinguished by the amplitude of his grasp, and by the delicacy of its tact. His speculations have none of the vagueness which is the common fault of political philosophy. On the contrary, they are strikingly practical. They teach us not only the general rule, but the mode of applying it to solve particular cases. In this respect they often remind us of the Discourses of Machiavelli. . . . His work is eminently judicial. Its whole spirit is that of the bench, not that of the bar. He sums up with a calm, steady, impartiality, turning neither to the right nor to the left, glossing over nothing, exaggerating nothing, while the advocates on both sides are alternately biting their lips to hear their conflicting mis-statements and sophisms exposed. On a general survey we do not scruple to pronounce the Constitutional History to be the most impartial book that we ever read.—MACAULAY, THOMAS

BABINGTON, 1828, *Hallam's Constitutional History, Critical and Miscellaneous Essays.*

The book is the production of a decided partisan; presenting not the history itself, but what is called the philosophy of history, and to be received with the more suspicion, because it deals in deductions and not in details. There are many ways in which history may be rendered insidious; but there is no other way by which an author can, with so much apparent good faith, mislead his readers. . . .

"Unto thee,
Let thine own times like an old story be,"
is the advice which Donne gives to him who would derive wisdom from the course of passing events. A writer of contemporary history could take no better motto. Mr. Hallam has proceeded upon a system precisely the reverse to this; and carried into the history of the past, not merely the maxims of his own age, as infallible laws by which all former actions are to be tried, but the spirit and the feeling of the party to which he has attached himself, its acrimony and its arrogance, its injustice and its ill-temper.—SOUTHEY, ROBERT, 1828, *Hallam's Constitutional History of England, Quarterly Review, vol.* 37, *pp.* 195, 260.

There are objectional passages, and even strange passages, more particularly in the notes, but they are of no consequence in a work of so vast a range, and of so much merit. And Mr. Hallam may have given offence, which could never have been his intention, to some good men, to whom their establishments are naturally so dear; but I see not how this was to be avoided, if he was to render equal justice to all persons and parties, all sects and churches in their turn; and if he was to do his duty, as he has nobly done, to the civil and religious liberties of his country.—SMYTH, WILLIAM, 1828-39, *Lectures on Modern History, Lecture* VI, *Note.*

Panizzi came in the evening, and there was a great deal of pleasant conversation. He had breakfasted the day before with Macaulay, whose "History" (the two next volumes) will not be ready for another year. Panizzi said Macaulay was very conscientious as to his authorities, and spared no pains to get at the truth, and willingly re-wrote any part of his book when he had any reason to believe that he had been in error as to facts. Of all living

English historians, Panizzi considered Hallam to be the most eminent, and that his book on the "Constitutional History of England" was not to be surpassed.—GREVILLE, HENRY, 1854, *Leaves from His Diary, Nov.* 12; *Second Series, ed. Enfield, p.* 139.

Taught our University students and our educated youth in general the true nature and the priceless worth of the free but orderly institutions, that have grown up in England during long centuries, expanding their popular organization and energy, as the people expanded its capacity to use them, but preserving their primary principles intact, and as abhorrent of anarchy as of despotism. It is not of course meant that the true character of the British Constitution was undiscovered before Hallam's time; but it was he, more than any other statesman or writer, who by his learning, his sagacity, his perfect fairness, his lucidness in statement, and his force in argument, brought those truths home to his readers' minds; and made sound constitutional knowledge one of the very groundworks of the education of the English upper and middle classes. . . . Party spirit made some of the organs of very high-flying Toryism attack these works on their first appearance, but this opposition soon died away, and the highest Conservatives now acknowledge Hallam's merits as freely as do all loyal Liberals.—CREASY, SIR EDWARD, 1875, *Memoirs of Eminent Etonians, Second Ed., pp.* 591, 592.

The author's literary style is so faulty that but for his great learning and good sense the work would long since have been condemned to obscurity. Its judicial spirit of fairness to all persons and parties makes it popular with judicious minds, in spite of all its shortcomings.—ADAMS, CHARLES KENDALL, 1882, *A Manual of Historical Literature, p.* 482.

INTRODUCTION TO THE LITERATURE OF EUROPE
1837-39

I have read Hallam's book, which is dry, meagre, and ill written, with a few misplaced patches of laboured rhetoric. So far from understanding any one *subject* well, he does not seem to understand any one book well. His text is a mere digest of compilations and biographical dictionaries. I believe that he knows a little German, for a governess who lived in his family went afterwards to Lady ————, who told me that Hallam had learnt of her. Probably he spells through a book by the help of a dictionary with about the same success that he translates "das Bücherwesen," "the being of books." It must be confessed that charlatanerie is marvellously successful.—LEWIS, SIR GEORGE CORNEWALL, 1837, *To E. W. Head, June 2; Letters to Various Friends, ed. Lewis, p.* 80.

The work of Mr. Hallam, now in progress of publication; the first volume of which,—the only one which has yet issued from the press,—gives evidence of the same curious erudition, acuteness, honest impartiality, and energy of diction, which distinguish the other writings of this eminent scholar. But the extent of his work, limited to four volumes, precludes any thing more than a survey of the most prominent features of the vast subject which he has undertaken. —PRESCOTT, WILLIAM HICKLING, 1839, *Chateaubriand's Sketches of English Literature, North American Review, vol.* 49, p. 319.

I am glad to find in it more unction than in his former writings—more to please as well as instruct. I am much pleased with his view of Luther, the hardest character, perhaps, to be understood in modern time, not from any inherent difficulty, but from the prejudices and passions awakened by his name.—CHANNING, WILLIAM ELLERY, 1839, *To Miss Aikin, April* 28; *Correspondence of William Ellery Channing and Lucy Aikin, ed. Le Breton, p.* 338.

The subject which he has now treated is one of more general interest than those discussed in his previous publications; and, as the work was known to embody the labors of many years, it was received with curiosity and respect, and is likely to establish for him a wide and enduring reputation. . . . We close with the expression of gratitude to him for undertaking an important and difficult task, and of respect for the ability, learning, and taste, with which it is executed.—BOWEN, FRANCIS, 1843, *Hallam's Introduction to the Literature of Europe, North American Review, vol.* 56, *pp.* 46, 89.

Mr. Hallam, a learned and elegant scholar, has written the history of European literature for three centuries,—a performance of great ambition, inasmuch as a judgment was to be attempted on every book. But his eye does not reach to the ideal standards: the verdicts are all dated from London; all new thought must be cast into the old moulds. The expansive element which creates literature is steadily denied. Plato is resisted, and his school. Hallam is uniformly polite, but with deficient sympathy; writes with resolute generosity, but is unconscious of the deep worth which lies in the mystics, and which often outvalues as a seed of power and a source of revolution all the correct writers and shining reputations of their day. He passes in silence, or dismisses with a kind of contempt, the profounder masters: a lover of ideas is not only uncongenial, but unintelligible. Hallam inspires respect by his knowledge and fidelity, by his manifest love of good books, and he lifts himself to own better than almost any the greatness of Shakspeare, and better than Johnson he appreciates Milton. — EMERSON, RALPH WALDO, 1856–84, *English Traits; Works, Riverside Ed., vol.* v, *p.* 233.

It shows the ability and the accomplishments of the authors to better advantage than either of his other productions. Its great qualities have been universally acknowledged. It displays conscientiousness, accuracy, good judgment, and great familiarity with the vast subject of which it treats. It comprehends within its scope the literature of poetry, history, romance, natural science, mathematics, physics, medicine, law and theology; and at all points the author shows himself, not merely a good descriptive writer, but also a fair and competent critic. The style is less faulty than that of Hallam's earlier works, as it is less involved and more uniform and straightforward.—ADAMS, CHARES KENDALL, 1882, *A Manual of Historical Literature, p.* 211.

Often written with great force, suffers from the enormous range. Hardly any man could be competent to judge with equal accuracy of all the intellectual achievements of the period in every department. Weaknesses result which will be detected by specialists; but even in the weaker departments it shows good sound sense, and is invaluable to any student of the literature of the time. Though many historians have been more brilliant, there are few so emphatically deserving of respect. His reading was enormous, but we have no means of judging what special circumstances determined his particular lines of inquiry.—STEPHEN, LESLIE, 1890, *Dictionary of National Biography, vol.* XXIV, *p.* 97.

A sober, sensible, learned work, but not effervescent. It is falling into disrepute, and if you ask why, you will probably be told by some young exquisite, who has never read it, that its author must have been a blockhead because he did not sufficiently admire Shakespeare's sonnets, and calls them remarkable productions, and goes so far as to wish Shakespeare had never written them. To display temper on such a subject is ridiculous. Replace Hallam, if you can, by a writer of equal learning and better judgment; but, till you have done so, the English student who wishes to get a general acquaintance with the course of European literature, will not do wrong to devote a few hours a week to the careful reading of this book, even though it does not bubble or sparkle.—BIRRELL, AUGUSTINE, 1895, *Good Taste, Scribner's Magazine, vol.* 17, *p.* 119.

If Hallam's "Introduction to the Literature of Europe," admirable as it is for its learning and good sense, were recast, revised, amended, and reduced from four large volumes to a single volume of three hundred pages, we should possess something which might at least serve as a stopgap until a better book were ready to take its place.—DOWDEN, EDWARD, 1895, *New Studies in Literature, p.* 421.

Perhaps the most successful of all attempts at a general history of literature.—GAYLEY, CHARLES MILLS, AND SCOTT, FRED NEWTON, 1899, *An Introduction to the Methods and Materials of Literary Criticism, p.* 256.

GENERAL

The extreme austerity of Mr. Hallam takes away something from the pleasure of reading his learned, eloquent, and judicious writings. He is a judge, but a hanging judge, the Page or Buller of the high court of literary justice. His black cap is in constant requisition. In the long calendar of those whom he has tried, there is hardly one who has not, in spite of evidence to character and recommendations to mercy, been sentenced and left for execution.—MACAULAY, THOMAS BABINGTON, 1834, *Sir James Mackintosh, Critical and Miscellaneous Essays.*

One of the most judicious minds of the day—a mind trained in the most exact and laborious historic research.—REED, HENRY, 1850-55, *Lectures on English Literature from Chaucer to Tennyson, p.* 222.

The cold academic style of Robertson may suit the comparative calmness of the eighteenth century, but the fervour and animation of its close communicated itself to the historical works of the next. Hallam was the first historian whose style gave token of the coming change; his works mark the transition from one age and style of literature to another. In extent and variety of learning, and a deep acquaintance with antiquarian lore, the historian of the Middle Ages may deservedly take a place with the most eminent writers in that style that Europe has produced; but his mind is more imaginative than those of his laborious predecessors, and a fervent eloquence, or poetic expression, often reveals the ardour which the heart-stirring events of his time had communicated to his disposition.—ALISON, SIR ARCHIBALD, 1853, *History of Europe, 1815-1852, ch.* v.

He has often essayed to criticise our greatest poets, and has displayed intimate knowledge of their writings, and of the ages in which they lived. But it is merely mechanical knowledge. He knows poets by *head*-mark, not by *heart*-recognition. He may see, but he scarcely feels, their beauties.—GILFILLAN, GEORGE, 1855, *A Third Gallery of Portraits, p.* 182.

Mr. Hallam's impartiality does not proceed from indifference as to the topics which he discusses, but from the moderation of his views, and the calmness of his judgment. Extreme opinions find little favor in his eyes. He was a Whig; but he was a Whig educated at Oxford, and this circumstance doubtless exerted a very fortunate influence on the character of his writings. Even when he expresses the strongest disapprobation of any system or policy, or pronounces the most unfavorable opinion as to the character of any individual, or any body of men, he never suffers himself to lapse into partisanship, and his language has the calmness and dignity of a judicial opinion. Unlike Mr. Carlyle, he never attempts to make a man odious by personal abuse, and in his delineation of character he uses other colors beside black and white. It is this moderation in his views—this inflexible determination to follow the narrow path between the mountain and the sea—which, as we conceive, constitutes Mr. Hallam's least questionable title to a place among the greatest historians who have written in our language. It is very easy to be a partisan: it is very hard to hold moderate opinions.— SMITH, C. C., 1861, *Hallam as an Historian*, *North American Review, vol.* 92, *p.* 169.

With the skill of an advocate he combines the calmness of a judge; and he has been justly called "the accurate Hallam," because his facts are in all cases to be depended upon. By his clear and illustrative treatment of dry subjects, he has made them interesting; and his works have done as much to instruct his age as those of any writer. Later researches in literature and constitutional history may discover more than he has presented, but he taught the new explorers the way, and will always be consulted with profit, as the representative of this varied learning during the first half of the nineteenth century.—COPPEÉ, HENRY, 1872, *English Literature, p.* 448.

Of Henry Hallam a writer of distinction observed, at the time of his death, that the reader of his weighty (not heavy) works, impressed with the judicial character of the style both of thought and expression, imagined him a solemn, pale student, and might almost expect to see him in a judge's wig; whereas the stranger would find him the most rapid talker in company, quick in his movements, genial in his feelings, earnest in narrative, rather full of dissent from what everybody said, innocently surprised when he found himself agreeing with anybody, and pretty sure to blurt out something awkward before the day was done— but never giving offence, because his talk was always the fresh growth of the topic, besides that his manners were those of a thoroughbred gentleman.—JACOX, FRANCIS, 1872, *Aspects of Authorship, p.* 412.

In 1830 George IV instituted two gold medals for the best historical works of his reign; and Hallam and Washington Irving were the historians that his Majesty delighted to honour. Hallam's works are praised for industrious research and dignified impartiality; his "Constitutional History" is accepted as the standard work on that subject. He had great reputation as a scholar; Byron calls him "Classic Hallam much renowned for Greek": but it may be doubted whether his "Introduction to the Literature of Europe" was not too ambitious

a work for any one man not possessed of the resources of Faust. Certainly his criticisms of English writers, though always expressed with elegance, will not always bear close examination, and too often give evidence of very superficial and secondhand knowledge. Ornate, dignified elegance is the characteristic of his style: for popular purposes it is perhaps too Latinised.—MINTO, WILLIAM, 1872-80, *Manual of English Prose Literature, p.* 524.

The subject of this memoir was never in Parliament, and never addressed his fellow countrymen by speech or by pen on any of the immediate questions of the day. He founded no association—he took no part in electioneering: he was not even proprietor or editor of a newspaper: and yet he has influenced the political opinions and conduct of the best and ablest classes of Englishmen, more than almost any other leader of thought that modern times have produced; and his influence is certain to be permanent.—CREASY, SIR EDWARD, 1875, *Memoirs of Eminent Etonians, Second Ed., p.* 590.

Henry Hallam was the first who wrote history in this country with so careful a love of truth, and with so accurate a judgment of the relative value of facts and things, that prejudice was excluded. His "Europe During the Middle Ages," and his "Literature of Europe" are distinguished for their exhaustive and judicial summing up of facts; and his "Constitutional History of England" set on foot a new kind of history in the best way.—BROOKE, STOPFORD A., 1876, *English Literature (Primer), p.* 132.

The greatest historical name in this period, and one of the most learned of our constitutional writers and critics. . . . With vast stores of knowledge, and indefatigable application, Mr. Hallam possessed a clear and independent judgment, and a style grave and impressive, yet enriched with occasional imagery and rhetorical graces. His "Introduction to the Literature of Europe" is a great monument of his erudition. His knowledge of the language and literature of each nation is critical, if not profound, and his opinions were conveyed in a style remarkable for its succinctness and perspicuity.—CHAMBERS, ROBERT, 1876, *Cyclopædia of English Literature, ed. Carruthers.*

No great historian ever wrote with less

passion, or was more anxious than Hallam to place the whole of his facts, for what they were worth, before his readers. In this respect, then, Hallam displays a marked contrast to Mitford. In elaborate research he was at least Mitford's equal. . . . It may be doubted whether three works of any other author contain the results of such extensive, varied, and careful reading.--WALPOLE, SPENCER, 1878, *A History of England from the Conclusion of the Great War in 1815, vol.* I, *p.* 343.

Was an historian of powers, perhaps, not originally superior to those of Mackintosh, but put to infinitely better account.— NICOLL, HENRY J., 1882, *Landmarks of English Literature, p.* 342.

Industrious, sober-minded, accomplished and as judicial in his views as was consistent with a certain want of catholicity of taste and with strong views in general politics, Hallam is an authority to be cautiously differed with. The style in him exactly corresponds to the thought.— SAINTSBURY, GEORGE, 1886, *Specimens of English Prose Style, p.* 312.

We have had a few other critics—they might be counted on one hand, and barely exhaust the fingers—who show flashes of finer insight. Even, however, from a born rhetorician like Lord Macaulay, Hallam extorted the praise that here only was the judge with one weight and one balance,— *justissimus unus.*—PALGRAVE, FRANCIS TURNER, 1888, *Chaucer and the Italian Renaissance, The Nineteenth Century, vol.* 24, *p.* 355.

The truth about Hallam seems to have been that books were more to him than men, and literature than life. The pulse of human feeling beats faintly in his writings, through which the reader moves as in a shadowy intellectual world inhabited by the departed actors of a real, indeed, but unresuscitated past. We feel that this is the land of shades, and the ghost of history, which needs to be clothed upon with flesh and blood. Hallam's works are a capital demonstration of the thesis that imagination is indispensable to the writing of history, whether social or political. It was the intellectual framework of things that interested him: action, passion, the busy world of moving humanity, for these he had no eye, or no reconstructive talent. The warmth, colour, and animation of the

brisk, humourous drama of life are not suggested on his canvas, and it would be difficult, perhaps, to recall a single scene or single character of which he speaks in words that betray a keen personal pleasure, sympathy or aversion. With one he deals as with another, much as the geometrician deals with his cubes and squares.—DIXON, W. MACNEILE, 1896, *English Prose, ed. Craik, vol.* V, *p.* 185.

Hallam represents, better perhaps than any other, the English intellect of the epoch in which the eighteenth century was passing into the nineteenth, when the age of "common-sense" was discredited but not extinct, and Romanticism was in the air, but not in the blood.—HERFORD, C. H., 1897, *The Age of Wordsworth, p.* 44.

Was full of all serenities of character— even under the weight of such private griefs as were appalling. He was studious, honest, staid—with a great respect for decorum; he would have gravitated socially —as he did—rather to Holland House than to the chambers where Lamb presided over the punch bowl. In describing the man one describes his histories; slow, calm, steady even to prosiness, yet full; not entertaining in a gossipy sense; not brilliant; scarce ever eloquent. If he is in doubt upon a point he tells you so; if there has been limitation to his research, there is no concealment of it; I think, upon the whole, the honestest of all English historians. In his search for truth, neither party, nor tradition, nor religious scruples make him waver. None can make their historic journey through the Middle Ages without taking into account the authorities he has brought to notice, and the path that he has scored.—MITCHELL, DONALD G., 1897, *English Lands Letters and Kings, The Later Georges to Victoria, p.* 171.

A brilliantly gifted writer on political history. . . . In his old age Hallam made a track through the previously pathless waste of general European literature. His gravity is supported by a vast basis of solid knowledge, his judgment is sane and balanced, and to his immediate contemporaries his style appeared remarkable for "succinctness and perspicuous beauty." But the modern writer is not so well pleased with Hallam, who begins to be the Georgian type of the falsely impressive. His felicities are those which Macaulay emphasised and carried to a further precision; his faults are his own, and they are a want of intuitive sympathy with the subject under discussion, and a monotonous and barren pomp of delivery which never becomes easy or flexible. The far-famed "judgment," too, of Hallam is not as wide as we could wish. He is safe only in the discussion of recognised types, and the reader searches his critical pages in vain for signs of the recognition of an eccentric or abnormal talent. The most laudible tendency of the historians of this age, seen in Hallam, indeed, but even more plainly in secondary writers.—GOSSE, EDMUND, 1897, *A Short History of Modern English Literature, pp.* 325, 326.

We seldom find any warmth in his works, his style lacks animation, and in his æsthetic views of poetry, he is a man of the eighteenth rather than the nineteenth century. His dry, cold manner reminds us of Ranke.—ENGEL, EDWARD, 1902, *A History of English Literature, rev. Bent, p.* 466.

William Hickling Prescott
1796–1859

Born, at Salem, Mass., 4 May 1796. Early education at Salem. At school in New York, Jan. 1803 to June 1808. Parents removed to Boston, 1808. To Harvard Coll., Aug. 1811; B. A., 1814. While at Harvard lost the sight of one eye through an accident; the other soon afterwards became seriously and permanently affected. At St. Michael's, Azores, for health, Oct. 1815 to April 1816. Travelled in Europe, 1816–1817. In Boston, winter 1817–1818. Married Susan Amory, 4 May 1820. Adopted literary career. Corresponding Member of French Academy, Feb. 1845. Corresponding Mem. Royal Soc. of Berlin, Feb. 1845. Visit to England, 1850. Died, in Boston, 28 Jan. 1859. Buried in St. Paul's Church, Boston. *Works:* "Life of Charles Brockden Brown," 1834; "History of the Reign of Ferdinand and Isabella" (3 vols.), 1838; "History of the Conquest of Mexico" (3 vols.), 1843; "Critical and Historical Essays," 1845; "History of the Conquest of Peru" (2 vols.), 1847; "Memoir of . . . J. Pickering," 1848; "The History of the Reign of Philip II," vols. I, II, 1855; vol. III, 1858; "Memoir of the Hon. A. Lawrence" (priv. ptd.), 1856; "The Life of Charles V after his Abdication" (vol. III of Robertson's "Hist. of the Reign of Charles V"), 1857. He *edited:* Mme. Calderon de la Bara's "Life in Mexico," 1843. *Life:* by G. Ticknor, 1863.—SHARP, R. FARQUHARSON, 1897, *A Dictionary of English Authors, p.* 232.

PERSONAL

This morning, as I was sitting at breakfast, a gentleman on horseback sent up word that I should come down to him. It was Prescott, author of "Ferdinand and Isabella." He is an early riser and rides about the country. There on his horse sat the *great author.* He is one of the best fellows in the world, and much my friend; handsome, gay, and forty; a great diner-out; gentle, companionable, and modest; quite astonished to find himself so famous.—LONGFELLOW, HENRY WADSWORTH, 1838, *Letter to George W. Greene, Oct.* 22; *Life of Henry Wadsworth Longfellow, ed. Longfellow, vol.* I, *p.* 300.

Prescott, the author of "Ferdinand and Isabella," a handsome, half-blind shunner of the vanities of the world, with some others who read and write a good deal, and no one the wiser for it.—GRATTAN, T. C., 1841, *Letter to Mrs. Trollope, What I Remember by Thomas Adolphus Trollope, p.* 503.

When Prescott comes to England, a Caspian Sea of soup awaits him.—SMITH, SYDNEY, 1845(?), *A Memoir of the Rev. Sydney Smith by Lady Holland.*

The Niagara steamer arrived this morning from Liverpool. In her came passenger William H. Prescott, our eminent historian, and excellent good fellow. I had a visit from him this morning at my office. He returns in good health and excellent spirits, after an absence of five months, during which time the greatest respect and attention were paid to him by the distinguished people of England, from the Queen down; as an evidence of which he told me (but without any vainglorious boasting) that he had, during his sojourn in London, twelve dinner invitations for one day. These highly merited compliments reflect equal honour on both parties. — HONE, PHILIP, 1850, *Diary, Sept.* 27; *ed. Tuckerman, vol.* II, *p.* 392.

There is little in the external aspect of this house in Beacon Street to distinguish it from the others in its immediate vicinity. It is one of a continuous but not uniform block. It is of brick, painted white, four stories high, and with one of those swelled fronts which are the characteristic of Boston. It has the usual proportion and distribution of drawing rooms, dining-room, and chambers, which are furnished with unpretending elegance and adorned with some portraits, copies of originals in Spain, illustrative of Mr. Prescott's writings. The most striking portion of the interior consists of an ample library, added by Mr. Prescott to the rear of the house, and communicating with the drawing-rooms. It is an apartment of noble size and fine proportions, filled with a choice collection of books, mostly historical, which are disposed in cases of richly-veined and highly-polished oak. This room, which is much used in the social arrangements of the household, is not that in which Mr. Prescott does his hard literary work. A much smaller apartment, above the library and communicating with it, is the working study—an arrangement similar to that adopted by Sir Walter Scott at Abbotsford.—HILLARD, GEORGE S., 1853-96, *Homes of American Authors*, ed. *Hubbard, p.* 86.

I have had the happiness to form and retain the friendship of many excellent men; no one has ever, considering the short personal intercourse which I enjoyed with him, and our but occasional correspondence, wakened such strong and lasting attachment. He found his way at once to the heart, and has there remained and ever will remain, during the brief period to which I can now look forward, as an object of the warmest esteem and affection. I think I should have loved the man if I had only known him as an author; his personal society only showed his cordial, liberal, gentle character in a more distinct and intimate form. That which was admiration became love. There is here but one feeling, among those who had not the good fortune to know him, as among those who knew him best,—deep regret for a man who did honor to the literature of our common language, and whose writings, from their intrinsic charm and excellence, were most popular, without any art or attempt to win popularity.—MILMAN, HENRY HART, 1859, *Letter to George Ticknor, Feb.* 19; *Life of Prescott by Ticknor, p.* 446.

Mr. Prescott's personal appearance itself was singularly pleasing, and won for him everywhere, in advance, a welcome and favor. His countenance had something that brought to the mind "the beautiful disdain" that hovers on that of the Apollo. But, while he was high-spirited, he was tender, and gentle, and humane. His voice was like music; and one could never hear enough of it. His cheerfulness reached and animated all about him. He could indulge in playfulness, and could also speak earnestly and profoundly; but he knew not how to be ungracious or pedantic. In truth, the charms of his conversation were unequalled, he so united the rich stores of memory with the ease of one who is familiar with the world.—BANCROFT, GEORGE, 1859, *Address Before the New York Historical Society, Feb.* 1.

Yes, it was your letter which first told me of Prescott's death. The next day I read it in the Paris papers. Taillandier announced it at the opening of his lecture. The current of grief and praise is everywhere unbroken. Perhaps no man, so much in people's mouths, was ever the subject of so little unkindness. How different his fate from that of others. Something of that immunity which he enjoyed in life must be referred to his beautiful nature, in which enmity could not live. This death touches me much. You remember that my relations with him had for years been of peculiar intimacy. Every return to Boston has always been consecrated by an evening with him. I am sad to think of my own personal loss.—SUMNER, CHARLES, 1859, *Letter to H. W. Longfellow, March* 4; *Memoir and Letters of Charles Sumner, ed. Pierce, vol.* III, *p.* 597.

I know not in what words to speak of Prescott. He was my oldest friend,—the last friend of my boyhood. Our fathers were intimate friends, and their intimacy fell to us as an inheritance. His genial face, and that cordial manner which was but the transparent vesture of his constant kindness, I shall meet no more. . . . Nor need I add my testimony to the universal recognition of the ability, the industry, the accurate learning, the admirable judgment, and the perfect taste which have placed him at the head of our literature and made him our pride.—PARSONS, THEOPHILUS, 1859, *Memoir of Chief-Justice Parsons, p.* 187.

Mr. Prescott was a true son of Boston; well-born, well-bred, of extremely dignified and agreeable manners, and with a delicate and nobly chiselled face. He was a perfect man of the world, fond of society, and with not the slightest touch of the pedant about him. I saw him frequently and intimately at his Nahant house and at the neighboring villa of his daughter, Mrs. Lawrence, who was an admirable hostess as well as a beautiful woman. Although he was past sixty when I first met him, he was still as attractive as a man of thirty in dress and manner, and with the added delight of his extremely cultivated mind. His infirmity of sight did not prevent his getting about alone and eating his dinner with the grace of a diplomatist. If he asked any one for the toast or the cream at one of his daughter's delicious country teas, it was really a pleasantry and a compliment, and he could make his infirmity of sight a joke. If the cream-pitcher turned up under his hand, he would thank the finder and say, "If it had been a bear it would have bit me." He asked my husband and myself to his "workshop," as he called his library, and showed us the apparatus which is used by the blind—a wire-ruled machine for guiding the hand.— SHERWOOD, MARY E. W., 1897, *An Epistle to Posterity, p.* 117.

His hours were so scrupulously laid out that when the appointed minute came for putting down a novel that was read aloud to the family circle, Prescott was inexorable, no matter where or how the hero and the heroine were to be left. If ten o'clock was his bed-time, he was capable, when the hour struck, of leaving a company of bachelor friends whom he was entertaining at dinner, telling them to call for whatever they desired, "and if you don't go home till morning, I wish you a merry night of it." In the morning when he was waked, he gave himself time to count twenty, and if he failed to jump out of bed when he had done so, he paid a fine of his own exaction to the servant who had called him. His tailor marked his clothes with the number of ounces each garment weighed and being told exactly where the thermometer stood, he dressed himself accordingly. Every morning for a long period, even in the coldest weather, he rode on his horse from Boston to watch the sunrise from a particular spot in Jamaica Plain. In his library the blue window shades were so arranged that the light could be kept at a uniform dimness, even as successive clouds crossed the sun. He "reckoned time," he said, "by eyesight, as distances on railroads are reckoned by hours." The catalogue of his rigours with himself might be lengthened to such an extent as to make him seem quite without the charm that springs from impulse, but justice forbids one to leave unmentioned the gentler graces of his life—the tender devotion to his parents, wife, and children, the social gift which made the acquaintance think himself a friend, and the friend know himself to be fortunate beyond most men in the friendship with such a man.—HOWE, M. A. DEWOLFE, 1898, *American Bookmen, p.* 139.

THE REIGN OF FERDINAND AND ISABELLA
1888

In every page we have been reminded of that untiring patience and careful discrimination which have given celebrity to the great, though not always impartial, historian of the "Decline and Fall of the Roman Empire."—PICKERING, JOHN, 1838, *Prescott's Ferdinand and Isabella, New York Review, April.*

The spirit and sentiment of the work is admirable; there is enough of reflection, and not too much; the narrative is lively and flowing; and great judgment is shown in the proportions assigned to the various topics on which he treats. It is entertaining, with every mark of strict adherence to truth, and instructive without deep philosophy indeed, or sententiousness of remark; but by means of a pervading spirit of candour, good sense and liberality, the interest of the subject hurries one on, at first reading, too fast, I believe, for the credit of the writer; and I have little doubt that a second perusal would disclose many fresh merits of detail.—AIKIN, LUCY, 1838, *To Dr. Channing, Nov.* 16; *Correspondence of William Ellery Channing and Lucy Aikin, ed. Le Breton, p.* 320.

By much the first historical work which British America has yet produced, and one that need hardly fear a comparison with any that has issued from the European press since this century began.— FORD, RICHARD, 1839, *Prescott's History of Ferdinand and Isabella, Quarterly Review, vol.* 54, *p.* 58.

We cannot but timidly flatter ourselves that, one day or another, our American aspirants for literary honors will get more into the way of spending some time in sowing and reaping their laurels, preparatory to tuning their voices for the Harvest Home. A very few examples, at all like the recent one of Mr. Prescott's brilliant success, cannot fail of producing a decided effect of this kind; and whoever, by showing what a mind of high endowments owes to itself, and what it may achieve, if it have but fair play, disposes our young scholars to be content to wait for applause till they have time to deserve it, has done a service to his country worthy of all grateful commemoration.—PALFREY, JOHN GORHAM, 1840, *Hillhouse's Poems and Discourses, North American Review, vol.* 50, *p.* 232.

It has taken the rank of a classic in our language, and in the emulous favor with which it has been received on each side of the Atlantic may be read an assurance of the unbiased judgment of posterity.— HILLARD, GEORGE S., 1844, *Prescott's History of the Conquest of Mexico, North American Review, vol.* 58, *p.* 158.

Mr. Prescott has proved himself in this work to be most indefatigable. His industry has been immense. His sources of information were widely scattered. To bring them together could be no common labour. For almost every statement, sometimes to the unimportant and even trivial, he is prepared with his corroboration. He has taken nothing upon report and general credulity. He works his way through mountains of conflicting testimony. . . . The principal fault of the publication is in its deficiency of philosophical generalization.—HAMILTON, R. W., 1845, *British Quarterly Review, Feb.*

Hardly nine years have passed since the publication of the "History of Ferdinand and Isabella" placed Mr. Prescott at once by universal consent both in England and America, in the front rank of English historians. — BOWEN, FRANCIS, 1847, *Prescott's Conquest of Peru, North American Review, vol.* 65, *p.* 366.

As the period which Mr. Prescott selected was that in which the modern system of Europe may be said to have taken its rise, and was in an especial degree encumbered with falsehood and sophistry, it was a subject which seemed at once to tempt the historian by its importance and repel him by his difficulties. . . . His work accurately reflects the spirit of the age and the character of his prominent actors; and

we have been especially struck with his felicity in developing character, not in an isolated analysis of qualities, but in the narration of the events which called them forth. He so blends character with events, that their mutual relation is distinctly seen. —WHIPPLE, EDWIN PERCY, 1848, *Prescott's Histories, Essays and Reviews, vol.* II, *p.* 214.

"Ferdinand and Isabella," — in my opinion his best work.—LIEBER, FRANCIS, 1855, *Letter to S. Austin Allibone, Oct.* 16; *Critical Dictionary of English Literature, vol.* II, *p.* 1667.

"The History of Ferdinand and Isabella" was published at the close of 1837, or the beginning of 1838; and, on my arrival in Europe in the summer of 1840, I found it extensively known and duly appreciated. . . . Calling one day on the venerable Mr. Thomas Grenville, whom I found in his library, (the second in size and value of the private libraries of England), reading Xenophon's "Anabasis" in the original, I made some passing remark on the beauty of that work. "Here," said he, holding up a volume of "Ferdinand and Isabella," "is one far superior." With the exception of the Nestor of our literature (Mr. Irving), no American writer appeared to me so widely known or so highly esteemed in England as Mr. Prescott; and when he visited that country, a few years later, the honours paid to him by all the cultivated classes of society, from the throne downward, were such as are seldom offered to the most distinguished visitant.—EVERETT, EDWARD, 1859, *Remarks at a Meeting of the Massachusetts Historical Society, Feb.* 10; *Proceedings, vol.* 4, *pp.* 200, 202.

Is one of the most comprehensive surveys of a great subject ever presented to the historical student. The condition and relations of the crown, the nobles, the clergy, the cities, and the commons, are painted with a masterly hand, and are presented in a picture at once clear, concise, and complete. The wily, able Ferdinand and the good Isabella, the model of womanly heroism, are portrayed with consummate skill and delicacy; and neither Robertson nor Irving has excelled in easy pace the narratives of the siege of Malaga and the crowning conquest of Granada.—STIRLING, WILLIAM, 1859, *Encyclopædia Britannica, Eighth Ed., vol.* XVIII.

It at once established his reputation in the

very first rank of living historians.—
YONGE, CHARLES DUKE, 1872, *Three Centuries of English Literature, p.* 159.

No such comprehensive view of Spain at
the zenith of her greatness has ever appeared in English. The proportion of its
parts and the justice of its estimates are
universally acknowledged, while hyper-
criticism of the style—graceful, correct,
and sufficiently varied—can only point
to the occasional possibility of greater
condensation. — NICHOL, JOHN, 1882-85,
American Literature, p. 148.

Though this history was the first written
by Prescott, it has scarcely been excelled
in merit by any of its successors. . . .
Prescott's writings are conspicuous for
thoroughness of research, keenness of insight, impartiality of judgment, picturesqueness of narration, exclusion of irrelevant matter, and correctness and elegance
of style. He had not much of the passion
of the politician or the imagination of the
poet; and therefore he is never quite able
to produce the highest dramatic effects in
narration, or arouse the highest enthusiasm
of the reader. But as an offset to this deficiency, if, indeed, it can be called such,
he has the far more than counterbalancing
merit of making his readers feel that they
are listening to a wise and learned judge
rather than to a skillful advocate. Prescott's good qualities are so marked and so
numerous that the best judges will hardly
hesitate to place him at the head of American historians.—ADAMS, CHARLES KEN-
DALL, 1882, *A Manual of Historical Literature, p.* 407.

THE CONQUEST OF MEXICO
1843

Mr. Prescott possesses high qualifications,
and some peculiar advantages, for the
execution of such a work. . . . In his
disquisitions on the political state and the
civilization of the Aztec kingdoms, he is
full and copious, without being prolix and
wearisome; his narrative is flowing and
spirited, sometimes very picturesque; his
style has dropped the few Americanisms
which still jarred on our fastidious ear in
his former work, and is, in general, pure
and sound English. Above all, his judgments are unaffectedly candid and impartial. . . . We conclude with expressing our satisfaction that Mr. Prescott
has given us an opportunity at this time of
showing our deep sympathy, the sympathy

of kindred and of blood, with Americans
who, like himself, do honour to our common literature. Mr. Prescott may take
his place among the really good English
writers of history in modern times, and
will be received, we are persuaded, into the
small community, with every feeling of
friendly and fraternal respect.—MILMAN,
HENRY HART, 1843, *Prescott's History of
the Conquest of Mexico, Quarterly Review,
vol.* 73, *pp.* 188, 235.

It is a noble work; judiciously planned
and admirably executed; rich with the
spoils of learning easily and gracefully
worn; imbued everywhere with a conscientious love of the truth, and controlled
by that unerring good sense, without which
genius leads astray with its false lights,
and learning encumbers with its heavy
panoply. It will win the literary voluptuary to its pages by the attractiveness of
its subject and the flowing ease of its style;
and the historical student will do honour to
the extent and variety of the research
which it displays, and to the thoroughness
with which its investigations have been
conducted. We can confidently predict
for it an extensive and permanent popularity. . . . It will take its place
among those enduring productions of the
human mind which age cannot stale, and
custom cannot wither.—HILLARD, GEORGE
S., 1844, *Prescott's History of the Conquest
of Mexico, North American Review, vol.* 58,
pp. 209, 210.

I doubt whether Mr. Prescott was aware
of the extent of the sacrifice I made. This
was a favorite subject, which had delighted
my imagination ever since I was a boy. I
had brought home books from Spain to aid
me in it, and looked upon it as the pendant
to my Columbus. When I gave it up to
him, I in a manner gave him my bread, for
I depended upon the profit of it to recruit
my waning finances. I had no other subject at hand to supply its place. I was
dismounted from my *cheval de bataille,* and
have never been completely mounted since.
Had I accomplished that work, my whole
pecuniary situation would have been
altered. When I made the sacrifice, it
was not with a view to compliments or
thanks, but from a warm and sudden impulse. I am not sorry for having made it.
Mr. Prescott has justified the opinion I
expressed at the time, that he would treat
the subject with more close and ample

research than I should probably do, and would produce a work more thoroughly worthy of the theme. He has produced a work that does honor to himself and his country, and I wish him the full enjoyment of his laurels.—IRVING, WASHINGTON, 1844, *To Pierre M. Irving, March* 24; *Life and Letters of Washington Irving, ed. Irving, vol.* III, *p.* 143.

I wrote to Prescott about his book, with which I was perfectly charmed. I think his descriptions masterly, his style brilliant, his purpose manly and gallant always. The introductory account of Aztec civilization impressed me exactly as it impressed you. From beginning to end the whole history is enchanting and full of genius.—DICKENS, CHARLES, 1844, *To Prof. Felton, Jan.* 2; *The Letters of Charles Dickens, ed. Dickens and Hogarth, vol.* III, *p.* 57.

Prescott is too much of an abstract, and perhaps of an eulogy, though generally very well and pleasingly written, which after all is the great point in such matters. But I must protest against the author's extravagant and, in my mind, *absurd and offensive* defence of the cruelties and tyranny of Cortez.—JEFFREY, FRANCIS LORD, 1845, *Letter to Napier, April* 22; *Selection from the Correspondence of Macvey Napier, ed. Napier, p.* 489.

It is an elegant and eloquent production, rich and copious in expression, yet distinguished by a grace and simplicity worthy of any English historian. It is in clearness and beauty of his style, and his conscientious and careful analysis of authorities, that Mr. Prescott's chief excellencies lie. We may travel with him confidently, and yield our faith without hesitation, whenever his conclusions are declared. We have reason to be proud of his production.—SIMMS, WILLIAM GILMORE, 1845, *Views and Reviews of American Literature, History and Fiction, p.* 151.

We shall not pretend to have examined a narrative which has given us so much pleasure, with the keen scrutiny of a severe criticism; but we can conscientiously affirm, that we remember little or nothing in the manner of its execution which we could have wished otherwise. Mr. Prescott appears to us to possess almost every qualification for his task. He has a pure, simple, and eloquent style—a keen relish for the picturesque — a quick and discerning judgment of character—and a calm, generous, and enlightened spirit of philanthrophy. There is no exaggeration in asserting, that his "Conquest of Mexico" combines—some allowance, where that is necessary, being made for the inferior extent and the importance of his subject—most of the valuable qualities which distinguish the most popular historical writers, in our own language, of the present day.—PHILLIPPS, CHARLES, 1845, *Prescott's Conquest of Mexico, Edinburgh Review, vol.* 81, *p.* 434.

Whatever may be the comparative merits of the four great histories he has already published, as intellectual efforts, there is little room to doubt that "The Conquest of Mexico" will continue to be the popular. It is justly remarked in the *Edinburgh Review*, that, considered merely as a work of amusement, it will bear a favourable comparison with the best romances in the language. The careful, judicious, and comprehensive essay on the Aztec civilization, with which it opens, is not inferior in interest to the wonderful drama to which it is an epilogue.—GRISWOLD, RUFUS WILMOT, 1847-70, *The Prose Writers of America, p.* 373.

Rarely has so splendid a theme been treated by an historian so fortunate at once in the possession of requisite materials and requisite capacity. Among the many characteristics of the work, that which will be most likely to strike and charm the general reader, is its picturesqueness of description, both as regards incidents and scenery. The freshness and vividness with which every thing is presented is a continual stimulant to attention; and there is a nerve in the movement of the style which gives to the narrative a continual vitality.—WHIPPLE, EDWIN PERCY, 1848, *Prescott's Histories, Essays and Reviews, vol.* II, *p.* 226.

We have heard some of his most extravagant admirers contend that the "Conquest of Mexico" is a magnificent poem. This is absurdity; we can, however, truly predicate that it possesses many of the chief ingredients. Till Mr. Prescott published his voluminous histories there was much vagueness in the knowledge possessed by the masses on the subjects of which he has treated; he seems suddenly to have illuminated the general world, and to have created a knowledge where before there was a darkness. This is seldom achieved without the possession of that peculiar power termed genius, and we consider ourselves within the bounds of demonstration when we say that in these respects we consider Mr. Prescott as deserving the rare distinction of having a genius for historical composition.—POWELL, THOMAS, 1850, *The Living Authors of America, p.* 177.

Mr. Prescott's rhetoric will never cease to charm, but the historical authority of this work has received a damaging shock from Mr. Wilson's criticisms. And so great is Mr. Prescott's reputation, and so long have the traditions which he narrates been told and credited, that comparatively little attention is paid to the critic, and so posterity will continue to believe, I suppose, that six hundred Spanish soldiers overran and conquered a country inhabited by some millions of people advanced in civilization and the arts.—BROWNE, IRVING, 1885, *Iconoclasm and Whitewash, p.* 15.

THE CONQUEST OF PERU
1847

What a fine accomplishment there is about it! And yet there is something wanting to me in the moral nerve. History should teach men how to estimate characters. It should be a teacher of morals. And I think it should make us *shudder* at the names of Cortez and Pizarro. But Prescott's does not. He seems to have a kind of sympathy with these inhuman and perfidious adventurers, as if they were his heroes. It is too bad to talk of them as the soldiers of Christ. If it were said of the Devil, they would have better fitted the character.—DEWEY, ORVILLE, 1847, *To Rev. William Ware, Aug.* 22; *Autobiography and Letters, ed. Dewey, p.* 190.

In the "Conquest of Mexico" and the "Conquest of Peru," and especially in the chapters on the civilization of the Aztecs and the Incas, Mr. Prescott displays great sagacity in assorting the scattered fragments of social edifices, which were destroyed before they could be intelligently delineated, and in recalling to their living forms the dry bones of the extinct races which inhabited them. He also appears to have shaken off the diffidence of a stranger in the historical field. His style betokens more self-confidence, and is bolder and more animated. His descriptions of scenery, in which he is always happy and never redundant, are more full

and vivid, and are elaborated with the greater care which was required by the strangeness of unfamiliar lands. Mexico spreads her matchless valley, her lake, and her imperial city before our eyes; and we wander through the royal gardens, beneath the giant cedars, of Tezcuco; the golden halls of the Inca and the blazing temples of the sun unfold themselves before us; we follow the silver-shod cavalry of Pizarro through the flowery dales of the Cordilleras; or we ascend through the pastures of the Llama or the stern regions where the condor hovers in the tropical sun around the peaks of the Andes. The account of the *triste noche,* the rueful night in which, after the death of Montezuma, Cortez and his band retreated across the lake and along the broken causeway, cutting their way through a nation in arms, is one of the finest pictures of modern historical painting.— STIRLING, WILLIAM, 1859, *Encyclopædia Britannica, Eighth Ed., vol.* XVIII.

While it was passing through the press, or just as the stereotyping was fairly begun, he made a contract with the Messrs. Harper to pay for seven thousand five hundred copies on the day of publication at the rate of one dollar per copy, to be sold within two years, and to continue to publish at the same rate afterwards, or to surrender the contract to the author at his pleasure; terms, I suppose, more liberal than had been offered for a work of grave history on this side of the Atlantic. In London it was published by Mr. Bentley, who purchased the copyright for eight hundred pounds, under the kind auspices of Colonel Aspinwall; again a large sum, as it was already doubtful whether an exclusive privilege could be legally maintained in Great Britain by a foreigner. . . . In five months five thousand copies of the American edition had been sold. At about the same time, an edition of half that number had been exhausted in England. It had been republished in the original in Paris, and translations were going on into French, German, Spanish and Dutch. A more complete success in relation to an historical work of so much consequence could, I suppose, hardly have been asked by any author, however much he might previously have been favored by the public.—TICKNOR, GEORGE, 1863, *Life of William Hickling Prescott, pp.* 248, 249.

Boys read his "Mexico" and "Peru" as

they read the "Arabian Nights"; critics can point to few flaws in the accuracy of his judgment.—NICHOL, JOHN, 1882-85, *American Literature, p.* 150.

THE REIGN OF PHILIP II
1855-58

I finished Prescott's "Philip the Second." What strikes me most about him is that, though he has had new materials, and tells his story well, he does not put anything in a light very different from that in which I had before seen it; and I have never studied that part of history deeply.— MACAULAY, THOMAS BABINGTON, 1855, *Journal, Nov.* 27; *Life and Letters, ed. Trevelyan, ch.* xiii.

Of the merits of this particular work, we have only to say, that they equal those of its predecessors. The style is, if anything, more easy and fluent, and all the parts show the same thorough preparation and uniform polish and finish. . . . The chapters on the Knights Hospitallers of St. John and the Siege of Malta are particularly interesting, and, like many other portions of these volumes, will undoubtedly always be ranked among the finest passages of modern history.—UPHAM, C. W., 1856, *Prescott as an Historian, North American Review, vol.* 83, *p.* 103.

The author's task was arduous in the highest degree. . . . Suffice it to say, for the present, that the difficulty of the achievement is but the measure of the genius and industry manifested in its successful accomplishment, and that expectations founded on the author's previous works are, if possible, more than realized in this.—PEABODY, ANDREW PRESTON, 1856, *Critical Notices, North American Review, vol.* 82 *p.* 571.

To this merit of a well-arranged history Mr. Prescott adds that of an easy, unaffected, though somewhat frigid, power of narration. He belongs to the historical school of Robertson, judicious rather than profound in its general views, and more remarkable for simplicity than for descriptive power. The pictures Mr. Prescott has given us are never wanting in truth, but they are sometimes wanting in life. History only becomes dramatic on two conditions; it must either have the passion of the politician or the imagination of the poet. Mr. Prescott has neither one nor the other; he is a calm and enlightened philosopher, an accomplished man of letters; he is well read in the history of Philip II, and he relates it with fidelity; but he has studied it after the lapse of three centuries in all the serenity of his own reflections and the tranquility of a New England study,—faithfully therefore, as these events and these personages are described by him, he leaves them where he finds them, in their tombs.— GUIZOT, FRANÇOIS PIERRE GUILLAUME, 1857, *Philip II and His Times, Edinburgh Review, vol.* 105, *p.* 44.

Two volumes of Philip II were published in 1855, and the third appeared only a few months ago. To the grace and vivacity of the narratives of the rebellion of the Moriscos, and of the battle of Lepanto and to the undiminished fire and power displayed in this last installment of the work, our current magazines and reviews have borne, and are still bearing, testimony. It will be long indeed ere a historian is found worthy to take up the thread where it has been so suddenly and so unhappily broken. —STIRLING-MAXWELL, SIR WILLIAM, 1859-91, *William Hickling Prescott, Miscellaneous Essays and Addresses, p.* 73.

"Philip II," Mr. Prescott's latest and unfinished work—with less brilliancy of colouring, as becomes the more sombre theme —is rendered even more weighty by the solidity of its judgments.—NICHOL, JOHN, 1882-85, *American Literature, p.* 150.

It is a monument of thorough study and research, of tolerant and dispassionate judgment, and a model of skill in narration.—ADAMS, CHARLES KENDALL, 1882, *A Manual of Historical Literature, p.* 408.

CHARLES V
1857

My "Charles the Fifth," or rather Robertson's, with my Continuation, made his bow to the public to-day, like a strapping giant with a little urchin holding on to the tail of his coat. I can't say I expect much from it, as the best and biggest part is somewhat of the oldest. But people who like a complete series will need it to fill up the gap betwixt "Ferdinand" and "Philip." —PRESCOTT, WILLIAM HICKLING, 1856, *Letter to George Ticknor, Dec.* 8; *Life of Prescott by Ticknor, p.* 379.

It bears all the characteristics of style and manner, all the tokens of elaborate research and philosophic vision, which it has been, and will, we trust, yet be our frequent privilege to record.—PEABODY, ANDREW PRESTON, 1857, *Critical Notices, North American Review, vol.* 87, *p.* 281.

A sequel in which he related, in his usual agreeable style, the true history of the emperor's retirement and death; events upon which recently-discovered documents have thrown so much light.—STIRLING, WILLIAM, 1859, *Encyclopædia Britannica, Eighth Ed., vol.* XVIII.

GENERAL

The style of Mr. Prescott's works, as might be expected from his character, is manly, perspicuous, picturesque, lucid, equally removed from stateliness and levity, disdaining all tawdry ornaments and stimulated energy, and combining clearness and simplicity with glow.—WHIPPLE, EDWIN PERCY, 1848, *Prescott's Histories, Essays and Reviews, vol.* II, *p.* 207.

We consider Prescott the most unobjectionable representative of that school of history, the ideal of which is correct and tasteful narrative. In other respects, he seems to us vastly overrated. We look in vain for that earnestness of purpose, that high and uncompromising tone of sentiment, that genuine love of humanity, which should distinguish the historian of the nineteenth century. Prescott is a kind of elegant trimmer in literature.—TUCKERMAN, HENRY THEODORE, 1849, *Characteristics of Literature, p.* 190.

In history there has been nothing done to which the world at large has not been eager to award the full meed of its deserts. Mr. Prescott, for instance, has been greeted with as much warmth abroad as here. We are not supposed to undervalue his industry and power of clear and elegant arrangement. The richness and freshness of his materials are such that a sense of enchantment must be felt in their contemplation. We must regret, however, that they should have been first presented to the public by one who possesses nothing of the higher powers of the historian, great leading views, or discernment as to the motives of action and the spirit of an era. Considering the splendour of the materials the books are wonderfully tame, and every one must feel that having once passed through them and got the sketch in the mind, there is nothing else to which it will recur. The absence of thought, as to that great picture of Mexican life, with its heroisms, its terrible but deeply significant superstitions, its admirable civic refinement, seems to be quite unbroken. Mr. Bancroft is a far more vivid writer; he has great resources and great command of them, and leading thoughts by whose aid he groups his facts.—OSSOLI, MARGARET FULLER, 1850(?), *American Literature; Art, Literature and the Drama, p.* 303.

Mr. Prescott was by far the first historian of America, and he may justly be assigned to a place beside the very greatest of modern Europe. To the indispensable requisites of such an author—industry, candour, and impartiality—he united ornamental qualities of the highest grade: a mind stored with various and elegant learning, a poetical temperament, and great, it may almost be said unrivalled, pictorial powers. These great qualities appeared not less strongly in his last production, the "History of the Reign of Philip the Second," than in the earlier works—the "History of the Reign of Ferdinand and Isabella," the "History of the Conquest of Mexico," and the "History of the Conquest of Peru," which won for him his world-wide fame. The death of such a man, in the prime of life, and in the meridian of his powers, is a loss not to his country alone, but to the whole human race, to whom his beautiful writings will always prove a source of instruction and enjoyment.—ALISON, SIR ARCHIBALD, 1859, *Letter to S. Austin Allibone, Critical Dictionary of English Literature, vol.* II, *p.* 1673.

Few historians, indeed, have evinced such praiseworthy scrupulousness in the composition of their writings. Far from starting with a system laid down *a priori*, and making the facts he had to deal with bend to it, Mr. Prescott thought that the first duty of a historian was to assemble all its existing documents, classifying and purifying them by a severe criticism, and to employ all his efforts for the discovery of truth. Like Augustin Thierry, he surmounted, by the force of his will, obstacles which seemed almost invincible and to exclude him from the researches of the historian. . . . Of a just and upright spirit, he had a horror of paradox. He never allowed himself to be drawn away by it, and often condemned himself to long investigation to refute even the most audacious assertions. His criticism, full at once of good sense and acuteness, was never deceived in the choice of documents, and his discernment is as remarkable as his good faith. If he may be reproached with often hesitating, even after a long investigation, to pronounce a definite judgment, we must at least acknowledge that he omitted nothing to prepare the way for it, that the author, too timid perhaps to decide, always leaves his reader sufficiently instructed to need no other guide.— MÉRIMÉE, M. PROSPER, 1859, *Revue des Deux Mondes, tome* XX, *p.* 600.

I had as great a regard for Mr. Prescott as for any man of whom I knew so little, and I think very highly of his works.— MACAULAY, THOMAS BABINGTON, 1859, *Letter to S. Austin Allibone, Critical Dictionary of English Literature, vol.* II, *p.* 1673.

Truth was his first aim, as far as he could detect it in the conflicting records of events; and the next aim was to impress this truth, in its genuine colors, upon the reader. The characters and motives of men were weighed in the scales of justice, as they appeared to him after careful research and mature thought. In all these qualities of an accomplished historian, we may safe'y challenge for him a comparison with any other writer.—SPARKS, JARED, 1859, *Remarks at a Meeting of the Massachusetts Historical Society, Feb.* 1; *Proceedings, vol.* 4, *p.* 173.

Wherever the English language is spoken, over the whole earth—his name is perfectly familiar. We all of us know what his place was in America. But I can also say, that in eight years (1851-1859) passed abroad I never met a single educated person, of whatever nation, that was not well acquainted with his fame, and hardly one who had not read his works. No living American name is so widely spread over the whole world.—MOTLEY, JOHN LOTHROP, 1859, *To William Amory, Rome, Feb.* 26; *Proceedings of the Massachusetts Historical Society, vol.* 4. *p.* 267.

It is a saying that "the style is the man"; and of no great author in the literature of the world is that saying more true than of him whose loss we mourn. For in the transparent simplicity and undimmed beauty and candour of his style were read the endearing qualities of his soul; so that his personal friends are found wherever literature is known, and the love for him is co-extensive with the world of letters,—

not limited to those who speak our Anglo-Saxon mother-language, to the literature of which he has contributed such splendid works, but co-extensive with the civilized languages of the human race.—FELTON, CORNELIUS CONWAY, 1859, *Remarks at a Meeting of the Massachusetts Historical Society, Feb.* 1; *Proceedings, vol.* 4, *p.* 185.

So long as in ages far distant, and not only in countries now refined and polished, but in those not yet brought into the domain of civilization, the remarkable epoch which he has described shall attract the attention of men, so long as the consolidation of the Spanish monarchy, and the expulsion of the Moors, the mighty theme of the discovery of America, the sorrowful glories of Columbus, the mail-clad forms of Cortez and Pizarro and the other grim *conquistadores*, trampling new-found empires under the hoofs of their cavalry, shall be subject of literary interest; so long as the blood shall curdle at the cruelties of Alva, and the fierce struggle of the Moslem in the East,—so long will the writings of our friend be read.—EVERETT, EDWARD, 1859, *Remarks at a Meeting of the Massachusetts Historical Society, Feb.* 10; *Proceedings, vol.* 4, *p.* 203.

The excellence of his productions is, in part, transparent to every reader. Compare what he has written with the most of what others have left on the same subjects, and Prescott's superiority beams upon you from the contrast. The easy flow of his language, and the faultless lucidity of his style, may make the reader forget the unremitting toil which the narrative has cost; but the critical inquirer sees everywhere the fruits of investigation rigidly and most perseveringly pursued, and an impartiality and soundness of judgment which give authority to every statement and weight to every conclusion.—BANCROFT, GEORGE, 1859, *Address Before the New York Historical Society, Feb.* 1.

But there was one charm in Mr. Prescott's style which, I think, was much felt, without being much understood by the great mass of his readers. He put not a little of his personal character into it; a great deal more, I think, than is common with writers of acknowledged eminence. The consequence was, that the multitudes who knew him in no way except as an author were yet insensibly drawn to him by the qualities that made him so dear to his friends as a man, and felt, in some degree, the attachment that is commonly the result only of personal intercourse. They seemed to know him more than they know other authors whom they have never seen; and, as most of us have favorite writers without always being able to explain why they are such, he became peculiarly so to many, who yet never stopped to inquire what was the cause of an interest so agreeable to them.—TICKNOR, GEORGE, 1863, *Life of William Hickling Prescott, p.* 212.

How well historiography in its stricter forms has been cultivated in America is proved by her historians, whose great excellence will be acknowledged by the severest critic. William Hickling Prescott must be mentioned before all others; his "History of Ferdinand and Isabella," and "History of Philip the Second," treat the most important periods of Spanish history in a masterly manner; and his works on the two great romantic episodes of American history—"History of the Conquest of Mexico" and "History of the Conquest of Peru"--are of equal excellence and beauty. —SCHERR, J., 1874, *A History of English Literature, tr. M. V., p.* 310.

I have a notion that no one can reach the finest harmonies of style who has not a musical ear. Prescott had no music.— WINTHROP, ROBERT C., 1880, *Journal, Nov.* 17; *A Memoir of Robert C. Winthrop, ed. Winthrop, p.* 303.

Historical literature in America finds its most eminent representative in the brilliant and genial Prescott, who, surpassed by others in vigor and profundity, is rarely equalled in power to win the fancy and to touch the heart.—WELSH, ALFRED H., 1883, *Development of English Literature and Language, vol.* II, *p.* 310.

In this field Prescott had been equalled only by Cooper and surpassed only by Parkman. The defects of his style are chiefly those of excess. The writer of graphic pictorial description must ever career upon the verge of a precipice, and Prescott, like Cooper, sometimes fell into the depths of bombast and fine writing. He delighted in battles and scenes of action, but he never, like Macaulay, sacrificed truth to rhetoric nor dragged in useless scenes to exhibit his mastery over them. His power was chiefly that of a skillful narrator. Stripped of their pictorial effects, his histories would still be valuable,

but they would lose the greater part of their charm.—PATTEE, FRED LEWIS, 1896, *A History of American Literature, p.* 309.

A critical, rather than a creative, age has charged him with being more interesting than accurate. This is the old charge against Herodotus, and against Thucydides; it is the charge made against Prescott's great English contemporary, Macaulay. What critic of either of these has won an equal place in literature?—THORPE, FRANCIS NEWTON, 1897, *Library of the World's Best Literature, ed. Warner, vol.* XX, *p.* 11767.

Prescott's attention was fastened upon the spectacle of life. He filled his wide canvas with splendid masses of figures, scenes of court and camp and tropical forest, battle-fields and strange barbaric pomp. Yet there was unity to the great design, and beauty of detail. The methods of work enforced by his disability aided rather than hindered the pictorial conception. His secretaries, blundering sadly over the Spanish, would read to him day after day and week after week, until his mind was fully stored. Then from the lonely brooding of the blind would leap the vivid chapter.—BATES, KATHARINE LEE, 1897, *American Literature, p.* 243.

Possessed in a wonderful degree not only the patient spirit necessary for careful and painstaking research, but also the imaginative power to present the dry facts thus discovered in a picturesque and delightful narrative. — PANCOAST, HENRY S., 1898, *An Introduction to American Literature, p.* 228.

Prescott's work, then, is often mentioned as rather romantic than scholarly. In this view there is some justice. The scholarship of his day had not collected anything like the material now at the disposal of students; and Prescott's infirmity of sight could not help limiting the range of his investigation. His style, too, always clear and readable, and often vivid, is somewhat florid and generally coloured by what seems a conviction that historical writers should maintain the dignity of history. For all this, his works so admirably combine substantial truth with literary spirit that they are more useful than many which are respected as authoritative. What he tells us is the result of thoughtful study. —WENDELL, BARRETT, 1900, *A Literary History of America, p.* 270.

Sydney Owenson Lady Morgan

1783(?)–1859

Born in Dublin, Ireland, about 1780; was the daughter óf an actor, who anglicized his name from McOwen, and was said to possess some literary ability. She published in 1797, a volume of poems, and afterward wrote two novels, which met with little success. In 1806 her novel, "The Wild Irish Girl, a National Tale," gained her a sudden popularity. This work introduced her into aristocratic English circles, and in 1812 she married Sir Thomas Charles Morgan, a distinguished physician. She continued for many years to write novels, songs, comic operas, biographies and works of travel. Among her more popular novels were "Florence Macarthy" (1812); "The O'Briens and the O'Flahertys" (1827); and "The Princess" (1835). In other departments her most celebrated works were probably the "Life and Times of Salvator Rosa" (1823), and "Woman and Her Master" (1840). Lady Morgan was long a leader in London literary society, where she gained warm friends and had no lack of bitter enemies. In the last year of her life she published "Passages from my Autobiography," (1858). Died in London, Apr. 13, 1859. An edition of her works was edited by herself 1855-56. She is said to have gained £25,000 by her writings, in addition to a pension of £300 conferred upon her by the ministry of Lord Grey.—BEERS, HENRY A., 1897, *rev. Johnson's Universal Cyclopœdia, vol.* v, *p.* 891.

PERSONAL

She vows vengeance against you as the supposed author of the article in the *Quarterly*, in which her atheism, profanity, indecency, and ignorance have been exposed. You are to be the hero of some novel of which she is about to be delivered.—PEEL, ROBERT, 1817, *Letter to Mr. Croker, Nov.* 22; *The Croker Papers, ed. Jennings, vol.* I, *p.* 109.

Thank you for your information about Lady Morgan. She, it seems, is resolved to make me read one of her novels. I hope I shall feel interested enough to be able to learn the language. I wrote the main part of the article in the *Quarterly*, but, as you know, was called away to Ireland when it was in the press; and I am sorry to say that some blunders crept in accidentally, and one or two were premeditatedly added, which, however, I do not think Lady Morgan knows enough either of English, French, or Italian to find out. If she goes on we shall have sport.—CROKER, JOHN WILSON, 1817, *Letter to Robert Peel, Nov.* 26; *The Croker Papers, ed. Jennings, vol.* I, *p.* 111.

Lady Morgan did not displease me till I reflected on her conversation. She seems good-natured as well as lively. She talked like one conscious of her importance and superiority.—ROBINSON, HENRY CRABB, 1824, *Diary, July* 1; *Diary, Reminiscences and Correspondence, ed. Sadler.*

She has no idea of *mauvaise honte* or embarrassment, her manners are not the most refined, and affect the *aisance* and levity of the fashionable world, which, however, do not sit calmly or naturally upon her. She has the English weakness, that of talking incessantly of fashionable acquaintances, and trying to pass for very *recherchée* to a degree quite unworthy of a woman of such distinguished talents. She is not at all aware how she thus underrates herself. She is not difficult to know, for with more vivacity than good taste she instantly professes perfect openness. . . . In her writings she is far more guarded and dignified than in her conversation. The satire of the latter is, however. not less biting and dexterous than that of her pen, and just as little remarkable for conscientious regard to truth.—PUECKLER-MUSKAU, 1832, *Tour of a German Prince, A Series of Letters to Mrs. Austin.*

The sum of my long experience in society leaves in its total a large balance in favour of what is good. I have no reason to complain of memory; I find in my efforts to track its records, guided by the fond feelings of my life, and warmed by the fancifulness of my Celtic temperament, bright hues come forward like the colours of the tesselated pavement of antiquity when the renovating water is flung upon them. . . . I have other links connecting me with the past; of the many kind and illustrious friends whom I have made through life, I have never lost one except by death; and I am now enjoying in the second and third generation of those who are gone, the distinction conferred upon me by the personal kindness of their grandsires. One of the chief temptations to present the principal facts of my life to the public, has been to

SYDNEY LADY MORGAN

ANNA JAMESON

prove the readiness with which society is willing to help those who are honestly and fervently ready to help themselves.—MORGAN, SYDNEY OWENSON LADY, 1857, *Memoir, Prefatory Address, vol.* I, *pp.* 2, 3.

"Facts" were anything but "stubborn things" for Lady Morgan. She had that disregard of truth which foolish people often attribute to "exuberance of imagination." As painted by the autobiography there never was a more brilliant and fascinating siren. Let us discount largely, and we may still believe that she was very attractive. It is so easy for an Irish woman to be charming! And this young Irishwoman was good-looking, quick, impulsive, not without a streak of genius, desirous of pleasing and of being pleased, singing Irish songs, playing the harp, telling droll stories, amusing society by her vivacity and vanity, and overshadowing no one by any eminent superiority: she alarmed no one by her learning or profundity; distressed no one by her cleverness. Her talents were essentially social; and were appreciable by the smallest intellects. The gay little Irish heart was warmly affectionate and sympathetic. Nor had she the failings in conduct which often accompany the Irish heart; underneath all the extravagance of an excitable temperament, there was the solid good sense and integrity of her English mother. She was thoroughly prudent in conduct, whatever she may have been in speech. She flirted freely, but kept out of scrapes.—JEWSBURY, GERALDINE ENDSOR, 1863, *Our Survey of Literature and Science, Cornhill, vol.* 7, *p.* 133.

She had about her all the natural kindness of her country people. She once by great personal exertion saved the life of a criminal. If it was a work of mercy or charity I never knew any one who went about it with more good will, or more perseveringly.—REDDING, CYRUS, 1867, *Personal Reminiscences of Eminent Men, vol.* III, *p.* 39.

One of the most peculiar and original literary characters whom I have ever known, was Sydney Lady Morgan, a composition of natural genius, acquired accomplishments, audacity that flew at the highest game, shrewd thought, and research at once intelligent and superficial; personal coquetries and affectations, balanced by sincere and strenuous family affections; extreme liberality of opinions, religious and political; extremely narrow literary sympathies, united with a delight in all the most tinsel pleasures and indulgences of the most inane aristocratic society; a genial love for Art, limited by the most inconceivable prejudices of ignorance; in brief, a compound of the most startling contradictions, impossible to be overlooked or forgotten, though possible to be described in two ways—both true, yet the one diametrically opposite to the other.—CHORLEY, HENRY FOTHERGILL, 1873, *Autobiography, Memoir and Letters, vol.* I, *p.* 230.

With her wit and vanity, poor French and fine clothes, good common sense and warm Irish heart, Lady Morgan was a most entertaining and original character—a spirited, versatile, spunky little woman, whose whole life was a grand social success. She was also one of the most popular and voluminous writers of her day; but, with all her sparkle and dash, ambition and industry, destined in a few generations more to be almost unknown, vanishing down that doleful "back entry" where Time sends so many bright men and women. . . . She was extremely sensitive in regard to her age, and if forced to state it on the witness-stand would doubtless have whispered it to the judge in a bewitching way.—SANBORN, KATE A., 1878, *Lady Morgan, Lippincott's Magazine, vol.* 22, *p.* 466.

Ah! she was a most pleasant Irish lady, proud of her country—so far as words went —and retaining a brogue to the last—the brogue that is never entirely lost. Why should it be? Lady Morgan did not seek to hide hers—perhaps because she knew she could not. . . . Her easy-chair was her throne at Knightsbridge; seated there she exacted homage, and received it—the queen of assembled satellites. Her youth had long passed; but she sought to hide the knowledge even from herself; her exact age was a secret carefully kept: from all letters, account-books, et cætera, dates were scrupulously removed.—HALL, SAMUEL CARTER, 1883, *Retrospect of a Long Life, p.* 345.

While Miss Austen only received a few hundreds for her inimitable novels, Lady Morgan counted her profits by thousands and thousands. She not only had a "gude conceit" of herself, but she persuaded other people to have the same. By a happy combination of circumstances she heard herself called "Lady," which tickled her ears and pleased her vanity. In short, the daring, careless, inaccurate, *insouciante* "Glorvina" had the fairy secret of success, though people of the present day may stare at the verdict that once pronounced her a genius.—HAMILTON, CATHARINE J., 1892, *Women Writers, First Series, p.* 226.

The centre of a certain literary society of which Mrs. Stewart became an intimate was Lady Morgan, a little old woman of such pungent wit, that Mr. Fonblanque, then the editor of the *Examiner*, used to say of her, "She is just a spark of hell-fire, and is soon going back to her native element."—HARE, AUGUSTUS J. C., 1895, *Biographical Sketches, p.* 145.

GENERAL

I have just read your "Wild Irish Girl," a title which will attract by its novelty, but which does not well suit the charming character of Glorvina. As a sincere and warm friend to Ireland, I return you my thanks for the just character which you have given to the lower Irish, and for the sound and judicious observations which you have attributed to the priest. The notices of Irish history are ingeniously introduced, and are related in such a manner as to induce belief amongst infidels.—EDGEWORTH, RICHARD LOVELL, 1806, *Letter to Sydney Owenson, Dec.* 23; *Lady Morgan's Memoir, vol.* I, *p.* 293.

Though by no means approving of some of the opinions in her later publications, yet I admired the ability shown in "O'Donnel," the only work of hers that I have ever read through.—GRANT, ANNE, 1825, *Letter to Mrs. Gorman, Mar.* 23; *Memoir and Correspondence, ed. Grant, vol.* III, *p.* 581.

I have amused myself occasionally very pleasantly during the last few days by reading over Lady Morgan's novel of "O'Donnel," which has some striking and beautiful passages of situation and description, and in the comic part is very rich and entertaining. I do not remember being so much pleased with it at first. There is a want of story, always fatal to a book the first reading—and it is well if it gets a chance of a second. Alas, poor novel!—SCOTT, SIR WALTER, 1826, *Journal, March* 14; *Life by Lockhart, ch.* lxviii.

Poor Lady Morgan! her "O'Briens and O'Flaherties" seems to have fallen dead, completely dead, from the press. The book is decidedly dull, but still her name ought to have carried an edition through. Colburn, I hear, swears that Jerdan's having discovered it was an improper book for ladies to read has cost him five hundred pounds, and really this is not impossible.—CROKER, CROFTON, 1828, *Letter to Blackwood, Jan.; William Blackwood and His Sons, ed. Oliphant, vol.* I, *p.* 520.

Lady Morgan has succeeded in adulterating her refinement; Thomas Moore unsuccessfully endeavored to refine his grossness. She has abundant *talent*; he has abundant *genius*: and whatsoever distinction those terms admit of, indicates, in my mind, their *relative* merit. This allowance, however, must be made—that the lady has contented herself with invoking only substantial beings and things of this sublunary world, while the gentleman has ransacked both heaven and hell, and "the half-way house," for figurative assistance.—I knew them both before they had acquired any celebrity, and after they had attained to much. I esteemed them then, and have no reason to disesteem them now: it is on their own account that I wish some of the compositions of both had never appeared; and I really believe, upon due consideration, they will themselves be of my way of thinking.—BARRINGTON, SIR JONAH, 1830, *Personal Sketches of His Own Times.*

In all she writes there is a genius, and that of very varied kind; there is wit, humour, tenderness, love of country, and a fine vein of agreeable fancy.—CUNNINGHAM, ALLAN, 1833, *Biographical and Critical History of the Literature of the Last Fifty Years.*

Whatever the novelist may be elsewhere, it is clear that as long as to have propped rising states can give it a claim to the title, she must be a "stateswoman" in Belgium. —THOMPSON, T. P., 1835, *Lady Morgan's Princess, Westminster Review, vol.* 22, *p.* 304.

And dear Lady Morgan! Look, look how she comes,
With her pulses all beating for freedom, like drums,—
So Irish, so modish, so *mixtish*, so wild,
So committing herself, as she talks, like a child,
So trim yet so easy, polite yet big-hearted,
That truth and she, try all she can, won't be parted.
She'll put on your fashions, your latest new air,
And then talk so frankly, she'll make you all stare:—
Mrs. Hall may say "Oh," and Miss Edgeworth say "Fie,"

But my lady will know all the what and the why.
Her books, a like mixture, are so very clever,
The god himself swore he could read them forever;
Plot, character, freakishness, all are so good;
And the heroine's herself playing tricks in a hood.
So he kissed her, and call'd her "eternal good wench";
But asked, why the devil she spoke so much French?
—HUNT, LEIGH, 1837, *Blue-Stocking Revels.*

Her style and her writings, as I have observed before, made no pretence to anything profound. They were lively sketches, more especially those touching upon Irish manners; but they had the merit of being faithfully drawn, and not without humour. . . . A fertile invention, and a lively imagination, with a habit of catching the salient points in what she heard or saw, and of depicting them in a vivacious manner, were the secrets of her success. . . . Some of her characters, essentially Irish, were sketched with a masterly hand, but in her inexperience she made her characters too imaginative. This, however, was amended by time, and a few female writers of England became more popular in their day.—REDDING, CYRUS, 1867, *Personal Reminiscences of Eminent Men, vol.* III, *pp.* 8, 12, 16.

The national tales of Ireland really commence with Lady Morgan. It is at her hands that we must seek for that true mirror of native society that enlarges into the reflection of all creeds and classes, as well as that humour and warmth of temperament needed to animate the reflex, and supply to every outline its due colour and reality. . . . (As in her books on France and Italy), she was no pretender as a novelist, and in two of her tales, at least, asserts her right to take her place in the front rank of national fiction.—BERNARD, BAYLE, 1874, *The Life of Samuel Lover, pp.* 160, 168.

Her writing, though slipshod and often inflated, contained much humorous observation, and when describing what she understood, the lower-class Irish, she was as good as Lever or Banim.—HAMILTON, J. A., 1894, *Dictionary of National Biography, vol.* XXXIX, *p.* 29.

Its phenomenal success ["Wild Irish Girl"] was due more to the fact that the Irish question was one of supreme interest than to its own intrinsic merits. It has not borne the test of time, and it is almost impossible now to read it without weariness.—GERARD, FRANCES A., 1897, *Some Fair Hibernians, p.* 183.

Rufus Choate
1799–1859

Born at Essex, Mass., Oct. 1, 1799: died at Halifax, Nova Scotia, July 13, 1859. A distinguished American lawyer, orator, and statesman. He was graduated at Dartmouth, in 1819, was admitted to the bar in 1823, was elected a representative to Congress from Massachusetts in 1830, and was reëlected in 1832, but resigned his seat in 1834. In 1841 he became the successor in the Senate of Daniel Webster, who accepted the office of secretary of state under President Harrison. He remained in the Senate until 1845, when Webster was reëlected.—SMITH, BENJAMIN E., ed., 1894–97, *The Century Cyclopedia of Names, p.* 247.

PERSONAL

In him "the elements were so combined," that all his acquaintances became his devoted friends. So far as I know, even party malevolence spared him. He was pure and incorruptible; and in all our intercourse I have never known him to utter or insinuate a sentiment respecting public affairs which was not of a high tone and elevated character.—BUCHANAN, JAMES, 1859, *Letter, July* 18; *The Works of Rufus Choate, ed. Brown, vol.* I, *p.* 249.

He was a scholar by instinct and by the determining force of his nature. All forms of high intellectual activity had charm and reward for his sympathetic and splendid intelligence. He especially delighted, however, in history, philosophy, eloquence, and the immense riches of the ancient literature. His library was peopled to him with loving minds. The critical and august procedures in history were as evident to him as processions in the streets. No inspiring and majestic voice had spoken from Athenian *bema,* in Roman forum, in English Parliament whose vital words, even whose tones, did not still echo in his ear. He would have made a Greek professor, elegant in scholarship, rich in acquisition, energetic and liberal in instruction. I am not aware that he ever made special study of theology. He simply took it up, I think, with a literary interest, when its great discussions came in his way; yet Professor Park once said of him, after a half day's conversation, that "If he had not been the first lawyer of his time, he might have been its most eminent theologian."—STORRS, R. S., 1884, *Letter, Memoirs of Rufus Choate by Joseph Neilson, p.* 280.

He was more than a father to me, and I loved him next to idolatry. I studied law with him in 1847 and 1848. The most striking of all his characteristics was his regard for the feelings of others. Whatever he might say in the excitement of a trial in regard to the opposite party, or even of witnesses whom he disbelieved, he was, in his office, and in all professional and social intercourse, most considerate of the feelings of others. I never heard him speak an impatient or angry word in my life. Especially to young men did he show this tender consideration. Webster's presence overawed a young man; Choate impressed the young man with his greatness, but he did so by lifting him for the time up to his own level. His genius seemed to be an inspiration to every young man who entered his presence; and those who had the honor of his acquaintance regarded him with an admiration akin to hero-worship. . . . One of Mr. Choate's characteristics was to idealize everything. His perception of subtile analogies tinged his mind, and appears in his utterances; in his mental atmosphere all things, however common or even unclean, became transformed, beautiful. Another feature was his charity. From those who would borrow he turned not away.— CARPENTER, MATTHEW H., 1884, *Letter, Memoirs of Rufus Choate by Joseph Neilson, pp.* 293, 294.

Mr. Choate was from boyhood a serious thinker, and a believer in the truth of Christianity, though I do not know that he ever became a member of any particular church. But the extreme sensitiveness, so characteristic of him, often led him to parry playfully any attempt on the part of the over-zealous to draw him into conversation on religious subjects. . . . I should say that one of Choate's most remarkable traits of character was his unresting, unflagging industry, coupled with a readiness to make any and every sacrifice of his own likings or enjoyment to the one great object of securing the highest position in his profession. This was with him no vulgar ambition, but simply a love of, and a desire for, perfection.—MARSH, GEORGE P., 1884, *Letter, Memoirs of Rufus Choate by Joseph Neilson, p.* 381.

A man only less than six feet in height, with a full, deep breast, high and unseemly shoulders, hips and legs slender and in appearance weak, arms long, hands and feet large and ill-formed, a head broad, chaste, symmetrical, covered with a luxuriant suit of black, glossy, wavy hair, a face intellectually handsome and equally attractive to men and to women, a complexion dark and bronzed as becomes the natives of the tropical isles of the East, a beard scanty and vagrant, mouth and nose large, lips thin and long, an eye black, gentle and winning in repose, but brilliant, commanding, and persuasive in moments of excitement—we shall have thus and now created an imperfect picture of Rufus Choate as he presented himself to his contemporaries when his physical qualities had not been wasted by disease nor impaired by age. . . . And to these charms of person and benignity of manners we are to super-add a voice that in conversation, debate, or oration was copious, commanding, sonorous, and emotional, responding like music to every change of thought, and, in its variety of tone and sweep of accent and emphasis, touching and influencing not only the sentiments and feelings but even the opinions and judgments of men. His vocabulary knew no limits except those set by the language itself; and such was his facility in its use as to extort from the stern Chief-Justice of the Supreme Judicial Court of Massachusetts the remark, when told that Webster's new dictionary contained many thousand additional words, "I beg of you not to let Choate hear of it."—BOUTWELL, GEORGE, 1887, *The Lawyer, Statesman and the Soldier, pp.* 1, 2.

Was all impetuosity—pouring out torrents of exquisite thought and brilliant language in utter disregard of the length of his sentences or the vehemence of his gesticulation. One might say of him, as Cicero said of Scævola, "Jurisperitorum eloquentissimus, eloquentium jurisperitissimus." He was certainly the most eloquent of our jurists, and the greatest jurist of our orators. — WINTHROP, ROBERT C., 1894, *Webster's Reply to Hayne, Scribner's Magazine, vol.* 15, *p.* 127.

How it was that such an exotic nature, so ardent and tropical in all its manifestations, so truly Southern and Italian in its impulses, and at the same time so robust and sturdy in its strength, could have been produced upon the bleak and barren soil of our northern cape, and nurtured under the chilling blasts of its east winds, is a mystery insoluble. . . . This love of study became a ruling passion in his earliest youth. To it he sacrificed all that the youth of our day— even the best of them—consider indispensable, and especially the culture and training of the body; and when we recall his pale face, worn and lined as it was in his later years, one of his most pathetic utterances is found in a letter to his son at school: "I hope that you are well and studious, and among the best scholars. If this is so, I am willing you should play every day till the blood is ready to burst from your cheeks. Love the studies that will make you wise, useful and happy when there shall be no blood at all to be seen in your cheeks or lips." He never rested from his delightful labors—and that is the pity of it —he took no vacations.—CHOATE, JOSEPH H., 1898, *Rufus Choate, An Address Delivered at the Unveiling of his Statue in the Court House in Boston, Oct.* 15; *The Green Bag, vol.* 10, *pp.* 506, 507.

LAWYER

Having been for more than twenty years after Mr. Choate came to this bar, his antagonist in forensic struggles, at the least, I believe, as frequently as any other member of it, I may well be competent to bear witness to his peculiar abilities, resources, and manners in professional service. And having, in the varied experiences of nearly forty years, not infrequently encountered some of the giants of the law, whose lives and memories have contributed to render this bar illustrious throughout the land,— among whom I may include the honored names of Prescott, Mason, Hubbard, Webster, and Dexter, and others among the dead, and those of others yet with us, to share in the sorrows of this hour,—I do no injustice to the living or the dead in saying, that for the peculiar powers desirable for a lawyer and advocate, for combination of accurate memory, logical acumen, vivid imagination, profound learning in the law,

exuberance of literary knowledge and command of language, united with strategic skill, I should place him at the head of all whom I have ever seen in the management of a cause at the bar.—LORING, CHARLES G., 1859, *Address at Meeting of the Suffolk Bar, The Works of Rufus Choate, ed. Brown, vol.* I, *p.* 250.

When approaching the argument of a great cause, or the delivery of an important speech, his mind was absolutely absorbed with it. The lights were left burning all night in his library, and after retiring he would frequently arise from his bed, and, without dressing, rush to his desk to note rapidly some thought which flashed across his wakeful mind. This was repeated sometimes ten or fifteen times in a night. . . . Every important and difficult cause took such possession of him that he would get no sound sleep till it was finished. His mind, to use his own illustration, became a stream that took up the cause, like a ship, and bore it on day and night till the verdict or judgment was reached. It is not surprising, then, that he came from a trial so much exhausted. Almost every considerable case was attended or followed with a severe attack of sick-headache. . . . No one could make a more clear, convincing and effective statement; none held all the resources of the language more absolutely at command. His power over the sympathies, by which, from the first word he uttered, you were drawn to him with a strange and inexplicable attraction, was wonderful. Court, jury, and spectators seemed fused into one mass of willing and delighted listeners. They could not *help* being influenced by him. Calming the hostility of his hearers by kindness, bending their will to his in delightful harmony, he moved on with irresistible force, boiling along his course. tumultuous but beautiful, lifting them bodily, bearing all with him, and prostrating all before him.—BROWN, SAMUEL GILMAN, 1862, *ed. The Works of Rufus Choate, Memoir, vol.* I, *pp.* 285, 286, 295.

Many of his admirers contend that he was the greatest lawyer ever living in any age, and there are many good reasons for the assertion. There are in the daily records of this eminent advocate's life, so many samples worthy the earnest emulation of the student, the lawyer, even the statesman. In reviewing his course of mental discipline, no better could be presented, in all that is required to make the ripe scholar, the thorough lawyer.—SCOTT, HENRY W., 1890, *Distinguished American Lawyers, p.* 149.

With the ordinary twelve men in a jury-box, Mr. Choate was a wizard. His knowledge of human nature, his wide and deep sympathies, his imagination, his power of statement, with his rich musical voice and his wonderful fascination of manner, made him a charmer of men and a master in the great art of winning verdicts. So far as the writer is able to form an opinion, there has never been at the English or American bar a man who has been his equal in his sway over juries.—STICKNEY, ALBERT, 1897, *Library of the World's Best Literature, ed. Warner, vol.* VI, *p.* 3653.

GENERAL

The style of Mr. Choate is the style of an orator, not of an author. It will hardly bear a minute criticism, founded on general principles of taste, but must be judged with reference to the character of the speaker and the object of his speech. The tone of his diction is pitched on too high a key for written composition. The same splendid oration which thrilled a popular assembly, or influenced the verdict of a jury, would lose a very important portion of its charm when subjected to the calm, cold judgment of the reader. Besides, it must be admitted, that Mr. Choate's immense wealth of language, and opulence of fancy, urge him into redundance of expression, and sometimes overload his style with shining words.—WHIPPLE, EDWIN PERCY, 1847, *Rufus Choate, Essays and Reviews, vol.* II, *p.* 175.

But he does not deal exclusively in those ponderous sentences. There is nothing of the artificial Johnsonian balance in his style. It is as often marked by a pregnant brevity as by a sonorous amplitude. He is sometimes satisfied, in concise epigrammatic clauses, to skirmish with his light troops and drive in the enemy's outposts. It is only on fitting occasions, when great principles are vindicated and solemn truths told, when some moral or political Waterloo or Solferino is to be fought,—that he puts on the entire panoply of his gorgeous rhetoric. It is then said that his majestic sentences swell to the dimensions of his thought,—that you hear afar off the awful roar of his rifled ordnance,—and—when he

has stormed the heights and broken the centre and trampled the squares and turned the staggering wings of his adversary,—that he sounds his imperial clarion along the whole line of battle, and moves forward with all his hosts in one overwhelming charge.—EVERETT, EDWARD, 1859, *Faneuil Hall, July* 22; *The Works of Rufus Choate, ed. Brown, vol.* I, *p.* 270.

Mr. Choate's mind was so complex, peculiar, and original,—so foreign in temperament and spirit to the more representative traits of New England character,—so large, philosophic, and sagacious in vision and survey of great questions, and so dramatic and vehement in their exposition and enforcement,—so judicial and conservative in always maintaining in his arguments the balance and relation of interdependent principles, and so often in details marring the most exquisite poetry with the wildest extravagancies in style,—so free from mere vulgar tricks of effect, and so full of imaginative trickiness and surprises, —so mischievous, subtle, mysterious, elusive, Protean,—that it is no wonder he has been more admired and more misunderstood than any eminent American of his time.—WOODMAN, H., 1860, *Rufus Choate, Atlantic Monthly, vol.* 6, *p.* 79.

What a strange, Oriental, enchanted style he has! What gleams of far-off ideas, flashes from the sky, essences from Arabia, seem unconsciously to drop into it! I have been reading him, in consequence of what you wrote. It is strange that with all his seeking for perfection in this kind he did not succeed better. But it would seem that his affluent and mysterious genius could not be brought to walk in the regular paces. He was certainly a very extraordinary person.—DEWEY, ORVILLE, 1864, *To Miss Catherine M. Sedgwick, May* 5; *Autobiography and Letters, p.* 273.

Charles Fox said that "no good speech ever read well," and, tried by this test alone, those contained in this ["Addresses and Orations"] volume must have been very good ones. Mr. Choate's speeches certainly do not read well; but if they have this mark of excellence they are disappointing in other and more important qualities. Two-thirds of this collection are historical or literary addresses called forth by special occasions; the rest are political speeches. The latter, contrary to what would naturally be expected, are much the best. All are disfigured by a very bad style. Now and then a passage occurs which is nervous, forcible, and simple, but the sentences are as a rule complex, involved, and of intolerable length. Some of them actually cover a page or more, and read like an unpunctuated catalogue. That Mr. Choate should have made these interminable paragraphs bearable to his listeners would have been an extraordinary feat. . . . Mr. Choate's rhetoric, though deeply overloaded and at times strained, is often brilliant, and is always remarkable for an apparently unbounded vocabulary. He was too fond of Latin derivatives, and never adhered sufficiently to strong Saxon words, the use of which by Mr. Webster he highly commends. Yet with all his faults in this respect no one can read this collection and not be struck by the variety and richness of the language.—LODGE, HENRY CABOT, 1878, *A Whig Orator, The Nation, vol. 27, p. 287.*

As a speaker he was copious, reiterative, and much given to illustrations useful in an argument; as a writer he was more simple and severe. But, however widely his methods differed, the same delicate and touching sensibility, the same vivid and picturesque beauty, the same wealth of thought and power of expression appeared in what was spoken and in what was written. In neither was his brilliant imagery used as a mere embellishment; the visions of beauty in his mind became articulate without effort; the musical flow and rhythm as inimitable as the melody of the murmuring brook. He evidently believed that from the harmony that could exist between a subject and the tone of its discussion might arise a sense of ideal and emotional beauty, pleasing to the mind; that a brilliant style was consistent with directness of thought and simplicity of speech; and that rhetorical and illustrative imagery, employed with taste and judgment, —pictures to the eye and to the mind,— might add to the spirit and force of an argument. Mr. Choate wrote with great freedom, and often spoke with vehemence and rapidity; the words waiting instantly and submissively on the thoughts. When the subject moved him strongly and was to be compressed within the limits of a single discourse, he sometimes rushed through one of those long sentences thought to be peculiar to him. However easy it may have been for him,—and it appeared to be easy,—the work in its nature was unique and difficult.—NEILSON, JOSEPH, 1884 *Memoirs of Rufus Choate, p. 112.*

Horace Mann
1796-1859

American Statesman and Educator, born at Franklin, Mass., May 4, 1796; was graduated at Brown university, Providence, and commenced the study of law. Elected to the legislature of Massachusetts in 1827, his first speech was in favor of religious liberty, and his second a plea for railways. He was an advocate of temperance, and a founder of the state lunatic asylum. Removing to Boston, he was elected, 1836, to the state senate, of which he became president. After editing the revised statutes of the state, he was for eleven years secretary of the board of education. He gave up business and politics and devoted his whole time to the cause of education, introduced normal schools and paid committees, and, in 1843, made a visit to educational establishments in Europe. His report was reprinted both in England and America. For eleven years he worked fifteen hours a day, held teachers' conventions, gave lectures, and conducted a large correspondence. In 1848 he was elected to Congress as the successor of ex-President John Quincy Adams, whose example he followed in energetic opposition to the extension of slavery. At the end of his term he accepted the presidency of Antioch college at Yellow Springs, Ohio, established for the education of both sexes, where he labored with zeal and success until his death Aug. 2, 1859. His principal works are his educational reports, and "Slavery Letters and Speeches."—PECK, HARRY THURSTON, ed. 1898, *The International Cyclopædia, vol. IX, p. 447.*

PERSONAL

One tends to idealize a character, which, during many years of the closest intimacy was never swayed by unworthy motives, or acted upon secondary principles, and over which the beauty of sacred affections poured an indefinable charm. I am aware, that, where others see faults, I see only virtues. When his is called a "rugged nature," because he could not temporize, and because he made great requisitions of men upon whom were laid great duties, I see only his demand for perfection in others as well as in himself; and no man ever made greater requisitions of self. He could forget his own interests when he worked for great causes; and he sometimes wished others, who had not his moral strength, to do likewise. But the very requisition often evolved self-respect to such a degree as to bring forth the power to do the duty, as many a man who has come under his influence can testify; and what greater honor can we do our fellow man than to expect of him the very highest of which he is capable? It is true of him, that he had not much charity for those who sinned against the light; but it is equally true, that his tenderness for the ignorant and the oppressed was never found wanting, and that the first motion of repentance in the erring melted his heart at once. Love of man was so essentially the impelling power in him, that it cost him no effort to exercise it; but he had no self-appreciation which made him feel that he could do what others could not if they would. Perhaps the most remarkable trait in his character was his modest estimate of himself.—MANN, MARY, 1865, *Life of Horace Mann by His Wife, Introduction, p. v.*

EDUCATOR

There is not a town nor a school district in Massachusetts, where his influence has not been felt; there is not one which has not largely profited by the spirit which he has excited, and by the improvements which he has introduced.—BOWEN, FRANCIS, 1845, *Teachers of the Boston Schools, North American Review, vol.* 60, *p.* 225.

I honor beyond all common names of respect the distinguished gentleman (Horace Mann), who for twelve years has devoted the uncommon powers of his mind, and the indomitable energy of his character, to this noble cause. He will be remembered till the history of Massachusetts is forgotten, as one of her greatest benefactors.—EVERETT, EDWARD, 1849, *Second Speech on Aid to Colleges, Orations and Speeches, vol.* II, *p.* 618.

The record of his life is that of a great thinker and an heroic and indefatigable worker for the mental and moral well-being of the youth of America. His mind was pure and lofty and far ahead of his time;

his devotion to the cause of learning and self-abnegation in his work was such as became rather an angel of light than a creature of earthly mold. . . . Horace Mann was a hero. He set a herculean task before himself and did it. He gave his life to the youth of America and we are all his debtors. The work which he did is imperishable. He lifted a nation upon his Atlantean shoulders and broke open the locked doors to hidden stores of wisdom. He built "monuments more enduring than brass" in uncounted thousands of young lives. He did for America what Froebel and Pestalozzi earlier did for western Europe. But Horace Mann was no saint, though he did a saintly work. His nature was delicately attuned and the sharp raspings of the world often struck out anything but heavenly melody.—KASSON, FRANK H., 1891, *Horace Mann, Education, vol.* 12 *pp.* 36, 37.

No other college president ever had before him a more susceptible body of students; and no other body of students ever had over them a more honored president, or one with greater power to impress himself. Those six years were years of sacrifice, filled with many petty annoyances and grievous disappointments to Mr. Mann; but at the same time they were years of great victory for the causes for which he was laboring. In those six years he did more for the higher education and for the elevation of women, than any other man, in any other place, ever did in a quarter of a century. In those six years he demonstrated to the world that men and women can be educated together with mutual advantage to both intellect and morals. In those six years he did more than any other man in a generation to demonstrate that women have equal intellectual capacity with men. In those six years he showed how a college can be Christian in the best sense in which that word can be used, and at the same time not sectarian. In those six years he did much to prove that conduct and character, rather than opinion, are the essential things in this life. In those six years he impressed his high ideals upon hundreds and hundreds of young people in such a way as to change the entire character of their after lives. His power to inspire was phenomenal. In those six years, outside college walls, in educational meetings and on the lecture platforms, in Ohio and other western states, by his magical power as a speaker he stimulated thousands of people to nobler thinking and higher living. In those six years he imbued Antioch college with a spirit that still pervades it; which stimulates to higher aims and nobler purposes everyone who is brought within the influence. Those six years were religious climax to one of the grandest lives this world has ever known.—BELL, W. A., 1896, *Horace Mann at Antioch College, Journal of Proceedings and Addresses of the Thirty-fifth Annual Meeting of the National Educational Association, p. 74.*

In conclusion I suggest again the thought of Mr. Mann as a character inspired with missionary zeal to reform society by means of the school system. It was this missionary zeal that led him to advocate in the Massachusetts legislature the first insane asylum, and secure its establishment—to favor the establishment of asylums for deaf, dumb, and blind; to secure normal schools, humane school discipline, methods of instruction that appeal to the child's interest and arouse him to self-activity, and finally to devote the evening of his life to the Antioch college experiment. It is this missionary zeal for the school that works so widely and in so many followers to-day. What enthusiastic teacher is not proud to be called a disciple of Horace Mann?—HARRIS, WILLIAM T., 1896, *Horace Mann, Educational Review, vol. 12, p. 119.*

He was the contemporary and equal of Charles Sumner. In fact, there was no man, with the exception of Daniel Webster, in Massachusetts, who, in prospects, stood ahead of Horace Mann. Everything in the way of fame and fortune was easily within his grasp. The question with him was, should he give up all these brilliant prospects and take up a cause that seemed lost and almost hopeless—that of the common schools? He accepted the position at one thousand dollars a year, and threw himself into his work with all his might and main.—PARKER, FRANCIS W., 1896, *Horace Mann, Educational Review, vol. 12, p. 68.*

The supreme work of Mr. Mann was the remodeling of the school system of Massachusetts. He introduced many of the features which are now widely accepted as invaluable elements of the school systems of the U. S., and to him as much as to any one person is due the founding of the normal schools in the U. S.—THURBER, C. H.,

1897, *Johnson's Universal Cyclopædia, vol. v, p. 523.*

No educational institution in America has a more prophetic story than Antioch. Here Horace Mann came in the zenith of his power, and his great heart flamed through a period of six years in the interest of his ideals. Here for the first time in the history of the world was the bold venture undertaken of establishing an institution of higher learning where the discriminations of sect, sex and race were to be of no value. It was an ideal worthy of the greatest prophet of education the United States has ever known. It was an ideal worthy the democracy dreamed of in the Declaration of Independence, in the minds of the Adamses and Jefferson. Back of him was the tide of prophecy, the rising interest in science, the growing freedom of thought, surely a backing that would seem to be inadequate, but in front of him were the stumps and the malaria, the crudeness of bigotry that still survived under the most promising pretensions, and Horace Mann fell at his post.—JONES, JENKIN LLOYD, 1898, *Unity, June 23.*

He was a great constructive pedagogist, a wise educational statesman, an eloquent tribune of the common school. He called upon the people of all classes, as with the voice of a herald, to raise their estimate of public instruction, and to provide better facilities by which it could be furnished. He devised or adopted new educational agencies, and persuaded the people to use them. He organized public opinion, and influenced the action of legislatures. He gave men higher ideas of the work and character of the teacher at the same time that he taught the teacher to magnify his office. He heightened the popular estimate of the instruments that are conducive and necessary to the existence of good schools. He elevated men's ideas of the value of ethical training, and made valuable suggestions looking to its prosecution.—HINSDALE, B. A., 1898, *Horace Mann (The Great Educators), p. 273.*

Mr. Mann's reputation for scholarship and zeal gave his opinions greater weight than those of almost any other man in the country. As a result, the most radical educational ideas were received from him with respect; and he carried forward the work of giving a practical embodiment to co-education, non-sectarianism, and the requirements of practical and efficient moral character, as perhaps no other educator could have done. His influence among people and the aspirations which he kindled in thousands of minds by public addresses and personal contact, did for the people of the Ohio valley a work, the extent and value of which can never be measured.—HUBBELL, GEORGE ALLEN, 1900, *Horace Mann in Ohio, p.* 50.

Horace Mann is by general consent the greatest educator that this Western hemisphere has produced. He was not the greatest scholar, was not the greatest teacher, was not the best beloved by the teachers of his day, yet he is everywhere known as the first among American educational leaders.—WINSHIP, ALBERT E., 1900, *Great American Educators, p.* 15.

GENERAL

To know him as a thinker, we must read his speeches made in Congress, his articles in *The Common School Journal*, and his reports as secretary of the Massachusetts Board of Education. These show the cumulative nature of his thought. To convince men was his purpose, not merely to illustrate his ideas, and to this end he was not satisfied with crushing opposition with the weight of his arguments, he would also bury it with their bulk. . . . He was not a seer, but a sayer and a doer. He was not a first-rate man. He was an organizer. The men who organize are always second-rate. He originated nothing, and did not pretend to do so. His test of truth was portability. He liked phrenology on this account, because it was so practical and business-like. He left other men to seek new truth. For himself, he went to work to see if he could embody some of that which was already in the world.—CHADWICK, JOHN W., 1867, *Horace Mann, The Nation, vol.* 4, *p.* 210.

The writings of Mann are full of good sense and apt illustration, and are clear, and often elegant in style.—UNDERWOOD,

FRANCIS H., 1872, *A Hand-Book of English Literature, American Authors, p.* 172.

Horace Mann's reports as secretary of the Massachusetts Board of Education rank with legislative documents, yet they are really eloquent treatises, full of matter, but of matter burning with passion and blazing with imagery.—WHIPPLE, EDWIN PERCY, 1876–86, *American Literature and Other Papers, ed. Whittier, p.* 136.

A great educator like Horace Mann left behind him no standard treatise on pedagogy, but a vitalizing influence in American schools. Literature got little from him; the nation, much.—RICHARDSON, CHARLES F., 1887, *American Literature, 1607–1885, vol.* I, *p.* 517.

Horace Mann does not walk by the sole light of political or social experience; his pedagogy is inspired by higher principles. This man of action, so positive in his views and in his methods, has his philosophy; and it is no amateur philosophy, good to charm a leisure hour. He lives in it, feeds upon it, applies it in everything; it is his inspirer and his mistress. All his teaching, his whole scheme of education, is penetrated with it, and does but translate it. Horace Mann is not a professional philosopher, no more than he is a systematic pedagogue; but he is still less an empiric, led solely by a happy instinct, by present and variable necessity, by isolated observations; he has his fixed ideas, his general ideas of the order of nature and of destiny.—PÉCAUT, FÉLIX, 1888, *Revue Pédagogique, March.*

Mr. Mann wrote with power and eloquence, but there was a want of chasteness and finish in his style.—PIERCE, EDWARD L., 1893, *ed. Memoir and Letters of Charles Sumner, vol.* III, *p.* 57.

Every word that Horace Mann has written can be read to-day by every teacher with the greatest profit.—PARKER, FRANCIS W., 1896, *Horace Mann, Educational Review, vol.* 12, *p.* 74.

Delia Bacon

1811–1859

Author; sister of Dr. Leonard Bacon; born at Tallmadge, Ohio, Feb. 2, 1811; wrote, besides "Tales of the Puritans" and a drama entitled "The Bride of Fort Edward," "The Philosophy of Shakespeare's Plays" (1857), in which she first threw out the startling hypothesis that these plays were really written by Francis Bacon, who simply used Shakespeare as a shield against the prejudices of the time. In support of this hypothesis, which became an infatuation, she visited England, met much repression, and her troubles impaired her health. Died at Hartford, Conn., Sept. 2, 1859. *See* "Delia Bacon; A Biographical Sketch" by Theodore Bacon (1888); and "Recollections of a Gifted Woman," in Hawthorne's "Our Old Home."—BEERS, HENRY A., 1897, *rev. Johnson's Universal Cyclopædia, vol.* I, *p.* 439.

PERSONAL

I have lately made one or two drafts on your goodness,—which I hate to do, both because you meet them so generously, and because you never give me an opportunity of revenge,—and mainly in the case of Miss Bacon, who has a private history that entitles her to high respect, and who could be helped only by facilitating her Shakespeare studies, in which she has the faith and ardor of a discoverer. Bancroft was to have given her one to Sir H. Ellis. Everett, I believe, gave her one to Mr. Grote; and when I told her what I remembered hearing of Spedding, she was eager to see him; which access I knew not how to secure, except through you. She wrote me that she prospers in all things, and had just received at once a summons to meet Spedding at your house. But do not fancy I send any one to you heedlessly; for I value your time at its rate to nations, and refuse many more letters than I give. I shall not send you any more people without good reason.— EMERSON, RALPH WALDO, 1853, *To Carlyle, Aug.* 10; *Correspondence of Carlyle and Emerson, ed. Norton, vol.* II, *p.* 257.

As for Miss Bacon, we find her, with her modest, shy dignity, with her solid character and strange enterprise, a real acquisition and hope we shall now see more of her, now that she has come nearer to us to lodge. I have not in my life seen anything so tragically *quixotic* as her Shakespeare enterprise: alas, alas, there can be nothing but sorrow, toil, and utter disappointment in it for her! I do cheerfully what I can;— which is far more than she *asks* of me (for I have not seen a prouder silent soul);—but there is not the least possibility of truth in the notion she has taken up: and the hope of ever proving it, or finding the least document that countenances it, is equal to that of vanquishing the windmills by stroke of lance. I am often truly sorry about the poor lady: but she troubles nobody with her difficulties, with her theories; she must try the matter to the end, and charitable souls must further her so far.—CARLYLE, THOMAS, 1853, *To Emerson, Sept.* 9; *Correspondence of Carlyle and Emerson, ed. Norton, vol.* II, *p.* 261.

She was rather uncommonly tall, and had a striking and expressive face, dark hair, dark eyes, which shone with an inward light as soon as she began to speak, and by-and-by a color came into her cheeks and made her look almost young. Not that she really was so; she must have been beyond middle age: and there was no unkindness in coming to that conclusion, because, making allowance for years and ill health, I could suppose her to have been handsome and exceedingly attractive once. —HAWTHORNE, NATHANIEL, 1863, *Recollections of a Gifted Woman, Our Old Home, p.* 123.

The first lady whom I ever heard deliver a public lecture was Miss Delia Bacon, who opened her career in Boston, as teacher of history, by giving a preliminary discourse, describing her method, and urging upon her hearers the importance of the study. I had called on her that day for the first time, and found her very nervous and anxious about her first appearance in public. She interested me at once, and I resolved to hear her speak. Her person was tall and commanding, her finely shaped head was well set on her shoulders, her face was handsome and full of expression, and she moved with grace and dignity. The hall in which she spoke was so crowded that I could not get a seat, but she spoke so well that I felt no fatigue from standing. She was at first a little embarrassed, but soon became so engaged in recommending the study of history to all present, that she ceased to think of herself, and then she became eloquent. — FARRAR, ELIZA WARE, 1866, *Recollections of Seventy Years, p.* 319.

This is the story of a life that was neither splendid in achievement or adventure, nor successful, nor happy. It began deep in a New World wilderness, in the simplicity of a refined and honored poverty; it continued for almost fifty years of labor and sorrow, and ended amid clouds of disappointment and distraction. Neither the subject of it, nor those to whom in her lifetime she was very dear by ties of kindred, would easily have consented that the world should know more of her than could be learned from her gravestone: that she was born and died. Yet because she was of rare intellectual force and acuteness, of absolute sincerity and truthfulness, of self-annihilating earnestness and devotion in whatever work she entered upon; and because the world is determined that it will speak of her as if it knew her, supplying its lack of knowledge with conjecture or with fable, I purpose to tell it something of Delia Bacon: of what she was, from inheritance and environment; and what she did.—BACON, THEODORE, 1888, *Delia Bacon, A Biographical Sketch*, p. iii.

The personal charm and refined enthusiasm of Miss Bacon fairly magnetized Hawthorne; it did not appear to him incredible that the vicar at Stratford-on-Avon, and the sexton, had given her—apparently if not really—opportunity to open the grave of Shakespeare, in the night, in search of documents which were to disprove his authorship of the plays. The potency of the imprecation on that grave was shown in the faltering of her own heart.—CONWAY, MONCURE D., 1890, *Life of Nathaniel Hawthorne (Great Writers)*, p. 157.

When this singular woman had exhausted all her financial means, when her family and friends declined to assist her unless she would give up her chimerical pursuit and return to America, she—almost despairingly — appealed to Hawthorne; and he responded in a manner that displayed his nobleness of heart, by the way in which he aided the forlorn enthusiast in her direst need. It gives one a higher estimate of human nature to hear of such unselfishness, such unwearied patience, and such rare delicacy as were exhibited by Hawthorne in extending the moral and material aid which she was too proud to solicit.— BRIDGE, HORATIO, 1893, *Personal Recollections of Nathaniel Hawthorne*.

GENERAL

I have often thought we had effects without cause in those works, if they were written by an uncultivated mind, or rather by a mind not cultivated and educated to the *last* possibility, and I have said "It is a miracle." Yet I could believe in a miracle. To add all these, however, to what Lord Bacon has avowedly done, is to make him such a prodigy as the world never before saw. But this I have room enough for also. What I want now is more and more and more of your detections, your proofs, your criticism. I have an insatiable hunger, and I shall be glad when these and all are in print, for just as sure as there comes a point of trembling interest, you begin to interline and I am driven wild. But this last manuscript is much plainer than the others. Mr. Hawthorne has gone to Routledge this morning to speak about them. I hope that he will have the wit to publish them, for, irrespective of their ulterior purpose, they are wonderful, magnificent.—HAWTHORNE, SOPHIA, 1856, *Letter to Miss Bacon; Delia Bacon by Theodore Bacon*, p. 226.

On this object, which she conceives so loftily, the author has bestowed the solitary and self-sustained toil for many years. The volume now before the reader, together with the historical demonstration which it pre-supposes, is the product of a most faithful and conscientious labour, and a truly heroic devotion of intellect and heart. No man or woman has ever thought or written more sincerely than the author of this book. She has given nothing less than her life to the work. . . . And now, at length, after many delays and discouragements, the work comes forth. It had been the author's original purpose to publish it in America; for she wished her own country to have the glory of solving the enigma of those mighty dramas, and thus adding a new and higher value to the loftiest productions of the English mind. It seemed to her most fit and desirable, that America —having received so much from England, and returned so little—should do what remained to be done towards rendering this great legacy available, as its authors meant it to be, to all future time. This purpose was frustrated; and it will be seen in what spirit she acquiesces. . . . I am not the editor of this work; nor can I consider myself fairly entitled to the honor (which, if I deserved it, I should feel to be a very high as well as a perilous one) of seeing my name associated with the author's on the title-page. My object has been merely to speak a few words, which might, perhaps, serve the purpose of placing my countrywoman upon a ground of amicable understanding with the public. She has a vast preliminary difficulty to encounter. The first feeling of every reader must be one of absolute repugnance towards the person who seeks to tear out of the Anglo-Saxon heart the name which for ages it has held dearest, and to substitute another name, or names, to which the settled belief of the world has long assigned a very different position.

What I claim for this work is, that the ability employed in its composition has been worthy of its great subject, and well employed for our intellectual interests, whatever judgment the public may pass upon the questions discussed.—HAWTHORNE, NATHANIEL, 1857, *The Philosophy of the Plays of Shakspere Unfolded by Delia Bacon, Preface, pp.* xii, xiii, xiv.

The subtlest critic of the last thirty years in America is Delia Bacon, who—devoting her life to the establishment of the thesis that Lord Bacon and Sir Walter Raleigh were the joint authors of the plays attributed to Shakespeare—has, amid the mass of confused infatuations, occasionally thrown a finer light on passages of those plays than any English writer since Coleridge. No one, as Nathaniel Hawthorne asserts, has cast a more beautiful wreath on the tomb of the world's "playwright" than the half insane woman of genius who almost denied his existence.—NICHOL, JOHN, 1882–85, *American Literature, p.* 451.

A biography of Delia Bacon can only be justified by a belief in the truth of the theory with which her life is identified.

Anything less than this is to stir the dust of the lunatic dead for commercial purposes; it is to exhibit her, straight-jacket and all, to an unsympathetic public, for a pecuniary consideration. If Delia Bacon was not insane when she framed and uttered that theory, if she was right in her views,—as right as Aristarchus of Samos was in his day,—then she deserves a hundred biographies to be written by tender and loving friends, with reverent eyes and enthusiastic admiration. If she was right, then was she, indeed, the profoundest thinker of her age, with a sweep of thought and depth of penetration a thousand miles beyond the shallow great ones of her generation. If she was right, she deserves to be honored as a martyr to the truth, who stood nobly up in the arena of the world until torn to pieces by the wild beasts of public opinion. There are many now who regard her as the greatest American yet born; they hope to see her biography yet written by some one who loves, honors, and believes in her.—DONNELLY, IGNATIUS, 1889, *Delia Bacon's Unhappy Story, North American Review, vol.* 148, *p.* 308.

Theodore Parker

1810–1860

Born, at Lexington, Mass., Aug. 24, 1810: died at Florence, Italy, May 10, 1860. A noted American clergyman, lecturer, reformer, and author. He studied at the Cambridge Divinity School 1834–36; became a Unitarian clergyman at Roxbury, Massachusetts, in 1837; became the head of an independent rationalistic society at the Melodeon (1846), and later at Music Hall, Boston; and was a conspicuous advocate of the abolition of slavery. Among his works are "Discourse on Matters Pertaining to Religion" (1842), "Sermons on Theism, Atheism, and the Popular Theology" (1853), "Ten Sermons of Religion" (1853), besides a large number of addresses, etc., and "Great Americans" (this was published after his death). His complete works were edited by F. P. Cobbe (12 vols. 1863–65).—SMITH, BENJAMIN E., ed., 1894–97, *The Century Cyclopedia of Names, p.* 782.

PERSONAL

No doubt my life is to be outwardly a life of gloom, and separation from old associates (I will not say friends). I know men will view me with suspicion, and ministers with hatred: That is not my concern. Inwardly, my life is and must be one of profound peace, of satisfaction and comfort that all words of mine are powerless to present. There is no mortal trouble that disturbs me more than a moment; no disappointment that makes me gloomy or sad or distrustful. All outward evils fall off me as snow from my cloak. I never thought of being so happy in this life as I have been these two years. The destructive part of the work I feel called on to do is painful, but is slight compared with the main work of building up. Don't think I am flattered, as some say, by seeing many come to listen. Nothing makes a real man so humble as to stand and speak to many men. The thought that I am doing what I know to be my duty is rich reward to me: I know of none so great. Besides that, however, I have the satisfaction of knowing that I have awakened the spirit of religion, of faith in God, in some twenty or twenty-five men, who, before that, had no faith, no hope, no religion. This alone, and the expression of their gratitude (made by word of mouth, or made by letters or by a friend), would compensate me for all that all the ministers in the world could say against me or do against me.—PARKER, THEODORE, 1843, *Letter to Rev. Chandler Robbins, Jan. 27; Theodore Parker by Frothingham, p. 171.*

Parker is a most hardy, compact, clever little fellow, full of decisive utterance, with humor and good humor; whom I like much. —CARLYLE, THOMAS, 1843, *To Emerson, Oct. 31; The Correspondence of Carlyle and Emerson, ed. Norton, vol. II, p. 44.*

Now P.'s creed than this may be lighter or darker,
But in one thing, 'tis clear, he has faith, namely
  —Parker;
And this is what makes him the crowd-drawing preacher,
There's a background of god to each hard-working feature;
Every word that he speaks has been fierily furnaced
In the blast of a life that has struggled in earnest:
There he stands, looking more like a plough-man than priest,
If not dreadfully awkward, not graceful at least,
His gestures all downright and same if you will,
As of brown-fisted Hobnail in hoeing a drill,
But his periods fall on you, stroke after stroke,
Like the blows of a lumberer felling an oak;
You forget the man wholly, you're thankful to meet
With a preacher who smacks of the field and the street,
And to hear, you're not over-particular whence,
Almost Taylor's profusion, quite Latimer's sense.
—LOWELL, JAMES RUSSELL, 1848, *A Fable for Critics.*

Saw Mr. Parker for the first time. He was lying in bed with his back to the light. Mrs. Parker brought me into the room. He took my hand tenderly and said in a low, hurried voice, holding it: "After all our wishes to meet, Miss Cobbe, how strange it is we should meet *thus.*" I pressed his hand, and he turned his eyes, which were trembling painfully and evidently seeing nothing, towards me and said, "You must not think you have seen *me.* This is not *me,* only the wreck of the man I was." Then, after a pause, he added: "Those who love me most can only wish me a quick passage to the other world. Of course I am not *afraid* to die (he smiled as he spoke) but there was so much to be done!"— COBBE, FRANCES POWER, 1860, *Journal, Apr. 28th; Life of Frances Power Cobbe by Herself, vol. II, p. 338.*

But it was in popularizing thought and knowledge that his great and wonderful power lay. Not an original thinker, in the same sense with Emerson, he yet translated for thousands that which Emerson spoke to hundreds only. . . . Thinkers might find no new thought in the new discourse, leaders of action no new plan, yet, after all that had been said and done, his was the statement that told upon the community. He knew this power of his, and had analysed some of the methods by which he attained it, though, after all, the best part was an unconscious and magnetic faculty. . . . Without grace or beauty or melody, his mere elocution was sufficient to produce effects which melody and grace and beauty might have sighed for in vain. . . . Surcharged with European learning, he yet remained at heart the Lexington farmer's-boy, and his whole atmosphere was indigenous, not exotic. Not haunted by any of the distrust and criticism which are apt to effeminate the American scholar, he plunged deep into the current of hearty national life around him, loved it, trusted it, believed in it; and the combining of his life with such tremendous criticism of public and private sins formed an irresistible power. He could condemn without crushing,—denounce mankind, yet save it from despair. . . . His conversational power was so wonderful that no one could go away from a first interview without astonishment and delight. . . . He lived his life much as he walked the streets of Boston,— not quite gracefully, nor yet stately, but with quick, strong, solid step, with sagacious eyes wide open, and thrusting his broad shoulders a little forward, as if butting away the throng of evil deeds around him, and scattering whole atmospheres of unwholesome cloud. Wherever he went, there went a glance of sleepless vigilance, an unforgetting memory, a tongue that never faltered, and an arm that never quailed. — HIGGINSON, THOMAS WENT-WORTH, 1860, *Theodore Parker, Atlantic Monthly, vol. 6, pp. 453, 454, 457.*

When some Americans die—when most Americans die—their friends tire the public with excuses. They confess this spot, they explain that stain, they plead circumstances as the half justification of that mistake, and they beg of us to rememer that nothing but good is to be spoken of the dead. We need no such mantle for the green grave under the sky of Florence,—no excuses, no explanations, no spot. Priestly malice has scanned every inch of his garment,—it was seamless; it could find no stain. History, as in the case of every other of her beloved children, gathers into her bosom the arrows which malice had shot at him, and says to posterity, "Behold the title-deeds of your gratitude!" We ask no moment to excuse, there is nothing to explain. What the snarling journal thought bold, what the selfish politician feared as his ruin,—it was God's seal set upon his apostleship. The little libel glanced across him like a rocket when it goes over the vault; it is passed, and the royal sun shines out as beneficent as ever.—PHILLIPS, WENDELL, 1860, *Address before the New England Anti-Slavery Convention, May* 31; *Speeches, Lectures and Letters, Second Series, p.* 424.

Mr. Parker, though strong in his convictions, was no dogmatist, and assumed no robes of infallibility. No man was more docile in regard to being taught, even by the lowliest. Mr. Phillips has done him no more than justice, when he said that he was willing and eager to obtain instruction from any quarter. Hence he was always inquiring of those with whom he came in contact, so that he might learn, if possible, something from them that might aid him in the great work in which he was engaged. When the question of "Woman's Rights" first came up for discussion, like multitudes of others, Mr. Parker was inclined to treat it facetiously, and supposed it could be put aside with a smile. Still it was his disposition to hear and to learn; and as soon as he began to investigate, and to see the grandeur and world-wide importance of the "Woman's Rights" movement, he gave to it his hearty support before the country and the world.—GARRISON, WILLIAM LLOYD, 1860, *Address before the New England Anti-Slavery Society, May.*

He never kept back the truth for fear to make an enemy. But, on the other hand, it was complained that he was bitter and harsh; that his zeal burned with too hot a flame. It is so difficult, in evil times, to escape this charge!—for the faithful preacher most of all. It was his merit— like Luther, Knox, Latimer, and John the Baptist, to speak tart truth when that was peremptory, and when there were few to say it. But his sympathy with goodness was not less energetic. One fault he had:

he overestimated his friends, I may well say it, and sometimes vexed them with the importunity of his good opinion, whilst they knew better the ebb which follows exaggerated praise. He was capable, it must be said, of the most unmeasured eulogies on those he esteemed, especially if he had any jealousy that they might not stand with the Boston public as high as they ought. His commanding merit as reformer is this, that he insisted, beyond all men in pulpits,—I cannot think of one rival,—that the essence of Christianity is its practical morals.—EMERSON, RALPH WALDO, 1860; *Address at the Commemoration Service, Boston, June.*

Theodore Parker possessed a power of acquisition, which few men, out of Germany, have had. He knew the contents of all the books in his library. He could take the substance out of a book in an incredibly short time. On that fatal winter which broke down his constitution and determined his fate (the winter which killed him), he was in the habit of filling a carpet-bag, not with novels, but with works of tough philosophy and theology, in Greek, Latin, German, in old black-letter print, and yellow parchment covers; and would study them, Monday, while riding in the cars, to lecture on Monday night; study them, Tuesday, while riding to lecture at another place on Tuesday night; and so on, studying all day and lecturing every night, till Friday. On Friday he would come home, write his Sunday's sermon on Saturday forenoon, visit the sick and suffering of his society on Saturday afternoon, preach Sunday morning to two or three thousand people, rest a little on Sunday afternoon, receive his friends on Sunday evening, and away again on Monday.—CLARKE, JAMES FREEMAN, 1860, *Memorials and Biographical Sketches, p.* 119.

When Mr. Parker went to Boston, he fitted up the fourth story of his house for a study, by lining the walls with shelves of the simplest description, without mouldings or ornaments, so as to save every inch of space for books. These shelves gradually crept over the door, the windows, and the chimney-pieces, thence into little adjoining rooms, and finally stepped boldly down the stairs, one flight at a time, for three flights, colonizing every room by the way, including the large parlor in the second story, and finally paused only at the dining-room close to the front door. The bathing-room, the closets, the attic apartments, were inundated with books. Unbound magazines and pamphlets lay in chests of drawers above-stairs; miscellaneous matter was sorted in properly labelled boxes; cupboards and recesses were stuffed full. He had evoked this inundating demon, but did not know the laying spell. In the centre of the study floor rose two or three edifices of shelves to receive the surplus which could find no other bestowment. No house was ever so adorned from basement to attic. To his eye, who knew so well the contents of each volume of the twelve thousand, the walls were frescoed with the ages of human thought, and the solemn tragedies of all the great souls, who counted life a little thing to exchange for the liberties of truth.—WEISS, JOHN, 1863, *Life and Correspondence of Theodore Parker, vol.* II, *p.* i.

This man was an organised conscience. The degree to which he quickened the perceptions of the American people to detect the subtlest distinctions between right and wrong cannot be told to those who did not live under his immediate influence. When the post-mortem examination of slavery takes place, the arrow of Theodore Parker will be found deepest in its heart. . . . He was not a man who had only fine words for humanity. When he was poor he divided with those who were poorer, and his charities grew with his means. He considered the poor as well as gave to them. He not only pleaded the cause of the hunted fugitive slaves, but protected them in his house, and fed them at his table. The negro of the far South knew his name, and on arriving in Boston after a perilous flight, came by night to his door. Two of these—man and maid betrothed—were concealed for some days in his study, while Parker sat outside the door with a pistol by his side, writing his next Sunday's discourse. Then he married the two, and giving the man a Bible and a dagger, exhorting him to die rather than let himself or his wife return to slavery, he with some others got them off to an English ship bound for London, where the two now reside.—CONWAY, MONCURE DANIEL, 1867, *Theodore Parker, Fortnightly Review, vol.* 8, *pp.* 143, 149.

At the foot of a cypress-tree, not far from the column of Frederick William, is the simple grave of Theodore Parker. A tangled flower bed inclosed within a stone border, a plain head and foot stone, and the simple inscription:

> **Theodore Parker,**
> **Born at Lexington, Mass.,**
> **United States of America,**
> **Aug. 24, 1810,**
> **Died at Florence May 10,**
> **1860.**

—SPENCER, O. M., 1873, *The Protestant Cemetery at Florence, Harper's Magazine, vol.* 47, *p.* 511.

While in Florence in the spring of 1883 I visited the old Protestant cemetery, where, under the cypresses and willows, lie the remains of celebrated English writers like Elizabeth Barrett Browning, Frances Trollope, Walter Savage Landor, and Arthur Hugh Clough, and of not a few almost equally famous Americans, including Theodore Parker, Richard Hildreth, and Lorimer Graham. These exiled graves were generally marked by memorials worthy of the literature their occupants enriched and of the land in which they died, with the then exception of those of Parker and Hildreth, whose rude tombstones certainly did scant credit either to American taste or national gratitude. I then and there resolved to do what I could to change this state of things at least in so far as concerned the grave of the great Boston divine. So shortly afterward I began collecting subscriptions among European friends and admirers of Parker, informing them that the money was to be used in beautifying his last resting-place. The responses were prompt, and the desire to do him honor spread from Europe to America. Among the many European subscribers were Frances Power Cobbe, Miss Jane Cobden, daughter of the great free trader; the late Paul Bert, the French scientist and statesman; M. Renan; the late M. Godin, creator of the Guise Social Palace; Mme. Jules Favre, widow of the celebrated French statesman and to-day Director of the State Superior Normal School for women at Sèvres; Björnstjerne Björnson, the Norwegian author and republican leader; M. Frederik Bajer, of the Danish Parliament; M. H. E. Bener, of the Norwegian Parliament; the Rev. James Martineau, D. D.; Prof. Albert Revillé, of the College of France; Prof. F. W. Newman, brother of the Cardinal; the late Richard A. Proctor, the astronomer, etc. The list of American subscribers contains many well-known names, but I have mislaid it and so hesitate to draw up from memory an incomplete one.—STANTON, THEODORE, 1891, *Theodore Parker's Grave, Open Court, vol. 5, p.* 3063.

Those who knew Parker only in the pulpit did not half know him. Apart from the field of theological controversy, he was one of the most sympathetic and delightful of men. I have rarely met any one whose conversation had such a ready and varied charm. His idea of culture was encyclopædic, and his reading, as might have been inferred from the size of his library, was enormous. The purchase of books was his single extravagance. One whole floor was given up to them, and in spite of this they overflowed into hall and drawing-room. He was very generous in lending them, and I often profited by his kindness in this respect. . . . I cannot remember that the interest of his sermons ever varied for me. It was all one intense delight. The luminous clearness of his mind, his admirable talent for popularizing the procedures and conclusions of philosophy, his keen wit and poetic sense of beauty,—all these combined to make him appear to me one of the oracles of God. Add to these his fearlessness and his power of denunciation, exercised in the community a great part of which seemed bound in a moral sleep. His voice was like the archangel's trump, summoning the wicked to repentance and bidding the just take heart. It was hard to go out from his presence, all aglow with the enthusiasm which he felt and inspired, and to hear him spoken of as a teacher of irreligion, a pest to the community.—HOWE, JULIA WARD, 1899, *Reminiscences*, 1819–1899, *pp.* 161, 167.

He was not a master of metaphysical refinements. . . . The fullness of Parker's mind and the vigor of his mental operations are, however, less admirable than his moral character, as displayed in all the personal relations of his life, in his unflagging industry, in the exigent interpretation that he gave to his ministerial office, in his courageous dealing with political iniquity, and especially in his devotion of himself with all his gifts and acquisitions to the furtherance of religious truth and social righteousness. His life was one of perfect consecration to the welfare of his fellow men.—CHADWICK, JOHN WHITE, 1900, *Theodore Parker, Preacher and Reformer, p.* 402.

GENERAL

The work, "A Discourse of Matters Pertaining to Religion," concludes with a "Discourse of the Church"; in which Ecclesiastical History is made to yield a series of social pictures, representing the actual agency of Christianity in its successive developments. The drawing has a breadth of boldness, and the colouring a warmth, that might tempt a careless critic to suspect more genius in the design than knowledge in the execution; but traces are not wanting, which show that we are running over the summary results of large reading, reproduced from a philosophical mind.—MARTINEAU, JOHN, 1857, *Strauss and Parker, The Westminster and Foreign Quarterly Review, vol.* 47, *p.* 173.

I heard that he was "poison." Then I like poison very well.—DICKINSON, EMILY, 1859, *Letters, ed. Todd, vol.* I, *p.* 194.

His early writings are much more rich and full than his later ones. His "Discourse on Religion"—his first printed book —remains his best one.—CLARKE, JAMES FREEMAN, 1860, *Memorials and Biographical Sketches, p.* 126.

He was a great and good man: the greatest and best, perhaps, which America has produced. He was great in many ways. In time to come his country will glory in his name, and the world will acknowledge all his gifts and powers. His true greatness, however, will in future ages rest on this: that God revealed Himself to his faithful soul in His most adorable aspect—that he preached with undying faith, and lived out in his consecrated life the lesson he had thus been taught—that he was worthy to be the *Prophet* of the greatest of all truths, the ABSOLUTE GOODNESS OF GOD; the centre truth of the universe.—COBBE, FRANCES POWER, 1863–71, *ed. Works of Theodore Parker, Introduction.*

He was far less a philosopher than he was a man of affairs, and far less a theologian than he was a practical reformer of society. The huge masses of his knowledge and experience were never organized in a system, or made to revolve in beautiful order about some central thought. The treasures amassed by his acquisitive power, and stored in the several departments of his mind, lay in separate heaps. He was a sturdy Puritan of New England, laden with the erudition of a German professor; but the Puritan could not absorb the professor, nor could the professor absorb the Puritan; nor could the Puritan and the professor combine in a single human consciousness. The Yankee and the transcendentalist could not quite coalesce. The realist by nature and the idealist by culture could not cordially embrace. The elements of opposite systems seemed to be side by side in his mind, and now one and now another of them had a preponderance. Here you would say decidedly that he was a Pantheist, immersing the whole universe of God; there you would say with equal confidence that he was a Theist separating the Maker in essence from his world. There are passages in which he speaks of the controlling influence of law, linking all events in a chain of destiny so closely woven that no room is left for an independent thought or a volition along the whole line of human development; and there are passages that speak of Providence, and the Divine care of the smallest things, with the tender unction of an old-fashioned Christian.—FROTHINGHAM, OCTAVIUS BROOKS, 1864, *Theodore Parker, North American Review, vol. 98, p.* 322.

Mr. Parker was not a man of genius, nor yet of an original mind. The doctrines with which he connected his name were not of his devising. They had come down from former generations of freethinkers. It was the freshness of illustration and the zeal and energy which he brought to their enforcement, together with the strong personal influence that went out from his —what we call in this country "magnetism"—that accounts for the stir he made among the dry bones, and the hold he had and still retains upon living souls.— QUINCY, EDMUND, 1871, *Parker's Historic Americans, The Nation, vol. 12, p.* 76.

His writings are generally strong and rugged in style. He addresses the reason, and makes few appeals to the feelings. But his love of nature was intense, and nearly every discourse has some tribute to the beauty of the seasons, and some illustration of spiritual truth drawn from the visible world. He excelled also in pathetic description, and gave to the ideas of home, parents, children, age, and death, a tender and impressive charm. His chief deficiency as a writer was in taste, the want of which often mars his general literary excellence.— UNDERWOOD, F. H., 1872, *A Handbook of English Literature, American Authors, p.* 339.

Mr. Parker's works have been republished and widely read in England, and have been lately translated into other languages for circulation in other European countries. No one can doubt the immense influence which he has exerted by his vigorous thought, his vast learning, his pithy and telling style, and his intense and unabated zeal, upon the mind of the age; while, however men may dissent from many of his theological views, it will be remembered to his eternal honor, that a Puritan of Puritans in his faith in God and in his strictness of moral character, he was the stalwart and ever faithful friend of wronged and oppressed humanity; rained down blows, thick and fast, upon every giant sin or evil of his day; and, at the time when most Christian pulpits were deaf and dumb to the demands of the hour, "preached righteousness in the great congregation."— PUTNAM, ALFRED P., 1874, *Singers and Songs of the Liberal Faith, p.* 296.

A born controversialist, who had the challenging chip always on his shoulder, which he invited both his Unitarian and his Orthodox brethren to knock off. There never was a man who more gloried in a fight. . . . He was the Luther of radical Unitarianism. When the Unitarian societies refused fellowship with his society, he organized a church of his own, and made it one of the most powerful in New England. There was nothing but disease which could check, and nothing but death which could close his controversial activity. . . . He was among the leaders in the attempt to apply the rigid maxims of Christianity to practical life; and many Orthodox clergymen, who combined with him in his assaults on intemperance, slavery, and other hideous evils of our civilization, almost condoned his theological heresies in the admiration of his fearlessness in practical reforms. He was an enormous reader and diligent student, as well as a resolute man of affairs. He also had great depth and fervency of piety. — WHIPPLE, EDWIN PERCY, 1876–86, *American Literature and Other Papers, ed. Whittier, pp.* 68, 69.

Parker's writings will not stand criticism so well as Channing's. If he is sometimes more impassioned, he is often florid, diffuse, and even noisy in his trumpets of revolt. He does not, like Emerson, take up a calm vantage ground of philosophical survey or scorn, "he roars beneath the walls of the

Jericho of orthodoxy, and expects them to fall."—NICHOL, JOHN, 1882–85, *American Literature, p.* 135.

Early years of excessive bodily and mental toil, of actual privation for one of his mental and physical calibre, of exhausting thought and study, a middle life spent in a desperate struggle for the strength to do his earnest work, and the most intense devotion to the cause of freedom of thought in every path of life, made the days of this great, earnest thinker and worker comparatively short, yet into his fifty years were crowded enthusiasm, the immense acquisition of knowledge, the ripened study of the four-score years of the Psalmist. It was an ideal life in its force and intensity— the spirit of the enthusiast and the exact knowledge of the scholar united in it a singular degree with the devotion to humanity which was so overpowering that the superficial and hasty multitude too often called him iconoclast, atheist, and many more opprobrious epithets because they thought in his love for mankind he forgot the Maker of all. . . . Thousands of minds feel Theodore Parker's influence, hundreds of writers and thinkers bear witness to his power; our library shelves teem with works upon his writings and his life, his name is one long to be remembered in our land.—OLIVER, GRACE A., 1883, *Story of Theodore Parker by Frances P. Cobbe, Introduction, pp* xlvii, xlviii

We may regard Parker as the clearest and most logical interpreter of Transcendental principles. "A Transcendental religion needs," he said, "a Transcendental theology." His posthumous essay, "Transcendentalism," and also his first work, "A Discourse on Matters Pertaining to Religion," admirably sum up the doctrines which inspired his whole life, and which he believed destined to become the religion of enlightened minds during the next thousand years. There must not be sought in them a rigorous analysis of the psychological phenomena which serve as the basis of philosophy of intuition. Parker has adopted as a starting-point the methods of the followers of Kant. Henceforth, therefore, he declines to discuss its underlying principles, and contents himself with the application of it, to the search for and the development of religious truth. To be sure, he rejects neither the control nor the support of external observation; but it is above all to internal phenomena that he turns in order to obtain decisive evidence for the existence of God and the doctrine of immortality.— ALVIELLA, COUNT GOBLET, 1885, *Contemporary Evolution of Religious Thought in England, America and India, tr. Moden, p.* 176.

It is much to be regretted that Parker is not better known here in England. Many of those who are familiar with his name look upon him mainly as an advanced religious thinker, who was more at home in opposing the claims of orthodoxy than in teaching spiritual religion. But as a matter of fact he spoke at times with the voice of an inspired poet, whose words glowed with holy fire.—MODEN, J., 1885, *tr., The Contemporary Evolution of Religious Thought in England, America and India by Count Goblet d'Alviella, p.* 178, *note.*

There is no more noticeable name, either for ability or for independence, among the American Unitarians than that of Theodore Parker.—DUFFIELD, SAMUEL WILLOUGHBY, 1886, *English Hymns, p.* 435.

The progress of liberal thought in Boston was greatly aided by him, and Boston's political conservatism was correspondingly weakened. To sum up his work, it may be said that it was a work of intensely aggressive theism, moving partly on Christian lines, towards religious and civil changes. His theism, in its character and force, is best illustrated in his volume of printed prayers—the only noteworthy contribution ever made in America to this once prominent department of literature. Parker was the last of the preachers whose words and works have had any general effect on American thought, in so far as that thought has concerned itself with movements associated with individual names. Parker was at times superficial, sensational, noisy, and indiscreet; but for mere discretion and prudence he had small liking, while his uproarious method of attack he deemed necessary, in his endeavour to overthrow ancient evils. His superfiacility was due to his boundless energy, which prematurely wore out his life, and to his desire to absorb all knowledge. But, after all, he was a characteristic American figure; and his position in the religion and politics of discreetly liberal Boston, before the war, is half pathetic, half comic.—RICHARDSON, CHARLES F., 1887, *American Literature, 1607–1885, vol.* I, *p.* 311.

I shall be happy to have my name figure in an act of homage paid to Theodore Parker. He is, among contemporary thinkers, the one who has treated religious truth in the most elevated manner.— RENAN, N., 1887, *Letter to Theodore Stanton, Theodore Parker's Grave, Open Court, vol. 5, p.* 3063.

Parker was much more an orator than a writer; and his published writings, with few exceptions, reflect two lights that flare upon the public stage. They are diffuse in matter, and loosely articulated in their form, in spite of the mechanical arrangement of their parts. What gives to them their greatest charm is a certain vivid homeliness of phrase, shaping itself upon the facts of nature and of our human life. Luther nor Latimer excelled him here. He wrote some beautiful hymns and other poems; but the best of his poetry will not be found in these, but in passages of his sermons, that go very near the tenderest joys and simplest tragedies of our experience. Not only was he so human that nothing human was foreign to him, but his sympathy was as keen as Wordsworth's with all natural things, and something of nature's wide inclusiveness and generous toleration was characteristic of his sympathy with universal life. It is suggestive of the homeliness of his affections that ninety-one of his words out of every hundred were Saxon, to eighty-five of Webster's and seventy-four of Sumner's; though in the range of his reading and scholarship he was incomparably inferior to either of these men. In praising another for "words so deep that a child could understand them," he was unconsciously giving a most apt description of his own.—CHADWICK, JOHN WHITE, 1897, *Library of the World's Best Literature, ed. Warner, vol.* XIX, *p.* 11076.

In real friendliness—of intention or of speech, he could give points to kings and outdo them. As for his intellectual resources, they were prodigious and imposing; but they had serious flaws. In what touched humanitarian questions, he reasoned—with his heart; his tenderness over and over, upset his logic, his tears put a mist into his pleas even at the Court of Heaven. Again, his sharp, keen memory for particular facts made him neglectful of accepted and accredited records; he had exaggerated trust in himself, in his instincts, his memory, his purposes. He looked down on most men; he had his slaps for Paul the Apostle—as for an over-confident boy; he looked up to none—save God.—MITCHELL, DONALD G., 1899, *American Lands and Letters, Leather-Stocking to Poe's "Raven," p.* 172.

There have been few men in New England whose learning has equalled his in range and in vitality. The manner in which his ardent nature impelled him to express himself, however, was so far from what is generally characteristic of scholars that in popular memory his scholarship has almost been forgotten. As a Unitarian minister, Parker is remembered mostly for having carried individual preaching to its most unflinching conclusions. So far as one can judge, this preaching was actuated by unswerving devotion to what he believed true. The range of his scholarship had made him familiar with thousands of facts which seemed inconsistent with many forms of Christian tradition. These he unhesitatingly preached with a fervid eloquence which even in his own days, when New England oratory was at its height, commanded unusual attention. His teaching consequently carried Unitarianism so far from orthodox Christianity, in days when the Higher Criticism was still to come, that he did more than any other man to frighten less daring spirits into the Episcopal communion, which now maintains alliance with the ancestral church of England.—WENDELL, BARRETT, 1900, *A Literary History of America, p.* 347.

Anna Jameson
1794–1860

Born [Anna Brownell Murphy], in Dublin, 17 May 1794. Family removed to England, 1798. Governess in Marquis of Winchester's family, 1810–14. Travelled with a pupil in France and Italy, summer of 1821 to 1822. Governess in family of Mr. Littleton, 1822–25. Married to Robert Jameson, 1825. Obtained legal appointment in Canada for her husband, 1833. To Germany same year; friendship with Major Noel, Ottilie von Goethe, Tieck, Schlegel, etc. Joined her husband in Canada, 1836; returned without him, 1838. Friendship with Lady Byron. Active literary life. Visit to Germany, 1845.

To Italy, with her neice (afterwards Mrs. Macpherson), 1847. Crown Pension, 1851. Quarrel with Lady Byron, about 1853. Died, at Ealing, 17 March 1860. *Works:* "A Lady's Diary" (anon.), 1826 (another edn., anon., called "The Diary of an Ennuyée, same year); "The Loves of the Poets" (anon.), 1829; "Memoirs of Celebrated Female Sovereigns" (2 vols.), 1831; "Characteristics of Women" (2 vols.), 1832; Letterpress to "Beauties of the Court of King Charles II." (illustrated by her father), 1833; Letterpress to "Fantasien," 1834; "Visits and Sketches" (4 vols.), 1834; "The Romance of Biography," 1837; "Sketches of Germany," 1837; "Winter Studies and Summer Rambles in Canada," 1838; "Handbook to the Public Galleries of Art in and near London," 1842; "Companion to the most celebrated Private Galleries in London," 1844; "Memoirs of the Early Italian Painters" (2 vols.), 1845; "Memoirs and Essays," 1846; Letterpress to "The Decorations of the Garden Pavilion, etc.," 1846; "Sacred and Legendary Art" (2 vols.), 1848; "Legends of the Monastic Orders," 1850; "Legends of the Madonna," 1852; "Handbook to the Court of Modern Sculpture in the Crystal Palace," 1854; "A Commonplace Book," 1854; "Sisters of Charity," 1855; "The Communion of Labour," 1856. *Posthumous:* "The History of Our Lord," completed by Lady Eastlake (2 vols.), 1864. She *translated:* Princess Amelia of Saxony's "Social Life in Germany," 1840; G. F. Waagen's "Peter Paul Rubens," 1840. *Life:* by Mrs. Macpherson, 1878.—SHARP, R. FARQUHARSON, 1897, *A Dictionary of English Authors, p.* 127.

PERSONAL

I called on Mrs. Jameson, author of "King Charles's Beauties." She is very clever, middle-aged, red-haired, and agreeable, though I suspect you would call her a conceited minx.—WILSON, JOHN, 1832, *Letter to His Wife, Christopher North, ed. Gordon, p.* 358.

In those young eyes, so keenly, bravely bent
To search the mysteries of the future hour,
There shines the will to conquer, and the pow'r
Which makes that conquest sure,—a gift heav'n-sent.
—BYRON, A. L. NOEL, 1841, *On A Portrait of Mrs. Jameson by her Father.*

There are few people whom I pity more than Mrs. Jameson. I always thought she had a great deal of good in her, but the finer elements in her character have become more apparent and valuable to me the longer I have known her; her abilities are very considerable, and her information very various and extensive; she is a devoted, dutiful daughter, and a most affectionate and generous sister, working laboriously for her mother and the other members of her family. . . . I compassionate and admire her much.—KEMBLE, FRANCES ANN, 1845, *Letter, Dec. 15; Records of Later Life, p.* 454.

The poor lady seems to be very lame; and I am sure I was grateful to her for having taken the trouble to climb up the seventy steps of our staircase, and felt pain at seeing her go down again. It looks fearfully like the gout, the affection being apparently in one foot. The hands, by the way, are white, and must once have been, perhaps now are,

beautiful, She must have been a perfectly pretty woman in her day,—a blue or gray eyed, fair-haired beauty. I think that her hair is not white, but only flaxen in the extreme.—HAWTHORNE, NATHANIEL, 1858, *Passages from the French and Italian Note-Books, p.* 195.

She had a pale, clear, intellectual blue eye, that could flash anger, or jealousy, or love; her hair was red, and her complexion very fair, and of the hue of an irate temper. Her arms, neck, and hands were beautiful, but her whole person wanted dignity; it was short, and of those dimensions that to ears polite are embonpoint—to the vulgar, fat. Her genius and accomplishments need no note of mine; they live in her books. I believe no woman has written more variously, and few, men or women, so well. She impressed me as the best talker I ever heard, and I have heard many gifted "unknown," and many known and celebrated. Mrs. Kemble, who has had far more extended opportunities than mine, as she has been familiar with men trained to talk in the London social arena, I have heard assign the first place to Mrs. Jameson.—SEDGWICK, CATHARINE, 1860, *Life and Letters, ed. Dewey, p.* 381.

Mr. Jameson was a man of considerable ability and legal accomplishment, filling with honor the posts of Speaker of the House of Assembly of Upper Canada, and the Attorney-General of the Colony, and he is spoken of with respect by his personal friends in England; but the marriage was a mistake on both sides. The husband and wife separated almost immediately, and for many years. In 1836, Mrs. Jameson joined her husband at Toronto; but it was for a very short time; and they never met again. . . . A warm-hearted and courageous woman, of indomitable sociability of nature, large liberalities, and deep prejudices.— MARTINEAU, HARRIET, 1860, *Biographical Sketches, pp.* 114, 119.

I well remembered her face,—"oh, call it fair, not pale!"—the whiteness of which was set off and intensified by her ruddy curls.—SEDGWICK, HENRY DWIGHT, 1895. *Reminiscences of Literary Berkshire, The Century, vol.* 50, *p.* 557.

One of the best and brightest women of the earlier years of the Victorian era. . . . She was a human Irish harp; to see her kindle into enthusiasm amidst the gorgeous natural beauty and the antique memorials and the sacred Christian relics of Italy was an experience not to be forgotten.—BELLOC, BESSIE RAYNER, 1895, *In a Walled Garden, p.* 67.

There were various legends regarding Mrs. Jameson's private history. It is said that her husband, marrying her against his will, parted from her at the church door, and thereafter left England for Canada, where he was residing at the time of her visit. I first met her at an evening party at the house of a friend. . . . She was of middle height, her hair red blond in color. Her face was not handsome, but sensitive and sympathetic in expression. The elegant dames of New York were somewhat scandalized at her want of taste in dress. I actually heard one of them say, "How like the devil she does look."—HOWE, JULIA WARD, 1899, *Reminiscences,* 1819–1899, *p.* 41.

GENERAL

Shepherd. "Mrs. Jameson's prose aye reminds me o' Miss Landon's poetry—and though baith hae their fawtes, I wou'd charactereese baith alike by the same epithet— rich. I hate a simple style, for that's only anither word for puir."—WILSON, JOHN, 1831, *Noctes Ambrosianæ, Nov.*

I have been much interested, too, in Mrs. Jameson's "Characteristics of Women," a work full of beauty, grace and feeling. I have not dared to recommend it, for the moral lies too deep for most readers. Most readers would gather from it that woman has no higher vocation than to *love;* that absorption in this passion, at the expense and sacrifice of every other sentiment and every duty, is innocent; and that she whose hope is blasted in this has nothing to live for, perhaps nothing to do but to die, like Juliet, by her own hand. I do not mean that these lessons are taught, but that such impression would be received by not a few readers from several parts. Mrs. J. discovers in her introduction so just an appreciation of woman, that I wonder a loftier, healthier tone does not decidedly characterize her book. Perhaps I am hypercritical, for in some of her characters she pays just homage to virtue and to the high destiny of her sex; and I feel almost ungrateful in finding fault with a lady who has delighted me so much by her fine perception of character, her richness of illustration, and felicities of style.—CHANNING, WILLIAM ELLERY, 1833, *To Miss Aikin, Aug.* 30; *Correspondence of William Ellery Channing and Lucy Aikin, ed.* LeBreton, *p.* 182.

In the present century, Coleridge and Schlegel, so nearly at the same time that the question of priority and even plagiarism has been mooted, gave a more philosophical, and at the same time a more intrinsically exact, view of Shakspeare than their predecessors. What has since been written has often been highly acute and æsthetic, but occasionally with an excess of refinement which substitutes the critic for the work. Mrs. Jameson's "Essays on the Female Characters of Shakspeare" are among the best. It was right that this province of illustration should be reserved for a woman's hand.—HALLAM, HENRY, 1837–39, *Introduction to the Literature of Europe, pt.* iii, *ch.* vi, *par.* 54.

Tell that charming writer, Mrs. Jameson, that I (being a little prudish) took great offence at seeing so much beautiful praise lavished on the beauties of Charles the Second's Court, whom I consider no better than they should be. But, afterwards, her strictures on Shakspeare's female characters delighted me. She invested them with all the properties that I had long studied and admired, without a hope of meeting with any one that would understand, far less explain my feelings. Pray thank her for me for melting the frost of age about my heart, and restoring to me the delights of loving and admiring excellence. I can never do her any good, but she has done a great deal to me; thank her for me, I entreat you.—GRANT, ANNE,

1838, *Letters, Apr.* 9; *Memoir and Correspondence,* ed. *Grant, vol.* III, *p.* 317.

Mrs. Jameson is an established favourite with the public. She is an accomplished woman, an elegant writer, and her refined taste and quick sensibility are good influences on her age. Her "Characteristics of Women" contain a searching analysis of character and fine criticism, such as ought to place her name among those of the greatest commentators of Shakspeare. Her exposition of the character of Cordelia is, in especial, beautifully true; and her perception of the intensity, and strength, and real dignity of soul in Helena (in "All's Well that Ends Well"), notwithstanding that the tenor of all the incidents and circumstances around her wound and shock, manifests the true power to look beyond the outward show of things and read the heart. The "Visits and Sketches at Home and Abroad" is a delightful book; accomplishing that rare task of rendering descriptions of works of art pleasant reading instead of dull catalogues.—HORNE, RICHARD HENGIST, 1844, *A New Spirit of the Age.*

Nor could we give a better instance of real description and opinions interwoven with a romance—though in no way needing this fictious interest—than another established favourite,—Mrs. Jameson's "Diary of Ennuyée."—EASTLAKE, ELIZABETH LADY, 1845, *Lady Travellers, Quarterly Review, vol.* 76, *p.* 105.

Mrs. Jameson's volume on the "Female Characters" is a most eloquent and impassioned representation of Shakspeare's women, and in many respects is an important contribution to critical literature. Its defects are so covered up in the brilliancy and buoyancy of its style, that they are likely to escape notice.—WHIPPLE, EDWIN PERCY, 1848, *Shakspeare's Critics; Essays and Reviews, vol.* II, *p.* 261.

It is especially in her descriptions of paintings ["Poetry and Legendary Art"] that Mrs. Jameson's great talents are displayed. Nowhere do we recollect criticisms more genial, brilliant, picturesque than those which are scattered through these pages. Often they have deeper merits, and descend to those fundamental laws of beauty and of religion by which all Christian art must ultimately be tested. Mrs. Jameson has certainly a powerful inductive faculty; she comprehends at once the idea

and central law of a work of art, and sketches it in a few vivid and masterly touches; and really, to use a hack quotation honestly for once, "in thoughts which breathe, and words which burn."—KINGSLEY, CHARLES, 1849, *The Poetry of Sacred and Legendary Art, Miscellanies, vol.* I, *p.* 254.

You have given me so much [pleasure] particularly in your last work, "Sacred and Legendary Art." How very precious it is to me! . . . It most amply supplies the cravings of the religious sentiment,—the spiritual nature within. It produces in my soul the same effect that great organists have produced by laying slight weights upon certain keys of their instruments,—thus keeping an unbroken flow of sound while their fingers are busy with other keys and stops. And there let these volumes lie,—pressing just enough upon my thoughts to make perpetual music. God bless you for this book!—LONGFELLOW, HENRY WADSWORTH, 1850, *Letter to Mrs. Jameson, Jan.; Life,* ed. *Longfellow, vol.* II, *p.* 158.

A few writers of refined sympathies and highly cultivated tastes have laboured effectively at the development of an Art Literature in this country. Next to Mr. Ruskin, its originator and best-known representative, stands Mrs. Jameson. Early instructed in the principles of Art, she devoted to the unfolding of its beauties an arduous but fertile literary career of more than thirty years. No writer has done so much to acquaint us with the productions of the Early Italian Masters.—SPALDING, WILLIAM, 1852, *A History of English Literature, p.* 433.

At first sight, a very winning book ["Characteristics of Women"]. Wherever the reader opened, the picture was charming; and the analysis seemed to be acute, delicate, and almost philosophical. After a second portrait the impression was somewhat less enthusiastic; and when, at the end of four or five, it was found difficult to bring away any clear conception of any, and to tell one from another, it was evident that there was no philosophy in all this, but only fancy and feeling. The notorious mistake in regard to Lady Macbeth, to whom Mrs. Jameson attributes an intellect loftier than that of her husband, indicates the true level of a work which is yet full of charm, from its suggestiveness, and frequent truth of sentiment. Mrs.

Jameson's world-wide reputation dates from the publication of this book.—MARTINEAU, HARRIET, 1860, *Biographical Sketches*, p. 116.

On the subject of art, her writing is next to that of Ruskin; to intense love of the beautiful, she adds a fine discriminating and cultivated taste with rich stores of knowledge.—CHAMBERS, ROBERT, 1876, *Cyclopædia of English Literature*, ed. *Carruthers*.

Mrs. Jameson was absolutely without knowledge or instinct of painting; and had no sharpness of insight for anything else; but she was candid and industrious, with a pleasant disposition to make the best of all she saw, and to say, compliantly, that a picture was good, if anybody had ever said so before.—RUSKIN, JOHN, 1887, *Prœterita, vol. II, ch.* vii.

Her "Sacred and Legendary Art" is a storehouse of delightful knowledge, as admirable for accurate research as for poetic and artistic feeling, and only marred to a slight extent by the authoress's limited acquaintance with the technicalities of painting. She appears to equal advantage when depicting her favourite Shakespearean heroines, or the brilliant yet unostentatious society she enjoyed so greatly in Germany—to greater advantage still, perhaps, in the graceful æsthetics and deeply felt moralities of her "Commonplace Book," or the eloquence of her "House of Titian," an essay saturated with Venetian feeling. Much of her early writing is feebly rhetorical, but constant intercourse with fine art and fine minds brought her deliverance.—GARNETT,

RICHARD, 1892, *Dictionary of National Biography, vol.* XXIX, *p.* 232.

A woman with much enthusiasm for art, and no inconsiderable power of literary expression, she had begun her literary career as a writer with other kinds of criticism, a work upon "The Female Characters of Shakespeare," having gained her much reputation, and taught the public to expect from her that kind of commentary and appreciation of beautiful things which was then considered especially suitable to feminine authors, the elegant literature of the boudoir and drawing-room, not very profound or original, but full of good, nay, fine feelings and much prettiness, both of language and sentiment.—OLIPHANT, MARGARET O. W., 1892, *The Victorian Age of English Literature*, p. 526.

In her "Winter Studies and Summer Rambles" she records her observations on Canada and the United States, as far as she traveled. The shadow over these original and spirited pictures is—unhappiness in wedded life! Everywhere she finds marriage a slavery, a sin, or a sorrow. The shaft in her own bosom she plants in that of every other married pair; like a person with a painful disease, she hears only of the afflicted, and fancies the world to be a hospital of incurables.—SAUNDERS, FREDERICK, 1894, *Character Studies*, p. 35.

Mrs. Anna Jameson was a better writer than Collier, and she enjoys an unclouded reputation. Her "Characteristics of Shakespeare's Women" still holds its ground as a fine example of the critical analysis of character.—WALKER, HUGH, 1897, *The Age of Tennyson*, p. 193.

George Payne Rainsford James

1801–1860

Born, in London, 9 Aug. 1801. Educated at school at Putney. Travelled on Continent in youth. Contributed to periodicals, and eventually adopted literary career. Historiographer Royal, 1839. British Consul at Massachusetts, 1850[?]–52; at Norfolk, Virginia, 1852–56; at Venice, 1856–60. Died, at Venice, 9 May, 1860. Buried in the Lido Cemetery. *Works:* "Life of Edward the Black Prince," 1822; "The Ruined City," 1828; "Adra," 1829; "Richelieu" (anon.), 1829; "Darnley" (anon.), 1830; "De L'Orme" (anon.), 1830; "Philip Augustus" (anon.), 1831; "Henry Masterton" (anon.), 1832; "History of Charlemagne," 1832; "Memoirs of Great Commanders," 1832; "The String of Pearls" (anon.), 1832; "Mary of Burgundy" (anon.), 1833; "Delaware" (anon.), 1833; "Life . . . of John Marston Hall," 1834; "One in a Thousand," 1835; "On the Educational Institutions of Germany," 1835; "My Aunt Pontypool" (anon.), 1835; "Gipsey," 1835; "The Desultory Man," 1836; "Attila," 1837; "Life . . . of Louis XIV," 1838; "The Huguenot," 1838; "The Robber" (anon.), 1838; "Brief Hist. of the U. S. Boundary Question," 1839; "Henry of Guise," 1839; "Charles

Tyrrell," 1839; "Blanche of Navarre," 1839; "The Gentleman of the Old School," 1839; "A Book of the Passions," 1839; "The King's Highway," 1840; "Man-at-Arms," 1840; "The Jacquerie," 1841; "The Ancient Regime," 1841; "Corse de Leon," 1841; "Some Remarks on the Corn Laws," 1841; "Morley Ernstein," 1842; "The Woodman," 1842; "Hist. of . . . Richard Cœur-de-Lion" (4 vols.), 1842–49; "Hist. of Chivalry," 1843; "The Commissioner" (anon.), 1843; "Forest Days," 1843; "The False Heir," 1843; "Eva St. Clair," 1843; "Arabella Stuart," 1844; "Rose D'Albret," 1844; "Agincourt," 1844; "Works" (collected; 21 vols.), 1844–49; "The Smuggler," 1845; "Arrah Neil," 1845; "The Stepmother," 1845; "Heidelberg," 1846; "Russell," 1847; "Life of Henry IV of France," 1847; "A Whim" (anon.), 1847; "The Convict," 1847; "The Castle of Ehrenstein," 1847; "The Last of the Fairies" [1848]; "Beauchamp," 1848; "Margaret Graham," 1848; "Cameralzaman," 1848; "Sir Theodore Broughton," 1848; "Delaware," 1848; "The Forgery," 1849; "The Fight of the Fiddlers," 1849; "An investigation of the Murder of John, Earl of Gowrie, and Alexander Ruthven, etc.," 1849; "John Jones's Tales for Little John Jones's," 1849; "Dark Scenes of History," 1849; "The Old Oak Chest" 1850; "Gowrie," 1851; "The Fate," 1851; "Henry Smeaton," 1851; "Pequinillo," 1852; "A Story Without a Name," 1852; "Revenge," 1852; "Adrian" (with M. B. Field), 1852;" "Agnes Sorrel," 1853; "The Vicissitudes of a Life," 1853; "Arabella Stuart," 1853; "An Oration on the . . . Duke of Wellington," 1853; "Ticonderoga," 1854; "Prince Life," 1856; "The Old Dominion," 1856; "Leonora d'Orco," 1857; "Lord Montagu's Page," 1858. *Posthumous:* "Bernard Marsh," 1864. He *edited:* "Memoirs of Celebrated Women," 1837; the "Vernon Letters," 1841; Ireland's "David Rizzio," 1849.—SHARP, R. FARQUHARSON, 1897, *A Dictionary of English Authors, p.* 146.

PERSONAL

We have not the means of verifying the number of Mr. James's publications, nor the period within which they were produced. But, we believe, we are sufficiently accurate for general purposes in saying that he commenced his career about fifteen years ago, and that from that time to the present, he has published nearly two novels of histories, annually. . . . If all these works were gathered together, and a scrivener employed to copy them, it would probably occupy him a longer period of fair average daily labour in the simple task of transcription than the author expended upon their composition. . . . How Mr. James, although he might compose faster than another person could copy, contrived both to compose and write so much within so short a period? But the problem is set at rest by the fact that Mr. James did not *write* any of his works. Like Cobbett, he employs an amanuensis, and all his long and brilliant array of historical narratives with which the public have been so pleasantly entertained for such a series of years have been dictated by the author, while he was walking up and down his study, one after another, or, sometimes, possibly, two or three at a time!—HORNE, RICHARD HENGIST, 1844, *A New Spirit of the Age.*

If he was sometimes a tedious writer, he was always the best story-teller that I ever listened to. He had known almost everybody in his own country, and he never forgot anything. The literary anecdotes alone which I have heard him relate would suffice to fill an ordinary volume. He was a big-hearted man, too—tender, merciful, and full of religious sentiment; a good husband, a devoted father, and a fast friend. If I dwell longer upon him than some others who occupy a higher niche in the temple of fame, it is because I knew him so well, and there always existed so affectionate a regard between us.—FIELD, MAUNSELL B., 1873, *Memoirs of Many Men and of Some Women, p.* 206.

In the same year [1850] G. P. R. James, whose first three initials were interpreted by George William Curtis as "George Prince Regent" (which interpretation was locally adopted), came to Stockbridge, where he lived till the end of 1852. He was a generous and public-spirited townsman, and gave a clock to the tower of the Episcopal Church. The industry for which he was so famous was conspicuous there, and he dictated romances to three or four secretaries simultaneously. Mr. James was a vigorous snuff-taker, and was one of the last in the society of that day to sport the red bandana, which that beguiling habit rendered indispensable.—SEDGWICK, HENRY DWIGHT, 1895, *Reminiscences of Literary Berkshire, The Century, vol.* 50, *p.* 562.

I caught sight of this great necromancer of "miniver furs," and mantua-making chivalry—in youngish days, in the city of New York—where he was making a little over-ocean escape from the multitudinous work that flowed from him at home; a well-preserved man, of scarce fifty years, stout, erect, gray-haired, and with countenance blooming with mild uses of mild English ale—kindly, unctuous—showing no signs of deep thoughtfulness or of harassing toil. I looked him over, in boyish way, for traces of the court splendors I had gazed upon, under his ministrations, but saw none; nor anything of the "manly beauty of features, rendered scarcely less by a deep scar upon the forehead,"—nor "of the gray cloth doublets slashed with purple;" a staunch, honest, amiable, well-dressed Englishman —that was all.—MITCHELL, DONALD G., 1897, *English Lands Letters and Kings, The Later Georges to Victoria, p.* 284.

GENERAL

North.—" 'Richelieu' is one of the most spirited, amusing, and interesting romances I ever read; character well drawn—incidents well managed—story perpetually progressive—catastrophe at once natural and unexpected—moral good, but not goody—and the whole felt, in every chapter, to be the work of a —Gentleman."— WILSON, JOHN, 1830, *Noctes Ambrosianæ, April.*

Mr. James may be regarded as not less fortunate in the choice of his subject than meritorious in its treatment; indeed, his work is not so much the best as the only "History of Charlemagne" which will hereafter be cited. For it reposes upon a far greater body of research and collation than has hitherto been applied even in France to this interesting theme; and in effect it is the first account of the great emperor and his times which can, with a due valuation of the term, be complimented with the title of a critical memoir.—DEQUINCEY, THOMAS, 1832, *Charlemagne, Collected Writings, ed. Masson, vol.* v, *p.* 362.

He belongs to the historical school of fiction, and, like the masters of the art, takes up a real person or a real event, and pursuing the course of history, makes out the intentions of nature by adding circumstances and heightening character, till, like a statue in the hands of the sculptor, the whole is in fair proportion, truth of sentiment, and

character. For this he has high qualities, —an excellent taste, extensive knowledge of history, a right feeling of the chivalrous, and a heroic and a ready eye for the picturesque: his proprieties are admirable; and his sympathy with whatever is high-souled and noble is deep and impressive. His best works are "Richelieu" and "Mary of Burgundy."— CUNNINGHAM, ALLAN, 1833, *Biographical and Critical History of the Literature of the Last Fifty Years.*

To genius of any kind, it seems to us that he has little pretension. In the solemn tranquility of his pages we seldom stumble across a novel emotion, and if any matter of deep interest arises in the path, we are pretty sure to find it an interest appertaining to some historical fact equally vivid or more so than in the original chronicles.—POE, EDGAR ALLAN, 1836, *Marginalia, Works, ed. Stedman and Woodberry, vol.* VII, *p.* 282.

Incomparably good and great in all his works, words, and thoughts.—LANDOR, WALTER SAVAGE, 1841, *Some Letters of Walter Savage Landor, Sept.* 12; *The Century, vol.* 35, *p.* 520.

For the last ten years, he has been repeating his own repetitions, and echoing his own echoes. His first novel was a shot that went through the target, and he has ever since been assiduously firing through the hole. To protect his person from critical assault, he might pile up a bulwark of books many volumes thick and many feet high. Yet the essence of all that he has written, if subjected to a refining process, might be compressed into a small space, and even then would hardly bear the test of time, and journey safely down to posterity. . . . As space has no limits, and as large portions of it are still unoccupied by tangible bodies, it seems not very philosophical to quarrel with any person who endeavors to fill up its wide chasms; yet in the case of Mr. James, we grudge the portion of infinite space which his writings occupy. We dispute his right to pile up matter, which is the type or symbol of so small an amount of spirit. We sigh for the old vacuum, and think, that though nature may have abhorred it in the days of Aristotle, her feelings must have changed since modern mediocrity has filled it with such weak apologies for substance and form.—WHIPPLE, EDWIN PERCY, 1844, *James's Novels Essays and Reviews, vol.* I, *pp.* 112, 113.

He is a picturesque writer, and paints

his canvas-deep figures in bright costume, and in the midst of excellent landscape. Often when I have been very unwell, I have been able to read his books with advantage, when I could not read better ones. You may read him from end to end without a superfluous beat of the heart,—and they are just the sort of intellectual diet fitted for persons "ordered to be kept quiet" by their physicians. Do not mistake, I am writing quite gravely, and not, I hope, ungratefully. I am grateful to Mr. James for many a still, serene hour. I have every respect for him as a sensible level writer—a very agreeable writer—pure-minded, and with talents in his own province. But to give him place as a romance writer over Bulwer, the prose poet of the day, and over Banim, the prose-dramatist, is, must be, a monstrous exaggeration of his actual claim.—BROWNING, ELIZABETH BARRETT, 1844, *Letters of Elizabeth Barrett Browning Addressed to Richard Hengist Horne, Jan.* 5, *Letter* xxxiv, *p.* 170.

The number of James's works is immense, but they bear among themselves a family likeness so strong, and even oppressive, that it is impossible to consider this author otherwise than as an ingenious imitator and copyist—first of Scott, and secondly of himself. . . . His great deficiency is want of real, direct, powerful human passion, and consequently of life and movement in his intrigues. There is thrown over his fictions a general air of good-natured, frank, and well-bred refinement, which, however laudable, cannot fail to be found rather tiresome and monotonous.—SHAW, THOMAS B., 1847, *Outlines of English Literature, pp.* 374, 375.

I read everything that is readable, old and new, particularly fiction, and philosophy, and natural history. . . . And hail every fresh publication of James, though I know half what he is going to do with his lady, and his gentleman, and his landscape, and his mystery, and his orthodoxy, and his criminal trial. But I am charmed with the new amusement which he brings out of old materials. I look on him as I should look upon a musician, famous for "variations." I am grateful for his vein of cheerfulness, for his singularly varied and vivid landscapes, for his power of painting woman at once lady-like and loving (a rare talent), for his making lovers to match, at once beautiful and well-bred, and for the

solace which all this has afforded me, sometimes over and over again, in illness and in convalescence, when I required interest without violence, and entertainment at once animated and mild.—HUNT, LEIGH, 1850–60, *Autobiography, vol.* II, *pp.* 294, 295.

There is a constant appeal in his brilliant pages not only to the pure and generous, but to the elevated and noble sentiments; he is imbued with the very soul of chivalry, and all his stories turn on the final triumph of those who are influenced by such feelings over such as are swayed by selfish or base desires. He possesses great pictorial powers and a remarkable facility of turning his graphic pen at will to the delineation of the most distant and opposite scenes, manners, and social customs. . . . Not a word or a thought which can give pain to the purest heart ever escapes from his pen; and the mind wearied with the cares, and grieved at the selfishness of the world, reverts with pleasure to his varied compositions, which carry it back, as it were, to former days, and portray, perhaps in too brilliant colours, the ideas and manners of the olden time.—ALISON, SIR ARCHIBALD, 1853, *History of Europe,* 1815–1852, *ch.* v.

The shelves of the circulating libraries still groan under his endless volumes; and there are readers of peculiar taste who enjoy his monotonous fictions. His great field is modern history; and perhaps his first historical novel, "Richelieu" (1829), is his best. But to read one of James's novels is to read all. His famous opening scene of two travellers winding on horseback down a mountain road, in the red light of sunset—the one dark and elderly, the other young and fair, &c., has been often turned into fun.—COLLIER, WILLIAM, FRANCIS, 1861, *A History of English Literature p.* 513.

We have all been accustomed to laugh at the time-honoured scene with which his stories were wont to open—where the last beams of the setting sun gilded the valley along which rode two horsemen, one of whom appeared to be some six or seven summers older than the other; but we have had time since then to become accustomed to even more bombastic and inflated styles, with perhaps even less literary merit to redeem them.—OLIPHANT, MARGARET O. W., 1892, *The Victorian Age of English Literature, p.* 15.

Flimsy and melodramatic as James's

romances are, they are highly popular. The historical setting is for the most part laboriously accurate, and though the characters are without life, the moral tone is irreproachable; there is a pleasant spice of adventure about the plots, and the style is clear and correct. The writer's grandiloquence and artificiality are cleverly parodied by Thackeray in "Barbazure, by G. P. R. James, Esq., &c.," in "Novels by Eminent Hands," and the conventional sameness of the openings of his novels, "so admirable for terseness," is effectively burlesqued in "The Book of Snobs," chaps. ii and xvi.—HAMILTON, J. A., 1892, *Dictionary of National Biography, vol.* XXIX, *p.* 210.

James wrote better than Ainsworth: his historical knowledge was of a much wider and more accurate kind, and he was not unimbued with the spirit of romance. But the sameness of his situations (it became a stock joke to speak of the "two horsemen" who so often appeared in his opening scenes), the exceedingly conventional character of his handling, and the theatrical feebleness of his dialogue, were always reprehended and open to reprehension.—SAINTSBURY, GEORGE, 1896, *A History of Nineteenth Century Literature, p.* 139.

Even more prolific than Ainsworth. . . . More perhaps than Ainsworth he has suffered from time, because he remains more constantly on a dead level of mediocrity. James trusted, and in his own day trusted not in vain, to adventure; but unless there is some saving virtue of style, or of thought, or of character, each generation insists on making its own adventures. James has sunk under the operation of this law, and he is not likely to be revived.—WALKER, HUGH, 1897, *The Age of Tennyson, p.* 78.

An excellent, industrious man, who drove his trade of novel-making—as our engineers drive wells—with steam, and pistons, and borings, and everlasting clatter.—MITCHELL, DONALD G., 1897, *English Lands Letters and Kings, The Later Georges to Victoria, p.* 283.

Had also a faint touch of Scott's romantic spirit; but almost all his novels are of that one inadmissible *genre* defined by the French critic as *le genre ennuyeux*. And the intolerable slowness of their movement as individual stories was hardly compensated by the speed with which they followed one another from his too prolific pen.—TRAILL, HENRY DUFF, 1897, *Social England, vol.* VI, *p.* 163.

Gen. Sir William Francis Patrick Napier

1785–1860

Born, at Celbridge, Co. Kildare, 17 Dec. 1785. Educated at Celbridge Grammar School. Ensign in Royal Irish Artillery, June 1800; Lieutenant, April 1801; Captain in 43rd Regt., 1804. Took part in expedition against Copenhagen, 1807; in Sir John Moore's campaign in Spain, winter of 1808–09. With his regiment in Portugal, spring of 1809 to autumn of 1811. Married Caroline Amelia Fox, Feb. 1812. In Peninsula with regiment, March 1812 to Jan. 1813; Major, May 1812. In England, Jan. to Aug., 1813. In Peninsula, Aug. 1813 to 1814. Brevet Lieut.-Colonel, Nov. 1813. Retired from active service, 1819. C. B., 1819. Settled in London; took great interest in fine arts, and contributed to various periodicals. Removed to Bromham, Cornwall, 1826; to Freshford, near Bath, 1831. Colonel, July 1830. Annual Grant for Distinguished Services, from May 1841. Major-General, Nov. 1841. Lieut.-Governor of Guernsey, Feb. 1842; removed thither, April 1842; resigned, 1847. K. C. B., 27 April 1848. Lieut.-General, Nov. 1851; General, Dec. 1859. Died, at Clapham Park, 10 Feb. 1860. Buried at Norwood. *Works:* "History of the War in the Peninsula" (6 vols.), 1828–40 (followed by five phamphlets in answer to objections to the History; viz., "A Reply to Lord Strangford's 'Observations,' " 1828; "A Reply to various Opponents," 1833; "Colonel Napier's Justification on his third volume," 1833; "A Letter to Gen. Lord Viscount Beresford," 1834; "Counter-Remarks to Mr. D. M. Perceval's Remarks," 1835); " Observations Illustrating Sir John Moore's Campaign," 1832 ; " Observations on the Corn Laws," 1841; "The Conquest of Scinde" (2 vols.), 1845; "Notes on the State of Europe," 1848; "Six Letters in vindication of the British Army," 1849; "History of Sir Charles Napier's Administration of Scinde," 1851; "Comments upon a Memorandum of the Duke of Wellington," 1854; "Life and Opinions of Gen. Sir C. J. Napier" (4 vols.), 1857; "Gen. Sir Charles Napier and the Directors of the East India Company," 1857. He *edited:* Admiral Sir C. Napier's "The Navy," 1851; General Sir C. J. Napier's "Defects, Civil and Military, of the Indian Government," 1853, and "William the Conqueror," 1858. *Life:* by Lord Aberdare, 1864.—SHARP, R. FARQUHARSON, 1897, *A Dictionary of English Authors, p.* 209.

PERSONAL

He had one son. Nine daughters were born to him, five of whom survive him. His life was happy in old age. His utterly fearless nature saved him from the suffering which most of us would undergo in provoking and sustaining hostile controversies. His wife, some unmarried daughters, many grandchildren, and all whom his benign domestic temper had attached to him, ministered to his ease, and to his intellect as well; so that his decline was gentle. Till a late stage of his life his accomplishments as an artist were a precious resource to him. Others besides his immediate friends will remember his statue—the Death of Alcibiades—in virtue of which he was made an honorary member of the Royal Academy. His paintings are no commonplace amateur daubs, but both explain and are explained by the splendid picture-gallery of his great historical work.—MARTINEAU, HARRIET, 1860, *Biographical Sketches, p.* 204.

He appears indeed to have excelled in all he attempted. Among his other acquirements, he was a first-rate billiard-player and very fond of the game; but he gave it up entirely from the fear that it might become too engrossing. . . . In appearance William Napier was one of the handsomest men of his time. Six feet high, formed in the most powerful mould it is possible to conceive as compatible with extraordinary grace and activity. He was able to jump six feet in height. The head of an Antinous covered with short clustering black curls—the square brow, both wide and high, the aquiline nose—the firm mouth and the square massive jaw, indicating indomitable firmness and resolution—the eye of that remarkable bluish grey, so terrible in anger, so melting in tenderness, so sparkling in fun. In his youth his head and face might have served for a portrait of the war god. In his latest years, with milk-white hair and beard, his appearance was that of a Jupiter.—BRUCE, H. A., 1864, *Life of Gen. Sir William Napier, vol.* I, *p.* 27.

There was an openness and manliness about Sir William that at once won confidence. It was felt that he was a man of principle. . . . There was in his bearing an openness highly agreeable. His scorn of chicane was perceptible at a first acquaintance, and this was particularly observable when he entered into earnest conversation.—REDDING, CYRUS, 1867, *Personal Reminiscences, vol.* III, *pp.* 154, 155.

Napier was noble and generous by nature, resembling his brother Charles in hatred of oppression and wrong, in a chivalrous defence of the weak, and a warm and active benevolence. He was an eloquent public speaker, but sometimes formed his judgments too hastily. He had a great love of art, and was no mean artist. His statuette of Alcibiades, in virtue of which he was made an honorary member of the Royal Academy, received the warm praise of Chantrey.—VETCH, R. H., 1894, *Dictionary of National Biography, vol.* XL, *p.* 86.

HISTORY OF THE WAR IN THE PENINSULA.
1828–40

I have finished Napier's "War in the Peninsula." It is written in the spirit of a Liberal, but the narrative is distinct and clear. He has, however, given a bad sample of accuracy in the case of Lord Strangford, where his pointed affirmation has been as pointedly repelled. It is evident he would require probing. His defence of Moore is spirited and well argued, though it is evident he defends the statesman as much as the general. As a *Liberal* and a military man, Napier finds it difficult to steer his course. The former character calls on him to plead for the insurgent Spaniards; the latter induces him to palliate the cruelties of the French. Good-even to him until next volume, which I shall long to see.—SCOTT, SIR WALTER, 1828, *Journal, May* 31; *Life by Lockhart, ch.* lxxvi.

I quite agree about Napier's book. I did not think that any man could venture to write so true, bold, and honest a book; it gave me a high idea of his understanding, and makes me very anxious about his *caractère.*—SMITH, SYDNEY, 1829, *To N. Fazakerly, Oct.; A Selection from the Letters of Sydney Smith, ed. Mrs. Austin.*

The "History of the Peninsular War" [by Southey] is already dead: indeed, the second volume was dead-born. The glory of producing an imperishable record of that great conflict seems to be reserved for Colonel Napier.—MACAULAY, THOMAS BABINGTON, 1830, *Southey's Colloquies on Society, Edinburgh Review, vol.* 50, *p.* 531.

As for Napier himself, his Spanish Campaigns are immortal.—WILSON, JOHN, 1831, *Audubon's Ornithological Biography, Blackwood's Magazine, vol.* 30, *p.* 248.

I have been exceedingly impressed with the evil precedent of Colonel Napier's "History of the Peninsular War." It is a specimen of the true French military school; not a thought for the justice of the war,—not a consideration of the damnable and damning iniquity of the French invasion. All is looked at as a mere game of exquisite skill, and the praise is regularly awarded to the most successful player. How perfectly ridiculous is the prostration of Napier's mind, apparently a powerful one, before the name of Buonaparte! I declare I know no book more likely to undermine the national sense of right and wrong in matters of foreign interference than this work of Napier's.—COLERIDGE, SAMUEL TAYLOR, 1831, *Table Talk, ed. Ashe, June* 26, *p.* 121.

He has produced a work which for vivid beauty of narrative may vie, I have heard good judges say, with Cæsar or Tacitus.—CUNNINGHAM, ALLAN, 1833, *Biographical and Critical History of the Literature of the Last Fifty Years.*

We observed, towards the close of our first article upon Colonel Napier's history, that to point out all its inaccuracies and expose fully the unjust partialities and systematic misrepresentations by which it is almost everywhere disfigured would require a work more voluminous than itself. The necessity for such a work is, however, daily diminishing; and even before the Colonel has finished his undertaking he will, we apprehend, discover that the sandy foundations on which he has rested his claims to lasting reputation, either as a writer of good taste, or as an accurate and judicious historian, have already given way. . . . We hope ere long to resume our exposure of this author's historical and professional blunders; and when we have concluded the examination of his book, we may probably give an article (which need not be a long one) to his (so-called) replies. —MURRAY, SIR GEORGE, 1838, *Napier's Peninsular War, Quarterly Review, vol.* 61, *pp.* 51, 96.

Colonel Napier's description of battles and the heart-stirring events of military warfare are superior to anything in the same style, not only in modern, but almost in ancient, history. . . . But the great defect of this brilliant work is the want of calmness in the judgment of political events, and undue crowding in the details of his work. He is far too minute in the account of inconsiderable transactions.—ALISON, SIR ARCHIBALD, 1844, *Michelet's France, Essays Political, Historical and Miscellaneous.*

Our English Thucydides, the historian of the Peninsular War.—LANDOR, WALTER SAVAGE, 1856, *On Orthography, Fraser's Magazine, vol.* 53, *p.* 244.

It is not because his "History of the Peninsular War" is the finest military history ever produced that his labors should be so spoken of, but because of the act of writing that narrative was a political service of incalculable importance. When he entered on his work Wellington was unwilling that the melancholy facts of the early part of the struggle should become known to the world, and if he, the conqueror, was unwilling, it may be imagined what was left by the obstructive officials who had done their utmost to crush the commander and his enterprise. Well as we understand it now, nobody knew at the close of the war that Wellington's greatest difficulties lay within the Cabinet and the War Office at home. Whether we ever should have learned the truth without Napier's help there is no saying; but we know that to him we owe the full and clear understanding that we have of the true scheme and character of the Peninsular War, of the ability, temper, and conduct of the Ministry of the time, and of the merits of our great general. That History has therefore modified our national policy, and our views, plans, spirit and conduct as a people. There are few on record which have effected such a work as this. It is this view of it which explains the wrath it excited.—MARTINEAU, HARRIET, 1860, *Biographical Sketches, p.* 200.

Is a work of the highest order.—ARNOLD, THOMAS, 1862–87, *A Manual of English Literature, p.* 490.

Writers of what may be called technical or professional history hardly come within the scope of a work on general literature. Yet the present century has been adorned by one author of that class of such preeminent merit that it can hardly be unseasonable to mention that the achievements in the Peninsular war of the greatest of British Generals have been described by an author who served under him, Colonel Napier of the 43rd Regiment, not only with the military knowledge and skill of an experienced soldier, but with a mastery of all the arts of composition, with a command over all the resources of the language, with an animation and vigour which few authors by profession have ever equalled; and that his narrative of the Conquest of Scinde by his own brother, an undertaking still more gratifying to his fraternal pride, rivals his greater and better known work in all the qualities which can confer renown on an author, and which deservedly procure for the writings in which they are displayed a longevity more durable, as the Roman poet affirms, than brass or marble. —YONGE, CHARLES DUKE, 1872, *Three Centuries of English Literature, p.* 176.

His "History" was not written for all time; and, with the exception of a few students of military affairs and a few lovers of good literature, the readers of our generation know it only by those isolated passages in which chronicle rises to the sublimity of epic poetry. . . . There are isolated passages in the book that will to the end sparkle among the most brilliant gems of literature, —passages that will always be read, and, whenever read, will make the hearts of the readers burn with them. But I do not believe that the book, as a whole, will continue to be read, at least by general readers. Forgotten it will never be: but its life will resemble the ghostly existence of the "Faery Queen," not the god-like immortality of the "Pilgrim's Progress." The truth is that for general readers, the book is far too long. Not the most skillful storyteller that ever lived, not even Macaulay himself, if he were alive, could induce our generation, much less future generations, to wade through a detailed narrative of the innumerable combats, sieges, marches, and the counter-marches of the Peninsular War. At the same time, it is probable that, if Napier had written with greater brevity, he would have given less satisfaction to that large portion of his public,—the soldiers who had themselves acted in the scenes which he described. No fair critic would think of finding fault with the length of his descriptions of such important events as the siege of Badajoz or the battle of Al-

buera. My complaint is, though I make it with diffidence, that he showed little sense of proportion, that he did not know when to contract his narrative.—HOLMES, T. R. F., 1885, *Sir William Napier, The National Review, vol.* 5, *pp.* 616, 625.

Southey said of Napier, "His history will be the standard *un*-literary history of his campaigns—mine the philosophical, moral, and popular one, of the Peninsular War." Southey was greatly deceived. His history is now comparatively unknown, while Napier's is not only the standard military authority, but by far the best literary work on the subject.—SMILES, SAMUEL, 1891, *A Publisher and his Friends, vol.* II, *p.* 239.

In the spring of 1840, Napier completed his "History" by the publication of the sixth volume. The French translation by Count Mathieu Dumas was completed shortly after, and translations appeared in Spanish, Italian, and German. The work steadily grew in popularity, and has become a classic of the English language, while the previous attempts of Captain Hamilton, of Southey, and of Lord Londonderry have been completely forgotten. It is commended to the general reader no less by its impartial admiration for the heroes on both sides than by the spontaneity of its style. Its accuracy was the more firmly established by the inevitable attacks of actors in the scenes described, who thought the parts they had played undervalued.—VETCH, R. H., 1894, *Dictionary of National Biography, vol.* XL, *p.* 84.

The famous description of the Battle of Albuera is only one of many showing eloquence without any mere fine writing, and with the knowledge of the soldier covering the artist's exaggeration.—SAINTSBURY, GEORGE, 1896, *A History of Nineteenth Century Literature, p.* 212.

Perhaps the greatest specimen of military history in any language, and have left it not only without equal, but without second in our own. His personal experience, though a great advantage, was the least of his qualifications. He could when the dry light of his intellect was not damped by passion, reason closely, and expound with admirable lucidity. When the principles of war, or the military causes of success and failure were the matter in hand, he gave his reason fair play. In this respect, however, he has been equalled by other military writers. Where he stands, it may be confidently affirmed, alone, is in this, that he brought to the history of war the imagination of a great romantic writer, and a poet's command of "simple, sensuous, and passionate images." His style is perfectly adapted to his subject—simple, swift, direct at times, and when under the stimulus of some heroic action, or heroic suffering, rising to a sonorous vehemence full of telling images, often conveyed by the power of a single word put in its place. He goes intrepidly to the very border of the turgid, but never over it. His qualities as a writer fully atone for his patent errors as a judge.—HANNAY, DAVID, 1896, *English Prose, ed. Craik, vol.* v, *p.* 276.

Is one of the rare masterpieces in modern military history.—HERFORD, C. H., 1897, *The Age of Wordsworth, p.* 44.

George Croly
1780–1860

An English divine and writer, was born in Dublin, Aug. 1780, and educated at Trinity College. After his ordination he went to London, and spent some years as a writer for the newspaper press. In 1835 he was appointed rector of St. Stephen's, Walbrook, and he occupied that parish with great credit, both as preacher and pastor, up to the day of his death, Nov. 24, 1860. Dr. Croly wrote several extravagant novels and tragedies, among them "Salathiel," "Marston" and "Catiline." His better reputation rests upon his fidelity and power as a preacher, after his appointment to St. Stephen's, and upon his religious writings, the more important of which are "Divine Providence, or the three Cycles of Revelation" (Lond. 1834, 8vo):—"The Apocalypse":—"Prophecy of the Rise, Progress, and Fall of the Church of Rome" (3rd. ed. Lond. 1838, 8vo): "The Popish Primacy," 2 sermons (Lond. 1850, 8vo):—"Sermons" (1848, 8vo). He also wrote a "Life of Burke," and a "Life of George IV," both reprinted in America.—M'CLINTOCK AND STRONG, *eds.*, 1869, *Cyclopædia of Biblical, Theological and Ecclesiastical Literature, vol.* II, *p.* 575.

PERSONAL

Croly is a fierce-looking Irishman, very lively in conversation, and certainly has considerable talent as a writer; his eloquence, like his person, is rather energetic than elegant, and though he has great power and concentration of thought, he wants the delicacy and discrimination of judgment which are the finest qualities in a critic.—ROBINSON, HENRY CRABB, 1813, *Diary, Apr.* 5; *Diary, Reminiscences and Correspondence.*

We dined with the Harnesses; Milman and Croly were among the guests. I like Mr. Milman; not so the other critic.—KEMBLE, FRANCES ANN, 1831, *Journal, Apr.* 21; *Records of a Girlhood, p.* 390.

He was a man of undoubted talent, but cold, imperious, and sarcastic.— PLANCHÉ, J. R., 1872, *Recollections and Reflections, vol.* I, *p.* 103.

He had a large and not prepossessing person, and a dashing and somewhat imperious manner; held violent Tory opinions; expressed them very energetically.—PROCTER, BRYAN WALLER, 1874 (?), *Recollections of Men of Letters, ed. Patmore, p.* 133.

Rev. George Croly was a somewhat severe and bitter political Tory partisan; but as the author of two enduring novels, a successful play, and a work that professes to interpret the Apocalypse of St. John, he holds higher rank as an author than he did as a clergyman of the Established Church—first as curate of a parish on barren, beautiful Dartmoor, then as, for a time, Chaplain to the Foundling Hospital, and subsequently as rector of one of the City churches—St. Stephen, Walbrook. During the mayoralty of his friend, Sir Francis Graham Moon, his parishioners presented him with a testimonial—a marble bust of himself. His was not a pleasant face to perpetuate, neither was his a genial nature to commemorate; a fierce politician, he hated his opponents with a hatred at once irrational and unchristian.—HALL, SAMUEL CARTER, 1883, *Retrospect of a Long Life, p.* 385.

GENERAL

There are many natural scenes, and passages tender and eloquent, but somewhat cold and stately; it ["Salathiel"] abounds in descriptions on which all the splendours of fancy and languages are lavished. . . . The author in his poem of "May Fair" was more at home; it contains passages which, for condensed vigour of thought and language, and sharp severity of rebuke, are not to be paralleled in the "Legion Club" of Swift.—CUNNINGHAM, ALLAN, 1833, *Biographical and Critical History of the Literature of the Last Fifty Years.*

Croly has a remarkable splendour of language; he is stately, dignified, and affluent in imagery; but sometimes, from condensation and inversions, obscure; and he is deficient in simplicity and tenderness, which is doubtless the principal reason why his works are so little read. He is not less distinguished as a prose writer than as a poet. His "Salathiel, a Story of the Past, the Present, and the Future," has hardly been surpassed in energy, pathos, or dramatic interest, by any romance of the time; and his "Tales of the Great St. Bernard" were nearly as attractive and popular.— GRISWOLD, RUFUS W., 1844, *The Poets and Poetry of England in the Nineteenth Century*, p. 317.

Hundreds of copies of verses from his indefatigable pen, some of them of surpassing excellence, lie scattered about—rich bouquets of unowned flowers—throughout the wide, unbounded fields of periodical literature. . . . A rich command of language, whether for the tender or the serious—an ear finely attuned to musical expression—a fertile and lucid conceptive power, and an intellect at once subtle and masculine.— MOIR, D. M., 1851–52, *Sketches of the Poetical Literature of the Past Half-Century, Lecture* iv.

Whose thoughts full of genius and lofty views, are conveyed in the purest and most classical English idiom. The ardent admirer of Burke, he has adopted his views, shared his fervor, and, in a great measure, imitated his style. But he has largely inhaled, also, the spirit, and profited by the lessons of the age in which he lived; the contemporary and observer of the French Revolution and its consequences, he has portrayed both in a philosophic spirit and with a poet's fire; and what Burke predicted from the contemplation of the Future, he has painted from the observation of the Present. — ALISON, SIR ARCHIBALD, 1853, *History of Europe*, 1815–1852, *ch.* v.

Few authors of the nineteenth century, who have written so much, have written so well as Dr. Croly. His prose style is clear, rich, idiomatic, and at times eloquent;

while as a poet he has many great and shining qualities.—CLEVELAND, CHARLES D., 1853, *English Literature of the Nineteenth Century*, p. 632.

Whose verse, more especially in his shorter pieces, sometimes surprises us with sudden felicities, although in general, perhaps, in everything at least except the sound, rather too like prose, as his prose certainly too much resembles verse.— CRAIK, GEORGE L., 1861, *A Compendious History of English Literature and of the English Language, vol.* II, p. 540.

Dr. Croly succeeded as a poet, as a writer of fiction, as an historian, as a literary editor, as a religious polemic. In this long list of works, there is scarcely one that at the time of its publication did not make its mark. His "Catiline" in poetry, his "Salathiel," in fiction, his "George IV" and "Edmund Burke," in history, fall little short of being of the first class in their several kinds.—HART, JOHN S., 1872, *A Manual of English Literature*, p. 448.

His works are numberless; from sermons to novels, from political pamphlets to romantic poems. The book by which he is best known is the singular romance of "Salathiel," embodying one of the legends of the Wandering Jew, and showing occasionally considerable power. This book made a distinct impression upon the mind of the time, and holds a fantastic place, if not on the same level as "Vathek," at least in a similar fanciful region; but it has not, like "Vathek," kept the reputation which in its day it obtained.—OLIPHANT, MARGARET O. W., 1882, *Literary History of England, XVIII–XIX Century, vol.* III, p. 217.

Croly is a characteristic example of the dominant literary school of his youth, that of Byron and Moore. The defects of this school are unreality and meretriciousness; its redeeming qualities are a certain warmth of colouring and largeness of handling, both of which Croly possessed in ample measure. His chief work, "Salathiel," is boldly conceived, and may still be read with pleasure for the power of the situations and the vigour of the language, although some passages are palpable imitations of De Quincey. He was less at home in modern life, yet "Marston" is interesting as a romance, and remarkable for its sketches of public men. In all his works, whether in prose or verse, Croly displays a lively and gorgeous fancy, with a total deficiency of creative imagination, humour, and pathos.—GARNETT, RICHARD, 1888, *Dictionary of National Biography, vol.* XIII, *p.* 136.

He was an eloquent speaker and writer,

and some passages from his poems have served the schoolmaster and the elocutionist well; but as a whole his poems lack interest.—MILES, ALFRED H., 1897, *The Poets and the Poetry of the Century, Sacred, Moral and Religious Verse, Appendix, p.* ix.

James Kirke Paulding
1779–1860

James Kirke Paulding, was born in Dutchess county, New York, August 22, 1779. A friend of Washington Irving, he wrote part of "Salmagundi." During the war of 1812 he published the "Diverting History of John Bull and Brother Jonathan," and in 1814 a more serious work, "The United States and England," which gained him an appointment on the Board of Naval Commissioners. He also wrote a successful novel, "The Dutchman's Fireside" (1831), "Westward Ho!" (1832), a "Life of Washington" (1835), and a defence of "Slavery in the United States" (1836). In 1837 he became Secretary of the Navy. He died 6th April 1860. See "Literary Life" by his son (1867).—PATRICK AND GROOME, *eds.,* 1897, *Chambers's Biographical Dictionary, p.* 725.

PERSONAL

Paulding was a man of great intellectual robustness: strong in his convictions, and inexorable in his prejudices; with great clearness of perception, but little inclination to the ideal; . . . rejoicing in sarcasm, though free from malignity both in his books and in his conversation; never yielding to the illusion of fancy or feeling, and expressing himself in language more remarkable for its grave irony and blunt vigour than for its amenity or elegance. No man ever stood up more stoutly or manfully in defence of that

"mother of a mighty race,"

when she was assailed from abroad, than James K. Paulding; nor did any man ever born on American soil entertain greater contempt for foreign example or criticism.—WILSON, JAMES GRANT, 1885, *Bryant and His Friends, p.* 129.

GENERAL

No two writers could be more thoroughly opposed in everything—disposition, habit, style—than were Irving and Paulding. The former was cheerful; pleasant, given to laughing at whatever he saw—not peevishly, satirically, or spitefully, but in real good humour: the latter—even while he *laughed* as Byron says of Lara—*sneered.* Irving would make us love human nature—wish it well—or pity it: Paulding would make us ashamed of it; or angry with it. One looks for what is good in everything; the other for what is bad.—NEAL, JOHN, 1825, *American Writers, Blackwood's Magazine, vol.* 17, *p.* 199.

We are convinced by a deliberate examination of the design, manner, and rich material of the work ["Life of Washington"] that, as it grows in age, it will grow in the estimation of our countrymen, and, finally, will not fail to take a deeper hold upon the public mind, and upon the public affections, than any work upon the same subject, or of a similar nature, which has been yet written—or, possibly, which may be written hereafter. Indeed, we cannot perceive the necessity of anything farther upon the great theme of Washington.—POE, EDGAR ALLAN, 1836, *Marginalia, Works, ed. Stedman and Woodberry, vol.* VII, *p.* 292.

Mr. Paulding's writings are distinguished for a decided nationality. He has had no respect for authority unsupported by reason, but on all subjects has thought and judged for himself. He has defended our government and institutions, and has embodied what is peculiar in our manners and opinions. There is hardly a character in his works who would not in any country be instantly recognised as an American. He is unequalled in a sort of quaint and whimsical humour, but occasionally falls into the common error of thinking there is humour in epithets, and these are sometimes coarse or vulgar. . . . He who pauses to invent its dress will usually find his invention exhausted before he attempts its body. He seems generally to have no regular schemes and premeditated catastrophes. He follows the lead of a free fancy and writes down whatever comes into his mind. He creates his characters, and permits circumstances to guide their conduct. — GRISWOLD, RUFUS WILMOT, 1847-70, *Prose Writers of America, p.* 144.

"Salmagundi" was manifestly written without the fear of criticism before the eyes of the authors, and to this sense of perfect freedom in the exercise of their genius is probably owing the charm and delight with which we still read it. Irving never seemed to place much value on the part he contributed to this work, yet I doubt whether he ever excelled some of those papers in "Salmagundi" which bear the most evident marks of his style; and Paulding, though he has since acquired a reputation by his other writings, can hardly be said to have written anything better than the best of those which are ascribed to his pen.—BRYANT, WILLIAM CULLEN, 1860, *Washington Irving, Orations and Addresses, p.* 110.

"The Backwoodsman" belongs to the old school of poetry, and met with but ordinary success at home, though translations of a portion were published and praised in a literary periodical of the time at Paris. . . . In almost all the writings of Paulding there is occasionally infused a dash of his peculiar vein of humorous satire and keen sarcastic irony. To those not familiarized with his manner, such is the imposing gravity, that it is sometimes somewhat difficult to decide when he is jesting and when he is in earnest. This is on the whole a great disadvantage in an age when irony is seldom resorted to, and has occasionally subjected the author to censure for opinions which he does not sanction. His most prominent characteristic is, however, that of nationality. He found his inspiration at home at a time when American woods and fields, and American traits of society, were generally supposed to furnish little if any materials for originality.—DUYCKINCK, EVERT A. AND GEORGE L., 1865-75, *Cyclopædia of American Literature, ed. Simons, vol.* II, *pp.* 3, 5.

In justice to the talents of the man, it should be observed that he was in no exact sense an author. Early involved in political disquisition, and in the discussion of principles which he considered as being the very foundation stones of our system, he devoted almost the whole of his mature life, that was not absorbed in official routine, to

newspaper writing upon subjects of this nature. His adventures in literature proper were rather the episodes of his intellectual activity than the real labors of his mind. Holding a prolific and facile pen, and working so much for immediate demand, he fell into a hasty and careless style, impatient of correction; and, accordingly, he never found nor made time to do himself justice. Notwithstanding this, throughout all his various productions and in the midst of his most heedless composition, occur passages of description, or little sketches of real or fictitious character or incident, or quaint vistas into the idiosyncrasies of his own mind, which, though dashed off *currente calamo,* are marked by a felicity of diction or originality of view which casts a new light or a novel grace over the most hackneyed subject.—PAULDING, WILLIAM J., 1867, *Literary Life of James K. Paulding, p.* 3.

He does not deserve a long biography, nor elaborate criticism, nor, briefly, remembrance. And in fact he has been very well forgotten. Between 1802, when he began contributing to Peter Irving's *Morning Chronicle,* and 1858, when he wrote some verses which were probably his last literary effort, he produced something like twenty-five volumes, and Griswold says that a complete collection of his more elaborate writings would fill about thirty volumes; but except "Salmagundi," the joint production of himself and Washington Irving, nothing of all this mass of matter is now read by anybody; hardly anybody knows the titles of any two of the volumes, and "Salmagundi" is known to ten persons by its title where it is known to one by its contents.—DENNETT, J. R., 1867, *James Kirke Paulding, The Nation, vol.* 4, *p.* 431.

"The Dutchman's Fireside." This is a genuine, life-like story, full of stirring incidents, of picturesque scenes and striking characters, for which the author's early experiences had furnished the abundant materials. The amiable and whimsical peculiarities of the Dutch settlers, the darker traits of Indian character, and the vicissitudes of frontier life have rarely been more powerfully sketched.—UNDERWOOD, FRANCIS H., 1872, *A Handbook of English Literature, American Authors, p.* 57.

Honest, pathetic Paulding, a rabid miso-Briton who burned to write something truly

American, and couldn't.—LATHROP, GEORGE PARSONS, 1876, *A Study of Hawthorne, p.* 315.

Most of his writings are now forgotten, though they evinced a somewhat strong though coarse vein of humor, which was not without its effect at the period when its local and political allusions and personalities were understood. A scene in one of his novels indicates the kind of comicality in which he excelled. The house of an old reprobate situated on the bank of a river is carried away by a freshet. In the agony of his fear he strives to recall some prayer which he learned when a child; but as he rushes distractedly up and down the stairs of his floating mansion he can only remember the first line of the baby's hymn, "Now I lay me down to sleep," which he incessantly repeats as he runs. — WHIPPLE,

EDWIN PERCY, 1876–86, *American Literature and Other Papers, ed. Whittier, p.* 53.

He united sentiment and humor, paid small heed to art, was vivacious and ephemeral.—HAWTHORNE, JULIAN, AND LEMMON, LEONARD, 1891, *American Literature, p.* 63.

His humour is always boisterous, never chaste and sensitive. Often it is crude and caustic, leaving behind it a rankling wound. The artistic sense, the delicate touch, the tender sympathy which made "Rip Van Winkle" immortal, are too often lacking in "The Dutchman's Fireside," and, in spite of its humor and its pathos, the book is forgotten.—PATTEE, FRED LEWIS, 1896, *A History of American Literature, p.* 128.

Paulding, at his best in "The Dutchman's Fireside," had Irving's glee without his grace.—BATES, KATHARINE LEE, 1897, *American Literature, p.* 292.

Elizabeth Barrett Browning
1806[?]–1861

Born [Elizabeth Barrett Moulton-Barrett], at Coxhoe, co. Durham, 6 March 1806. [Date disputed, but this probably correct]. Early life at Hope End, Herefordshire. Delicate health owing to accident to spine while at Hope End. Poem, "Battle of Marathon," printed for her by her father, 1820. First publication, 1826. At Sidmouth, 1831–33. First contrib. to "Athenæum," 1 July 1837. "Contrib. to Finden's Tableaux," same year. To Torquay for health, 1838; brother drowned there, 11 July 1840. Returned to London, summer of 1841. Married to Robert Browning, 12 Sept. 1846. To Paris and Italy. Settled in Florence, winter of 1847. Son born, 9 March 1849. Visit to Rome, 1850; to England, 1851; winter and spring in Paris; to London summer of 1852; return to Florence in autumn. Winter of 1853–54 in Rome. Visit to Normandy, July 1858. To Rome, winter of 1859–60, and 1860–61. Died, at Florence, 29 June 1861. *Works:* "An Essay on Mind" (anon.), 1826; "Prometheus Bound," 1833; "The Seraphim," 1838; "Poems" (2 vols.), 1844 (reprinted at New York as "A Drama of Exile, etc.," 1845); "The Runaway Slave at Pilgrim's Point," 1849; "Casa Guidi Windows," 1851; "Two Poems: by E. Barrett and R. Browning," 1854; "Aurora Leigh," 1857 [1856]; "Poems before Congress," 1860. *Posthumous:* "Last Poems," 1862; "The Greek Christian Poets and the English Poets," 1863; "Selected Poems," ed. by Robert Browning (2nd series), 1866, 1880; "Letters to R. H. Horne" (2 vols.), 1877 [1876]; "Earlier Poems, 1826–33," 1877 [1878]; "The Battle of Marathon" (in type-facsimile, privately printed), 1891. She *edited:* Chaucer's Works (with R. H. Horne and others), 1841. *Collected Works:* (2 vols.), New York, 1871; London, 1890. *Life:* by J. H. Ingram ("Eminent Women" series), 1888.—SHARP, R. FARQUHARSON, 1897, *A Dictionary of English Authors, p.* 34.

PERSONAL

We are ignorant of her lineage, her education, her tastes, and (last not least, where a lady is concerned) her personal attractions. We know nothing more of her, than can be gathered from her poetry, except the solitary fact, which we have heard on good authority, that her first volume was published when the writer was but seventeen years old; and, as that bears the year

eighteen hundred and twenty-five upon the title-page, a shrewd guess may be given as to her age at the present time.—HILLARD, GEORGE S., 1842, *Recent English Poetry, North American Review, vol.* 55, *p.* 202.

I read without principle. I have a sort of unity indeed, but it amalgamates instead of selecting—do you understand? When I had read the Hebrew Bible, from Genesis to Malachi, right through, and was never stopped by the Chaldee—and the Greek poets, and Plato, right through from end to end—I passed as thoroughly through the flood of all possible and impossible British and foreign novels and romances, with slices of metaphysics laid thick between the sorrows of the multitudinous Celestinas. It is only useful knowledge and the multiplication table I never tried hard at. And now—what now? Is this matter of exultation? Alas, no! Do I boast of my omnivorousness of reading, even apart from the romances? Certainly no!—never, except in joke. It's against my theories and ratiocinations, which take upon themselves to assert that we *all* generally err by *reading too much*, and out of proportion to what we *think*. I should be wiser, I am persuaded, if I had not read half as much— should have had stronger and better exercised faculties, and should stand higher in my own appreciation. The fact is, that the *ne plus ultra* of intellectual indolence is this reading of books. It comes next to what the Americans call "whittling."— BROWNING, ELIZABETH BARRETT, 1843, *Letters of Elizabeth Barrett Browning addressed to Richard Hengist Horne, Dec. 20; Letter lvii.*

Probably no living individual has a more extensive and diffuse acquaintance with literature—that of the present day inclusive—than Miss Barrett. Although she has read Plato, in the original, from beginning to end, and the Hebrew Bible from Genesis to Malachi (nor suffered her course to be stopped by the Chaldean), yet there is not probably a single good romance of the most romantic kind in whose marvellous and impossible scenes she has not delighted, over the fortunes of whose immaculate or incredible heroes and heroines she has not wept; nor a clever novel or fanciful sketch of our own day, over the brightest pages of which she has not smiled inwardly, or laughed outright, just as their authors themselves would have desired.—HORNE, RICHARD HENGIST, 1844, *A New Spirit of the Age.*

My true initials are E. B. M. B.—my long name, as opposed to my short one, being Elizabeth Barrett Moulton Barrett!— there's a full length to take away one's breath!—Christian name. . . Elizabeth Barrett:—surname, Moulton Barrett. So long it is, that to make it portable, I fell into the habit of doubling it up and pack-

ing it closely, . . . and of forgetting that I was a *Moulton*, altogether. One might as well write the alphabet as all four initials. Yet our family name is *Moulton Barrett*, and my brothers reproach me sometimes for sacrificing the governorship of an old town in Norfolk with a little honourable verdigris from the Herald's Office. — BROWNING, ELIZABETH BARRETT, 1845, *Letter to Robert Browning, Dec. 20; Letters of Robert Browning and Elizabeth Barrett, vol. I, p. 343.*

I have also here a poet and a poetess— two celebrities who have run away and married under circumstances peculiarly interesting, and such as render imprudence the height of prudence. Both excellent; but God help them! for I know not how the two poet heads and poet hearts will get on through this prosaic world. I think it possible I may go on to Italy with them.— JAMESON, ANNA, 1846, *Letter from Paris, Sept.; Memoirs. ed. Macpherson, p. 228.*

She is little, hard-featured, with long, dark ringlets, a pale face, and plaintive voice—something very impressive in her dark eyes and her brow. Her general aspect puts me in mind of Mignon—what Mignon might be in maturity and maternity.— COLERIDGE, SARA, 1851, *To Ellis Yarnall, Aug. 28; Memoir and Letters, ed. her Daughter, p. 516.*

My first acquaintance with Elizabeth Barrett commenced about fifteen years ago [1836]. She was certainly one of the most interesting persons that I had ever seen. Everybody who then saw her said the same; so that it is not merely the impression of my partiality or my enthusiasm. Of a slight, delicate figure, with a shower of dark curls falling on either side of a most expressive face, large tender eyes richly fringed by dark eye-lashes, a smile like a sunbeam, and such a look of youthfulness that I had some difficulty in persuading a friend, in whose carriage we went together to Chiswick, that the translatress of the "Prometheus" of Æschylus, the authoress of the "Essays on Mind," was old enough to be in company, in technical language was *out*. Through the kindness of another invaluable friend, . . . I saw much of her during my stay in town. We met so constantly and so familiarly that in spite of the difference of age, intimacy ripened into friendship, and after my return into the country, we corresponded freely and frequently, her letters being just what they

ought to be—her own talk put upon paper.
MITFORD, MARY RUSSELL, 1851, *Recollections of a Literary Life, p.* 170.

Dined at home, and at eight dressed to go to Kenyon. With him I found an interesting person I had never seen before, Mrs. Browning, late Miss Barrett,—not the invalid I expected; she has a handsome oval face, a fine eye, and altogether a pleasing person. She had no opportunity of display, and apparently no desire.—ROBINSON, HENRY CRABB, 1852, *Diary, Oct.* 6; *Diary, Reminiscences and Correspondence,* ed. *Sadler.*

Mrs. Browning is in many respects the correlative of her husband. As he is full of manly power, so she is a type of the most sensitive and delicate womanhood. She has been a great sufferer from ill health, and the marks of pain are stamped upon her person and manner. Her figure is slight, her countenance expressive of genius and sensibility, shaded by a veil of long, brown locks; and her tremulous voice often flutters over her words, like the flame of a dying candle over the wick. I have never seen a human frame which seemed so nearly a transparent veil for a celestial and immortal spirit. She is a soul of fire enclosed in a shell of pearl. Her rare and fine genius needs no setting forth at my hands. She is also, what is not so generally known, a woman of uncommon, nay, profound learning. . . . Nor is she more remarkable for genius and learning, than for sweetness of temper, tenderness of heart, depth of feeling, and purity of spirit. It is a privilege to know such beings singly and separately, but to see their powers quickened, and their happiness rounded, by the sacred tie of marriage, is a cause for peculiar and lasting gratitude. A union so complete as theirs— in which the mind has nothing to crave nor the heart to sigh for—is cordial to behold and soothing to remember.—HILLARD, GEORGE STILLMAN, 1853–55, *Six Months in Italy, p.* 114.

Oh! she is indeed a precious gem! With all her varied and profound learning and high poetic gift, she is as simple and unassuming in manner as a child. What a visit of joy it was to me, in their love-sanctified and art-beautified home. Their union seems perfect in happiness, the mind as well as the heart having met its own affinity. When we parted, after some hours of delightful conversation, wherein the bright and tender nature of Elizabeth Browning shone like soft beams of light, I felt as though years of pleasant acquaintance had passed between us.—LEVERT, OCTAVIA WALTON, 1855, *Souvenirs of Travel, vol.* II, *p.* 229.

The Brownings are long gone back now, and with them one of my delights,—an evening resort where I never felt unhappy. How large a part of the real world, I wonder, are those two small people?—taking meanwhile so little room in any railway carriage, and hardly needing a double bed at the inn. —ROSSETTI, DANTE GABRIEL, 1856, *Letters to William Allingham, p.* 189.

Mr. Milnes introduced me to Mrs. Browning, and assigned her to me to conduct into the breakfast-room. She is a small, delicate woman, with ringlets of dark hair, a pleasant, intelligent, and sensitive face, and a low, agreeable voice. She looks youthful and comely, and is very gentle and ladylike. . . . She is of that quickly appreciative and responsive order of women with whom I can talk more freely than with any man; and she has, besides, her own originality, wherewith to help on conversation, though, I should say, not of a loquacious tendency.—HAWTHORNE, NATHANIEL,1856, *English Note-Books, vol.* II, *pp.* 103, 104.

Mrs. Browning met us at the door of the drawing-room, and greeted us most kindly, —a pale, small person, scarcely embodied at all; at any rate, only substantial enough to put forth her slender fingers to be grasped, and to speak with a shrill, yet sweet, tenuity of voice. Really, I do not see how Mr. Browning can suppose that he has an earthly wife any more than an earthly child; both are of the same elfin race, and will flit away from him some day when he least thinks of it. She is a good and kind fairy, however, and sweetly disposed towards the human race, although only remotely akin to it. It is wonderful to see how small she is, how pale her cheeks, how bright and dark her eyes. There is not such another figure in the world; and her black ringlets cluster down into her neck, and make her face look the whiter by their sable profusion. I could not form any judgment about her age; it may range anywhere within the limits of human life or elfin life. When I met her in London at Lord Houghton's breakfast-table, she did not impress me so singularly; for the morning light is more prosaic than the dim illumination of their great tapestried drawing room; and, besides, sitting next to her, she did not have occasion to raise her voice in speaking, and I was not sensible what a slender voice she has. It is marvellous to me how so extraordinary, so acute, so sensitive a creature can impress us, as she does, with the certainty of her benevolence. It seems to me that there were a million chances to one that she would have been a miracle of acidity and bitterness.—HAWTHORNE, NATHANIEL, 1858, *Passages from the French and Italian Note-Books, June 9; p. 294.*

This noble woman, confined to her sick chamber for years, for the most part confined to her bed by actual illness, nevertheless devoted herself to the unwearied pursuit of truth and excellence, making of her couch of pain the very seed-ground for the highest and noblest thoughts.—SMILES, SAMUEL, 1860, *Brief Biographies, p. 455.*

The main comfort is that she suffered very little pain, none besides that ordinarily attending the simple attacks of cold and cough she was subject to—had no presentiment of the result whatever, and was consequently spared the misery of knowing she was about to leave us: she was smilingly assuring me she was "better," "quite comfortable—if I would but come to bed," to within a few minutes of the last. . . . Through the night she slept heavily and brokenly—that was the bad sign; but then she would sit up, take her medicine, say unrepeatable things to me, and sleep again. At four o'clock there were symptoms that alarmed me; I called the maid and sent for the doctor. She smiled as I proposed to bathe her feet, "Well, you *are* determined to make an exaggerated case of it!" Then came what my heart will keep till I see her again and longer—the most perfect expression of her love to me within my whole knowledge of her. Always smilingly, happily, and with a face like a girl's, and in a few minutes she died in my arms, her head on my cheek. These incidents so sustain me that I tell them to her beloved ones as their right; there was no lingering, nor acute pain, nor consciousness of separation, but God took her to Himself, as you would lift a sleeping child from a dark, uneasy bed into your arms and the light. Thank God! Annunziata thought, by her earnest ways with me, happy and smiling as they were, that she must have been aware of our part-

ing's approach, but she was quite conscious had words at command, and yet did not even speak of Peni, who was in the next room. Her last word was, when I asked, "How do you feel?" "Beautiful."—BROWNING, ROBERT, 1861, *Letter to Miss Haworth, July 20; Life and Letters of Robert Browning, ed. Orr, vol. II, p. 361.*

I praised thee not while living; what to thee
  Was praise of mine? I mourned thee not
    when dead;
  I only loved thee,—love thee! oh thou fled
Fair spirit, free at last where all are free,
I only love thee, bless thee, that to me
  For ever thou hast made the rose more red,
  More sweet each word by olden singers said
In sadness, or by children in their glee.
—GREENWELL, DORA, 1861, *Elizabeth Barrett Browning.*

This day week, at half-past four o'clock in the morning, Mrs. Browning died. . . . Probably there never was a greater instance of the power of genius over the weakness of the flesh. . . . For nearly fifteen years Florence and the Brownings have been *one* in the thoughts of many English and Americans; and Casa Guidi, which has been immortalized by Mrs. Browning's genius, will be as dear to the Anglo-Saxon traveller as Milton's Florentine residence has been heretofore. Those who now pass by Casa Guidi fancy an additional gloom has settled upon the dark face of the old palace, and grieve to think that those windows from which a spirit-face witnessed two Italian revolutions, and those large mysterious rooms where a spirit-hand translated the great Italian Cause into burning verse, and pleaded the rights of humanity in "Aurora Leigh," are hereafter to be the passing homes of the thoughtless or the unsympathizing. Those who have known Casa Guidi as it was could hardly enter the loved rooms now and speak above a whisper. They who have been so favored can never forget the square anteroom, with its great picture and piano-forte, at which the boy Browning passed many an hour,—the little dining-room covered with tapestry, and where hung medallions of Tennyson, Carlyle, and Robert Browning,—the long room filled with plaster casts and studies, which was Mr. Browning's retreat, —and, dearest of all, the large drawing-room, where *she* always sat. It opens upon a balcony filled with plants, and looks out upon the old iron-gray church of Santa Felice. There was something about this room that seemed to make it a proper and especial haunt for poets. The dark shadows and subdued light gave it a dreamy look, which was enhanced by the tapestry-covered walls and the old pictures of saints that looked out sadly from their carved frames of black wood.—FIELD, KATE, 1861, *Elizabeth Barrett Browning, Atlantic Monthly, vol. 8, pp.* 368, 369.

The white-rose garland at her feet,
   The crown of laurel at her head,
Her noble life on earth complete,
   Lay her in the last low bed
For the slumber calm and deep:
   "He giveth His belovéd sleep."
Soldiers find their fittest grave
   In the field whereon they died;
So her spirit pure and brave
   Leaves the clay it glorified
To the land for which she fought
With such grand impassioned thought.
Keats and Shelley sleep at Rome,
   She in well-loved Tuscan earth;
Finding all their death's long home
   Far from their old home of birth.
Italy, you hold in trust
Very sacred English dust.
—THOMSON, JAMES, 1861, *E. B. B.*

Strong-hearted lover of the sore-oppressed!
Thou sleepest now by Arno's wayward stream;
And in that sleep perchance thy life's fond dream
Of comfort for the suffering haunts thy rest;
Still wouldst thou grasp lone children to thy breast,
Still wouldst thou make earth's blessings richly teem
For those who want, nor judge things as they seem,
Nor choose the path of riches, for the best.
Through a sad life of duty nobly done
Rose the rich music of thy Poet-voice
For struggling childhood. Sleep serenely now,
The fight is o'er! the victory is won!
Through pain and tears, the saddest hearts rejoice
To weave the eternal laurel for thy brow!
—ROSSLYN, EARL, 1861, *Mrs. E. Barrett Browning.*

A life of suffering ended in peace. A frail body, bearing the burden of too great a brain, broke at last under the weight. After six days' illness, the shadows of night fell upon her eyes for the last time, and half an hour after daybreak she beheld the Eternal Vision. Like the pilgrim in the dream, she saw the heavenly glory before passing through the gate. "It is beautiful," she exclaimed, and died; sealing these last words upon her lips as the fittest inscription that could ever be written upon her

life, her genius, and her memory. In the English burial-ground at Florence lie her ashes.—TILTON, THEODORE, 1862, *Last Poems of Mrs. Browning, Memorial Preface.*

She was slight and fragile in appearance, with a pale, wasted face, shaded by masses of soft chestnut curls which fell on her cheeks, and serious eyes of bluish-gray. Her frame seemed to be altogether disproportionate to her soul. This, at least, was the first impression: her personality, frail as it appeared, soon exercised its power and it seemed a natural thing that she should have written the "Cry of the Children" or the "Lady Geraldine's Courtship." I also understood how these two poets, so different both intellectually and physically, should have found their complements in each other. The fortunate balance of their reciprocal qualities makes them an exception to the rule that the intermarriage of authors is unadvisable.—TAYLOR, BAYARD, 1862, *Home and Abroad, Second Series, p.* 414.

O lyric Love, half-angel and half-bird
And all a wonder and a wild desire,—
Boldest of hearts that ever braved the sun,
Took sanctuary within the holier blue,
And sang a kindred soul out to his face,—
Yet human at the red-ripe of the heart—
When the first summons from the darkling earth
Reached thee amid thy chambers, blanched their blue,
And bared them of the glory—to drop down,
To toil for man, to suffer or to die,—
This is the same voice: can thy soul know change?
Hail then, and hearken from the realms of help!
Never may I commence my song, my due
To God who best taught song by gift of thee,
Except with bent head and beseeching hand—
That still, despite the distance and the dark,
What was, again may be; some interchange
Of grace, some splendour once thy very thought,
Some benediction anciently thy smile:
—Never conclude, but raising hand and head
Thither where eyes, that cannot reach, yet yearn
For all hope, all sustainment, all reward,
Their utmost up and on,—so blessing back
In those thy realms of help, that heaven thy home,
Some whiteness which, I judge, thy face makes proud,
Some wanness where, I think, thy foot may fall!
—BROWNING, ROBERT, 1869, *The Ring and the Book,* v. 1391–1416.

A more timid nature was never joined to a bolder spirit than in Elizabeth Browning. She fairly shrunk from observation, and could not endure mixed company, though in her heart kind and sympathetic with all. Her timidity was both instinctive and acquired; having been an invalid and student from her youth up, she had lived almost the life of a recluse; thus it shocked her to be brought face to face with inquisitive strangers, or the world in general.—KINNEY, ELIZABETH C., 1870, *A Day With the Brownings at Pratolino, Scribner's Monthly, vol.* 1, *p.* 186.

I have never seen one more nobly simple, more entirely guiltless of the feminine propensity of talking for effect, more earnest in assertion, more gentle yet pertinacious in difference, than she was. Like all whose early nurture has chiefly been from books, she had a child's curiosity regarding the life beyond her books, co-existing with opinions accepted as certainties concerning things of which (even with the intuition of genius) she could know little. She was at once forbearing and dogmatic, willing to accept differences, resolute to admit no argument; without any more practical knowledge of social life than a nun might have, when after long years, she emerged from her cloister and her shroud.—CHORLEY, HENRY FOTHERGILL, 1873, *Autobiography, Memoirs and Letters, vol.* II, *p.* 35.

The monument of Mrs. Browning, though beautiful in design, is painfully suggestive of an unstable equilibrium. It consists of a sarcophagus of white marble of mediæval form, supported by six composite columns resting upon an ornamental base, the whole protected by a stone border surmounted by an iron rail. One end of the sarcophagus is decorated with a lyre in bass-relief, while on one side is a medallion of the poetess, with the simple inscription,

E. B. B. OB. 1861.

—SPENCER, O. M., 1873, *The Protestant Cemetery at Florence, Harper's Magazine, vol.* 47, *p.* 511.

It curiously happens that I first met Mrs. Browning at Rome in 1859, where and when Hawthorne also first made her acquaintance, I believe. I remember going through the Vatican with him, and the then ex-President Pierce, during my sojourn in Rome, in the spring of that year. Though we both saw Mrs. Browning last in that year, my impressions are very distinct that her hair was a dark-chestnut. It did not curl naturally; but, by one of those artifices of the toilet which all of her sex and some of mine understand, it was worn, as it has usually been painted, in side ringlets. Hawthorne's constitutional propensity to take sombre views of things may account for the liberty he seems to have taken with Mrs. Browning's hair.—BIGELOW, JOHN, 1882, *The Critic, vol.* 2, *p.* 254.

Those among us who only know Mrs. Browning as a wife and as a mother have found it difficult to realise her life under any other conditions, so vivid and complete is the image of her peaceful home, of its fireside where the logs are burning, and the mistress established on her sofa, with her little boy curled up by her side, the door opening and shutting meanwhile to the quick step of the master of the house, and to the life of the world without, coming to find her in her quiet corner. We can recall the slight figure in its black silk dress, the writing apparatus by the sofa, the tiny inkstand, the quill-nibbed pen-holder, the unpretentious implements of her work. "She was a little woman; she liked little things." Her miniature editions of the classics are still carefully preserved, with her name written in each in her sensitive fine handwriting, and always her husband's name added above her own, for she dedicated all her books to him: it was a fancy that she had.—RITCHIE, ANNIE THACKERAY, 1886, *Dictionary of National Biography, vol.* VII, *p.* 79.

The date and place of Mrs. Browning's birth have been variously stated. For some years biographers wavered between London and Hope End, Herefordshire, as her natal place. Quite recently Mrs. Richmond Ritchie, authorized by Mr. Browning, declared Burn Hall, Durham, the place, and March 6, 1809, the date of Mrs. Browning's birth. My researches have enabled me to disprove these statements. In "The Tyne Mercury," for March 14, 1809, is announced for March 4, "In London, the wife of Edward M. Barrett, Esq., of a daughter." Having published my data, their accuracy was challenged by Mr. Browning, who now asserted that his wife was "born on March 6, 1806, at Carlton Hall, Durham, the residence of her father's brother." Carlton Hall was not in Durham, but in Yorkshire, and, I am authoritatively informed, did not become the residence of Mr. S. Moulton

Barrett until some time after 1810. Mr. Browning's latest suggestions cannot, therefore, be accepted.—INGRAM, JOHN H., 1888, *Elizabeth Barrett Browning, p.* 263.

I saw the flat stone which covers the grave of Landor; I passed the monument of Arthur Hugh Clough; I read the names of Hiram Powers and Theodore Parker; and finally I came to the tomb of Mrs. Browning. Handfuls of lilies of the valley had been strewed between the low columns that support the sarcophagus, either early that hot morning or late the day before, for they were wilted with the sun. On seeing these evidences of affection to the poetess I wondered to myself whether it were possible nowadays to read her poetry; and, with this in my mind, stopped at a bookshop and bought a volume of selections from her poems. Yes, they could indeed be read, often with pleasure and sometimes with surprise.—SCHUYLER, EUGENE, 1888–1901, *Mrs. Browning, Italian Influences, p.* 189.

That my visits to Casa Guidi were valued by me as choice morsels of my existence, is to say not half enough. I was conscious even then of coming away from those visits a better man, with higher views and aims. And pray, reader, understand that any such effect was not produced by any talk or look or word of the nature of preaching, or anything approaching to it, but simply by the perception and appreciation of what Elizabeth Barrett Browning was; of the immaculate purity of every thought that passed through her pellucid mind, and the indefeasible nobility of her every idea, sentiment, and opinion.—TROLLOPE, THOS. ADOLPHUS, 1888, *What I Remember, p.* 392.

No intelligible, certainly no reasonably consistent, account of the early life of the writer of these books has yet reached us. Delicate from her birth, and always an invalid, she is represented as suffering from a mysterious malady, which may or may not have been caused by a fall from her horse, which she herself appears to have forgotten, or from a cough which she remembered. Some declare that she was confined to her room for years, unable in fact, to leave her bed for months at a time. Others state that during this period she was occasionally met in society. She was always lying at death's door, and always writing letters and poems.—STODDARD, RICHARD HENRY, 1891, *A Box of Autographs, Scribner's Magazine, vol.* 9, *p.* 221.

Of Mrs. Browning I never saw much. Sundry visits we paid to each other missed, and when I did find her at home in Casa Guidi we did not fall on congenial themes. I was bubbling over with enthusiasm for her poetry, but had not the audacity to express my admiration (which, in truth, had been my special reason for visiting Florence), and she entangled me in erudite discussions about Tuscan and Bolognese schools of painting, concerning which I knew little and, perhaps, cared less. But I am glad I looked into the splendid eyes which *lived* like coals, in her pain-worn face, and revealed the soul which Robert Browning trusted to meet again on the threshold of eternity. Was there ever such a testimony as their *perfect* marriage—living on as it did in the survivor's heart for a quarter of a century—to the possibility of the eternal union of Genius and Love?—COBBE, FRANCES POWER, 1894, *Life by Herself, vol.* II, *p.* 344.

I knew but little of his wife; she died comparatively early. I never saw her in society, but at her own fireside she struck me as very pleasing and exceedingly sympathetic. Her physique was peculiar: curls like the pendent ears of a water-spaniel, and poor little hands—so thin that when she welcomed you she gave you something like the foot of a young bird; the Hand that made her great had not made her fair. But she had striking eyes, and we forgot any physical shortcomings—they were entirely lost sight of in what I may call her incomparable sweetness, I might almost say affectionateness; just as, while we are reading it, we lose sight of the incompleteness of her poetry—its lack of artistic control. She vanquishes by her genius and her charm.—LOCKER-LAMPSON, FREDERICK, 1895, *My Confidences, p.* 157.

How often M. Milsand has told me of his charming conversations with this exquisite woman, whose shining superiority was always concealing itself under her unconscious goodness and lovely simplicity. Neither Mrs. Sutherland Orr nor Miss Thackeray had yet written about her, and everything was new to me that he told me of this life, so imprisoned in suffering and only free in thought, until the day when so kind and robust a *génie* had come to break the bonds, and carry her in his arms through the years that lay before them.—BENTZON, TH. (MME. BLANC), 1896, *A French Friend of Browning, Scribner's Magazine, vol.* 20, *p.* 112.

It was on June 29, 1861,that Mrs. Browning died. She was buried at Florence, where her body rests in a sarcophagus designed by her friend and her husband's friend, Frederic Leighton, the future President of the Royal Academy. At a later date, when her husband was laid to rest in Westminster Abbey, her remains might have been transferred to England, to lie with his among the great company of English poets in which they had earned their places. But it was thought better, on the whole, to leave them undisturbed in the land and in the city which she had loved so well, and which had been her home so long. In life and in death she had been made welcome in Florence. The Italians, as her husband said, seemed to have understood her by an instinct; and upon the walls of Casa Guidi is a marble slab, placed there by the municipality of Florence, and bearing an inscription from the pen of the Italian poet, Tommaseo:—

Qui scrisse e mori
ELISABETTA BARRETT BROWNING
che in cuore di donna conciliava
scienza di dotto e spirito di poeta
e fece del suo verso aureo anello
fra italia e inghilterra.
pone questa lapide
firenze grata
1861.

—KENYON, FREDERIC G., 1897, *ed., The Letters of Elizabeth Barrett Browning, vol.* II, *p.* 452.

A DRAMA OF EXILE
1844

We rank the "Drama of Exile" among the least successful of her efforts. Although the poem for which she has professed the most partiality, we think it will scarcely gain the acceptation in any quarter for which her preface eloquently but humbly pleads. While fullest of her peculiar faults, it has the fewest of her surpassing beauties. She writes with sincerity, and as sincerely as she writes do we believe that in no one reader will it produce the impression she desires;—less as she tells us for her own fame than for their spiritual progress. We regret the misadventure of so excellent an intent,—but the public are too much indebted to the rich bounteousness of her genius in other poems to justify a single reproach for incompleteness or failure.—ADAMS, S. F., 1844, *Poems by Elizabeth Barrett, Westminster Review, vol.* 42, *p.* 382.

In the plot of the drama of Miss Barrett it is something even worse than incongruity which affronts: a continuous mystical strain of ill-fitting and exaggerated allegory—if, indeed, allegory is not much too respectable a term for it.—POE, EDGAR ALLAN, 1845, *Miss Barrett's "A Drama of Exile," Works,* ed. *Stedman and Woodberry, vol.* VI, *p.* 295.

Cannot hesitate to rank her, in vigour and nobleness of conception, depth of spiritual experience, and command of classic allusion, above any female writer the world has yet known. . . . She has the imagination all compact—the healthy archetypal plant from which all forms may be divined, and, so far as now existent, understood. Like Milton, she sees the angelic hosts in real presence; like Dante, she hears the spheral concords and shares the planetary motions. But she cannot, like Milton, marshal the angels so near the earth as to impart the presence other than by sympathy. He who is near her level of mind may, through the magnetic sympathy, see the angels with her. Others will feel only the grandeur and sweetness she expresses in these forms. Still less can she, like Dante, give, by a touch, the key which enables ourselves to play on the same instrument. She is singularly deficient in the power of compression. There are always far more words and verses than are needed to convey the meaning, and it is a great proof of her strength, that the thought still seems strong, when arrayed in a form so Briarean, clumsy and many-handed.—OSSOLI, MARGARET FULLER, 1845-50, *Miss Barrett's Poems, Art, Literature, and the Drama, pp.* 198, 200.

The intellect displayed in this noble production is stupendous. The conception is massive: the treatment of the prominent idea truly consistent and powerful: the pathos such as only a woman could have written: and the moral tone of the work most lofty and pure. But, in spite of all these excellencies, the poem often fatigues us. It keeps the mind too much on the stretch; requires an unceasing exercise of our deepest thoughts; and while we never fail at last to see the extreme beauty of the writer's ideas, we grow tired in studying them.—ROWTON, FREDERICK, 1848, *The Female Poets of Great Britain, p.* 502.

As a whole, the poem is strained, extravagant, and unequal to its theme. . . . The "Drama of Exile" contains many noble passages. Some of its conceptions give evidence of great originality and power. But passages in a poem written upon such a subject, which excite a reader's laughter by their extravagance, are fatal to its claims to be considered a great work of the imagination. Homer sometimes nods, but he never rants. It has been the unanimous voice of criticism, and cannot fail to be the opinion of every candid and intelligent reader, that in the "Drama of Exile" Mrs. Browning very often and very laughably rants.—HINCKS, EDWARD·Y., 1868, *Elizabeth Barrett Browning, Eminent Women of the Age, p. 231.*

Her chief work, "A Drama of Exile," is a vision in lyrical dramatic form, a mystery, in which man's loss of the ideals of his youth is beautifully typified by Adam and Eve's expulsion from paradise. Eve is a figure of truly ethereal loveliness.—SCHERR, J., 1874, *A History of English Literature, tr. M. V., p. 267.*

In the "Drama of Exile" she aimed at the highest, and failed; but such failures are impossible to smaller poets. It contains wonderfully fine passages; is a chaotic mass, from which dazzling lustres break out so frequently that a critic aptly spoke of the "flashes" of her "wild and magnificent genius," the "number and close propinquity of which render her book one flame."—STEDMAN, EDMUND CLARENCE, 1875-87, *Victorian Poets, p. 128.*

Notwithstanding a few fine passages, "A Drama of Exile" cannot be considered a successful effort. The scheme of the poetess was imperfectly developed, and many of the colloquies of Adam and Eve, and of Lucifer and Gabriel, are forced and unnatural. The lyrics interspersed throughout the poem are often harsh and unmusical, and the whole drama is deficient in action and interest.—CHAMBERS, ROBERT, 1876, *Cyclopœdia of English Literature, ed. Carruthers.*

The theme of the "Drama of Exile" is so daring, and the execution, despite innumerable faults, so excellent, that either condemnation or praise is hard to award. The great defect in what the poetess intended should be her masterpiece is that, notwithstanding the introduction of Adam and Eve, and the self-sacrificing love of the latter for her partner in sorrow, it is almost entirely devoid of human interest. Admiration is frequently compelled by bursts of true lyrical beauty; but the heart never throbs with hope nor thrills with terror for the poetic phantasmata whose weeping and wailing fill so many pages of the drama. There are, it is true, some magnificent passages of poetry in the work, notably Lucifer's description of the effect of the curse upon animal creation.—INGRAM, JOHN H., 1888, *Elizabeth Barrett Browning, p.* 115.

LADY GERALDINE'S COURTSHIP
1844

"Lady Geraldine's Courtship," as a transcript from the "red-leaved tablets of the heart"—as a tale of love, set to the richest music—as a picture of the subtle workings, the stern reasonings, and the terrible bursts of passion—is above praise. How like a volcano does the poet's heart at length explode! How first all power is given him in the dreadful trance of silence, and then in the loosened tempest of speech! What a wild, fierce logic flows forth from his lips, in which, as in that of Lear's madness, the foundations of society seem to quiver like reeds, and every mount of conventionalism is no longer found; and in the lull of that tempest, and in the returning sunshine, how beautiful, how almost superhuman, seem the figures of the two lovers, seen now and magnified through the mist of the reader's fast flowing tears. It is a tale of successful love, and yet it melts you like a tragedy, and most melts you in the crisis of the triumph. On Geraldine we had gazed as on a star, with dry-eyed and distant admiration; but when that star dissolves in showers at the feet of her poet lover, we weep for very joy. Truly a tear is a sad yet beautiful thing; it constitutes a link connecting us with distant countries, nay, connecting us with distant worlds.—GILFILLAN, GEORGE, 1847, *Female Authors, Tait's Magazine, vol.* 14, *p.* 623.

With the exception of Tennyson's "Locksley Hall," I have never read a poem combining so much of the fiercest passion with so much·of the most delicate imagination, as the "Lady Geraldine's Courtship" of Miss Barrett. I am forced to admit, however, that the latter work *is* a palpable imitation of the former, which it surpasses in thesis, as much as it falls below it in a certain calm energy, lustrous and indomitable —such as we might imagine in a broad river of molten gold.—POE, EDGAR ALLAN, 1849, *A Chapter of Suggestions, Works, ed. Stedman and Woodberry, vol.* VIII, *p.* 343.

It is impetuous and passionate, and the action is carried forward with immense vehemence. . . . Probably the most characteristic specimen of Mrs. Browning's peculiar powers and genius.—SMILES, SAMUEL, 1860, *Brief Biographies, p.* 459.

"Lady Geraldine's Courtship" was the ballad, which gained her a sudden repute among lay-readers. It is said that she composed it in twelve hours, and not improbably; for, although full of melodious sentiment and dainty lines, the poem is marred by common places of frequent occurrence. Many have classed it with "Locksley Hall," but, while certain stanzas are equal to Tennyson's best, it is far from displaying the completeness of that enduring lyric. I value it chiefly as an illustration of the greater freedom and elegance to which her poetic faculty had now attained, and as her first open avowal, and a brave one in England, of the democracy which generous and gifted spirits, the round world over, are wont to confess. As for her story, she only succeeds in showing how meanly a womanish fellow might act, when enamored of one above him in social station, and that the heart of a man possessed of healthy self-respect was something she had not yet found out.— STEDMAN, EDMUND CLARENCE, 1875–87, *Victorian Poets, p.* 130.

If Mrs. Browning's intelligent readers were asked to name her most characteristic poem, they would probably fix upon "Lady Geraldine's Courtship." The choice would lie between that and "The Duchess May." The finest wine of her genius, the intensest elixir of her poetic sympathy, the very essence of her womanly pride, and not less of her womanly ecstasy of self surrendering humility, as well as her most original imagery, puissant thought, and splendid language, are present in both poems. I should not, for my own part, undertake to say which of the two is the more characteristic; but I should pronounce it impossible for any one to have a right insight into these two without possessing a fairly accurate idea of the distinctive character of her genius. . . . "Lady Geraldine's Courtship" is steeped in melody,—the language, the imagery, the sentiment, the thought, all instinct with music, floating and flowing and rippling along in an element of liquid harmony and modulated brilliance.— BAYNE, PETER, 1881, *Two Great Englishwomen, pp.* 60, 71.

THE CRY OF THE CHILDREN
1844

Full of a nervous, unflinching energy—a horror sublime in its simplicity—of which a far greater than Dante might have been proud. . . . In some cases it is nearly impossible to determine what metre is intended. "The Cry of the Children" cannot be scanned: we *never saw* so poor a specimen of verse.—POE, EDGAR ALLAN, 1845, *Miss Barrett's "A Drama of Exile," Works,* ed. Stedman and Woodberry, vol. VI, pp. 302, 312.

Will always form a worthy companionpiece to Hood's "Song of the Shirt," losing nothing by the comparison. It is full of a thrilling energy of thought, clothed in simple, nervous language.—SMILES, SAMUEL, 1860, *Brief Biographies, p.* 459.

The poetry of Mrs. Browning is not only that of the poet's inspiration, but it has the influence of exquisite and extended culture. Her genius was that of the highest order— the spiritualisation of intellect. She is the first woman who has expressed the pathos of struggling and repressed life in poetry, as Millet has expressed it in painting. She felt, as did Hood, that the lover's song, and even that the intimations of nature, are less appealing than the grinding toil that submerges the uncomforted poor. To her was given the task to arouse England and the modern world, indeed, to a sense of the child suffering in factory life. Her poem "The Cry of the Children" appeared almost simultaneously with Lord Shaftesbury's great speech in Parliament on child labour. The poem and eloquence together aroused England, nor has the echo lessened with the years.—WHITING, LILIAN, 1896, *Elizabeth Barrett Browning, The Bookman, vol.* 3, *p.* 38.

CASA GUIDI WINDOWS
1851

I have lately read again with great delight Mrs. Browning's 'Casa Guidi Windows." It contains, amongst other admirable things, a very noble expression of what I believe to be the true relation of the religious mind to the past.—ELIOT, GEORGE, 1862, *Journal, Feb.* 17; *George Eliot's Life as Related in her Letters and Journals,* ed. *Cross, vol.* II, *p.* 243.

This poem exhibits Mrs. Browning in her greatest intellectual strength. The fabric is solid and enduring; the poem as sustained as anything which she has written, and more perfect than her remaining longer one. Clearly her feeling was in this work as well as her imagination, and the combined powers have given us something which cannot fail to live.—SMITH, GEORGE BARNETT, 1875, *Elizabeth Barrett Browning, Poets and Novelists, p.* 95.

AURORA LEIGH
1856

The most successful book of the season has been Mrs. Browning's "Aurora Leigh." I could wish some things altered, I confess; but as it is, it is by far (a hundred times over) the finest poem ever written by a woman. We know little or nothing of Sappho—nothing to induce comparison—and all other wearers of petticoats must courtesy to the ground.—PROCTER, BRYAN WALLER, 1856, *Letter to James T. Fields, "Barry Cornwall" and Some of His Friends, Harper's Magazine, vol.* 52, *p.* 63.

Yet with all my knowledge I have felt something like a bug ever since reading "Aurora Leigh." Oh, the wonder of it! and oh, the bore of writing about it.—ROSSETTI, DANTE GABRIEL, 1856, *Letters to William Allingham, p.* 189.

I am greatly delighted with Mrs. Browning's "Aurora Leigh." It is full of strong things, and brilliant things, and beautiful things. And how glad I am to see modern literature tending so much toward the breaking down of social distinctions!—CHILD, LYDIA MARIA, 1856, *To Mrs. S. B. Shaw, Dec.* 8; *Letters of L. M. Child, p.* 87.

Although . . . Mrs. Browning's "Aurora Leigh" is her finest work, there are many among her admirers whom her earlier poems will still move the most deeply. Comparatively few can follow, with full sympathy, her entire course. Perhaps most of those whose spiritual life has actually begun, stand yet upon the stage of sorrow and longing. While such gaze with admiration on the shining path of their poet, they will yet feel the deepest sympathy with her, as she is still walking among the shadows, and cheering them with her songs. It appears to us, also, that the "Aurora Leigh" is not to be reckoned among the works destined for immortality. The universal element in it is too much mingled with the peculiarities of our time, to admit of its becoming naturalized in another age. This need not, however, lessen our enjoyment of it; as we should not find the blossom of the century-plant less beautiful for the thought that the entire age had been needed for its production, and that it yet would wither, very shortly, before our eyes.—EVERETT, CHARLES CARROLL, 1857, *Elizabeth Barrett Browning, North American Review, vol.* 85, *p.* 441.

It is a unique, wonderful and immortal poem; astonishing for its combination of masculine power with feminine tenderness; for its novelty, its facility, its incessant abundance of thought, and expression; its being an exponent of its age, and a prophetic teacher of it, its easy yet lofty triumph over every species of common place; and its noble and sweet avowal, after all, of a participation of error; its lovely willingness to be no loftier, or less earthly, than something on an equality with love.—HUNT, LEIGH, 1857, *Letter to Robert Browning, Jan.* 1; *Cornhill Magazine, vol.* 76, *p.* 739.

I am reading a poem full of thought and fascinating with fancy: Mrs. Browning's "Aurora Leigh." In many pages, and particularly 126 and 127, there is the wild imagination of Shakespeare. I have not yet read much farther. I had no idea that any one in this age was capable of so much poetry. I am half drunk with it. Never did I think I should have a good hearty draught of poetry again; the distemper had got into the vineyard that produced it. Here are indeed, even here, some flies upon the surface, as there always will be upon what is sweet and strong. I know not yet what the story is. Few possess the power of construction.—LANDOR, WALTER SAVAGE, 1857, *Letter to John Forster, Walter Savage Landor, a Biography by John Forster, bk.* ii, *note.*

We are reading "Aurora Leigh" for the third time, with more enjoyment than ever. I know no book that gives me a deeper sense of communion with a large as well as beautiful mind.—ELIOT, GEORGE, 1857, *To Sara Hennell, June* 8; *George Eliot's Life as Related in her Letters and Journals, ed. Cross, vol.* I, *p.* 331.

With here and there a pure strain of sentiment, a genuine touch of nature, the effect of the whole is unpleasant with the faults of the worst school of modern poetry,—the physically intense school, as I should be inclined to call it, of which Mrs. Browning's "Aurora Leigh" is the worst example, whose muse is a *fast* young woman with the lavish ornament and somewhat overpowering perfume of the demi-monde, and which pushes expression to the last gasp of sensuous exhaustion. --LOWELL, JAMES RUSSELL, 1866-90, *Swinburne's Tragedies, Prose Works, Riverside Ed., vol.* II, *p.* 122.

An extraordinary work, which is also a masterpiece; I repeat that space fails me in order that I may state, after having perused it twenty times, how beautiful I consider it to be. It contains the confession of a generous, heroic, and impassioned spirit, one superabounding in genius, of which the culture has been complete, of a philosopher and a poet dwelling amid the loftiest ideas, and surpassing the elevation of her ideas by the nobility of her instincts, wholly modern by her education, by her high-mindedness, by her daring, by the perpetual vibration of her strained sensibility, wound up to such a pitch that the slightest touch awakens in her a vast orchestra and a most wonderful symphony of concords. It is all soul, and the inward monologue, the sublime song of a young girl's and artist's great heart, attracted and irritated by an enthusiasm and a pride as strong as her own; the sustained contrast of the masculine and feminine utterance, which, amid the outbursts and the variations on the same theme, continually become separated and opposed in greater measure, till at last, suddenly combining, they unite in a prolonged, mournful and exquisite duo, of which the strain is so lofty and so penetrating as to be wholly unsurpassable.— TAINE, H. A., 1872, *Notes on England, tr. Rae, p.* 344.

An audacious, speculative freedom pervades it, which smacks of the New World rather than the Old. . . . As a poem, merely, it is a failure, if it be fair to judge it by accepted standards.—STEDMAN, EDMUND CLARENCE, 1875-87, *Victorian Poets, p.* 141.

Our own view of it is that, as a whole, it is somewhat inconsequent; it lacks unity, for a poem of such magnitude; but even in these higher respects, though not perfect, it is little beneath anything produced by this generation. When we come to regard it in other aspects, however, our praise is almost necessarily unbounded. It is a poem which we could imagine Shakspeare dropping a tear over for its humanity.—SMITH, GEORGE BARNETT, 1875, *Elizabeth Barrett Browning, Poets and Novelists, p.* 103.

What is "Aurora Leigh," by the greatest poetess of our century, if not all time, but one long and carefully elaborated lesson of life?--HOLLAND, J. G., 1876, *Every-Day Topics, First Series, p.* 55.

I cannot state with equal precision what book contributed to the formation of my views on the Woman question. On one side of it, Professor Stuart's "New Abolitionists," describing Mrs. Butler's crusade against the Police des Mœurs, had a great influence. On the other, that of equality and justice, I can hardly say. Mill on the Subjection of Woman had, I think, much less influence than Mrs. Browning's "Aurora Leigh."—STEAD, W. T., 1887, *Books Which Have Influenced Me, p.* 35.

It probes to the bottom, but with a hand guided by purity and justice, those social problems which lie at the root of what are known as women's questions. Her intense feeling that the honour of manhood can never be reached while the honour of womanhood is sullied; her no less profound conviction that people can never be raised to a higher level by mere material prosperity, make this book one of the most precious in our language. She herself speaks of it in the dedication as "The most mature of my works, and the one into which my highest convictions upon Life and Art have entered." If she had written nothing else, she would stand out as one of the epoch-making poets of the present century.— FAWCETT, MILLICENT GARRETT, 1889, *Some Eminent Women of our Times, p.* 115.

Mrs. Barrett Browning, who, with all her weaknesses of style, towers above all women-poets of the first half of the Victorian Era, has eloquently written upon the stunting effects of ordinary life upon women in "Aurora Leigh," that wonderful book, so strong and at the same time so full of blemishes.—SHARP, ELIZABETH A., 1890, *Women Poets of the Victorian Era, Preface, p.* xxx.

Concerning "Aurora Leigh" there will always be differences of opinion and feeling, for it exhibits the poet's weakness not less manifestly than her strength. Its form is defective, its inspiration intermittent, its style unequal; it is greater in parts than as a whole; but if we regard its finest details of description and characterisation, if we weigh the nuggets of imaginative thought which we turn over on nearly every page, we may fairly pronounce it, with all its faults, one of the fullest and most opulent poems produced in this century by any English poet.—NOBLE, JAMES ASHCROFT, 1892, *The Poets and the Poetry of the Century, Joanna Baillie to Mathilde Blind, ed. Miles, p.* 163.

The most complete monument perhaps of her genius. The remarkable thing in this work is its energy and strong poetical vitality, the rush and spring of life which is in a narrative, often lengthy, and of which the subject and the story are not sufficient for the fervour and power of utterance. . . . There are really admirable pieces of description and bursts of feeling in this poem, but it is throughout a little rhetorical, and its great quality is, as we have said, the remarkable sustained energy and vitality of the long volume of verse.—OLIPHANT, MARGARET O. W., 1892, *The Victorian Age of English Literature, pp.* 232, 233.

It is a difficult volume to work through. It is the kind of book that one begins to read for the first time with intense enjoyment, congratulating oneself after the first hundred pages that there are still three-hundred to come. Then the mood gradually changes; it becomes difficult to read without a marker; and at last it goes back to the shelf with the marker about three-fourths of the way through.—BENSON, ARTHUR CHRISTOPHER, 1896, *Essays, p.* 227.

I was sixteen, and I read "Aurora Leigh." A grown person may smile—but, no; no gentle-minded man or woman smiles at the dream of a girl. What has life to offer that is nobler in enthusiasm, more delicate, more ardent, more true to the unseen and the unsaid realities which govern our souls, or leave us sadder forever because they do not? There may be greater poems in our language than "Aurora Leigh," but it was many years before it was possible for me to suppose it; and none that ever saw the hospitality of fame could have done for that girl what that poem did at that time. I had never a good memory—but I think I could have repeated a large portion of it; and know that I often stood the test of haphazard examinations on the poem from half-scoffing friends, sometimes of the masculine persuasion. Each to his own; and what Shakespeare or the Latin Fathers might have done for some other impressionable girl, Mrs. Browning—forever bless her strong and gentle name!—did for me.—PHELPS, ELIZABETH STUART, 1896, *Chapters from a Life, p.* 65.

Mrs. Browning herself considered "Aurora Leigh," published in 1856, the most mature of her works, and the one into which her highest convictions upon Life and Art had entered. Her view was supported by its great popularity with the general public, but the critics have been more discriminating in their praise. They have been ready to acknowledge the abundance of poetical material, the moments of high suggestion, the many beautiful passages which this poem contains, but they have also pointed out its want of method, its ignorance of real life, its numerous digressions and frequent lapses into prose. Neither the situations nor the characters are dramatically conceived or well delineated.—GRAHAM, RICHARD D., 1897, *Masters of Victorian Literature, p.* 325.

The piercing and terrible pathos of the story is as incomparable and as irresistible as the divine expression of womanly and motherly rapture which seems to suffuse and imbue the very page, the very print, with the radiance and the fragrance of babyhood. There never was, and there never will be, such another baby in type as that. Other poets, even of the inferior sex, have paid immortal tribute to the immortal Godhead incarnate in the mortal and transitory presence of infancy; the homage of one or two among them, a Homer or a Hugo, may have been worthy to be mistaken for a mother's; but here is a mother's indeed; and "the yearlong creature" so divinely described must live in sight of all her readers as long as human nature or as English poetry survives. No words can ever be adequate to give thanks for such a gift as this.—SWINBURNE, ALGERNON CHARLES, 1898, *ed. Aurora Leigh, p.* 277, *note.*

Even her dear faults as an artist are those of a woman, and not such as surely befall to the woman who fails to write out of the depths of her womanly consciousness and experience. What these faults are, the author of "Aurora Leigh" knows full well; and knows, also, that the woman-artist shall not escape them even by the knowing of them! It has, of late years, been urged that this poem, by reason of its length, transcends the good reader's patience. I do not agree with this lazy consensus.—THOMAS, EDITH M., 1900, *Elizabeth Barrett Browning, The Critic, vol.* 37, *p.* 516.

SONNETS

I am disposed to consider the "Sonnets from the Portuguese" as, if not the finest, a portion of the finest subjective poetry in our literature. Their form reminds us of an English prototype, and it is no sacrilege to say that their music is showered from a higher and purer atmosphere than that of the Swan of Avon. . . . The most exquisite poetry hitherto written by a woman, and of themselves justify us in pronouncing their author the greatest of her sex,—on the ground that the highest mission of a female poet is the expression of love, and that no other woman approaching her in genius has essayed the ultimate form of that expression.—STEDMAN, EDMUND CLARENCE, 1875-87, *Victorian Poets, pp.* 137, 138.

It is we imagine, almost universally accepted that to write the sonnet excellently is about the most difficult performance in the domain of poetry. At any rate, it is the one branch of the art least frequently successfully achieved. It is questionable whether we have more than three or four English poets who can be credited with the highest execution in this respect. But to these three or four must be added the name of Mrs. Browning. After Shakspeare, we should be inclined to maintain that she is the equal of any.—SMITH, GEORGE BARNETT, 1875, *Elizabeth Barrett Browning, Poets and Novelists, p.* 97.

Of these far more truly than of Shakspeare's "Sonnets" may it be affirmed that "each is an autobiographical confession." —MAIN, DAVID M., 1879, *ed., A Treasury of English Sonnets, p.* 441, *note.*

The poems which, from what may be called a technical point of view, may be counted irreproachable, may, if we except the Sonnets, almost be reckoned on the fingers. Her sonnets are among the very best work she has produced. Perhaps indeed her greatest poetic success is to be found in the "Sonnets from the Portuguese,"—sonnets, it need hardly be said, which are not "from the Portuguese" at all, but are the faintly disguised presentment of the writer's most intimate experience. Into the "sonnet's narrow room" she has poured the full flood of her profoundest thought, and yet the minuteness and exquisiteness of the mould has at the same time compelled a rigorous pruning alike of superabundant imagery and of harmonious verbosity, which has had the happiest results. She is one of the greatest sonnet writers in our language, worthy for this at all events to be ranked side by side with Milton and with Wordsworth.—

ARNOLD, WILLIAM T., 1880, *The English Poets, ed. Ward, vol.* IV, *p.* 566.

Most dear and memorable of all those nightingale melodies, those resonant heart-throbs wrought into a divine music, those ecstasies of love and grief and high aspiration, which have been left as an immortal legacy by Elizabeth Barrett Browning.— NOBLE, JAMES ASHCROFT, 1880-92, *The Sonnet in England, p.* 4.

The last half of the third century of the English sonnet need not detain us, for, amid the multitude of singers who have illustrated it, I find but one who seems to me to rank with the great masters of this species of composition,—Mrs. Browning.—STODDARD, RICHARD HENRY, 1881, *The Sonnet in English Poetry, Scribner's Monthly, vol.* 22, *p.* 921.

There is a quality in them which is beyond words; an echo from afar which belongs to the highest human expression of feeling.—RITCHIE, ANNIE THACKERAY, 1886, *Dictionary of National Biography, vol.* VII, *p.* 79.

No more impassioned soul ever found expression in rhythmical speech than Elizabeth Barrett Browning, and there is nothing in her poetry which is finer than that famous love-record, the so-called "Sonnets from the Portuguese." Impetuous as was her genius, hasty and frequently careless as was she in production, she never found the archetypal sonnet too circumscribed for her. The pathetic beauty, the fascinating personality, the pure poetry displayed in these sonnets, have touched many and many a heart since the tired singer was laid to rest under the cypresses not far from that beloved river whose flow she had so often followed in thought down the far-off Pisan sea. Only those who have thoroughly studied contemporary poetry, and not only the poetry which is familiar to many but that also which is quite unknown, and by minor writers of no reputation or likelihood of reputation, can realise the potency of Mrs. Browning's influence, especially among women.—SHARP, WILLIAM, 1886, *Sonnets of this Century, Introduction, p.* lxx.

It was in the "Sonnets from the Portuguese" that the first living soul was breathed into Mrs. Browning's poetry. Sonnets they are not, for they err against all the canons; but they are passionate expressions of love, and a few lines will show their drift. . . .

And love, whether timid or ardent, gave Mrs. Browning an insight to her husband's character which, it may be doubted, his biographers would not express as strongly.—SCHUYLER, EUGENE, 1888-1901, *Mrs. Browning, Italian Influences, pp.* 195, 196.

> Sweet poet! sweetest lover! unto thee
> The great world bows in fond idolatry,
> Holding thy love most sacred, thee most dear
> Of all its poet-lovers; for so free,
> So passion-pure a love without a fear,
> Ne'er mingled with such rare humility.
> —CROSS, ALLEN EASTMAN, 1889, *Sonnets from the Portuguese, Poet Lore, April.*

These "Sonnets" reach the highest poetic tide of her genius—the modest *abandon* of a heart overflowing with tenderness, and that surprise of delight as of the primal creation, which the true poet finds in each new thing that meets his sight and experience, but still more strongly in what was almost, in this particular case, a resurrection from the dead.—OLIPHANT, MARGARET O. W., 1892, *The Victorian Age of English Literature, p.* 231.

In these sonnets (which it is hardly necessary to say are not translations) she speaks the universal language; to her other graces had now been added that which she had somewhat lacked before, the grace of content; and for these probably she will be longest and most gratefully admired. Any one who steps for the first time through the door into which he has seen so many enter, and finds that poets and lovers and married folk, in their well-worn commonplaces, have exaggerated nothing, will love these sonnets as one of the sweetest and most natural records of a thing which will never lose its absorbing fascination for humanity. To those that are without, except for the sustained melody of expression, the poetess almost seems to have passed on to a lower level, to have lost originality—like the celebrated lady whose friends said that till she wrote to announce her engagement she had never written a commonplace letter.—BENSON, ARTHUR CHRISTOPHER, 1896, *Essays, p.* 213.

LETTERS

Her letters make Cowper's poor. In a hurried note, whose hurry is evident in the handwriting, she drops . . . incidental, but brilliant words—just as if the jewels in her rings, jarred by her rapid fingers, had been suddenly unset and fallen out on the paper. No other handwriting is like hers; it is strong, legible, singularly un-English and more like a man's than a woman's.—TILTON, THEODORE, 1862, *Last Poems of Mrs. Browning, Memorial Preface.*

Her letters ought to be published. In power, versatility, liveliness, and *finesse;* in perfect originality of glance, and vigour of grasp at every topic of the hour; in their enthusiastic preferences, prejudices, and inconsistencies, I have never met with any, written by men or by women, more brilliant, spontaneous, and characteristic.—CHORLEY, HENRY FOTHERGILL, 1873, *Autobiography, Memoirs and Letters, vol.* II, *p.* 33.

The spiritual strength of Miss Barrett's letters, combined with modest self estimate, and temporary forgetfulness of her dangerous state of health, which they evince, renders them unique. The struggle, not only for emancipation from solitude but for life itself, during which they were written, gives them psychological as well as literary value in the key they supply to her mind as expressed in her powers.—MAYER, S. R. TOWNSEND, 1876, *ed., Letters of Elizabeth Barrett addressed to Richard Hengist Horne, Prefatory Note, vol.* I, *p.* vi.

Mrs. Browning as a letter writer is disappointing; again and again there is a touch of true feeling, a noble thought, but with all this there is a want of incisiveness, a wearisome seriousness, which of all qualities is the one that ought not to obtrude itself, a strange lack of humour, a certain strain—a *scraping* of the soul, as Turgenief has it.—BENSON, ARTHUR CHRISTOPHER, 1896, *Essays, p.* 208.

These letters, familiarly written to her private friends, without the smallest idea of publication, treating of the thoughts that came uppermost in the ordinary language of conversation, can lay no claim to make a new revelation of her genius. On the other hand, perhaps because the circumstances of Mrs. Browning's life cut her off to an unusual extent from personal intercourse with her friends, and threw her back upon letter writing as her principal means of communication with them, they contain an unusually full revelation of her character. And this is not wholly unconnected with her literary genius, since her personal convictions, her moral character, entered more fully than is often the case into the composition of her poetry.—KENYON, FREDERIC G., 1897, *ed., The Letters of Elizabeth Barrett Browning, Preface, vol.* I, *p.* x.

GENERAL

A young lady then, whom to miss were a
    caret
In any verse-history, named, I think, Barrett,
(I took her at first for a sister of Tennyson)
Knelt, and receiv'd the god's kindliest benison.
—"Truly," said he, "dost thou share the blest
    power
Poetic, the fragrance as well as the flower;
The gift of conveying impressions unseen,
And making the vaguest thoughts know what
    they mean."
—HUNT, LEIGH, 1837, *Blue-Stocking Revels.*

The principal poem in this volume is an
"Essay on Mind," occupying some ninety
pages. Viewing this as the production of a
young lady of sixteen or seventeen, it is a
remarkable, nay, extraordinary performance, to which the records of early genius
can furnish very few parallels. It is a
metaphysical and reflective poem, showing
uncommon power of patient and discriminating thought, a wide range of reading, and
a ripe judgment. The versification is easy
and vigorous. It blends together, in a
very happy combination, the forms of
philosophic thought and the vivid hues of
poetical fancy. It is especially remarkable
for its freedom from any of those morbid
elements, which are so apt to be attendant
upon precocity of genius, especially in
women. There is no exaggeration of personal feeling, no overwrought sensibility, no
extravagance of thought and expression,
and no sickly melancholy. It seems to be
written by one whose mind had been
healthy and naturally developed, and whose
symmetry had not been impaired by rapid
growth.—HILLARD, GEORGE S., 1842, *Recent English Poetry, North American Review, vol.* 55, p. 202.

Poetry has been as serious a thing to me
as life itself; and life has been a very serious
thing; there has been no playing at skittles
for me either. I never mistook pleasure
for the final cause of poetry; nor leisure,
for the hour of the poet. I have done my
work, so far, as work,—not as mere hand
and head work, apart from the personal being,—but as the completest expression of
that being to which I could attain,—and as
work I offer it to the public,—feeling its
shortcomings more deeply than any of
my readers, because measured from the
height of my aspiration,—but feeling also
that the reverence and sincerity with which
the work was done should give it some protection with the reverent and sincere.—

BROWNING, ELIZABETH BARRETT, 1844,
Poems, Preface, p. xiv.

Probably the greatest female poet that
England has ever produced, and one of the
most unreadable, is Elizabeth B. Barrett.
In the works of no woman have we ever observed so much grandeur of imagination,
disguised, as it is, in an elaborately infelicitous style. She has a large heart and a
large brain; but many of her thoughts are
hooded eagles. That a woman of such
varied acquirements, of so much delicacy of
sentiment and depth of feeling, of so much
holiness and elevation of thought, possessing, too, an imagination of such shaping
power and piercing vision, should not consent always to write English, should often
consent to manufacture a barbarous jargon
compounded of all languages, is a public
calamity. "The Cry of the Human" to her,
is, "Be more intelligible." . . . A number
of her poems are absolutely good for nothing, from their harshness and obscurity of
language. Her mind has taken its tone and
character from the study of Æschylus,
Milton, and the Hebrew poets; and she is
more familiar with them than with the
world. Vast and vague imaginations, excited by such high communion, float duskily
before her mind, and she mutters mysteriously of their majestic presence; but she
does not always run them into intelligible
form.—WHIPPLE, EDWIN PERCY, 1845,
*English Poets of the Nineteenth Century,
Essays and Reviews, vol.* I, p. 345.

That Miss Barrett has done more, in
poetry, than any woman, living or dead,
will scarcely be questioned:—that she has
surpassed all her poetical contemporaries of
either sex (with a single exception) is our
deliberate opinion—not idly entertained,
we think, nor founded on any visionary
basis.—POE, EDGAR ALLAN, 1845, *Miss Barrett's "A Drama of Exile," Works, ed. Stedman and Woodberry, vol.* VI, p. 316.

Among my holiday gifts was Miss Barrett's poems. She is a woman of vigorous
thought, but not very poetical thought, and
throwing herself into verse involuntarily becomes honied and ornate, so that her verse
cloys. It is not natural, quite. . . . Burrill
did not see why I called Miss Barrett purple.
It was because her highly colored robe was
not harmonious with her native style of
thought.—CURTIS, GEORGE WILLIAM, 1845,
To Dwight, Jan. 12; *Early Letters to John S.
Dwight, p.* 200.

In selecting Mrs. Hemans as our first specimen of Female Authors, we did so avowedly, because she seemed to us the most feminine writer of the day. We now select Mrs. Browning for the opposite reason, that she is, or at least is said by many to be, the most masculine of our female writers. . . . To say that Mrs. Browning has more of the man than any female writer of the period, may appear rather an equivocal compliment; and its truth even may be questioned. We may, however, be permitted to say, that she has more of the *heroine* than her compeers. Hers is a high heroic nature, which adopts for the motto at once of its life and of its poetry, "Perfect through suffering." . . . To do Mrs. Browning justice, she has not complained of neglect nor of injury at all. But she has acknowledged herself inspired by the genius of suffering. And this seems to have exerted divers influences upon her poetry. It has, in the first place, taught her to rear for herself a spot of transcendental retreat, a city of refuge in the clouds. Scared away from her own heart, she has soared upwards, and found a rest elsewhere. To those flights of idealism in which she indulges, to those distant and daring themes which she selects, she is urged less, we think, through native tendency of mind, than to fill the vast vacuity of a sick and craving spirit.— GILFILLAN, GEORGE, 1847, *Female Authors, Tait's Magazine, vol.* 14, *pp.* 620, 621.

The most imaginative poetess that has appeared in England, perhaps in Europe, and who will attain to great eminence if the fineness of her vein can but outgrow a certain morbidity, reminds her readers of the peculiarities of contemporary genius. She is like an ultra-sensitive sister of Alfred Tennyson.—HUNT, LEIGH, 1847, *British Poetesses; Men, Women, and Books, vol.* II, *p.* 96.

The poems of this lady are marked with strength of beauty and beauty of strength. She is deeply read, being familiar with the original of the great ancients (the Greek dramatists having been her particular study), and with the more attractive of the Christian fathers. Her translation of the untranslatable "Prometheus Bound" of Æschylus received high praise as a worthy attempt; and her various writings show that she has drunk true inspiration from the fountain to which she has so often resorted with the graceful vase of her natural genius. Miss Barrett is singularly bold and adventurous. Her wing carries her, without faltering at their obscurity, into the cloud and the mist, where not seldom we fail to follow her, but are tempted, while we admire the honesty of her enthusiasm, to believe that she utters what she herself has but dimly perceived. Much of this, however, arises from her disdain of carefulness. Her lines are often rude, her rhymes forced, from impatience rather than affectation; and for the same reason, she falls into the kindred fault of verboseness, which is always obscure. She forgets the advice which Aspasia gave a young poet, "to sow with the hand, and not with the bag." Her Greek studies should have taught her more sculptor-like finish and dignity; but the glowing, generous impulses of her woman's heart are too much for the discipline of the classics. Hence it is that we like her less as a scholar than as a woman; for then she compels our sympathy with her high religious faith, her love of children, her delight in the graceful, and beautiful, her revelations of feminine feeling, her sorrow over the suffering, and her indignation against the oppressor.—BETHUNE, GEORGE WASHINGTON, 1848, *The British Female Poets, p.* 452.

I think it may be said that she is chief amongst the learned poetesses of our land: at least, I know of no British female writer who exhibits so intimate an acquaintance with the *spirit* of both antique and modern philosophy, or so refined a perception of intellectual purity and beauty. Her poetry is the poetry of pure reason.—ROWTON, FREDERIC, 1848, *The Female Poets of Great Britain, p.* 500.

She has more poetic genius than any other woman living—perhaps more than any other woman ever showed before, except Sappho. Still there is an imperfectness in what she produces; in many passages the expressions are very faulty, the images forced and untrue, the sentiments exaggerated, and the situations unnatural and unpleasant. Another pervading fault of Mrs. Browning's poetry is rugged, harsh versification, with imperfect rhymes, and altogether that want of art in the department of metre which prevents the language from being an unobstructive medium for thought.—COLERIDGE, SARA, 1851, *To Ellis Yarnall, Aug.* 28; *Memoir and Letters, ed. her Daughter, p.* 516.

Gifted with a fine and peculiar genius, what Mrs. Browning might have achieved, or may yet achieve, by concentration of thought and rejection of unworthy materials, it is impossible to say; but most assuredly she has hitherto marred the effect of much she has written by a careless self-satisfaction. Instead of being a comet that "from its horrid hair shakes pestilence and war," she might have been, and I trust is destined yet to be, a constellation to twinkle for ever in silver beauty amid the blue serene.—MOIR, D. M., 1851-52, *Sketches of the Poetical Literature of the Past Half-Century, Lecture* vi.

My moon of poets!—BROWNING, ROBERT, 1855, *One Word More.*

Her poems were to me, in my sick-room, marvellously beautiful: and, now that from the atmosphere of the sick-room, my life has been transferred to the free open air of real, practical existence, I still think her poetry wonderfully beautiful in its way, while wishing that she was more familiar with the external realities which are needed to balance her ideal conceptions. —MARTINEAU, HARRIET, 1855-77, *Autobiography,* ed. Chapman, vol. I, p. 315.

What a treasure-house of thought that woman is! Some of the boxes are locked, and you must turn the key with a will; but when you *have* opened, you are rich for life. —BROOKS, CHARLES WILLIAM SHIRLEY, 1860, *The Gordian Knot.*

Mrs. Browning's Death is rather a relief to me, I must say: no more Aurora Leighs, thank God! A woman of real Genius, I know: but what is the upshot of it all? She and her Sex had better mind the Kitchen and their Children; and perhaps the Poor: except in such things as little Novels, they only devote themselves to what Men do much better, leaving that which Men do worse or not at all.—FITZGERALD, EDWARD, 1861, *To W. H. Thompson, July 15; Letters and Literary Remains,* ed. Wright, vol. I, p. 280.

The long study of her sick-bed (and her constant chafing against the common estimate of the talents and genius of her sex) overcharged her works with allusions and thoughts relating to books, and made her style rugged with pedantry. She was often intoxicated, too, with her own vehemence. "Aurora Leigh" sets out determined to walk the world with the great Shakespearian stride, whence desperate entanglement of feminine draperies and blinding swirls of dust. The sonnets entitled "From the Portuguese" reveal better her inmost simple nature.—THOMSON, JAMES ("B. V."), 1864, *The Poems of William Blake, Biographical and Critical Sketches,* p. 267.

Mrs. Browning's works are distinguished by their intellectuality and their freedom from that weak sentimentalism which is too often the fault of female writers, as well as by their lively interest in the great questions of the age in which she lived, which made her an enthusiastic, rather than a wise partisan, and not always on the right side. Like Browning, she paid too little attention to form and finish; and many of her poems, especially of later years, seem intentionally strained in language and rugged in versification. In depth of thought, however, she is perhaps unequalled among English female poets.—JOHNSTON, RICHARD MALCOLM, AND BROWNE, WILLIAM HAND, 1872, *English Literature,* p. 382.

She, at any rate, has demonstrated what emotional poetry really means, in contradistinction to the poetry of simple art; and it cannot be said, either, that she has altogether come short in the matter of design —the design which stamps the greatest poets. Sensibility and intuition, those endowments of supereminent importance to individuals whose greatness is to grow in proportion to their understanding and interpretation of human life, were in her united in a degree seldom witnessed.— SMITH, GEORGE BARNETT, 1875, *Elizabeth Barrett Browning, Poets and Novelists,* p. 66.

Her *taste* never seemed quite developed, but through life subordinate to her excess of feeling. So noble, however, was the latter quality, that the critics gave her poetry their attention, and endeavoured to correct its faults of style. For a time she showed a lack of the genuine artist's reverence, and not without egotism followed her wilful way. The difficulty with her obsolete words was that they were introduced unnaturally, and produced a grotesque effect instead of an attractive quaintness. Moreover, her slovenly elisions, indiscriminate mixture of old and new verbal inflections, eccentric rhymes, forced accents, wearisome repetition of favored words to a degree that almost implied poverty of thought,—such matters justly were held to be an outrage upon the beauty and dignity of metrical art.—STEDMAN, EDMUND CLARENCE, 1875-87, *Victorian Poets, p.* 126.

The highest place among our modern poetesses must be claimed for Mrs. Browning, formerly Miss Barrett. In purity and loftiness of sentiment and feeling, and in intellectual power, she is excelled only by Tennyson, whose best works, it is evident, she had carefully studied. Her earlier style reminds us more of Shelley, but this arises from similarity of genius and classical tastes, not imitation.—CHAMBERS, ROBERT, 1876, *Cyclopædia of English Literature, ed. Carruthers.*

Leigh Hunt called her the "Sister of Tennyson," and another writer, more daringly, the "Daughter of Shakespeare." I think she was worthy of that high parentage.—STODDARD, RICHARD HENRY, 1877, *ed. Letters of Elizabeth Barrett Browning Addressed to Richard Hengist Horne, Memoir, p.* xxxvii.

The best English poetess.—MORLEY, HENRY, 1879, *A Manual of English Literature, ed. Tyler, p.* 648.

Her rhymes are often illegitimate, her words are often far-fetched, and occasionally even ungrammatical. The splendid dash and energy with which she throws herself at a difficult piece of work should not blind us to the fact that after all its difficulties are sometimes evaded rather than met.—ARNOLD, WILLIAM T., 1880, *The English Poets, ed. Ward, vol.* IV, *p.* 564.

Apparently poured off hastily, without any attempt at correction or curtailment, her poems contain many flaws—faults of language, and faults of thought, but they also show genuine lyric impetuosity, true pathos, and unfailing freshness and force.—NICOLL, HENRY J., 1882, *Landmarks of English Literature, p.* 408.

Her poetry as a whole is an uneven production, full of prosaic episodes, with much that is forced and unnatural, a chaos from which rare lustres break out.—WELSH, ALFRED H., 1883, *Development of English Literature, vol.* II, *p.* 369.

The notes of Mrs. Browning's poetry are emotion, purity, pathos, intense earnestness, sympathy with every form of suffering, with everything great and good, hatred of everything evil, specially of all oppression. Her want of humour, a few rough and careless rhymes, and occasional forcing of sense and phrase, have made some critics

of word and style complain; but students may rely on it, that to know Mrs. Browning as she reveals herself in her works is a liberal education, and to enter into her spirit one of the most ennobling pursuits that a man can undertake.—FURNIVALL, FREDERICK JAMES, 1887, *Celebrities of the Century, p.* 181.

Mrs. Browning will probably be longest remembered by her incomparable sonnets and by her lyrics, which are full of pathos and passion. Perhaps her two finest poems in this kind are the "Cry of the Children" and "Cowper's Grave." All her poems show an enormous power of eloquent, penetrating, and picturesque language; and many of them are melodious with a rich and wonderful music.—MEIKLEJOHN, J. M. D., 1887, *The English Language: Its Grammar, History and Literature, p.* 358.

Apart from Dante and Shakspeare, it would be difficult to meet with so great a condensation of thought, such abridged yet complete characterization, as is frequently met with in this marvellous poem; and yet, all things considered, it is not perhaps very strange that the "Vision of Poets" has failed to elicit the applause of critics, and indeed to find that many of them have refrained from speaking of it at all. In the whole range of literature it would be difficult to parallel, in prose or verse, such concise yet descriptive portraiture as the poem contains.—INGRAM, JOHN H., 1888, *Elizabeth Barrett Browning, p.* 117.

Mrs. Browning's poetry awakened in me the very greatest and deepest interest from the time of her first introduction to the American public as Elizabeth Barrett. That her educational influence over me was as great as that of Wordsworth I should not like to assert, but her emotional was certainly greater. She was eminently the religious, the Christian poet, and so she sounded every depth of feeling. She had learned in suffering what she taught in song, and so she won our sympathy. She was a woman, feminine in all her tastes and feelings, but masculine in the breadth of her attainments and the strength of her intellect.—PITMAN, ROBERT C., 1888, *Books that Have Helped Me, The Forum, vol.* 4, *p.* 607.

If ever any poet stood in the white light of the beauty which we call poetry, it was Mrs. Browning. Her thoughts were as fire

and her words were as fire.—EGAN, MAU-
RICE FRANCIS, 1889, *Lectures on English
Literature, p.* 135.

Mrs. Browning, in her studies of Greek
Dramatists, displayed nothing less than a
genius for form, so that her first and most
unstudied utterances were always her best.
—HUNT, THEODORE W., 1890, *Studies in
Literature and Style, p.* 54.

The stifling air of the sick-chamber is
oppressive in these writings of hers—writings wherein the strength of her mind is
seen engaged in a life and death struggle
with the weakness of her body, where she
is always ambitious and straining after
effect, where her language, though forcible,
is violent, and her imagination, never well
in hand, runs riot.—STODDARD, RICHARD
HENRY, 1891, *A Box of Autographs, Scribner's Magazine, vol.* 9, *p.* 221.

Mrs. Browning, with all her noble idealism and her profound sense of responsibility, was most depressingly indifferent about
form, and was quite a law to herself in the
matter of rhymes. — REPPLIER, AGNES,
1891, *Points of View, p.* 38.

Her success, it must be admitted, grows
every day more dubious. Where she strove
to be passionate she was too often hysterical; a sort of scream spoils the effect of all
her full tirades. She remains readable
mainly where she is exquisite, and one
small volume would suffice to contain her
probable bequest to posterity.—GOSSE, ED-
MUND, 1893, *Christina Rossetti, The Century, vol.* 46, *p.* 211.

Many of her poems are weighted with a
dragging moral; many of them fly with a
broken wing, stopping and rising again, dispersing and returning with a kind of pur-
poseless persistency, as if they were incapable of deciding where to have done.
Poems with passage after passage of extraordinary depth of thought and amazing
felicity of expression, every now and then
droop and crawl like the rain on a November day, which will not fall in a drenching
shower nor quite desist, but keeps dropping,
dropping from the sky out of mere weakness or idleness.—BENSON, ARTHUR CHRIS-
TOPHER, 1896, *Essays, p.* 219.

In the spirituality of life that characterised Elizabeth Barrett Browning, genius
assumes its highest form and it is in this
spiritualisation of human life that Mrs.
Browning is seen apart from all other great

modern poets. In her expression she has
embodied a potency of influence which the
world is only beginning to recognise and
estimate aright. Among women poets she
easily stands supreme, and there are passages in her work which surpass anything
that has been given to the world since
Shakespeare. Nor is this assertion a mere
trick of phrasing that should shrink abashed
before so lofty a presence. It is but a single
expression of truth.—WHITING, LILIAN,
1896, *Elizabeth Barrett Browning, The Bookman, vol.* 3, *p.* 35.

The poetesses of the world form a company so small that the retrospective eye is
hardly arrested till it reaches the shadowy
and fragmentary Sappho; and to vote a
niche to Elizabeth Barrett Browning in so
nearly empty a temple may seem but a
doubtful honour. . . . The technical defects
of her verse are numerous and occasionally
flagrant, and her literary taste was far from
irreproachable; but she had a passionate
sense of beauty in all its forms, and she
sounds at her best moments a note of thrilling and poignant pathos which not many
poets of her own or any time have matched.
—TRAILL, HENRY DUFF, 1897, *Social England, vol.* VI, *p.* 277.

She who was so profoundly acquainted
with the life of her day, who understood
and pitied its miseries and misfortunes, this
most distinguished artist who longs to join
a Faculty of Arts in promoting the welfare
of humanity, knew also how to frame
stanzas of a limpid confidence in which her
most intimate emotions are revealed. No
one can read certain poems of Mrs. Browning without perceiving in them that peculiar
and tender frankness of which only a
woman's heart is capable. — MOLMENTI,
POMPEO, 1898, *Elizabeth Barrett Browning,
Living Age, vol.* 219, *p.* 39.

Mrs. Browning's technique is uncertain,
and she never freed herself from her characteristic faults of vagueness and unre-
straint. But her sympathy with noble
causes, the elevation and ardor of her
moods of personal emotion, and the distinction of her utterances at its best, out-
balance these negative considerations. She
shares her husband's strenuousness and
optimism, but she speaks always from the
feminine vantage-ground.—MOODY, WILL-
IAM VAUGHN, AND LOVETT, ROBERT MORSS,
1902, *A History of English Literature,
p.* 332.

Arthur Hugh Clough

1819–1861

Arthur Hugh Clough was born in Liverpool, England, January 1, 1819. When a small boy he accompanied his father on a business visit to the United States. In 1828 he was sent to Rugby, where he soon excelled in scholarship and was a leading contributor to the "Rugby Magazine." From Rugby he went to Oxford, where he gained a scholarship at Balliol, and afterward a fellowship at Oriel. While at Oxford he wrote a long poem entitled "The Bothie of Tober-na-Vuolich," which was published in 1848. Clough gave up his fellowship in 1848, and travelled in France and Italy. On his return he was appointed principal of University Hall, and professor of English literature, in University College, London. In 1852 he resigned this chair, crossed the Atlantic, and became a private tutor in Cambridge, Massachusetts. In 1853 he returned to England to accept a place in the Education department of the Privy Council, married, and settled in London, devoting himself for several years to the hard work of his office, and giving his leisure hours to a revision of Dryden's translation of Plutarch, which was published in 1859. In 1861 his health gave way, and he went to travel on the Continent; but he died at Florence, Italy, November 13, and was buried there. His "Amours de Voyage," a story in verse, was published in the "Atlantic Monthly" in 1858. His collected poems, with a memoir by Charles Eliot Norton, were published in Boston in 1862, and his complete works, with a life by his widow, in London, in 1869.—JOHNSON, ROSSITER, 1875, *Little Classics, Authors,* p. 56.

PERSONAL

Here was a man who loved truth and justice, not coldly and afar off, as most, but with passion and intensely; . . . who walked the world's way as matter of duty, living a life, meanwhile, hidden with higher and holier things. . . . Plainer living and higher thinking were the texts on which he gave us many a humorous and admirable lesson. . . . His influence was always towards whatever should incline others to a liberal view of the questions of the day, of the claims of the feeble, and the feelings of the poor.—PALGRAVE, FRANCIS TURNER, 1847, *Letter, Journals and Memories of his Life, ed. Palgrave,* p. 31.

People seem very fond of Arthur, and to think a great deal of him; but Arthur does not seem to mind much about people here; they don't seem to suit him exactly, and he gets wearied and worn out with the continual talking about religious matters; and I think, too, the pomp and grandeur trouble him. He does not appear at all to fancy coming to live in London.—CLOUGH, ANNE JEMIMA, 1849, *Journal, Memoir, ed. Blanche Athena Clough,* p. 73.

Clough came in the afternoon. I like him exceedingly; with his gentleness, and his bewildered look, and his half-closed eyes.—LONGFELLOW, HENRY WADSWORTH, 1852, *Journal, Dec.* 30; *Life, ed. Longfellow, vol.* II, p. 230.

I was glad to see Clough here, with whom I had established some kind of robust work-

ing-friendship, and who had some great permanent values for me. Had he not taken me by surprise and fled in a night, I should have done what I could to block his way. I am too sure he will not return. The first months comprise all the shocks of disappointment that are likely to disgust a newcomer. The sphere of opportunity opens slowly, but to a man of his abilities and culture—rare enough here—with the sureness of chemistry. The Giraffe entering Paris wore the label, "Eh bien, messieurs, il n'y a qu'une bête de plus!" And Oxonians are cheap in London; but here, the eternal economy of sending things where they are wanted makes a commanding claim. Do not suffer him to relapse into London. He had made himself already cordially welcome to many good people, and would have soon made his own place. He had just established his valise at my house, and was to come—the gay deceiver—once a fortnight for his Sunday; and his individualities and his nationalities are alike valuable to me.—EMERSON, RALPH WALDO, 1853, *To Carlyle, Aug.* 10; *Correspondence of Carlyle and Emerson, ed. Norton, vol.* II, p. 257a.

That is a loss which I shall feel more and more as time goes on, for he is one of the few people who ever made a deep impression upon me, and as time goes on, and one finds no one else who makes such an impression, one's feeling about those who did make it gets to be something more and more distinct and unique. Besides, the object of it no longer survives to wear it out himself by becoming ordinary and different from what he was. People were beginning to say about Clough that he never would do anything now, and, in short, to pass him over. I foresee that there will now be a change, and attention will be fixed on what there was of extraordinary promise and interest in him when young, and of unique and imposing even as he grew older without fulfilling people's expectations.—ARNOLD,MATTHEW, 1861, *To His Mother, Nov.* 20; *Letters, ed. Russell, vol.* I, *p.* 176.

A man of very shy demeanour, of largish build about the head and shoulders, with a bland and rather indolent look, and a noticeable want of alertness in his movements—such, to a stranger meeting him casually, appeared that Arthur Hugh Clough, of whom, till his death the other day at the age of forty-two, all those who knew him intimately were wont to speak in terms of such unusually high regard. Many persons to whom the name of Clough was only beginning to be adequately known when a premature death removed him will now take up with interest the beautiful little volume in which his "Poems" are first collected, and in which they are introduced by a brief "Memoir" from the pen of his friend, Mr. F. T. Palgrave.—MASSON, DAVID, 1862, *The Poems of Arthur Hugh Clough, Macmillan's Magazine, vol.* 6, *p.* 318.

It irk'd him to be here, he could not rest.
He loved each simple joy the country yields,
He loved his mates; but yet he could not keep,
For that a shadow lower'd on the fields,
Here with the shepherds and the silly sheep.
Some life of men unblest
He knew, which made him droop, and filled his
head.
He went; his piping took a troubled sound
Of storms that rage outside our happy ground;
He could not wait their passing, he is dead.
—ARNOLD, MATTHEW, 1866, *Thyrsis.*

Clough was five feet ten in height, well made, inclining to burliness; he had a handsome frank face, dark-eyed, full-chinned and ruddy complexioned, the nose being straight and rather short; his head, which was early bald, ran deep from front to back, and showed a graceful domed outline. In manner he was quiet, grave, and reticent; usually speaking little, by no means from want of sympathy, but in part, we should say, from a wish both to hear and reply with gravity and exactness, and also from a feeling of instinct of personal dignity

and refinement which belonged to him in high degree. He carefully avoided all risk of intrusion, either on his own part or his interlocutor's, and kept in constant check every merely impulsive movement. It is probable that a more than commonly sensitive temperament was controlled and calmed into this habitual quietude of demeanour, which was not at all of the drowsy or thick-skinned sort, but living and palpitating. It would have been hard to find a readier friend, in little matters or great.— ALLINGHAM, WILLIAM, 1866, *Arthur Hugh Clough, Fraser's Magazine, vol.* 74, *p.* 535.

He lies buried in the little Protestant cemetery, just outside the walls of Florence, looking towards Fiesole and the hills which he loved and which he had gazed on as he entered Florence, little thinking he should leave it no more. "Tall cypresses wave over the graves, and the beautiful hills keep guard around"; nowhere could there be a lovelier resting-place. The memory of Arthur Clough will be safe in the hearts of his friends. Few beyond his friends have known him at all; his writings may not reach beyond a small circle; but those who have received his image into their hearts know that something has been given them which no time can take away, and to them we think no words will seem fitter than those of the poet, happily also his friend, which have cherished the memory of another beautiful soul:—

So, dearest, now thy brows are cold,
We see thee as thou art, and know
Thy likeness to the wise below,
Thy kindred with the great of old.
—CLOUGH, MRS. ARTHUR HUGH, 1869, *ed. Prose Remains of Arthur Hugh Clough, p.* 55.

He our passing guest,
Shy nature, too, and stung with life's unrest,
Whom we too briefly had but could not hold,
Who brought ripe Oxford's culture to our board,
    The Past's incalculable hoard,
Mellowed by scutcheoned panes in cloisters old,
Seclusions ivy-hushed, and pavements sweet
With immemorial lisp of musing feet;
Young head, time-tonsured smoother than a
        friar's,
Boy face, but grave with answerless desires,
Poet in all that poets have of best.
—LOWELL, JAMES RUSSELL, 1874, *Agassiz, Heartsease and Rue.*

He had a beautiful, spiritual face and delicate, shy manners; such a face and such manners as are dimly seen in morning dreams. One may be sure that such a rare being, if real flesh and blood, would at some time be found at Elmwood.—UNDERWOOD, FRANCIS H., 1881, *James Russell Lowell, A Biographical Sketch, p.* 159.

Of Clough Carlyle had formed the very highest opinion, as no one who knew him could fail to do. His pure beautiful character, his genial humour, his perfect truthfulness, alike of heart and intellect—an integrity which had lead him to sacrifice a distinguished position and brilliant prospects, and had brought him to London to gather a living as he could from under the hoofs of the horses in the streets—these together had recommended Clough to Carlyle as a diamond sifted out of the general rubbish-heap.—FROUDE, JAMES ANTHONY, 1884, *ed. Thomas Carlyle, A History of his Life in London, vol.* I, *p.* 390.

The memory of Clough remains, with those who had the happiness of knowing him in life, distinct and precious. It is that of one of the highest and purest souls. Sensitive, simple, tender, manly, his figure stands as one of the ideal figures of the past, the image of the true poet, the true friend, the true man. He died too young for his full fame, but not too young for the love which is better than fame. — NORTON, CHARLES ELIOT, 1897, *Library of the World's Best Literature, ed. Warner, vol.* VII, *p.* 3828.

Apart from the gifts of imagination and mental analysis, Clough was of a noble, pure, and self-controlling nature. His friends felt certain that the temptations to excess which assail young men, at Universities and elsewhere, had by him been resolutely and victoriously resisted. His clear black eyes, under a broad, full, and lofty forehead, were often partly closed, as if through the pressure of thought; but when the problem occupying him was solved, a glorious flash would break from the eyes, expressive of an inner joy and sudden illumination, which fascinated any who were present. For though his sense of humour was keen, the spirit of satire was absent; benevolence in his kindly heart never never finding a difficulty in quelling ill-nature. It will be said that there are many satirical strokes in "Dipsychus," and this is true; but they are aimed at classes—their follies and hypocrisies—never at any individual, except himself. His mouth was beautifully formed, but both it and the chin were characterised by some lack of determination and firmness. This deficiency, however, so far as it existed, was harmful only to himself; those who sought his counsel or help found in him the wisest of advisers, the steadiest and kindest of friends. . . . On the moral side he was firm as a rock. — THOMAS, ARNOLD, 1898, *Arthur Hugh Clough,. Nineteenth Century, vol.* 43, *pp.* 105, 115.

He whom all his contemporaries counted certain to take a commanding place in the higher life of England sank into comparative insignificance. He began by failing of that First Class, which was the undoubted meed due to his knowledge and ability. He went on always hoping, longing to do some great thing, yet never doing it. For years he held his tutorship and fellowship, doubting whether he ought not to give them up since he no longer held the faith supposed to be their indispensable condition. At last he resigned them both, but not to give his splendid talents work to do for any high ends outside the circle of the university. One petty appointment after another he held—petty, that is, in comparison with what his intellectual endowments qualified him for—but always questioning whether this was or was not what he ought to be at. At last peace seems to have come to him only by giving up finally and forever all such noble ambitions for the bettering of the world as had inspired his early youth, quietly settling down into a useful, if somewhat narrow, government office, and taking all his joy from the homely love of wife and children. And yet this was a good man, a religious man, of whom I have been speaking, a man far better and more religious than many who have shone conspicuously as patriots and heroes, a man in the highest degree lovable, a man who inspired others to a strenuousness of which he himself failed, a man whose intellect was held in honor by the most intellectual.—ARMSTRONG, RICHARD A., 1898, *Faith and Doubt in the Century's Poets.*

Mr. Clough arrived in Boston, furnished with excellent letters of introduction both for that city and for the dignitaries of Cambridge. My husband at once invited him to pass some days at our house, and I was very glad to welcome him there. In appearance I thought him rather striking. He was tall, tending a little to stoutness, with a beautifully ruddy complexion and dark eyes which twinkled with suppressed humor. His sweet, cheery manner at once attracted my young children to him, and I was amused, on passing near the open door of his room, to see him engaged in conversation with my little son, then some five or six years of age.—HOWE, JULIA WARD, 1899, *Reminiscences, 1819-1899, p.* 185.

THE BOTHIE OF TOBER-NA-VUOLICH
1848

I write to you now merely to thank you for having given me a great and unexpected pleasure, by leaving with me "The Bothie of Tober-na-Vuolich," which Mrs. Arnold, too, had recommended me to read. I was very unwilling to commence it, for I detest English hexameters, from Surrey's to Southey's; and Mr. Clough's spondaic lines are, to my ear, detestable too,—that is, to begin with. Yet I am really charmed with this poem. There is a great deal of mere prose in it, and the worse, to my taste, for being prose upon stilts; but, take it for all in all, there is more freshness of heart and soul and sense in it than it has been my chance to find and feel in any poem of recent date,—perhaps I ought to say than in any recent poem of which the author is not yet much known; for I have no mind to depreciate Alfred Tennyson, nor any other man who has fairly won his laurel.—QUILLINAN, EDWARD, 1849, *Letter to Henry Crabb Robinson, Jan.* 12; *Diary, Reminiscences and Correspondence of Henry Crabb Robinson, ed. Sadler.*

Why did you not send me word of Clough's hexameter poem, which I have now received and read with much joy. But no, you will never forgive him his metres. He is a stout, solid, reliable man and friend, —I knew well; but this fine poem has taken me by surprise. I cannot find that your journals have yet discovered its existence.—EMERSON, RALPH WALDO, 1849, *To Carlyle, Jan.* 23; *Correspondence of Carlyle and Emerson, ed. Norton, vol.* II, *p.* 204.

His "Bothie" is a rare and original poem, quite Homeric in treatment and modern to the full in spirit. I do not know a poem more impregnated with the nineteenth century or fuller of tender force and shy, delicate humor.—LOWELL, JAMES RUSSELL, 1853, *To C. F. Briggs, June* 10; *Letters, ed. Norton, vol.* I, *p.* 202.

Here certainly was as healthy a burst as Goethe himself could have desired to see, out of the "subjective" into the "objective." Who does not know the "Bo-

thie"—in its form, a new feat in our literature, inasmuch as it really settled in the only true way, namely, by a capital example, the question, still argued, whether hexameter verse will do in English; in its matter, such a hearty and delightful story of the adventures of a reading party of young Oxonians, who have gone, with their tutor, to the Highlands for the long vacation, and, in particular, of the marriage theories of one of them, Philip Hewson, ending in his love for the demure Highland maiden Elspie, whom he at last marries and takes with him to New Zealand? Or, if there are any of our readers who do not yet know the "Bothie," they are to be envied the pleasure which remains for them of a first acquaintance with it.—MASSON, DAVID, 1862, *The Poems of Arthur Hugh Clough, Macmillan's Magazine, vol.* 6, *p.* 327.

There is no weakness in his longer poems. "The Bothie of Tober-na-Vuolich," which was the first of these to appear, is an idyl of country-life, as fresh as a breeze in summer, into which is woven a social problem of love-making such as Clough was fond of introducing into his more ambitious poems. With even its decided merits, it is less characteristic of the author than one piece written in the succeeding year, 1849, which first saw light, nine years later, in the earliest pages of "The Atlantic."—PERRY, THOMAS SERGEANT, 1875, *Arthur Hugh Clough, Atlantic Monthly, vol.* 36, *p.* 413.

His "Bothie of Tober-na-Vuolich," which bears the reader along less easily than the billowy hexameters of Kingsley, is charmingly faithful to its Highland theme, and has a Doric simplicity and strength. His shorter pieces are uneven in merit, but all suggestive and worth a thinker's attention. If he could have remained in the liberal American atmosphere, and have been spared his untimely taking-off, he might have come to greatness; but he is now no more, and with him departed a radical thinker and a living protest against the truckling expedients of the mode.—STEDMAN, EDMUND CLARENCE, 1875-87, *Victorian Poets, p.* 244.

In spite of many artistic shortcomings, this poem is so healthy, human, and original, that it can scarcely fail to survive when a good deal of far more fashionable verse shall have disappeared from men's memories. The one infallible note of a true poet—the power of expressing himself in rhythmical movements of subtility and sweetness which baffle analysis—is also distinctly manifest in passages of the "Bothie," passages the music of which was, we fancy, lingering in the ear of Tennyson when he wrote certain parts of "Maud." The originality of this idyl is beyond question. It is not in the least like any other poem, and an occasionally ostentatious touch of the manner of "Herman and Dorothea" seems to render this originality all the more conspicuous in the main.—PATMORE, COVENTRY, 1889-98, *Principle in Art*, p. 111.

His "Bothie of Tober-na-Vuolich" is his chief title to fame. It is the narrative, in hexameters, a style exceedingly difficult to manage in English. — OLIPHANT, MARGARET O. W., 1892, *The Victorian Age of English Literature*, p. 436.

GENERAL

I quite agree in what you say of poor Clough. A man more vivid, ingenious, veracious, mildly radiant, I have seldom met with, and in a character so honest, modest, kindly. I expected very considerable things of him.—CARLYLE, THOMAS, 1860, *Letter to Froude, Thomas Carlyle, A History of his Life in London*, ed. Froude, vol. II, p. 207.

Clough's work, in tone, more resembles the great masters of simplicity and majesty to whom he always turned with increasing reverence—Homer, or Sophocles, or Milton, or that earlier Englishman who in the "Tales" renewed, or seemed to renew, the very genius of the "Odyssey." Nor, however vast the difference in realized poetry, is his poem unworthy these splendid models. A sense of fresh, healthy manliness; a scorn of base and selfish motives; a beauty and tenderness of nature; a frank acceptance of common life; a love of earth, not "only for its earthly sake," but for the divine and the eternal interfused in it— such, and other such, are the impressions left. These noble qualities are rare in any literature; they have a charm so great that, like Beauty before the Areopagus, they almost disarm the judgment. Viewed in that aspect, Clough's work is wanting in art; the language and the thought are often unequal and incomplete; the poetical fusion into a harmonious whole, imperfect. Here, and in his other writings, one feels a doubt whether in verse he chose the right vehicle,

the truly natural mode of utterance. His poetry, in a word, belongs to that uncommon class in which the matter everywhere far outruns the workmanship.—PALGRAVE, FRANCIS TURNER, 1862, *Arthur Hugh Clough, Fraser's Magazine*, vol. 65, p. 529.

Of one metre, however,—the hexameter, —we believe the most accomplished judges, and also common readers, agree that Mr. Clough possesses a very peculiar mastery. . . . Whether any consummate poem of great length and sustained dignity can be written in this metre, and in our language, we do not know: until a great poet has written his poem, there are commonly no lack of plausible arguments that seem to prove he cannot write it; but Mr. Clough has certainly shown that in the hands of a skilful and animated artist, it is capable of adapting itself to varied descriptions of life and manners, to noble sentiments, and to changing thoughts. It is perhaps the most flexible of English metres. Better than any others, it changes from grave to gay without desecrating what should be solemn, or disenchanting that which should be graceful. And Mr. Clough was the first to prove this, by writing a noble poem in which it was done. . . . The sort of conversation for which he was most remarkable rises again in the "Amours de Voyage," and gives them, to those who knew him in life, a very peculiar charm. It would not be exact to call the best lines a pleasant cynicism; for cynicism has a bad name, and the ill-nature and other offensive qualities which have given it that name were utterly out of Mr. Clough's way. Though without much fame, he had no envy.—BAGEHOT, WALTER, 1862, *Mr. Clough's Poems, Works*, ed. Morgan, vol. I, pp. 196, 197.

From the higher mind of cultivated, all-questioning, but still conservative England, in this our puzzled generation, we do not know of any utterance in literature so characteristic as the poems of Arthur Hugh Clough, "sometime fellow of Oriel College, Oxford." Freely he thinks and speaks; yet always as an Englishman. His sympathies are general, but his tastes and standards are still national.—ALLINGHAM, WILLIAM, 1866, *Arthur Hugh Clough, Fraser's Magazine*, vol. 74, p. 535.

He was greatly beloved by those who knew best the rare qualities of his genius, and his friendships were with the best men and women. There was an attractive blending of scholarly shyness, melancholy, and geniality in the impression he made; and he had the fullest sympathy with the freedom and the promise of American life. But his sad self was relentless. He could not escape the old wonder and questioning. What he wrote in poetry and prose had a strain of sincere, child-like pathos, wholly unsurpassed in contemporary literature. And it characterizes all his writings. It is not a pathos of sighs and sobs, and elegiac weeping and wailing, but a melancholy like that of the Autumn in Nature, a primeval sadness. — CURTIS, GEORGE WILLIAM, 1868, *The Old and the New, Putnam's Magazine, vol.* 11, *p.* 7.

The whole range of our literature shows no poet whose writings so fully and faithfully represent the man as those of Clough. We know none who so freely and entirely gives us himself. There is not one of his poems in which we do not find the personal outcome of his nature. His songs he sings out of his own heart. To give expression to his own thoughts and feelings was the *motive* of his music. No doubt his deep and genuine feeling for all that was human, and his marvellous power of analysis, could not fail to make him capable of entering into the characters of others. The portraits of the Trevellyns (though sketchy, and meant to be no more), of Hobbes, of Elspie, of "the grave man nicknamed Adam," are all true and forcible; while, of the voyagers in "Mari Magno," the lawyer, and "the rural dean," are as perfect in their way as any of the Canterbury pilgrims. Yet in none is there that complete reticence of self which is demanded by the best descriptive, as well as the best dramatic, poetry. In every character there is something of Clough himself. We find among his verses few or no "dramatic lyrics," little of the working of the historical imagination, that delights to place itself in other conditions, and to speak with other tongues. Even in the poems cast in a quasi-dramatic mould,—"The Mystery of the Fall" and "Dipsychus,"— it is, for the most part, Clough who, in varying moods, utters himself by turns through the mouths of each of the interlocutors. It is not merely form and colour, but material substance, that are supplied from within. Hence the study of his poems is the study of Clough himself.—DOWDEN, JOHN, 1869, *Arthur Hugh Clough, Contemporary Review, vol.* 12, *p.* 513.

The oftener I return to Clough's unfinished but striking poems, the more I am struck by something in their fresh natural handling, and a certain lustre of sunlight on their surface, which suggests to me a modern and intellectualized Chaucer; and I think the same homely breadth and simplicity were strongly marked in his countenance. . . . I do not think that any competent judge who really studies Clough's Remains will doubt for a moment that he was one of the most original men of our age, and perhaps its most intellectual, and buoyant, though very far, of course, from its richest, most musical and exquisite poet. There is a very peculiar and unique attraction about what I may call the physical and almost animal buoyancy of these subtly intellectual rhythms and verses, when once the mass of the poet's mind—by no means easy to get into motion—is fairly under way.— HUTTON, RICHARD HOLT, 1869, *Arthur Hugh Clough, Essays in Literary Criticism, pp.* 169, 178.

Clough's "Dipsychus" I consider the most really remarkable contribution we have had; but the poetry, like all else, is going post-haste to the Devil just now.— FROUDE, JAMES ANTHONY, 1870, *Letter to John Skelton, Feb.* 10; *The Table-Talk of Shirley, ed. Skelton, p.* 141.

There will always be a great charm, especially for Oxford men, in the "Long Vacation Pastoral," "The Bothie of Toberna-Vuolich." Humour, pathos, clear character-drawing, real delight in nature and a power of rendering her beauties, above all a sense of life, of "the joy of eventful living" —it has all these, and over the whole is thrown, through the associations of the hexameter, a half-burlesque veil of academic illusion that produces the happiest effect. . . . Clough holds a high and permanent place among our poets, not only because, as Mr. Lowell says, he represents an epoch of thought, but because he represents it in a manner so rare, so individual. He is neither singer nor prophet; but he is a poet in virtue of the depth and sincerity with which he felt certain great emotions, and the absolute veracity with which he expressed them.—WARD, THOMAS HUMPHRY, 1880, *The English Poets, vol.* IV, *p.* 591.

Of "Dipsychus" in its entirety, we must confess that it is, when beheld in its present state, simply a *cul-de-sac;* — or if the reader prefer it, a suite of richly-adorned

chambers, but not a perfect palace. If
Clough had lived he might, like Goethe,
have gradually, through a period of thirty
years, developed his works, and at the age
of sixty have delighted the world with
the publication of another masterpiece,—
another palace of art, or "lordly pleasure-
house" for the soul.—WADDINGTON, SAM-
UEL, 1882, *Arthur Hugh Clough, p.* 241.

He failed to carry out any large design,
and his poetry is deficient in form and
polish; yet it has a greater charm for congenial minds than much poetry of superior
refinement and more exquisite workmanship. It reveals, without self-consciousness, a character of marked sweetness,
humour, and lofty moral feeling. Though
Clough was in part a disciple of Wordsworth, he shows the originality of true
genius in his descriptions of scenery, and in
his treatment of the great social and philosophical problems of his time. If several
contemporaries showed greater artistic
skill, no one gave greater indications of the
power of clothing serious contemplation in
the language of poetry.—STEPHEN, LESLIE,
1887, *Dictionary of National Biography, vol.*
XI, *p.* 128.

Clough worshipped Truth with more
than the passion of a lover, and his writings
are, for the most part, the tragic records of
a life-long devotion to a mistress who steadily refused his embraces; but as it is greatly
better to have loved without attaining than
to have attained without loving, so Clough's
ardent and unrewarded stumblings in the
dark towards his adored though unseen
divinity are greatly more attractive and
edifying to those who have shared, successfully or not, the same passion, than is that
complacent fruition of her smiles which she
often accords to those who are contented to
be no more than her speaking acquaintances. — PATMORE, COVENTRY, 1889-98,
Principle in Art, p. 106.

Clough expresses the changes which the
Christian faith has undergone, and the per-
plexities of conduct.—SYMONDS, JOHN ADD-
INGTON, 1890, *Essays Speculative and Suggestive, vol.* II, *p.* 246.

Even more out of place in such good company is the weary and wearisome laureate
of Oxonicules and Bostonicules, the late
Mr. Lowell's realised ideal and chosen representative of English poetry at its highest
in the generation of Tennyson and Browning. Literary history will hardly care to

remember or to register the fact that there
was a bad poet named Clough, whom his
friends found it useless to puff: for the public, if dull, has not quite such a skull as belongs to believers in Clough.—SWINBURNE,
ALGERNON CHARLES, 1891, *Social Verse,
The Forum, vol.* 12, *p.* 182.

Arthur Hugh Clough united in happy and
sympathetic association, healthy mental
and physical life. Though given to psychological inquiry and introspective analysis
he took the keenest delight in the enjoyment of the physical world, and so maintained in even balance the two parts of
his remarkably vigorous and harmonious
nature. In an equipment so complete a
sense of humour could not be lacking, and
Clough gives ample evidence of possessing
it in a rare degree.—MILES, ALFRED H.,
1894, *The Poets and the Poetry of the Century, Humour, Society, Parody and Occasional Verse, p.* 409.

There are few names in this century
which have had, for young men especially,
greater attractive power than that of
Arthur Hugh Clough. This power has never
been widely, but in many cases it has been
deeply, felt. It has its source more in the
nature of the man and in the conditions of
his life than in his work, although the latter
is full of the elevation, the aspiration, and
the beauty of a very noble mind. But it is
not as a finished artist, as a singer whose
message is clear and whose note is resonant,
that Clough attracts; it is rather as a child
of his time, as one in whom the stir and
change of the century were most distinctly
reflected. There was an intense sympathy
with his age in the heart of Clough, a sensitiveness to the tidal influences of thought
and emotion, which made his impressionable nature, for a time at least, a prey to
agitation and turmoil; and there is no more
delicate registry of the tempestuous weather
of the second quarter of the century than
that which is found in his work.—MABIE,
HAMILTON WRIGHT, 1894, *My Study Fire,
Second Series, p.* 101.

Far less polished than Arnold's, Clough's
poetry yet shows in some respects a freer
and broader power. His outlook on modern
society is more manly, as more specific in
severity; and his pungent gift of mockery
is foreign to Arnold's pensive grace and
musical despair. But the spiritual attitude
of the two is wider apart than their artistic
or social temper. We read Arnold's laments

over the past, his intense longing for steadfastness and peace, and the conviction grows upon us that his keenest regret is not faith but assurance, less the truth which the world has forfeited than the tranquility which the truth produced. He craves with an almost querulous desire the unquestioning and serene spirit, which has fled never to return. Passing to the pages of his friend, we find pain of a different order—the agonized desire for a faith that is lost, and for a distant God. Tranquility is the supreme end of Arnold's ambition; the Truth alone could satisfy the soul of Clough.—SCUDDER, VIDA D., 1895, *The Life of the Spirit in the Modern English Poets, p.* 266.

Mentally sane, honest, intrepid to the last degree—so his life and his words alike describe him: a clear and direct thinker; a man impatient of shams and figments of every kind; frank with himself no less than with others; intolerant of self-deception; with a temperamental horror of the vague, the mawkish, the sentimental; always resolutely determined to see fact and to make the best of it;—such was Arthur Hugh Clough—in the noblest sense of that much-abused term, a genuine seeker after truth. . . . It may be pointed out in passing that Clough's poetry as a whole is naturally marked by a persistent sense of impermanence, instability, and transition—by the forward-reaching spirit of a man who, himself falling upon an epoch of upheaval, experiment, and widespread intellectual unrest, stands tiptoe to catch if may be some hint of unrealized things. It is a poetry of anticipation, dominated throughout by the presentiment of the morrow—the keen foretaste of impending and inevitable change. . . . The note of fluctuation, the attitude of eager watchfulness, the mood of inquiry, thus become characteristics of the great body of Clough's work in verse. . . . His poetry is the poetry of moods—moods of comparative hopefulness, moods of weariness and despair, moods of mere inquiry and deliberate reserve. To the superficial reader, turning over the pages of his collected works, there might even seem to be the strangest inconsistencies in the utterances of some of his shorter poems; for his sensitive nature catches up and repeats, though always in tempered tones, now the sad wail of some who mourn over the rapid dissolution of the world's great heritage of belief, and now again the glad shout of

others who, boldly and trustfully, press forward to meet the coming day. But the wail and the shout—the song of sorrow and the song of promise — alike belong to the man himself, and, far from being discordant or incompatible, are in their own ways equally expressive of his relation to the great issues of the time.—HUDSON, WILLIAM HENRY, 1896, *Studies in Interpretation, pp.* 91, 114, 115, 117.

On the whole, Clough is one of the most unsatisfactory products of that well-known form of nineteenth century scepticism which has neither the strength to believe nor the courage to disbelieve "and have done with it." He hankers and looks back, his "two souls" are always warring with each other, and though the clash and conflict sometimes bring out fine things, . . . though his "Latest Decalogue" has satirical merit, and some of his country poems, written without undercurrent of thought, are fresh and genial, he is on the whole a failure. But he is a failure of a considerable poet, and some fragments of success chequer him.—SAINTSBURY, GEORGE, 1896, *A History of Nineteenth Century Literature, p.* 309.

His nature was of rare superiority alike of character and intellect. His moral integrity and sincerity imparted clearness to his imagination and strength to his intelligence, so that while the most marked distinction of his poems is that which they possess as a mirror of spiritual conditions shared by many of his contemporaries, they have hardly less interest as the expression and image of his own individuality. . . . It became impossible for him to accept, however they might be interpreted, the doctrines of any church. He would not play tricks with words nor palter with the integrity of his soul. This perfect mental honesty of Clough, and his entire sincerity of expression, were a stumbling-block to many of his more conventional contemporaries, and have remained as a rock of offense to many of the readers of his poetry, who find it disturbing to be obliged to recognize in his work a test of their own sincerity in dealing with themselves. With how few are conviction and profession perfectly at one! The difficulty of the struggle in Clough's case, the difficulty of freeing himself from the chains of association, of tradition, of affection, of interest, which bound him to conformity with and acceptance of the popular creed in one or the other of its forms, has led superficial critics of his life and poetry to find in them evidence that the struggle was too hard for him and the result unsatisfactory. There could not be a greater error. Clough's honest acceptance of the insolubility of the vain questions which men are perpetually asking, and his recognition of the insufficiency of the answers which they are ready to accept or to pretend to accept, left him as regards his most inward soul one of the serenest of men.—NORTON, CHARLES ELIOT, 1897, *Library of the World's Best Literature,* ed. *Warner, vol.* VII, *pp.* 3821, 3823.

Arthur Hugh Clough was in no respect a "man of letters." Literature was not his business. It does not fall to the lot of those who may have to deal with his life and his work to be compelled to trace out a perhaps sordid and coarse personality beneath the robes of an almost regal success in the world of letters. There is little that Clough has left us that is not transparent and natural. But within this we find so attractive a personality that we may perhaps be in some danger of exaggerating the merely literary importance of the forms through which that personality expressed itself. We find that personality ever most sensitively alive to everything in nature that is gentle and beautiful, ever tenderly tolerant towards every kind of human defect or shortcoming, but at the same time severely and inexorably just towards itself. It is this mixing of tenderness and severity, coupled as it is with the utmost sensitiveness to every beautiful and ennobling impression, that gives the distinctive charm to one of the very few men of the present century who can claim to be studied, not for what they did, but for what they were.—STATHAM, F. REGINALD, 1897, *Arthur Hugh Clough, National Review, vol.* 29, *p.* 201.

Clough was a most fascinating character, thoroughly genuine, but so oppressed with the problems of life that it was difficult ever to get a smile out of him; and if one did, his round ruddy face with the deep heavy eyes, seemed really to suffer from the contortions of laughter. He took life very seriously, and made greater sacrifices to his convictions than the world ever suspected. He was poor, but from conscientious scruples gave up his fellowship, and was driven at last to go to America to make himself independent without giving up the independence of his mind. With a little more sun-shine above him and around him he might have grown to a very considerable height, but there was always a heavy weight on him, that seemed to render every utterance and every poem a struggle. His poems are better known and loved in America, I believe, than in England, but in England also they still have their friends, and in the history of the religious or rather theological struggles of 1840-50 Clough's figure will always be recognised as one of the most characteristic and the most pleasing.—MÜLLER, F. MAX, 1898, *Auld Lang Syne, Literary Recollections, p.* 127.

Clough proved that the world cannot satisfy the conscientious spirit. He expressed sovereign contempt for those who sought to nourish themselves upon the ashes of this life and of the senses; such seemed to him to be abandoned to the most deceptive dreams. He found society and traffic full of falsehood and dissimulation, covering ruthless selfishness, and this discord between the real and ideal, between what things and relations are in social life and what they ought to be, falling upon his highly developed conscience and acute intellect, struck from them some of the most cutting satire of his day.—WHITE, GREENOUGH, 1898, *Clough's Poetry, Matthew Arnold and the Spirit of the Age, p.* 12.

There is perhaps no poet of the Victorian era in whom the Agnostic spirit has found more distinct and articulate utterance than in Arthur Hugh Clough. To him, the very essence of all religion worth having consists in the firm, resolute, unswerving conviction that nothing can be known of the Supreme. Providential schemes, creeds and certainties are all in his estimation a profane pretence of knowledge, and are to be strenuously resisted, as so many temptations to Baalism and idolatry. The only recipe he feels himself justified in prescribing, and he is never weary of recommending it, is "contentedness not to know."— WILSON, S. LAW, 1899, *The Theology of Modern Literature, Introduction, p.* 17.

Clough's work is controlled by no prevailing sense of beauty, like Goethe's; he has movements of greatness, and may perhaps still claim to have written three or four of the finest English hexameters; but it is almost as certain that he has to answer for a hundred or more of the worst.—HERFORD, CHARLES HAROLD, 1902, *English Tales in Verse, Introduction, p.* lv.

John Lord Campbell
1779–1861

John, Baron Campbell, Lord Chancellor of England, was born, 15th September 1779, at Cupar-Fife, a son of the parish minister. He studied for the ministry at St. Andrews University, became (1798) a tutor in London, joined Lincoln's Inn (1800), read law and acted as reporter and made dramatic critic to the *Morning Chronicle*, and was called to the bar in 1806. His *nisi prius* "Reports" (1808), brought him into notice, and by 1824 he was leader of the Oxford circuit. He became king's counsel in 1827, Whig M. P. for Stafford in 1830, and for Dudley in 1832, in which year he was made solicitor-general and knighted. Attorney-general in 1834, he was defeated at Dudley, but returned for Edinburgh. He became Lord Campbell (1841), and for six weeks Lord Chancellor of Ireland, next, Chancellor of the Duchy of Lancaster (1846), Chief-justice of the Queen's Bench (1850), and Lord Chancellor of England (1859). He died 22nd June 1861. He was a courteous and painstaking judge; he carried statutes on defamation, compensation for death by accident, and against obscene publications. His "Lives of the Chief-justices" (1849–57) and of the "Lord Chancellors" (1845–47), though readable, are disfigured by the obtrusion of himself, and in the later volumes by misrepresentation and inaccuracy.—PATRICK AND GROOME, *eds.*, 1897, *Chambers's Biographical Dictionary, p.* 173.

PERSONAL

Sir John Campbell is a stout athletic man. He rejoices in a pair of good round shoulders: he would certainly have made an able-bodied labourer had fate made him a "working"-man. His personal appearance is rather uncouth. In walking you would fancy he was some farmer measuring distances on his lands, by means of what are called "paces." His head generally droops on his shoulder, as if the neck were tired of the burden; and he usually looks towards the ground on which he walks, as if lost in profound meditation. His complexion is pale: his eyes have little lustre in them. The whole expression of his countenance is that of a care-worn man;—though why he should be so, I cannot exactly understand; for he has no reason to complain of want of success, either as a politician or as a professional man.—GRANT, JAMES, 1837, *The Bench and Bar, vol.* II, *p.* 47.

He is a fine, noble-looking man, with an impressive manner, and clear tone of voice. He is deemed one of the most excellent jurists in the three kingdoms, and likewise a statesman. I was deeply interested in him, for I was told he had been the architect of his own fortune. — LE VERT, OCTAVIA WALTON, 1853, *Souvenirs of Travel, vol.* I, *p.* 17.

In my London days, Lord Campbell was "Plain John Campbell": but Plain John was wonderfully like the present Lord;—facetious, in and out of place, politic, flattering to an insulting degree, and prone to moralising in so trite a way as to be almost insulting. He was full of knowledge, and might have been inexhaustibly entertaining if he could have forgotten his prudence and been natural. When his wife, Lady Stratheden, was present, there was some explanation of both the worldly prudence and the behaviour to ladies,—as if they were spoiled children,—which Plain John supposed would please them.—MARTINEAU, HARRIET, 1855–77, *Autobiography, ed. Chapman, vol.* I, *p.* 255.

An act of cruelty has been committed by an English judge, and I have arraigned the perpetrator before the bar of public opinion, because that is the only tribunal to which he is amenable. His son, by pleading on his behalf, has recognised the jurisdiction. It remains for me to consider his reply; it will finally remain for the public to decide on its validity. If it is valid, the charge falls to the ground; the accused is absolved; and I, as the accuser, am covered with confusion. If it is not valid, the failure of the defence will strengthen the force of the accusation, and even they who wish to favour the judge will be compelled to allow, that what they would fain have palliated, as the momentary ebullition of an arbitrary temper, swells into far graver matter, when, instead of being regretted, it is vindicated with stubborn pertinacity, and in an obstinate and angry spirit.—BUCKLE, HENRY THOMAS, 1859, *Letter to a Gentleman Respecting Pooley's Case, Miscellaneous and Posthumous Works, ed. Taylor, vol.* I, *p.* 72.

It has been well said of him in explanation of his success, that he lived eighty years and preserved his digestion unimpaired. He had a hard head, a splendid constitution, tireless industry, a generally judicious temper. He was a learned, though not a scientific lawyer, a faithful political adherent, thoroughly honest as a judge, dutiful and happy as a husband. But there was nothing admirable or heroic in his nature. On no great subject did his principles rise above the commonplace of party, nor had he the magnanimity which excuses rather than aggravates the faults of others. His life is the triumph of steady determination unaided by a single brilliant or attractive quality.—SMITH, W. C., 1876, *Encyclopædia Britannica, Ninth Ed., vol.* IV.

Campbell was indeed only a clever, shrewd lawyer of the hard and narrow class. He never made any pretension to statesmanship, or even to great political knowledge.—MCCARTHY, JUSTIN, 1879, *A History of Our Own Times from the Accession of Queen Victoria to the Berlin Congress, ch.* V.

On Friday he was kept very late in the House. But on Saturday morning, June the 22nd, he appeared perfectly well. He drove to Lincoln's Inn, accompanied by two of his daughters, and sat in Court till the afternoon, when he went to Downing Street for a meeting of the Cabinet. Thence he walked home to Stratheden House, and, having some spare time before preparing for a dinner party, he sat down to his desk and wrote a judgment. . . . Throughout the evening he conversed with his usual animation, and when the guests had departed, remained having a last talk with his children, and bade them Good-night at about twelve o'clock. At eight next morning his servant went into his room and found him seated in an armchair with no appearance of life. Medical advice was instantly called in, but he had gone to his last rest, and, in his own words, was "honourably released from the labours and anxieties of the Great Seal." . . . His body was carried to Hartrigge, and on Saturday, June the 29th, we laid it beside that of our dear mother in the Abbey at Jedburgh; carrying out the wish he had expressed at the time of his brother's funeral, that the English Burial Service might be used, when "his remains should be deposited in the resting place secured to him in very holy ground."—HARDCASTLE, MARY SCARLETT, 1880, *ed., Life of John, Lord Campbell, vol.* II, *pp.* 409, 410.

He was an admirable example of what may be done by perseverance, energy and industry, combined with shrewdness and sagacity. He should have a section to himself in the next edition of "Self Help." In his readiness to turn his hand to anything that could be turned to advantage—to write dramatic criticisms or undertake the department of wit, to learn dancing or teach French—he rivalled the man who, being asked whether he could play on the fiddle, replied that he didn't know but he would try. If there were a bump in the phrenological system for the get-on faculty, there would be one of the biggest on Campbell's cranium. But he did not abide implicitly by the well-known Scotch maxim. He got on honestly. He used his opportunities without abusing them, and he was enabled to do so by being always prepared for them when they occurred. He was never before or after the time, never in or out of the way, when preferment or promotion was in the air.—HOWARD, ABRAHAM, 1881, *Lord Campbell Lord Chief Justice and Lord Chancellor, Quarterly Review, vol.* 151, *p.* 39.

North of the Tweed,—and in some places south of the Tweed, too,—it has for many years been a commonplace with those who preach Self-Help, or who discuss the phenomena and the philosophy of Getting On, to point to the career of Lord Campbell. By extraordinary industry: by rigorous self-denial: by steadfastly keeping his end in view: by great ability no doubt and great learning: all seconded by wonderful good luck; the St. Andrews student of Divinity, the son of good old Dr. Campbell, parish minister of Cupar, who had no great connections and no powerful friends to back him; was Solicitor-general at the age of fifty-three; Attorney-general at fifty-four; was raised to the bench as Lord Chief Justice of England; and finally became Lord Chancellor of Great Britain. Nor is it enough to say he held these great places: no one can deny that he proved himself equal to the duties of each. He was a strong Attorney-general. He was one of the most eminent of Chief Justices. And, though raised to the Woolsack at four-score, he was a thoroughly sufficient Chancellor.—BOYD, ANDREW K. H., 1881, *Lord Campbell, Fraser's Magazine, vol.* 103, *p.* 334.

GENERAL

You *are*, indeed, in a proper scrape, if you must do such an act—of what shall I call it?—as review Jack Campbell's Speeches.

Are you aware that they are the standing jest of the whole town, both in and out of the profession? No one has, of course, read them, but only seen them cited in newspapers. However, it was not necessary to read, or even to see that much. The very fact of *his* publishing his speeches was what raised endless ridicule in all quarters.— BROUGHAM, HENRY LORD, 1842, *To Napier, Aug. 3; Selections from the Correspondence of Macvey Napier, ed. Napier, p. 402.*

But of all the sins against Francis Bacon, that of Lord Campbell is the last and worst. I wish to speak with respect of so bold and great a man as our present Lord Chancellor. He is one who has swept up the slope of fame by native power of heart and brain; in the proud course of his life, from the Temple to the Peerage, from the Reporters' Gallery to the Woolsack, I admire the track of a man of genius,—brave, circumspect, tenacious, strong; one not to be put down, not to be set aside; an example to men of letters and men of law. But the more highly I rank Lord Campbell's genius, the more I feel drawn to regret his haste. In such a case as the trial of Bacon's fame he was bound to take pains; to sift every lie to its root; to stay his condemning pen till he had satisfied his mind that in passing sentence of infamy he was right, beyond risk of appeal. A statesman and a law-reformer himself, he ought to have felt more sympathy for the just fame of a statesman and law-reformer than he has shown. Not that Lord Campbell finds fault with Bacon where he speaks by his own lights. Indeed, there he is just. He has no words too warm for Bacon's reforms as a lawyer, for his plans as a minister, for his rules as a chancellor. When Lord Campbell knows his subject at first hand, his praise of his hero rings out clear and loud. But there is much in the life of Bacon which he does not know. He has not given himself time to sift and winnow. Like an easy magistrate on the bench, he has taken the pleas for facts. That is his fault, and in such a man it is a very grave fault.—DIXON, WILLIAM HEPWORTH, 1861, *Personal History of Lord Bacon, p. 5.*

His energy now devoted itself to literature; and he began to bring out his "Lives" of the Chancellors." In that work he has described himself better than any one else could describe him. The style is entertaining, the facts anything that he chose to make them, and the spirit depreciatory to

the last degree. The late Sir Harris Nicolas, the highest possible authority in antiquarian memoirs, accidentally examined some old MSS., which expressly contradicted Lord Campbell's painful account of Sir Christopher Hatton; and was so struck by the easy style of statement in Lord Campbell's life of that Chancellor that he made further investigations among State papers, and established and published a case of malversation of materials which will not easily be forgotten. The same process was afterward carried on, with the same result, by the *Westminster Review,* which entirely overthrew the value of the work as History or Biography, while stamping upon it the imputation of libel on the reputation of personages long gone where the voice of praise or censure cannot reach them. Lord Campbell certainly saw Sir H. Nicolas's exposures; for he omitted a few statements, qualified others, and inserted "it is said" in yet other instances; leaving, however, a considerable number uncorrected, to pass through successive editions, and become History if no vigilant curator of the fame of the dead does not take measures to preclude an evil so serious.—MARTINEAU, HARRIET, 1861–69, *Biographical Sketches, p. 244.*

The merits of his "Lives" are very considerable. They are eminently readable. The style is lively though rough, careless, and incorrect; every incident is presented effectively; they are full of good stories, and they contain a great deal of information about the history of law and lawyers which is not easily to be found elsewhere. The later volumes, moreover, both of the "Chancellors" and the "Chief Justices," have the freshness and interest of personal memoirs. For all these qualities Campbell has received due and sufficient recognition. Nor has time worn away the merits of his books; they still find many readers, and there is little probability that they will be displaced by anything more entertaining written on the same subject. None the less are they among the most censurable publications in our literature. . . . The tone of laborious research which pervades every volume is delusive. No writer ever owed so much to the labours of others who acknowledged so little. . . . Literary morality in its other form, the love of historical truth and accuracy, he hardly understood. No one who has ever followed him to the sources of his information will trust him more; for not only was he too hurried and careless to sift such evidence as he gathered, but even plain statements of fact are perverted, and his authorities are constantly misquoted.—MACDONELL, G. P., 1886, *Dictionary of National Biography, vol.* VIII, *p.* 383.

These biographies are carelessly written in an extremely slovenly style, and are in many cases inaccurate and unjust; but they never fail to keep up their interest, and especially in the latest volumes, where Campbell is writing of his own time, are full of vivacity,—of prejudice, too, it is said, perhaps more than the previous ones, —but one can safely say of all Campbell's biographical work, that the unpardonable sin of dulness is not included in the list of his transgressions.—OLIPHANT, MARGARET O. W., 1892, *The Victorian Age of English Literature, p.* 200.

David Gray
1838–1861

Born at Duntiblæ, a small village on the Luggie, some eight miles from Glasgow. The son of a weaver, he began to write verses when a boy, and through the influence of Sydney Dobell, with whom he had carried on some correspondence, visited London in 1860, where he was introduced to Lord Houghton. Some months later, signs of consumption having showed themselves, he persistently refused to avail himself of the medical treatment tendered by his London friends, and returned home, where he shortly afterwards died. Through the influence of Lord Houghton, arrangements had been completed for the publication of his descriptive poem "The Luggie"; but Gray did not live to see it printed. It was published in 1862, under the title of "The Luggie and Other Poems," and includes "In the Shadows," a series of sonnets written during his closing days.—RANDOLPH, HENRY FITZ, 1887, *ed., Fifty Years of English Song, Biographical and Bibliographical Notes, vol.* I, *p.* xxii.

PERSONAL

THIS MONUMENT OF
AFFECTION, ADMIRATION AND REGRET,
IS ERECTED TO
DAVID GRAY,
THE POET OF MERKLAND,
BY FRIENDS FROM FAR AND NEAR,
DESIROUS THAT HIS GRAVE SHOULD BE RE-
MEMBERED
AMID THE SCENES OF HIS RARE GENIUS
AND EARLY DEATH,
AND BY THE LUGGIE, NOW NUMBERED WITH
THE STREAMS
ILLUSTRIOUS IN SCOTTISH SONG.
Born 29th January, 1838; *Died 3rd December,* 1861.
—INSCRIPTION ON MONUMENT, 1865, "*Auld Aisle*" *Burying Ground, Kirkintilloch.*

I am in London and dare not look into the middle of next week. What brought me here? God knows, for I don't. *Alone* in such a place is a horrible thing. I have seen Dr. Mackay, but it's all up. People don't seem to understand me. . . . Westminster Abbey! I was there all day yesterday. If I live I shall be buried there—so help me God! A completely defined consciousness of *great* poetical genius is my only antidote against utter despair and despicable failure.—GRAY, DAVID, 1860, *Letter to Sydney Dobell.*

Below lies one whose name was traced in sand.
He died, not knowing what it was to live:
Died, while the first sweet consciousness of manhood
And maiden thought electrified his soul,
Faint beatings in the calyx of the rose.
Bewildered reader! pass without a sigh,
In a proud sorrow! There is life with God,
In other kingdom of a sweeter air;
In Eden every flower is blown: Amen.
—GRAY, DAVID, 1861, *My Epitaph, Sept.* 27.

'Tis near a year since Andrew went to sleep—
A winter and a summer. Yonder bed
Is where the boy was born, and where he died,
And yonder o'er the lowland is his grave:
The nook of grass and gowans where in thought
I found you standing at the set o' sun. . . .
The Lord content us—'tis a weary world.
. . . And you think weel of Andrews' book?
You think
That folk will love him, for the poetry's sake,
Many a year to come ? We take it kind,
You speak so weel of Andrew.
—BUCHANAN, ROBERT, 1868, *Poet Andrew.*

Foam-flecks of day on murmuring streams of life,
Gloom woven thick with mist of silky white,
Rare sounds of joy in waves of pain, a strife
Subdued, a storm made beautiful with light!

"Ah, nay!" thou sayest, weary of his wound!
"These are but echoes of a fight still on,
Wailed accents hiding in a worried sound,—
The lustre of a day forever gone."
Perhaps.   Yet he believed the stars within the
    night
Were pale with dawn; and he must sing his
    way to light.
—GUNSAULUS, FRANK W., 1891, *Lines Writ-
ten In a Copy of the Poems of David Gray,
Phidias and Other Poems.*

Days passed, weeks passed, months
passed, and he knew that he could not live.
He was ready to die, his life had been such a
failure; but he was not willing to die until
he was sure his poems would be published.
He worked over them, he copied them, he
wrote to his friends about them—wrote so
earnestly, so yearningly, so sadly, that they
raised money enough to publish them, Lord
Houghton subscribing five pounds, and Mr.
Dobell and other friends other sums.   So
they were placed in the hands of the printer,
and a specimen page that began "How
beautiful!" was sent to him.   It reached
him on December 2, 1861.   When he saw it,
his face lighted up, and the fame for which
he had struggled was won.   "It is good
news," he said.   The next day he died, his
last words being, "God has love, and I have
faith!"—STODDARD, RICHARD HENRY, 1892,
Under the Evening Lamp, p. 161.

GENERAL

Oh, rare young soul! Thou wast of such a mould
As could not bear the poet's painful dower!
Hence, in the sweet spring-tide of opening
    power,
Ere yet the gathering breeze of song had roll'd
Out on the world its music manifold,
Death gently hushed the harp, lest storm or
    shower—
Which surely life had brought some later hour—
Should snap the quivering strings or dim their
    gold.
Yet not the less shall tender memories dwell
In those sweet notes—and sad as sweet they
    seem—
Which from the burning touch of boyhood fell;
For long as little Luggie winds her stream,
And the twin Bothlin prattles down the dell,
Thither shall many a pilgrim turn and dream!
—HILL, ALSAGER HAY, 1863, *"In Memor-
iam," David Gray; A Scholar's Day-Dream,
Sonnets, and Other Poems.*

I would recommend the readers of these
Poems to keep in mind how deeply they are
based on the few phenomena of nature that
came within the Poet's observation.   He
revels in the frost and snow until the winter
of his own sorrow and sickness becomes too

hard for him to bear, and then he only asks
for
    "One clear day, a snowdrop, and sweet air."
The lost illusion of the cuckoo, when it was
transformed into
    "A slender bird of modest brown,"
is missed, as something he cannot afford to
spare in his scanty store of natural delights.
The "Luggie" itself ever remains the simple
stream that it really is, and is not decked-
out in any fantastic or inharmonious coloring.—MILNES, RICHARD MONCKTON (LORD
HOUGHTON), 1865, *Poems of David Gray,
Introductory Notice, p.* xiii.

David Gray's poetical susceptibility was
of the most conspicuous description.   He
had a most refined perception of the beautiful; he had a perception of an interminable
vista of beauty and truth.   He had noble
and pure thoughts, and he had been enabled
to express those noble and pure thoughts in
very noble and pure language.   "The Luggie" is a most remarkable poem, containing many very fine passages, inspired partially, no doubt, by a careful perusal of
Thomson's "Seasons" and Wordsworth's
"Excursion," and not, therefore, so entirely original as some of the author's subsequent poems; but with passages breaking out in it every now and then which
neither Thomson nor Wordsworth suggested, and which are entirely the conceptions of David Gray's own genius. . . . The
series of sonnets entitled "In the Shadows"
—written by the poet during his last illness
—many of them bearing relation to his own
condition, his own life, and his own prospects—appear to me to possess a solemn
beauty not surpassed by many of the finest
passages in Tennyson's "In Memoriam,"
totally distinct and unlike the "In Memoriam," but as genuine, as sincere, as heart-
stirring, and often as poetical.—BELL,
HENRY GLASSFORD, 1865, *Address at the Inauguration of Gray's Monument, July* 29.

Tho' the world could turn from you,
    This, at least, I learn from you:
Beauty and Truth, though never found, are
    worthy to be sought,
    The singer, upward-springing,
    Is grander than his singing,
And tranquil self-sufficing joy illumes the dark
    of thought.
    This, at least, you teach me,
    In a revelation:
That gods will snatch, as worthy death, the soul
    in its aspiration.
—BUCHANAN, ROBERT, 1868, *To David in
Heaven, st.* xiv.

The touching story and writings of poor Gray—who lived just long enough to sing his own dirges, and died with all his music in him—reveal a sensitive temperament unsustained by co-ordinate power. Possibly we should more justly say that his powers were undeveloped, for I do not wholly agree with those who deny that he had genius, and who think his work devoid of true promise. The limitless conceit involved in his estimate of himself was only what is secretly cherished by many a bantling poet, who is not driven to confess it by the horror of impending death. His main performance, "The Luggie," shows a poverty due to the want of proper literary models in his stinted cottage-home. It is an eighteenth-century poem, suggested by too close reading of Thomson and the like. Education, as compared with aspiration, comes slowly to low-born poets. The sonnets entitled "In the Shadows," written during the gradual progress of Gray's disease, are far more poetical, because a more genuine expression of feeling. They are indeed a painful study. Here is a subjective monody, uttered from the depths, but rounded off with that artistic instinct which haunts a poet to the last.—STEDMAN, EDMUND CLARENCE, 1875-87, *Victorian Poets, p.* 264.

"The Luggie," with its sense of natural beauty, and its promise of didactic and descriptive power, constitutes Gray's chief claim as a poet, but his sonnets are remarkable in substance, and several of them are felicitous in structure and expression.—BAYNE, THOMAS, 1890, *Dictionary of National Biography, vol.* XXIII, *p.* 5.

To gauge the potentialities of his genius is as impossible as it would be to describe the petals of an unopened bud. We can, however, see that the bud is itself a thing of beauty. With some cadences echoed from the poets whom he best loved, "The Luggie" has a music and a vision of its own; and those who read the noble sonnets written "in the twilight" may well lament the songs of the noontide which remain for ever unsung.—NOBLE, JAMES ASHCROFT, 1896, *The Poets and the Poetry of the Century, William Morris to Robert Buchanan, ed. Miles.*

His verse however is pleasant, and it might have acquired power. It retains a pathetic interest on account of the author's fate.—WALKER, HUGH, 1897, *The Age of Tennyson, p.* 258.

Catherine Grace Gore

1799–1861

Born, [Catherine Grace Frances Moody] at East Retford, 1799. Early literary precocity. Married to Capt. Charles Arthur Gore, 15 Feb. 1823. "The School for Coquettes" produced at Haymarket Theatre, 1831; "Lords and Commons," at Drury Lane; "The King's Seal," 1835; "King O'Neil," 1835; "The Queen's Champion," 1835; "The Maid of Croissy," 1835. Actively employed in novel-writing, also composed music. Lived in France for some years from 1832. Comedy, "Quid pro Quo," won £500 prize offered by Webster at Haymarket Theatre; produced there, 18 June 1844. Died, at Lyndhurst, Hampshire, 29 Jan. 1861, buried in Kensal Green cemetery. *Works:* "Theresa Marchmont," 1824; "The Bond," 1824; "The Lettre de Cachet" (anon.), 1827; "The Reign of Terror" (anon.), 1827; "Hungarian Tales" (anon.), 1829; "Romance of Real Life" (anon.), 1829; "Women as they are; or, the Manners of the Day" (anon.), 1830 (2nd edn. same year); "Pin Money" (anon.), 1831; "The Tuileries" (anon.), 1831; "Mothers and Daughters" (anon.), 1831; "The Historical Traveller," 1831; "The Fair of May Fair" (anon.), 1832; "The Opera" (anon.), 1832; "The Sketch-Book of Fashion" (anon.), 1833; "Polish Tales" (anon.), 1833; "The Hamiltons" (anon.), 1834; "The Maid of Croissy," 1835; "King O'Neil," 1835; "The Diary of a Désennuyée" (anon.), 1836; "Mrs. Armytage" (anon.), 1836; "Memoirs of a Peeress" (anon.), 1837; "Stokeshill Place" (anon.), 1837; "The Heir of Selwood" (anon.), 1838; "Mary Raymond," 1838; "The Rose Fancier's Manual," 1838; "The Woman of the World" (anon.), 1838; "The Cabinet Minister" (anon.), 1839; "The Courtier of the Days of Charles II.," 1839; "Dacre of the South," 1840; "The Dowager," 1840; "Preferment," 1840; "Cecil" (anon.), 1841; "Cecil a Peer" (sequel to preceding), 1841; "Greville," 1841; "The Soldier of Lyons," 1841; "The Ambassador's Wife," 1842; "The Man of Fortune," 1842; "Ormington" (anon.), 1842; "The Banker's Wife," 1843; "The Inundation," 1843; "Modern Chivalry" 1843; "The Money-Lender," 1843; "Quid pro Quo" (under initials: C. F. G.).

1844; "Agathonia" (anon.), 1844; "The Birthright," 1844; "The Popular Member," 1844; "Self" (anon), 1845; "The Snow Storm," 1845; "The Story of a Royal Favourite," 1845; "The Débutante," 1846; "New Year's Day," 1846 (2nd edn. same year); "Men of Capital," 1846; "Peers and Parvenus," 1846; "Sketches of English Character," 1846; "The Queen of Denmark," 1846; "Castles in the Air," 1847; "Temptation and Atonement," 1847; "The Diamond and the Pearl," 1848; 'The Inundation," [1848]; "A Good Night's Rest," 1852; "The Dean's Daughter," 1853; "The Lost Son," 1854; "Progress and Prejudice," 1854; "Mammon," 1855; "A Life's Lessons," 1856; "The Two Aristocracies," 1857; "Heckington," 1857. She *contributed* to: "The Tales of all Nations," 1827; "Heath's Picturesque Annual," 1832; "The Edinburgh Tales" (vols. i–iii.), 1845; "The Tale Book," 1859. *Posthumous:* "The Royal Favourite," 1863. She *edited:* "The Lover and the Husband," 1841; "The Woman of a Certain Age," 1841; "Fascination," 1842; "Modern French Life," 1842; "The Queen of Denmark," 1846; and probably was the translator of Saintine's "Picciola," 1837.—SHARP, R. FARQUHARSON, 1897, *A Dictionary of English Authors, p.* 115.

GENERAL

Many of Mrs. Gore's novels are works in which the present state of society and manners is more or less clearly impressed; they are pictures of the time and no more.—CUNNINGHAM, ALLAN, 1833, *Biographical and Critical History of the Literature of the Last Fifty Years.*

"Mrs. Gore." Phœbus open'd his arms, with a face,
In the gladness of which was the coming embrace.
"For her satire," he said, "wasn't evil, a bit;
But as full of good heart, as of spirits and wit;
Only somewhat he found, now and then, which dilated
A little too much on the fashions it rated,
And heaps of 'Polite Conversation' so true,
That he, once, really wish'd the three volumes were two;
But not when she dwelt upon daughters or mothers;
Oh, then the three made him quite long for three others."
—HUNT, LEIGH, 1837, *Blue-stocking Revels.*

By the way, how is it that your certainly very clever friend, Mrs. Gore, cannot do more for me than skim along the surface? I never knew so much real talent in seizing the outside of characters, and drawing magic lantern pictures, so entirely fail in creating permanent interest. I have sent home "Mrs. Armytage" a second time, without getting quite half through, and yet how clever the individual portraits!—WARD, R. PLUMER, 1841, *Letter to P. G. Patmore, Oct.* 20; *My Friends and Acquaintance by P. G. Patmore, vol.* II, *p.* 190.

It is well known in the literary circles that Mrs. Gore is the author of that clever, but surpassingly impudent book, "Cecil." We believe she has never avowed it, and has rather, on the contrary, kept up a little mystification about it. But there is really no doubt on the subject. She wrote the story, and Mr. Beckford helped her to the learning. The public have been often perplexed by Mrs. Gore's Greek and Latin, which, although they were never paraded so impertinently as the polyglot pretensions of Lady Morgan, were still remote enough from the ordinary course of female accomplishments to startle the public. Where they came from on former occasions we know not; but in this instance they may be referred to Mr. Beckford, together with the still more recondite scraps of far-off tongues that are scattered through the work. "Cecil" is a perfect representation of the worst, but certainly the most dazzling aspect of Mrs. Gore's genius. It abounds in flashy, high-mettled fashionable slang, and is thrown off in such a vein of upsetting egotism, with such a shew of universal knowledge, and in a style of such dashing effrontery, that it carries the multitude fairly off their legs. There never was a novel written at such a slapping pace. The fearlessness of the execution diverts attention from its deficiencies as a work of art, and helps in a great degree to conceal the real poverty of the conception. But books of this class will not endure the test of re-perusal. Their shallowness becomes palpable at the second reading, even to those who have not sufficient discernment to detect it at once. As there is nothing so intolerable as dulness, so there is nothing so attractive as vivacity. And this is the predominant quality which has ensured the success of "Cecil." The unflagging gaiety by which the story is lighted up, puts the reader into the best possible humour with himself and the author.—HORNE, RICHARD HENGIST, 1844, *A New Spirit of the Age.*

Is one of the most popular of the living female novelists of England; the number of her works would give her celebrity, had she no other claim. She is, however, a powerful and brilliant writer, and it seems almost a paradox to assert, that her surprising fertility of imagination should be an obstacle to her attaining the high literary reputation she merits. But her works are so unfailingly presented to the public, so constantly poured out, that they are received like the flowers and fruits, acceptable and delightful, but not to be sought for and praised, as some rare occasional production. We revel in our showers of roses, but they are commonplace, while we make a wonder of some prickly production of a foreign bed.—HALE, SARAH JOSEPHA, 1852, *Woman's Record*, p. 676.

The success of this popular novelist in her sketches of the prevailing tone of fashionable society is admitted by the ablest critics.—ALLIBONE, S. AUSTIN, 1854-58, *A Critical Dictionary of English Literature*, vol. I, p. 708.

Mrs. Gore long continued to furnish one or two novels a year. She had seen much of the world both at home and abroad, and was never at a loss for character or incident. The worst of her works must be pronounced clever. Their chief value consists in their lively caustic pictures of fashionable and high society. Besides her long array of regular novels, Mrs. Gore contributed short tales and sketches to the periodicals, and was perhaps unparalleled for fertility. All her works were welcome to the circulating libraries. They are mostly of the same class—all pictures of existing life and manners; but the want of genuine feeling, of passion and simplicity, in her living models, and the endless frivolities of their occupations and pursuits, makes us sometimes take leave of Mrs. Gore's fashionable triflers in the temper with which Goldsmith parted from Beau Tibbs—"The company of fools may at first make us smile, but at last never fails of rendering us melancholy."—CHAMBERS, ROBERT, 1876, *Cyclopædia of English Literature*, ed. *Carruthers.*

Her writings are characterised by great cleverness in invention, lively satire, shrewd insight into character, and keen observation of life. Their popularity at the time was great, and they possess historic value as a faithful picture of the life and pursuits of the English upper classes during a partic-

ular period. George IV observed respecting "The Manners of the Day, or Women as they are," that it was "the best bred and most amusing novel published in his remembrance."—BOASE, G. C., 1890, *Dictionary of National Biography*, vol. XXII, p. 237.

She still continued to write during the earlier portion of the Victorian period, but her style and manner were essentially of the past. The fashionable novel, as she understood and executed it, was of Almacks and that transition period between the wild days of the Regency and the newborn decorum of the young Queen's purified court.—OLIPHANT, MARGARET O. W., 1892, *The Victorian Age of English Literature*, p. 303.

The fashionable novel proper came, however, after a while, to be almost stereotyped as to certain of its features. The stock incidents included duels and elopements, and the third volume always ended with a wedding. There was of necessity a hero, who was *de rigueur* handsome and morally perfect, and a heroine who was beautiful and good; in most cases a villain was added, who invariably came to a bad end. One of the first to elevate this type of writing to almost the highest level whereto it could attain, was Mrs. Catherine Grace Gore.—RUSSELL, PERCY, 1894, *A Guide to British and American Novels*, p. 151.

Where is that witty old ghost of the Silver Fork school, Mrs. Gore.—LOCKER-LAMPSON, FREDERICK, 1895, *My Confidences*, p. 334.

The novel of high life that thus skimmed the surface of things fell into the hands of women, and degenerated into trash and rhapsody. . . . The best of the class are the one hundred or more novels and tales written by Mrs. Catherine Gore between 1824 and 1862. About many of them that have come in my way is an air of profound learning. Not infrequently three languages are represented in a motto standing at the head of a chapter; while the language within is a mixture of aristocratic English and stock French phrases. Mrs. Gore's subject was commonly club life, ennui, fribbledom, and the political questions of the hour. The writer who had rejuvenated this kind of fiction, and given it a political bias, transformed it.—CROSS, WILBUR L., 1899, *The Development of the English Novel*, p. 174.

Sir Francis Palgrave

1788-1861

Sir Francis Palgrave (born 1788, died 1861), historian, was the son of a Jewish stock-broker named Cohen, and changed his name in 1823 on embracing the Christian faith. The failure, and consequent poverty, of his father compelled him to become a solicitor's clerk in 1803, but in 1821 he was employed under the Record Commission in the publication of original documents. He was called to the bar in 1827, and practised his profession for some years, obtaining distinction in pedigree cases before the House of Lords. In 1832 knighthood was the reward bestowed for important contributions to historical and anti-quarian literature. From 1833-5 he served on the Municipal Corporation Commission; and in 1838 was appointed deputy-keeper of her Majesty's Records, a post he held until his death. Of his voluminous writings and editions the most important are his "Par-liamentary Writs" (1827-34); "History of England" (1831); "Rise and Progress of the English Commonwealth" (1832); "Rotuli Curiæ Regis" (1835); "Calendars and In-ventories of the Exchequer" (1836); "The Merchant and the Friar" [Marco Polo and Friar Bacon] (1837); "History of Normandy and of England" (1851-64).—SANDERS, LLOYD C., ed., 1887, Celebrities of the Century, p. 806.

GENERAL

The work of my learned and gifted friend, Sir Francis Palgrave, replete with omni-farious reading and fearless spirit, though not always commanding the assent of more skeptical tempers.—HALLAM, HENRY, 1848, Views of the State of Europe During the Middle Ages, Preface to Supplemental Notes.

The works of Palgrave and Alison gave earnest of that conscientious zeal and pains-taking attention to detail which are char-acteristic of the best histories of the period. The most valuable labours of Sir Francis Palgrave were directed to the elucidation of early English history, and supply, in an agreeable style, fuller and more accurate in-formation than was formerly possessed re-garding the Saxons and the Normans.—SPALDING, WILLIAM, 1852, A History of English Literature, p. 420.

No account of the historians of early Eng-land could be regarded as complete, if hon-orable mention is not made of Sir Francis Palgrave, whose antiquarian lore is so great and withal so accurate, that we not only have obtained the same light from his labors on the past which we enjoy on the present, but feel equal confidence in threading our way through the one which we do in thread-ing the other.—ALISON, SIR ARCHIBALD, 1853, History of Europe, 1815-1852, ch. v.

Few living men have equalled him in the extent of his reading. Still fewer have sur-passed him in sincere and independent in-quiry. He has won the deep gratitude of every historical student by the new light which he has thrown upon the ancient in-stitutions of our own land. He has at least

deserved, if he has not always won, a grati-tude deeper still for being the first to find the key to the great riddle of general mediæ-val history. The man who discovered that the Roman Empire did not terminate in A. D. 476, but that the still living and act-ing imperial power formed an historical centre for centuries later, merits a place in the very highest rank of historical in-quirers.—FREEMAN, EDWARD A., 1859, Sir F. Palgrave's Normandy and England, Ed-inburgh Review, vol. 109, p. 486.

Some fanciful positions and generalisa-tions have been adopted by Sir Francis Pal-grave, but few have dug so deep into the dark mines of our early history, and the nation owes him gratitude for the light he has thrown on the origin of the British people and institutions. — CHAMBERS, ROBERT, 1876, Cyclopædia of English Literature, ed. Carruthers.

The first really critical inquiry into the earlier ages of English history, and even had he achieved less himself, would be worthy of high praise for his services as a pioneer in clearing the ground for those who came after. His "History of Normandy and England," which was not completed at his death in 1861, is, however, a work of ac-knowledged merit.—OLIPHANT, MARGARET O. W., 1892, The Victorian Age of English Literature, p. 179.

There can be no question as to his serv-ices both in popularising and in promoting the critical study of mediæval history in England.—WROTH, WARWICK, 1895, Dic-tionary of National Biography, vol. XLIII, p. 108.

Theodore Winthrop

1828–1861

Born at New Haven, Conn., Sep. 22, 1828; killed at the battle of Big Bethel, June 10, 1861. An American author, and officer (of New York Volunteers) in the Civil War. He was military secretary to General Butler, with the rank of major. He wrote "Cecil Dreeme" (1861), "John Brent" (1862), "Edwin Brothertoft" (1862), "The Canoe and the Saddle" (1862), "Life in the Open Air" (1863).—SMITH, BENJAMIN E., ed., 1894–97, *The Century Cyclopedia of Names, p.* 1067.

PERSONAL

Theodore Winthrop's life, like a fire long smouldering, suddenly blazed up into a clear, bright flame, and vanished. Those of us who were his friends and neighbors, by whose firesides he sat familiarly, and of whose life upon the pleasant Staten Island, where he lived, he was so important a part, were so impressed by his intense vitality, that his death strikes us with peculiar strangeness, like sudden winter-silence falling upon these humming fields of June. As I look along the wooded brook-side by which he used to come, I should not be surprised, if I saw that knit, wiry, light figure moving with quick, firm, leopard tread over the grass,—the keen gray eye, the clustering fair hair, the kind, serious smile, the mien of undaunted patience. If you did not know him, you would have found his greeting a little constrained,—not from shyness, but from genuine modesty and the habit of society. You would have remarked that he was silent and observant rather than talkative; and whatever he said, however gay or grave, would have had the reserve of sadness upon which his whole character was drawn. If it were a woman who saw him for the first time, she would inevitably see him through a slight cloud of misapprehension; for the man and his manner were a little at variance. The chance is that at the end of five minutes she would have thought him conceited. At the end of five months she would have known him as one of the simplest and most truly modest of men.—CURTIS, GEORGE WILLIAM, 1861, *Theodore Winthrop, Atlantic Monthly, vol.* 8, *p.* 242.

GENERAL

Our American life lost by his death one who, had he lived, would have represented it, reported it to the world, soul and body together; for he comprehended its spirit, as well as saw its outer husk; he was in sympathy with all its manifestations. That quick, intelligent eye saw everything; that kindly, sympathetic spirit comprehended always the soul of things; and no life, however common, rugged, or coarse, was to him empty. If he added always something of his own nobility of heart, if he did not pry out with prurient eyes the meannesses of life around him, the picture he drew was none the less true,—was, indeed, it seems to me, all the more true. Therefore I say that his early death was a loss to American literature, or, to speak more accurately, to that too small part of our literature which concerns itself with American life.—NORDHOFF, CHARLES, 1863, *Theodore Winthrop's Writings, Atlantic Monthly, vol.* 12, *p.* 154.

There has been perhaps no loss to the literature of the nation from the war so severe as that of Theodore Winthrop. It is at the same time—and it is one of the remarkable occurrences which mark a period in every respect exceptional—almost certain that we owe the gift of his writings to the public to the war. The sacrifice of the soldier secured the fame of the author. . . . "John Brent," his second novel, carries us across the Plains from California in a style such as pen has never crossed them before. The book should have been called "Don Fulano," in honor of the matchless steed who so faithfully bears his master to the redressal of wrong and setting up of right, at eventful crises. A horse has seldom been so admirably described, so sharply individualized. It is a work to rank with the great masters of the chisel and the palette as well as of the pen. The descriptions of prairie life, of the mountain passes, the wavy landscape, the far-off approach of caravans, are admirable. So too is the individualization of the characters, the fresh, vigorous overland mail-carriers, the Oregon frontiersman, the disgusting rabble of Mormons from Lancashire.—DUYCKINCK, EVERT A., AND GEORGE L., 1865–75, *Cyclopædia of American Literature, ed. Simons, vol.* II, *pp.* 824, 825.

Mr. Winthrop's writings show a freshness, a versatility, and a vigor which make his early death a loss greatly to be deplored.

HENRY DAVID THOREAU

From an Engraving by F. T. Stuart.

THEODORE PARKER

Engraving by S. A. Schoff.   From a
Daguerreotype by Allen & Horton.

Had he lived, there can be little doubt that he would have become one of the greatest lights of American letters.—HART, J. S., 1872, *A Manual of American Literature, p.* 477.

The last sentence, in evident deprecation of the charge of partiality, points to the fact that Winthrop's wandering life was a hindrance to the concentration of his energies; even to the perfection of his style. . . . On the other hand, the adventurous activity of his nature is the source of much of the charm of his work, which, like that of Sidney, to whom Mr. Curtis is fond of comparing him, was more than a mere promise. His claim to recognition lies not merely in his having been an actor as well as a dreamer, but in the fact that he has done substantial and peculiar though imperfectly-appreciated, work. He belonged in part to the class of the older writers in whose minds incident predominated, but he was also an analyst of the school of Hawthorne, and might, with length of years have been his most legitimate successor. The first phase is represented by his novel, "John Brent," in great measure a graphic record of his experiences in the Far West, mingled with imaginative romance. The descriptive passages in this book, especially that of the chase, rivet our attention because they are brought into contact with scenes of emotion and passion, and are not mere transcripts of still life, such as we find on the gaudily-printed papers of old inn walls. "Edwin Brothertoft" is a tale of the Revolutionary War, which only misses being a classic by its frequent crudity of expression and ultraferocity of plot.—NICHOL, JOHN, 1882-85, *American Literature, p.* 371.

They are strong stories, full of action and passion, but are written in a self-conscious, abrupt style; the sentiment is forced and the characterization unnatural. . . . Winthrop lacked experience, and in aiming to be original, became cramped and artificial: but he aimed high, and there are germs of good possibilities in his pages.—HAWTHORNE, JULIAN, AND LEMMON, LEONARD, 1891, *American Literature, p.* 216.

His novels, though in parts crude and immature, have a dash and buoyancy—an outdoor air about them—which give the reader a winning impression of Winthrop's personality. The best of them is, perhaps, "Cecil Dreeme," a romance that reminds one a little of Hawthorne, and the scene of which is the New York University building on Washington Square, a locality that has been further celebrated in Henry James's novel of "Washington Square."—BEERS, HENRY A., 1895, *Initial Studies in American Letters, p.* 192.

Henry David Thoreau
1817–1862

Born at Concord, Mass., July 12, 1817: died at Concord, May 6, 1862. An American writer. He graduated at Harvard in 1837, taught school, and afterward became a landsurveyor. He lived alone on the shore of Walden Pond, Concord, 1845–47. He was a transcendentalist, and a friend of Emerson, Alcott, etc.; stood out for the rights of the individual; and was at one time imprisoned for his refusal to pay taxes. Among his works are "A Week on the Concord and Merrimac Rivers" (1849), "Walden, or Life in the Woods" (1854), "Excursions in Field and Forest" (1863: with a memoir by Emerson), "The Maine Woods" (1864), "Cape Cod" (1865), "Letters to Various Persons" (1865: with a notice by Emerson), "A Yankee in Canada, etc." (1866). He wrote for the leading periodicals, and was the author of several poems.—SMITH, BENJAMIN E., *ed.,* 1894-97, *The Century Cyclopedia of Names, p.* 993.

PERSONAL

He is a little under size, with a huge Emersonian nose, bluish gray eyes, brown hair, and a ruddy, weather-beaten face, which reminds me of some shrewd and honest animal's—some retired philosophical woodchuck or magnanimous fox. He dresses very plainly, wears his collar turned over like Mr. Emerson and often an old dress-coat, broad in the skirts, and by no means a fit. He walks about with a brisk, rustic air, and never seems tired.—SANBORN, FRANK B., 1855, *Diary, Henry D. Thoreau (American Men of Letters), p.* 199.

There was somewhat military in his nature not to be subdued, always manly and able, but rarely tender, as if he did not feel himself except in opposition. He wanted a fallacy to expose, a blunder to pillory, I may say required a little sense of victory, a roll of the drum, to call his powers into full exercise. It cost him nothing to say No; indeed, he found it much easier than to say Yes. It seemed as if his first instinct on hearing a proposition was to controvert it, so impatient was he of the limitations of our daily thought. This habit, of course, is a little chilling to the social affections; and though the companion would in the end acquit him of any malice or untruth, yet it mars conversation. Hence, no equal companion stood in affectionate relations with one so pure and guileless. "I love Henry," said one of his friends, "but I cannot like him; and as for taking his arm, I should as soon think of taking the arm of an elm-tree." Yet, hermit and stoic as he was, he was really fond of sympathy, and threw himself heartily and childlike into the company of young people whom he loved, and whom he delighted to entertain, as he only could, with the varied and endless anecdotes of his experiences by field and river. And he was always ready to lead a huckleberry-party or a search for chestnuts or grapes. . . . There is a flower known to botanists, one of the same genus with our summer plant called "Life-Everlasting," a *Gnaphalium* like that which grows on the most inaccessible cliffs of the Tyrolese mountains, where the chamois dare hardly venture, and which the hunter, tempted by its beauty, and by his love, (for it is immensely valued by the Swiss maidens), climbs the cliffs to gather, and is sometimes found dead at the foot, with the flower in his hand. It is called by botanists the *Gnaphalium leontopodium*, but by the Swiss *Edelweiss*, which signifies *Noble Purity*. Thoreau seemed to me living in the hope to gather this plant, which belonged to him of right. The scale on which his studies proceeded was so large as to require longevity, and we were the less prepared for his sudden disappearance. The country knows not yet, or in the least part, how great a son it has lost. — EMERSON, RALPH WALDO, 1862, *Thoreau, Atlantic Monthly, vol.* 10, *pp.* 240, 249.

Thoreau was a stoic, but he was in no sense a cynic. His neighbors in the village thought him odd and whimsical, but his practical skill as a surveyor and in woodcraft was known to them. No man was his enemy, and some of the best men were his fastest friends. But his life was essentially solitary and reserved. Careless of appearances in later days, when his hair and beard were long, if you had seen him in the woods you might have fancied Orson passing by; but had you stopped to talk with him, you would have felt that you had seen the shepherd of Admetus's flock, or chatted with a wiser Jacques. For some time past he had been sinking under a consumption. He made a journey to the West a year ago, but in vain; and returned to die quietly at home.—CURTIS, GEORGE WILLIAM, 1862, *The Easy Chair, Harper's Magazine, vol.* 25, *p.* 270.

To him no vain regrets belong,
Whose soul, that finer instrument,
Gave to the world no poor lament,
But wood-notes ever sweet and strong.
O lonely friend! he still will be
A potent presence, though unseen,—
Steadfast, sagacious, and serene:
Seek not for him,—he is with thee.
—ALCOTT, LOUISA M., 1863, *Thoreau's Flute, Atlantic Monthly, vol.* 12, *p.* 281.

He was short of stature, well built, and such a man as I have fancied Julius Cæsar to have been. Every movement was full of courage and repose; the tones of his voice were those of Truth herself; and there was in his eye the pure bright blue of the New England sky, as there was sunshine in his flaxen hair. He had a particularly strong aquiline-Roman nose, which somehow reminded me of the prow of a ship.—CONWAY, MONCURE DANIEL, 1866, *Thoreau, Fraser's Magazine, vol.* 73, *p.* 461.

If any American deserves to stand as a representative of the experience of recluseness, Thoreau is the man. His fellow-feelings and alliances with men were few and feeble; his disgusts and aversions many, as well as strongly pronounced. All his life he was distinguished for his aloofness, austere self-communion, long and lonely walks. He was separated from ordinary persons in grain and habits, by the poetic sincerity of his passion for natural objects and phenomena. As a student and lover of the material world he is a genuine apostle of solitude, despite the taints of affectation, inconsistency, and morbidity which his writings betray. . . . There was uncommon love in him, but it felt itself repulsed, and, too proud to beg or moan, put on stoicism and wore it until the mask became the face. His opinionative stiffness and contempt were his hurt self-respect protecting itself against the conventionalities and scorns of those who despised what he revered and revered what he despised. His interior life, with the relations of thoughts and things, was intensely tender and true, however sorely ajar he may have been with persons and with the ideas of persons. If he was sour, it was on a store of sweetness; if sad, on a fund of gladness.—ALGER, WILLIAM ROUNSEVILLE, 1866, *The Solitudes of Nature and of Man, pp.* 329, 337.

His readers came many miles to see him, attracted by his writings. Those who could not come sent their letters. Those who came when they could no more see him, as strangers on a pilgrimage, seemed as if they had been his intimates, so warm and cordial was the sympathy they received from his letters. If he also did the duties that lay nearest and satisfied those in his immediate circle, certainly he did a good work; and whatever the impressions from the theoretical part of his writings, when the matter is probed to the bottom, good sense and good feeling will be detected in it. A great comfort in him, he was eminently reliable. No whim of coldness, no absorption of his time by public or private business, deprived those to whom he belonged of his kindness and affection. He was at the mercy of no caprice: of a reliable will and uncompromising sternness in his moral nature, he carried the same qualities into his relation with others, and gave them the best he had, without stint. He loved firmly, acted up to his love, was a believer in it, took pleasure and satisfaction in abiding by it. . . . In height, he was about the average; in his build, spare, with limbs that were rather longer than usual, or of which he made a longer use. His face, once seen, could not be forgotten. The features were quite marked: the nose aquiline or very Roman, like one of the portraits of Cæsar (more like a beak, as was said); large, overhanging brows above the deepest set blue eyes that could be seen, in certain lights, and in others gray,—eyes expressive of all shades of feeling, but never weak or near-sighted; the forehead not unusually broad or high, full of concentrated energy and purpose; the mouth with prominent lips, pursed up with meaning and thought when silent, and giving out when open a stream of the most varied and instructive sayings. His hair was a dark brown, exceedingly abundant, fine and soft; and for several years he wore a comely beard. His whole figure had an active earnestness, as if he had no moment to waste.—CHANNING, WILLIAM ELLERY, 1873, *Thoreau: The Poet-Naturalist, pp.* 18, 25.

Both admirer and censor, both Channing in his memoir, and Lowell in his well-known criticism, have brought the eccentricities of Thoreau into undue prominence, and have placed too little stress on the vigor, the good sense, the clear perceptions, of the man. I have myself walked, talked, and corresponded with him, and can testify that the impression given by both these writers is far removed from that ordinarily made by Thoreau himself. While tinged here and there, like most New England thinkers of his time, with the manner of Emerson, he was yet, as a companion, essentially original, wholesome, and enjoyable. Though more or less of a humorist, nursing his own whims, and· capable of being tiresome when they came uppermost, he was easily led away from them to the vast domains of literature and nature, and then poured forth endless streams of the most interesting talk. He taxed the patience of his companions, but not more so, on the whole, than is done by many other eminent talkers when launched upon their favorite themes. It is hard for one who thus knew him to be quite patient with Lowell in what seems almost wanton misrepresentation. Lowell applies to Thoreau the word "indolent": but you might as well speak of the indolence of a self-registering thermometer; it does not go about noisily, yet it never knows an idle moment. Lowell says that Thoreau "looked with utter contempt on the august drama of destiny, of which his country was the scene, and on which the curtain had already risen"; but was it Thoreau, or Lowell, who found a voice when the curtain fell, after the first act of that drama, upon the scaffold of John Brown? Lowell accuses him of a "seclusion which keeps him in the public eye," and finds something "delightfully absurd" in his addressing six volumes under such circumstances to the public, when the fact is that most of these volumes were made up by friends, after Thoreau's death, from his manuscripts, or from his stray papers in newspapers and magazines.—HIGGINSON, THOMAS WENTWORTH, 1879-88, *Short Studies of American Authors, p. 22.*

From my first introduction, Thoreau seemed to me a man who had experienced Nature as other men are said to have experienced religion. An unmistakable courage, sincerity, and manliness breathed in every word he uttered.—WHIPPLE, EDWIN PERCY, 1882, *Some Recollections of Ralph Waldo Emerson, Harper's Magazine, vol. 65, p. 581.*

Thoreau was, probably, the wildest civilized man this country has produced, adding to the shyness of the hermit and woodsman the wildness of the poet, and to the wildness of the poet the greater ferity and elusiveness of the mystic. An extreme product of civilization and of modern culture, he was yet as untouched by the worldly and commercial spirit of his age and country as any red man that ever haunted the shores of his native stream. He put the whole of Nature between himself and his fellows. A man of the strongest local attachments—not the least nomadic, seldom wandering beyond his native township, yet his spirit was as restless and as impatient of restraint as any nomad or Tartar that ever lived. He cultivated an extreme wildness, not only in his pursuits and tastes, but in his hopes and imaginings. — BURROUGHS, JOHN, 1882, *Henry D. Thoreau, The Century, vol. 24, p. 371.*

Thoreau's thin, penetrating, big-nosed face, even in a bad woodcut, conveys some hint of the limitations of his mind and character. With his almost acid sharpness of insight, with his almost animal dexterity in act, there went none of that large, unconscious geniality of the world's heroes. He was not easy, not ample, not urbane, not even kind; his enjoyment was hardly smiling, or the smile was not broad enough to be convincing; he had no waste lands nor kitchen-midden in his nature, but was all improved and sharpened to a point.— STEVENSON, ROBERT LOUIS, 1882, *Henry David Thoreau, Familiar Studies of Men and Books.*

Thoreau "built himself in Walden woods a den" in 1845,—after his return from tutoring in the family of Emerson's brother at Staten Island; here he wrote most of "Walden" and the "Week on the Concord and Merrimac Rivers," and much more that has been posthumously published; from here he went to jail for refusing to pay a tax on his poll, from here he made the excursion described in "The Maine Woods." He finally removed from Walden in the autumn of 1847, to reside in the house of Emerson during that sage's absence in Europe. An old neighbor of Thoreau's, who had often watched his "stumpy" figure as he hoed the beans, and had even once or twice assisted him in that celestial agriculture, tells us that Thoreau's hut was removed by a gardener to the middle of the bean-field and there occupied for some years. Later it was purchased by a farmer, who set it upon wheels and conveyed it to his farm some miles distant, where it has decayed and gone to pieces.—WOLFE, THEODORE F., 1895, *Literary Shrines, p. 71.*

Thoreau lived very near to nature; nothing escaped his notice, and over birds, beasts and fishes his influence was almost magical. He had simplified life till he had realized the fine savage in himself. His mind was as pure as that of a child, and the high attainments of the scholar never caused him to think less reverently of human life. He had a moral nature both strong and generous.—WARREN, INA RUSSELLE, 1895, *Henry David Thoreau, The Magazine of Poetry, vol. 7, p. 421.*

Another peculiar spirit now and then haunted us, usually sad as a pine tree—Thoreau. His enormous eyes, tame with religious intellect and wild with the loose rein, making a steady flash in this strange unison of forces, frightened me dreadfully at first. . . . When he died, it seemed as if an anemone, more lovely than any other, had been carried from the borders of a wood into its silent depths, and dropped in solitude and shadow, among the recluse ferns and mosses which are so seldom disturbed by passing feet. Son of freedom and opportunity that he was, he touched the heart by giving to nature's peacefulness like the saints, and girding upon his American sovereignty the hair-shirt of service to self-denial. He was happy in his intense discipline of the flesh, as all men are when they have once tasted power—if it is the power which awakens perception of the highest concerns. His countenance had an April pensiveness about it; you would never have guessed that he could write of owls so jocosely. His manner was such as to suggest that he could mope and weep

with them. I never crossed an airy hill or
broad field in Concord, without thinking of
him who had been the companion of space
as well as of delicacy; the lover of the
wood-thrush, as well as of the Indian.
Walden woods rustled the name of
Thoreau whenever we walked in them.—
LATHROP, ROSE HAWTHORNE, 1897, *Memories of Hawthorne, p.* 420.

WALDEN
1854

There is nothing of the mean or sordid
in the economy of Mr. Thoreau, though to
some his simplicity and abstemiousness
may appear trivial and affected; he does
not live cheaply for the sake of saving, nor
idly to avoid labor; but, that he may live
independently and enjoy his great thoughts;
that he may read the Hindoo scriptures
and commune with the visible forms of
nature. We must do him the credit to
admit that there is no mock sentiment, nor
simulation of piety or philanthropy in his
volume. He is not much of a cynic, and
though we have called him a Yankee
Diogenes, the only personage to whom he
bears a decided resemblance is that good-
humored creation of Dickens, Mark Tapley,
whose delight was in being jolly under
difficulties.—BRIGGS, CHARLES F., 1854, *A
Yankee Diogenes, Putnam's Magazine, vol.*
4, *p.* 445.

In describing his hermitage and his forest
life, he says so many pithy and brilliant
things, and offers so many piquant, and,
we may add, so many just comments on
society as it is, that his book is well worth
reading, both for its actual contents and
its suggestive capacity.—PEABODY, AN-
DREW PRESTON, 1854, *Critical Notices,
North American Review, vol.* 79, *p.* 536.

The oddity of its record attracted universal attention. . . . As in the author's
previous work, the immediate incident
is frequently only the introduction to
higher themes. The realities around him
are occasionally veiled by a hazy atmosphere of transcendental speculation,
through which the essayist sometimes
stumbles into abysmal depths of the
bathetic. We have more pleasures, however, in dwelling upon shrewd humors of
the modern contemplative Jacques of the
forest, and his fresh, nice observation of
books and men, which has occasionally
something of a poetic vein. He who would
acquire a new sensation of the world about

him, would do well to retire from cities to
the banks of Walden pond, and he who
would open his eyes to the opportunities of
country life, in its associations of fields and
men, may loiter with profit along the
author's journey on the Merrimack, where
natural history, local antiquities, records,
and tradition, are exhausted in vitalizing
the scene.—DUYCKINCK, EVERT A., AND
GEORGE L., 1855-65-75, *Cyclopædia of
American Literature, ed. Simons, vol.* II, *pp.*
601, 602.

From whatever point of view it be regarded, "Walden" is undoubtedly Thoreau's
masterpiece; it contains the sum and essence of his ideal and ethical philosophy; it
is written in his most powerful and incisive
style, while by the freshness and *naïveté* of
its narrative it excites the sympathy and
imagination of the reader, and wins a popularity far exceeding that of his other
writings.—SALT, H. S., 1890, *The Life of
Henry David Thoreau, p.* 153.

Thoreau showed in a very marked degree
the influence of Emerson. His biographer,
who knew him personally, says that he
imitated Emerson's tones and manners so
that it was annoying to listen to him. Unconsciously he acquired Emerson's style of
writing. He became a master of the short,
epigrammatic sentence. Yet there is often
a rudeness and an inartistic carelessness
about Thoreau's style that is not at all like
Emerson. No one has ever excelled him in
the field of minute description. His acute
powers of observation, his ability to keep
for a long time his attention upon one thing,
and his love of nature and of solitude, all
lend a distinct individuality to his style.—
PATTEE, FRED LEWIS, 1896, *A History of
American Literature, p.* 226.

Like every real book "Walden" is for its
own hours and its own minds; a book for
those who love books, for those who love
nature, for those who love courageous thinking, courageous acting, and all sturdy,
manly virtues; a book to be read through;
a book, also, to be read in parts, as one uses
a manual of devotion; a tonic book in the
truest sense; a book against meanness,
conformity, timidity, discouragement, unbelief; a book easily conceived of as marking an era in a reader's life; a book for the
individual soul against the world.—TOR-
REY, BRADFORD, 1897, *Walden, Introduction, p.* xxiii.

He is an author who has fallen into that

abeyance, awaiting all authors, great or small, at some time or another; but I do think that with him, at least in regard to his most important book, it can be only transitory. I have not read the story of his hermitage beside Walden Pond since the year 1858, but I have a fancy that if I should take it up now, I should think it a wiser and truer conception of the world than I thought it then. It is no solution of the problem; men are not going to answer the riddle of the painful earth by building themselves shanties and living upon beans and watching ant-fights; but I do not believe Tolstoy himself has more clearly shown the hollowness, the hopelessness, the unworthiness of the life of the world than Thoreau did in that book.—HOWELLS, WILLIAM DEAN, 1900, *Literary Friends and Acquaintance, p.* 57.

GENERAL

A vigorous Mr. Thoreau,—who has formed himself a good deal upon one Emerson, but does not want abundant fire and stamina of his own;—recognizes us, and various other things, in a most admiring great-hearted manner; for which, as for *part* of the confused voice from the jury-box (not yet summed into a verdict, nor likely to be summed till Doomsday, nor needful to sum), the poor prisoner at the bar may justly express himself thankful! In plain prose I like Mr. Thoreau very well; and hope yet to hear good and better news of him.—CARLYLE, THOMAS, 1847, *To Emerson, May* 18; *Correspondence of Carlyle and Emerson, ed. Norton, vol.* II, *p.* 160.

He was not a strong thinker, but a sensitive feeler. Yet his mind strikes us as cold and wintry in its purity. A light snow has fallen everywhere in which he seems to come on the track of the shier sensations that would elsewhere leave no trace. We think greater compression would have done more for his fame. A feeling of sameness comes over us as we read so much. Trifles are recorded with an overminute punctuality and conscientiousness of detail. He records the state of his personal thermometer thirteen times a day. . . . His better style as a writer is in keeping with the simplicity and purity of his life. We have said that his range was narrow, but to be a master is to be a master. He had caught his English at its living source, among the poets and prose-writers of its best days; his literature was extensive

and recondite; his quotations are always nuggets of the purest ore; there are sentences of his as perfect as anything in the language, and thoughts as clearly crystallized; his metaphors and images are always fresh from the soil; he had watched Nature like a detective who is to go upon the stand; as we read him, it seems as if all-out-of-doors had kept a diary and become his own Montaigne; we look at the landscape as in a Claude Lorraine glass; compared with his, all other books of similar aim, even White's "Selborne," seem dry as a country clergyman's meteorological journal in an old almanac.—LOWELL, JAMES RUSSELL, 1866-90, *Thoreau; Works, Riverside Ed., p.* 378, 380.

Of all our moralists, he seemed the wholesomest, the busiest, and the best republican citizen in the world; always at home minding his own affairs. A little over-confident by genius, and stiffly individual, dropping society clean out of his theories, while standing friendly in his strict sense of friendship, there was in him an integrity and love of justice that made possible and actual the virtues of Sparta and the Stoics,—all the more welcome in his time of shuffling and pusillanimity. . . . A scholar by birthright, and an author, his fame had not, at his decease, travelled far from the banks of the rivers he described in his books; but one hazards only the truth in affirming of his prose, that in substance and pith, it surpasses that of any naturalist of his time; and he is sure of large reading in the future. . . . More primitive and Homeric than any American, his style of thinking was robust, racy, as if Nature herself had built his sentences and seasoned the sense of his paragraphs with her own vigor and salubrity. Nothing can be spared from them; there is nothing superfluous; all is compact, concrete, as nature is.—ALCOTT, A. BRONSON, 1869, *Concord Days, pp.* 13, 14, 16.

Singular traits run through his writing. His sentences will bear study; meanings not detected at the first glance, subtle hints which the writer himself may not have foreseen, appear. It is a good English style, growing out of choice reading and familiarity with the classic writers, with the originality adding a piquant humor and unstudied felicities of diction. He was not in the least degree an imitator of any writer, old or new, and with little of his times or their opinions in his books. Never eager, with a pensive hesitancy he steps about his native fields, singing the praises of music and spring and morning, forgetful of himself. No matter where he might have lived, or in what circumstance, he would have been a writer; he was made for this by all his tendencies of mind and temperament; a writer because a thinker and even a philosopher, a lover of wisdom. . . . He had that pleasant art of convertibility, by which he could render the homely strains of Nature into homely verse and prose, holding yet the flavor of their immortal origins; while meagre and barren writers upon science do perhaps intend to describe that quick being of which they prose, yet never loose a word of happiness or humor.—CHANNING, WILLIAM ELLERY, 1873, *Thoreau: The Poet-Naturalist, pp.* 31, 234.

There are certain writers in American literature who charm by their eccentricity as well as by their genius, who are both original and originals. The most eminent, perhaps, of these was Henry D. Thoreau— a man who may be said to have penetrated nearer to the physical heart of Nature than any other American author. Indeed, he "experienced" nature as others are said to experience religion. . . . He was so completely a naturalist that the inhabitants of the woods in which he sojourned forgot their well-founded distrust of man, and voted him the freedom of their city. His descriptions excel even those of Wilson, Audubon, and Wilson Flagg, admirable as these are, for he was in closer relation with the birds than they, and carried no gun in his hand. In respect to human society, he pushed his individuality to individualism; he was never happier than when absent from the abodes of civilization, and the toleration he would not extend to a Webster or a Calhoun he extended freely to a robin or a wood-chuck. With all this peculiarity, he was a poet, a scholar, a humorist, also, in his way, a philosopher and philanthropist; and those who knew him best, and entered most thoroughly into the spirit of his character and writings, are the warmest of all the admirers of his genius.—WHIPPLE, EDWIN PERCY, 1876-86, *American Literature and Other Papers, ed. Whittier, p.*111.

All I claim for Thoreau is a disinterested and not a one-sided and prejudiced hearing.

Because he hated the hypocrisies and make-shifts of our modern social life, and plainly said so, do not let us therefore conclude that he was *only* morbid and stoical; let us do him justice as the patriot and reformer also; and try to discover how it was that the man who held society in such despite on some accounts was so eager to purify it from the worst incubus that probably ever rested upon it. It was Thoreau's love of Nature that formed the basis of his peculiar simplicity and dislike of what was involved, doubtful, and morally tortuous: if we get to understand that, much in his character which is otherwise puzzling, may become clear to us.—JAPP, ALEXANDER H. (H. A. PAGE), 1877, *Thoreau: His Life and Aims, Preface, p.* ix.

"The man who goes alone can start to-day," was one of his sayings; "but he who travels with another must wait till that other is ready, and it may be a long time before they get off." It is this self-contained and self-sustaining temper which gives zest to all that Thoreau does and says, and makes him so thoroughly original.—HUGHES, THOMAS, 1878, *The Academy.*

Whatever question there may be of his talent, there can be none, I think, of his genius. It was a slim and crooked one, but it was eminently personal He was imperfect, unfinished, inartistic; he was worse than provincial—he was parochial; it is only at his best that he is readable.—JAMES, HENRY, 1880. *Nathaniel Hawthorne (English Men of Letters), p.* 94.

It is what Thoreau clearly whispered that Whitman so up-roariously bawls.—STEVENSON, ROBERT LOUIS, 1882, *Henry David Thoreau, Familiar Studies of Men and Books.*

Thoreau brought to his intellectual tasks an originality as marked as Emerson's, if not so brilliant and star-like—a patience far greater than his, and a proud independence that makes him the most solitary of modern thinkers.—SANBORN, FRANK B., 1882, *Henry D. Thoreau (American Men of Letters), p.* 149.

Thoreau appeals to many of us who want to live their own lives in their own way, and who do not want to discover, when they come to approach their long home, that they have never lived. He was a great listener to Nature's voice; he was a keen observer and faithful recorder; he watched Nature with a big ledger in his hand; he was very patient.—PURVES, JAMES, 1882, *The Academy, vol.* 22, *p.* 272.

His English, we might judge, was acquired from the poets and prose-writers of its best days. His metaphors and images have the freshness of the soil. His range was narrow, but within his limits he was a master. He needed only a tender and pervading sentiment to have been a Homer. Pure and guileless, and fond of sympathy, he yet was cold and wintry. . . . His works are replete with fine observations, finely expressed. One cannot fail to see the resemblance of his style to Emerson's and Alcott's. Nothing that he wrote can be spared.—WELSH, ALFRED H., 1883, *Development of English Literature and Language, vol.* II, *p.* 413.

Among students and lovers of out-door nature Thoreau has no exact counterpart. It could not be said of him what Isaak Walton said of himself, that his humour was to be "free, and pleasant, and civilly merry." In some respects he reminds us of Gilbert White; but there was this important difference between them—that White loved the study of animals and plants, while Thoreau studied them because he loved them. White desired to know, did not speculate, scarcely wondered; but facts were valuable to Thoreau only in relation to ideas. White once described the author of "The Seasons" as "a nice observer of natural occurrences." The phrase is very good as a description of White himself, but it would be quite inapplicable to Thoreau. Thoreau's interest centred not in nature, but in man. He was a student of life. He chose the woods because existence there seemed to him simpler and truer than in the town; yet every object was to him a symbol having reference to the life of man.—LEWIN, WALTER, 1884, *The Academy, vol.* 26, *p.* 193.

Thoreau's poetry is not of the kind that will lift the reader by any lyric sweep of prodigious exaltation, but it appeals rather to the inner spirit, like the lines of Wordsworth and Emerson. It brings with it no drum and fife; it expresses, instead, the rapture and fervor and ecstasy of the still, small voice. It carries with it the unconscious melody of the brook's ripple and the jocund spirit of the bird's song.—BENTON, JOEL, 1886, *The Poetry of Thoreau, Lippincott's Magazine, vol.* 37, *p.* 500.

It may be doubted whether any other name, in the pleasant company of American writers on nature, is worthy of mention beside his. . . . The writings of Thoreau are comprised in nine volumes—a little library of words written from, to, and in nature. Behind his descriptions is a thoughtful mind, and his observations are strengthened by a decent culture, begun at college and aided by constant reading of a few books. By the bole of the elm-tree Plato seems to stand, and Greek summer hovers over Massachusetts winter. Here is the life of nature, and back of the life, the mind of nature. One of Thoreau's biographers was right in calling him a "poet-naturalist." He was too much a poet to forget the soul of things, the ideal behind the real; and too much a naturalist to neglect the constant habit of accurate observation. He might have said to the forests and streams of Concord, to its fauna and flora: "A chiel's amang ye, takin' notes." His notes of nature and natural history were taken because he loved his subjects, and not because he wanted to rush into print.—RICHARDSON, CHARLES F., 1887, *American Literature,* 1607-1885, *vol.* I, *pp.* 384, 387.

The interest in his books has steadily grown, and of late years many other writers have followed his footsteps in the woods and fields. But no one has rivalled Thoreau; the native power and fertility of his mind, his sturdy independence and originality, his keen perception of nature, and of the poetry of nature, the extent of his reading, and the delightful qualities of his style, combine to render him the ablest and most attractive of the writers of this century upon his chosen themes. He must be an author among ten thousand for whom so much has to be ignored or tolerated, and who yet is everywhere read with delight, in spite of passages on which some pitying angel should have dropped a tear.—UNDERWOOD, FRANCIS H., 1888, *Henry David Thoreau, Good Words, vol.* 29, *p.* 452.

One of the most strongly-marked individualities of modern times. . . . Thoreau's fame will rest on "Walden," the "Excursions," and his "Letters," though he wrote nothing which is not deserving of notice. Up till his thirtieth year he dabbled in verse, but he had little ear for metrical music, and he lacked the spiritual impulsiveness of the true poet. He had occasional flashes of insight and could record beautifully, notwithstanding: his little poem "Haze" is surcharged with concentrated loveliness. His weakness as a philosopher is his tendency to base the laws of the universe on the experience-born, thought-produced convictions of one man—himself. His weakness as a writer is the too frequent striving after antithesis and paradox. If he had had all his own originality without the itch of appearing original, he would have made his fascination irresistible. As it is, Thoreau holds a unique place. He was a naturalist, but absolutely devoid of the pedantry of science; a keen observer, but no retailer of disjointed facts. He thus holds sway over two domains: he has the adherence of the lovers of fact and of the children of fancy. He must always be read, whether lovingly or interestedly, for he has all the variable charm, the strange saturninity, the contradictions, austerities, and delightful surprises, of Nature herself.—SHARP, WILLIAM, 1888, *Encyclopædia Britannica, Ninth Ed., vol.* XXIII.

In his moral and intellectual growth and experience, Thoreau seems to have reacted strongly from a marked tendency to invalidism in his own body. He would be well in spirit at all hazards. What was this neverending search of his for the wild but a search for health, for something tonic and antiseptic in nature? Health, health, give me health, is his cry. He went forth into nature as the boys go to the fields and woods in spring after wintergreens, black-birch, crinkle-root, and sweetflag; he had an unappeasable hunger for the pungent, the aromatic, the bitter-sweet, for the very rind and salt of the globe. He fairly gnaws the ground and the trees in his walk, so craving is his appetite for the wild. He went to Walden to study, but it was as a deer goes to a deer-lick; the brine he was after did abound there. Any trait of wildness and freedom suddenly breaking out in any of the domestic animals as when your cow leaped your fence like a deer and ate up your corn, or your horse forgot that he was not a mustang on the plains, and took the bit in his mouth, and left your buggy and family behind high and dry, etc., was eagerly snapped up by him. Ah, you have not tamed them, you have not broken them yet! He makes a most charming entry in his journal about a little boy

he one day saw in the street, with a home-made cap on his head made of a wood-chuck's skin. He seized upon it as a horse with the crib-bite seizes upon a post. It tasted good to him. — BURROUGHS, JOHN, 1889, *Indoor Studies, p.* 13.

There has always been to me something fascinating about this out-door idealist. I never have been, and probably never shall be, a sympathizer with the view which makes Thoreau a skulker, as Carlyle calls him, or a loafer, as most of our typical American business men, if they know anything about him at all, would probably dub him. At the same time, I will confess that the man's asceticism has less fascination for me than the persistency with which he harps upon the idea that nine-tenths or ninety-nine one-hundredths of our people waste their time in making money; touch Thoreau at any point with regard to business policy or business life, and he fairly bristles with sarcasm and jibes. It has been a life-long wonder to me that the man has not been valued more highly even in this community devoted to matters of fact, and that so few outside of a narrow circle of writers and thinkers know anything about him. I am convinced that the time will come when the name of Henry David Thoreau will stand high in American annals. He was our first noted Protestant —passionate, earnest, persistent, honest,— against the sordid materialism of this country.—HUBERT, PHILIP G., JR., 1889, *Liberty and a Living, p.* 171.

It is the close alliance or unity of Thoreau's genius and personal character which gives such power to his words for the purpose I have in view, namely, to awaken or revive our interest in the worthiest things, to lift us above the world of care and sadness into that fairer world which is always waiting to receive us.—BLAKE, H. G. O., 1890, *ed. Thoreau's Thoughts, Introduction, p.* v.

It has been claimed for Thoreau by some of his admirers, never by himself, that he was a man of science, a naturalist. Certainly, in some respects, he had in him the material for an almost ideal naturalist. His peculiar powers of observation, and habits of noting and recording natural facts, his patience, his taste for spending his days and nights in the open air, seem to furnish everything that is required. Nor would his morbid dislike of dissection have been any serious bar, for the least worked but by no means the least important portion of natural history is the study of living forms, and for this Thoreau seems to have been peculiarly adapted; he had acquired one of the rarest of arts, that of approaching birds, beasts and fishes, and exciting no fear. There are all sorts of profoundly interesting investigations which only such a man can profitably undertake. But that right question which is at least the half of knowledge was hidden from Thoreau; he seems to have been absolutely deficient in scientific sense. His bare, impersonal records of observations are always dull and unprofitable reading; occasionally he stumbles on a good observation, but, not realizing its significance, he never verifies it or follows it up. His science is that of a fairly intelligent school-boy—a counting of birds' eggs and a running after squirrels. Of the vital and organic relationship of facts, or even of the existence of such relationships, he seems to have no perception. Compare any of his books with, for instance, Belt's "Naturalist in Nicaragua," or any of Wallace's books: for the men of science, in their spirit of illuminating inquisitiveness, all facts are instructive; in Thoreau's hands they are all dead. He was not a naturalist: he was an artist and a moralist. —ELLIS, HENRY HAVELOCK, 1890-92, *The New Spirit, p.* 93.

Thoreau's Mysticism, though born out of due time, is pure Darwinian. In that Walden wood he stands as the most wonderful and sensitive register of phenomena, finer and more exact than any cunningly devised measure. He is vision and learning, touch, smelling, and taste incarnate. Not only so, but he knows how to preserve the flashing forest colours in unfading light, to write down the wind's music in a score that all may read, to glean and garner every sensuous impression.—GRAHAM, P. A., 1891, *Nature in Books.*

Of his published works it is not easy to state which is most emphatically characteristic of the man. "Walden" and "A Week" are his most literary productions, and upon the whole, represent him at his highest level, although one may not forget his breezy "Excursions," nor innumerable poetic and lovely pages of his journals. From these we may gather violets during winter, or be encased with ice-crystals and hoar-frost in the fervid midsummer noon. It were likewise difficult to find Nature and

philosophy so poetically interfused as in his week's sojourn on the Concord and Merrimack rivers; and had he accomplished naught save the results of his two years' isolation at Walden, his life had been a most eventful one, prolific in the riches bequeathed to posterity. . . . He is self-conscious and splenetic, full of antipathies and whimsical fancies; and when he would be oracular he ruffles up his feathers after the manner of his beloved Walden owl. A strange embodiment of the cynical and the spiritual, of the cosmical and the translunary, together with a strain of the savage, existed in his character,— a certain element of the ghostly and uncanny, as of one who moved in a different sphere from that of his fellow-men, and whose soul was not actually human, but had absorbed some occult influence from the moon and the night.—ELLWANGER, GEORGE H., 1895, *Idyllists of the Country-Side, pp.* 183, 186.

He was a chief of the poet naturalists, and he was not only intimate with nature but friendly. One who knew him said that he talked "about Nature just as if she'd been born and brought up in Concord." He was always more poet than naturalist, for his observation, interesting as it ever is, is rarely novel. It is his way of putting what he has seen that takes us rather than any freshness in the observation itself. His sentences have sometimes a Greek perfection; they have the freshness, the sharpness, and the truth which we find so often in the writings of the Greeks who came early into literature, before everything had been seen and said. Thoreau had a Yankee skill with his fingers, and he could whittle the English language in like manner; so he had also a Greek faculty of packing an old truth into an unexpected sentence. He was not afraid of exaggeration and paradox, so long as he could surprise the reader into a startled reception of his thought. He was above all an artist in words, a ruler of the vocabulary, a master phrase-maker. But his phrases were all sincere; he never said what he did not think; he was true to himself always.—MATTHEWS, BRANDER, 1896, *An Introduction to the Study of American Literature, p.* 192.

His especial greatness is that he gives us standing ground below the surface, a basis not to be washed away. A hundred sentences might be quoted from him which make common observers seem superficial and professed philosophers trivial, but which, if accepted, place the realities of life beyond the reach of danger. He was a spiritual ascetic to whom the simplicity of nature was luxury enough; and this, in an age of growing expenditure, gave him an unspeakable value. To him life itself was a source of joy so great that it was only weakened by diluting it with meaner joys. —HIGGINSON, THOMAS WENTWORTH, 1898, *American Prose, ed. Carpenter, p.* 342.

One can hardly know this author, except by reading him thoroughly, up and down and across, in every light, every season, every labor. The truths of nature quiver in his talk, as color quivers on a chameleon; and when we have caught the changing tints—by how much are we wiser? Full-paced naturalists tell us that he is not always to be relied upon for naming of common facts; and the uncommon ones in his story are largely so, because they radiate (for the time) his *shine* of emotion, of impulse, of far-away comparisons. Yet what tender particularity in his "Excursions" not showing us great wonders; no more does White of Selborne; yet what large country love and yearning! 'Tis a grandchild, telling us of the frosty beard and the quaking voice of the grandpapa. How true is that snowy foliage of his— "answering leaf for leaf to its summer dress!" . . . Unlike many book-making folk, this swart, bumptious man has grown in literary stature since his death; his drawers have been searched, and cast-away papers brought to day. Why this renewed popularity and access of fame? Not by reason of newly detected graces of style; not for weight of his *dicta* about morals, manners, letters; there are safer guides than all these. But there is a new-kindled welcome for the independence, the tender particularity, and the outspokenness of this journal-maker. . If asked for a first-rate essayist, nobody would name Thoreau; if a poet, not Thoreau; if a scientist, not Thoreau; if a political sage, not Thoreau; if a historian of small socialities and of town affairs, again not Thoreau. Yet we read him—with zest, though he is sometimes prosy, sometimes overlong and tedious; but always—Thoreau.—MITCHELL, DONALD G., 1899, *American Lands and Letters, Leather-Stockings to Poe's "Raven," pp.* 277, 278.

It cannot be denied, I think, that Thoreau fascinates. To begin with a minor reason: he is blunt. He attracts a young man because he is an iconoclast. He is no respector of persons, and he says what he thinks. Often we find that he thinks things we should like to think if we only dared. He is very plain-spoken with his reader. In life such treatment would not be tolerated; in a book it is, on the whole, pleasant. The free-handed way in which he criticises the world and the conventions it has learned to work with is delicious. He has no time to waste upon the things most persons have been taught they have to do. He says those things are unnecessary, and he proceeds to do as he pleases. A man who has found time to do that in this world is to be listened to. It does not matter whether what he pleases is what we please; it does not even matter whether his ways are the best ways or the practical ones; so long as he has the courage of his convictions he is an inspiration. But there are men in plenty who have such a possession and are bankrupt at that. With Thoreau one soon begins to find that the better things lie deeper.—SMITH, FREDERICK M., 1900, *Thoreau, The Critic, vol.* 37, *p.* 60.

Thoreau's individuality is often so assertive as to repel a sympathy which it happens not instantly to attract; but that sympathy must be unwholesomely sluggish which would willingly resist the appeal of his communion with Nature. If your lot be ever cast in some remote region of our simple country, he can do you, when you will, a rare service, stimulating your eye to see, and your ear to hear, in all the little commonplaces about you, those endlessly changing details which make life everywhere so unfathomably, immeasurably wonderous. . . . Nor is Thoreau's vitality in literature a matter only of his observation. Open his works almost anywhere,—there are ten volumes of them now,—and even in the philosophic passages you will find loving precision of touch. He was no immortal maker of phrases. Amid bewildering obscurities, Emerson now and again flashed out utterances which may last as long as our language. Thoreau had no such power; but he did possess in higher degree than Emerson himself the power of making sentences and paragraphs artistically beautiful.

Read him aloud, and you will find in his work a trait like that which we remarked in the cadence of Brockden Brown and of Poe; the emphasis of your voice is bound to fall where meaning demands. An effect like this is attainable only through delicate sensitiveness to rhythm.—WENDELL, BARRETT, 1900, *A Literary History of America*, *pp*. 334, 335.

In an attempt at an extreme statement Thoreau was very unlikely to fail. Thanks to an inherited aptitude and years of practice there have been few to excel him with the high lights. In his hands exaggeration becomes one of the fine arts. We will not call it the finest art; his own best work would teach us better than that; but such as it is, with him to hold the brush, it would be difficult to imagine anything more effective.... The sympathetic reader—the only reader—knows what is meant, and what is not meant, and finds it good; as he finds it good when he is bidden to turn the other cheek to the smiter, or to distribute all his living among the poor.—TORREY, BRADFORD, 1899, *Thoreau's Attitude toward Nature, Atlantic Monthly, vol.* 84, *p*. 706.

His writings cleave so closely to the man that they can hardly be studied wholly apart, nor is it necessary so to consider them at length here. What is most remarkable in them is their wild "tang," the subtlety and the penetrative quality of their imaginative sympathy with the things of field, forest, and stream. The minuteness, accuracy, and delicacy of the observation and feeling are remarkable; while mysticism, fancy, poetic beauty, and a vein of shrewd humor often combine with the other qualities to make a whole whose effect is unique. Thoreau's verse is much like Emerson's on a smaller scale and a lower plane, having the same technical faults and occasionally the same piercing felicity of phrase. On the whole, Thoreau must be classed with the minor American authors; but there is no one just like him, and the flavor of his best work is exceedingly fine.—BRONSON, WALTER C., 1900, *A Short History of American Literature, p.* 213.

The greatest by far of our writers on Nature, and the creator of a new sentiment in literature. . . . Much of his writing, perhaps the greater part, is the mere record of observation and classification, and has not the slightest claim on our remembrance,—unless, indeed, it possesses some scientific value, which I doubt. Certainly the parts of his work having permanent interest are just those chapters where he is less the minute observer, and more the contemplative philosopher. Despite the width and exactness of his information, he was far from having the truly scientific spirit; the acquisition of knowledge, with him, was in the end quite subordinate to his interest in the moral significance of Nature, and the words he read in her obscure roll were a language of strange mysteries, sometimes of awe. It is a constant reproach to the prying, self-satisfied habits of small minds to see the reverence of this great-hearted observer before the supreme goddess he so loved and studied.—MORE, PAUL ELMER, 1901, *A Hermit's Notes on Thoreau, Atlantic Monthly, vol.* 87, *p.* 860.

Henry Thomas Buckle

1821–1862

Henry Thomas Buckle was born at Lee, in Kent, 24th November 1821, the son of a London shipowner, a Tory and a staunch churchman. A sickly child, he was for a very short time at an academy in Kentish-Town; no other school and no university claims credit for his education, which yet was liberal in the highest degree. In 1840 he found himself master of £1500 a year; by 1850 he knew eighteen foreign languages, and had amassed a library of 22,000 volumes, chosen mostly to help him in a *magnum opus*, which gradually took shape as "The History of Civilisation in England" (vols. i., ii., 1857–61). His health had been meantime shattered by the loss of an idolised mother; and on 29th May 1862, after six months' wandering in Egypt and Palestine, he died of typhoid fever at Damascus. For over twenty years he had been reckoned one of the first chess players in the world. Buckle's "Miscellaneous and Posthumous Works" were edited by Miss Helen Taylor (1872, new ed. by Grant Allen, 1885). See his Life by A. H. Huth (2 vols. 1880); and "Buckle and his Critics," by J. M. Robertson (1896).—PATRICK AND GROOME, eds., 1897, *Chambers's Biographical Dictionary, p.* 148.

PERSONAL

I dined with Grote yesterday to meet Mr. Buckle, the literary lion of the day. He is not prepossessing in appearance, but he talks very well and makes a great display of knowledge and extensive reading, though without pedantry or dogmatism. There was a small party of literary men to meet him, and Lady William Russell and I acted the part of gallery. — GREVILLE, CHARLES C. F., 1858, *A Journal of the Reign of Queen Victoria from 1852 to 1860, ed. Reeve, March 10, p. 424.*

I live merely for literature; my works are my only actions; they are not wholly unknown, and I leave it to them to protect my name. If they cannot do that, they are little worth. I have never written an essay, or even a single line anonymously, and nothing would induce me to do so, because I deem anonymous writing of every kind to be an evasion of responsibility, and consequently unsuited to the citizen of a free country. Therefore it is that I can easily be judged. I have myself supplied the materials, and to them I appeal. So far from despising public opinion, I regard it with great, though not with excessive respect; and I acknowledge in it the principal source of such influence as I have been able to wield.—BUCKLE, HENRY THOMAS, 1859, *Letter to a Gentleman Respecting Pooley's Case, Miscellaneous and Posthumous Works, ed. Taylor, vol. I, p. 71.*

Buckle, of course, was the card. He talked with a velocity and fulness of facts that was wonderful. The rest of us could do little but listen and ask questions. And yet he did not seem to be lecturing us; the stream of his conversation flowed along easily and naturally. Nor was it didactic; Buckle's range of reading has covered everything in elegant literature, as well as the ponderous works whose titles make so formidable a list at the beginning of his History, and, as he remembers everything he has read, he can produce his stores upon the moment for the illustration of whatever subject happens to come up. — HALE, CHARLES, 1862, *Personal Reminiscences of the Late Henry Thomas Buckle, Atlantic Monthly, vol. 11, p. 489.*

Mr. Buckle's costume was an old black dress-coat his butler, he said, would not have worn, a double-breasted cloth waistcoat, and winter trousers, all over thick flannel under-garments; a wide-awake, with an ample puggery, crowned his spare, stooping figure, covered his bald head, and shaded his unshaven face. He often further endeavoured to protect himself from the sun in a black burnous. I hinted once that all this was rather warm clothing for the Arabian deserts. He replied that, though the commoner sort of Arabs certainly wore nothing but a short shirt yet the great chiefs had several robes.—GLENNIE, J. S. S., 1863, *Mr. Buckle in the East, Fraser's Magazine, vol. 68, p. 175.*

I wish to say a word or two about the eminent person whose name is connected with this way of looking at History, and whose premature death struck us all with such a sudden sorrow. Many of you, perhaps, recollect Mr. Buckle as he stood not so long ago in this place. He spoke more than an hour without a note,—never repeating himself, never wasting words; laying out his matter as easily and as pleasantly as if he had been talking to us at his own fireside. We might think what we please of Mr. Buckle's views, but it was plain enough that he was a man of uncommon power; and he had qualities also—qualities to which he, perhaps, himself attached little value—as rare as they were admirable.—FROUDE, JAMES ANTHONY, 1864, *The Science of History, Short Studies on Great Subjects, vol. I, p. 7.*

Nature had gifted him with a superlative aptitude for the game of chess, and he brought the powers of a rare intellect— clear, penetrating, and sagacious beyond that of most men—to bear upon it. His imagination was that of the poet, "all compact," but subservient to the dictates of a logical judgment. His combinations accordingly, under such guidance, seldom, if ever, exhibited a flaw, and were characterized by exactitude of calculation and brilliant device. He excelled in pawn play, which he conducted with an ingenuity and deadly accuracy worthy of the renowned pawn general, Szen. He gave large odds, such as Rook and Knight, with wonderful skill and success, appearing to have a sort of intuitive knowledge of a strange opponent's chess idiosyncrasy, which enabled him precisely to gauge the kind of risks he might venture to run. The rendering of heavy odds, as every experienced chess player knows, necessitates hazardous and unsound play on the part of the giver. These contests of his at odds, were always full of interest and entertainment to lookers-on, and a gallery two or three deep often surrounded his board in the Strand Divan, where it was his "custom in the afternoon" to recreate himself with his favourite game. I have occasionally seen roars of laughter elicited from the spectators by the crestfallen aspect of some poor discomfited Rook-player, who, with much care and solicitude, having obtained, as he fondly believed, an impregnable position, and suddenly found his defences scattered like chaff, and himself accommodated with a mate, after the sacrifice, by his keen-witted opponent, of two or three pieces in succession. Whether winning or losing, Mr. Buckle was a courteous and pleasant adversary, and sat quietly before the board, smoking his cigar, and pursuing his game with inflexible steadiness.—KENNEDY, CAPTAIN H. A., 1873, *Mr. Buckle as a Chess Player, Westminster Papers, vol.* 6.

During many years' wanderings throughout the world, I have never met any one, whose general knowledge or conversational power could be compared for a moment with that of Buckle; whether in botanizing up Sinai, or geologizing at Petra, in astronomy, medicine, chemistry, theology or languages, everything and every subject appeared to me handled as if by a professional. And yet, however much one differed from him, his kindly mode of reasoning with me against what he believed to be erroneous views was always so pleasant and fascinating that I could not resist returning again and again to his arguments.—GRAY, ALEXANDER HILL, 1880, *The Life and Writings of Henry Thomas Buckle by Alfred Henry Huth, vol.* II, *p.* 201.

There is hardly another instance in history of so great a leap from the complete literary obscurity to the highest pinnacle of literary fame. From the east and the west poured inquiries as to the antecedents of the gifted author, his fame was noised abroad, and in a few years there was hardly an educated man in the world who did not know his name, and what he had done. . . . By the year 1850, the total number of languages he knew was nineteen; namely,— 1. English, 2. French, 3. German, 4. Italian, 5. Spanish, 6. Portuguese, 7. Dutch, 8. Danish, 9 Walloon, 10. Flemish, 11. Swedish, 12. Icelandic, 13. Frisiac, 14. Maorian, 15. Russian, 16. Anglo-Saxon, 17. Hebrew, 18. Greek, 19. Latin. All of them distinct languages, as he observed, though

some of them are similar to each other. The first seven he knew well, and could converse in them or write them with ease. With the rest he had a sufficient acquaintance to be able to read them without trouble; and indeed, he never cared for a knowledge of any language excepting as a key to its literature.—HUTH, ALFRED HENRY, 1880, *The Life and Writings of Henry Thomas Buckle, vol.* I, *pp.* 1, 38.

HISTORY OF CIVILIZATION
1857–61

This volume is certainly the most important work of the season; and it is perhaps the most comprehensive contribution to philosophical history that has ever been attempted in the English language. It is full of thought and original observations; but it is no speculative creation of a brilliant theorist. It is learned in the only true sense of the word. A mere glance at the matter accumulated in the notes will show the labour and reading which it has cost to quarry the materials. These are as judiciously selected as they have been widely sought, and make the volume, besides its proper merits, a most instructive repertory of facts. The style of the text is clear, and always easily followed. It is too diffuse and a little cumbrous; but it is never tedious.—PATTISON, MARK, 1857–89, *History of Civilization in England, Essays, ed. Nettleship, vol.* II, *p.* 396.

I read Buckle's book all day, and got to the end, skipping of course. A man of talent and of a good deal of reading, but paradoxical and incoherent. He is eminently an anticipator, as Bacon would have said. He wants to make a system before he has got the materials; and he has not the excuse which Aristotle had, of having an eminently systematizing mind. The book reminds me perpetually of the Divine Legation.—MACAULAY, THOMAS BABINGTON, 1858, *Journal, March* 24; *Life and Letters, ed. Trevelyan, ch.* xiv, *note.*

It is a remarkable book, as you say, and shows an astonishing amount of knowledge for a man of his years, and a power of generalization remarkable at any age. His views of what is connected with our spiritual nature are, no doubt, unsound, and his radicalism is always offensive. I have seldom read a book with which I have so often been angry, and yet I have learnt, I think, a great deal from it, and had my mind waked up by it upon many matters, for it has suggested to me a great variety of points for inquiry, of which I might otherwise never have thought.—TICKNOR, GEORGE, 1858, *To Robert H. Gardiner, June 25; Life, Letters and Journals of George Ticknor, vol.* II, *p.* 410.

This is the most important work, in its line, from a British hand, which the world has seen for many a year. . . . Mr. Buckle has given us one of the most important contributions which any Englishman has yet made to the philosophy of human history. We wish we had adequate space to point out its excellencies in detail. . . . We congratulate the author on his success. We are sure the thoughtful world will give him a thoughtful welcome, and if his future volumes, which we anxiously look for, shall equal this, he is sure of a high place in the estimation of mankind.—PARKER, THEODORE, 1858, *Buckle's History of Civilization, Christian Examiner, vol.* 64, *pp.* 233, 276.

In truth, the title of the work, as far as it has proceeded, is a misnomer. It is not a history of civilization or of anything else but the statement of a system of doctrine borrowed in great part from the Positive Philosophy of Comte, and supported by a series of illustrations drawn at random from the history of all nations and all ages, and from the records of literature and science. Hence the work is eminently discursive and ill-digested, and might be prosecuted through a dozen more thick volumes, filled with the fruits of the author's desultory reading, but having no more connection with the history of England than with that of China, and affording not even a glimpse of the writer's theory respecting the nature of civilization. In point of mere style, the merits of the book are considerable, and even the rambling and desultory nature of its contents is a source of attractiveness and power. The language is clear, animated and forcible, sometimes rising very nearly to eloquence, and marked with the earnestness of one who thoroughly believes the doctrine which he expounds. Even the cool dogmatism of Mr. Buckle's assertions, and his entire confidence in the truth of his opinions and the force of his arguments, are often as amusing as they are unreasonable. One who has no doubts to express, and no qualifications or exceptions to state, has a great advantage in point of liveliness of manner. Like his great master, Hobbes,

he betrays a good deal of egotism also, a quality which adds much to the freshness and raciness of his style.—BOWEN, FRANCIS, 1861–80, *Gleanings from a Literary Life, p.* 249.

It is long since any hand has taken such a grip of the thistle; it is long since the fierce little land has received such a rouser. Not, by any means, that it is all onslaught. . . . Mr. Buckle has been praised for his summaries of history; but I must say I think his summary of Scottish History as far as the fifteenth century exceedingly poor. . . . Now I challenge any one who knows anything of Scotland and the Scotch to say whether, in Mr. Buckle's outline of Scottish History to the fifteenth century, there is any vision, any gleam, any wink, of Scotland and the Scotch at all. The sketch is featureless, feeble, confused. A few pages of Scott's easiest slipshod, a few pages of old Barbour, or of Blind Henry, are, for the purpose of sheer science even, worth a score of it. . . . In two respects, it seems to me, he deserves the honour of real distinction among his literary contemporaries. In the first place, though not a rich thinker—though rather a man of three or four ideas which he uses as a constant and pronglike apparatus than a man of fertile invention from moment to moment — yet he is a thinker, and a thinker of real force. All that he writes is vertebrate, if one may so express it, with some distinct proportion or other, true or false; and there is consequently the same kind of pleasure in reading anything he writes that there is in reading a dissertation by Mr. John Stuart Mill, or Mr. Herbert Spencer, or others of that select class. In the second place, he is characterized, in a singular degree, by moral fearlessness, by a boldness in speaking right out whatever he thinks.—MASSON, DAVID, 1861, *Mr. Buckle's Doctrine as to the Scotch and their History, Macmillan's Magazine, vol.* 4, *pp.* 178, 183, 186, 189.

The most effective sketch of the intellectual and social state of France in the last century is given in Buckle's "History of Civilisation," vol. i; especially in ch. 8, 11, 12, and 14. His narrative only sets forth the dark side of the picture, and the Christian reader frequently feels pained at some of his remarks; but it is generally correct so far as it goes, and the references are copious to the original sources which the author used. I have therefore frequently rested content with quoting this work without indicating further sources.—FARRAR, ADAM STOREY, 1862, *A Critical History of Free Thought, p. 164, note.*

His style is flowing, but lax and utterly wanting in precision. He has not produced a single follower. His book, though readable, is already dead. The public have forgotten Mr. Buckle and Mr. Buckle's speculations. That the public estimate of his work has changed is certain. Is the change just? . . . Mr. Buckle is in some respects now underrated as he was overrated sixteen years ago, but the verdict of 1873 is far more just than the verdict of 1857.—DICEY, A. V., 1873, *Mr. Buckle, The Nation, vol.* 16, *p.* 270.

It is seldom that so brilliant a success as Mr. Buckle's has been even temporarily achieved by such superficial thinking and such slender scholarship. The immense array of authors cited in his book bears witness to the extent of his reading, but the loose, indiscriminate way in which they are cited shows equally how uncritical and desultory his reading was. . . . We find in Mr. Buckle's book sundry commonplace reflections of quite limited value or applicability, such as the statements that skepticism is favourable to progress, or that over-legislation is detrimental to society. No doubt such commonplaces might be so treated as to acquire the practical value of new contributions to history. But to treat them so required subtle analysis of the facts generalized, and all that Mr. Buckle did was to collect miscellaneous evidences for the statements in their rough, ready-made form. Of generalizations that go below the surface of things, such as Comte's suggestive though indefensible "Law of the Three Stages," we find none in Mr. Buckle. The only attempt at such an analytic theory is the generalization concerning the moral and intellectual factors in social progress, wherein Mr. Buckle's looseness and futile vagueness of thought is shown perhaps more forcibly than anywhere else in his writings. It is not of such stuff as this that a science of historic phenomena can be wrought.—FISKE, JOHN, 1876–85, *Postscript to Mr. Buckle, Darwinism and Other Essays, pp.* 212, 216.

Buckle had a high ideal of the historian's duties, and he laboriously endeavored to realize it; but he fancied himself far more successful in the attempt than he really

was, and greatly underrated what had been accomplished by others. He brought a vast amount of information from the most varied and distant sources to confirm his opinions, and the abundance of his materials never perplexed or burdened him in his argumentation, but examples of well-conducted historical inductions are rare in his pages. He sometimes altered and contorted the facts; he very often unduly simplified his problems; he was very apt when he had proved a favorite opinion true to infer it to be the whole truth. His intellect was comprehensive and vigorous, but neither classically cultured nor scientifically disciplined; it was amazingly stored with facts, but not rich in ideas; it was ambitious in inspiration, confident to excess in its own powers, and exceptionally unconscious of where its knowledge ceased and its ignorance began. It was deficient in imagination, poetical feeling, and sympathy.—FLINT, R., 1877, *Encyclopædia Britannica, Ninth Ed., vol.* IV.

The author's want of systematic training was itself an advantage for the immediate effect of his work; he knew nothing but the prejudices he had escaped, the facts he had accumulated, and the doctrines he had marshalled them to support; he addressed a public as ignorant as he had been, and as acute as his father had been. He had followed the scientific movement of his day, and observed with prophetic insight that the discussion of the transmutation of species was the weak point in Lyell's great work on Geology, but he had not busied himself with the speculative movement then mainly political or theological. If he had done so he would have been in danger of losing himself in side issues. As it was he stated and illustrated clearly and weightily, so that the work will not have to be done again for any section of the Western world, the conception of an orderly movement of human affairs depending upon ascertained facts of all degrees of generality. This is his great service; his special theories were of value chiefly as they furnished headings under which facts could be classified.—SIMCOX, GEORGE AUGUSTUS, 1880, *Henry Thomas Buckle, Fortnightly Review, vol.* 33, *p.* 276.

It would have been impossible to tell beforehand what view of history would be taken by the studious son of an English merchant, whose opinions were formed during the great agitation for free-trade.

But, when we know by experience what view he actually did take, the theory seems to be in perfect harmony with a social environment of which it was most interesting, though not the most highly organised nor the most enduring expression. In endeavouring to represent Buckle's philosophy as something more than a mere product of individual genius, I have been faithful, amid all differences, to that most general principle which it shares with every philosophy worthy of the name, and which it has contributed so powerfully to enforce. Twenty-five years ago the idea of law, universal and unbroken, was almost a paradox. It is now almost a commonplace; and among those by whose efforts so vast a change in public opinion was accomplished must be placed the name of this noble thinker, whose learning and eloquence have not often been singly equalled, and, in their combination, have never, to my knowledge, been approached.—BENN, ALFRED W., 1881, *Buckle and the Economics of Knowledge, Mind, vol.* 6, *p.* 259.

The appearance of the first volume of this celebrated work in 1857 raised the author at once from obscurity to literary and social renown. The book was everywhere talked of as a phenomenal work of a new genius. Nor was it until after the author's death, in 1862, that the reading world recovered its equanimity sufficiently to estimate the work at its real value. . . . Though these volumes show great breadth and acuteness of reasoning, as well as an almost unrivalled amount of learning, it must be admitted that the more carefully they are read, the more inadequate do the proofs appear. Not only that, but they are not free from inconsistencies fatal to successful argumentation. . . . But, in spite of these defects, some portions of the work have great value. The chapters in the first volume on "France before the Revolution" may be read with profit by every student of that period. It should also be added that many students who even reject the author's general conclusions have been filled by him with a glowing enthusiasm for historical study.—ADAMS, CHARLES KENDALL, 1882, *A Manual of Historical Literature, pp.* 57, 59.

The "History of Civilisation in England" won for its author a reputation which has hardly been sustained. The reasons are obvious. Buckle's solitary education deprived him of the main advantage of schools and universities—the frequent clashing with independent minds—which tests most searchingly the thoroughness and solidity of a man's acquirements. Specialists in every department of inquiry will regard him as a brilliant amateur rather than a thorough student.—STEPHEN, LESLIE, 1886, *Dictionary of National Biography, vol.* VII, *p.* 211.

A work singularly effective in style, which failed of permanent influence mainly through the author's ignorance of the theory of evolution. He had grasped too hastily at conclusions derived from mere statistics, and died ere he could remodel his book by the light kindled while its composition had absorbed him.—GARNETT, RICHARD, 1887, *The Reign of Queen Victoria, ed. Ward, vol.* II, *p.* 474.

Buckle had many of the distinctive faults of a young writer; of a writer who had mixed little with men, and had formed his mind almost exclusively by solitary, unguided study. He had a very imperfect appreciation of the extreme complexity of social phenomena, an excessive tendency to sweeping generalizations, and an arrogance of assertion which provoked much hostility. His wide and multifarious knowledge was not always discriminating, and he sometimes mixed good and bad authorities with a strange indifference. This is a long catalogue of defects, but in spite of them Buckle opened out wider horizons than any previous writer in the field of history. No other English historian had sketched his plan with so bold a hand, or had shown so clearly the transcendent importance of studying not merely the actions of soldiers, politicians, and diplomatists, but also those great connected evolutions of intellectual, social, and industrial life on which the type of each succeeding age mainly depends. To not a few of his contemporaries he imparted an altogether new interest in history, and his admirable literary talent, the vast range of topics which he illuminated with a fresh significance, and the noble enthusiasm for knowledge and for freedom that pervades his work, made its appearance an epoch in the lives of many who have passed far from its definite conclusions.—LECKY, WILLIAM EDWARD HARTPOLE, 1890, *Formative Influences, The Forum, vol.* 9, *p.* 388.

Curiously enough, however, this book of limited perceptions and scholastic origin struck the world with that sudden accidental and moral effect which sometimes makes a man with no particular right to distinction, awake to find himself famous.—OLIPHANT, MARGARET O. W., 1892, *The Victorian Age of English Literature, p.* 419.

The book attained at once, and for some time kept, an extraordinary popularity which has been succeeded by a rather unjust depreciation. Both are to be accounted for by the fact that it is in many ways a book rather of the French than of the English type, and displays in fuller measure than almost any of Buckle's contemporaries in France itself, with the possible exception of Taine, could boast, the frank and fearless, some would say the headlong and headstrong, habit of generalisation—scorning particulars, or merely impressing into service such as are useful to it and drumming the others out—on which Frenchmen pride themselves. . . . The worst fault of Buckle was the Voltairianism above referred to, causing or caused by, as is always the case, a deplorable lack of taste, which is not to be confined to religious matters.—SAINTSBURY, GEORGE, 1896, *A History of Nineteenth Century Literature, pp.* 243, 244

In accounting for Buckle's failure, stress has often been laid upon the fact that his education was private. This is a little pedantic. Grote, whose history has been accepted at the universities as the best available, was of no university. Mill, one of the men who have most influenced thought in this century, was of none either. Gibbon, perhaps the greatest of historians, has put on record how little he owed to Oxford; and Carlyle has told us with characteristic vigour how unprofitable he thought his university of Edinburgh. The men who did not go to a university have done good work; and the men who did go to one have declared that they owed little or nothing to the education there received. In the face of such facts it is impossible to account so for the failure of Buckle. The real reason, besides the cardinal fact that the attempt was premature, is that Buckle, though he had the daring of the speculator's temperament, had neither its caution nor its breadth.—WALKER, HUGH, 1897, *The Age of Tennyson, p.* 133.

It is admittedly the result of a unique range of reading, and displays brilliant generalising powers. The question that has exercised critics is whether the generalisa- tions are of a really scientific kind. Whether accepted or not, many of them have become familiar in current thought, and have had a decidedly stimulating effect.—WHITTAKER, T., 1897, *Social England, ed. Traill, vol.* VI, *p.* 327.

But the two volumes that were all of the author's colossal plan he lived to execute, are crude and unsatisfactory.—GRAHAM, RICHARD D., 1897, *The Master of Victorian Literature, p.* 221.

To the reader, who takes it up with a serious determination to understand its contents, it is extremely difficult, not indeed for want of clearness, for Buckle's style, like that of most Englishmen, is very clear, but on account of the amount of thought which he crowds into a small space. In order to write one line, Buckle must often have been obliged to work his way through several volumes. The footnotes give but a slight indication of the enormous learning of the author.—ENGEL, EDWARD, 1902, *A History of English Literature, rev. Hamley Bent, p.* 469.

GENERAL

A great thinker, a great writer, and a great scholar.—DICKENS, CHARLES, 1870, *Speeches and Sayings, p.* 86.

It may be inferred with tolerable certainty that it was during these eight years —from 1842 to 1850—that his gradually amassed knowledge of the great outlines of modern history, together with the experience he was acquiring of the tendencies of his own mind, led him to the choice of his subject. His literary style seems also to have been completely formed by this time, for all its main characteristics are to be found in the fragments on the reign of Elizabeth, written at least as early as 1850. One of its most marked characteristics, and one which principally contributes to its energy and above all, to its picturesque charm, is his frequent use of those metaphors and of those rhetorical forms of speech to which all the world is accustomed, and which have become common places in the language.—TAYLOR, HELEN, 1872, *ed., Miscellaneous and Posthumous Works of Henry Thomas Buckle, Biographical Notice, vol.* I, *p.* 16.

Buckle, forsooth, bears witness. . . . Quote if you choose publicans on liquor laws, or slave-drivers on the capacities of blacks; cite Martial as a witness to purity, or Bacchus to sobriety; put Danton to conduct a bloodless revolution, or swear in the Gracchi as special constables; but do not set up Mr. Buckle as an arbiter of judicial measure or precision, nor let the fame of anything that is called a religion or a clergy depend upon his nod.—GLADSTONE, WILLIAM EWART, 1876, *Macaulay, Gleanings of Past Years, vol.* II, *p.* 333.

A poor book—a very erroneous book—is sometimes the very best provocative of thought. Who is better for this than Mr. Buckle, and who is fuller of crude paradoxes and undigested knowledge? Of him unfortunately that was true which Bentley said of Warburton, that "there never was a man with so great an appetite and so bad a digestion." You say Mr. Buckle himself was a great commonplace-book maker. Yes, but he didn't half digest his commonplaces. Take them and digest them yourself.—ATKINSON, WILLIAM P., 1878, *The Right Use of Books, p.* 62.

James Sheridan Knowles

1784–1862

Born, at Cork, 12 May 1784. At his father's school there, 1790–93. Family removed to London, 1793. Left home on his father's second marriage, 1800. Served as ensign in Wilts Militia, 1804; in Tower Hamlets Militia, 1805–06. Studied medicine. M. D., Aberdeen, 1808. Resident Vaccinator to Jennerian Soc., 1808. First appeared on the stage, at Bath, 1809. Married Maria Charteris, 25 Oct. 1809. Play "Leo," produced by Edmund Kean at Waterford, 1810. "Brian Boroihme" produced at Belfast, 1811 (at Covent Garden, 20 April 1837); "Caius Gracchus," at Belfast, 13 Feb. 1815; at Covent Garden, 18 Nov. 1823. Kept a school at Belfast, 1812–16; at Glasgow, 1816–28. "Virginius" produced at Glasgow, 1820; at Covent Garden, 17 May 1820; "William Tell," Covent Garden, 1825. On staff of Glasgow "Free Press," Jan. 1823 to Dec. 1824. "The Beggar's Daughter of Bethnal Green" produced at Drury Lane, 28 May 1828. Removed from Glasgow to Newhaven, near Edinburgh, 1830. Contrib. to "Literary Souvenir," "Keepsake," and other periodicals. "Alfred the Great" produced at Drury Lane, 28 April 1831; "The Hunchback," Covent Garden, 5 April 1832; "The Wife," Covent Garden, 24 April 1833. Acted in America, 1834. "The Daughter," Drury Lane, 29 Nov. 1836; "The Bridal," Haymarket, 26 June 1837; "The Love Chase," Haymarket, 10 Oct. 1837; "Woman's Wit," Covent Garden, 23 May 1838; "Maid of Mariendorpt," Haymarket, 9 Oct. 1838; "Love," Covent Garden, 4 Nov. 1839; "John of Procida," Covent Garden, 19 Sept. 1840; "Old Maids," Covent Garden, 2 Oct. 1841. Wife died, Feb. 1841. Married Miss Elphinstone, 1842. "The Rose of Arragon," Haymarket, 4 June 1842; "The Secretary," Drury Lane, 24 April 1843. Retired from stage, 1843. Contrib. to various periodicals. Civil List Pension, 1848. One of committee for purchase of Shakespeare's Birthplace, 1848. Joined the Baptists about this time. Entertained at banquet in Cork, May 1862. Died, at Torquay, 30 Nov. 1862. Buried in Glasgow Necropolis. *Works:* "The Welch Harper" [1796]; "Fugitive Pieces," 1810; "The Senate" (under pseud. "Selim"), 1817; "Virginius," 1820 (third edn. same year); "Caius Gracchus," 1823; "The Elocutionist," 1823; "William Tell," 1825; "The Beggar's Daughter of Bethnal Green," 1828 (second edn., called "The Beggar of Bethnal Green," 1834); "Alfred the Great," 1831; "The Hunchback," 1832; "The Magdalen," 1832; "A Masque" [on the death of Sir Walter Scott], 1832; "The Wife," 1833; "The Daughter," 1837 (second edn. same year); "The Love Chase," 1837; "The Bridal" (from Beaumont and Fletcher), [1837]; "Woman's Wit," 1838; "Dramatic Works," 1838; "The Maid of Mariendorpt," 1838; "Love," 1840; "John of Procida," 1840; "Old Maids," 1841; "The Rose of Arragon," 1842; "The Secretary," 1843; "Dramatic Works" (3 vols.),[1]1843; "George Lovell," 1847; "Fortescue" (from "Sunday Times") 1847 (priv. ptd., 1846); "The Rock of Rome," 1849; "The Idol Demolished by its own Priest," 1851; "The Gospel Attributed to Matthew is the Record of the Whole Original Apostlehood," 1855; "Dramatic Works," 1856. *Posthumous:* "True unto Death," 1866 (another edn., called "Alexina," same year); "Brian Boroihme," 1872 (priv. ptd., 1871); "Lectures on Dramatic Literature" (2 vols.), 1873; "Various Dramatic Works" (priv. ptd.) 1874. He *edited:* J. A. Mason's "Treatise on the Climate," 1850. *Life:* by R. B. Knowles, revised edn., 1872.—SHARP, R. FARQUHARSON, 1897, *A Dictionary of English Authors, p.* 159.

PERSONAL

Twelve years ago I knew thee, Knowles, and
then
Esteemed you a perfect specimen
Of those fine spirits warm-soul'd Ireland
    sends,
To teach us colder English how a friend's
Quick pulse should beat. I knew you brave,
    and plain,
Strong-sensed, rough-witted, above fear or
    gain;
But nothing further had the gift to espy.
—LAMB, CHARLES, 1820, *To J. S. Knowles,
Esq., on his Tragedy of Virginius.*

When Mr. James Sheridan Knowles shall
die, the newspapers will mourn the loss of
the best, most successful dramatist of the
day; they will discourse pathetically of the
many ills, which, during life, he suffered at
the hands of a public. A goodly number of
obituary notices will appear, and in the
place of his burial, there will be erected, by
the beneficently disposed, a monument, to
perpetuate the memory of so popular a
dramatist. No matter if the cost of this
monument would, while he lived, have relieved his distress; no matter if even then
his plays shall be acted, to thin houses, for
the benefit of his widow and children.—
BENJAMIN, PARK, 1835, *Sheridan Knowles,
North American Review, vol.* 40, *p.* 142.

Of all the eccentric individuals I ever encountered, Sheridan Knowles was, I think,
the greatest. Judge, gentle reader, if the
following anecdotes may not justify my assertion. Walking one day with a brother-
dramatist, Mr. Bayle Bernard, in Regent's
Quadrant, Knowles was accosted by a gentleman in these terms:—"You're a pretty
fellow, Knowles! After fixing your own day
and hour to dine with us, you never make
your appearance, and from that time to
this not a word have we heard from you!"
"I couldn't help it, upon my honour," replied Knowles; "and I've been so busy ever
since I haven't had a moment to write or
call. How are you all at home?" "Oh
quite well, thank you; but come now, will
you name another day, and keep your
word?" "I will—sure I will." "Well, what
day? Shall we say Thursday next?"
"Thursday? Yes, by all means—Thursday
be it." "At six?" "At six. I'll be there
punctually. My love to 'em all." "Thank
ye. Remember, now. Six next Thursday."
"All right, my dear fellow; I'll be with
you." The friend departed and Knowles,
relinking his arm with that of Bayle Ber-

nard, said, "Who's that chap?" not having
the least idea of the name or residence of
the man he had promised to dine with on
the following Thursday, or the interesting
"family at home," to whom he had sent
his love.—PLANCHÉ, J. R., 1872, *Recollections and Reflections, vol.* II, *p.* 32.

He lived a long life, and did not waste it.
Up to a good old age he was healthy and
hearty. Macready described to me their first
interview, when the actor received the dramatist in the green-room. Sheridan Knowles
presented himself—a jolly-looking fellow,
with red cheeks, a man obviously full of
buoyancy and good-humor—and read to the
great manager his tragedy of "Virginius."
"What!" cried Macready, half-pleasantly,
half-seriously, when the reading was over,
"you the author of that tragedy—you?
Why you look more like the captain of a
Leith smack!" Nature had endowed Sheridan Knowles with a rare gift, but it was not
improved by learning or study, and he owed
little, if anything, to his great predecessors
in dramatic art. In his later days, as I have
remarked, the celebrated dramatist became a Baptist minister. I regret now that
I never heard him preach, although I am
told it was a performance that one might
have been satisfied to witness only once.
But I am sure that, whatever and wherever
he was, in the pulpit or on the stage, Sheridan Knowles was in earnest—simple,
honest, and hearty always. His was a
nature that remained thoroughly unspoiled
by extraordinary success.—HALL, SAMUEL
CARTER, 1883, *Retrospect of a Long Life, p.*
388.

I have seen my old friend Sheridan
Knowles on the stage only on one or two
occasions. There was much fervour and
sincerity in his acting, which, however, did
not greatly impress me. His emotion
seemed to be always at boiling-point.
Through a want of relief and transition, his
style soon became tedious. Excitement at
times interfered with the clearness of his
utterance, which did not gain in charm by
the addition of a strong Irish brogue. His
unmistakable earnestness, however, recommended him to audiences with whom, moreover, he was highly popular on account of
his success as a dramatist. They evidently
felt, both in his plays and in his acting, that
"his heart was in the right place." Occasionally he gave lectures on elocution, with
illustrative recitations. I liked him better

on the platform than on the stage. On the latter he was comparatively calm, and there his delivery had more discrimination and variety.—MARSTON, JOHN WESTLAND, 1888, *Our Recent Actors, vol.* II, *p.* 122.

VIRGINIUS
1820

Almost without the aid language affords,
Your piece seems wrought. That huffing medium, *words,*
(Which in the modern Tamburlaines quite sway
Our shamed souls from their bias) in your play
We scarce attend to. Hastier passion draws
Our tears on credit: and we find the cause
Some two hours after, spelling o'er again
Those strange few words at ease, that wrought the pain.
Proceed, old friend; and, as the year returns,
Still snatch some new old story from the urns
Of long-dead virtue. We, that knew before
Your worth, may admire, we cannot love you more.
—LAMB, CHARLES, 1820, *To J. S. Knowles, Esq., on his Tragedy of Virginius.*

The only way in which Mr. Knowles personifies our age, is in his truly domestic feeling. The age is domestic, and so is he. Comfort—not passionate imaginings,—is the aim of everybody, and he seeks to aid and gratify this love of comfort. All his dramas are domestic, and strange to say, those that should be most classic, or most chivalric, most above and beyond it, are the most imbued with this spirit. In what consists the interest and force of this popular play of "Virginius"? The domestic feeling. The costume, the setting, the decorations are heroic. We have Roman tunics, but a modern English heart,—the scene is the Forum, but the sentiments those of the "Bedford Arms." The affection of the father for his daughter—the pride of the daughter in her father, are the main principles of the play.—HORNE, RICHARD HENGIST, 1844, *A New Spirit of the Age, p.* 239.

It was about three o'clock one day that I was preparing to go out, when a parcel arrived containing a letter from Tait and the MS. of "Virginius." After some hesitation I thought it best to get the business over, to do at once what I had engaged to do, and I sat down determinedly to my work. The freshness and simplicity of the dialogue fixed my attention; I read on and on, and was soon absorbed in the interest of the story and the passion of its scenes, till at its close I found myself in such a state of excitement that for a time I was undecided

what step to take.—MACREADY, W C., 1873, *Reminiscences, ed. Pollock, p.* 157.

In the scene in which the client of Appius attempts to possess himself of her, Virginia remains absolutely mute. She is mute also in the great scene of the judgment, and she seems, moreover, to have understood nothing of what has been happening, for she asks her father if he is going to take her home. From the angels and furies of Shakespeare and Corneille we have come down to a virtuous idiot, and we are told that this is a return to Nature.—FILON, AUGUSTIN, 1897, *The English Stage, tr. Whyte, p.* 52.

THE HUNCHBACK
1832

After my riding lesson, went and sat in the library to hear Sheridan Knowles's play of "The Hunchback." Mr. Bartley and my father and mother were his only audience, and he read it himself to us. A real play, with real characters, individuals, human beings, it is a good deal after the fashion of our old playwrights, and does not disgrace its models. I was delighted with it; it is full of life and originality; a little long, but that's a trifle. There is want of clearness and coherence in the plot, and the comic part has really no necessary connection with the rest of the piece; but none of that will signify much, or, I think, prevent it from succeeding. I like the woman's part exceedingly, but am afraid I shall find it very difficult to act.—KEMBLE, FRANCES ANN, 1831, *Journal, Apr.* 23; *Records of A Girlhood, p.* 390.

A play made up of the rarest qualities of literary genius; a production which has shed a golden light on the cold and comfortless gloom of the modern theatre; a mental achievement that places its author in "the forehead of the times," that will embalm his memory with the highest dramatic genius of England, mighty and glorious as she is in that genius—"The Hunchback," which has acted as a dream, a talisman, on the intellect of the vast metropolis.—JERROLD, DOUGLAS, 1832, *The English Stage, The Life and Remains of Douglas Jerrold, ed. Blanchard Jerrold, Appendix, p.* 423.

"The Hunchback" is the most original and the most successful of all the productions of Knowles. . . . The part of *Julia* in "The Hunchback" has always been a favorite part with our actresses, and we have had as many *Julias* on our stage as we have had leading ladies, or ladies who so considered themselves, to play it. In no other part, perhaps, have so many aspirants for dramatic fame tried their 'prentice hand as in *Julia*, and to no other do they seem to return so fondly. It is regarded as a sort of test part, and the rising star thinks if she can shine as *Julia* that she need fear no further eclipse.—HUTTON, LAURENCE, 1875, *Plays and Players, pp.* 146, 147.

No wonder the character of Julia is so popular, and so often selected by a débutante. There is an infinite variety in it; there is a double crucial test by which the actress can be judged. In the early acts, opportunities are given for the display of the highest comedy acting—the country girl, content and happy with her country life; then a change—her head is turned by the gay and novel scenes in which she finds herself placed in that first London season. The whirl of pleasure has turned her into a woman of fashion. All this wants refinement, elegance of carriage, grace in movement; in fact, all the attributes which make your Lady Townleys and your Lady Teazles.—GORDON, WALTER, 1882, *"The Hunchback," The Theatre, vol.* 8, *p.* 146.

GENERAL

Ignorant alike of rules, regardless of models, he follows the steps of truth and simplicity, and strength, proportion, and delicacy are the infallible results. By thinking of nothing but his subject, he rivets the attention of the audience to it. All his dialogue tends to action, all his situations form classic groups. There is no doubt that "Virginius" is the best acting-tragedy that has been produced on the modern stage.—HAZLITT, WILLIAM, 1825, *The Spirit of the Age.*

The poetry of his dialogue is the poetry of passion; it is kindled up in him by the collision of events, and seems less proper to the man than to the scene: his language is to the purpose; it is but little ornamented. His dramas are full of impressive groupings, domestic incidents, the bustle of business, the activity of life: he subdues subject, scene, and language to the purpose and aim of his play. In this he differs from many writers, and differs for the better. His strength lies in home-bred affections: his "Virginius," his "Beggar's Daughter," and his "Wife of Mantua," all bear evidence of this, and contain scenes of perfect truth and reality, such as no modern dramatist sur-

passes. He teaches the heart and is safe.—CUNNINGHAM, ALLAN, 1833, *Biographical and Critical History of the Literature of the Last Fifty Years.*

The first dramatist of modern days; . . .
His is a wizard wand. Its potent spell
Broke the deep slumber of the patriot Tell!
And placed him on his native hills again,
The pride and glory of his fellow men!
The poet speaks—for Rome Virginia bleeds!
Bold Caius Gracchus in the forum pleads!
Alfred—the Great, because the good and wise—
Bids prostrate England burst her bonds and rise!
Sweet Bess, the Beggar's Daughter, beauty's queen,
Walks forth the joy and wonder of the scene!
The Hunchback enters—kindly—fond—severe—
And last, behold the glorious Wife appear!
    These are the bright creations of a mind
Glowing with genius, chastened and refined.
In all he's written, be this praise his lot,
"Not one word, dying, would he wish to blot!"
—MORRIS, GEORGE P., 1834, *Addresses for the benefit of James Sheridan Knowles.*

We have seen many a barrister famed for cross-examination unable to comprehend, till the piece was half over, the drift of Sheridan Knowles's dramas. — ALISON, SIR ARCHIBALD, 1846, *The Romantic Drama, Blackwood's Magazine, vol.* 60, *p.* 164.

Now finish, my song, with one visitor more;
The good old boy's face—how it bloom'd at the door!
Hazlitt, painting it during its childhood, turn'd grim,
Saying, "D—n your fat cheeks!" then out louder, "Frown, Jim."
Those cheeks still adorn'd the most natural of souls,
Whose style yet was not so—James Sheridan Knowles.
His style had been taught him in those his green days;
His soul was his own, and brought crowds to his plays.
—HUNT, LEIGH, 1859, *The Feast of the Poets.*

This play, ["Caius"] although not one of the best from the gifted author's pen, abounds in passages of lofty thought, and is marked by the impress of his genius with that truth of character so constantly observable in his writings. But among scenes of striking power, pathetic situations, and bursts of heroic passion, there is great inequality. Whole pages are given to the cavillings of the plebeians, who in their contentions neither sustain the dignity of tragedy nor recall the idea of the Roman people. Indeed the mob, though advancing the action but little, is too prominent an agent, whilst the familiar language of their altercations often descends to vulgarity. But in the poet's conception and draught of Cornelia we see before us the mother of the Gracchi, the ideal of the Roman matron. . . . Though instances of power and pathos may be multiplied from the poet's page, yet it must be admitted there is a want of sustained progressive interest in the plot, the fluctuation of party triumph not very actively agitating the hopes and fears of the auditors. The death of Gracchus, stabbing himself with the dagger concealed under the folds of his toga, is nobly concieved, and was startling in its effect. In Caius the passion of the more energetic parts and the tenderness of the domestic interviews laid strong hold on my sympathies, and I gave myself to the study of the part with no ordinary alacrity and ardour.—MACREADY, W. C., 1873, *Reminiscences, ed. Pollock, pp.* 220, 221.

Wrote some dramas suitable for the stage and not at all wanting in poetic conception. In his historical pieces, "Virginius," "Gracchus," "Alfred," the talent of the poet does not quite come up to his subject; but his comedies "The Love Chase" and "The Hunchback," are altogether satisfactory. —SCHERR, J., 1874, *A History of English Literature, tr. M. V.,* p. 268.

Although his style as a poet was but weakly imitative of our elder drama, Sheridan Knowles had skill in the construction of his plots, and that quick sense of stage effect which gratifies an actor who must needs think of the figure he will make upon the stage.—MORLEY, HENRY, 1881, *Of English Literature in the Reign of Victoria with a Glance at the Past,* p. 347.

Judged by literary tests alone, Knowles's plays cannot lay claim to much distinction. His plots are conventional, his style is simple, and, in spite of his Irish birth, his humour is not conspicuous. Occasionally he strikes a poetical vein, and his fund of natural feeling led him to evolve many effective situations. But he is a playwright rather than a dramatist.—SAUNDERS, T. BAILEY, 1892, *Dictionary of National Biography, vol.* XXXI, p. 299.

Knowles' plays were a great success upon a stage which could not hold the dramatic works of much greater poets. Setting aside the dramas written for the library, a long list might be made of the plays written by greater poets—from Coleridge to Tennyson —and meant to be acted, which cannot be credited with a tithe of the success that those of Sheridan Knowles achieved. That his dramatic instinct was far greater than his poetic gift is clear, and that his success was due rather to his dramatic skill than to his poetic force is doubtless true; and yet, taking his work as it stands, it can hardly be disputed that he demonstrated the possibility of making the poetic drama acceptable to nineteenth century audiences. . . . His dialogue, though sometimes marred by conceits and extravagances, is generally simple, direct and vigorous, and ever bright and rapid enough to excite and sustain interest. He had a wide range in his choice of subject, and a large command of dramatic situation. . . . His work, whether treating of classical or modern themes, always deals with men and women, and being instinct with human interest does not fail to interest the human. He worked simply, with simple means, and depended for his success upon the natural excitement of natural emotions. —MILES, ALFRED H., 1892, *The Poets and the Poetry of the Century, Southey to Shelley, pp.* 265, 266.

Independently of his technical knowledge, Knowles really had that knowledge of human nature without which drama is impossible, and he could write very respectable English. But the fatal thing about him is that he is content to dwell in decencies for ever. There is no inspiration in him; his style, his verse, his theme, his character, his treatment are all emphatically mediocre, and his technique as a dramatist deserves only a little, though a little, warmer, praise.—SAINTSBURY, GEORGE, 1896, *A History of Nineteenth Century Literature,* p. 422.

The respectable, but absolutely undistinguished, productions of Sheridan Knowles.—TRAILL, HENRY DUFF, 1897, *Social England, vol.* VI, p. 519.

As literature, his plays are far from remarkable. His tragedies are of little interest, and his comedies, while ingenious, are pieces of skilful mechanism rather than works inspired by the poetic spirit.— WALKER, HUGH, 1897, *The Age of Tennyson,* p. 46.

William Makepeace Thackeray

1811–1863

Born, at Calcutta, 18 July 1811. Brought to England at his father's death, 1816. At Charterhouse School, 1822–28. Matric., Trin. Coll., Camb., Feb. 1829. Left Cambridge, 1830; took no degree. Travelled on Continent, 1830–31. Lived in Hare Court, Temple, and studied Law, 1831–32. Edited "National Standard," May to Dec. 1833. After severe monetary losses, removed to Paris, Dec. 1833. Contrib. to "Fraser's Mag." from about 1833. Married Isabella Gethin Creagh Shawe, 20 Aug. 1836. Settled in London. Contrib. to "Fraser's Mag.," "New Monthly Mag.," "Ainsworth's Mag.," "Times," "Westminster Rev.," etc. Separation from his wife, 1840. Travelled in East, Aug. to Oct. 1844. Contrib. to "Punch," 1842–50. Called to Bar at Middle Temple, 26 May 1848. First lectured in London, 1851. In America lecturing, Dec. 1852 to spring of 1853; again, Dec. 1855 to April 1856. Lectured in England and Scotland, 1856. Stood as M. P. for City of Oxford, 1857; was defeated. Edited "Cornhill Mag.," Nov. 1859 to March 1862. Died, in London, 24 Dec. 1863. Buried at Kensal Green. *Works:* "The Yellow-plush Correspondence" (anon.), 1838; "The Paris Sketch-book" (under pseud. "Mr. Titmarsh"), 1840; "An Essay on the Genius of George Cruikshank" (anon.), 1840; "Comic Tales and Sketches" (under pseud. "Michael Angelo Titmarsh"), 1841; "The Second Funeral of Napoleon" (under pseud. "M. A. Titmarsh"), 1841; "The Irish Sketch-Book" (2 vols.), 1843; "The Luck of Barry Lyndon," 1844; "Notes of a Journey from Cornhill to Cairo," 1846; "Mrs. Perkin's Ball" (under pseud. "M. A. Titmarsh"), [1847]; "The Book of Snobs," 1848; "Vanity Fair," 1848; "Our Street" (under pseud. "M. A. Titmarsh"), 1848; "Dr. Birch and his Young Friends" (under pseud. "M. A. Titmarsh") 1849; "The History of Samuel Titmarsh; and the Great Hoggarty Diamond," 1849; "An Interesting Event" (under pseud. "M. A. Titmarsh"), 1849; "The History of Pendennis" (2 vols.), 1849–1850; "Rebecca and Rowena" (under pseud. "M. A. Titmarsh"), 1850; Text to "Sketches after English Landscape Painters," 1850; "The Kickleburys on the Rhine" (under pseud. "M. A. Titmarsh"), 1851; "The History of Henry Esmond," 1852; "The English Humourists of the Eighteenth Century," 1853; "Men's Wives," 1853; "The Newcomes" (2 vols.), 1854–55; "Miscellanies" (4 vols.), 1854–57; "Ballads," 1855; "The Rose and Ring" (under pseud. "M. A. Titmarsh"), 1855; "The Virginians" (2 vols.), 1858–59; "Lovel the Widower," 1861; "The Four Georges," 1861; "The Adventures of Philip," 1862; "Roundabout Papers," 1863 [1862]. *Posthumous:* "Dennis Duval," 1867; "Ballads and Tales," 1869; "The Orphan of Pimlico," 1876; "Etchings while at Cambridge," 1878; "The Chronicle of the Drum," 1886; "A Collection of Letters . . . 1847–1855", 1887; "Sultan Stork, etc.," 1887. *Collected Works:* in 26 vols., 1869–86.— SHARP, R. FARQUHARSON, 1897, *A Dictionary of English Authors, p.* 279.

PERSONAL

What a misfortune it is to have a broken nose, like poor dear Thackeray! He would have been positively handsome, and is positively ugly in consequence of it. John and his friend Venables broke the bridge of Thackeray's nose when they were school-boys playing together. What a mishap to befall a young lad just beginning life.— KEMBLE, FRANCES ANN, 1832, *Journal, Jan.* 17; *Records of a Girlhood, p.* 490.

By the by, there is a friend of mine that I promised to introduce to you. He is the cleverest of all the London writers, I think, —his name is Thackeray; a gentleman, a Cambridge man. I told him he had better not waste his time with inferior magazines when he writes the best things (he is the Yellow Plush of *Fraser* and the Major Gaha-

gan of the *New Monthly*), but go at once to you. He is shy, I suppose, for he said he wished you would *invite* him to contribute. If you will let me know whether you wish to hear from him I will communicate your reply; or if you wish to see him, he lives No. 13 Great Coram Street, Russell Square. He is also literary reviewer in the *Times*.— WHITE, REV. JAMES, 1838, *Letter to Robert Blackwood, William Blackwood and His Sons, ed. Oliphant, vol.* II, *p.* 196.

Went to Thackeray's lecture on the "Humorists" at Willis's Rooms. It was a very large assembly, including Mrs. Carlyle, Dickens, Leslie, and innumerable note-worthy people. Thackeray is a much older-looking man than I had expected; a square powerful face, and most acute and sparkling eyes, grayish hair and eyebrows. He

WILLIAM MAKEPEACE THACKERAY

Engraving by J. C. Armytage. From a
Drawing by Samuel Laurence.

WALTER SAVAGE LANDOR

Engraving by H. W. Smith. From a
Portrait by Alfred D'Orsay.

reads in a definite, rather dry manner, but makes you understand thoroughly what he is about. The lecture was full of point, but the subject was not a very interesting one, and he tried to fix our sympathy on his good-natured, volatile, and frivolous hero rather more than was meet. "Poor Dick Steele" one ends with, as one began; and I cannot see, more than I did before, the element of greatness in him.—FOX, CAROLINE, 1851, *Memories of Old Friends, ed. Pym; Journal, June 12, p. 292.*

We think there was no disappointment with his lectures. Those who knew his books found the author in the lecturer. Those who did not know his books were charmed in the lecturer by what is charming in the author—the unaffected humanity, the tenderness, the sweetness, the genial play of fancy, and the sad touch of truth, with that glancing stroke of satire which, lightning-like, illumines while it withers. The lectures were even more delightful than the books, because the tone of the voice and the appearance of the man, the general personal magnetism, explained and alleviated so much that would otherwise have seemed doubtful or unfair. For those who had long felt in the writings of Thackeray a reality quite inexpressible, there was a secret delight in finding it justified in his speaking; for he speaks as he writes—simply, directly, without flourish, without any cant of oratory, commending what he says by its intrinsic sense, and the sympathetic and humane way in which it was spoken. Thackeray is the kind of "stump orator" that would have pleased Carlyle. He never thrusts himself between you and his thought. If his conception of the time and his estimate of the men differ from your own, you have at least no doubt what his view is, nor how sincere and necessary it is to him.—CURTIS, GEORGE WILLIAM, 1853-94, *Thackeray in America, Literary and Social Essays, p.* 130.

Thackeray has very rarely come athwart me since his return: he is a big fellow, soul and body; of many gifts and qualities (particularly in the Hogarth line, with a dash of Sterne super-added), of enormous *appetite* withal, and very uncertain and chaotic in all points except his *outer breeding*, which is fixed enough, and *perfect* according to the modern English style. I rather dread explosions in his history. A *big, fierce,* weeping, hungry man; not a strong one. *Ay de mi!*—CARLYLE, THOMAS, 1853, *To Ralph Waldo Emerson, Sept.* 9; *Correspondence of Carlyle and Emerson, ed. Norton, vol.* II, *p.* 262.

Thackeray has a dread of servants, insomuch that he hates to address them or to ask them for anything. His morbid sensibility, in this regard, has perhaps led him to study and muse upon them, so that he may be presumed to have a more intimate knowledge of this class than any other man.—HAWTHORNE, NATHANIEL, 1855, *English Note-Books, vol.* I, *p.* 240.

The first drawback in his books, as in his manners, is the impression conveyed by both that he never can have known a good and sensible woman. I do not believe he has any idea whatever of such women as abound among the matronage of England, —women of excellent capacity and cultivation applied to the natural business of life. It is perhaps not changing the subject to say next what the other drawback is. Mr. Thackeray has said more, and more effectually, about snobs and snobbism than any other man; and yet his frittered life, and his obedience to the call of the great are the observed of all observers. As it is so, so it must be; but "Oh! the pity of it! the pity of it!"—MARTINEAU, HARRIET, 1855-77, *Autobiography, ed. Chapman, vol.* II, *p.* 61.

I breakfasted this morning with Fowler of Lincoln, to meet Thackeray (the author) who delivered his lecture on George III in Oxford last night. I was much pleased with what I saw of him; his manner is simple and unaffected: he shows no anxiety to shine in conversation, though full of fun and anecdote when drawn out. He seemed delighted with the reception he had met with last night—the undergraduates seem to have behaved with most unusual moderation.—DODGSON, CHARLES LUTWIDGE, 1856, *The Journal of Lewis Carroll.*

Mr. Thackeray is forty-six years old, though from the silvery whiteness of his hair he appears somewhat older. He is very tall, standing upwards of six feet two inches and as he walks erect, his height makes him conspicuous in every assembly. His face is bloodless, and not particularly expressive but remarkable for the fracture of the bridge of the nose, the result of an accident in youth. He wears a small grey whisker but otherwise is clean shaven. No one meeting him could fail to recognize in him a gentleman: his bearing is cold and uninviting, his style of conversation either openly cynical or affectedly good-natured and benevolent; his *bonhommie* is forced, his wit biting, his pride easily touched—but his appearance is invariably that of the cool, *suave*, well-bred gentleman, who, whatever may be rankling within, suffers no surface display of emotion.—YATES, EDMUND, 1858, *Town Talk.*

I believe you have never seen Thackeray, he has the appearance of a colossal infant—smooth white shiny ringletty hair, flaxen, alas! with advancing years, a roundish face with a little dab of a nose, upon which it is a perpetual wonder how he keeps his spectacles, a sweet but rather piping voice, with something of the childish treble in it, and a very tall, slightly stooping figure—such are the characteristics of the great "snob" of England. His manner is like that of England—nothing original, all planed down into perfect uniformity with that of his fellow-creatures. There was not much more distinction in his talk than in his white choker, or black coat and waistcoat.—MOTLEY, JOHN LOTHROP, 1858, *To his Wife, May* 28; *Correspondence, ed. Curtis, vol.* I, *p.* 229.

He was a cynic! By his life all wrought
Of generous acts, mild words, and gentle ways;
His heart wide open to all kindly thought.
His hand so quick to give, his tongue to praise!
He was a cynic! You might read it writ
In that broad brow, crowned with its silver hair,
In those blue eyes, with childlike candour lit,
In that sweet smile his lips were wont to wear
He was a cynic! By the love that clung
About him from his children, friends, and kin;
By the sharp pain light pen and gossip tongue
Wrought in him, chafing the soft heart within!
—BROOKS, SHIRLEY, 1863, *Punch.*

This great writer—our greatest novelist since Scott, (and in some senses greater, because deeper, more to the quick, more *naked* than he), our foremost wit and man of letters since Macaulay—has been taken from us with an awful unexpectedness. He was found dead in bed this morning. This is to us so great a personal as well as public calamity, that we feel little able to order our words aright or to see through our blinding tears. Mr. Thackeray was so much greater, so much nobler than his works, great and noble as they are, that it is difficult to speak of him without apparent excess. . . .

We know of no death in the world of letters since Macaulay's which will make so many mourners,—for he was a faithful friend. No one, we believe, will ever know the amount of true kindness and help, given often at a time when kindness cost much, to nameless, unheard-of suffering. A man of spotless honor, of the strongest possible home affections, of the most scrupulous truthfulness of observation and of word, we may use for him his own words to his "faithful old gold pen":

"Nor pass the words as idle phrases by;
Stranger! I never writ a flattery,
Nor signed the page that registered a lie."
—BROWN, JOHN, 1863-66, *Thackeray's Death, Spare Hours, Second Series, pp.* 229, 234.

My conviction was, that beneath an occasional affectation of cynicism, there was a tenderness of heart which he was more eager to repress than to exhibit; that he was no idolater of rank in the sense in which Moore was said dearly to love a lord, but he had his best pleasures in the society of those of his own social position—men of letters and artists; and that, however fond of "the full flow of London talk," his own home was the centre of his affections. He was a sensitive man, as I have seen on more than one occasion.—KNIGHT, CHARLES, 1863, *Passages of a Working Life during Half a Century, p.* 444.

With the first grasp of his broad hand, and the first look of his large, serious gray eyes, I received an impression of the essential manliness of his nature,—of his honesty, his proud, almost defiant candor, his ever-present, yet shrinking tenderness, and that sadness of the moral sentiment which the world persisted in regarding as cynicism. This impression deepened with my further acquaintance, and was never modified. Although he belonged to the sensitive, irritable genius, his only manifestations of impatience, which I remember were when that which he had written with a sigh was interpreted as a sneer. When so misunderstood, he scorned to set himself right. "I have no brain above the eyes," he was accustomed to say; "I describe what I see." He was quick and unerring in detecting the weaknesses of his friends, and spoke of them with a tone of disappointment sometimes bordering on exasperation: but he was equally severe upon his own short-comings. He allowed no friend to think him better than his own deliberate estimate made him, I have never known a man whose nature was so immovably based on truth.—TAYLOR, BAYARD, 1864–80, *Critical Essays and Literary Notes, p. 135.*

It is no part of this little Memorial to refer to what may be called his public relations, and his success as a lecturer. I merely record my recollection of the peculiar voice and cadence; the exquisite manner of reading poetry; the elocution, matchless in its simplicity; his tranquil attitude—the only movement of his hands being when he wiped his glasses as he began and turned over the leaves of his manuscript; his gentle intonations. There was sweet music in his way of repeating the most hackneyed lines, which freshened them anew. I seem still to hear him say,—

"And nightly to the listening earth
Repeats the story of her birth."

—REED, WILLIAM BRADFORD, 1864, *Haud Immemor, A Few Personal Recollections of Mr. Thackeray in Philadelphia.*

Though he said witty things now and then, he was not a wit, in the sense in which Jerrold was, and he complained, sometimes, that his best things occurred to him after the occasion had gone by! He shone most —as in his books,—in little subtle remarks on life, and little descriptive sketches suggested by the talk. We remember in particular, one evening, after a dinner party at his house, a fancy picture he drew of Shakespeare during his last years at Stratford, sitting out in the summer afternoon watching the people, which all who heard it, brief as it was, thought equal to the best things in his Lectures. But it was not for this sort of talent,—rarely exerted by him,—that people admired his conversation. They admired, above all, the broad sagacity, sharp insight, large and tolerant liberality, which marked him as one who was a sage as well as a story-teller, and whose stories were valuable because he was a sage.—HANNAY, JAMES, 1864, *A Brief Memoir of the Late Mr. Thackeray.*

His medical attendants attributed his death to effusion on the brain. They added that he had a very large brain, weighing no less than 58½ oz. He thus died of the complaint which seemed to trouble him least.— HOTTEN, JOHN CAMDEN (THEODORE TAYLOR), 1864, *Thackeray the Humorist and the Man of Letters, p. 180.*

I am surprised almost to find how much I am thinking of him; so little as I had seen him for the last ten years; not once for the last five. I have been told—by you, for one—that he was spoiled. I am glad therefore that I have scarce seen him since he was "old Thackeray." I keep reading his "Newcomes" of nights, and as it were hear him saying so much in it; and it seems to me as if he might be coming up my Stairs and about to come (singing) into my Room, as in old Charlotte Street, etc., thirty years ago.—FITZGERALD, EDWARD, 1864, *Letter to Samuel Laurence, Jan. 7; Letters and Literary Remains, vol. II, p. 171.*

The last line he wrote, and the last proof he corrected, are among these papers through which I have so sorrowfully made my way. The condition of the little pages of manuscript where Death stopped his hand, shows that he had carried them about, and often taken them out of his pocket here and there, for patient revision and interlineation. The last words he corrected in print, were, "And my heart throbbed with an exquisite bliss." God grant that on that Christmas Eve when he laid his head back on his pillow and threw up his arms as he had been wont to do when very weary, some consciousness of duty done and Christian hope throughout life humbly cherished, may have caused his own heart so to throb, when he passed away to his Redeemer's rest! He was found peacefully lying as above described, composed, undisturbed, and to all appearance asleep, on the twenty-fourth of December, 1863. He was only in his fifty-third year; so young a man, that the mother who blessed him in his first sleep, blessed him in his last. . . . On the bright wintry day, the last but one of the old year, he was laid in his grave at Kensal Green, there to mingle the dust to which the mortal part of him had returned, with that of a third child, lost in her infancy years ago. The heads of a great concourse of his fellow-workers in the Arts, were bowed around his tomb.— DICKENS, CHARLES, 1864, *In Memoriam, Cornhill Magazine, vol. 9, pp. 131, 132.*

I have been this Sunday afternoon on pilgrimage to Thackeray's tomb at Kensal Green; the great master would have smiled at the break-down of my devotion. "You'll find it by the great red brick tomb of Mr. Cheese" was the direction. I found the last resting place of the lamented Cheese, red and brick as they had said;

Thackeray'ϱ I could not find. I wandered, sick at heart, amongst sarcophagi and mausolea and truncated columns and obelisks and urns. "Where do you bury the Christians?" I asked, as I gazed round on the symbols of paganism. "We buries the Dissenters, sir," blandly replied the policeman, "in the t'other side of the Cimitiry!"—GREEN, JOHN RICHARD, 1864, *To W. Boyd Dawkins, Feb.* 1; *Letters, ed. Stephen, p.* 138.

Lord Macaulay rests at the foot of the statue of Addison, whose character and genius none had painted as he. . . . And whilst. from one side of that statue, his bust looks toward the Royal Sepulchres, in the opposite niche is enshrined that of another no less profound admirer of the "Spectator," who had often expressed his interest in the spot as he wandered through the transept—William Makepeace Thackeray. —STANLEY, ARTHUR PENRHYN, 1868, *Historical Memorials of Westminster Abbey, pp.* 319, 320.

Thackeray was remarkable both for the clearness of his handwriting and for the general neatness of his manuscripts.— SETON, GEORGE, 1869, *Gossip about Letters and Letter-Writers, p.* 215.

He was essentially of a nervous temperament, and altogether deficient in that vigorous self-possession which enables a man to shine in public assemblies; for it was absolute pain to him to be called upon to make a speech, and even in ordinary conversation he showed no particular desire to hold a prominent place. But, the above considerations apart, it would be easier to know many men in a few days than it would be thoroughly to understand Thackeray in the same number of years. . . . He never became energetic, but spoke with that calm deliberation which distinguished his public readings; and there was one peculiarity which, among others, I especially remarked, viz., that when he made a humorous point, which inevitably caused me to laugh, his own countenance was unmoved, like that of the comedian Liston, who, as is well known, looked as if he wondered what had occurred to excite the risibility of his audience.— HODDER, GEORGE, 1870, *Recollections of William Makepeace Thackeray, Harper's Magazine, vol.* 41, *pp.* 262, 263.

I had the opportunity, both in England and America, of observing the literary habits of Thackeray, and it always seemed to me that he did his work with comparative ease, but was somewhat influenced by a custom of procrastination. Nearly all his stories were written in monthly instalments for magazines, with the press at his heels. He told me that when he began a novel he rarely knew how many people were to figure in it, and, to use his own words, he was always very shaky about their moral conduct. He said that sometimes, especially if he had been dining late and did not feel in remarkably good-humor next morning, he was inclined to make his characters villainously wicked; but if he arose serene with an unclouded brain, there was no end to the lovely actions he was willing to make his men and women perform. When he had written a passage that had pleased him very much he could not resist clapping on his hat and rushing forth to find an acquaintance to whom he might instantly read his successful composition. . . . The most finished and elegant of all *lecturers*, Thackeray often made a very poor appearance when he attempted to deliver a set speech to a public assembly. He frequently broke down after the first two or three sentences. He prepared what he intended to say with great exactness, and his favorite delusion was that he was about to astonish everybody with a remarkable effort. It never disturbed him that he commonly made a woful failure when he attempted speech-making, but he sat down with such cool serenity if he found that he could not recall what he wished to say, that his audience could not help joining in and smiling with him when he came to a stand-still.—FIELDS, JAMES T., 1871, *Yesterdays with Authors, pp.* 15, 18.

A member of "The Garrick," who was specially unpopular with the majority of the members, was literally *drawn* out of the club by Thackeray. His figure, being very peculiar, was sketched in pen and ink by his implacable persecutor. On every pad on the writing-tables, or whatever paper he could venture to appropriate, he presented him in the most ridiculous and derogatory situation that could be imagined, always with his back towards you; but unmistakable. His victim, it must be admitted, bore this desecration of his "lively effigies" with great equanimity for a considerable period; but at length, one very strong—perhaps too strong—example of the artist's graphic and satirical abilities, combined with the conviction that he was generally objectionable, induced him to retire from the club.—PLANCHÉ, JAMES ROBINSON, 1872, *Recollections and Reflections, vol.* I, *p.* 171.

Thackeray was, even to his latest day, and after considerable experience, an uncertain speaker. The idea that he had to make a speech on any occasion disturbed his mind, and worked upon his nerves. . . . Sometimes he would suddenly break down: at others, his words would flow placidly from him to the end; but he never managed a peroration, nor rose to eloquence. He gossiped in his own delightful way with his audience—when he was in the mood; and when he could not do this easily, he collapsed. The set phrases, the rhetorical flights, the clap-traps of a chairmanship, were impossible to him.—JERROLD, WILLIAM BLANCHARD, 1873, *Best of all Good Company.*

Having been most kindly received, he took umbrage at some hard rallying, perhaps rather of others than himself, and not only declined her [Lady Ashburton] invitations, but spoke of her with discourtesy and personal dislike. After some months, when the angry feeling on his part had had time to die out, he received from her a card of invitation to dinner. He returned it with an admirable drawing on the back, representing himself kneeling at her feet with his hair all aflame from the hot coals she was energetically pouring on his head out of an ornamental brazier. This act of contrition was followed by a complete reconciliation, and much friendship on her part towards him and his family.—MILNES, RICHARD MONCKTON (LORD HOUGHTON),1873, *Monographs, Personal and Social, p.* 224.

His voice, as I recall it, was at once low and deep, with a peculiar and indescribable cadence; his elocution was matchless in its simplicity. His attitude was impressive and tranquil, the only movement of his hands being when he wiped his glasses as he turned over the leaves of his manuscript. He read poetry exquisitely.—STODDARD, RICHARD HENRY, 1874, *William Makepeace Thackeray, Harper's Magazine, vol.* 49, *p.* 544.

His remarks, with an occasional touch of satiric humor, were in their general spirit genial and benevolent; and it was easy to see that his disposition was charitable, however shrewd and even caustic his expressions may sometimes have been. I do not think he struck me as being what is technically called a *conversationist*—that is, one who would be invited to dinner for the purpose of keeping up the round of talk—and there was not the least shadow of attempt to show himself off; and though what he said was always sensible and to the point, it was the language of a well-bred and accomplished gentleman, who assumed no sort of superiority, but seemed naturally and simply at ease with his companions of the moment.—LAMB, GEORGE, 1877, *Recollections of Thackeray, Harper's Magazine, vol.* 54, *p.* 259.

My recollection of him, though fresh enough, does not furnish much material for biography. He came to school young—a pretty, gentle, and rather timid boy. I think his experience there was not generally pleasant. Though he had afterwards a scholarlike knowledge of Latin, he did not attain distinction in the school; and I should think that the character of the headmaster, Dr. Russell, which was vigorous, unsympathetic, and stern, though not severe, was uncongenial to his own. With the boys who knew him, Thackeray was popular; but he had no skill in games, and, I think, no taste for them.—VENABLES, GEORGE, 1879, *Letter to Anthony Trollope, Thackeray (English Men of Letters), p.* 4.

A tall, ruddy, simple-looking Englishman, who cordially held out his hand, and met me with a friendly smile. There was nothing like a scowl on his face, and it was neither thin, bilious, nor ill-natured, but plump, rubicund, and indicative of an excellent digestion. . . . In person he was a "large man"—his height I think was over six feet. His eyes were mild in expression, his hair nearly gray, his dress plain and unpretending. Everything about the individual produced the impression that pretense was hateful to him. . . . His face and figure indicated a decided fondness for roast beef, canvas-back ducks—of which he spoke in terms of enthusiasm—plum-pudding, "Bordeaux," of which he told me he drank a bottle daily at his dinner, and all the material good things of life.—COOKE, JOHN ESTEN, 1879, *An Hour With Thackeray, Appleton's Journal, vol.* 22, *pp.* 249, 250.

It was because Thackeray so desired the respect of others, was so anxious for the social consideration of the people he was meeting, that he thought so much about snobs and snobbishness. . . . He looked at the snobbish mind so closely and with such interest, because that mind had been directed upon himself. He examined it as a private soldier examines the cat-o'-nine-tails. It was the quickness of his sensibility to disrespect or unkindness, it was his keenly sympathetic consciousness of the hostile feelings of people toward himself, which awakened a rather indolent mind to such energetic perception of the snobbish moods. It was this which caused him to look with such power upon a snob. During his fifty years of life he had conned a vast number of snobbish thoughts, and must have accumulated a great quantity of snob lore. No doubt, he thought too much about snobs.—NADAL, EHRMAN SYME, 1881–82, *Thackeray's Relations to English Society, Essays at Home and Elsewhere, pp.* 93, 94.

Thackeray came to Washington while I was there. He gave his course of lectures on the "English Humorists of the Eighteenth Century." His style, especially in his earlier writings, had one quality which the critics did not seem to notice; it was not conventional, but spun out of the brain. With the power of thought to take hold of the mind, and a rich, deep, melodious voice, he contrived, without one gesture, or any apparent emotion in his delivery, to charm away an hour as pleasantly as I have ever felt it in a lecture. What he told me of his way of composing confirms me in my criticism on his style. He did not dash his pen on paper, like Walter Scott, and write off twenty pages without stopping, but, dictating to an amanuensis,—a plan which leaves the brain to work undisturbed by the pen-labor,—dictating from his chair, and often from his bed, he gave out sentence by sentence, slowly, as they were moulded in his mind.—DEWEY, ORVILLE, 1882 (?), *Autobiography and Letters, ed. Dewey, p.* 114.

On Christmas Day, 1863, we were startled by the news of Thackeray's death. He had then for many months given up the editorship of the *Cornhill Magazine*—a position for which he was hardly fitted either by his habits or temperament—but was still employed in writing for its pages. I had known him only for four years, but had grown into much intimacy with him and his family. I regard him as one of the most tender-hearted human beings I ever knew, who, with an exaggerated contempt for the foibles of the world at large, would entertain an almost equally exaggerated sympathy with the joys and troubles of individuals around him. He had been unfortunate in early life—unfortunate in regard to money—unfortunate with an afflicted wife—unfortunate in having his home broken up before his children were fit to be his companions. This threw him too much upon clubs, and taught him to dislike general society. But it never affected his heart, or clouded his imagination. He could still revel in the pangs and joys of fictitious life, and could still feel—as he did to the very last—the duty of shewing to his readers the evil consequences of evil conduct.—TROLLOPE, ANTHONY, 1882–83, *An Autobiography.*

That Christmas of 1863 was saddened by the news of Thackeray's death. I had seen him the last time in November in Trafalgar Square, looking strong and full of life. I remember walking back after him to see him again. It has been one of the regrets of my life not to have known Thackeray. "Esmond" had been my favourite novel, and I loved the creator of Colonel Newcome, although I had never spoken to him.— GOWER, RONALD LORD, 1882, *My Reminiscences, vol.* I, *p.* 167.

He was a *bon vivant*: fond of a nice little dinner, a connoisseur of wines, the devotee of a good cigar, a willing receiver of many little pleasures which an ascetic judgment would pronounce wasteful and slothful. . . . No reproach of excess or grossness of any kind attaches to his character. Though perhaps he was self-indulgent, he was not a voluptuary. His pleasure was as innocent as that of Colonel Newcome when he visited the smoky depths of Bohemia with young Clive, and the dinner was but the means of sociability and hospitality, the preparation for a more intellectual treat, a key to the fetters which keep some hearts and minds in this oddly-constituted and misgiving world from the openness and confidence of brotherhood.—RIDEING, WILLIAM H.,1885, *Thackeray's London, p.* 70.

As I was standing in my office, I heard heavy footsteps on the stairs leading from the street. Presently the door was opened; and Charles Sumner walked in, followed by William M. Thackeray, a man of such lofty stature and proportionate stoutness that he actually made the Massachusetts senator look comparatively small.—BRAINARD, CHARLES H., 1885, *Recollections of Thackeray, Some Noted Princes, Authors, and Statesmen of our Time, ed. Parton, p.* 52.

Thackeray, with all his good-nature, varied as it was by occasional bursts of the opposite quality, thought it fair to caricature other people, but very unfair for other people to caricature him. When Mr. Edmund Yates wrote and published a not particularly flattering, but not ill-natured description of him, derived solely from the knowledge he had acquired of him in the Garrick Club, of which they were both members, he forgot the similar case of Fowker, in which he was the offending party, and vowed such social vengeance against Mr. Yates as it was possible for him to take. The result was a literary *fiasco*, which led to the withdrawal of Mr. Yates from the Club, and threatened to lead to the withdrawal of Charles Dickens also. Happily for the Club, and perhaps for Thackeray also, this consummation of a dispute, which Mr. Thackeray ought never to have instigated, was averted.—MACKAY, CHARLES, 1887, *Through the Long Day, vol.* II, *p.* 63.

When Thackeray was here on his last visit I was presented to him, at the old theatre at the corner of Broome Street and Broadway. I thought him, with his great height, his spectacles, which gave him a very pedantic appearance, and his chin always carried in the air, the most pompous, supercilious person I had ever met; but I lived to alter that opinion, and in a very short time. . . . Thackeray then lived with a very great and dear friend of mine and my father's, and they had rooms together in Houston Street. I had a house next door but one to them, and this is how I became so intimate with Thackeray. . . . Thackeray, I suppose, took a fancy to me; at any rate it was understood every night when I came home from acting that if I saw a light in a certain window I was to go in. . . . When I did find them in, we never parted until half-past two or three in the morning. Then was the time to see Thackeray at his best, because then he was like a boy; he did not attempt to be the genius of the party. . . . Such an unsophisticated, gentle-hearted creature as he was.—WALLACK, LESTER, 1888, *Memoirs of Fifty Years, pp.* 205, 206.

The two key-secrets of Thackeray's great life, as I take it, were these—Disappointment, and Religion. The first was his poison; the second was his antidote. And, as always, the antidote won. No wonder that he was disappointed. First a man of for-

tune, then a ruined and a struggling artist, then a journalist, recognised to the full as such even by the brothers of the craft, but, like them, very little beyond it—then at last the novelist and the famous man.— MERIVALE, HERMAN, 1891, *Life of W. M. Thackeray (Great Writers), p.* 13.

A writer like Mr. Thackeray gave himself to the world in his art, and with rather too little than too much reserve. Anyone can read a melancholy chapter of his life "a living sorrow," in the "Hoggarty Diamond." Who wants the details except the lover of tattle? Anybody can tell that he has loved unhappily, or what are the fortunes of Clive Newcome, of the elder George Warrington, of Henry Esmond derived from? They are written in tears. Everyone sees that Mr. Thackeray was not particularly happy at school, that he enjoyed himself at college, that he lived a good deal in Paris, that he often heard the chimes at midnight, that he had lost money at cards. We have the evidence of Mr. Deuceace, of Blundell Blundell, of Pendennis, of Captain Costigan. He had met and studied minxes, or he could not have given us Becky and Betty. What do the names of the minxes of real life matter to us? I could a tale, or a tradition unfold concerning one of these ladies but this is not a column of the New Journalism. What Mr. Thackeray thought of that glorious institution we can read in his remarks on "Young Grub Street"; he is as frank about his animosities as about his dinners and his liking for a good dinner. All his experience he gave us, all his loves, hates, hopes and fears, his religion, his devotion to good letters, his generosity, his little bouts of impatience and petulance. What more, I ask, do we want? . . . Some thought him a snob; some called him a cynic; one declared that "there is a want of heart in all he writes"; that "his style of conversation is either openly cynical or affectedly good-natured and benevolent." We only see, feel, and understand in proportion as we have eyes, hearts, and brains. All these may be exercised on the Thackeray who declares himself in his books, just as well as on any Thackeray of a stout, well-padded biography.—LANG, ANDREW, 1891, *At the Sign of the Ship, Longman's Magazine, vol.* 17, *pp.* 673, 674.

Thackeray spent a good deal of his time on stilts. He wrote, too, as he talked; but then, he was a very disagreeable companion to those who did not want to boast that they knew him. In his society people had to do two things when one would have been quite enough; they had to smile titteringly as well as to listen.—HAKE, GORDON, 1892, *Memoirs of Eighty Years, p.* 86.

He came
Among us, and went from us, and we knew
Only the smoke and ash that hid the flame,
Only the cloak and vestment of his soul;
And knew his priesthood only by his stole
And, thus unknown, he went his journey through.
Yet there were some who knew him, though his face
Was never seen by them; although his hand
Lay never warm in theirs, they yet had grace
To see, past all misjudgment; his true heart
Throbbed for them in the creatures of his art,
And they could read his words and understand.
—BUNNER, H. C., 1892, *On Reading Certain Published Letters of W. M. T.*

I first met Thackeray at dinner, when I was staying with Leech. . . . I was introduced by our host, and for his sake he gave me a cordial greeting. "We must be about the same height," he said; "we'll measure." And when, as we stood *dos-à-dos*, and the bystanders gave their verdict, "a dead heat" (the length was six feet three inches). . . . He said so many good things, being the best talker I have ever listened to. —HOLE, S. REYNOLDS, 1893, *Memories, pp.* 69, 70, 71.

It need not be told here that Thackeray loved the great world and the strange, noble, and even ignoble creatures it contains; he loved delightful women always, and "liked to see them straight," as he says somewhere; and would have said to his favorites, as Dr. Johnson said to Mrs. Thrale; "Be brisk, and be splendid, and be publick"; but he loved above all his fireside corner and his "little girls," and the friends they drew about them. Not the least characteristic incident of his life is his flight home from America, leaving his engagements to lecture and everything else to take care of themselves, because he saw Christmas approaching and stockings which might be otherwise unfilled. He bravely said he was homesick; and with no excuse to anyone he stepped on board a Boston steamer, and vanished thus from the centre of his admirers.—FIELDS, ANNIE, 1894, *A Third Shelf of Old Books, Scribner's Magazine, vol.* 16, *p.* 359.

I had a sincere regard for Thackeray. I well remember his striking personality—striking to those who had the ability to recognise it: the look of the man, the latent power, and the occasional keenness of his remarks on men and their actions, as if he saw through and through them. Thackeray drew many unto him, for he had engaging as well as fine qualities. He was open-handed and kind-hearted. He had not an overweening opinion of his literary consequence, and he was generous as regarded the people whom the world chose to call his rivals. . . . If I am not much mistaken, the man Thackeray was melancholy—he had known tribulation, he had suffered. He was not a light-hearted wag or a gay-natured rover, but a sorrowing man. He could make you a jest, or propound some jovial or outrageous sentiment, and imply, "Let us be festive," but the jollity rarely came. However, I ought to say that though Thackeray was not cheerily, he was at times grotesquely, humorous. Indeed, he had a weakness for buffoonery. I have seen him pirouette, wave his arm majestically, and declaim in burlesque—an intentionally awkward imitation of the ridiculous manner that is sometimes met with in French opera. — LOCKER - LAMPSON, FREDERICK, 1895, *My Confidences, pp.* 297, 304.

Thackeray's genius was the flowering of a century and a half of family culture; a culture of which the beautiful after-efflorescence still blooms in "Old Kensington," the "Story of Elizabeth," and the "Village on the Cliff." Thackeray's robustness of character, his hatred of shams, his scorn of all things base, had their roots deep down in the manly life of the old Yorkshire moorland. The power of producing high-class mental work to order, when work must needs be done, came to him from a century of later ancestors who had made their bread by their brains. . . . The clerical traditions of a family, with nineteen parsons among them, made Thackeray, quite apart from his intellectual convictions, the friend of true churchmen, and filled his imagination with the poetry of the rites of the Church. "How should he who knows you," he wrote, "not respect you or your calling? May this pen never write a pennyworth again if it ever cast ridicule upon either." . . . But the greatest single influence of Thackeray's life-work was still his mother. My earliest portrait of him is that of a little child clinging to his mother, her arm around his neck, and the father sitting close by. At any rate it is something that the best of Bengal civilian families in the last century furnished the mother of Thackeray. The lofty tenderness for women which he learned from that mother he lavished on his wife, until parted from her by her dark malady; it overflowed to his daughters, and breathes in his works.—HUNTER, SIR WILLIAM WILSON, 1897, *The Thackerays in India and some Calcutta Graves, pp.* 180, 181, 182.

He was a complete success [1852]. He was as delightful as his own literary personages are, and so "like his writings" that every one spoke of it. His allusions, his voice, his looks, were all just what we had expected. Never did a long-hoped-for hero fill the bill so thoroughly. His loving and life-giving genius spoke in every word. Wonderful examples of excellence those papers on "The Four Georges," and delivered in a clear, fine, rich voice. Their simplicity was matchless, and the fun in him came out as he described the fourth George, and then stopped, not smiling himself, while we all laughed. He silently stood, his head tipped back, and then calmly wiped his spectacles and went on. He had a charm as a speaker which no one has since caught: it defies analysis, as does his genius. It was Thackerayian. . . . A kind-hearted, noble, tender man; a generous, sincere gentleman; a healthy, good liver, and with a fine grip to his hearty hand. He was a big man and heavy, and walked with a strong step; a healthful, broad-shouldered Englishman, whose jollity and fun seemed to forbid reticence on his part, but who could and did, at the touch of humbug or affectation, retreat into himself, turn away with an expression of polished irony on his face, and, with a singular movement of the head, assure the bore that he was no longer needed.—SHERWOOD, MARY E. W., 1897, *An Epistle to Posterity, pp.* 79, 81.

In May, his third child, Harriet Marion——afterwards Mrs. Leslie Stephen—was born, and his wife became very ill. The illness eventually affected her mind, and Thackeray, who regarded this as only a natural sequence of the illness, which would pass away in time, when her health was restored, threw all business aside, sent his children to their grandparents at Paris, and for many months travelled with his wife from watering-place to watering-place, as

the doctors as a last resource had recommended, hoping against hope that the cloud on her intellect would dissolve. . . . At last Thackeray was compelled to realise the truth—that his poor wife would never recover sufficiently to undertake the duties of a mother and a wife. She was unable to manage her life, though she took interest in any pleasant things around her, especially in music; but it was essential that she should be properly cared for, and, with this object, she was placed with Mr. and Mrs. Thompson at Leigh, in Essex. She outlived her husband by so many years that it was with a shock, having already been dead to the world for nearly forty years, that the announcement of her death, in January, 1894, at the age of seventy-five, was read. She was interred in the same grave at Kensal Green cemetery as her husband.—MELVILLE, LEWIS, 1899, *The Life of William Makepeace Thackeray, vol.* I, *p.* 129.

Thackeray shocked Charlotte Brontë sadly by the fashion of his talk on literary subjects. The truth is, Charlotte Brontë's heroics roused Thackeray's antagonism. He declined to pose on a pedestal for her admiration, and with characteristic contrariety of nature he seemed to be tempted to say the very things that set Charlotte Brontë's teeth, so to speak, on edge, and affronted all her ideals. He insisted on discussing his books very much as a clerk in a bank would discuss the ledgers he had to keep for a salary. But all this was, on Thackeray's part, an affectation; an affectation into which he was provoked by what he considered Charlotte Brontë's highfalutin'. Miss Brontë wanted to persuade him that he was a great man with a "mission"; and Thackeray, with many wicked jests, declined to recognise the "mission."—SMITH, SIR GEORGE MURRAY, 1901, *In the Early Forties, The Critic, vol.* 38, *p.* 58.

ART

We well remember, ten or twelve years ago, finding him day after day engaged in copying pictures in the Louvre, in order to qualify himself for his intended profession. It may be doubted, however, whether any degree of assiduity would have enabled him to excel in the money-making branches, for his talent was altogether of the Hogarth kind, and was principally remarkable in the pen-and-ink sketches of character and situation, which he dashed off for the amusement of his friends.—HAYWARD, ABRAHAM,

1848, *Thackeray's Writings, Edinburgh Review, vol.* 87, *p.* 49.

He had a genuine gift of drawing. The delicious "Book of Snobs" is poor without his own woodcuts; and he not only had the eye and the faculty of a draughtsman, he was one of the best of art critics. He had the true instinct and relish, and the nicety and directness, necessary for just as well as high criticism: the white light of the intellect found its way into this as into every region of his work.—BROWN, JOHN, 1863-66, *Thackeray's Death, Spare Hours, Second Series*, p. 232.

Thackeray has been called a "lesser Hogarth," and, since he himself has included Hogarth among the humorists rather than among artists, we may admit, I think, the comparison so far; in their humour the two have a considerable amount in common. That Thackeray can in any true sense be called an artist—confining the term to pictorial art,—I do not for a moment believe. In drawing, as in writing, he had an inimitable gift of humorous conception; he had a wonderful power of catching a fit expression and fixing it in three or four strokes, and a fine capacity for humorous detail, but of *technique* he is absolutely innocent; "touching" as in Madame's hand in the last sketch, was ever anything so impossible? And we must remember, in this connection, that Thackeray could not claim to be an untaught genius, since he started his career by studying for an artist.—FIENNES, GERARD, 1894, *Some Notes upon Thackeray, New Review, vol.* 10, *p.* 339.

All his life he preferred the pencil to the pen. As I have already said, he often found writing wearisome and the strain of composition irksome; there were times even when he almost hated the chain that held him to the desk. But he always turned to the drawing-board with pleasure. . . . He was at his best when illustrating his own writings. There has hardly been an artist who could make his drawings so helpful to the text. His characters are as truly depicted by the pencil as by the pen, and they tell the story together. His drawing may not always have been quite accurate, the perspective may have occasionally been wrong, and an arm may have slightly resembled a fin, or leg have been slightly out of correct drawing; but for quaint fancy and humour they have rarely been surpassed.—MELVILLE, LEWIS, 1899, *The Life of William Makepeace Thackeray, vol.* II, *pp.* 200, 210.

How ill we could spare Thackeray's illustrations. Who can forget the sense of fitness which has recommended to him these drawings, weak and insufficient in themselves, but so evidently imbued with the living literary conception? That he could not satisfactorily illustrate the thoughts of others we have abundant evidence, but where have we ever seen book illustrations more helpful to the right understanding of the author's thought than those in "The Christmas Books," "Dr. Birch," "Our Street," and "The Kickleburys on the Rhine"?—LAYARD, GEORGE SOMES, 1899, *Our Graphic Humourists: W. M. Thackeray, The Magazine of Art, vol.* 23, *p.* 260.

BARRY LYNDON
1844

In imagination, language, construction, and general literary capacity, Thackeray never did anything more remarkable than "Barry Lyndon."—TROLLOPE, ANTHONY, 1879, *Thackeray (English Men of Letters), p.* 69.

"Barry Lyndon," the autobiography of the Irish adventurer, gambler, and scoundrel is a masterpiece. It is a worthy precursor of "Esmond" in the difficult piece of the historical novel. The hero is a scamp of the last century, not of ours. The world in which he moves is a world of long ago, a world as yet unshrivelled in the fire of the French Revolution. And it is a real world. We never feel doubt or hesitation about that. The characters, adventures, surroundings, all produce on us the impression of life. In the telling of the story, too, what witchery of style. How eloquent, for instance, the passage in which Barry Lyndon defends gambling—how admirable the long episode of the ill-fated love of the Princess Olivia, and of her terrible end! "Barry Lyndon" appeared in *Fraser* during the greater part of 1844, and one may legitimately wonder that the world did not then discover that a great novelist was writing for its amusement and edification. And perhaps an even greater work was to follow.—MARZIALS, FRANK T., 1891, *Life of W. M. Thackeray (Great Writers), p.* 131.

Certainly a master-piece.—LILLY, WILLIAM SAMUEL, 1895, *Four English Humourists of the Nineteenth Century, p.* 55.

In Barry Lyndon there is imagined to the

life a scoundrel of such rare quality that he never supposes for a moment but he is the finest sort of a gentleman; and so, in fact, he was, as most gentlemen went in his day. Of course, the picture is over-colored; it was the vice of Thackeray, or of Thackeray's time, to surcharge all imitations of life and character, so that a generation apparently much slower, if not duller than ours, should not possibly miss the artist's meaning. But I do not think it is so much surcharged as Esmond; Barry Lyndon is by no manner of means so conscious as that mirror of gentlemanhood, with its manifold self-reverberations; and for these reasons I am inclined to think he is the most perfect creation of Thackeray's mind.—HOWELLS, WILLIAM DEAN, 1895, *My Literary Passions, p.* 135.

I cannot tell how often I have read the "Scarlet Letter" and "Smoke," "Henry Esmond" and "Pere Goriot," the "Rise of Silas Lapham" and the "Adventures of Huckleberry Finn." To make a choice of them is frankly impossible, or even to say that these six are the favorite half dozen. But if a selection is imperative, I am ready for the moment at least, to declare that Thackeray is the novelist I would rather discuss here and now, well aware that no favourite has a right to expect a long continuance in grace. And the reason why I pick out Thackeray from among the other novelists I like as well as I like him (if not better) is that I may thus call attention to a book of his which I believe to be somewhat neglected. I hold this book to be his best artistically, the one most to be respected, if not the one to be regarded with the most warmth. It is perhaps the only story of Thackeray's which the majority of his readers have never taken up. It is the tale of his telling which most clearly reveals some of his best qualities and which most artfully masks some of his worst defects. It is the "Memoirs of Barry Lyndon, Esq., Written by Himself." . . . "Barry Lyndon" is neither insipid nor dull; yet its secret history would be interesting enough. It was written when Thackeray was not yet thirty-five years of age—for he flowered late, like most of the greater novelists. . . . As Thackeray paints the portrait, it is worthy to hang in any rogues' gallery—as the original was worthy to be hanged on any scaffold. The villain double-dyed is very rare in modern fiction, and Barry Lyndon is an altogether incomparable scoundrel, who be-

lieves in himself, tells us his own misdeeds, and ever proclaims himself a very fine fellow—and honestly expects us to take him at his own valuation, while all our knowledge of his evil doings is derived from his own self-laudatory statements!-MATTHEWS, BRANDER, 1897-1901, *On A Novel of Thackeray's, The Historical Novel and Other Essays, pp.* 151, 152, 157.

"Barry Lyndon !"—the greatest of all these stories and the first in which the author's genius shines unfettered.—MELVILLE, LEWIS, 1899, *The Life of William Makepeace Thackeray, vol.* I, *p.* 210.

BOOK OF SNOBS
1848

Never was satire so keen and unflinching. It is the boldest book ever written by a man who had no personal pique to gratify. We are not surprised that the author of it should have been blackballed at the clubs; the wonder rather is, that the doors of private mansions do not "grate harsh thunder" when he stands before them, and that "Jeames" does not positively refuse to take up his name.—KIRK, JOHN FOSTER, 1853, *Thackeray as a Novelist, North American Review, vol.* 77, *p.* 218.

I regard as a master-piece of humour. Its playfulness is, of course, of the satiric kind. The keen and vivacious satire of an accomplished man of the world is Thackeray's distinctive note as a humourist. . . . There is exaggeration, there is caricature, in the "Book of Snobs." But it is substantially true. It is a very direct, a very amusing, and I will add, a very philosophical indictment of a specially English vice—a dominant vice, we may say, of the English mind, an unreasonable deference for artificial superiorities.—LILLY, WILLIAM SAMUEL, 1895, *Four English Humourists of the Nineteenth Century, p.* 56.

The "Snob Papers" had a very marked effect, and may be said to have made Thackeray famous. He had at last found out how to reach the public ear. The style was admirable, and the freshness and vigour of the portrait painting undeniable. It has been stated (Spielmann, p. 319) that Thackeray got leave to examine the complaint books of several clubs in order to obtain material for his description of club snobs. He was speaking, in any case, upon a very familiar topic, and the vivacity of his sketches naturally suggested identification with particular individuals. These must be in any case doubtful, and the practice was against Thackeray's artistic principles.—STEPHEN, LESLIE, 1898, *Dictionary of National Biography, vol.* LVI, *p.* 96.

VANITY FAIR
1848

I brought away the last four numbers of "Vanity Fair," and read one of them in bed, during the night. Very good, indeed, beats Dickens out of the world.—CARLYLE, JANE WELSH, 1847, *To Thomas Carlyle, Sept.* 16; *Letters and Memorials, ed. Froude, vol.* I, *p.* 296.

You mentioned Thackeray and the last number of "Vanity Fair." The more I read Thackeray's works the more certain I am that he stands alone—alone in his sagacity, alone in his truth, alone in his feeling (his feeling, though he makes no noise about it, is about the most genuine that ever lived on a printed page), alone in his power, alone in his simplicity, alone in his self-control. Thackeray is a Titan, so strong that he can afford to perform with calm the most herculean feats; there is the charm and majesty of repose in his greatest efforts; *he* borrows nothing from fever, his is never the energy of delirium—his energy is sane energy, deliberate energy, thoughtful energy. The last number of "Vanity Fair" proves this peculiarly. Forcible, exciting in its force, still more impressive than exciting, carrying on the interest of the narrative in a flow, deep, full, resistless, it is still quiet—as quiet as reflection, as quiet as memory; and to me there are parts of it that sound as solemn as an oracle. Thackeray is never borne away by his own ardour —he has it under control. His genius obeys him—it is his servant, it works no fantastic changes at its own wild will, it must still achieve the task which reason and sense assign it, and none other. Thackeray is unique. I *can* say no more, I *will* say no less. —BRONTË, CHARLOTTE, 1848, *Letter to W. S. Williams, March* 29; *Charlotte Brontë and Her Circle, ed. Shorter, p.* 411.

An attempt, somewhat after the manner of Fielding, to represent the world as it is, especially the selfish, heartless, and cunning portion of it. The author has Fielding's cosy manner of talking to his readers in the pauses of his narrative, and, like Fielding, takes his personages mostly from ordinary life. The novel, though it touches often upon topics which have been worn threadbare and reproduces many commonplace types

of character, is still, on the whole, a fresh and vigorous transcript of English life, and has numerous profound touches of humanity and humor.—WHIPPLE, EDWIN PERCY, 1848, *Novels of the Season, Essays and Reviews, vol.* II, *p.* 368.

I can read nothing but "Vanity Fair," over and over again, which fills me with delight, wonder, and *humility.* I would sooner have drawn Rawdon Crawley than all the folks I ever drew.—KINGSLEY, CHARLES, 1850, *Letter to his Wife, Charles Kingsley, his Letters and Memoirs of his Life, ed. his Wife, vol.* II, *p.* 25, *note.*

I confess to being unable to read "Vanity Fair," from the moral disgust it occasions.—MARTINEAU, HARRIET, 1855–77, *Autobiography, ed. Chapman, vol.* II, *p.* 60.

His greatest work, one of the great masterpieces of genius in our, or indeed in any language, without doubt is "Vanity Fair." —BROWN, JOHN, 1863–66, *Thackeray's Death, Spare Hours, Second Series, p.* 230.

I once made a pilgrimage with Thackeray (at my request, of course, the visits were planned) to the various houses where his books had been written; and I remember when he came to Young Street, Kensington, he said, with mock gravity, "Down on your knees, you rogue, for here 'Vanity Fair' was penned! And I will go down with you, for I have a high opinion of that little production myself." He was always perfectly honest in his expressions about his own writings, and it was delightful to hear him praise them when he could depend on his listeners. A friend congratulated him once on that touch in "Vanity Fair" in which Becky *"admires"* her husband when he is giving Steyne the punishment which ruins *her* for life. "Well," he said, "when I wrote the sentence, I slapped my fist on the table and said, '*That is* a touch of genius!' "— FIELDS, JAMES T., 1871, *Yesterdays with Authors, p.* 27.

The tale may be said to have been in some degree deceptive, for the novel certainly had a heroine, Miss Rebecca, or, as she is profanely but more commonly called, Becky Sharp. No one, however, stopped to criticise the title; it was acknowledged at once to be a great work, not indeed of the very highest class, such as "Ivanhoe" or "Woodstock," but rather of the school of Fielding, and worthy of the master, being indeed much such a work as he himself, if polished into decorum by the more refined civilization of the nineteenth century, would have written.—YONGE, CHARLES DUKE, 1872, *Three Centuries of English Literature, p.* 631.

If I were called upon to name the saddest incident and the most tragic touch in modern fiction, I should select the close of the thirty-second chapter of "Vanity Fair."— STODDARD, RICHARD HENRY, 1874, *William Makepeace Thackeray, Harper's Magazine, vol.* 49, *p.* 541.

When we speak now of "Vanity Fair," it is always to Becky that our thoughts recur. She has made a position for herself in the world of fiction, and is one of our established personages.—TROLLOPE, ANTHONY, 1879, *Thackeray (English Men of Letters), p.* 97.

How did Thackeray achieve his effects? Becky Sharp is a unique and permanent figure in literature, a subtle embodiment of duplicity, ambition, and selfishness. She is avaricious, hypocritical, specious, and crafty. Though not malignant nor to a certainty criminal, she is a conscienceless little malefactor, whose ill deeds are only limited by the ignoble dimensions of her passions. She lies with amazing glibness, is utterly faithless to her hulking husband, and utterly indifferent to her child. Her mendacity is superlative, and double-dealing enters into all her transactions. But she is so shrewd, so vivacious, so artful, so immensely clever and good-humoured, she has so much prettiness of manner and person, that, while we despise her, and have not the least pity for her when retribution falls heavily upon her, our indignation against her is not so great as we feel that it ought to be, principally because her sins have a certain feminine archness and irresponsibility in them, which keeps them well down to the level of comedy. When we close the book we know her through and through, and thoroughly understand all the complex workings of her strategic mind. How do we know her so well?· Thackeray is not exegetical, and does not depend on elaborate analysis for his effects. The actions of the characters are themselves fully expository, and do not call for any outside comments or enlargement on the part of the author. This is the case to such an extent that, when we examine the completeness with which the characters are revealed to us, we are inclined to believe that Thackeray's art is of the very highest kind, and that, though in

form it is undramatic, intrinsically it is powerfully dramatic.—RIDEING, WILLIAM H., 1885, *Thackeray's London, p.* 34.

We have been to the show. What now are our reflections? What higher and braver thoughts have come to our minds when, wearied with toil and the witness of life's discordant realities, we turned aside to dream of the unreal? What encouragement have we gained for efforts at well-doing by the sight of honest work and patient endurance rewarded? Or what warning have we had from the contemplation of vice and intrigue overtaken by disaster, or at least by disappointment? Instead of these we have found—and to some extent been ashamed to find—ourselves admiring a creation that is as seductive as it is evil. Added to this we were conscious of a loss of some portion of that which it is most calamitous to lose. Woe to him who parts from his trust in mankind, who does not believe that in this world there is goodness beyond that which he has never found in his own being the capacity to practise! In this book the artist—and he was an eminently great artist —seemed to have endeavored to drive mankind to their own unaided struggles, taking away from them all good examples, and leaving them to conclude that nothing is real but folly and perfidy.—JOHNSTON, RICHARD MALCOLM, 1886, *The Extremity of Satire, Catholic World, vol.* 42, *p.* 688.

I do think that any boy—at least any boy who is genuine, and has not prematurely learnt to feign liking for what he thinks he ought to like—can really enjoy "Vanity Fair." The full beauty of Becky (I can honestly say that I always saw some of it) is necessarily hidden from him; he can not taste the majesty of the crowning scene with Lord Steyne, or the even finer, though less dramatic, negotiations which avert the duel; his knowledge of life is insufficient to allow him to detect the magnificent thoroughness and the more magnificent irony of the general treatment. On the other hand, he is sure, if he is good for anything, to be disgusted with the namby-pambyness of Amelia, with the chuckle-headed goodness of Dobbin, with the vicious nincompoopery and selfishness of George Osborne. For these are things which, though experience may lead to the retraction of an opinion that any of the three is unnatural, leave on some tolerably mature judgments the impression that they are one-sided and out of

composition, if not of drawing.—SAINTS-
BURY, GEORGE, 1895, *Corrected Impressions,*
p. 2.

After reading "Pendennis" I went to
"Vanity Fair," which I now think the poorest of Thackeray's novels—crude, heavy-
handed, caricatured.—HOWELLS, WILLIAM
DEAN, 1895, *My Literary Passions, p.* 132.

George Osborn ought to be the hero of
"Vanity Fair," and in truth is handsome
and outwardly attractive enough; but in
almost all the higher qualities he is almost beneath contempt. What more can
be said in his praise than that he won and
retained the love of one of the sweetest and
purest of women? Major Dobbin, with
whom he is contrasted, is everything externally that the conventional hero of fiction ought not to be—uncouth and ridiculous, rough and forbidding. It is, however, within this ungainly casket that
Thackeray places a truly beautiful soul,
honest and brave, patient and unselfish,
true and faithful. With the fortunes of
these four persons the story is mainly concerned. But there are besides many others
—Joseph Sedley, the older Osborne, and the
Crawleys—all drawn to the life, and with a
pencil that never falters. Whether we like
his views of life and of society or not, we
cannot help feeling that these pictures are
as true in outline as they are faithful in detail. Thackeray never fails in his purpose
to amuse, but in the exercise of his sterner
functions as a moralist and censor, he may
sometimes arouse a sentiment of pity for
the puppets of his fancy on whom he has
brought down with such terrible effect the
lash of his retributory satire.—GRAHAM,
RICHARD D., 1897, *The Masters of Victorian
Literature, p.* 27.

I cannot help thinking that although
"Vanity Fair" was written in 1845 and the
following years, it was really begun in 1817,
when the little boy, so lately come from India, found himself shut in behind those
filigree iron gates at Chiswick, of which he
writes when he described Miss Pinkerton's
establishment. Whether Miss Pinkerton
was, or was not, own sister to the great
Doctor at the head of the boarding-school
for young gentlemen on Chiswick Mall, to
which "Billy boy" (as the author of "Vanity Fair" used to be called in those early
days) was sent, remains to be proved. There
is certainly a very strong likeness between
those two majestic beings, the awe-inspir-

ing Doctor and the great Miss Pinkerton
whose dignity and whose Johnsonian
language marked an epoch in education.
. . . My brother-in-law has some of the
early MS. of "Vanity Fair." It is curious
to compare it with that of "Esmond," for
instance, which flows on straight and with
scarcely an alteration. The early chapters
of "Vanity Fair" are, on the contrary,
altered and rewritten with many erasures
and with sentences turned in many different
ways.—RITCHIE, ANNE ISABELLA THACK-
ERAY, 1898, ed. *Vanity Fair, Introduction,
pp.* xv, xxxvii.

The story is none too engrossing, but the
strength lies in the truth of the characters.
It is indeed a novel "without a hero," devoid of thrilling occurrences or adventures,
without a murder, or a forged will and with
no lofty virtues or monstrous vices, for
"Becky Sharp," Thackeray's most celebrated character, is no tigress, only a cat,
or it may be a tiger-cat. The book is a
thorough picture of English middle-class
life. Thackeray is merciless in his treatment of this mediocrity, the spoilt child of
the English novelist. The mean and ignoble
standard of second-rate morality, too timid
to be vicious, too indolent to be virtuous, is
exposed in a number of characters that
may be regarded as typical. "Vanity Fair"
is the author's masterpiece; witness the
delicacy and quiet reserve in the most
touching scenes: the parting of George
Osborne and Amelia, the battlefield of
Waterloo and the death of Osborne—all depicted in a few brief memorable lines.—
ENGEL, EDWARD, 1902, *A History of English
Literature, rev. Hamley Bent, p.* 454.

HISTORY OF PENDENNIS
1849–50

A book which, with all its wealth of wit,
humor, and worldly knowledge, still leaves
the saddest impression on the mind of all
of Thackeray's works. It is enjoyed while
we are engaged in reading its many-peopled
pages; the separate scenes and incidents
are full of matter; but it wants unity and
purpose, and the wide information of the
superficies of life it conveys is of the kind
which depresses rather than exhilarates.—
WHIPPLE, EDWIN PERCY, 1866, *Thackeray,
Character and Characteristic Men, p.* 211.

I can easily believe that a girl should be
taught to wish to love by reading how
Laura Bell loved Pendennis. Pendennis
was not, in truth, a very worthy man, nor

did he make a very good husband; but the girl's love was so beautiful, and the wife's love, when she became a wife, so woman-like, and at the same time so sweet, so un-selfish, so wifely, so worshipful—in the sense in which wives are told that they ought to worship their husbands—that I cannot believe that any girl can be injured, or even not benefited, by reading of Laura's love.—TROLLOPE, ANTHONY, 1882-83, *An Autobiography.*

The "History of Pendennis"—more veracious than many a history of more pre-tension—is at once the delight and the de-spair of all young men who seek to lead the literary life. Indeed, one may often won-der how many men there are now getting on in years, who have taken to literature as the honest trade whereby they were to get their bread, after a youthful reading of those wonderful chapters which tell the entranc-ing tale of Pen's spending an evening in writing "The Church Porch" up to a plate in an annual, and which set forth the start-ing of the "Pall Mall Gazette," written by a gentleman for gentlemen. And who is there to say that "Pendennis" is better or more beautiful or more captivating than "Henry Esmond" or "Vanity Fair" or "The Virginians." When I recall certain pages of those books and of their fellows, "The Newcomes," and the incomparable "Barry Lyndon," I am ready to break out into dithyrambic rhapsodies of enthusiasm, and I know I had best be silent. The dithyrambic rhapsodist is not a fashionable critic, just now.—MATTHEWS, BRANDER, 1888, *Books That Have Helped Me*, p. 80.

Here, as in "Vanity Fair," the heroism has been found a little insipid; and there may be good ground for finding Laura Pen-dennis dull, though she has a spirit of her own. In later books she becomes, what Thackeray's people very seldom are, a tire-some as well as uninviting person. Costigan is unique, and so is Major Pendennis, a type which, allowing for differences of period and manners, will exist as long as society does, and which has been seized and de-picted by Thackeray as by no other novelist. His two encounters, from both of which he comes out victorious, one with Costigan in the first, the other with Morgan in the sec-ond volume, are admirable touches of genius. In opposition to the worldliness of the Major, with which Pendennis does not escape being tainted, we have Warrington,

whose nobility of nature has come un-scathed through a severe trial, and who, a thorough gentleman if a rough one, is really the guardian of Pendennis's career. There is, it should be noted, a characteristic and acknowledged confusion in the plot of Pendennis, which will not spoil any intel-ligent reader's pleasure.—POLLOCK, WAL-TER H., 1888, *Encyclopædia Britannica, Ninth Ed., vol.* XXIII.

It is a delightful, a great book, and con-tains some of the best scenes that Thack-eray ever described, some of the best char-acters he ever painted. Among the latter comes, first and foremost, an old flame of mine, and probably of many men who are now no longer young—I mean, of course, Laura Bell. Thackeray was not usually at his happiest when dealing with good women.—MARZIALS, FRANK T., 1891, *Life of W. M. Thackeray (Great Writers)*, p. 153.

I think it was "Pendennis" I began with, and I lived in the book to the very last line of it, and made its alien circumstance mine to the smallest detail. I am still not sure but it is the author's greatest book, and I speak from a thorough acquaintance with every line he has written, except the "Vir-ginians," which I have never been able to read quite through; most of his work I have read twice, and some of it twenty times.— HOWELLS, WILLIAM DEAN, 1895, *My Liter-ary Passions*, p. 131.

In the same way perhaps that "Vanity Fair" was begun at Chiswick in the year 1818, some of the early chapters of "Penden-nis" must have been written within the first quarter of the century, and Fairoaks and Charteris are certainly to be found be-tween the folded sheets which travelled from Charterhouse and Cambridge to the mother at Larkbeare by Ottery St. Mary's. Some one ery like Helen Pendennis was the mistress of Larkbeare, where my father spent his holidays as a boy; and there was a little orphan niece called Mary Graham, who also lived in the old house, with its seven straight windows and its background of shading trees. Major Pendennis, most assuredly, was *not* to be found there. I have heard my father describe the bitter journey in winter-time, when he drove from Charterhouse to Larkbeare upon the top of the snowy Exeter coach. On one occa-sion my grandmother told me he had to be lifted down, so benumbed was he with the cold. The journey from Cambridge must have been longer still, but he was older and better able to stand it, nor was it always winter-time then, any more than it is now. Between 1824 and 1825, after his fight with Mr. Venables and the accident which broke the bridge of his nose, my father left Penny's house and went to live in Charterhouse Square with Mrs. Boyes, who took in boys belonging to Charterhouse and Merchant Tailors. It was a low brick house with a tiled roof; he once pointed it out to us, and he took us across the playground and into the old chapel.—RITCHIE, ANNE ISABELLA THACKERAY, 1898, ed. *Pendennis, Introduction, p.* xiii.

In "Pendennis," begun almost immediately after finishing "Vanity Fair," Thackeray took his stand by Fielding, defending "the Natural in Art," and announcing that he was going to present the public with a new "Tom Jones." His specific intent was an exact account of the doings of a young man, at school, at college, in the inns of court, and at the clubs, as he had observed them. But if "Pendennis" be compared with its prototype, certain points of difference are clear. Tom Jones yields to temptation. Arthur Pendennis and George Warrington, bundles of high manly qualities and very great weaknesses, are for a time led astray by passions which they afterward overcome. Thackeray admits frankly that there are some passages in the careers of his gentlemen that will not bear telling. Fielding concealed nothing; "Tom Jones" is a study in the nude. Thackeray reluctantly draped his figures, out of respect to conventions he was inclined from time to time to ridicule.—CROSS, WILBUR L., 1899, *The Development of the English Novel, p.* 204.

HENRY ESMOND
1852

Though I have had to run to London several times, I generally ran back as fast as I could; much preferring the fresh air and the fields to the smoke and "the wilderness of monkeys" in London. Thackeray I saw for ten minutes: he was just in the agony of finishing a Novel: which has arisen out of the Reading necessary for his Lectures and relates to those Times—of Queen Anne, I mean. He will get £1000 for his Novel. He was wanting to finish it, and rush off to the Continent, I think, to shake off the fumes of it.—FITZGERALD, EDWARD, 1852, *Letter to F. Tennyson, June* 8; *Letters and Literary Remains, vol.* II, *p.* 2.

There is abundance of incident in the book, but not much more plot than in one of Defoe's novels: neither is there, generally speaking, a plot in man's life, though there may be and often is in sections of it. Unity is given not by consecutive and self-developing story, but by the ordinary events of life blended with those peculiar to a stirring time acting on a family group, and bringing out and ripening their qualities; these again controlling the subsequent events, just as happens in life. The book has the great charm of reality.—BRIMLEY, GEORGE, 1852-58, "*Esmond,*" *Essays, ed. Clark, p.* 254.

"Esmond," appears to me *the* book of the century, in its department. I have read it three times; and each time with new wonder at its rich ripe wisdom, and at the singular charm of Esmond's own character. The power that astonishes me the most in Thackeray is his fertility, shown in the way in which he opens glimpses into a multitudinous world as he proceeds. The chief moral charm is in the paternal vigilance and sympathy which constitute the spirit of his narration.—MARTINEAU, HARRIET, 1855-77, *Autobiography, ed. Chapman, vol.* II, *p.* 60.

For myself, I own that I regard "Esmond" as the first and finest novel in the English language. Taken as a whole, I think that it is without a peer. There is in it a completeness of historical plot, and an absence of that taint of unnatural life which blemishes, perhaps, all our other historical novels, which places it above its brethren. And, beyond this, it is replete with a tenderness which is almost divine,—a tenderness which no poetry has surpassed. Let those who doubt this go back and study again the life of Lady Castlewood. In "Esmond," above all his works, Thackeray achieves the great triumph of touching the innermost core of his subject, without ever wounding the taste. We catch all the aroma, but the palpable body of the thing never stays with us till it palls us. Who ever wrote of love with more delicacy than Thackeray has written in Esmond?—TROLLOPE, ANTHONY, 1864, *W. M. Thackeray, Cornhill Magazine, vol.* 9, *p.* 136.

"Esmond" was from the first most liked among literary men who can appreciate a style having no resemblance to the fashion of the day; but there was a vein of tenderness and true pathos in the story which, in spite of some objectionable features in the plot, and of a somewhat wearisome genealogical introduction, have by degrees gained for it a high rank among the author's works.—HOTTEN, JOHN CAMDEN (THEODORE TAYLOR), 1864, *Thackeray the Humorist and the Man of Letters, p.* 140.

Amongst all these transformed novels will appear a single genuine one, elevated, touching, simple, original, the history of Henry Esmond. Thackeray has not written a less popular nor a more beautiful story.—TAINE, H. A., 1871, *History of English Literature. tr. Van Laun, vol.* II, *bk.* v, *ch.* ii, *p.* 395.

If I could possess only *one* of his works, I think I should choose "Henry Esmond." To my thinking, it is a marvel in literature, and I have read it oftener than any of the other works.—FIELDS, JAMES T., 1871, *Yesterdays with Authors, p.* 16.

"Henry Esmond," which was given to the world complete, should be read, if possible, at a sitting, when its completeness, as a whole, will, I think, be felt. As a work of art, it is Thackeray's masterpiece; as the reproduction of a past age—as a historical novel—it is unrivaled. There is nothing like it, nothing so perfect, in English fiction.—STODDARD, RICHARD HENRY, 1874, *William Makepeace Thackeray, Harper's Magazine, vol.* 49, *p.* 543.

There are few productions in the world of fiction which exhibit the finish of "Esmond," for the author has not only drawn his characters with unusual skill, but delighted the reader with repeated bursts of natural, unaffected eloquence, in language sedulously borrowed from the age of Steele and Addison.—SMITH, GEORGE BARNETT, 1875, *William Makepeace Thackeray, Poets and Novelists, p.* 22.

In Beatrix Esmond, the broad marks in the character of an ambitious and brilliant woman are well given by the incidents of the novel, and that scene in which she and the Prince are found together by Esmond at Castlewood is highly true and dramatic. But Thackeray does not make the wilfulness and brilliancy of the woman as dazzling and charming as he had wished them to be, or, perhaps, had conceived them to be. His imagination has flagged, and he altogether fails in his obvious efforts to goad it into a fresh apprehension of the character.—NADAL, EHRMAN SYME, 1881–82, *Thack-eray's Relations to English Society, Essays at Home and Elsewhere, p.* 99.

Of Thackeray's works certainly the most remarkable and perhaps the best is "Esmond." Many novelists following in the wake of Scott have attempted to reproduce for us past manners, scenes, and characters; but in "Esmond" Thackeray not only does this—he reproduces for us the style in which men wrote and talked in the days of Queen Anne. To produce the forgotten phraseology, to remember always not how his age would express an idea, but how Steele, or Swift, or Addison would have expressed it, might have been pronounced impossible of accomplishment. Yet in "Esmond" Thackeray did accomplish it, and with perfect success. The colouring throughout is exquisite and harmonious, never by a single false note is the melody broken.—NICOLL, HENRY J., 1882, *Landmarks of English Literature, p.* 389.

A perfect fiction.—PATER, WALTER, 1888, *Appreciations, with an Essay on Style, p.* 14.

A reader of light novels may find it difficult to acquire a taste for Thackeray. It requires good taste to appreciate the marvellous art shown in every line of "Henry Esmond." It is worth taking pains to reach to that taste. Once gained, it is gained forever. Once gained, the meretricious in literature is easily discovered by the sense so refined.—EGAN, MAURICE FRANCIS, 1889, *Lectures on English Literature, p.* 181.

"Esmond" is beyond doubt the first of Thackeray's novels as a work of art. There is something in the exquisite finish and the harmony of this which we can only express by the epithet, artistic; it is a pure combination of perfect taste and perfect workmanship, which puts it in a separate class, in which many of the greatest literary works have no claim to rank. . . . As a composition "Esmond" is almost without a flaw. The details of the execution are all worked out in the same masterly manner, and the language is perfect. We may take, as one instance of the exquisite finish of the minor points, the little explanation of Esmond's prejudice against Marlborough.—OLIPHANT, MARGARET O. W., 1892, *The Victorian Age of English Literature, p.* 278.

It is difficult to think of Esmond as of a character in fiction. His story is so perfectly set in a framework of history, that one can scarcely believe that he did not really exist as he is represented, side by side with Addison, Steele, General Webb, Lord Mohun, and the Chevalier of St. George. For the same reason, it is impossible to regard the book which tells Esmond's story in the light of a mere novel. It is a novel, undoubtedly, but it is also more. It is a history, and that of the best kind, for it deals with the social rather than the political side of events. It is a history of English people of the period in which the action of the story is laid—namely, in the reigns of William III and Anne. It presents us with a series of pictures of their life and manners, dealing also, as true history always must, with the state of religion and literature. . . . The characters of Henry Esmond and of Lady Castlewood are such as grow upon one with every fresh reading of the book. The author is too great an artist to make either of them flawless. In the lady, especially, we mark those particular defects which we are sometimes inclined to think Thackeray must have believed inseparable from all charming women. But when these are subtracted, we feel that in Esmond and his mistress we have before us a perfect gentleman and lady, in the best sense of the words.—RAIKES, E., 1893, *Great Characters of Fiction, ed. Townsend, pp. 23, 26.*

The greatest book in its own special kind ever written.—SAINTSBURY, GEORGE, 1896, *A History of Nineteenth Century Literature, p. 152.*

The book shows even more than the lectures how thoroughly he had imbibed the spirit of the Queen Anne writers. His style had reached its highest perfection, and the tenderness of the feeling has won perhaps more admirers for this book than for the more powerful and sterner performances of the earlier period. The manuscript, now in the library of Trinity College, Cambridge, shows that it was written with very few corrections, and in great part dictated to his eldest daughter and Mr. Crowe. Earlier manuscripts show much more alteration, and he clearly obtained a completer mastery of his tools by long practice. He took, however, much pains to get correct statements of fact, and read for that purpose at the libraries of the British Museum and the Athenæum.— STEPHEN, LESLIE, 1898, *Dictionary of National Biography, vol.* LVI, *p.* 99.

The artistic perfection of "Henry Esmond"—the single and striking exception among his works.—BROWNELL, W. C.,1899, *William Makepeace Thackeray, Scribner's Magazine, vol.* 25, *p.* 236.

To be sure she [Beatrix Esmond] is never directly seen, but always through the eyes of that intolerable prig, Henry Esmond, which are fixed mainly upon his own perfections. Even if she had been directly seen, however, I doubt if there would have been much real drama in her, though plenty of theatre. Several *coups de théâtre* there are in her career, and chiefly that when Esmond and her brother find her at Castlewood with the young Pretender, and prevent her for the time from giving her worthlessness to his worthlessness. If one reads the story in cold blood it is hard to believe in it at all, it is at every moment so palpably and visibly fabricated; and perhaps Beatrix is no more a doll than those other eighteenth-century marionettes; but compared with Becky Sharp a doll she certainly is. It is only in her avatar of Madame Bernstein, in "The Virginians," that she begins to persuade you she is at best anything more than a nineteenth-century actress made up for her part. She suffers, of course, from the self-parade of Esmond, and has not, poor girl, half a chance to show herself for what she is. Her honest, selfish worldliness is, however, more interesting than her mother's much-manipulated virtues.— HOWELLS, WILLIAM DEAN, 1901, *Heroines of Fiction, vol.* I, *p.* 198.

ENGLISH HUMOURISTS
1853

A lecture should not read like an essay; and, therefore, it surprises me that these lectures so carefully prepared, so skilfully adapted to meet the requirements of oral delivery, should be such agreeable reading. As *lectures*, they wanted only a little more point, and emphasis and animation on the part of the speaker: as *essays*, they atone in eloquence and earnestness for what they want in finish and purity of style.—JAMESON, ANNA, 1853, *A Commonplace Book of Thoughts, Memories and Fancies, p.* 270.

Next to Macaulay and Hazlitt, he is the most entertaining of critics. You read his lectures with quite as much gusto as you do "Pendennis," and with infinitely more than you do such dull mimicry of the past as is to be found in "Esmond." Clever, too, of course, sagacious often, and sometimes powerful, are his criticisms, and a geniality not frequent in his fictions, is often here. Sympathy with his subject is also a quality he possesses and parades ; indeed, he appears as one born out of his proper time, and seems, occasionally, to sigh for the age of big-wigs, bagnios, and sponging - houses. — GILFILLAN, GEORGE, 1855, *A Third Gallery of Portraits, p.* 218.

He gave his lectures on "The English Humourists" to large audiences in Carusi's saloon. The interest of these lectures was in their matter, and in their author, but not in their manner of delivery; for he was utterly wanting in those graces of oratory which add so much to the pleasure of listening to the reading of a genuinely literary performance. He was closely confined to his manuscript, which he read in a monotone; yet he was always audible, and he commanded the closest attention of his auditors.—BRAINARD, CHARLES H., 1885, *Recollections of Thackeray; Some Noted Princes, Authors and Statesmen of Our Time, ed. Parton, p.* 54.

By judicious selection, by innuendo, here a pitying aposiopesis, there an indignant outburst, the charges are heaped up. Swift was a toady at heart, and used Stella vilely for the sake of that hussy Vanessa. Congreve had captivating manners—of course he had, the dog! And we all know what that meant in those days. Dick Steele drank and failed to pay his creditors. Sterne —now really I know what Club life is, ladies and gentlemen, and I might tell you a thing or two if I would: but really, speaking as a gentleman before a polite audience, I warn you against Sterne.—QUILLER-COUCH, A. T., 1891, *Adventures in Criticism, p.* 95.

A good deal of fault has lately been found with Thackeray's lecture on Swift. We still think it both delightful and just. The rhapsody about Stella is not to our mind. Rhapsodies about real women are usually out of place. Stella was no saint, but a quick-witted, sharp-tongued hussy, whose fate it was to win the love and pacify the soul of the greatest Englishman of his time —for to call Swift an Irishman is sheer folly. But, apart from this not unnatural slip, what, we wonder, is the matter with Thackeray's lecture, regarded, not as a storehouse of facts, or as an estimate of Swift's writings, but as a sketch of character? Mr. Collins says quite as harsh things about Swift as are to be found in Thackeray's lecture, but he does not attempt, as Thackeray does, to throw a strong light upon this strange and moving figure. It is a hard thing to attempt—failure in such a case is almost inevitable; but we do not think Thackeray wholly failed. An ounce of mother-wit is often worth a pound of clergy. Insight is not the child of study. But here, again, the matter should be brought to the test by each reader for himself. Read Thackeray's lecture once again.—BIRRELL, AUGUSTINE, 1894, *Essays about Men, Women and Books, p.* 12.

Thackeray knew not only the literature but the life of the eighteenth century as few have known it. In minute acquaintance with facts he has doubtless been surpassed by many professional historians; but there is no book to be compared to "Esmond" as a picture of life in the age of Queen Anne; and the lectures on the humourists are saturated, as "Esmond" is, with the eighteenth century spirit. The figures of the humourists live and move before our eyes. We may not always agree with the critic's opinion, but we can hardly fail to understand the subject better through his mode of treatment. Strong objection has been taken, perhaps in some respects with justice, to his handling of Swift. Yet, much as has been written about Swift, where does there exist a picture of him so vivid, so suggestive and so memorable? Who else has done such justice to Steele? Who has written better about Hogarth? Thackeray succeeded because he not only knew the work of these men but felt with them. He was at the bottom of the eighteenth century type. Much of Swift himself, softened and humanised, something of Fielding, whom he justly regarded as a model, and a great deal of Hogarth may be detected in Thackeray.—WALKER, HUGH, 1897, *The Age of Tennyson, p.* 92.

THE NEWCOMES
1854-55

This is by far the best of Thackeray's stories. — PEABODY, ANDREW PRESTON, 1856, *Critical Notices, North American Review, vol.* 82, *p.* 284.

"The Newcomes" is perhaps the most genial of the author's works, and the one which best exhibits the maturity and the range of his powers. It seems written with a pen diamond-pointed, so glittering and incisive is its slightest touch.—WHIPPLE, EDWIN PERCY, 1866, *Thackeray, Character and Characteristic Men, p.* 214.

Generally accounted his masterpiece; and

which, if less sparkling than "Vanity Fair," and less severely testing the artistic skill of the author than "Esmond," yet deserves its fame by presenting us, in Colonel Newcome and Ethel, with the most beautiful pictures both of man and woman that he ever drew.—YONGE, CHARLES DUKE, 1872, *Three Centuries of English Literature, p.* 632.

Thackeray rose to the perfection of his art in fiction in "The Newcomes"; and it is such books as this which show us what a fine teacher and instructor the novel may become in the hands of genius. In the representation of human nature this story is worthy of Richardson or Fielding. It is the *chef-d' œuvre*, in our opinion, of its author.— SMITH, GEORGE BARNETT, 1875, *William Makepeace Thackeray, Poets and Novelists, p.* 26.

One day, while the great novel of "The Newcomes" was in course of publication, Lowell, who was then in London, met Thackeray on the street. The novelist was serious in manner, and his looks and voice told of weariness and affliction. He saw the kindly inquiry in the poet's eyes, and said, "Come into Evans's, and I'll tell you all about it. *I have killed the Colonel.*" So they walked in and took a table in a remote corner, and then Thackeray, drawing the fresh sheets of MS. from his breast pocket, read through that exquisitely touching chapter which records the death of Colonel Newcome. When he came to the final *Adsum*, the tears which had been swelling his lids for some time trickled down his face, and the last word was almost an inarticulate sob.—UNDERWOOD, FRANCIS HENRY, 1881, *James Russell Lowell, Harper's Magazine, vol.* 62, *p.* 265.

There has been a diversity of opinion about Thackeray, his temper, and principles; and they who did not understand him have made some cruel mistakes. Whoever desires to know what sort of man he was, his love of goodness, and his contempt of evil, let him read "The Newcomes."— HOLE, S. REYNOLDS, 1893, *Memories, p.* 76.

"The Newcomes" was written in the years that came between my father's first and second journey to America. He began the preface at Baden on the 7th of July 1853, he finished his book at Paris on the 28th of June 1855, and in the autumn of that year he returned to America. The story had been in his mind for a long time. While still writing "Esmond" he speaks of a new novel "opening with something like Fareham and the old people there," and of "a hero who will be born in India, and have a half-brother and sister." And there is also the description to be read of the little wood near to Berne, in Switzerland, into which he strayed one day, and where, as he tells us, "the story was actually revealed to him."—RITCHIE, ANNE ISABELLA THACKERAY, 1898, *ed. The Newcomes, Introduction, p.* xxii.

It is an epitome of human life in its manifold variety of social and individual phrases unmatched, I think, in fiction. Its range is extraordinary for the thread of a single story to follow. Yet all its parts are as interdependent as they are numerous and varied. It is Thackeray's largest canvas, and it is filled with the greatest ease and to the borders. It stands incontestably at the head of the novels of manners. And it illustrates manners with an unexampled crowd of characters, the handling of which, without repetition or confusion, without digression or discord, exhibits the control of the artist equally with the imaginative and creative faculty of the poet—the "maker." The framework of "The Newcomes" would include three or four of Balzac's most elaborate books, which compared with it, indeed, seem like studies and episodes, lacking the large body and ample current of Thackeray's epic.—BROWNELL, W. C., 1899, *William Makepeace Thackeray, Scribner's Magazine, vol.* 25, *p.* 245.

THE VIRGINIANS
1858–59

"The Virginians" is the most carefully planned of his novels, and the most mature as regards his ideas, but the work has not been carried out so perfectly as some others.—SCHERR, J., 1874, *A History of English Literature, tr. M. V., p.* 277.

"The Virginians," Thackeray told Motley "was devilish stupid, but at the same time most admirable"; and the criticism, paradoxical as it may seem, possesses an element of truth. "Devilish stupid" the book, of course, is not. But it is thoroughly ill "composed," to borrow the art critic's term. The first half and the second half scarcely hang together; the interest is divided, somewhat clumsily, between the two brothers—and I, for one, confess to be very sorry when George comes to life again, and is installed as hero *vice* Henry deposed. But, with all drawbacks, the hand of the great master is there, in the matchless style, the admirable scenes, the excellent delineations of character, the exact reproduction of the life of the last century. All this is on the "most remarkable" side.—MARZIALS, FRANK T., 1891, *Life of W. M. Thackeray (Great Writers), p.* 194.

I have never quite understood the common depreciation of "The Virginians" which contains things equal, if not superior, to the very finest of its author's other work, and includes the very ripest expression of his philosophy of life. For though indeed I do not approve a novel more because it contains the expression of a philosophy of life, others do. So, too, the irregularity and formlessness of plot which characterised most of Thackeray's work undoubtedly appear in it; but then, according to the views of our briskest and most modern critics, plot is a very subordinate requisite in a novel, and may be very well dispensed with. Here again I do not agree, and I should say that Thackeray's greatest fault was his extreme inattention to construction, which is all the more remarkable inasmuch as he was by no means a very rapid or an extremely prolific writer.—SAINTSBURY, GEORGE, 1895, *Corrected Impressions, p.* 17.

THE FOUR GEORGES
1861

I have heard Thackeray's four lectures on the four Georges, truculent enough in their general satire,—though not much beyond the last half-volume of "Harry Esmond" about Queen Anne,—but full of generous passages about individuals. The sketches of the German princes of the seventeenth century, and down to the middle of the eighteenth, with which he opened, amused me more than anything else. They were capital. The passage most applauded was a beautiful tribute of loyalty to Queen Victoria, and the tone and manners of her Court. It was given, on his part, with much feeling, and brought down the house— always crowded—very fervently. . . . His audience was the best the city could give, and about twelve hundred strong, besides which, he repeated the lecture about George III to an audience of two thousand, two or three evenings ago.—TICKNOR, GEORGE, 1855, *To Sir Edmund Head, Dec.* 23; *Life, Letters and Journals of George Ticknor, vol.* II, *p.* 294.

I heard one of Thackeray's lectures, the one on George III, and thought it better than good—fine and touching. To what is it that people are objecting? At any rate, they crowd and pay.—BROWNING, ELIZABETH BARRETT, 1856, *Letter to Mary Russell Mitford, Jan.* 7.

No one succeeded better than Mr. Thackeray in cutting his coat according to his cloth: here he flattered the aristocracy, but when he crossed the Atlantic, George Washington became the idol of his worship, the "Four Georges" the objects of his bitterest attacks. These last-named Lectures have been dead failures in England, though as literary compositions they are most excellent.—YATES, EDMUND, 1858, *Town Talk.*

Thackeray's lectures on "The Four Georges" are a piece of history, written in the spirit of Macaulay. But he may escape the censure which Macaulay, to some extent justly, incurred, because he is not, like Macaulay, a professional historian. In proportion as his work is less pretentious, his responsibility to claims and ideals of scientific history is less serious. He takes a small field of the historian's province. We have only to ask how he acquits himself within these narrow limits.—FOWLER, J. H., 1897, *XIX-Century Prose, p.* 92.

POEMS

The greatest of living satirists. . . . This collection contains nothing more mirth-provoking than the "Ballads of Policeman X," by Mr. Thackeray.—PARTON, JAMES, 1856-84, *ed., The Humorous Poetry of the English Language, p.* 687.

We should not forget his verses,—he would have laughed if they had been called poems; but they had more imaginative *vis,* more daintiness of phrase, more true sensibility and sense, than much that is called so by its authors and the public.—BROWN, JOHN, 1863-66, *Thackeray's Death, Spare Hours, Second Series, p.* 232.

With all his wonderful finish there was not the same width in Praed as in Thackeray; and had he not achieved one of the highest reputations as a novelist, the latter would have gained no inconsiderable place as a singer of every-day life. Imagination was absent in him; but humour, satire, playfulness, tenderness, were abundant.—SMITH, GEORGE BARNETT, 1875, *English Fugitive Poets, Poets and Novelists, p.* 404.

I am not disposed to say that Thackeray will hold a high place among English poets.

He would have been the first to ridicule such an assumption made on his behalf. But I think that his verses will be more popular than those of many highly reputed poets, and that as years roll on they will gain rather than lose in public estimation.—TROLLOPE, ANTHONY, 1879, *Thackeray (English Men of Letters), p.* 180.

Little has yet been said of Thackeray's performances in poetry. They formed a small but not the least significant part of his life's work. The grace and apparent spontaneity of his versification are beyond question. Some of the more serious efforts, such as "The Chronicle of the Drum" (1841), are full of power, and instinct with true poetic feeling. Both the half-humorous half-pathetic ballads and the wholly extravagant ones must be classed with the best work in that kind; and the translations from Béranger are as good as verse translations can be. He had the true poetic instinct, and proved it by writing poetry which equalled his prose in grace and feeling.—POLLOCK, WALTER H., 1888, *Encyclopædia Britannica, Ninth Ed., vol.* XXIII.

Another great name here somewhat wofully misrepresented is that of Thackeray; whose "White Squall" is now and then rather too provocative of such emotions as nature's might provoke in the digestive economy of a bad sailor. To make the gorge rise at it is hardly the sign or the property of elegance in verse: and if indecency, which means nothing more than unseemliness, is very properly considered as a reason for excluding from elegant society the most brilliant examples of the most illustrious writers ever touched by so much as a passing shade of it, the rule should be applied equally to every variety of the repulsive and the unbecoming—not by any means only to matters of sexual indecorum and erotic indelicacy. To none of the other selections from the lighter work of the same illustrious hand is any such objection or suggestion applicable: but not one of them shows Thackeray at his very best as a comic poet.—SWINBURNE, ALGERNON CHARLES, 1891–94, *Social Verse, Studies in Prose and Poetry, p.* 106.

His so-called ballads have the charm that belongs to the wholly or half-playful exercises, the recreations in rhyme, of a supreme literary craftsman. They are not verses of society; they are either too richly humorous, or too sharply satiric, or too deeply coloured by feeling. Through them, as all through his prose, mirth glides by the easiest transitions into sadness, mockery trembles into tenderness, to the strain of boon goodfellowship succeeds the irrepressible reminder that all below is vanity. Carelessly as they seem to have been penned, they abound in happy rhymes and turns of phrase, they show the hand of the writer born to work in metre no less than in prose. "The White Squall" is a really wonderful *tour de force* of vivid, rattling description and novel, dexterous rhyming; there is the true martial note in the rough swinging verses of "The Chronicle of the Drum"; and as for the Irish Ballads, they seem bound to amuse till the drying up of the fountain of laughter. Since Burns wrote the "Ordination," no more telling, mirth-provoking bit of satire has been done in rhyme than the immortal "Battle of Limerick"; and where could there be found a more delicious revel of vocables, all honeyed by the Milesian usage, than in Mr. Maloney's account of the ball that was given to the Nepaulese ambassador?—WHYTE, WALTER, 1894, *The Poets and the Poetry of the Century, Humour, Society, Parody, and Occasional Verse, ed. Miles, p.* 321.

What an admirable gift had Thackeray! Who is so genial, tender, and humorous? Why, the very negligence of his verse has its charm! Read his Horatian "Wait till you come to Forty Year."—LOCKER-LAMPSON, FREDERICK, 1895, *My Confidences, p.* 298.

GENERAL

There is a man in our own days whose words are not framed to tickle delicate ears; who, to my thinking, comes before the great ones of society much as the son of Imlah came before the throned kings of Judah and Israel; and who speaks truth as deep, with a power as prophet-like and as vital—a mien as dauntless and as daring. Is the satirist of "Vanity Fair" admired in high places? I cannot tell; but I think if some of those amongst whom he hurls the Greek fire of his sarcasm, and over whom he flashes the levin-branch of his denunciation, were to take his warnings in time, they or their seed might yet escape a fatal Ramoth-Gilead. Why have I alluded to this man? I have alluded to him, reader, because I think I see in him an intellect profounder and more unique than his contemporaries have yet recognized; because I regard him as the first social regenerator of the day—as the very master of that working corps who would restore to rectitude the warped system of things; because I think no commentator on his writings has yet found the comparison that suits him, the terms which rightly characterise his talent. They say he is like Fielding; they talk of his wit, humor, comic powers. He resembles Fielding as an eagle does a vulture; Fielding could stoop on carrion, but Thackeray never does. His wit is bright, his humor attractive, but both bear the same relation to his serious genius, that the mere lambent sheet-lightning, playing under the edge of the summer cloud, does to the electric death-spark hid in its womb.—BRONTË, CHARLOTTE, 1847, *Jane Eyre, Preface.*

He is a nice discerner and skillful delineator—so skillful that, if there were a detective police for the follies and infirmities of human nature, he would be elected chief by acclamation. But I have no affinities for this sagacity, and no great admiration for his detective revelations. I prefer those nice analyses that find sustenance instead of detecting poison; the one work is for our Channings, the other for Thackeray and the wise in their generation.—SEDGWICK, CATHARINE M., 1852, *Letter to Dr. Dewey, Nov.* 27; *Life and Letters, ed. Dewey, p.* 343.

Mr. Thackeray's humour does not mainly consist in the creation of oddities of manner, habit, or feeling; but in so representing actual men and women as to excite a sense of incongruity in the reader's mind—a feeling that the follies and vices described are deviations from an ideal of humanity always present to the writer. The real is described vividly, with that perception of individuality which constitutes the artist; but the description implies and suggests a standard higher than itself, not by any direct assertion of such a standard, but by an unmistakable irony. The moral antithesis of actual and ideal is the root from which springs the peculiar charm of Mr. Thackeray's writings; that mixture of gaiety and seriousness, of sarcasm and tenderness, of enjoyment and cynicism, which reflects so well the contradictory consciousness of man as a being with senses and passions and limited knowledge, yet with a conscience and a reason speaking to him of eternal laws and a moral order of the universe. It is this that makes Mr. Thackeray a profound moralist, just as Hogarth showed his

knowledge of perspective by drawing a landscape throughout in violation of its rules. . . . No one could be simply amused with Mr. Thackeray's descriptions or his dialogues. A shame at one's own defects, at the defects of the world in which one was living, was irresistibly aroused along with the reception of the particular portraiture. But while he was dealing with his own age, his keen perceptive faculty prevailed, and the actual predominates in his pictures of modern society.—BRIMLEY, GEORGE, 1852-58, *"Esmond," Essays, ed. Clark, pp.* 255, 256.

Thackeray all cynicism, with an affectation of fashionable experience.—MITFORD, MARY RUSSELL, 1853, *To Mr. Starkey, June* 31; *The Friendships of Mary Russell Mitford, ed. L'Estrange.*

In Dickens, the lower part of "the World" is brought into the Police Court, as it were, and there, after cross-examination, discharged or committed, as the case may be. The characters are real and low, but are facts. That is one way. Thackeray's is another and better. One of his books is like a Dionysius ear, through which you hear the World talking, entirely unconscious of being overheard.—LOWELL, JAMES RUSSELL, 1854, *To C. F. Briggs, Feb.* 15; *Letters, ed. Norton, vol.* I, *p.* 211.

Thackeray finds that God has made no allowance for the poor thing in his universe, —more's the pity, he thinks,—but 'tis not for us to be wiser; we must renounce ideals and accept London.—EMERSON, RALPH WALDO, 1856-84, *English Traits; Works, Riverside Ed., vol.* V, *p.* 234.

If it were asked what one aspect of life Mr. Thackeray has distinctively exhibited, the answer could be given in one word,— the trivial aspect. The characters he draws are neither the best of men nor the worst. But the atmosphere of triviality which envelopes them all was never before so plainly perceivable. He paints the world as a great Vanity Fair, and none has done that so well. The realism of Thackeray can hardly fail to have a good effect in fictitious literature. It represents the extreme point of reaction against the false idealism of the Minerva Press. It is a pre-Raphaelite school of novel writing. And as pre-Raphaelitism is not to be valued in itself, so much as in being the passage to a new and nobler ideal, the stern realism of Thackeray may lead the way to something better than itself.—BAYNE,

PETER, 1857, *Essays in Biography and Criticism, First Series, p.* 391.

Our own opinion is, that his success is on the wane; his writings never were understood or appreciated even by the middle classes; the aristocracy have been alienated by his American onslaught on their body, and the educated and refined are not sufficiently numerous to constitute an audience; moreover, there is a want of heart in all he writes, which is not to be balanced by the most brilliant sarcasm and the most perfect knowledge of the workings of the human heart.—YATES, EDMUND, 1858, *Town Talk.*

No one can read Mr. Thackeray's writings without feeling that he is perpetually treading as close as he dare to the border line that separates the world which may be described in books from the world which it is prohibited so to describe. No one knows better than this accomplished artist where that line is, and how curious are its windings and turns. The charge against him is that he knows it but too well; that with an anxious care and a wistful eye he is ever approximating to its edge, and hinting with subtle art how thoroughly he is familiar with and how interesting he could make the interdicted region on the other side. He never violates a single conventional rule, but at the same time, the shadow of the immorality that is not seen is scarcely ever wanting to his delineation of the society that is seen,—every one may perceive what is passing in his fancy.—BAGEHOT, WALTER, 1858, *Charles Dickens, Works, ed. Morgan, vol.* II, *p.* 266.

Thackeray's success is almost solely owing to his moral influence. Much as we respect his intellectual powers, we have a far higher admiration of his heart—that noble, courageous generosity for which language has no word. He is emphatically the true gentleman of our generation, who has appealed to our best and most chivalric sympathies, and raising us from the slough and pollution of the Regency has made us once more "a nation of gentlemen."—JEAFFRESON, JOHN CORDAY, 1858, *Novels and Novelists from Elizabeth to Victoria, vol.* II.

Mr. Thackeray, I believe, is as perfect a master in his kind of art as is to be found in the whole series of British prose writers; a man in whom strength of understanding, acquired knowledge of men, subtlety of perception, deep philosophic humour, and exquisiteness of literary taste, are combined in a degree and after a manner not seen in any known precedent.—MASSON, DAVID, 1859, *British Novelists and Their Styles, p.* 249.

Thackeray's range is limited. His genius is not opulent, but it is profuse. He does not create many types, but he endlessly illustrates what he does create. In this he reminds a traveler of Ruysdael and Wouvermann, the old painters. There are plenty of their pictures in the German galleries, and there is no mistaking them. This is a Ruysdael, how rich and tranquil! this is a Wouvermann, how open and smiling! are the instinctive words with which you greet them. The scope, the method, almost the figures and the composition are the same in each Ruysdael, in each Wouvermann, but you are not troubled. Ruysdael's heavy tree, Wouvermann's white horse, are not less agreeable in Dresden than in Berlin, or Munich, or Vienna. And shall we not be as tolerant in literature as in painting? Why should we expect simple pastoral nature in Victor Hugo, or electrical bursts of passion in Scott, or the "ideal" in Thackeray?— CURTIS, GEORGE WILLIAM, 1862, *The Easy Chair, Harper's Magazine, vol.* 25, *p.* 423.

O gentler Censor of our age!
Prime master of our ampler tongue!
Whose word of wit and generous page
Were never wrath, except with Wrong.

Fielding—without the manner's dross,
Scott—with a spirit's larger room,
What Prelate deems thy grave his loss?
What Halifax erects thy tomb?

But, may be, He,—who so could draw
The hidden Great,—the humble Wise,
Yielding with them to God's good law.
Makes the Pantheon where he lies.

—MILNES, RICHARD MONCKTON, (LORD HOUGHTON), 1863, *Historical Contrast, Cornhill Magazine, vol.* 9, *p.* 133.

The clear, transparent simplicity of the boy at the Charterhouse never deserted him. In fact he often reminded me of a boy. On this very day of which I am speaking he wore an old shooting-coat much too short for him: it sat upon the giant as a boy's jacket would fit an ordinary mortal. And then the contrast would strike one. This mighty, vehement, white-headed boy had written the simplest, purest, most idiomatic English; he had sketched, with a touch incomparably delicate and finished, the intricate mental relations of a meditative but feverish age, of an active yet pensive society; he was a master of that implied and constructive irony which is the last refinement of banter, that irony which is a feature of our modern literature, of which, to repeat what I have said elsewhere, we see no sign in that emphatic satire of Dryden, only an occasional trace in the polemical poetry of Pope and the polemical prose of Bolingbroke, but which bursts into perfect flower in the serious books of Mr. Thackeray and the satirical speeches of Mr. Disraeli.— SKELTON, JOHN, 1863-83, *Essays in History and Biography*, p. 294.

Have we exchanged a word about Thackeray since his Death? I am quite surprised to see how I sit moping about him: to be sure, I keep reading his Books. Oh, the Newcomes are fine! And now I have got hold of Pendennis, and seem to like that much more than when I first read it. I keep hearing him say so much of it; and really think I shall hear his Step up the Stairs to this Lodging as in old Charlotte Street thirty years ago. Really, a grand figure has sunk under Earth.—FITZGERALD, EDWARD, 1864, *To George Crabbe, Jan.* 12; *Letters and Literary Remains, ed. Wright, vol.* I, *p.* 295.

Running as he did, a literary race with another eminent humorist, it was his *spécialité* to be able to paint a gentleman with all his faults without caricaturing him into something which no other gentleman ever saw. Again, we are eminently a practical people. Even in our hours of relaxation we carry with us our love for what "can be" rather than what "might be." We love a Hogarth better than a Watts, and the lecturer who proves his case by practical experiment better than one who wanders into theory and foretells important but, until proved, to us problematical results. When we read books of amusement we would rather have a good description of a schoolboy's feelings than the ideal passion of an Othello or a Hamlet. That is our normal state of taste, and Thackeray suited the market; nor did he suit by the supply of a low description of goods. If through want of imagination he fell far short of the great names in the world of art, he followed in the footsteps of two of the master-spirits, Goethe and Shakespeare, in the delineation of his characters. He affected to have no heroes; but taking such as he gave us to be heroes in the sense of the principals in his story, we invariably find that they had

much infirmity of mind and temper, and that he maintains our interest in a man or a woman, even after we have ceased to respect them. — BERDMORE, S., 1864-83, *Thackeray, A Scratch Team of Essays.*

Thackeray, who, apart from all question as to his truth or as to his power, most certainly possessed one of the richest minds with which a novelist has ever been gifted, it was said more frequently than of men who can boast not one tithe of his genius, that he lacked variety.—DALLAS, E. S., 1866, *The Gay Science, vol.* II, *p.* 289.

No author is more fertile in dissertations; he constantly enters his story to reprimand or instruct us; he adds theoretical to active morality. . . . Of all satirists, Thackeray, after Swift, is the most gloomy. Even his countrymen have reproached him with depicting the world uglier than it is. Indignation, grief, scorn, disgust, are his ordinary sentiments. When he digresses, and imagines tender souls, he exaggerates their sensibility, in order to render their oppression more odious. The selfishness which wounds them appears horrible, and this resigned sweetness is a mortal insult to their tyrants: it is the same hatred which has calculated the kindliness of the victims and the harshness of the persecutors. . . . He does as a novelist what Hobbes does as a philosopher. Almost everywhere, when he described fine sentiments, he derives them from an ugly source. Tenderness, kindness, love, are in his characters the effect of the nerves, of instinct, or of a moral disease. . . . He does not animate beings, he lets puppets act. He only combines their actions to make them ridiculous, odious, or disappointing. After a few scenes we recognise the spring, and thenceforth we are always forseeing when it is going to act. —TAINE, H. A., 1871, *History of English Literature, tr. Van Laun, vol.* II, *bk.* v, *ch.* ii, *pp.* 371, 374, 380, 392.

In fiction, out of 1,000 volumes issued recently in a single day, no fewer than 55 were by Thackeray, and 25 by Scott. The steady advance of the popular relish for Thackeray is unmistakable. Every year the admirers of this noblest among novelists are multiplied, and the librarian finds it more and more difficult to satisfy their applications.—HASSARD, JNO. R. G., 1871, *The New York Mercantile Library, Scribner's Monthly, vol.* 1, *p.* 364.

But surely Thackeray must be held the

prince of Carthusians, seeing that he has illustrated in his works every part of our house?—IRVINE, JOHN W., 1872, *Brethren and Companions, A Sermon Preached in the Chapel of the Charterhouse on Founder's Day, Dec.* 12.

For myself, I honestly confess that I never could learn anything from Thackeray; there is a certain feeble amiability even about his best characters, which, if it is free from the depressing influence of his bad ones, is certainly anything but bracing.—BLACKIE, JOHN STUART, 1873, *On Self-Culture.*

Ranks as the third master of the novel of modern manners and morals. . . . He was made to be a satirist; his gaze penetrated to the very hearts of men, and the caustic acuteness of his description cut into and laid open the most secret blemishes with the inexorable accuracy of a dissecting-knife. Scarcely ever has a great satirist proved so great a narrator as Thackeray.— SCHERR, J., 1874, *A History of English Literature, tr. M. V., p.* 276.

Thackeray, whom I in vain tried to vindicate from the charge of a prevailing "spirit of caustic cynicism," Mr. de Quincey appeared to regard as simply a crotchety illusion or a blind partiality my remonstrances in favour of the author of "Pendennis. . . . It has always been a puzzle to me how such a gracious nature, so delicately responsive to every fine touch, so acutely predisposed to the appeals of genuine pathos, should have missed the force and beauty of what is tender in Thackeray. —JACOX, FRANCIS, 1877, *Recollections of De Quincey, Thomas De Quincey by Alexander H. Japp, vol.* I, *p.* 385.

With satire's poignant spear he loved to fight,
And flocks of scampering falsehoods to disband,
So sinewy were the savage blows he planned,
So sweeping yet so accurate his keen sight!
Than he no man more loyally loved the right,
No man could wrong more valiantly withstand,
Who shook the old human web with such fierce hand
That half fraud's ambushed vermin swarmed to light!
How forcefully could he paint the proud grandee;
The skilled adventuress, with her game, sly-played;
The toadying snob, in triple brass arrayed;
The dissolute fop; the callous debauchee;
And dowagers, in rouge, feathers and brocade,
Sneering at life across their cards and tea!
—FAWCETT, EDGAR, 1878, *Fantasy and Passion, p.* 184.

Thackeray in "Esmond," exhibited powers which vindicated for their possessors a very rare infusion of that higher poetic spirit which might have made of both something greater than the painters of the manners of a day and a class. But to paint the manners of a day and a class as Dickens and Thackeray have done is to deserve fame and the gratitude of posterity. The age of Victoria may claim in this respect an equality at least with that of the reign which produced Fielding and Smollett; for if there are some who would demand for Fielding a higher place on the whole than can be given either to Dickens or to Thackeray, there are many on the other hand who would not say that either Dickens or Thackeray is distinctly superior to Smollett. The age must claim a high place in art which could in one department alone produce two such competitors. Their effect upon their time was something marvellous. People talked Dickens or thought Thackeray. — MC-CARTHY, JUSTIN, 1879, *A History of Our Times, from the Accession of Queen Victoria to the Berlin Congress, ch.* xxix.

Unsteadfast, idle, changeable of purpose, aware of his own intellect but not trusting it, no man ever failed more generally than he to put his best foot foremost. Full as his works are of pathos, full of humour, full of love and charity, tending, as they always do, to truth and honor, and manly worth and womanly modesty, excelling, as they seem to me to do, most other written precepts that I know, they always seem to lack something that might have been there. There is a touch of vagueness which indicates that his pen was not firm while he was using it. He seems to me to have been dreaming ever of some high flight, and then to have told himself, with a half-broken heart, that it was beyond his power to soar up into those bright regions. I can fancy, as the sheets went from him every day, he told himself, in regard to every sheet, that it was a failure.— TROLLOPE, ANTHONY, 1879, *Thackeray (English Men of Letters), p.* 19.

Thackeray's ideal of life is really childlike in its purity. In "Vanity Fair" he took, like Fielding whom he did not study in vain, a broad canvas on which to paint an image of the world. As Fielding, in Tom Jones, and Blifil, represented the two opposite poles about which our world turns, so Thackeray contrasted Becky Sharp and the Crawley side of the world with the side of Major Dobbin and Amelia. When it was said that his good people were innocent babies, that was his praise; for a childlike innocence, remote enough from the conception of the cynic, was Thackeray's ideal to the last. If Major Dobbin seemed too weak, Thackeray mended the fault in Colonel Newcome, to whom he gave the same feature of unworldly simplicity and innocence. Thackeray's sensibility made him, perhaps, a little too much afraid of the conscious idlers who consider themselves men of the world. Being himself tenderly framed, he took refuge like the hermit crab in a shell that was not his own but served well for protection. He certainly was, in his younger days, somewhat too much in awe of the conventions of society; for there is an implied bowing down before them in some of the Snob papers that is saved only by its honest origin from being not conventionally but essentially vulgar.—MORLEY, HENRY, 1881, *Of English Literature in the Reign of Victoria with a Glance at the Past*, p. 380.

The somewhat slack and, I always think, somewhat low-pitched satirist.—LANIER, SIDNEY, 1881, *The English Novel*, p. 196.

In his delineation of character, in the perfect naturalness with which all his personages act out their respective parts, no novelist is more realistic than Thackeray. . . . Some readers will receive that impression from Thackeray's novels; but they will be those who think that the evil and the unhappiness predominate. So thought the author himself. But the world in general think differently, and agree to look upon Thackeray as a satirist.—TUCKERMAN, BAYARD, 1882, *A History of English Prose Fiction*, p. 300.

Thackeray, with some remarkable slovenliness (he is probably the last writer of the first eminence of whom the enemy "and which" has made a conquest), elaborated, rather it would seem by practice and natural genius, than in the carrying out of any theory, a style which for the lighter purposes of literature has no rival in urbanity, flexibility, and width of range since Addison, and which has found the widest acceptance among men of letters.—SAINTSBURY, GEORGE, 1886, *Specimens of English Prose Style*, p. 33.

He is to the age of Victoria what Addison and Steele were to the age of Anne—its painter; not like his disciple, Anthony Trollope, its photographer. His own temperament deeply influences his pictorial handling: to assume the absolute accuracy of his pictures would be like inferring, from the too exclusive study of some modern painters, that the men and women of the Victorian epoch invariably lived in rooms hung with yellow.—GARNETT, RICHARD, 1887, *The Reign of Queen Victoria, ed. Ward, vol.* II, p. 465.

This social life which Trollope does not penetrate, which Reade exaggerates, look at it with a curious, sceptical eye, sharpened by a wearied heart; be superior to all the fine illusions of existence, by defect of spiritual insight as well as by the subtility of external observation; lay bare all the hypocrisies and rascalities of "proper" people, without losing faith in the possibility of virtue; survey men and women in their play rather than in their real struggle and work; bring all the resources of keen observation, incisive wit, and delicate humor to the task of exhibiting the frailties of humanity, without absolutely teaching that it is hopelessly vicious and effete—and you have Thackeray, a kindly man of genius, honestly forced by his peculiar intellect and experience to inculcate the dreadful doctrine that life does not pay.—WHIPPLE, EDWIN PERCY, 1887, *In Dickens-Land, Scribner's Magazine, vol. 2*, p. 743.

My pleasure in reading fiction is limited to a very few authors. Scott I know intimately, but there is not any novelist whom I appreciate so heartily except Thackeray, whose masterpieces I have read over and over again; indeed, I never tire of them.—HAMERTON, PHILIP GILBERT, 1887, *Books Which Have Influenced Me*, p. 59.

With Thackeray, as with Michael Angelo, the art which conceals art is characteristic. The simplest of means produce the largest of effects. In the fewest words, in the plainest sentences, without the ghost of visible effort or the slightest strain after effect, Thackeray has in "Vanity Fair" given us the most living and Homeric picture of the "Battle of Waterloo" that exists. In scenes of domestic pathos, he is a household Æschylus at times. I know nothing of the 100-book school, as I have said, and don't want to know anything. But if I were to advise those who are learned amongst us as to a course for study, I should select passages, I think, rather than books, for very especial attention. And I would have them know those passages almost by heart. Amongst them, for the simplicity of sublimity, for that same quality of massiveness, for homely pathos and quiet power, I would refer readers to one than which I think English prose can rise no higher. Of tears in the voice we have all heard; this I should call "tears in the pen." It is the story of the death of Helen Pendennis; where in the last and beautiful reconciliation between the estranged mother and son, he kneels like a child to say the Lord's Prayer at her feet, sobs out that wonderful message of love and faith to "generations of sinful and humbled men," and sees her die. If Thackeray could write such prose as this, it is because he was a poet. Happy the novelist who has any of that sacred fire to keep alive in him, for he has ten chances to one in his favour against all comers, when it comes to a bid for greatness.—MERIVALE, HERMAN, 1888, *About Two Great Novelists, Temple Bar, vol.* 83, *p.* 199.

Thackeray had a quarrel with himself and a quarrel with society; but his was not a temper to push things to extremes. He could not acquiesce in the ways of the world, its shabbiness, its shams, its snobbery, its knavery; he could not acquiesce, and yet it is only for born prophets to break with the world and go forth into the wildnerness crying, "Repent!" . . . Thackeray had not the austerity and lonely strength needful for a prophet; he would not be a pseudo prophet; therefore he chose his part—to remain in the world, to tolerate the worldlings, and yet to be their adversary and circumventer, or at least a thorn in their sides. —DOWDEN, EDWARD, 1888, *Victorian Literature, Transcripts and Studies, pp.* 168, 171.

Personally, he scarce appeals to us as the ideal gentleman; if there were nothing else, perpetual nosing after snobbery at least suggests the snob; but about the men he made, there can be no such question of reserve. And whether because he was himself a gentleman in a very high degree, or because his methods were in a very high degree suited to his class of work, or from the common operation of both causes, a gentleman came from his pen by the gift of nature. He could draw him as a character part, full of pettiness, tainted with vulgarity, and yet still a gentleman, in the inimitable Major Pendennis. He could draw him as the full-blown hero in Colonel Esmond. He could draw him—the next thing to the work of

God—human and true and noble and frail in Colonel Newcome. If the art of being a gentleman were forgotten, like the art of staining glass, it might be learned anew from that one character.—STEVENSON, ROBERT LOUIS, 1888–95, *Some Gentlemen in Fiction, Miscellaneous Papers, p.* 371.

A friend of mine tells me that once, when he was a little boy, he was sitting under a table, reading "Vanity Fair." A tall, white-haired old gentleman came in and said, "What are you reading? 'Vanity Fair'? That's not a book for *you.*" The tall gentleman was Thackeray. He might have said every day to me, in my boyhood, "That's not the book for you." But they were all the books for me, beloved books, full of the kindest friends, the noblest gentlemen, the purest ladies, the wittiest, best-hearted people, with a few wicked noblemen to hate, a few campaigners to avoid. People may say that Thackeray makes one too sentimental, too tolerant. They may urge similar objections against a well-known passage in the letters of Paul of Tarsus. In the matter of style Thackeray is inimitable, and not to be imitated. But no writer except Fielding, perhaps, and George Sand, gives a young student so brilliant an example of what style may be, had one time to think of it.— LANG, ANDREW, 1888, *Books That Have Helped Me, p.* 36.

No one ever wrote with more perfect frankness than Thackeray. If he felt happy he said so brightly; if he felt sad he openly betrayed his dejection. And underlying all the humorous drollery of his letters is a strain of profound weariness, of utter lassitude and depression. He, too, like Amiel, lacked the courage to be light-hearted in the incessant warfare of life. . . . The very fulness of his life at times wearies and repulses him. He cries out impatiently that idleness is best, and that a blessed repose of mind and body is worth all the troublesome turmoil of success. It is plain that he enjoys very little of that solid satisfaction which most authors derive from a perpetual contemplation of their own laurels; and this loss, irreparable indeed to him, is not wholly without compensation to his readers. . . . We admire Thackeray none the less after reading this bundle of letters; and, in view of the disastrous revelations too often forced upon the world by the publication of a writer's correspondence, there can be no stronger praise than to add that we love him a great deal more.—REPPLIER, AGNES, 1888, *Letters of Thackeray, Catholic World*, vol. 46, p. 602.

Thackeray is the young man's first love. —BARRIE, JAMES MATTHEW, 1889, *An Edinburgh Eleven*, p. 117.

The great modern master of novelists, him of the big heart and the generous sympathy, that great lay preacher and critic of manners, who has written such classic prose and given such grand character-studies in "Vanity Fair" and "Pendennis" and "Henry Esmond" and "The Newcomes." —MULLANY, PATRICK FRANCIS (BROTHER AZARIAS), 1889, *Books and Reading*, p. 52.

Esmond apart, there is scarce a man or a woman in Thackeray whom it is possible to love unreservedly or thoroughly respect. That gives the measure of the man, and determines the quality of his influence. He was the average clubman *plus* genius and a style. And, if there is any truth in the theory that it is the function of art not to degrade but to ennoble—not to dishearten but to encourage—not to deal with things ugly and paltry and mean but with great things and beautiful and lofty—then, it is argued, his example is one to depreciate and to condemn. . . . He may not have been a great man but assuredly he was a great writer; he may have been a faulty novelist but assuredly he was a rare artist in words. Setting aside Cardinal Newman's, the style he wrote is certainly less open to criticism than that of any other modern Englishman. He was neither super-eloquent like Mr. Ruskin nor a Germanised Jeremy like Carlyle; he was not marmoreally emphatic as Landor was, nor was he slovenly and inexpressive as was the great Sir Walter; he neither dallied with antithesis like Macaulay nor rioted in verbal vulgarisms with Dickens; he abstained from technology and what may be called Lord Burleighism as carefully as George Eliot indulged in them, and he avoided conceits as sedulously as Mr. George Meredith goes out of his way to hunt for them. He is a better writer than any one of these, in that he is always a master of speech and of himself, and that he is always careful yet natural, and choice yet seemingly spontaneous.—HENLEY, WILLIAM ERNEST, 1890, *Views and Reviews*, pp. 15, 16.

William Makepeace Goliath, white waistcoat and all.—QUILLER-COUCH, A. T.,1891, *Adventures in Criticism*, p. 98.

It is precisely because Thackeray, discerning so well the abundant misery and hollowness in life, discerns also all that is not miserable and hollow, that he is so great. He has neither the somewhat bestial pessimism of M. Zola, nor the fatuous gaiety of M. Ohnet. Like any classic, he stands the test of experience, of psychology. We have mentioned together Swift, Addison, and Steele, we might take Lucretius, Virgil, and Horace. Each has left a picture of patrician life, glittering and tedious. Lucretius, contrasting the splendour without and the gloom within; Virgil, the restlessness and haste with the placid peace of the country; Horace, content to let it all go by, neither envying nor despising. Something of each, again, is in Thackeray: an English classic not less true and real. than the classic Romans.—JOHNSON, LIONEL, 1891, *The Academy, vol*. 39, *p*. 227.

Thackeray's readers were and are limited by the limitations of his subjects, by nothing else. He did much that Scott did not attempt and that Dickens could not ever have conceived; but for every million that can understand Scott and Dickens there are probably only a thousand that can understand Thackeray. His minute observation of the upper classes of his day is lost on persons to whom those classes are not familiar, partly because such persons do not recognize what he is dealing with, and partly because they are not interested in the questions with which he is most preoccupied. Indeed, of all great novelists Thackeray is the narrowest, not because the range of his vision is confined to the upper classes, for these viewed comprehensively form a complete microcosm and in many ways exhibit the problems and possibilities of life better than any other class; but because, accepting the upper classes as the world, he views them from one position only, and his view of them is extremely partial. Only a few of his characters he knows from the inside; all the rest he knows from the outside only. Men who were clients of the world or its victims, who were struggling with it or hostile to it—these men Thackeray knew from the inside. But the world itself, which for him meant the aristocratic class as a body—he was familiar with its aspect, but he never understood its spirit. . . . A more important question is whether the interest with which he is read now is as fresh and vital as that with which he was read originally. I should say it was **not**; and I should say so for this reason, that as compared with Scott and Dickens he lacked the qualities by which the vitality of his work could be perpetuated. He lacked their extraordinary breadth and their extraordinary variety; he lacked the qualities that made them so peculiarly and so comprehensively national. They each gave us a nation—a nation which still lives; Thackeray gave us a fragment of a generation, which already is almost past.—MALLOCK, WILLIAM HURREL, 1892, *Are Scott, Dickens, and Thackeray Obsolete? The Forum, vol.* 14, *pp.* 512, 513.

Some people have a quiet way of testing the quality of a man's literary culture and determining the presence or absence of the instinct for literature by his feeling for Thackeray; and it is certainly true that no one of our novelists has given us so much literature in proportion to the mass of his writing as this splendid artist, whose briefest and most hurried notes disclose the touch of a master in every line. Thackeray's point of view is, however, widely misunderstood, and the deep and beautiful tenderness which underlies so much of his work does not make itself felt at the first glance. —MABIE, HAMILTON W., 1893, *The Most Popular Novels in America, The Forum, vol.* 16, *p.* 513.

> To him who in the fields of life
> > Quickly discerned the vulgar chaff,—
> And knew it void of honest grain,
> > And blew it from him with a laugh.
> To him whose laughter none the less
> > Was not wild mirth nor wanton jeer,
> But oftenest of that rare fine ring
> > That finds its echo in a tear.
> To him whose pen was never still,
> > Who for three decades thought and wrote;
> Who told of life, of love, of death,
> > And never struck an untrue note.

—ROGERS, ROBERT CAMERON, 1894, *Thackeray's Birthday.*

Thackeray, with a fine and sympathetic soul, had a creative imagination that was far stronger on the darker and fouler sides of life than it was on the brighter and purer side of life. He saw the bright and pure side: he loved it, he felt with it, he made us love it. But his artistic genius worked with more free and consummate zest when he painted the dark and the foul. His creative imagination fell short of the true equipoise, of that just vision of *chiaroscuro*, which we find in the greatest masters of the human heart. This limitation of his genius

has been visited upon Thackeray with a heavy hand. And such as it is, he must bear it. — HARRISON, FREDERIC, 1895, *Studies in Early Victorian Literature, p.* 126.

I owe him a debt of gratitude which it would be difficult to over-estimate. He saved me from no end of dangerous follies by kindling in me a spark of sobering self-criticism, which enabled me to catch little side-glimpses of myself, when I was on the verge of committing a *bêtise*. He aroused in me a salutary scepticism as to the worth of much which the world has stamped with its approval. He blew away a good deal of that romantic haze which hid reality from me and prevented me from appraising men and things at their proper value.—BOYESEN, HJALMAR HJORTH, 1895, *The Great Realists and the Empty Story-Tellers, The Forum, vol.* 18, *p.* 727.

I admire Thackeray's style, and the pathetic quality in his writings; in this he never faltered. I like his sardonic melancholy. Thackeray, in a passing mood, might quite well have said: "Who breathes must suffer, and who thinks must mourn, and he alone is blest who ne'er was born." He shows knowledge with human nature and much acquaintance with life—not a wide acquaintance, but complete within its limits. The vernacular of his Fokers and his Fred Bayhams is classical, and so is their slang.—LOCKER-LAMPSON, FREDERICK, 1895, *My Confidences, p.* 302.

On the rare occasion when I met him in the snuggery at Onslow Square, or elsewhere, I found him one of the gentlest of satirists. At the same time he was extremely outspoken; he had a childish inability to conceal, and, like a child, he sometimes repeated what was not intended for repetition.—SKELTON, JOHN, 1895, *The Table-Talk of Shirley, p.* 25.

His appeal was mainly if not quite exclusively to the refined and educated class of readers; and it was among their interests and occupations that he sought the material of his art. He has left the field of the stronger and more primitive passions, the *votum, timor, ira* of humanity, to others; and it is from the *voluptas, gaudia, discursus*—the pleasures, ambitions, pursuits of society, with the activities they stimulate, the weaknesses they foster, and the virtues which occasionally redeem them, that he collected the *farrago* of his books. But among these he moves a supreme and unapproachable master; the possessor of a far more limited domain than Dickens, but traversing it with a far surer foot and surveying it with a far more penetrating eye.— TRAILL, HENRY DUFF, 1897, *Social England, vol.* VI, *p.* 282.

Thackeray was a finished novelist; but, alas! he was nearly forty years of age, and he was to die at fifty-two. The brief remainder of his existence was crowded with splendid work; but Thackeray is unquestionably one of those writers who give us the impression of having more in them than accident ever permitted them to produce. Fielding had escorted the genius of Thackeray to the doors of success. . . . But Thackeray was no consistent disciple of Fielding, and when we reach his masterpieces—"Esmond," for instance—the resemblance between the two writers has become purely superficial. Thackeray is more difficult to describe in a few words than perhaps any other author of his merit. He is a bundle of contradictions—slipshod in style, and yet exquisitely mannered; a student of reality in conduct, and yet carried away by every romantic mirage of sentiment and prejudice; a cynic with a tear in his eye, a pessimist that believes the best of everybody. The fame of Thackeray largely depends on his palpitating and almost pathetic vitality; he suffers, laughs, reflects, sentimentalises, and meanwhile we run beside the giant figure, and, looking up at the gleam of the great spectacles, we share his emotion. His extraordinary power of entering into the life of the eighteenth century, and reconstructing it before us, is the most definite of his purely intellectual claims to our regard.—GOSSE, EDMUND, 1897, *A Short History of Modern English Literature, p.* 353.

Eleven years before, young Thackeray had married Miss Isabella Shawe, the daughter of a colonel in the army. He had three children, two of whom—Mrs. Ritchie, whose work is so well known, and Mrs. Leslie Stephen—grew up to be the greatest delight to him, as if in compensation for his terribly unhappy married life. After the birth of her third daughter, his wife became ill, and lost her mind. At first Thackeray would not believe that it was anything but illness, and night after night, after his work at the office of *Fraser's* or *Punch* was over, he would sit up with the poor demented

creature, when everybody but the devoted husband could see that there was no cure for her. It was finally necessary to put her into an asylum, where she lived, hopelessly insane, long after her husband's death. It was during these terrible years that Thackeray was writing the sense and nonsense, the fun and satire, which, with John Leach's pictures, were making the reputation of *Punch.* Into every joke there must have gone an aching heart.—LEACH, ANNA, 1897, *Glimpses of Thackeray, Munsey's Magazine, vol.* 17, *p.* 414.

Once convince a young man that Thackeray's world is the real world, that vulgarity, meanness, trickery, and fraud abound, and you put him in a yoke from which he shall never free himself. This is the yoke of base expectation. . . . Thackeray has no faith; he does not entertain high expectations. His characters do shameless things, and Thackeray says to the reader, "Be not surprised, injured-seeming friend; you would have done the like under the like temptation." At first you contradict, you resent, but little by little Thackeray's opinion of you inoculates you; the virus takes; you lose your conviction that you would have acted differently; you concede that such conduct was not impossible, even for you,—no, nor improbable,—and, on the whole, after reflection, that the conduct was excusable, was good enough, was justified, was inevitable, was right, was scrupulously right, and only a Don Quixote would have acted otherwise.—SEDGWICK, HENRY D., JR., 1898, *Some Aspects of Thackeray, Atlantic Monthly, vol.* 82, *p.* 708.

One always recognises in Thackeray the powerful artist, who, like a Japanese painter, will with a few lines place a living man or woman before you, never to be forgotten.—MÜLLER, FRIEDRICH MAX, 1898, *Auld Lang Syne, p.* 125.

In all of these writings we are struck with the honesty, earnestness, and commonsense of the critic, even though we may occasionally fail to recognise the big view of the statesman. Yet Thackeray was more of a statesman than his colleague Douglas Jerrold, who for years was practically *Punch's* Prime Minister. It was, moreover, greatly on a question of statesmanship that he left *Punch* (just as Doyle had left it on a question of religion); for he did not choose to identify himself with the "savageness" of the particular colleague first-mentioned, whose political writings he believed to be against the interests of the country as well as against the dignity of the paper. Yet this repugnance of his for violence has been cited as a reproach. He was not fierce enough, we are told—not vehement enough in his denunciations of human folly; and it is evidently reckoned for unrighteousness that he preferred irony as a flail for the evil-doer, to burning wrath and hot denunciation. Perhaps the famous old lady who considered Thackeray "an uncomfortable writer" was the first to discover him to be a Cynic. Perhaps she was right—but, in that case, a Cynic after Thackeray's own heart.—SPIELMANN, M. H., 1899, *The Hitherto Unidentified Contributions of W. M. Thackeray to "Punch," Introduction, p. i.*

He is already a classic. He is the representative English man of letters of his time, and one of the few great novelists of the world.—BROWNELL, W. C., 1899, *William Makepeace Thackeray, Scribner's Magazine, vol. 25, p. 236.*

Apart from the high intellectual level of Thackeray's writings, nothing would induce him to abate one jot of his prejudices to suit the taste of the public, though no one knew better than he what would suit the majority of novel-readers. — MELVILLE, LEWIS, 1899, *The Life of William Makepeace Thackeray, vol. I, p. 202.*

Thackeray I take to have been an author whose native bent was towards reality in fiction. But he lived in a literary time when it was all but impossible for one to be directly true; one must somehow bring the truth in circuitously, apologetically, almost shamefacedly. A direct rendering of life was then supposed to be wanting in "imagination," and though Thackeray despised and mocked the false in fiction as much as any man who ever lived, he could not help being a man of his time. He put on a fine literary air of being above his business; he talked of fiction as fable-land, when he ought to have known it and proclaimed it the very home of truth, where alone we can see men through all their disguises; he formed the vicious habit of spoiling the illusion, or clouding the clear air of his art, by the intrusion of his own personality; and in fine he showed himself in spite of his right instincts a survival of the romanticistic period whose traces in others (especially Bulwer and Disraeli) he knew how so de-

liciously to burlesque. I shall affront some of those who like Thackeray most (but not most wisely), by saying that he came short of his great possibilities by his willingness to dawdle (and shall I say twaddle?) over his scene when it was strictly his affair to represent it, and by his preference of caricature to character, and sentimentality to sentiment. All the same he was a great talent, and the Ever-Womanly knew his ultimate truth so well that she revealed herself to him as she had not to any other English novelist since Jane Austen's time.— HOWELLS, WILLIAM DEAN, 1901, *Heroines of Fiction, vol. I, p. 191.*

Character-drawing, mastery of style, humor, pathos, passion—all these Thackeray had. One thing he lacked—high poetic imagination. "I have no brains above my eyes," Prof. Beers has quoted him as saying: "I describe what I see." None knew more fully the world in which men love and fear and flatter and hate and sorrow, but beyond his horizon lay the forest of Arden and the seacoast of Bohemia. —NETTLETON, GEORGE HENRY, 1901, *Specimens of the Short Story, p. 112.*

Thackeray took no print from the romantic generation; he passed it over, and went back to Addison, Fielding, Goldsmith, Swift. His masters were the English humorists of the eighteenth century. He planned a literary history of that century, a design which was carried out on other lines by his son-in-law, Leslie Stephen. If he wrote historical novels, their period was that of the Georges, and not of Richard the Lion Heart. It will not do, of course, to lay too much stress on Thackeray, whose profession was satire and his temper purely anti-romantic. —BEERS, HENRY A., 1901, *A History of English Romanticism in the Nineteenth Century, p. 397.*

If, then, we find that in all great walks of life—in the Church, in war, in commerce, and in diplomacy—Mr. Thackeray has nothing but abuse and sneers for success; if we find that he loves to portray the ludicrous and the discreditable only, is it unfair to say that he is the apostle of Mediocrity? Mediocre ways of life, mediocre thoughts, mediocre inclinations (miscalled passions) mediocre achievements—these, if not positively enjoined, as they sometimes are, are in effect all that is left to one who takes Mr. Thackeray for his guide. For the rest, never had a mean gospel so doughty an Apostle.

—LORD, WALTER FREWEN, 1902, *The Apostle of Mediocrity, The Nineteenth Century, vol.* 51, *p.* 410.

One mark of Thackeray's realism is his refusal to take his art seriously. In his view an author is but the master of a set of puppets with which he can represent real life, if he please, but over whose movements it is absurd to pretend that he has not absolute control. Hence Thackeray jests at his art in a tone that was most unpleasant to minor craftsmen. This tone has done him a disservice with later readers, and belies the essential importance of his work; for though the world which he pictures is a bit antique in our eyes, its problems are ours, and granting the thirty years' difference in time, Thackeray treats them in a way as significant for us as that of Meredith or Ibsen.—MOODY, WILLIAM VAUGHN, AND LOVETT, ROBERT MORSS, 1902, *A History of English Literature, p.* 369.

Richard Whately
1787–1863

Richard Whately, D. D., (born 1787, died 1863), an eminent thinker and writer, entered at Oriel College, Oxford, in 1805, and took his M. A. in 1812. He became a fellow of Oriel in 1811, and after a short experience of a country living at Halesworth, in Suffolk (1822-5), was appointed principal of St. Alban's Hall, Oxford, in 1825. In 1819 he brought out his "Historical Doubts relative to Napoleon Bonaparte," an ingenious attempt to show by parody the absurdity of sceptical criticism; and in 1822 he was Bampton lecturer, publishing his addresses under the title of "The Use and Abuse of Party Feeling in Religion." The lively interest he had taken in social subjects well qualified him for the post of professor of political economy at Oxford, to which he was appointed in 1830, and in the following year his nomination to the Archbishopric of Dublin was severely commented on by certain sections of the English Church. A good appointment, however, it turned out to be and he was of immense service in organising a national system of education in Ireland. Archbishop Whately was the author of:—"Elements of Rhetoric" (1828); "The Elements of Logic" (1826), upon which several strictures have been passed by Hamilton; "Introduction to Political Economy" (1831); "Sermons" (1835); "Essays on Some of the Dangers to Christian Faith which may arise from the Teaching or the Conduct of its Professors" (1839); "Kingdom of Christ" (1841), and other works.—SANDERS, LLOYD C., *ed.* 1887, *Celebrities of the Century, p.* 1042.

PERSONAL

Now I am sure that in point of real essential holiness, so far as man can judge of man, there does not live a truer Christian than Whately; and it does grieve me most deeply to hear people speak of him as of a dangerous and latitudinarian character, because in him the intellectual part of his nature keeps pace with the spiritual—instead of being left, as the Evangelicals leave it, a fallow field for all unsightly weeds to flourish in. He is a truly great man—in the highest sense of the word,—and if the safety and welfare of the Protestant Church in Ireland depend in any degree on human instruments, none could be found, I verily believe, in the whole empire, so likely to maintain it.—ARNOLD, THOMAS, 1831, *To Rev. G. Cornish, Dec.* 23; *Life and Correspondence, ed. Stanley, vol.* I, *p.* 275.

He is tall, rather awkward, constantly in motion, constantly talking very rapidly, with a good deal of acuteness and a great variety of knowledge, not without humor, and indulging frequently in classical allusions and once or twice venturing a Greek quotation. He is not prepossessing in manner, and Rogers, from the constant motion of his person from side to side, calls him the "White Bear"; but you always feel, in talking with him, that you are in the grasp of a powerful mind.— TICKNOR, GEORGE, 1835, *Journal, July* 16; *Life, Letters and Journals, vol.* I, *p.* 412.

The Bishop's movements* were sometimes as graceful as those of a girl, and at other times as sharp and fierce as those of an angry sibyl; his face never lost its amenity, nor his voice its sweetness—a sweetness which increased when his compliments were most keenly edged with insinuations. His speech was throughout ingenious; but as a whole it was a blunder. There is an inspiration of common sense, as well as one of genius; and crafty men often miss both forms of it.—DEVERE, AUBREY, 1845, *Letter, Recollections, p.* 137.

*Speech in Parliament.

He (Dr. Lloyd) talked of Whately, who is much injured by being the centre of a clique who flatter and never contradict him, hence he becomes very despotic. He is a most generous creature, and full of knowledge. He wriggles his limbs about in an extraordinary manner, and once pronounced the benediction with one leg hanging over the reading-desk in church; and in society he will sit balancing his chair, occasionally tipping over backwards. One of his chaplains, during a walk with him, stated that fungus was very good eating, upon which the archbishop insisted on his then and there consuming a slice, which the poor chaplain resisting, the archbishop jerked it into his mouth. A doctor who was with them was in ecstasies of mirth at the scene, which the archbishop perceiving said, "Oh, doctor! you shall try it too: it is very important for you to be able to give an opinion." "No, thank you, my lord," said the doctor; "I am not a clergyman, nor am I in your lordship's diocese."—FOX, CAROLINE, 1846, *Memories of Old Friends, ed. Pym, p.* 230.

I met the Archbishop of Dublin, Whately, at dinner yesterday at Raikes Currie's. I don't think him at all agreeable; he has a skimble-skamble way of talking as if he was half tipsy, and the stories he tells are abominably long and greatly deficient in point.— GREVILLE, CHARLES C. F., 1847, *A Journal of the Reign of Queen Victoria from* 1837 *to* 1852, *ed. Reeve, March* 31*st; vol.* II, *p.* 218.

There were a few bishops; — Whately, with his odd, overbearing manners, and his unequal conversation, — sometimes rude and tiresome, and at other times full of instruction, and an occasional drollery coming out amidst a world of effort. Perhaps no person of all my acquaintance has from the first appeared to me so singularly overrated as he was then. I believe it is hardly so now.—MARTINEAU, HARRIET, 1855-77, *Autobiography, ed. Chapman, vol.* I, *p.* 255.

There is scarcely anyone whom in memory I love more than Whately, even now. How gladly would I have called upon him in Dublin, except that, again and again by his friends and my own, I have been warned off. He is now pursuing me in his new publications, without my having any part in the provocation. In 1836 he was most severe upon me in relation to the Hampden matter. In 1837 he let me call on him when he was in Oxford; I have never seen him since.

I ever must say he taught me to think.— NEWMAN, JOHN HENRY, 1860, *Letters and Correspondence of John Henry Newman During his Life in the English Church, vol.* I, *p.* 124, *note.*

I have scrambled through the second volume of the Archbishop's "Life," and while the old impression of the sifting and clearing power (up to a certain point) of his mind and conversation has been wonderfully revived, I have found, too, something touching and spiritual which very much moves and interests me, and which gives me a sense of depth and rest in the man which his writings never give, and personal intercourse with him seldom, I think, gave.—ARNOLD, MATTHEW, 1866, *To his Mother, Nov.* 3; *Letters, ed. Russell, vol.* I, *p.* 396.

We have read lately "Whately's Life." Good, but dry: the man remaining as he was, or a trifle better—honest, prosaic, dogmatic, vain, still an able man.—WILLIAMS, ROWLAND, 1866, *Journal-Notes, Dec.* 26; *Life and Letters, ed. his Wife, vol.* II, *p.* 251.

An industrious student, a deep thinker, an acute reasoner, a learned mind, a correct and at times elegant writer—these are titles of honour with the mere outside-world, travelling in its flying railway-carriage, will gladly award to the late Archbishop of Dublin (Dr. Whately). Not so familiar are certain minor and more curious gifts, which he kept by him for his own and his friends' entertainment, which broke out at times on more public occasions. He delighted in the oddities of thought, in queer quaint distinctions; and if an object had by any possibility some strange distorted side or corner, or even point, which was undermost, he would gladly stoop down his mind to get that precise view of it, nay, would draw it in that odd light for the amusement of the company. Thus he struck Guizot, who described him as "startling and ingenious, strangely absent, familiar, confused, eccentric, amiable, and engaging, no matter what unpoliteness he might commit, or what impropriety he might forget." In short, a mind with a little of the Sydney Smith's leaven, whose brilliancy lay in precisely these odd analogies. It was his recreation to take up some intellectual hobby, and make a toy of it.—TIMBS, JOHN, 1866, *English Eccentrics and Eccentricities, vol.* II, *p.* 240.

A figure somewhat above the ordinary height, and strongly framed, though rather loosely put together. The features of the face have certainly escaped the "fatal gift of beauty." It is essentially a hard-featured face, with but small amount of color to aid its expressiveness. The eyes are of a pale grayish blue; and the hair is rather sparse and of a pale, sandy tint. The forehead is large and square, and the chin has the pronounced development which indicates abundance of what the French call *caractère*. The *tout ensemble* of face, figure, manner and movement is as wholly devoid of graciousness or gracefulness as can easily be imagined. The outward wrappages and integuments which so frequently furnish a key to the character of the human being that is inside them correspond with very complete accuracy to that of the man in question. His black waistcoat bears the marks of having been copiously besprinkled with snuff. His academic gown hangs from his shoulders all awry. His bands are probably not in their proper place in front of his neck. His doctor's hood hangs similarly out of its due position behind it. And all these trappings, instead of being borne along with pompous elegance which would befit the time and place, are worn with an air that seems to say unmistakably that in the wearer's opinion they are stupid encumbrances and annoyances, which he would fain get rid of if it were possible. But, withal, there is that about the head and face which to any competent observer would give the unmistakable assurance that there walked a man of no ordinary power and energy of intellect; and the springy activity of gait, apparently repressed with difficulty to the sober pace befitting the occasion, and the superfluous amount of motion with which every part of the person seems to be instinct, give an equal impression of vigor and force.—TROLLOPE, THOMAS ADOLPHUS, 1874, *Recollections of Archbishop Whately, Lippincott's Magazine, vol.* 14, *p.* 106.

He was of a gigantic size and a gaunt aspect, with a strange unconsciousness of the body; and, what is perhaps the next best thing to a perfect manner, he had no manner. What his legs and arms were about was best known to themselves. His rank placed him by the side of the lord lieutenant's wife when dining at the Castle, and the wife of one of the lord lieutenants has told me that she had occasionally to remove the archbishop's foot out of her lap. His life has been written in two volumes,

but without any attempt to represent his powers as appearing in conversation, always vigorous and significant, often delightfully epigrammatic. He never wasted a thought upon his dignity. If he had, the dignity would have been an unwelcome weight; but, without any intentional arrogance, he was accustomed to assume the intellectual dictatorship of every company in which he found himself. There could be no greater mistake than to infer from this that there was any tincture in him of ecclesiastical intolerance. He was, in reality, intolerant of intolerance, and of not many things beside.—TAYLOR, SIR HENRY, 1885, *Autobiography, vol.* I, *p.* 266.

If there was a man easy for a raw, bashful youth to get on with it was Whately—a great talker, who endured very readily the silence of his company, original in his views, lively, forcible, witty in expressing them, brimful of information on a variety of subjects—so entertaining that, logician as he was, he is said sometimes to have fixed the attention of a party of ladies to his conversation, or rather discourse, for two or three hours at a stretch; free and easy in manners, rough indeed and dogmatic in his enunciation of opinion, but singularly gracious to undergraduates and young masters who, if they were worth anything, were only too happy to be knocked about in argument by such a man. And he on his part professed to be pleased at having cubs in hand whom he might lick into shape, and who, he said, like dogs of King Charles's breed, could be held up by one leg without yelling.—MOZLEY, ANNE, 1890, *ed., Letters and Correspondence of John Henry Newman During his Life in the English Church, Autobiographical Memoir, vol.* I, *p.* 92.

As his eloquence was a good deal beyond my infantine capacity, I am glad to have heard his Grace at a later period, though I should not say public speaking was his *forte*. His voice was not well adapted to the requirements of even a moderately spacious building; it was scarcely what could be called clear-sounding, and his tone was apt to become monotonous. His manner was not remarkable for energy or spirit, and his personal appearance, though he was tall and well-built, was somewhat heavy. His discourses, however, were never wearisome, because not too "long drawn out." Archbishop Whately's strong point, as is well known, was logic, and this pre-eminence could scarcely be denied to a man clever enough to argue with such subtlety that he could prove Napoleon never existed.— BYRNE, MRS. WILLIAM PITT, 1898, *Social Hours with Celebrities, ed. Miss R. H. Busk, vol.* I, *p.* 366.

The burden of his office [Archbishop of Dublin] was not lightened by popularity. His English birth and breeding and his well-known antipathy to evangelical principles made him an object of jealousy and suspicion to both clergy and laity. His preaching was unpalatable. His chaste, clear-cut, unimpassioned, argumentative style failed to move his hearers, even if his matter did not, as to some it sometimes did, savour of heresy, not to say infidelity.—RIGG, J. M., 1899, *Dictionary of National Biography, vol.* LX, *p.* 425.

GENERAL

I should say that the book ["Treatise on Logic"] was the restoration of an unjustly deposed art.—MACKINTOSH, SIR JAMES, 1827, *Letter to George Moore, May* 13; *Memoirs, ed. Mackintosh, vol.* II, *p.* 435.

In reality, there is not a section of his work which has not furnished us with occasion for some profitable speculations; and we are, in consequence, most anxious to see his *Logic,*—which treats a subject so much more important than *Rhetoric,* and so obstinately misrepresented that it would delight us much to anticipate a radical exposure of the errors on this subject taken up from the days of Lord Bacon. . . . Dr. Whately's is incomparably the best book of its class since Campbell's "Philosophy of Rhetoric." —DEQUINCEY, THOMAS, 1828–59, *Rhetoric, Collected Writings, ed. Masson, vol.* X, *pp.* 132, 133.

That he is bold and somewhat rash, must be admitted. That his style is often awkward and ungainly is no less true. But to question his originality or argumentative ability would occur to no one but a partisan. Whoever is acquainted with his "Rhetoric" and "Logic" must be well aware that however great his faults may be, they cannot be imputed to deficiency of intellect. There is sometimes an apparent incoherence in his arguments, which, on reading further, will be found to have arisen from the very depth and compass of his logical design. Of one thing our readers may be well assured, that, when they hear this ["Kingdom of Christ"] or any other work of Whately set aside as empirical and superficial, they may safely attribute it to a sad want either of discrimination or of candour in the critic. From some of his opinions on church government we utterly dissent, for we are neither prelatists nor independents; but we laugh at the idea of decrying him as one who is unworthy of a hearing, and we certainly enjoy the opportunity of seeing how the words of an apostle can be treated by apostle-worshippers.—ALEXANDER, J., 1842, *Whately's Kingdom of Christ, Princeton Review, vol.* 14, *p.* 597.

It is somewhat surprising, that, with his high claims to distinction, writing upon many of the most interesting questions in a style singularly attractive, his work should have been made so little the subjects of contemporary criticism. Whatever celebrity he has acquired is in no degree owing to the Reviews. He is scarcely at all mentioned by any of the prouder and more august arbiters of destiny, and journalists of humbler pretentions have been slow to notice his publications, and generally they have been niggardly of their encomiums. Like some other great names we could mention, he has risen into celebrity amidst the silence of the heralds of renown. . . . In turning over Archbishop Whately's volumes, one of the first qualities that strikes us, is the great intellectual *energy* they display. This is shown in the number and variety of the works he has published, evincing a mind ready to take an interest in everything, and quick to exhibit that interest in a practical manner. Logic, rhetoric, political economy, theology —nothing comes wrong to him. Great or small, he has something *distinctive* to say of it; and he does not much care where he says it, provided it be the fitting channel—in the Saturday Magazine, or in the Quarterly; in a half-penny tract, or in a twelve-shilling volume.—WELSH, D., 1844, *Archbishop Whately's Works, North British Review, vol.* 1, *p.* 489.

Touching Whately's "Rhetoric," I have read it twice, first when it came out, and again within the last few years, and I think of it, as of his other works, that it is full of ideas, and would make a good article in itself, but still more so if the occasion were taken for a general estimate of the man and his writings. . . . Whately is certainly a very remarkable and even eminent man, and one whose merits and faults are both very important to be pointed out.—MILL, JOHN STUART, 1846, *To Napier, May* 1;

Selections from the Correspondence of Macvey Napier, ed. Napier, p. 527.

We . . . venture to express our conviction . . . that, though this lucid and eloquent writer may, for obvious reasons, be most widely known by his "Logic" and "Rhetoric," the time will come when his theological works will be, if not more widely read, still more highly prized. To great powers of argument and illustration, and delightful transparency of diction and style, he adds a higher quality still—and a very rare quality it is,—an evident and intense honesty of purpose, an absorbing desire to arrive at the *exact truth*, and to state it with perfect fairness and with the just limitations.—ROGERS, HENRY, 1849, *Reason and Faith, Edinburgh Review, vol.* 90, *p.* 301.

The dogmatical and crotchety Archbishop Whately.—MILNES, RICHARD MONCKTON (LORD HOUGHTON), 1854, *To the Chevalier Bunsen, Oct.* 26; *Life, Letters and Friendships, ed. Reid, vol.* I, *p.* 498.

The writings of Dr. Whately are uniformly characterized by clearness of thought, and precision and transparency of style. If one would not *indorse* all his sentiments, with the slightest attention he may, at least, *comprehend* them.—FISH, HENRY C., 1857, *Pulpit Eloquence of the Nineteenth Century, p.* 752.

Archbishop Whately's "Elements of Logic" exhibit, with beautiful precision of statement and felicity of illustration, the Aristotelian logic in an English dress.—ARNOLD, THOMAS, 1862-87, *A Manual of English Literature, p.* 504.

We do not know that any of his works more effectually exhibits the characteristics of his mind. It ["Errors of Romanism"] has the spirit and air of originality which attend upon sublime good sense; and the freshness thus cast around a subject supposed to be worn out is a sample of the vigor which in those days animated everything he said and did. Its fault was the fault of its author's life—its want of thoroughness. Its reasonings and illustrations stop short at the point where their application to his own Church would be inconvenient; and thus the work was eagerly seized on by the Dissenters, and its omissions supplied. — MARTINEAU, HARRIET, 1863-69, *Biographical Sketches, p.* 173.

Whately rendered the most important service to free thought in his generation, and contributed largely in ways direct and indirect to the promotion of speculative activity.—PORTER, NOAH, 1873, *Philosophy in Great Britain and America, History of Philosophy by Friedrich Ueberweg, vol.* II, *p.* 437.

Gave a new life to the study of logic, as was admitted by Sir William Hamilton, who combated some of his doctrines, and it has long since taken its place as a standard in the library of mental science. Whately said his mind had for fourteen years brooded over the leading points of his work on Logic. —CHAMBERS, ROBERT, 1876, *Cyclopædia of English Literature, ed. Carruthers.*

Whately had a very good saying about the majority of preachers. "They aim at nothing, and they hit it." Is it possible to describe better his own episcopate?—MOZLEY, THOMAS, 1882, *Reminiscences Chiefly of Oriel College and the Oxford Movement, vol.* I, *p.* 272.

In theology, as in other things, Whately was an active and fertile thinker, animated by an insatiable love of finding the truth and plainly stating it. In sheer grasp of faculty—in laying hold of "some notion" which he considered practically important, and following it out in all its details, beating it plain till no one could fail to see it as he himself saw it—he was unrivalled. Clearness, common sense, honesty and strength of intellect were his great characteristics, and it is in virtue of these rather than in any depth of richness of new or living thought that he became a power first at Oxford and then in the theological world. Whereas Coleridge brought to the interpretation of Christianity the light of a fresh spiritual philosophy, and sought some synthesis of thought by which religion in its highest form should be seen not only to be in harmony with human nature, but to be its only perfect flower and development, its true philosophy, Whately—taking the prevailing philosophy as he found it—brought the daylight of ordinary reason and of historical fact to play upon the accumulated dogmas of traditionary religion, and to show how little they had, in many cases, to say for themselves. He was a subverter of prejudice and commonplace—of what he believed to be religious as well as irreligious mistake, more than anything else.—TULLOCH, JOHN, 1885, *Movement of Religious Thought in Britain During the Nineteenth Century, p.* 35.

As a writer, his style, though wholly without grace, was admirable in its lucidity. He had a singular felicity of illustration, and especially of metaphor, and a rare power of throwing his thoughts into terse and pithy sentences; but his many books, though full of original thinking and in a high degree suggestive to other writers, had always a certain fragmentary and occasional character, which prevented them from taking a place in standard literature. He was conscious of it himself, and was accustomed to say that it was the mission of his life to make up cartridges for others to fire. — LECKY, WILLIAM EDWARD HARTPOLE, 1890, *Formative Influences, The Forum, vol. 9, p. 382.*

Whately was a man of clear intellect, happy humour, and benevolent heart, but not a learned theologian. His best known book is his "Logic," constructed upon Aristotelian principles, which was once largely used in English colleges and universities. He carried his sound common sense into theological questions also, and found that not a few orthodox dogmas have no foundation in the Scriptures. . . . The unwearied diligence with which Whately devoted himself to his ecclesiastical duties, to promoting the education of the lower classes, and unostentatiously assisting the poor, both Protestant and Catholic, of his diocese in Ireland, reflects favourably on his practical and rational theology, which was not either in philosophy or in history and criticism profound. In the latter respect there is much affinity between it and the Rationalistic (Kantian) supernaturalism, as it was represented in Germany in the first decades of the century by not a few theologians deserving of all respect.—PFLEIDERER, OTTO, 1890, *The Development of Theology in Germany since Kant, and its Progress in Great Britain since 1825, tr. Smith, pp. 369, 370.*

His clear, cold, penetrating intellect, which was not tempered by any sympathy with an emotional religion of any kind, caused him to be more in his element when he was engaged in destructive than in constructive work; but it is a great mistake to regard him as an irreligious man. He had a very firm belief in the fundamental truths of Christianity, and he rendered valuable service to the Church by his masterly confutations of unbelief in its various forms; but he could never be mistaken

for a High Churchman or a Low Churchman; theologically as well as politically he was a Liberal of Liberals. . . . He does not seem to me to have had anything sufficiently positive and definite to offer, in lieu of the Evangelicalism on the one side, which he did his best to upset, or the High Churchmanship on the other, from which he drifted further and further away. At the same time, it is surely a mistaken, not to say suicidal, policy of the defenders of Christianity to persist in regarding him as an enemy, and not as an ally, and a very effective ally, as far as he went. In the literature of the period, his works occupy a prominent place; and, as will be shown in a future chapter, they are all on the side of belief *versus* unbelief; and a time which was by no means rich in apologetic literature can ill afford to reject the sincerely proffered aid of one who possessed one of the most luminous and powerful intellects of the day.—OVERTON, JONH HENRY, 1894, *The English Church in the Nineteenth Century, pp.* 118, 120.

Whately, who had some points in common with Sydney Smith, was, like him, in part the victim of the extreme want of accuracy and range in the Oxford education of his youth; but his mental and literary powers were great.—SAINTSBURY, GEORGE, 1896, *A History of Nineteenth Century Literature, p.* 356.

Whately, as to his point of view and general spirit as a religious thinker, has been fitly likened to Grotius. He handled with clearness and logical strength whatever subject he took up.—FISHER, GEORGE P. 1896, *History of Christian Doctrine, p.* 450.

In the Oxford of his day Whately's was a name to mention with bated breath. He was known to be "noetic," anti-evangelical, and anti-Erastian. He was accordingly credited with the authorship of the anonymous "Letters on the Church by an Episcopalian" (London, 1826, 8vo.), which, by the vigour of their argument for the autonomy of the church, caused no small stir in clerical circles. Through Newman, whom they profoundly influenced, the "Letters" contributed to the initiation of the tractarian movement. By Whately they were neither acknowledged nor disavowed; but neither were they claimed by any one else. The style is undoubtedly Whatelian; but the high view of apostolical succession which they embody is countenanced in none, and expressly repudiated in one, of Whately's mature works. On the whole it is most probable that they were written by Whately, but written without an exact appreciation of the ultimate consequences of their principles.—RIGG, J. M., 1899, *Dictionary of National Biography, vol.* LX, *p.* 424.

Frances Milton Trollope
1780–1863

Born Frances Milton at Heckfield vicarage, Hants; in 1809 married Thomas Anthony Trollope, barrister and fellow of New College. In 1827, her husband having fallen into the direst embarrassment, she went out to Cincinnati, and during a residence in the United States amassed the materials of her "Domestic Manners of the Americans" (1832), much resented by Americans. Left a widow in 1835, she settled in Florence. She wrote industriously novels of society and impressions of travel. Of her novels the most successful was, perhaps, "The Widow Barnaby" (1839), with its sequel, "The Widow Married" (1840). Her works (115 vols.) deserved their popularity, but are well-nigh forgotten.— PATRICK AND GROOME, *eds.,* 1897, *Chambers's Biographical Dictionary, p.* 925.

PERSONAL

With her politics were always an affair of the heart, as, indeed, were all her convictions. Of reasoning from causes, I think that she knew nothing. Her heart was in every way so perfect, her desire to do good to all around her so thorough, and her power of self-sacrifice so complete, that she generally got herself right in spite of her want of logic; but it must be acknowledged that she was emotional. I can remember now her books, and I can see her at her pursuits. The poets she loved best were Dante and Spenser. But she raved also of him of whom all such ladies were raving then, and rejoiced in the popularity and wept over the persecution of Lord Byron. She was among those who seized with avidity on the novels as they came out, of the then unknown Scott, and who could still talk of the triumphs of Miss Edgeworth. With the literature of the day she was familiar, and with the poets of the past. Of other reading I do not think she had mastered much. Her life, I take it, though latterly clouded by many troubles, was easy, luxurious, and idle, till my father's affairs and her own aspirations sent her to America. She had dear friends among literary people, of whom I remember Mathias, Henry Milman, and Miss Landon; but till long after middle life she never herself wrote a line for publication. . . . She continued writing up to 1856, when she was seventy-six years old, and had at that time produced one hundred and fourteen volumes, of which the first was not written till she was fifty. Her career offers great encouragement to those who have not begun early in life, but are still ambitious to do something before they depart hence. She was an unselfish, affectionate, and most industrious woman, with great capacity for enjoyment, and high physical gifts. She was endowed, too, with much creative power, with considerable humor, and a genuine feeling for romance. But she was neither clear-sighted nor accurate; and in her attempts to describe morals, manners, and even facts, was unable to avoid the pitfalls of exaggeration.—TROLLOPE, ANTHONY, 1882-83, *An Autobiography.*

Her mind was one of the most extraordinary constituted in regard to recuperative power and the capacity of throwing off sorrow that I ever knew or read of. Any one who did not know her, as her own son knew her, might have supposed that she was deficient in sensibility. No judgment could be more mistaken. She felt acutely, vehemently. But she seemed to throw off sorrow as, to use the vulgar phrase, a duck's back throws off water, because the nature of the organism will not suffer it to rest there. How often have I applied to her the words of David under a similar affliction!—TROLLOPE, THOMAS ADOLPHUS, 1888, *What I Remember, p.* 174.

What an iron frame this woman must have had; what an indomitable will, and, better than all, what a tender and loving heart; her sympathies extend even beyond her own children, for we find her gentle care and solicitude bestowed upon others also. . . . Frances Trollope never possessed sufficient leisure for the production of perfect work, and so, perhaps, cannot be classed among our great writers. She was something, however, more admirable, more worthy of love and praise—she was, in the highest sense, a good woman.—NEWCOME, GEORGE, 1896, *The Academy, vol.* 49, *p.* 172.

DOMESTIC MANNERS OF THE AMERICANS
1832

This is exactly the title-page we have long wished to see, and we rejoice to say that, now the subject has been taken up, it is handled by an English *lady* of sense and acuteness, who possesses very considerable power of expression, and enjoyed unusually favourable opportunities for observation. — LOCKHART, JOHN GIBSON, 1832, *Domestic Manners of the Americans, Quarterly Review, vol.* 47, *p.* 39.

Her observations on society appear to have been confined to what she saw in the stage-coaches, steamboats, and taverns. What insight this would give her into domestic manners need not be said.—EVERETT, EDWARD, 1833, *Prince Pückler Muscau and Mrs. Trollope, North American Review, vol.* 36, *p.* 41.

Mrs. Trollope's *stories* might, for the most part, suit manners nearer home just as well as they do those of Tennessee.—FOSTER, AUGUSTUS J., 1841, *Notes on the United States.*

If she had been an ordinary discontented tourist, her adventures in America would not be worth the trouble of discussing; but her slanderous book made such exposures necessary.—MARTINEAU, HARRIET, 1855–77, *Autobiography, ed. Chapman, vol.* I, *p.* 240.

"The Domestic Manners of the Americans" was the first of a series of books of travels, of which it was probably the best, and was certainly the best known. It will not be too much to say of it that it had a material effect upon the manners of the Americans of the day, and that that effect has been fully appreciated by them. No observer was certainly ever less qualified to judge of the prospects or even of the happiness of a young people. No one could have been worse adapted by nature for the task of learning whether a nation was in a way to thrive. Whatever she saw she judged, as most women do, from her own standing-point. If a thing were ugly to her eyes, it ought to be ugly to all eyes—and if ugly, it must be bad. What though people had plenty to eat and clothes to wear, if they put their feet upon the tables and did not reverence their betters? The Americans were to her rough, uncouth, and vulgar— and she told them so. Those communistic and social ideas, which had been so pretty in a drawing-room, were scattered to the winds. Her volumes were very bitter; but they were very clever, and they saved the family from ruin.—TROLLOPE, ANTHONY, 1882-83, *An Autobiography.*

Of all books of travel that have appeared during the twelve-month, this sixty-year-old classic ought to be read with the greatest avidity by Americans, for it is history in its most taking form. The style is that of a bright, cultivated Englishwoman, with a "conscious incapacity for description," but with a very unusual capacity for it, nevertheless. She writes not from memory but from notes made on the spot, and with a manifest desire to be moderate and truthful.—GARRISON, W. P., 1894, *The Nation, vol.* 59, *p.* 345.

Although her criticisms and assertions were engendered in disappointment, national animosity, and revenge, they were essentially true, and however chagrined we were, we acknowledged them as such by essaying to correct our manners; as was afterward universally demonstrated whenever one in public fell within the range of her criticisms as the cry of "Trollope! Trollope! Trollope!" was immediately vociferated. . . . It gave pleasure to the English, but profit to us, however much we may have been annoyed by it at first.—HASWELL, CHARLES H.,1896, *Reminiscences of an Octogenarian, pp.* 276, 277.

The authoress's opportunities for producing a valuable book were considerable. She had spent four years in the country, travelled in nearly every part of it, associated with all classes, and unremittingly exercised a keen faculty for observation. If it notwithstanding fails to offer a completely authentic view of American manners, the reason is no want of candour or any invincible prejudice, but the tendency, equally visible in her novels, to dwell upon the more broadly humorous, and consequently the more vulgar, aspects of things. Mrs. Trollope was personally entirely exempt from vulgarity, but she knew her forte to lie in depicting it. Americans might therefore justly complain that her view of their country conveyed a misleading impression as a whole, while there is no ground for questioning the fidelity of individual traits, or for assuming the authoress's pen to have been guided by dislike of democratic institutions. Much of the ill will excited by the book was occasioned by the freedom of her strictures on slavery, which Americans outside New England were then nearly as unanimous in upholding as they are now in denouncing.—GARNETT, RICHARD, 1899, *Dictionary of National Biography*, *vol.* LVII, *p.* 244.

GENERAL

I have been reading Bulwer's novels and Mrs. Trollope's libels, and Dr. Parr's works. I am sure *you* are not an admirer of Mrs. Trollope's. She has neither the delicacy nor the candour which constitute true nobility of mind, and her extent of talent forms but a scanty veil to shadow her other defects.—BROWNING, ELIZABETH BARRETT, 1832, *To Mrs. Martin, Dec.* 14; *Letters, ed. Kenyon, vol.* I, *p.* 17.

Speaking of travellers, I have amused myself with looking over Mrs. Trollope's "Paris." She is certainly clever at observing the surface, but, like other superficial book-makers, leaves you about as wise as she found you. You see through the whole that she is plotting future visits to Paris, and means to be well received. The tone of fearless truth, which cares not for giving offence, is singularly wanting. I was quite amused with her Toryism. It aims to be authoritative and dignified, but cannot rise above scolding.—CHANNING, WILLIAM ELLERY, 1836, *To Miss Aikin, May* 10; *Correspondence of William Ellery Channing and Miss Aikin, ed. Le Breton, p.* 267.

The class to which she belongs is, fortunately, very small; but it will always be recruited from the ranks of the unscrupulous, so long as a corrupt taste is likely to yield a trifling profit. She owes everything to that audacious contempt of public opinion, which is the distinguishing mark of persons who are said to *stick at nothing*. Nothing but this sticking at nothing could have produced some of the books she has written, in which her wonderful impunity of face is so remarkable. Her constitutional coarseness is the natural element of a low popularity, and is sure to pass for cleverness, shrewdness, and strength, where cultivated judgment and chaste inspiration would be thrown away. Her books of travel are crowded with plebeian criticisms on works of art and the usages of courts, and are doubtless held in great esteem by her admirers, who love to see such things overhauled and dragged down to their own level. The book on America is of a different class. The subject exactly suited her style and her

taste, and people looked on at the fun as they would at a scramble of sweeps in the kennel; while the reflecting few thought it a little unfair in Mrs. Trollope to find fault with the manners of the Americans. Happily for her she had such a topic to begin with. Had she commenced her literary career with Austria or France, in all likelihood she would have ended it there. . . . We have heard it argued on the behalf of Mrs. Trollope, that her novels are, at all events, drawn from life. So are sign-paintings. It is no great proof of their truth that centaurs and griffins do not run loose through her pages, and that her men and women have neither hoofs nor tails. The tawdriest wax-works, girt up in paste and spangles are also "drawn from life"; but there ends the resemblance.—HORNE, RICHARD HENGIST, 1844, *A New Spirit of the Age.*

A tendency to artificial sentiment was certainly not the fault of Mrs. Frances Trollope as a novelist. There was a practical heartiness in her work that gave pleasure to the readers of her own generation, and her name lives for the next generation of readers also in two sons who maintain its credit.—MORLEY, HENRY, 1881, *Of English Literature in the Reign of Victoria with a Glance at the Past, p.* 181.

That Mrs. Trollope had no sympathy with the Romantic school will not excite surprise. Lamennais and Victor Hugo she stigmatizes as *décousus* of the worst kind, and places them in the same rank as Robespierre. The genius of Victor Hugo, so vast, so elevated, and so profound, she could not understand; she could see only its irregularities, like a certain "æsthete" who, when contemplating the water-floods of Niagara, directed his attention to a supposed defect in their curve! . . . In truth, she is seldom happy in her literary criticisms. She speaks of Béranger as "a meteor." . . . We have hinted that Mrs. Trollope's strength lay in her faculty of observation, and her strong, pungent humour. Occasionally, however, she ventures on a vein of reflection, and not without success.—ADAMS, W. H. DAVENPORT, 1883, *Celebrated Women Travellers of the Nineteenth Century, pp.* 393, 394, 399.

She wrote a great deal at this period, and survived till 1863; but her work hardly survived as long as she did. It has, however, been said, and not without justice, that much of the more vivid if coarser substance of her younger son's humour is to be traced in it.—SAINTSBURY, GEORGE, 1896, *A History of Nineteenth Century Literature, p.* 329.

Mrs. Trollope's success in a particular department of her art has been injurious to her general reputation. She lives by the vigour of her portraits of vulgar persons, and her readers cannot help associating her with the characters she makes so entirely her own. . . . She writes not only like a woman of sense, but like a woman of feeling. Though shrewd and observant, she could hardly be termed intellectual, nor was she warmly sympathetic with what is highest in literature, art, and life. But she was richly provided with solid and useful virtues—"honest, courageous, industrious, generous, and affectionate," as her character is summed up by her daughter-in-law. As a writer, the most remarkable circumstance in her career is perhaps the late period at which she began to write. It can but seldom have happened that an author destined to prolonged productiveness and some celebrity should have published nothing until fifty-two.—GARNETT, RICHARD, 1899, *Dictionary of National Biography, vol.* LVII, *p.* 245.

Frederick William Faber
1814–1863

Born at Calverley, Yorkshire, and educated at Harrow. In 1832 he entered Balliol College, Oxford, and three years later, University College, having obtained one of his scholarships, and in 1836 gained the Newdigate prize by his poem, "The Knights of St. John." He graduated A. B. in 1836, and the following year obtained a Fellowship and the Johnson Divinity Scholarship. While at Oxford he had come under the influence of the Tractarian movement, and was a diligent attendant at the Church at St. Mary's, Oxford, of which Dr. (afterwards Cardinal) Newman was the incumbent; and after graduation translated the seven books of Opatus for the "Library of the Fathers." He was ordained deacon in 1837, and priest two years later, and in 1843 was presented to the living of Elton, Huntingdonshire. After a visit to Rome, and an interview with Pope Gregory XVI, he was, in 1845, received into the Church of Rome. Three years later he was received into the Oratory of St. Philip Neri, and in October of the following year was appointed Superior of the Oratory in London. He published "Hymns," 1848; "Jesus and Mary," 1849; "Jesus and Mary," new and enlarged edition, 1852; "The Oratory Hymn Book," 1854; "Hymns," 1861.—RANDOLPH, HENRY FITZ, 1887, *ed., Fifty Years of English Song, Biographical and Bibliographical Notes, vol.* IV, *p.* xviii.

PERSONAL

He incidentally declared his indifference to Whigs, Tories, and Radicals, having no predilections; and so far from being hostile to *born* Dissenters, as such, he thought any serious orthodox Dissenter ought to pause, and consider well what he did, before he departed from "the state into which Providence had called him"; and he exonerates all born Dissenters from the sin of schism. This same regard to the will of Providence influences him in his feelings towards the Church of Rome. He is certain he will never go over to Rome, though he rather regrets not having been born in that communion. He believes both the Roman and Anglican churches to be portions of the Catholic Church. On my objecting to the manifold corruptions of the Romish Church, he admitted these, but held that they did not invalidate its authority. There are trials of the faith of the believer. This same idea of the trial of faith he applied to other diffi-culties, and to the seeming irrationality of certain orthodox doctrines. A revelation ought to have difficulties. It is one of the signs of its Divine origin that it seems incredible to the natural man.—ROBINSON, HENRY CRABB, 1842, *Diary, Dec.* 30; *Diary, Reminiscences and Correspondence, ed.* Sadler.

The house abounds with photographs of him. I could not help myself, notwithstanding all these facts (quoted in the letter), discerning something of the *baby* in them—an absence of that solid intelligence which is the natural result of a thoughtful life. As for influence upon others, that is a question which I have not solved.—MOZLEY, JAMES BOWLING, 1864, *Letters, ed. His Sister, p.* 261.

He was remarkable for his habits of order and neatness, and once, when a father remarked upon the tidiness of his room, he replied, "The napkin in the sepulchre was found *folded* at the resurrection." As might be imagined from the narrative of his life, he was always distinguished for gentleness; and Father Bowden remarks that he never was severe in the manner of correcting the faults of his spiritual subjects, except possibly in matter connected with the ceremonial of divine worship. Any defect of demeanour during service, or inattention to the requirements of the rubric, he rebuked with marked severity. In the church he would have everything of the best, whether it could be seen by the congregation or not. When the new high altar of marble was put up in the Oratory, he was much dissatisfied because the back was not finished like the front, and he found fault with the altar rails for the same reason, complaining that "the side next our Lord" was not ornamented. He was very fond of children, and his correspondence contains some striking evidences of his tenderness to them. We have already spoken of his love of humor—a sense which seems naturally to accompany the poetic instinct. His room was at all hours the frequent resort of his brethren who looked upon it as a renewal of St. Philip's "School of Christian Mirth."—HEWIT, A. F., 1869, *The Life of Father Faber, Catholic World, vol.* 10, *p.* 160.

In person, he was extremely prepossessing—of good height, slender figure, fair complexion, bright blue eyes, well-formed features, almost feminine grace. . . . Evening after evening, in Frederick Faber's rooms, we spent together in reading, and comparing our impressions of our favourite poets; . . . was a poet himself; a man of genius, though not of that kind in which strength predominates. His nature was tender and emotional; he thought and felt in superlatives; and, though his thoughts and feelings were real and true, they were surrounded by a *nimbus* of artificial light. . . . His usual flow of spirits was great; and in conversation he was positive, sometimes paradoxical. There was in his mental nature an element of waywardness and inconstancy of which in his earlier years he was conscious. It manifested itself sometimes in a rapid change of opinion from one extreme to another; and at other times (though this never happened to myself), in his relations to particular persons. —PALMER, ROUNDELL (EARL OF SELBORNE), 1888–96, *Memorials, Part I, Family and Personal, vol.* I, *pp.* 136, 137, 138.

The friendship with F. W. Faber was at its height during these years. They had known each other at Oxford since 1833, but had not been very intimate there. They now drew together, in the thorough and enthusiastic line which they adopted in matters of Catholic devotion; and Faber was Ward's "spiritual director" from 1853 to the end of his life. Faber threw all the gifts of high imagination and musical utterance, which had made Wordsworth recognise him early as one who should be a great poet, into the service of the Catholic Church; giving up all effort on the lines which lead to literary fame. Mr. Ward always held that the events of 1845 transformed him; and that a nature which had seemed in early years to have something of the dilettante in it, revealed at last quite unexpected depths. Few had looked in the Oxford Faber for the almost unique influence as a spiritual guide at the London Oratory, which is still in the memory of many.—WARD, WILFRID, 1893, *William George Ward and the Catholic Revival, p.* 61.

POETRY

His verses, less labored and polished than Keble's, quite make up in natural warmth what they lack in artistic finish; and we find in them always that ease of expression which we miss in the highly wrought poems of Keble.—SPALDING, MARTIN JOHN, 1855, *Miscellanea.*

The hymns which he wrote were collected and published in 1848. There were not many of them. The edition of 1849 was much enlarged, and that of 1852 contained sixty-six pieces. In 1861 the number had risen to one hundred and fifty. These hymns are so truly devotional in spirit, and so eminently appropriate to the religious use of all Christians, that they have been for a long time among the treasures of English hymnody. Editions of them have been issued, from which those that belong to the exclusive service of the Church of Rome have been eliminated, and in which the touching and exquisite lyrics which are so dear to all believers have been retained. This is in full accordance with the large desire of their author, who says this much and more in his preface.—DUFFIELD, SAMUEL WILLOUGHBY, 1886, *English Hymns, p.* 507.

There is one hymn writer to whom we owe much, and who went out from among us, with so many others, now nearly forty years ago—Frederick William Faber. Some of his beautiful hymns are spoiled by a strange sentimentalism; some are good and noble poetry. Faber was one of a family distinguished in literature.—PRESCOTT, J. E., 1893, *Christian Hymns and Hymn Writers,* p. 178.

Faber enjoyed for a number of years the friendship of Wordsworth, to whom, as we have seen, he dedicated one of his early volumes. Upon hearing of Faber's determination to enter the Church, Wordsworth wrote him: "I do not say you are wrong, but England loses a poet." Whether Faber would ever have justified the application of the term poet in the high sense in which we should expect Wordsworth to use it may be doubted; but judged by any standard which it is proper to apply to sacred poetry, as such the best of his verse will take honourable rank. In "Carl Ritter," "The Heiress of Gösting," and the "Dream of King Crœsus," one of his best poems, he showed some faculty for narrative verse, but he lacked originality; and when not dealing with a classical or legendary theme showed want of resource and invention. Some of his hymns, however, have become very popular, and some contain the more enduring qualities not always found in popular work.—MILES, ALFRED H., 1897, *The Poets and the Poetry of the Century, Sacred, Moral and Religious Verse,* p. 300.

GENERAL

In his numerous devotional books, in all his correspondence, and in his hymns, almost all of which are of the highest order for beauty, tenderness, and spirituality, there breathes sweet humility, childlike trust in Jesus as the Savior of the lost, and the most loving submission to the Divine will. Some of his hymns have found their way into Protestant collections, such as "Hymns of the Ages," and have met with much favour. The first of his remarkable series of spiritual books, entitled, "All for Jesus," is the one on which his reputation as an author mainly rests; but all his books were eagerly welcomed at the time of their publication, and were immediately translated into different languages. And there is much in them which is fitted to excite healthfully the devotional feelings of the pious who are not of the Church to which he belonged, and who have no sympathy with it, to suggest to them profitable thought, and to incite them to faithfulness in the performance of duty. That which is false in them can easily be discriminated,

and separated from that which is good and true.— SCRIBNER, WILLIAM, 1871, *Life and Letters of Faber, Princeton Review, vol.* 43, p. 515.

He was no Gallican, no rigorist, no advocate of anything that might be called Neo-Catholic or Anglo-Catholic. Even in regard to minor and accessory matters, to modes and ways in which there is great room for variation in opinion and practice, he preferred those which characterize the genius of the Italian and Spanish nations, and which seem to the colder and more reserved temperament of the English to be the most remote and foreign to their tastes and intellectual habits. He endeavored to divest himself of everything which bore the semblance of conformity even in accidentals to Anglicanism, and to throw his whole soul in what he considered to be the most perfectly Catholic mould. He outran in this many both of the old English Catholics and of his fellow-converts. Especially in regard to the devotion to the Blessed Virgin Mary, he made himself the champion of the most exalted views concerning the power and glory of the Mother of God, and the importance of her cultus in the practical teaching and piety which is directed to the end of the conversion and perfection of souls. He followed St. Bernardine of Sienna, St. Alphonsus, and the V. Louis Grignon de Montfort, and his entire spiritual doctrine is derived from similar sources, as it were flowing from the very topmost heights of mystic contemplation, above the clouds, and far remote from the paths and ken of ordinary mortals. In his theology, which is remarkable both for accuracy and depth, he always follows those authors whose doctrine accords with the strictest criterion of Roman orthodox—HEWIT, A. F., 1871, *The Princeton Review on Dr. Faber, Catholic World, vol.* 14, *p.* 412.

As a spiritual pathologist F. W. Faber stands without a rival. Old Ames, in the preface to his sagacious and most practical treatise, "De Conscientia," observes that in this department the Romanists are superior to our own writers. This certificate, coming from the author of one of the most effective polemics against Rome, the "Bellarminus Enervatus," may be unhesitatingly accepted. Certainly it is true of Faber. The whole human subject lies open to his scrutiny. With the skill of the trained anatomist he cuts down upon the spot he wishes to lay bare, and dissects away all obstructing material. He speaks with his eye steadily on the object. He sees the reality and he tells what he sees in one of the most lucid and racy styles ever employed by an English writer. The gravity of his subject and the austerity of his judgment are relieved by the tender sympathy of a man who knows the difficulty of holy living, and by a humour which does not so much leap out in sudden flashes, as maintains throughout a steady brightness. His therapeutics are, of course, mixed—strangely mixed. . . . In a word, the reader must discount his Romanism; but having done so he feels he is in the company of a man who knows him as if he had lived with him all his days, and to whom the spiritual life is an actuality of vital importance. The cure of the soul is, in Faber, reduced to something like a science. He does not fall into the mistake of some writers on experimental religion, who treat the soul mechanically, and leave in the mind the impression that all one needs to do in order to attain perfection is to attend to certain rules. But hopefulness springing from a sounder source breathes through all Faber's writings, and counsels suggested by an unrivalled knowledge of men's actual infirmities convey encouragement and last-

ing help. In pure theology, also, Faber has rare excellences. His "The Creator and the Creation" is a presentation of the love of God so affecting as to be irresistible. The material which his theological insight and learning gather is transfused by his poetic genius into a form all aglow with finely controlled emotion.—DODS, MARCUS, 1887, *Books which Have Influenced Me, p.* 111.

By his unceasing labours in connection with the London Oratory, by his persuasive eloquence in the pulpit, and by his numerous publications, Faber rendered signal service to the Roman Catholic cause in England. He introduced Italian forms of prayer and pious practices, some of which were at first distasteful to English Catholics of the old school, and he constantly inculcated devotion to the pope as an essential part of christian piety. The light and charming style of his spiritual treatises, which unite mystical devotion with profound theological learning, obtained for them an extraordinary popularity. His longer poetical works possess considerable merit, and the use of his beautiful hymns is almost universal in catholic churches wherever the English language is spoken.—COOPER, THOMPSON, 1889, *Dictionary of National Biography, vol.* XVIII, *p.* 110.

Sir George Cornewall Lewis

1806–1863

Born in London, 21st April 1806, son of Sir T. F. Lewis, Bart., of Harpton Court, Radnorshire, and was educated at Eton and Christ Church, Oxford, where in 1828 he took a first-class in classics and a second-class in mathematics. He was called to the bar in 1831, and became a Poor-law Commissioner in 1839. He was Liberal M. P. for Herefordshire 1847–52, and for the Radnor Boroughs from 1855. He rose to be financial secretary to the Treasury, Chancellor of the Exchequer under Palmerston 1855–58, Home Secretary 1859–61, and then War Secretary. He succeeded his father as second baronet in 1855, and died at Harpton Court, 13th April 1863. He wrote "Origin of the Romance Languages" (1835), "Inquiry into the Credibility of Ancient Roman History" (1855—against Niebuhr), "Astronomy of the Ancients" (1859), "Dialogue on the Best Form of Government" (1859), &c. He was editor of the *Edinburgh Review* from 1852 to 1855. See his "Letters" (1870) and Bagehot's "Literary Studies" (1879).—PATRICK AND GROOME, *eds.*, 1897, *Chambers's Biographical Dictionary, p.* 589.

PERSONAL

Gladstone seems bent on leading Sir George Lewis a weary life, but Lewis is just the man to encounter and baffle such an opponent, for he is cold-blooded as a fish, totally devoid of sensibility or nervousness, of an imperturbable temper, calm and resolute, labourious and indefatigable, and exceedingly popular in the House of Commons from his general good humor and

civility, and the credit given him for honor, sincerity, plain dealing, and good intentions.—GREVILLE, CHARLES C. F., 1857, *A Journal of the Reign of Queen Victoria, from 1852 to 1860, ed. Reeve, Feb.* 8; *p.* 346.

Few more curious sights were, not long since, to be seen in London than that of Sir G. C. Lewis at the War Office. What is now a melancholy recollection was, when we used to see it, an odd mixture of amusing anomalies. The accidental and bit-by-bit way in which all minor business is managed in England has drifted our public offices into scattered, strange, and miscellaneous places; it has drifted the war minister into the large drawing-room of an old mansion, which is splendid enough to receive fashionable people and large enough to receive a hundred people. In this great and gorgeous apartment sat, a few months since, a homely scholar in spectacles, whose face bore traces of secretary labor, and whose figure was bent into the student stoop. Such a plain man looked odd enough in such a splendid place, but it was much more odd to think that that man in that place supremely regulated the War Department of England. The place should have been a pacific drawing-room, and the man was a pacific student: he looked like a conveyancer over deeds, like a scholar among treatises, like a jurist making a code; he looked like the last man to preside over martial pomp and military expeditions. . . . No German professor, from the smoke and study of many silent years, has ever put forth books more bristling with recondite references, more exact in every technicality of scholarship, more rich in matured reflection, than Sir George Lewis found time, mind, and scholarlike curiosity to write in the very thick of eager English life: and yet he was never very busy, or never seemed so. In the extremity of the "Trent" difficulty—when, as he was inclined to think, a war with America was impending, when a war minister might be pardoned for having no time for general reflection—Sir George Lewis found time, at three o'clock on a busy parliamentary day, to discuss with the writer of these lines for some twenty minutes the comparative certainty (or rather *un*certainty) of the physical and moral sciences. It was difficult to know what to make of such a man.—BAGEHOT, WALTER, 1863, *Sir George Cornewall Lewis, Works, ed. Morgan, vol.* III, *pp.* 222, 223.

Of course I knew him but little, but there was one quality of his mind of vast consequence to him as a statesman, and to his country, which was very quickly apparent; I mean his *instinctive fairness.* He was singularly able and willing to change his opinion, when new facts came to unsettle his old one. He seemed to do it, too, without regret. This struck me the first time I

saw him, which was at breakfast at Lord Stanhope's, in July, 1856, and it was still more strongly apparent the next morning at breakfast at his own house; the conversations on both occasions having been much on American affairs. . . . And so it continued, I think, every time I saw him that summer, and the next, down to the last dinner at his house, when we were together. I remember that I used to think that he had the greatest respect for *facts* of any man I ever saw, and an extraordinary power of determining, from internal evidence, what were such. I suppose this meant, that the love of truth was the uppermost *visible* quality in his character.— TICKNOR, GEORGE, 1863, *To Sir Edmund Head, May* 12; *Life, Letters and Journals of George Ticknor, vol.* II, *p.* 462.

Lord Bacon tells us, "Reading makes a full man, writing a correct man, and speaking a ready man"; and as Sir Cornewall Lewis had ample experience of the three systems, he was naturally expected to take a high position. In an eminent degree he abounded with the materials out of which good speaking might be made. His main fault was a tendency to be doctrinaire, to forget the feelings and prejudices of Englishmen, to reason too much like the philosopher in his closet, and to forget to make allowance for the infirmities of human nature.—RITCHIE, J. EWING, 1869, *British Senators: or, Political Sketches Past and Present, p.* 414.

He was one of the most profound scholars of his day. He was not only an eminent statesman, but might, as Dean Milman said, "have done honour as Professor of Greek to the most learned university in Europe." In hours snatched from public business he performed "feats of scholarship which might try the erudition and research of the most recluse student." His "Babrius" is the perfection of classsical editing. He wrote notable books on Roman history, ancient astronomy, international law, methods of political reasoning and forms of government. His essays on the administration of Great Britain from 1783 to 1830 are an important historical contribution, modestly put forth in the form of reviews. Looking back on all this variety of work, and work of such a high order, it certainly strikes one at first sight as strange that it should have attracted so little attention from his contemporaries. They took it all very much as a matter of course, like any common incident of nature—daylight or the flowing of the tide—very wonderful when one thinks of it, but which one doesn't think about at all. . . . He worked with the coldness and precision of machinery, and to casual observers seemed rather a system or intellectual process than a man.—FYFE, J. H., 1870, *Sir George Cornewall Lewis, Macmillan's Magazine, vol.* 21, *p.* 465.

Sir George Lewis's was no ordinary character: there was mixed with his clear intelligence and capacity for profound and distinct thought a peculiar singleness and simplicity with which such qualities are rarely found in union. A part of this simplicity was his entire freedom from vanity. Aware of his own superiority he could hardly fail to be, but on no occasion was he ever tempted to make a display of it, either in order to obtain praise or gain an advantage. Neither did he on any occasion take offence: he never felt animosity towards persons who misunderstood and disparaged him, nor dislike to those who treated him slightingly because in some common-place matters they were more efficient than himself. He was gentle and unassuming, calm, dispassionate, and just, and was consequently beloved in private and respected in public life. . . . The love of letters was, in Sir George Lewis's mind, the dominant passion, and that for its own sake. It was this quality which rendered his commerce so delightful to his learned associates. Ever ready to plunge into discussions of grave questions, bringing to them stores of heaped-up knowledge, with a candid appreciation of opinions at variance with his own, no man was more sought after as a converser by the distinguished members of the literary republic. — LEWIS, SIR GILBERT FRANKLAND, 1870, *ed., Letters of the Right Hon. Sir George Cornewall Lewis, Preface, pp.* v, vii.

Few recent lives of Englishmen are so worthy to be set on record for the example of posterity as that of Sir George Cornewall Lewis. It was so balanced and sustained; such an honest life of work, gradually and surely winning its own reward, and demonstrating that the race is not always to the swift, nor the battle to the strong. A weak physique never suggested to him an excuse for indolence; a singular modesty never interfered with the earnest pursuit of high aims in his works and acts; a consistent gentleness and dislike of giving offence never prevented his holding his own opinion and holding it so that, sooner or later, he was generally found to be in the right. And what animated his whole career was rather perseverance than genius; there were no brilliant *coups*, though there were manifold instances of the triumph of plain sound judgment based on a careful survey of precedents. Gifted with a clear head, a spirit of research, and a calm judicial mind, he achieved by industry, system, and steadfast conscientiousness, an eminence far higher than the high station in which he was born, and left behind him a name, of which his country is justly proud, in the annals of its statesmanship and its literature.—DAVIES, JAMES, 1872, *Sir G. C. Lewis's Letters, The Contemporary Review, vol.* 20, *p.* 803.

He was a singular man; his manners were dry and phlegmatic, though too simple to be supercilious; he was thoroughly honest-minded; he was of an imperturbable temper, though cynical; and, externally frigid as he was, he had two or three attachments of which the secret strength was to be inferred from an unvarying constancy. His success in political life never received a check; and it showed how unessential popular manners are to such success in this country, so long as integrity and sincerity are unquestioned; proving also that coldness and comparative indifference, with the requisite conscientiousness and intellectual power, may inspire more general and durable confidence than political ardors, howsoever patriotic. His well-known saying that "life would be tolerable enough but for its amusements" was genuinely characteristic; and I doubt whether politics were much more congenial to him than amusements; or work in his office, whether as chancellor of the exchequer or secretary of state, equally acceptable with work in his study. Even when in his office he seemed to prefer laborious literary research and the composition of able, but dry, literary works to administrative industries; though for these also he was well fitted by the largeness of his understanding; for, with all his devotion to learning and scholastic literature, his mind was in no sense pedantic. He had a highly cultivated logical faculty; but he knew that faculty to be instrumental only—designed to serve the higher reason, not to master it. What limitation there was of his intellect was on the imaginative side. His mind was essentially prosaic.—TAYLOR, SIR HENRY, 1885, *Autobiography, vol.* I, *p.* 258.

If George Lewis had taken care of himself he might possibly have been alive now, but he was of a skeptical turn of mind, and even disbelieved in what is the center of truth to so many, his own country doctor. Hence, an illness, I believe easily curable at first, rapidly got worse, and no one attended to it, till too late. And so he died prematurely. His loss has been a very great one, and we feel it more and more every day, for he stands as one of those honest and independent Liberals, whose political fibre was not relaxed by his constantly feeding himself upon sentimental platitudes. He really loved his native land better than his party or his own personal interests, so that whenever a duty to England showed itself before him, he might safely have been depended upon.—DOYLE, SIR FRANCIS HASTINGS, 1886, *Reminiscences and Opinions, p.* 72.

GENERAL

It is as a writer, as a clear-headed and fearless though thoughtful inquirer into abstruse problems of Polity and Jurisprudence, that he will be best remembered. His Essays "On the Use and Abuse of Political Terms," "On the Influence of Authority in Matters of Opinion;" "On the Government of Dependencies;" and "On the Method of Observation and Reasoning in Politics," show his characteristic merits. He has also left us a short but very valuable work, "On the Extradition of Criminals;" a difficult subject, which continually forces itself on the attention of those who have to deal with International law.—CREASY, SIR EDWARD, 1857, *Memoirs of Eminent Etonians, Second Ed., p.* 578.

Most of his books are too full of citations and explanations, and to the last he would have been more read and more influential if he had thought often of Sydney Smith's precept, "Now, remember Noah, and be *quick.*" But though a tendency to overlay a subject with superfluous erudition was one of Sir George Lewis's defects, the possession of that available erudition was one of his greatest powers.—BAGEHOT, WALTER, 1863, *Sir George Cornewall Lewis, Works, ed. Morgan, vol.* III, *p.* 234.

The author was one of the wisest as well as one of the most learned men of the last generation.—ADAMS, CHARLES KENDALL, 1882, *A Manual of Historical Literature, p.* 527.

The most remarkable characteristic of Lewis was the great variety of his literary activity. Yet he was by no means a versatile man; and in his speculations he ever preserved the clearness, method, regularity, and industry that characterised his political life. With strong limitations, and with but plain and homely qualities, he succeeded in making his influence widely felt in several departments of letters.—TOUT, T. F., 1887, *The Celebrities of the Century, ed. Sanders, p.* 675.

A somewhat incongruous figure to appear in this company has nevertheless a right to be mentioned in connection with Roman history. . . . He was also a prolific writer, chiefly upon more or less political questions. . . . This class of writing is seldom entertaining, and in Sir George Lewis's hands becomes exceedingly dry; but there is more life in the more important work which leads us to class the author among the students of ancient history, a ruthless attack upon all manner of legends and traditions, entitled an "Inquiry into the Credibility of the Early Roman History." We have small sympathy, as a rule, with the demolishers of traditions. It is certainly not a work of mercy, and seldom of necessity; indeed, it usually reminds us, especially when carried out with undue violence, of the unnecessary efforts of Panard's stage hero.

> "J'ai vu Roland dans sa colère
> Exercer l' effort de son bras
> Pour pouvoir arracher de terre
> Des arbres—qui n'y tenait pas."

But there is certainly in this author a refreshing vivacity of attack, hitting out all round, not only at the good, easy legend by which children are lured on to think there must really be something to read in history, but with equal force assailing the calm assumptions of the scientific Niebuhr, —which gives a somewhat pleasurable sensation to the reader.—OLIPHANT, MARGARET, O. W., 1892, *The Victorian Age of English Literature, pp.* 191, 192.

His writings are more remarkable for scholarly research than for any elegance of style, and are distinguished by the same practical good sense, as well as the same absence of any desire for popularity, which were so noticeable in his parliamentary career. Lewis had a tendency to overestimate the effects of education, and was firmly convinced that "a well-educated man was competent to undertake any office and write on any subject." His characteristic assertion that "life would be tolerable but for its amusements," though familiar to many, is frequently misquoted.—BAR-

KER, G. F. RUSSELL, 1893, *Dictionary of National Biography, vol.* XXXIII, *p.* 181.

A keen scholar and a fastidious writer.— SAINTSBURY, GEORGE, 1896, *A History of Nineteenth Century Literature, p.* 206.

Extensive knowledge, combined with a clearness of intellect and independence of judgment, gives value to his work.— WALKER, HUGH, 1897, *The Age of Tennyson, p.* 169.

Lyman Beecher
1775–1863

Born at New Haven, Conn., Oct. 12, 1775; graduated at Yale College in 1797; studied theology under President Dwight; and became in 1810 minister of the Congregational church at Litchfield, Conn. He was a popular preacher, and acquired great influence among the orthodox churches. To oppose the rapid progress of Unitarian doctrines he removed to Boston about 1826, and preached in the Hanover Street church. He was president of Lane Seminary at Cincinnati 1832–51. Here he was brought to a stormy trial for heresy; and, although not condemned by the presbytery, this event was one of the great factors in the separation of the New from the Old School Presbyterians in 1837. He published, beside other works, "Views in Theology" and "Sermons on Temperance," which had a great circulation. He was a man of very energetic character. Died at Brooklyn, N. Y., Jan. 10, 1863. His works were published in three volumes (Boston, 1852).— ADAMS, CHARLES KENDALLL, *ed.*, 1897, *Johnson's Universal Cyclopædia, vol.* I, *p.* 559.

PERSONAL

A calm and comprehensive estimate of all his sermons, letters, and actions must convince a candid mind what is true, namely, that if he went into controversy, he went into it because he felt that his business of saving souls was in some way obstructed, and he must remove the obstruction. If he attacked either systems, or institutions, or men with severity, it was because he felt that the eternal interests of immortal souls were at stake.—BEECHER, CHARLES, 1863, *ed. Autobiography, Correspondence, etc., of Lyman Beecher, Introduction, vol.* II, *p.* 10.

Friends and children were able and willing to see to it that the brave old veteran of fourscore years should be fully provided for. The Lane arrears were paid up; a house was purchased for him in Brooklyn, close by that of his most famous son; and here, with an annuity sufficient for his wants, he passed the last seven years of his life, ministered to by his children by blood and marriage. Month by month the veil between him and the outward world grew thicker fold by fold. The connection between him and the world grew weaker and weaker. Memory was gone, language was gone—or seemed to be so. Yet now and then were strange flashes which seemed to say that the strong mind was curtained,

not blinded. "Dr. Beecher," said some one to him, "you know a great deal: tell us what is the greatest of all things." For a moment the curtain seemed to be rent, and he replied, with his old vigor, terseness, and earnestness: "It is not theology, it is not controversy; but it is to save souls." Then the curtain fell again, and he was lost to human sight behind its folds. For the last year of his life all the organs of communication between him and the world without appeared to fail, except indistinct phrases seemed to indicate that the mental life existed. Still his eye was bright, and his face bore an expression of strength and sweetness. Yet even to the very close there were moments when the veil was for a moment parted.—GUERNSEY, A. H., 1865, *Lyman Beecher, Harper's Magazine, vol.* 30, *p.* 709.

It is said, that he would return from a funeral and send forth the quickest airs from his fiddle. He was of the most cheerful temperament, as I, who knew him for thirty years, can well testify. Few clergymen—probably none—have been more noted, more able, and I may add more useful than Dr. Beecher. He was then in his prime. It was in Litchfield, the year after I left there, that he delivered his celebrated lectures on temperance. It was a good place to begin work, for Litchfield had several able and distinguished men, who died or lost their influence by intemperance. Dr. Beecher was called the "great gun of Calvinism," and it seemed to me the very irony of fate to see him tried ten years after by the Presbytery of Cincinnati for heresy in Calvinic Theology. . . . Dr. Beecher was so far superior to all other preachers of that section, that all the students who went to church at all went to his church. I was always a regular attendant, not losing, I think, more than two or three Sundays while I was there. Dr. Beecher was remarkable for great irregularity in what may be called the quality of his sermons. There was none inferior, but there were times when he was dull. A friend said to me once that he had heard much of Dr. Beecher, and went to hear him, but he never heard a duller sermon. I can realize that might have been, but Dr. Beecher was at times exceedingly eloquent. His spells of eloquence seemed to come on by fits.—MANSFIELD, F. D., 1879, *Personal Memories, p.* 139.

Was one of the leading preachers, reformers, and controversialists of his day. Sturdy in body and mind, full of sensibility, aflame with enthusiasm, devoted to the highest aims and utterly unselfish in life, a Christian in whom deep spirituality and strong common sense were happily blended, he was just the man to transmit excellent qualities to his children; a father to be enjoyed while living, and to be remembered with love and reverence after his death.— BEECHER, WILLIAM C., AND SCOVILLE, SAMUEL, 1888, *A Biography of Henry Ward Beecher, p.* 17.

I had known Dr. Beecher before I left New England as one of the vigorous assailants of Unitarianism, and I had expected to find him uncongenial if not austere; but he proved to be one of the most social and agreeable of men. He spent a number of days at my house, and I became strongly attached to him. I had known him in the pulpit as an earnest, intolerant, and always logical preacher. It did not take me long to discover that out of it he abounded in sympathy, in geniality, in good-will for everybody. . . . Dr. Beecher had the reputation of being the father of more brains than any other man in the country. As far as I know he merited the reputation. His six sons and four daughters were very unlike in talents and in their

leading characteristics; but there was not an ordinary one among them.—McCULLOCH, HUGH L., 1888, *Men and Measures of Half a Century, pp.* 149, 150.

He was one of the lights—technically speaking, the "blue-light"—of orthodoxy. He was a powerful preacher to a devoted congregation, and indulged in sectarian denunciation beyond what are generally considered the bounds of good taste. . . . I believe that Dr. Lyman Beecher was one of the most conscientious preachers among those who adorned the Boston pulpit, but his name cannot be mentioned without recalling the immense stride in liberal theology which has been made between his day and our own.—TUCKERMAN, CHARLES K., 1895, *Personal Recollections of Notable People at Home and Abroad, vol.* I, *pp.* 46, 47.

GENERAL

The names of few men among the American clergy now living, have stood out so long in bold relief as that of Lyman Beecher. . . . As a preacher, Dr. Beecher has possessed uncommon power. When his own emotions were thoroughly aroused, and his thoughts were transfused with the most fervid moral and social emotion, with vigorous tongue, in original phrase, interlaced with short and glancing illustrations, which glowed and ripened into the boldest metaphors, his power was electrical; and the audience was swayed to his sonorous voice, as trees in a forest to the rushing of autumnal winds. . . . The famous sermons on Intemperance were occasioned by the inebriety of a very dear friend; and were thus born of a full heart. And, although they did not save the man whose case inspired them, they have doubtless saved millions of others, as they initiated a great moral enterprise, and are still read in almost every language of the civilized world. —FISH, HENRY C., 1857, *Pulpit Eloquence of the Nineteenth Century, p.* 409.

Notwithstanding all that has been written and published since on this great theme, these sermons ["Temperance Sermons"] yet remain unrivalled.—CLEVELAND, CHARLES D., 1859, *A Compendium of American Literature, p.* 207.

The Autobiography of the Rev. Dr. Lyman Beecher, edited by his son Charles, awakens vividly our recollection of a venerable man seen not long ago walking the streets of Brooklyn, or rising to speak in

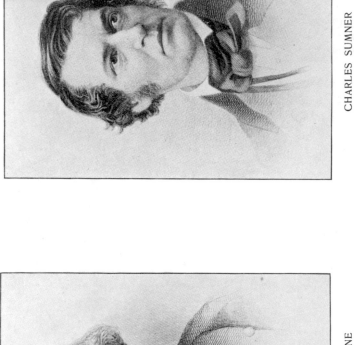

NATHANIEL HAWTHORNE

CHARLES SUMNER

Engraving by J. A. J. Wilcox.

From a Daguerreotype taken for Edward L. Pierce in 1853.

the prayer-meetings at Plymouth Church, or sitting an attentive listener in the great congregation; his silvery hair falling low upon his shoulders; his fine appearance half disguising his infirmities. . . . The present book is something of a novelty in book-making—an autobiography not written by its subject but snatched from his lips at intervals by his questioning family, and penned on the spot; many of the pages standing in the form of question and answer, the interrogator's name indicated by initials, making altogether an inartistic, loosely-joined, unsatisfactory, yet fascinating record—resembling, in parts, the report of a cross-examination in a law trial.— TILTON, THEODORE, 1865-69, *Lyman Beecher and Roxana Foote, Sanctum Sanctorum, p.* 106.

His writings are not numerous, as compared with those of his still more illustrious descendents, but are marked by great boldness, vigor, and clearness, both of thought and expression, with occasional outbursts of passionate eloquence. . . As a thinker, Dr. Beecher was bold to the point of audacity, and it was this feature of his character probably, more than any positive errors, that made him a subject of anxiety to the more conservative class of theologians. He was one of the earliest and most eloquent advocates of the temperance movement.— HART, JOHN S., 1872, *A Manual of American Literature, p.* 275.

His name for the years of his Boston residence, and previous to them, was the synonym for Trinitarianism in the pulpit, as Channing's was for Unitarianism. In preaching, more than in book-making, appeared his force and fire.—RICHARDSON, CHARLES F., 1887, *American Literature,* 1607-1885, *vol.* I, *p.* 295.

Nathaniel Hawthorne
1804–1864

Born, in Salem, Mass., 4 July 1804. At school there. At Raymond, Maine, 1818-19. At Salem, 1819-21. Issued weekly paper, "The Spectator," Aug. to Sept., 1820. To Bowdoin Coll., Brunswick, 1821; B. A., 1825. At Salem, engaged in literary pursuits, 1825-37. Contrib. to "The Token," 1831-38; "New England Mag.," 1834-35; "Knickerbocker," 1837. Editor of "The American Mag. of Useful and Entertaining Knowledge," 1836. Contrib. to the "Democratic Review," 1838-46. Weigher and Gauger of Customs at Boston, 1839-41. Joined the "Arcadia" settlement at Brook Farm, April 1841. Married Sophia Amelia Peabody, July 9, 1842. Lived at the Old Manse, Concord, Mass., 1842-46. At Salem, as Surveyor of Customs, 1846-49. Removed to Lennox, Mass., 1850; to West Newton, near Boston, 1851; to Concord, 1852. American Consul at Liverpool, 1853-57; travelled on Continent, 1857-59; returned to America, 1860. Contrib. to "Atlantic Monthly," 1860-64. Died, at Plymouth, N. H., 18 May, 1864. Buried at Concord. *Works:* "Fanshawe" (anon.), 1828; "Twice-Told Tales," 1st series, 1837; 2nd series, 1842; "Grandfather's Chair," (pt. i.), 1841; ("Famous Old People," 1841, and "Liberty Tree," 1842, extracted from preceding); "Biographical Stories for Children," 1842; "Mosses from an Old Manse" (2 vols.), 1846; "The Scarlet Letter," 1850; "The House of the Seven Gables," 1851; "True Stories from History and Biography," 1851; "The Wonder Book," 1851; "The Snow Image, etc.," 1851; "The Blithedale Romance," 1852; "Life of Franklin Pierce," 1852; "The Tanglewood Tales," 1853; "A Rill from the Town Pump," 1857; "The Marble Faun" (English edn. called "Transformation"), 1860; "Our Old Home," 1863; "Pansie," [1864]. *Posthumous Works:* "Tales" (2 vols.), 1866; "Passages from the American Note-books of Hawthorne," 1868; "Passages from the English Note-books of Hawthorne," 1870; "Passages from the French and Italian Note-books of Hawthorne," 1871; "Septimus Felton," 1872; "The Dolliver Romance," 1876; "Tales of the White Hills," 1877; "A Virtuoso's Collection, etc.," 1877; "Legends of New England," 1877; "Legends of the Province House," 1877; "Dr. Grimshawe's Secret," 1883; "Sketches and Studies," 1883. He *edited:* H. Bridge's "Journal of an African Cruiser," 1865.—SHARP, R. FARQUHARSON, 1897, *A Dictionary of English Authors, p.* 127.

PERSONAL

I have not yet concluded what profession I shall have. The being a minister is of course out of the question. I should not think that even you could desire me to choose so dull a way of life. Oh, no, mother,

I was not born to vegetate forever in one place and to live and die as calm and tranquil as—a puddle of water. As to lawyers, there are so many of them already that one half of them (upon a moderate calculation) are in a state of actual starvation. A physician, then, seems to be "Hobson's choice"; but yet I should not like to live by the diseases and infirmities of my fellow-creatures. And it would weigh very heavily on my conscience, in the course of my practice, if I should chance to send any unlucky patient "ad inferum," which being interpreted is, "to the realms below." Oh that I was rich enough to live without a profession! What do you think of my becoming an author, and relying for support upon my pen? Indeed, I think the illegibility of my handwriting is very author-like. How proud you would feel to see my works praised by the reviewers, as equal to the proudest productions of the scribbling sons of John Bull. But authors are always poor devils, and therefore Satan may take them. I am in the same predicament as the honest gentleman in "Espriella's Letters,"

"I am an Englishman, and naked I stand here,
A-musing in my mind what garment I shall
wear."

—HAWTHORNE, NATHANIEL, 1821, *Letter to his Mother, Nathaniel Hawthorne and His Wife*, ed. *Hawthorne, vol.* I, *p.* 107.

When nature was shaping him, clay was not
granted
For making so full-sized a man as she wanted,
So, to fill out her model, a little she spared,
From some finer-grained stuff for a woman prepared,
And she could not have hit a more excellent
plan
For making him fully and perfectly man.

—LOWELL, JAMES RUSSELL, 1848, *A Fable for Critics.*

And Hawthorne, too, I remember as one with whom I sauntered, in old heroic times, along the banks of the Scamander, amid the ruins of chariots and heroes. Tell him not to desert, even after the tenth year.—THOREAU, HENRY D., 1848, *Letter to R. W. Emerson, July* 8; *Familiar Letters of Thoreau*, ed. *Sanborn, p.* 110.

The offices in Massachusetts have all gone most rigorously according to party service and party caste. Even Hawthorne, who never attended a political meeting or wrote a political article, has been ejected from his small retreat in the Salem custom house.—SUMNER, CHARLES, 1849, *To George Sumner, July* 17; *Memoir and Letters of Charles Sumner*, ed. *Pierce, vol.* III, *pp.* 44, *note.*

During Hawthorne's first year's residence in Concord I had driven up with some friends to an æsthetic tea at Mr. Emerson's. It was in the winter, and a great wood-fire blazed upon the hospitable hearth. There were various men and women of note assembled; and I, who listened attentively to all the fine things that was said, was for some time scarcely aware of a man who sat upon the edge of the circle, a little withdrawn, his head slightly thrown forward upon his breast, and his bright eyes clearly burning under his black brow. As I drifted down the stream of talk, this person, who sat silent as a shadow looked to me as Webster might have looked had he been a poet, —a kind of poetic Webster. He rose and walked to the window, and stood quietly there for a long time, watching the dead-white landscape. No appeal was made to him, nobody looked after him, the conversation flowed steadily on, as if everyone understood that his silence was to be respected. It was the same thing at table. In vain the silent man imbibed æsthetic tea. Whatever fancies it inspired did not flower at his lips. But there was a light in his eye which assured me that nothing was lost. So supreme was his silence, that it presently engrossed me, to the exclusion of everything else. There was very brilliant discourse, but this silence was much more poetic and fascinating. Fine things were said by the philosophers, but much finer things were implied by the dumbness of this gentleman with heavy brows and black hair. When he presently rose and went, Emerson, with the "slow, wise smile" that breaks over his face like day over the sky, said, "Hawthorne rides well his horse of the night."—CURTIS, GEORGE WILLIAM, 1854-94, *Homes of American Authors, Literary and Social Essays, p.* 43.

Should you ask me, "Who is Hawthorne?
Who this Hawthorne that you mention?"
I should answer, I should tell you,
"He's a Yankee, who had written
Many books you must have heard of;
For he wrote the 'Scarlet Letter'
And 'The House of Seven Gables,'
Wrote, too, 'Rappacini's Daughter,'
And a lot of other stories;—
Some are long, and some are shorter;
Some are good, and some are better.
And this Hawthorne is a Consul,

Sitting in a dismal office,—
  Dark and dirty, dingy office,
Full of mates, and full of captains,
  Full of sailors and of niggers,—
And he lords it over Yankees."
. . . .
Do you ask me, "Tell me further
Of this Consul, of this Hawthorne?"
  I would say, "He is a sinner,—
Reprobate and churchless sinner,—
  Never goes inside a chapel,
Only sees outsides of chapels,
  Says his prayers without a chapel!
I would say that he is lazy,
  Very lazy, good-for-nothing;
Hardly ever goes to dinners,
  Never goes to balls or soirees:
Thinks one friend worth twenty friendly;
  Cares for love, but not for liking;
Hardly knows a dozen people."
—BRIGHT, HENRY, 1855, *Song of Consul Hawthorne, Dec. 25; Nathaniel Hawthorne and his Wife, ed. Hawthorne, vol.* II, *pp.* 78, 79.

The personal appearance and demeanor of these two gifted men, at the early period of which I speak, was also in striking contrast. Willis was slender, his hair sunny and silken, his cheek ruddy, his aspect cheerful and confident. He met society with a ready and welcome hand, and was received readily and with welcome. Hawthorne on the contrary, was of a rather sturdy form, his hair dark and bushy, his eye steel-gray, his brow thick, his mouth sarcastic, his complexion stony, his whole aspect cold, moody, distrustful. He stood aloof, and surveyed the world from shy and sheltered positions.—GOODRICH, SAMUEL GRISWOLD, 1856, *Recollections of a Lifetime, vol.* II, *p.* 269.

I sent my letter at once; from all that I had heard of Mr. Hawthorne's shyness, I thought it doubtful if he would call, and I was therefore very much pleased when his card was sent in this morning. Mr. Hawthorne was more chatty than I had expected, but not any more diffident. He remained about five minutes, during which time he took his hat from the table and put it back once a minute, brushing it each time. The engravings in the books are much like him. He is not handsome, but looks as the author of his books should look; a little strange and odd, as if not of this earth. He has large, bluish-gray eyes; his hair stands out on each side, so much so that one's thoughts naturally turn to combs and hair-brushes and toilet ceremonies as one looks at him.—

MITCHELL, MARIA, 1857, *Journal, Aug.* 5; *Life, Letters and Journals, ed. Kendall, p.* 89.

Alas! it was no "author's excuse" which was published in the *Atlantic*, but a most sad and serious truth. Mr. Hawthorne has really been very ill all winter, and not well, by any means, for a much longer time; not ill in bed, but miserable on a lounge or sofa, and quite unable to write a word, even a letter, and lately unable to read. I have felt the wildest anxiety about him, because he is a person who has been immaculately well all his life, and this illness has seemed to me an awful dream which could not be true. But he has wasted away very much, and the suns in his eyes are collapsed, and he has had no spirits, no appetite, and very little sleep. Richard was not himself, and his absolute repugnance to see a physician, or to have any scientific investigation of his indispositon, has weighed me down like a millstone. I have felt such a terrible oppression in thinking that all was not doing for his relief that might be done, that sometimes I have scarcely been able to endure it —at moments hardly able to fetch my breath in apprehension of the possible danger. But, thank Heaven, Mr. Ticknor has taken him out of this groove of existence, and intends to keep him away until he is better. He has been in New York at the Astor House since last Tuesday night, a week from to-day. I have had six letters, five from Mr. Ticknor, and one at last from my husband, written with a very tremulous hand, but with a cheerful spirit. . . . The state of our country has, doubtless, excessively depressed him. His busy imagination has woven all sorts of sad tissues. You know his indomitable, untamable spirit of independence and self-help. This makes the condition of an invalid peculiarly irksome to him. He is not a very manageable baby, because he has so long been a self-reliant man; but his innate sweetness serves him here, as in all things, and he is very patient and good.—HAWTHORNE, SOPHIA A., 1864, *Letter to Horatio Bridge, April 5; Personal Recollections of Nathaniel Hawthorne, pp.* 189, 191.

You will have seen, with profound sorrow the announcement of the death of the dearest and most cherished among our early friends. . . . He had been more or less infirm for more than a year. I had observed particularly within the last three or four months, evidences of diminished strength whenever we met. The journey, which was terminated by Mr. Ticknor's sudden death at Philadelphia, was commenced at the urgent solicitation of friends, who thought change essential for him. Mr. Ticknor's death would have been a great loss and serious shock to H. at any time, but the effect was undoubtedly aggravated by the suddenness of the event and H.'s enfeebled condition. About three weeks since I went to Concord (Mass.), and made arrangements to take a journey to the lakes, and thence up the Pemigewasset with my carriage, leaving time and details of the trip to be settled by circumstances *en route*. . . . We arrived at Plymouth about six o'clock. After taking a little tea and toast in his room, and sleeping for nearly an hour upon the sofa, he retired. A door opened from my room to his, and our beds were not more than five or six feet apart. I remained up an hour or two after he fell asleep. He was apparently less restless than the night before. The light was left burning in my room—the door open—and I could see him without moving from my bed. I went, however, between one and two o'clock to his bedside, and supposed him to be in a profound slumber. His eyes were closed, his position and face perfectly natural. His face was towards my bed. I awoke again between three and four o'clock, and was surprised—as he had generally been restless—to notice that his position was unchanged—exactly the same as it was two hours before. I went to his bedside, placed my hand upon his forehead and temple, and found that he was dead. He evidently had passed from natural sleep to sleep from which there is no waking, without suffering, and without the slightest movement.— PIERCE, FRANKLIN, 1864, *Letter to Horatio Bridge, May* 21; *Personal Recollections of Nathaniel Hawthorne, pp.* 176, 178.

Late in the afternoon of the day before he left Boston on his last journey I called upon him at the hotel where he was staying. He had gone out but a moment before. Looking along the street, I saw a form at some distance in advance which could only be his,—but how changed from his former port and figure! There was no mistaking the long iron-gray locks, the carriage of the head, and the general look of the natural outlines and movement; but he seemed to have shrunken in all his dimensions, and faltered along with an uncertain, feeble step,

as if every movement were an effort. I joined him, and we walked together half an hour, during which time I learned so much of his state of mind and body as could be got at without worrying him with suggestive questions,—my object being to form an opinion of his condition, as I had been requested to do, and to give him some hints that might be useful to him on his journey. His aspect, medically considered, was very unfavorable. There were persistent local symptoms, referred especially to the stomach,—"boring pain," distension, difficult digestion, with great wasting of flesh and strength. He was very gentle, very willing to answer questions, very docile to such counsel as I offered him, but evidently had no hope of recovering his health. He spoke as if his work were done, and he should write no more. With all his obvious depression, there was no failing noticeable in his conversational powers. There was the same backwardness and hesitancy which in his best days it was hard for him to overcome, so that talking with him was almost like love-making, and his shy, beautiful soul had to be wooed from its bashful prudence like an unschooled maiden. The calm despondency with which he spoke about himself confirmed the unfavorable opinion suggested by his look and history. —HOLMES, OLIVER WENDELL, 1864, *Hawthorne, Atlantic Monthly, vol.* 14, *p.* 99.

Now I look back, and meadow, manse, and stream
  Dimly my thought defines;
I only see—a dream within a dream—
  The hill-top hearsed with pines.
I only hear above his place of rest
  Their tender undertone,
The infinite longings of a troubled breast,
  The voice so like his own.
There in seclusion and remote from men
  The wizard hand lies cold,
Which at its topmost speed let fall the pen,
  And left the tale half told.
Ah! who shall lift that wand of magic power,
  And the lost clew regain?
The unfinished window in Aladdin's tower
  Unfinished must remain!
—LONGFELLOW, HENRY WADSWORTH,1864, *Hawthorne, Flower-de-Luce, Poetical Works, Cambridge Ed., p.* 289.

Your father was lame a long time from an injury received while playing bat-and-ball. His foot pined away, and was considerably smaller than the other. He had every doctor that could be heard of; among the rest, your grandfather Peabody. But it was "Dr.

Time" who at last cured him. I remember he used to lie upon the floor and read, and that he went upon two crutches. Everybody thought that, if he lived, he would be always lame. Mr. Joseph E. Worcester, the author of the "Dictionary," who at one time taught a school, in Salem, to which your father went, was very kind to him; he came every evening to hear him repeat his lessons. It was during this long lameness that he acquired his habit of constant reading. Undoubtedly he would have wanted many of the qualities which distinguished him in after life, if his genius had not been thus shielded in childhood.—HAWTHORNE, ELIZABETH, 1865 (?), *Letter to Una Hawthorne, Nathaniel Hawthorne and his Wife*, ed. *Hawthorne, vol.* I, *p.* 100.

This marked love of cases of conscience, this taciturn, scornful cast of mind; this habit of seeing sin everywhere, and hell always gaping open; this dusky gaze bent always upon a damned world, and a nature draped in mourning; these lonely conversations of the imagination with the conscience; this pitiless analysis resulting from a perpetual examination of one's self, and from the tortures of a heart closed before men and open to God—all these elements of the Puritan character have passed into Mr. Hawthorne, or, to speak more justly, have filtered into him, through a long succession of generations.—MONTÉGUT, EMILE, 1866, *Contes étranges imités d'Hawthorne par E. A. Spoll, précédés d'une étuade.*

Hawthorne was of the darker temperament and tendencies. His sensitiveness and sadness were native, and he cultivated them apparently alike by solitude, the pursuits and studies in which he indulged, till he became almost fated to know gayer hours only by stealth. By disposition friendly, he seemed the victim of his temperament, as if he sought distance, if not his pen, to put himself in communication and possible sympathy with others, with his nearest friends even. His reserve and imprisonment were more distant and close, while the desire for conversation was livelier, than any one I have known. There was something of strangeness even in his cherished intimacies, as if he set himself afar from all and from himself with the rest. The most diffident of men, as coy as a maiden, he could only be won by some cunning artifice, his reserve was so habitual, his isolation so entire, the solitude so vast. How distant people were

from him, the world they lived in, how he came to know so much about them, by what stratagem he got into his own house or left it, was a marvel. Fancy-fixed, he was not to be jostled from himself for a moment, his mood was so persistent. There he was in the twilight, there he stayed.—ALCOTT, A. BRONSON, 1869, *Concord Days, p.* 193.

No man had more of the feminine element than he. He was feminine in his quick perceptions, his fine insight, his sensibility to beauty, his delicate reserve, his purity of feeling. No man comprehended woman more perfectly; none has painted woman with a more exquisite and ethereal pencil. And his face was as mobile and rapid in its changes of expression as is the face of a young girl. His lip and cheek heralded the word before it was spoken. His eyes would darken visibly under the touch of a passing emotion, like the waters of a fountain ruffled by the breeze of summer. — HILLARD, GEORGE S., 1870, *The English Note-Books of Nathaniel Hawthorne, Atlantic Monthly, vol.* 26, *p.* 258.

A most genial and original man, full of life, full of humour, in no respect shy. He agreed at once to pass a day with me. I gave him the option of a party or no party. He chose the latter alternative. A pleasanter day than the one in question is not in my "Golden" Book. I think I have never heard any one, save my honoured friend Carlyle, laugh so heartily as did Hawthorne. It is generally a nervous business to receive those to whom one has long looked up; but it was not the least so in his case. The impression I received was one of a man genial, and not over sensitive, even when we could make merry on the subject of national differences and susceptibilities.—CHORLEY, HENRY FOTHERGILL, 1870, *Autobiography, Memoirs and Letters,* ed. *Hewlett, vol.* II, *p.* 247.

The rarest genius America has given to literature,—a man who lately sojourned in this busy world of ours, but during many years of his life

"Wandered lonely as a cloud,"—

a man who had, so to speak, a physical affinity with solitude. . . . His religion was deep and broad, but it was irksome for him to be fastened in by a pew-door, and I doubt if he heard often an English sermon. He very rarely described himself as *inside* a church, but he liked to wander among the graves in the churchyards and read the epitaphs on the moss-grown slabs.   He liked better to meet and have a talk with the *sexton* than with the *rector.* . . . He was unlike any other author I have met, and there were qualities in his nature so sweet and commendable, that, through all his shy reserve, they sometimes asserted themselves in a marked and conspicuous manner.   I have known rude people, who were jostling him in a crowd, give way at the sound of his low and almost irresolute voice, so potent was the gentle spell of command that seemed born of his genius.— FIELDS, JAMES T., 1871, *Yesterdays with Authors, pp.* 41, 74, 87.

Hawthorne's superb head was by all odds the finest in the room.   He looked genial, and, *mirabile dictu!* appeared at his ease.   To me, who had not seen him since he lived at Lenox, in Massachusetts, this transformation appeared marvelous.   I sat down by his side, and he talked brilliantly for half an hour, without exhibiting any of the shyness which for years had made him a perfect recluse.   It was said that he was still unapproachable in his Consulate at Liverpool, but he appeared completely humanized at Mrs. Hall's.—FIELD, MAUN-SELL B., 1873, *Memoirs of Many Men and Some Women, p.* 145.

A simple stone, with the single word "Hawthorne" cut upon it, was placed above him.   He had wished that there should be no monument.   He liked Words-worth's grave at Grasmere, and had writ-ten: "It is pleasant to think and know that he did not care for a stately monument." Longfellow and Lowell and Holmes, Emer-son and Louis Agassiz, and his friends Pierce, and Hillard, with Ellery Channing, and other famous men, assembled on that peaceful morning to take their places in the funeral train. . . . The orchards were blossoming; the roadside-banks were blue with violets, and the lilies of the valley, which were Hawthorne's favorites among the flowers, had come forth in quiet com-panies to look their last on his face, so white and quiet too.   So, while the batteries that had murdered him roared sullenly in the distant South, the rites of burial were ful-filled over the dead poet.   Like a clear voice beside the grave, as we look back and listen, Longfellow's simple penetrating chant re-turns upon the ear.—LATHROP, GEORGE PARSONS, 1876, *A Study of Hawthorne, p.* 325.

The author's college life was prophetic of the after years, when he so dwelt apart from the mass of men, and yet stirred so deeply the world's sensibilities and delighted its fancy.   His themes were written in the sustained, finished style that gives to his mature productions an inimitable charm. The late Professor Newman, his instructor in rhetoric, was so impressed with Haw-thorne's powers as a writer, that he, not in-frequently, summoned the family circle to share in the enjoyment of reading his com-positions.   The recollection is very distinct of Hawthorne's reluctant step and averted look, when he presented himself at the Pro-fessor's study, and with girlish diffidence submitted a composition which no man in his class could equal.—PACKARD, GEORGE THOMAS, 1876, *Bowdoin College, Scribner's Monthly, vol.* 12, *p.* 52.

The beauty of his countenance was re-markable.   Crayon portraits and photo-graphs preserve the fine outline of his head and face, but fail to give his vivid coloring and varying expression.   His eyes, fringed with dark lashes, gleamed like tremulous sapphires.   Whenever their look encount-ered mine, they seemed to say: "This sens-itive soul prays the world not to be rough or rude." — HOWE, JULIA WARD, 1881, *Two Glimpses of Hawthorne, The Critic, vol.* 1, *p.* 158.

Colonel Higginson mentions Hawthorne's gray eyes; while the present writer, who once studied them attentively, found them mottled gray and brown, and at that time indescribably soft and winning.   That they were sometimes *accipitral* we can readily be-lieve.—UNDERWOOD, FRANCIS H., 1882, *James Russell Lowell, a Biographical Sketch, p.* 150.

That most lovable of writers was also—to those who knew him intimately—one of the most lovable of men.   My acquaintance with him was slight; but it has left on my mind a vivid impression of his painful shyness in general society, and the retiring—nay, mor-bid delicacy—with which he shrank from notice, instead of courting, or rather com-manding, it, as was the manner of his brother-novelist.—HALL, SAMUEL CARTER, 1883, *Retrospect of a Long Life, p.* 420.

She [Mrs. Nathaniel Hawthorne] believed in his inspiration; and her office was to pro-mote, so far as in her lay, the favorableness of the conditions under which it should manifest itself.   As food and repose nourish

and refresh the body, so did she refresh and
nourish her husband's mind and heart. Her
feminine intuition corresponded to his masculine insight; she felt the truth that he
saw; and his recognition of this pure faculty
in her, and his reverence for it, endowed his
preception with that tender humanity in
which otherwise it might have been deficient. Her lofty and assured ideals kept
him to a belief in the reality and veracity of
his own. In the warmth and light of such
companionship as hers, he could not fall
into the coldness and gloom of a selfish intellectual habit. She revived his confidence
and courage by the touch of her gentle
humor and cheerfulness; before her unshak-
able hopefulness and serenity, his constitutional tendency to ill-foreboding and discouragement vanished away. Nor was she
of less value to him on the merely intellectual side. Her mental faculties were finely
balanced and of great capacity; her taste
was by nature highly refined, and was rendered exquisitely so by cultivation. . . Mr.
Hawthorne never was a teetotaler, any
more than he was an abolitionist or a thug;
but he was invariably temperate. During
his lifetime he smoked something like half a
dozen boxes of cigars, and drank as much
wine and spirits as would naturally accompany that amount of tobacco. Months and
sometimes years would pass without his
either drinking or smoking at all; but when
he would resume those practices, it was not
to "make up for lost time," his moderation was not influenced by his abstention.
Though very tolerant of excesses in others,
he never permitted them in himself; and his
conduct in this respect was the result not
more of moral prejudice than of temperamental aversion. He would have been sober if he had had no morality.— HAW-
THORNE, JULIAN, 1885, *Nathaniel Hawthorne and His Wife, vol.* I, *pp.* 40, 87.

May his memory be forever loved and
honored, in the annals of this our country,
for his goodness to Delia Bacon!—DON-
NELLY, IGNATIUS, 1889, *Delia Bacon's Unhappy Story, North American Review, vol.*
148, *p.* 317.

There are few authors with whom the
world is more intimate than the one supposed to have most shunned its intimacy.
But Nathaniel Hawthorne, though his peculiar sensibility shrank from men, loved
mankind, and described his earliest writings
as "attempts to open an intercourse with

the world." In his works he has occasionally taken the world into his confidence in
matters which most men of the world would
veil—as in the opening chapter of "The
Scarlet Letter." Like his own Hilda, in
"Transformation," he was spiritually compelled to descend from his aërial hermitage,
and unburden his heart in the world's con-
fessional.—CONWAY, MONCURE DANIEL,
1890, *Life of Nathaniel Hawthorne (Great
Writers), p.* 9.

As the chairman of the Salem Lyceum, it
was my privilege to entertain such men as
R. W. Emerson, George W. Curtis and
others. Thomas Starr King, when he lectured in Danvers, drove over to my house
and spent the rest of the evening. Nathaniel Hawthorne I used to meet frequently on the street. I often saw Mrs.
Hawthorne leading her children by the
hand. Mr. Hawthorne, who was in Salem
from 1846 to 1849, was remarkable for his
shyness. His favorite companions were
some Democratic politicians, who met
weekly at the office of one of them, where he
occupied himself in listening to their talk,
but he avoided cultivated people. On one
occasion a friend of mine asked us to meet
him at dinner; twice he went to remind his
guest of the engagement. The hour arrived,
the dinner was kept waiting half an hour
for Mr. Hawthorne to come. He said but
little during the dinner, and immediately
afterward got up and went away; his reluctance to meet people overcoming his
sense of propriety.—FROTHINGHAM, OCTA-
VIUS BROOKS, 1891, *Recollections and Impressions, p.* 42.

Hawthorne used to stay at Bixby's.* He
was a moody man, who sat by the stove and
spoke to no one.—LELAND, CHARLES GOD-
FREY, 1893, *Memoirs, p.* 204.

Hawthorne was a slender lad, having a
massive head, with dark, brilliant, and
most expressive eyes, heavy eyebrows, and
a profusion of dark hair. . . . Hawthorne's
figure was somewhat singular, owing to his
carrying his head a little on one side; but
his walk was square and firm, and his manner self-respecting and reserved. A fashionable boy of the present day might have seen
something to amuse him in the new student's appearance; but had he indicated
this he would have rued it, for Hawthorne's
clear appreciation of the social proprieties
and his great physical courage would have

* A hotel in New York.

made it as unsafe to treat him with discourtesy then as at any later time. Though quiet and most amiable, he had great pluck and determination.—BRIDGE, HORATIO, 1893, *Personal Recollections of Nathaniel Hawthorne, pp.* 4, 5.

But I desire to speak of Nathaniel Hawthorne as I remember him about 1854, rather than presume to be his critic. In society he was one of the most painfully shy men I ever knew. I never had the privilege of an unbroken *tête-à-tête* with him, and am under the impression that with a single listener he must have been a very interesting talker; but in the small social circle in which I first met him—it was at the house of Mr. Bennoch to whom I have before alluded—it really seemed impossible to draw him out. We were only five or six intimate friends, sitting round the fire, and with a host remarkable for his geniality and tact; but Hawthorne fidgeted on the sofa, seemed really to have little to say, and almost resented the homage that was paid to him. Though I say this, my reverence for him and admiration of his genius remain unchanged, for the true man is in his works— there he reveals himself as the deep thinker, the true philosopher, the charitable sympathizer with his fellow-creatures—in short, the prose-poet.—CROSLAND, MRS. NEWTON, (CAMILLA TOULMIN), 1893. *Landmarks of a Literary Life, p.* 211.

Abutting upon the back yard of Hawthorne's birthplace is the old Manning homestead of his maternal ancestors, the home of his own youth and middle age and the theatre of his struggles and triumph. It is known as number twelve Herbert Street, and is a tall, unsightly, erratic fabric of wood, with nothing pleasing or gracious in its aspect or environment. The ugly and commonplace character of his surroundings here during half his life must have been peculiarly depressing to such a sensitive temperament as Hawthorne's, and doubtless accounts for his mental habits. That he had no joyous memories of this old house his letters and journals abundantly show. Its interior arrangement has been somewhat changed to accommodate the several families of laborers who have since inhabited it, and one front room seems to have been used as a shop; but it is not difficult to identify the haunted chamber which was Hawthorne's bed-room and study. This little, dark, dreary apartment under the eaves,

with its multipaned window looking down into the room where he was born, is to us one of the most interesting of all the Hawthorne shrines. Here the magician kept his solitary vigil during the long period of his literary probation, shunning his family, declining all human sympathy and fellowship, for some time going abroad only after nightfall; here he studied, pondered, wrote, revised, destroyed, day after day as the slow months went by; and here, after ten years of working and waiting for the world to know him, he triumphantly recorded, "In this dismal chamber FAME was won." Here he wrote "Twice-Told Tales" and many others, which were published in various periodicals, and here, after his residence at the old Manse,—for it was to this Manning house that he "always came back, like the bad halfpenny," as he said,—he completed the "Mosses." This old dwelling is one of the several which have been fixed upon as being the original "House of the Seven Gables," despite the novelist's averment that the Pyncheon mansion was "of materials long in use for constructing castles in the air."—WOLFE, THEODORE F., 1895, *Literary Shrines, p.* 131.

If Thoreau was a recluse, Hawthorne was an anchorite. He brought up his children in such purity and simplicity as is scarcely credible,—not altogether a wise plan. It was said that he did not even take a daily paper. In the following year Martin F. Conway, the first United States representative from Kansas, went to Concord to call on Emerson, and Emerson invited Hawthorne to dine with them. Judge Conway afterwards remarked that Mr. Hawthorne said very little during the dinner, and whenever he spoke be blushed. Imagine a man five times as sensitive as a young lady in her first season, with the will of a Titan, and a mind like a crown-glass mirror, and you have Nathaniel Hawthorne. While he was in a state of observation, the expression of his face reflected everything that was going on about him; in his reflective moods, it was like looking in at the window of a dark room, or perhaps a picture-gallery; and if any accident disturbed him his look was something like a cracked pane of glass. Moreover there was something unearthly or superterrestrial about him, as if he had been born and brought up in the planet Saturn. Wherever he went he seemed to carry twilight with him. He walked in perfect silence, looking furtively about for fear he might meet some one that he knew. His large frame and strong physique ought to have lasted him till the year 1900. There would seem to be something strange and mysterious about his death, as there was in his life. His head was massive, and his face handsome without being attractive. The brow was finely chiseled, and the eyes beneath it were dark, luminous and fathomless. I never saw him smile, except slightly with his eyes. — STEARNS, FRANK PRESTON, 1895, *Sketches from Concord and Appledore, p.* 54.

It seemed to me a terrible thing that one so peculiarly strong, sentient, luminous, as my father should grow feebler and fainter, and finally ghostly still and white. Yet when his step was tottering and his frame that of a wraith, he was as dignified as in the days of greater pride, holding himself, in military self-command, even more erect than before. He did not omit to come in his very best black coat to the dinner-table, where the extremely prosaic fare had no effect upon the distinction of the meal. He hated failure, dependence, and disorder, broken rules and weariness of discipline, as he hated cowardice. I cannot express how brave he seemed to me. The last time I saw him, he was leaving the house to take the journey for his health which led suddenly to the next world. My mother was to go to the station with him,—and she who, at the moment when it was said that he died, staggered and groaned, though so far from him, telling us that something seemed to be sapping all her strength; I could hardly bear to let my eyes rest upon her shrunken, suffering form on this day of farewell. My father certainly knew, what she vaguely felt, that he would never return. Like a snow image of an unbending but an old, old man, he stood for a moment gazing at me. My mother sobbed, as she walked beside him to the carriage. We have missed him in the sunshine, in the storm, in the twilight, ever since.—LATHROP, ROSE HAWTHORNE, 1897, *Memories of Hawthorne, p.* 480.

His son Julian, though eighteen years old when his father died, read none of Hawthorne's books until after that time, and then could not understand how such a man as the father he had known was their author.—HOWE, M. A. DEWOLFE, 1897–98, *American Bookmen, p.* 201.

I had the honor of meeting with the distinguished author for the first time. . . . The time was April of 1853; a journey southward had brought me to Willard's Hotel in Washington. Hawthorne was a fellow-lodger, in company with his cheery publisher William D. Ticknor. . . . Mr. Hawthorne was then nearing fifty—strong, erect, broad-shouldered, alert—his abundant hair touched with gray, his features all cast in Greek mould and his fine eyes full of searchingness, and yet of kindliness; his voice deep, with a weighty resounding quality, as if bearing echoes of things unspoken; no arrogance, no assurance even, but rather there hung about his manner and his speech a cloud of self-distrust, of *mal-aise,* as if he were on the defensive in respect of his own quietudes, and determined to rest there. Withal, it was a winning shyness; and when —somewhat later—his jolly friend Ticknor tapped him on the shoulder, and told him how some lad wanted to be presented, there was something painful in the abashed manner with which the famous author waited a school-boy's homage—cringing under such contact with conventional usage, as a school-girl might.—MITCHELL, DONALD G., 1899, *American Lands and Letters, Leather-Stocking to Poe's "Raven," p.* 244.

The news of Mrs. Hawthorne's death reminded me of a happy evening spent beneath the roof of that most gracious and lovable woman, at a time when for me to visit Hawthorne's house was to make a pilgrimage to a shrine. . . . After their children had left us for the night, we sat and talked together; or rather I questioned and she answered, telling me of her husband's home life and also of his intercourse with strangers; saying, what touched but did not surprise me, that men who had committed great crimes or whose memories held tragic secrets would sometimes write to him or would even come great distances to see him, and unburden their souls. This was after the publication of the "Scarlet Letter," which made them regard him as the father-confessor for all hidden sins. . . . She said that it was not her husband's custom to sit with her while he wrote, or to tell her about any literary work till it was finished, but that then he was always impatient to read it to her. In writing the "Wonder-Book," to be sure, he liked to read his day's work to the children in the evening, by way of test.—HIGGINSON,

THOMAS WENTWORTH, 1899, *An Evening with Mrs. Hawthorne, Contemporaries, pp.* 102, 104.

The door was opened to my ring by a tall, handsome boy whom I suppose to have been Mr. Julian Hawthorne; and the next moment I found myself in the presence of the romancer, who entered from some room beyond. He advanced carrying his head with a heavy forward droop, and with a pace for which I decided that the word would be *pondering.* It was the pace of a bulky man of fifty, and his head was that beautiful head we all know from the many pictures of it. But Hawthorne's *look* was different from that of any picture of him that I have seen. It was sombre and brooding, as the look of such a poet should have been; it was the look of a man who had dealt faithfully and therefore sorrowfully with that problem of evil which forever attracted, forever evaded Hawthorne. . . . In the face that confronted me there was nothing of keen alertness; but only a sort of quiet, patient intelligence, for which I seek the right word in vain. It was a very regular face, with beautiful eyes; the mustache, still entirely dark, was dense over the fine mouth. Hawthorne was dressed in black, and he had a certain effect which I remember, of seeming to have on a black cravat with no visible collar. He was such a man that if I had ignorantly met him anywhere I should have instantly felt him to be a personage. . . . My memory of him is without alloy one of the finest pleasures of my life. In my heart I paid him the glad homage that I paid Lowell and Holmes, and he did nothing to make me think that I had overpaid him. This seems perhaps very little to say in his praise, but to my mind it is saying everything, for I have known but few great men, especially of those I met in early life, when I wished to lavish my admiration upon them, whom I have not the impression of having left in my debt.— HOWELLS, WILLIAM DEAN, 1900, *Literary Friends and Acquaintance, pp.* 51, 52, 55.

Proud was the day for Berkshire which added the name of Nathaniel Hawthorne to the roll of those who have caused the lustre of their achievement to shine resplendently upon the country they honored, and proud will be the day when the hallowed site of the red house by the lake where Hawthorne wrought some of his mightiest creations shall be appropriately marked with some memorial to this master workman.—MALLORY, R. DEWITT, 1902, *Lenox and the Berkshire Highlands, p.* 160.

FANSHAWE
1828

"Fanshawe" is a work which derives its interest wholly from the author's later masterpieces. It has the slightest possible plot, and the characters are imperfectly presented, the descriptions are commonplace to the verge of tameness, yet one who reads the story carefully will easily detect the weak and timid presence of all Hawthorne's peculiar powers.—TAYLOR, BAYARD, 1876, *Nathaniel Hawthorne, Critical Essays and Literary Notes, p.* 355.

"Fanshawe" was published in 1828 by Marsh and Capen, at Boston, without the author's name but at his expense, one hundred dollars being the sum paid; it failed, and Hawthorne looked on it with so much subsequent displeasure that he called in all the copies he could find and destroyed them, and thus nearly succeeded in sinking the book in oblivion, but the few copies which survived secured its republication after his death. The novel is brief, with a melodramatic plot, well-marked scenes, and strongly contrasted character; the style flows on pleasantly; but the book is without distinction. . . . In fact, notwithstanding what Hawthorne had taken from his own observation and feelings, this provincial sketch, for it is no more, is a Scott story, done with a young man's clever mastery of the manner, but weak internally in plot, character, and dramatic reality. It is as destitute of any brilliant markings of his genius as his undergraduate life itself had been, and is important only as showing the serious care with which he undertook the task of authorship.—WOODBERRY, GEORGE E., 1902, *Nathaniel Hawthorne (American Men of Letters), pp.* 31, 32.

TWICE TOLD TALES
1837-42-52

It is a singular fact that, of the few American writers by profession, one of the very best is a gentleman whose name has never yet been made public, though his writings are extensively and favorably known. We refer to Nathaniel Hawthorne, Esq., of Salem, the author of the "Gentle Boy," the "Gray Champion," etc., etc., all productions of high merit, which have appeared in the annuals and magazines of the last three or four years. Liberally educated, but bred to no profession, he has devoted himself exclusively to literary pursuits, with an ardor and success which will, ere long, give him a high place among the scholars of this country. His style is classical and pure; his imagination exceedingly delicate and fanciful, and through all his writings there runs a vein of sweetest poetry. Perhaps we have no writer so deeply imbued with the early literature of America; or who can so well portray the times and manners of the Puritans.—BRIDGE, HORATIO, 1836, *For Boston Post, Personal Recollections of Nathaniel Hawthorne, p.* 70.

When a new star rises in the heavens, people gaze after it for a season with the naked eye, and with such telescopes as they may find. In the stream of thought, which flows so peacefully deep and clear, through the pages of this book, we see the bright reflection of a spiritual star, after which men will be fain to gaze "with the naked eye and with the spy-glasses of criticism." This star is but newly risen; and ere long the observations of numerous star-gazers, perched up on arm-chairs and editors' tables, will inform the world of its magnitude and its place in the heaven of poetry, whether it be in the paw of the Great Bear, or on the forehead of Pegasus, or on the strings of the Lyre, or in the wing of the Eagle. Our own observations are as follows. To this little work we would say, "Live ever, sweet, sweet book." It comes from the hand of a man of genius. Everything about it has the freshness of morning and of May. These flowers and green leaves of poetry have not the dust of the highway upon them. They have been gathered fresh from the secret places of a peaceful and gentle heart. There flow deep waters, silent, calm, and cool; and the green trees look into them, and "God's blue heaven." The book, though in prose, is written nevertheless by a poet. He looks upon all things in the spirit of love, and with lively sympathies; for to him external form is but the representation of internal being, all things having a life, an end and aim.—LONGFELLOW, HENRY WADSWORTH, 1837, *Hawthorne's Twice Told Tales, North American Review, vol.* 45, *p.* 59.

Of Mr. Hawthorne's "Tales" we would say, emphatically, that they belong to the highest region of Art—an Art subservient to genius of a very lofty order. — POE, EDGAR ALLAN, 1842, *Literary Criticism,*

Works, ed. Stedman and Woodberry, vol. VII, *p.* 33.

From the press of Munroe & Co., Boston, in the year 1837, appeared "Twice-Told Tales." Though not widely successful in their day and generation, they had the effect of making me known in my own immediate vicinity; insomuch that, however reluctantly, I was compelled to come out of my owl's nest and lionize in a small way. Thus I was gradually drawn somewhat into the world, and became pretty much like other people. My long seclusion had not made me melancholy or misanthropic, nor wholly unfitted for the bustle of life; and perhaps it was the kind of discipline which my idiosyncrasy demanded, and chance and my own instincts, operating together, had caused me to do what was fittest.—HAWTHORNE, NATHANIEL, 1853, *Letter to Richard Henry Stoddard, Nathaniel Hawthorne and His Wife, ed. Hawthorne, vol.* I, *p.* 98.

First, then, on this special shelf stand Nathaniel Hawthorne's "Twice - Told Tales." It is difficult to explain why I like these short sketches and essays, written in the author's early youth, better than his later, more finished, and better-known novels and romances. The world sets greater store by "The Scarlet Letter" and "Transformation" than by this little book —and, in such matters of liking against the judgment of the world, there is no appeal. I think the reason of my liking consists in this—that the novels were written for the world, while the tales seem written for the author; in these he is actor and audience in one. Consequently, one gets nearer him, just as one gets nearer an artist in his first sketch than in his finished picture.—SMITH, ALEXANDER, 1863, *Dreamthorp, p.* 190.

His bitterness is without abatement, and his bad opinion of man is without compensation. . . . His little tales have the air of confessions which the soul makes to itself, they are so many little slaps which the author applies to our face.—MONTÉGUT, EMILE, 1866, *Contes étranges imités d'Hawthorne par E. A. Spoll, précédés d'une étude.*

There is a propriety in Hawthorne's fantasy to which Poe could not attain. Hawthorne's effects are moral where Poe's are merely physical. The situation and its logical development and the effects to be got out of it are all Poe thinks of. In Hawthorne the situation, however strange and weird, is only the outward and visible sign of an inward and spiritual struggle. Ethical consequences are always worrying Hawthorne's soul; but Poe did not know that there were any ethics.—MATTHEWS, BRANDER, 1888, *Pen and Ink*, p. 79.

MOSSES FROM AN OLD MANSE
1846

Hawthorne walked with me yesterday afternoon, and not until after our return did I read his "Celestial Railroad," which has a serene strength which we cannot afford not to praise, in this low life.—EMERSON, RALPH WALDO, 1843, *Letter to Thoreau; Familiar Letters of Thoreau, ed. Sanborn*, p. 143.

In description, narration, allegory, humor, reason, fancy, subtlety, inventiveness, they exceed the best productions of Addison; but they want Addison's sensuous contentment, and sweet and kindly spirit.—WHIPPLE, EDWIN PERCY, 1860, *Nathaniel Hawthorne, Character and Characteristic Men*, p. 225.

Such concentration of frightful truth do these most graceful and exquisitely-wrought creations contain, that the intensity becomes almost poisonous. — LATHROP, GEORGE PARSONS, 1876, *A Study of Hawthorne*, p. 203.

The truth of these sketches is their prime quality, for Hawthorne wrote them with the familiar affection and home-attachment of one who had fleeted the golden time of his youth amid these scenes of common day, and prolonged it far into manhood, and should never quite lose its glow of mere existence, its kindliness for humble things, its generous leisure for the perishable beauty of nature dotted here and there with human life.—WOODBERRY, GEORGE E., 1902, *Nathaniel Hawthorne (American Men of Letters)*, p. 129.

THE SCARLET LETTER
1850

We are glad that "The Scarlet Letter" is, after all, little more than an experiment and need not be regarded as a step necessarily fatal. It is an attempt to rise from the composition of petty tales, to the historical novel; and we use the expression *an attempt*, with no disparaging significance, for it is confessedly a trial of strength only just beyond some former efforts, and was designed as part of a series. It may properly be called a novel, because it has all the ground-work, and might have been very easily elaborated into the details, usually included in the term; and we call it *historical*, because its scene-painting is in a great degree true to a period of our Colonial history, which ought to be more fully delineated. We wish Mr. Hawthorne would devote the powers which he only partly discloses in this book, to a large and truthful portraiture of that period, with the patriotic purpose of making us better acquainted with the stern old worthies, and all the *dramatis personæ* of those times, with their yet surviving habits, recollections, and yearnings, derived from maternal England.—COXE, ARTHUR CLEVELAND, 1851, *The Writings of Hawthorne, The Church Review, vol. 3*, p. 503.

The frivolous costume and brisk action of the story of fashionable life are easily depicted by the practised sketcher, but a work like "The Scarlet Letter" comes slowly upon the canvas, where passions are commingled and overlaid with the masterly elaboration with which the grandest effects are produced in pictorial composition and coloring. It is a distinction of such works that while they are acceptable to the many, they also surprise and delight the few who appreciate the nicest arrangement and the most high and careful finish. "The Scarlet Letter" will challenge consideration in the name of Art, in the best audience which in any age receives Cervantes, Le Sage, or Scott.—GRISWOLD, RUFUS WILMOT, 1851, *Nathaniel Hawthorne, International Magazine, vol. 3*, p. 157.

These excellent writers have been long before the public; but a new star has lately sprung into light in the Western horizon, who in a totally different manner—and nothing is more remarkable among all these American novelists than their utter difference from each other—will hardly fail to cast a bright illumination over both hemispheres. It is hardly two years since Mr. Hawthorne until then known only by one or two of those little volumes which the sagacious hold as promise of future excellence, put forth that singular book, "The Scarlet Letter," *àpropos* to which, Dr. Holmes, who so well knows the value of words, uses this significant expression:

I *snatch* the book, along whose burning leaves
His scarlet web our wild romancer weaves.

And it is the very word. We do *snatch* the book; and, until we have got to the end, very few of us, I apprehend, have sufficient strength of will to lay it down. . . . Detestable as the husband is and with all the passionate truth that Mr. Hawthorne has thrown into the long agony of the seducer, we never, in our pity for the sufferer, lose our abhorrence of the sin.—MITFORD, MARY RUSSELL, 1851, *Recollections of a Literary Life, pp.* 517, 518.

It is admirably written. Not having any great sympathy with a custom-house—nor, indeed, with Salem, except that it seems to be Hawthorne's birth-place—all my attention was concentrated on the *style,* which seems to me excellent.—PROCTER, BRYAN WALLER, 1853, *Letter to James T. Fields, "Barry Cornwall" and some of His Friends, Harper's Magazine, vol.* 52, *p.* 59.

With all the care in point of style and authenticity which mark his lighter sketches, this genuine and unique romance may be considered as an artistic exposition of Puritanism as modified by New England colonial life. In truth to costume, local manners, and scenic features, the "Scarlet Letter" is as reliable as the best of Scott's novels; in the anatomy of human passion and consciousness it resembles the most effective of Balzac's illustrations of Parisian or provincial life; while in developing bravely and justly the sentimental of the life it depicts, it is as true to humanity as Dickens.—TUCKERMAN, HENRY T., 1853, *The Prose Poet; Nathaniel Hawthorne, Mental Portraits.*

It presents more vividly than any history the gloomy picturesqueness of early New England life. There is no stain in our literature so characteristic or more real than that which Hawthorne has successfully attempted in several of his earlier sketches, and of which "The Scarlet Letter" is the great triumph. It became immediately popular, and directly placed the writer of stories for a small circle among the world's masters of romance.—CURTIS, GEORGE WILLIAM, 1854–94, *Homes of American Authors, Literary and Social Essays, p.* 49.

Speaking of Thackeray, I cannot but wonder at his coolness in respect to his own pathos, and compare it with my emotions, when I read the last scene of "The Scarlet Letter" to my wife just after writing it,— tried to read it rather, for my voice swelled and heaved, as if I were tossed up and down on an ocean as it subsides after a storm. But I was in a very nervous state then, having gone through a great diversity of emotion, while writing it, for many months. I think I have never overcome my own adamant in any other instance.— HAWTHORNE, NATHANIEL, 1855, *English Note-Books, vol.* I.

There is something extraordinarily fascinating in this book; we read on even while we shrink from it. The mystery of the poor woman, Hester Prynne,—she who wears the badge of disgrace,—stands prominent in every page; in strange contrast with her elfin child, little Pearl. We hang over that remarkable scene between the faithless priest and the guilty woman in the deep shadow of the primeval forest—while the mysterious child plays near at hand by the brookside, with a deeply riveted interest. Then that picture of the wronged husband, silently pursuing his revenge— how terrible it is! Yet, harrowing though the subject be, there is nothing prurient or feverish about it. The whole story is told with a simple power. The work is pure, severe, and truthful; and it holds every reader in thrall until the end of the dark story is reached.—SMILES, SAMUEL, 1860, *Brief Biographies, p.* 266.

It may be said that it "captivated" nobody, but took everybody captive. Its power could neither be denied nor resisted. There were growls of disapprobation from novel-readers, that Hester Prynne and the Rev. Mr. Dimmesdale were subjected to cruel punishments unknown to the jurisprudence of fiction,—that the author was an inquisitor who put his victims on the rack,—and that neither amusement nor delight resulted from seeing the contortions and hearing the groans of these martyrs of sin; but the fact was no less plain that Hawthorne had for once compelled the most superficial lovers of romance to submit themselves to the magic of his genius.— WHIPPLE, EDWIN PERCY, 1860, *Nathaniel Hawthorne, Character and Characteristic Men, p.* 227.

I believe and am sure that "The Scarlet Letter" will endure as long as the language in which it is written; and should that language become dead, the wonderful work will be translated. Mr. S. C. Hall says I am to tell you that your works will live when marble crumbles into dust. I can well understand that even genius stands breathless in silence, watching events; still, master you must send us forth some fresh enchantment ere long, though you have done so much. Forgive my freedom, dear Mr. Hawthorne, and imagine me the reader you speak of in the preface to "Transformation."—AIKIN, BERKELEY (FANNY AIKIN KORTRIGHT), 1862, Letter to Hawthorne, Nathaniel Hawthorne and His Wife, ed. Hawthorne, vol. II, p. 305.

We behold in it the greatest embodiment of remorse ever achieved. Terrible in its gloom, the spirit of the reader asks again and again for some relief. Even the writer of it had experienced the same feeling, but found it impossible to relieve the shadow of the story with so much light as he would gladly have thrown in.—SMITH, GEORGE BARNETT, 1875, Nathaniel Hawthorne, Poets and Novelists, p. 174.

"The Scarlet Letter" is, on the English side of the water, perhaps the best known. It is so terrible in its pictures of diseased human nature as to produce most questionable delight. The reader's interest never flags for a moment. There is nothing of episode or digression. The author is always telling his one story with a concentration of energy which, as we can understand, must have made it impossible for him to deviate. The reader will certainly go on with it to the end very quickly, entranced, excited, shuddering, and at times almost wretched. —TROLLOPE, ANTHONY, 1879, The Genius of Nathaniel Hawthorne, North American Review, vol. 129, p. 208.

It is densely dark, with a single spot of vivid color in it; and it will probably long remain the most consistently gloomy of English novels of the first order. But I just now called it the author's masterpiece, and I imagine it will continue to be, for other generations than ours, his most substantial title to fame. . . . The faults of the book are, to my sense, a want of reality and an abuse of the fanciful element—of a certain superficial symbolism. The people strike me not as characters, but as representatives, very picturesquely arranged, of a single state of mind; and the interest of the story lies, not in them, but in the situation, which is insistently kept before us, with little progression, though with a great deal, as I have said, of a certain stable variation; and to which they, out of their reality, contribute little that helps it to live and move. —JAMES HENRY, 1880, Hawthorne (English Men of Letters), pp. 106, 110.

In the concluding chapter of this, the most profound, the boldest, the most riveting analytical romance of our tongue, in our century—followed, I think, at an interval by "Wuthering Heights," and by "Silas Marner"—the author goes farther, and trenches on the ground of George Sand's "Lelia" and Goethe's "Elective Affinities."—NICHOL, JOHN, 1882-85, American Literature, p. 339.

As a mere story, it is not altogether cheerful reading; a nameless feeling of melancholy, an indefinable foreboding, a consciousness of supernatural influence, seems to follow us—we cannot explain why—from the very beginning. But we would search long ere we should find a story constructed with more artistic skill, with purer graces of style, more refined in sentiment, superior in characterization and delicate psychological insight. It is the book for the student, the thinker, the artist; but to the superficial novel reader whose reading is merely for amusement it will be a disappointment.—BALDWIN, JAMES, 1883, English Literature and Literary Criticism, Prose, p. 236.

It will rank as one of those great creations of pure art that hover on the borderland between the natural and the supernatural, like the Caliban or Ariel, or Coleridge's Geraldine.—JOHNSON, CHARLES F., 1885, Three Americans and Three Englishmen, p. 147.

Most perfect and finished as works of Art are the novels of the late Nathaniel Hawthorne, most finished of all "The Scarlet Letter," an effusion of terrible and stupefying gloom, but wonderfully finely wrought. If Victor Hugo had been fettered by an art as rigid as that of Hawthorne, and had restricted his canvas accordingly, he would have escaped all those mad splashes of the brush which disfigure his best painting. Confined to the compass of the "Scarlet Letter," "Les Travailleurs de la Mer" would have been double its present value. BUCHANAN, ROBERT, 1886, A Look Round Literature, p. 37.

"The Scarlet Letter" is beyond doubt the foremost story yet written on this continent, and the fact that it holds the third place in this long list is both suggestive and encouraging. "The Marble Faun" follows close upon its greater companion; for, however fascinating the later book in its subtle psychologic insight and however beautiful its art, it remains true that the earlier story surpasses it in closeness of construction and in depth and intensity of human interest. That a book of such quality finds so wide a reading shows that the finest art does not fail to charm when it allies itself with the deepest life.—MABIE, HAMILTON W., 1893, *The Most Popular Novels in America, The Forum, vol.* 16, *p.* 512.

"The Scarlet Letter," a work of far grander aim and profounder intensity of genius than any other of Hawthorne's romances—a work, indeed, which, if not the most artistic outcome of his powers, is supremely beautiful, daring, and original in conception, and finished in workmanship. The little group of figures—a group worthy to have been portrayed by the powerful and discerning art of Rembrandt—in whom the interest of the story centres, are conceived with consummate vigour, delicacy, and imaginative suggestiveness.— BRADFIELD, THOMAS, 1894, *The Romances of Nathaniel Hawthorne, The Westminster Review, vol.* 142, *p.* 207.

A bit of New England history is brought before us with a dramatic impressiveness that has rarely, if ever, been rivalled; and the power, the mystery, the deathless judical zeal which are inseparable attributes of the human conscience, imprint themselves upon our senses in lines that affright and agonise like fire.—SELBY, THOMAS G., 1896, *The Theology of Modern Fiction, p.* 75.

No reader can have felt imaginatively the passionate spiritual struggles of Arthur Dimmesdale without being thereafter more sensitive to good influences and less tolerant of self-deception and concealed sin.— BATES, ARLO, 1897, *Talks on the Study of Literature, p.* 201.

The novel of the "Scarlet Letter" is one of the links in the development of the novel from a means of portraying single phases of emotion to a vehicle of highest expressional power. It was written by a psychological student of the problems which harass the human soul. . . . It is a tragedy—a tragedy sombre, intense, unrelieved. It is almost a fatalistic tragedy; almost as stern as if it had been written by Æschylus. It is not a love story; it is not a story of youth; it is not a story of contemporaneous life; it is not a story of eager hope. . . . The "Scarlet Letter" is not alone an interpretation of personality. It is the first suggestion and forerunner of the Novel of Purpose and of the Novel of Problem. It is the convincing proof of the greatness of the art of

Hawthorne that the "Scarlet Letter" is thus at once a presentation and a prophecy —STODDARD, FRANCIS HOVEY, 1900, *The Evolution of the English Novel, pp.* 76, 77, 83.

Consider for a moment "The Scarlet Letter;" the pathos of the subject, and the tragic scenes portrayed. All the world agrees that here is a masterpiece of mortal terror and remorse; we are lost in the admiration of the author's insight into the suffering human heart; yet has any one ever shed a tear over that inimitable romance? I think not. The book does not move us to tears; it awakens no sense of shuddering awe such as follows the perusal of the great tragedies of literature; it is not emotional, in the ordinary acceptance of the word, yet shallow or cold it certainly is not. . . . Why, then, we ask, should we have tears ready for "The Newcomes," and none for "The Scarlet Letter," although the pathos of the latter tale can so stir the depths of our nature as it did the author's? What curious trait in his writing, what strange attitude of the man toward the moral struggles and agony of human nature is this that sets him apart from other novelists?—MORE, PAUL ELMER, 1901, *The Solitude of Nathaniel Hawthorne, Atlantic Monthly, vol.* 88, *pp.* 588, 589.

From the first there is no affectation of shadowy uncertainty in the setting of the great tragedy of "The Scarlet Letter." As nearly as can be, the scenes of the several events are ascertained, and are identified with places in actual Boston. With a like inward sense of strong reality in his material, and perhaps compelled to its expression by that force in the concept, each detail of the drama, in motive, action, and character, is substantiated, so that from first to last it is visible, audible, tangible. From Hester Prynne in her prison—before she goes out to stand with her unlawful child in her arms and the scarlet letter on her breast before the Puritan magistracy and ministry and people, and be charged by the child's own father, as her pastor, to give him up to like ignominy—to Hester Prynne, kneeling over her dying paramour, on the scaffold, and mutely helping him to own his sin before all that terrible little world, there is the same strong truth beating with equal pulse from the core of the central reality, and clothing all its manifestations in the forms of credible, of indisputable personality. In its kind the romance remains sole, and it is hard to see how it shall be surpassed, or even companioned.—HOW-ELLS, WILLIAM DEAN, 1901, *Heroines of Fiction, vol.* I, *p.* 164.

"The Scarlet Letter" is a great and unique romance, standing apart by itself in fiction; there is nothing else quite like it. Of all Hawthorne's works it is most identified with his genius in popular regard, and it has the peculiar power that is apt to invest the first work of an author in which his originality finds complete artistic expression. It is seldom that one can observe so plainly the different elements that are primary in a writer's endowment coalesce in the fully developed work of genius; yet in this romance there is nothing either in method or perception which is not to be found in the earlier tales; what distinguishes it is the union of art and intuition as they had grown up in Hawthorne's practice and had developed a power to penetrate more deeply into life.—WOODBERRY, GEORGE E., 1902, *Nathaniel Hawthorne, p.* 189.

The appearance of the "Scarlet Letter" is probably, then, the largest event thus far in American literature. Here, for the first time, a life, or a group of intertwined lives, is revealed, with entrancing skill, in an environment and with an atmosphere all the artist's own, yet impressing us as ideally true to human nature.—LAWTON, WILLIAM CRANSTON, 1902, *Introduction to the Study of American Literature, p.* 164.

THE HOUSE OF THE SEVEN GABLES
1851

"The House of the Seven Gables" was finished yesterday. Mr. Hawthorne read me the close last evening. There is unspeakable grace and beauty in the conclusion, throwing back upon the sterner tragedy of the commencement an ethereal light, and a dear home-loveliness and satisfaction. How you will enjoy the book,—its depth of wisdom, its high tone, the flowers of Paradise scattered over all the dark places, the sweet wall-flower scent of Phœbe's character, the wonderful pathos and charm of old Uncle Venner. I only wish you could have heard the Poet sing his own song, as I did; but yet the book needs no adventitious aid,—it makes its own music, for I read it all over again to myself yesterday, except the last three chapters.—HAW-THORNE, SOPHIA, 1851, *Letter, Jan.* 27; *Nathaniel Hawthorne and His Wife, ed. Hawthorne, vol.* I, *p.* 383.

The "House of the Seven Gables" in my opinion, is better than "The Scarlet Letter;" but I should not wonder if I had refined upon the principal character a little too much for popular appreciation; nor if the romance of the book should be found somewhat at odds with the humble and familiar scenery in which I invest it. But I feel that portions of it are as good as anything I can hope to write, and the publisher speaks encouragingly of its success.—HAW-THORNE, NATHANIEL, 1851, *Letter to Bridge, Mar.* 15; *Personal Recollections of Nathaniel Hawthorne by Horatio Bridge, p.* 125.

I think we have no romancer but yourself, nor have had any for this long time. I had become so set in this feeling, that but for your last two stories I should have given up hoping, and believed that all we were to look for in the way of spontaneous growth were such languid, lifeless, sexless creations as in the view of certain people constitute the chief triumphs of a sister art as manifested among us. But there is rich blood in Hester, and the flavor of the sweet-fern and the bayberry are not truer to the soil than the native sweetness of our little Phœbe! The Yankee mind has for the most part budded and flowered in pots of English earth, but you have fairly raised yours as a seedling in the natural soil.—HOLMES, OLIVER WENDELL, 1851, *Letter to Hawthorne, April* 9; *A Study of Hawthorne by G. P. Lathrop, p.* 232.

I have been so delighted with "The House of the Seven Gables" that I cannot help sitting down to tell you so. I thought I could not forgive you if you wrote anything better than "The Scarlet Letter;" but I cannot help believing it a great triumph that you should have been able to deepen and widen the impression made by such a book as that. It seems to me that the "House" is the most valuable contribution to New England history that has been made. It is with the highest art that you have typified (in the revived likeness of Judge Pyncheon to his ancestor the Colonel) that intimate relationship between the Present and the Past in the way of ancestry and descent, which historians so carefully overlook.—LOWELL, JAMES RUSSELL, 1851, *Letter to Hawthorne, April* 24; *Nathaniel Hawthorne and His Wife, ed. Hawthorne, vol.* I, *p.* 390.

The contents of this book do not belie its clustering romantic title. With great enjoyment we spent almost an hour in each separate gable. This book is like a fine old chamber, abundantly but still judiciously furnished with precisely that sort of furniture best fitted to furnish it. There are rich hangings, whereon are braided scenes from tragedies. There is old china with rare devices, set about on the carved beaufet; there are long and indolent lounges to throw yourself upon; there is an admirable sideboard, plentifully stored with good viands; there is a smell of old wine in the pantry; and finally, in one corner, there is a dark little black-letter volume in golden clasps, entitled "Hawthorne: A Problem."—MELVILLE, HERMAN, 1851, *Letter to Hawthorne, A Study of Hawthorne by G. P. Lathrop, p.* 231.

It is not less original, not less striking, not less powerful, than the "Scarlet Letter." We doubt indeed whether he has elsewhere surpassed either of the three strongly-contrasted characters of the book. . . . The "House of Seven Gables" is the purest piece of imagination in our prose literature. —GRISWOLD, RUFUS WILMOT, 1851, *Nathaniel Hawthorne, International Magazine, vol. 3, p.* 159.

Accept my most cordial thanks for the little volume you have had the kindness to send me. I prize it as the right hand of fellowship extended to me by one whose friendship I am proud and happy to make, and whose writings I have regarded with admiration as among the very best that have ever issued from the American press.—IRVING, WASHINGTON, 1852, *Letter to Hawthorne, Nathaniel Hawthorne and His Wife,* ed. *Hawthorne, vol.* I, *p.* 440.

The scenery, tone, and personages of the story are imbued with a local authenticity which is not for an instant impaired by the imaginative charm of romance. We seem to breathe, as we read, the air, and be surrounded by familiar objects, of a New England town. . . . We may add that the same pure, even, unexaggerated, and perspicuous style of diction that we have recognised in his previous writings is maintained in this.—TUCKERMAN, HENRY T., 1853, *The Prose Poet; Nathaniel Hawthorne, Mental Portraits.*

No one should read the "House of Seven Gables" for the sake of the story, or neglect to read it because of such faults as I have described. It is for the humor, the satire, and what I may perhaps call the philosophy which permeates it, that its pages should be turned. Its pages may be turned on any day and under any circumstances. To "The Scarlet Letter" you have got to adhere till you have done with it; but you take this volume by bits, here and there, now and again, just as you like it. There is a description of a few poultry, melancholy unproductive birds, running over four or five pages, and written as no one but Hawthorne could have written it. There are a dozen pages or more in which the author pretends to ask why the busy Judge does not move from his chair,—the Judge the while having dree'd his doom and died as he sat. There is a ghastly spirit of drollery about this which would put the reader into full communion with Hawthorne if he had not read a page before, and did not intend to read a page after. To those who can make literary food of such passages as these, "The House of the Seven Gables" may be recommended. To others it will be caviare.—TROLLOPE, ANTHONY, 1879, *The Genius of Nathaniel Hawthorne, North American Review, vol.* 129, *p.* 216.

The fun has gone out of "Vanity Fair," and the "House of the Seven Gables" is a hotel with seven hundred beds.—HARRISON, FREDERIC, 1893, *The Decadence of Romance, The Forum, vol.* 15, *p.* 222.

In "The House of Seven Gables" the problem of heredity is dealt with. The predisposition to mysterious and fatal disease, the passionate championship of a wrong cause, and the curse cleaving to ill-gotten possessions may be handed on to succeeding generations, just as obviously as ancestral lineaments; and the entail of the curse can be cut off only by the reconciliation of those who have inherited, as disastrous heirlooms, the grudges and grievances of their forefathers.—SELBY, THOMAS G., 1896, *The Theology of Modern Fiction, p.* 75.

If there are probably no four books of any author among which, for a favorite, readers hesitate longer than between Hawthorne's four longest stories, there are at any rate many for whom this remains distinctly his largest and fullest production. Suffused as it is with a pleasant autumnal haze, it yet brushes more closely than its companions the surface of American life, comes a trifle nearer to being a novel of manners. The manners it shows us indeed are all interfused with the author's special tone, seen in a slanting afternoon light; but detail and illustration are sufficiently copious; and I am tempted for my own part to pronounce the book, taking subject and treatment together, and in spite of the position as a more concentrated classic enjoyed by "The Scarlet Letter," the closest approach we are likely to have to the great work of fiction, so often called for, that is to do us nationally most honor and most good. . . . "The House of the Seven Gables," I may add, contains in the rich portrait of Judge Pyncheon a character more solidly suggested than—with the possible exception of the Zenobia of "The Blithedale Romance"—any other figure in the author's list.—JAMES, HENRY, 1897, *Library of the World's Best Literature,* ed. *Warner, vol.* XII, *pp.* 7056, 7057.

If not his best book (as the author thought it in his serener moods), it is certainly next best. If Dante had ever told a story of the crime and mysteries which saturated some old country house upon the Euganean hills, I think it would have had much of the color, and much of the high, fierce lights which blaze about the gables of the Pyncheons! Yet it is all his own;—change as his theme may, the author is redolent everywhere of his own clean and complete selfhood; he is not like the rare Stevenson of our day, on whose close-thumbed pages we encounter—now, Defoe with his delicious particularity and *naïveté*—now, find him egotizing, as does Montaigne, or lapsing into such placid humors as embalm the periods of Lamb; or, yet again, catching in smart grip the trumpet of some old glorified Romancer, and summoning his knights (who are more than toy-knights) to file down once more from their old mediæval heights upon the dusty plains of today. No such golden memorial-trail enwraps the books of the Master of Puritan Romance; but, always the severe, unshaken, individual note was uppermost.—MITCHELL, DONALD G. 1899, *American Lands and Letters, Leather-Stocking to Poe's "Raven,"* p. 236.

There is, of course, a choice in Hawthorne's romances, and I myself prefer "The Blithedale Romance" and "The Scarlet Letter" to "The Marble Faun," and "The House of the Seven Gables." The last, indeed, I have found as nearly tiresome as I could find anything of Hawthorne's. I do not think it is censuring it unjustly to say that it seems the expansion

of a short story motive to the dimensions of a novel; and the slight narrative in which the concept is nursed with whimsical pathos to the limp end, appears sometimes to falter, and alarms the sympathetic reader at other times with the fear of an absolute lapse. The characters all lack the vitality which the author gives the people of his other books. . . . Hawthorne could not help giving form to his work, but as nearly as any work of his could be so "The House of the Seven Gables" is straggling. There is at any rate no great womanly presence to pull it apart powerfully together, and hold it in the beautiful unity characteristic of "The Blithedale Romance" and "The Scarlet Letter."—HOWELLS, WILLIAM DEAN, 1901, *Heroines of Fiction, vol.* I, *p.* 163.

THE BLITHEDALE ROMANCE
1852

It is enough for me that you have put another rose into your chaplet, and I will not ask whether it outblooms or outswells its sister flowers. Zenobia is a splendid creature, and I wish there were more such rich and ripe women about. I wish, too, you could have wound up your story without killing her, or that at least you had given her a drier and handsomer death. Priscilla is an exquisite sketch. I don't know whether you have quite explained Hollingsworth's power over two such diverse natures. Your views about reform and reformers and spiritual rappings are such as I heartily approve. Reformers need the enchantment of distance. Your sketches of things visible, detached observations, and style generally, are exquisite as ever. May you live a thousand years, and write a book every year!—HILLARD, GEORGE S., 1852, *Letter to Hawthorne, July 27; Nathaniel Hawthorne and His Wife,* ed. *Hawthorne, vol.* I, *p.* 448.

"The Blithedale Romance" is a work of no ordinary power, and indicative of all its author's mental affluence. In character-painting, he has overtaken his highest previous skill in Hollingsworth, and exceeded it in Zenobia. Then, of lesser personages, who could fail to recognise, in Silas Foster, the agricultural foreman of the farm, a marvellously accurate type of the New England yeoman of the generation just now passing the meridian of manhood? The descriptions of the kitchen, the table, the style of dress, the manner of labor, and the Sunday habits of the Blithedale community, attractive as they are in themselves, are doubly so, as being beyond a question the portions in which observation and experience, rather than fancy, furnished the material for the narrative.—PEABODY, ANDREW PRESTON, 1853, *Nathaniel Hawthorne, North American Review, vol. 76, p. 241.*

I should be ashamed to tell you how often I have read "The Marble Faun," or "The Blithedale Romance." The latter is, I think, of all your pieces the one I like best.—CHANNING, WILLIAM ELLERY, 1860, *Letter to Hawthorne, Sep. 3; Nathaniel Hawthorne and His Wife, vol. II, p. 265.*

Contrary, perhaps, to the general verdict we are almost impelled to the conclusion that the most perfect work left by Hawthorne is the "Blithedale Romance." . . . As regards composition alone, it may be pronounced a perfect work. The masterpiece of Oliver Goldsmith is brought to mind whilst reading it, though the two novels differ in most respects as widely as possible. In each, however, there is a charming style, whose easy flow has never been excelled, while in Hawthorne's story there is a poetic beauty which is not to be found in the "Vicar of Wakefield." The drawing of character is also very satisfactory. The *dramatis personæ* are few in number, but all are realized with extraordinary vividness.—SMITH, GEORGE BARNETT, 1875, *Nathaniel Hawthorne, Poets and Novelists, p. 181.*

The special characteristic of "The Blithedale Romance" seems to me to be its appearance of unlabored ease, and a consequent breeziness of effect distinguishing its atmosphere from that of any of the other romances. The style is admirably finished, and yet there is no part of the book that gives the same impression of almost unnecessary polish which occasionally intervenes between one's admiration and the "Seven Gables." On this score, "Blithedale" is certainly the most consummate of the four completed romances.—LATHROP, GEORGE PARSONS, 1876, *A Study of Hawthorne, p. 241.*

The book, indeed, is a mixture of elements, and it leaves in the memory an impression analogous to that of an April day—an alternation of brightness and shadow, of broken sun-patches and sprinkling clouds.—JAMES, HENRY, 1880, *Hawthorne (English Men of Letters), p. 128.*

MARBLE FAUN, OR TRANSFORMATION
1860

I've finished *the* book, and am, I think, more angry at your tantalizing cruelty than either "Athenæum" or "Saturday Review." I want to know a hundred things you do not tell me,—who Miriam was, what was the crime in which she was concerned and of which all Europe knew, what was in the packet, what became of Hilda, whether Miriam married Donatello, whether Donatello got his head cut off, etc. Of course you'll say I ought to *guess;* well, if I do guess, it is but a guess, and I want to *know.* Yesterday I wrote a review of you in the "Examiner," and in spite of my natural indignation, I hope you will not altogether dislike what I have said. In other respects I admire "Monte Beni" more than I can tell you; and I suppose no one now will visit Rome without a copy of it in his hand. Nowhere are descriptions to be found so beautiful, so true, and so pathetic. And there are little bits of *you* in the book which are best of all,—half moralizing, half thinking aloud. There is a bit about *women sewing* which Harriet raves about. There are bits about Catholicism and love and sin, which are marvellously thought and gloriously written.—BRIGHT, HENRY, 1860, *Letter to Hawthorne, Nathaniel Hawthorne and His Wife, ed. Hawthorne, vol. II, p. 240.*

Smith and Elder certainly do take strange liberties with the titles of books. I wanted to call it "The Marble Faun," but they insisted upon "Transformation," which will lead the reader to anticipate a sort of pantomime. They wrote some days ago that the edition was nearly all sold, and that they were going to print another; to which I mean to append a few pages, in the shape of a conversation between Kenyon, Hilda, and the author, throwing some further light on matters which seem to have been left too much in the dark. For my own part, however, I should prefer the book as it now stands.—HAWTHORNE, NATHANIEL, 1860, *Letter to Henry Bright; Nathaniel Hawthorne and His Wife, ed. Hawthorne, vol. II, p. 241.*

The style of the book is perfect of its kind, and, if Hawthorne had written nothing else, would entitle him to rank among the great masters of English composition. . . . Hawthorne not only writes English, but the sweetest, simplest, and clearest English that ever has been made the vehicle of equal depth, variety, and subtility of thought and emotion. His mind is reflected in his style, as a face is reflected in a mirror; and the latter does not give back its image with less appearance of effort than the former. His excellence consists not so much in using common words as in making common words express uncommon things. —WHIPPLE, EDWIN PERCY, 1860, *Nathaniel Hawthorne, Character and Characteristic Men, p.* 239.

The minuteness and the closeness of his analysis of the secret workings of the human heart with guilt for a companion, and withal the extreme delicacy with which the subject is handled, is something marvelous, and has perhaps never been equalled by any writer.—SMILES, SAMUEL, 1860, *Brief Biographies, p.* 269.

Everything that you have ever written, I believe, I have read many times, and I am particularly vain of having admired "Sights from a Steeple," when I first read it in the Boston *Token*, several hundred years ago, when we were both younger than we are now; of having detected and cherished, at a later day, an old Apple-Dealer, whom, I believe, you have unhandsomely thrust out of your presence, now that you are grown so great. But the "Romance of Monte Beni" has the additional charm for me that it is the first book of yours that I have read since I had the privilege of making your personal acquaintance. My memory goes back at once to those walks (alas, not too frequent) we used to take along the Tiber, or in the Campagna; . . . and it is delightful to get hold of the book now, and know that it is impossible for you any longer, after waving your wand as you occasionally did then, indicating where the treasure was hidden, to sink it again beyond plummet's sound. . . . With regard to the story, which has been somewhat criticised, I can only say that to me it is quite satisfactory. I like those shadowy, weird, fantastic, Hawthornesque shapes flitting through the golden gloom, which is the atmosphere of the book. I like the misty way in which the story is indicated rather than revealed; the outlines are quite definite enough from the beginning to the end to those who have imagination enough to follow you in your airy flights; and to those who complain, I suppose that nothing

less than an illustrated edition, with a large gallows on the last page, with Donatello in the most pensile of attitudes,—his ears revealed through a white night-cap,—would be satisfactory.—MOTLEY, JOHN LOTHROP, 1860, *Letter to Hawthorne, March* 29; *A Study of Hawthorne by G. P. Lathrop, p.* 261.

We are not to accept this book as a story; in that respect it is grievously deficient. The characters are utterly untrue to nature and to fact; they speak, all and always, the sentiments of the author; their words also are his; there is no one of them for which the world has furnished a model.—HALL, SAMUEL CARTER, 1860, *Reviews, Art Journal, vol.* 12, *p.* 127.

One of the most perfect works of art in literature, whose marvellous spell begins with the very opening words.—CURTIS, GEORGE WILLIAM, 1864–94, *The Works of Nathaniel Hawthorne, Literary and Social Essays, p.* 79.

His "Marble Faun," whether consciously or not, illustrates that invasion of the æsthetic by the moral which has confused art by dividing its allegiance, and dethroned the old dynasty without as yet firmly establishing the new in an acknowledged legitimacy.—LOWELL, JAMES RUSSELL, 1866, *Swinburne's Tragedies, Prose Works, Riverside Ed., vol.* II, *p.* 125.

To Perugia, as well as to Rome, Hawthorne has given a new interest; and it is not until the tourist who journeys northward from Rome has crossed over Monte Beni—on the road from Florence to Bologna—that he passes beyond a region which owes one of its chiefest charms to the rare genius of the author of the "Marble Faun."—ALDEN, WILLIAM L., 1871, *Scenes from the Marble Faun, Scribner's Monthly, vol.* 2, *p.* 494.

The most characteristic instance of Hawthorne's power in studying combinations of emotions that are, as it were, at once abhorrent to nature and true to life.—HUTTON, RICHARD HOLT, 1871, *Nathaniel Hawthorne, Essays in Literary Criticism.*

No more pathetic story could well be conceived, and no plainer moral indicated, than we find here.—SMITH, GEORGE BARNETT, 1875, *Nathaniel Hawthorne, Poets and Novelists, p.* 199.

There are few books put so often into the hands of English and American visitors to

Rome as Hawthorne's "Marble Faun," or as it is more generally known here, "Transformation," from the cheap and widely circulated Tauchnitz edition, which has followed the English style. Pilgrimages are made to what is now generally known as Hilda's Tower; and when young ladies go to the Capuchin church to see the picture of Guido, they almost dread to find a dead monk laid out and bleeding from the nostrils. The book gives a strong impression of local colour.—SCHUYLER, EUGENE, 1889–1901, *The Italy of Hawthorne, Italian Influences, p.* 308.

I cannot recall a writer more successful in this union of ornamental detail and organic structure. It is like the pediment end of the Doric order, whose beauty is not applied but wrought in. Whenever this is true, a style, whether in literature or architecture, painting or sculpture, gains immensely in dignity and unity. I do not say that it is not true of "The Marble Faun," nor that its local color is less natural than that of Hawthorne's New England novels; but that mingled with what is strictly necessary to the scenic effect is a great deal of information which belongs to the guide-book rather than the work of art. Hawthorne's analysis of a painting or interpretation of a statue is often vital to the story, and has a value apart from its relation to it; but there is much of description and history which belongs rather to a work like Irving's "Alhambra" than to a romance.—HARDY, ARTHUR SHERBURNE, 1889. *Hawthorne's Italian Romance, The Book Buyer, vol.* 6, *p.* 428.

Hawthorne's genius is expressed equally in other works, but it is in "Transformation" that his inner history is told,—and therein all the evolutionary years of New England, whereof he was the characteristic flower. Having come so far the book reaches far: it has the phenomenal success of becoming at once the tourist's guide and the scholar's interpreter.—CONWAY, MONCURE DANIEL, 1890, *Life of Nathaniel Hawthorne* (*Great Writers*), *p.* 162.

One vital mistake has been made by many. They have taken "The Marble Faun" as a guide to Rome; almost as a picture of Italy. It gives neither Rome nor Italy. Read it by the light of those Note-Books and you will see that Hawthorne never fully appreciated Italy; therefore he could not portray that country "which

most have considered the second in the world, thus really proving it the first." A man who could place Powers's Eve above the Venus di Milo, because its skin is smooth and its members sound; a man who gazed, again and again, upon the Venus di Medici, —which is no goddess, but a dainty Greek girl claiming love as her lawful right,—yet seldom visited the Medici Chapel whose giant forms writhe in a powerless passion as they give eternity limited by earth, could not really love Florence for her best, much less Rome for her grandest.—CURTIS, JESSIE KINGSLEY, 1892, *The Marble Faun, Andover Review, vol.* 18, *p.* 139.

"Transformation" is the most unsatisfactory although in some parts the most richly descriptive of the longer stories.— BRADFIELD, THOMAS, 1894, *The Romances of Nathaniel Hawthorne, The Westminster Review, vol.* 142, *p.* 210.

The longest of his fictions and the richest in descriptive beauty. The theme of this was the development of the soul through the experience of sin. There is a haunting mystery thrown about the story, like a soft veil of mist, veiling the beginning and the end. There is even a delicate teasing suggestion of the preternatural in Donatello, the Faun, a creation as original as Shakespeare's Caliban or Fouqué's Undine, and yet quite on this side the border-line of the human.—BEERS, HENRY A., 1895, *Initial Studies in American Letters, p.* 122.

In "The Marble Faun" his pure and tranquil grace of style is at its best. The economy of incident is not so strict as in the statuesque simplicity of the "Scarlet Letter" groupings, nor is the dramatic intensity so keen; but there is Hawthorne's own rich subdued, autumnal coloring, with the first soft shadows deepening into sable. —BATES, KATHERINE LEE, 1897, *American Literature, p.* 314.

As for the plot, we may be wrong, ideally in demanding anything more than the ethereal or spiritual solution,—the completion of Donatello's education, but there is much truth in the complaint, that all imaginative literature heretofore, as Hawthorne's own stories, and even hints in the course of these scenes themselves, had led us to expect some final explanation as to Donatello's deed and his punishment, which would satisfy—I will not say our curiosity, for we know he is a creature of Hawthorne's, after all, but—our sense of artistic justice and finish. The reluctant final chapter of the second edition, we may all well agree with Hawthorne himself, is worthless. It only shows that in regard to these questions as to Miriam's earlier history as well, he had himself nothing to offer us.—LAWTON, WILLIAM CRANSTON, 1898, *The New England Poets, p.* 92.

It has but four characters, and a single sin. Two of the characters, Hilda and Kenyon, are Bostonian: Miriam is portrayed from a Jewess whom Hawthorne had met in London; and if Donatello has any distinct prototye it is that curious New England Saint Francis who lived near to nature's heart—Henry David Thoreau. A visit to Whitby—to the abbey of St. Hilda, suggested the name of the spotless heroine who represents as well as may be the New England Puritanism. Kenyon, the artist, stands for Reason. Donatello is the innocent child of nature, a type of the early Greek. And thus the characters, as always in Hawthorne's romances, fade into symbols.—SMYTH, ALBERT H., 1900, *Critical Studies in American Literature, The Chautauquan, vol.* 30, *p.* 523.

SEPTIMUS FELTON

There still remain little roughnesses, which the author's delicate revision would have swept away; as the enumeration of "beautiful flowers" under the head of "tender greenness" in the very third line of the story;—the ungrammatical "and which," at the bottom of the first page; the seeming to include Rose Garfield among her own progenitors, on the second; the awkward occurrence of "now" and "then," "before" and "floor," in ungraceful proximity on the third page;—and just below, the abrupt "so it was" and "passed through Cambridge" (college);—these trifles and such as these have interest because they prove, what I for one never doubted, that Hawthorne's pages owed something of their delicious smoothness to the use of the file.— HIGGINSON, THOMAS WENTWORTH, 1872, *Hawthorne's Last Bequest, Scribner's Monthly, vol* 5, *p.* 105.

It is plain to any reader that "Septimus Felton," as it stands, with its roughness, its gaps, its mere allusiveness and slightness of treatment, gives us a very partial measure of Hawthorne's full intention; and it is equally easy to believe that this intention was much finer than anything we find

in the book. Even if we possessed the novel in its complete form, however, I incline to think that we should regard it as very much the weakest of Hawthorne's productions. — JAMES, HENRY, 1880, *Hawthorne (English Men of Letters), p.* 172.

In the unfinished story of "Septimus," we have an example of one of Hawthorne's stories in the making, and it seems to indicate how entirely Hawthorne always framed his work on facts. The Note-books show how precise an observer he was, and whatever he presented to the world was constructed on these observations. The author says of "Septimus," "our story is an internal one, dealing as little as possible with outward events, and taking hold of these only where it cannot be helped, in order, by means of them, to delineate the history of a mind." Yet it actually is, as it stands, far more full of action and incident than any of its predecessors. Here and there the narrative is broken; something was to have been filled in—something ghostly or speculative, perhaps. If Hawthorne had lived to complete this book, it is easy to believe the frame-work would have been so wrought upon that, in its final shape, the story would have ranked among the most weird of his romances.—LEWIN, WALTER, 1890, *The Academy, vol.* 38, *p.* 286.

NOTE-BOOKS

It is hard to conceive the existence of so much pettiness in a man so great and real; of such a resolution to brood over fancied slights and strange formalities, yet, withal, to generalize so widely on such narrow premises; of such vulgarity in one who had written for the public so exquisitely. It is difficult to accept such a writer's criticisms on "the steaks and sirloins" of English ladies. I still remember Hester Prynne and Pearl, in the "Scarlet Letter," and Phœbe and Hepzibah, in the "House of the Seven Gables," and ask myself how far the case in point proves the adage that there is nothing so essentially nasty as refinement. The tone of these English journals is as small and peevish as if their writer had been thwarted and overlooked, instead of waited on by hearty offers of service, which in most cases were declined almost as persistently as if they had been so many affronts. A more puzzling case of inconsistency and duality has never come before me.—CHORLEY, HENRY F. 1870, *Autobiography, Memoirs and Letters, ed. Hewlett, vol.* II, *p.* 248.

We owe to Hawthorne's consular life two books, "Our Old Home" and "The English Note-Books." They are alike, but with a difference. They resemble each other as an English flower-garden—in which the walks are swept and the lawn is mowed every day, where not a leaf is allowed to moulder where it falls, where every flower seems to glow with richer hues as if conscious of its privileges and anxious to make a grateful return for the care bestowed upon it—resembles an English park, where, though the shaping and restraining hand of Art is everywhere seen, Nature is yet allowed a certain range and scope. In both the style is exquisite,—the happiest combination possible of grace, harmony, flexibility, and strength; but in the former work there is more of elaboration, in the latter more of ease. Hawthorne's English is absolutely unique; very careful and exact, but never studied; with the best word always in the best place; pellucid as crystal; full of delicate and varied music; with gleams of poetry, and touches of that peculiar humor of his, which is half smile and half sigh. His style can only be matched by that of the best writers in France. . . . His style is not stiff, not pedantic; it is free from mannerism, caricature, and rhetoric; it has a sap and flavour of its own; it is a peculiar combination of ease and finish. The magic of style is like the magic of manner: it is felt by all, but it can be analyzed and defined by few.—HILLARD, GEORGE S., 1870, *The English Note-Boooks of Nathaniel Hawthorne, Atlantic Monthly, vol.* 26, *p.* 264.

The finish and deliberation of the style in these fragmentary chronicles, fitly known under the name of Note-Books, are very likely to mislead any one who does not constantly recall the fact that they were written *currente calamo*, and merely as superficial memoranda, beneath which lay the author's deeper meditation, always reserved in essence until he was ready to precipitate it in the plastic forms of fiction. Speaking of "Our Old Home," which—charming though it be to the reader—was drawn almost wholly from the surface deposit of his "English Note-Books," Hawthorne said: "It is neither a good nor a weighty book." And this, indirectly, shows that he did not regard the journals as concentrating the profounder substance of his genius.—LATHROP, GEORGE PARSONS, 1876, *ed. Passages from the American Note-Books.*

A very singular series of volumes; I doubt whether there is anything exactly corresponding to them in the whole body of literature. . . . I have just re-read them carefully, I am still at a loss to perceive how they came to be written—what was Hawthorne's purpose in carrying on for so many years this minute and often trivial chronicle. . . . He rarely takes his Note-Book into his confidence, or commits to its pages any reflections that might be adapted for publicity; the simplest way to describe the tone of these extremely objective journals is to say that they read like a series of very pleasant, though rather dullish and decidedly formal, letters, addressed to himself by a man who, having suspicions that they might be opened in the post, should have determined to insert nothing compromising. They contain much that is too futile for things intended for publicity; whereas, on the other hand, as a receptacle of private impressions and opinions, they are curiously cold and empty.—JAMES, HENRY, 1880, *Hawthorne (English Men of Letters), pp.* 39, 40.

To his death also we owe a book,—six volumes of crude miscellaneous notes—the publication of which must have made that exquisite writer and fastidious critic turn in his otherwise quiet grave.—NICHOL, JOHN, 1882-85, *American Literature, p.* 329.

GENERAL

The most pleasing writer of fanciful prose, except Irving, in the country.—BENJAMIN, PARK, 1835, *New England Magazine.*

Another characteristic of this writer is the exceeding beauty of his style. It is as clear as running waters are. Indeed he uses words merely as stepping-stones, upon which, with a free and youthful bound, his spirit crosses and recrosses the bright and rushing stream of thought.—LONGFELLOW, HENRY WADSWORTH, 1837, *Hawthorne's Twice-Told Tales, North American Review, vol.* 45, *p.* 63.

And here, though we cannot do him justice, let us remember the name of Nathaniel Hawthorne, deserving a place second to none in that band of humorists whose beautiful depth of cheerful feeling is the very poetry of mirth. In ease, grace, delicate sharpness of satire,—in a felicity of touch which often surpasses the felicity of Addison, in a subtelty of insight which often reaches further than the subtlety of

Steele,—the humor of Hawthorne presents traits so fine as to be almost too excellent for popularity, as, to every one who has attempted their criticism, they are too refined for statement.—WHIPPLE, EDWIN PERCY, 1846–71, *The Ludicrous Side of Life, Literature and Life, p.* 154.

He has the purest style, the finest taste, the most available scholarship, the most delicate humor, the most touching pathos, the most radiant imagination, the most consummate ingenuity; and with these varied good qualities he has done *well* as a mystic. But is there any one of these qualities which should prevent his doing doubly as well in a career of honest, upright, sensible, prehensible, and comprehensible things? Let him mend his pen, get a bottle of visible ink, come out from the Old Manse, cut Mr. Alcott, hang (if possible) the editor of the *Dial,* and throw out of the window to the pigs all his odd numbers of the *North American Review.*—POE, EDGAR ALLAN, 1847, *Literary Criticism, Works, ed. Stedman and Woodberry, vol.* VII, *p.* 38.

I am altogether entranced with Hawthorne; though I find few to enter into my ecstasies.—GREENWELL, DORA, 1850, *Letter, Memoirs, ed. Dorling, p.* 34.

Can you possibly get a Daguerreotype of Hawthorne to be engraved for the *International?* I want to do Hawthorne (who is, as I have printed it a dozen times, decidedly the greatest living literary man in this country, greatest, in romance, now writing the English language). I want to do Hawthorne's life for the occasion of a reviewal of the "Seven Gables."—GRISWOLD, RUFUS W., 1850, *To James T. Fields, Jan.* 24; *Passages from the Correspondence and Other Papers, p.* 257.

To Hawthorne, if we judge him in his best mood, may justly be ascribed the merit of reflective powers habitually active, connected with a style that is taking, apparently unstudied, and generally perspicuous and expressive. He has been compared with Irving; but though in some respects he is not injured by the experiment he must be considered, in others, as decidedly inferior. Irving is the better artist, and that not only in the choice of words, but in the arrangement of details, the production of effect, and the breadth and completeness of design; but had Hawthorne the taste and discrimination, and something more of the instinctive delicacy of Irving,

we are not sure that the latter would long be left lonely in his preëminence.—COXE, ARTHUR CLEVELAND, 1851, *The Writings of Hawthorne, The Church Review, vol.* 3, *p.* 499.

You write as if you wrote for Germany. The equality before the law—the moral law as well as the juridicial—is the great wish of the women of my country; and you have illustrated this point with the skill of an artist, and a deep knowledge of man's secret motives and feelings. We know "The House of the Seven Gables," which is a lesson to family pride,—a frailty which must lie deep in human natures, since you have been able to trace it even in a free country. What it is with us, with our old aristocracy, —penniless beggars with long names,—you scarcely can imagine. Nevertheless, such a picture as you have drawn is a useful lesson, and will do good here if known in the right quarter. This is unfortunately not now the case, and it is the fault of the translators. Your passages are long, you do not write a racy style to carry on the reader, and in bad language it is impossible to get on with it. Instead of curtailing, they have spun out the matter, and have made two volumes of one ; and the consequence is that the second remains unread. We must prevent this for the future. Those who read English are enchanted with it; but their number is not large, and ladies are almost alone proficient in foreign languages, and at the the same time ladies have no position in Germany. Believe me that I truly appreciate your great talent, and sincerely wish that you might come to a sort of fusion and longed-for Literature of the World.— BÖTTA, AMELIA, 1852, *Letter to Hawthorne, July* 7; *Nathaniel Hawthorne and His Wife, ed. Hawthorne, vol.* I, *p.* 442.

Hawthorne is a grand favorite of mine, and I shall be sorry if he do not go on surpassing himself.—ELIOT, GEORGE, 1852, *To Mrs. Peter Taylor, Aug.* 19; *George Eliot's Life as related in her Letters and Journals, ed. Cross, vol.* I, *p.* 208.

Imagine such an anatomizer of the human heart as Balzac, transported to a provincial town of New England, and giving to its houses, streets, and history the analytical power of his genius, and we realize the triumph of Hawthorne. Bravely adopting familiar materials, he has thrown over them the light and shadow of his thoughtful mind, eliciting a deep significance and a prolific beauty; if we may use the expression, he is ideally true to the real. His invention is felicitous, his tone magnetic; his sphere borders on the supernatural, and yet a chaste expression and a refined sentiment underlie his most earnest utterance; he is more suggestive than dramatic. The early history of New England has found no such genial and vivid illustration as his pages afford. At all points his genius touches the interests of human life, now overflowing with a love of external nature as gentle as that of Thomson, now intent upon the quaint or characteristic in life with a humor as zestful as that of Lamb, now developing the horrible or pathetic with something of John Webster's dramatic terror, and again buoyant with a fantasy as aerial as Shelley's conceptions. And in each instance, the staple of charming invention is adorned with the purest graces of style.—TUCKERMAN, HENRY T., 1852, *A Sketch of American Literature.*

If I were to meet you face to face, I should not say a word to you about the great pleasure we have derived from your works; but on paper may I not do so without offence? Of course you know the delight you have given to thousands. But you do not know how exquisite to our taste is all your minute detail,—your working out a character by Pre-Raphaelian touches, as it were,—if you understand my phrase; your delicate touch upon touch, which produces such a finished whole,—so different from the slap-dash style of writing so common nowadays. Yes, I assure you that independently of the intrinsic interest with which we read your books at first, we now refer again and again to them as exquisite works of art, the elaborate finish and detail of which are never exhausted. When I say *we*, I mean myself and my husband—now an antipode—and my daughter.—HOWITT, MARY, 1854, *Letter to Hawthorne, May 14; Nathaniel Hawthorne and His Wife*, ed. *Hawthorne, vol.* II, *p.* 48.

Hawthorne is remarkable for the delicacy of his psychological insight, his power of intense characterization, and for his mastery of the spiritual and the supernatural. His genius is most at home when delineating the darker passages of life, and the emotions of guilt and pain. He does not feel the necessity of time or space to realize his spells, and the early history of New England and its stern people have found no

more vivid illustration than his pages afford. The style of Hawthorne is the pure colorless medium of his thought; the plain current of his language is always equable, full and unvarying, whether in the company of playful children, among the ancestral associations of family or history, or in grappling with the mysteries and terrors of the supernatural world.—BOTTA, ANNE C. LYNCH, 1860–84, *Hand-Book of Universal Literature, p.* 521.

He is quiet, fanciful, quaint, and his humour is shaded by a meditativeness of spirit. Although a Yankee, he partakes of none of the characteristics of a Yankee. His thinking and his style have an antique air. His roots strike down through the visible mould of the present, and draw sustenance from the generations under ground. The ghosts that haunt that chamber of his mind are the ghosts of dead men and women. He has a strong smack of the Puritan; he wears around him, in the New England town, something of the darkness and mystery of the aboriginal forest. He is a shy, silent, sensitive, much ruminating man, with no special overflow of animal spirits. He loves solitude, and the things which age has made reverent.. There is nothing modern about him. Emerson's writing has a cold, cheerless glitter, like the new furniture in a warehouse, which will come of use by and by; Hawthorne's, the rich, subdued color of furniture in a Tudor mansion house which has winked to long-extinguished fires, which has been toned by the usage of departed generations.—SMITH, ALEXANDER, 1863, *Dreamthorp, p.* 190.

Hawthorne was a genius. As a master of prose, he will come in the first class of all who have written the English language. He had not the grand style, but who has had a delicacy of touch superior to his?—SUMNER, CHARLES, 1864, *To Henry W. Longfellow, May* 21; *Memoir and Letters, ed. Pierce, vol.* IV, *p.* 202.

The death of Nathaniel Hawthorne is a national event. In original creative genius no name in our literature is superior to his; and while everybody was asking whether it were impossible to write an American novel, he wrote romances that were hardly possible elsewhere, because they were so purely American. There was never, certainly, an author more utterly independent than Hawthorne of the circumstances that surrounded him. In his style, even, which, for a rich, idiomatic raciness, is unsurpassed, there was no touch of any of the schools of his time. It was as clear and simple as Thackeray's and as felicitious; but there was a flush of color in it, sometimes, of which Thackeray has no trace.—CURTIS, GEORGE WILLIAM, 1864, *Editor's Easy Chair, Harper's Magazine, vol.* 29, *p.* 405.

The Puritanism of the past found its unwilling poet in Hawthorne, the rarest creative imagination of the century, the rarest in some ideal respects since Shakespeare.—LOWELL, JAMES RUSSELL, 1865–90, *Thoreau, Prose Works, Riverside Ed. vol.* I, *p.* 365.

A writer of singular purity and simplicity. His writings are principally denoted by their fine poetical imagery, originality of thought and expression. His pleasant fancies are philosophical, and his keen reflections not too metaphysical.—HUNT, EPHRAIM, 1870, *Literature of the English Language, p.* 175.

The devotee of Hawthorne is unrelenting in certain moody prejudices, epicurean in his taste and aspirations, and dreamy and uncertain in his theory of this life and the next. —PORTER, NOAH, 1870, *Books and Reading, p.* 230.

Hawthorne has been called a mystic, which he was not,—and a psychological dreamer, which he was in very slight degree. He was really the ghost of New England,—I do not mean the "spirit," nor the "phantom," but the ghost in the older sense in which that term is used, the thin, rarified essence which is to be found somewhere behind the physical organization: embodied, indeed, and not by any means in a shadowy or diminutive earthly tabernacle, but yet only half embodied in it, endowed with a certain painful sense of the gulf between his nature and its organization, always recognising the gulf, always trying to bridge it over, and always more or less unsuccessful in the attempt. His writings are not exactly spiritual writings, for there is no dominating spirit in them. They are ghostly writings. Hawthorne was, to my mind, a sort of sign to New England of the divorce that has been going on there (and not less perhaps in old England) between its people's spiritual and earthly nature, and of the difficulty which they will soon feel, if they are to be absorbed more and more in that shrewd, hard earthly sense which is one of their most striking characteristics, in even *communicating* with their former self.—HUTTON, RICHARD HOLT, 1871,

Nathaniel Hawthorne, Essays in Literary Criticism, p. 98.

Hawthorne seems to me the most of a Man of Genius America has produced in the way of Imagination: yet I have never found an Appetite for his Books.—FITZGERALD, EDWARD, 1872, *To W. F. Pollock, Nov.; Letters and Literary Remains, ed. Wright, vol.* I, *p.* 347.

On the whole, Hawthorne must be esteemed the foremost writer of prose among Americans; and it would not be easy to select a name from the crowded annals of English literature that is more closely and honorably associated with the marriage of fine thoughts to fine language, which constitutes the charm of prose. As a romancist, he stands alone and unapproached. His psychological insight was simply marvelous, and gave a distinguishing and inimitable character to all his writings.—CATHCART, GEORGE R., 1874, *Literary Reader, p.* 155.

As a writer of short stories which are not mere episodes, but which have all the elements of a complete romance, condensed and therefore intensified, Hawthorne has no equal. He produced dozens of such, and he wrote the cleanest and most effective English of any American who has ever put pen to paper.—JOHNSON, ROSSITER, 1875, *Little Classics, p.* 121.

No modern writer has the same skill in so using the marvellous as to interest without unduly exciting our incredulity. He makes, indeed, no positive demands on our credulity. The strange influences which are suggested rather than obtruded upon us are kept in the background, so as not to invite, nor indeed to render possible, the application of scientific tests. . . . In fact Hawthorne was able to tread in that magic circle only by an exquisite refinement of taste, and by a delicate sense of humour, which is the best preservative against all extravagance. Both qualities combine in that tender delineation of character which is, after all, one of his greatest charms. His Puritan blood shows itself in sympathy, not with the stern side of the ancestral creed, but with the feebler characters upon whom it weighed as an oppressive terror. He resembles in some degree, poor Clifford Pyncheon, whose love of the beautiful makes him suffer under the stronger will of his relatives and the prim stiffness of their home. He exhibits the

suffering of such a character all the more
effectively because, with his kindly compassion there is mixed a delicate flavour of
irony. The more tragic scenes affect us, perhaps, with less sense of power; the playful,
though melancholy, fancy seems to be less
at home when the more powerful emotions
are to be excited; and yet once, at least, he
draws one of those pictures which engrave
themselves instantaneously on the memory.
—STEPHEN, LESLIE, 1875, *Hours in a Library, vol.* I, *pp.* 95, 97.

It is impossible, as we have seen, to fix
an absolute ratio between these writers.
Irving has a more human quality than Poe,
but Poe is beyond dispute the more original
of the two. Each, again, has something
which Hawthorne does not possess. But,
if we must attempt at all to reduce so intricate a problem to exact terms, the mutual position of the three may be stated in
the equation, Poe *plus* Irving *plus* an unknown quantity equals Hawthorne.—LA-
THROP, GEORGE PARSONS, 1876, *A Study of
Hawthorne, p.* 317.

What sybil to him bore
The secret oracles that move and haunt?
At night's dread noon he scanned the enchanted
glass,
Ay, and himself the warlock's mantle wore,
Nor to the thronging phantoms said Avaunt,
But waved his wand and bade them rise and
pass.
. . . .
But he whose quickened eye
Saw through New England's life her inmost
spirit—
Her heart, and all the stays on which it leant—
Returns not, since he laid the pencil by
Whose mystic touch none other shall inherit.
—STEADMAN, EDMUND CLARENCE, 1877,
Hawthorne.

The subtle analysis of spiritual moods,
which made him at home in the darkest recesses of the human heart, long reflection
upon the motives and moods and processes
in minds conscious of crimes, sure intuition
of the laws that govern them, a profound,
perhaps melancholy, thoughtfulness upon
the problems of good and evil, guilt and
sorrow, life and death—these are but new
growths in later times of those dark-veined
leaves that grew of old upon the Puritan
stalk. . . . In psychological insight he is
unrivalled among the men of our time.—
SYMONDS, J. A., 1878, *Hawthorne, An Oration.*

Holds the first place in the ranks of American writers of fiction. He is most fascinat-

ing, possessing delicacy of taste and finish
of style, combined with an insight into the
human mind most remarkable. He wrote
many stories illustrating character, the subjects being taken from New England life at
different periods.—PATTON, J. H., 1879,
*Brooke's English Literature (Primer) Ap-
pendix, p.* 181.

Hawthorne appalls—entices.—DICKIN-
SON, EMILY, 1879, *To T. W. Higginson, Letters, ed. Todd, vol.* II, *p.* 329.

One of the most characteristic of Hawthorne's literary methods is his habitual use
of guarded under-statements and veiled
hints. It is not a sign of weakness, but of
conscious strength, when he surrounds each
delineation with a sort of penumbra, takes
you into his counsels, offers hypotheses, as,
"May it not have been?" or, "Shall we not
rather say?" and sometimes, like a con-
jurer, urges particularly upon you the card
he does not intend you to accept. He seems
not quite to know whether Arthur Dimmesdale really had a fiery scar on his breast, or
what finally became of Miriam and her
lover. He will gladly share with you any
information he possesses, and, indeed, has
several valuable hints to offer; but that is
all. The result is that you place yourself
by his side to look with him at his characters
and gradually share with him the conviction that they must be real. Then, when
he has you thus in possession, he calls your
attention to the profound ethics involved
in the tale, and yet does it so gently that
you never think of the moral as being
obtrusive.— HIGGINSON, THOMAS WENT-
WORTH, 1879–88, *Short Studies of American
Authors, p.* 8.

The writings of Hawthorne are marked
by subtle imagination, curious power of
analysis, and exquisite purity of diction. He
studied exceptional developments of character, and was fond of exploring secret
crypts of emotion. His shorter stories are
remarkable for originality and suggestiveness, and his larger ones are as absolute
creations as "Hamlet" or "Undine." Lacking the accomplishment of verse, he was in
the highest sense a poet. His work is pervaded by a manly personality, and by an
almost feminine delicacy and gentleness.
He inherited the gravity of his Puritan ancestors without their superstition, and
learned in his solitary meditations a knowledge of the night side of life which would
have filled them with suspicion. A pro-

found anatomist of the heart, he was singularly free from morbidness, and in his darkest speculations concerning evil was robustly right-minded. He worshipped conscience with his intellectual as well as his moral nature; it is supreme in all he wrote. Besides these mental traits, he possessed the literary quality of style—a grace, a charm, a perfection of language which no other American writer ever possessed in the same degree, and which places him among the great masters of English prose.—STODDARD, RICHARD HENRY, 1879, *Encyclopædia Britannica, Ninth Ed., vol.* XI.

Hawthorne was melancholy, laborious, reflective—one of the greatest of modern novelists. His works are so richly adorned with all the vivid ornaments of fancy that they seem poems truly epic; he wrote them with intense feeling, lost in his own fine visions. When he had finished the Scarlet Letter, and read it to his wife, he was racked by an intense excitement, he relates, and at its close burst into tears. Writing, to him, was no holiday recreation, but a violent labor that stirred the very sources of his life. We may imagine Homer weeping as he described the sorrows of Priam; it was thus that Hawthorne felt with his own characters. His disposition was too sad to resemble altogether that of the manly Greek poet; he might have stood almost for Milton's *Il Penseroso.* He was fond of the dark, mysterious, gloomy, he was a conservative who seemed to care little for the future; he studied spiritualism, and examined the old and forgotten; he is never very cheerful.— LAWRENCE, EUGENE, 1880, *A Primer of American Literature, p.* 110.

I would advise no man, unless his faith in the greatness and purity of Hawthorne is established beyond the possibility of disturbance, to investigate too closely into the muck-heaps of local prejudice which even to this day are found to exist among certain cliques and coteries of his native town. [Salem] Persons of intelligence and respectability are met who actually regard their illustrious townsman with feelings of strong personal aversion. I have endeavored honestly and patiently to look into this strange matter for the purpose of discovering, if I could, the cause of an animosity so pronounced that were I to repeat here the sentiments of rancor and bitterness toward Hawthorne which I have heard spoken, the record would be read with as-

tonishment and incredulity. I rejoice to say, however, that these people are in a very small minority, and that to most Hawthorne is a bright, particular star, dwelling aloft beyond the reach of detraction.—HOLDEN, GEORGE H., 1881, *Hawthorne Among his Friends, Harper's Magazine, vol.* 63, *p.* 263.

In every higher qualification of the artist, he easily excels. His style is masterly in ease, grace, clearness,—the winning, absorbing, entrancing quality. His skill in hinting in ideal and spiritual elements is the most perfect in our day. His mastery of light and shade—the power of deepening gloom by sunshine and intensifying sunshine by means of darkness—is of the finest order, at once the gift of original perception and the result of most assiduous practice. Probably few writers ever made so many successes that were failures, or so many failures that were successes; that is, few ever did so much that was to others artistically perfect in order that they might do something artistically perfect to themselves.—MORSE, JAMES HERBERT, 1883, *The Native Element in American Fiction, The Century, vol.* 26, *p.* 294.

His fictions, in conception and performance, are always and essentially romances. Yet have they a character of fundamental trueness to spiritual laws, of harmony with time, place, and circumstance,—of realism existing in an ideal atmosphere, or invested with a halo of a poetic medium. We have not the worn out paraphernalia of abbeys, castles, courts, gentry, aristocracy, and sovereigns; but we have types, mental conditions,—beyond the sphere of habitual existence, indeed, yet belonging profoundly to spirit and to man. No civilization has produced a romantic genius at all comparable in power to his. Other writers have been more learned, more dramatic, more versatile, more comprehensive. His stories are generally deficient in converging unity. His personages seldom reveal themselves; but, as in the "Marble Faun," we are told what they are, in page upon page of description, keen, minute, finished,—marvellous workmanship. No one ever depended so little upon plot or incident. Facts are subordinated to the influences with which they are charged. He is not a portrait painter who sets forth a complete individuality. His forte is not in adventure, not in movement; but in the depicture of the rare and the occult, in the operation and results of involved and conflicting motives, feelings, and tendencies. He is here a solitary original in English letters. It may be questioned whether the "Scarlet Letter," as an example of imaginative writing, has its parallel in any literature.—WELSH, ALFRED H., 1883, *Development of English Literature and Language, vol.* II, *p.* 512.

A correspondent asks me if I do not like the work of Mr. Howells. Of course one cannot choose but like his writing. But one cannot also avoid comparing his work with that of his countryman, Nathaniel Hawthorne, who added to the charm of style the interest of a romantic and exciting story.—BESANT, SIR WALTER, 1884, *The Art of Fiction, p.* 28, *note.*

Hawthorne had no "authorities," and we are fain to be content with the belief that he was not able to solve his own riddles. . . The greatest genius America has yet produced. — LODGE, HENRY CABOT, 1884, *Studies in History, pp.* 23, 354.

There is a propriety in Hawthorne's fantasy to which Poe could not attain. Hawthorne's effects are moral, where Poe's are merely physical. The situation and its logical development, and the effects to be got out of it, are all Poe thinks of. In Hawthorne the situation, however strange and weird, is only the outward and visible sign of an inward and spiritual struggle. Ethical consequences are always worrying Hawthorne's soul: but Poe did not know that there were any ethics. . . . As to which of the two was the greater, discussion is idle; but that Hawthorne was the finer genius, few would deny. . . . In all his most daring fantasies Hawthorne is natural; and, though he may project his vision far beyond the boundaries of fact, nowhere does he violate the laws of nature. He had at all times a wholesome simplicity, and he never showed any trace of the morbid taint which characterises nearly all Poe's work. Hawthorne, one may venture to say, had the broad sanity of genius, while we should understand any one who might declare that Poe had mental disease raised to the nth.— MATTHEWS, BRANDER, 1885–1901, *The Philosophy of Short-story, pp.* 39, 41, 43.

Dramatist or no dramatist, there can be no question that Hawthorne was a consummate artist. His characters may often be wanting in opaqueness and solidity, but nothing can interfere with the extraordinary felicity and power of his scenes. The personages do not always stand out with distinctness, but the management of the incidents, the grouping of the accessories, the natural background of colour and tone and scenery, and all the "staging," so to speak, of the piece are alike admirable. Further than this, the insight into emotion and the perception of the contrasts of passion, though they often appear arbitrary and unnatural, strike the imagination with rare force and mastery.—COURTNEY, W. L., 1886, *Hawthorne's Romances, Fortnightly Review, vol.* 46, *p.* 520.

He stood apart—but as a mountain stands
In isolate repose above the plane;
Robed in no pride of aspect, no disdain,
Though clothed with power to steep the sunniest lands
In mystic shadow. At the mood's demands,
Himself he clouded, till no eye could gain
The vanished peak—no more, with sense astrain,
Than trace a foot-print on the surf-washed sands.
Yet hidden within that rare, sequestered height,
Imperially lonely, what a world
Of splendor lay! What pathless realms untrod!
What rush and wreck of passion! What delight
Of woodland sweets! What weird wind, phantom-whirled!
And over all, the immaculate sky of God!
—PRESTON, MARGARET J., 1886, *Hawthorne, The Critic, July* 10.

He was a great writer—the greatest writer in prose fiction whom America has produced.—LANG, ANDREW, 1886, *Letters to Dead Authors, p.* 149.

The people are gaining upon Nathaniel Hawthorne's works. A century hence, when the most popular authors of to-day are forgotten, he will probably be more widely read than ever.—ROE, EDWARD P., 1888, *The Forum, vol.* 5, *p.* 229.

Hawthorne's was a long and lonely vigil before the world found him out. When it did find him, it discovered no novice, but a ripe artist. . . . Hawthorne was imagination in the flesh. Imagination and fancy load his most fragile theme; and to strip them away would be to leave a skeleton one would hardly deem it possible to so build on and vivify as to make it a thing of beauty. —CHENEY, JOHN VANCE, 1891, *The Golden Guess, pp.* 269, 272.

But far greater in genius than the idealist Emerson was the mystic and recluse, Nathaniel Hawthorne. His actual life was of the simplest. He was born in quaint Salem, Massachusetts, in 1804; he graduated from Bowdoin College, held in the course of his career two political offices, shunned publicity and wrote novels which met at the time with no remarkable sale. But from this simple career came the weirdest, most imaginative and most profound tales in American, if not in all Anglo-Saxon literature.—MABIE, HAMILTON W., 1892, *The Memorial Story of America, p.* 595.

To men of our time, beyond doubt, his work seems generally not fantastic but imaginative, and surely not meretricious but in its own way beautiful. Nor is this the whole story: almost alone among our writers, we may say, Hawthorne has a lasting native significance. For this there are surely two good reasons. In the first place, he is almost the solitary American artist who has phrased his meaning in words of which the beauty seems sure to grow with the years. In the second place, what marks him as most impregnably American is this: when we look close to see what his meaning really was, we find it a thing that in the old days, at last finally dead and gone, had been the great motive power of his race. What Hawthorne really voices is that strange, morbid, haunting sense of other things that we see or hear, which underlay the intense idealism of the emigrant Puritans, and which remains perhaps the most inalienable emotional heritage of their children. It is Hawthorne, in brief, who finally phrases the meaning of such a life as Theophilus Eaton lived and Cotton Mather recorded.—WENDELL, BARNETT, 1893, *Stelligeri and other Essays Concerning America, p.* 139.

His best work deals with abnormal life in New England, and is written in a style of quaint simplicity, truthfulness, and beauty akin to that of Charles Lamb.—ROBERTSON, J. LOGIE, 1894, *A History of English Literature, p.* 355.

Hawthorne is, perhaps, the most truly creative of American novelists, and some passages in the "Scarlet Letter," and other of his fiction, belong to the higher planes of art.—RUSSELL, PERCY, 1894, *A Guide to British and American Novels, p.* 282.

He is psychologic rather than moral, an observer and analyzer of moral problems, and coldly critical, not sympathetic in his treatment of them.—VEDDER, HENRY C., 1895, *American Writers of To-day, p.* 270.

New England, in Hawthorne's work, achieved perfection in romance; but the romance is always an allegory; and the novel is a picture in which the truth to life is suffered to do its unsermonized office for conduct; and New England yet lacks her novelist, because it was her instinct and her conscience to be true to an ideal of life rather than to life itself.—HOWELLS, WILLIAM DEAN, 1895, *Literary Boston Thirty Years Ago, Harper's Magazine, vol.* 91, *p.* 868.

In truth, for many persons his great, his most touching sign will have been his aloofness wherever he is. He is outside of everything, and an alien everywhere. He is an æsthetic solitary. His beautiful, light imagination is the wing that on the autumn evening just brushes the dusky window. It was a faculty that gave him much more a terrible sense of human abysses than a desire rashly to sound them and rise to the surface with his report. On the surface—the surface of the soul and the edge of the tragedy—he preferred to remain. He lingered to weave his web, in the thin exterior air. This is a partial expression of his characteristic habit of dipping, of diving just for sport, into the moral world without being in the least a moralist. He had none of the heat nor of the dogmatism of that character; none of the impertinence, as we feel he would almost have held it, of any intermeddling. He never intermeddled; he was divertedly and discreetly contemplative, pausing oftenest wherever, amid prosaic aspects, there seemed most of an appeal to a sense for subtleties. But of all cynics he was the brightest and kindest, and the subtleties he spun are mere silken threads for stringing polished beads. His collection of moral mysteries is the cabinet of a dilettante.—JAMES, HENRY, 1897, *Library of the World's Best Literature, ed. Warner, vol.* XII, *p.* 7061.

Of the moderns, Hawthorne possesses in a remarkable degree the power of impressing unity on his creations. His hand is firm. He never wavers in style, standpoint, aim, or subject by a hair's-breadth. His plots are simple, his motives more so; in fact, no people ever were dominated by so few impulses as are the characters in Hawthorne's romances. There is something Greek in their simplicity, although they are as unlike a Greek conception of humanity as are Caliban or Ariel. But they never waver. Such as the author conceived them in the first chapter, they remain to the end. There is no growth or development of character. This gives his tales an atmosphere which is never blown away by any nineteenth-century wind, and a unity which insures them a place in the literature which endures. There is a certain sameness about his style which might become monotonous in spite of its wonderful charm, and a limited experience of life which might become uninteresting, and an impress of a poverty-stricken and repellant external world which might become disheartening, but the unity is so thoroughly artistic that the pleasure received far outweighs the annoyance which is caused by the depressing and fatalistic atmosphere which envelopes some of his romances.—JOHNSON, CHARLES F., 1898, *Elements of Literary Criticism, p.* 34.

Hawthorne's work you may read from end to end without the temptation to transfer so much as a line to the commonplace book. The road has taken you through many interesting scenes, and past many a beautiful landscape; you may have felt much and learned much; you might be glad to turn back straightway and travel the course over again; but you will have picked up no coin or jewel to put away in a cabinet. This characteristic of Hawthorne is the more noteworthy because of the moral quality of his work. A mere story-teller may naturally keep his narrative on the go, as we say,—that is one of the chief secrets of his art; but Hawthorne was not a mere story-teller. He was a moralist,—Emerson himself hardly more so; yet he has never a moral sentence. The fact is, he did not make sentences; he made books. The story, not the sentence, nor even the paragraph or the chapter, was the unit. The general truth—the moral—informed the work. Not only was it not affixed as a label; it was not

given anywhere a direct and separable verbal expression. If the story does not convey it to you, you will never get it. Hawthorne, in short, was what, for lack of a better word, we may call a literary artist. . . . His work is all of a piece, woven in his own loom. As nobody quotes him, so he quotes nobody. Inverted commas are as scarce on his pages as November violets are in the Concord meadows. You will find them, but you will have to search for them.—TORREY, BRADFORD, 1899, *Writers that are Quotable, Atlantic Monthly, vol.* 83, *pp.* 407, 410.

The story of Hawthorne is only half told when we say he refined Gothic art and fashioned it to high ethical purposes. As in the case of Poe, one of his great charms is his workmanship in structure and style. In the technique of the short tale, Poe was at least his equal; in the longer tale, where Poe left many loose ends, Hawthorne succeeded twice—in "The Scarlet Letter" and "The House of the Seven Gables." Poe modelled his style on Defoe and De Quincey, now suggesting the one and now the other. Hawthorne by laborious practice acquired a more individual style; the good taste of Addison and Irving are visible in it, and the brooding and dreamy fancy of Tieck, disguised however in the fusion.—CROSS, WILBUR L., 1899, *The Development of the English Novel, p.* 165.

Nathaniel Hawthorne has been well called "The ghost of New England." In him all that is weird and romantic in the superstitions of Puritanism flowers into the finest art. He is familiar with every mood of the austere Puritan life.—SMYTH, ALBERT H., 1900, *Critical Studies in American Literature, The Chautauquan, vol.* 30, *p.* 522.

To one who reads Hawthorne carefully, his work seems to fall together like the movements of a great symphony built upon one imposing theme.—MORE, PAUL ELMER, 1901, *The Solitude of Nathaniel Hawthorne, Atlantic Monthly, vol.* 88, *p.* 589.

Walter Savage Landor
1775–1864

Born, at Warwick, 30 Jan. 1775. At school at Knowle, 1779–85; at Rugby, 1785–91. With private tutor, 1791–93. Matric. Trin. Coll., Oxford, 13 Nov. 1792; rusticated, 1794; did not return to Oxford. Visit to Paris, 1802. Settled at Bath, 1805; intimacy with Southey begun, 1808. In Spain, Aug. to Nov., 1808. Settled at Llanthony Abbey, Monmouthshire, 1809. Married Julia Thuillier, May 1811. Removed to Jersey, and thence to Tours, 1814. To Italy, Sept. 1815. Lived at Como, 1815–18. At Pisa, 1818–21. At

Florence, 1821–35. Visit to England 1832. Quarrelled with his wife and went to England, 1835. Returned to Florence, 1858. Died there, 17 Sept. 1864. *Works:* "Poems," 1795; "Moral Epistle respectfully dedicated to Earl Stanhope," 1795; "Gebir" (anon.), 1798 (Latin version, by Landor, 1803); "Poems from the Arabic and Persian" (anon.), 1800; "Poetry" (anon.), 1802; "Simonidea" (anon.), 1806; "Three Letters to D. Francisco Riqueline," 1809; "Count Julian" (anon.), 1812; "Commentary on the Memoirs of Mr. Fox" (anon.), 1812; "Idyllia Heroica," 1814 (enlarged edn., 1820); "Poche Osservazioni sullo stato attuale di que' popoli che vogliono governarsi per mezzo delle Rappresentanze," 1821: "Imaginary Conversations," vols. i, ii, 1824; vols. iii, iv, 1828; vol. v, 1829; "Gebir. Count Julian, and other Poems," 1831; "Citation and Examination of William Shakespeare" (anon.), 1834; "The Letters of a Conservative," 1836; "Terry Hogan" (anon., attrib. to Landor), 1836; "Pericles and Aspasia," 1836; "A Satire on Satirists," 1836; "The Pentameron and Pentalogia" (anon.), 1837; "Andrea of Hungary and Giovanna of Naples," 1839; "Fra Rupert," 1840; "Works" (collected 2 vols.), 1846; "Hellenics," 1847; "Poemata et Inscriptiones," 1847; "Imaginary Conversation of King Carlo Alberto and the Duchess Belgoioiso," 1848; "Italics," 1848; "'Popery, British and Foreign," 1851; "Imaginary Conversations of Greeks and Romans," 1853; "The Last Fruit off an Old Tree," 1853; "Letters of an American," 1854; "Letter . . . to R. W. Emerson," [1856]; "Antony and Octavius," 1856; "Dry Sticks," 1858; "Hebrew Lyrics" (anon.), 1859; "Savonarola e il Priore di San Marco," 1860; "Heroic Idyls, with additional poems," 1863. *Collected Works:* in 8 vols., 1876. *Life:* by J. Forster, 1869; by Sidney Colvin, 1881.—SHARP, R. FARQUHARSON, 1897, *A Dictionary of English Authors, p.* 162.

PERSONAL

Differing as I do from him in constitutional temper, and in some serious opinions, he is yet of all men living the one with whom I feel the most entire and cordial sympathy in heart and mind; were I a single man, I should think the pleasure of a week's abode with him cheaply purchased by a journey to Florence, though, pilgrim-like, the whole way were to be performed on foot.—SOUTHEY, ROBERT, 1824, *Letter, Nov.* 13; *The Correspondence of Robert Southey with Caroline Bowles, ed Dowden, p.* 71.

Mr. Landor, who has long been known to scholars as a Latin poet beyond the elegance of centos, and has lately shown himself one of our most powerful writers of prose, is a man of a vehement nature, with great delicacy of imagination. He is like a stormy mountain pine, that should produce lilies. After indulging the partialities of his friendships and enmities, and trampling on Kings and ministers, he shall cool himself, like a Spartan worshipping a moon-beam, in the patient meekness of Lady Jane Grey. . . . Mr. Landor's conversation is lively and unaffected, as full of scholarship or otherwise as you may desire, and dashed now and then with a little superfluous will and vehemence, when he speaks of his likings and dislikes. His laugh is in peals, and climbing: he seems to fetch every one from a higher story.—HUNT,

LEIGH, 1828, *Lord Byron and Some of His Contemporaries, vol.* II., *p.* 377, 380.

Met today [1830] the one man living in Florence whom I was anxious to know. This was Walter Savage Landor, a man of unquestionable genius, but very questionable good sense; or rather, one of those unmanageable men,—

"Blest with huge stores of wit,
Who want as much again to manage it."

He was a man of florid complexion, with large, full eyes, and altogether a *leonine* man, and with a fierceness of tone well suited to his name; his decisions being confident, and on all subjects, whether of taste or life, unqualified; each standing for itself, not caring whether it was in harmony with what had gone before or would follow from the same oracular lips. But why should I trouble myself to describe him? He is painted by a master hand in Dickens' novel, "Bleak House," now in course of publication, where he figures as Mr. Boythorn. The combination of superficial ferocity and inherent tenderness, so admirably portrayed in "Bleak House," still at first strikes every stranger—for twenty-two years have not materially changed him—no less than his perfect frankness and reckless indifference to what he says.—ROBINSON, HENRY CRABB, 1830-52, *Diary, Reminiscenses and Correspondence, ed. Sadler.*

Landor, as usual, with the very finest man's head I have ever seen, and with all his Johnsonian disposition to tyrannise and lay down the law in his talk, restrained and refined by an old-world courtesy and deference towards his bright hostess, for which *chivalry* is the only right word.— CHORLEY, HENRY FOTHERGILL, 1838, *Autobiography, Memoir and Letters, ed. Hewlett, p.* 190.

The high breeding and urbanity of his manners, which are very striking, I had not been taught to expect. . . . His avoidance of general society, though courted to enter it, his dignified reserve when brought in contact with those he disapproves, and his fearless courage in following the dictates of a lofty mind, had somehow or other given the erroneous impression that his manners were, if not somewhat abrupt, at least singular. This is not the case, or, if it be, the only singularity I can discern is a more than ordinary politeness towards women. . . . The politeness of Landor has nothing of the troublesome officiousness of a *petit-maître*, nor the oppressive ceremoniousness of a fine gentleman of *l'ancien régime*; it is grave and respectful, without his ever losing sight of what is due to himself, when most assiduously practising the urbanity due to others. There is a natural dignity which appertains to him that suits perfectly with a style of his conversation and his general appearance.—BLESSINGTON, MARGUERITE COUNTESS, 1839, *Idler in Italy, p.* 283.

A tall, broad, burly man, with gray hair, and large fierce-rolling eyes; of the most restless, impetuous vivacity, not to be held in by the most perfect breeding,—expressing itself in high-colored superlatives, indeed in reckless exaggeration, now and then in a dry, sharp laugh not of sport but of mockery; a wild man, whom no extent of culture had been able to tame! His intellectual faculty seemed to me to be weak in proportion to his violence of temper; the judgment he gives about anything is more apt to be wrong than right,—as the inward whirlwind shows him this side or the other of the object; and *sides* of an object are all he sees. He is not an original man; in most cases one but sighs over the spectacle of common-place torn to rags.—CARLYLE, THOMAS, 1840, *To Emerson, April* 1; *Correspondence of Carlyle and Emerson, ed. Norton, vol.* I, *p.* 303.

Of all the literary men with whom Lady Blessington came in contact—and they certainly were not few or undistinguished—

at home and abroad, the person whom she looked upon with the most respect, honour and affectionate regard, was Walter Savage Landor. — MADDEN, RICHARD ROBERT, 1855, *Literary Life and Correspondence of the Countess Blessington, vol.* II, *p.* 102.

On the 15th May [1833] I dined with Mr. Landor. I found him noble and courteous, living in a cloud of pictures at his Villa Gherardesca, a fine house commanding a beautiful landscape. I had inferred from his books, or magnified from some anecdotes, an impression of Achillean wrath,—an untamable petulance. I do not know whether the imputation were just or not, but certainly on this May day his courtesy veiled that haughty mind and he was the most patient and gentle of hosts. He praised the beautiful cyclamen which grows all about Florence; he admired Washington; talked of Wordsworth, Byron, Massinger, Beaumont and Fletcher. To be sure, he is decided in his opinions, likes to surprise, and is well content to impress, if possible, his English whim upon the immutable past. . . . . Mr. Landor carried to its height the love of freak which the English delight to indulge, as if to signalize their commanding freedom. He has a wonderful brain, despotic, violent and inexhaustible, meant for a soldier, by what chance converted to letters; in which there is not a style or a tint not known to him, yet with an English appetite for action and heroes. The thing done avails, and not what is said about it. An original sentence, a step forward, is worth more than all the censures. Landor is strangely undervalued in England; usually ignored and sometimes savagely attacked in the Reviews. The criticism may be right or wrong, and is quickly forgotten; but year after year the scholar must still go back to Landor for a multitude of elegant sentences; for wisdom, wit and indignation that are unforgettable.—EMERSON, RALPH WALDO, 1856, *English Traits; Works, Riverside Ed., vol.* V, *pp.* 11, 13.

We left Mr. Landor in great comfort. I went to see his apartment before it was furnished. Rooms small, but with a look out into a little garden; quiet and cheerful and he doesn't mind a situation rather out of the way. He pays four pound ten (English) the month. Wilson has *thirty* pounds a year for taking care of him, which sounds a good deal; but it *is* a difficult position. He has excellent, generous, affectionate impulses, but the impulses of the tiger every now and then. Nothing coheres in him, either in his opinions, or I fear, affections. It isn't age; he is precisely the man of his youth, I must believe. Still, his genius gives him the right of gratitude on all artists at least, and I must say that my Robert has generously paid the debt. Robert always said that he owed more as a writer to Landor than to any contemporary. At present, Landor is very fond of him; but I am quite prepared for his turning against us as he has turned against Forster, who has been so devoted for years and years. Only one isn't kind for what one gets by it, or there wouldn't be much kindness in this world.—BROWNING, ELIZABETH BARRETT, 1859, *To Miss Browning, Dec.; Letters, ed. Kenyon, vol.* II, *p.* 353.

He who is within two paces of his ninetieth year may sit down and make no excuses; he must be unpopular, he never tried to be much otherwise; he never contended with a contemporary, but walked alone on the far eastern uplands, meditating and remembering.—LANDOR, WALTER SAVAGE, 1863, *Heroic Idyls with Additional Poems, Preface; Works, vol.* VIII, *p.* 305.

He had in him a strong faculty of admiration; and a deep, pure, fresh current of tenderness and sweetness ran under the film of gall which Nature unhappily shed over his existence at the fountain. This was one of the contradictions of which this paradoxical being was made up; and it is, with the rest, worthy of some contemplation; not because paradoxical persons or the paradoxes they produce are choice objects of study in a striving and practical age like ours, but because Landor achieved some things that were great, and many that were beautiful, in spite of the paradoxical elements of his life and character.—MARTINEAU, HARRIET, 1864-69, *Biographical Sketches,* p. 121.

Though followed by two younger brothers, as soon as they could be received at Rugby, there remains nothing worth recording till he was twelve years old,—when a violent fit of the gout—gout which might have qualified him for an alderman—restored him to his mother's care at Warwick. Never was there a more impatient sufferer; and his imprecations, divided equally between the gout and his nurses, were heard afar. It is also strange that there was never any return of this disorder. Our father suf-

fered from it, and all three of the younger brothers; but though Walter's appetite much surpassed the best of ours (or the worst) he escaped it during more than seventy years. However active at dinner, he was always temperate after it; and I never saw the smallest sign of excess, though he greatly enjoyed two or three glasses of light wine.—LANDOR, ROBERT, 1865, *Letter to Mr. Forster; Walter Savage Landor, A Biography by John Forster, bk.* i.

For a moment I recall the well-remembered figure and face, as they first became known to me nearly thirty years ago. Landor was then upwards of sixty, and looked that age to the full. He was not above the middle stature, but had a stout stalwart presence, walked without a stoop, and in his general aspect, particularly the set and carriage of his head, was decidedly of what is called a distinguished bearing. His hair was already silvered gray, and had retired far upward from his forehead, which, wide and full but retreating, could never in the earlier time have been seen to such advantage. What at first was noticeable, however, in the broad white massive head, were the full yet strangely-lifted eyebrows; and they were not immediately attractive. They might have meant only pride or self-will in its most arrogant form, but for what was visible in the rest of the face. In the large gray eyes there was a depth of composed expression that even startled by its contrast to the eager restlessness looking out from the surface of them; and in the same variety and quickness of transition the mouth was extremely striking. The lips that seemed compressed with unalterable will would in a moment relax to a softness more than feminine; and a sweeter smile it was impossible to conceive. What was best in his character, whether for strength or gentleness, had left its traces there. It was altogether a face on which power was visibly impressed, but without the resolution and purpose that generally accompany it. . . . The eye is fine; but black hair covers all the forehead, and you recognize the face of the later time quite without its fulness, power and animation. The stubbornness is there, without the softness; the self-will, untamed by any experience; plenty of energy, but a want of emotion. The nose was never particularly good; and the lifted brow, flatness of cheek and jaw, wide upper lip, retreating mouth and chin, and heavy neck, peculiarities necessarily prominent in youth, in age contributed only to a certain lion-look, he liked to be reminded of, and would confirm with a loud, long laugh hardly less than lionine. Higher and higher went peal after peal, in continuous and increasing volleys, until regions of sound were reached very far beyond ordinary human lungs.—FORSTER, JOHN, 1865-69, *Walter Savage Landor, A Biography, bk.* i.

It was impossible to be in Landor's society a half hour and not reap advantage. His great learning, varied information, extensive acquaintance with the world's celebrities, ready wit, and even readier repartee, rendered his conversation wonderfully entertaining. He would narrate anecdote after anecdote with surprising accuracy, being possessed of a singularly retentive memory, that could refer to a catalogue of notables far longer than Don Giovanni's picture-gallery of conquests. Names, it is true, he was frequently unable to recall, and supplied their place with a "God bless my soul, I forget everything;" but facts were indelibly stamped upon his mind. He referred back to the year *one* with as much facility as a person of the rising generation invokes the shade of some deed dead a few years.—FIELD, KATE, 1866, *Last Days of Walter Savage Landor, Atlantic Monthly, vol.* 17, *p.* 391.

The arms were very peculiar. They were rather short, and were curiously restrained and checked in their action at the elbows; in the action of the hands, even when separately clenched, there was the same kind of pause, and a noticeable tendency to relaxation on the part of the thumb. Let the face be never so intense or fierce, there was a commentary of gentleness in the hands, essential to be taken along with it. . . . In the expression of his hands, though angrily closed, there was always gentleness and tenderness; just as when they were open, and the handsome old gentleman would wave them, with a little courtly flourish that sat well upon him, as he recalled some classic compliment that he had rendered to some reigning Beauty, there was a chivalrous grace about them such as pervades his softer verses.—DICKENS, CHARLES, 1869, *Landor's Life, All the Year Round, vol.* 22, *p.* 182.

I met him first in 1847, when he was seventy-three years of age. . . . I was visiting Mr. Brabant in Bath, and we were at Mr. Empson's "old curiosity shop," when we saw what seemed a noble-looking old man, badly dressed in shabby snuff-colored clothes, a dirty old blue necktie, unstarched cotton shirt— with a front more like a night-gown than a shirt—and "knubbly" applepie boots. But underneath the rusty old hat brim gleamed a pair of quiet and penetrating gray-blue eyes; and the voice was sweet and masterly; the manner that of a man of rare distinction.—LINTON, ELIZA LYNN, 1870, *Reminiscenses of Walter Savage Landor, Fraser's Magazine, vol.* 82, *p.* 119.

He had a stately and agreeable presence, and the men of letters from different countries who brought introductions to him spoke of his affectionate reception, of his complimentary old-world manners, and of his elegant though simple hospitality. But it was his conversation that left on them the most delightful and permanent impression; so affluent, animated and coloured, so rich in knowledge and illustration, so gay and yet so weighty—such bitter irony and such lofty praise uttered with a voice fibrous in all its tones, whether gentle or fierce—it equalled, if not surpassed, all that has been related of the table-talk of men eminent for social speech. It proceeded from a mind so glad of its own exercise, and so joyous in its own humor, that in its most extravagant notions and most extravagant attitudes it made argument difficult and criticism superfluous. And when memory and fancy were alike exhausted, there came a laughter so pantomimic yet so genial, rising out of a momentary silence into peals so cumulative and sonorous, that all contradiction and possible affront were merged forever.—MILNES, RICHARD MONCKTON (LORD HOUGHTON), 1873, *Monographs, Personal and Social, pp.* 47, 61.

Landor was to all intents and purposes, in the narrowest as well as in the broadest sense of the word, a gentleman. He was a gentleman by birth, by association, by his tastes and habits; and not only a gentleman, but a refined, elegant and classical scholar by education. Yet he was one of the most determined h-murderers that I ever heard speak. He talked always of his 'ouse, his 'orse and his 'ome. I do not think that he went upon the compensation principle of introducing the unfortunate letter where it ought not to be heard.—TROLLOPE, THOMAS ADOLPHUS, 1874, *Some Recollections of Walter Savage Landor, Lippincott's Magazine, vol.* 13, *p.* 439.

The Prince of Carpi said of Erasmus he was so thin-skinned that a fly would draw blood from him. The author of the "Imaginary Conversations" had the same infirmity. A very little thing would disturb him for hours, and his friends were never sure of his equanimity. There were three things in the world that received no quarter at his hands, and when in the slightest degree he scented *hypocrisy, pharisaism,* or *tyranny,* straightway he became furious, and laid about him like a mad giant.—FIELDS, JAMES T. 1875, *"Barry Cornwall" and some of his Friends, Harper's Magazine, vol.* 51, *p.* 784.

High from his throne in heaven Simonides,
Crowned with wild aureole of memorial tears
That the everlasting sun of all time sees
All golden, molten from the forge of years,
Smiled, as the gift was laid upon his knees
Of songs that hang as pearls in mourners' ears,
Mild as the murmering of Hymettian bees
And honeyed as their harvest, that endears
The toil of flowery days;
And smiling perfect praise
Hailed his one brother mateless else of peers.
The mightiest heart since Milton's leapt,
The gentlest since the gentlest heart of Shakespeare slept. . . .
All sweet, all sacred, all heroic things,
All generous names and loyal, and all wise,
With all his heart in all its wayfarings
He sought, and worshiped, seeing them with his eyes
In very present glory, clothed with wings
Of words and deeds and dreams immortal, rise
Visible more than living slaves and kings,
Audible more than actual vows and lies.
—SWINBURNE, ALGERNON CHARLES, 1880, *Song for the Centenary of Walter Savage Landor, Studies in Song, pp.* 21, 30, 43.

Dashed by his volcanic temperament and his blinding imagination into collision with facts, he suffered shipwreck once and again. But if we apply to his character and career the measure not of results, but of intention, we shall acknowledge in Landor a model on the heroic scale of many noble and manly virtues. He had a heart infinitely kind and tender. His generosity was royal, delicate, never hesitating. In his pride there was no moroseness, in his independence not a shadow of jealousy.

From spite, meanness or uncharitableness he was utterly exempt. He was loyal and devoted in friendship, and, what is rare, at least as prone to idealize the virtues of his friends as the vices of his enemies. Quick as was his resentment of a slight, his fiercest indignations were never those which he conceived on personal grounds, but those with which he pursued an injustice or an act of cruelty; nor is there wanting an element of nobleness and chivalry in even the wildest of his breaches with social custom. He was no less a worshipper of true greatness than he was a despiser of false. He hated nothing but tyranny and fraud, and for those his hatred was implacable. His bearing under the consequences of his own impracticability was of an admirable courage and equanimity.—COLVIN, SIDNEY, 1881, *Landor (English Men of Letters), p.* 217.

In 1811 he married a very pretty girl aged seventeen, Miss Julia Thuillier. She was a moneyless damsel, of noble Swiss family, and was remarkable for the rich abundance of her curls; her tone of mind, romantic and self-indulgent; her charms of person, coupled with much youthful amiability. Landor married her for her good looks, and perhaps little true sympathy existed between them. There were quarrels and reconciliations, and the poet, in the earlier years of his marriage, showed as much forebearance as was consistent with one of the least forebearing and intolerant, imperious, liberty-loving characters on record. At last, after they had had four children, Landor left his wife behind in Fiesole, near Florence, returned to England, and would never see her again; the motive was probably nothing more unbearable than what he would now at length no longer bear, incompatibility of temper. He relinquished to her his Italian villa and almost the whole of his fortune. In advanced age, towards 1855, he returned to Florence; but he lived in lodgings, and there he died in 1864, aged eighty-nine. His wife outlived him till the spring of 1879, dying at the age of eighty-five.—ROSSETTI, WILLIAM M., 1881, *The Wives of Poets, Atlantic Monthly, vol.* 47, *p.* 521.

Ranking high among the men of genius to whom the nineteenth century has given fame, his career as a man of letters points a moral indeed, but it is by showing that vicious propensities are sure to produce wretchedness, for his misery was entirely of his own creating; his life was a perpetual wrangle, notwithstanding the advantages he inherited, and might have enjoyed, from the cradle to the grave—his many rich gifts of fortune and of nature. Handsome in his youth, of goodly presence when I knew him in 1836, of great physical as well as intellectual strength, inheriting large property; well if not nobly born, with natural faculties of a high order duly trained by an excellent education—these advantages were all rendered not only futile, but positive sources of evil, by a vicious disposition, ruled by a temper that he himself described as "the worst beyond comparison that man was ever cursed with," but which he made no effort to guide, restrain or control.—HALL, SAMUEL CARTER, 1883, *Retrospect of a Long Life, p.* 333.

You felt yourself in the presence of one who was emphatically a Man, not the image of a man; so emphatically, indeed, that even Carlyle thought the journey to Bath not too dear a prize to pay for seeing him, and found something royal in him. When I saw him he was in his seventy-eighth year, but erect and vigorous as in middle life. There was something of challenge even in the alertness of his pose, and the head was often thrown back like that of a boxer who awaits a blow. He had the air of the arena. I do not remember that his head was large, or his eyes in any way remarkable.— LOWELL, JAMES RUSSELL, 1888, *Some Letters of Walter Savage Landor, The Century, vol.* 35, *p.* 513.

In the north Park Cemetery of Calcutta there is a black marble slab containing the inscription:

IN MEMORY OF
THE HONOURABLE
ROSE WHITWORTH AYLMER,
WHO DEPARTED THIS LIFE MARCH 2D, A. D.
1800.
AGED 20 YEARS.

This name calls to mind the most romantic period of the life of Walter Savage Landor. Landor left Oxford in 1797. He spent some time on the Welsh coast, where he made the acquaintance of Lord Aylmer's family. An attachment sprang up between Rose, the daughter of Lord Aylmer, and young Landor. One day she loaned him a book from the Swansea Circulating Library. It was a romance by Clara Reeve. Here he found an Arabic tale which so profoundly

impressed him that it suggested his first great work, "Gebir." . . . Landor, in his poem, "Abertawy," indicates both her unwillingness to go and his own sorrow at her departure.—HURST, JOHN FLETCHER, 1891, *English Writers in India, Harper's Magazine, vol.* 82, *p.* 358.

Landor's character is sufficiently marked by his life. Throughout his career he invariably showed nobility of sentiment and great powers of tenderness and sympathy, at the mercy of an ungovernable temper. He showed exquisite courtesy to women; he loved children passionately, if not discreetly; he treated his dogs (especially "Pomero" and "Bath") as if they had been human beings, and loved flowers as if they had been alive. His tremendous explosions of laughter and wrath were often passing storms in a serene sky, though his intense pride made some of his quarrels irreconcilable. He was for nearly ninety years a typical English public school boy, full of humors, obstinacy, and Latin verses, and equally full of generous impulses, chivalrous sentiment, and power of enjoyment. In calmer moods he was a refined epicurean; he liked to dine alone and delicately; he was fond of pictures, and unfortunately mistook himself for a connoisseur. He wasted large sums upon worthless daubs, though he appears to have had a genuine appreciation of the earlier Italian masters when they were still generally undervalued. He gave away both pictures and books almost as rapidly as he bought them. He was generous even to excess in all money matters. Intellectually he was no sustained reasoner, and it is a mistake to criticise his opinions seriously. They were simply the prejudices of his class. In politics he was an aristocratic republican, after the pattern of his great idol Milton. He resented the claims of superiors, and advocated tyrannicide, but he equally despised the mob and shuddered at all vulgarity. His religion was that of the eighteenth-century noble, implying much tolerance and liberality of sentiment, with an intense aversion for priestcraft. Even in literature his criticisms, though often admirably perceptive, are too often wayward and unsatisfactory, because at the mercy of his prejudices. He idolized Milton, but the mediævalism of Dante dimmed his perception of Dante's great qualities. Almost alone among poets he always found

Spenser a bore.—STEPHEN, LESLIE, 1892, *Dictionary of National Biography, vol.* XXXII, *p.* 60.

When, resolute not to pay the damages cast against him in a trial for libel, a libel which the quick-tempered old poet ought not to have uttered, although indeed it was not uncalled for, Landor sold off all he had and quitted England to end his days in Italy, he left in my hands a pile of leaflets to be distributed in justification of his action. It was really a repetition of the libel, and, thinking such a course unworthy of so great a man, I burned the leaflets, every one. Some while after he sent to Browning, as a present for me, a large picture he supposed to be by Michael Angelo. Landor at one time had a large collection of pictures, supposed to be genuine, but seldom if ever of any worth. This "Angelo" might be of that sort. I called on Browning (the only time I ever saw him) to look at and to speak about the picture. It was a "Last Judgment," a poor and very unpleasant composition, too large and too unpleasant to be hung in a private house, a gift as of a white elephant, neither to be accepted nor refused.—LINTON, WILLIAM JAMES, 1894. *Three-Score and Ten Years, p.* 156.

Another of our *habitués* on my first visit to Florence was Walter Savage Landor. At that time he was, with his dear Pomeranian dog, Giallo, living alone in very ordinary lodging in Florence, having quarrelled with his family and left his villa in their possession. He had a grand, leonine head with long white hair and beard, and to hear him denouncing his children was to witness a performance of "Lear" never matched on any stage. He was very kind to me, and we often walked about odd nooks of Florence together, while he poured out reminiscences of Byron and Shelley, some of which I have recorded, and of others of the older generation whom he had known, so that I seemed in touch with them all. He was then about eighty-eight years of age, and perhaps his great and cultivated intellect was already failing. Much that he said in wrath and even fury seemed like raving, but he was gentle as a child to us women, and to his dog whom he passionately loved.—COBBE, FRANCES POWER, 1894, *Life by Herself, vol.* II, *p.* 348.

Landor's face put me in mind of the portraits of Hogarth. He had a diabolical laugh—a prolonged mockery, with apparently no heart or happiness in it, and when you thought he had done he went on and on; perhaps his extreme age was the cause of his prolongation, but not of its *timbre*. He gave me *an aperçu* of his views on art, politics and literature. I suppose he was a very wrong-headed man, and that his fierce individuality (Welsh choler) made his acquaintance as uncomfortable as his friendship was perilous. Every now and then the Tuscan States rang with his 'larum, and at one time he made Florence too hot to hold him. A parodoxical old Jacobin, it seemed to me that there was nothing really genial about the man Landor. Alfred Tennyson tells me he used to meet him at Mr. John Forster's chambers in Lincoln's Inn Fields; that one day, while Landor was reciting some poetry, a member of the company tumbled down stairs and broke his leg, and that Landor the while went on spouting without showing any special concern.—LOCKER-LAMPSON, FREDERICK, 1895, *My Confidences, p.* 162.

We cannot wonder that the Italians failed to understand this imperious and eccentric Englishman. Strange stories about him were current among the people. He was believed to have challenged the Secretary of Legation for whistling in the street when Mrs. Landor passed; to have walked up to the judges in a court of justice, with a bag of dollars in his hand, asking how much was necessary to obtain him a favourable verdict; to have thrown his cook out of the window, for neglect of a dinner, and while the man lay groaning on the ground with a broken limb, thrust his head out with the exclamation "Good God, I forgot the violets!"—FYVIE, JOHN, 1895, *Walter Savage Landor, Temple Bar, vol.* 105, *p.* 256.

Landor lies under a flat white marble stone in the English Cemetery here, on the left of, and not very far from, the entrance. The inscription simply bears his name and records the fact that it is "The Last Sad Tribute of his Wife and Children."—HUTTON, LAURENCE, 1897, *Literary Landmarks of Florence, p.* 58.

My mother's near relationship to the Rose Aylmer of his boyish romance was the first link in the chain of this long friendship, for he remembered her as a little girl running by her sister, Rose Alymer's side. They never met after that until 1835 at Florence, and the intimacy continued which ceased only with their lives. It must have been to the charm of that inherited name that I am indebted for the many lovely verses—then so carelessly appreciated, now so deeply valued—with which he honoured a young and ignorant girl. . . . He was as full of fun as a boy; but if sometimes his boisterous spirits outran his discretion a reproving look would instantly restore his balance. These letters may not add one laurel to his brow, but their tenderness and grace will cling round his memory like the perfume of the gracious cyclamen, the flower he loved so well.—GRAVES-SAWLE, ROSE C., 1898, *Letter to Mr. Wheeler, Feb.*; *Letters of Walter Savage Landor, Private and Public, ed. Wheeler, Introduction, p.* X.

GEBIR
1798

At Bristol I met with the man of all other whom I was most desirous of meeting— the only man living of whose praise I was ambitious, or whose censure would have humbled me. You will be anxious to know who this could be. Savage Landor, the author of "Gebir," a poem which, unless you have heard me speak of it, you have probably never heard of at all.—SOUTHEY, ROBERT, 1808, *To C. C. Bedford, Apr.* 26; *Life and Correspondence of Robert Southey, ch.* XIV.

Mr. Walter Savage Landor, a very worthy person, I believe, and author of an epic piece of gossiping called "Gebir," upon the strength of which Mr. Southey dedicated to him his "Curse of Kehama." There is really one good passage in " Gebir " about a sea-shell, and the author is one of those dealers in eccentric obscurity, who might promise to become something if they were boys; but these gentlemen have now been full-grown for some time, and are equally too old and too stubborn to alter. I forbear to rake up the political allusions in a poem which nobody knows.—HUNT, LEIGH, 1814-15, *The Feast of the Poets, p.* 117, *note.*

His first work was a poem, viz. "Gebir;" and it had the sublime distinction, for some time, of having enjoyed only two readers; which two were Southey and myself. It was on first entering at Oxford that I found "Gebir" printed and *published,—i. e.* nominally made *public,* whereas all its advertisements of birth and continued existence were but so many notifications of its in-tense privacy. Not knowing Southey at that time, I vainly conceited myself to be the one sole purchaser and reader of this poem. I even fancied myself to have been pointed out in the streets of Oxford, where the two Landors had been well known in times preceding my own, as the one inexplicable man authentically known to possess "Gebir," or even (it might be whispered mysteriously) to have read "Gebir." It was not clear but this reputation might stand in lieu of any independent fame, and might raise me to literary distinction.— DE QUINCEY, THOMAS, 1847-58, *Notes on Walter Savage Landor, Works, ed. Masson, vol.* XI, *p.* 399.

Its merit lies apart from either intention or construction, style and treatment constituting the charm of it. It presents many splendours of imagination, in a setting of unusual strength and range of mind. The characteristics preëminent in it are the intellect and reflection which pervade and interfuse its passion; the concentration yet richness, of its descriptive power; the vividness with which everything in it is presented to sight as well as thought; the wealth of its imagery; and its marvels of language. Everywhere as real to the eye as to the mind are its painted pictures, its sculptured forms, and the profusion of its varied but always thoughtful emotion. These qualities have not even yet had general acknowledgement; but the effect produced by the poem upon a few extraordinary men was such as to more than satisfy any writer's ambition. The mark it made in Landor's life will constantly recur; and of the manner in which his genius affected his contemporaries, not by influencing the many, but by exercising mastery over the few who ultimately rule the many, no completer illustration could be given.—FORSTER, JOHN, 1865-69, *Walter Savage Landor, a Biography, bk.* II.

Never was there a swifter stride made than from Landor's prenticework to "Gebir," which displayed his royal poetic genius in full robes. Where now be his politics and polemics? Henceforth his verse, for the most part, is wedded to pure beauty, and prose becomes the vehicle of his critical or controversial thought. In "Gebir," art, treatment, imagination, are everything; argument very little; the story is of a remote, Oriental nature, a cord upon which he strings his extraordinary language, imagery, and versification. The structure is noble in the main, though chargeable, like Tennyson's earlier poetry, with vagueness here and there; the diction is majestic and sonorous, and its progress is specially marked by sudden, almost random, outbursts of lofty song. I do not hesitate to say that this epic, as poetry, and as a marvelous production for the period and for Landor's twenty-two years, stands next to that renowned and unrivalled torso, composed so long afterward, the "Hyperion" of John Keats.—STEDMAN, EDMUND CLARENCE, 1875-78, *Victorian Poets*, p. 40.

The transitions from one theme to another are effected with more than Pindaric abruptness, and the difficulty of the poem is further increased by the occurrence of grammatical constructions borrowed from the Latin, and scarcely intelligible to those ignorant of that language. It is only after considerable study that the reader succeeds in taking in "Gebir" as a whole, however much he may from the first be impressed by the power of particular passages. Next to the abruptness and the condensation of "Gebir," its most striking qualities are breadth and vividness of imagination. Taken severally, and without regard to their sequence and connection, these colossal figures and supernatural actions are presented with masterly reality and force. As regards style and language, Landor shows that he has not been studying the great masters in vain. He has discarded Bellona and the Zephyrs, and calls things by their proper names, admitting no heightening of language that is not the natural expression of heightened thought. For loftiness of thought and language together, there are passages in "Gebir" that will bear comparison with Milton. There are lines, too, that for majesty of rhythm will bear the same comparison; but majestic as Landor's blank verse often is, it is always too regular; it exhibits none of the Miltonic variety, none of the inventions in violation or suspension of ordinary metrical law, by which that great master draws unexampled tones from his instrument.—COLVIN, SIDNEY, 1881, *Landor (English Men of Letters)*, p. 27.

"Gebir" is jeweled with lines that are faultless, alike in rounded beauty of expression and majesty of rhythm. Nevertheless, "Gebir" is not exactly easy reading. The plot is at once dull and fantastic; the story drags; the breath of life is not in the characters.—WHYTE, WALTER, 1892, *The Poets and the Poetry of the Century, Robert Southey to Percy Bysshe Shelley*, ed. Miles, p. 95.

If Landor had had, at this earlier period, greater artistic poise and sureness, "Gebir" and not the "Lyrical Ballads" might now be held to signalize the triumph of the new romantic poetry. But the poem is incoherent and immature, and in spite of many beauties, is a failure. It lies outside Landor's characteristic work, as do likewise the efforts which he made during the next twenty-five years in the romantic drama.—MOODY, WILLIAM VAUGHN, AND LOVETT, ROBERT MORSS, 1902, *A History of English Literature*, p. 305.

COUNT JULIAN
1812

I have finished "Count Julian" this evening. . . . It will have many defects; but I did not imagine I could do so well as I have done. The *popularis aura*, though we are ashamed or unable to analyse it, is requisite for the health and growth of genius. . . I believe I am the first man who ever wrote the better part of a tragedy in a concert room. . . It cannot be well done, written with such amazing rapidity. In forty hours I have *done* a thousand lines. Little of the original plan is retained, but about three-hundred verses are unaltered, or nearly so. When my fingers are fairly well again, I will transcribe the whole for you, that the eye may take in all at a time. I ought to have it acted, as an indemnity for the sleeve of a new coat which it has actually made threadbear. Do not whisper to anyone that I have written a tragedy. My name is composed of unlucky letters. But if you know of any poor devil who can be benefited by the gift of one, he may have it—profit, fame and all; and what is more, if it is not successful, he may say it is mine. At all events, it will have a better chance with him than with me.—LANDOR, WALTER SAVAGE, 1811, *Letter to Southey, Jan. 21; Walter Savage Landor, a Biography by John Forster*, bk. III; *note.*

I am not disappointed in Count Julian; it is too Greek for representation in these times, but it is altogether worthy of you. The thought and feeling which you have frequently condensed in a single line is unlike anything in modern composition. The conclusion, too, is Greek. . . . Never was a character more finely conceived than Julian. That image of his seizing the horses is in the very first rank of sublimity; it is the grandest image of power that ever poet produced.—SOUTHEY, ROBERT, 1811, *Letter to Landor, Feb.* 12; *The Life and Correspondence of Robert Southey, ed. C. C. Southey, ch.* XVI.

I have a tragedy of Landor's in my desk, of which Count Julian is the hero; it contains some of the finest touches, both of passion and poetry, that I have ever seen.— SOUTHEY, ROBERT, 1812, *Letter to Sir Walter Scott; Walter Savage Landor, a Biography by John Forster, bk.* III, *note.*

I must read again Landor's "Julian." I have not read it for some time. I think he must have failed in Roderick, for I remember nothing of him, nor of any distinct character as a character—only fine sounding passages.—LAMB, CHARLES, 1815, *Letters.*

The position of Count Julian is one which might indeed be "majestically described," and is worthy of the hand which showed us Hamlet and Othello, each in the centre of a world which had crumbled about him, undermined by that falsehood which is the death of every possibility. . . . Is such a hero as demands the hand of the highest genius.—OLIPHANT, MARGARET O. W., 1882, *Literary History of England,* XVIII-XIX *Century, vol.* I, *p.* 314.

The sublimest poem published in our language between the last masterpiece of Milton and the first masterpiece of Shelley —one equally worthy to stand unchallenged beside either for poetic perfection as well as moral majesty—the lofty tragedy of "Count Julian," which appeared in 1812, without the name of its author. No comparable work is to be found in English poetry between the date of "Samson Agonistes" and the date of "Prometheus Unbound;" and with both these great works it has some points of greatness in common. The superhuman isolation of agony and endurance which encircles and exalts the hero is in each case expressed with equally appropriate magnificence of effect. The style of "Count Julian," if somewhat deficient in dramatic ease and the fluency of natural dialogue, has such might and purity and majesty of speech as elsewhere we find only in Milton so long and so steadily sustained.—SWINBURNE, ALGERNON CHARLES,

1882, *Encyclopædia Britannica, Ninth Ed., vol.* XIV.

It shows the same defects of structure as "Gebir," and the characters are unimpressive.—WALKER, HUGH, 1887, *Celebrities of the Century, ed. Sanders, p.* 652.

POEMS

That deep-mouthed Bœoian "Savage Landor." —BYRON, LORD, 1823, *Don Juan, Canto* II.

What is it that Mr. Landor wants, to make him a poet? His powers are certainly very considerable, but he seems to be totally deficient in that modifying faculty, which compresses several units into one whole. The truth is he does not possess imagination in its highest form,—that of stamping *il più nell' uno.* Hence his poems, taken as wholes, are unintelligible; you have eminences excessively bright, and all the ground around and between them in darkness. Besides which, he has never learned with all his energy, how to write simple and lucid English.—COLERIDGE, SAMUEL TAYLOR, 1834, *Table Talk, ed. Ashe, Jan.* 1, *p.* 268.

He writes criticism for critics, and poetry for poets; his drama, when he is dramatic, will suppose neither pit nor gallery, nor critics, nor laws. He is not a publican among poets—he does not sell his Amreeta cups upon the highway. He delivers them rather with the dignity of a giver to ticketed persons; analyzing their flavour and fragrance with a learned delicacy, and an appeal to the esoteric. His very spelling of English is uncommon and theoretic. And as if poetry were not, in English, a sufficiently unpopular dead language, he has had recourse to writing poetry in Latin; with dissertations on the Latin tongue, to fence it out doubly from the populace. *Odi profanum vulgus et arceo.*—BROWNING, ELIZABETH BARRETT, 1844, *Letter to R. H. Horne, Contemporary Review, vol.* 23, *p.* 809.

The poetry of Savage Landor has not been so much read as his prose. His "Imaginary Conversations" have eclipsed his verse. Yet there is a great vigor, much satire, and much tender feeling in his poems which should render them acceptable to all lovers of manly writing.—HOWITT, WILLIAM, 1847, *Homes and Haunts of the Most Eminent British Poets, vol.* II, *p.* 373.

The style, tone, idiom and manner of Landor are all quite un-English. He never acquired the Saxon geniality of his mother-tongue; and his "Gebir," "Count Julian," and many of his other poems, read exactly like translations, closely rendered. . . . . With many high excellencies, Landor's poetry must ever remain "a sealed book" to the multitude; for whoever prefers to the obviously sublime, beautiful and true, the grotesque, the visionary, and the involved, must submit to be admired by the capricious select, who can alone relish such elements in composition.—MOIR, D. M., 1851-52, *Sketches of the Poetical Literature of the Past Half-Century, Lecture* II.

The difficulty in selecting from his works is the abundance; but I prefer the "Hellenics," that charming volume, because, few, very few, have given such present life to classic subjects. I begin with the Preface, so full of grace and modesty.—MITFORD, MARY RUSSELL, 1851, *Recollections of a Literary Life*, p.304.

Walter Savage Landor is of all English modern poets the one least read by the public, and the one whom the fewest impostors care even to pretend they have read. The reasons for this are twain: he achieved a literary position so many years ago, that the new generation have never known him; and his poetry has not at any time been the fashion, its austere simplicity rendering it unintelligible to the mass of men. He himself has aptly compared it to the wood of the olive-tree, which is known when it burns by the purity of its flame and the paucity of its ashes.—COLLINS, MORTIMER, 1871, *Landor's Country, Belgravia, vol.* 13, *p.* 435.

We place Landor, who was greater, even, as a prose-writer, among the foremost poets, because it was the poetry within the man that made him great; his poetry belongs to a high order of that art, while his prose, though strictly prosaic in form—he was too fine an artist to have it otherwise—is more imaginative than other men's verses. Radically a poet, he ranks among the best essayists of his time; and he shares this distinction in common with Milton, Coleridge, Emerson, and other poets, in various eras, who have been intellectual students and thinkers. None but sentimentalists and dilettanti confuse their prose and verse,—tricking out the former with a cheap gloss of rhetoric, or the false and effeminate jingle of a bastard rhythm. . . . Landor belonged, in spite of himself, to the Parnassian aristocracy; was, as he has said, a poet for

poets, and one who personally impressed the finest organizations. Consider the names of those who, having met him and known his works, perceive in him something great and worshipful.—STEDMAN, EDMUND CLARENCE, 1875-78, *Victorian Poets, p.* 37.

There is something glowing, soft, and Oriental about Landor's genius. He stands alone in his gifts as clearly as any poet. Some of his minor works are worthy of a place in the Greek anthology.—SMITH, GEORGE BARNETT, 1875, *English Fugitive Poets, Poets and Novelists, p.* 406.

Though a great wit, a great thinker, a great Hellenist, rather than a great poet, Landor has written some verses distinguished by singular transparency of style and elevation of thought.—EDWARDS, AMELIA BLANDFORD, 1878, *ed. A Poetry Book, Second Series, The Modern Poets, p.* 323, *note.*

The consummate grace of many of Landor's smaller pieces will ever recommend them to the general reader, but the bulk of his poetry can only be appreciated by those who possess cognate tastes and something of similar acquisitions. There remains, however, a just interest in this signal example of the enduring dominion of the old classic forms of thought, not only over the young imagination, but over the matured and most cultivated intelligence.—MILNES, RICHARD MONCKTON (LORD HOUGHTON), 1880, *The English Poets, ed. Ward, vol.* IV, *p.* 472.

Landor was the earliest of our modern poets specially characterised by their devotion to ideal beauty and to classical associations. With classical literature his name has long been intimately joined, not only by many an "Imaginary Conversation," in which the heroes, poets, and philosophers of antiquity are invoked from the shades, but yet more by his poetry, formed as that was, after a classical model,—his English poetry, not less than that written with such signal merit in the Latin language. . . . Landor's poetry has sometimes been charged with a deficiency of pathos. It is true that in general he loves rather to exhibit human life in the exhilarating and equable light of day, than tinged with the lights of a low horizon, and clouded with the shadows of eve. His pathos has, notwithstanding, a peculiar depth and tenderness; and though unostentatious, is very far from being infrequent. The "Death of Artemidora" may serve as a specimen.—DE VERE, AUBREY, 1887, *Landor's Poetry, Essays Chiefly on Poetry, vol.* II, *pp.* 143, 156.

Landor, notwithstanding his success in presenting objects of artistic beauty—and his poetry is full of exquisite delineations of them—failed to interest men; nor could his skill in expressing thought, although he was far more intellectual than his successors, save his reputation. Landor mistook a few of the marks of art for all. His work has the serenity, the remoteness, that characterize high art, but it lacks an intimate relation with the general life of men; it sets forth formal beauty, as painting does, but that beauty remains a sensation, and does not pass into thought. This absence of any vital relation between his art and life, between his objects and ideas, denotes his failure.—WOODBERRY, GEORGE EDWARD, 1890-1900, *Makers of Literature, p.* 81.

As a poet Landor cannot rank with the greatest men of his time; he cannot, one need hardly say, stand beside Shelley and Keats and Wordsworth and Byron. But he did a kind of work unlike the work of any of these, and he did it almost perfectly. From the writings of greater poets, the finest spirits of their day, the deepest lovers of art, will again and again turn for change and refreshment to Landor's idyllic verse. He was himself aware that his greatest work was done in prose.—WHYTE, WALTER, 1892, *The Poets and the Poetry of the Century, Robert Southey to Percy Bysshe Shelley, ed. Miles, p.* 96.

Come hither, who grow cloyed to surfeiting
With lyric draughts o'ersweet, from rills that rise
On Hybla not Parnass mountain: come
With breakers rinsed of the dulcifluous wave
Hither, and see a magic miracle
Of happiest science, the bland Attic skies
True-mirrored by an English well; no stream
Whose heaven-belying surface makes the stars
Reel with its restless idiosyncrasy;
But well unstirred, save when at times it takes
Tribute of lover's eyelids, and at times
Bubbles with laughter of some sprite below.
—WATSON, WILLIAM, 1893, *On Landor's "Hellenics," Poems, p.* 25.

Landor's Greek tales are written with a severity which in other hands would seem frigid and artificial; but his native grandeur of mind, his mingled passion and tenderness, triumph over this obstacle; the verse is hard and inflexible as marble, but it breathes and burns. He renders the hurly-burly of battle not, like Scott, by a sympathetic rush and tumult of style, but like a sculptor, by an intense and passion-fraught repose. — HERFORD, CHARLES HAROLD, 1902, *English Tales in Verse, Introduction, p.* lii.

PERICLES AND ASPASIA
1836

There is another characteristic of Landor's writings, which I mention the more distinctly from the fact that it seems not to have much attracted the admiration even of his admirers,—and that is the depth and tenderness of feeling which they breathe. "Pericles and Aspasia," especially, is full of the sweetest and truest expressions of sensibility; and so are many of the dialogues. We are frequently forced to drop the book and surrender ourselves to the visions and memories, soft or sad, which his words awaken and cause to pass before the mind. —HILLARD, GEORGE STILLMAN, 1856, *Selections from the Writings of Walter Savage Landor, Preface.*

As an exhibition of intellectual beauty, may be termed the masterpiece of Landor's whole career. Critics are not wanting who maintain "Pericles and Aspasia" to be the purest creation of sustained art in English prose. . . . Is clear as noonday, a book for thinkers,—but a book for lovers also, and should be as immortal as the currents which flow between young hearts.—STEDMAN, EDMUND CLARENCE, 1875-78, *Victorian Poets, pp.* 51, 54.

"Pericles and Aspasia," like some of the classical "Conversations," has the misfortune of being weighted with disquisitions too learned for the general reader, and not sound enough for the special student. But for this drawback, the book is throughout in Landor's best manner. It is full of variety and invention; we pass from the performance of "Prometheus" before the assembled Athenians to Aspasia's account of the dawn of love between herself and Pericles, and of the fascination and forwardness of the boy Alcibiades, to letters which reveal the love-frenzy of the unhappy Xeniades; then to others containing criticisms, accompanied by imaginary specimens, of various greater or minor Greek poets; and thence to original exercises in poetry by the correspondents themselves.—COLVIN, SIDNEY, 1881, *Landor (English Men of Letters), p.* 153.

PENTAMERON
1837

I have just finished reading Landor's "Pentameron." It is full of interest for the critical and poetical mind, but is sullied by some *Landorisms*, which are less like weeds in a fine flower-bed than some evil ingredient in the soil, revealing itself here and there by rankish odors, or stains and blotches on leaf and petal.—COLERIDGE, SARA, 1846, *To Aubrey De Vere, Aug.* 31; *Memoir and Letters, ed. her Daughter, p.* 285.

Petrarch and Boccaccio were highly esteemed by Landor, who did not sympathize with Lord Chesterfield in his opinion that the former deserved his *Laura* better than his *lauro*. The best evidence of this predilection is Landor's great work, "The Pentameron," second only to his greatest, "Pericles and Aspasia." Its *coleur locale* is marvellous. On every page there is a glimpse of cloudless blue sky, a breath of warm sunny air, a sketch of Italian manner. The masterly *gusto* with which the author enters into the spirit of Italy would make us believe him to be "the noblest Roman of them all," had he not proved himself a better Grecian. Margaret Fuller realized this when, after comparing the Pentameron and Petrarca together, she wrote: "I find the prose of the Englishman worthy of the verse of the Italian. It is a happiness to see such marble beauty in the halls of a contemporary." — FIELD, KATE, 1866, *Last Days of Walter Savage Landor, Atlantic Monthly, vol.* 17, *p.* 550.

A hundred volumes of travels and a thousand biographical and antiquarian dissertations would not place so vividly or graphically before the reader, with their appropriate framing of local scenery, the Tuscan peasant and the Tuscan priest as they were, and with small changes are still, and the Tuscan man of letters as he was in the middle ages. It is impossible to doubt that Landor had made himself thoroughly acquainted with the locality. But he has erred, or more probably has chosen to modify the real facts in his treatment of his fiction, in representing Boccaccio's house to have been a "*villetta* hard by Certaldo," and in that delicious account of Ser Francisco's ride to his Sunday's morning mass at the church of Certaldo. For the house is, as has been said, in the main street of the town, and within a hundred yards of the church. If, however, a more

accurate accordance with the particulars of the locality had been the means of depriving us of the "crowned martyr's" ride, and of the saddling of the canonico's nag by the joint efforts of himself and Assuntina, we should have lost infinitely more than we could have gained in minuteness of matter of fact information.—TROLLOPE, THOMAS ADOLPHUS, 1874, *Some Recollections of Walter Savage Landor, Lippincott's Magazine, vol.* 13, *p.* 447.

In the "Pentameron" Landor is again at his very best. All his study of the great Italian writers of the fourteenth century, and all his recent observations of Tuscan scenery and Tuscan character, are turned to skillful and harmonious account. Landor loved and understood Boccaccio through and through; and if he overestimated that prolific and amiable genius in comparison with other and greater men, it was an error which for the present purpose was almost an advantage. Nothing can be pleasanter than the intercourse of the two friendly poets as Landor had imagined it; nothing more classically idyllic than the incidental episodes. Even the humor of the piece is successful, in all at least that has to do with the characters of the sly parish priest, the pretty and shrewd servant-maid Assuntina, and her bashful lover.—COLVIN, SIDNEY, 1881, *Landor (English Men of Letters), p.*156.

IMAGINARY CONVERSATIONS

Now for twenty years we have still found the "Imaginary Conversations" a sure resource in solitude, and it seems to us as original in its form as in its matter. Nay, when we remember his rich and ample page wherein we are always sure to find free and sustained thought, a keen and precise understanding, an affluent and ready memory familiar with all his chosen books, an industrious observation in every department of life, an experience to which nothing has occurred in vain, honor for every just and generous sentiment and a scourge like that of furies for every oppressor, whether public or private,—we feel how dignified is the perpetual censor in his curule chair, and we wish to thank a benefactor of the reading world.—EMERSON, RALPH WALDO, 1843, *Walter Savage Landor, Papers from the Dial; Works, Riverside Ed., vol. XII, p.* 204.

Landor's "Conversations," among the most charming, profound, and delicate productions I have ever read.—DICKENS,

CHARLES, 1845, *To the Countess of Blessington, May 9; The Letters of Charles Dickens,* ed. *Dickens and Hogarth, vol.* III, *p.* 72.

In our own time Walter Savage Landor has adopted and improved upon the model of Lyttelton and when his heroes talk they are certain to say something new.—LAWRENCE, EUGENE, 1855, *The Lives of the British Historians, vol.* I, *p.* 384.

Well as he succeeded in hitting the mode of thought of many of his discoursing personages, it was by means of his learning and not of his sympathies, that he did so. They were all raised from the dead in their habits as they lived; but it was in order to be possessed by Landor in every case—his spirit speaking through their brains, perhaps, as well as through their lips—but always his spirit and no other. Hence his failures in the case of Milton, and partly, even in that of Cromwell; though there he might have been expected to succeed pre-eminently.—MARTINEAU, HARRIET, 1864-69, *Biographical Sketches, p.* 123.

His "Imaginary Conversations" are absolutely unique in their way, and betray an insight into the characters of men which no writer except Shakespeare has surpassed. These marvellous productions, sparingly read at present, will certainly outlive most of the imaginative literature of our time. To read them is like entering the stately halls and magical gardens of Alcinous, in the company of the lovely Nausicaa. The genius which enables Landor to comprehend and depict the characters of past history is so amazing, that we are apt to forget the splendid scholarship on which it is based. . . . He writes our language, in both prose and verse, with a strength and purity unrivalled in the present century.—COLLINS, MORTIMER, 1871, *Landor's Country, Belgravia, vol.* 13, *p.* 435.

They have passed into literature and their influence and charm are undying. . . . Their personages are as noble as those of Sophocles, as sage and famous as Plutarch's, as varied as those of Shakespeare himself.—STEDMAN, EDMUND CLARENCE, 1875-78, *Victorian Poets, p.* 50.

His "Imaginary Conversations" are full of fine thoughts, expressed in a style so finished, so eloquent, so clearly bearing the impress of genius and cultivated taste, so felicitous in imagery and in diction, that one wonders why they are in general so little read. The reason probably is that their subjects have little interest to people in general, and that their tone of sentiment does not for the most part appeal to the ordinary sympathies and emotions of humanity.—NICOLL, HENRY J., 1882, *Landmarks of English Literature, p.* 374.

There is, doubtless, something of labor in reading Landor's "Conversations" if one is not conversant with high thinking, and if one is but slenderly endowed with historic imagination, but the labor is not in the writing. The very form of conversation permits a quickness of transition and sudden shifting of subject and scene which enliven the art and give an inexhaustible variety of light and shade. One returns to passages again and again for their exceeding beauty of expression and their exquisite setting. To one accustomed to the glitter of current epigrammatic writing, the brilliancy of some of Landor's sentences may not at first be counted for its real worth, but to go from Landor to smart writers is to exchange jewels for paste. What I have said may serve partly to explain the limited audience which Landor has had and must continue to have. If it is a liberal education to read his writings, it requires one to receive them freely. The appeal which Landor makes to the literary class is very strong, and apart from a course of study in the Greek and Latin classics, I doubt if any single study would serve an author so well as the study of Landor. Indeed, there is perhaps no modern work which gives to the reader not familiar with Greek or Latin so good an idea of what we call classical literature. Better than a translation is the original writing of Landor for conveying the aroma which a translation so easily loses. The dignity of the classics, the formality, the fine use of sarcasm, the consciousness of an art in literature,—all these are to be found in the "Imaginary Conversations;" and if a reader used to the highly seasoned literature of recent times complains that there is rather an absence of humor, and that he finds Landor sometimes dull, why, Heaven knows we do not often get hilarious over our ancient authors, and Landor, for his contemporaries, is an ancient author with a very fiery soul. . . . Landor is sometimes characterized as arrogant and conceited; stray words and acts might easily be cited in support of this, but no one can read his "Conversations" intelligently and not perceive how noble was his scorn of mean men, how steadfast his admiration of great men.—SCUDDER, HORACE E., 1887, *Men of Letters, pp.* 102, 104.

I began to be not quite sure whether the balance of his sentences, each so admirable by itself, did not grow wearisome in continuous reading,—whether it did not hamper his freedom of movement, as when a man poises a pole upon his chin. Surely he has not the swinging stride of Dryden, which could slacken to a lounge at will, nor the impassioned rush of Burke. Here was something of that cadenced stalk which is the attribute of theatrical kings. And sometimes did not his thunders also remind us of the property-room? Though the flash failed, did the long reverberation ever forget to follow?—LOWELL, JAMES RUSSELL, 1888, *Some Letters of Walter Savage Landor, The Century, vol.* 35, *p.* 73.

One of the great charms of the "Conversations" is their unexpectedness, and want of visible sequence; one never knows whither the writer's quickly changing moods will take him, or what surprises are not in store for the reader. . . . When Landor leaves the domain of what he has himself witnessed and experienced, he becomes wild, absurd and too often trivial. The conversations between ancient Greeks and Romans should be excepted, because of the fitness and propriety of these the judgment of the reader must be guided by a great familiarity with the classics, which Landor had, and by a large experience of humanity, in which he was notably deficient. What I particularly refer to are the Conversations, the scene of which is laid in Russia, Poland, or the East, on which his authorities were imperfect, and the spirit of which he by his nature could not understand. — SCHUYLER, EUGENE, 1888-1901, *Italian Influences, pp.* 69, 71.

Landor was happy, too, in selecting the form of "Imaginary Conversations" between distinguished men of different ages and opinions. None other would have so well suited his mind, and brought into such perfect play his wide knowledge of men and books. His mind had a tendency, after a time, to run off any one direct track of thought into paradox and contradiction, and the form he selected gave scope to this peculiarity, without weakening the force of his views. These "Imaginary Conversations" abound with noble arguments and

thoughts, worthy of the characters of those into whose mouths they are put, and I read them with great pleasure as well as profit.—STORY, WILLIAM WETMORE, 1890, *Conversations in a Studio, vol.* II, *p.* 437.

No finer specimens of dignity in letters can be seen than that evinced in the pages of this author's "Imaginary Conversations," in which, as he represents the greatest authors of all history holding high converse on exalted themes, he himself is in fullest sympathy with the theme and adds dignity to dignity by the personal decorum of his manner.—HUNT, THEODORE W., 1890, *Studies in Literature and Style, p.* 51.

To me, two of the most delightful features of the "Imaginary Conversations" are the tenderness so frequently displayed, and the delicate but sure handling of female character. I know of no more exquisite pathos, no more refined expression of the love of man and woman, no more truth to woman's subtler instincts, than are to be found in such conversations as those between Æsop and Rhodope, between Epicurus, Leontion, and Ternissa, between Achilles and Helena, between Agamemnon and Iphigenia, between Dante and Beatrice.—ANDERSON, MELVILLE B., 1892, *Landor, The Dial, vol.* 13, *p.* 72.

Which have given him his chief fame; but which, very possibly, may be outlived in the popular mind by the wonderful finish and the Saxon force which belong to many of his verselets. . . . There are seven great volumes of it all—which must belong to all considerable libraries, private or other, and which are apt to keep very fresh and uncut. . . . . It is a great, wide, eloquent, homely jumble; one bounces from rock to rock, or from puddle to puddle (for there are puddles) at the will of this great giant driver of the chariot of imaginary talk.—MITCHELL, DONALD G., 1897, *English Lands Letters and Kings, The Later Georges to Victoria, pp.* 132, 133, 134.

The "Conversations" display, in stiff and attic form, dramatic aptitudes, for confirmation of which we search in vain the pages of his academic plays. These historic dialogues, strange as it seems, were refused by publisher after publisher; but, at length, in 1824, two volumes of them were issued, and the world was gained. This great series of stately colloquies holds a unique position in English literature. The style of Landor is too austere, too little provided with ornament, too strenuously allusive to please the running reader. But in a mingling of dignity and delicacy, purity and vehemence, into what is an amalgam of all the rarer qualities of thought and expression, Landor ranks only just below the greatest masters of language. His genius is impeded by a certain haughty stiffness; he approaches majestically, and sometimes nimbly, but always protected from the reader by a suit of mail, always rendered inaccessible by an unconquerable shyness.— GOSSE, EDMUND, 1897, *A Short History of Modern English Literature, p.* 324.

GENERAL

There is little moral courage in our literary world. Few will speak what they think; and they gather what they think from conduits and common sewers rather than from springs and fountains. They do not guide the mass, but are moved along and soon confounded with it. In all other countries the literary part of the community is the best; in England, I am sorry to say, it is guided by spleen, fashion, and interest.— LANDOR, WALTER SAVAGE, 1838, *To Leigh Hunt, Feb.* 6; *Correspondence of Leigh Hunt, ed. his Son, vol.* I, *p.* 319.

Two new tragedies of his that I read lately are the fatalest stuff I have seen for long: not an ingot; ah, no, a distracted coil of wire-drawings salable in no market.—CARLYLE, THOMAS, 1840, *To Emerson, April* 1; *Correspondence of Carlyle and Emerson, ed. Norton, vol.* I, *p.* 304.

Yet it is not as an artist that Mr. Landor commends himself to us. He is not epic or dramatic, he has not the high, overpowering method by which the master gives unity and integrity to a work of many parts. He is too wilful, and never abandons himself to his genius. His books are a strange mixture of politics, etymology, allegory, sentiment, and personal history; and what skill of transition he may possess is superficial, not spiritual. His merit must rest, at last, not on the spirit of the dialogue or the symmetry of any of his historical portraits, but on the value of his sentences. Many of these will secure their own immortality in English literature; and this, rightly considered, is no mean merit. These are not the plants and animals, but the genetical atoms of which both are composed. All our great debt to the Oriental world is of this

kind, not utensils and statues of the precious metal, but bullion and gold-dust. Of many of Mr. Landor's sentences we are fain to remember what was said of those of Socrates; that they are cubes, which will stand firm, place them how or where you will.— EMERSON, RALPH WALDO, 1843, *Walter Savage Landor, Papers from the Dial; Works, Riverside Ed., vol.* XII, *p.* 211.

Mr. Landor is a man of genius and learning, who stands in a position unlike that of any other eminent individual of his time. He has received no apparent influence from any one of his contemporaries; nor have they or the public received any apparent influence from him. The absence of any fixed and definite influence upon the public is actually as it seems; but that he has exercised a considerable influence upon the minds of many of his contemporaries is inevitable, because so fine a spirit could never have passed through any competent medium without communicating its electric forces, although from the fineness of its elements, the effect, like the cause, has been of too subtle a nature to leave a tangible or visible impress. . . . Every sarcasm, irony, jest, or touch of humor, is secreted beneath the skin of each tingling member of his sentences. His wit and his humor are alike covered up amidst various things, apparently intended to lead the reader astray, as certain birds are wont to do when you approach the nests that contain their broods. Or, the main jests and knotty points of a paragraph are planed down to the smooth level of the rest of the sentences, so that the reader may walk over them without knowing anything of the matter. All this may be natural to his genius; it may also result from pride, or perversity. So far from seeking the public, his genius has displayed a sort of apathy, if not antipathy, to popularity; *therefore,* the public must court it, if they would enjoy it; to possess yourself of his wit you must scrutinize; to be let into the secret of his humor you must advance "pointing the toe." Such are the impressions derivable from Mr. Landor's writings. —HORNE, RICHARD HENGIST, 1844, *A New Spirit of the Age.*

We know no author whose writings breathe a more conscious presence of nobility. His thought is perfect and entire, calm, clear, independent: it does not attempt to make you a convert; it is there without any declamation of apology, for you to return to it or not, as you choose; but you do return to it, fascinated by its brightness and single grandeur. Landor presents himself to us in his writings as a proud, intellectual man, an inflexible lover of truth, though not insensible to prejudice; of a native nobility of soul, quickly impressed by the show of manliness and worth; a sincere friend, and what, with a man of his temperament, is its correlative, a good hater; a fastidious, educated man, who carries his moral sensitiveness into the world of literature; a lover of poetry, he himself a poet. Mr. Landor's poetry, however, is the poetry of the intellect rather than the heart.— GRISWOLD, RUFUS W., 1844, *The Poets and Poetry of England in the Nineteenth Century, p.* 101.

Is it not true that Landor, too, is one of the men who carry their passions about with them into everything, as a boy would pebbles, muddying every clear water, with a stone here and a stone there? The end is, that we lose the image of himself in the serene depth, as we might have had it— and the little stone comes to stand for him. How unworthy of such a man as Landor, such weakness is! To *think* with one's temper! One might as well be at once Don Quixote, and fight with a warming pan.—BROWNING, ELIZABETH BARRETT, 1846, *Letters of Robert Browning and Elizabeth Barrett, 1845-1846, vol.* II, *p.* 313.

Mr. Landor, who always rises with his subject, and dilates like Satan into Teneriffe or Atlas when he sees before him an antagonist worthy of his powers, is probably the one man in Europe that has adequately conceived the situation, the stern self-dependency, and the monumental misery of Count Julian. That sublimity of penitential grief, which cannot accept consolation from man, cannot hear external reproach, cannot condescend to notice insult, cannot so much as *see* the curiosity of bystanders,—that awful carelessness of all but the troubled deeps within his own heart, and of God's spirit brooding upon their surface, and searching their abysses.— DE QUINCY, THOMAS, 1847-58, *Notes on Walter Savage Landor; Works, ed. Masson, vol.* XI, *p.* 433.

Though he could not be deprived of his daily bread for his sins of plain speaking, yet he has had his share of the malevolence of the low and selfish. The reptiles have bitten, and no doubt have stung, at times,

deeply, when he has trodden them beneath his feet, or flung among them his scalding and clinging Greek fire. But he knows that the fruit of his life will not be lost. Already he has lived long enough to see that the tide of opinion and reform is setting in strongly in the direction which he has indicated. It is amazing what progress the truth has made within the last twenty years; and a man like Landor knows that at every future step it must derive fresh strength from his writings. He has pandered to no corruption, he has flattered no fashion; his efforts are all directed to the uprooting of error and the spread of sound reason; and, therefore, the more the latter prevails the more his writings will grow into the spirit of the age. There are those who say that Landor's writings never can be popular. They are greatly mistaken. There is a large reading class, every day becoming larger, in which, were they made cheap enough, they would find the most lively acceptation. It is the class of the uncorrupted people itself. His opinions, and his manly, uncompromising spirit, are just what fall on the popular spirit like showers in summer. They are drank in with a thirsty avidity, and give at once life and solace. In this respect I do not hesitate to place them among the very first of the age.—HOWITT, WILLIAM, 1847, *Homes and Haunts of the Most Eminent British Poets, vol.* II, *p.* 373.

Having proposed to himself to be a labourer in literature, Mr. Landor's first care has been to make himself master of his implements. His success has been signally great. . . . His language is finished, yet perfectly natural. Although always visibly correct, and always terse, it is still free, never stiff, never pedantic. His words are singularly choice; and they seem as if they came unsought for, and from every department of our composite language. His composition has less of the air of a student's— less of the disciple's of any school—less of the professed writer's, than that of any other recent English author we can call to mind. For the most part, it is that of one intent merely on uttering his thoughts, which it does after no set or favourite form, but in a varying manner, suited to the matter to be delivered. And with a most remarkable readiness, his diction takes the character of the ideas to be expressed, doing its work always promptly, always effectively, and always with ease, sometimes with admirable gracefulness and beauty. This is high praise, but well deserved, and sincere as great.—TAYLOR, I., 1847, *Landor's Works, North British Review, vol.* 6, *p.* 80.

Look at Walter Savage Landor! No one can doubt that he is intensely and essentially a poet, and that his prose and verse contain little bursts of glorious poetic music. But they are brief; they are broken; they are not sustained; they are perpetually intermingled with harsh and harrow-like paragraphs, and both his prose and verse conjoin in proving that he never could have elaborated any long, linked, and continuous harmony.—GILFILLAN, GEORGE, 1855; *A Third Gallery of Portraits, p.* 137.

No style surely bears such testimony as his, by its calmness and proportion, its freedom and its severity, to the influence of the best authors upon him, and to his own power of coping with them and mastering them. It is, moreover, adapted to this century, no copy of Taylor or Milton's, of South's or Addison's, though benefitted and enriched by them all; still more by his classical reading, not corrupted nor made the least pedantic by it. His style is never obtrusive, seldom leads you to think about it, but it always suggests a man of whose mind it must be the utterance. The dialogue was the rightly chosen instrument of such a mind. He required it that he might present the different aspects of his own character; it kept up the balance of powers, each of which was always tending to excess.— MAURICE, FREDERICK DENISON, 1869, *Walter Savage Landor and Henry Crabb Robinson, Macmillan's Magazine, vol.* 20, *p.* 358.

More than any he reminds of Shakespeare in dramatic power; of Plato, in his mastery of dialogue; in epic force, of Æschylus. He seems to have been one of the demigods, cast down, out of place, out of his time, restless ever, and indignant at his destiny.

" Heaven's exile straying from the orb of light." —ALCOTT, A. BRONSON, 1869, *Concord Days, p.* 197.

His prose writings are better known than his poetry; yet it is probably his poetry that is the most secure basis of his reputation. His crowning excellence is sublimity of conception: the character of Count Julian is his masterpiece, and it is ranked by so sober a judge as De Quincey with the Satan of Milton and the Prometheus of Æschylus. In his "Imaginary Conversations," as was to be expected from so eager an egotist, dramatic exhibition of character is no part of their excellence. Some critics, indeed, profess to see a great deal of character in some of the dialogues. But the concession is made that it is not impossible that in many cases he first wrote the opinions and then looked about for a passably consistent mouthpiece; and in many cases personages are credited with opinions that they are very unlikely to have entertained. The "Conversations" are interesting not from their dramatic propriety or significance, but as the vehicles of Landor's own opinions. He does not attempt to imitate the style of literary interlocutors; in the dialogue between Sir Philip Sidney and Fulke Greville, Greville talks the language of Sidney's "Arcadia," and Sidney the language of Walter Landor. In his prose style two points of excellence may be singled out— the aphoristic force of his general propositions, and the felicitous force of his imagery. In the opinion of many, his style has too much *force*. In addition to the vigor and occasional vehemence of the meaning, the minute observer will remark that the words are studiously chosen for emphatic articulation, containing an unusual proportion of energetic "labials," a choice doubtless apt and consistent, but, like all obtrusive arts, liable to be overdone.—MINTO, WILLIAM, 1872-80, *Manual of English Prose Literature, p.* 537.

Nowhere in the range of the English language are the glory and happiness of moderation of mind more nobly preached and powerfully illustrated than in the writings of this most intemperate man; nowhere is the sacredness of the placid life more hallowed and honoured than in the utterances of this tossed and troubled spirit; nowhere are heroism and self-sacrifice and forgiveness more eloquently adored than by this intense and fierce individuality, which seemed unable to forget for an instant its own claims, its own wrongs, its own fancied superiority over all its fellow-men. . . . His style is so natural an outgrowth of a rich imaginative mind, and so clear a representative of thought, that its study is not likely to lead to any servile imitation, while it conveys the most distinct impression of the charm and power of Form. Abounding in strong, even passionate diction, it is never vague or convulsive; magniloquent as declamation can demand, it is never pompous or turgid; humorous throughout, it avoids contortions and abhors caricature. In strange contradiction to the temper of the writer, its chief characteristic is self-command, and it bears a weight or paradox with as much ease and dignity as ordinary writing its lightest commonplace. —MILNES, RICHARD MONCKTON (LORD HOUGHTON), 1873, *Monographs, Personal and Social, pp.* 67, 141.

Another flaring beacon of the rock, on which great wits are often wrecked for want of a little kindly culture of unselfishness, is Walter Savage Landor, the most finished master of style, perhaps, that ever used the English tongue; but a person at the same time so imperiously wilful, and so majestically cross-grained, that, with all his polish, style and pointed thought, he was constantly living on the verge of insanity.—BLACKIE, JOHN STUART, 1874, *On Self-Culture.*

As an artist he was, like a maple, swift of development, but strong to hold it as an elm or oak; while many poets have done their best work under thirty, and ten years after have been old or dead, the very noon-tide of Landor's faculties was later than his fiftieth year. We could not regard him as a tyro, had he died, like Keats, at twenty-five, not as a jaded old man, dying, as he did, at ninety; for he was as conservative in youth as he ever grew to be, and as fiery and forward-looking in age as in youth. He attained the summit early, and moved along an elevated plateau, forbearing as he grew older to descend the further side, and at death flung off somewhere into the ether, still facing the daybreak and worshipped by many rising stars.—STEDMAN, EDMUND CLARENCE, 1875-78, *Victorian Poets, p.* 35.

No man ever lived whose life seemed so utterly beyond any law but his own caprice; no man ever wrote whose course of thought upon all great subjects was more strictly subordinated to universal law. In his life he was the ungoverned Berserker of the Scandinavian sagas; in his writings he is the sage and philosopher who might have given lessons to Plato or Cicero.—GUERNSEY, A. H., 1875, *Walter Savage Landor, The Galaxy, vol.* 20, *p.* 743.

If ever that sovereign power of perfection was made manifest in human words, such words assuredly were his, whether English or Latin, who wrote that epitaph on the martyred patriots of Spain, as far exceeding in its majesty of beauty the famous inscription for the Spartan three-hundred as the law of the love of liberty exceeds all human laws of mere obediance; who gave back Iphigenia to Agamemnon forever, and Vipsania for an hour of Tiberius. Before the breath of such a spirit as speaks in his transcendent words, the spirit of a loyal-minded man is bowed down as it were at a touch and melted into burning tears, to be again raised up by it and filled and kindled and expanded into something —or he dreams so—of a likeness for the moment to itself.—SWINBURNE, ALGERNON, CHARLES, 1877, *A Note on Charlotte Brontë, p.* 67.

Few men have ever impressed their peers so much, or the general public so little, as Walter Savage Landor. Of all celebrated authors, he has hitherto been one of the least popular. Nevertheless he is among the most striking figures in the history of English literature; striking alike by his character and his powers. . . . The place occupied by Landor among English men of letters is a place apart. He wrote on many subjects and in many forms, and was strong both in imagination and criticism. He was equally master of Latin and English, and equally at home in prose and verse. He cannot properly be associated with any given school, or, indeed, with any given epoch of our literature, as epochs are usually counted, but stands alone, alike by the character of his mind and by the tenour and circumstances of his life. . . . Everything he says must be his own, and nothing but his own. On the other hand, it is no part of Landor's originality to provoke attention, as many even of illustrious writers have done, by emphasis or singularity of style. Arbitrary and vehement beyond other men in many of his thoughts, in their utterance he is always sober and decorous. He delivers himself of whatever is in his mind with an air, to borrow an expression of his own, "majestically sedate."—COLVIN, SIDNEY, 1881, *Landor (English Men of Letters), pp.* 1, 2.

Landor was not one of our modern dressing-gown-and-slippers kind of authors. He always took pains to be splendid, and preferred stately magnificence to chatty familiarity.—BIRRELL, AUGUSTINE, 1887, *Obiter Dicta, Second Series, p.* 206.

To some of us Landor's imagination is not only inferior in kind but poverty-stricken in degree; his creative faculty is limited by the reflection that its one achievment is Landor's; his claim to consideration as a dramatic writer is negatived by the fact that, poignant as are the situations with which he loved to deal, he was apparently incapable of perceiving their capacities: inasmuch as he has failed completely and logically to develop a single one of them; inasmuch, too, as he has never once succeeded in conceiving, much less in picturing, such a train of conflicting emotions as any one of the complications from which he starts might be supposed to generate. To many there is nothing Greek about his dramatic work except the absence of stage directions; and to these that quality of "Landorian abruptness" which seems to Mr. Sidney Colvin to excuse so many of its shortcomings is identical with a certain sort of what in men of lesser mould is called stupidity.— HENLEY, WILLIAM ERNEST, 1890, *Views and Reviews*, p. 164.

In Landor's eight volumes there are more fine thoughts, more wise apothegms, than in any other discursive author's works in English literature; but they do not tell on the mind. They bloom like flowers in their gardens, but they crown no achievement. At the end, no cause is advanced, no goal is won. . . . His prose is rather the monologue of a seer. In reading his works one feels somewhat as if sitting at the feet of Coleridge. Landor has the presence that abashes companions. His manner of speech is more dignified, more ceremonial, his enunciation is more resonant, his accent more exquisite, than belong to the man of the world. He silences his readers by the mere impossibility of interrupting with a question so noble and smooth-sliding a current of words. The style is a sort of modern Miltonic; it has the suggestion of the pulpit divine in Hooker, the touch of formal artificiality that characterizes the first good English prose. — WOODBERRY, GEORGE EDWARD, 1890-1900, *Makers of Literature*, pp. 73, 85.

His own literary quality is to a great extent independent of the quality of his subjects, but none the less real for that. Like other original writers, he has to create the taste by which he is to be enjoyed. Judicial criticism has often affirmed his obvious faults, mentioning his merits parenthetically. It is the subtle merits that need affirmation, for it is by them that he differs from other writers. By them he may, in the long run, come to be known. For, whereas Dickens, George Eliot, and Browning show signs of losing, from lack of a sense of form, the pre-eminence which their strength seemed to command, Landor is perhaps gaining recognition as the possessor of a faculty which in them was subordinate. Not that he is gaining many readers nor that his writings can all be read by anybody. His best is unmatched in its kind, however; not to know it is to be a loser. Its chance in the struggle for existence rests on the likelihood of there being in future generations a few men with Emerson's unjaded taste for "pure literature."—CLYMER, W.B. SHUBRICK, 1890; *Landor Once More, Scribner's Magazine, vol.* 10, *p.* 128.

I have sometimes wondered whether Walter Savage Landor did not really meditate writing an historical novel at some time during the evolution of the "Imaginary Conversations." More than one work of the kind, and assuredly of the highest order, must have presented itself to his mind, since he possessed in a supreme degree the power most necessary to the historical novelist, that of seizing the dramatic points in the lives of historical personages and of creating splendid dramatic dialogues without at any time compromising undoubted facts. In other words, he knew how to combine the romantic and the real in such true and just proportions as to demonstrate clearly that they may and should go hand in hand.—CRAWFORD, F. MARION, 1893, *The Novel, What is It?; p.* 74.

Born in the decade which gave us Wordsworth, Coleridge, Southey, and Scott, at his maturity, when the fervid generation of Keats, Shelley and Byron were in full tide of song, Landor was as secluded and solitary as a mountain tarn. His long life of well-nigh ninety years included the entire Romantic movement of modern times. He stood in relations of personal friendship with the English poets who gave a new impulse and direction to the national imagination; he was a young man when the Schlegels, Novalis, and Tieck were recalling the enchantments of the Middle Ages in Germany; he was at the full maturity of his power when Lamartine published the "Meditations" and Victor Hugo routed the French Classicists on the stage of the Theatre

Français with his drama of "Hermani."
Through this tumultuous age, so intensely
modern in spirit that for the moment the
antique seemed wholly obliterated, Landor
preserved a calmness, a moderation, a self-
possession that were born of hourly companionship with a world of classical repose
and strength. To study him is to get in
clear perspective the proportions of his contemporaries, and to feel what is easily apprehended but not so easily described—
the difference between the Classical and the
Romantic manner.—MABIE, HAMILTON
WRIGHT, 1893; *Short Studies in Literature*,
p. 139.

Landor is uneven in the matter of unity.
He can keep severely to one topic, but he
forgets. He will begin an important paragraph on, say, Laura's decreasing coldness
towards Petrarca, and, after illustrating
this point by a remarkably inapposite account of the lady being kissed at a ball by
Charles of Luxemburg, will proceed to tell
you in the same paragraph of Petrarca's
travels and visits in the following summer.
Generally, however, Landor's frequent digressions proceed by whole paragraphs.
In the matter of proportion Landor has
very considerable merits, though by no
means the highest. He pays little attention to proportion by bulk; but he uses the
semicolon and the period with great skill to
secure right distribution of emphasis.
Here, however, the principle of euphony
often interferes. No author ever surpassed
Landor in such tricks of melody as introducing at the end of a resounding period a
very brief colon clause for cadence. These
skilful variations sometimes misplace the
thought emphasis. When, however, the
two principles coincide in the application,
the effect is perfect. The felicitous combination occurs oftener in the short than in
the long paragraphs. In the longer ones we
sometimes feel that the writer is caring
nothing for precision—only for the infinite
variety of prose modulation which he himself describes—that "amplification of harmonies, of which even the best and most
varied poetry admits but few." Landor's
style is intuitive and segregating; the incoherence of it is its weakest point.—LEWIS,
EDWIN HERBERT, 1894, *The History of the
English Paragraph, p.* 133.

It is not Landor's influence, by any means,
which is felt in the random dialogues of to-
day. He is an author more praised than

loved, more talked about than read, and his
unapproachable delicacy and distinction
are far removed from all efforts of facial
imitation.—REPPLIER, AGNES, 1894; *Dialogues, The Cosmopolitan, vol.* 17, *p.* 380.

Landor is the great solitary of English
literature. So strangely were the elements
mixed in him, that, with many of the qualities that endear men to their fellows, to
keep on terms with society was too severe a
tax upon his temper. Nor are the friends of
the author much more numerous than were
those of the man. He was content to keep
his way apart in life and content too that
the path he trod as a writer should be little
traveled. "I shall dine late," he said, "but
the dining-room will be well lighted, the
guests few and select." They are few and
select, and Landor, who was not a man of
his time, will never be the people's man.
At an epoch, when the cold fires of the classic ritual of eighteenth-century literature
began to pale before the passion and colour
and mystery of the mediæval revival, with
singular indifference to contemporary fashion he began to speak English with a purer
classic accent than had yet been heard in
the modern world. . . . Without achieving
success Landor by reason of his style takes
undisputed place among the masters of
English prose. The majestic march, the
solemn cadences and sustained harmonies
of his Roman period are among the golden
joys of the student of literature. Landor's
was the art of the statuary. His instinct
was for that form of excellence which consists in firmly outlined intellectual drawing,
and "words that fit the thing." To achieve
distinction in this manner is to be subject to
no changes of fashion and to be numbered
among those in whose quiet gardens, as in
the courts of some ancient college, the artist
loves to linger, to recall and meditate the
past, secure from the bustle of the crowd
and the faces of anxious men.—DIXON, W.
MACNEILE, 1896, *English Prose, ed. Craik,
vol.* v, *pp.* 197, 199.

Supreme genius Landor had not. His
brain was not a great brain, and he did not
possess the exquisite alertness to his own
weaknesses, or the stubborn knack of confinement to things suitable to him, which
some natures much smaller than the great
ones have enjoyed. But he had the faculty
of elaborate style—of style elaborated by a
careful education of the best models and vivified by a certain natural gift—as no one

since the seventeenth century had had it, and as no one except Mr. Ruskin and the late Mr. Pater has had since. Also, he was as much wider in his range and more fertile in his production than Mr. Pater as he was more solidly grounded on the best models than Mr. Ruskin. Where Landor is quite unique is in the apparent indifference with which he was able to direct this gift of his into the channels of prose and poetry—a point on which he parts company from both the writers to whom he has been compared, and in which his only analogue, so far as I am able to judge, is Victor Hugo. The style of no Englishman is so unlike in the two harmonies as is that of Landor. And it is perhaps not surprising that, this being the case, he shows at his best in prose when he tries long pieces, in verse when he tries short ones.—SAINTSBURY, GEORGE, 1896, *A History of Nineteenth Century Literature, p.* 102.

He is stiff in opinion, not because his vision of truth is so dazzling, but because he has the bull-dog's instinct of hanging-on to whatever comes beneath the teeth. "Mama says so," remarked the once famous child in "Punch;" "and if Mamma says so it *is* so, even if it isn't!" That was the opinion of Walter Savage Landor about Walter Savage Landor's opinions—even when he recommended the Greeks to fight the Turks with bows and arrows instead of firearms. Let us be thankful that a certain genius

makes them not too seldom right and that a classical style allied with a strong personality makes them always interesting. In no intellectual quality, perhaps, can he be called great; but he has written some of the best prose in the English language.—THOMPSON, FRANCIS, 1897, *Academy Portraits, The Academy, vol.* 51, *p.* 259.

The heroic ideals of Landor's imagination, derived in part from communion with the greatest natural aristocrats of all time, helped to save his verse and his prose from the violence and egotism which often confused his life, and which often cleared away as suddenly, like clouds before the wind and sun. He toiled indeed at his art with an intemperate rage that exhausted him; but it was to produce a form of marmoreal purity and permanence, to discover the laws and the lines of ideal majesty or ideal grace.—DOWDEN, EDWARD, 1897, *The French Revolution and English Literature, p.* 259.

Whose noble monumental style, far more truly and successfully Greek than his attempted Hellenisings in verse, has reconciled many a reader to as perversely ill-sorted a set of political and literary opinions as was ever begotten of the union of Tory prejudices and Jacobin theories in the same person, and to as arrogantly defiant a dogmatism as over-weening pride of intellect ever brought to their support.—TRAILL, HENRY DUFF, 1897, *Social England, vol.* VI, *p.* 29.

Adelaide Anne Procter
1825–1864

Born in London, and daughter of Byran Waller Procter (Barry Cornwall). Her earliest literary work consisted of poetical contributions published under the pseudonym of Miss Mary Berwick, in *Household Words,* conducted by Charles Dickens. Dickens himself had no suspicion of the real authorship of the poems until the warm approval expressed by him to Mr. and Mrs. Procter, of a poem by Miss Berwick, published in the Christmas number of *Household Words,* 1854, led Miss Procter to disclose her identity. Some years before her death, Miss Procter became a Roman Catholic, and took great interest in charitable work in London. It was for the benefit of a lodging house for homeless women in London that her "Chaplet of Verses" was written. She published "'Legends and Lyrics," 1858, and an enlarged edition, 1861; "A Chaplet of Verses," 1862.—RANDOLPH, HENRY FITZ, 1887, *ed. Fifty Years of English Song, Biographical and Bibliographical Notes, vol.* IV, *p.* 25.

PERSONAL

I took Mrs. Montague up in the carriage on my way to church, and after service drove her home, and went up to see Mrs. Procter, and found baby (Adelaide Procter) at dinner. That child looks like a poet's child, and a poet. It has something "doomed" (what

the Germans call "fatal") in its appearance —such a preternaturally thoughtful, mournful expression for a little child, such a marked brow over the heavy blue eyes, such a transparent skin, such pale-golden hair. John says the little creature is an elf-child. I think it is the prophecy of a poet.—KEMBLE,

FRANCES ANN, 1832, *Journal, Jan.* 29; *Records of a Girlhood, p.* 499.

A beautiful girl of eight or nine years, the "golden-tressed Adelaide," delicate, gentle and pensive, as if she was born on the lip of Castaly, and knew she was a poet's child, completed the picture of happiness.—WILLIS, NATHANIEL PARKER, 1835, *Pencillings by the Way, Letter* CXX.

In the spring of the year 1853, I observed, as conductor of the weekly journal, *Household Words,* a short poem among the proffered contributions, very different, as I thought, from the shoal of verses perpetually setting through the office of such a periodical, and possessing much more merit. Its authoress was quite unknown to me. She was one Miss Mary Berwick, whom I had never heard of; and she was to be addressed by letter, if addressed at all, at a circulating-library in the Western district of London. Through this channel, Miss Berwick was informed that her poem was accepted, and was invited to send another. She complied, and became a regular and frequent contributor. Many letters passed between the journal and Miss Berwick, but Miss Berwick herself was never seen. How we came to gradually establish at the office of *Household Words* that we knew all about Miss Berwick, I have never discovered. But we settled somehow, to our complete satisfaction, that she was governess in a family; that she went to Italy in that capacity, and returned; and that she had long been in the same family. We really knew nothing whatever of her, except that she was remarkably business-like, punctual, self-reliant, and reliable; so I suppose we insensibly invented the rest. For myself, my mother was not a more real personage to me than Miss Berwick the governess became. This went on until December, 1854, when the Christmas number, entitled "The Seven Poor Travellers," was sent to press. Happening to be going to dine that day with an old and dear friend, distinguished in literature as "Barry Cornwall," I took with me an early proof of that number, and remarked as I laid it on the drawing-room table, that it contained a very pretty poem, written by a certain Miss Berwick. Next day brought me the disclosure that I had so spoken of the poem to the mother of its writer, in its writer's presence; that I had no such correspondent in existence as Miss Berwick; and that the name had been assumed by

Barry Cornwall's eldest daughter, Miss Adelaide Anne Procter.—DICKENS, CHARLES, 1865, *Adelaide Anne Procter, Atlantic Monthly, vol.* 16, *p.* 739.

Ilicet! let her go! though it were brave,—
  In the hot vintage, where the strongest fail
Weeding God's grapes from thistles—still to have
  Her silver hymns o'er weariness prevail!
Ilicet! Otherwhere they need those strains,
  Sounding so true for men—albeit low;
A throne was vacant (though its steps were pains,)
  For a soul, tried, pure, perfect—let her go!
—ARNOLD, SIR EDWIN, 1880, *Adelaide Anne Procter, "Ilicet," Poems, p.* 187.

Of the gifted eldest daughter the mother was intensely proud, and well may she have been, for a more vital spirit never inhabited a finely wrought frame. Adelaide Anne Procter was so curiously unlike her poems, and yet so distinct in individuality, that it is a pity she was not painted by an artist capable of rendering her singular and interesting face. There was something of Dante in the contour of its thin lines, and the coloring was a pale, delicate brown, which harmonized with the darker hair, while the eyes were blue, less intense in hue than those of Shelley; and like his also was the exquisitely fine, fluffy hair, which when ruffled stood out in a halo round the brow. A large oil painting of her exists, done, I believe, by Emma Galiotti, and it is like her as she appeared in a conventional dress and a most lugubrious mood, but the real woman was quite different. She had a forecast of the angel in her face and figure, but it was of the Archangel Michael that she made one think. There was something spirited and almost militant in her aspect, if such a word can be applied to one so exquisitely delicate and frail.—BELLOC, BESSIE RAYNER, 1895, *In a Walled Garden, p.* 167.

If Miss Brontë did not talk much, as was usual with her, she kept her eyes open. One of Mr. Thackery's guests was Miss Adelaide Procter, and those who remember that lady's charming personality will not be surprised to learn that I was greatly attracted by her. During our drive home I was seated opposite to Miss Brontë; and was startled by her leaning forward, putting her hands on my knees, and saying, "She would make you a very nice wife." "Whom do you mean?" I replied. "Oh, you know whom I mean," she said, "and we relapsed into silence. Though I admired Miss Procter very much, it was not the case of love at first sight, as Miss Brontë supposed.—SMITH, SIR GEORGE MURRAY, 1901, *In the Early Forties, The Critic, vol.* 38, *p.* 57.

GENERAL

Adelaide Anne Procter, even had she been the most pushing and irrepressible of blue stockings, with every vantage ground of circumstance, was not appreciated as she deserved. But, in addition to the original sin of being a woman, several reasons peculiar to herself concurred to render her, what we think she has been, one of the most underrated writers of her day. First, she was an Englishwoman. Had she not been, she might never have been anything; but once being something, we do not think it was an utterly inestimable advantage. For, as being English, every one took for granted that she must be a Protestant, and every one was disappointed and provoked to find her a Catholic.—RUDD, F. A., 1867, *Adelaide Anne Procter, The Catholic World, vol.* 5, *p.* 555.

Read her "Two Worlds," "The Warrior to his Dead Bride," "The Story of the Faithful Soul"— read, in fact, almost everything she has ever written—and you will find only pity for the world, a contempt of death, and a yearning, without any admixture of doubt, for the home beyond the grave.—AUSTIN, ALFRED, 1870, *The Poetry of the Period, p.* 187.

It is like telling one's beads, or reading a prayer-book, to turn over her pages,—so beautiful, so pure and unselfish a spirit of faith, hope and charity pervades and hallows them. These women, with their melodious voices, spotless hearts, and holy aspirations are priestesses of the oracle. Their ministry is sacred; in their presence the most irreverent become subdued.—STEDMAN, EDMUND CLARENCE, 1875-87 *Victorian Poets p.* 280.

Miss Procter, on the publication of her "Legends and Lyrics," at once assumed a high place in popular estimation; and that place she has maintained year after year, and still maintains without any diminution, the present demand for her poems being far in excess of that for the writings of any living poet, except Mr. Tennyson.—PATMORE, COVENTRY, 1877, *ed. Bryan Waller Procter, an Autobiographical Fragment and Biographical Notes, p.* 98.

She was very unobtrusive as a literary personage. She did not claim for herself any particular place or mission among her brothers and sisters of the pen. Her poems were not efforts. They were spontaneous productions of a sweet, wholesome nature, designed solely to brighten the lives of ordinary people. If she pleased the many readers of "Household Words," apparently her ambition was largely satisfied. We know, also, that while by nature she was endowed in many artistic ways, and while among her friends she was full of that sunshiny character which endears its possessor more than talent, her real life was not in the higher realms of imagination or in the intercourse of society, but was a secret devotion to piety. To be sure, the fact that this piety led her into the Roman Catholic Church shocked and perhaps prejudiced many who had early admired her writings. Still, there is a nun-like charm about the portrait of her which hearsay has handed down to us. And this peculiar charm hangs about her poetry also.—ROBERTSON, ERIC S., 1883 *English Poetesses, p.* 226.

Wherever she treats distinctly of peculiar Catholic doctrines, as in "The Chaplet," she is inferior to herself; but she has a heart and mind for broad and deep Christianity, and the two poems from "The Chaplet" which are nearly free from a narrower aim are really perfect, as much so as Dr. Newman's exquisite lines, "Lead, Kindly Light." The pieces to which I refer are . . . . "Ministering Angels" and "Per Pacem ad Lucem."—TAYLOR, EMILY, 1884, *Memories of Some Contemporary Poets, p.* 163

Her poetry may be classified as narrative, lyrical, and devotional, though, as we have already observed, the deeply religious and devotional cast of their author's mind is manifest in all of them. Nor is their purpose unapparent, though their didacticism is kept under admirable restraint. All of them faithfully reflect the deeper convictions of her mind, and it is matter of observation that though she lived till 1864, in the midst of intellectual people, many of whom must have been profoundly influenced by the scepticism, the unrest, the despair, of the time, no trace of it is to be discovered in her writings,—a remarkable fact in connection with the work of one so eager, so sympathetic, so impetuous. . . . Adelaide Procter is never obscure. She never struggles to find entrance for any "perplexed meanings;" all she says is clear, simple, direct. On the other hand, it is not often that she touches a very deep note in the human heart . . . . One of her best and most characteristic pieces is, undoubtedly, "The Story of the Faithful Soul." To compare her for a moment with another sweet religious singer of this century, —Keble—it might be said that, while she instills the same precepts and inculcates the same duties, she has never attained to his height.—GIBBS, H. J., 1892, *The Poets and the Poetry of the Century, Joanna Baillie to Mathilde Blind, ed. Miles, pp.* 361, 364.

It remains to say a few words about her poems. Since for years they had a larger sale than those of any other poet save Tennyson, they must have penetrated into every reading household in Great Britain. Of late, however, their popular fame seems chiefly to repose on "The Lost Chord," nobly set to music by Sir Arthur Sullivan. It is wonderful to see the enthusiasm infused by this song. The vast audience of St. James's Hall thrills as one man when it is given. But in the beauty of the narrative poems, and in the profound depth of feeling of those which have an autobiographical source, the student of Victorian literature will, I'm convinced, find permanent delight; and that many verses and many lines will survive may be inferred from the perfection of form which is essential to lasting fame. Miss Procter always used the plainest words to convey her thought, the simplest, choicest words to express her feeling. Some of those which deal with the human heart are wonderfully sweet and subtle.—BELLOC, BESSIE RAYNER, 1895, *In a Walled Garden, p.* 172.

Miss Procter, if not a great poet, had a gift for verse, and expressed herself with distinction, charm and sincerity. She borrowed little or nothing, and showed to best advantage in her narrative poems. "The Angel's Story," the "Legend of Bregenz," the "Legend of Provence," the "Story of a Faithful Soul," are found in numerous poetical anthologies. Her songs, "Cleansing Fires," "The Message," and "The Lost Chord," are well known, and many of her hymns are in common use. Her poems were published in America, and also translated into German. In 1877 the demand for Miss Procter's poems in England was in excess of those of any living writer except Tennyson. —LEE, ELIZABETH, 1896, *Dictionary of National Biography, vol.* XLVI, *p.* 416.

Though all of Adelaide Procter's poems are characterized by an earnestness of purpose which gives them a religious tone, her actual output of definitely religious verse is very small. The poem "Thankfulness," . . . . has given voice to the religious feelings of so many that it certainly deserves a place in any collection of the religious poetry of the time.—MILES, ALFRED H., 1897, *The Poets and the Poetry of the Century, Sacred, Moral and Religious Verse, p.* 736.

There is a certain grace in her verse, but it is altogether destitute of weight and power of thought.—WALKER, HUGH, 1897, *The Age of Tennyson, p.* 260.

John Clare

1793–1864

John Clare, peasant poet, the son of a poor labourer, was born at Helpstone, near Peterborough, July 13, 1793. After some scanty schooling, he began to do outdoor work in his seventh year, and for eleven months was an under-gardener at Burghley Park; meanwhile he studied Thomson's "Seasons," and began to cultivate verse writing. He enlisted in the militia (1812), associated with Gypsies, in 1817 worked at a lime-kiln, but was discharged for wasting his time in scribbling, and had to apply for parish relief. His "Poems, descriptive of Rural Life" (1821), had a good reception; but though the Marquis of Exeter and other patrons secured him £45 a year, he continued unfortunate. He died in the lunatic asylum, Northampton, 20th May 1864.—PATRICK AND GROOME, *eds.* 1897, *Chambers's Biographical Dictionary, p.* 218.

PERSONAL

For the boisterous sports and amusements which form the usual delight of village youth, Clare had neither strength nor relish; his mother found it necessary to drive him from the chimney corner to exercise and to play, whence he quickly returned, contemplative and silent. His parents—we speak from knowledge—were apprehensive for his mind as well as his health; not knowing how to interpret, or to what cause to refer these habits so opposite to those of other boys of his condition; and when, a few years later, they found him hourly employed in writing—and writing verses, too, —"he gear was not mended" in their estimation. "When he was fourteen or fifteen," says Dame Clare, "he would show me a piece of paper, printed sometimes on one side, and scrawled all over on the other, and he would say, 'Mother, this is worth *so* much; and I used to say to him, 'Aye, boy, it looks as if it warr!'—but I thought he was wasting his time". . . . The clouds which had hung so heavily over the youth of Clare, far from dispersing, grew denser and darker as he advanced toward manhood. His father, who had been the constant associate of his labours, became more and more infirm, and he was constrained to toil alone, and far beyond his strength, to obtain a mere subsistence. It was at this cheerless moment, he composed "What is Life?" in which he has treated a common subject with an earnestness, a solemnity, and an originality deserving of all praise: some of the lines have a terseness of expression and a nervous freedom of versification not unworthy of Drummond, or of Cowley.—SOUTHEY, ROBERT 1820, *Clare's Poems, Quarterly Review, vol.* 23, *pp.* 168, 169.

We recently visited him by the courteous permission of the medical superintendent, who generally refuses the same favor to others, because he deems, and rightly too, that his patients should not be made an "exhibition" of. Passing through several of the wards, we were ushered into what we at first deemed to be a gentleman's private sitting-room, but which was the ordinary sitting-chamber of the better class of patients and which appeared very cosy and comfortable with its mahogany chairs, table, and couch, warm soft carpets, and cheerful fire. Several patients were lounging about, and in a recess formed by one of the windows, which command a beautiful view of the large and spacious gardens belonging to the establishment, sat John Clare. Time had dealt gently with the poet, who—making allowances for his increased years—bore a very striking resemblance to the portrait of him prefixed to "The Village Minstrel." He was rather short in stature, with a very large forehead, and mild, benevolent-looking features. On our approaching him, we found him to be extremely taciturn, but the attendant informed us that in general Clare was good humored, obedient, and cheerful.

—PLUMER, JOHN, 1861, *A Forgotten Poet, Once a Week.*

In the spring of 1864, in the Northamptonshire General County Lunatic Asylum, after a sad incarceration of about twenty-three years, an appendix to a previous incarceration in a private asylum, from which he escaped, died John Clare. In the lucid intervals which shone upon him, he had always expressed a wish to sleep his last sleep in the churchyard of his native village, Helpstone. Accordingly, when his spirit had fled, the superintendent of the asylum wrote to the Earl Fitzwilliam, one of the great peers of England, and whose property lies immediately in the neighborhood of Helpston, asking for the grant of a small sum to carry the wish of the poor deceased into effect. The illustrious peer briefly replied by a refusal, implying that the deceased died as a pauper, and should be buried in the pauper's burial-ground. There were others who judged more generously than the noble earl, and it is a satisfaction to feel that this great indignity was not perpetrated towards the remains of one of the sweetest village nightingales that ever warbled the notes of pastoral melody in English verse. A requisite burial fund was raised in a few days; the poet's body was conveyed to Helpstone, and now lies beneath the shade of a sycamore tree, tombed over only by the green grass and the eternal vault of the sky. . . . Never have literature and labour been more remarkably combined than in the instance of John Clare, the Northamptonshire peasant; perhaps none who have attained any degree of eminence in literature from the lowly walks of life ever had to contend with difficulties more stern and severe than this singularly beautiful soul. — HOOD, EDWIN PAXTON, 1870, *The Peerage of Poverty.*

I recall him, poor fellow, with his huge, over-burdening head, that might have dreamed dreams and seen visions, but obviously was not the throne of productive thought. His life was cheerless, or gladdened only by a brief ray of sunshine that speedily gave way to blacker and blacker clouds of calamity, under the gloomy influence of which his mind sank: and after long years of confinement he died in the insane asylum at Northampton, the town with which his name is inseparably associated—though not to its honor. He was not buried in a pauper's grave; a few pounds were kindly subscribed to preserve his body from that indignity; that, and a small annuity purchased for him by subscription, while he was yet free from the most terrible of maladies, is the sum of what his country did for the poor peasant-boy who lived through penury and suffering to leave his mark in the literary annals of his time.—HALL, SAMUEL CARTER, 1883, *Retrospect of a Long Life, p.* 409.

GENERAL

Clare has latterly been patronized with a degree of liberality which does credit to the taste and benevolence of those who have so kindly interested themselves in his behalf. Injudicious friends have placed him by the side of Bloomfield and Burns; but he is many removes from either; although, at the same time, we admit that some of his effusions . . . evince great nature, and considerable sweetness of versification.—RYAN RICHARD, 1826, *Poetry and Poets, vol.* II, *p.* 275.

John Clare often reminds us of James Grahame. They are two of our most artless poets. Their versification is mostly very sweet, though rather flowing forth according to a certain fine natural sense of melody, than construed on any principles of music. So, too, with their imagery, which seems seldom selected with much care; so that, while it is always true to nature, often possesses a charm from its appearing to rise up of itself, and with little or no effort on the poet's part to form a picture, it is not unfrequently chargeable with repetition—sometimes, perhaps, with a sameness which, but for the inherent interest in the objects themselves, might be felt a little wearisome—there is so much still-life. They are both most affectionately disposed towards all manner of birds. Grahame's "Birds of Scotland" is a delightful poem; yet its best passages are not superior to some of Clare's about the same charming creatures—and they are both ornithologists after Audubon's and our own heart.—WILSON, JOHN, 1831–42, *Christopher North's Recreations; An Hour's Talk About Poetry.*

His poems were not the mere reflexes of his reading. He had studied for himself in the fields, and in the woods, and by the side of brooks. I very much doubt if there could be found in his poems a single commonplace image, or a description made up of hackneyed elements. In that respect, his poems are original, and have even a separate value, as a sort of calendar (in extent, of course, a very limited one) of many rural appearances, of incidents in the fields not elsewhere noticed, and of the loveliest flowers most felicitously described. The description is often true even to a botanical eye; and in that, perhaps, lies the chief defect; not properly in the scientific accuracy, but that, in searching after this too earnestly, the feeling is sometimes too much neglected. However, taken as a whole, his poems have a very novel quality of merit, though a quality too little, I fear, in the way of public notice. — DE QUINCEY, THOMAS, 1840, *Literary Reminiscenses; Works, ed. Masson, vol.* III, *p.* 144.

His third publication, too, "The Rural Muse," in spite of its unpromising title, more than justified all that had been done for him. The improvement was most remarkable. That he should gain a greater command over language, a choicer selection of words, and the knowledge of grammatical construction, which he had wanted before, was to be expected; but the habit of observation seemed to have increased in fineness and accuracy in proportion as he gained the power of expression, and the delicacy of his sentiment kept pace with the music of his versification. What can be closer to nature than his description of the nightingale's nest?—MITFORD, MARY RUSSELL, 1851, *Recollections of a Literary Life, p.* 116.

Clare is Bloomfield's successor, but he is very far his superior, dwelling among the ever-varying scenes of nature. He is not merely a rustic poet or a rural bard; such poets take merely the impression of a georgic world, but they do not reflect themselves; their bucolics abound in prettinesses and generalities, without the boldness of generalization. Clare has more fully individualized his scenery than any poet of his class, always excepting Burns. It is the poetry of rural life and taste, but rural life with the dignity of the man, not with the rudeness or manners of the clown. It is worth some inquiry what makes the evident distinction between the methods of Cowper and Wordsworth, and Keats and Tennyson, in describing nature; and between these, again, and our humbler friend of whom we are now speaking. All love the country, but few love it as Clare loves it; yet it seems indispensable to the proper appreciation of rural scenery that we should not only take our walks there, but find our work there. The poems of Clare are now, even in literary circles, almost unknown, and quite unreferred to. Their purity, their excessive modesty, their intense devotion to nature in the woods and fields, in an age when the woods and fields have been comparatively forsaken: these may be assigned as some of the reasons for the obscurity which has gathered round the name of one of the sweetest singers of the children of labour—one of the saddest names in the Peerage of Poverty.—HOOD, EDWIN PAXTON, 1859-70, *The Peerage of Poverty.*

John Clare is entitled to a high place, if not to the highest, among the "uneducated" poets of England. His keen observation of nature amounted to a genius; his delicacy in painting natural objects, whether a flower, a tree, a sunset, or a spring scene, was next to marvelous. He owed little to books, but wrote from his heart. He saw things with the eye of a true poet, and as he observed, so did he write.—SMILES, SAMUEL, 1860, *Brief Biographies, p.* 438.

Clare, in his humble way, and not consciously sharing in it, was a helper in that reaction against the conventionality and stiff formalism of the Johnsonian era in English poetry, which was led by such men as Wordsworth and Coleridge and Scott. He was not a mannerist nor an imitator. Perhaps, if he had possessed a wider knowledge of books when he began to write, he might have been less original; as it was, his verses aimed only to describe what a genuine lover of nature saw and felt—not merely her more obvious and general aspects, but many such minute charms as no other poet to this day has thought worthy of embalming. The ant, at its toil; the lady-bug, preening its gay wings on the bending grass-spear; the felled tree, that he fain would have left to "grow old in picturesque decay;" the frog, wetting his freckled sides as he leaped across the dewy meadow; the evening daisies, that "button into buds;"—the rain-dripping oaks, that "print crimpling dimples" on the lake; the glow-worm, apostrophized as a
"Tasteful illumination of the night,
Bright, scattered, twinkling star of spangled earth":
all these and thousands more of such minor beauties, employed his muse, and attested his close and loving observation.—AVERY, BENJAMIN P., 1873, *Relics of John Clare, The Overland Monthly, vol.* 10, *p.* 136.

Clare's sonnets are irregular in structure, and in a sense they are only fourteen-line poems. They might as well as not be better, or worse, for being two or three lines shorter or longer. There is no *inevitableness* about them: one feels that the choice of vehicle has been purely arbitrary,—in a word, that they have not that essential characteristic—adequacy of sonnet-motive. Like all his work, however, they are characterised by the same winsome affection for and knowledge of the nature amidst which he spent his life. Clare's poetry is often like a sunny and windy day bursting through the gloom of late winter.—SHARP, WILLIAM, 1886 *Sonnets of this Century, p.* 284, *note.*

Between Clare and Burns there is the difference (besides that of intrinsic power) between the most depressed English labourer and the independent Scottish farmer. Clare's poetry is modeled upon that of the cultivated classes, instead of expressing the sentiments of his own class. Lamb advised him to avoid his rustic "slang," and recommended Shenstone's "Schoolmistress" in preference to "Goody's own language." Clare becomes less vernacular in his later poems, and the advice may have suited the man. . . Though Clare shows fine natural taste, and has many exquisite descriptive touches, his poetry does not rise to a really high level; and, though extraordinary under the circumstances, requires for its appreciation that the circumstances should be remembered.—STEPHEN, LESLIE, 1887, *Dictionary of National Biography, vol.* x, *p.* 386.

The poetry of Clare is what might have been expected from his long familiarity with rural scenery, and his intimate knowledge of country life. Simple as the song of a bird, it is best described by Milton's phrase, "native wood-notes wild," for art it has none, and only such music as lingered in the memory of Clare from the few poets that he had read. It abounds with picturesque details, which declare the naturalist as well as that of the poet; it sparkles with happy epithets, and to those who delight in nature for its own sake, and not for the human quality which the present race of poets are striving to infuse into it, it is winsome and charming. It is not the kind of poetry to criticise, for it is full of faults, but to read generously and tenderly, remembering the lowly life of Clare, his want of education, his temptations, his struggles, his sorrow and suffering, and his melancholy end.— STODDARD, RICHARD HENRY, 1892, *Under the Evening Lamp, p.* 132.

This poetry has a very distinctive value of its own. Its minute and loving observation of nature is exceptionally accurate; and its pictures of the English peasant in his everyday life, agricultural pursuits, rural sports, fairy lore, hopes, fears, and hard struggles for daily bread, are those of one who, born in that class, had the soul and exceptionally keen sensibility of a poet. The verse is like a tender, modest, wild flower, with the dew of morning fresh upon it—like the note of a bird among green leaves. You are in the open air while you read this poetry, with the pulse stirred and the sense quickened. Yet it was not until he had acquired range and fluency of expression from books that he gave this deep intuition voice—though in the "Shepherd's Calendar," and even in the "Village Minstrel" volume, he occasionally did.—NOEL, RODEN, 1894, *The Poets and the Poetry of the Century, Keats to Lytton, p.* 81.

It is pure landscape painting, like that of Keats in youth, though beneath that in power. Such is the landscape of his early "Summer Evening." . . . This may seem an easy style, almost a mere catalogue. Let those who think so, try! That delicate minute truth to fact; that pure simple sincerity of touch, and every word in its natural place; yet the indescribable something that makes poetry, poetry preserved; by inborn gift only, not labour ever so strenuous, can this be effected. But the unhappy poet's best gifts in song came during the twenty years and more of later life which he spent in an asylum. During that long but inevitable imprisonment sanity seems to have returned to him at times; but accompanied as it was by consciousness of where he was, and why he was there, I know not whether such recovery can be counted gain. No poetry known to me has a sadness more absolute than Clare's asylum songs, reverting with what pathetic yearning to the village scenes of his hard-worked youth!—PALGRAVE, FRANCIS TURNER, 1896, *Landscape in Poetry, pp.* 206, 207.

George Pope Morris
1802–1864

Born at Philadelphia, Oct. 10, 1802; died at New York, July 6, 1864. An American journalist and poet. With Samuel Woodworth he established the "New York Mirror" in 1823 (discontinued in 1842), with N. P. Willis the "New Mirror" in 1843, and shortly after the "Evening Mirror." In 1845 he founded the "National Press." Its name was changed in a few months to "The Home Journal." This he edited with Willis till shortly before his death. He wrote "Briarcliff" (1825), etc., and edited "American Melodies" and, with N. P. Willis, "The Prose and Poetry of America" (1845). Among his best-known poems are "Woodman, Spare that Tree" and "My Mother's Bible."—SMITH, BENJAMIN E., ed. 1894–97, *The Century Cyclopedia of Names, p.* 708.

PERSONAL

He was about five feet two or three inches high, or, perhaps, a few inches more, not much more, however. His face was genial and pleasant. Short, crisp, dark curly hair, thinly streaked with silver threads, encircled a high, well-formed forehead, beneath which was a pair of bright, twinkling black eyes. The nose was well-shaped, and the mouth and chin cast in delicate moulds, the latter being slightly dimpled. The complexion was fresh and florid; altogether the aspect of the face was decidedly intellectual; not your pseudo-pensive, thoughtful sort of expression—that mock sentimentalism of look which certain young gentlemen, with turn-down collars, rejoice in, but a pleasant, vivacious, sparkling Tom Moore-ish look, which at once convinced you that its owner was open-hearted, as well as open-faced.

The gentleman, too, had a semi-military air and carriage, albeit, he had by no means a martial figure.—DIX, JOHN ROSS, 1854, *Bungay's Crayon Sketches and Off-Hand Takings, p.* 44.

It happened one day that I was driving in the vicinity of New York with George Morris, the American poet. We turned into Bloomfield Road, then a woodland lane of great natural beauty, to view at Morris's request a stately old tree, which had been planted by the poet's grandfather. I well remember the ring of genuine pathos in Morris's voice as he told me, on our way towards the tree, of the tender recollections associated with the old homestead to which it was contiguous. His happy boyhood in the old home, surrounded by father, mother, and sisters, all came back to him at the mention of that old tree. Little did we dream of the drama that was to follow. As we neared the homely cottage that had once housed the Morris family, my friend noticed an old man with his coat off, sharpening an axe. "What are you going to do?" asked the poet, with a tremor of apprehension in his tone. "You surely do not intend to cut down that tree?" "Yes, siree," was the blunt reply of the old man, who was evidently the occupant of one of the cottages. Morris and I descended from our trap to hold a parley with the old fellow. In conversation it transpired that the old man did not fancy having the tree so near his house. Besides, he wanted it for firewood. We asked him how much the wood would be worth, and he replied, "About ten dollars." So a bargain was speedily made; the money was paid to him, and the daughter of the woodman pledged her word that the tree should stand as long as she lived. Now this incident made a deep impression upon me, and I suggested it to Morris as a fine subject for poetic treatment. He took the hint and wrote the now well-known poem, "Oh, Woodman, Spare that Tree," which I immediately set to music.—RUSSELL, HENRY, 1895; *Cheer! Boys, Cheer! p.* 63.

No poet of his generation was more loved both in Europe and America.—PATTEE, FRED LEWIS, 1896, *A History of American Literature, p.* 171.

GENERAL

Morris is, very decidedly, our best writer of songs—and, in saying this, I mean to assign him a high rank as *poet.*—POE, EDGAR ALLAN, 1849, *George P. Morris, Works, ed. Stedman and Woodberry, vol.* VIII, *p.* 275.

Morris is the best known poet of the country, by acclamation, not by criticism. He is just what poets would be if they sang, like birds, without criticism; and it is a peculiarity of his fame, that it seems as regardless of criticism, as a bird in the air. Nothing can stop a song of his. It is very easy to say that they are easy to do. They have a momentum, somehow, that is difficult for others to give, and that speeds them to the far goal of popularity—the best proof consisting in the fact, that he can, at any moment, get fifty dollars for a song unread, when the whole remainder of the American Parnassus could not sell one to the same buyer for a shilling. It may, or may not, be one secret of his popularity, but it is the truth—that Morris's heart is at the level

of most other people's and his poetry flows out by that door. He stands breast-high in the common stream of sympathy, and the fine oil of his poetic feeling goes from him upon an element it is its nature to float upon, and which carries it safe to other bosoms, with little need of deep diving or high-flying. His sentiments are simple, honest, truthful and familiar; his language is pure and eminently musical, and he is prodigally full of the poetry of every-day feeling.—WILLIS, NATHANIEL PARKER, 1851, *George P. Morris the Song-Writer, Hurry-Graphs.*

In our judgment, there is no professed writer of songs in this day who has conceived the true character of this delicate and peculiar creation of art with greater precision and justness than Mr. Morris, or been more felicitous than he in dealing with the subtle and multiform difficulties that beset its execution.—WALLACE, HORACE BINNEY, 1852–56, *Literary Criticisms and Other Papers.*

George P. Morris, among the honored contributors to American poetry, whose pieces are familiar, is recognised as the song-writer of America. — TUCKERMAN, HENRY T., 1852, *A Sketch of American Literature.*

The most genuine lyric poet who has yet honored American literature, was George P. Morris. His songs are almost as familiar to American and English households as the music of birds, and they are ever welcome guests, for they are chaste in language and sentiment. They are magnetic because of their sympathy with the finer feelings of human nature. The author's genial humor, and kindliness of heart were ever manifest in his writings; and these qualities gave him hosts of friends among those even who never looked upon his ruddy face and sparkling black eyes. . . . It was not as a journalist that General (he held the office of brigadier) Morris won his widest popularity. It was chiefly and most substantially by his songs. These were ever sought after; and Balfe, Sir John Stephenson, Sir Henry Bishop and other English composers wedded them to sweet melodies, when they were sung by Malibran, Braham, Russell, Dempster, Anna Bishop and other noted vocalists, at public concerts. Millions of copies of "Woodman, Spare that Tree" were sold; and other songs, such as "We were Boys Together," "My Mother's Bible," "Origin of Yankee Doodle," "Long Time Ago," were sources of great profit to author and publisher, because of their popularity.—LOSSING, BENSON J., 1855-86, *Eminent Americans, pp.* 419, 420.

He has written odes and songs for a wide diversity of occasions, temperaments, and modes of feeling, from grave to gay, without ever pandering to a low taste, or giving voice to an unworthy sentiment. The popularity of his lyrics is the surest testimony to their poetic worth. . . . Mr. Morris has an easy command of rhythm and metre. His verses are music to the ear, as well as poetry to the inward sense. They are not such verses as feebly suit existing melodies, but such as would of themselves inspire and reward the musical composer, and could not fail to prescribe and enforce at his hand, each its appropriate style of treatment. They commonly seize on the one central idea of the occasion or theme, give perfect unity to its expression, and group around it just those subsidiary thoughts that render it more emphatic.—PEABODY, ANDREW P., 1858, *Critical Notices, North American Review, vol.* 87, *p.* 277.

The songs of Mr. Morris have been produced at intervals during the whole term of his literary career. They have been successfully set to music, and popularly sung on both sides of the Atlantic. The themes include most varieties of situation, presenting the love ballad, the patriotic song, the expression of patriotism, of friendship, and numerous occasional topics.—DUYCKINCK, EVERT A., AND GEORGE L., 1865-75, *Cyclopædia of American Literature, ed. Simons, vol.* II, *p.* 157.

It is chiefly as a song writer that Morris will be best remembered. Some of his lyrics such as "Woodman, Spare that Tree," and "Near the Lake where Drooped the Willow," are compositions of which any poet might be proud. A proof of the great popularity of Morris as a poet is the fact that for above a score of years he could, any day, exchange one of his songs unread for a fifty-dollar cheque, when none of the *literati* of New York could at that time sell one for the fifth part of that sum. Between 1838, the year that he published "The Deserted Bride, and Other Poems," and 1860, when the last edition of his poetical writings appeared, several collections of his songs, ballads, and poems were issued by some of the best New York publishers. His military title, . . . comes from his connection with the state militia.—WILSON, JAMES GRANT, 1886, *Bryant and his Friends, p.* 403.

Morris is strong in the expression of simple sentiments, such as are assured of the ready sympathy of the people. Of his poems, "Woodman, Spare that Tree!" is the best known; of others, his "Song of Marion's Men" is meritorious as a stirring and native ballad. These two poems and a few others will live with the songs of the nation, while his more ambitious efforts are already forgotten.—SIMONDS, ARTHUR B., 1894, *American Song, p.* 155.

Henry Rowe Schoolcraft

1793–1864

American ethnologist, born in Albany county, N. Y. In 1817-18 visited the mining region west of the Mississippi (described in his *Journal*), and in 1820 went with General Cass to Lake Superior as geologist. In 1822 he became Indian agent for the tribes about the lakes, and in 1823 married a wife of Indian blood. In 1832 he commanded an expedition which discovered the sources of the Mississippi (*Narrative*, 1834). While superintendent for the Indians, he negotiated treaties by which the government acquired 16,000,-000 acres. In 1845 he collected the statistics of the Six Nations ("Notes on the Iroquois," 1848). For government, he prepared his "Information respecting the Indian Tribes of the United States" (6 vols. 1851-57). His other works include poems, a Life of Cass, "Algic Researches" (1839), "The Red Race of America" (1847), "Thirty Years with the Indian Tribes" (1851), etc.—PATRICK AND GROOME, *eds.*, 1897, *Chambers's Biographical Dictionary, p.* 831.

PERSONAL

Mr. Schoolcraft was a conspicuous figure in the scientific life of the early part of the century. A pioneer in some fields, the immediate follower of the pioneers in others, he was, in all the branches of research to which he gave attention, earnest, ready, diligent, sagacious, original, and modest. As among his titles to be remembered, the biographer who prefaces his Personal Memoirs names the early period at which he entered the field of observation in the United States as a naturalist; the enterprise he manifested in exploring the geography and geology of the great West; and his subsequent researches as an ethnologist in investigating the Indian languages and history. —YOUMANS, WILLIAM JAY, *rev. and ed.* 1896, *Pioneers of Science in America, p.* 300.

GENERAL

We believe Mr. Schoolcraft, at first, feeling some distrust whether the Tales would be acceptable or popular in their present shape, thought of submitting them to some polished pen, which, like the pencil in respect to many of the Indian portraits that have been given to the public eye, would have detracted from their merit in proportion to the embellishment thrown over them. It is fortunate for the public, that he did not yield to this idea. The standard which we now have for measuring Indian intellect, and judging of the Indian imagination and powers of invention, of Indian mythological notions and superstitions,—a true standard, as we are fain to believe,—would have been falsified and erroneous. We should still have been left a prey to the fancies of authors, who could paint the Red man *enbeau*, with little chance, among their readers, of discriminating the creatures of the brain from the realities of the forest.—WHITING, H., 1839, *Schoolcraft's Indian Tales and Legends, North American Review, vol.* 49, *p.* 360.

Mr. Schoolcraft's ethnological writings are among the most important contributions that have been made to the literature of this country. His long and intimate connection with the Indian tribes, and the knowledge possessed by his wife and her family of the people from whom they were descended by the maternal side, with his power of examining their character from the European point of view, have enabled him to give us more authentic and valuable information respecting their manners, customs, and physical traits, and more insight into their moral and intellectual constitution, than can be derived, perhaps, from all other authors. His works abound in materials for the future artist and man of letters, and will on this account continue to be read when the greater portion of the popular literature of the day is forgotten.— GRISWOLD, RUFUS WILMOT, 1847-70, *The Prose Writers of America, p.* 300.

We have the highest authority for stating that Baron Humboldt, having had occasion to examine the work, expressed in strong

terms his opinion that it was a crude and worthless compilation, and his great surprise that it should be allowed to appear with the sanction and at the expense of the government of the United States. . . . The appropriation of nearly thirty thousand dollars a volume for the ill-digested and valueless compilation that lies before us ["The Indian Tribes"], rich though it be in its exterior and costly in its illustrations, is enough to discredit the whole system of publishing works at the government expense. We have done our share in exposing the nature of the evil; it is for Congress to do the rest.—BOWEN, FRANCIS, 1853, *Schoolcraft on the Indian Tribes, North American Review, vol.* 77, *p.* 262.

It may be fairly said that by this great national and Christian undertaking ["The Indian Tribes"], which realizes the aspirations of President Jefferson and carries out to their full extent the labours and efforts of a Secretary of the Treasury, the Hon. Albert Gallatin, the government of the United States has done more for the antiquities and language of a foreign race than any European government has hitherto done for the language of their ancestors. Certainly scarcely any single man has done more for collecting and digesting the materials than Mr. Schoolcraft, whose own observations and inquiries form the most important part of that publication.— BUNSEN, CHRISTIAN KARL JOSIAS BARON, 1854, *Outlines of the Philosophy of Universal History.*

To Henry Rowe Schoolcraft the world is more indebted for a variety of knowledge of Indian history, ethnology, archæology, character, customs and costumes, than to any other man.—LOSSING, BENSON J., 1855-86, *Eminent Americans, p.* 423.

The various and valuable writings of Mr. Schoolcraft, to whom the literary world is greatly indebted for his indefatigable zeal in rescuing from oblivion so much of the legendary lore of the Indians.—LONGFELLOW, HENRY WADSWORTH, 1857, *Works, p.* 398.

His great work is his "Historical Information concerning the Indian Tribes, etc.," published by act of Congress, in six large quarto volumes, profusely and handsomely illustrated. The work contains an immense amount of information upon everything relating to Indian manners, mythology, antiquities, language, etc., but so poorly digested and so deficient in philosophic method as to be, in the words of Humboldt, "almost worthless." The volumes are a mine from which the gold is yet to be extracted by some future explorer.—HART, JOHN S., 1872, *A Manual of American Literature, p.* 314.

The great thesaurus of information ("History, Condition, and Prospects of the Indian Tribes of the United States") ,concerning the Indian races east of the Rocky Mountains. The author was an enthusiast in the study of the habits and character of the Indian; and his huge volumes will be a permanent monument to his name. The labors of the author were carried on under the patronage of the government; and, although the work is more picturesque than scientific, it can never cease to have considerable value.—ADAMS, CHARLES KENDALL, 1882, *A Manual of Historical Literature, p.* 575.

The total number of his publications, as his widow informed the writer, was thirty-one; and as the historian of the American Indians, he will always be considered the leading authority.—LANMAN, CHARLES, 1885, *Haphazard Personalities, p.* 367.

Josiah Quincy
1772–1864

Born at Boston, Feb. 4, 1772: died at Quincy, Mass., July 1, 1864. An American statesman, orator, and historian: son of Josiah Quincy (1744–75). He was a Federalist member of Congress from Massachusetts 1805–13; opposed the embargo, the admission of Louisiana, and the War of 1812; was a member of the Massachusetts legislature; was mayor of Boston 1823–28; and was president of Harvard 1829–1845. He wrote a "History of Harvard University" (1840), "Municipal History of Boston" (1852), "Life of J. Q. Adams" (1858).—SMITH, BENJAMIN E., ed. 1894–97, *The Century Cyclopedia of Names, p.* 836.

PERSONAL

Few men have acquired so just a distinction for unspotted integrity, fearless justice, consistent principles, high talents, and extensive literature. Still fewer possess the merit of having justified the public confidence by the singleness of heart and purpose, with which they have devoted themselves to the best interests of society. In every station, to which you have been called by the free suffrages of the people, you have discharged its duties with the most exemplary ability, fidelity, and conscientiousness. In your present exalted station, to which you were invited by the combined voice of the guardians of the University, under the most flattering circumstances, every act of your life has conduced to establish the importance and wisdom of the choice.—STORY, JOSEPH, 1835, *Letter to Josiah Quincy, Oct.; Life and Letters, ed. Story, vol.* II, *p.* 216.

It was a noble spectacle to see this venerable man of eighty-five with his memory and all his powers about him, grand, stately, simple, a relic of great times gone by, born before the battle of Bunker Hill, six years old at the Declaration of Independence, whose father had died in the Cause, a member of Congress under Jefferson's administration.—DANA, RICHARD HENRY, 1855, *Journal, March; Richard Henry Dana by C. F. Adams, vol.* I, *p.* 342.

This great and good man, and true patriot. He has held no office which he did not fill with singular fidelity, wisdom, and zeal. With an ardor of temperament and energy of soul seldom equalled, he has ever enlisted these high characteristics in the cause of truth, justice, liberty, humanity: always pursuing the right rather than the seemingly expedient, convinced that in the long run the right *is* the expedient. His rare moral courage has more than once been put to the test, when he has stood alone, braving any amount of obloquy for pursuing what he deemed the truth, and what duty demanded of him.—CLEVELAND, CHARLES D., 1859, *A Compendium of American Literature, p.* 181.

Mr. Quincy had many qualities calculated to win favor with the young,—that one above all which is sure to do it, indomitable pluck. With him the dignity was in the man, not in the office. He had some of those little oddities, too, which afford amusement without contempt, and which rather tend to heighten than diminish personal attachment to superiors in station. His punctuality at prayers, and in dropping asleep there, his forgetfulness of names, his singular inability to make even the shortest off-hand speech to the students,—all the more singular in a practised orator,—his occasional absorption of mind, leading him to hand you his sand-box instead of the leave-of-absence he had just dried with it,—the old-fashioned courtesy of his, "Sir, your servant," as he bowed you out of his study,— all tended to make him popular. He had also a little of what is somewhat contradictorily called dry humor, not without influence in his relations with the students. In taking leave of the graduating class, he was in the habit of paying them whatever honest compliment he could. Who, of a certain year which shall be nameless, will ever forget the gravity with which he assured them that they were "the *best-dressed* class that had passed through college during his administration? . . . One great element of his popularity with the students was his *esprit de corps.* However strict in discipline, he was always on *our* side as respected the outside world.—LOWELL, JAMES RUS-SELL, 1871, *A Great Public Character, My Study Windows, pp.* 109, 110.

Mr. Quincy had a more intense and efficient will-power than any other man that I ever knew. He combined the sturdy uprightness of purpose and strenuousness of action which are commonly—I will not say how aptly—termed Roman, with the pure and high ethical standard, and the generous regard for human well-being, which are distinctively Christian. He was, by nature and by hereditary right, of the genuine aristocracy, born to rule; and, could the world's governing and care-taking be in the hands of men of his type, there would be no yearning for democratic institutions.—PEABODY, ANDREW P., 1888, *Harvard Reminiscenses, p.* 20.

M. A grand, heroic character of the ancient type, whose courage was as great as his patriotism was pure; who kept the enthusiasm of his youth and his faith in the future to the last; who was no sad praiser of the past, no "laudator temporis acti me puero," but who breathed encouragement to all with his words, and animated youth by his counsel, and never despaired when clouds gathered around the State.

B. I knew him well, and all you say of him is just; his uncorrupted and incorruptible principles, his true honesty, his large and liberal sentiments, his fresh-heartedness made him dear and honored by all men. I would we had many such in the councils of the nation.—STORY, WILLIAM WETMORE, 1890, *Conversations in a Studio, vol.* I, *p.* 135.

GENERAL

Quincy's "Life of Josiah Quincy" ranks high among the best biographical memoirs that have appeared in our language, and is generally received as a classical book in that department.—FLINT, TIMOTHY, 1833, *Sketches of the Literature of the United States, London Athenæum.*

In the "History of Harvard University," the progress of that distinguished seat of learning, which has had so great and beneficent an influence upon the character and condition of this nation, is traced with minuteness and fidelity through the two centuries which had elapsed since its formation. His style is perspicuous and elegant, and the narrative animated, generally well proportioned and interesting.—GRISWOLD, RUFUS WILMOT, 1847-70, *The Prose Writers of America, p.* 130.

It ["Life of Josiah Quincy"] well deserves a place in every American library, and it is greatly to be hoped that a new edition of it may be forthcoming at no distant day from the same filial hand;—a hand still untrembling under the ceaseless industry of more than four-score years, and never weary of doing another, and still another, labor of love for his kinsfolk, his fellow-citizens, or his country.—WINTHROP, ROBERT C., 1859, *Luxury and the Fine Arts, Addresses and Speeches on Various Occasions, vol.* II, *p.* 452.

Mr. Quincy's greatest occasion was the two-hundredth anniversary of the founding of the college, in 1836, when he delivered the commemorative address, which was the nucleus of his subsequent two-volume history of Harvard College. In this, as always, he showed himself the master of an English style, pure, rich, and vigorous. His elocution, when he had a manuscript before him, retained, with the weight and impressiveness, the fervor which had marked his eloquence in deliberative assemblies; but he no longer, if ever, sustained the even flow of unwritten discourse. When he felt the most strongly, his words seemed at first to be struggling for utterance, and then were poured out in spasmodic jets, with prolonged intervening pauses. — PEABODY, ANDREW P., 1888, *Harvard Reminiscences, p.* 34.

Benjamin Silliman
1779–1864

"The Nestor of American Science" (*Edward Everett*), is universally known by his works on Chemistry and as the founder of *Silliman's Journal of Science and Art*. Professor Silliman was born in North Stratford, Ct., and graduated at Yale, in the class of 1796. He was Professor of Chemistry, Mineralogy, and Geology, in Yale, from 1804 to 1855, a little over half a century. By the brilliancy of his lectures, his eminence as a man of science, and the genial and pervading goodness of heart which formed a prominent trait in his character, he contributed largely to the prosperity of the institution. Besides his scientific works, Professor Silliman wrote several attractive works of Travel: "A Journal of Travels in England, Holland, and Scotland," 3 vols., 8vo.; "Remarks on a Short Tour between Hartford and Quebec," 2 vols.; and "A Narrative of a Visit to Europe in 1851," 2 vols. He wrote also a work called "The Consistency of Discoveries in Modern Geology with the Sacred History of the Creation and Deluge," and numerous special addresses. His "Life and Correspondence," by Professor Fisher, 2 vols., 8vo., consists to a great extent of Professor Silliman's own writings.—HART, JOHN S., 1872, *A Manual of American Literature*, p. 245.

PERSONAL

I accordingly called, and met Professor Silliman for the first time. As the friend of Professor Dana I was kindly received, and not only furnished with what information I sought, but was soon engaged in a frank and pleasant conversation, chiefly upon topics of a scientific character, in which whole hours almost insensibly glided by. On leaving I was pressed so cordially to return that I did not hesitate to avail myself of the courtesy. This interview took place shortly after Professor Silliman's last visit to Europe, the recollections of which constantly crowded upon his mind, and were pleasantly interspersed through his conversation. At this time he had retired from the more active duties of life, to repose upon the laurels of a well-earned scientific reputation. He bore evident marks of advancing years, but yet was possessed of a naturally vigorous constitution and full physique, upon which the inroads of time had made less impression than is usually the case. He resembled so much the portrait painted by Wilson—to be found in his European tour, published in 1853—that I should have had no difficulty in recognizing him under any circumstances; but meeting him as I did, under the shelter of his own roof and amidst the scenes of his life-long labors, his face seemed at the moment of recognition as that of an old and familiar friend. Through his writings, and the periodic return of his *Journal*, I had for years been apparently as well acquainted with him as if he had existed before me with an animated form and an articulated voice; and the transition from my acquaintance with him as the conductor of an able scientific journal to a personal one seemed so slight as to scarcely be recognized.—WYNNE, JAMES, 1862, *Benjamin Silliman, Harper's Magazine, vol. 25*, p. 480.

As a lecturer he was almost unsurpassed. Without a severe logical method, he threw so much zeal into his discourse, expressed himself with such an attractive rhetoric, and supported his doctrine by experiments of such almost unfailing beauty and success that all audiences delighted to hear him; so that for years no lecturer so attractive could address an assembly, whether gathered in the walls of a college or from the people of crowded cities. In his own lecture-room the students felt the genial sway of his oratory. No other such instructions were given, uniting at once pleasure and improvement. Hence for many years the study of chemistry was, perhaps, the most popular one in the institution. In the latter years of his professional life the science of geology seemed to take the largest share of his interest. And, here, the grandeur of the subject-matter seemed especially fitted to kindle and exalt his fervor. The mighty agencies that have moulded the earth over and over, as clay is moulded in the hands of the potter, the immense ages which almost appall the imagination, this vast framework of the earth, the theatre of such sublime displays, and over all, before the eye of faith, the Divine Architect carrying the great building forward, until it had become a fit dwelling-place for his immortal creature, man—these grand objects inspired him, and he threw the inspiration into his audiences, wherever they were gathered.—WOOLSEY, THEODORE DWIGHT, 1864, *Funeral Discourse, p. 8.*

His life was a continued course of sunshine, the brightness of his mid-day answering to the brilliant promise of the morning, and passing by gentle transitions into the serene and softened glow of a cloudless sunsetting. His death was a veritable *euthanasia*, quiet, peaceful, sudden—a literal breathing away of the spirit in love to man and in praise to God. . . . The example of such a man in so long a life is a legacy of inspiration to the young men of the country, and not least valuable or important to the devotees of science, to lift them above the sordid and material aims, the petty rivalries, and the selfish ends from which even the most accomplished culture and the largest attainments and the widest acquaintance with men are not certain to deliver them.—PORTER, NOAH, 1866, *Professor Silliman's Memoirs, The Nation, vol. 2, pp.* 629, 630.

GENERAL

His "Journal" represents England to the Americans as it is, and exhibits to the English a fair specimen of the real American character. . . . Mr. Silliman is a good representative of the best American character.—SOUTHEY, ROBERT, 1816, *Works on England, Quarterly Review, vol.* 15, *pp.* 555, 556.

Of the American travelers who have published accounts of England, the work of Professor Silliman has been hitherto the best.—TUDOR, WILLIAM, 1816, *Louis Simond's Travels in England, North American Review, vol.* 2, *p.* 242.

His "Letters from England;" or "Silliman's Tour," a book published in America, after his return from a tour through England, Scotland, Wales, and Holland, is highly credible to his temper, heart, and good sense. It is a very fair picture of what he saw here; and a work which deserves to be, as it is, popular, in his country.—His "Tour in Canada" is contemptible; a piece of egregious book-making.—We think very highly of Professor Silliman, as a writer; as a mineralogist; as a geologist; and as a chemist; but very humbly, as a book-maker.—NEAL, JOHN, 1825, *American Writers, Blackwood's Magazine, vol.* 17, *p.* 201.

In 1818, Professor Silliman founded the "American Journal of Science and Arts,"—a work which has done more than any other to raise the reputation of our country for science, and to make her known and honored abroad; while it has placed the learned editor in the very front rank of scientific

men, and will ever remain a permanent monument to his zeal and perseverance in his favorite studies. Besides communicating with the public on scientific subjects through the press, he has frequently given courses of scientific lectures to popular audiences in our cities and towns, and always with great acceptance. His easy and dignified manners bespeak the gentleman born and bred; while his happy talent at illustration, and tact in communicating knowledge, always render his lectures as pleasing as they are instructive. . . . Professor Silliman has fitly been called the "Father of American Periodical Science;" and, although others of his countrymen preceded him in the study of nature, no man probably has done so much as he to awaken and encourage students of science, to collect and diffuse the researches of American naturalists, and to arouse in all classes of the community a respect for learning and a desire for its advancement.—CLEVELAND, CHARLES D., 1859, *A Compendium of American Literature, pp.* 233, 234.

His first edition of "Henry's Chemistry" appeared in 1808, with the modest announcement,—"to which are added notes by a Professor of Chemistry in this country." As soon as Gay Lussac's method of obtaining potassium by the decomposition of its hydrate by heat in an iron tube, was known in this country, Professor Silliman repeated the process with success, obtaining potassium for the first time, it is believed, in America. He was the first to notice and record the effect of a powerful voltaic battery in volatilizing carbon and transferring it from the positive to the negative pole in a state of vapor. His paper on this subject is full of curious interest, and was a long way in advance of the then existing state of knowledge. Professor Silliman labored zealously with the oxy-hydrogen blow-pipe of Dr. Hare, to determine the fusibility of different substances, and made interesting discoveries in this direction. His investigation in reference to the Western Meteor has already been mentioned. Such labors indicate that he was not indifferent or inactive in respect to the progress of the sciences which he taught. But his fame rests upon his work as a pioneer, opening the way in this country for new branches of science, and securing for them countenance and respect, and as a teacher who inculcated scientific truth in a way to interest, in an almost unexampled degree, his auditors. —FISHER, GEORGE P., 1866, *Life of Benjamin Silliman, vol.* II, *p,* 319.

The young man thus chosen was not mainly, or even largely an investigator; that was not the first thing needed. He obeyed the logic of his situation. What was first needed was an apostle of science to make known throughout the Republic an existing revelation, to make men listen to it, and, of those willing to listen, to stimulate the brightest and best to develop the work still further. It is no more disparagement to say that Benjamin Silliman was not a great original investigator than to say that a King is not a cabinet minister. When Sir Charles Lyell writes from the South expressing amazement at the numbers of men whom he found in most remote parts of the country who had received an impulse in scientific studies from Silliman, he had a vision of the real work of his honored friend. At this pioneer work he wrought for half a century. In his laboratory and lecture-room on these grounds, at centers of thought in all parts of the country, through the journal which he founded, through his correspondence, abroad and at home, he, more than any other man of his time, gave an impulse to scientific investigation throughout this country, which has never been lost.— WHITE, ANDREW, D. 1884, *Address at the Unveiling of the Bronze Statue of Professor Benjamin Silliman at Yale College, June* 24.

Thomas Starr King

1824–1864

Thomas Starr King, born in New York, Dec. 16, 1824; died in San Francisco, Cal., Mar. 4, 1864. His father was a Universalist minister in Charlestown, Mass. From 12 till 20 he labored first as clerk in a store, afterward as a teacher, preparing himself in leisure hours for the ministry. His first preaching was in Woburn, Mass., his first settlement in Charlestown, over his father's parish. In 1848 he accepted a call to the Unitarian church in Hollis st., Boston, and remained there till the spring of 1860, when he went to California to take charge of the Unitarian church in San Francisco. The outbreak of the civil war roused all his remarkable powers as a writer, speaker, and man, and to his influence is ascribed the change of public opinion in the State from lukewarmness toward the Northern cause to devoted loyalty. Through his exertions the United States Sanitary Commission obtained the generous sums of money that enabled it to carry on its work at the critical period of the war. He contributed frequently to the *Universalist Quarterly*, but he published but one book, "The White Hills, their Legends, Landscapes, and Poetry." A few of his papers were collected after his death—"Patriotism, and other Papers."—BARNARD AND GUYOT, *eds.* 1885, *Johnson's New General Cyclopædia, vol.* I, *p.* 727.

PERSONAL

Came the Relief. "What, Sentry, ho!
　How passed the night through thy long
　　waking?"
"Cold, cheerless, dark—as may befit
　The hour before the dawn is breaking."
"No sight? no sound?" "No; nothing, save
　The plover from the marshes calling;
And in yon western sky about
　An hour ago, a Star was falling."
"A star? There's nothing strange in that."
　"No, nothing; but, above the thicket
Somehow it seemed to me that God
　Somewhere had just relieved a picket!"
—HARTE, FRANK BRET, 1864, *Relieving Guard—March 4th*; *King Memoriam, p.* 15.

A noble Soul! a living well
　That knew not drought, nor ice, nor wall;
Whose healthful waters leapt and fell
　Broadly and brightly over all.
A King indeed! but one who kept
　His people's pleader next the throne;
Nor while the meanest suitor wept,

Had room for causes of his own.
Who were his people? Ask the Tent,
　The Field, the Hospital—for he
Not only blew "*To arms!* " but sent
　After the blast his largess free.
Who were his people? Ask the slave
　Now standing up in manhood's day;
Or him who once beside the grave
　Of Asian fathers knelt to pray.
For in the market-place he stood,
　Where Gold was Truth, and Self was God,
And cried: "Love Manhood! God is good!
　Unloose the shackle! break the rod!"
Nor cried he all in vain; for though
　Still toils uncitizened Cathay,
Afric hath broke her bolts; and lo!
　That great pure soul hath half his way.
—LUDLOW, FITZ-HUGH, 1864, *Abest*; *Surrexit*; *King Memoriam, p.* 16.

The great work laid upon his two-score years
Is done, and well done. If we drop our tears,
Who loved him as few men were ever loved,
We mourn no blighted hope, nor broken plan

With him whose life stands rounded and ap-
proved
In the full growth and stature of a man.
Mingle, O bells! along the western slope,
With your deep toll a sound of faith and hope!
Wave cheerily still, O banner! half-way down,
From thousand-masted bay and steepled town!
Let the strong organ with its loftiest swell
Lift the proud sorrow of the land, and tell
That the brave sower saw his ripened grain.
O East and West! O morn and sunset twain
No more forever!—has he lived in vain,
Who, priest of freedom, made ye one, and told
Your bridal service from his lips of gold!
—WHITTIER, JOHN GREENLEAF, 1864,
Thomas Starr King.

Was widely distinguished as an eloquent preacher and lecturer; but perhaps the affection and admiration which were attracted to him as a rare example of Christian manhood do more justice to his character than even these discourses can do to the intellect which was the offshot and expression of it. Nobody more quickly converted chance acquaintances into warm friends. To know him was to love him. . . . The funeral of Mr. King was a touching ceremony, for it expressed the genuine grief of a great city at the departure of its greatest citizen. There is always a tendency, in the public funeral of an eminent man, to convert the occasion into a mere imposing spectacle for crowds to gaze at; but in this instance the formalities were identical with the realities of sorrow. It was universally felt that a vital force, pledged to the cause of all that was noble, generous, and good, and which could not be replaced, had been withdrawn in the full sweep of its beneficent activity. To the throngs of persons who hastened to take a last look at the beloved pastor or friend, there was something indescribably pathetic in the placid smile on the dead face —the smile which was on the features when death approached, and which death itself had not power to efface. The flags at half-mast all over the city and in the shipping in the harbor; the tolling bells; the melancholy minute-guns fired by direction of the authorities at Washington; the crowd of citizens, which not only filled the church, but occupied in a dense mass every avenue to it,—all attested the grief of a community which really felt itself bereaved. That silent, respectful sorrow, hushing for the time the noise of traffic, and indicating that thousands of people who were utterly unknown to him mourned his death as though

they had lost a personal friend, was the most fitting tribute that could have been rendered to Mr. King's genius and virtues. —WHIPPLE, EDWIN PERCY, 1877, *ed. Christianity and Humanity, pp. 7, 8.*

I may safely say that no man in New England, since Edward Everett and Buckminster, won a general reputation for eloquence so young. He was hardly twenty-four years old when he was asked to become the minister of Hollis Street Church, and that connection began which continued so fortunately for him and for the church for nearly twelve years. . . . Absolutely well as I knew him,—and I believe I knew him as well as one man can know another,— I can say, and I ought to say, that I never heard him, under any circumstances, even of the most light-hearted recreation, say a word or do a thing which you were sorry to have had said by a living prophet of a living God. So it was that he never came into the room but you were delighted to see him.—HALE, EDWARD EVERETT, 1888, *Reminiscences of Thomas Starr King, The Unitarian Review, vol. 29, p. 312.*

GENERAL

Having for ten years, in winter as well as summer, viewed its grace and glory, he embodies the result of his experience in a noble volume, entitled "The White Hills,—their Legends, Landscape, and Poetry.". . . This production is far more than a description of the White Hills: its rich descriptions of every variety of landscape apply to all natural scenes, and bring out their inmost meaning. There is much of himself in this volume, of his rare spiritual insight,—much of what his cultured and reverent eye saw in the beauty and the grandeur that God is creating every day.—FROTHINGHAM, RICHARD, 1864, *A Tribute to Thomas Starr King, p. 147.*

The critical reader will feel that some paragraphs in these printed sermons are too perplexed and involved in their expression. The occasions, however, are few, where this criticism can be made. The unity of the central thought and the general strain of eloquence by which it is enforced will strike the critic more than the occasional deviations from a scrupulous rhetoric. King's mode of composition led him into using long sentences. He seemed to have a special delight in lingering on dashes, commas, and semicolons, and to avoid as long as he decently could the pause of the period.—WHIPPLE, EDWIN PERCY, 1877, *ed. Christianity and Humanity, p.* lix.

The first impression made by these volumes upon a competent reader is the very opposite of that brilliant and seductive superficiality with which his name may have been associated by those who knew him least. Outside the essays of Emerson, we shall look in vain for volumes more remarkable for breadth of thought and loftiness of spiritual vision in our national literature. The very titles of these lectures and sermons are a challenge to the most generous thinking and the most profound insight into the most vital themes. Indeed, the one theme of all his conversation, discourse, and living was the spiritual life of man, his relations to Nature, to humanity, and God. Whether in the form of lecture, sermon, essay, stump speech, talk in the cars, or anniversary platform extravaganza, he instinctively drove at one topic and stuck to his text with a persistence that no temptation could shake. A most accomplished literary critic, he only spoke of books to light up their authors. Thoroughly at home in the whole range of ancient and modern philosophy, he never philosophized except to illustrate the nature, duties, and destiny of man.—MAYO, A. D., 1877, *Thomas Starr King, Unitarian Review, vol.* 8, *p.* 638.

James Frederick Ferrier
1808–1864

James Frederick Ferrier, metaphysician, was born in Edinburgh, 16th June, 1808. His father was a brother of Miss Ferrier, the novelist; his mother, a sister of Christopher North. He graduated B. A. at Oxford in 1831, and next year was admitted to the Scottish bar, but never practised. In 1842 he became professor of History at Edinburgh, in 1845 of Moral Philosophy at St. Andrews. Ferrier early attracted notice by his metaphysical essays in *Blackwood's Magazine.* In his "Institutes of Metaphysics" (1854) he endeavours to construct a system of idealism in a series of propositions demonstrated after the manner of Euclid. He died at St. Andrews, 11th June, 1864. See Life by his son-in-law, Sir Alexander Grant, prefixed to his "Lectures on Greek Philosophy" (1866).—PATRICK AND GROOME, *eds.,* 1897, *Chambers's Biographical Dictionary, p.* 362.

PERSONAL

The only other thing I am "not to forget" is that of the "Essay on Consciousness" in *Blackwood.* The writer of those Papers is one Ferrier, a nephew of the Edinburgh Miss Ferrier who wrote "Marriage" and some other novels; nephew also of Professor Wilson (Christopher North), and married to one of his daughters. A man of perhaps five-and-thirty; I remember him in boyhood, while he was boarding with an Annandale clergyman; I have seen him since manhood, and liked him well: a solid, square-visaged, dark kind of man, more like your Theodore Parker than any mutual specimen I can recollect. He got the usual education of an Edinburgh Advocate; but found no practice at the bar, nor sought any with due anxiety, I believe; addicted himself to logical meditations;—became, the other year, Professor of Universal History, or some such thing, in the Edinburgh University, and lectures with hardly any audience; a certain *young* public wanted *me* to be that Professor there, but I knew better.— Is this enough about Ferrier?— CARLYLE, THOMAS, 1844, *To Emerson, April* 3; *The Correspondence of Carlyle and Emerson, ed. Norton, vol.* II, *p.* 62.

The most ancient of the northern universities is associated with the name of the latest Scotch philosopher, and the most brilliant philosophical professor of his time in Scotland. Those who admire speculative genius will long be attracted to a place now associated with him, and may be touched by the story of his withdrawal, too soon for his work, from this strange life of sense, to which his thinking has helped to add intellectual charm. His philosophy had its root in his life, and his life found expression in his philosophy; while there is a continuous identity connecting his earliest with his latest writings, which, taken all together, form a unity of which I think we have no other example more complete in the history of British philosophy.—FRASER A. C., 1868, *The Philosophical Life of Professor Ferrier, Macmillan's Magazine, vol.* 17, *p.* 198.

Ferrier is described by his friends and colleagues as a man of singular personal charm. A manner of much dignity was combined with fine literary taste, wide culture, and thorough gentleness and kindness of heart. He was a man of finely strung nerves, and could be combative in defense of his opinions, but of a tolerant and chivalrous nature. His style is admirably clear and direct. He was a keen metaphysician, and comparatively indifferent to ethical and other applications of his doctrine. His whole aim was to establish his theory of knowing and being. He says that "his philosophy is Scottish to the very core." He was well acquainted with Spinoza, Kant and the later German philosophy, and greatly admired Hegel; but he differed radically from the applications made by his friend, Sir William Hamilton. He was profoundly influenced by Berkeley, and his theory seems to be a development of Berkeley in the light of later discussions.— STEPHEN, LESLIE, 1889, *Dictionary of National Biography, vol.* XVIII, *p.* 390.

GENERAL

The most interesting philosophical personage whom Scotland has given us to contemplate in these years. He preserved the charm of a genial spirit during a lifelong pilgrimage in the land of abstractions; as entirely self-dedicated to curious thinking about the world in which all are feeling and acting as any recluse in the annals of philosophy. And his works are the signal example in Scotland of an alliance of an artistic beauty with abstract philosophy. Notwithstanding, even those who profess to speculate are only now beginning to penetrate into his meaning, and to recognize his chivalrous devotion to abstract truth, in

sublime disregard, one may say, of its consequences or of its utility.—FRASER, A. C., 1868, *The Philosophical Life of Professor Ferrier, Macmillan's Magazine, vol.* 17, *p.* 194.

Ferrier has perhaps never had any disciples, but his book is still remembered with respect, and instanced as a remarkable example of excellence in that department of speculative thought which for some time appeared to have lost entirely its attraction for at least the English school of thinkers. —OLIPHANT, MARGARET O. W., 1892, *The Victorian Age of English Literature, p.* 407.

Too strong a Hamiltonian influence (not in style but in some other ways), and an attempt at an almost Spinozian rigidity of method, have sometimes been held to have marred Ferrier's philosophical performance; but it is certain that he had the making of a great metaphysician, and that he was actually no small one.— SAINTSBURY, GEORGE, 1896, *A History of Nineteenth Century Literature, p.* 351.

In the domain of purely metaphysical thought was probably the most gifted man of his time. Ferrier describes his own philosophy as Scottish to the core. There is in it, nevertheless, a considerable tincture from the German, and Ferrier deserves the credit of being one of the earliest professional philosophers who really grappled with German thought. He was also a master of a very clear and attractive style, which makes the reading of his philosophy a pleasure rather than a toil.—WALKER, HUGH, 1897, *The Age of Tennyson, p.* 167.

Abraham Lincoln

1809–1865

Born in Hardin County, Ky., Feb. 12, 1809: died at Washington, D. C., April 15, 1865. The sixteenth President of the United States. He was descended from a Quaker family, of English origin, residing in the middle of the 18th century in Berks County, Pennsylvania. His grandfather emigrated from Virginia to Kentucky about 1780. His father, Thomas Lincoln, settled with his family in Indiana in 1816, and in Illinois in 1830. His mother was Nancy Hanks, Thomas Lincoln's first wife. He left his father's home soon after settling in Illinois, and after following various occupations, including those of a farm laborer, a salesman, a merchant, and a surveyor, was admitted to the bar in 1836, and began the practice of law at Springfield in 1837. He served first as a captain and afterward as a private in the Black Hawk war in 1832; was a Whig member of the Illinois State legislature 1834–42; and was a Whig member of Congress from Illinois 1847–1849. In 1858, as Republican candidate for United States senator, he held a series of joint discussions throughout Illinois with the Democratic candidate, Stephen A. Douglas, in which he took a pronounced stand against the institution of slavery. This debate attracted the attention of the country, and in 1860 he was nominated as candidate for President by the

Republican party. The disunion of the Democratic party secured for him an easy victory. He received 180 electoral votes against 72 for John C. Breckenridge, candidate of the Southern Democrats; 39 for John Bell, candidate of the Constitutional Union party; and 12 for Stephen A. Douglas, candidate of the Northern Democrats; and was inaugurated on March 4, 1861. His election was the signal for the secession, one after another, of the slave States of the South, and for the organization of the Confederate States. Hostilities began with an attack by the Secessionists of South Carolina on the Federal troops at Fort Sumter, April 12, 1861. The fort surrendered on the 13th. On the 15th a call was issued by the President for 75,000 volunteers, and the control of events passed from the cabinet to the camp. He proclaimed a blockade of the Southern ports April 19, 1861; and Sept. 22, 1862, issued a proclamation emancipating all slaves in States or parts of States which should be in rebellion on Jan. 1, 1863. He was re-elected president by the Republican party in 1864, receiving 212 electoral votes against 21 for George B. McClellan, candidate for the Democratic party. He began his second term of office March 4, 1865. He entered Richmond with the Federal army April 4, 1865, two days after the flight of the Confederate government; and was occupied with plans for the reconstruction of the South when he was shot by John Wilkes Booth at Ford's Theatre, Washington, April 14, 1865, and died the following day. Numerous biographies of Lincoln have been published, the most comprehensive of which is that by J. G. Nicolay and John Hay (1890).—SMITH, BEN-JAMIN E., ed. 1894–97, *The Century Cyclopedia of Names, p.* 612.

PERSONAL

In the course of a recent visit to the United States, the writer of this article had a short interview with President Lincoln, then just re-elected. . . . The president's face and figure are well known by likenesses and caricatures. The large-boned and sinewy frame, six feet four inches in height, is probably that of the yeoman of the north of England—the district from which Lincoln's name suggests that his fore-fathers came—made spare and gaunt by the climate of America. The face, in like manner, denotes an English yeoman's solidity of character and good sense, with something super-added from the enterprising life and sharp habits of the Western Yankee. The brutal fidelity of the photograph, as usual, has given the features of the original, but left out the expression. It is one of kindness, and, except when specially moved to mirth, of seriousness and care. The manner and address are perfectly simple, modest, and unaffected, and therefore free from vulgarity in the eyes of all those who are not vulgar themselves.—SMITH, GOLDWIN, 1865, *President Lincoln, Macmillan's Magazine, vol.* 11, *p.* 300.

He bore the nation's perils, and trials, and sorrows, ever on his mind. You know him, in a large degree, by the illustrative tories of which his memory and his tongue were so prolific, using them to point a moral, or to soften discontent at his decisions. But this was the mere badinage which relieved him for the moment from the heavy weight of public duties and re-

sponsibilities under which he often wearied. Those whom he admitted to his confidence, and with whom he conversed of his feelings, knew that his inner life was checkered with the deepest anxiety and most discomforting solicitude. Elated by victories for the cause which was ever in his thoughts, reverses to our arms cast a pall of depression over him. One morning over two years ago, calling upon him on business, I found him looking more than usually pale and careworn, and inquired the reason. He replied, with the bad news he had received at a late hour the previous night, which had not yet been communicated to the press—he had not closed his eyes or breakfasted; and, with an expression I shall never forget, he exclaimed, "How willingly would I exchange places to-day with the soldier who sleeps on the ground in the Army of the Potomac!"—COLFAX, SCHUYLER, 1865, *Funeral Oration, Chicago, Ill.*

Upon thousands of hearts great sorrows and anxieties have rested, but not on one such, and in such measure, as upon that simple, truthful, noble soul, our faithful and sainted Lincoln. Never rising to the enthusiasm of more impassioned natures in hours of hope, and never sinking with the mercurial in hours of defeat to the depths of despondency, he held on with unmovable patience and fortitude, putting caution against hope that it might not be premature, and hope against caution that it might not yield to dread and danger. He wrestled ceaselessly, through four black and dreadful purgatorial years, wherein God was cleansing the sins of his people as by fire.—BEECHER, HENRY WARD, 1865, *Patriotic Addresses, p.* 702.

O Captain! my Captain! our fearful trip is done,
The ship has weather'd every rack, the prize we
    sought is won,
The port is near, the bells I hear, the people all
    exulting,
While follow eyes the steady keel, the vessel
    grim and daring;   •
    But O heart! heart! heart!
        O the bleeding drops of red,
            Where on the deck my Captain lies,
                Fallen cold and dead.
O Captain! my Captain! rise up and hear the
    bells;
Rise up—for you the flag is flung—for you the
    bugle trills,
For you boquets and ribbon'd wreaths—for you
    the shores a-crowding,
For you they call, the swaying mass, their
    eager faces turning;
    Here Captain! dear father!
        This arm beneath your head!
            It is some dream that on the deck,
                You've fallen cold and dead.
My Captain does not answer, his lips are pale
    and still,
My father does not feel my arm, he has no pulse
    nor will,
The ship is anchor'd safe and sound, its voyage
    closed and done,
From fearful trip the victor ship comes in with
    object won;
    Exult O shores, and ring O bells!
        But I with mournful tread,
            Walk the deck my Captain lies,
                Fallen cold and dead.
—WHITMAN, WALT, 1865, *O Captain! My Captain!*

It has been the business of my life to study the human face, and I have said repeatedly to friends that Mr. Lincoln had the saddest face I ever attempted to paint. During some of the dark days of the spring and summer of 1864, I saw him at times when his care-worn, troubled appearance was enough to bring tears of sympathy into the eyes of his most bitter opponents. I recall particularly one day, when, having occasion to pass through the main hall of the domestic apartments, I met him alone, pacing up and down a narrow passage, his hands behind him, his head bent forward upon his breast, heavy black rings under his eyes, showing sleepless nights—altogether such a picture of the effects of sorrow and care as I have never seen—CARPENTER FRANK B., 1865, *Anecdotes and Reminiscences of President Lincoln.*

Latterly Mr. Lincoln's reading was with the humorous writers. He liked to repeat from memory whole chapters from these books; and on such occasions he always preserved his own gravity though his auditors might be convulsed with laughter. He said that he had a dread of people who could not appreciate the fun of such things; and he once instanced a member of his own Cabinet, of whom he quoted the saying of Sydney Smith, "that it required a surgical operation to get a joke into his head." The light trifles spoken of diverted his mind, or, as he said of his theatre-going, gave him refuge from himself and his weariness. But he also was a lover of many philosophical books, and particularly liked Butler's "Analogy of Religion," Stuart Mill on Liberty, and he always hoped to get at President Edwards on the Will. These ponderous writers found a queer companionship in the chronicler of the Mackerel Brigade, Parson Nasby, and Private Miles O'Reilly. The Bible was a very familiar study with the President, whole chapters of Isaiah, the New Testament, and the Psalms being fixed in his memory, and he would sometimes correct a misquotation of Scripture, giving generally the chapter and verse where it could be found. He liked the Old Testament best, and dwelt on the simple beauty of the historical books.—BROOKS, NOAH, 1865, *Personal Recollections of Abraham Lincoln, Harper's Magazine, vol.* 31, *p.* 229.

A laboring man, with horny hands,
Who swung the axe, who tilled his lands,
    Who shrank from nothing new,
    But did as poor men do!
One of the People! Born to be
Their curious Epitome;
    To share, yet rise above
    Their shifting hate and love.
Common his mind (it seemed so then),
His thoughts the thoughts of other men:
    Plain were his words, and poor—
    But now they will endure!
—STODDARD, RICHARD HENRY, 1865, *Abraham Lincoln, Ode.*

In his character Lincoln was through and through an American. . . . The habits of his mind were those of meditation and inward thought, rather than of action. He delighted to express his opinons by an apothegm, illustrate them by a parable, or drive them home by a story. He was skilful in analysis, discerned with precision the central idea on which a question turned, and knew how to disengage it and present it by itself in a few homely, strong old English words that would be intelligible to all. He excelled in logical statement more than in executive ability. He reasoned clearly, his reflective judgment was good, and his purposes were fixed; but, like the Hamlet of his only poet, his will was tardy in action, and, for this reason, and not from humility or tenderness of feeling, he sometimes deplored that the duty which devolved on him had not fallen to the lot of another. . . . Lincoln was one of the most unassuming of men. In time of success, he gave credit for it to those whom he employed, to the people, and to the Providence of God. He did not know what ostentation is; when he became President he was rather saddened than elated, and his conduct and manners showed more than ever his belief that all men are born equal. — BANCROFT, GEORGE, 1866, *Memorial Address on the Life and Character of Abraham Lincoln*, *Feb.* 12, *pp.* 43, 45.

He was no inspired Elijah or John Baptist, emerging from the awful desert sanctified by lonely fastings and wrestlings with Satan in prayer, to thrill loving, suppliant multitudes with unwonted fires of penitence and devotion; he was no royal singer of Israel, touching at will his harp and sweeping all the chords of emotion and aspiration in the general heart; he was simply a plain, true, earnest, patriotic man, gifted with eminent common-sense, which in its wide range gave a hand to shrewdness on the one hand, humor on the other, and which allied him intimately, warmly, with the masses of mankind. I doubt whether any woman, or child, white or black, bond or free, virtuous or vicious, accosted or reached forth a hand to Abraham Lincoln, and detected in his countenance or manner any repugnance or shrinking from the proffered contact, any assumption of superiority or betrayal of disdain. No one was ever more steeped in the spirit of that glorious lyric of the inspired Scotch ploughman—

A man's a man, for a' that.

. . . When I last saw him, some five or six weeks before his death, his face was haggard with care, and seamed with thought and trouble. It looked care-ploughed, tempest-tossed, and weather-beaten, as if he were some tough old mariner, who had for years been beating up against wind and tide, unable to make his port or find safe anchorage. Judging from that scathed, rugged countenance, I do not believe he could have lived out his second term had no felon hand been lifted against his priceless life. . . . He was not a born king of men, ruling by the resistless might of his natural superiority, but a child of the people, who made himself a great persuader, therefore a leader, by dint of firm resolve, and patient effort, and·dogged perseverance. He slowly won his way to eminence and renown by ever doing the work that lay next to him— doing it with all his growing might—doing it as well as he could, and learning by his failure, when failure was encountered, how to do it better.—GREELEY, HORACE, 1868 (?) –1891, *An Estimate of Abraham Lincoln*, ed. Benton, *Century Magazine*, vol. 42, pp. 381, 382.

Lincoln was himself a man of much quaint humour, curiously expressed in tales of Kentucky and Illinois life, told in their broadest form of American speech. These he brought into connection with events seeming to require a graver illustration, yet which could not really have been better illustrated. Of the six Presidents of the United States whom I have known, including Andrew Johnson, he seemed to me the only one gifted with this faculty. I recollect sitting with him and Mr. Seward over a log-fire in the White House (the Federal forts and General Lee's dismantled villa seen from the windows across the Potomac), a few hours only after intelligence had been received of the first disastrous battle of Chattanooga. The conversation at first centred on this event; but the cheerful temperament of these two remarkable men gradually transferred it to other topics; and the President amused himself and us by some of those racy anecdotes which so often convey more of practical truth than any dry reasoning can afford—now and then stopping for a moment to put a fresh log on the fire. The possession of this simple and genial humour, not alloyed by any personal asperities, helped greatly that popularity which was mainly due to the honesty and consistency of the man, in times of unforseen and perilous trial to his country.— HOLLAND, SIR HENRY, 1871, *Recollections of Past Life*, p. 277.

Surely if there were to be chosen a figurehead for America it must be this! There was something undeniably grotesque about the face (1858), and yet not a coarse line; it was battered and bronzed, but the light of an eye, both gentle and fiery, kept it from being hard. The nose was a good strong buttress—such as Bonaparte would have valued—to a solid brow; and the forehead rose to its greatest height in the region assigned to the benevolent and the conscientious organs, declining along those of firmness and self-esteem into what I should call a decidedly feeble occiput. But never was there a case in which the sage's request —"Speak, that I may see you"—had more need to be repeated; for a voice more flexible, more attuned to every kind of expression, and to carry truth in every tone, was never allotted to mortal. Although he seemed to me oddly different from any other man whom I had seen, he seemed also related to them all, and to have lineaments characteristic of every section of the country; and this is why I thought he might well be taken as its figure-head. His manner of speaking in public was simple, direct, and almost religious; he was occasionally humorous, but rarely told anecdotes as he did in private conversation; and there was no sarcasm, no showing of the teeth. I had not listened to him long, on the occasion to which I refer, before I perceived that there was a certain artistic ability in him as a public speaker, which his audience would least recognise when it was most employed. . . . I have often wondered that Mr. Lincoln's power as an orator—surpassed as it is by that of only one other American—is so little known or thought of in Europe; and I have even found the impression that he was, as a speaker, awkward, heavy, and ungrammatical. It is a singular misjudgment. For terse, well-pronounced, clear speech; for a careful and easy selection of the fit word for the right place; for perfect tones; for quiet, chaste, and dignified manner,—it would be hard to find the late President's superior. — CONWAY, MONCURE DANIEL, 1873, *Personal Recollections of President Lincoln, Fortnightly Review, vol.* 1, *p.* 58.

Unassuming and unpretentious himself, Mr. Lincoln was the last person to wear borrowed honors. He was not afflicted with the petty jealousy of narrow minds, nor had he any apprehension that others would deprive him of just fame. He gave to Mr. Seward, as to each of his council, his generous confidence, and patiently listened if he did not always adopt or assent to the suggestions that were made. To those who knew Abraham Lincoln, or who were at all intimate with his Administration, the representation that he was subordinate to any member of his Cabinet, or that he was deficient in executive or administrative ability, is absurd.—WELLES, GIDEON, 1873, *Mr. Lincoln and Mr. Seward, The Galaxy, vol.* 16, *p.* 518.

A man who was at home and welcome with the humblest, and with a spirit and a practical vein in the times of terror that commanded the admiration of the wisest. His heart was as great as the world, but there was no room in it to hold the memory of a wrong.—EMERSON, RALPH WALDO, 1876, *Greatness, Letters and Social Aims; Works, Riverside Ed., vol.* VII, *p.* 301.

Lincoln was not a type. He stands alone —no ancestors, no fellows, and no successors. He had the advantage of living in a new country, of social equality, of personal freedom, of seeing in the horizon of his future the perpetual star of hope. He preserved his individuality and his self-respect. He knew and mingled with men of every kind; and, after all, men are the best books. He became acquainted with the ambitions and hopes of the heart, the means used to accomplish ends, the springs of action and the seeds of thought. He was familiar with nature, with actual things, with common facts. He loved and appreciated the poem of the year, the drama of the seasons. . . . Lincoln never finished his education. To the night of his death he was a pupil, a learner, an inquirer, a seeker after knowledge. . . . Wealth could not purchase, power could not awe, this divine, this loving man. He knew no fear except the fear of doing wrong. Hating slavery, pitying the master—seeking to conquer, not persons, but prejudices—he was the embodiment of the self-denial, the courage, the hope, and the nobility of a nation. He spoke, not to inflame, not to upbraid, but to convince. He raised his hands, not to strike, but in benediction. He longed to pardon. He loved to see the pearls of joy on the cheeks of a wife whose husband he had rescued from death. Lincoln was the grandest figure of the fiercest civil war. He is the gentlest memory of our world.—INGERSOLL, ROBERT G., 1885, *Motley and Monarch, North American Review, vol.* 141, *pp.* 528, 529, 531.

If we gained nothing else by our long association with Mr. Lincoln, we hope at least that we acquired from him the habit of judging men and events with candor and impartiality.—NICOLAY, JOHN G., AND HAY, JOHN, 1886-90, *Abraham Lincoln, A History, vol.* I, *p.* 13.

In determining Lincoln's title to greatness we must not only keep in mind the times in which he lived, but we must, to a certain extent, measure him with other men.   Many of our great men and our statesmen, it is true, have been self-made, rising gradually through struggles to the topmost round of the ladder; but Lincoln rose from a lower depth than any of them. His origin was in that unknown and sunless bog in which history never made a footprint.—HERNDON, WILLIAM H., 1888, *Abraham Lincoln, The True Story of a Great Life, Preface, vol.* I, *p.* vii.

Mr. Lincoln's nature was one of almost child-like sweetness.   He did not "put you at your ease" when you came into his presence.   You felt at your ease without being put there.   He never assumed superiority over anybody in the ordinary intercourse of life.—WHITE, HORACE, 1892, *Abraham Lincoln, by Herndon and Weik, Introduction, vol.* I, *p.* xxiii.

> Close to the ground what if his life began,
>   In rude bucolic self-denial keyed,
> Fed on realities, yet hearing Pan
>   Along the brookside blow a charmed reed!
> O flocks of Hardin, you remember well
>   The awkward child, and had he not a look
> Of one forechosen of grand destiny?
>   In field or forest dell
> Did he not prophesy to bird and brook,
>   And shape vague runes of what was yet to be?

—THOMPSON, MAURICE, 1894, *Lincoln's Grave,* XV.

Joined to these strong mental and moral qualities was that power of immediate action which so often explains why one man succeeds in life while another of equal intelligence and uprightness fails.   As soon as Lincoln saw a thing to do he did it.   He wants to know, here is a book—it may be a biography, a volume of dry statutes, a collection of verse; no matter, he reads and ponders it until he has absorbed all it has for him.   He is eager to see the world; a man offers him a position as a "hand" on a Mississippi flatboat; he takes it without a moment's hesitation over the toil and exposure it demands.   John Calhoun is willing to make him deputy surveyor; he knows nothing of the science; in six weeks

he has learned enough to begin his labors. Sangamon County must have representatives; why not he? And his circular goes out. Ambition alone will not explain this power of instantaneous action.   It comes largely from that active imagination which, when a new relation or position opens, seizes on all its possibilities and from them creates a situation so real that one enters with confidence upon what seems to the unimaginative the rashest undertaking.   Lincoln saw the possibilities in things, and immediately appropriated them.—TARBELL, IDA M., 1896, *The Early Life of Abraham Lincoln, p.* 221.

While he was great in genius, in character, and in opportunities, he was even greater in sanity of heart and elevation of spirit. While he was entirely human, there was no mean fiber in his composition, no base, petty, selfish impulse in his soul.—DANA, CHARLES ANDERSON, 1896, *Lincoln and His Cabinet, p.* 70.

It is now forty years since I first saw and heard Abraham Lincoln, but the impression which he left on my mind is ineffaceable. After his great successes in the West he came to New York to make a political address. He appeared in every sense of the word like one of the plain people among whom he loved to be counted.   At first sight there was nothing impressive or imposing about him—except that his great stature singled him out from the crowd; his clothes hung awkwardly on his giant frame, his face was that of a dark pallor, without the slightest tinge of color; his seamed and rugged features bore the furrows of hardship and struggle; his deep-set eyes looked sad and anxious; his countenance in repose gave little evidence of that brain power which had raised him from the lowest to the highest station among his countrymen; as he talked to me before the meeting, he seemed ill at ease, with that sort of apprehension which a young man might feel before presenting himself to a new and strange audience, whose critical disposition he dreaded.   It was a great audience, including all the noted men—all the learned and cultured—of his party in New York: editors, clergymen, statesmen, lawyers, merchants, critics. . . . His style of speech and manner of delivery were severely simple. What Lowell called "The grand simplicities of the Bible," with which he was so familiar, were reflected in his discourse.

With no attempt at ornament or rhetoric, without parade or pretence, he spoke straight to the point. If any came expecting the turgid eloquence or the ribaldry of the frontier, they must have been startled at the earnest and sincere purity of his utterances. It was marvellous to see how this untutored man, by mere self discipline and the chastening of his own spirit, had outgrown all meretricious arts, and found his own way to the grandeur and strength of absolute simplicity.—CHOATE, JOSEPH H., 1900, *Abraham Lincoln, Address, Nov.* 13.

STATESMAN

Our hearts lie buried in the dust
With him so true and tender,
The patriot's stay, the people's trust,
The shield of the offender.

—HOLMES, OLIVER WENDELL, 1865, *For the Service in Memory of Abraham Lincoln.*

With the least possible personal hatred; with too little sectional bitterness, often forgetting justice in mercy; tender-hearted to any misery his own eyes saw; and in any deed which needed his actual sanction, if his sympathy had limits,—recollect he was human, and that he welcomed light more than most men, was more honest than his fellows, and with a truth to his own convictions such as few politicians achieve. With all his shortcomings, we point proudly to him as the natural growth of democratic institutions. Coming time will put him in that galaxy of Americans which makes our history the day-star of the nations.—PHILLIPS, WENDELL, 1865, *Abraham Lincoln, Address, April 23rd; Speeches, Lectures and Letters, Second Series, ed. Pease, p.* 448.

The results of the policy pursued by Mr. Lincoln during his administration thus far are its own best justification. The verdict of the future is not to be foreshown. But there can be little doubt that history will record the name of Abraham Lincoln as that of a pure and disinterested patriot. She may find in his course many errors; she may point out in his character many defects; she will speak of him as a man who had to contend against the disadvantages of imperfect culture, of self-education, and of little intercourse with men of high-breeding. But she will speak also of the virtues which the hard experience of early life had strengthened in him; of his homely sincerity and simplicity; of his manly frankness and self-respect; of his large, humane, and tender sympathies; of his self-control and good temper; of his truthfulness and sturdy honesty. She will represent him as actuated by an abiding sense of duty, as striving to be faithful in his service of God and of man, as possessed with deep moral earnestness, and as endowed with vigorous common-sense and faculty for dealing with affairs. She will tell of his confidence in the people, and she will recount with approval their confidence in him. And when she has told all this, may she conclude her record by saying that to Abraham Lincoln more than to any other man is due the success which crowned the efforts of the American people to maintain the Union and the institutions of their country, to widen and confirm the foundations of justice and liberty, on which those institutions rest, and to establish inviolable and eternal peace within the borders of their land.— NORTON, CHARLES ELIOT, 1865, *Abraham Lincoln, North American Review, vol.* 100, *p.* 20.

"Forgive them, for they know not what they do!"
He said, and so went shriven to his fate,—
Unknowing went, that generous heart and true.
Even while he spoke the slayer lay in wait,
And when the morning opened Heaven's gate
There passed the whitest soul a nation knew.
Henceforth all thoughts of pardon are too late;
They, in whose cause that arm its weapon drew,
Have murdered Mercy. Now alone shall stand
Blind Justice, with the sword unsheathed she wore.
Hark, from the eastern to the western strand,
The swelling thunder of the people's roar:
What words they murmur,—Fetter not her hand!
So let it smite, such deeds shall be no more!

—STEAMAN, EDMUND CLARENCE, 1865, *Abraham Lincoln.*

In one respect President Lincoln achieved a wonderful success. He maintained, through the terrible trials of his Administration, a reputation with the great body of the people, for unsullied integrity of purpose and of conduct, which even Washington did not surpass, and which no President since Washington has equalled. He had command of an army greater than that of any living monarch; he wielded authority less restricted than that conferred by any other constitutional government; he disbursed sums of money equal to the exchequer of any nation in the world; yet no man, of any party, believes him in any instance to have aimed at his own aggrandizement, to have been actuated by personal ambition, or to have consulted any other interest than the welfare of his country, and the perpetuity of its Republican form of government.—RAYMOND, HENRY J., 1865, *The Life and Public Services of Abraham Lincoln, p.* 716.

A character so unique that he stood alone without a model in history, or a parallel among men. . . . He was one of the few great rulers whose wisdom increased with his power, and whose spirit grew gentler and tenderer as his triumphs were multiplied. This was the man, and these his associates, who look down upon us from the canvas.—GARFIELD, JAMES ABRAM, 1878, *Lincoln and Emancipation, Address, Feb.* 12; *Works, ed. Hinsdale, pp.* 536, 537.

There never has been a President in such constant and active contact with the public opinion of the country, as there never has been a President who, while at the head of the government, remained so near to the people. Beyond the circle of those who had long known him, the feeling steadily grew that the man in the White House was "honest Abe Lincoln" still, and that every citizen might approach him with complaint, expostulation, or advice, without danger of meeting a rebuff from power-proud authority, or humiliating condescension; and this privilege was used by so many and with such unsparing freedom that only superhuman patience could have endured it all. There are men now living who would to-day read with amazement, if not regret, what they then ventured to say or write to him. But Lincoln repelled no one whom he believed to speak to him in good faith and with patriotic purpose. No good advice would go unheeded. No candid criticism would offend him. No honest opposition, while it might pain him, would produce a lasting alienation of feeling between him and the opponent. It may truly be said that few men in power have ever been exposed to more daring attempts to direct their course, to severer censure of their acts, and to more cruel misrepresentation of their motives. And all this he met with that good-natured humor peculiarly his own, and with untiring effort to see the right, and to impress it upon those who differed from him.—SCHURZ, CARL, 1891, *Abraham Lincoln, Atlantic Monthly, vol.* 67, *p.* 743.

Chained by stern duty to the rock of state,
His spirit armed in mail of rugged mirth,
Ever above, though ever near to earth,
Yet felt his heart the cruel tongues that sate
Base appetites, and foul with slander, wait
Till the keen lightnings bring the awful hour
When wounds and suffering shall give them
    power.
Most was he like to Luther, gay and great,
Solemn and mirthful, strong of heart and
    limb.
Tender and simple too; he was so near
To all things human that he cast out fear,
And, ever simpler, like a little child,
Lived in unconscious nearness unto Him
Who always on earth's little ones hath
    smiled.
—MITCHELL, S. WEIR, 1891, *Lincoln, Collected Poems, p.* 251.

Tested by the standard of many other great men, Lincoln was not great, but tested by the only true standard of his own achievements, he may justly appear in history as one of the greatest of American statesmen. Indeed, in some most essential attributes of greatness I doubt whether any of our public men ever equaled him. We have had men who could take a higher intellectual grasp of any abstruse problem of statesmanship, but few have ever equaled, and none excelled, Lincoln in the practical common-sense, and successful solution of the gravest problems ever presented in American history. He possessed a peculiarly receptive and analytical mind. He sought information from every attainable source. He sought it persistently, weighed it earnestly, and in the end reached his own conclusions. When he had once reached a conclusion as to a public duty, there was no human power equal to the task of changing his purpose. He was self-reliant to an uncommon degree, and yet as entirely free from arrogance of opinion as any public man I have ever known.—MC-CLURE, A. K., 1892, *Abraham Lincoln and Men of War-Times, p.* 69.

His greatest, his most distinctive, and most abiding trait was his humanness of nature; he was the expression of his people; at some periods of his life and in some ways it may be that he expressed them in their uglier forms, but generally he displayed them in their noblest and most beautiful developments; yet, for worse or for better, one is always conscious of being in close touch with him as a fellow-man. People often call him the greatest man who ever lived; but, in fact, he was not properly to be compared with any other. One may set up a pole and mark notches upon it, and label them with the names of Julius Cæsar, William of Orange, Cromwell, Napoleon, even Washington, and may measure these men against each other, and dispute and discuss their respective places. But Lincoln cannot be brought to this pole, he cannot be entered in any such competition.—MORSE, JOHN T., JR., 1893, *Abraham Lincoln, vol.* II, *p.* 356.

Whether it was in the small things or in the great things with which he had to deal, he was equally matchless. And all this was born in him. Neither education nor experience nor example had anything to do with the production of this great central, controlling force in the greatest of all the crises that ever came upon the nation. His development kept pace with the multiplying exigencies which confronted him, and he was never found wanting.—DAWES, HENRY L., 1895, *Abraham Lincoln, ed. Ward, p.* 6.

It requires the most gracious pages in the world's history to record what one American achieved. The story of this simple life is the story of a plain, honest, manly citizen, true patriot, and profound statesman, who believing with all the strength of his mighty soul in the institutions of his country, won because of them the highest place in its government—then fell a precious sacrifice to the Union he held so dear, which Providence had spared his life long enough to save. . . . What were the traits of character which made Abraham Lincoln prophet and master, without a rival, in the greatest crisis in our history? What gave him such mighty power? To me the answer is simple: Lincoln had sublime faith in the people. He walked with and among them. He recognized the importance and power of an enlightened public sentiment and was guided by it. Even amid the vicissitudes of war, he concealed little from public review and inspection. In all he did, he invited, rather than evaded, examination and criticism. He submitted his plans and purposes, as far as practicable, to public consideration with perfect frankness and sincerity. There was such homely simplicity in his character that it could not be hedged in by the pomp of place, nor the ceremonials of high official station. He was so accessible to the public that he seemed to take the whole people into his confidence.—

McKINLEY, WILLIAM, 1896, *Abraham Lincoln, Address, Feb.* 12.

GENERAL

Homely, dispassionate, showing all the rough-edged process of his thought as it goes along, yet arriving at his conclusions with an honest kind of every-day logic, he is so eminently our representative man, that, when he speaks, it seems as if the people were listening to their own thinking aloud. The dignity of his thought owes nothing to any ceremonial garb of words, but to the manly movement that comes of settled purpose and an energy of reason that knows not what rhetoric means. There has been nothing of Cleon, still less of Strepsiades striving to underbid him in demagogism, to be found in the public utterances of Mr. Lincoln. He has always addressed the intelligence of men, never their prejudice, their passion, or their ignorance. —LOWELL, JAMES RUSSELL, 1864, *Abraham Lincoln, My Study Windows, p.* 176.

That he is something more than a boor his address at the dedication of the cemetery at Gettysburg will in itself be sufficient to prove. . . . There are one or two phrases here, such as "dedicated to the proposition," which betray a hand untrained in fine writing, and are proofs that the composition is Lincoln's own. But, looking to the substance, it may be doubted whether any king in Europe would have expressed himself more royally than the peasant's son. And, even as to the form, we cannot help remarking that simplicity of structure and pregnancy of meaning are the true characteristics of the classical style. Is it easy to believe that the man who had the native good taste to produce this address would be capable of committing gross indecencies—that he would call for comic songs to be sung over soldiers' graves?—SMITH, GOLDWIN, 1865, *President Lincoln, Macmillan's Magazine, vol.* 11, *p.* 302.

His finest effort, the immortal Gettysburg speech,—which brief as it is, will be read and remembered long after Edward Everett's ambitious oration, which occupied hours in the delivery, shall have been forgotten,—was prepared with extraordinary care. According to the statement of Mr. Noah Brooks, his friend, it was written and re-written many times.—MATHEWS, WILLIAM, 1878, *Oratory and Orators, p.* 444.

Lincoln excelled in the art of putting

things aptly and concisely, and, like many old Romans, would place his whole argument in a brief droll narrative, the point of which would render his whole meaning clear to the dullest intellect. In their way, these were like the illustrated proverbs known as fables. Menenius Agrippa and Lincoln would have been congenial spirits.—LELAND, CHARLES GODFREY, 1879, *Abraham Lincoln, p.* 237.

The contrast between these two well-known funeral orations could not have been more marked. Everett's was long, Lincoln's short; Everett's drew allusions from classic history, Lincoln's went no farther back than the record of American nationality; Everett's displayed the culture of the Boston university man and the European resident; Lincoln's was the plain speech of an unlettered native of Kentucky and citizen of Illinois. The range and ultimate direction of American literature—to which both orations clearly belong—could not have been better illustrated than by their various methods and similar results. . . . There are, however, manifest advantages in that simple method illustrated by President Lincoln's Gettysburg address, which the newer school of orators may well make a model for imitation. — RICHARDSON, CHARLES F., 1887, *American Literature,* 1607–1885, *vol.* I, *pp.* 238, 240.

Though anything but a literary man, was among America's history-makers, and whose inaugural and farewell addresses, and commemorative speech at Gettysburg, are unsurpassed for dignity, simplicity and lofty and manly sentiment.—HAWTHORNE, JULIAN, AND LEMMON, LEONARD, 1891, *American Literature, p.* 80.

Each of Lincoln's paragraphs is an organism. Each is knit together by perfect logical sequence, perfect unity. There is no modulation of emphasis, for by the nature of the subject there can be none. The letter is a challenge. Each sentence is meant to go home like a shot. The whole appeal is to the will, and in cases of this sort it may be of the very essence of style to eschew the fine shades of meaning that should exist in an intellectual type of discourse.—LEWIS, EDWIN HERBERT, 1894, *The History of the English Paragraph, p.* 155.

Perhaps no point in the career of Abraham Lincoln has excited more surprise or comment than his remarkable power of literary expression. It is a constant puzzle to many men of letters how a person growing up without the advantages of schools and books could have acquired the art which enabled him to write the Gettysburg address and the second inaugural. At first view, indeed, the question appears to be an educational one; and when men who devote their days and nights to rules, theories, and text-books find themselves baffled in such an acquirement, they naturally wonder how a laboring frontiersman could have gained it.—NICOLAY, JOHN G., 1894, *Lincoln's Literary Experiments, Century Magazine, vol.* 47, *p.* 823.

In prose the chief productions inspired by the war were, without question, two or three addresses delivered by President Lincoln. His address at the dedication of the National Cemetery on the battlefield of Gettysburg, Nov. 19, 1863, and his second inaugural address, delivered March 4, 1865, stand with the great orations of the century. . . . His oratory is in marked contrast with that of Webster and Everett and the early school of orators; it has no studied periods and elaborately wrought climaxes; it has little of ornament or of inspiration; it is simply the words of a man whose heart was deeply stirred, who, speaking as Whittier sang, without a thought of art or of effect, poured out words that are unsurpassed in simple beauty, dignity, and even grandeur. . . . Lincoln's orations are short when compared with the labored efforts of a Webster or a Choate, and they were not written with literary intent, yet few productions in American literature are more certain of immortality.—PATTEE, FRED LEWIS, 1896, *A History of American Literature, pp.* 347, 348.

The second of the American statesmen holding high rank as a man of letters was Abraham Lincoln, whose later state papers are models, not only in insight and in tact but in expression also. His masterpiece is the short speech delivered on the battlefield of Gettysburg at the dedication of the national cemetery in November, 1863. Lofty in thought, deep in feeling, simple in language, this speech has a Greek perfection of form.—MATTHEWS, BRANDER, 1896, *An Introduction to the Study of American Literature, p.* 222.

Lincoln had humor and pathos and Douglas possessed neither. Lincoln's faculty of being at once at home with his audience in the easy familiarity which makes them both friendly and receptive was the genius of popular oratory. But with these elements he had a singularly lucid power of statement and was master of logic. Unlike Douglas, he was weak unless he knew he was right. His whole nature must be stirred with the justice of his cause for him to rise above the commonplace. But once convinced that he was battling for right and truth and he was irresistible. He became logical, epigrammatic and eloquent. Convincing as was his speech to those who listened, it was more powerful when read in cold type. . . . The great-hearted, broad-souled, wise-brained man of love and charity.—DEPEW, CHAUNCEY M., 1896, *Address, Oct. 7.*

The flawless sublimity of Lincoln's Gettysburg address comes not merely from its concentrated truth, its crystal clarity, its involuntary rhythm of emotion, the moral intensity of every syllable, but from the silence of that sleeping battle-host. The Scriptural cadences of the Second Inaugural are weighted with a nation's agony and upborne upon a nation's faith.—BATES, KATHARINE LEE, 1897, *American Literature, p.* 257.

Mr. Lincoln had a style—a distinctive, individual, characteristic form of expression. In his own way he gained an insight into the structure of English, and a freedom and skill in the selection and combination of words, which not only made him the most convincing speaker of his time, but which have secured for his speeches a permanent place in literature. One of those speeches is already known wherever the English language is spoken; it is a classic by virtue not only of its unique condensation of the sentiment of a tremendous struggle into the narrow compass of a few brief paragraphs, but by virtue of that instinctive felicity of style which gives to the largest thought the beauty of perfect simplicity. The two Inaugural Addresses are touched by the same deep feeling, the same large vision, the same clear, expressive, and persuasive eloquence; and these qualities are found in a great number of speeches, from Mr. Lincoln's first appearance in public life. In his earliest expressions of his political views there is less range; but there is the structural order, clearness, sense of proportion, ease, and simplicity which give classic quality to the latter utterances. Few speeches have so little of what is commonly regarded as oratorical quality; few have approached so constantly the standards and character of literature.—MABIE, HAMILTON WRIGHT, 1897, *Library of the World's Best Literature, ed. Warner, vol.* XVI, p. .

A great debater, as his campaign struggle with Stephen A. Douglas proved, has left one masterpiece of brief, pregnant political oratory, in the purest English, his address at the dedication of the Gettysburg monument.—BRONSON, WALTER C., 1900, *A Short History of American Literature, p.* 276.

Edward Everett
1794–1865

Edward Everett (1794–1865), born at Dorchester, Mass., graduated at Harvard in 1811 and in 1815 was elected professor of Greek there. In 1820 he became editor of the *North American Review,* and in 1824 a member of the U. S. congress. In 1835–38 he was four times governor of Massachusetts, and in 1841–45 minister at the court of St. James. While in England he was made D. C. L. by Oxford, and LL. D. by Cambridge and Dublin. He was president of Harvard 1846–49, and 1852 succeeded Daniel Webster as secretary of state, and in 1853 was returned to the U. S. senate. His chief works are "A Defence of Christianity" (1814); several poems; his "Orations and Speeches" (1836–59); and the memoir prefixed to Daniel Webster's works (1852).—PATRICK AND GROOME, *eds.* 1897, *Chambers's Biographical Dictionary, p.* 350.

PERSONAL

I have been attending Professor Everett's lectures, which he has begun to deliver in this city, upon Antiquities. I am as much enamored as ever with the incomparable manner of my old idol, though much of his matter is easily acquired from common books. We think strong sense to be his distinguishing feature; he never commits himself, never makes a mistake.—EMERSON, RALPH WALDO, 1823, *Letter to John B. Hill, Jan. 3; Memoir, ed. Cabot, vol.* I, p. 95.

What I desire, is, that, in addition to the many beautiful, ay, exquisitely beautiful specimens of your genius, which we have had upon occasional topics, you would now meditate some great work for posterity, which shall make you known and felt through all time, as we, your contemporaries, now know and esteem you. This should be the crowning future purpose of your life. *Sat verbum sapienti.* If I should live to see it, I should hail it with the highest pleasure. If I am dead, pray remember that it was one of the thoughts which clung most closely to me to the very last.—STORY, JOSEPH, 1840, *Letter to Edward Everett, May 30; Life and Letters, ed. Story, vol. II, p. 334.*

Edward Everett is one of the most remarkable men living. He is a native of Massachusetts, and was born about 1796. At nineteen he had already acquired the reputation of an accomplished scholar, and was drawing large audiences as a Unitarian preacher. At twenty-one (the age at which Roger Ascham achieved a similar distinction) he was appointed Professor of Greek in Harvard University, and soon afterwards he made a tour of Europe, including Greece. M. Cousin, who was with him in Germany, informed a friend of ours that he was one of the best Grecians he ever knew, and the translator of Plato must have known a good many of the best. On his return from his travels he lectured on Greek literature with the enthusiasm and success of another Abelard—we hope, without the Heloise. . . . It is admitted, however, that he failed in Congress; and his addresses literary and commemorative, are rather eloquent pieces of writing than orations in the popular acception of the term.—HAYWARD, ABRAHAM, 1840, *American Orators and Statesmen, Quarterly Review, vol. 67, p. 39.*

Mr. Everett's manuscript is a noble one. It has about it an air of deliberate precision emblematic of the statesman, and a mingled grace and solidity betokening the scholar. Nothing can be more legible, and nothing need be more uniform. The man who writes thus will never grossly err in judgment or otherwise; but we may also venture to say that he will never attain the loftiest pinnacle of renown.—POE, EDGAR ALLAN, 1841, *A Chapter of Autography, Works ed. Stedman and Woodberry, vol. IX, p. 210.*

Everett, the American Minister, has been here at the same time with my eldest brother. We all liked him, and were confirmed in our good opinion of him. A sensible, unassuming man, always wise and reasonable.—SMITH, SYDNEY, 1844, *Letter to Mrs. Grote, Jan. 31; Memoir, ed. Holland.*

If Webster is the Michael Angelo of American oratory, Everett is the Raphael. In the former's definition of eloquence, he recognises its latent existence in the occasion as well as in the man and in the subject. His own oratory is remarkable for grasping the bold and essential; for developing, as it were, the anatomical basis—the very sinews and nerves of his subject—while Everett instinctively catches and unfolds the grace of occasion, whatever it be; in his mind the sense of beauty is vivid, and nothing is more surprising in his oratory than the ease and facility with which he seizes upon the redeeming associations of every topic, however far removed it may be from the legitimate domain of taste or scholarship.—TUCKERMAN, HENRY THEODORE, 1851, *The Orator, Characteristics of Literature, Second Series.*

Edward Everett, the man of letters *par excellence,* burning incense to the south, and insulting abolitionists while they are few and weak, endeavouring to propitiate them as they grew strong, and finally breaking down in irretrievable disgrace under a pressure to which he had exposed himself by ambition, but which he had neither courage nor conscience to abide. I early saw in him the completest illustration I met with of the influences of republican life upon a man of powers without principle, and of knowledge without wisdom. He was still worshipped through vanity, when I knew him, though his true desserts were well enough understood in private: he had plenty of opportunity to retrieve his political character afterwards: he obtained in England, when ambassador, abundance of the admiration which he sacrificed so much to win; and then at last, when the hour arrived which must test his quality, he sank, and must abide for the rest of his life in a slough of contempt from which there was no rescue. This is precisely what was anticipated twenty years ago by (not his enemies, for I believe he then had none, but) friends who mourned over his quitting a life of scholarship, for which he was eminently qualified, for one of political aspiration. They knew that he had not self-reliance or courage enough for effective ambition, nor virtue enough for a career of

independence. It is all over now; and the
vainest of men, who lives by the breath of
praise, is placed for the sad remnant of his
days between the scorn of the many and
the pity of the few. Vindicators he has
none; and I believe no followers.—MARTIN-
EAU, HARRIET, 1855–77, *Autobiography, ed.
Chapman, vol. I, p. 375.*

So fell our Everett; more like some great elm,
   Lord of the grove, but something set apart,
That all the tempests could not overwhelm,
   Nor all the winters of his seventy years,
But on some peaceful midnight bursts his heart,
   And in the morning men behold the wreck,
(Some with gray hairs, who cannot hold their
      tears),
   But in the giant timber find no speck
Nor unsound spot, but only wholesome wood.
   No secret worm consuming at the core
The stem that ever seemed so fair and good:
   And aged men that knew the tree of yore
When but a sapling, promising full well,
   Say to each other, "This majestic plant
Came to full growth; it made no idle vaunt;
   From its own weight, without a flaw, it fell!"
—PARSONS, THOMAS WILLIAM, 1865, *Ever-
ett, Poems, p. 68.*

There was refinement in the very substance of his being; by a necessity of his
constitution he disposed everything he perceived into some orderly relations to ideas
of dignity and grace; he instinctively
shunned what was coarse, discordant, uncomely, unbecoming; and that internal
world of thoughts, sentiments, and dispositions, which each man forms or re-forms
for himself, and in which he really lives, in
his case obeyed the law of comeliness, and
came out as naturally in his manners as in
his writings, in the beautiful urbanity of his
behavior, as in the cadenced periods of his
eloquence.—WHIPPLE, EDWIN PERCY, 1865,
*Edward Everett, Character and Characteris-
tic Men, p. 244.*

Mr. Everett's speeches were generally
written, and with great care in his forms of
expression. Words were selected in respect to their measure and sound, as well as
their meaning, and their precise effect upon
the ear often determined by rehearsal.
He sometimes, I think, sacrificed the power
of thought to the euphony of words. Mr.
Webster, on the other hand, ordinarily
speaking without notes, sought to express
his thoughts clearly, directly, and nothing
more. . . . Mr. Everett's manner in speaking was elaborate and studied. It was
artistic till the appearance of art was lost in
its perfection. There was an exquisite

adaptation of voice, tone, position and
gesture to sentiment, and yet so great was
the charm which he threw around his subject, by his perfect knowledge of it, in all its
relations, bearings and history, and by the
beauty of his illustrations, that his auditors
forgot the auditor in the theme. Here he
felt the advantages of his extended studies
and critical research, in which he was immeasurably the superior of his distinguished
friend.—DAVIS, THOMAS T., 1865, *Eulogy
on Edward Everett, May 12th.*

He never missed an opportunity to do a
kind office to a fellow man, especially to a
man of letters. All his life long he was true
to this quality in his nature. . . . He never
doled out scant praise. He never withheld
from any one the applause that was due. I
never could discern in him the slightest
vestige of envy. His heart expanded at observing merit in others; and if sometimes he
was too forbearing or too complacent
toward mediocrity, he gloriously redeemed
that foible by the keenest and most willing
perception of all kinds of excellence. . . .
His manner of life was marked by liberality
and elegance; but he was simple in his habits and was never given to ostentation; and
by the fruits of his own exertion he was
able to be of service to those who were akin
to him and to others. There were those
whom he never ceased to care for, even
when the burden became very heavy for
him to bear. Here is another leading trait
in his character; he gave away money not
thoughtlessly but freely, always with reflecting judgment, as befitted one who
had much to spare and who desired to do
the most good; he kept up his habit of
generosity always; and in proportion to his
own income, there was perhaps no one who
gave more, or showed himself more free
from everything that is sordid.—BANCROFT,
GEORGE, 1865, *Edward Everett.*

Mr. Edward Everett was at that time
[1843] our Minister at the Court of St.
James. I was the bearer to him of a letter
of introduction from Mr. Benjamin F. Butler, who had been Attorney-General of the
United States under President Van Buren.
I found Mr. Everett as frigid as an iceberg.
His reserve was constitutional. He was as
polished as his own writings, but equally
cold. To a young man just out of college,
this sort of reception operated like a wet
blanket. After my first call, I never ventured upon him again. I feared taking

cold.—FIELD, MAUNSELL B., 1873, *Memories of Many Men and of Some Women, p. 13.*

As early as 1820 he had established a reputation, such as few men in later days have enjoyed, as an orator. He was frequently invited, as other public men are invited in America, to deliver an "oration" on one or another public topic of historical or other interest. With him these "orations," instead of being the ephemeral entertainments of an hour, became careful studies of some important theme, so that the collected edition of them is now one of the standard books of reference in an American's library. Eager to avert, if possible, the impending conflict of arms, Everett prepared an "oration" on Washington, which he delivered in every part of America. In a printed note accompanying the published edition of it, he names nearly one hundred and twenty-five occasions, in almost every State in the Union, in every section but the extreme Southwest, where it was repeated. This exception was caused only by illness in his family, after he had received invitations to go to that quarter also. He travelled really as an ambassador of peace among irritated States. The eagerness to hear him was so great that, from the first, his hosts arranged, almost always, that tickets should be sold to all auditors, and as he travelled wholly at his own charges, the audiences thus contributed more than one hundred thousand dollars for the purchase of the old home of Washington at Mount Vernon, and the securing it as a shrine for American patriotism.— HALE, EDWARD EVERETT, 1878, *Encyclopædia Britannica, Ninth Ed., vol.VIII, p.* 647.

Edward Everett, of Massachusetts, was the ideal of public and private virtue. He was placid, cool, exact, and conscientious, yet always imaginative, and sometimes impassioned. . . . The illustrious Everett looked the character he was. Gentle, courteous, kind, with a musical voice, a face of singular benevolence, a figure erect and graceful, and an air of high yet modest culture, his conversation was exceedingly fascinating.—FORNEY, JOHN W., 1881, *Anecdotes of Public Men, vol. II, pp.* 11, 13.

"Then Mr. Everett pronounced an oration which surpassed all I had ever heard. When, toward the conclusion, he alluded to the noble conduct of our guest in procuring a ship for his own transportation, at a time when all America was too poor to offer him a passage to her shores, the scene was overpowering. *Every man in the assembly was in tears.*" *In Journal, August* 26, 1824. I believe that this last expression was literally true. I have heard the great orators of my day at their best; but it was never given to any one of them to lift up an audience as Everett did upon this occasion. I can conceive of nothing more magnificent in the way of oratory. Many who have listened to Mr. Everett's polished periods during the latter part of his life may question the supreme effect he produced. They will say that he was by nature a conservative, seldom in sympathy with the heart of popular feeling, and that there was always a suspicion of a chill upon his matchless rhetoric. I can only say that the words he spoke that day in the venerable church in Cambridge were as full of fire as of music.— QUINCY, JOSIAH, 1883, *Figures of the Past from the Leaves of Old Journals, p.* 107.

Notwithstanding his ready fluency of speech, I never heard him utter a sentence that needed correction for the press.— KEYES, GEN. E. D., 1884, *Fifty Years' Observation of Men and Events, p.* 37.

At times he was almost electrical in his utterances; his reasoning was logical and luminous, and his remarks always gave evidence of careful study. As a politician Mr. Everett was not successful. The personification of self discipline and dignity, he was too much like an intellectual icicle to find favor with the masses, and he was deficient in courage when any bold step was to be taken.—POORE, BEN: PERLEY, 1886, *Reminiscences, vol. I, p.* 80.

Edward Everett was then second only to Mr. Webster as an orator. In scholarship and manner of speaking, he was Mr. Webster's superior. He was perhaps the finest classical scholar of the day, the greatest linguist that ever went to Congress, except Caleb Cushing. . . . Mr. Everett did not maintain his high reputation in Congress. He was an orator, not a debater, and he was too refined in character, too much of a gentleman to be perfectly at home in the lower House of Congress.—McCULLOCH, HUGH, 1888, *Men and Measures of Half a Century, p.* 24.

Of Edward Everett's eloquence—consummate of its kind—delivery, description, narration and illustration, historical incident and classical allusion, were the most notable and noteworthy features. "It is hardly too much to say of him"—if I may borrow from my own tribute to him at Faneuil Hall a day or two after his death— "it is hardly too much to say of him that he established a new standard of American eloquence; that he was the founder of a new school of occasional oratory, of which he was at once the acknowledged master and the best pupil, and in which we were all proud to sit at his feet as disciples." Delivering his principal orations avowedly from memory, every sentence and every gesture were studied to produce the most striking effect. And they did produce it. He was as dramatic at times as Kean or Macready, and his audiences hung with rapture on his lips.—WINTHROP, ROBERT C., 1894, *Webster's Reply to Hayne, Scribner's Magazine, vol.* 15, *p.* 127.

I was scarcely less an admirer of Edward Everett, whose cold, classical, and studied style was in marked contrast to the massive warmth and energy of his great rival in public oratory. The one struck the quarry with the emphasis of a discoverer; the other chiselled the marble with the delicacy of a finished sculptor. To listen to Webster was to be warmed with an unexpected emotion; to hang upon the periods of Everett was to feel the charms of cultured rhetoric.— TUCKERMAN, CHARLES KEATING, 1895, *Personal Recollections of Notable People, vol.* I, *p.* 30.

Mr. Everett was one of the most graceful and polished speakers of modern times. He was called the "golden-mouthed orator" by his friends and contemporaries, Choate, Webster and Phillips. In preparing his speeches no detail was too minute to escape his care—invention, arrangement of matter, expression, intonation and gesture—all received the greatest attention. Mr. Everett's eloquence was of the Ciceronian order— copious, graceful, and flowing. He also resembled Cicero in the variety—and extent of his knowledge. His memory was very retentive. His sensibilities were refined. His imagination rich and sparkling. His gestures were graceful, and appropriate, and the tones of his voice clear, sweet and melodious. His manner was elegant and persuasive. It is said that no one could listen to him without being moved, instructed, and delighted.—HARDWICKE, HENRY, 1896, *History of Oratory and Orators, p.* 358.

GENERAL

The great charm of Mr. Everett's orations consists not so much in any single and strongly-developed intellectual trait as in that symmetry and finish which, on every page, give token of the richly-endowed and thorough scholar. The natural movements of his mind are full of grace; and the most indifferent sentence which falls from his pen has that simple elegance which it is as difficult to define as it is easy to perceive. His level passages are never tame, and his fine ones are never superfine. His style, with matchless flexibility, rises and falls with his subject, and alternately easy, vivid, elated, ornamented, or picturesque; adapting itself to the dominant mood of the mind, as an instrument responds to the touch of a master's hand. His knowledge is so extensive, and the field of his allusions so wide, that the most familiar views in passing through his hands, gather such a halo of luminous illustrations, that their likeness seems transformed, and we entertain doubts of their identity.—HILLARD, GEORGE STILLMAN, 1837, *Everett's Orations and Speeches, North American Review, vol.* 44, *p.* 139.

We should have no hesitation, therefore, in placing in the hands of young American citizens these volumes ["Orations and Speeches"] as containing the best developments of the genius of free institutions; the noblest expositions of the lofty duties by which the citizen of a free State is bound; the most spirit-stirring representations of the greatness of the illustrious founders of our commonwealths, now living immortal in the monuments of genius and patriotic wisdom they have left behind them.—FELTON, CORNELIUS C., 1850, *Everett's Orations and Speeches, North American Review, vol.* 71, *p.* 456.

It is curious to follow the public life of such a man, and that is easy to do in the two volumes before us. Here, as in all of his literary works and political harangues, as well as in all the discourses pronounced by Mr. Everett for the last thirty years, he is found *en rapport* with his fellow-citizens. The subjects are naturally very various, but the thought is always the same, and returns to one point, intellectual education, the morality and the patriotism of the people. This unity is in the word as well as in the life of the author.—LABOULAYE, ÉDOUARD RENÉ, 1853, *Journal des Debats, Oct.*

This was a mind so rounded, so complete,
No partial gift of Nature in excess,
That, like a single stream where many meet,
Each separate talent counted something less.

. . . .

Servant of all his powers, that faithful slave,
Unsleeping Memory, strengthening with his toils,
To every ruder task his shoulder gave,
And loaded every day with golden spoils.
Order, the law of Heaven, was throned supreme
O'er action, instinct, impulse, feeling, thought;
True as the dial's shadow to the beam,
Each hour was equal to the charge it brought.
Too large his compass for the nicer skill
That weighs the world of science grain by grain;
All realms of knowledge owned the mastering will
That claimed the franchise of its whole domain.
—HOLMES, OLIVER WENDELL, 1865, *Edward Everett*.

The "Defence of Christianity," which he then published, is of value, chiefly as a piece of controversy belonging to the history of opinion in this neighborhood at that moment. Controversy has long since taken other grounds. For that purpose, at that moment, the book did its work completely. It exhausted the points which Mr. English raised, and exhausted them in a way which required very patient study. Mr. Everett once said that to compile the chapter on the quotations of the Old Testament by the New Testament writers, he went through the whole of the Mischna in the edition of Surenhusius, in six volumes folio. This chapter, I may say in passing, is the chapter of most permanent value in the "Defence." Now this "Defence," the work of a boy of twenty years of age, was written in the midst of the demands made upon the popular preacher in one of the largest parishes in Boston, in a few months' time,—sent to the printer chapter by chapter. And Mr. Everett said of it, in after-life, that, if it did not seem like affectation, he would say that it was relaxation from the work he was doing in the pulpit. I have no doubt it was.—HALE, EDWARD EVERETT, 1865, *Edward Everett, Atlantic Monthly, vol. 15, p. 343.*

He stood undoubtedly at the head of men of letters of New England, and perhaps I might say at the head of the men of letters of America. True, Longfellow excelled him in poetry, and Hawthorne in romance, and Prescott in history, and the incomparable Irving in his own peculiar walks; but in power of rapid and exact acquisition of knowledge, in variety and comprehensiveness of research, in the perfectly methodical arrangement of his learning, in the sovereign command over the vast mass of his resources, in the warmth and rich coloring of style, in correctness, in the use of words, in the finished neatness of composition, he excelled all.—BANCROFT, GEORGE, 1865, *Edward Everett.*

Everett never impresses you, as do Webster and Clay, with the feeling that the man is more puissant than his periods. His expressions do not suggest a region of thought, a dim vista of imagery, an oceanic depth of feeling, beyond what is compassed by his sentences. He never seems to struggle with language in order to wrest from it words enough for his wealth of thought. It is not an example of "Strength, half leaning on its own right arm," but of Beauty endowed with every natural and artificial charm. Nevertheless, let us not fail to do justice to Mr. Everett's real merits, for he has many and great ones. The great charm of his orations does not lie in any one trait, but in their symmetry and finish, the proofs they exhibit on every page that they are the products of the most careful culture. The style seems to us the very perfection of the epideictic, or demonstrative style. Artificial it undoubtedly is, and occasionally, though rarely, may betray the artist's tooling; but it is a style formed by the most assiduous painstaking, and polished by a taste as exquisitely sensitive as a blind man's touch.—MATHEWS, WILLIAM, 1878, *Oratory and Orators, p. 341.*

The elegant volume by which he is best remembered, twenty-seven "Orations," selected and published in 1836, shows his strength and weakness, his learning, frequent fancy, and fair judgment, on the one side; his ambition beyond his powers, early overtasked, on the other. Discoursing on a wide range of subjects—of which the refrains are America and Greece, the Mayflower, Patriotism, Reform, the Progress of Discovery, Concord, Lexington, and the inevitable Bunker Hill—these speeches are always able, but only by fits inspiring. They are "too long," and smell of the lamp. The writer exhausts his hearers by ransacking history and literature with an approach to pedantry. In his great address on the Republic, delivered August 26, 1824, before the Phi-Beta-Kappa Society, we have, at one opening of the book, the Parthenon, the Theseum, the Alexandrian and Periclean ages, Callimachus, Pindar, Lycophron, Sophocles, Aristotle, Aristophanes of Byzantium, Apollonius of Rhodes, Alcæus, Menander, Horace, Lucretius, Tacitus, Constantine, Dante, Petrarch, Boccaccio, Machiavelli, Guicciardini, Galileo, Ariosto, Tasso, Cervantes, Corneille, and Racine— all doubtless illustrating the orator's position, but heaped up with bewildering rapidity. Everett's work, carefully elaborated and richly adorned, is that of the first of rhetoricians rather than a genuine orator.— NICHOL, JOHN, 1882-85, *American Literature, p.* 130.

Edward Everett, in his best literary work, was second to no eminent author of his day in the quiet majesty of his presence and address, so that all who came within the circle of his influence were chastened and uplifted.—HUNT, THEODORE W., 1890, *Studies in Literature and Style, p.* 52.

The great euphemist of that age; he studied and polished his speeches until they reached a pitch of rhetorical perfection unexampled since the days of Greek and Latin oratory. The fashion has gone by for such elaborate art and artifice, but it was precisely suited to the audiences to which Everett appealed. He appeared to remain always in a state of admiring contemplation of pensive reminiscence, of glowing premonition over something, it mattered little what. His smooth-flowing, musical sentences have nowhere a hitch or a discord; he rang all the changes on sweetness, pathos, sentiment, optimistic prophecy. He ex-

ploited the requirements of culture to the ultimate degree of fastidiousness; even religion and morality, under his touch, are made to seem pretty, touching and graceful, rather than searching or sublime. There was a ladylike quality in his deliverances— a deficiency of rugged and resonant masculine fibre—which removes them somewhat from the sympathies of to-day.—HAWTHORNE, JULIAN, AND LEMMON, LEONARD, 1891, *American Literature, p.* 79.

Throughout these four volumes ["Orations and Speeches"], comprising the utterances of more than forty years, every paragraph seems a studied, masterly work of art. Everett's natural feeling was warm and spontaneous; but he had acquired and he unswervingly maintained that incessant self-control which his generation held among the highest ideals of conduct. So whatever he publicly uttered, and still more whatever he suffered himself to print, was deliberately considered to the minutest detail.—WENDELL, BARRETT, 1900, *A Literary History of America, p.* 255.

With the exception of his reply to English, his lives of Washington, John Stark, and John Lovell, and the Mount Vernon Papers, the great preponderance of all that Everett allowed to go to print, consisted of addresses and orations; these were gathered into four volumes, issued at intervals during a period of twenty years. On these public utterances, and on his reputation rather than on his performances as a scholar, rests Everett's claim to be considered as an American man of letters. The claim, however, must be allowed, in spite of the fact that no single work of great repute is credited to him.—SWIFT, LINDSAY, 1900, *Our Literary Diplomats, The Book Buyer, vol.* 20.

· Elizabeth Cleghorn Gaskell

1810-1865

Born [Elizabeth Cleghorn Stevenson], in Chelsea, 29 Sept. 1810. Mother died Oct. 1810. Lived with her aunt in youth. At school at Stratford-on-Avon, 1825-27. Married to Rev. William Gaskell, 30 Aug. 1832. Lived in Manchester. Intimacy with William and Mary Howitt, and Dickens. Contrib. to "Household Words" from first no., March 1850. Friendship with Charlotte Brontë begun, 1850. Active literary life. Died suddenly, at Holybourne, Hampshire, 12 Nov. 1865. Buried at Knutsford. *Works:* "Clopton Hall," in Howitt's "Visits to Remarkable Places," 1840; "Mary Barton" (anon.), 1848; "The Moorland Cottage" (anon.), 1850; "Ruth" (anon.), 1853; "Cranford" (anon.), 1853; "North and South" (anon.), 1855; "Lizzie Leigh" (anon.), 1855; "Life of Charlotte Brontë," 1857 (2nd and 3rd edns. same year); "Round the Sofa," 1859; "My Lady Ludlow," 1859; "Right at Last," (anon.), 1860; "Lois the Witch," 1861; "A Dark Night's Work," 1863; "Sylvia's Lovers," 1863 (2nd and 3rd edns. same year); "The Grey Woman," 1865; "Hand and Heart," 1865; "Cousin Phyllis," 1865. *Posthumous:* "Wives and Daughters," 1866. She *edited*: "Mabel Vaughan," 1857; C. A. Vecchi's "Garibaldi at Caprera," 1862. Collected Works: in 7 vols., 1873.—SHARP, R. FARQUHARSON, 1897, *A Dictionary of English Authors, p.* 110.

PERSONAL

She is remarkably pleasing, unaffected, and easy in her manners, with a melodious voice in speaking.—GREVILLE, HENRY, 1856, *Leaves from his Diary, Oct.* 21; *Second Series, ed. Enfield, p.* 392.

Mrs. Gaskell seems lovely at home, where besides being a writer she proves herself to be a first-class housekeeper, and performs all the duties of a minister's wife.—STOWE, HARRIET BEECHER, 1857, *Letter to her Daughters, Life and Letters, ed. Fields, p.* 235.

Report says that she was most beautiful to behold [1829]. There are, however, I believe no portraits of her at that time of life. The friends who knew her intimately in later years describe her face as possessing extreme interest rather than rare beauty. In a photograph taken shortly before her death, which one of her old pupils had the goodness to show me, she is seated at a table with a lace shawl thrown lightly over the figure. Rare refinement and delicacy of feature are the points which strike one at the first glance. One sees at once that she was a cultivated and high-souled woman. Her mouth is most delicately curved, and the eyes are of an exquisite shape. The same lady favoured me with the following detailed verbal description of Mrs. Gaskell from memory: "Her face was most interesting, with very delicately-cut features, and a specially fine brow. Her hair was dark, and her hazel eyes had an unusual brightness and animation when their owner was engaged in conversation. Her mouth was firm but kind, and almost always playing into a smile. She was of the medium height, graceful and dignified in her bearing." This description, given by one who frequently saw her at the head of her own table, and also while she was engaged in teaching at the Sunday School, may, I think, be accepted, and justifies the idea entertained of her early beauty.—HOMPES, MAT, 1895, *Mrs. Gaskell, Gentlemen's Magazine, vol.* 279, *p.* 127.

Mrs. Gaskell was a very beautiful young woman. I heard her described only the other day by a friend who remembered her in her youth. She had a well-shaped head,

regular, finely-cut features; her mien was bright and dignified, almost joyous, so my informant said, and among her many other gifts was that of delightful companionship. She was very young when she was married to the Reverend William Gaskell, minister of the Cross Street Unitarian Chapel in Manchester. She was married from her aunt's house at Cranford at the Parish Church, and not in the beautiful old Unitarian Chapel, with its ivy-clad walls and its latticed windows, dating from Oliver Cromwell's time. In those days marriages were only solemnised in the Parish Church.—RITCHIE, ANNE THACKERAY, 1898, *ed. Cranford, Preface, p.* XVI.

MARY BARTON
1848

Although pre-eminently a moralist in the sense of being a writer whose works touch the heart rather than the imagination or the philosophical intellect, Mrs. Gaskell is not to be numbered among the preachers. No one, however impatient of reproof and correction, need be frightened away from her novels by the fear of having to listen to didactic homilies. She prefixed a little sermon, pithy and well-timed, by way of preface to "Mary Barton," extracting from it a lesson for the day; but the lesson is not formulated and expounded in the novel, which is, what it professes to be, a tale—a representation of life. It is shaped and coloured by the author's good-natured wisdom but it is not stiffened and distorted as a work of art by any hard specific moral purpose. Mrs. Gaskell was, indeed, a born story-teller, charged through and through with the story-teller's peculiar element, a something which may be called suppressed gipsiness, a restless instinct which impelled her to be constantly making trial in imagination of various modes of life.—MINTO, WILLIAM, 1878, *Mrs. Gaskell's Novels, Fortnightly Review, vol.* 30, *p.* 366.

Of all Mrs. Gaskell's books her earliest has enjoyed the most widespread reputation. It has been translated into French and German and many other languages, including Finnish; while at home the author became an established favourite. Some of the chief employers of labour in the Manchester district, however, complained that they were unjustly treated, and that she spoke rashly of some "burning questions of social economy." She was accused in the Manchester "Guardian" (28 Feb. and 7 Mar. 1849) of "maligning" the manufacturers. Much of the same position was taken in W. R. Greg's "Essay on Mary Barton" (1849), which he thought worth reprinting many years afterward (1876), in his volume entitled "Mistaken Aims and Attainable Ideals of the Artisan Class." Without discussing the point here, it may be observed, as Prof. Minto has done, that John Barton must not be taken too hastily as a type of his whole class; that the book refers to the period of distress (1842) which suggested Disraeli's "Sybil;" and that it has unquestionably contributed to the growth of sentiments which have helped to make the manufacturing world and Manchester very different from what they were forty years ago. The sincerity of its pathos and insight into the very hearts of the poor are of enduring value. Its humour is marked by the rather patriarchal flavour characteristic of Lancashire humour in general; nothing is more striking in Mrs. Gaskell's literary life than the ease and rapidity with which, in this respect, her genius contrived to emancipate itself. — WARD, ADOLPHUS WILLIAM, 1890, *Dictionary of National Biography, vol.* XXI, *p.* 50.

Is one of the most powerful and moving stories in the whole literature of English fiction.—TRAILL, HENRY DUFF, 1897, *Social England, vol.* VI, *p.* 283.

This powerful and fascinating story at once set Mrs. Gaskell in the first rank of English novelists. People differed as to the views set forth in the book, but all were agreed as to its literary force and its great merits. Like "Alton Locke," it has done much to break down class barriers and make the rich try to understand the poor; and when we see the great advance in this direction that has been made since the date of its publication, we are able partly to realise how startling the first appearance of such a book must have been. . . . "Mary Barton," which for nearly half a century has been influencing people all over the world, owes its vitality very largely to the fact that Mrs. Gaskell knew the working people of Manchester, not as a professional doler out of tracts or charitable relief, not in any detestable, patronizing way, but

knew them as *friends.*—BAYLY, ADA ELLEN (EDNA LYALL), 1897, *Women Novelists of Queen Victoria's Reign, pp.* 133, 134.

In 1847 she had finished that noble book, "Mary Barton," that book with a "sob in it," as the French critic says. *Ah! quelle musique douloureuse dans un sanglot.* But there is something far beyond a sob in "Mary Barton." The writer is writing of what she has lived, not only of what she has read or even looked at as she passed her way.—RITCHIE, ANNE THACKERAY, 1898, *ed. Cranford, Preface, p.* xvii.

RUTH
1853

Of course you have read "Ruth" by this time. Its style was a great refreshment to me, for its finish and fulness. How women have the courage to write, and publishers the spirit to buy, at a high price, the false and feeble representations of life and character that most feminine novels give, is a constant marvel to me. "Ruth," with all its merits, will not be an enduring or classical fiction—will it? Mrs. Gaskell seems to me to be constantly misled by a love of sharp contrasts—of "dramatic" effects. She is not contented with the subdued coloring, the half-tints, of real life. Hence she agitates one for the moment, but she does not secure one's lasting sympathy; her scenes and characters do not become typical. But how pretty and graphic are the touches of description! That little attic in the minister's house, for example, which, with its pure white dimity bed-curtains, its bright-green walls, and the rich brown of its stained floor, remind one of a snowdrop springing out of the soil. Then the rich humor of Sally, and the sly satire in the description of Mr. Bradshaw. Mrs. Gaskell has, certainly, a charming mind, and one cannot help loving her as one reads her books.—ELIOT, GEORGE, 1853, *To Mrs. Peter Taylor, Feb.* 1; *George Eliot's Life as related in her Letters and Journals, ed. Cross, vol.* I, *p.* 219.

I am told, to my great astonishment, that you have heard painful speeches on account of "Ruth;" what was told me raised all my indignation and disgust. Now I have read only a little (though, of course, I know the story) of the book; for the same reason that I cannot read "Uncle Tom's Cabin," or "Othello," or "The Bride of Lammermoor." It is too painfully good, as I found before I had read half a volume. But this I can tell you, that among all my large acquaintance I never heard, or have heard, but one unanimous opinion of the beauty and righteousness of the book, and that, above all, from real *ladies*, and really good women. If you could have heard the things which I heard spoken of it this evening by a thorough High Church fine lady of the world, and by her daughter, too, as pure and pious a soul as one need see, you would have no more doubt than I have, that whatsoever the "snobs" and the bigots may think, English people in general, have but one opinion of "Ruth," and that is, one of utter satisfaction.—KINGSLEY, CHARLES, 1853, *To Mrs. Gaskell, July 25; Charles Kingsley, Letters and Memories of his Life, ed. his Wife, vol.* I, *p.* 370.

Tell me if you have read Mrs. Gaskell's "Ruth." That's a novel which I much admire. It is strong and healthy at once, teaching a moral frightfully wanted in English society. . . . By the way, "Ruth" is a great advance on "Mary Barton," don't you think so?—BROWNING, ELIZABETH BARRETT, 1853, *To Mrs. Martin, Oct.* 5; *Letters, ed. Kenyon, vol.* II, *p.* 141.

We have grown serious in considering the scope and influence of this book, because it is so very sad. Like an autumn day, full of a low wailing wind, and a nameless sorrow, the tale sweeps on with its wan sunlights and long mournful shadows to the end. . . . The book is mellow, mature and sober. Its landscape painting is equally beautiful and characteristic. Those who know the woods, and waters, and country life, and small town life, and the lonely seashore life, will recognize in the descriptions of this book the heart and hand of one who has also felt them as they are.—CURTIS, GEORGE WILLIAM, 1853, *Villette and Ruth, Putnam's Magazine, vol.* 1, *p.* 539.

"Ruth," her second great work in order of publication, is, as regards style and power, inferior to "Mary Barton," perhaps to all her sustained effort. But it stands out from the rest, as the handling by a woman of a side of life which is unfortunately too often either ignored in real life and in fiction, or treated in a light, flippant manner. —HOMPES, MAT, 1895, *Mrs. Gaskell, Gentleman's Magazine, vol.* 279, *p.* 133.

CRANFORD
1853

No short tale could be more delightful; the early chapters describe the quiet, aris-

tocratic country life of the female population of the little town, and are full of the richest humor. All is so telling and yet so good-natured, for Mrs. Gaskell is telling us about the worthy people among whom she passed the happy days of her girlhood.— HOMPES, MAT, 1895, *Mrs. Gaskell, Gentlemen's Magazine, vol.* 279, *p.* 133.

In "Cranford" (1853) Mrs. Gaskell passed into a more serene atmosphere, in which, describing under this name the Knutsford of her early acquaintance, she lovingly sets forth the genteel poverty, the innocent self-respecting pride, the quaint humours, and the gentle charities of a society of elderly spinsters and widows without children. Nothing could be done more simply, exquisitely, or with a higher air of truth. To have read "Cranford" is to have personally known the sleepy old place, to have come forever under the power of its charm, to have taken part in its innumerable tea-drinkings and games of Preference, to have trembled at the uncanny feats of Signor Brunoni, and to have fallen irrevocably in love with dear, old, pathetic Miss Matty.— GRAHAM, RICHARD D., 1897, *The Masters of Victorian Literature, p.* 84.

I am sure Cranford existed in the quarter in Paris where my own early youth was passed. I can remember it in Kensington also, though we did not quite go the length of putting our cows into gray flannel dressing-gowns, as Miss Betsy Barker did. Perhaps Cranford did not even stop at Kensington, but may have reached farther afield, taking Chiswick on its way. Miss Deborah, as she preferred to be called, is certainly first cousin to Miss Pinkerton; can either of these ladies have been connected with the unrivalled Miss Seward herself? I do not quite know upon what terms Miss Seward and Dr. Johnson happened to be, but I could imagine the great lexicographer driving them all before him and Miss Pinkerton's turban, or Miss Jenkyns in her little helmet-like bonnet. Miss Deborah and Miss Pinkerton belong to an altogether bygone type, but all the rest of the ladies in Cranford are as modern and as much alive as if they had been born in the 60's.—RITCHIE, ANNE THACKERAY, 1898, *ed. Cranford, Preface, p.* VIII.

One province she discovered and made her own—feminine society in out-of-the-way towns and villages before the encroachment of railroads and penny postage. Of this life

Cranford is the classic. Here is described the old-style etiquette, the genteel poverty, the formal calls, and evening parties, of a village wholly in the possession of the Amazons—widows and spinsters—where no men are tolerated, except the country doctor, who is allowed to stay there occasionally over-night when on his long circuit. Old maids spent their time in tea-drinking and stale gossip, and in chasing sunbeams from their carpets. Before going to bed they peep beneath the white dimity valance or roll a ball under it, to be sure no Iachimo with "great fierce face" lies concealed there. So ends the day of trivialities and Gothic fears.—CROSS, WILBUR L., 1899, *The Development of the English Novel, p. 234.*

It was discovered long ago that the place "Cranford," described in Mrs. Gaskell's famous story, was Knutsford—in England, of course. To the old house on the heath in Knutsford, the baby, Elizabeth Cleghorn Stevenson, came when only a few weeks old to be brought up by her aunt; and there she lived till she grew to womanhood. In the parish church she was married, and in the quiet graveyard on the sloping bankside by Brook Street her ashes rest. Thus it is that Knutsford is identified with the personality of Mrs. Gaskell and, besides, she has put it into many of her books. It is "Cranford" most of all.—JENKINS, HOWARD M., 1901, *The Real "Cranford," Ladies' Home Journal, vol. 18, No. 11, p. 9.*

NORTH AND SOUTH
1855

It ["North and South"] is one of Mrs. Gaskell's ablest and most interesting books. It exhibits, at least till near the close, a notable advance in constructive powers; the characters are drawn with unprecedented firmness, and in some cases tinged with true humour, and though there is no loss of sympathy for the artisan the judgment of social problems shows greater impartiality and riper reflections. Her experience was widened and her interest in politics had grown deeper. She had made acquaintance with many able philanthropists, and in the company of Susanna Winkworth had moved about a good deal among the working classes, listened to discussions of workmen's clubs, and made herself the confidante of many a poor girl. Dickens was warm in his congratulations to Mrs. Gaskell "on the vigorous and powerful accomplishment of an anxious labour." But for some defects of

construction, due perhaps in part to the piecemeal method of weekly publication which the authoress heartily disliked, "North and South" might safely be described as her most effective narrative fiction.—WARD, ADOLPHUS WILLIAM, 1890, *Dictionary of National Biography, vol.* XXI, *p.* 51.

LIFE OF CHARLOTTE BRONTË
1857

Let me renew our long-interrupted acquaintance by complimenting you on poor Miss Brontë's "Life." You have had a delicate and a great work to do, and you have done it admirably. Be sure that the book will do good. It will shame literary people into some stronger belief that a simple, virtuous, practical home-life is consistent with high imaginative genius; and it will shame, too, the prudery of a not over cleanly, though carefully white-washed age, into believing that purity is now (as in all ages till now) quite compatible with the knowledge of evil. I confess that the book has made me ashamed of myself.—KINGSLEY, CHARLES, 1857, *To Mrs. Gaskell, May* 14; *Charles Kingsley, Letters and Memories of his Life, ed. his Wife, vol.* II, *p.* 24.

Patrick Branwell Brontë was no domestic demon—he was just a man moving in a mist, who lost his way. More sinned against, mayhap, than sinning, *at least* he proved the reality of his sorrows. They killed him, and it needed not that his memory should have been tarnished, much, as I think, to the detriment of the "Biography" of his sister. I am desirous to be anything rather than a hostile critic of the memoir. Mrs. Gaskell was an intimate friend of my family, and her husband at one time my father's colleague in the ministry. I admire "Mary Barton" and her other Novels greatly. Towards her memory I have the kindest feeling; but *Fiat justitia!* and I must say what I can in favour of my old friend.—GRUNDY, FRANCIS H., 1879, *Pictures of the Past, p.* 92.

The substantial accuracy of the picture drawn by Mrs. Gaskell of her heroine's life and character, and of the influences exercised upon them by her personal and local surroundings, has not been successfully impugned. As to her literary skill and power and absolute uprightness of intention as a biographer there cannot be two opinions. She expressly disclaimed having made any attempt at psychological analysis; but she was exceptionally successful in her endeavor to bring before her readers the picture of a very peculiar character and altogether original mind.—WARD, ADOLPHUS WILLIAM, 1890, *Dictionary of National Biography, vol.* XXI, *p.* 52.

Mrs. Gaskell set an example in this book which has added a new terror to death and a new danger to those whose lives fall under that fierce light which beats not only upon thrones, but on many less exalted regions in these curious and all-inquiring days.— OLIPHANT, MARGARET O. W., 1892, *The Victorian Age of English Literature, p.* 309.

In the whole of English biographical literature there is no book that can compare in wide-spread interest with the "Life of Charlotte Brontë" by Mrs. Gaskell. It has held a position of singular popularity for forty years; and while biography after biography has come and gone, it still commands a place side by side with Boswell's "Johnson," and Lockhart's "Scott." As far as mere readers are concerned, it may indeed claim its hundreds as against the tens of intrinsically more important rivals. There are obvious reasons for this success. Mrs. Gaskell was herself a popular novelist, who commanded a very wide audience, and "Cranford," at least, has taken a place among the classics of our literature. She brought to bear upon the biography of Charlotte Brontë all those literary gifts which had made the charm of her seven volumes of romance. And these gifts were employed upon a romance of real life, not less fascinating than anything which imagination could have furnished. . . . It is quite certain that Charlotte Brontë would not stand on so splendid a pedestal to day but for the single-minded devotion of her accomplished biographer.—SHORTER, CLEMENT K., 1896, *Charlotte Brontë and her Circle, pp.* 1, 20.

Mrs. Gaskell's book was avowedly incomplete in so far as she was unable to give the names of many persons and places, indeed, in some cases she cannot have known them, as Miss Nussey eliminated many of them from the letters she lent Mrs. Gaskell. But when these are filled in, and, apart from what Mary Taylor called the declamation, which is practically confined to the Branwell-Robinson episode, it is difficult to conceive a biography of Charlotte Brontë, which, even with all the new facts before the writer, would be an improvement on

Mrs. Gaskell's. A few minor details might be added, but her main facts and conclusions have in no instance been proved wrong, and they are presented in such a way as to give a true and vivid picture of the life and character of the subject of her memoir which is hardly surpassed by any biography in the English language.—WILLETT, B. W., 1901, *ed. The Life of Charlotte Brontë by E. C. Gaskell, Introduction, p.* XV.

WIVES AND DAUGHTERS
1865

The story of Molly Gibson's life is so uneventful, and at the same time her character is so fully and delicately described, that only the most careful analysis can do it justice. There is the same minute realism in the picture of daily life as we find in Jane Austen; but there is, we think, a finer perception and deeper insight. Not only is every shade of conduct and character noted and described, but subtle and tender feelings are discerned, and the atmosphere is no longer that of genteel comedy.—COLERIDGE, CHRISTABEL, 1893, *Great Characters of Fiction, ed. Townsend, p.* 215.

Worthy to be placed beside "John Halifax, Gentleman," that modern epic of the true Christian life, is Mrs. Gaskell's "Wives and Daughters." Few if any novels can vie with this in naturalness and in the evolution of really entrancing interest out of the most ordinary and matter-of-course incidents of English life. Molly Gibson, the loved and loving daughter of the country doctor, who is drawn into a second marriage by the ex-governess and curate's widow, is one of the most finished studies of girlhood in English fiction. The step-mother, Mrs. Gibson, is drawn to the life, and then the old squire in his relations to his very diverse sons is equally real. The whole reads like what it is—a most faithful transcript from nature itself. Amid so much that is most amusing here, we have ever and anon a deep full note of humanity in its more passionate phases; and there are passages such as those where Squire Hamley grieves for his wife, and especially where he utters his exceedingly bitter cry over the death of his first-born, which draw tears from the eyes of the old as well as the young, and such tears as show through their mist some gleams of immortality and heaven. What is most remarkable, too, about this novel is that it moves the reader without employing the machinery of anything in the least

abnormal, unnatural, or even unlikely.—
RUSSELL, PERCY, 1894, *A Guide to British
and American Novels*, p. 159.

GENERAL

The authoress was a prose Crabbe—earnest, faithful, and often spirited in her delineations of humble life. By confining herself chiefly to the manufacturing population, she threw light on conditions of life,
habits, and feelings comparatively new and
original in our fictitious literature.—CHAM-
BERS, ROBERT, 1876, *Cyclopædia of English
Literature*, ed. *Carruthers*.

No one would dream of ranking Mrs. Gaskell as a novelist beside Dickens or Thackeray, but she deserves a very high place
among those who are comparatively unam-
bitious in their efforts, and who, having a
just measure of their own powers, succeed
perfectly in what they undertake. She
never attempted high flights, but pursued
her way steadily and surely at a moderate
elevation. Her style has not the magnificent reach of her friend, Charlotte Brontë;
it is homely, as suited her subjects. It was
natural that art such as hers, working earnestly within a definite field, without straining to get beyond it, and never wasting its
strength against the precipices, should become more perfect as she went on.—MINTO,
WILLIAM, 1878, *Mrs. Gaskell's Novels,
Fortnightly Review*, vol. 30, p. 368.

When, after the strain to which Mrs.
Gaskell had been subjected by the publication of her "Life of Charlotte Brontë," a
master-piece, in spite of all early cavils and
later supplements, she returned to fiction,
she proved to have finally formed the style
which is inalienably her own. Its exquisite
delicacy of texture and tender grace,
subduing but not concealing an irony
which is the secret of the finest
of English humorous prose, characterise each of her last three fictions.
. . . . The biography of Mrs. Gaskell we
know, is likely to remain unwritten; and
though literary criticism must chafe against
conditions which impair its force, the re-
striction may in this instance not prove
wholly disadvantageous. Something may
be learnt by guessing, instead of being
taught in detail, how a self-control which
matured a literary style as strong as it is
tender, and as subtle as it is sweet, reflected
the wondrously diversified experiences of a
pure and disciplined woman's life.—WARD,
ADOLPHUS WILLIAM, 1896, *English Prose,
ed. Craik*, vol. V, p. 524.

She has written one or two short books
which are technically faultless, and might
be taken as types of the novel form. Strange
to say, the recognition of her delicate and
many-sided genius has never been quite
universal, and has endured periods of
obscuration. Her work has not the personal
interest of Thackeray's, nor the intense
unity and compression of Charlotte Brontë's.
It may even be said that Mrs. Gaskell suffers
from having done well too many things.
She wrote, perhaps, a purer and a more exquisite English than either of her rivals,
but she exercised it in too many fields.—
GOSSE, EDMUND, 1897, *A Short History of
Modern English Literature*, p. 355.

Few writers, we think, have exercised a
more thoroughly wholesome influence over
their readers than Mrs. Gaskell.—BAYLY,
ADA ELLEN (EDNA LYALL), 1897, *Women
Novelists of Queen Victoria's Reign*, p. 144.

Mrs. Gaskell saw everything in the light
of a sympathetic humour. It is this quality
that has served hitherto as salt to her books
and has preserved their flavour while that
of a great deal of more ambitious literature
has been lost. If her humour is not equal to
the best specimens of that of George Eliot,
it is more diffused; if less powerful, it is gentler and quite as subtle. In style she is
easy and flowing; and her later books show
more freedom than her first attempt. At
the same time, her writing rarely rises to
eloquence. She had more talent than genius.
She has created many good, but no great
characters; and she stands midway between
Thackeray and Dickens, who are emphatically men of genius, and writers like Trollope who, with abundant talent and exhaustless industry, have no genius whatever.—WALKER, HUGH, 1897, *The Age of
Tennyson*, p. 108.

Hardly aspiring to the title of novelist,
she frequently reminded her public that she
was writing only tales. These tales were
told in the first person, and for the moral
edification of her own sex. In form and aim
they were accordingly of the Edgeworth
type. Indeed Mrs. Gaskell may be said, in
a general way, to have performed in them
the same noble service to her contemporaries that Maria Edgeworth did to hers.
She entered into the thoughts and wayward moods of children with true insight;
she gave us the first English nurses and

housekeepers of hard common sense and racy wit, the Nancys and the Sallys.— CROSS, WILBUR L., 1899, *The Development of the English Novel, p.* 234.

Mrs. Gaskell's short prose compositions would, in a writer of less eminence, themselves constitute a title to distinction; and their having failed to command the recognition they deserve is undoubtedly due to their inequality, so flawless a gem as "Cousin Phillis" being found with the collection that includes the common place production called "Hand and Heart " But some of the tales, notably "Cousin Phillis" and "The Crooked Branch," the one for grace and perfection of workmanship, the other for powerful and dramatic presentation, have never been surpassed by any of the longer novels written by Mrs. Gaskell. . . . Judged by the present arbitrary rules which prevail amongst modern crititcs, as to the nature and essentials of the short story, Mrs. Gaskell's tales would be weighed and found wanting; but they submit satisfactorily to tests that are likely to be more universal and permanent, and display their authoress as a perfect mistress in this branch of fiction,

whose art adequately satisfies and responds to the reader's instincts and demands. Mrs. Gaskell has a story to tell, some phenomena of human nature or life to present, and she sets them forth with perfect unity and completeness. . . . The varied range of powers exhibited by Mrs. Gaskell, her capacity for delineating the most diverse phenomena of human life and nature, ranging from an exquisite idyll flowing in the softest measures, to a concentrated tragedy of terrible and profound emotion, is completed by the delightful little piece called "Mr. Harrison's Confessions." The mere incidents narrating the arrival of a young and lively and nicelooking doctor in a town full of ladies, mostly old and gossiping are nothing; but the play of light and genial humour which is shed around them, the good-humoured satire free of every touch of acerbity or judgment, with which their foibles and habits are painted, and the capital portraiture of certain old-fashioned and fast-dying types are only to be matched in the pages of Addison at his brightest and best.—LOWE, FRANCES H., 1899, *Mrs. Gaskell's Short Tales, Fortnightly Review, vol.* 72, *pp.* 633, 641.

Nicholas Patrick Wiseman

1802–1865

Cardinal-priest and Roman Catholic Archbishop of Westminster, was, according to the German translator of his "Horæ Syriæ" (1828), "descended from an Irish family, born in Spain, educated in England, consecrated in Italy, Syrian scholar." He entered the Catholic College at Ushaw, near Durham, in 1810, and was removed to the English College at Rome in 1818. He was made D. D. in 1824, he was promoted to the priesthood in 1825, and became, in 1827, professor of Oriental literature, and afterwards, in 1828, rector of the English College. In 1835 he lectured in the Catholic Chapel at Lincoln's Inn Fields on "The Principal Doctrines and Practice of the Catholic Church." In 1840 he was chosen bishop-coadjutor to Dr. Walsh, the Vicar Apostolic of the Central District in England, and was consecrated Bishop of Melipotamus *in partibus* at Rome by Cardinal Frenzoni. He soon arrived at Oscott, and presided over St. Mary's College till 1847, when he was removed to the London district. In 1850, on the establishment of the hierarchy, he was nominated Archbishop of Westminster, and was made cardinal-priest of the title of St. Pudenziana. His conciliatory attitude during the storm that followed was highly commended by several of the leaders of the Whig party, and throughout his life he was the object of the deep veneration of all Roman Catholics. Cardinal Wiseman has been characterised as a great Biblical scholar, a profound divine, a judicious critic, an able linguist, and a scientist of note. The *Gentleman's Magazine* for May, 1865, gives a complete list of his works, in which appear:—"The Connection between Science and Revealed Religion" (1836); "Real Presence" (1836); "Lives of Five Saints Newly Canonised" (1839); "Prayers for the Conversion of England" (1840); "Papal and Royal Supremacy Contrasted" (1850); "The Hierarchy" (1850); and "Fabiola" (1854).—SANDERS, LLOYD C., *ed.* 1887, *Celebrities of the Century, p.* 1062.

PERSONAL

The evening I passed with the Trevelyans who had asked Dr. Wiseman, the head of

the English College here, and an eloquent preacher, to meet me. He seemed a genuine priest, not without talent, very good-looking

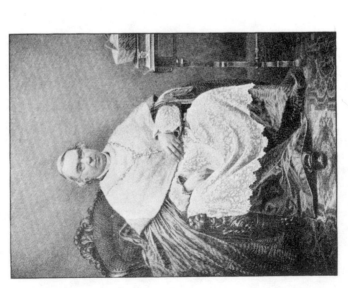

NICHOLAS PATRICK WISEMAN

Engraving by D. J. Pound. From a Photograph by Simonton & Millard.

HENRY LORD BROUGHAM

Engraving from a Photograph by W. & D. Downey.

and able-bodied, and with much apparent practice in the world. He talked well, but not so well as I expected.—TICKNOR, GEORGE, 1837, *Journal, Feb.* 16; *Life, Letters, and Journal, vol.* II, *p.* 73.

> Pius with Wiseman tries
> Our English Church to ban;
> O Pius, man unwise!
> O impious Wiseman!

—SCOTT, ROBERT, 1850, *On the Appointment of Cardinal Wiseman by Pope Pius to the Titular Archbishopric of Westminster.*

Yesterday I saw Cardinal Wiseman and heard him speak. It was at a meeting for the Roman Catholic Society of St. Vincent de Paul; the Cardinal presided. He is a big portly man something of the shape of Mr. Morgan; he has not merely a double but a treble and quadruple chin; he has a very large mouth with oily lips, and looks as if he would relish a good dinner with a bottle of wine after it. He came swimming into the room smiling, simpering, and bowing like a fat old lady, and sat down very demure in his chair and looked the picture of a sleek hypocrite. He was dressed in black like a bishop or dean, in plain clothes, but wore scarlet gloves and a brilliant scarlet waistcoat. A bevy of inferior priests surrounded him, many of them very dark-looking and sinister men. The Cardinal spoke in a smooth, whining manner, just like a canting Methodist preacher. The audience seemed to look up to him as to a god. A spirit of the hottest zeal pervaded the whole meeting.—BRONTË, CHARLOTTE, 1851, *Letter to Rev. P Bronte, June* 17; *Charlotte Bronte and her Circle, ed. Shorter, p.* 461.

Manning took me today to see Cardinal Wiseman, who lives in a plain house. His library is good and contains all the standard Catholic works. We found him clad in a black gown with a red band about his neck. He has a fine, imposing figure, wears gold glasses, is cautious and measured in his utterance, and looks more like a well-fed Italian prelate, fond of good living, than like an ascetic. The impression upon me was not pleasant. He impressed me not as a winning amiability but of calculating shrewdness. His face is almost entirely lacking in spirituality and intellectuality, both of which his writings would lead you to look for. He betrayed almost total ignorance of German theology.—SCHAFF, PHILIP, 1854, *Diary; Life of Philip Schaff by David S. Schaff, p.* 194.

The Cardinal is portly, with a feeble sweet voice, and most beautiful hands, which were always in movement. He did not give a very able lecture; it was confused and illogical, though in parts very clever and eloquent. He took me captive at first, for he began by expatiating on the admirable proposal of the Committee for the Prince's Memorial, of a hall to unite the purposes of science and art; then he read a few lines from the Report. He told, also, some good stories, showing his aptitude for humour, which his slight Irish tone makes one expect. His lecture, like his sermons, I suppose, was meant for an illogical audience, and brevity was as little studied as close reasoning, for instead of one hour he was just two.—EASTLAKE, ELIZABETH RIGBY LADY, 1863, *Journal, Jan.* 31; *Journals and Correspondence, ed. Smith, vol.* II, *p.* 175.

His life and education had been somewhat cosmopolitan. Some German translator of his "Horæ Syriacæ" had described him in one many-syllabled word as the "from-an-Irish-family-descended-in-Spain-born-in-England-educated-in - Italy - consecrated Syrian Scholar," but he showed no inclination to merge his British nationality in his sacerdotal or scholastic character. — MILNES, RICHARD MONCKTON (LORD HOUGHTON), 1873, *Monographs, Personal and Social, p.* 39.

In the life of Cardinal Wiseman we find a new exemplification of the inscrutable justice of the Divine Power. Here is a boy, an orphan, whose ancestors had to fly their native land for their devotion to the Catholic faith; raised up, nurtured, and trained in the center of Christendom and sent to recall to a knowledge of God the very nation that had so cruelly persecuted his forefathers. In the early ages, Ireland sent many holy and zealous men to convert the Anglo-Saxons, but it is very doubtful if any among them were more learned, more earnest, or more successful in their mission than the illustrious bishop whose body lies mouldering without the confines of the English capital.—MCGEE, JAMES E., 1874, *Lives of Irishmen's Sons, p.* 211.

Nor must we omit to mention the death of Cardinal Wiseman, on February 15, 1865. Cardinal Wiseman had outlived the popular clamour once raised against him in England. There was a time when his name would have set all the pulpit-drums of no-popery rattling; he came at length to be respected and admired everywhere in England as a scholar and a man of ability. He was a devoted ecclesiastic, whose zeal for his church was his honour, and whose earnest labour in the work he was set to do had shortened his busy life.—McCARTHY, JUSTIN, 1880, *A History of Our Own Times, from the Accession of Queen Victoria to the General Election of 1880, vol.* III.

The great variety of his pursuits might seem at first sight suggestive of the *dilettante*. Over and above his professional duties, we have seen him occupied with Oriental studies, with art, with literature, with the Tractarian Movement, at one time on a diplomatic mission on behalf of the liberal Pope, at another lecturing to a London audience on the Crimean war; then again busy with practical reforms among the poor, and soon afterwards offering suggestions as to the hanging of a national portrait gallery. Yet his intimate friends are unanimous as to the unity of his work and purpose. The key to the explanation of this apparent contradiction is, I think, found in a saying of his friend Father Whitty, in a letter to Henry Edward Manning, written just after Wiseman's death. The cause of Wiseman's influence did not lie, Father Whitty said, only in his talents and acquirements, considerable as they were, but in his being in his tastes, in his policy and work, and in his writings, a faithful representative of the Catholic Church—*not*, he adds, as a Saint represents her, solely on the ethical side, but as a national poet represents the all-round genius of a particular country in his various poems.—WARD, WILFRID, 1897, *The Life and Times of Cardinal Wiseman, vol.* II, *p.* 151.

Of the ecclesiastics who have illustrated this century, there is one to whom none has refused, or could refuse, the recognition of his brilliant qualifications as a man of learning, of letters and of science, nor yet of his fitness for the high and responsible position he held in ecclesiastical authority, yet whose grand character, broad views and private virtues are too little known to the general public. . . . I am quite sure that all who were so fortunate as to enjoy his personal acquaintance will bear me out in my testimony to his admirable qualities of heart and mind, his winning manners, habitual forbearance, never-failing consideration for others, and his courteous and cordial hospitality. I may venture to say I knew Cardinal Wiseman *intus et in cute*, and might record instance upon instance of his universal benevolence, of his kindness to the sick generally, his thoughtfulness, and also tenderness in visiting them, his cheery tone in talking to them, and also the personal attention he has often been known to bestow on those who, whether from falling ill in a foreign country, or from other causes, have had no relations or friends at hand; with such he has not hesitated to watch through the night, to administer medicines and apply lotions, and no trained nurse could show more skill in dressing blisters, manipulating leeches, or applying bandages.—BYRNE, MRS. WILLIAM PITT, 1898, *Social Hours with Celebrities, vol.* I, *pp.* 308, 309.

We have several times cited passages in which Cardinal Wiseman is called a *great Englishman*, but it would be very unjust did we terminate this notice of his life without pointing out that he was also a *great Irishman!* For his mother was Irish, and it is a question physiology has by no means decided in the negative whether a mother has not a much larger share in determining the innermost nature and the essential character of a son than has his father. The geniality, the kindness, the ready eloquence, and—when not in pain and suffering—the light-heartedness of Wiseman are surely genuinely "Irish;" and genuinely "Irish," also, was the reception given him when, in 1858, he made a tour in the Island of St. Patrick. . . . We knew Nicholas Wiseman from the spring of 1844, for more than twenty years; and we have no recollection, as to that intercourse, of anything which it is not a pleasure to recollect, save alone that physical suffering and occasional mental depression by which he was from time to time so severely tried.—MIVART, ST. GEORGE, 1898, *Cardinal Wiseman, The American Catholic Quarterly Review, vol.* 23, *pp.* 380, 381.

My recollections of England's great Cardinal-Archbishop of Westminster, Nicholas Wiseman, are strong and vivid. His relations with Dr. Newman, and with that crowd of converts which clustered around that great founder of the English Oratory as their natural leader in the current of conversions to the old and only true Faith, has no signs of weakness in it. My judgment will not tolerate any theory which imputes any weakness to Wiseman's will. No theory of that kind can ever be made to hold water.

It is contrary to Wiseman's natural disposition, which in the recollection of too many living men that once knew him towers above all suggestion of such weakness.—WALWORTH, C. L., 1899, *Reminiscenses of a Catholic Crisis in England Fifty Years Ago, Catholic World, vol.* 70, *p.* 247.

Wiseman's reputation was worldwide. He was conspicuous for rare intellect and abilities, for "the general justice of his mind," for the suavity of his demeanour, and the wide range of his literary and artistic knowledge and sympathies. As a linguist and scholar he was especially distinguished. He was often called the English Mezzofanti. Speaking of his linguistic facility to the present writer, he once said that, if he were allowed to choose his own path westwards, he could talk all the way from the most eastern point of the coast of Asia to the most western point of the coast of Europe. The poet Browning attempted an unfavourable interpretation of Wiseman's character in his "Bishop Blougram's Apology" (first published in Browning's "Men and Women," 1855); "Sylvester Blougram," Browning's bishop, was undoubtedly intended for Wiseman, but Blougram's worldly and self-indulgent justification of his successful pursuit of the clerical career in the Roman catholic church, although dramatically most effective, cannot be accepted as a serious description of Wiseman's aims in life or conduct. According to Father Prout, Wiseman in "The Rambler" temperately reviewed "Men and Women" on its publication, and favourably noticed "Bishop Blougram's Apology," as a masterly intellectual achievement, although he regarded it as an assault on the groundworks of religion.—KENT, CHARLES, 1900, *Dictionary of National Biography, vol.* LXII, *p.* 246.

FABIOLA
1854

In the first place I must inform you that your little work "Fabiola" is most highly appreciated by the Catholics of Germany, and some influential persons on reading this admirable description of the "Church in the Catacombs" have come to the conclusion that you alone are capable of giving the same life, and colouring, to the two or three other tales in illustration of the different periods of Church history, to which you allude in your preface. I could not, therefore, refuse the aid of my humble pen to lay at the feet of your Eminence the petition of those

whose wish (so entirely in accordance with mine) is, that you will continue what you have so happily begun, and not trust to weaker hands the completion of a work so highly calculated to advance the cause of truth, and for which we are all convinced you alone have the learning, knowledge of the localities, and talent requisite for rendering the whole series such as we should wish it to be, in order to produce the deepest impression on the public mind.—RIO, APOLLONIA, 1855, *Letter to Cardinal Wiseman, Oct.* 10; *The Life and Times of Cardinal Wiseman by Wilfrid Ward, vol.* II, *p.* 104.

Translations of "Fabiola" appeared in Italian, French, Spanish, Portuguese, Hungarian, German, Danish, Polish, Slavonian, and Dutch. There were seven Italian versions, and I find among his papers several requests to translate it into Spanish, and many to render it into French and German. It has been impossible to read all the "appreciations" which, especially in France and Italy, it drew forth both in public and in private.—WARD, WILFRID, 1897, *The Life and Times of Cardinal Wiseman, vol.* II, *p.* 101.

GENERAL

This ["Connection between Science and Revealed Religion"] is one of the most entertaining as well as valuable works which learning and ingenuity have produced for confirming the truth of the Holy Scriptures.—HORNE, THOMAS HARTWELL, 1839, *A Manual of Biblical Bibliography, p.* 391.

Wiseman's answer is also just out, and, I confess, seems to me very powerful. He has greatly the advantage of Palmer in style and temper—though quite as *cutting*, yet more quietly so; and as Palmer's tone was certainly enough to provoke an opponent, one must let a man have his revenge; at least it is ὑπὲρ ἄνθρωπον not to give tit-for-tat.— MOZLEY, JAMES BOWLING, 1841, *To Thomas Mozley, May* 19; *Letters, ed. his Sister, p.* 119.

He is a man of great natural abilities, considerable scholarship, and no little taste, when his critical palate is not tempted to excess. But disingenuous statements, and gorgeous and luxuriating descriptions, whether of art or nature, are not calculated to remove certain impressions respecting scarlet ladies from the severe English mind; and it would have done no harm to the credit given him, and I dare say justly given him, for consideration towards others when speaking in his own person, if he had spared his fellow-readers of the English poets the necessity of charging him with false accusations of their common benefactors.—HUNT, LEIGH, 1859, *English Poetry versus Cardinal Wiseman, Fraser's Magazine, vol.* 60, *p.* 766.

Besides his theological works, and his numerous controversial pamphlets, Cardinal Wiseman published many occasional lectures and essays on subjects connected with literature and art. These lectures and essays showed broad views and generous culture, and gained for the author a lasting place in the respect of his countrymen outside of his own communion. He writes with singular grace and elegance, and his thoughts are often strikingly beautiful.—HART, JOHN S., 1872, *A Manual of English Literature, p.* 581.

These discourses ["Connection Between Science and Revealed Religion"] were most interesting to all who heard them, and, though, perhaps, the wide range they took created some distrust in the perfect accuracy of the author, yet his acknowledged eminence in one portion of Oriental philology fairly suggested the inference that he would not run the risk of careless assertions or inadequate knowledge in other portions of his work. . . . His style never became agreeable to ordinary English taste; the foreign education of his young manhood damaged the force and even the correctness of his diction, and a certain natural taste for richness of form and colour encumbered his writings with superfluous epithets and imagery. . . . Dr. Wiseman, in the ordinary course of his profession, would have exercised a very wide moral influence by the general justice of his mind and the sweetness of his disposition. If he had to be intolerant, it was against the grain; and perhaps he gladly took refuge in a somewhat pompous rhetoric from the necessity of plainly expressing unpalatable truths and harsh conclusions. — MILNES, RICHARD MONCKTON (LORD HOUGHTON), 1873, *Monographs, Personal and Social, pp.* 47, 50, 58.

Cardinal Wiseman wrote in a clear and polished style, sometimes too much in the florid Italian manner; but often too with a calm eloquence peculiarly suited to the English temperament.—JENKINS, O. L., 1876, *The Student's Handbook of British and American Literature, p.* 348.

He was a prelate of the largest sympathies, of a broad and highly cultivated and many-sided mind.—VAUGHAN, HERBERT, 1892, *Reply of the Archbishop-Elect to the Address of the Clergy and Laity of the Diocese of Westminster, p.* 6.

One great cause of the interest felt in him was the work he had written "On the Connection between Science and Revealed Religion," which was first made known in the form of lectures, delivered in Cardinal Weld's rooms at Rome in the Lent of 1835, and which were speedily published. Devoted as they were to the consideration of the difficulties which were then felt with regard to various questions which had arisen concerning physical science and criticism, they were welcomed and read with extraordinary avidity. In the present day some of his arguments are, of course, out of date, owing to the advance of science; but they have an historical interest, and an especial interest for us who seek to understand Wiseman. They show that he had a real sympathy for science as well as art, that his mind was a broad one, that he deprecated most earnestly anxious fears with respect to human intellectual progress, and that his great desire was that Churchmen should show themselves to be sympathetic with science, and the Church to be evidently an aid to, instead of a check upon, intellectual advancement in all directions.—MIVART, ST. GEORGE, 1898, *Cardinal Wiseman, The American Catholic Quarterly Review, vol.* 23, *p.* 361.

Except in the beauty of some of his imagery, Wiseman's language does not bear many signs of Taylor's influence. Wiseman is more verbose and intricate in the composition of his sentences. Yet this is rather the peculiarity of the sermons composed between the years 1827 and 1837 than of his later discourses. It belongs to the time rather than to the person. . . . Mr. Ward also blames Wiseman's style as being "overcharged with imagery," and elsewhere speaks of his "usual exuberance of metaphor." Had he said "occasional," Wiseman's greatest admirer must have allowed the censure. Yet it must not be misunderstood. It is very seldom that Wiseman introduces a mixed metaphor; though sometimes his images press so closely one upon the other as to produce the effect of a Dutch painting of tulips and fruit. More commonly, however, he imitated the Japanese artist who displays one lovely plant alone on his polished panel.—BRIDGETT, T. E., 1898, *Monuments to Cardinal Wiseman, Dublin Review, vol. 122, pp.* 259, 260.

It was in 1854 that he published his historical romance, "Fabiola;" "a good book which had all the success of a bad one," the Archbishop of Milan wittily said. It was speedily translated into almost all European languages, and new editions of it are still appearing in England and on the Continent. —LILLY, WILLIAM SAMUEL, 1898, *Mr. Wilfrid Ward's "Cardinal Wiseman," Fortnightly Review, vol.* 69, *p.* 300.

His verse is loose in texture, but flowing and melodious. His style lacked compression. It could never be said of him, in Landor's phrase, that he "inspissated his yellows into blacks." There was ever the something too much of facile genius. He loved, in diction as in life, splendor for its own sake.

He liked his state as Prince of the Church. He graciously vested himself in his official robes to furnish Charles Kean the correct costume for Cardinal Wolsey. . . . He was rich in humor, which diffused itself through his genial demeanor. Above all, he was an honest man, pure and good, a worthy dignitary. His spirit was devout. His mood was of faith and worked by love. The Roman church may well be proud of giving him birth and nurture, of recognizing his gifts, and setting him in her high places of authority. It may be questioned if every Protestant denomination could breed just such a man, or would know precisely what to do with him. The Roman Catholic Church has its narrow doors and cramped vestibules, but there seems room and verge enough for those who are fairly inside.—RICHARDS, C. A. L., 1898, *A Great Roman Prelate, The Dial, vol.* 24, *p.* 257.

Richard Cobden
1804–1865

Born at Heyshott, near Midhurst, Sussex, England, June 3, 1804: died at London, April 2, 1865. An English statesman and political economist, especially noted as an advocate of free trade and of peace, and as the chief supporter of the Anti-Corn-Law League 1839–46. He began, in partnership with others, the business of calico-printing in 1831; entered Parliament in 1841; visited the United States in 1854; and negotiated an important commercial treaty between England and France 1859–60. During the Civil War in the United States he was a supporter of the cause of the North. His "Political Writings" were published in 1867; his "Speeches on Questions of Public Policy" (ed. Bright and Rogers) in 1870.—SMITH, BENJAMIN E., *ed.*, 1894–97, *The Century Cyclopedia of Names, p.* 262.

PERSONAL

Went to the House of Commons and heard Cobden bring on his arbitration motion to produce universal peace. He has a good face, and is a clear, manly speaker. A French lady who was with us in our little box, informed us that she was staying at his house, that she had travelled with him and his wife in Spain, and concluded by accepting him as her standard of perfection.— FOX, CAROLINE, 1849, *Memories of Old Friends, ed. Pym, Journal, June* 12, *p.* 265.

Cobden in physiognomy and appearance might almost pass for an American, and has a certain New England sharpness and shrewdness in his way of dealing with a subject. His address was argumentative, and yet there was a certain popular clearness about it, a fertility of familiar illustrations, and an earnest feeling which made it uncommonly impressive.—BRYANT, WILLIAM CULLEN, 1850, *Letters of a Traveler.*

Cobden is a man of an extremely interest-

ing mind; quite the opposite of an Englishman in this respect, that you never hear him talk commonplaces, and that he has few prejudices.—MÉRIMÉE, PROSPER, 1860, *Correspondence.*

Take him all in all, Mr. Cobden is a man of rare intelligence, of unswerving industry, and of spotless integrity. In qualities of head and heart, we believe him to be excelled by few men. His conscientiousness is of the highest order. Though he has had much political enmity to encounter, no one has ever charged him with doing a mean thing, or prostituting the great power he unquestionably wielded to subserve any personal or selfish end. His eloquence—or rather his persuasiveness—is remarkable. He practises none of the graces of the orator. His style is simple, almost homely, but thoroughly logical and convincing; and his matter is always full of facts. He emphatically hits the nail on the head, clinching it at both sides. In person he is pale lean, and wiry, of melancholic features; and his voice is thin, and sounds somewhat nasal. Yet, with these personal disadvantages, the influence which he exercises as a speaker is something extraordinary. We believe the secret to lie in his immense fund of common sense, his great practical sagacity and shrewdness, his evident honesty of purpose and earnest straightforwardness, and, at the same time, the clearness and simplicity of speech which enables him to bring his reasonings and his facts completely home to the judgment, and appeal so powerfully to the silent judge in every man's bosom.—SMILES, SAMUEL, 1860, *Brief Biographies, p.* 115.

Not even the tragedy here can make me indifferent to the death of Richard Cobden, who was my personal friend and the friend of my country. I felt with you entirely in the touching words which you uttered in Parliament. I wish he could have lived to enjoy our triumph and to continue his counsels. His name will be cherished here as in England. History will be for him more than Westminster Abbey.—SUMNER, CHARLES, 1865, *To John Bright, April* 18; *Memoir and Letters of Charles Sumner, ed. Pierce, vol.* IV, *p.* 239.

Few who were living, and of sufficiently matured powers of observation at the time, will ever forget the sad and general impression made by the tidings of Mr. Cobden's peaceful release, throughout the whole land, amongst all classes of its citizens, and in the great countries of Europe and in the New World. Mr. Cobden, with a patriotism as undeniable and unquenchable as ever animated a human breast, had nevertheless been the great apostle of kindliness and conciliation in international relations. And one consequence was, that he was more beloved and popular out of his own land, than ever statesman was in the history of the world. Englishmen—even those who had admired him most warmly whilst living—were astounded when they came, after his death, to realise the beauty of his character, the magnitude of his services, and the amount of what they had lost by his somewhat early departure. — McGILCHRIST, JOHN, 1865 *Richard Cobden, p.* 255.

What the qualities of Mr. Cobden were in the House all present are aware; yet, perhaps, I may be permitted to say that as a debater he had few equals. As a logician he was close and complete; adroit, perhaps even subtle;

yet at the same time he was gifted with such a degree of imagination that he never lost sight of the sympathies of those whom he addressed, and so, generally avoiding to drive his arguments to extremity, he became as a speaker both practical and persuasive. I believe that when the verdict of posterity shall be recorded on his life and conduct, it will be said of him that he was, without doubt, the greatest political character the pure middle class of this country has yet produced—an ornament to the House of Commons, and an honour to England.—DISRAELI, BENJAMIN (EARL OF BEACONSFIELD), 1865, *Speech in House of Commons, April* 3, 1865.

Mr. Cobden spoke after me [1847], and was received with unbounded enthusiasm. He then for the first time broached the doctrine about the advent of universal peace, which was so signally belied by the events of the following spring. Mr. Cobden appeared to me to be quite a monomaniac; his eye was wild, and his style of speaking was nothing more than chatting with the audience in a very business-like and effective way.—ALISON, SIR ARCHIBALD, 1867 (?), *Some Account of my Life and Writings, vol.* I, *p.* 566

I recollect him only as an eloquent but intolerant talker; impatient of the speech and opinions of others; very inconsecutive, and putting forth with a plethora of words misty dogmas in theology and metaphysics, partly of German origin, which he never seemed to me to clear up to his own understanding or to that of others. What has come out posthumously of his philosophy has not removed this imputation upon it.— HOLLAND, SIR HENRY, 1871, *Recollections of Past Life, p.* 205.

Though he was amply endowed with that practical wisdom which Aristotle describes as the first quality of the man who meddles with government, all his aims, his sympathies, his maxims were as open and transparent as the day. Nobody could be more free from the spirit of Machiavellian calculation. He had in a full measure the gift of tact, but it came from innate considerateness and good feeling, and not either from social art or from hidden subtlety of nature. . . . In his own house, where public men do not always seek the popularity that is the very breath of their nostrils abroad, he was tender, solicitous, forbearing, never exacting. Most of his preparation for speeches and pamphlets was done amid the bustle of a young household, and he preferred to work amid the sociable play of his little children. His thoroughly pleasant and genial temper made him treat everybody who approached him as a friend. Few men have attracted friends of such widely different type. The hard-headed man of business and the fastidious man of letters were equally touched by the interest of his conversation and the charm of his character. There must have been something remarkable about one who won the admiration of Prosper Mérimée, and the cordial friendship of Mr. Goldwin Smith, and the devoted service of strenuous practical men like Mr. Slagg and Mr. Thomasson. His exceeding amiability was not insipid. He was never bitter, but he knew how to hit hard, and if a friend did wrong and public mischief came of it, Cobden did not shrink from the duty of dealing faithfully with him.—MORLEY, JOHN, 1881, *The Life of Richard Cobden, vol.* II, *p.* 475.

Mr. Morley says that he has asked scores of persons who knew him, Conservatives as well as Liberals, what the secret was of his influence and success as an orator, and they all agreed in using the word *"persuasiveness"* as Cobden's most marked characteristic. His power of *extempore* argument was wonderful; simple, lucid, cogent, full of facts, he was never dry nor abstract, nor over terse; while all he said was carried home, to use Mr. Bright's words, by "the absolute truth that shone in his eye and in his countenance."—MORISON, JAMES COTTER, 1882, *The Life of Richard Cobden by John Morley, Macmillan's Magazine, vol.* 45, *p.* 213.

When he was thirty years old, which was about the time of the Reform Bill revolution, Cobden was one of the most learned men in England; and yet in the jargon of conceited scholarship he was called "an uneducated man," that is to say, a man whom the colleges did not know. The truth is, that although he had little schooling, few of his critics had read as many books or as many men as he had read. The best scholar is not the man who learns the most, but the man who forgets the least, and Cobden forgot little. There was not a man at Oxford who had read as many chapters in the Book of Realities as Richard Cobden had. He had studied man as a moral, intellectual,

spiritual, social, agricultural, manufacturing and mercantile being, in his relations to this moral, intellectual, spiritual, social, agricultural, manufacturing, and mercantile world. His political wisdom grew out of a vast accumulation of useful knowledge; and herein it was that when he entered Parliament at thirty-seven years of age, there was not a man in the House of Commons so well equipped with political information, not one so competent in debate. . . . . His eulogy may be condensed into this: He gave more food and better clothes, higher wages, and shorter hours of labor to all the workingmen of England.—TRUMBULL, M. M., 1892, *Richard Cobden, The American Journal of Politics, vol.* I, *pp.* 3, 15.

Cobden himself had a large share of the qualities which Englishmen rightly reverence. He was upright, honourable, and disinterested; kindly and affectionate in his private life; an excellent father, husband, and brother; sedulous in his work, simple in his habits, pleasantly free from ostentation and self-seeking ambition; and no one can question his courage, or the conscientious industry and self-sacrificing energy, with which he served the cause of humanity, according to his lights.—LOW, SIDNEY, 1896, *The Decline of Cobdenism, The Nineteenth Century, vol.* 40, *p.* 184.

GENERAL

On Saturday week I read in the newspapers the speech Cobden made at Manchester abusing the Duke of Wellington, and scouting the national defenses. On Wednesday I wrote a letter to him in the *Times*, which has had great success. I have received innumerable compliments and expressions of approbation about it from all quarters, and the old Duke is pleased. I had no idea of making such a *hit*, but the truth is, everybody was disgusted at Cobden's impertinence and (it may be added) folly. His head is turned by all the flattery he has received, and he has miserably exposed himself since his return to England, showing that he is a man of one idea and no statesman.—GREVILLE, CHARLES C. F., 1848, *A Journal of the Reign of Queen Victoria from* 1837 *to* 1852, *ed. Reeve, Feb.* 8, *vol.* II, *p.* 262.

I deem him one of the most privileged, as he deserves to be one of the most honoured of his race. No man has ever been called in to exercise more important functions, and no man's exertions have been more successful in their issue, or more unpretending in their display.... His strength has always been found in his advocacy of sound principles to be carried out in their full extension. No surrender of a truth—no compromise with an error. Yet he has always been willing to take reasonable instalments towards the payment of a just debt, he has never sacrificed an obtainable good in the pursuit of an unapproachable better, but has felt that every step forward is progress, leaving less to be done than if that step had not been taken.—BOWRING, SIR JOHN, 1861, *Autobiographical Recollections, pp.* 300, 301.

Very rarely, if even ever, in history has a man achieved so much by his words, been victor in what was thought at the time to be a class struggle, and yet spoken so little evil as Mr. Cobden. There is hardly a word to be found, perhaps, even now, which the Recording Angel would wish to blot out. We may on other grounds object to an agitator who lacerates no one; but no watchful man of the world will deny that such an agitator has vanquished one of life's most imperious and difficult temptations.—BAGEHOT, WALTER, 1865, *Mr. Cobden, Works,* ed. *Morgan, vol.* III, *p.* 415.

It is the duty of those to whom the memory of Richard Cobden is the memory of a greatness, not only beyond question and almost beyond rivalry, but of a wholly original kind—a greatness which, while it filled a vast chasm in political philosophy, was rich in a new promise and possibilities hitherto unimagined for the happiness of mankind, and which, at the same time, neither was nor is generally appreciated or understood—to see that his name appears in history, not under the light of a fictitious and common-place distinction, but in its own peculiar and enduring lustre, and takes its appropriate place in the hearts and in the minds of men.—HOBART, LORD, 1873, *The "Mission" of Richard Cobden, p.* 29.

In 1835 he published his first pamphlet, entitled "England, Ireland and America, by a Manchester Manufacturer." It attracted great attention, and ran rapidly through several editions. It was marked by a breadth and boldness of views on political and social questions which betokened an original mind. In this production Cobden advocated the same prin-

ciples of peace, non-intervention, retrenchment, and free trade to which he continued faithful to the last day of his life. . . . His abhorence of war amounted to a passion. Throughout his long labors in behalf of unrestricted commerce he never lost sight of this, as being the most precious result of the work in which he was engaged,—its tendency to diminish the hazards of war and to bring the nations of the world into closer and more lasting relations of peace and friendship with each other. He was not deterred by the fear of ridicule or the reproach of Utopianism from associating himself openly, and with all the ardor of his nature, with the peace party in England. . . . It has already been remarked that Cobden's efforts in furtherance of free trade were always subordinated to the highest moral purposes—the promotion of peace on earth and good-will among men. This was his desire and hope as respects the Commercial Treaty with France. He was therefore deeply dissappointed and distressed to find the old feeling of distrust towards our neighbors still actively fomented by the press and some of the leading politicians of the country. He therefore, in 1862, published his pamphlet entitled "The Three Panics," the object of which was to trace the history and expose the folly of those periodical visitations of alarm as respects the design of our neighbors with which this country had been afflicted for the preceding fifteen or sixteen years.—RICHARD, HENRY, 1877, *Encyclopædia Britannica, Ninth Ed., vol.* VI, *pp.* 85, 87, 88.

Cobden believed that the real interests, of the individual, of the nation, and of all nations are identical; and that these several interests are all in entire and necessary accord with the highest interests of morality. With this belief, an economic truth acquired with him the dignity and vitality of a moral law, and, instead of remaining a barren doctrine of the intellect, became a living force, to move the hearts and consciences of men.—MALLET, SIR LOUIS, 1878, *Writings of Cobden, Introduction.*

Cobden made his way to men's hearts by the union they saw in him of simplicity, earnestness, and conviction, with a singular facility of exposition. This facility consisted in a remarkable power of apt and homely illustration, and a curious ingenuity, in framing the argument that happened to be wanting. Besides his skill in thus hitting on the right argument, Cobden had the oratorical art of presenting it in the way that made its admission to the understanding of a listener easy and undenied. . . . He always seemed to have made the right allowance for the difficulty with which men follow a speech, as compared with the ease of following the same argument on a printed page. . . . Then men are attracted by his mental alacrity, by the same readiness with which he turned round to grapple with a new objection. Prompt and confident, he was never at a loss, and he never hesitated. This is what Mr. Disraeli meant when he spoke of Cobden's sauciness.— MORLEY, JOHN, 1881, *The Life of Richard Cobden, vol.* I, *pp.* 194, 195.

The man whose name is and always will be by far the most celebrated among the apostles of Free Trade.—NICOLL, HENRY J., 1881, *Great Movements and Those who Achieved Them, pp.* 226, 238.

His radicalism from the first was the radicalism of a class, and such in all essentials it remained to the end. His lack of the historic sense was not compensated by any great scientific or speculative power. Much as he saw to disapprove of in the existing condition of England, he never framed a large and consistent theory of the methods by which it was to be improved. Outside the narrow bounds of the economics of trade he had political projects, but no coherent political system; so that if he was too theoretical to make a good minister of state, he was too fragmentary and inconsistent to make a really important theorist. —BALFOUR, ARTHUR JAMES, 1882, *Morley's "Life of Cobden," The Nineteenth Century, vol.* 11, *p.* 54.

He had a mastery over every part of the great Free Trade controversy, such as no other could pretend to; and in the number of speeches which he made on this one subject he showed a boundless fertility of illustration, and an inexhaustible ingenuity in varying the arrangement and the form of his arguments. He succeeded in fighting and winning the battle of Free Trade almost against hope. Time vindicated his principles, and his merits and services were ultimately acknowledged even by his opponents.—SMITH, GEORGE BARNETT, 1887, *Celebrities of the Century, ed. Sanders, p.* 265.

Cobden was one of those noble men whose whole thoughts and work and life are devoted to the welfare of their fellow-creatures, and especially to the welfare of the largest and least prosperous classes among them; but who, at the same time, pursue those objects without fawning, fear or flattery, and who care little for the momentary favour of the people they most desire to serve. In the great Corn Law struggle his first and most eager desire was to carry the working classes with him in working out their own salvation; and it was, as he has told us, only when they rejected the object he thought all-important, in favour of the points of the Charter, that he and his friends were compelled to turn to the middle class for support, and to make the agitation a middle-class struggle. In all his subsequent efforts for Education, for Free Trade, and for Peace, it was the welfare of the working classes which lay nearest to his heart—and whether they agreed with him or not, this was the object which he steadily pursued. Peace, above all things: Peace, which is the best friend of industry, was his one great object—an object so overwhelmingly important that he perhaps sometimes allowed it to obscure the actual conditions of imperfect human nature.—FARRER, THOMAS HENRY LORD, 1894, *Reminiscences of Richard Cobden, Compiled by Mrs. Salis Schwabe, Preface, p.* x.

"Hurrah! hurrah! the Corn Bill is law, and now my work is done." So wrote Richard Cobden to his wife just fifty years ago: on the 26th of June, 1846. It is perhaps fortunate for the earnest and sanguine champion of the Manchester school that he did not live long enough to take part in the chastened festivities with which a few of his followers have endeavored to celebrate the "jubilee" of Peel's great measure of fiscal revolution. Assuredly if his work was done in 1846, he would have been forced to acknowledge that a good deal of it has been undone by 1896. Indeed, as the Cobdenite jubilators have sadly to admit, the time is one singularly unpropitious for rejoicing on their part. . . . It is possible that if Cobden were alive today, and face to face with the conditions of latter-day industrialism and international competition, he might be a Cobdenite no longer. It is certain that so acute an explorer of the currents of public opinion would have perceived that such projects as that of an Imperial Customs Union would have to be dealt with on their merits, political and social, as well as financial. And he would have understood that they could not be disposed of by being called "veiled Protectionism," or by an appeal to an economic pontificate that has lost its sanctity.—LOW, SIDNEY, 1896, *The Decline of Cobdenism, The Nineteenth Century, vol. 40, pp.* 173, 186.

William Edmondstoune Aytoun

1813–1865

Born, at Edinburgh, educated for the law, and called to the Scottish bar in 1840. In 1848 he was appoined Regius professor of English literature in the University of Edinburgh, and the following year married the youngest daughter of Professor John Wilson. He was promoted to the Shrievalty of Orkney and Shetland in1852. From 1845 to the time of his death, Aytoun was one of the leading contributors to *Blackwood*. He published "Poland and other Poems," 1831; "The Lays of Scottish Cavaliers," 1848; "Bothwell," 1856; "Firmilian: a Spasmodic Tragedy," 1858. In conjunction with his friend Sir Theodore Martin he published "Bon Gaultier's Book of Ballads," and an edition of translations of several minor poems of Goethe. He was also the author of various tales.—RANDOLPH, HENRY FITZ, 1887, *ed. Fifty Years of English Song, Biographical and Bibliographical Notes, vol.* I, *p.*19.

PERSONAL

The Radicals have set up a silly person of the name of Aytoun, a briefless advocate, as their candidate. He has no chance, but we have made good use of him in our attacks on the Whigs, and great numbers of his voters will go over to Mr. Blair in preference to Jeffrey, and still more in preference to Abercromby. — BLACKWOOD, WILLIAM, 1833, *Letter to his son William, Sept.* 2; *William Blackwood and his sons, ed. Oliphant, vol.* II, *p.* 109.

It is to ourselves a source of great though melancholy pleasure to look back on our long intercourse with him, which was never interrupted by any differences of opinion or estrangement of feeling. It is rare, indeed, that the relations of business become a source of so much heart-felt pleasure and familiar intimacy; and we cannot think without painful emotion that all this happiness is at an end.—BLACKWOOD,WILLIAM, 1865, *Blackwood's Magazine.*

He was the warmest and most loyal of friends, and, because he was so, he was most happy in his friendships. He was beloved as a son, a brother, and a husband. He had a side for all men; he understood and could make allowance for all peculiarities; and he was quick to appreciate and frank to acknowledge merit of every kind. He was singularly gentle, just, considerate, and forbearing to everything but meanness, vulgarity, and conceit; and even when most provoked by these, he would, out of his large charity, find excuses for "the weak but well-meaning creatures" in whom they had been offensively shown. His duties, public and private, he discharged with conscientious zeal, and with the chivalrous courtesies of a true-hearted gentleman. Therefore he died honoured by his fellow-citizens, and deeply mourned by those who had the happiness to know him as a friend.—MARTIN, SIR THEODORE, 1867, *Memoir of William Edmondstoune Aytoun, p.* 250.

All who knew Aytoun seem to have liked and felt kindly towards him, and to have remembered him as a pleasant, genial, courteous man, refined and cultured, tolerant, warm-hearted and sympathetic, and bringing sunshine wherever he went by his vivacity and good temper. The stories of his ready wit are numerous. — MASSON, ROSALINE, 1898, *Pollok and Aytoun (Famous Scots Series), p.* 151.

LAYS OF THE SCOTTISH CAVALIERS

1848

Professor Aytoun has selected his ballad themes from striking incidents and from stirring scenes in our mediæval Scottish history—some remote as the field of Flodden, others as recent as that of Drummossie Muir; and he has thrown over them the light of an imagination at once picturesque and powerful. . . . The *perfervidum ingenium Scotorum*—that burning, irrepressible energy of character which, whether directed towards good or towards evil, has ever distinguished our country—breathes throughout all his "Lays," and lends even stern fact the etherealising hues of fiction. —MOIR, D. M., 1851-52, *Sketches of the*

Poetical Literature of the Past Half-Century,
Lecture VII.

Here are eight ballads, or "lays," reminding one, by that name, of Mr. Macaulay's idea of reconstructing ballad from history; reversing the process by which ancient history makes itself from legendary ballad. Assuming the position of a bard near the time of the action of his several poems, Mr. Aytoun writes his ballads, as we might almost say none but a Scotchman can. In the midst of their very easy flow, of the very careful language, of the true, elaborate poetical dress, there is retained the real *tang* of the Scotch ballad,—its simplicity, its pathos, its point, and its fire. —HALE, E. E., 1852, *Lays of the Scottish Cavaliers, Christian Examiner, vol.* 52, *p.* 226.

Fashions in poetry may alter, but so long as the themes with which they deal have an interest for his countrymen, his "Lays" will find, as they do now, a wide circle of admirers. His powers as a humorist were perhaps greater than as a poet. They have certainly been more widely appreciated. His immediate contemporaries owe him much, for he has contributed largely to that kindly mirth without which the strain and struggle of modern life would be intolerable. Much that is excellent in his humorous writings may very possibly cease to retain a place in literature from the circumstance that he deals with characters and peculiarities which are in some measure local, and phases of life and feeling and literature which are more or less ephemeral. But much will certainly continue to be read and enjoyed by the sons and grandsons of those for whom it was originally written; and his name will be coupled with those of Wilson, Lockhart, Sidney Smith, Peacock, Jerrold, Mahony, and Hood, as that of a man gifted with humour as genuine and original as theirs, however opinions may vary as to the order of their relative merits.—MARTIN, SIR THEODORE, 1867, *Memoir of William Edmondstoune Aytoun, p.* 249.

Established his fame as a poet of the Walter Scott school. This collection, in which of all his works his chivalrous ardour is most contagious, the impetuous swing of his muse most felt, has required about thirty distinct issues to satisfy the craving of readers.—ROBERTSON, J. FORBES, 1887, *Celebrites of the Century, ed. Sanders. p.* 78.

The "Lays of the Scottish Cavaliers," on which his chief serious claim must rest, is an interesting book, if hardly a great one. The style is modelled with extreme closeness upon that of Scott, which even Sir Walter, with all his originality and genius, had not been able always to preserve from flatness. In Aytoun's hands the flats are too frequent, though they are relieved and broken at times by really splendid bursts, the best of which perhaps are "The Island of the Scots" and "The Heart of the Bruce." For Aytoun's poetic vein, except in the lighter kinds, was of no very great strength; and an ardent patriotism, a genuine and gallant devotion to the Tory cause, and a keen appreciation of the chivalrous and romantic, did not always suffice to supply the want of actual inspiration.—SAINTSBURY, GEORGE, 1896, *A History of Nineteenth Century Literature, p.* 303.

GENERAL

Has evinced early in life the very highest talents for lyric poetry, and enriched the literature of his country with a volume of ballads, which exceed the strains of Tyrtæus in patriotic spirit, while they rival the odes of Dryden in fire and pathos. So great, indeed, is their merit, and so varied the talent and powers of their accomplished author, that no hesitation need be felt in predicting for him, if his life is spared, the highest destiny in the realms of poetry, as well as the less inviting fields of political discussion.— ALISON, SIR ARCHIBALD, 1853, *History of Europe, 1815–1852, ch.* V.

If you should happen to lift the first volume of Professor Aytoun's "Ballads of Scotland," the book of its own accord will open at "Clerk Saunders," and by that token you will guess that the ballad has been read and re-read a thousand times. And what a ballad it is! The story in parts is somewhat perilous to deal with, but with what instinctive delicacy the whole matter is managed! Then what tragic pictures, what pathos, what manly and womanly love!— SMITH, ALEXANDER, 1863, *Dreamthorp, p.* 200.

Aytoun's humour and poetry stand quite apart. Between the broad fun of "How I became a Yeoman"—another of his best *Blackwood* papers—and the fife and kettledrum liveliness of the "Lays," there is no moral connection visible. In short, all we ever read or saw of Aytoun induces us to think of him as a shrewd, able Scot, with a strong vein of the national humour, but whose poetry was mere cleverness exercised on the traditionary material of his political school. His white rose was not waxen—we do not say that. But we do say that it had a very faint smell; that though his poetic Jacobite romanticism was real as far as it went, it did not go very far. . . . His mind, though of good quality, was not fertile.— HANNAY, JAMES, 1866, *Recent Humorists, North British Review, vol. 45, p. 83.*

Bothwell was not a hero about whom it was possible to feel any concern. Whatever gloss might be put upon his character, the main fact was not to be got over, that he was a thoroughly selfish, worthless villain, "bloody, bold, and resolute," and the last man either to feel or to talk, as men must feel and talk who are to engage our sympathies in verse. It was, therefore, clearly impossible to keep faith with history, and at the same time be in harmony with the laws of poetic art. Bothwell, as a character in a drama, would have given splendid scope for poetical handling. Bothwell in a dungeon, telling his own story, was a mistake. Aytoun struggled gallantly against these difficulties, but they were too much for him. The result was a poem full of passages of great beauty and picturesque force, but the ultimate verdict of the public has declared it unsatisfactory as a whole.—MARTIN, SIR THEODORE, 1867, *Memoir of William Edmondstoune Aytoun, p. 169.*

No more remarkable representative than Aytoun to the last of what we have called the afterglow from the spirit of Scott.— MASSON, DAVID, 1889–92, *Edinburgh Sketches and Memories, p. 431.*

His finest poetical work shows clearly how largely he was influenced by the same spirit which influenced Scott—the spirit of romanticism aroused by the study of the old ballads. As a poet his powers were considerable, although most of his poems exhibit the same general characteristics. The undeniable animation of his verse, and his frequent flashes of descriptive power, cause him to be credited with more imaginative fire than in reality he possesses. But none can deny its presence in those fine lines which depict the exploits of the Scottish exiles at the passage of the Rhine, or in some of the stanzas (hardly, however, so good)

which depict the massacre of Glencoe. Undoubtedly he possessed, also, the enviable faculty, rare even among men of genius, of knowing where his real strength lay. Hence he avoided fruitless waste of literary energy and did the best work of which he was capable. The chief quality of his poetry is its picturesqueness; it reproduces very vividly one aspect of the Scottish sentiment which belonged to a by-gone age.— BELL, MACKENZIE, 1892, *The Poets and the Poetry of the Century, Frederick Tennyson to Arthur Hugh Clough, ed. Miles, p. 395.*

His racy and overflowing humour was occasionally extravagant and uproarious. In his prose tales he carried exaggeration to excess, and upset probability in a riot of ludicrous fancy. But he had the keenest appreciation of the comic foibles of his countrymen, and especially of the Western Scott.—WHYTE, WALTER, 1894, *The Poets and the Poetry of the Century, Humour, Society, Parody and Occasional Verse, ed. Miles p. 388.*

It is not, of course, contended that Aytoun was a profound inquirer or a great thinker; he was no Bagehot, nor, in all probability, had he ever reasoned out for himself any abstract system of politics. All that can be claimed for him is a very exceptional measure of ability, good sense and acuteness, combined with a gift of clear and lively writing. . . . Whatever is to be thought of the "Lays of Ancient Rome," the "Lays of the Scottish Cavaliers" and "Bothwell" (which is nothing but a protracted lay) share few of their excellencies and exaggerate all their defects. With little true strength and little true feeling, they abound in violence and in stagey rhetoric. The conventional simplicity, directness, and movement of the old ballads are scarce attempted; the monotonous jingle of the verse is scarce ever varied. Of technical finish, in a sense, there is plenty; that is to say, there are no doubtful rhymes or superfluous syllables. Yet too many epithets, and even lines, cry aloud that their presence is due to no intrinsic propriety of their own, but to the exigencies of rhyme and metre. —MILLAR, J. H., 1896, *William Edmondstoune Aytoun, The New Review, vol. 14, pp. 105, 108.*

During his later life-time, Professor Aytoun ranked as one of the leading literary men in Scotland, especially after Professor Wilson's death, when the mantle of Christopher North had fallen on his shoulders. It is true that there were not many to shred the mantle with him; and he himself modestly attributed his fame and popularity entirely to this state of matters. It is perhaps a pity that, after having established his reputation and influence, Aytoun continued to spend so much of his time on clever little squibs and satires, whose themes were absolutely of the place and moment, instead of concentrating himself on some greater work that would to this day have been associated with his name. Much of his writing was on current politics, and writing of this sort is apt to share the fate of yesterday's newspaper. His "Bothwell" failed to be a masterpiece, and, owing perhaps mainly to the clumsy form of a prolonged monologue into which he cast it, reads very heavily. His only novel, though full of beautiful descriptive writing, hung fire, and has never become popular. Yet it should be remembered that both of them were written towards the end of his life, after trouble and ill-health had deadened his spirit.—MASSON, ROSALINE, 1898, *Pollok and Aytoun (Famous Scots Series)*, p. 152.

Francis Wayland

1796–1865

Educator, born in New York, Mar. 11, 1796, of English parents; graduated at Union College, 1813; studied medicine and began practice at Troy, but having joined the Baptist church (1816), devoted himself to the ministry; studied theology one year at Andover; was tutor in Union College 1817–21; pastor of the First Baptist church at Boston, Mass., 1821–26; became president of Brown University Feb., 1827, having previously filled for some months the professorship of Mathematics and Natural History in Union College; retired from the presidency in 1855, and was for fifteen months (1857–58) acting pastor of the First Baptist church at Providence, and was highly distinguished as a pulpit orator. Died at Providence, R. I., Sept. 30, 1865. He was the author of several volumes of sermons and addresses; "Elements of Moral Science" (1835); "Elements of Political Economy" (1837); "Limitations of Human Reason" (1840); "Thoughts on the Collegiate System of the United States" (1842); "Elements of Intellectual Philosophy" (1854); "Life of Rev. Adoniram Judson, D.D." (2 vols., 1853); and other works. His "Life" was written by his sons Francis and H. L. Wayland (2 vols., 1867), also by Prof. J. O. Murray of Princeton (Boston, 1890).—BALDWIN, J. M., 1897, rev. *Johnson's Universal Cyclopædia, vol.* VIII, *p.* 676.

PERSONAL

The personal appearance of Dr. Wayland is stately and majestic, well befitting the noble intellect within. The whole aspect of the man is such as would arrest attention in the largest assembly. He is, in stature, a little above the medium height, square built, and massive. His head has been spoken of as one which a sculptor might have taken as a model for Jupiter; and the dark piercing eyes gleam out from beneath bushy black brows, which in their turn are surmounted by a broad forehead, overtopped by iron-gray hair.—FISH, HENRY C., 1857, *Pulpit Eloquence of the Nineteenth Century, p.* 457.

He had a religious horror of waste. He once expressed the opinion that, in the millenium, people would so conduct their cooking, and all their household arrangements, as to secure perfect economy. All these things, which would have been petty if their end had been selfish accumulation, were ennobled by the object which he had in view. It was by economy that he was enabled to practice benevolence. He was never wealthy. Those who thought otherwise were deceived by the largeness of his donations. During many years he gave away more than half of his entire income. After his salary as president ceased, the amount of his contributions was necessarily diminished. With his later years he inclined to bestow his benefactions without the intervention of a society, "seeking out the cause that he knew not," and enhancing the value of the gift by the sympathy which accompanied it.—WAYLAND, FRANCIS AND H. L., 1867, *A Memoir of the Life and Labors of Francis Wayland, vol.* II, *p.* 353.

As an orator, Dr. Wayland cannot, in the

popular sense of that word, be called great; yet, if to have the gift of speaking with fluency and elegance, and of stirring an audience to the very depths of emotional feeling is eloquence, he certainly possessed that quality in a remarkable degree.— STONE, WILLIAM L., 1868, *Reminiscences of Dr. Wayland, Galaxy, vol. 5, p.* 182.

Dr. Wayland does not appear to us to have been at all a man of genius, nor was his own education of a large or liberal type. The faults and the excellences of his character were strongly marked. He was hampered by a narrow creed; but his deep religious earnestness went far towards atoning for its imperfections. He was not a very learned man; but he had to the highest degree the power of using the learning he possessed. He was a born teacher and administrator; and he had those qualities which gain the confidence and conciliate the good-will of young men,—an honest simplicity of character, a hearty hatred of all pretence, an inflexible will, and an untiring perseverance. . . . He was emphatically a genuine man, honest, straightforward, sagacious, and sincere,—a man of great simplicity, and of too much real dignity of character ever to need any of that false dignity which small men in high places are wont to assume. He cured his ministerial dyspepsia by sawing Deacon Lincoln's wood, and he dug his own presidential garden, and was not afraid to be seen going home from the presidential study with his boys on his back.—ATKINSON, W. P., 1868, *Life and Labors of Francis Wayland, North American Review, vol.* 106, *pp.* 701, 704.

One of the leaders in the religious thought of America. . . . The greater part of Dr. Wayland's life was spent in the work of education. Yet he was none the less on that account a leader in religious thought. It was religious thought mainly as to the practical working of Christianity, not as to its dogmatic statements. He had no theory of education which admitted of any divorce between it and religion, nay, between it and the Christian faith. He was distinctively a religious teacher all his life, in the classroom, on the platform, through the press, and in the pulpit. Dr. Arnold, of Rugby, moulded the religious thinking of his pupils, and so ultimately that of wide circles in England. The same may be said of Dr. Wayland in America.—MURRAY, JAMES O., 1890, *Francis Wayland, Preface, p.* vi.

EDUCATOR

But extraordinary as were Dr. Wayland's mental endowments, his greatness and his influence were more conspicuously moral than intellectual. His imperial will, his ardent love of the simple truth, his tender sympathy for the oppressed and the suffering, his generosity to the poor, his unconquerable love of soul liberty, his hatred of spiritual despotisms, his unflinching devotion to duty, his sublime unselfishness, his spirit of unquestioning filial obedience to God, his abiding faith in Jesus Christ and him crucified, these were the great elements of his character, the impelling forces of that splendid intellect, and the sources of his mighty power. He believed with all his soul that life is made up of duties, duties to man and to God. This idea he was ever holding up in all possible lights, and impressing on his hearers with all his power. It lent shape and coloring to all his instructions as professor, and to all his acts as president, lifted the college to a lofty plane, and gave earnestness and purpose to the lives of his pupils. . . . As his moral power predominated over his intellectual, he was more successful both in investigating and in teaching moral than intellectual philosophy. —ANGELL, JAMES BURRITT, 1865, *Hours at Home, Dec.*

As a teacher, Dr. Wayland had preëminent gifts. If he did not, like Socrates, follow up his pupil with a perpetual cross-examination, he set before himself the same end, that of eliciting the pupil's own mental activity. He aimed to spur him to the work of thinking for himself and of thinking soundly. He had a spice of humor in his nature, and this lent an additional zest to his terse, colloquial expressions in the classroom. The truth that there is nothing new under the sun, as far as the essential traits of man are concerned, he embodied in the saying that "human nature has very few new tricks." On one occasion he had listened with his usual patience to the persistent questioning of a pupil as to *how* we know a certain intuitive truth or axiom. At length, his previous answers not having silenced the inquirer, he broke out with the emphatic response: "How? by our innate *inborn gumption.*" In these amicable conflicts with his pupil, he never took unfair advantage or contended for victory. On the contrary, he seemed desirous, as he really was, to do full justice to every objection, and in alluding to writers who differed from him, to speak of them with personal respect.—FISHER, GEORGE P., 1866, *The Late President Wayland, New Englander, vol. 25, p.* 139.

Dr. Wayland carried the function of the teacher beyond the mere mental discipline of studies pursued. The preparation of his pupils for actual life measured for him his responsibility as a teacher. He brought, perhaps, less of learning to the class-room than some of his contemporaries. He was never spoken of as a learned man in philosophy, or ethics, or political economy. He had mastered the essential principles in all these departments of knowledge, and was abundantly equipped for teaching them. But his class-room was made the place where constant lessons were given on the conduct of life, which, unlike Mr. Matthew Arnold, he made the whole and not a fraction of it.—MURRAY, JAMES O., 1890, *Francis Wayland, p.* 190.

GENERAL

It is seldom that we have met with sounder views, or with sentiments more just and liberal on some important topics, than are contained in these discourses ["On the Duties of an American citizen"]. . . . The above extracts will serve as a specimen of Mr. Wayland's mode of thinking and writing, although it would not be fair to judge of the entire merits of his discourses, from the very imperfect outline, which we have here presented. As an exhibition of strong powers of intellect, united with a wide reach of inquiry and liberality of sentiment, few performances of a similar kind are worthy of higher commendation. We object to nothing but some of the author's remarks on the Romish church, which would have been more applicable three centuries ago, than at the present time.—SPARKS, JARED, 1825, *On the Duties of An American Citizen, North American Review, vol.* 21, *pp.* 360, 368.

We are bound to declare, that the preceding remarks have been suggested by the defects of Dr. Wayland's book, considered as a manual of instruction. In other respects, it presents many of those features, which have gained for the author's work on Ethics a well merited popularity. The arrangement and division of the subject are almost faultless. We find the same closeness and severity of argument and equal

conciseness and purity of style. The author avows, that he has not aspired to originality, and of course the leading opinions are those maintained in the ablest works of the English Economists. But the order and expression are varied to advantage, and some of the maxims are made to rest on a novel and satisfactory train of reasoning. Sometimes, indeed, the writer forgets that his work is addressed to youthful pupils, to whom a more lively manner would have imparted a deeper interest in the subject, and an abundance of examples and facts have reconciled to abstract and dry inquiries. The great fault of the work is its want of American character,—of adaptation to our peculiar circumstances and institutions. Practically considered, few principles of the science, as they appear in most treatises, are universally true. We have shown, that they must be cautiously reduced to practice, when the attendant circumstances are different from those, which the author or discoverer had in view. Dr. Wayland has hardly attempted to state the exceptions to the rules, or to limit the enunciation; and the usefulness of his book in this country is proportionably diminished.—BOWEN, FRANCIS, 1838, *Wayland's Political Economy, Christian Examiner, vol.* 24, *p.* 57.

Few works which have so little ornament are as attractive and agreeable as those of this able thinker. They have the natural charm which belongs to the display of active, various and ready strength. Everything that proceeds from his pen has a character of originality.—GRISWOLD, RUFUS WILMOT, 1847-70, *Prose Writers of America, p.* 365.

Dr. Wayland's volume of "Sermons" recently issued well sustains his reputation as a thinker and a preacher. They are characterized by the analytical power, the clearness and force of statement, and, in general, by the soundness of logic, which we are accustomed to expect from him. Though the topics are suited to any pulpit, they are often treated in a manner peculiarly adapted to a university pulpit. The preacher does not forget the character of the audience before him, and avails himself of every fair opportunity of applying the doctrine he discusses to what may be supposed to be their condition and wants. His discourses consist of serious and earnest expositions of his views of Christian truth, and could not fail to be impressive and edifying, especially to those who concurred with him in opinion It is well that the head of a university thus should occupy the highest place of instruction in it, and to the authority of his office add that of a spiritual guide.—PALFREY, C., 1849, *Wayland's Sermons, The Christian Examiner, vol.* 46, *p.* 399.

He has a vigorous and logical mind, and writes with clearness and energy. He has a wide range and strong grasp of thought, and a power both of intellectual construction and analysis.   His deep religious convictions, and his sensibilities to moral beauty, save his writings from the dryness which is apt to characterize the productions of minds of so much logical acuteness.—HILLARD, GEORGE S., 1856, *ed. First-Class Reader, p.* 397.

The writings of Dr. Wayland are, in respect of style, models of pure, crystalline, Anglo-Saxon simplicity.—FISH, HENRY C., 1857, *Pulpit Eloquence of the Nineteenth Century, p.* 458.

Dr. Wayland's admirable treatise on ethics.—HORNE, THOMAS HARTWELL, 1858, *Letter to S. Austin Allibone, July* 5; *Dictionary of English Literature, vol.* III, *p.* 2617.

Besides the great ability and thoroughness conspicuous in all his writings, Dr. Wayland has shown true independence in thought and action.—CLEVELAND, CHARLES D., 1859, *A Compendium of American Literature, p.* 430.

Dr. Wayland's "Sermon on the Moral Dignity of the Missionary Enterprise" remains unequalled for grandeur of thought and style. Its periods roll on as if fraught full with the glory of a regenerated world. It sent a glow of zeal and joy through the Christian hearts of the land, and, if we remember aright, was reproduced in other tongues.—PEABODY, ANDREW P., 1862, *The American Board of Foreign Missions, North American Review, vol.* 94, *p.* 472.

Seventy-five bound volumes, written and published by Dr. Wayland during his life, including discourses, reviews, lectures and magazine articles, attest the industry of the man. All are replete with thought and varied information, and, it is believed, have accomplished the purposes for which they were designed.   The works, however, on which his reputation will rest as a vigorous and original writer, are his "Moral Science," "Political Economy," and "Intellectual Philosophy"—works which still retain their place as text books, both in this country and in Europe.—STONE, WILLIAM L., 1868, *Reminiscences of Dr. Wayland, Galaxy, vol.* 5, *p.* 183.

Dr. Wayland was a man of remarkable power and originality of thought, and his tastes and studies inclined him to the pursuit of fundamental truths. His style was a reflex of his mental traits, clear, cogent, and direct.   His greatest work was his "Elements of Moral Science," which has long been a standard text book.—UNDERWOOD, FRANCIS H., 1872, *A Hand-Book of English Literature, American Authors, p.* 187.

In general it may be said of Dr. Wayland's authorship that it was controlled by a dominant aim to secure practical results. Toward the end of his "Political Economy," he has a short section "On consumption for the gratification of desire," which seems to be almost purely an ethical discussion. Indeed, one charm which the study of Political Economy had for him was his view that in some of its bearings it was closely related to Moral Science. His books never wandered into any region of speculation.   They show no wide reading, never suggest *learned* authorship. In fact, he had read more widely than his works would show.   But they one and all move with practical purpose to a practical end. Their direct, lucid, serious style is fitted to this end, and to reach it seems to have been his only ambition in the field of authorship.— MURRAY, JAMES O., 1890, *Francis Wayland p.* 227.

Lydia Huntley Sigourney

1791–1865

Mrs. Lydia Huntley Sigourney, author, born in Norwich, Conn., 1st September, 1791, and died in Hartford, Conn., 10th June, 1865. She was the daughter of Ezekiel Huntley, a soldier of the Revolution. She was a very precocious child. At the age of three years she read fluently, and at seven she wrote verses. She was educated in Norwich and Hartford, and she taught a private girl's school in Hartford for five years. In 1815 she published her first volume, "Moral Pieces in Prose and Verse." In 1819 she became the wife of Charles Sigourney, a literary and artistic man, of Hartford. She then devoted herself to literature. Her books became very popular. In her posthumous "Letters of Life," published in 1866, she names forty-six separate works from her pen, besides two thousand articles contributed to three-hundred periodicals. . . . She was active in charity and philanthrophy, and she had many pensioners. In 1840 she visited Europe, and in 1842, she described her journey in "Pleasant Memories of Pleasant Lands." While in London, Eng., she published two volumes of poetry. Her best works are: "Traits of the Aborigines of America," a poem (1822); "Sketch of Connecticut Forty Years Since"(1824); "Letters to Young Ladies" (1833, twentieth American and fifth English edition in 1853); "Letters to Mothers" (1838, with several English editions); "Pocahontas and Other Poems" (1841); "Scenes in My Native Land" (1844); "Voice of Flowers" (1845); " Weeping Willow" (1846); "Water Drops" (1847); "Whisper to a Bride" (1849); "Letters to My Pupils" (1850); "Olive Leaves" (1851); "The Faded Hope," a memorial of her only son, who died at the age of nineteen years (1852); "Past Meridian" (1854); "Lucy Howard's Journal" (1857); "The Daily Counselor" (1858); "Gleanings," poetry (1860), and "The Man of Uz, and Other Poems" (1862). Her whole married life, with the exception of the time she spent in Europe, was passed in Hartford.—MOULTON, CHARLES WELLS, 1893, *A Woman of the Century, ed. Willard and Livermore, p.* 656.

PERSONAL

She is free from any the least pretension, and shines in my eye far more in private than in her books. I have never talked with a more sensible or a more unassuming woman.—ALEXANDER, JAMES W., 1845, *Forty Years' Familiar Letters, vol.* II, *p.* 27.

Few persons living have exercised a wider influence than Mrs. Sigourney; no one that I know can look back upon a long and earnest career of such unblemished beneficence. —GOODRICH, SAMUEL GRISWOLD, 1856, *Recollections of a Lifetime, vol.* II, *p.* 125.

Were any intelligent American citizen now asked to name the American woman, who, for a quarter of a century before 1855, held a higher place in the respect and affections of the American people than any other woman of the times had secured, it can hardly be questioned that the prompt reply would be, Mrs. Lydia Huntley Sigourney.—HUNTINGTON, E. B., 1868, *Eminent Women of the Age, p.* 85.

She was a mild, sweet, and gentle woman, of an essentially feminine nature, and gifted with a high order of mind. Those who knew her well bear testimony to her many noble and lovable qualities.—HALL, SAMUEL CARTER, 1883, *Retrospect of a Long Life, p.* 421.

GENERAL

Her writings in blank verse are remarkable for the music of their flow. In their style of thought and expression, they remind us of those passages of Cowper, where the movement of the verse is in perfect keeping with the gravity and tenderness of the subject. Like him, she is attracted only by Nature's soothing and gentle aspects; her spirit holds no communion with the elements in their wrath; she takes no delight in witnessing the whirlwind and the storm; she looks on all the seasons, as they change, not to people them with images of gloom, but to draw from them whatever of happiness and instruction they can give. A voice of praise is uttered in her Winter Hymn; the beautiful drapery of the woods in autumn reminds her less of approaching decay, than the newness of life which is to follow. We could not desire that the moral influence of her writings should be other than it is; while she pleases the fancy, she elevates the heart. — PEABODY, WILLIAM BOURNE OLIVER, 1835, *Mrs. Sigourney and Miss Gould, North American Review, vol.* 41, *p.* 447.

Freedom, dignity, precision, and grace, without originality, may be properly attributed to her. She has fine taste, without genius.—POE, EDGAR ALLAN, 1841, *A Chapter in Autography, Works, ed. Stedman and Woodberry, vol.* IX, *p.* 195.

The poems of Mrs. Sigourney include almost every variety of subject, yet all are happily made to subserve a high moral sentiment. They are characterized by harmonious measure, felicitous rhyme, great powers of expression, and an almost unrivalled purity of thought. A heart of the liveliest and tenderest susceptibilities has thrown a charm into her verse, which has won not only admiration, but esteem and love, alike in the highest literary circles, and, we may venture to say, in every village and hamlet of the land.—EVEREST, CHARLES W., 1843, *The Poets of Connecticut*, p. 196.

The moral character of her writings is unexceptionable. She possesses great facility in versification, and is fluent both in thoughts and language. But much that she has written is deformed by the triteness and irregularity consequent upon hasty composition and hardly does justice to her real powers. " Niagara," " The death of an infant," "Winter," and "Napoleon's Epitaph," are favourable specimens of her talents.—WHIPPLE, EDWIN PERCY, 1844, *Griswold's Poets and Poetry of America*, *North American Review, vol.* 58, *p.* 34.

Mrs. Sigourney has acquired a wider and more pervading reputation than many women will receive in this country. The times have been favorable for her, and the tone of her works such as is most likely to be acceptable in a primitive and pious community. Though possessing but little constructive power, she had a ready expression, and an ear naturally so sensitive to harmony that it has scarcely been necessary for her to study the principles of versification in order to produce some of its finest effects. She sings impulsively from an atmosphere of affectionate, pious, and elevated sentiment, rather than from the consciousness of subjective ability. . . . Whether there is in her nature the latent energy and exquisite susceptibility that, under favorable circumstances, might have warmed her sentiment into passion, and her fancy into imagination; or whether the absence of any deep emotion and creative power is to be attributed to a quietness of life and satisfaction of desires that forbade the development of the full force of her being, or whether benevolence and adoration have had the mastery of her life, as might seem, and led her other faculties in captivity, we know too little of her secret experiences to form an opinion: but the abilities displayed in "Napoleon's Epitaph" and some other pieces in her works, suggest that it is only because the flower has not been crushed that we have not a richer perfume.—GRISWOLD, RUFUS WILMOT, 1848, *The Female Poets of America, p.* 93.

Of her prose works we can only indicate that which most clearly establishes the writer's rank among our very best prose writers of the age. Her "Past Meridian," given to the world in her sixty-fifth year, which has now reached its fourth edition, is one of our most charming classics. One cannot read those delightful pages, without gratitude that the gifted author was spared to give us such a coronal of her useful authorship. It were easy to collect quite a volume of the most enthusiastic commendations of this charming work; but we must leave it, with the assurance that it gives a new title to its beloved author to a perpetual fame in English Literature.—HUNTINGTON, E. B., 1868, *Eminent Women of the Age*, *p.* 98.

Mrs. Sigourney's poems have a musical flow, and are inspired with a deep religious feeling; her thoughts are not profound, but are expressed in clear phrase, and are frequently enlivened by poetic fancy. Many of her productions have the qualities that should preserve them, and a judicious collection would undoubtedly be welcome, especially with religious readers.—UNDERWOOD, FRANCIS H., 1872, *A Hand-Book of English Literature, American Authors, p.* 123.

Mrs. Sigourney, voluminous and mediocre, is amusing because so absolutely destitute of humor, and her style, a feminine *Johnsonese*, is absurdly hifalutin and strained.—SANBORN, KATE, 1885, *The Wit of Women, p.* 48.

A gentle and pious womanhood shone through her verse; but her books are undisturbed and dusty in the libraries now, and likely to remain so.—CONE, HELEN GRAY, 1890, *Woman in American Literature, The Century, vol.* 40, *p.* 922.

There is absolutely nothing of any high order of merit in her poems. . . . The one great characteristic of Mrs. Sigourney's verse is its uniform propriety. It is pure, chaste, and insipid, highly moral but lowly poetical. —ONDERDONK, JAMES L., 1899–1901, *History of American Verse pp.* 155, 156.

Obtained the coveted title of "the American Mrs. Hemans"; she is still useful as an index to the taste of the times, which left its impress upon greater writers as well, and helps to explain some of their artistic shortcomings.—BRONSON, WALTER C., 1900, *A Short History of American Literature*, *p.* 171.

Richard Hildreth

1807–1865

An American journalist and historian, was born in Deerfield, Mass., June 28, 1807. He graduated at Harvard in 1826, and, while studying law, contributed numerous articles to magazines. Admitted to the bar in Boston in 1830, he abandoned the legal profession at the expiration of two years, to accept the position of associate editor of the "Boston Atlas," which soon became one of the ablest Whig journals in New England. His health having failed, he spent the year 1835 in Florida, and while there wrote "Archy Moore," an anti-slavery novel. It was republished and favourably reviewed in England, and an enlarged edition, under the title of "The White Slave," was issued in the United States in 1852. In 1837 he furnished to the columns of the "Atlas" a series of articles which contributed powerfully towards defeating schemes then on foot for the annexation of Texas. He took a conspicuous part in the Presidential canvass which resulted in the nomination and election of General Harrison. He also gave to the public during this period his "Despotism in America," an able review of the social, political, and economical aspects of slavery in the United States, to which he added in 1854 a chapter on the "Legal Basis of Slavery." His health having again failed, he embarked in 1840 for British Guiana, and, during a residence of three years at Georgetown, the capital, wrote his "Theory of Morals," published in 1844, and "Theory of Politics, or an Inquiry into the Foundation of Governments and the Causes and Progress of Political Revolutions," issued in 1853. Mr. Hildreth is best known, however, by his "History of the United States of America," from the discovery of the continent to the close of the Sixteenth Congress in 1820, (6 vols., 8vo., 1849-52). It was projected while the author was a student at Harvard. The work has been variously criticised, but all agree in classing it among the standard histories of our country. Died at Florence in July, 1865.—THOMAS, JOSEPH, 1901, *Lippincott's Universal Pronouncing Dictionary of Biography and Mythology, Third Ed., vol.* II, *p.* 1286.

PERSONAL

A bold, blunt, hard-headed, and resolute man, caustic in temper, keen in intellect, indefatigable in industry, and blessed with an honest horror of shams.—WHIPPLE, EDWIN PERCY, 1876–86, *American Literature and Other Papers ed. Whittier, p.* 92.

HISTORY OF THE UNITED STATES
1849-52

If a plain and well-written narrative of public events, mostly in the order of their occurrence, without any attempt to generalize them, or to deduce from them broader lessons of experience, is all that constitutes a good history, then Mr. Hildreth's work deserves its name, and has fair claims to respectful notice. It is easy to see however, that this is not all, and that history written on such a plan must needs be imperfect and untrustworthy. . . . Nothing can be more cold and naked than his recital of any facts which are honourable to the memory of the first settlers of New England; if they do not occupy a very prominent place on the common record he forgets to mention them at all. When they are forced upon his notice he dismisses them as rapidly as possible. He has not a word of praise for their conscientiousness, their heroism, or their self-denial; though the first alone caused them

to emigrate, so that it was the seminal principle of the New England colonies, while the second and third sustained their settlements through many years of danger and privation.—BOWEN, FRANCIS, 1851, *Hildreth's History of the United States, North American Review, vol.* 73, *pp.* 411, 414.

As a book of reference, this history still remains as the best in our catalogues of works on American history. The style is concise, the facts happily combined, the judgments generally good; and while justice is done to our great men, there is everywhere observable an almost vindictive contempt of persons who have made themselves "great" by the arts of the demagogue. Hildreth studied carefully all the means of information within his reach; but his plan did not contemplate original research on the large scale in which it was prosecuted by Bancroft.—WHIPPLE, EDWIN PERCY, 1876–86, *American Literature and other Papers, ed. Whittier, p.* 92.

Hildreth's "History of the United States" may be studied with constant improvement, and will always retain its place in letters.—LAWRENCE, EUGENE, 1880, *A Primer of American Literature, p.* 117.

These volumes, completed as early as 1850, still probably form the most valuable single work on American history. But, though they have genuine merits, they also are not without somewhat serious defects. They have the advantage of describing a longer period than does the work of Bancroft, the only history with which Hildreth's may properly be compared. The author's style is free from irrelevant discursiveness, is direct, is devoid of imagination and fancy, is often so bald in its methods as to be dry, and sometimes is even so careless as to be ungrammatical. It never rises to anything like fervor, nor does it exhibit the slightest capacity for the graphic or picturesque. A still further defect is the absence of foot-notes and references to authorities, though for this deficiency the author has made partial atonement by publishing a long list of works used in the preparation of the volumes. But these somewhat grave defects are more than counterbalanced by the general accuracy and sterling qualities of the author's judgment. The peculiarities named make the work less a favorite with the general reader than with the serious student.—ADAMS, CHARLES KENDALL, 1882, *A Manual of Historical Literature, p.* 533.

Its real literary merit is small. It is a plain, unvarnished narrative of facts as they were understood by its author, devoid of all attempts at rhetorical finish or philosophical digression. The partisanism of Hildreth is even more marked than that of Bancroft; in narrating the vicissitudes of parties and the prejudices of factions he is too prone to hide the faults of his friends and to parade those of his enemies. His history will be found valuable mainly as a work of reference.—BALDWIN, JAMES, 1883, *English Literature and Literary Criticism, Prose, p.* 83.

Hildreth's "History of the United States" cannot be called a hasty or superficial production. His material was ample, he had studied it and arranged it with care, and though, at the last, he wrote rapidly, he had been preparing to write all his life, and merely transcribed the records stored in a full mind. If he was politician as well as historian, the same might be said of his rival Bancroft, whose democracy was as intense, though not as aggressive, as Hildreth's whiggism. . . . The history is clear, though it cannot be called readable; the art of picturesque writing was not known to Hildreth; and even his characterization, contrasts, and denunciations do not quicken

the reader's pulse. His statements of facts are trustworthy; they cover a period still undescribed in any other work of the same size; and they are marked by the courage of conviction and an intrepid desire to state the truth. It would be idle to claim that his pages are untinged by political prejudice; but certainly the author did not consciously yield to that prejudice.—RICHARDSON, CHARLES F., 1887, *American Literature,* 1607-1885, *vol.* I, *p.* 472.

Hildreth's own work came later,—late enough to feel the force of increasing sectional animosities, and to show the effects of them in an unfortunate degree. A man of very decided convictions, and ardently interested in politics, the Whig editor wrote the "History of the United States" with a strong partisan bias. In the first three volumes, bringing the story down to the close of the Revolution, this naturally finds less place, and the lucidity, directness, and accuracy of the writer made his book one of much value, though a little dry to the general reader. But in the last three volumes, treating the history of our national politics down to 1821, its partisanship of the Federalists is so manifest that all its lucidity, directness, and general accuracy cannot wholly redeem it.—JAMESON, J. FRANKLIN, 1891, *The History of Historical Writing in America, p.* 112.

Richard Hildreth's name will be remembered chiefly from his "History of the United States," and the solid and judicial qualities of that work will make it endure for many years to come. He will never be popular with the general reader, however. His narrative is too prosy, not vivid enough for a moment to enwrap the attention of the casual reader; and his occasional attempts at picturesqueness or descriptions of pageantry are very painful. The historian never arouses us with his enthusiasm, nor makes people and events live anew for us by the power of his inspiration. Nor is his writing in the least philosophical. Other historians make us see clearly the great sweeps and curves of the nation in its onward march, and they point out how its various trendings have led hither and thither. But Hildreth leaves us to trace out for ourselves the great highway, while he stops to explore some undiscovered and overgrown by-path, bestowing upon it the same painstaking research that he gives to conspicuous and important events. Yet in spite of all these negatives, Hildreth will always—and rightly—command attention and admiration. His work is full of purpose, and has in it the energy of a forceful and zealous student. It is direct, untrammeled, and courageous. If it grows dull for the casual reader, it is a delight to the close student. The primitive historical instinct in its most finished state filled him; for in spite of its surface faults, his narration, in straightforwardness, accuracy, and firmness, is an admirable work of high and solid merit.— WARNER, CHARLES DUDLEY, 1897, *ed. Library of the World's Best Literature, vol.* XIII, *p.* 7372.

Three volumes are devoted to the period before 1783. An annalistic work. Often poorly arranged. Often every dry. It is, however, very accurate as to names and dates, and this gives it its place. The volumes dealing with the period from 1783 to 1821 are written from the federalist point of view, and are intensely hostile to Jefferson and his supporters.—CHANNING, EDWARD, 1902, *The Literature of American History, ed. Larned, p.* 282.

Thomas Chandler Haliburton
1796–1865

Thomas Chandler Haliburton, "Sam Slick," born at Windsor, Nova Scotia, in December 1796, and was called to the bar in 1820, and became a member of the House of Assembly, chief-justice of the common pleas (1828), and judge of the supreme court (1842). In 1856 he retired and settled in England, in 1858 was made D. C. L. by Oxford, and in 1859–65 was Conservative M. P. for Launceston. He is best known as the author of "Sam Slick," a sort of American Sam Weller, whose quaint drollery, unsophisticated wit, knowledge of human nature, and aptitude in the use of "soft sawder" have given him a fair chance of immortality. The newspaper sketches in which this character first appeared were collected in 1837–40 as "The Clockmaker, or Sayings and Doings of Samuel Slick of Slickville," continued as "The Attache, or Sam Slick in England" (1843–44). Haliburton's other works include "A Historical and Statistical Account of Nova Scotia" (1825–29); "Bubbles of Canada" (1839); "The Old Judge, or Life in a Colony" (1843); "Traits of American Humour" (1843); and "Rule and Misrule of the English in America" (1850). He died at Isleworth, 27th August 1865. See "Memoir" by F. B. Crofton (1889).—PATRICK AND GROOME, eds. 1897, *Chambers's Biographical Dictionary, p.* 452.

PERSONAL

Among other frequenters of it, my diary makes frequent mention of Judge Haliburton, of Nova Scotia, better known to the world as Sam Slick, the Clockmaker. He was, as I remember him, a delightful companion—for a limited time. He was in this respect exactly like his books—extremely amusing reading if taken in rather small doses, but calculated to seem tiresomely monotonous if indulged in at too great length. He was a thoroughly good fellow, kindly, cheery, hearty, and sympathetic always; and so far always a welcome companion. But his funning was always pitched in the same key, and always more or less directed to the same objects. His social and political ideas and views all coincided with my own, which, of course, tended to make us better friends. In appearance he looked entirely like an Englishman, but not at all like a Londoner. Without being at all too fat, he was large and burly in person, with gray hair, a large ruddy face, a humorous mouth, and bright blue eyes always full of mirth. He was an inveterate chewer of tobacco, and, in the fulness of comrade-like kindness, strove to indoctrinate me with that habit. But I was already an old smoker, and preferred to content myself with that mode of availing myself of the blessing of tobacco.—TROLLOPE, THOMAS ADOLPHUS, 1888, *What I Remember, p.* 250.

Played a very important part in the history of Nova Scotia for a period of over thirty years. He figured in political, in legal, and in literary affairs, and in each sphere of action he acquired very considerable repute. The reputation which he won as a legislator is greater than his reputation as a lawyer and judge; and the success of his literary work far surpassed the utmost measure of his success at the bar, on the bench, in the legislature of his native Province, or in the House of Commons of England. It is indeed as the author of the "Sam Slick" papers, that his name is most likely to be long preserved. . . . As the most illustrious man of letters that Canada has so far produced, Judge Haliburton will be long remembered.—CHISHLOM, J. A., 1895, *Thomas Chandler Haliburton, The Green Bag, vol.* 7, *pp.* 489, 494.

GENERAL

On this point we speak with some confidence. We can distinguish the real from the counterfeit Yankee, at the first sound of the voice, and by the turn of a single sentence; and we have no hesitation in declaring that Sam Slick is not what he pretends to be; that there is no organic life in him; that he is an impostor, an impossibility, a nonentity. A writer of genius, even if he write from imperfect knowledge, will, as it were, breathe the breath of life into his creations. Sam Slick is an awkward and highly infelicitous attempt to make a character, by heaping together, without discrimination, selection, arrangement, or taste, every vulgarity that a vulgar imagination can conceive, and every knavery that a man blinded by national and political prejudice can charge upon neighbors whom he dislikes.—FELTON, CORNELIUS CONWAY, 1844, *Sam Slick in England, North American Review, vol.* 58, *p.* 212.

It is a piquant curiosity ["Sam Slick"], a book and an excellent book, composed, printed, and published in one of the most unknown cities of the world, between Cape Breton and the Appalachian mountains, on the shores of the Atlantic, in the lap of a slumbering civilization, discouraged, strangled, deadened by the neighborhood of the United States. . . . Mr. Haliburton's book,"The Clockmaker," gives at a glance all the American elegancies. I have said, it is a remarkably good book. It is not a romance, history, drama, philosophic treatise, voyage, story, or declamation; this patois-book, written by a colonist of Halifax, full of adages à la Sancho Panza, and of stories worthy of Bonaventure Desperiers, is simply an admirable book. The author explains the sketchy, existing civilization of the United States; the rickety, unhealthy civilization of Canada, and the profound torpor of the neighboring British provinces. He enters into the secret details of private life, and exhibits all which English travellers have left in shadow. . . . Since the personages of Sir Walter Scott, nothing has been better done than this character of Sam Slick.—CHASLES, PHILARÈTE, 1852, *Anglo-American, Literature and Manners, pp.* 222 224, 227.

Author of a series of amusing works illustrative of American and colonial manners marked by shrewd, sarcastic remarks on political questions, the colonies, slavery, domestic institutions and customs, and almost every familiar topic of the day. The first series—which had previously been inserted as letters in a Nova Scotia paper—appeared in a collected form under the title of "The Clockmaker, or the Sayings and Doings of Sam Slick of Slickville." A second series was published in 1838, and a third in 1840. "Sam Slick" was a universal favourite, and in 1843 the author conceived the idea of bringing him to England. "The Attaché, or Sam Slick in England," gives an account of the sayings and doings of the clockmaker when elevated to the dignity of the "Honourable Mr. Slick, Attaché of the American Legation of the court of St. James's." There is the same quaint humour, acute observation, and laughable exaggeration in these volumes as in the former but, on the whole, Sam is most amusing on the other side of the Atlantic.—CHAMBERS, ROBERT, 1876, *Cyclopædia of English Literature, ed. Carruthers.*

Haliburton, writing as Sam Slick, told his countrymen many home truths. Those who laughed at Sam Slick's jokes did not always relish his outspoken criticisms, and his popularity as a writer was far greater out of Nova Scotia than in it; his fame, however, became general. None of his writings are regularly constructed stories, but the incidents and the characters are always spirited and mostly humourous. "Sam Slick" had a very extensive sale, and notwithstanding its idiomatic peculiarities was translated into several different languages. . . . Haliburton was the first writer who used the American dialect, and was pronounced by Artemus Ward to be the founder of the American school of humour.—BOASE, G. C., 1890, *Dictionary of National Biography, vol.* XXIV, *p.* 44.

As a humorist, Haliburton's chief qualifications were a keen appreciation of the ludicrous, an excellent memory for absurdities, the faculty of hitting off quaint and fancy-tickling phrases, and a most lively imagination. All these characteristics are copiously illustrated in the multitudinous yarns which his characters spin upon the smallest provocation. Indeed, it is evident that he often moots a subject merely to introduce an anecdote; and the very slight main plot of each of the four books narrating Mr. Slick's career is little more than a thread to string his tales and talks upon. The same may be said of "The Old Judge" and "The Season Ticket." . . . As an historian, Haliburton's style is generally clear and classical, although it has not the uniform polish of a master of style, and sometimes deviates into ponderosity. His reflections are mostly shrewd and philosophical, if sometimes biased by his strong conservatism and love for British institutions.

. . . For a man who began life as a provincial lawyer and politician, Haliburton's horizon was remarkably, almost phenomenally, wide. He intuitively recognized the tendencies of the age, noted all the currents of public opinion, and gauged their volume and force with approximate exactness. Indeed the time may come when his fame as a political and ethical thinker, and forecaster of events and movements, may exceed his fame as a humorist.—CROFTON, F. BLAKE, 1892, *Thomas Chandler Haliburton, Atlantic Monthly, vol.* 69, *pp.* 356, 359, 360.

John Keble
1792–1866

Born at Fairford, entered Corpus Christi, Oxford, in 1806, having obtained a scholarship, and was elected a Fellow of Oriel College in 1811. He was ordained in 1815, became a college tutor in 1818, and in 1825 accepted a curacy at Fairford. In 1831 he was elected Professor of Poetry in Oxford, and occupied that chair for ten years. During the term of his professorship he took a prominent part in the organization of the Tractarian movement, to which he was inclined by both his High Church views and personal interest in many of the leaders of that movement, especially in Hurrell Froude, who had been his favorite pupil at Fairford. In 1835 he was appointed to the vicarage of Hursley, which he held to the time of his death. In 1845 he had attempted to secure the foundation in Oxford of a "Poor Man's College," designed for the education of priests for the English Church; but the scheme was at the time wholly unsuccessful, except that a plot of land was purchased on the top of Headington Hill as a site. After his death, however, the project was revived, and pushed forward with great rapidity, and in 1870 Keble College Oxford, was opened as a memorial of him. In addition to numerous works in prose, he published "The Christian Year," 1827; "Lyra Innocentium," 1845; "Poems" (posthumously). He was also one of the contributors to the "Lyra Apostolica," 1836.—RANDOLPH, HENRY FITZ, 1887, ed. *Fifty Years of English Song, Biographical and Bibliographical Notes, vol.* IV, *p.* 19.

PERSONAL

Talking of sacred poets, I hope you have read and often recur to the "Christian Year," written by a most holy man, an acquaintance of mine at Oxford, Mr. Keble. He is a man the most meek, the most humble, and yet the most gifted with genius and learning, of any I ever met with. He went to Oxford at fourteen, and carried away all the honours and prizes; and lately refused to stand for the Headship of his College, though almost certain of succeeding, that he might be the comfort and support of his aged father, and relieve him from the cares of his parish by acting as his curate.—HOOK, WALTER FARQUHAR, 1833, *To W. P. Wood, June* 1; *Life and Letters, ed. Stephens, p.* 167.

He has the simplest and most childlike mind conceivable, playing with his nephew and a son of Davison's on the shore, as if he had never a higher thought in his head than how he should make 2 boys happiest.—WILBERFORCE, SAMUEL, 1836, *To C. Anderson, Aug.* 19; *Life by Ashwell.*

I can hardly tell you what conversation was about; Keble lets everything take its course, and never sets any subject going of a continuous kind—probably would rather interfere with it if any one else did. You must not suppose by all this that I do not like K.'s manner or am disappointed. On the contrary, it really takes with me; only if I were a friend of his I should be afraid sometimes of *others* being offended by it and not understanding him.—MOZLEY, JAMES BOWLING, 1838, *To his Sister, April* 27; *Letters, ed. his Sister, p.* 77.

Nothing could be more simple and unaffected than his manner; and yet, in a word, it was as if George Herbert had risen from his grave, and were talking with me in a familiar way.—COXE, ARTHUR CLEVELAND, 1855, *Impressions of England.*

Keble died lately—his wife a week after. His death moved me less than it once would, from his age, my own change of sentiment, and specially from his prominence of late in movements of persecuting repression, for which, indeed, he had always, or often, as in the Hampden case, betrayed a culpable inclination. Still, he was a master in his kind, and it was given to him to achieve, what few men do—one work of the highest excellency.—WILLIAMS, ROWLAND, 1866, *Journal, May 21; Life and Letters, vol.* II, *p.* 249.

I have received a printed letter, signed by your Grace, inviting me to contribute to the Keble Memorial. Under ordinary circumstances such an appeal would have been most congenial to my feelings of respect, and I may say of old affection, for Keble. I must confess that I have long wondered, not without some shame, and expressed my wonder (though not publicly), that, while the dignities and honors of the Church were lavished on many certainly not very distinguished men, no dignity, not even a barren honour, as far as I know, was ever bestowed on the author of the "Christian Year" and the editor of Hooker. I cannot but think that this is not to the credit of those who for nearly fifty years have had the disposal of those dignities and honours.—MILMAN, HENRY HART, 1866, *Letter to Archbishop Longley, July 9; Henry Hart Milman, Dean of St. Paul's, ed. his Son, p.* 216.

The same devout mind which had done so much to restore the Church of England to the faith and zeal of former days, was ever active for good in the parish of Hursley. The sick were tended with loving care; the poor were helped in soul and body; the ignorant and ungodly were diligently sought after, warned, and instructed. Clubs and societies were formed for the good of the labouring classes; children were carefully and lovingly trained for God's service. . . . He spared no pains to reclaim those who went astray, and to guide those who needed guidance. In many a dark winter's night, after he had passed the usual span of man's life, he would walk alone, with a lantern in his hand, to some distant part of the widely-scattered parish of Hursley to prepare a few of his flock for confirmation or communion. He would have one or two at a time for instruction, that he might teach them more impres-

sively than he could with many together, and he would never grudge hours spent in repeating the same things over and over again to those who were dull and unapt in learning. If friends were staying with him whose society he wished to enjoy, still he cheerfully left them that he might attend to the poor lads who came to him for instruction.—MOOR, JOHN FREWEN, 1866, *Memoir and Notes of John Keble.*

Keble had not regular features; he could not be called a handsome man, but he was one to be noticed anywhere, and remembered long; his forehead and hair beautiful in all ages; his eyes, full of play, intelligence and emotion, followed you while you spoke; and they lighted up, especially with pleasure, or indignation, as it might be, when he answered you.—COLERIDGE, SIR JOHN TAYLOR, 1868, *A Memoir of the Rev. John Keble, p.* 548.

Once, if my memory serves, I remember to have seen him in the University pulpit at St. Mary's, but his voice was not strong, and did not reach many of the audience. . . . . All that was known of Keble at that time to the outer world of Oxford was vague and scanty. The few facts here added are taken from what has since been made public by two of his most attached friends, Sir John Coleridge and Dr. Newman, the former in his beautiful letters, memorial of Keble, the latter in his "Apologia." Yet these facts, though few, are well worthy of attention, both because Keble's character is more than his poetry, and because his poetry can only be rightly understood in the light of his character. For there is no poet whose poetry is more truly an image of the man himself, both in his inner nature and in his outward circumstances.—SHAIRP, JOHN CAMPBELL, 1868–72, *Studies in Poetry and Philosophy, pp.* 219, 220.

Mr. Keble, the "sweet singer of Israel," and a true saint, if this generation has seen one.—GLADSTONE, WILLIAM EWART, 1868, *A Chapter of Autobiography, Gleanings from Past Years, vol.* VII, *p.* 141.

A purer or more blameless character it would be impossible to imagine. Those who knew him best thought him almost faultless. To himself it seemed far otherwise. From early years to old age his life had been one which can only be described in the words of Scripture—he "walked with God." This was evidently the secret and mainspring of all: and the result of that converse was, as it must ever be, *humility.* He was ever trying himself by the one perfect standard and finding himself deficient. An exquisitely sensitive modesty was natural to him; but this natural endowment had been refined and deepened into the corresponding Christian grace in its most perfect form. He had, indeed, *humbled himself, and become as a little child.* There was no effort, far less any affectation, in his constant rejection of all praise, and acknowledgment of sin and failure.— VAUGHAN, E. T., 1869, *The Life of Keble, Contemporary Review, vol.* 2, p. 274.

I heard Keble's Life read, but I felt it waterish. The entire want of any theology provokes me.—ERSKINE, THOMAS, 1869, *To Miss Wedgwood, March* 13; *Letters, ed. Hanna, p.* 491.

It is not generally known that much of the poetry and tender human feeling of Mr. Keble's life took its origin from this stay at Sidmouth. Yet, now that more than sixty years have passed away, it can violate no sanctities to reveal that the depths of his nature were stirred by one whose acquaintance he then first made; and though she was at that time very young, his interest in Cornelia Sarah Cornish, the sister of his friend, ripened in after days into a deep and tender, though rejected, love. One who knew well whereof he spoke, and who more than any had a right to speak of those dim, distant days, wrote: "I believe much of the pathos of the whole book—' The Christian Year' —had its source in his love for her." It is, indeed, impossible to read "The Christian Year" without being sure that the varied stops of human feeling had all been tuned and exercised before such true harmony of its kind flowed from his soul. It was this early love which called out such tenderness towards a younger Cornelia— or "Keenie"—Cornish, who became the wife of his nephew; and the chord once struck still sounded in these words, under date of 1840.—PAUL, C. KEGAN, 1869-83, *Biographical Sketches, p.* 40.

To his immediate friends he was genial, affectionate. and possibly instructive, but he had no faculty for winning the unconverted. If he was not bigoted he was intensely prejudiced. If you did not agree with him there was something morally wrong with you, and your "natural man" was provoked into resistance. To speak habitually with authority does not necessarily indicate an absence of humility, but does not encourage the growth of that quality. If there had been no "movement," as it was called, if Keble had remained a quiet country clergyman, unconscious that he was a great man, and uncalled on to guide the opinions of his age, he would have commanded perhaps more enduring admiration. The knot of followers who specially attached themselves to him show traces of his influence in a disposition not only to think the views which they hold sound in themselves, but to regard those who think differently as their intellectual inferiors. Keble was incapable of vanity in the vulgar sense. But there was a subtile self-sufficiency in him which has come out more distinctly in his school.—FROUDE, JAMES ANTHONY, 1881, *The Oxford Counter-Reformation, Short Studies on Great Subjects, vol.* IV, *p.* 175; *Good Words, vol.* 22, *p.* 101.

Was always a shy man, and on the rare occasions on which he revisited Oxford, he preferred some quiet domestic hearth to Oriel commonroom. . . . Yet everybody who visited Oriel inquired after Keble, and expected to see him. It must be added that he was present in everybody's thoughts, as a glory to the college, a comfort and a stay, for the slightest word he dropped was all the more remembered for there being so little of it, and from it seeming to come from a different and holier sphere. His manner of talking favoured this, for there was not much continuity in it, only every word was a brilliant or a pearl.—MOZLEY, THOMAS, 1882, *Reminiscenses Chiefly of Oriel College and the Oxford Movement, vol.* I, *pp.* 36, 37.

Keble is undoubtedly to be looked upon as the flower of the Oxford movement—for in Newman the movement moved beyond itself. Keble's theology, Keble's churchmanship, Keble's rectory and life and character, and the whole constitution of his mind, are the precise fulfillment of the Tractarian ideal. The intimate relation between his thought and character is striking. The character is certainly one of rare beauties; and let the thought have credit for all it can do. In that crowded and exciting time we think of no other whose life was so completely a mirror of his doctrine, and whose doctrine was so completely a mirror of his life, save only Arnold.—MEAD, EDWIN DOAK, 1884, *Arnold of Rugby and the Oxford Movement, The Andover Review, vol.* 1, *p.* 508.

Mr. Keble was the man on whom, if he had been resident at Oxford, and had not shrunk from all forms of self-assertion, the mantle of Newman would naturally have fallen. But he lived at Hursley, near Winchester; and though his influence was felt by many individual minds, most of them knew him chiefly as the author of the "Christian Year," a book which reflected the uncontroversial side of his mind and opinions, and on some points did not reflect his later opinions at all. Those (and they were not few) who turned to him as their adviser and guide, did so generally by private correspondence for their own personal benefit, rather than as disciples in an intellectual school. He was, by affection and habit, strongly attached to the Church of England; modest in temperament, unaffectedly humble in spirit and manner, but firm as a rock within, with a strong and very tenacious grasp of the opinions which he took up. He did, I think, drift some considerable way from his original moorings; but his feeling for the church of his baptism and of his parents, and for his people and his pastoral work among them, was stronger than any influence which might have tended to draw him after Newman; though there were signs, as he grew older, of increasing sympathy with that line of thought which had landed Newman in Rome.—PALMER, ROUNDELL (EARL OF SELBORNE), 1888–96, *Memorials, Part I, Family and Personal, vol. I, p.* 397.

He [Isaac Williams] had before him all day long in John Keble a spectacle which was absolutely new to him. Ambitious as a rising and successful scholar at college, he saw a man, looked up to and wondered at by every one, absolutely without pride and without ambition. He saw the most distinguished academic of his day, to whom every prospect was open, retiring from Oxford in the height of his fame to bury himself with a few hundreds of Gloucestershire peasants in a miserable curacy. He saw this man caring for and respecting the ignorant and poor as much as others respected the great and the learned. He saw this man who had made what the world would call so great a sacrifice, apparently unconscious that he had made any sacrifice at all, gay, unceremonious, bright, full of play as a boy, ready with his pupils for any exercise, mental or muscular—for a hard ride, or a crabbed bit of Æschylus, or a logic fence

with disputatious and paradoxical undergraduates, giving and taking on even ground. These pupils saw one, the depth of whose religion none could doubt, "always endeavouring to do them good as it were unknown to themselves and in secret, and ever avoiding that his kindness should be felt and acknowledged;" showing in the whole course of daily life the purity of Christian love, and taking the utmost pains to make no profession or show of it.—CHURCH, RICHARD WILLIAM, 1891, *The Oxford Movement, p.* 59.

He was humble and self-depreciatory almost to excess. This lowly sense of unworthiness, this penitential attitude of soul, was all the more prominent after the great troubles that overtook the Oxford movement. He felt, as it were, the chastening hand of God, and humbled himself beneath it. He used language about his own unworthiness that, to superficial persons, might appear either exaggerated or else significant of some grave shortcomings. In some of his letters to Newman this was so prominent that, before they were handed over for publication, the Cardinal erased certain sentences, lest, as he said, they should be misunderstood and create an entirely wrong impression. ... As a preacher, Keble could be learned and scholarly before a University congregation. But he set himself deliberately to speak with simple plainness of thought and language to his village flock. He did not shrink from bringing before them the highest truths of Christianity. He explained fully, yet very simply, the sacraments of the church, and the great fundamental doctrines of the Incarnation and the Atonement. But he more and more brought himself to use homely illustrations, taken from the daily life of his hearers, to convey to them the deep lessons of the gospel.—DONALDSON, AUG. B., 1899, *Five Great Oxford Leaders, pp.* 46, 47.

THE CHRISTIAN YEAR
1827

I have Keble lying open before me. The hymns for the holy week are beautiful,— Monday is exquisite: I think that I like it best of them all. The use made of Andromache's farewell is quite filling to the heart, and the theology of the fourth stanza, "Thou art as much his care," etc., is worth, in my mind, the whole Shorter and Longer Catechisms together.—ERSKINE, THOMAS,

1829, *To Miss Rachel Erskine, March* 11;
Letters, ed. Hanna, p. 111.

> For its golden fraught
> Of prayer and praise, of dream and thought,
> Where Poesy finds fitting voice
> For all who hope, fear, grieve, rejoice,
> Long have I loved, and studied long,
> The pious minstrel's varied song.

—PRAED, WINTHROP MACKWORTH, 1836,
*To Helen, with Keble's "Christian Year,"
Feb.* 12.

The "Christian Year" made its appearance in 1827. It is not necessary, and scarcely becoming, to praise a book which has already become one of the classics of the language. When the general tone of religious literature was so nerveless and impotent, as it was at that time, Keble struck an original note, and woke up in the hearts of thousands a new music, the music of a school long unknown in England. Nor can I pretend to analyse, in my own instance, the effect of religious teaching so deep, so pure, so beautiful. I have never till now tried to do so, yet I think I am not wrong in saying that the two main intellectual truths which it brought home to me were the same two which I had learned from Butler (in his "Analogy"), though recast in the creative mind of my new master. The first of these was what may be called, in a large sense of the word, the sacramental system; that is, the doctrine that material phenomena are both the types and the instruments of real things unseen.—NEWMAN, JOHN HENRY, 1864, *Apologia pro Vitâ Suâ, p.* 77.

If we were asked to assign in a few words the causes of the great power which the "Christian Year" has exercised over such different classes of readers, we should say that Mr. Keble has done for religious poetry what Wordsworth did for poetry in general. First, he has shown us, what many were beginning to doubt, that poetry is a requirement, or at all events a high enjoyment of, the religious mind; and secondly, that it is limited to no one class of feelings, or language, or doctrines. Writing himself under the influence of a distinctly theological and orthodox spirit, he has yet understood the still higher art of touching those springs of moral and religious feeling which lie deep in the hearts of all good Christians, whatever their creed; and in the temper of a higher Master he has made everything in nature,—the flowers of the field, our homes and paths, the very "murky lanes" of our

cities,—dear to the religious heart. It is this simplicity and reality which has made him the favourite, as Wordsworth became, of all thoughtful and cultivated minds, and emphatically the religious poet of the age. Men of the most opposite convictions have drawn an almost daily inspiration from his writings; and he has been the teacher, the domestic companion, almost the religious philosopher, alike of Arnold, of Newman, and of Robertson. . . . It is chiefly as the poet of the religious affections, of God's love to man and man's answering love to God, that Mr. Keble seems to us unrivalled, at once in the depth and beauty of feeling which he displays, and the manner in which he connects this feeling with everything in nature and life. Here again we believe that it is no mere fancy to say that he is the poet of his time, and has remarkably met its wants, and even supplied an important link of its religious philosophy, by the power with which he has made us realize the personal love of "One unseen, yet ever nigh."—LAKE, WILLIAM CHARLES, 1866, *Mr. Keble and the "Christian Year," Contemporary Review, vol.* 2, *pp.* 324, 331.

If there is one quality which more than any other may be said to mark his writings, it is their intense and absolute veracity. Never for a moment is the very truth sacrificed to effect. I will venture to say with confidence that there is not a sentiment to be found elevated or amplified beyond what he really felt, nor, I would add, even an epithet that goes beyond his actual and true thought. What he was in life and character, that he was transparently in every line he wrote—entirely, always, reverentially true.—MOBERLEY, GEORGE, 1869, *ed. Keble's Miscellaneous Poems, Preface, p.* XVII.

It stands alone in literature; for though George Herbert's poems and Bishop Heber's hymns each present some points of resemblance, we should be inclined to rate Herbert far higher as a poet, and Heber far lower. Herbert's verse can only be read with pleasure when the mind is attuned to feelings of personal devotion in which none others can share: Heber's hymns can be sung by mixed congregations: while "The Christian Year" fits itself to the closet or the drawing-room, not to singing in church; can be read aloud, when to read Herbert were profanation; can be enjoyed for its poetry by those who object to its theology; while its theology has gained an admission for poetic thoughts into the minds of many wooden-headed people.—PAUL, C. KEGAN, 1869–83, *Biographical Sketches, p.* 43.

It taught because his own soul was moved so deeply; the stream burst forth, because the heart which poured it out was full; it was fresh, deep, tender, and loving because himself was such; it disclosed to souls secrets which they knew not, but could not fail to own when known, because it was so true, and thought aloud: and conscience everywhere responded to the voice of conscience.—PUSEY, EDWARD BOUVERIE, 1876, *Sermon at Keble College, p.* 6.

The force of the book lies in its sincerity. Its music is the music of a well-harmonized life; the devotion is real; the quiet sense of nature is real. There are no tricks of style, though there are no flashes of genius. Keble laid stress on the authority and customs of the church; he was what in the language of party is called a high churchman; but the true man, whichever his side and whatever his cause, belongs to all and is a help to all.—MORLEY, HENRY, 1881, *Of English Literature in the Reign of Victoria with a Glance at the Past, p.* 287.

High Churchmanship has been hitherto dry and formal; Keble carried into it the emotions of Evangelicalism while he avoided angry collision with Evangelical opinions. Thus all parties could find much to admire in him, and little to suspect. English religious poetry was generally weak — was not, indeed, poetry at all. Here was something which in its kind was excellent; and every one who was really religious, or wished to be religious, or even outwardly and from habit professed himself and believed himself to be a Christian, found Keble's verses chime in his heart like church bells.—FROUDE, JAMES ANTHONY, 1881, *The Oxford Counter-Reformation, Short Stories on Great Subjects, vol.* IV, *p.* 173.

It is by the "Christian Year" that Keble won the ear of the religious world, and will retain it. It was a happy thought that dictated the plan of the book, to furnish a meditative religious lyric for each Sunday of the year, and for each saint's day and festival of the English Church. . . . 1. The peculiar tone of religious feeling that pervades it, at once deep, pure, and tender, sober, and severely self-denying. . . . 2. A second note of the "Christian Year" is reverence for the church, and for the pastoral office within it,—a solemn sense of its dignity and its awful responsibility. . . . 3. A third note is the strong and tender affection for home and friends, the filial and fraternal piety, which everywhere pervades it. . . . 4. A prevailing spirit of modesty and of delicate reserve, very unlike the vanity with which poets are often credited. Combined with this is a special tenderness for those persons and things which the world thinks least of—for those who pine forgotten in hidden nooks, for the downtrodden and the despised. . . . 5. Besides these qualities of Keble's heart as a man, there are others which belong to him especially as a poet. Prominent among these is his love of nature, particularly for the more ordinary and unnoticed features of English landscape.—SHAIRP, JOHN CAMPBELL, 1882, *Encyclopædia Britannica, Ninth Ed., vol.* XIV, *pp.* 27, 28.

His poetic and gracious gifts are embalmed in the "Christian Year," which has touched so many hearts. There is an ineffable sweetness in its verse. Christian experience may outgrow the savor, but it lingers like a delightful fragrance in the memory.—TULLOCH, JOHN, 1885, *Movements of Religious Thought in Britain during the Nineteenth Century, p.* 66.

Perhaps the best test of the "accurate learning" displayed by Mr. Keble is to be found in the extremely small number of lapses amongst a crowd of beautiful fitnesses and coincidences. Indeed, after the conscientious correction of one or two minute errors in later editions, there remains scarcely a drawback to the exact and admirable descriptions, allusive or in detail, strewn throughout the "Christian Year;" and the charmed reader may repose in the conviction that he is under the influence of a picture as faithful as it is graceful of any scene with which the several narratives or meditations are conversant.—GRANT, ALEXANDER H., 1887, *ed. The Christian Year, Biographical Sketch of John Keble, p.* 51.

Who will dare to say that the "Christian Year" is not a true, perhaps a great poetical work? It has carried hope and happiness and support to hearts that cannot be numbered; but it says little or nothing to me. Poetry has been somewhere or other called "idealised utterance." I do not quite understand this definition (definitions of poetry indeed are always more or less unintelligible), but accepting it as an approach to the truth, and judging Keble by that definition, I should say that he commonly stammered rather than spoke. But yet, his power of influencing beautiful souls, and filling them with unfading joy and peace, is so great a gift, that to talk of him without due reverence seems something like a blasphemy.—DOYLE, SIR FRANCIS HASTINGS, 1887, *Reminiscences and Opinions, p.* 183.

The "Christian Year" was published anonymously in two volumes in 1827. His father's desire to see it in print before he died partly gave the impulse. No one, and least of all Keble himself, anticipated its great success. Before his death it had passed through ninety-five editions and by the next year the number had reached 109. The editions contained three thousand and even five thousand copies; nor is there yet any sign of the decline of its popularity. Keble said that he aimed at bringing men's thoughts and feelings into more entire unison with the prayer-book. The suggestiveness of the book, the writer's intimate knowledge of the Bible and power of presenting its most poetic incidents, the accuracy of its descriptions of natural scenery, the sweetness of its melody, the happiness of its general diction and particular expressions, its exquisite taste, its scholarly tone, its beautiful spirit of unaffected piety, were all appreciated. Its defects were also recognized from the first. Its ruggedness of metre and awkwardness of construction in some parts were so marked that the poet Wordsworth (Dr. Pusey tells us) "proposed to the author that they should go over the work together with a view to correcting the English." Its obscurity was also complained of. But it was favorably received even by those who did not share its author's views.—OVERTON, JOHN HENRY, 1892, *Dictionary of National Biography, vol.* XXX, *p.* 293.

Certainly the language of Homer has inspired some of the best poems of the "Christian Year." Or was it Scott, to whom he goes back so frequently in the "Prælectiones," and of whom he speaks so lovingly in his review of Lockhart's life? Certainly either Homer with his idealization of the heroic age, or Scott with that of the age of chivalry, would kindle his own love of the recollections of childhood or the glories of the early Church, though the very sense of such dependence would keep him on his guard against direct imitation of their form. In the earlier poems, indeed, Southey's influence of form and thought is perceptible, and in a less degree that of Scott and Wordsworth, but he had shaken himself free and has a style that is independent and entirely his own in the "Christian Year." It is marred from time to time by want of smoothness of metre, by obscurity in the connection of the thought between verse and verse, but on the whole it is spontaneous, melodious, and clear. . . . Its most permanent value lies in this power to soothe. . . . The poems awe and stir and soothe alike, because they are so real; they have so vivid a sense of the spiritual world, with all its terrors as well as its beauty and grace. He is the prophet of the fear of God no less than the poet of His love.—LOCK, WALTER, 1892, *John Keble, pp.* 53, 71, 72.

With its poetry, so good within its own range, so weak beyond it, was the source of many books of poems of a similar but inferior character.—BROOKE, STOPFORD A., 1896, *English Literature, p.* 247.

Keble's evening hymn has far outstripped in general use his morning hymn. Although the "Christian Year" has gone through one hundred editions, the last of which placed the bulk of it before one hundred thousand readers, this hymn is known not to thousands, but to millions, and the music of its verse is familiar in every nook and corner of the English-speaking world. —STEAD, W. T., 1897, *Hymns that Have Helped, p.* 206.

GENERAL

Mr. Keble, for example, has translated him for women; he has himself told us that he owed to Wordsworth the tendency *ad sanctiora* which is the mark of his own writings; and in fact he has but adapted the tone and habit of reverence, which his master applied to common objects and the course of the seasons, to sacred objects and the course of the ecclesiastical year,—diffusing a mist of sentiment and devotion altogether delicious to a gentle and timid devotee —BAGEHOT, WALTER, 1852, *Works, ed. Morgan, vol.* I, *p.* 78.

I do not expect a general agreement in opinion with me, when I say that the "Lyra Innocentium," if not equal to the "Christian

Year," as a whole, is at least more than equal in some parts, and on the whole worthy of its author. Though very successful in comparison with the generality of such works, it has not had a circulation at all proportionate to that of the "Christian Year;" it has not become a *manual* in general use, and has not consequently been studied, and is not known in the same degree. I may therefore be excused a few words upon it. . . . No one, perhaps, but a parent, can fully enter into all parts of it, and yet he who wrote it did not marry young, and was never a father.—COLERIDGE, SIR JOHN TAYLOR, 1868, *A Memoir of the Rev. John Keble, pp.* 311, 312.

There can be no doubt that Keble had, in even an eminent degree, some of the higher qualities which make the true poet. His fancy was lively and fertile in images full of beauty. His observation of outward nature, such as it may be seen in the rich lowlands of England was accurate; and his feeling for the quiet and tender beauty of grove and stream, and field and English wild flowers was exquisitely quick and true. His sympathy with all that is pure and sweet in home affections, with the joys and sorrows of family life, with the ways and the feelings of children, was almost unequalled. His deep personal piety harmonized all these natural endowments, and cast upon all he saw and felt those solemn lights and shades from the world above and beyond, which glorified the play of natural fancy and feeling, gave it unity and purpose, and often elevated his poetry into the region of imagination as distinguished from the lower province of mere fancy. He had learnt, too, from Cowper and Wordsworth in England, and from the early poets of ancient Greece, whom he loved so well, to express his thought by preference directly and truthfully, avoiding artificial "poetic diction."—VAUGHAN, E. T., 1869, *The Life of Keble, Contemporary Review, vol.* 11, *p.* 276.

This edition of Hooker occupied him five years, from 1831 to 1836. Of all his prose works the introduction to this edition seems to us far the ablest. It shows great critical power both in the minuter questions which concern the authenticity of certain portions of the ecclesiastical policy, and in the broader subject of what Hooker's real opinions were upon the turning points of the long controversy he held with the puritan writers, and

what the influences were by which they were shaped. This was a work to which his whole heart was given. For though he would call no man master, not even Richard Hooker, and where they differed stated with all boldness and sincerity the difference and its cause, yet he could not but perceive in Hooker's times of opposition and reproach that which shadowed forth to his inner consciousness the likeness of his own work in his own generation. This consciousness often re-appears in his pages, and adds a most life-like reality to them.—WILBERFORCE, SAMUEL, 1869, *Keble's Biography, Quarterly Review, vol.* 127, *p.* 119.

He was a poet; he was a man of eminent goodness; and he was a great Christian thinker and theologian. Of these characters the first has mainly riveted the attention of the world. The name of the author of the "Christian Year" is known to thousands who know nothing, whatever they may infer, about his life and character. And a scarcely smaller number who are aware that he was a man of singular purity and simplicity of life have no idea that his intellect was one of unusual strength and beauty, and that he wielded decisive influence at a crisis pregnant with consequences to the religious future of his country. "The poet Keble!" The phrase is used, often indeed as a title of honour, but sometimes also to imply that he was only a maker of religious verses, and not properly a leader or guide of men.—LIDDON, HENRY PARRY, 1876–94, *Clerical Life and Work, p.* 335.

Keble was not a sacred, but in the best sense of the word, a secular poet. It is not David only, but the Sibyl, whose accents we catch in his inspirations. The "sword in myrtle drest" of Harmodius and Aristogeiton, "the many-twinkling smile of ocean" from Æschylus, are images as familiar to him as "Bethlehem's glade," or "Carmel's haunted strand." Not George Herbert, or Cowper, but Wordsworth, Scott, and perhaps more than all, Southey, are the English poets that kindled his flame, and coloured his diction. The beautiful stanza, "Why so stately, maiden fair?" and the whole poem on "May Garlands," might have been written by the least theological of men. . . . Though Keble's pastoral life was retired and his ecclesiastical life narrow, as a poet he not only touched the great world of literature, but he was also a free-minded, free-speaking thinker. Both in form and in doctrine his poetry has a broad and philosophical vein, the more striking from its contrasts to his opposite tendencies in connection with his ecclesiastical party.—STANLEY, ARTHUR PENRHYN, 1880, *The English Poets, ed. Ward, vol.* IV, *pp.* 504, 505.

His poetry was for a long time only for himself and his intimate friends; his indulgence in poetical composition was partly playful, and it was not till after much hesitation on his own part and also on theirs, and with a contemptuous undervaluing of his work, which continued to the end of his life, that the anonymous little book of poems was published which has since become familiar wherever English is read, as the "Christian Year." His serious interests were public ones. Though living in the shade, he followed with anxiety and increasing disquiet the changes which went on so rapidly and so formidably, during the end of the first quarter of this century, in opinion and in the possession of political power.—CHURCH, RICHARD WILLIAM, 1891, *The Oxford Movement, p.* 22.

After 1840, when the craving for spiritual guidance came to be widely felt, many turned to the elderly author of the "Christian Year." They were met with the most embarrassing condescension, the tenderest sympathy, and sure and ready insight; they were not led to make any great venture or scale any great heights; he did not attempt to impose or inspire the very considerable austerities which he practised; his guidance was often hesitating and never peremptory. Probably most who trusted him enough to persevere in acting on his hints did learn to possess their souls in patience, to expend their emotions in safe ways, and in some measure to purify their hearts. His self-depreciation did not affect his happiness or the esteem of two generations. He was loved and honored to the last, though he lived to call himself a testy old clerk. Perhaps he will be remembered, like Shelley, as "a beautiful ineffectual angel;" but Keble's wings were never smirched.—SIMCOX, GEORGE AUGUSTUS, 1893, *The Academy, vol.* 43, *p.* 235.

If his writings were not poetry, we may be thankful that for more than half a century there have been spirits so high, so refined, so devoted, as to have been misled by his spiritual ardour, the lofty sublimity

of his ideals, as to mistake his refined and enthusiastic utterance for the voice of the genuine bard.—BENSON, ARTHUR CHRISTOPHER, 1896, *Essays, p.* 204.

Keble has a deeper strain of thought than Lyte; he is in closer harmony with Wordsworth; and the rare fragments of landscape which his train of subjects has admitted are worthy of the Master—true to Nature, dignified, instinct with serious thought and feeling.—PALGRAVE, FRANCIS TURNER, 1896, *Landscape in Poetry, p.* 250.

With Herbert and Miss Rossetti, Keble ranks as the greatest of English writers in sacred verse, the irregular and unequal efforts of Vaughan and Crashaw sometimes transcending, oftener sinking below the three. If Keble has not the exquisite poetical mysticism of Christina Rossetti he is more copious and more strictly scholarly, while he escapes the quaint triviality or the triviality sometimes not even quaint, which mars Herbert. The influence of Wordsworth is strongly shown, but it is rendered and redirected in an entirely original manner. The lack of taste which mars so much religious poetry never shows itself even for a moment in Keble; yet the correctness of his diction, like the orthodoxy of his thought is never frigid or tame. There are few poets who so well deserve the nickname of a Christian Horace, though the phrase may seem to have something of the paradox of "prose Shakespeare." The careful melody of the versification and the exact felicity of the diction exclude, it may be, those highest flights which create most enthusiasm, at any rate in this century. But for measure, proportion, successful attainment of the proposed end, Keble has few superiors.—SAINTSBURY, GEORGE, 1896, *A History of Nineteenth Century Literature, p.* 363.

Notwithstanding drawbacks, however, Keble stands admittedly among the foremost of the sacred poets of the century, and he does so by reason of his superior poetic equipment. Many writers of sacred verse employ poetic forms for didactic purposes, because they find them effective for inculcating doctrine and disseminating truth: they are churchmen first and poets afterwards. But Keble was much more than a writer of hymns and poems upon sacred subjects. Nature made him a poet, and circumstances made him a churchman; and had circumstances predisposed him otherwise he would still have been a poet, and might still have won distinction by his verse.—MILES, ALFRED H., 1897, *The Poets and the Poetry of the Century, Sacred, Moral, and Religious Verse, p.* 122.

Keble's influence was essentially personal, and was due to his saintly life more than to anything he wrote, even in poetry. The Tractarian movement took its rise in a longing for saintliness, of which Keble furnished a living example. He was not to any considerable extent an originator of theory. Certain germs of theory about the church, about its relation to pre-Reformation times, about authority in religion, were in the air and they became absorbed in Keble's system. But his was not a creative mind, and his disposition at the head of the Anglo-Catholic movement was little more than an accident. He was like a child who by a thrust of his hand sends a finely-poised rock thundering down a hill. In his literary aspects he is disappointing. A brilliant boy and a most blameless man, he remains throughout too little of this world. The pale perfection of his life is reflected in his works. He would have been better had he been less good; he would have been much better had he been less feminine.—WALKER, HUGH, 1897, *The Age of Tennyson, p.* 145.

The charm of Keble's best poetry lies chiefly in its purity, its serenity, its deep transparency of thought and feeling, its calmness of expression, its consoling spirit. His theory was that "the utterance of high or tender feeling, controlled or modified by a certain reserve, is the very soul of poetry." His imagination is illuminating rather than creative; in this he differs from Henry Vaughan, to whom in many things he is so near of kin. Of fancy, and of that striking, inventive power of expression which usually goes with fancy, he has little or nothing; in this he differs from his brother preacher-poet, George Herbert. In broad, buoyant, vigorous emotion, such as finds an utterance in the noblest hymns, wherein we hear the sound of many voices triumphantly praising God, Keble was deficient; he was too reflective, too secluded in spirit, to be among the great hymn-writers. Keble's real master in poetry—though he himself gave the highest praise and admiration to Scott among the moderns—his real master was Wordsworth.—VAN DYKE, HENRY, 1897, *Aids to the Devout Life, Outlook, vol.* 57, *p.* 663.

William Whewell

1794-1866

A clergyman and professor of the Church of England, was born at Lancaster, England, in 1794. He graduated from Trinity College in 1816, and received the degree of D. D.; was ordained deacon in 1820, and priest in the following year; became master of Trinity College, Cambridge, 1841, and was vice-chancellor of the university. Previous to this he was fellow and tutor of Trinity College, and from 1828 to 1832 was professor of mineralogy in the university; from 1838 to 1855 he was professor of moral theology. Dr. Whewell died at Cambridge, March 6, 1866. As an author he was prolific; among his works being, "An Elementary treatise on Mechanics" (1819)—which passed through seven editions:— "Analytical Statics" (1826):—"Architectural Notes on German Churches" (1830):— "Principles of University Education" (1831):—"First Principles of Mechanics" (1832):— "Doctrine of Limits" (eod.):—"Treatise of Dynamics" (1832–36):—"Astronomy and General Physics" (1834):—"Mechanical Euclid" (1837):—"History of the Inductive Sciences" (eod. 3 vols.):—"The Mechanics of Engineering" (1841):—"Liberal Education" (1845):—"Verse Translations from German" (1847):—"Lectures on the History of Moral Philosophy" (1852):—"Systematic Morality" (1846):—"Elements of Morality" (1848). He was also editor of an edition of Newton's "Principia," first three sections (1846); of Butler's "Human Nature" (1843); of Butler's "Moral Subjects" (1849); and of various other scientific works. He was also the author of various scientific articles in leading periodicals, and published many pamphlets and numerous sermons.—M'CLIN-TOCK, JOHN, AND STRONG, JAMES, eds., 1881, *Cyclopædia of Biblical, Theological and Ecclesiastical Literature, vol.* X, *p.* 979.

PERSONAL

This day was rendered interesting by a visit from one of the most remarkable of our scholars and men of science, Professor Whewell. He breakfasted with me and my nephew. The occasion of his visit was, that I might look over his translation of "Hermann and Dorothea" with the original, with a view to some suggestions I had made. His pursuits are very multifarious. To some one who said, "Whewell's forte is science,"—"Yes," said Sydney Smith, "and his foible is omni-science."—ROBINSON, HENRY CRABB, 1840, *To Wordsworth, May 22; Diary, Reminiscences and Correspondence, ed. Sadler.*

The immediate object of my writing to you is that I have been your trumpeter, in my best fashion, I hope, with an "éloquence vraiment britannique," in announcing your forthcoming great work, particularly at a great *déjeûner* given to us this morning by Humboldt. I ventured to mention of what great use your book would be to him before he launched his "Cosmos," and I hope you will send him one of your first copies, through his relative Baron Bülow. He expressed great regret at never having made your acquaintance, which feeling I augmented by telling him you were the English Humboldt.—MURCHISON, SIR RODERICK IMPEY, 1840, *Letter to Whewell, May 28; Life by Geikie, vol. I, p. 294.*

He is a very manly person, and I should think above all mean feelings of jealousy.—DEVERE, AUBREY, 1847, *Letter to Sir W. R. Hamilton, Feb. 23; Life of Hamilton by Graves, vol. II, p. 559.*

Dr. Whewell's accession to the Mastership of Trinity might well have been an era in the history of that "royal and religious foundation." The new head was a gentleman of most commanding personal appearance, and the very sound of his powerful voice betokened no ordinary man. He was a remarkably good rider even in a country of horsemen, and the anecdote was often told, and not altogether repudiated by him, how, in his younger days, about the time of his ordination, a pugilist, in whose company he accidentally found himself while travelling, audibly lamented that such lusty thews and sinews should be thrown away on a parson. With these physical advantages was combined a knowledge almost literally universal. Some people are said to know a little of everything; he might be truly said to know a great deal of everything.—BRISTED, CHARLES ASTOR, 1852, *Five Years in an English University.*

The master is a man to be noted, even physically. He is much above ordinary size, and, though now gray-haired, would be extraordinarily handsome if it were not for an expression of ill-temper about the mouth. An Englishman is proud; a Cambridge man is the proudest of Englishmen; and Dr. Whewell, the proudest of Cambridge men. In the opinion of a Cambridge man, to be master of Trinity, is to be master of the world! . . . . Dr. Whewell's self-respect and immense self-esteem led him to imperiousness of manner which touches the border of discourtesy. He loves a good joke, but his jests are serious. He writes verses that are touchingly beautiful, but it is difficult to believe, in his presence, that he writes them.—MITCHELL, MARIA, 1857, *Journal; Life, Letters and Journals, ed. Kendall, pp. 114, 118.*

We spent two days at Carclew with Dr. Whewell and his wife, Lady Afleck. He was as urbane and friendly as needs be, and seemed determined to live down Sydney Smith's quiz about astronomy being his forte, and omniscience his foible; for he rarely chose to know more about things than other people, though we perseveringly plied him with all manner of odds and ends of difficulties. There is a capital element of fun in that vast head of his; witness his caricatures of Sedgwick in his Cornish Sketch-Book. He made me notice the darkness of sky between two rainbows, a fact only lately secured, and a part, he says, of the whole theory of the rainbow. Speaking of some book he had written with a touch of architecture in it, he said, "There are many wise things in it, but I'm wiser still!" which he hoped was a modest way of stating the case.—FOX, CAROLINE, 1859, *Memories of Old Friends, ed. Pym, Journal, Sept. 4, p. 345.*

I am sorry to say Whewell is beaten by his terrible foe. It is only a question of hours now. The feeling here is deep and solemn. Men say he was the leader in progress and reform, when such were a persecuted minority. He was the regenerator of Trinity; he is connected with every step forward that the University has made for years past. Yes. He was a very great man: and men here feel the awful suddenness of it. He never was better or pleasanter than on the Thursday, when I dined there, and he was asking me for my "dear wife." His manner with women was always charming. He was very kind to me, and I was very fond of him.—KINGSLEY, CHARLES, 1866, *Letters, Charles Kingsley, Letters and Memories of his Life, ed. his Wife, vol. II, p. 227.*

In intellectual eminence we cannot follow him. But the moral qualities which clustered about his mental power may be imitated even by the least gifted. The unflagging energy which overcame all disadvantages, the manly courage which ever disdained unworthy applause, the simple faith in God through Christ, which in him was thrown into stronger relief by his large acquaintance with all branches of human knowledge; such qualitie as these are not beyond the reach of any. His example supplies a fresh incentive as it imposes a fresh responsibility.—LIGHTFOOT, J. B., 1866, *Funeral Sermon Preached in Trinity College Chapel.*

Any one may point out his failings, which were accidental and external; but a man must be as great and strong as he was adequately to gauge his essential greatness and strength. In the judgment of all who knew him, his life was throughout one of exemplary purity. The temptations of youth left him unscathed and unstained. Pure in deed, he was also pure in word. Even in his youth, when a bad fashion corrupted many, he religiously abstained from the use of profane oaths, and from the utterance of any word unbefitting Christian lips. . . . Bold and confident as he was in all that he considered legitimate matter for speculation, he was humble and reverent in matters of faith. His orthodoxy was the expression of a sincere and unwavering belief. At the same time he was tolerant and charitable towards those of a different creed, and never was heard to impute unworthy motives to men who doubted what he believed. . . . His munificence was extraordinary. Though no one could charge him, like the Cardinal, with being unsatisfied in getting, yet in bestowing he was, like him, most princely. Besides devoting the main part of his fortune for the benefit of the University and the College, he gave largely in private charities, and lent considerable sums to persons who had as little claim upon him as prospect of repaying.—CLARK, W. G., 1866, *William Whewell, Macmillan's Magazine, vol.* 13, *pp.* 550, 551.

The master of Trinity was conspicuous as a rough customer, an intellectual bully, an overbearing disputant; the character was as well established as that of Sam Johnson. But there was a marked difference. It was said of Johnson that if his pistol missed fire, he would knock you down with the butt end of it; but Whewell, in like case, always acknowledged the miss, and loaded again or not, as the case might be. He reminded me of Dennis Brulgruddery, who says to Dan, "pacify me with a good reason, and you'll find me a dutiful master." I knew him from the time when he was my teacher at Cambridge, more than forty years. As a teacher, he was anything but dictatorial, and he was perfectly accessible to proposal of objections. He came in contact with me in his slashing way twice in our after joint lives, and on both occasions he acknowledged himself overcome, by that change of manner, and apologetic mode of continuance, which I had seen him employ towards others under like circumstances. . . . I have said that Whewell was gentle with his pupils; it was the same with all who wanted teaching: it was only on an armed enemy that he drew his weapon.— DEMORGAN, AUGUSTUS, 1871 (?), *A Budget of Paradoxes, pp,* 415, 416.

During our long friendship I never remember hearing him speak unkindly of any one behind his back, though he was free enough and bold enough spoken wher he had you face to face. He was wonderfully fond of his friends, whom he never forgot. I remember his having made one of them sit for his picture to Lonsdale, and then his having given the portrait which he paid for to a third party, a mutual friend. But it would be endless to tell instances of his generous spirit. And, in fact, it was that, no doubt which gained him the friendship of so many who were incompetent to profit by his extraordinary intellectual powers. He conciliated all but proud, self-conceited people, who did not like to be put down by a word or two from him.—DIGBY, KENELM, 1872, *Letter to Mrs. Stair Douglas, Feb.* 12; *Life of Dr. Whewell, p.* 38.

I do not think adequate justice can be rendered to Dr. Whewell's vast knowledge and power by any person who did not know him intimately, except by the examination of his extensive correspondence; such an examination cannot fail to raise the opinion formed of him by the study of his published works, however high that opinion may be. —TODHUNTER, ISAAC, 1876, *William Whewell, Nature, vol.* 24, *p.* 138.

The same ardour which distinguishes his intellectual temperament belonged in an even greater degree to his affections. They bound him with filial fondness to his remote Lancashire home, to his family, to the picturesque town of Lancaster itself, to his old schoolmaster, Joseph Rowley. They bound him with great tenacity and appreciative esteem to persons from whom he differed in opinion on almost every point. They bound him with the most indulgent tenderness to younger relations who could contribute nothing but love and gratitude to the unequal friendship. And they bound him also with a loyalty and fidelity which no shock of disagreement, no strain of separation, could permanently impair, to the "friends of a lifetime," as he delighted to call Herschel, Jones, Sedgwick, Worsley, Peacock, Kenelm Digby, Airy, Henslow, Forbes, and others, whose friendship he reckoned amongst the greatest blessings of his life.—DOUGLAS, MRS. STAIR, 1881, *The Life and Selections from the Correspondence of William Whewell, Introductory, p.* viii.

A controversy used to exist in Cambridge as to the proper pronunciation of Whewell's name. He was described in a newspaper article as a man whose name it was more easy to *whistle* than to *spell;* and in practice the pronunciation was somewhat various, some saying You-ell, others Woo-ell, or perhaps rather Whoo-ell. On a public occasion, when he recited his own name, I remember that his own pronunciation corresponded nearly to the last of these three, which therefore I presume may be regarded as the correct rendering of the name. . . . When I was a young man in Cambridge, Whewell was in the prime of his powers. His "History of the Inductive Sciences" was published while I was an undergraduate; and I remember him well in the University pulpit, when he preached his course of sermons on the "Foundation of Morals." I have always thought that the appearance of Whewell in St. Mary's was one of the most impressive that I have ever seen; his commanding person, his grand brow, his massive head, the very impersonation of physical and mental strength—it is difficult to conceive a more noble picture.—CARLISLE, HARVEY, 1881, *William Whewell, Macmillan's Magazine, vol.* 45, *pp.* 139, 140.

The great doctor was not, in undergraduate eyes—or, at all events, in the eyes of those like myself who were about "only not to disgrace themselves by taking an ordinary degree"—an agreeable person. His

manners were rough, and his temper, when he troubled himself to keep it at all, of the shortest. . . . Most people in his eyes were *wuthless* who were not acquainted with the Inductive Sciences. His presence was majestic; he made an admirable figure-head for the collegiate ship; but, though I speak of course as a cabin-boy, I never heard of his troubling himself about the crew.—PAYN, JAMES, 1884, *Some Literary Recollections, pp.* 43, 44.

By dint of sheer ability and force of character he fought his way up to the very highest place in the University of Cambridge—certainly a much more democratic institution than that of Oxford,—becoming in succession Fellow and Tutor of his college, Professor of Mineralogy, Professor of Moral Philosophy, and Master of Trinity. In this last capacity Whewell was emphatically king, or rather pope, of Cambridge. The authority that he exercised was of the manner of a paternal despotism, the chief thing postulated from his subjects being that they should agree with him. To strangers—especially unargumentative strangers,—and to dutiful subjects,—no potentate could be more gracious, but the rebellious spirits who set up theories of their own were apt to be somewhat roughly treated. Whewell was conscious of the enormous extent of his knowledge and perhaps too anxious to prove that nothing was omitted from it; as was wittingly said of him. "Science was his forte and omniscience his foible."—OLIPHANT, MARGARET O. W., 1892, *The Victorian Age of English Literature, p.* 403.

My reminiscences of the great Dr. Whewell, Master of Trinity College, Cambridge, and author, among other books, of the famous "History" and of the "Philosophy of the Inductive Sciences," are chiefly those of the days when I was an undergraduate, a scholar, and a young fellow of the great college over which he presided. . . . Only a few favored youths, chiefly scholars, were invited to what were called "the standups" —that is, to parties at the master's lodge, where no undergraduate was ever supposed to take the awful liberty of sitting down. . . . I vividly recall the fine and stately presence of the master, which (as another myth related) made a prize-fighter deplore that so splendid a physique, and such thews and sinews, should be thrown away on a mere clergyman! I remember him especially in the college chapel. He was an unfeignedly religious man.—FARRAR, FREDERICK W., 1897, *Men I Have Known, pp.* 126, 128.

Whewell was a man of splendid physical development. A Cambridge legend told of a prize-fighter who had exclaimed, "What a man was lost when they made you a parson!" His face showed power rather than delicacy, and a massive brow gave special dignity to his appearance. His masculine vigour implied certain unattractive qualities. His friend Hare felt it a duty to remonstrate with him upon his "vehemence" and impatience, and held up as examples the sweetness of William Wilberforce, Bishop Otter and Manning. Whewell received the advice good-temperedly, and admitted that in so "eminent a station" as the mastership he was especially bound not to be "overbearing." He did not, however, quite admit the facts alleged in proof. He loved an argument, and his position as a great man in a small circle tended to make the argument one-sided. He was popular as a tutor; but for some time he provoked a good deal of hostility as master. In early days he had little chance of acquiring social refinement; and, though he was anxious to be hospitable, his sense of the dignity of his position led to a formality which made the drawing-room of the lodge anything but a place of easy sociability. In later years age and sorrow made him conspicuously milder, and the object not only of the pride but of the warm affection of the University. Though rough at times, he was from the first magnanimous; he never cherished resentment and admitted defeat frankly, and received the opinions of young and insignificant persons with remarkable courtesy. Few men, too, have had more friends or retained their friendships more carefully. He had many controversies, but no personal quarrels. His domestic life was perfect, and he always respected and attracted women. STEPHEN, LESLIE, 1899, *Dictionary of National Biography, vol.* LX, *p.* 460.

HISTORY OF THE INDUCTIVE SCIENCES
1837

Mr. Whewell appears on all occasions to be fully alive to the extent of these pretensions, and the consequent importance and dignity of his task. There is, however, no arrogance in the tone in which they are put forward—and, so far as we can perceive, no partiality in the bias, and assuredly no levity in the temper, of his decisions on the many delicate and difficult points on which, as an historian and a philosopher, he has to pass judgment—not merely as to simple personal questions of priority, but as to the substantial merits and value of inductions and discoveries themselves. . . . Its chief characters are a remarkable occasional point and felicity of expression, and the almost systematic adoption, as a mode of illustration, of a great assemblage and variety of metaphorical allusion, much greater indeed than we should like to see adopted by an author less thoroughly imbued with his own meaning, and less capable of curbing the exuberance of a lively fancy into an entire subordination to his reason. . . . Among our author's various and brilliant accomplishments not one of the least remarkable is his poetical talent, of which we have specimens in the mottoes prefixed to the several books of his "History."—HERSCHEL, SIR J. F. W., 1841, *Whewell on Inductive Sciences, Quarterly Review, vol.* 68, *pp.* 183, 238.

One attempt—a bold and successful one—has been made in our own day to unite two or three of the departments,—I mean the History and the Philosophy of the Inductive Sciences. An English philosopher, of wonderful versatility, industry, and power, has erected a permanent monument to his reputation in a voluminous work bearing the preceding title.—FORBES, J. D., 1853, *Encyclopædia Britannica, Eighth Ed.*

The ablest historian of Natural Science. —OWEN, RICHARD, 1859, *Address before the British Association for the Advancement of Science, p.* 7.

In a work of so much merit as Dr. Whewell's, it is important that these errors should be indicated, because we have no other book of value on the general history of the sciences; and many authors have deceived themselves and their readers, by implicitly adopting the statements of this able and industrious writer. I would particularly caution the student in regard to the physiological part of Dr. Whewell's "History," where, for instance, the antagonism between the methods of Cuvier and Bichat is entirely lost sight of, and while whole pages are devoted to Cuvier, Bichat is disposed of in four lines.—BUCKLE, HENRY THOMAS, 1861, *History of Civilization in England, vol.* II, *ch.* VII, *note.*

The excellence of the book as a whole is wonderful, if we consider the rapidity with which it was composed. We learn on good authority that it was sent to the press chapter by chapter as it was written. He worked with the hot haste of a parliamentary reporter. For this haste there was no apparent reason; no reason indeed, except such as sprang from his own ardent temperament. Other yet unexplored fields of knowledge were tempting him, and he was eager to be done with the mechanical drudgery imposed by the task in hand. He had none of that "long patience" which, according to Cuvier, is "genius." But few will deny that he had genius, and his example alone would suffice to prove that Cuvier's definition is not universally true.—CLARK, W. G., 1866, *William Whewell, Macmillan's Magazine, vol.* 13, *p.* 547.

Let any man read so common a book as Whewell's "History of the Inductive Sciences," and instead of rising from the perusal with the idea that science is "exact," "certain," and "stable," he will be much more likely to institute a comparison between it and the ever-changing sands on the shores of the ocean than with the fixed and ever-lasting hills.—BARNES, ALBERT, 1868, *Lectures on the Evidences of Christianity, p.* 88.

Happily for me, Dr. Whewell, early in this year, published his "History of the Inductive Sciences." I read it with eagerness, and found in it a considerable approximation to what I wanted. Much, if not most, of the philosophy of the work appeared open to objection; but the materials were there, for my own thoughts to work upon; and the author had given to those materials that first degree of elaboration, which so greatly facilitates and abridges the subsequent labour. I had now obtained what I had been waiting for.—MILL, JOHN STUART, 1873, *Autobiography.*

This may properly be called one of the great books of the last half-century. The author was a man whose prodigious learning made him one of the intellectual wonders of the last generation; but what was scarcely less remarkable than his learning was the subordination in which his attainments were held by his good sense and good judgment. . . . To the general student, the book on the scientific ideas prevailing in the Middle Ages will probably be found of most especial interest and value. The additions incorporated in the third edition are of much importance.—ADAMS, CHARLES KENDALL, 1882, *A Manual of Historical Literature, pp.* 55, 56.

GENERAL

I am reading Whewell, and admire all his observations on the mystical taste and studies of the Middle Ages, and his illustrations of the manner in which their mode of reasoning retarded the progress of Science.—EDGEWORTH, MARIA, 1838, *Letter to Sir W. R. Hamilton, Feb.* 15; *Life of Hamilton by Graves, vol.* II, *p.* 243.

The reputation of Dr. Whewell for energy of understanding and variety of attainment led us to his work on morals ["Elements of Morality"] with no little eagerness of hope. We forgot for the moment the questionable symptoms presented in his former works. We forgot his republication of Mackintosh's "Essay,"—an essay so pleasant in its gossips so slender in its philosophy. We remembered only his position as professor at Cambridge, and his judgment as an admirer of Butler: and expected to find the hints of that great writer worked out at length into a consistent theory of human duty. The expectation has been wholly disappointed. . . . . When Dr. Whewell forgets what is expected of him as a metaphysician, and writes out his unelaborated sentiments on the actual interest and pending questions of the world,—Slavery, Church Establishments, Public Education,—there is a vigor and directness in his treatment which, though sometimes vehement and overbearing, is never inefficient. But in our estimation there is something inexpressibly ungainly in all his movements "on the *a priori road.*" With constant exercise he makes no way; but after the boldest feats of verbal conjuring, in which energy of resolve is more remarkable than subtlety of execution, remains, so far as common eyes can measure, precisely where he was.—MARTINEAU, JAMES, 1845, *Whewell's Morality; Essays, Philosophical and Theological, vol.* II, *pp.* 4, 5.

Have you read Dr. Whewell (of Cambridge) on Morality and Polity? He has taken much from my "Ethics" without even mentioning the work, and even asked me, when I breakfasted with him, whether I had any objection to his using words I had formed, in order to express certain ideas, without acknowledging the source. I answered that he as a gentleman would know what was just and proper. The work has since been published. He uses my technical expressions, and, as I said, does not even mention my work.—LIEBER, FRANCIS, 1846, *To Mittermaier, April* 6; *Life and Letters, ed. Perry, p.* 204.

Professor Whewell is well known as an author, who has made science in its various branches and its highest relations his constant and anxious study. He is a plain and even dry writer, seldom eloquent, indulging in few flights of fancy, in no captivating theories, and in no charms of diction; but his sober and accurate reasoning and profound knowledge of his subject, make him a high authority and a safe guide, in comparison of those flowery and seductive writers whose shallow draughts at the Pierian spring have served only to intoxicate them, and to give them presumption in proportion to their incapacity.—BREWSTER, SIR DAVID, 1846, *Whewell's Indications of the Creator, North British Review, vol.* 4, *p.* 364.

They say in Cambridge that Dr. Whewell's book, "Plurality of Worlds," reasons to this end: The planets were created for this world; this world for man; man for England; England for Cambridge; and Cambridge for Dr. Whewell!—MITCHELL, MARIA, 1857, *Journal*; *Life, Letters and Journals, ed. Kendall, p.* 121.

Speaking generally it may be said that Whewell was not really great as a mathematician. There are indications in his writings of a certain rude strength, but he had not the true mathematical instinct; he had no taste for the more refined methods of modern analysis, and so far as I know he made

no real mathematical advance. The history and philosophy of science were more practicable to him; he took a keen interest in watching the course of science, and in certain branches, especially that of the theory of tides, he attempted to make contributions; but any addition to our physical knowledge which he may have made bears no comparison with the greatness of his mental endowment, and must not be taken as a measure of the man.—CARLISLE, HARVEY, 1881, *William Whewell, Macmillan's Magazine, vol.* 45, *p.* 140.

He was rather a bully, and his work has no extraordinary merit of style, but it is interesting as being among the latest in which science permitted her votaries not to specialize very much, and rather to apply the ancient education to the new subjects than to be wholly theirs.—SAINTSBURY, GEORGE, 1896, *A History of Nineteenth Century Literature, p.* 356.

Whewell's strong point is his great knowledge of the history of science. His inductive theory is somewhat loose. It amounts to no more than a succession of tests of hypotheses; and of these tests the most stringent, prediction and consilience of inductions, are open to the fatal objection that they are not and cannot be applied to all inductions.—WALKER, HUGH, 1897, *The Age of Tennyson, p.* 166.

Whewell did great service to the cause of scientific thought. His was a bold attempt to reduce to something like coherence the confused mass of scientific knowledge. Underlying the book was the idea of the organic unity of the sciences; and if he failed to realize his ideal, the reason lay not in his lack of insight, but in the fact that scientists had not then discovered by observation and experiment the marvelous unity of nature. —MACPHERSON, HECTOR, 1900, *Spencer and Spencerism, p.* 21.

Thomas Love Peacock
1785–1866

Born, at Weymouth, 18 Oct. 1785. At a school at Englefield Green, 1793–98. To London, 1801, Sec. to Sir Home Riggs Popham, winter of 1808–09. Friendship with Shelley begun, 1812; visit to Edinburgh with him, 1813. Appointed to post in East India House, 1819; Chief Examiner, 1836. Married Jane Gryffydh, 20 March 1820. Settled at Lower Halliford, 1823. Retired from East India House, March 1856. Died, at Halliford, 23 Jan. 1866. Buried in Shepperton Cemetery. *Works:* "The Monks of St. Mark," 1804; "Palmyra," 1806; "The Genius of the Thames," 1810; "The Philosophy of Melancholy," 1812; "Sir Proteus" (under pseudonym: "P. M. O'Donovan, Esq."), 1814; "Headlong

Hall" (anon.), 1816; "Melincourt" (anon.), 1817; "Nightmare Abbey" (anon.), 1818; "Sir Hornbrook" (anon.), 1818; "Rhododaphne" (anon.), 1818; "Maid Marian" (anon.), 1822; "The Misfortunes of Elphin" (anon.), 1829; "Crotchet Castle" (anon.), 1831; "Paper Money Lyrics," 1837; "Gryll Grange" (anon.), 1861. He *translated*: "Gli Ingannat; and Ælia Lælia Crispis," 1862. *Collected Works:* ed., with *memoirs*, by Sir H. Cole (3 vols.) 1873; by R. Garnett (10 vols.), 1891.—SHARP, R. FARQUHARSON, 1897, *A Dictionary of English Authors, p.* 224.

PERSONAL

Did you ever read "Headlong Hall" and "Maid Marian"? —a charming lyrical poet and Horatian satirist he was when a writer; now he is a white-headed jolly old worldling, and secretary to the E. India House, full of information about India and everything else in the world.—THACKERAY, WILLIAM MAKEPEACE, 1850, *Collection of Letters, p.* 100.

I met Peacock; a clever fellow, and a good scholar. I am glad to have an opportunity of being better acquainted with him. We had out Aristophanes, Æschylus, Sophocles and several other old fellows, and tried each other's quality pretty well. We are both strong enough in these matters for gentlemen. But he is editing the Supplices. Æschylus is not to be edited by a man whose Greek is only a secondary pursuit.—MACAULAY, THOMAS BABINGTON, 1851, *Journal, Dec.* 31; *Life and Letters, ed. Trevelyan, ch.* xii.

I saw a good deal of Mr. Peacock about this time, and enjoyed his society extremely, He was utterly unlike anybody I have ever seen before or since, and is best represented, to those who never knew him, by "Gryll Grange"—surely one of the brightest, as well as the most fantastic, books that has appeared in our time.—DUFF, SIR MOUNTSTUART E. GRANT, 1853, *Notes from a Diary, April* 1, *vol.* i, *p.* 53.

The portrait prefixed to the collected edition of his works conveys a very good idea of the man as I first saw him—a stately old gentleman with hair as white as snow, a keen, merry eye, and a characteristic chin. His dress was plain black, with white neckcloth, and low shoes, and on his head he wore a plaited straw hat. One glance at him was enough to reveal his delightful character, that of his own Dr. Opimian. "His tastes in fact were four: a good library, a good dinner, a pleasant garden, and rural walks." This was the man who, as a beautiful boy, had been caught up and kissed by Queen Caroline; who, when

he grew up to manhood, had been christened "Greeky Peeky," on account of his acquirement in Greek. . . . Age had mellowed and subdued the "cameo leopard," but the "fine wit," as I very speedily discovered, was as keen as ever. His life had been passed in comparative peace and retirement. . . . He had his "good library," and it *was* a good one—full of books it was a luxury to handle, editions to make a scholar's mouth water, bound completely in the old style in suits as tough as George Fox's suit of leather. . . . Knowing Peacock only from his books, I was not prepared to find in him that delightful *bonhomie* which was in reality his most personal characteristic, in old age at least; and when we became acquainted, and read and talked together, I was as much astonished at the sweetness of his disposition as amused and captivated by his quaint erudition. In that green garden, in the lanes of Halliford, on the bright river, in walks and talks such as "brightened the sunshine," I learned to know him, and although he was so much my senior he took pleasure (I am glad to say) in my society, partly because I never worried him with "acrimonious dispute," which he hated above all things.— BUCHANAN, ROBERT, 1886, *A Look Round Literature, pp.* 165, 166, 167, 168.

Peacock's literary style was elaborately polished, and he disliked writing letters, lest he should fall into any fault in hasty composition. . . . If, in conclusion, I may supplement these imperfect memories and family traditions from the sources of Peacock's books and the memoirs of his granddaughter, I should say that he was a kindhearted, genial, friendly man, who loved to share his enjoyment of life with all around him; and he was self-indulgent without being selfish. His ideals of life were noble and generous, and in "Melincourt" they temper with seriousness, even sadness, the boyish love of fun and caricature which never fail him. And if we see in "The Misfortunes of Elphin" and "Crotchet Castle" increased intellectual power accompanied by a more

worldly tone of thought, the natural consequence of prosperous enjoyment of life as
he found it, it is pleasant to recognise signs
in "Gryll Grange," the child of his old age,
a softer and better morality than that which
characterises the two last-named books.—
STRACHEY, SIR EDWARD, 1891, *Recollections
of Thomas Love Peacock.*

Peacock's character is well delineated in
a few words by Sir Edward Strachey: "A
kind-hearted, genial, friendly man, who
loved to share his enjoyment of life with all
around him, and self-indulgent without being selfish." He is a rare instance of a man
improved by prosperity; an element of
pedantry and illiberality in his earlier writings gradually disappears in genial sunshine
although with the advance of age, obstinate
prejudice takes its place, good humoured
but unamenable to argument.—GARNETT,
RICHARD, 1895, *Dictionary of National Biography, vol.* XLIV, *p.* 146.

POETRY

His fine wit
Makes such a wound the knife is lost in it;
A strain too learned for a shallow age,
Too wise for selfish bigots; let his page
Which charms the chosen spirits of the time,
Fold itself up for the serener clime
Of years to come, and find its recompense
In that just expectation.
—SHELLEY, PERCY BYSSHE, 1820, *Letter to
Maria Gisborne.*

The poetry of Peacock is neither the poetry of sentimental namby-pambyism nor of
burning passion. If he does not glow with
the fire of Shelley, he does not pall with the
sickly maunderings of later nerveless versi-
fiers, whose genius has had some difficulty
in crawling through its long clothes. While
our author's verse is liquid and musical, it
is never weak and faltering. He is able to
endow his creations with some amount of
life-breathing power. It can scarcely be
said that he was happier in his poetry than
his prose; rather, indeed, must the reverse
be admitted. His intellectual and dissecting strength was greater than his emotional.
He knew, probably, that the general reader
would take no delight in his verse; but that
mattered little to him; he could give him
none other—consequently all his work in
this direction betrays rather the thinking
than the feeling man.—SMITH, GEORGE
BARNETT, 1875, *Thomas Love Peacock,
Poets and Novelists, p.* 144.

The fame of Peacock as a prose humorist
of incomparable vivacity has tended to
overshadow and stunt his reputation as a
poet. It is time, however, that his claims in
verse should be vindicated, and a place demanded for him as an independent figure in
the crowded Parnassus of his age,—a place
a little below the highest, and somewhat
isolated, at the extreme right of the composition. He has certain relations, not wholly
accidental, with Shelley, who stands above
him, and with such minor figures as Horace
Smith and Thomas Haynes Bayly, who
stand no less obviously below him; but in
the main he is chiefly notable for his isolation. His ironical and caustic songs are
unique in our literature, illuminated by too
much fancy to be savage, but crackling
with a kind of ghastly merriment that inspires quite as much terror as amusement.
In parody he has produced at least one specimen, "There is a fever of the spirit," which
does not possess its equal for combined
sympathy and malice. When we pass to his
serious and sentimental lyrics, our praise
cannot be so unmeasured.—GOSSE, ED-
MUND, 1880, *The English Poets, ed. Ward,
vol.* IV, *p.* 417.

The riper and richer humour of Peacock,
as superior to Praed's as dry champagne to
sweet, or a Sultana grape to a green goose-
berry, is excellently represented by the
masterly and generous satire of "Rich and
Poor, or Saint and Sinner;" his deeper and
sweeter gift of grave and tender song, by
the matchless elegiac idyl of "Youth and
Age."—SWINBURNE, ALGERNON CHARLES,
1891-94, *Social Verse, Studies in Prose and
Poetry, p.* 101.

Why, after having scored a brilliant success in prose, as he certainly did in his novels
he should have gone back to verse in "Rhododaphne" is one of those puzzles with which
the lives of men of genius abound, and which
weaken, if they do not destroy, our belief in
their self-knowledge. "Rhododaphne"
was a delusion, and an aberration on the
part of Peacock, in whom, at the age of
thirty-three, it was inexcusable. It possesses no interest in itself, and is only interesting in the history of modern English
poetry when compared with the "Endymion" of Keats, which was written at the
same time. There was no comparison between the two men; for Peacock was a Grecian, and Keats was not. But he was better

than a Grecian—he was a Greek, as Landor said, and, better still, he was a great poet.— STODDARD, RICHARD HENRY, 1892, *Under the Evening Lamp, p.* 236.

Thomas Love Peacock wrote for respectable and sentimental England five of the very best drinking-songs ever given to an ungrateful world. No thought of possible disapprobation vexed his soul's serenity. He lived in the nineteenth century, as completely uncontaminated by nineteenth-century ideals as though Robinson Crusoe's desert island had been his resting place. The shafts of his good-tempered ridicule were leveled at all that his countrymen were striving to prove sacred and beneficial. His easy laugh rang out just when everybody was most strenuous in the cause of progress. His wit was admirably calculated to make people uncomfortable and dissatisfied. And in addition to these disastrous qualities, he apparently thought it natural and reasonable and right that English gentlemen—sensible, educated, *married* English gentlemen—should sit around their dinner-tables until the midnight hour, drinking wine and singing songs with boyish and scandalous joviality.—REPPLIER, AGNES, 1897, *Varia, p.* 146.

GENERAL

Peacock has married a Welsh turtle, and is employed at present in devising inextinguishable lanterns: which he puffs at with a pair of bellows.—BEDDOES, THOMAS LOVELL, 1824, *To Thomas Forbes Kelsall, April* 17; *Letters, ed. Gosse, p.* 24.

A new generation rose around him, to many of whose name—the name of one who had written novels when Bulwer and Disraeli were children—was unknown. His vigorous and versatile mind employed itself in new directions. He planned vessels which weathered the Cape, as he had produced books which will weather the century; but so far was he from abandoning letters, that his genius had an Indian summer not a whit less full of life and colour than the summer of its prime. "Gryll Grange," published in "Fraser" some six or seven years ago, when Peacock was more than seventy years of age, is quite as fresh as any book of the "Headlong Hall" series, and even more remarkable than the best of them, for ingenuity, liveliness of humor, genial vigour of wit, and wide reading in literature. What is no less interesting about

"Gryll Grange" is its similarity in tone and character to the author's novels of half a century before. His favorite views are not altered, only strengthened and confirmed. —HANNAY, JAMES, 1866, *Recent Humourists, North British Review, vol.* 45, *p.* 92.

It would, perhaps, be too much to aver that without his classicism, without his constant resort to the rich bank of ancient authors for the loan of thoughts and images, his novels would have been devoid of a residuary charm; for Peacock had a strong vein, a rare lyrical faculty, some invention, and a large and decided bent for satire: but the grace which harmonized these, and lent a spirit of "long, long ago" to the quaint modern figures, with which he loved to people his halls and granges, abbeys, castles, and green woods, was derived from those intellectual repasts of Greek and Latin authors which furnished to him a perpetual banquet.—DAVIES, JAMES, 1875, *Thomas Love Peacock, Contemporary Review, vol.* 25, *p.* 736.

His vast learning, his precise style, his great research, his boundless sarcasm, his intense abhorrence of cant, are all so many claims upon our regard. With the ordinary novelists he has little in common; in most respects he cannot be put into competition with them; for, whilst he has many virtues which they do not possess, he exhibits few of their vices.—SMITH, GEORGE BARNETT, 1875, *Thomas Love Peacock, Poets and Novelists, p.* 150.

In this ironic banter and *reductio ad absurdum* Peacock has no superior. His books themselves will probably seem tedious to the hasty reader, but even he will find in them innumerable suggestions which subsequent writers have made capital of. His wine and beasts have helped us to many feasts since his day.—OLIPHANT, MARGARET O. W., 1882, *The Literary History of England, XVIII–XIX Century, vol.* III, *p.* 155.

Smile as we may at the formality and pedantry of the eighteenth century, there were giants in those days; and Peacock resembled them in intellectual stature. His books will live, if only for their touches of quaint erudition; but they abound in delicious little pictures, such as that of Mr. Falconer and his seven Vestal attendants in "Gryll Grange," or those of Coleridge and Shelley in "Nightmare Abbey." Sir Oran Haut-ton is perfect, a masterpiece of characterisation, and as for Dr. Opimian, he is as sure of immortality as "my Uncle Toby" himself.—BUCHANAN, ROBERT, 1886, *A Look Round Literature*, p. 183.

Peacock's novels are unlike those of other men: they are the genuine expressions of an original and independent mind. His reading and his thinking ran together; there is free quotation, free play of wit and satire, grace of invention, too, but always unconventional. The story is always pleasant, although always secondary to the play of thought for which it gives occasion.—MORLEY, HENRY, 1887, ed. *Crotchet Castle, Introduction*, p. 6.

When his robust independence is associated with a congenial subject, the effect is very agreeable,—it is like being made thoroughly at home by one who is thoroughly at home himself. Peacock seldom responded to the mere call of a publisher or editor, for such a call was seldom addressed to him. He was neither popular enough nor needy enough to be frequently diverted from his own bent, and thus exempt from taskwork, he could always be fresh and vigorous.—GARNETT, RICHARD, 1891, ed. *Calidore and Miscellanea, Introduction*, p. 7.

Peacock's prose is what Matthew Arnold maintained poetry should be—a criticism of life, not life in the abstract, but life in the concrete—the social, political, national life of his own people and period.—STODDARD, RICHARD HENRY, 1892, *Under the Evening Lamp*, p. 241.

There is no obscurity in Peacock; there is no gush; and there is a great deal of very active and poignant ridicule of gush, of obscurity, and of affectation. . . . He began by making fun of the times of our grandfathers, he ended by making fun of the times which are almost, if not quite our own; and if, as perhaps he did, he showed himself rather obstinately blind to many of the higher aspects of life in general, he saw what he did see with an unmatched clearness of vision, and expressed the ironic results of his sight with powerful distinction and scholarship. . . . Peacock had a more poetical, a more ironic, and a less popular temperament than Macaulay's: but there was a good deal in him which might be called Macaulayish, on the negative side. He was nearly as knock-down in his depreciation as Macaulay was in his eulogism of progress and reform; he was, also like Macaulay, an omnivorous reader, and he had to a great extent the same clear, emphatic, unshadowed and unclouded caste of thought. Being, as has been said, an unpopular Macaulay, he never pushes his positiveness even in the negative direction to the extent of Philistinism; but he is open to the charge of being as hard if not as hollow as Macaulay at his worst. His special merits, however, will always, while they indispose towards him those whom Macaulay fully satisfies, enchant those who, while they fully admit the merits of Macaulay, are half disgusted by his demerits.—SAINTSBURY, GEORGE, 1896, *English Prose*, ed. Craik, *vol.* V, *pp.* 286, 287.

Jared Sparks
1789–1866

Born at Willington, Conn., May 10, 1789: died at Cambridge, Mass., March 14, 1866. An American historian. He graduated at Harvard in 1815, and became a Unitarian clergyman. He was pastor of a church in Baltimore 1819–23; was editor of the "North American Review" 1824–31; was professor of history at Harvard 1839–49; and was president of Harvard 1849–53. He was also the founder and first editor of the "American Almanac and Repository of Useful Knowledge" (Boston, 1830–61). He wrote, among other works, the "Life of John Ledyard" (1828), and the "Life of Gouverneur Morris" (1832), and edited "Diplomatic Correspondence of the American Revolution" (12 vols. 1829–30), "Writings of George Washington, with a Life of the Author" (12 vols. 1834–38), "Library of American Biography" (1834–38: writing the lives of Arnold, Ethan Allen, Marquette, La Salle, etc.), "Works of Benjamin Franklin, with a Life of the Author" (10 vols. 1836–40), and "Correspondence of the American Revolution" (1854), etc.—SMITH, BENJAMIN E., 1894–97, ed. *The Century Cyclopedia of Names*, p. 949.

PERSONAL

His manuscript has an unusually odd appearance. The characters are large, round, black, irregular, and perpendicular—the signature being an excellent specimen of his chirography in general. In all the letters now before us the lines are as close together as possible, giving the idea of irretrievable confusion; still, none of them are illegible upon close inspection.—POE, EDGAR ALLAN, 1841, *A Chapter on Autography, Works, ed. Stedman and Woodberry, vol.* IX, *p.* 218.

In personal appearance Mr. Sparks had a noble presence, a firm, bold, massive head, which, as age crept on, sometimes seemed careworn and impassive, but never lost its intellectual power. His portraits show that in his prime his face was remarkable for dignified, manly beauty. His manners were winning; and, though undemonstrative and rather reticent among strangers, with friends he was always cheerful and hearty.—MAYER, BRANTZ, 1867, *Memoir of Jared Sparks, p.* 27.

But it was not those only on his own social plane who were impressed by the sweetness and benignity of his character. He won the affection of all who came into any sort of relation or intercourse with him, and it seemed impossible for him to overlook or omit an occasion of performing a kindness. One day shortly before his death, I overtook him with a large bundle of clothes from a laundress in his hand, and a little girl, in shabby raiment, tottering at his side. I found on inquiry that he had overtaken the child staggering with a weight too heavy for her, and was going out of his way to relieve her. This seemingly slight act was typical of the temper and habit of his whole life.—PEABODY, A. P., 1893, *Life and Writings of Jared Sparks, ed. Adams, vol.* II, *p.* 572.

GENERAL

Mr. S. was chaplain to Congress for a time, but, much to the credit of his good sense, after two or three years of trial, has given up the pulpit—a place, for which he was not well qualified, (as a speaker, we should say,) and has betaken himself to writing, a business for which he *is* qualified—save when he forgets himself—and presumes to be rhetorical, warm, or generous.—NEAL, JOHN, 1825, *American Writers, Blackwood's Magazine, vol.* 17, *p.* 202.

Upon the whole, we dismiss his work ["Life of Washington"] with unqualified satisfaction. Its extent required a patience of labor, which few men could have brought to the task. To these have been added rigid literary as well as moral integrity, and that love of his theme which engaged him in supplementary and illustrative researches in this country and Europe, of the most important and interesting character. Mr. Sparks must not look for his reward to pecuniary compensation. Notwithstanding Mr. Moore's recent complimentary remarks on the splendid dowry which literature now brings to those who espouse her, we doubt not he has been as well paid for the lightest of his own graceful effusions by the Mæcenas of Albemarle Street as Mr. Sparks will be for his ten years of unrelaxing and conscientious labor. His reward has been already in part enjoyed; it must be found in the consciousness of laboriously and worthily performing a noble work;—in the conviction that he has contributed to give a wider diffusion, and a more abiding permanence, to the fame of Washington; and that, whenever the authority of the greatest and best of chieftains and patriots is appealed to in all coming time, it will be in some associations with his own name and labors.—EVERETT, EDWARD, 1838, *Sparks's Life and Writings of Washington, North American Review, vol.* 47, *p.* 381.

It may well be believed that Mr. Sparks has selected a noble subject in the history of a man like this ["Life of La Salle"], and he has treated it in a manner worthy of his own reputation. His task was not a light one.—PEABODY, O. W. B., 1844, *Sparks's American Biography, North American Review, vol.* 59, *p.* 99.

In the "Life of Franklin" we have another proof of Mr. Sparks's fitness for the work he has chosen. While in that of Washington we had a picture of the harmonious union of the patriot, warrior and statesman, formed upon the only sure basis of the Christian gentleman, we have, in the biography of the great printer, as admirable a likeness of the patriot philosopher combined with the legislator. What one did from loftiness of soul the other did from a love of utility.—POWELL, THOMAS, 1850, *The Living Authors of America, p.* 358.

I have also made frequent use of "Washington's Writings," as published by Mr. Sparks; a careful collation of many of them with the originals having convinced me of the general correctness of the collection, and of the safety with which it may be relied upon for historical purposes; and I am happy to bear this testimony to the essential accuracy of one whom I consider among the greatest benefactors to our national literature; and to whose writings and researches I acknowledge myself largely indebted throughout my work.—IRVING, WASHINGTON, 1855, *Life of George Washington, Preface, p.* VI.

Mr. Sparks whom we regard as an extremely well informed and fair writer. . . . An expert in manuscripts, . . . one of those diligent collators and investigators whom nothing would escape . . . a discriminating, candid, and singularly fair man.—RANDALL, HENRY STEPHENS, 1857, *The Life of Thomas Jefferson, vol.* I, *p.* 318, *vol.* II, *p.* 370.

Not a few of his contemporaries in the field of American authorship have prosecuted their historical researches and found the heroes of their story in distant realms and in a remote past. But it has been one of the peculiarities of his career that it has been occupied exclusively with topics connected with his native land. In the crowded gallery of portraits which have owed their execution, directly or indirectly, to the untiring industry of Jared Sparks, and which include so great a variety of character and so wide a range of service, there is not one, I believe, which is not associated prominently, if not exclusively, with the colonial or the national history of our own country. Nor can any one write that history, now or hereafter, without acknowledging a deep indebtedness, at every step, to his unwearied researches.—WINTHROP, ROBERT C., 1866, *Proceedings of the Massachusetts Historical Society, Life and Writings of Jared Sparks, ed. Adams, vol.* II, *p.* 586.

Even over the piled-up volumes which contain the work that he performed, we must say, as over the end of the career of every good and great man, that he left more of his purposes and his resolutions unaccomplished. And yet these volumes do substantially contain the "American History" which Dr. Sparks desired and intended to write. The reader of them may trace in them the rise and development of this republic. Their pages carry him over the whole territory which it originally embraced, and recognize the agency of all the leading actors, all the important events, the enterprises, discomfitures, and successes which entered into its organization and its full establishment. When we consider the number and variety of the biographies in his works, both those which are full and elaborate and those which offer only condensed sketches of ascertained facts, and remember that the writer was scrupulously careful to present accurately the opinions and the actions of his subjects, we are tempted to ask, what was there for him to do more?—

ELLIS, GEORGE E., 1868, *Proceedings of the Massachusetts Historical Society, Life and Writings of Jared Sparks, ed. Adams, vol.* II, *p.* 588.

His merits as an author would probably stand out in higher relief were they not to some extent overtopped by his still greater merits as a dispassionate, laborious, and judicious investigator.—HART, JOHN S., 1872, *A Manual of American Literature.*

The most indefatigable of all explorers into the unpublished letters and documents illustrating the history of the United States was Jared Sparks. His voluminous editions of "The Life and Writings of Washington and Franklin," his "Diplomatic Correspondence of the Revolution," and other books devoted to the task of adding to the authentic materials of American history, are mines of information to the students of history; but Mr. Sparks, though a clear and forcible writer, had not the gift of attractiveness; and the results of his investigations have been more popularly presented by Irving in his " Life of Washington," and Parton in his "Life of Franklin," than by his own biographies of those eminent men, based on the results of tireless original research extending through many years.—WHIPPLE, EDWIN PERCY, 1876–86, *American Literature and Other Papers, ed. Whittier, p.* 89.

To Jared Sparks, himself a rather unimaginative man, I owe the early conviction, confirmed by reading Hawthorne, that imagination is a desirable quality for an historian.—HIGGINSON, THOMAS WENTWORTH 1886, *How I was Educated, The Forum, vol.* 1, *p.* 178.

With Jared Sparks, though not in him, appeared the latest and highest development of historical study and writing in America. Not an investigator of the highest order, not a writer who could set forth historical statements with the best rhetorical skill, and not the author of any single work to be compared with the masterpieces of his greater contemporaries, Sparks shared and promoted in good measure the later studies from which so valuable results were attained. . . . Jared Sparks was not a historian in the higher sense, though it is customary to rank him with the better American writers. He was not an analyst like Bancroft; he lacked the rhetorical and descriptive power of Prescott; nor, of course, could he be analyst and painter in one, like Motley. He was by nature a collector and arranger of materials, rather than one who, like Gibbon, could draw from them a connected story. His lives of Washington and Franklin are but extended prefaces to his collections of their writings. He left no original work of the highest class to which the student can point as Sparks' own achievement. Again, he lacked the power of sharply separating the good and the bad in a man's character, and of describing both in an impartial and instructive manner. He was unduly fond of eulogizing his subjects; —the besetting sin of American writers "before the war," a sin not yet fully atoned and corrected. But without his useful labors later writers would have lacked a needed helper. Valuable material might have perished; and historical study, both in the author's library and at the reader's table, would have lost a great stimulus. Patience and industry, with an unfaltering determination to discover and preserve all original documents of importance, were qualities which marked Sparks' mind and directed his life-work.— RICHARDSON, CHARLES F., 1887, *American Literature*, 1607–1885, *vol.* I, *pp.* 454, 458.

Mr. Sparks' letters show characteristic formality and attention to details. His letter-books contain copies, in another hand, of his most important answers to historical and other questions that were submitted to him. These letters and the wealth of knowledge which they contain are memorials of those quiet but useful years from 1853 to 1866. The extent, variety, and more or less occasional character of these writings do not admit their reproduction in the limited space of these closing chapters of a memorial volume. Suffice it to say, they all served the end for which they were written; they have entered into the thought and literary compositions of other men. The names of Mr. Sparks' contemporaries, who sought historical aid from him or his collections, indicate something of the living currents into which the tributary influence of his knowledge flowed. The speeches and books of other men bear witness to his friendly coöperation. Among those who most frequently turned to Mr. Sparks for help or suggestion were Edward Everett, George Bancroft, Charles Sumner, Robert C. Winthrop, George Ticknor, William E. Prescott, and Francis Lieber.—ADAMS, HERBERT B., 1893, *The Life and Writings of Jared Sparks, vol.* II, *p.* 556.

Though not educated in Germany, Sparks, with his untiring energy in the accumulating and arrangement of material, and his unusual power of making other people work systematically, was very like a sound German scholar. He really established a large historical factory; with skilled help, he collected all the raw material he could find; and he turned out something like a finished article in lengths to suit,—somewhat as his commercial contemporaries spun excellent cotton. In a mechanical way his work was admirable; he really advanced New England scholarship; and he may be said to have founded that school of earnest historical study which to this day remains so energetic and distinguished at the college of which he was a faithful professor and president. If neither Ticknor nor Sparks contributed to permanent literature, the names of both are closely connected with that of the first man in New England who wrote history in a spirit as literary as that of Gibbon or Macaulay.—WENDELL, BARRETT, 1900, *A Literary History of America, p.* 268.

Until a few years ago the writings of Washington were as much in need of a new editor as ever Shakespeare's were. Original manuscripts had been tampered with seriously, and there had come to light a vast store of new and significant material. Our demands of editors and publishers had much altered since the times of Jared Sparks. Textual integrity and the whole story have been exacted with relentless precision. Discretion in an editor has ceased to have the meaning it had formerly, scrupulous devotion to the text has so greatly modified the nature and extent of his function. The custom of abusing Sparks when opportunity offers fails to take sufficient account of this change. He lived in times different from ours. Not only was he hampered by the limited mass of material then accessible; the needs and requirements of the public imposed limitations upon him. These were of the simplest kind. Irving's commendation of Sparks illustrates this. For the most part the work of Sparks was pioneer work in the truest sense. We can only appreciate the extent and value of it all when we consider the state our history would be in if he had failed to do the work which we are now wont to abuse him for not doing better.—HALSEY, FRANCIS WHITING, 1902, *Our Literary Deluge and Some of Its Deep Waters, p.* 65.

John Pierpont

1785–1866

John Pierpont was born in Litchfield, Conn., April 6, 1785. He was graduated at Yale College in 1804, and went to South Carolina as a private tutor. He returned in 1809, studied law at Litchfield, and settled in Newburyport, Mass. A few years later he was in business in Baltimore with John Neal, and they became bankrupt in 1816. Mr. Pierpont then studied theology, completing his course at Harvard, and in 1819 was ordained pastor of the Hollis Street Congregational Church in Boston. In 1845 he accepted a call to the Unitarian Church in Troy, N. Y., and in 1849 to Medford, Mass., which last pastorate he resigned in 1856. He was chaplain of a Massachusetts regiment in 1861, but in the same year was appointed to a clerkship in the Treasury Department, which he held till his death. This took place in Medford, Mass., August 27, 1866. Mr. Pierpont published "Airs of Palestine" in 1816, and reissued it with additions, under the title "Airs of Palestine, and other Poems," in 1840. He read a long poem at the Litchfield Centennial in 1851, and published several sermons and addresses.—JOHNSON, ROSSITER, 1875, *Little Classics, Authors, p.* 198.

PERSONAL

The mightiest of the Hebrew seers,
Clear-eyed and hale at eighty years,
From Pisgah saw the hills and plains
Of Canaan, green with brooks and rains.
Our poet, strong in frame and mind,
Leaves eighty well-spent years behind;
And forward looks to fields more bright
Than Moses saw from Pisgah's height.
Yet be our Pierpont's voice and pen
Long potent with the sons of men;
And late his summons to the shore
Where he shall meet his youth once more.

—BRYANT, WILLIAM CULLEN, 1865, *To the Rev. John Pierpont on his Eightieth Birthday, April* 6.

He was tall, straight, and spare—six feet, I should say, and rather ungraceful, in fact, though called by the women of his parish not only the most graceful but the most finished of gentlemen. That he was dignified, courteous, and prepossessing, very pleasant in conversation, a capital story-teller, and a tolerable—no, intolerable—punster, exceedingly impressive both in the pulpit and elsewhere, when much in earnest, and in after life a great lecturer and platform speaker, I am ready to acknowledge; but he wanted ease of manner—the readiness and quiet self-possession of a high-bred man, who cannot be taken by surprise, and is neither afraid of being misunderstood nor afraid of letting himself down—till after he had passed the age of threescore. The first impression he made on me was that of a country schoolmaster, or of a professor, on his good behavior, who had got his notions of the polite world from Chesterfield; though, when I knew him better, and learned that he had been a tutor in the Alston family of South Carolina, I detected the original type

of his perpendicularity, serious composure, and stateliness,—the archetype.—NEAL, JOHN, 1866, *John Pierpont, Atlantic Monthly, vol.* 18, *p.* 655.

Mr. Pierpont united within himself the characteristics of two very distinct persons. One was graceful, cultivated, delicate, fastidious to the last degree, careful of etiquette, studious, dignified; with a certain loftiness of dignity, indeed, which strangers were apt to find somewhat frigid, but genial and expansive with his friends, and beautifully tender and loving with children. This was the clergyman and the poet. The other was an ardent knight, armed for battle, and seeking it far and near,—battle to the death with everything that was foul and mean; 'and the ancient oath of chivalry, by which the young knight vowed to "protect the distressed, maintain right against might, and never by word or deed to stain his character as a knight and a Christian," was no unfit or exaggerated expression of the spirit in which this modern champion took on his armor. Quick to discover injustice, he no sooner unearthed a new wrong than he attacked it with the fiery ardor of a nature whose enthusiasm was but the hotter for the restraint which the habits and tastes of the scholar ordinarily imposed upon it. He used all his weapons at once,—logic, sarcasm, invective, poetry, pathos,—and sharpened them all with a stern "Thus saith the Lord." This was John Pierpont the Reformer; and twenty-five years ago, few names rang wider throughout the careless, prosperous land than this.—CUMMINGS, C. A., 1866, *John Pierpont, Christian Examiner, vol.* 81, *p.* 375.

He was tall, strong-limbed and energetic,

possessing a very original mind and a directness of purpose which was never turned aside by questions of self-interest. Even to the verge of offence, and finally beyond it, he preached the duty of men to God and to each other, fearless of personal consequences. . . . . As an honest and fearless preacher, he was an honour to the pulpit; as a poet, his verses will always be included in any collection that fairly represents the lyrical talent of the period; as a promoter of education, his school-books were in use in every New England academy; and as a practical inventor, the "Pierpont stove," and even a very serviceable razor-strop attested his claims to the title of "universal genius."—TUCKERMAN, CHARLES K., 1895, *Personal Recollections of Notable People, vol.* I, *p.* 42, 43.

AIRS OF PALESTINE
1816

Had it been an indifferent poem, we should have noticed it in a more summary way, and passed over faults we despaired of correcting; but it has too much taste and beauty to be made the mere basis of an essay and dismissed without scrutiny; and if this superiority has given a proportionate prominence to its defects, Mr. Pierpont must be content to suffer the common penalty of eminence. Yet though we have endeavored to speak of it with perfect impartiality, we fear, on looking back on our remarks, we have not said so much in its praise as it deserves; we have passed without notice many of its beauties, and if our censures have in any instance done injustice to Mr. Pierpont, our readers who may be induced to purchase the book will at least acquit us of disappointing them by unmerited praise.—DEXTER, F., 1817, *Airs of Palestine, North American Review, vol.* 4, *p.* 420.

It is tame, badly arranged, incomplete—and worse than all—afflicted with plagiarism, imitation, and alliteration. Yet, is it, nevertheless, full of beauty—with a few eloquent—a few good—and a few great, passages in it.—NEAL, JOHN, 1825, *American Writers, Blackwood's Magazine, vol.* 17, *p.* 200.

The "Airs of Palestine" have been favorably known to the literary community for many years. On a subject — the effects of music — often enough handled by the poets, from Pindar down to Gray, Mr. Pierpont, nothing daunted by the mighty names who have preceded him, has certainly given us one of the most pleasing poems which yet adorn our literature. The beauty of the language, the finish of the versification, the harmony of the numbers, secure it an undisputed place among the few American classical works.—PALFREY, JOHN GORHAM, 1840, *Pierpont's Poems, North American Review, vol.* 51, *p.* 479.

For beauty of language, finish of versification, richness of classical and sacred allusions, and harmony of numbers, we consider that it takes rank among the very first of American poems and will be among those that will survive their century. But Mr. Pierpont has aimed at something more than gratifying his own scholarly tastes and charming his readers with the love of the beautiful. He is a reformer, a whole-hearted and a fearless one; and a large number of his fugitive pieces have been written to promote the holy causes of temperance and freedom.—CLEVELAND, CHARLES D., 1859, *A Compendium of American Literature, p.* 292.

GENERAL

His rhythm is at least equal in strength and modulation to that of any poet in America. Here he resembles Milman and Croly.—POE, EDGAR ALLAN, 1841, *A Chapter on Autography, Works, ed. Stedman and Woodberry, vol.* IX, *p.* 200.

The religious sublimity of the sentiments, the beauty of the language, and the finish of the versification, placed it ["Airs of Palestine"] at once, in the judgment of all competent to form an opinion on the subject, before any poem at that time produced in America. As a work of art, it would be nearly faultless, but for the occasional introduction of double rhymes, a violation of the simple dignity of the ten-syllable verse, induced by the intention of the author to recite it in a public assembly. . . . Mr. Pierpont has written in almost every metre, and many of his hymns, odes, and other brief poems are remarkably spirited and melodious. Several of them, distinguished alike for energy of thought and language, were educed by events connected with the moral and religious enterprises of the time, nearly all of which are indebted to his constant and earnest advocacy for much of their prosperity.—GRISWOLD, RUFUS WILMOT, 1842, *The Poets and Poetry of America, pp.* 52, 53.

Wrote numerous hymns and odes for

religious and national occasions, remarkable for their variety of difficult metres, and for the felicity both of the rhythm, sentiment, and expression. His "Airs of Palestine," a long poem of heroic verse, has many eloquent passages; and several of his minor pieces, especially those entitled "Passing Away" and "My Child," are striking examples of effective versification. The most popular of his occasional poems is "The Pilgrim Fathers," an ode written for the anniversary of the landing at Plymouth, and embodying in truly musical verse the sentiment of the memorable day.—TUCKERMAN, HENRY T., 1852, *A Sketch of American Literature.*

A complete collection of Mr. Pierpont's verses would contain much that was not poetry, but only measured prose. But it would also contain a dozen pieces in which the thought is wholly divorced from any moral or political motive, and in which the imagination is so bright and pure, and the expression so graceful and happy, as to entitle their author to a very high place among the poets of the century. First among these is, of course, the little dream called "Passing Away." We have no desire to exaggerate, but we are strongly of the opinion, that no poem has yet been written by any American author which possesses in so high a degree as this the qualities of true imaginative poetry. The poetry, we grant, is not of the highest order. The thought is but commonplace. But the succession of pictures is painted in colors at once so vivid and so harmonious, that we must go back to Keats for a parallel; and with a tenderness and purity of feeling which Wordsworth could not surpass.—CUMMINGS, C. A., 1866, *John Pierpont, Christian Examiner, vol.* 81, *p.* 377.

Mr. Pierpont was one of the best hymnwriters of America. He was a genuine poet, as well as a powerful preacher and stern reformer. His imagination took a bold, strong wing, and his fine lyric verse was inspired with the ardor and nobleness of his own great soul. Fiery as some of his pieces are in their rebuke and denunciation of injustice and cruelty, yet there are others which are remarkable for their tenderness and pathos, and betray the sweetness and love that lay hidden beneath his rugged face, and imperial, war-like manner. His songs as well as his sermons throb with intense devotion to truth and goodness, to country and humanity, and to that better church of God, that is yet to be.—PUTNAM, ALFRED P., 1875, *ed. Singers and Songs of the Liberal Faith, p.* 30.

Whatever else may have been his qualifications, he was a real poet, and also a wit. I have always thought that some parts of his "Airs of Palestine" were among the best specimens of American poetry.—MANSFIELD, E. D., 1879, *Personal Memories, p.* 126.

A most zealous reformer. Pierpont powerfully advocated the anti-slavery and temperance causes . . . In addition to his numerous poems, Pierpont published many addresses and discourses, and edited a popular series of school readers. A short time before his death, at Medford, in his native state, the writer spent an evening with the well-preserved old poet and his second wife, and found him at fourscore still in the enjoyment of vigorous health and strength. When I asked Pierpont which he preferred among his many poems, he replied, "The one called 'Passing Away,'"—which is certainly among the sweetest in American literature; I once heard it read by the elder Vandenhoff, the "passing away" sounding like the echoes of a distant bell.—WILSON, JAMES GRANT, 1886, *Bryant and his Friends, p.* 381.

His "Airs of Palestine," 1816, gave him a wide popularity. He wrote very voluminously both in prose and verse, his poems being chiefly hymns and odes written for various occasions, but his fame, like the refrain of his best-known poem, is "passing away."—PATTEE, FRED LEWIS, 1896, *A History of American Literature, p.* 168.

His patriotic lyrics are among the best and most spirited in our literature. His hymns and odes for anniversary and other celebrations are all in clear, vigorous, Saxon English. "The Fugitive Slave's Apostrophe to the North Star," "The Gag" and "The Tocsin" are among the best of our anti-slavery lyrics. "A Word from a Petitioner" is memorable as containing one of our "familiar quotations." He has given at least one beautiful lyric, which, as a creation of pure fancy as distinguished from imagination, is unsurpassed in American poetry. His "Passing Away," in its fanciful conception and melodious diction, suggests what its author was capable of doing in the direction of pure literature.—ONDERDONK, JAMES L., 1899–1901, *History of American Verse, p.* 128.

Francis Mahony

(Father Prout)

1805–1866

Born at Cork and educated in his native city, and afterwards at a college of the Jesuits abroad, where he acquired the intimate knowledge of Latin which was such a prominent characteristic of his scholarship. He entered the Roman Catholic priesthood, but practised his profession for only about two years, officiating during that time at the Chapel of the Bavarian Legation, London. In 1834 he commenced to contribute to *Fraser's Magazine* the "Prout Papers," which were modelled on the "Noctes Ambrosianæ" of *Blackwood*, and had for their *non de plume* the name of a Roman Catholic priest, who had lived for many years at Watergrass Hill in the County of Cork. In 1864 he visited Rome as the special correspondent of the London *Daily News*, and during the last years of his life was the foreign correspondent of the London *Globe* at Paris.—RANDOLPH, HENRY FITZ, 1887, ed. *Fifty Years of English Song, Biographical and Bibliographical Notes, vol.* IV, *p.* 21.

PERSONAL

He (Thackeray) said Father Prout was "good but dirty!"—FIELDS, JAMES T., 1859, *Diary, Biographical Notes and Personal Sketches, p.* 69.

The loneliness and celibacy of his life developed a certain oddity which always belonged to him. His dress was curiously negligent. He looked up at you with his keen blue eyes, over his spectacles, turning his head to one side, like some strange old bird; told an anecdote, or growled out a sarcasm, or quoted "Horace," with a voice still retaining a flavour of the Cork brogue; then, making no salutation of any kind and sticking his hands in his coat-pockets, he shot off, and his dapper little black figure disappeared around the corner. There was a half-cynical indifference to life, and even to literature, about the old Father in his last years; but, as the evening wore on, a strange little well of sentiment would bubble up in his talk, and remind you that he was the author of the "Bells of Shandon," as well as of endless epigrams.—HANNAY, JAMES, 1866, *Recent Humourists, North British Review, vol.* 45, *p.* 103.

I would do much when appealed to in the name of our common friend Mahony. How can I make the very nothings I shall be able to tell you—which yet are all I remember and like "characteristic points" in the man whom I knew so little, and liked so much—into something worthy of record? I met him first at Emerson Tennent's, many years ago. We talked and agreed about Rabelais and Erasmus, disagreeing as notably when he undervalued Spenser. I henceforth continued to meet him about town, generally in Regent Street. I never knew where he lived; he used to disappear and return as

unexpectedly, and our communication was a Latin word or two of greeting: "Where have you been?" His answer, "at Constantinople,"—"at Rome,"—a classical goodbye, and there an end.—BROWNING, ROBERT, 1868, *Letter to Blanchard Jerrold, June 5; Final Relics of Father Prout, p.* 61.

Of the manner of man he was, the space he filled in intellectual society at home and abroad; his quaint sayings; his genial outbursts of sentiment, sometimes more candid than courtly; his stern sense of right; his reverence for religion, and hatred of scoffers; his unqualified religious toleration, which caused him, whilst they were proud of him, to be looked on coldly by the men of his cloth; his rare gifted and discriminating mind; his most sympathetic heart—all these traits and features of his personal character and history may be traced through the various anecdotes and sketches supplied to this volume by friends who knew him long and intimately.—JERROLD, BLANCHARD, 1876, *ed. The Final Reliques of Father Prout, Preface, p.* xiii.

Francis Mahony—or, as he called himself, O'Mahony, better known as Father Prout—was a kindred spirit, with the same mixture of fun, learning, and fluency which distinguished Maginn. The fact that he was a priest, with something of an academical aspect even at his wildest, lent a certain piquancy to the strange Bohemian with his fine and delicate countenance, and the touch of sentiment which mellowed his mirth. He is called by somebody "an Irish potato seasoned with Attic salt," and the comparison has a certain appropriateness.—OLIPHANT, MARGARET O. W., 1882, *Literary History of England, XVIII-XIX Century, vol.* III, *p.* 220.

"Father Prout" spent most of his latter years in Paris, living the life of a mingled anchorite and sensualist. He occupied an attic there, where I once saw him, toasting a mutton-chop on which he was about to dine, while on a corner of his table, among letters and MSS., was laid a not very clean *serviette*—his table-cloth. But in these later years of Mahony's life his room of reception was the reading room at Galignani's, where, however, he seldom held any intercourse with his kind, usually entering, remaining for an hour or two, and departing without exchanging a word with any one; and if earth gave him any sources of enjoyment they were not those to which the good, the generous, the sympathetic resort for happiness. He was not often a visitor to London; but I believe he was rarely in the metropolis without paying a visit to us. Yet he never came with any apparent motive in view, and sometimes his conversation as to past, present, and future, was limited to half a dozen sentences. Occasionally he would enter our drawing-room, keep his hands in his pockets, look all about him, make some such observation as, "You have changed your curtains since I was here last," bid us good-morning, and retire, his visit, from first to last, having perhaps occupied some three minutes. Few, I imagine, looked on Mahony with regard—none, probably, with respect. His was an unlovely as well as a lonely life.—HALL, SAMUEL CARTER, 1883, *Retrospect of a Long Life, p. 382.*

When I knew him there was still a touch of the clerical in his costume, as he was always in black, but he had ceased to be a Jesuit in anything but name. He could not be called a denizen of the London Bohemia, but was domiciled in its outskirts, visiting occasionally the haunts of the more reputable of its inhabitants, for even the Bohemia of those days had its class distinction. He invited me to have a chat with him in the old office of the *Globe*, then a Liberal organ, to the staff of which he was attached, and for which the malicious averred he wrote, without stirring from the Strand, what professed to be correspondence from Rome. He was a genial, kindly little man, whose blue eyes looked at you over his spectacles, and who spoke in an undertone with a slightly Milesian accent. In a dark and dingy room of the *Globe* office he poured into my willing ears the early story of *Fraser's Magazine*, with racy anecdotes of

its founders, all of which were reproduced in the *Critic*. In his last years he was Paris correspondent of the *Globe*, and did really write his letters in Paris, where he died. They buried him in his native Cork, within earshot of those "bells of Shandon" of which he sang in still-remembered rhymes.— ESPINASSE, FRANCIS, 1893, *Literary Recollections and Sketches, p. 369.*

GENERAL

If Francis Mahony, otherwise Prout, has preferred all along the service of literature to that of his Church, he has paid homage to his spiritual mother all the same. One of his best essays is on "Literature and the Jesuits," where he cordially recognises and pleasantly describes what the Order which bred him has done for the field of action which tempted him. Nay, he pays a handsome compliment to his Church by choosing to embody himself in this very figure of a priest in the county of Cork, by which he is pleased to be represented. No man can separate himself from his traditions and early associations even if he tries. But a wise and generous man does not choose to try. He adores his own Sparta, though he may grumble at her modern government, and be tired of her black broth. There is no separating Carlyle altogether from Scotch Presbyterianism; and the cosmopolitan Mahony, known as well at Rome as at London, and at Paris as at either, has the kind of genius and accomplishments natural to an Irish Catholic and an Irishman of the South.— HANNAY, JAMES, 1860, *Father Prout, The Universal Review, Feb.*

Nothing is more disappointing to the Irish reader of the volume before us than the marked absence of Irish flavour in its pages. Were we to judge from this volume alone we should boldly assert that the sayings of the great Irish wit were neither wit nor Irish. There is some humour in the fragment which forms chapter IV. There is much interesting information and acute observation in the letters from Rome. But as for wit, there is none. Still worse, the laboured attempts at it are remarkable either for savageness or stupidity. I fear the former quality, associated with some vanity, was often shown by the great Padre. . . . In the next place, even jokes of general interest, and of cosmopolitan charcter, are often nothing when severed from the connection in which they occur, from the temper of the company and from the general tone of the conversation which led up to them. These considerations are sufficient to make us pronounce no general verdict on Father Prout from these his recorded conversations; nay, rather, the great repute of the man leads us to believe that he was far wittier and more brilliant in talking than in writing, and that, as with most Irishmen, his pen was weaker than his tongue. . . . Father Mahony was a very clever *litterateur*, a happy translator into various languages, a very brilliant essayist, an unmatched correspondent; but as an original thinker or poet he has left no mark beyond his own circle.—MAHAFFY, JOHN PENTLAND, 1875, *The Final Reliques of Father Prout, The Academy, vol.* 8, *pp.* 645, 646.

Mahony was rather possessed of his learning than the master of it like Maginn, and entirely lacked the vigor, conciseness, and strength of the latter. His illustrations and quotations were, however, sometimes happy as well as curious, and one of his translations, a paraphrase of Béranger's "Le Grenier," is among the happiest in the English language, having both the grace and spirit of the original, and a felicity of rhythm that thoroughly accented it in the mind. There have been many translations of the poem, but none that rivals this of Mahony.—WILLIAMS, ALFRED M., 1881, *The Poets and Poetry of Ireland, p.* 280.

We may quote, however, one snatch of characteristic verse, which has something in it of the visionary home-sickness and tender longing of an exile. To have heard Mahony sing this, an old man, leaning his fine old head, like a carving in ivory, against the mantelshelf, in a cracked and thready voice which had once been fine, is a pathetic memory. Between the melodious commonplace of Moore's melodies and the wild and impassioned ravings of the Shan Van Voght this more temperate type of Irish verse with its characteristic broken melody, its touch of mockery, its soul of tender if not profound resemblance, is wholesome and grateful, though it has no pretension to be great.—OLIPHANT, MARGARET O. W., 1882, *Literary History of England, XVIII–XIX Century, vol.* III, *p.* 220.

I had a deference for Mahony from what I had been told of his courageous discharge of his duties as a priest during the prevalence of an epidemic in St. Giles's, and I had an admiration for him because of his sprightly, scholarly, daintily-lettered style. When he died, a gentleman, whose name I choose to forget, had the hardihood to think he could replace and reproduce him. He stepped into his shoes but did not fill them. What a lamentable misfit! Mahony's writing had the fresh scent of learned allusion, spontaneously springing from the text. This gentleman's smelt offensively of the concordance.—O'SHEA, JOHN AUGUSTUS, 1885, *Leaves from the Life of a Special Correspondent, vol.* I, *p.* 117.

Mahony had personally less amiability than is proverbial with Irish humorists, and his cosmopolitan culture often obscured in his more scholarly essays the character of his nationality. But vivacity was rarely absent, and in both his prose and verse he grew at times so hilarious as to bring him on the verge of nonsense. Elsewhere, as in his essay on "Dean Swift's Madness," he showed himself capable of pathetic eloquence. He himself claimed to be "a rare combination of the Teian lyre and Irish bagpipe; of the Ionian dialect, blending harmoniously with the Cork brogue; an Irish potato, seasoned with Attic salt."—LEE, SIDNEY, 1893, *Dictionary of National Biography, vol.* XXXV, *p.* 338.

Nathaniel Parker Willis

1806–1867

Nathaniel Parker Willis, poet and essayist, born Portland, Me., 1806; died "Idlewild," near Newburgh, N. Y., 1867. Won at Yale, where he was graduated, 1827, a prize for the best poem. His earliest verses appeared in the "Youth's Companion" and "Boston Recorder," both founded by his father. In 1829, he established the "American Monthly Magazine," afterwards the "New York Mirror." In 1831 he visited Europe and the East, contributing letters to the "Mirror." A rebuke from Capt. Marryat in the "Metropolitan Magazine," for reporting private interviews, led to a bloodless duel. In 1839 he published the "Corsair," to which Thackeray contributed. In 1846 he founded, with G. P. Morris, the "Home Journal," remaining associate editor till his death, at the estate on the Hudson which he purchased in 1846 and named "Idlewild." Published

"Poetical Scripture Sketches," 1827; "Melanie, and Other Poems," "Lady Jane, and Other Poems," 1844; and many volumes of brilliant prose sketches, letters, travels, etc. A complete edition of his poems appeared in 1868.—STEDMAN, EDMUND CLARENCE, *ed.* 1900, *An American Anthology, Biographical Notes, p.* 832.

PERSONAL

Agreeable I found Mr. Willis, and kindly in his way, though flimsy in his acquirements and flashy in his manners—a thorough literary getteron, but a better-natured one than many I have since known.—CHORLEY, HENRY FOTHERGILL, 1834, *Autobiography, Memoir and Letters, p.* 171.

He makes invidious, uncharitable, and ill-natured remarks upon authors and their works; all of which he dispatches for the benefit of the reading public of America, and, at the same time that he has thus stabbed them behind their backs, he is requesting to be introduced to them—bowing, smiling, and simpering. . . . Although we are well acquainted with the birth, parentage, and history of Mr. Willis, previous to his making his continental tour, we will pass them over in silence; and we think that Mr. Willis will acknowledge that we are generous in so doing. . . . It is evident that Mr. Willis has never, till lately, been in good society, either in England or America. —MARRYAT, FREDERICK, 1836, *Metropolitan Magazine.*

I have just returned from bidding Willis farewell, and feel nearly as much regret as on leaving home; for I never met with one in my life who has won my regard and esteem in so short a time. . . . I will talk a little more about Willis. Griswold intended giving me a letter of introduction, but had no time. I called at his house, and on telling my name he knew me instantly. On apologizing for calling without a letter, he said it was unnecessary, as we knew each other already, and began conversing as familiarly as if we had been old friends. . . · I have been at his house three or four times, and when, this afternoon, he gave me his parting "God bless you," I felt as if I had left a true friend. I have not time now to give you much of his conversation, but it is daguerreotyped on my memory. He looks very much like the portrait in "Graham's Magazine," but not quite so young, although at times, when he becomes animated, you would not take him to be more than twenty-four; dresses with neatness and the most perfect taste, and has the very *beau idéal* of a study,—you can conceive of nothing more elegant. In fact, his poetry is visible in everything around him. —TAYLOR, BAYARD, 1844, *Letter to J. B. Phillips, June* 30; *Life and Letters, ed. Taylor and Scudder, vol.* I, *pp.* 39, 40.

He is yet young, and, without being handsome, in the ordinary sense, is a remarkably well-looking man. In height he is, perhaps, five feet eleven, and justly proportioned. His figure is put in the best light by the ease and assured grace of his carriage. His whole person and personal demeanor bear about them the traces of "good society." His face is somewhat too full, or rather heavy, in its lower portions. Neither his nose nor his forehead can be defended; the latter would puzzle phrenology. His eyes are a dull bluish gray, and small. His hair is of a rich brown, curling naturally and luxuriantly. His mouth is well cut; the teeth fine; the expression of the smile intellectual and winning. He converses little, *well* rather than fluently, and in a subdued tone.—POE, EDGAR ALLAN 1846, *The Literati, Works, ed. Stedman and Woodberry, vol.* VIII, *p.* 19.

I lately made a day's excursion up the Hudson, in company with Mr. and Mrs. M— G— and two or three others, to visit Willis in his poetical retreat of Idlewild. It is really a beautiful place, the site well chosen, commanding noble and romantic scenery; the house commodious and picturesque, and furnished with much taste. In a word, it is just such a retreat as a poet would desire. I never saw Willis to such advantage as on this occasion. . . . Willis talks and writes much about his ill-health, and is really troubled with an ugly cough; but I do not think his lungs are seriously affected, and I think it likely he will be like a cracked pitcher, which lasts the longer for having a flaw in it, being so much the more taken care of.—IRVING, WASHINGTON, 1854, *To J. P. Kennedy, Aug.* 31; *Life and Letters, ed. Irving, vol.* IV, *p.* 175.

He is a tall, dashing looking fellow, dressed rather in the extreme of fashion, yet in good taste, and with an air of fashionable languor about him. Nodding familiarly to the General [Morris], who smilingly returns his salute, he drops into a chair, stretches out his well-shaped legs, and, coquetting with a cigar, appears to watch the circling blue rays of smoke that soar to the ceiling. The stranger might be called handsome; certainly he *has* been so, but time and the pen have left their traces on his face; evidently he cultivates the Graces, although the enemy has thinned his curling locks, which are jauntily disposed over a fine forehead. His eyes are blue, and have much vivacity in their expression, but at their outer angles are those unmistakable evidences of coming age—crows'-feet. The cheeks are not so plump and fresh-looking as they must have appeared ten years ago, and they have a yellowish tinge, which travel or good living might have caused. The nose is short and slightly *retroussé*, the mouth delicately curved and the chin systematically chiselled. The shape of the face is round, and when the "dew of youth" rested on it, it must have been intellectually handsome, despite the dash of effeminacy that characterises it.—DIX, JOHN ROSS, 1854, *Bungay's Crayon Sketches and Off-Hand Takings, p.* 47.

I have simply stated the facts because, in the first place, I do not wish to be considered one of Mr. Willis's friends; and, in the next, it may be useful, and conducive to justice, to show, by a practical instance, what Mr. Willis's pretensions to intimacy are worth. His countrymen and countrywomen accept, in simplicity, his accounts of our aristocracy as from the pen of one of their own coterie; and they may as well have the opportunity of judging for themselves whether their "Penciller" is qualified to write of Scotch Dukes and English Marquises, and European celebrities of all kinds in the way he has done.—MARTINEAU, HARRIET, 1855-77, *Autobiography, ed. Chapman, vol.* I, *p.* 386.

I had the pleasure of meeting Mr. Willis on many occasions at Gore House, to which reference is made in the rather too celebrated "Pencilings by the Way," and also at the soirées of the late Lady Charleville, in Cavendish Square. Mr. Willis was an extremely agreeable young man in society, somewhat overdressed, and a little too demonstrative, but abounding in good spirits, pleasing reminiscences of Eastern and Continental travel, and of his residence there for some time as attaché to a foreign legation. He was observant and communi-

cative, lively and clever in conversation, having the peculiar art of making himself agreeable to ladies, old as well as young; degagé in his manner, and on exceedingly good terms with himself and with the élite of the best society wherever he went.—MADDEN, RICHARD ROBERT, 1855, *The Literary Life and Correspondence of the Countess of Blessington, vol.* II, *p.* 329.

I knew Mr. Willis very well indeed, and have passed many delightful hours at his house, while he resided in New York. He had committed many errors in his life—as who has not? But, unlike some, age purified him. I recollect meeting him one day in Broadway, when his salutation to me was, "I am sixty years old to-day!" I first became acquainted with him in New Haven, when I was a mere boy, and he was at the zenith of his fame. . . . . He was always an immense dandy, and there was a college tradition that while there he dressed in white broadcloth, which he had imported expressly for himself from England. —FIELD, MAUNSELL B., 1873, *Memories of Many Men and of Some Women, p.* 225.

Procter could sometimes be prompted into describing that brilliant set of men and women who were in the habit of congregating at Lady Blessington's, and I well recollect his description of young N. P. Willis as he first appeared in her *salon.* "The young traveler came among us," said Procter, "enthusiastic, handsome, and good-natured, and took his place beside D'Orsay, Bulwer, Disraeli, and the other dandies as naturally as if he had been for years a London man about town. He was full of fresh talk concerning his own country, and we all admired his cleverness in compassing so aptly all the little newnesses of the situation. He was *ready* on all occasions, a little too ready, some of the *habitués* of the *salon* thought, and they could not understand his cool and quite-at-home manners. He became a favorite at first trial, and laid himself out determined to please and be pleased. His ever kind and thoughtful attention to others won him troops of friends, and I never can forget his unwearied goodness to a sick child of mine, with whom, night after night, he would sit by the bedside and watch, thus relieving the worn out family in a way that was very tender and self-sacrificing.—FIELDS, JAMES T., 1875, "*Barry Cornwall" and Some of His Friends, Harper's Magazine, vol.* 51, *p.* 782.

Once in a while, a tall, slim-waisted, broad-shouldered young fellow of a little more than thirty [1840], with curling, light-brown hair, trained a little in the direction of ringlets, an affectation of foreign beard, and somewhat more of other affectation than boded well for his eventual reputation, dropped in on the circle. He had also an addiction to colored coats and D'Orsay neckties, and was named Nat Willis—Nathaniel P. Willis, as he should have written the name; N. Parker Willis as he did write it generally. . . . Englishmen, then, and even earlier, knew him far better than they knew any other American; and it is betraying no secret to say that they disliked him not a little because he observed too closely. A rather affected but very charming talker, whose affectations were smoothed if not hidden by his evident talent and coveted wide experience—undeniably handsome, and knowing the fact far too well—really warm-hearted, though many mistook the cold polish for the heart it covered —a wise fool, who had and has many brothers on the earth, not all of them with the same redeeming qualities—such was Nat Willis, whom Father Prout was already lampooning as "Nick Willis," when the writer met him first in these reunions.— MORFORD, HENRY, 1880, *John Keese, His Intimates; Morford's Magazine, June.*

I also remember two men who graduated in the class of 1827, that were frequently pointed out to me as its most conspicuous members. One was the son of a very prominent statesman, which, in fact, explained the notice he attracted; but there was enough of individuality about John Van Buren to command attention. He had already revealed the traits which distinguished him in after life,—easy and careless in manner, bold in character, and of an aggressive turn of mind. His rival in notoriety had no hereditary claims to support him, but he was gifted with a rare poetical talent that had already secured him distinction both in and out of college. His tone and bearing were aristocratic, not unmixed with *hauteur*, and though admired for his abilities he never commanded the sympathies of his comrades. Such was N. P. Willis, and such he remained to the end of his life.—WIKOFF, HENRY, 1880, *Reminiscences of an Idler.*

Nathaniel Parker Willis was in full bloom when I opened my first Portfolio. He had made himself known by his religious poetry, published in his father's paper, I think, and signed "Roy." He had started the "American Magazine," afterwards merged into the "New York Mirror." He had then left off writing scripture pieces, and taken to lighter forms of verse. He had just written

"I'm twenty-two, I'm twenty-two,—
    They idly give me joy,
As if I should be glad to know
    That I was less a boy."

He was young, therefore, and already famous. He came very nearly being very handsome. He was tall; his hair, of light brown colour, waved in luxuriant abundance; his cheek was as rosy as if it had been painted to show behind the footlights; he dressed with artistic elegance. He was something between a remembrance of Count D'Orsay and an anticipation of Oscar Wilde. There used to be in the gallery of the Luxembourg a picture of Hippolytus and Phædra, in which the beautiful young man, who had kindled a passion in the heart of his wicked step-mother, always reminded me of Willis, in spite of the shortcomings of the living face as compared with the ideal. The painted youth is still blooming on the canvas, but the fresh-cheeked, jaunty young author of the year 1830 has long faded out of human sight. I took the leaves which lie before me as I write, from his coffin, as it lay just outside the door of Saint Paul's Church; on a sad, overclouded winter's day, in the year 1867. At that earlier time, Willis was by far the most prominent young American author.— HOLMES, OLIVER WENDALL, 1885–95, *A Mortal Antipathy, Works, Riverside Ed., vol.* VII, *p.* 4.

He never renounced definitely his Christian belief. He never became skeptical; was not at any time, in fact, a thinker on such themes and subject to the speculative doubts which beset the thinker. He remained through life easily impressible in his religious emotions.—BEERS, HENRY A., 1885, *Nathaniel Parker Willis (American Men of Letters), p.* 96.

A tall and elegant figure, with rosy cheeks and a luxuriance of clustering hair, which upwards of fifty winters had failed to whiten, enters with the easy grace of a man of the world, and we see before us our friend the master of the mansion.—WILSON, JAMES GRANT, 1885, *Bryant and His Friends, p.* 312.

Willis was a dandy of the first water, in manners, dress, and conversation, while he was also a hard worker, after his fashion of literary work, but he was not a student. Willis at this time [1827], drove a square-topped gig, being that two-wheeled vehicle known as a Boston "chaise," but with a square instead of a bellows top, the leather sides of which were rolled up in fine weather, disclosing short green silk curtains on the inside. His horse, which he named Thalaba, was a tall, high-stepping bay, as showy as his master. His whip was the fashionable "bow whip" of the period, common enough now, to be sure, with a long lash, tapering down to a fine silk "snapper" on the end.— CURTIS, GEORGE TICKNOR, 1890, *Reminiscences of N. P. Willis and Lydia Maria Child, Harper's Magazine, vol.* 81, *p.* 718.

Next door to us lived a family in which were four daughters who grew up to be famous belles. It is said that when the poet N. P. Willis visited them, one of these young ladies, who was familiar with his works, was so overcome that she fainted. Forty years after Willis distinctly recalled the circumstance. Fainting was then fashionable. — LELAND, CHARLES GODFREY, 1893, *Memoirs, p.* 4.

POETRY

Mr. N. P. Willis enjoys, we believe, some reputation in his own country as a writer of verses. A volume of his rhymes was lately reprinted here, under the auspices of Mr. Barry Cornwall; but notwithstanding that editor's authority, the contents seemed to us of very slender merit—much upon a par with the young ladies' imitations of Wordsworth, Byron, and Moore, which crowd the gilded pages of our own *Annuals.*—LOCKHART, JOHN GIBSON, 1835, *Willis's Pencillings by the Way, Quarterly Review, vol.* 54, *p.* 455.

Upon a general view of these poems, we think we are justified in pronouncing Mr. Willis a poet of great and varied powers. In some attributes of the poetic character, we should hardly know where to look for his superior. His sensibility to beauty, whether of external nature, or of the human form, is ever alive. He enjoys richly and freely the breath of heaven, the sunshine, and the splendor of the star-crowned night; earth and sky are perpetual ministers to his imagination. His language is almost always choice, and descriptive. By the power of

finely selected words, he brings every variety of landscape before us; and the myriad voices of Nature seem to be uttered in his magical tones. Such is the richness, so captivating the sweetness of his verse, that many readers fail to discover the depth, variety, and power of his poetry. There is sometimes an over-daintiness of expression that naturally enough makes a fastidious delicacy, rather than strength, to be regarded as his leading characteristic. . . . The dramatic sketch of "Lord Ivon and his Daughter," and the Scripture piece, "Hagar in the Wilderness," show his power of entering into, and nobly expressing, the higher passions of human nature. Still it must be acknowledged, that Mr. Willis has too strong an inclination for finely turned lines, and repeats too often a few favorite expressions.—FELTON, CORNELIUS CONWAY, 1836, *Willis's Writings, North American Review, vol.* 43, *p.* 406.

The prose and poetry of Mr. Willis are alike distinguished for exquisite finish and melody. His language is pure, varied, and rich; his imagination brilliant, and his wit of the finest quality. Many of his descriptions of natural scenery are written pictures; and no other author has represented with equal vivacity and truth the manners of the age. His dramatic poems have been the most successful works of their kind produced in America. They exhibit a deep acquaintance with the common sympathies and passions, and are as remarkable as his other writings for affluence of language and imagery, and descriptive power. His leading characteristics are essentially different from those of his contemporaries. Dana and Bryant are the teachers of a high, religious philosophy; Halleck and Holmes excel in humour and delicate satire; Longfellow has a fine imagination and is unequalled as an artist; but Willis is more than any other the poet of society.—GRISWOLD, RUFUS WILMOT, 1842, *The Poets and Poetry of America, p.* 277.

We think highly of the drama ["Tortesa"] as a whole, and have little hesitation in ranking it before most of the dramas of Sheridan Knowles. Its leading faults are those of the modern drama generally—they are not peculiar to itself—while its great merits *are*.—POE, EDGAR ALLAN, 1845, *The American Drama, Works, ed. Stedman and Woodberry, vol.* VI, *p.* 219.

Mr. Willis first became popular with a

class on account of his sacred poems. These are still much admired. Our first impression was with his admirers, but our more matured judgment is bound to state that they lack the very soul of sacred poetry, simplicity and earnestness. They are too elegant to be sublime, and breathe more of the perfumer's shop than the fragrant incense of the altar.—POWELL, THOMAS, 1850, *The Living Authors of America, p.* 81.

Though Mr. Willis's prose writings are full of beauty and wit, of rich paintings of natural scenery, and delicate and humorous touches of the various phases of social life, it is by his poetry, especially by his sacred poetry, that he will be chiefly known and prized by posterity. There is a tenderness, a pathos, and a richness of description in it which give him a rank among the first of American poets.—CLEVELAND, CHARLES D., 1859, *A Compendium of American Literature, p.* 555.

There was that in his Scripture poems that suited the popular taste, which was caught by their melodious versification and their picturesque description. That they were precisely what they should not have been, —were artificial when they should have been simple, and pretty when they should have been severe,—in other words, that they violated the spirit of the old Biblical narratives of which they were a recension, —was of no consequence, since their admirers were not critical. He wrote finer poems in "Saturday Afternoon," in "The Annoyer," and his lines "To a Belfry Pigeon," but they were less highly thought of. Young as he was when these compositions flowed from his pen, he was better equipped for the literary profession than any of his contemporaries. He knew enough to serve the purpose he had in view,—had an instinctive tact that supplied his lack of experience, insight that divined what would be acceptable, and capacity to create it if it did not exist, cleverness, adroitness, versatility.—STODDARD, RICHARD HENRY, 1890, *Nathaniel Parker Willis, Lippincott's Magazine, vol.* 45, *p.* 109.

GENERAL

In Mr. Willis's case, the result has been, that while visiting about in London and in our provinces as a young American sonneteer of the most ultra-sentimental delicacy, he was all the time the regular paid correspondent of a New-York journal, in which, week after week, appeared his prose reports of what he saw and heard in British society—these same fifty letters which now lie collected on our table, and which, we greatly fear, will tend to throw obstacles in the path of any American traveller who may happen to honour England with his presence during the next season or two. Mr. Willis's prose is, we willingly admit, better than his verse: it has many obvious faults, especially those of exaggeration and affectation; but it is decidedly clever, and the elements of what might be trained into a really good style are perceptible. He has depicted some of our northern "scenes" in a not unpleasing manner; and his descriptions of "customs and manners" are often amusing—bearing the impress of shrewdness and sagacity, but deriving their power of entertainment chiefly from the lights which they reflect on the customs and manners of the author's own country.—LOCKHART, JOHN GIBSON, 1835, *Willis's Pencillings by the Way, Quarterly Review, vol.* 54, *p.* 456.

"Pencillings by the Way" is a very spirited book. The letters, out of which it is constructed, were written originally for the New York "Mirror," and were not intended for distinct publication. From this circumstance, the author indulged in a freedom of personal detail, which we must say is wholly unjustifiable, and we have no wish to defend it. This book does not pretend to contain any profound observations or discussions on national character, political condition, literature, or even art. It would be obviously impossible to carry any one of these topics thoroughly out, without spending vastly more time and labor upon it, than a rambling poet is likely to have the inclination to do. . . . There are passages in it of graphic eloquence, which it would be difficult to surpass from the writings of any other tourist whatever. The topics our author selects, are, as has been already stated, not those which require long and careful study to appreciate and discuss; they are such as the poetic eye would naturally dwell upon, and a poetic hand rapidly delineate, in a cursory survey of foreign lands. Occasionally, we think, Mr. Willis enters too minutely into the details of the horrible. Some of his descriptions of the cholera, and the pictures he gives us of the catacombs of the dead, are ghastly. But the manners of society he draws with admirable tact; and personal peculiarities of distinguished men, he renders with a most life-like vivacity. — FELTON, CORNELIUS CONWAY, 1836, *Willis's Writings, North American Review, vol.* 43, *pp.* 407, 410.

It has been the fate of this gentleman to be alternately condemned *ad infinitum* and lauded *ad nauseam*, a fact which speaks much in his praise. We know of no American writer who has evinced greater versatility of talent, that is to say, of high talent, often amounting to genius, and we know of none who has more narrowly missed placing himself at the head of our letters.—POE, EDGAR ALLAN, 1841, *A Chapter on Autography, Works, ed. Stedman and Woodberry, vol.* IX, *p.* 197.

There is Willis, all *natty* and jaunty and gay,
Who says his best things in so foppish a way,
With conceits and pet phrases so thickly o'er-
    laying 'em,
That one hardly knows whether to thank him
    for saying 'em;
Over-ornament ruins both poem and prose,
Just conceive of a Muse with a ring in her nose!
His prose had a natural grace of its own,
And enough of it, too, if he'd let it alone;
But he twitches and jerks so, one fairly gets
    tired,
And is forced to forgive where he might have
    admired;
Yet whenever it slips away free and unlaced,
It runs like a stream with a musical waste,
And gurgles along with the liquidest sweep;—
'Tis not deep as a river, but who'd have it
    deep?
—LOWELL, JAMES RUSSELL, 1848, *A Fable for Critics.*

There is a want of naturalness in Mr. Willis's writings which will inevitably affect their continuance, and we have doubts whether any of his numerous prose works will remain permanent portions of Literature.—POWELL, THOMAS, 1850, *The Living Authors of America, p.* 78.

I almost passed by Willis—"ah, *miboy*
Foine morning! da-da!" Faith I wish him
    joy—
He's forty-three years old—in good condi-
    tion—
And, positively, he has gained "position."
Gad! what a polish "upper-ten-dom" gives
This executioner of adjectives;
This man who strangles English worse than
    Thuggists,
And turns "the trade" to trunk-makers or
    druggists;
Labors on tragic plays that draws no tears—
Writes under bridges, and tells tales of peers;
His subjects Whey—his language sugared
    curds;

Gods! What a dose!—had he to "eat his
    words!"
His "Sacred Poems," like a rogue's confes-
    sions,
Gain him indulgence for his worst transgres-
    sions:
His "Fugitive Attempts" will doubtless live,
Oh! that more works of his were fugitive!
Fate to his fame a ticklish place has given,
Like Mahomet's coffin, 'twixt the earth and
    heaven;
But be it as it will—let come what may—
Nat is a star, his works—the Milky Way!
—DUGANNE, AUGUSTINE J. H., 1851, *Parnassus in Pillory.*

Beyond most writers of our country, he adorns whatever he touches; that without claiming to fathom the depths of philosophy, or yielding often to the tide of passion, he possesses a certain subtle alchemy of genius, resting on a basis of acute and just observation, which transmutes the most commonplace topic, and invests it with grace and beauty. — KENDRICK, ASAHEL CLARK, 1860, *The Life and Letters of Mrs. Emily C. Judson, p.* 99.

The tales and prose sketches of N. P. Willis are characterized by genial wit, and a delicate rather than a powerful imagination, while beneath his brilliant audacities of phrase there is a current of original thought and genuine feeling. Commanding all the resources of passion, while he is at the same time master of all the effects of manner, in the power of ingenious and subtle comment on passing events, of sketching the lights and shadows which flit over the surface of society, or playful and felicitous portraiture of individual traits, and of investing his descriptions with the glow of vitality, this writer is unsurpassed.—BOTTA, ANNE C. LYNCH, 1860, *Hand-Book of Universal Literature, p.* 521.

It ["Letters from Under a Bridge"] showed all his graceful ease, with something nearer to thought than he elsewhere gave his readers.—HIGGINSON, THOMAS WENTWORTH, 1874, *Charles Dudley Warner, Scribner's Monthly, vol.* 7, *p.* 332.

We can imagine no good to come from "attaining" a style by studying other men, except, perhaps, to cover up the literary coxcombry of such writers as Willis.—HOLLAND, JOSIAH GILBERT, 1876, *Every-Day Topics, First Series, p.* 22.

Though marred by occasional affectation, the sketches of Willis are light, graceful compositions.—CHAMBERS, ROBERT, 1876,

Cyclopædia of English Literature, ed. *Carruthers*.

His early Scripture sketches, written when he was a student of Yale, gave him the reputation of a promising genius; and though the genius did not afterward take the direction to which its first successes pointed, it gained in strength and breadth with the writer's advancing years. In his best poems he displayed energy both of thought and imagination; but his predominant characteristics were keenness of observation, fertility of fancy, quickness of wit, shrewdness of understanding, a fine perception of beauty, a remarkable felicity in the choice of words, and a subtle sense of harmony in their arrangement, whether his purpose was to produce melodious verse or musical prose. But he doubtless squandered his powers in the attempt to turn them into commodities.—WHIPPLE, EDWIN PERCY, 1876-86, *American Literature and other Papers*, ed. *Whittier*, p. 83.

Laying aside all question of appeal to that formidable tribunal, posterity, the many contemporaries who have owed hours of refined enjoyment to his graceful talent will join heartily with Thackeray in his assertion: "It is comfortable that there should have been a Willis."—BEERS, HENRY A., 1885, *Nathaniel Parker Willis* (*American Men of Letters*), p. 352.

In the library catalogues we find a long list of works attributed to his pen. Most of these are volumes made up from his ceaseless contributions to magazines and to his own journal. Of these, the "Pencillings by the Way" have still an interest for us; and they may, perhaps, be read by posterity. The volume of his poems, and that alone, enjoys considerable popularity. For the benefit of young writers, I may add that Mr. Willis never slighted his work, but bestowed upon every thing he did, even upon slight and transient paragraphs, the most careful labor, making endless erasures and emendations. On an average, he erased one line out of every three that he wrote; and, on one page of his editorial writing, there were but three lines left unaltered. He wrote very legibly, too, and gave no printer cause to complain of him. Even his erasures were made with a certain wavy elegance, and done so effectually that one could make out what had been written.— PARTON, JAMES, 1885, *Some Noted Princes, Authors and Statesmen of Our Time*, p. 311.

What an eye that man had for colour, and what an ear for music!—MORRISON, A. H., 1886, *The Art Gallery of the English Language*, p. 187.

Even the fop of American letters, shallow, frivolous, clever Willis, always wrote smoothly and with an air of good breeding. — MABIE, HAMILTON W., 1892, *The Memorial Story of America*, p. 588.

Nathaniel P. Willis, with his smooth and shallow versifications of Scripture, his animated, amiable letters, held a large and edified audience. — BATES, KATHARINE, LEE, 1897, *American Literature*, p. 105.

For our own generation it cannot be said that Willis himself has any vital importance, yet he cut a prodigious figure in his own time. . . . The contrast between Willis and Poe, in the nature of the men and of their work, is sufficiently striking; yet Willis in many ways is separated as distinctly from the two men whose names are always linked together in American literary annals, Fitz-Greene Halleck and Joseph Rodman Drake. Willis does not seem to have felt that it was better to live by one poem than to die with many books; at least he did not proceed upon such a theory, and to-day there is not one thing he wrote which is even as well known as his name.—HOWE, M. A. DeWOLFE, 1897-98, *American Bookmen*, pp. 99, 113.

Much of his work was brilliant persiflage; it shrunk under critical touch. Nor was it easy to sketch knowingly this poet's contacts with social life, and his ambitions and triumphs there, and at the same time weigh understandingly his higher tastes and accomplishments. Those accomplishments were indeed very real, though of a special quality. It might almost be said that his accomplishments undid him. In his latter years—for the behest of admiring readers—he was over-fond of always putting his thought (or rather his observations and suggestions) into a finical millinery of language; charging and fatiguing himself, to avoid plainness of speech—as much as ever an accredited modiste (who has studied colors all her life) wearies and worries herself to kill simplicities by the aggregation of her tints and furbelows.—MITCHELL, DONALD G., 1899, *American Lands and Letters, Leather-Stocking to Poe's "Raven,"* p. 98.

Satirists ridiculed his foppery, but he outlived the satirists. No American writer was more eagerly sought by the editors or more eagerly read by the public. His unfortunate choice of subjects, his diffusiveness, his flippancy, and what some regarded as his snobbishness, were matters with which the public concerned itself but little. He wrote to please, and succeeded. He struck a comparatively new vein in American poetry, and worked it to the utmost advantage. Whatever his faults, hypocrisy was not one of them. He detested the hard, barren realism of rural life, and refused to join the general chorus that was forever chanting the beauties of rustic simplicity. . . . He possessed no broad, general culture, indeed slight intellectual force, and still slighter poetic imagination. But he gave us much of the best in his time. Many of his lines have become household phrases, and he unquestionably enriched our literature by contributing some of its best lighter lyrics. —ONDERDONK, JAMES L., 1899–1901, *History of American Verse, pp.* 145, 147.

He was a man of far wider social experience than Bryant or Cooper, probably indeed than Irving himself; and those who personally knew him remember him, as Dr. Holmes did, pleasantly and kindly. Yet, after all, one feels in him rather the quality of a dashing adventurer, of an amiably honourable Bohemian, than such secure sense of personal distinction as marked Bryant and Irving and their contemporaries in New England. A school of letters in which a man of Willis's quality could attain the eminence which for years made him conspicuous was certainly declining.—WENDELL, BARRETT, 1900, *A Literary History of America, p.* 228.

Typical of the fate of the most brilliant of ephemeral writers is the fate that has overwhelmed Nathaniel Parker Willis. It has been the fashion of a generation to speak slightingly of him and of his work, and that fashion has been revived whenever his writings have been called to public attention. If the remoteness of Willis from our times has served somewhat to soften the terms in which judgement was formerly passed, the essential verdict remains what it was thirty or forty years ago. If ever a man of letters was a writer for his own day and for no other day, it was Willis. Not only his topics and his personality, but his peculiar mental constitution, seem to have been such as made it impossible he should do anything entitled to survive even for fifty years. If he had any of the qualities of genius, it was capacity for work, which indeed he had in considerable abundance, and yet what he did appears always to have been done with so much ease that one is tempted to qualify the importance even of this quality. . . . The writings of Willis have fallen into neglect; that was predestined from the nature of them, and in the main this was quite deserved. His prose writings are, I believe, out of print, though his poems still have some sale—about two hundred copies annually. . . . If Willis chose to write what he could sell at good price, than write what he believed would live,—in other words, if he preferred Willis's way to Hawthorne's way,—perhaps it is only the stern moralist who would condemn him. He at any rate had small literary ambition, and scarcely pretended to be more than he was, for which some credit is due to him. He was no rival of the men who have survived him. But surely this was not the fault of Willis; he was incapable of becoming their rival. He had talents, but lacked noble ambition. Therein lies the pathos of his life.—HALSEY, FRANCIS WHITING, 1902, *Our Literary Deluge and some of its Deep Waters, pp.* 94, 102, 103.

Fitz-Greene Halleck
1790–1867

Fitz-Greene Halleck was born in Guilford, Conn., July 8, 1790. He received a common school education, and became clerk in a store in Guilford. From 1811 till 1832 he was employed in a banking-house in New York City. He then entered the service of John Jacob Astor, of whose business and estate he kept the accounts till Astor's death, in 1848. Astor left him an annuity of $200. In 1849 he retired to Guilford, to live with an unmarried sister, and resided there during the remainder of his life. He never married. Halleck's earliest poem which has been preserved is "Twilight," which appeared originally in the New York "Evening Post," in 1818. In March, 1819, he formed a literary partnership with Joseph Rodman Drake, and they wrote the papers which in that year appeared in the "Post" under the signature of "Croaker & Co." Later in the year Halleck wrote his longest poem, "Fanny," a satire, which was very popular in its day.   The lines on Drake appeared originally in the "Evening Post." . . . Halleck travelled in Europe in 1822–23, and in 1827 published anonymously a volume containing "Marco Bozzarris," "Burns," and "Alnwick Castle."   In 1832 he edited an edition of Byron, and in 1840 "Selections from the British Poets."   He died in Guilford, Nov. 17, 1867.   A complete edition of his works has been prepared by James Grant Wilson, who has also written his life.—JOHNSON, ROSSITER, 1875, *Little Classics, Authors, pp.* 113, 114.

PERSONAL

Personally, he is a man to be admired, respected, but more especially beloved. His address has all the captivating *bonhomie* which is the leading feature of his poetry, and, indeed, of his whole moral nature. With his friends he is all ardor, enthusiasm, and cordiality; but to the world at large he is reserved, shunning society, into which he is seduced only with difficulty, and upon rare occasions.   The love of solitude seems to have become with him a passion.   He is a good modern linguist, and an excellent belles-lettres scholar; in general, has read a great deal, although very discursively.   He is what the world calls *ultra* in most of his opinions, more particularly about literature and politics, and is fond of broaching and supporting paradoxes.   He converses fluently, with animation and zeal; is choice and accurate in his language, exceedingly quick at repartee, and apt at anecdote.   His manners are courteous, with dignity and a little tincture of Gallicism. His age is about fifty.   In height he is probably five feet seven.   He *has been* stout, but may now be called well-proportioned.   His forehead is a noble one, broad, massive, and intellectual, a little bald, about the temples; eyes dark and brilliant, but not large; nose Grecian; chin prominent; mouth finely chiselled and full of expression, although the lips are thin; his smile is peculiarly sweet.—POE, EDGAR ALLAN, 1846, *The Literati, Works, ed. Stedman and Woodberry, vol.* VIII, *p.* 56.

I give to my friend Fitz-Greene Halleck an annuity of two hundred dollars, commencing at my decease, and payable half-yearly for his life, to be secured by setting apart so much of my personal estate as may be necessary; which I intend as a mark of regard for Mr. Halleck.—ASTOR, JOHN JACOB, 1848, *Will.*

With such advantages of physiognomy and manners, so winning a look and voice, how is it that Fitz-Greene Halleck has never let himself be known to audiences? With his well-won fame as the poet whom

everybody is ready to admire, he retires to his remote home in Connecticut, coming to New York only as the most retiring of visitors to the most secluded of hotels— thus "biding his time," while hundreds upon hundreds of those who appreciate and fervently admire him do not even know him by sight!   Halleck's genial countenance, and, still more, his full and genial cadences of voice, suited him especially for a lecturer. What a pity that so admirably-formed a creature should die (as he is likely to!) without the eye-and-ear homage for which Nature gifted him!—WILLIS, NATHANIEL PARKER, 1864, *Letters from Idlewild, Home Journal, June.*

Halleck was a bachelor, living in modest lodgings, and avoiding society, regular in his habits, even, it is said, to the stated number of glasses of brandy-and-water; but I have met few men who talked better, or who lighted up in conversation with a finer enthusiasm.   A wit and a *bon vivant,* he was also deeply religious, and, though educated a Connecticut Puritan, was a zealous Roman Catholic, and maintained that every man who really thought upon the matter must come to the same conviction.—NICHOLS, THOMAS L., 1864–75, *Forty Years of American Life.*

Our friend is gone, and to those of us who knew him the world seems the dimmer for his departure.—BRYANT, WILLIAM CULLEN, 1869, *Fitz-Greene Halleck, Orations and Addresses, p.* 193.

With the few whom Fitz-Greene Halleck liked, and with whom he associated on equal terms, he was genial, graceful, never wanton of speech, and always full of chat and pleasant humor; apt always and prompt at reply; with that spirit of repartee and easy wit which makes so much of the charm and spirit of the "Croaker" epistles.   His geniality, with such a circle, was always active; and he relished nothing better than a snug and select party, "fit though few." He was both socially and politically a natural aristocrat, and did not cheapen himself by any too easy entrance into society. He required to respect men, *mentally*, before associating with them, and seemed to me to revolt from all associations of trade, in spite of all his life-long connection with it, and, perhaps, because of that connection.—SIMMS, WILLIAM GILMORE, 1869, *To James Grant Wilson, Life and Letters of Fitz-Greene Halleck, ed. Wilson, p. 544.*

Mr. Halleck never received any compensation for the poems he contributed to the *Evening Post, National Advocate,* and other journals and magazines, extending over a period of nearly twenty years—years during which his most admired productions were published. Halleck appears to have written with the most unselfish indifference to fame or pecuniary reward, for, up to the year 1839, neither on the title-pages of his published volumes, nor with his single contributions to the press, did his name appear. . . . The whole sum received by Mr. Halleck for the various editions of his poems, including his poetical contributions to periodicals, was sixteen thousand dollars. If to this are added one thousand for editing Byron's works, and half that amount for making his selections from the British poets, we have a total of seventeen thousand five hundred dollars as the amount received by the poet for the literary labors of a lifetime.—WILSON, JAMES GRANT, 1869, *Life and Letters of Fitz-Greene Halleck, pp. 442, 532.*

> We o'er his turf may raise
> Our notes of feeble praise,
> And carve with pious care for after eyes
> The stone with "Here he lies;"
> He for himself has built a nobler shrine,
> Whose walls of stately rhyme
> Roll back the tides of time,
> While o'er their gates the gleaming tablets shine
> That wear his name inwrought with many a golden line!

—HOLMES, OLIVER WENDELL, 1869, *Poem —At the Dedication of the Halleck Monument, July 8.*

I used very often to see the poet Fitz-Greene Halleck, but had not a personal acquaintance with him. He was stiff, angular, and clean-shaved; wore a high, standing shirt-collar, and in the finest weather carried a green cotton umbrella under his arm.— FIELD, MAUNSELL B., 1873, *Memories of Many Men and of Some Women, p. 223.*

His features were not handsome, but the clear, mellow manliness of his expression made them seem so. His forehead, however, was nobly arched, indicating a large and well-proportioned brain, and it was balanced by a finely formed chin. He was a little under the medium height, but his erect carriage, even as an old man, and his air of natural dignity, had the effect of adding somewhat to his stature. I have never seen a man who was so simply and inevitably courteous; he was an incarnate *noblesse oblige.* — TAYLOR, BAYARD, 1877, *Fitz-Greene Halleck, North American Review, vol. 125, p. 64.*

He was a great favorite in society; was constantly noticed by magazines and newspapers at home and abroad; was the recipient of frequent public honors; but was so modest that he could hardly be persuaded to speak. . . . He was very happy in conversation, and could be infinitely satirical. Even out of his limited means, he was generous to a fault. In religion his toleration was supreme; and, though not a Catholic, he frequently attended the Catholic services.—FORNEY, JOHN W., 1881, *Anecdotes of Public Men, vol. II, pp. 269, 270.*

Something about him, I can scarcely say what, reminded me of Lamb, whose odd and fantastic tastes I sometimes fancied I detected in his whimsical talk. He was courtly and liberal in his literary opinions, except with regard to two English poets who then stood highest in popular favor, and who, for reasons which were incomprehensible to me, were his aversion. He had a conventional, last-century intellect, and found nothing to admire, but much to deride, in Tennyson and Browning. Campbell still possessed the early charm for him, and I shall never forget the warmth with which he defended the character of that poet from the aspersions which had been cast upon it by his whilom understrapper in the management of the *New Monthly Magazine,* Cyrus Redding, to which I somewhat injudiciously drew his attention. . . . He was fluent and animated in his conversation, which was rather in the vein of monologue than dialogue, but not so distinct in his enunciation as I could have wished. There was still a brightness in the eye over which age was beginning to draw its filmy curtain, and which sometimes seemed to emit sparks in the heat of talk. There was that within him which "o'er-informed this tenement of clay," though it did not wear out his pygmy body. For Halleck, as I recall his figure through the lapse of years, was somewhat diminutive in stature and slight of build; and if at one time I was reminded of Lamb, I was reminded at another of Barry Cornwall, whose sensitive, delicately-chiselled features he appeared to possess.—STODDARD, RICHARD HENRY, 1889, *Fitz-Greene Halleck, Lippincott's Magazine, vol.* 43, *pp.* 895, 896.

FANNY
1819

I do not think much of the merits of the work, the plague of correcting the proof-sheets, etc., having put me out of conceit with it, and I fear that its localities will render it almost entirely uninteresting to you. The book-seller stated to me that I was the only writer in America, Irving excepted, whose works he would risk publishing. This opinion was founded, of course, upon the popularity of "The Croakers." I do not anticipate the same popularity for this work. "The Croakers" cost the public nothing, this costs them fifty cents, which will have, no doubt, an effect in limiting the number of readers.—HALLECK, FITZ-GREENE, 1820, *To his Sister, Jan.* 1; *Life and Letters of Fitz-Greene Halleck, ed. Wilson, p.* 232.

Your pieces, if, as I suppose, you are the author of those signed "Croaker," have been read in the newspapers with great interest, but "Fanny" is of a higher order, and for its easy conversational wit, and poetry of descriptions, must go alongside of Lord Byron's and Mr. Rose's productions in the same way. It is the admiration of your poetical talents which has led me to make this communication to you, and to request, if you feel inclined to give your pieces a circulation among your Eastern brethren, you would sometimes select the *Club-Room* as the medium of communication. I find no difficulty as the editor in obtaining compositions in prose, but it is otherwise in poetry, which, as it is not necessary to publish, we feel unwilling to publish unlesss it is particularly good, and I know of no source from which I could be so likely to obtain this as from the author of "Fanny."—PRESCOTT, WILLIAM H., 1820, *To Halleck, March* 15; *Life and Letters of Fitz-Greene Halleck, ed. Wilson, p.* 239.

If we except a certain gentlemanly ease and insouciance, with some fancy of illustration, there is really very little about this poem to be admired. There has been no positive avowal of its authorship, although there can be no doubt of its having been written by Halleck. He, I presume, does not esteem it very highly.—POE, EDGAR ALLAN, 1846, *The Literati, Works, ed. Stedman and Woodberry, vol.* VIII, *p.* 52.

"Fanny," Halleck's longest poem, and one which was the perpetual delight of John Randolph of Roanoke, was published anonymously in December, 1819, and, though suggested by the current topics, incidents, and public men of that day, still retains to a remarkable degree the popularity which it at once acquired on its first appearance. . . . It has frequently been called a parody or imitation of "Don Juan," but Mr. Halleck assured me that it was written before he saw Lord Byron's poem, published the same year. He adopted the versification of "Beppo," one of Byron's minor poems. . . . The popularity of "Fanny" was so great, that the publisher offered Halleck five hundred dollars for another canto, an offer which he accepted, and in 1821 a second edition appeared, enlarged by the addition of fifty stanzas. Before its appearance, the poem had become so scarce that it sold for fabulous prices—ten dollars having been frequently paid for a copy of the thin pamphlet of forty-nine pages, originally published at fifty cents. Its authorship was attributed to a number of prominent literary men, but, except in a few instances, suspicion never rested upon Mr. Halleck.—WILSON, JAMES GRANT, 1869, *Life and Letters of Fitz-Greene Halleck, pp.* 230, 231, 234.

I confess, to me it is the flattest, tamest, dreariest of comic poems that have won any note. It was thought by some to have been inspired by "Don Juan;" but the fine distinction has latterly been made that it resulted from a perusal of Byron's "Beppo," a poem in the same style and stanza. "Beppo," however, has a plot, and therefore finishes itself; and Halleck failed to imitate it in this advantageous particular. The second part which he afterward provided does not remedy the defect. A more serious objection is that the wit is thin and scattered. Then the poem is so much taken up with wandering that it has no time for poetry. I find the intercalated song of the Horse-Boat a total enigma, when considered in the light of the praise it has received. Neither does the description of New York as seen from Weehawken appear to sustain the honors which have been bestowed upon it. . . . It was probably the surprise which people felt at seeing provincial Manhattan treated in verse of any sort that captivated the early readers of "Fanny."—LATHROP, GEORGE PARSONS, 1877, *Fitz-Greene Halleck, Atlantic Monthly, vol.* 39, *pp.* 721, 722.

There is no story in "Fanny," or none to speak of; and the most that one can say of it is that it is an imaginary sketch of the social experiences of its heroine, the daughter of a shopkeeper in Chatham Street, who having amassed what was then considered a comfortable little fortune, proceeded to make a brilliant brief splurge in society, and concluded his career by going where the woodbine twineth. To depict the mortifying experiences of a parvenu's daughter ought not to have been difficult, but it was more than the unpractised pen of Halleck could accomplish; for, flimsy in intention and feeble in execution, "Fanny" was dreary reading, because the author after writing what he probably considered a poetic passage immediately spoiled it by sticking his tongue in his cheek. A certain amount of antiquarian interest attaches to his pointless verse, and there is a pretty description of Weehawken, which was one of his favorite suburban resorts. What the subject-matter of such a poem as "Fanny" could be in the hands of a true poet was shown at a later period by Thomas Hood in "Miss Kilmansegg."—STODDARD, RICHARD HENRY, 1889, *Fitz-Greene Halleck, Lippincott's Magazine, vol.* 43, *p.* 892.

MARCO BOZZARIS
1827

"Marco Bozzaris" has much lyrical without any great amount of *ideal* beauty. Force is its prevailing feature,—force resulting rather from well-ordered metre, vigorous rhythm, and a judicious disposal of the circumstances of the poem than from any of the truer lyric material. I should do my conscience great wrong were I to speak of "Marco Bozzaris" as it is the fashion to speak of it, at least in print. Even as a lyric or ode it is surpassed by many American and a multitude of foreign compositions of a similar character.—POE, EDGAR ALLAN, 1846, *The Literati, Works, vol.*VIII, *p.* 54.

The corner-stone of his glory.—CLEVELAND, CHARLES D., 1859, *A Compendium of American Literature, p.* 407.

When Doctor Mott visited Europe, he met Rosa, the youngest daughter of Marco Bozzaris, justly styled "the Epaminondas of modern Greece," who bore a striking resemblance to the hero. She was studying the English language, that she might read Halleck's poems in the original, and with charming frankness and *naïveté* said she had an ardent desire to go to America expressly to see the poet who had immortalized her father.—WILSON, JAMES GRANT, 1869, *Life and Letters of Fitz-Greene Halleck, p.* 291.

Halleck was so much an amateur that if he had not been so much more a real workman, he would have fallen into the third rank. It was amateurish, his failure to know at once, on finishing "Marco Bozzaris," that he had written a great poem. He handed it to a business companion, asking, "Will that do?" But when we read it, *we* say, "Cannot this man do everything?" There is brilliant, perfect workmanship in it; there is splendid command of the sympathies. Is not the writer a master? One hour's crowned session on the throne makes a king; but I do not think that one effort of power, even so impressive as this, gives a right to the title of master, in poetry. Halleck gives us too many blurred pages and broken staves. — LATHROP, GEORGE PARSONS, 1877, *Fitz-Greene Halleck, Atlantic Monthly, vol.* 39, *p.* 728.

GENERAL

As a poet, Mr. Halleck ranks very high. He has not written much, but what he has written is almost faultless. If tenderness and warmth of feeling, playfulness of fancy, imagery, not abundant, but appropriate, and great copiousness and invariable euphony of language, constitute a claim to excellence, his effusions are excellent.— LEGGETT, WILLIAM, 1828, *New York Mirror, Jan.* 26.

Dear Halleck, Nature's favorite and mine,
Cursed be the hand that plucks a hair of thine:
Accept the tribute of a muse inclined
To bow to nothing, save the power of mind.
Bard of Bozzaris, shall thy native shore
List to thy harp and mellow voice no more?
Shall we, with skill like thine so nigh at hand,
Import our music from a foreign land?
While Mirror Morris chants in whimpering note
And croaking Dana strains his screech-owl throat;
While crazy Neal to metre shakes his chains,
And fools are found to listen to his strains;

While childish Natty P. the public diddles,
And Lunt and Rockwell scrape his second
  fiddles;
While Brooks, and Sands, and Smith, and
  either Clark,
In chase of Phœbus howl and yelp and bark,
Wilt thou be silent? Wake, O Halleck, wake!
Thine and thy country's honor are at stake!
Wake and redeem the pledge—thy vantage
  keep;
'Tis pity one like thee so long should sleep!
—SNELLING, JOSEPH, 1831, *Truth, A New
Year's Gift for Scribblers.*

The purest fountain of poetical inspiration, in the loftier strain of "Alnwick
Castle," tuned by a bard of our own native
land.—ADAMS, JOHN QUINCY, 1836, *Speech
in the House of Representatives, Jan.* 14.

Sometimes in the midst of a strain of
harmonious diction, and soft and tender
imagery, he surprises by an irresistible
stroke of ridicule, as if he took pleasure in
showing the reader that the poetical vision
he had raised was but a cheat. Sometimes,
with that aërial facility which is his peculiar
endowment, he accumulates graceful and
agreeable images in a strain of irony so fine
that, did not the subject compel the reader
to receive it as irony, he would take it for
a beautiful passage of serious poetry—so
beautiful that he is tempted to regret that
he is not in earnest, and that phrases so exquisitely chosen, and poetic coloring so
brilliant, should be employed to embellish
subjects to which they do not properly belong. At other times he produces the effect
of wit by dexterous allusion to contemporaneous events, introduced as illustrations
to the main subject, with all the unconscious gracefulness of the most animated
and familiar conversation. He delights in
ludicrous contrasts, produced by bringing
the nobleness of the ideal world into comparison with the homeliness of the actual;
the beauty and grace of Nature with the
awkwardness of Art. He venerates the
past, and laughs at the present. He looks
at them through a medium which lends to
the former the charm of romance, and exaggerates the deformity of the latter.—
BRYANT, WILLIAM CULLEN, 1836, *New York
Mirror.*

Mr. Halleck is the only one of our poets
who possesses a decided local popularity.
With the subjects of "Fanny," the "Croakers," and some of his other pieces, every
person in NewYork is in some degree acquainted, and his name is cherished in that
city with fondness and enthusiasm. His
humorous poems are marked with an uncommon ease of versification, a natural, unstudied flow of language, and a careless
playfulness and felicity of jest. . . . Halleck's serious poems are as admirable as his
satirical. There are few finer martial lyrics
than "Marco Bozzaris;" "Burns" and
"Red Jacket" are distinguished for manly
vigour of thought and language; and several
of his shorter pieces have rarely been excelled in melodiousness of versification or
quiet beauty of imagery.—GRISWOLD, R.W.,
1842, *The Poets and Poetry of America, p.* 172.

The name of Halleck is at least as well
established in the poetical world as that of
any American. Our principal poets are,
perhaps, most frequently named in this order—Bryant, Halleck, Dana, Sprague,
Longfellow, Willis, and so on—Halleck
coming second in the series, but holding, in
fact, a rank in the public opinion quite
equal to that of Bryant. The accuracy of
the arrangement as above made may, indeed, be questioned. For my own part I
should have it thus—Longfellow, Bryant,
Halleck, Willis, Sprague, Dana.—POE, ED-
GAR ALLAN, 1846, *The Literati, Works, ed.
Stedman and Woodberry, vol.* VIII, *p.* 50.

There goes Halleck, whose Fanny's pseudo
  Don Juan,
With the wickedness out that gave salt to the
  true one,
He's a wit, though, I hear, of the very first or-
  der,
And once made a pun on the words soft Re-
  corder;
More than this, he's a very great poet, I'm told,
And has had his works published in crimson
  and gold,
With something they call "Illustrations," to
  wit,
Like those with which Chapman obscured Holy
  Writ. . . .
In his verse a clear glimpse you will frequently
  find,
If not of a great, of a fortunate mind,
Which contrives to be true to its natural loves
In a world of back-offices, ledgers, and stoves.
When his heart breaks away from the brokers
  and banks,
And kneels in its own private shrine to give
  thanks,
There's a genial manliness in him that earns
Our sincerest respect (read, for instance, his
  "Burns"),
And we can't but regret (seek excuse where we
  may)
That so much of a man has been peddled away.
—LOWELL, JAMES RUSSELL, 1848, *A Fable
for Critics.*

My Dear Halleck: I must send you a line to report to you the substance of a delightful conversation I had with Rogers about you last week. He asked Lady Davy, at one of his breakfasts, if she had read your poems; she answered no. "Shame on you," said he; "he has written some things which no poet living has surpassed, and you shall not be ignorant of him any longer." The book was brought, and Rogers read in his best manner several passages from "Alnwick Castle," the greater part of "Marco Bozzaris," and a few of the shorter pieces. He then laid down the volume and entertained us with a beautiful tribute to your merit as a poet.—COGSWELL, JOSEPH G., 1849, *To Halleck, June 15; Life and Letters of Fitz-Greene Halleck, ed. Wilson, p.* 273.

The author of "Fanny" possesses many qualities calculated to make him a popular poet; he also has one or two which may, as time rolls on, peril his existence as part of the enduring national literature of America. He has fancy, versification, a keen eye for the incongruous, and a taste for the beautiful; but against these gifts must be set off his want of earnestness. We are never certain he feels his subject; he writes about it well and wittily; and in some of his poems he displays a truthfulness and depth worthy of any poet, but the mood seems to pass away, and he becomes the Mephistophelian jester at the various passions and pursuits of the world.—POWELL, THOMAS, 1850, *The Living Authors of America, p.* 222.

In his serious poems he belongs to the same school as Campbell, and in his lighter pieces reminds us of "Beppo" and the best parts of "Don Juan." "Fanny," conceived in the latter vein, has the point of a fine local satire gracefully executed. "Burns," and the lines on the death of Drake, have the beautiful impressiveness of the highest elegiac verse. "Marco Bozzaris" is perhaps the best martial lyric in the language, "Red Jacket" the most effective Indian portrait, and "Twilight" an apt piece of contemplative verse; while "Alnwick Castle" combines his grave and gay style with inimitable art and admirable effect. As a versifier, he was an adept in that relation of sound to sense which embalms thought in deathless melody. An unusual blending of the animal and intellectual with that full proportion essential to manhood, enables him to utter appeals that wake responses in the universal

heart. An almost provoking mixture of irony and sentiment is characteristic of his genius.—TUCKERMAN, HENRY T., 1852, *A Sketch of American Literature.*

No American author, probably, has been more sedulously devoted to the pursuit of mental cultivation, or with better results to the public in the quality of his writings; yet he purchased the leisure of authorship by the surrender of a great portion of life to the uncongenial occupation of a banker's clerk; summing up the enormous wealth of others, contenting himself with airy poetic numbers. . . . To the separate poems, which long composed the only acknowledged volume of Mr. Halleck's writings, "Alnwick Castle," "Marco Bozzaris," and the rest, it is hardly necessary to allude. They are familiar to every school-boy and school-girl in the land. They were so well received that Halleck, like Campbell, for a time "afraid of the shadow of his reputation," refused to add others to the number, lest he should fall short of his own standard. After a long silence, however, in 1864 he ventured before the public with a poem, or rather group of poems entitled "Young America;" which, if it did not increase, certainly did not diminish his fame. It was his last appearance in print.—DUYCKINCK, E. A., 1868, *Fitz-Greene Halleck, Putnam's Magazine, vol.* 11, *pp.* 231, 234.

Became popular by his humorous poem "Fanny," which is a clever copy of Byron's style in "Don Juan;" and he became a still greater favourite by his battle-scene "Marco Bozzaris." Next to Oliver Wendell Holmes, the master of irony, Halleck is considered the wittiest poet of America.—SCHERR, J., 1874, *A History of English Literature, tr. M. V., p.* 301.

One of the puzzles which arrest the attention of a historian of American literature is to account for the strange indifference of Halleck to exercise often the faculty which on occasions he showed he possessed in superabundance. All the subjects he attempted—the "Croaker Papers," "Fanny," "Burns," "Red Jacket," "Alnwick Castle," "Connecticut," the magnificent heroic ode, "Marco Bozzaris"—show a complete artistic mastery of the resources of poetic expression, whether his theme be gay or grave, or compounded of the two. His extravagant admiration of Campbell was founded on Campbell's admirable power of compression. Halleck thought that Byron was a mere rhetorician in comparison with his favorite poet.—WHIPPLE, EDWIN PERCY, 1876–86, *American Literature and Other Papers*, ed. *Whittier*, p. 51.

On the 15th of May (1877) the first monumental statue of an American author was unveiled in the Central Park of New York. It is not a fortunate specimen of our native art. The posture is ungraceful, the face over-conscious to the verge of ostentation, and the general character of the figure is so theatrical that few of those who knew the poet will immediately recognize him. . . . Why should the first distinction fall upon Fitz-Greene Halleck, an author whose period of activity was so brief, whose good works are so few, and whose name has scarcely passed beyond his country's borders? . . . After Drake's death, Halleck's trip to Europe and his ardent Philohellenic sympathies prolonged his poetic activity for a time; but the ten years, from 1817 to 1827, begin and complete his season of productiveness. Nothing that he wrote before or after that period possesses any vitality; and it is probable, in fact, that he will only be known to later generations by six poems, which I venture to name in the order of their excellence: "Marco Bozzaris," "Burns," "Red Jacket," "Alnwick Castle," "The Field of the Grounded Arms," and "On the Death of Drake." His "Fanny" may still be read with interest, but its original charm faded away with the surprise of its first appearance; some of the other brief lyrics and songs are unaffected, graceful, and either tender or mocking. . . . He certainly knew no imaginative or spiritual woes; he even seemed to be incapable of comprehending them in others. His faculty acted freely, soaring or sinking into silence at its own good-will, taking the facts of life as something inevitable, without prying into the mystery of Evil, or beating its wings bloody against that barrier of transparent adamant which separated it from so much possible Good. He never attempted to express anything higher than the principle of Manhood, and his verses sprang from the source of that principle in his own being.—TAYLOR, BAYARD, 1877, *Fitz-Greene Halleck, North American Review, vol.* 125, *pp.* 60, 61, 63.

> He toiled and sang; and year by year
>   Men found their homes more sweet,
> And through a tenderer atmosphere
>   Looked down the brick-walled street.

> The Greek's wild onset Wall Street knew;
>   The Red King walked Broadway;
> And Alnwick Castle's roses blew
>   From Palisades to Bay.
> Fair City by the Sea! upraise
>   His veil with reverent hands;
> And mingle with thy own the praise
>   And pride of other lands.
> Let Greece his fiery lyric breathe
>   Above her hero-urns;
> And Scotland, with her holly, wreathe
>   The flower he culled for Burns.

—WHITTIER, JOHN GREENLEAF, 1878, *Fitz-Greene Halleck, The Vision of Echard and Other Poems*.

Whose verse is a mixture of serious thought and emotion with playful and careless fancies,—manly, clear, vivid, warm with feeling, or sparkling with wit.—WELSH, ALFRED H., 1883, *Development of English Literature and Language, vol.* II, *p.* 378.

A natural lyrist whose pathos and eloquence were inborn, and whose sentiment, though he wrote in the prevailing English mode, was that of his own land. As we read those favorites of our schoolboy days, "Burns" and "Red Jacket" and "Marco Bozzaris," we feel that Halleck was within his bounds, a national poet. Circumstances dulled his fire, and he lived to write drivel in his old age. But the early lyrics remain, nor was there anything of their kind in our home-poetry to compete with them until long after their first production.—STEDMAN, EDMUND CLARENCE, 1885, *Poets of America, p.* 40.

I still read Halleck, or portions of Halleck, with pleasure, and, while I am keenly alive to his faults, which are mainly technical, I wish that the vein of sterling sense which runs through his best work was one of our present excellencies. He had something to say, and he said it. That he was a poet in any large sense is not true, neither is it true that he was a poet in any recondite sense. He should be read, as I read him, with a regard to the time at which he wrote, and the then condition of American song.—STODDARD, RICHARD HENRY, 1889, *Fitz-Greene Halleck, Lippincott's Magazine, vol.* 43, *p.* 887.

His own character may still better keep him a lasting name. He lacked, however, the intellectual independence and the creative genius which is unhindered by the wearing and destructive effect of drudgery. . . . Bryant, whose criticism of his intimates was sometimes less sure than friendly, has praised Halleck highly, but he is hardly read now. A few of his poems, however, such as "Burns," are full of fine, manly passages; and of his nobility as a man his memorial exists in the reminiscences and in the biographies of him by his friends.— SIMONDS, ARTHUR B., 1894, *American Song,* pp. 136, 143.

Was for years probably the most popular American poet. His clear lucid style, easy diction and good-natured raillery, appealed at once to the public sentiment, and gave him a temporary prestige in literary circles hardly equalled in our history. His odes, lyrics, and satires were the most polished of their kind, written in a strain at once to catch the popular fancy. Even those of a transient character, with allusions now for the most part of little interest, show the same graceful, poetic spirit that enlivens the more important works. He had that excellent command of language that enabled him to express his meaning in the most felicitous terms, without the slightest apparent effort. It is certainly no rash prediction to assert that his more familiar lyrics, though few in number, will last as long as any short poems in our literature.— ONDERDONK, JAMES L., 1899-1901, *History of American Verse, p.* 134.

Charles Farrar Browne
Artemus Ward
1834-1867

An American humorist, best known as "Artemus Ward." He was born at Waterford, Maine, April 26, 1834. He began life as a printer in the office of the *Skowhegan Clarion,* and at fifteen was a compositor for a comic weekly journal in Boston, *The Carpet Bag,* to which he made occasional contributions. He then became reporter of the *Cleveland Plain Dealer,* and conceiving the idea of writing in the character of a showman, be began a series of "Artemus Ward's Sayings," intentionally atrocious in spelling, but of humor that soon gained him notoriety. In 1860 he moved to New York, and joined the editorial staff of *Vanity Fair.* The first of his humorous lectures, "The Babes in the Wood," was delivered in Brooklyn, and proved so successful that he abandoned journalism for the platform. In 1862 he visited California and Utah, gathering materials for a series of comic lectures on the Mormons, "whose religion is singular but their wives are plural." These lectures, with a panoramic accompaniment, attained great popularity in America. Consumption attacked Browne in 1864, and for two years he withdrew from the public. In 1866, his health improving, he undertook a professional tour in England, where he lectured with very great success for three months, almost to the eve of his death, which occurred at Southampton, March 6, 1867. His lectures and humorous writings are collected as "Artemus Ward, His Book" (1865); "Artemus Ward, His Travels" (1865); "Artemus Ward in London" (1867). There is an edition of the "Works," with a biographical sketch by Melville D. Landon (1875).—GILMAN, PECK, AND COLBY, *eds.* 1902, *The New International Encyclopædia, vol.* III, *p.* 500.

PERSONAL

Personally Charles Farrar Browne was one of the kindest and most affectionate of men, and history does not name a man who was so universally beloved by all who knew him. It was remarked, and truly, that the death of no literary character since Washington Irving caused such general and widespread regret. In stature he was tall and slender. His nose was prominent,—outlined like that of Sir Charles Napier, or Mr. Seward; his eyes brilliant, small, and close together; his mouth large, teeth white and pearly; fingers long and slender; hair soft, straight, and blonde; complexion florid; mustache large, and his voice soft and clear. In bearing, he moved like a natural-born gentleman. In his lectures he never smiled —not even while he was giving utterance to the most delicious absurdities; but all the while the jokes fell from his lips as if he was unconscious of their meaning. While writing his lectures, he would laugh and chuckle to himself continually. There was one peculiarity about Charles Browne—*he never made an enemy.*—LANDON, MELVILLE D. (ELI PERKINS), 1875-98, *The Complete Works of Artemus Ward, Biography, p.* 24.

Browne's personal appearance was anything but prepossessing, and he is remembered by Clevelanders as one of the most verdant-looking youths that ever set foot within the city. He wore a slouch hat, from beneath which protruded a mass of straight and unmanageable yellow hair. He had long limbs, and was lean and lank. His features were prominent, and set off by a nose that was decidedly Tennysonian, and was an oddity in itself. His clothes were seedy and ill-fitting. The ends of his coat-sleeves coquetted with his elbows, while his trowsers made vain endeavors to reach the tops of his shoes. His stockings lapped over and gave him a slovenly appearance. He walked with a loose, shambling gait, and a person unfamiliar with his appearance would naturally feel inclined to laugh at the spectacle. After he had been in the city some time he began to pay more attention to his toilet, and at last even became foppish. When he began lecturing he became more particular than ever, and his fondness for dress and display developed into a weakness. He even took with him a hair-dresser to curl his hair,—which nature intended should be worn uncurled,—and affected a large diamond pin and an immense diamond ring.—RUTHRAUFF, C. C., 1878, *Artemus Ward at Cleveland, Scribner's Monthly, vol.* 16, *p.* 790.

In person he was tall, very thin, agile, with face of Norman type, a high aquiline nose, with sharp bent, and with quick, discerning eyes. He had the delicate, fair hand of woman—the most beautiful hand they ever saw, his friends say. He was slow and halting in speech, with soft, sweet voice, the tone often of gentle pleading and persuasion. When not directly engaged, he was inclined to abstraction. With all his play of wit, there was a tinge of melancholy, a suppressed expression of suffering or sorrow. . . . His manner of composing and writing, as described by Mr. George Hoyt and others of his associates in the *Plain-Dealer* office, was as peculiar as anything else about the man. He searched everywhere for funny things, and when he found them, or originated them, he seemed himself to enjoy them more than any one else. He had for his desk a rickety old table, and being an inveterate whittler, it was notched and gashed until it looked as though the lightning had gone through it. His chair was a fit companion thereto,—"a wabbling, unsteady affair, sometimes with four and sometimes with three legs." When writing, one leg hung over the arm of the chair like a great hook, and when a funny idea came to him he would laugh "with a guffaw which seemed to shake him from his heels up-ward." Sometimes he would "pound the table with his fists, slap the long, thin leg that hung over the arm of the chair, and explode with laughter." Upon these occasions he would also call his associates, and read to them what he had written. He laughed nearly all the time he was writing. —SEITZ, DON C., 1881, *Artemus Ward; His Home and Family, Scribner's Monthly, vol.* 22, *pp.* 52, 53.

Poor Artemus! I shall not see his like again, as he appeared for a few short weeks before an English audience at the Egyptian Hall, Piccadilly. Sometimes, as to looks, profoundly dejected, at others shy or reproachful; nervously anxious to please (apparently), yet with a certain twinkle at the back of his eye which convinced you of his perfect *sang froid;* and one thing always—full, unescapably full, of fun. The humour of Artemus was delicate, evanescent, and personal to an irritating degree. "I have bin troying," said the impetuous Irishman, after hearing Macready, "for an hour to spake it out, loike that man, but, be-gohrra! I cannot at all—at all!" And no one ever yet succeeded in "spaking it out" like Artemus Ward. . . . Artemus Ward was a worthy and lovable man; he was sound, blameless, shrewd, sensitive, and affectionate. — HAWEIS, HUGH REGINALD, 1882, *American Humorists, pp.* 137, 144.

He was a shrewd, naïf, but at the same time modest and unassuming young man. He was a native of Maine, but familiar with the West. Quiet as he seemed, in three weeks he had found out everything in New York.—LELAND, CHARLES GODFREY, 1893, *Memoirs, p.* 235.

GENERAL

Among the humorists who rose to eminence during the American War, Artemus Ward was the raciest. Among the satirists of the period he was the gentlest and the most genial.—HINGSTON, EDWARD P., 1870, *The Genial Showman, vol.* I, *p.* 15.

He, like Nasby, Billings, and company, hid under bad orthography and worse grammar the neatest nonsense and the broadest satire. While he had not so keen and critical a sense of the dialect or patois as Russell Lowell shows in the character of Hosea Bigelow—while he had not the pointed wit of Holmes or Saxe, whose verses are a fit frame for their exquisite artistic humor, yet Artemus, next to Mark Twain and Bret

Harte, hit the very midriff of American humor.—COX, S. S., 1875, *American Humor*, *Harper's Magazine, vol. 50, p. 847.*

The writings of Artemus Ward are most expressive of the society of the United States. His genius is very national. Such a character as Artemus Ward could not have existed in any other than a democratic community. The freedom with which he approaches everybody and everything would be possible only to an American, or to some member of society as democratic as ours. In what he has to say about the leading persons of the day, he does not at all take into account the fact that he is an obscure and uneducated youth; that he has never been at college; that he is only a reporter for a county paper; that he was yesterday a typesetter or a farmer's lad. No, he is an intellect, a judgment, which has arrived at a certain degree of power,—by what means it matters not,—and which looks about it with that freedom from corporeal modifications which might belong to an immaterial intelligence. Ward's humour has many traits which are national. . . . Ward's sketches, though caricatures, are extremely lively representations of American society. He draws a society strongly marked by alert selfishness and good nature. He describes admirably the civility which is half kindness and half policy, the prudence, and the humbug of such a society.—NADAL, EHRMAN SYME, 1880–82, *Artemus Ward, Essays at Home and Elsewhere, pp. 19, 24.*

Probably no writer in America—or out of it, for that matter—ever attained such universal notoriety, in such a brief space of time, as did that king of American humorists, Artemus Ward. His career was short but successful, and his fame will live as long as does the English language. . . . Despite his looks, Browne was a brilliant and ready writer. He became involved in numerous journalistic quarrels, and his cutting remarks and timely rebukes to his contemporaries soon made known the fact that he could not be mastered.—CLEMENS, WILL M., 1882, *Famous Funny Fellows, pp. 24, 25.*

He was the natural foe of bigotry, Pecksniffianism, and immorality of every kind. There are many hard hits at hypocrites, formalists, shams, and religious scoundrels; but throughout the whole of his works you will not find one sneer at virtue or religion, and in spite of a few broad jokes not quite in European taste, there is not one really loose or unguarded thought. — HAWEIS, HUGH REGINALD, 1882, *American Humorists, p. 144.*

We have no wish to detract from the literary merit, or to disparage the memory, of the amiable and generally-regretted "Artemus Ward," the most celebrated of the lighter or broader school of western humorists. There was nothing in his genius of the tragic element that made almost pathetic the representations of the unapproachable actor Robson; but Mr. Browne is affectionately remembered as a man of wit and talent, whose refinement of manner conciliated the severest critics. His work is only the perfection of a spurious art; but he wins our regard by the good-humour that smiles alongside of the satire that scathes; disarms censure by laughing at himself, and eludes all suspicion of vulgarity, by never pretending to be other than he was—the son of an old New-England Jackson democrat of the middle-class, who saw through the braggadocio and corruption of either party, and did good service by exposing them in his vivid caricatures. We have no call to criticise minutely, or frequently to quote from, the often irresistible pages of this popular favourite. Who is not familiar with the showman, to whose show editors were "as welcome as flowers in May," with his "wax-figgurs" running up and down the States; denounced as a "man of sin" by the Shaker Elder; imposed on by the Octoroon; listening to the Union orators and to Piccolomini; entertained by the Mormons; interviewing Albert Edward, President Lincoln, beset by "orfice seekers coming down the chimney," and Prince Napoleon; confiscated by the "screaming eagle" of the Confederacy; escaping home to Betsey Jane; willing to surrender to his country "even his wife's relations," and ready with such good advice as, "Always live within your income, even if you have to borrow money to do so."—NICHOL, JOHN, 1882–85, *American Literature, p. 417.*

Artemus Ward anticipated Mark Twain as a representative of calm American irreverence, ready to ridicule every thing not in a high degree sacred or lovable; but, like Mark Twain's, his lampoons were either made for the sake of fun alone, or for the ridicule of solemn pretence and hypocrisy. —RICHARDSON, CHARLES F., 1886, *American Literature, 1607–1885, vol. I, p. 523.*

He flashed like a brilliant meteor across the sky of American literature—emerging from obscurity, having a brief and brilliant career, and then vanishing, amid universal exclamations of regret. . . . Wit, such as his—so thoroughly spontaneous, so entirely *suigeneris*—can scarcely be said to have had a model. And yet he himself has said that Seba Smith's writings served to some extent as patterns for him. And it is almost beyond a doubt that his long connection with Messrs. Saxe and Halpine, on the staff of the *Carpet Bag*, greatly influenced him, and perhaps contributed to form the characteristics of his style. But granting all this is only to admit that the same things which influence us, and go to make us what we are, affected Charles Browne also. This does not alter the fact that though the manner might be an unconscious partial imitation of the style of a contemporary, yet the matter was unique, spontaneous, and as true an outflow of genius as it was possible to be. The unexpected way in which misspelt words confront one in his writings constitute in no small degree an element of their humor. . . . Artemus Ward was something more than a sparkling humorist. He was a man of character and principle. He was neither an adventurer nor a speculator. Throughout the whole of his works there will not be found one sneer at virtue or religion, and no profanity whatever. He says himself, and this is one of the times when Charles Browne, not Artemus Ward, speaks; "I rarely stain my pages even with mild profanity. It is wicked in the first place, and not funny in the second." There may be an occasional joke not quite in good taste; but in judging this we must consider the difference between the canons of good taste in England and in America.— NORTHCROFT, GEORGE J. H., 1888, *Artemus Ward the Baldinsville Showman, Time.*

Was a man whose mind was as quaintly put together as were those of Shakespeare's clowns. He was an involuntary—though by no means an unconscious—fun-maker: his conceits were in his marrow, and were not more the result of intellectual effort than his breathing was. To his eye, the universe was not a universe, but a great incoherency. Wherever he looked, he beheld a manifest absurdity. Standards of behavior, habits of thought, modes of life, appeared to him inverted, arbitrary, illusive: he was impelled to reverse all precedent and order, and to make the planet roll from east to west. Had his mind stopped here, he would simply have been insane; but, in fact, he was a duplex phenomenon; few men had so clear a perception as he himself had of his own perversity. Hence he was a born humorist, and— if such a thing be predicable of fun-making—a born genius. . . . This showman—Artemus—by the way, is one of the solidest figures in the gallery of American fiction. To the public, for whom Browne wrote, he is still a much more real person than is Charles Farrar Browne himself. Certainly there could not be a contrast greater than that between the blatant, vulgar, impudent old buffoon of the book, and the quiet, delicate, pensive, sensitive-looking young gentleman of the lecture-platform. And yet, before he had been speaking five minutes, you could understand how and why the creator of "Artemus" was his creator.—HAWTHORE, JULIAN, AND LEMMON, LEONARD, 1891, *American Literature,* pp. 312, 313.

It is vain to attempt to analyze the fun of Artemus Ward. Why did he make some people laugh till they cried, while others were all untouched? His secret probably was almost entirely one of manner, a trick of almost idiotic *naïveté*, like that of Lord Dundreary, covering real shrewdness. He had his rustic chaff, his Puritan profanity; his manner was the essence of his mirth. It was one of the ultimate constituents of the ludicrous, beyond which it is useless to inquire.—LANG, ANDREW, 1892, *Lost Leaders,* p. 75.

May be regarded as typical of the entire class of humorous journalists and speakers who have followed him. Certainly he has not been denied the homage of imitation, and certainly the writings he has left behind him are enough more than mere "comic copy" to give him his place as a representative figure. . . . It may be thought that an inordinate space has been devoted to a person who stood related to literature as *bouffe* to grand opera. Yet Artemus Ward represented conspicuously a class of writers which must not be overlooked in any general survey of American letters. Indeed, it would not be unprofitable to scrutinise the career and work of other men who stood less upon the dignity than the drollery of their productions; for if their appeal has not always been to the most fastidious, they have often meant more to "the great body of the plain people" than graver bookmen who escape the humourist's penalty of writing, as a rule, for one generation or decade.—HOWE, M. A. DEWOLFE, 1897-98, *American Bookmen, pp.* 163, 171.

When we remember that a large part of Browne's mature life was taken up in learning the printer's trade, in which he became a master, we must decide that he had only entered on his career as humorous writer. Much of what he wrote is simply amusing, with little depth or power of suggestion; it is comic, not humorous. He was gaining the ear of the public and training his powers of expression. What he has left consists of a few collections of sketches written for a daily paper. . . . He was more than a joker, as under the cap and bells of the fool in Lear we catch a glimpse of the face of a tender-hearted and philosophic friend. Browne's nature was so kindly and sympathetic, so pure and manly, that after he had achieved a reputation and

was relieved from immediate pecuniary pressure, he would have felt an ambition to do some worthy work and take time to bring out the best that was in him. As it is, he had only tried his 'prentice hand.— JOHNSON, CHARLES F., 1897, *Library of the World's Best Literature,* ed. *Warner, vol.* V, *p.* 2464.

As much of Browne's success depended on his personality, he is practically in the position of many a by-gone orator whose fame is kept up by tradition, not by his published works. The men and women who heard Browne are alone competent to judge him, yet when one has read what his admirers have written about him, and has avoided underrating the true wit and the fantastic humor of his writings, one is tempted to play the judge one's self and to declare that, as a whimsical genius, not as a broad, hearty humorist, he has had no equal in America.—TRENT, WILLIAM P., 1903, *A History of American Literature, p.* 535.

Catharine Maria Sedgwick
1789–1867

Author; daughter of Judge Theodore Sedgwick; born at Stockbridge, Mass., Dec. 28, 1789; undertook after her father's death (in 1813) the management of a private school for the education of young ladies, and continued in that employment fifty years. She published her first work of fiction, "A New England Tale," in 1822, the success of which decided her to continue the career of authorship; brought out "Redwood" (2 vols., 1824), which was reprinted in England, translated into French, Italian, German, and Swedish, and compared favorably with the novels of Cooper, to whom, indeed, it was attributed in the French version; and was the author of other popular works, including "The Traveller" (1825); "Hope Leslie, or Early Times in Massachusetts" (2 vols., 1827), reputed her best work; "Clarence, a Tale of our Own Times" (1830); "The Linwoods" (1835); "The Poor Rich Man and the Rich Poor Man" (1836); "Live and Let Live" (1837); "Means and Ends, or Self-Training" (1838); "Stories for Young Persons" (1840); "Letters from Abroad to Kindred at Home" (1841); "Morals and Manners" (1846); "Facts and Fancies" (1848); "Married or Single?" (1857); and "Letters to my Pupils" (1862). Died near Roxbury, Mass., July 31, 1867. See her "Life and Letters," by Mary E. Dewey (New York, 1871).—ADAMS, CHARLES KENDALL, *ed.,* 1897, *Johnson's Universal Cyclopædia, vol.* VII, *p.* 410.

PERSONAL

She is decidedly the pleasantest American woman I have ever seen. . . . The twang, to be sure, there is in plenty; and the toilette is the dowdiness (not the finery) of the backwoods; but then she is lively, kind, heart-warm; and I feel, somehow or other, almost on friendly terms with her, though I never spoke more than twenty consecutive words to her.—CHORLEY, HENRY FOTHERGILL, 1839, *Autobiography, Memoir and Letters, vol.* I, *p.* 279.

She is about the medium height, perhaps a little below it. Her forehead is an unusually fine one; nose of a slight Roman curve; eyes dark and piercing; mouth well-formed and remarkably pleasant in its expression. . . . Her manners are those of a high-bred woman, but her ordinary manner vacillates, in a singular way, between cordiality and a reserve amounting to hauteur.—POE, EDGAR ALLAN, 1846, *The Literati, Works, ed. Stedman and Woodberry, vol.* VIII, *p.* 121.

I had a great admiration of much in Miss

Sedgwick's character, though we were too opposite in our natures, in many of our views, and in some of our principles, to be very congenial companions. Her domestic attachments and offices were charming to witness; and no one could be further from all conceit and vanity on account of her high reputation in her own country. Her authorship did not constitute her life; and she led a complete life, according to her measure, apart from it: and this is a spectacle which I always enjoy, and especially in the case of a woman. The insuperable difficulty between us,—that which closed our correspondence, though not our good will, was her habit of flattery;—a national weakness, to which I could have wished that she had been superior. But her nature was a timid and sensitive one; and she was thus predisposed to the national failing;— that is, to one side of it; for she could never fall into the cognate error,—of railing and abuse when the flattery no longer answers. She praised or was silent. The mischief was that she praised people to their faces, to a degree which I have never considered it necessary to permit.—MARTINEAU, HARRIET, 1855–77, Autobiography, ed. Chapman, vol. I, p. 377.

Your aunt did me the honor to call on me soon after my arrival in New York, and was among my first American acquaintances, and was my first American friend. She was then, I suppose, between thirty and forty years old, of a slight and graceful figure, the movements of which were remarkably light and elastic, and with a countenance in which bright intelligence, a keen sense of humor, and an almost pathetic tenderness of expression were charmingly combined. None of these winning attributes had departed from my dear friend's form and face up to the last time of my seeing her, and it is some consolation to me for my separation from her during the last years of her life that my latest vision of her was (considering the interval between them) but little different from the earliest; the graceful figure had not grown heavy, nor the tender countenance harsh, nor had the liberal mind become narrowed, nor the warm heart chilled under the touch of Time. —KEMBLE, FRANCES ANN, 1869, Letter to Mrs. William Minot, Jr., April 25; Life and Letters of Catharine M. Sedgwick, ed. Dewey, p. 415.

Admirable as it was, her home life was more so; and beautiful as were the examples set forth in her writings, her own example was, if possible, still more beautiful. Her unerring sense of rectitude, her love of truth, her ready sympathy, her active and cheerful beneficence, her winning and gracious manners, the perfection of high breeding, make up a character, the idea of which, as it rests on my mind, I would not exchange for any thing in her own interesting works of fiction.—BRYANT, WILLIAM CULLEN, 1871, Reminiscences of Miss Sedgwick, Life and Letters of Catharine M. Sedgwick, ed. Dewey, p. 446.

The story of her life is a simple tale as regards outward circumstances. No striking incidents, no remarkable occurrences will be found in it, but the gradual unfolding and ripening amid congenial surroundings of a true and beautiful soul, a clear and refined intellect, and a singularly sympathetic social nature. She was born eighty years ago, when the atmosphere was still electric with the storm in which we took our place among the nations, and passing her childhood in the seclusion of a New England valley, while yet her family was linked to the great world without by ties both political and social, early and deep foundations were laid in her character of patriotism, religious feeling, love of nature, and strong attachment to home, and to those who made it what it was. And when, later in life, she took her place among the acknowledged leaders of literature and society, these remained the central features of her character, and around them gathered all the graceful culture, the active philanthropy, the social accomplishment which made her presence a joy wherever it came.—DEWEY, MARY E., 1871, ed. Life and Letters of Catharine M. Sedgwick, p. 10.

GENERAL

A very good female writer; simple, chaste, and very sensible; without pretension.— NEAL, JOHN, 1825, American Writers, Blackwood's Magazine, vol. 17, p. 201.

Her delineations of character are generally striking and happy, and the national peculiarities are hit off with great dexterity and effect, though perhaps, in some instances, they are brought out a little too broadly. There is, however, very little overcharging and exaggeration; the actors in the plot do not come upon the scene in their stage dresses, ready, on every occasion that offers, as in duty bound, to display, resolutely, and with all their might, the supposed peculiarities of the personages they represent, but they are made to look and act like people in the world about us. The characters are not only thus chastely drawn, but they are varied with exceeding art and judgment, and this variety is, for the most part, founded on essential differences.—BRYANT, WILLIAM CULLEN, 1825, *Redwood, North American Review, vol. 20, p. 256.*

"Hope Leslie" is the last of this lady's three larger works, and, in our judgment, the best. It bears the lineaments of the two others, so far as to entitle them to claim a family resemblance to it; but it is written with an easier, freer spirit than the others; its chain of beauty is less frequently interrupted; it contains a greater number of prominent characters; its style is more matured. In the whole three, however, there is the same purity and delicacy; the same generous, lofty sentiment; the same deep and solemn breathings of religion without parade, and of piety without cant or censoriousness; the same love of the grand and the lovely in nature, together with the same power so to express that love as to waken it up ardently, devotionally in others; the same occasional touches of merry wit and playful satire; the same glowing fancy; and, spread through all, and regulating all, the same good sense, leading to a right apprehension of human life and motives, restraining genius from extravagance, giving an air of reality to the narrative, and securing our constant respect for the narrator.—GREENWOOD, P. W. B., 1828, *Hope Leslie, North American Reveiw, vol. 26, p. 411.*

She writes English with uncommon elegance and purity. . . . She has the rare merit of never being common-place. . . . Her style is perfectly feminine. . . . Almost the only fault of style we have noticed, is an occasional diffuseness, the easily besetting sin of female writers.—HILLARD, W., 1831, *Clarence, North American Review, vol. 32, p. 75.*

If her literary power be somewhat less than that of her illustrious English prototype, Miss Edgeworth, the moral strain of her writings is of a yet higher cast. There are some appearances in the present state of learning, which seem to show that the ladies are taking the department of novel-writing into their own hands, and if they would all manage it with the ability, taste and discretion of our author, we cannot say that we should deeply regret the revolution.—EVERETT, ALEXANDER HILL, 1836, *The Linwoods, North American Review, vol. 42, p. 194.*

In speaking of the great worth of Miss Sedgwick's writings, in a moral and political point of view, as inculcating and exciting the self-respect and mutual respect, which make the distinctive nobility of the republican character,—that is, of the character of man, in a condition of society where he may fully act out the man, —we have implied our sense of their high literary excellence; since if her pictures were not radiantly true and vivid, they would not charm and move leaders as they do. We remarked that, in this series of tales, she was working the true vein of her own power. She has also, we believe, fallen upon the vein, from which the treasures of our future literature are to be wrought. . . . Miss Sedgwick's imaginations have such vigor and bloom, because they are no exotics. She paints scenes, as she has looked upon them; characters, as she has known them; the energy of passion and principle, as they have impelled or crossed each other under her own view; the pressure and the encouragement of circumstance, as American life exhibits it. She writes of minds and hearts, as they muse and beat, not in ancient Rome, nor modern Cumberland, but in the streets of our marts, and the retirement of our villages. — PALFREY, JOHN GORHAM, 1837, *Miss Sedgwick's Tales, North American Review, vol. 45, p. 481.*

As to Miss Sedgwick, I have not read the particular work. And the reason why I have not read that and several others of Miss S—'s works is that she never interests me in her *books*. She wants refinement, deep thought, knowledge of human nature; her men and women all stand on one leg—I mean one apiece; and her views, political and religious, are superficial and erroneous. In private life I like her exceedingly for her simplicity and kindness, and for not wearing blue stockings, but I never care to see her in print. — DANA, RICHARD HENRY, 1838, *Letter to Dr. Henry, May.*

Miss Sedgwick has been returning the compliment of all English journalists, by putting us all round on paper, to a degree which is too bad. She asked, it seems, poor dear Miss Mitford's servants what wages they received, and the like; and, I hear, has written that which is likely most sadly to compromise some of the Italian refugees in America, who were negotiating with the Austrian Government for a restoration to their families. I liked her so well in private, as an honest-minded, simple-mannered, cultivated woman, that I am really more vexed than there is any occasion for. I fear the next cage of Trans-atlantic birds will not run much chance of being very liberally dinnered and soiréed here; only everything passes off like a nine-days' wonder!—CHORLEY, HENRY FOTHERGILL, 1841, *Autobiography, Memoir and Letters, vol.* I, *p.* 280.

Strong common-sense and a masculine disdain of mere ornament.—POE, EDGAR ALLAN, 1841, *A Chapter of Autography, Works, ed. Stedman and Woodberry, vol.* IX, *p.* 212.

Though a multitude of attempts have been made, the only successful novel that we remember, founded on the early history of Massachusetts, is Miss Sedgwick's "Hope Leslie."—BOWEN, FRANCIS, 1849, *Merry-Mount, North American Review, vol.* 68, *p.* 205.

The best trait of Miss Sedgwick's writings is the amiable home-sentiment which runs through them: her pen is always intent to improve life and cultivate its refinements; but besides this practical trait she has cultivated the imaginative element in American fiction with success. The Indian character in "Hope Leslie" is identified in the local feeling with the streams and mountain scenery of the region in which the author resides.—DUYCKINCK, EVERET A., AND GEORGE L., 1865–75, *Cyclopædia of American Literature, ed. Simons, vol.* II, *p.* 82.

The most renowned of the female novelists of the earlier period, Miss Catharine M. Sedgwick, from her home at Stockbridge, gave to the world an excellent series of native tales.—LAWRENCE, EUGENE, 1880, *A Primer of American Literature, p.* 65.

Another almost forgotten writer. Her "Hope Leslie," a novel, was among the most popular in the circulating libraries in 1842, although written fifteen years previously. As an American novelist Miss Sedgwick showed great skill in choosing American subjects. The local traditions, scenery, manner, and costume being thus entirely familiar, she had greater freedom of the creative faculty.—GUILD, CURTIS, 1896, *A Chat about Celebrities, p.* 83.

Although the day of the leisurely two-volume novel has nearly passed, Miss Sedgwick's novels are still readable. Her greatest defect is the sermonizing tendency of her day, which filled her novels with diffuse and tedious pages. Her excellencies are the quiet, truthful pictures of her native Massachusetts home life.—PATTEE, FRED LEWIS, 1896, *A History of American Literature, p.* 148.

What Irving was pleased to designate as "the classic pen of Miss Sedgwick" vied in favor with Cooper's stronger quill. Her "Redwood," remembered for Debby Lennox, its Yankee spinster, was reprinted in England and translated into French. Her "Hope Leslie," a story of the early Colonial days, ran through edition after edition, and "The Linwoods," depicting Revolutionary times, accomplished the feat of wringing copious tears from her publisher, one of the Harper brothers, as he read the proof-sheets.—BATES, KATHARINE LEE, 1897, *American Literature, p.* 104.

Henry Timrod
1829–1867

Born in Charleston, S. C., 1829; died Columbia, S. C., 1867. Son of the bookbinder, William Henry Timrod, who published a volume of verse. Slender means prevented the son from taking the full course at the University of Georgia, and he became a tutor in the family of a Carolina planter. During the Civil War he was a correspondent of the Charleston "Mercury." and assistant editor of the Columbia "South Carolinian." The death of a favorite child and the destruction wrought by Sherman's troops in Columbia broke up his little home, and after a severe struggle with poverty he fell a prey to disease. His poems, having the misfortune to appear in 1860, had attracted less attention than they deserved; but in 1873 they were republished, with a sketch of the author by Paul H. Hayne, and a revised edition has appeared, 1899.—STEDMAN, EDMUND CLARENCE, 1900, *ed. An American Anthology, p.* 827.

PERSONAL

Poor Timrod is the very Prince of Dolefuls, and swallowed up in distresses. He now contemplates separation from his wife, that she may go forth as a governess and he as a tutor, in private families. He can earn nothing where he is [Columbia]; has not a dollar, goes to bed hungry every night, and suffers from bad health. It is the mortifying thing to all of us, that *none of us can* help him. Burns and myself are both living from hand to mouth, and not unfrequently the hand carries nothing to the cavernous receptacle.—SIMMS, WILLIAM GILMORE, 1867, *Letter to Paul Hamilton Hayne*, Oct. 22.

Nature, kinder to his senseless ashes than ever Fortune had been to the living man, is prodigal around his grave—unmarked and unrecorded though it be—of her flowers and verdant grasses, of her rains that fertilize, and her purifying dews. The peace he loved, and so vainly longed for through stormy years, has crept to him at last, but only to fall upon the pallid eyelids, closed forever; upon the pulseless limbs, and the breathless, broken heart. Still it is good to know that

"After life's fitful fever he sleeps well."

Yet, from this mere material repose, this quiet of decaying atoms, surely the most skeptical of thinkers, in contemplation of *such* a life and *such* a death, must instinctively look from earth to heaven; from the bruised and mouldering clod to the spirit infinitely exalted, and radiant in redemption. — HAYNE, PAUL HAMILTON, 1873, *Poems of Henry Timrod, Memorial Ed., Introduction*, p. xxx.

See where he lies—his last sad home
    Of all memorial bare,
Save for a little heap of leaves
    The winds have gathered there!
One fair frail shell from some far sea
    Lies lone above his breast,
Sad emblem and sole epitaph
    To mark his place of rest.

—MCKINLEY, CARL, 1877, *At Timrod's Grave.*

No poet could have found a more unpropitious time for graceful love-songs, and for lyrics in praise of spring and woodland, —to fit "a green thought in a green shade," —than that in which the shy young poet began to sing. Repose had gone from the troubled South, and the ominous days were carrying it nearer and nearer to war. It was

no time for music, and Timrod was not one to draw the gaze of busy men. Later, when the fever of war heated his verse, men carried his stirring songs in their hearts, but forgot the singer. Later still, when they came back crushed and heart-broken, yet ready to take up manfully the struggle of life anew, it was still less the fortunate hour for the poet.—TOOKER, L. FRANK, 1898, *Timrod the Poet, The Century*, vol. 55, p. 932.

Timrod, though dwelling in the shadow of consumption, was healthily in love with life. Poverty, pain, lack of general appreciation, did not cloud, did not even dim, his high spirit. He died beautifully like a Greek philosopher and poet, with a Christian's faith, receiving the sacrament.—AUSTIN, HENRY, 1899, *Henry Timrod, The Bookman*, vol. 9, p. 343.

GENERAL

His verses show him to have been as well convinced of the justice of the Southern cause as were any of his contemporaries; as patriotic and as confident of success. But although he once predicts that grass will grow in the streets of New York, and several times stigmatizes the Northern soldier as a Hun and a Goth, and a "ruffian foe," he does such things less frequently than most other writers of his political creed; and nowhere, we believe, does he exhibit that indiscriminate bloodthirstiness of reprobation and disgust, the apparently sincere expression of which used to cause a good deal of sincere surprise among Northern people, and which, even to a good part of the Southern public itself, must, we imagine, have now and again caused the writing of its poets to seem fatiguing. . . . It would, however, be an injustice to Mr. Timrod to test his ability as a poet by the lyrics extorted from him by a savage commotion, for partaking in which his sensitive nature entirely unfitted him.—DENNETT, J. R., 1873, *The Poems of Henry Timrod, The Nation*, vol. 16, p. 151.

Timrod's ode, sung on the occasion of decorating the graves of the Confederate dead, is, in its simple grandeur, the noblest poem ever written by a Southern poet.—WHIPPLE, EDWIN PERCY, 1876–86, *American Literature and Other Papers*, ed. *Whittier*, p. 131.

The South has been unfortunate in the loss of promising writers. One such as Timrod, whose handiwork was skilful and often imaginative and strong. Timrod's "Cotton Boll" was a forerunner of the method of a still finer poet than he, whose career was equally pathetic.—STEDMAN, EDMUND CLARENCE, 1885, *Poets of America.*

A man capable of painting so eloquently in words could hardly expect to be rich in more substantial ware!—MORRISON, A. H., 1886, *The Art Gallery of the English Language, p.* 185.

His little book of verse is so good in its martial and general work, that it makes us speculate on the possibilities which might have come in a longer life of one whose inspiration was so vivid that he half expected the incarnate spirit of springtide to appear in rosy flesh before him, in his woodland walks, exclaiming,

"Behold me! I am May!"
—RICHARDSON, CHARLES F., 1888, *American Literature*, 1607–1885, *vol.* II, *p.* 231.

Timrod's was probably the most finely endowed mind to be found in Carolina, or indeed in the whole South, at this period. His German blood and his inherited qualities had given him a greater artistic endowment than any other Southern writer, save Poe, had been blessed with. He was able, except in the case of his sonnets, in which he evidently came under Simms's influence, to control himself; was able to devote time and patience to the polishing and perfection of his verse; and, more than all, was able to distinguish between subjects that were proper and subjects that were alien to his art. In these respects he was slightly, but only slightly, superior to Hayne. But where Hayne and the generality of Southern poets possessed a delicate fancy, for the most part exercised on subjects not far removed from the commonplace, Timrod possessed an imagination which, if not lofty and wide embracing, was within its narrow range characterized by a singular intensity. He has not left much work behind him, and that work is marred by the effects which constant sickness and poverty and the stress of war necessarily had upon his genius; but he has left a few singularly beautiful poems, and one at least, the ode written for the occasion of the decoration of the Confederate graves in Magnolia Cemetery, that approximates perfection,—the perfection of Collins, not that of Lovelace. That he was dominated by Tennyson, just as Hayne was dominated by Tennyson and William Morris, and Simms

by Wordsworth, is perfectly true; but his poetic powers were not only greater than those of his brothers, but also more akin to the powers of the great model he set himself.—TRENT, WILLIAM P., 1892, *William Gilmore Simms* (*American Men of Letters*).

His thin volume has many lovers; for if his muse is in less degree than Hayne's—

"A serious angel, with entrancèd eyes
Looking to far-off and celestial things,"

she has a rosier flush of human beauty.—BATES, KATHARINE LEE, 1897, *American Literature, p.* 188.

In spite of his impracticability, he is not an impractical poet; he is essentially a sane and masculine thinker. Approaching him, we suspect provincialism, but find a genial breadth that surprises us. His gamut of feeling is wide, and even in his war-songs, where one expects little restraint, we find this admirable self-control and breadth.—TOOKER, L. FRANK, 1898, *Timrod the Poet, The Century, vol.* 55, *p.* 934.

The first thing that impresses a student of Timrod's work is its quiet possession of the absolute and abiding charm of spontaneity. This man sang because he had to sing. One never feels that he selected his themes; that he ever said to himself: "Here's a good subject to festoon with rhymes;" but, on the contrary, the things came to him, craving expression—and found it. . . . Few, very few, traces of the influences of other poets appear in the mass of Timrod's work. That he had absorbed the finest aromas of Tennyson's carefully weeded garden one may not doubt; but his own growths have their own beauty, their own perfume; and in his war-songs there is a fervour, a fire, which is lacking in the martial measures of the stately master-craftsman.—AUSTIN, HENRY, 1899, *Henry Timrod, The Bookman, vol.* 9, *pp.* 341, 342.

He gave us probably the best of the war lyrics written in the South.—ONDERDONK, JAMES L., 1899–1901, *History of American Verse, p.* 262.

How shall we praise him save with his own song?
The distant note, the delicate strain is there,
Of bees and sedge, of fields dim and apart;
Then, keen with men, affairs, loss, glory, wrong,
A various music storms along the air,
Sweeps past the years, and shakes us to the heart!
—REESE, LIZETTE WOODWORTH, 1900, *Timrod, Atlantic Monthly, vol.* 85, *p.* 138.

MICHAEL FARADAY

Likeness from a Photograph from Life.

RICHARD COBDEN

Likeness from an Authentic Photograph from Life.

A poet born but not a poet made, and, therefore, despite the timeworn adage, not a thorough poet after all. This is what the impartial critic feels upon laying down the small volume. . . . Not a thorough poet, and yet with a very real poetic nature, and with many of the poet's gifts. The pathos and the tragedy of his brief career find expression in words which he wrote not long before his death concerning his poetry:

"I would consign every line of it to eternal oblivion for—one hundred dollars in hand!" It was the cry of a starving man; and in it may be read the secret of his failure to reach the mark of a high attainment. Very near it he came; often touched it; in his work we find very seldom the perfect whole, often the flashes of a rare genius. — BOWEN, ROBERT ADGER, 1901, *Henry Timrod's Poetry, The Book-buyer, vol. 22, p. 385.*

Michael Faraday
1791–1867

Was pre-eminent in his day as a chemist. Faraday was the son of a blacksmith, and apprenticed to a bookbinder. His early education was very limited, but he had from the first a strong bias towards chemical science. Having an opportunity to attend the last four lectures of Sir Humphry Davy, he took notes and wrote out a sketch of the lectures, and sent it to Sir Humphry. Sir Humphry was so struck with the character of these notes that he recommended the appointment of young Faraday as an assistant in the laboratory of the Royal Institution. From that time Faraday devoted himself entirely to chemical research, and for many years before his death he was the most eminent authority in the world on that subject. His researches and discoveries were published in the "Philosophical Transactions," and have been republished in 3 vols. as "Experimental Researches in Chemistry." For the last forty years of his life, he delivered annual Lectures on Chemistry at the Royal Institution. These lectures were celebrated, not only for their eminent scientific character, but for the extraordinary fascinations of style which held the auditors spell-bound. One of his most popular publications was "Chemistry of a Candle, a Course of Six Lectures."—HART, JOHN S., 1872, *A Manual of English Literature, p. 556.*

PERSONAL

Sir Humphry Davy has the honor to inform the managers that he has found a person who is desirous to occupy the situation in the Institution lately filled by William Payne. His name is Michael Faraday. He is a youth of twenty-two years of age. As far as Sir H. Davy has been able to observe or ascertain, he appears well fitted for the situation. His habits seem good; his disposition active and cheerful, and his manner intelligent. He is willing to engage himself on the same terms as given to Mr. Payne at the time of quitting the Institution.—DAVY, SIR HUMPHRY, 1813, *To the Managers of the Royal Institution, March* 18.

My time has lately been much occupied with Faraday, the great English chemist, who has lately acquired a very high celebrity indeed. He fears that his time will not permit him to visit the Observatory; so at dinner, where I met him on Friday last, we agreed that I should breakfast with him this morning at the Bilton Hotel, which I accordingly did. I had lately been reading enough of chemistry, and especially of its connexion with electricity, to enjoy hearing Faraday talk on this subject. But what I

most enjoyed was the finding that he, who has been proceeding entirely by induction and experiment, and who is the most distinguished *practical* chemist in England, has been led to almost as anti-material a view as myself who have proceeded altogether in the opposite direction, and from the other pole of mind. He finds more and more the conception of matter an incumbrance and complication in the explanation of phenomena, instead of an assistance. He sees no proofs from chemical facts, or from the phenomena of definite proportions, for the existence of those little bulks or bricks, of which so many fancy the outward world to be built up. And as to his chief study, electricity, after having long given up the fancy of *two fluids*, he now sees no need nor use for even *one*, and seems to regard the electrical current as only a transference of *power*—nearly as, in modern optics, we regard the transmission of light as consisting in the motion of a motion.—HAMILTON, SIR WILLIAM ROWAN, 1834, *Letter to his Sister, June* 30; *Life, ed. Graves, vol.* II, *p. 95.*

I was unexpectedly introduced to Faraday just before the lecture; pleasant man, with a very quick and lively expression of countenance. The lecture was on Electrical Eels, etc.; most elegant lecturer he is; brilliant and rapid experimenter. I hope to hear him again.—GRAY, ASA, 1839, *Journal, Jan.* 18; *Letters, ed. Gray, vol.* I, *p.* 114.

In the evening heard a lecture by Faraday. What a contrast to Carlyle! A perfect experimentalist,—with an intellect so clear! Within his sphere, *un uomo compito.* How great would that man be who could be as wise on Mind and its relations as Faraday is on Matter!—ROBINSON, HENRY CRABB, 1840, *Diary, May* 8; *Diary, Reminiscences and Correspondence, ed. Sadler.*

Faraday was one of a small band who added to our scientific knowledge a whole continent of truth, who have done for the future peace and wealth of the nation more than conquerors of kingdoms, or heroes of battlefields. . . . While earning countless wealth for the nation, Faraday's own income seems never, but in one year, to have exceeded the modest bounds of £300. On that noble testimony of a nation's gratitude we left him to live and die.—RUSSELL, J. SCOTT, 1868, *Faraday a Discoverer, Macmillan's Magazine, vol.* 18, *p.* 191.

It is but little for me to remind you that a greater philosopher than Michael Faraday has rarely been known among us within the memory of recent times; but I am bold to add that never have we known a man who more perfectly exhibited the meekness, the peaceableness, the humility, the blamelessness, of the true child of God. I am not consciously exaggerating when I say that there went forth a virtue from that Christian man, which made those who had come from his presence feel happier, and, I may venture to say, even better men. Think not I am thus striving to laud the creature; I am rather praising the Creator by whose Divine Spirit our Faraday was made what he was. Nevertheless this great and good man never obtruded the strength of his faith upon those whom he publicly addressed; upon principle he was habitually reticent on such topics, because he believed they were ill suited for the ordinary assemblages of men. Yet on more than one occasion when he had been discoursing on some of the magnificent pre-arrangements of Divine Providence, so lavishly scattered in nature, I have seen him struggle to repress the emotion which was visibly striving for utterance; and then, at last, with

one single far-reaching word, he would just hint at his meaning rather than express it. On such occasions he only who had ears to hear, could hear.—PRITCHARD, CHARLES, 1868, *Analogy of Intellectual Progress to Religious Growth.*

Attended Tyndall's lecture (on Faraday, his genius and merits), which Tyndall treated as quite heroic. A full and somewhat distinguished audience, respectful, noiselesss, attentive, but not fully sympathetic, I should say; such, at least, was my own case, feeling rather that the eulogy was perhaps overdone. As to myself, "the grandeur of Faraday's discoveries," &c., excited in me no real enthusiasm, nor was either his faculty or his history a matter I could reckon heroic in that high degree. In sad fact, I cared but little for these discoveries—reckoned them uncertain—to my dark mind, and not by any means the kind of "discoveries" I wanted to be made at present. "Can you really turn a ray of light on its axis by magnetism? and if you could, what should I care?"—CARLYLE, THOMAS, 1868, *Journal, June* 27; *Thomas Carlyle, A History of His Life in London, ed. Froude, vol.* II, *p.* 312.

As a man, the beauty and the nobleness of his character was formed by very many great qualities. Among these the first and greatest was his truthfulness. His noble nature showed itself in his search for truth. He loved truth beyond all other things; and no one ever did or will search for it with more energy than he did. His second great quality was his kindness (agapê). It was born in him, and by his careful culture it grew up to be the rule of his life; kindness to every one, always—in thought, in word, and in deed. His third great quality was his energy. This was no strong effort for a short time, but a lifelong lasting strife to seek and say that which he thought was true, and to do that which he thought was kind. Some will consider that his strong religious feeling was the prime cause of these great qualities; and there is no doubt that one of his natural qualities was greatly strengthened by his religion. It produced what may well be called his marvellous humility. —JONES, BENCE, 1870, *ed. The Life and Letters of Faraday, vol.* II, *p.* 484.

His name, even after his active labours had ceased, ennobled the Royal Institution both at home and abroad—a name scarcely more eminent from the great discoveries attached to it than from those private virtues and affections which endeared him to all who knew him. His love for science was as pure as all his other affections, wholly unalloyed by jealousy, seeking only for truth. His earnestness and natural eloquence as a lecturer will ever be remembered by those, young as well as old, who crowded to listen to him in that building which was his home for more than fifty years. The infirmity which came upon him during the last year or two of his life, touched not the moral part of his nature, which remained unaltered to the very last.—HOLLAND, SIR HENRY, 1871, *Recollections of Past Life, p.* 218, *note.*

We think of Michael Faraday, the chemist and electrician, who knew so well how to reconcile the boldest researches into the heights and deeps of science with the sincerest spirit of faith and devotion; the memory of whose delightful improvisations on the science he loved to expound must remain for ever with all who had the privilege of hearing the unrivalled lecturer deliver his annual discourses at the Royal Institution.—McCARTHY, JUSTIN, 1879, *A History of Our Own Times from the Accession of Queen Victoria to the Berlin Congress, ch.* XXIX.

For relaxation of mind, he frequently visited the theatres. His food was simple but generous. At his two o'clock dinner he ate his meat and drank his wine. He began the meal by lifting both hands over the dish before him, and in tones of a son addressing a father of whose love he was sure, asked a blessing on the food. To those whom he knew to be animated by something higher than mere curiosity, he talked freely of religion; but he never introduced the subject himself. Nearer than anybody known to the writer he came to the fulfilment of the precept. "Take no thought for the morrow." He had absolute confidence that, in case of need, the Lord would provide. A man with such feeling and such faith was naturally heedless of laying by for the future. His faith never wavered; but remained to the end as fresh as when in 1821 he made his "confession of sin and profession of faith." In reply to a question from Lady Lovelace, he described himself as belonging to "a very small and despised sect of Christians, known—if known at all—as Sandemanians; our hope is founded on the faith as it is in Christ." He made a strict severance of his religion from his

science. Man could not, by reasoning, find out God. He believed in a direct communication between God and the human soul, and these whisperings and monitions of the Divinity were in his view qualitatively different from his data of science. Faraday was a man of strong emotions. He was generous, charitable, sympathising with human suffering. His five-pound note was ever ready for the meritorious man who had been overtaken by calamity. The tenderness of his nature rendered it difficult for him to refuse the appeal of distress. Still, he knew the evil of indiscriminate almsgiving, and had many times detected imposture; so that he usually distributed his gifts through some charity organisation which assured him that they would be well bestowed.—TYNDALL, JOHN, 1889, *Dictionary of National Biography, vol.* XVIII, *p.* 201.

GENERAL

An essay ["Conservation of Force"] full of thought and power, and which should be carefully studied by every one who wishes to understand the direction which the highest speculations of physical science are now taking.—BUCKLE, HENRY THOMAS, 1862-66, *History of Civilization in England, vol.* III, *p.* 363, *note.*

Mr. Faraday's researches and discoveries have raised him to the highest rank among European philosophers, while his high faculty of expounding, to a general audience, the result of recondite investigations, makes him one of the most attractive lecturers of the age. He has selected the most difficult and perplexing departments of physical science, the investigation of the reciprocal relations of heat, light, magnetism, and electricity; and by many years of patient and profound study, has tended greatly to simplify our ideas on these subjects. It is the hope of this philosopher that, should life and health be spared, he will be able to show that the imponderable agencies just mentioned are so many manifestations of one and the same force.—KEDDIE, WILLIAM, 1854, *ed. Cyclopædia of Literary and Scientific Anecdote, p.* 67.

In Faraday it would seem in an eminent degree the case, that the moral controlled and gave force to the intellectual being; the emotional nature became one with the intelligence; and, as is always the case where this is, gave grandeur and eminent dignity to the intellect. Hence Dr. Tyndall notices with admiration his love of truth; of course we do not mean in the mere inferior sense, that of course, but in the unhappiness produced in Faraday's mind by all doubtful knowledge. He hated what is called doubtful knowledge, he could not condescend to reason upon data which admitted of doubt, and he hastened to transfer such either to the region of definite ignorance, or to show its certainty, and to permit it to be doubtful no more. Be one thing or other, he seemed to say to all unproved hypothesis; either come out as a solid truth, or disappear as a convicted lie. His mind moved in a marvellous region of hypothesis, and yet the habitual caution of his nature ever prevented him from being deceived himself, and still more faithfully held him from deceiving others. — HOOD, EDWIN PAXTON, 1859-70, *The Peerage of Poverty.*

The year 1855 closed the series of experimental researches in electricity. It began in 1831 with his greatest discoveries, the induction of electric currents, and the evolution of electricity from magnetism; then it continued with terrestrial magneto-electric induction; then with the identities of electricity from different sources; then with conducting power generally. Then came electro-chemical decomposition; then the electricity of the voltaic pile; then the induction of a current on itself; then static induction; then the nature of the electric force or forces, and the character of the electric force in the gymnotus; then the source of power in the voltaic pile; then the electricity evolved by friction of steam; then the magnetisation of light and the illumination of magnetic lines of force; then new magnetic actions, and the magnetic condition of all matter; then the crystalline polarity of bismuth and its relation to the magnetic form of force; then the possible relation of gravity to electricity; then the magnetic and diamagnetic condition of bodies, including oxygen and nitrogen; then atmospheric magnetism; then the lines of magnetic force, and the employment of induced magneto-electric currents as their test and measure; and lastly the constancy of differential magnecrystallic force in different media, the action of heat on magne-crystals, and the effect of heat upon the absolute magnetic force of bodies. The record of this work, which he has left in his manuscripts and republished in his three volumes of "Electrical Researches," from the papers in the "Philosophical Transactions," will ever remain as his noblest monument—full of genius in the conception—full of finished and most accurate work in execution—in quantity so vast that it seemes impossible one man could have done so much; and this amount of work appeared still more remarkable to those who knew that Anderson's help might be summed up in two words—blind obedience. The use of magneto-electricity in induction machines, in electrotyping, and in lighthouses, are the most important practical applications of the "Experimental Researches in Electricity;" but it is vain to attempt to measure the stimulus and the assistance which these researches have given, and will give, to other investigators.— JONES, BENCE, 1870, *ed. The Life and Letters of Faraday, vol.* II, *p.* 348.

The most exact of natural philosophers. —EMERSON, RALPH WALDO, 1876, *Poetry and Imagination, Letters and Social Aims; Works, Riverside Ed., vol.* VII, *p.* 10.

Slenderly educated, and never quite mastering the amount of mathematics necessary for fully understanding the researches of more abstruse writers, he was gifted with an admirable literary style, so clear and simple that it is hard to say whether Faraday has done more to advance science by popularising his own and other men's knowledge, than by adding to the actual amount of hitherto unknown data His lectures on the chemistry of a candle, and on the non-metallic elements, are models of addresses delivered before a non-scientific audience, while his work on chemical manipulation is so valuable that, in spite of the advance of late years, it is still regarded as a classic.—BROWN, ROBERT, 1887, *Celebrities of the Century, ed. Sanders, p.* 411.

There are many branches of science into which it would be absurd for us to penetrate with our present object. Chemistry, for instance, brings before us the illustrious name of Michael Faraday; but Faraday, though one of the most charming of lecturers, wrote little, and was, in the little that he did write, too technical for our purpose. —OLIPHANT, MARGARET O. W., 1892, *The Victorian Age of English Literature, p.* 391.

As a lecturer on natural science he had few equals, from a happy gift of lucid exposition and illustration.—ROBERTSON, J. LOGIE, 1894, *A History of English Literature, p.* 379.

In genius he [Davy] was unquestionably superior to Faraday; in true nobility of character he was far below him. It is almost impossible to avoid comparing him with Faraday. Indeed it is one of the penalties of his position that he has to be tried by so severe a standard, and it may well be that his good name, which, as Bacon says, is the proper inheritance of the deceased, has suffered unduly in consequence. His true place in the history of science is defined by his discoveries; it is a sad reflection that the lustre of his fame has been dimmed rather than heightened by what has been styled the greatest of them all—Faraday. But there has undoubtedly been injustice in the comparisons which have been made. What Davy was to Faraday, Faraday would have been the first to admit. Davy made himself what he was by the sheer force of his unaided genius; what Faraday became was in large measure due to his connection with Davy, and the germs of his greatest works are to be traced to this association. This fact has been frankly acknowledged by Faraday. To the end of his days he regarded Davy as his true master,

preserving to the last, in spite of his knowledge of the moral frailties of Davy's nature, the respect and even reverence which is to be seen in his early lecture notes and in his letters to his friend Abbott. Faraday was not easily roused to anger, but nothing so effectually moved him as any aspersion of Davy's character as a man of science, or any insinuation of ungenerous treatment of himself by Davy.—THORPE, T. E., 1896, *Humphry Davy, Poet and Philosopher.*

Nor does the rank of prince of experimenters do Faraday full justice, for he was far more than a mere experimenter. He had not, perhaps, quite the intuitive insight of Davy, and he utterly lacked the profound mathematical training of Young. None the less was he a man who could dream dreams on occasion, and, as Maxwell has insisted, think in mathematical channels if not with technical symbols. Only his wagon must always traverse earth though hitched to a star. His dreams guided him onward, but ever the hand of experiment kept check over the dreams. —WILLIAMS, HENRY SMITH, 1900, *The Story of Nineteenth-Century Science, p. 208.*

Alexander Smith

1830–1867

Born, at Kilmarnock, Ayrshire, 31 Dec. 1830. Worked for some years in a lace factory in Glasgow. Contrib. verses to the "Glasgow Citizen," 1850. Sec. to Edinburgh Univ., 1854–67. Married Flora MacDonald, 1857. Contributor to "Encyclopædia Brit.," "National Mag.," "Macmillan's Mag.," "The Quiver," and other periodicals. Died, at Wardie, near Edinburgh, 5 Jan. 1867. *Works:* "A Life-Drama," 1852; "Poems," 1853 (2nd edn. same year); "Sonnets on the War" (with Sydney Dobell), 1855; "City Poems," 1857; "Edwin of Deira," 1861; "Dreamthorp," 1863; "A Summer in Skye" (2 vols.), 1865; "Alfred Hagart's Household," 1866; "Miss Oona McQuarrie," 1866. *Posthumous:* "Last Leaves," ed. by P. P. Alexander, with *memoir*, 1868. He *edited:* Burns' Poetical Works, 1865; J. W. S. Hows' "Golden Leaves from the American Poets," 1866.—SHARP, R. FARQUHARSON, 1897, *A Dictionary of English Authors, p. 260.*

PERSONAL

Attention to duty was one of his noblest characteristics. Though largely endowed with the poetic sensitiveness and imagination, he was as careful, honest, and industrious, in the discharge of whatever task-work he had to do, as the most prosaic of men could be. Considering the brilliance of this literary *avatar*, and the flattering testimonies that greeted his reception into the high circle of poets, his unaffected humility was not less rare and beautiful. All the pæans of his admirers had no effect whatever in disturbing the serene balance of his nature, resting as it did on a solid basis of

common sense. No ambitious dreams ever shook his faith in honest work, as the lot of every man, poet or clown, and the ultimate test of his worth. In this respect his life and character are full of instruction to young literary aspirants, especially those who believe themselves poets, with a special mission to sing, and that only. . . . Of all the men whom I have known that drew forth love as well as admiration, Alexander Smith was the most lovable. It was impossible not to love him, as impossible as it was to provoke him to do or say anything mean or unkind. Unlike many, whose whole goodness and fine sentiment is put into their books, his life and character were as beautiful as anything he wrote. The modesty of many men is but another form of pride: it was not so with him. He knew that he was gifted above his fellows, but he neither felt nor showed the pride of superiority, nor ever dreamed that he was privileged in any way, or absolved from the common work and duties of humanity. He was exquisitively sensitive, but as free from irritability as it is possible for a poet to be.— NICOLSON, ALEXANDER, 1867, *Alexander Smith, Good Words, vol. 8, pp.* 173, 177.

His noblest monument is that which he himself erected—his life. Seldom if ever, indeed, has one so eminently gifted with a poetic temperament and genius, manifested such self-government, or lived a life so well balanced, beautiful, and blameless. That life is the best lesson he has taught us. It is a valuable legacy to all, but especially to aspiring young men and all candidates in literature.—BRISBANE, THOMAS, 1869, *The Early Years of Alexander Smith, p.* 203.

As a matter of fact, Alexander Smith was one of the most modest of men. The appearance of his "Life Drama" had evoked a tumult of acclaim sufficient to have turned the heads of most men of his age: a pattern-drawer at some commercial house in Glasgow, he awoke one morning to find himself the most bepraised of poets; but it altered his simple character not one whit; and when the pendulum swung the other way, he took detraction with the same good-natured philosophy. "At the worst," he said, quoting from his own poem, "it's only a gingerbeer bottle burst." The epithet "spasmodic," so freely applied to him by the critics of the day, was singularly out of place; he was full of quiet commonsense, mingled with a certain Lamb-like humor. In these respects, though of a widely different character, he resembled another Edinburgh notoriety of that day— the gentle and hospitable Dean Ramsay.— PAYN, JAMES, 1884, *Some Literary Recollections, p.* 135.

A LIFE DRAMA
1852

We rejoice to learn that he is no *improvisatore* in composition; that he loves to write slowly; that he enjoys the labor of the file; that almost every line in his "Life Drama" was written several times—rejoice in this, because it assures us that his next work shall be no hasty effusion,

patched up by the heat of success, but that it shall be a calm and determined trial of his general and artistic strength.—GILFILLAN, GEORGE, 1855, *A Third Gallery of Portraits, p.* 141.

He speaks well,—without exaggeration or bombast; like a highly cultivated Englishman, to say the least. The man who wrote these poems is fluent, even eloquent; he has a happy knack of expressing himself; many of his brief sayings are pregnant and Shakspearian; *that* judgment all men of common candour, and who are not soured by professional jealousy must pronounce. And that he is more, his noble idealization of Glasgow, throughout which there is no effort, no strain, though it moves in lofty numbers and at a difficult altitude, is sufficient in itself, we think, to prove. No man except a born poet could have written that poem. No amount of mere literary cultivation could have succeeded. We do not speak of the workmanship; it is, no doubt, cleanly cut, finely chiselled; but these are things that labour, without genius, may accomplish; it is the imaginative fire which lights up that vast throng of gloomy and swarthy faces, and melts them into one towering form of woe and pain, like the lurid figure of the Destroyer, with his whetted sword hanging over the accursed city, in Lorenzo's picture, that indicates the poet, and the poet alone.—SKELTON, JOHN, 1858, *Northern Lights, Fraser's Magazine, vol.* 57, *p.* 110.

It is admitted by most who are familiar with the poetry of Alexander Smith that in the art and beauty of modulation, his untrained imagination was lacking in sure and effective balance, and that he, himself, felt keenly this blemish; these faulty, half utterances hindered and fettered his spirit. . . . If it were immaturity only with Alexander Smith, his early volume, entitled "A Life Drama and Other Poems," exhibited this, indeed, both in thought and art, but it exhibited more: there was a vagrant abandon of expression in his poetry, a persistent extravagance in the heedless huddling of thoughts and fancies, that could not have failed, as it did not, to challenge the critical and public taste, especially at a time when the exquisite lyrics of Tennyson, and his perfect idyls, like a magic flute, had captivated the poetic ear of the reading world; such tones as these, rendered so long, and without rival, made the minor songsters self-distrustful and chary. — THAYER, STEPHEN HENRY, 1891, *Alexander Smith, Andover Review, vol. 15, pp. 165, 166.*

A poem not without considerable merit, but steeped in the purple and gold of poetical metaphor and simile.—OLIPHANT, MARGARET O. W., 1892, *The Victorian Age of English Literature, p. 245.*

DREAMTHORP
1863

In 1863 appeared "Dreamthorp," published by Strahan, a collection of Essays, for the most part new. This volume alone would entitle Smith to a place among the best writers of English prose. It was well received; but will probably be more read and admired now that he is dead. Many things seem less weighty and admirable from the lips of a living man, especially a young man, than they do afterwards, when he has joined the immortals, and will speak to us no more. Some of the essays in this volume are worthy of comparison with those of our most classical authors. The "Lark's Flight" might have been owned by De-Quincey, and "Dreamthorp" by Washington Irving.—NICOLSON, ALEXANDER, 1867, *Alexander Smith, Good Words, vol. 8, p. 175.*

His chief prose work is "Dreamthorp," a volume of essays having few equals in the English language. In it he celebrates the praises of the country, as in his poems he had done those of the town. It is by this volume that he will live longest as an exquisite prose writer, and on it his fame in that department of literature will mainly depend. It gained for him the name of Essayist.—BRISBANE, THOMAS, 1869, *The Early Years of Alexander Smith, p. 198.*

GENERAL

An extraordinary faculty, although I think he is a phenomenon of a very dubious character.— ARNOLD, MATTHEW, 1853, *To Mrs. Foster, April* 14; *Letters, ed. Russell, vol.* I, *p. 33.*

Alexander Smith I know by copious extracts in reviews, and by some MSS. once sent to us by friends and readers. Judging from those he must be set down as a true poet in opulence of imagery, but defective, so far (he is said to be very young) in the intellectual part of poetry. His images are flowers thrown to him by the gods, beautiful and fragrant, but having no root either in Enna or Olympus. There's no unity and holding together, no reality properly so called, no thinking of any kind. I hear that Alfred Tennyson says of him: "He has fancy without imagination." Still, it is difficult to say at the dawn what may be written at noon. Certainly he is very rich and full of colour; nothing is more surprising to me than his favourable reception with the critics. I should have thought that his very merits would be against him.—BROWNING, ELIZABETH BARRETT, 1853, *To Mr. Westwood, Sept.; Letters, ed. Kenyon, vol.* II, *p. 138.*

The models whom this young poet has followed have been, it would appear, predominantly, if not exclusively, the writers of his own immediate time, *plus* Shakspeare. The antecedents of the "Life-Drama," the one long poem which occupies almost the whole of his volume are to be found in the "Princess," in parts of Mrs. Browning, in the love of Keats, and the *habit* of Shakspeare. There is no Pope, or Dryden, or even Milton; no Wordsworth, Scott, or even Byron to speak of. We have before us, we may say, the latest disciple of the school of Keats, who was indeed no well of English undefiled, though doubtless the fountain-head of a true poetic stream. Alexander Smith is young enough to free himself from his present manner, which does not seem his simple and natural own. He has given us, so to say, his Endymion; it is certainly as imperfect, and as mere a promise of something wholly different, as was that of the master he has followed. . . . Alexander Smith lies open to much graver critical carping. He writes, it would almost seem, under the impression that the one business of the poet is to coin metaphors and similes. He tells them out as a clerk might sovereigns at the Bank of England.—CLOUGH, ARTHUR HUGH, 1853, *Prose Remains, pp. 355, 374.*

Now, let it be fairly understood, Mr. Alexander Smith is not the object of our reproaches: but Mr. Alexander Smith's models and flatterers. Against him we have nothing whatsoever to say; for him, very much indeed. Very young, as is said, self-educated, drudging for his daily bread in some dreary Glasgow prison-house of brick and mortar, he has seen the sky, the sun and moon—and, moreover, the sea, report says, for one day in his whole life; and this is nearly the whole of his experience in natural objects. And he has felt, too painfully for his peace of mind, the contrast between his environment and that of others—his means of culture and that of others—and, still more painfully, the contrast between his environment and culture, and that sense of beauty and power of melody which he does not deny that he has found in himself, and which no one can deny who reads his poems fairly. . . . Mr. Smith does succeed, not in copying one poet, but in copying all, and very often in improving on his models. Of the many conceits which he has borrowed from Mr. Bailey, there is hardly one which he has not made more true, more pointed and more sweet; nay, in one or two places, he has dared to mend John Keats himself. But his whole merit is by no means confined to the faculty of imitation. Though the "Life Drama" itself is the merest cento of reflections and images, without coherence or organization, dramatic or logical, yet single scenes, like that with the peasant and that with the fallen outcast, have firm self-consistency and clearness of conception; and these, as a natural consequence, are comparatively free from those tawdry spangles which deface the greater part of the poem.—KINGSLEY, CHARLES, 1853, *Alexander Smith and Alexander Pope, Miscellanies, vol.* I, *pp.* 271, 275.

It is what the first work of a very young and very genuine poet is most likely to be, the exuberant expression of his passionate delight in the spectacle and the suggestion of nature. . . . We are not struck by any want of thought in this poetry. It is so evidently the first run of the self-pressed fruit, that we expect to find it honey-like and almost cloying. It is so satisfactory and natural in its kind, that we feel no right to challenge it, nor complain that it is not something else and greater. Can any higher evidence be adduced of the universal impression of its genuineness, than its immediate reference by the critics to the loftiest standard? Critics assert that Alexander Smith has not yet grappled with the realities of life, and that his experience has been thus far thin and superficial—that they find no penetrating sadness in his music, and do not rise from it chastened and bettered. But of the June roses that are just falling, did they ask more than roses? or of the May-blossoming trees the fruit that only autumn ripens?—CURTIS, GEORGE WILLIAM, 1853, *The Poems of Alexander Smith, Putnam's Monthly, vol.* 2, *pp.* 98, 100.

Smith's distinguishing characteristic is wealth of imagery, and a markedly youthful over-richness of language. "You scarce can see the grass for flowers." He did much to conquer his besetting fault, and to gain simplicity; but not with complete success. His tendency is to string fancies on a thread of thought too thin for the weight it bears. The sense is oppressed as with kaleidoscopic colours, and the main lines of plan are too little defined. In separate passages you meet with promise of strength, dramatic insight, and self-mastery; and in a few of his shorter poems,—"Glasgow," for example—he is strong; but even in "Edwin of Deira," his last large poetic work, and by far the most compacted, there are loose threads, evidences that the material has not been completely assimilated and mastered. Crude passages alternate with strong ones. You feel that the thing, as a whole, has not been fused and shapen glowing; but rather put together bit by bit, and with too much exercise of conscious ingenuity in spite of wealth of imagery, and the warmth and glow of separate parts.—JAPP, ALEXANDER H., 1892, *The Poets and the Poetry of the Century, Charles Kingsley to James Thomson, ed. Miles, p.* 424.

He contributed to periodicals essays of sterling merit. He wrote a tale, partly autobiographical, and above all, "A Summer in Skye," the picturesqueness and poetry of which have sent many a Southron as well as many a Scotchman to contemplate the savage grandeur of the misty Cuchullins.—ESPINASSE, FRANCIS, 1893, *Literary Recollections and Sketches, p.* 398.

A poet deeply unknown to the present generation, but then acclaimed immortal by all the critics, and put with Shakespeare, who must be a good deal astonished from time to time in his Elysian quiet by the companionship thrust upon him. I read this now dead-and-gone immortal with an ecstasy unspeakable; I raved of him by day, and dreamed of him by night; I got great lengths of his "Life-Drama" by heart, and I can still repeat several gorgeous passages from it; I would almost have been willing to take the life of the sole critic who had the sense to laugh at him, and who made his wicked fun in *Graham's Magazine*, an extinct periodical of the old extinct Philadelphian species. I cannot tell how I came out of this craze, but neither could any of the critics who led me into it, I dare say. The reading world is very susceptible of such lunacies, and all that can be said is that at a given time it was time for criticism to go mad over a poet who was neither better nor worse than many another third-rate poet apotheosized before and since. What was good in Smith was the reflected fire of the poets who had a vital heat in them; and it was by mere chance that I bathed myself in his second-hand effulgence.—HOWELLS, WILLIAM DEAN, 1895, *My Literary Passions.*

The present generation, which has been unjust to Dobell, has dealt still more hardly with Alexander Smith. The Nemesis of excessive praise is unjust depreciation, and both have been Smith's lot. He has been denied the title of poet altogether; but he is a poet, and even a considerable one. He shares both the defects and the excellences of Dobell, never sinking so low, and, on the other hand, never rising as high. His execution is unequal, he rants, he uses metaphor to excess, he is by no means free from affectation. But though the "Life Drama" is crude and unequal, there is plenty of promise in it. There was ground to hope that the spirit from which it proceeded was like a turbid torrent which would by-and-by deposit its mud and flow on strong and clear. To those who hoped thus "Edwin of Deira" was disappointing. A good deal of the mud had been deposited, the execution was more perfect, but there was less strength and less volume of thought than might have been expected. It is in his minor pieces and in occasional lines and passages that Smith shows best.—WALKER, HUGH, 1897, *The Age of Tennyson, p.* 250.

There are periods in the history of all the arts when the public seems to tire for a while of its old and well-established favourites, and to seek perversly enough for some one to supplant them; and during the interval between "Maud" and "Idylls of the King," Alexander Smith stood in much the same relation to Tennyson as "Master" Betty stood at an earlier date to John Kemble. He was the "young Roscius" of poetry, who, after being temporarily elevated to the same, if not to a higher, pedestal than that of its greatest living master, is now as clean forgotten as his dramatic prototype.—TRAILL, HENRY DUFF, 1897, *Social England, vol.* VI, *p.* 279.

In "Edwin of Deira," Smith writes an attractive and spirited poem, exhibiting commendable self-restraint and a chastened method. Unfortunately, the poem challenged attention almost simultaneously with Tennyson's "Idylls of the King," and it is surprising that, under such a disadvantage, it reached a second edition in a few months. Still, Smith did not escape the old charge of plagiarism and imitation. He was even blamed for utilising Tennyson's latest work, though his poem was mainly, if not entirely, written before the "Idylls" appeared. Envious comparisons thus instituted were inevitably detrimental, and a fine poem has probably never received its due.—BAYNE, THOMAS, 1898, *Dictionary of National Biography, vol.* LIII, *p.* 14.

Sir Archibald Alison

1792–1867

Born at Kenley, Shropshire, 29th September 1792, he entered Edinburgh University in 1805, and in 1814 was called to the Scottish bar. Within three years he was making £600 a year, which allowed him to form a fine library, and make four continental tours, till, in 1822, he was appointed advocate-depute, an office he held till 1830. He now began to appear as a writer on law, politics, and literature. Appointed sheriff of Lanarkshire in 1834, and in 1852 created a baronet, he died at Possil House, Glasgow, 23d May 1867. His "History of Europe during the French Revolution" (10 vols. 1833–42) was continued under the title of "The History of Europe from the Fall of Napoleon to the Accession of Louis Napoleon" (9 vols. 1852–59). He also published Lives of Marlborough and Castlereagh, "Principles of the Criminal Law of Scotland" (2 vols. 1832–33), &c., besides contributing to "Blackwood's Magazine" a series of Tory articles. See his Autobiography.—PATRICK AND GROOME, *eds.,* 1897, *Chambers's Biographical Dictionary, p.* 24.

PERSONAL

I rose at eight, and heard my son his lessons till half-past nine. Breakfast was over at ten, and from that hour till half-past eleven I wrote at my History. I then walked in to Glasgow, which I reached at twelve, and worked at my law till half-past four or five, when I walked home and dined at six.

Between dinner and tea I walked in the flower-garden, in winter read the newspaper or some light work, and at eight o'clock I began again at my History, and wrote till ten, or sometimes eleven. From either of these hours till the hour of retiring to rest arrived, at half-past eleven or twelve, I was reading either books and authorities connected with my work, or classical authors, such as Livy, Sallust, Tacitus, and Thucydides, on which I was anxious to form if possible its style. So far from feeling this allotment of time fatiguing, I found it the greatest alleviation of fatigue: recreation to an active mind is to be sought not so much in rest as in change of occupation. I never found that I could do more, either at law or literature, by working at it alone the whole day, than by devoting half my time to the other. The fatigue of the two was quite different, and neither disqualified for undergoing the opposite one. Often on returning home, after sitting twelve hours in the small-debt court, and finding no alleviation of the sense of fatigue by lying on the sofa, I rose up and said, "I am too tired to rest; I must go and write my History."— ALISON, SIR ARCHIBALD, 1867(?) *Some Account of My Life and Writings, vol.* I, *p.* 355.

Alison was thoroughly amiable and loved in his domestic life, and preserved health and strength, having given up writing after dinner on finishing the "History" in 1842. He notes that on 9 Sept. 1862, that is, at the age of seventy, he walked twenty miles in five hours without fatigue. He enjoyed great popularity in Glasgow; attended to his duties on 10 May, 1867, was taken ill next day, and closed a singularly industrious and thoroughly honourable life on 23 May. His funeral was attended by a crowd from 100,000 to 150,000 of the people of Glasgow.—STEPHEN, LESLIE, 1885, *Dictionary of National Biography, vol.* I, *p.* 290.

GENERAL

Alison deserves all anybody can say of his negligence, and also of his coxcombical pomposity and preachification, and worst of all, his affectation of liberalism here and there by way of extenuating to the wicked his really good principles, political and religious. But he *is* a good old Tory, and a good, honest, amiable man, and he has spent twenty years on this big book, and looks to it (he thinks not in vain) for pecuniary help to a large family. I think,

therefore, it would meet your wishes to be gentle to him—and certainly the contrary line would give me personal pain, we being very old acquaintances, and he the sheriff of my county, whom I must meet often whenever I go to Scotland. It occurs to me that you might do him a real kindness by pointing out his blunders; but it might be done in terms of respect and civility, and without any expression of severity mingled with regret. This is, however, *if* you *could* speak with general respect of his work—and I fear you could not; and if you could not— why, the article is all alive with interest and can spare a note, however good and however amusing. Is not he led wrongly by some prior writer or writers who might be shown up with a long whip, without calling the heavy sheriff by name into the ring?— LOCKHART, JOHN GIBSON, 1843, *Letter to Mr. Croker, Dec.* 6; *The Correspondence and Diaries of John Wilson Croker, ed. Jennings, vol.* III, *p.* 12.

A book to bend an omnibus,
 A style like Hullah's Chorus;
Rome may put up with *Tacitus,*
 But Glasgow boasts *Sonorous.*

—LOCKHART, JOHN GIBSON, 1848, *On Alison's History of Europe, Life and Letters, ed.* Lang, vol. II, *p.* 321.

The fundamental stratum on which Sir Archibald Alison's character, with all its feelings and faculties, is based, is that which is in all cases indispensable, but which in many instances has been wanting. That basis is thorough, fervent, well-applied honesty. He is a man who believes with the whole power of his soul. He is not cold and formal as Robertson; he is not tainted in his whole nature, as was Gibbon, by mistaking a sinewless phantom, called "philosophy"—evoked, like some Frankenstein, from vacancy, by the literary necromancy of French savants—for an embodiment of celestial truth: friends and foes alike respect the genuine fervor, linked with earth and with heaven, which pervades and animates the writings of Sir Archibald Alison. This it is which must, we think, make his works essentially pleasing to every honest man. In one place, we may question an inference; in another, we may detect an imperfect analogy; here we may smile at the identification of the advocates of organic reform (revolution) with the powers of hell; and there we may think the laws of chaste and correct imagery infringed; but we always feel that the company of this man is safe—that his breast holds no malice or guile—that he believes really, and believes in a reality. Such is the base of Sir Archibald's character—a basis of adamant.— BAYNE, PETER, 1858, *Essays in Biography and Criticism, Second Series, p.* 89.

Very little exception has been taken to the accuracy of his facts, as regards either omission or positive error—less than has been taken in the case of Macaulay's "History of England;" adverse critics have confined themselves principally to his opinions. His style has been exposed to considerable animadversions: grammarians have cited from his pages numerous violations of grammar, and the "Edinburgh Review" charges him with verbosity, and with excessive pomp in the enunciation of his general reflections. These, however, are faults that occur chiefly to the critic and the cynic; and the critics of Sir Archibald's style do not appear to have sufficiently accounted for the extraordinary world-wide popularity of the work. The "History of Europe," widely circulated at home, has been translated into all European languages, and also into Arabic and Hindustani: in a work designed for general reading, such popularity may be taken as a proof of excellence, unless good reasons can be assigned to the contrary. The intrinsic interest of the events narrated, absorbing as that undoubtedly was, and the author's industrious accuracy, great as that was, do not constitute a sufficient explanation; the interesting story is undeniably told with high narrative skill. When we disregard minute errors of structure, and look to general effects, we find many excellences of style that help to explain his popularity. The historian possesses a flowing command of simple and striking language, always equal to the dignity and spirit of the events related, and enlivened by happy turns of antithesis and epigram. He had a feeling for dramatic contrasts, and introduces them with striking effect. He visited the scenes of all the important engagements, and his descriptions have the freshness and animation of pictures drawn from nature. Finally, what is of prime importance in such a work, though he deals with highly complicated affairs involving the interaction of several different powers, he keeps the concurring streams of events lucidly distinct, and brings the reader without perplexity to their joint con-

clusion.—MINTO, WILLIAM, 1872-80, *Manual of English Prose Literature, p.* 525.

Alison, as a historian, was one of the last of the school of writers who told a piece of history through, according to their bias of opinion, with some generalization, little or no original research, and superstitious belief in a way of writing that was once supposed to befit the dignity of the historian. His book covers one of the most important periods in human history, and has its use. His facts are arranged in a clear sequence, and fully set forth, although they are diffusely told by an interpreter without any conception of their meaning.—MORLEY, HENRY, 1881, *Of English Literature in the Reign of Victoria, with a Glance at the Past, p.* 263.

This history is not only the most valuable in our language on the period described, but, although it is not without faults, it is a production of many good qualities. It was prepared with the utmost care, and its descriptions have the merits of minuteness and honesty. It would not be easy to show that any fact is suppressed or given less than its true force in order to strengthen the author's position. But while the author obviously endeavors to be entirely fair in his statements of facts, he allows his political sympathies, those of a high Tory, to pervade every part of the production and give color to his interpretations. His strong prejudices draw him often into ardent political discussions, and the work is written in a style that shows a constant tendency to run into exaggerated and frothy declamation. But the thoughtful student has only to keep these characteristics in mind, in order to profit greatly by the work. As a description of the great events that intervened between the two Napoleons there is no other book in our language comparable with it.— ADAMS, CHARLES KENDALL, 1882, *A Manual of Historical Literature, p.* 204.

Sir Archibald Alison was not, by his own showing, a man of letters, or a moralist, or even an historian in the popular or the scientific sense. He was a man with "a mission" akin to that of Burke and Wordsworth before his time and of Mr. Mallock in our own day. . . . Altogether, Sir Archibald Alison appears to have been a kindly, well-intentioned gentleman and a diligent student, with a fair, if not a rich, mind. No student of the period covered by his historical works omits to read them, and no investigator of the social history of England during the earlier half of the present century will pass over his autobiography.—WALLACE, WILLIAM, 1882, *The Academy, vol.* 22, *pp.* 445, 446.

It ["History"] is laborious and honest, though not unprejudiced. Disraeli sneeringly said that "Mr. Wordy" had proved by his twenty volumes that Providence was on the side of the Tories.—WALKER, HUGH, 1897, *The Age of Tennyson, p.* 141.

Alison's great book was being published in successive volumes, and, large and cumbrous though it was, met with a constant and steady sale, as happens to some books which are the books of their time, even though their literary qualities are not of the first order.—OLIPHANT, MARGARET O. W., 1897, *William Blackwood and His Sons, vol.* II, *p.* 206.

He had energy and industry; he was much less inaccurate than it was long the fashion to represent him; a high sense of patriotism and the political virtues generally,

a very fair faculty of judging evidence, and a thorough interest in his subject were his. But his book was most unfortunately diffuse, earning its author the *sobriquet* of "Mr. Wordy," and it was conspicuously lacking in grasp, both in the marshalling of events and in the depicting of characters. Critics, even when they sympathised, have never liked it; but contrary to the wont of very lengthy histories, it found considerable favour with the public, who, as the French gibe has it, were not "hampered by the style," and who probably found in the popular explanation of a great series of important and interesting affairs all that they cared for. Nor is it unlikely that this popularity rather exaggerated the ill-will of the critics themselves. Alison is not quotable; he is, even after youth, read with no small difficulty; but it would be no bad thing if other periods of history had been treated in his manner and spirit.—SAINTSBURY, GEORGE, 1898, *A History of Nineteenth Century Literature, p.* 218.

Henry Lord Brougham
1779–1868

A British statesman, born in Edinburgh Sept. 19, 1779. He graduated at the University of Edinburgh, and was admitted to the bar in 1800. In 1802 he was associated with Francis Jeffrey and Sydney Smith in founding the "Edinburgh Review," to which he contributed largely for many years. In 1808 he removed to London and entered upon successful practice as an advocate, and in 1810 was returned to Parliament of which he continued to be a member until 1830, distinguishing himself as a legal reformer and promoter of education. He was the leading counsel in the defense of Queen Caroline, wife of George IV., in 1820–21, and it was owing to a significant threat of his that the prosecution was abandoned. In 1830 he was made lord chancellor in the Whig ministry, and was raised to the peerage under the title of Baron Brougham and Vaux. He retired from the ministry, with his colleagues, in Nov. 1834, after which he pursued an independent political course in the House of Lords. Among his works are "The Objects, Advantages, and Pleasures of Science" and "Statesmen of the Time of George IV." He left an "Autobiography," which was published, by his directions, soon after his death. Died at Cannes, France, May 9. 1868.—BARNARD AND GUYOT, *eds.,* 1885, *Johnson's New General Cyclopædia, vol.* I, *p.* 145,

PERSONAL

I do more justice to Brougham than you imagine. I am aware that his present manner and habits do not proceed from his character, but from circumstances—from his not being naturally placed in the situation which his ambition, his feelings, and his taste equally make necessary to him, and which his intellect tells him is his due. His whole mind is so set on securing the means necessary for this purpose that everything and everybody who cannot in some manner help him, are neglected, or unnoticed, or indifferent to him. Above the mean arts of

actual adulation of those he despises, he selects the best he can among those most fitted for his purpose, and consoles himself for the weaknesses his quickness must see, and his prudence not notice in their characters, by being doubly severe on the characters of others. When he shall have secured the independence and distinction to which his abilities in this country must soon raise him we shall see him more generally attentive to merit, less severe to the want of it, judging of persons as they really are, and not as they can or may be useful to him, and, above all, getting rid of a certain sort of affected reserve in his conversation, and of childish gravity in his behaviour. We shall see him acquiring an unaffected popular manner which may better make his superior talents be forgiven by the trifling and the dull.—BERRY, MARY, 1808, *Letters.*

Brougham is a man of the most splendid talents and the most extensive acquirements, and he has used the ample means which he possesses most usefully for mankind. It would be difficult to overrate the services which he has rendered the cause of the slaves in the West Indies, or that of the friends to the extension of knowledge and education among the poor, or to praise too highly his endeavours to serve the oppressed inhabitants of Poland. How much is it to be lamented that his want of judgment and of prudence should prevent his great talents, and such good intentions, from being as great a blessing to mankind as they ought to be.—ROMILLY, SIR SAMUEL, 1816, *Diary, March* 20; *Memoirs of Life, ed. his Sons, vol.* III, *p.* 237.

Mr. Brougham, on the contrary, had an apparent restlessness, a consciousness, not of superior powers, but of superior activity, a man whose heart was placed in what should have been his head: you were never sure of him—you always doubted his sincerity. — COLERIDGE, SAMUEL TAYLOR, 1818–22? *Table Talk, ed. Ashe, p.* 316.

Brougham, whom I knew in society, and from seeing him both at his chambers and at my own lodgings, is now about thirty-eight, tall, thin and rather awkward, with a plain and not very expressive countenance, and simple or even slovenly manners. He is evidently nervous, and a slight convulsive movement about the muscles of his lips gives him an unpleasant expression now and then. In short, all that is exterior in him, and all that goes to make up the first impression, is unfavorable. The first thing that removes this impression is the heartiness and good-will he shows you, whose motive cannot be mistaken, for such kindness can come only from the heart. This is the first thing, but a stranger presently begins to remark his conversation. On common topics, nobody is more commonplace. He does not feel them, but if the subject excites him, there is an air of originality in his remarks, which, if it convinces you of nothing else, convinces you that you are talking with an extraordinary man. He does not like to join in a general conversa-

tion, but prefers to talk apart with only two or three persons, and, though with great interest and zeal, in an undertone. If, however, he does launch into it, all the little, trim, gay pleasure-boats must keep well out of the way of his great black collier, as Gibbon said of Fox. He listens carefully and fairly—and with a kindness that would be provoking, if it were not genuine—to all his adversary has to say, but when his time comes to answer, it is with that bare, bold, bullion talent which either crushes itself or its opponent. . . . Yet I suspect the impression Brougham generally leaves is that of a good-natured friend. At least, that is the impression that I have most frequently found, both in England and on the continent.—TICKNOR, GEORGE, 1819, *Journal, Life, Letters and Journals, vol.* I, *p.* 266.

You are aware that the only point of exception to Wilson may be, that, with the fire of genius, he has possessed some of its eccentricities; but, did he ever approach to those of Henry Brougham, who is the God of Whiggish idolatry?—SCOTT, SIR WALTER, 1820, *Letter to J. G. Lockhart, March* 30; *Life by Lockhart, ch.* xlviii.

Late in the evening Brougham, his hair and beard grown, looking like an orangoutang.—GRANVILLE, HARRIET COUNTESS, 1820, *To Lady G. Morpeth, Dec.* 21; *Letters, ed. Gower, vol.* I, *p.* 200.

Who, though he remains a lawyer, presents the singular spectacle of a lawyer, equally active in his lesser calling and his greater, and consenting, perhaps, to realize the gains of the one, only that he may secure the power of pursuing the noblest of all ambitions in the other. Mr. Brougham was "meant for mankind;" and luckily he has not been prevented by the minuter demands on his eyesight, from looking abroad and knowing it. His world is the world it ought to be,—the noble planet, capable of being added to the number of other planets which have perhaps worked out their moral beauty; —not a mere little despairing corner of it, entitled a court of justice.—HUNT, LEIGH, 1828, *Lord Byron and Some of his Contemporaries, vol.* I, *p.* 319, *note.*

This is the man, the only man, whose powers I contemplate with *wonder.* In society he has the artless gaity of a good-humoured child. Never leading the conversation, never canvassing for audience (in truth he has no need) he catches the ball as it flies with a careless and unrivalled skill. His little narratives are inimitable; the touch-and-go of his remarks leaves a trail of light behind it. On the tritest subjects he is now without paradox and without effort, simply, as it seems, because nature has interdicted him from commonplace. With that tremenduous power of sarcasm which he has so often put forth in public, he is the sweetest tempered man in private life, the kindliest in its relations, the most attracting to his friends—in short, as amiable as he is great.—AIKIN, LUCY, 1830, *To Dr. Channing, Dec. 14; Correspondence of William Ellery Channing and Lucy Aikin, ed. Le Breton, p. 58.*

I then came into parliament. I do not complain that he should have preferred Denman's claims to mine, and that he should have blamed Lord Lansdowne for not considering him. I went to take my seat. As I turned from the table at which I had been taking the oaths, he stood as near to me as you do now, and he cut me dead. We never spoke in the House excepting once, that I can remember, when a few words passed between us in the lobby. I have sat close to him when many men of whom I knew nothing have introduced themselves to me to shake hands and congratulate me after making a speech, and he has never said a single word. I know that it is jealousy, because I am not the first man whom he has used in this way. . . . He is, next to the King, the most popular man in England. There is no other man whose entrance into any town in the kingdom would be so certain to be with huzzaing and taking off of horses. At the same time he is in a very ticklish situation, for he has no real friends, Jeffrey, Sydney Smith, Mackintosh, all speak of him as I now speak to you. I was talking to Sydney Smith of him the other day, and said that, great as I felt his faults to be, I must allow him a real desire to raise the lower orders, and do good by education and those methods upon which his heart has been always set. Sydney would not allow this or any other merit. Now, if those who are called his friends feel towards him, as they all do, angry and sore at his overbearing, arrogant and neglectful conduct, when those reactions in public feeling which must come, arrive, he will have nothing to return upon, no place of refuge, no band of such tried friends as Fox and Canning had to support him. You will see

that he will soon place himself in a false position before the public. His popularity will go down, and he will find himself alone. —MACAULAY, THOMAS BABINGTON, 1831, *To Margaret Macaulay, Nov.* 27; *Life and Letters, ed. Trevelyan, ch.* iv.

I should wonder little to see one day a second Cromwell. He is the cunningest and the strongest man in England now, as I construe him, and with no better principle than a Napoleon has—a worship and self-devotion to power. God be thanked that I had nothing to do with his University and its committees. — CARLYLE, THOMAS, 1831, *Letter to John Carlyle, Thomas Carlyle, a History of the First Forty Years of His Life, ed. Froude, vol.* II, *p.* 116.

Tickler. "Brougham in his robes! Lord High Chancellor of England! Stern face, and stalwart frame—and his mind, people say, is gigantic. They name him with Bacon. Be it so; the minister he and the interpreter of Nature! Henry Brougham, in the eye of his idolators, is also an Edmund Burke. Be it so; at once the most imaginative and the most philosophical of orators that ever sounded lament over the decline and fall of empires, while wisdom, listening to his lips, exclaimed,
'Was ne'er prophetic sound so full of wo !' "
—WILSON, JOHN, 1832, *Noctes Ambrosianæ, Nov.*

That Lord Brougham is one of this favoured class, perhaps, few of his contemporaries will be hardy enough to dispute. He has risen in the course of comparatively a few years from obscurity to the highest honours of the state—the very acmé of political power and popularity. And in this, he owes nothing to birth, fortune, or family connections; he has been the architect of his own fame; and the honours he has attained have been won honourably. Let us search history where we may, we shall find few examples of a statesman having passed to office by a broader and more straightforward road—few instances of an individual having more closely connected the public interests with his own, than the present Lord Chancellor of England. He does not derive his present greatness from his superiority to other men in any one single line of excellence, whether it be learning, eloquence, a profound acquaintance with jurisprudence, or political sagacity—but from the universality of his genius and talents, and from the felicitous combination of the whole of the afore-mentioned excellencies meeting in his character.—JONES, WILLIAM, 1832, *Biographical Sketches of the Reform Ministers, vol.* I, *p.* 68.

He has attained a vast renown upon a very slender foundation. His failures— and they have been many—have proceeded from two causes. He has pretended to too much, and he wants moral courage. By attempting everything, he is unable to deal with any subject effectually. He knows nothing to the bottom. His incessant activity surprises the fools, but has ruined his own mind. . . . Present approbation is the very breath of his nostrils. To obtain this approbation he will sacrifice anything and everything.—ROEBUCK, JOHN ARTHUR, 1833, *Tait's Magazine, Dec.*

I was talking yesterday with Stephen about Brougham and Macaulay. He said he had known Brougham about thirty years and well remembers walking with him down to Clapham, to dine with old Zachary Macaulay, and telling him he would find a prodigy of a boy there of whom he must take notice. This was Tom Macaulay. Brougham afterward put himself forward as the monitor and director of the education of Macaulay, and I remember hearing of a letter he wrote to the father on the subject, which made a great noise at the time; but he was like the man who brought up a young lion, which finished by biting his head off. Brougham and Macaulay dislike each other. Brougham could not forgive his great superiority in many of those accomplishments in which he thought himself unrivaled; and being at no pains to disguise his jealousy and dislike, the other was not behind him in corresponding feelings of aversion. It was unworthy of both, but most of Brougham, who was the aggressor, and who might have considered the world large enough for both of them, and that a sufficiency of fame was attainable by each.—GREVILLE, CHARLES C. F., 1836, *Journal, Feb.* 9; *A Journal of the Reigns of King George IV. and King William IV., vol.* II, *p.* 458.

His Lordship took very little wine—less than I have seen any gentleman take at the head of his table in England; but if he have not that vice, which has been attributed to him,—and I fully believe that he has it not, —he has another which is, perhaps, as bad; certainly it is bad and vulgar beyond expression,—I mean *swearing.* I have dined in company nearly *every* day since I have

been in England, and I do not remember to have met a person who swore half so much as Lord Brougham;—and all this in conversation with an aged clergyman! His manner was rapid, hurried, and his voice very loud. He seemed uneasy and restless; and, of course, made me feel the same. His language, as you may well suppose, was vigorous and to the point. . . . I am almost sorry that I have seen Lord B., for I can no longer paint him to my mind's eye as the pure and enlightened orator of Christianity, civilization and humanity. I see him now, as before, with powers, such as belong to angels: why could I not have found him with an angel's purity, gentleness and simplicity? I must always admire his productions as models of art; but I fear that I shall distrust his sincerity and the purity of his motives. —SUMNER, CHARLES, 1838, *To George S. Hillard, Sept.* 6; *Memoir and Letters of Sumner, ed. Pierce, vol.* I, *pp.* 350, 352.

I called on Lord Brougham. It is strange that, in his presence, I forgot all my grounds of complaint against him.—ROBINSON, HENRY CRABB, 1840, *Diary, Dec.* 23; *Diary, Reminiscences, and Correspondence, ed. Sadler.*

He began his literary and political life with a scanty store of many small commodities. Long after he set out, the witty and wise Lord Stowell said of him that he wanted only a little law to fill up the vacancy. His shoulders were not over-burdened by the well-padded pack he bore on them; and he found a ready sale, where such articles find the readiest, in the town of Edinburgh. Here he entered into a confederacy (the word *conspiracy* may be libellous) to defend the worst atrocities of the French, and to cry down every author to whom England was dear and venerable. A better spirit now prevails in the "Edinburgh Review," from the generosity and genius of Macaulay. But in the days when Brougham and his confederates were writers in it, more falsehood and more malignity marked its pages than any other journal in the language. And here is the man who cries out he is wounded! The recreant who, screaming for help, aims a poisoned dagger at the vigorous breast that crushes him to the ground. . . . What other man within the walls of Parliament, however hasty, rude and petulant, hath exhibited such manifold instances of bad manners, bad feelings, bad reasonings, bad language and bad law?—LANDOR, WALTER SAVAGE, 1843, *Lord Brougham and the Examiner, Letters, ed. Wheeler, pp.* 259, 260.

There was something very charming in Lord Brougham's conversation. It was playful, varied, wise, witty, full of anecdote and novelty, and overflowing with vanity. His forgetfulness was extreme. He once asked me to breakfast. I went, but he had gone out long before the breakfast hour and told the servants they were not to expect him till dinner, and he afterwards, when I reminded him of his invitation, and of my disappointment, said with great simplicity that he had forgotten it wholly.—BOW-RING, SIR JOHN, 1853, *Autobiographical Recollections, p.* 295.

I needed no one to point out Lord Brougham. I knew him at once from the not flattering pictures of *Punch.* He is wonderfully like General Taylor, our military President.—LEVERT, MADAME OCTAVIA WAL-TON, 1853, *Souvenirs of Travel, vol.* I, *p.* 24.

The first sight of Brougham, then just seated on the wool-sack, and the object of all manner of expectation which he never fulfilled, was an incident to be remembered. I had not previously shared the general expectation of great national benefits from him. I believe that much of his effort for popular objects, even for education, was for party and personal purposes; and that he had no genuine popular sympathy, or real desire that the citizens at large should have any effectual political education. I distrusted his steadiness, and his disinterestedness, and his knowledge of the men and interests of his own time. I believed him too vain and selfish, and too low in morals and unrestrained in temper, to turn out a really great man when his day of action came. . . . . He talked excessively fast, and ate fast and prodigiously, stretching out his long arm for any dish he had a mind to, and getting hold of the largest spoons which would dispatch the most work in the shortest time. He watched me intently and incessantly when I was conversing with anybody else. For my part, I liked to watch him when he was conversing with gentlemen,-and his mind and its manifestations really came out. This was never the case, as far as my observation went, when he talked with ladies. . . . His swearing became so incessant and the occasional indecency of his talk so insufferable, that I have seen even coquettes and adorers turn pale,

and the lady of the house tell her husband that she could not undergo another dinner party with Lord Brougham for a guest. I, for my part, determined to decline quietly henceforth any small party where he was expected; and this simply because there was no pleasure in a visit where everybody was on thorns as to what any one guest might say and do next. My own impression that day was that he was either drunk or insane. Drunk he was not, for he had been publicly engaged in business till the last moment. All manner of protestations have been made by his friends, to this day, and he is, with all his eccentricities, "sane enough," but my impression remains that no man who conducted himself as he did that summer day in 1834 could be sane and sober.—MARTINEAU, HARRIET, 1855-77, *Autobiography, ed. Chapman, vol.* I, *pp.* 233, 235.

Strange fellow! His powers gone. His spite immortal. A dead nettle.—MACAU-LAY, THOMAS BABINGTON, 1857, *Journal; Life and Letters, ed. Trevelyan, ch.* XIV.

Notwithstanding the very large space which, while living, he has occupied in the public eye, a considerate man may doubt whether his permanent fame will be great in proportion. By seeking distinction in almost every department of genius, he has failed to establish a great name in any. He accomplished nothing as a statesman; he cannot be said to have extended the bounds of human knowledge by philosophical discovery; his writings, although displaying marvelous fertility, are already falling into neglect; his speeches, which when delivered nearly set the world on fire, when perused in print cause disappointment and weariness; and he must chiefly be remembered by the professional and party struggles in which he was engaged, and by the juridical improvements which he assisted to introduce. . . . He was very desirous of being considered a distinguished statesman, philosopher, orator, fine writer, and lawyer, but much more desirous of being believed to be "Brougham of that ilk,"—the representative of a great family, who derived their name from the name of the landed estate of which they had immemorially been in possession. His weakness upon this point was almost incredible, and I am afraid to repeat what I have heard him gravely state respecting the antiquity and splendour of his race.—CAMPBELL, LORD JOHN, 1859-68,

Lives of Lord Lyndhurst and Lord Brougham p. 214.

Lord Brougham has long since quitted the ranks of party, but whenever the real interests of the people were to be served he has always put forth his strength on either side. The spectator of present and the reviewer of past events, wide as may be the differences of opinion he may entertain from him on many political questions, regards with sincere admiration and respect a long life spent in avocations having for their object the advancement of freedom, the equalization of justice, and the elevation of the humbler classes of the community to a higher rank than hitherto in the scale of social happiness.—EARDLEY-WILMOT, SIR JOHN E., 1860, *ed. Lord Brougham's Law Reforms, Preface, p.* VI.

In private society no one could be more delightful than Lord Brougham. His kindliness of manner and simplicity of demeanor won every heart. Conversation with him flowed naturally, as it was suggested by topics started often by others, without either effort or anxiety for effect. It was very delightful to see this in a man past eighty, who for more than half a century had occupied an important position in the public eye, and had in many ways acquired such extensive fame. He spoke, like Mrs. Norton, much about himself; but that was readily forgiven in him, as in her, from the interesting matter which that subject contained.—ALISON, SIR ARCHIBALD, 1867?-83, *Some Account of My Life and Writings, vol.* II, *p.* 284.

It may truly be said of Lord Brougham, that none more completely represented his age, and no one more contributed to the progress of the times in which he lived. He had two qualities, almost in excess, which are rarely combined in the same person—one was energy, and the other versatility. The influence which creative power gave him, combined with strength of character, alone sustained him in a career which for its duration, as well as for its dazzling feats, has rarely been equalled in Europe.— DISRAELI, BENJAMIN (EARL OF BEACONS-FIELD), 1868, *Speech in House of Commons, July* 27,

Lord Brougham was at his chateau at Cannes when the first introduction of the daguerreotype process took place there; and an accomplished neighbor proposed to take a view of the chateau, with a group of guests in the balcony. The artist explained the necessity of perfect immobility. He only asked that his Lordship and friends would keep perfectly still "for five seconds;" and his Lordship vehemently promised that he would not stir. He moved about too soon, however, and the consequence was—a blur where Lord Brougham should be; and so stands the daguerreotype view to this hour. There is something mournfully typical in this. In the picture of our century, as taken from the life by History, this very man should have been a central figure; but now, owing to his want of steadfastness, there will be forever—a blur where Brougham should have been.—MARTINEAU, HARRIET, 1868-69, *Biographical Sketches, p.* 402.

The personal man, the bodily man, the private man did not vary. From 1830 to 1866—the period between his brightest glow of fame and his mental eclipse,—he was always the same gaunt, angular, raw-boned figure, with the high cheek-bones, the great, flexible nose, the mobile mouth, the shock head of hair, the uncouthly-cut coat with the velvet collar, the high black stock, the bulging shirt front, the dangling bunch of seals at his fob, and the immortal pantaloons of checked tweed. It is said that one of his admirers in the Bradford Cloth Hall gave him a bale of plaid trousering "a 'oo'" in 1825, and that he continued to the day of his death to have his nether garments cut from the inexhaustible store. I have seen Lord Brougham in evening dress and in the customary black continuations; but I never met him by daylight without the inevitable checks. This was the man bodily, as you might see him in the House of Peers, in the Gothic consulting room apportioned to him as a law lord in the palace at Westminster, in the Temple Church on Sundays, or stepping into his antique yellow carriage at the door of his solemn old mansion in Grafton street, Piccadilly.—SALA, GEORGE AUGUSTUS, 1868, *Lord Brougham, Temple Bar, vol.* 23, *p.* 427.

We very much doubt if, in the course of his fourscore years, Brougham ever wittingly did a kind or generous act. He was an intensely hard, selfish man. With talents of the highest order, with opportunities that fall to the lot of but few human beings, he passed through life without ever making a friend, and went to a grave unmoistened by a tear. He was intensely proud, and, what is uncommon with *proud* men, overbearing and tyrannical to his inferiors. . . . He was a willing referee in all cases where his legal knowledge and early-acquired habits of brow-beating plaintiff or defendant could aid in keeping cases of domestic scandal from public scrutiny.—CONSTABLE, A. G., 1874, *Archibald Constable and his Friends, Harper's Magazine, vol.* 48, *p.* 505.

John Mill, who early conceived a repugnance to Brougham, states that his father's attachment to him was for the sake of his public usefulness; but he acknowledged in private to myself that Brougham's fascination was very great when he set himself to gain any one, and that his father always succumbed under the influence. Not that he overlooked Brougham's faults.—BAIN, ALEXANDER, 1882, *James Mill, A Biography, p.* 76.

All that made Canning attractive Brougham lacked—so far as regards the outer man. Careless to a blamable extent of personal appearance, his clothes hung loosely about him, as if his tailor, when he made them, had neglected to take his measure. His action was the reverse of graceful; his features coarse and somewhat awry, the well-remembered twitching of the nose giving to them rather a repulsive character; the eyes were not expressive, except when animated, and then they rather reminded one of the vulture than the eagle—sly in their fierceness and little indicating the strength of expression so paramount in his flexible and powerful voice. It was not the eye of the Ancient Mariner that compelled the bystander to listen; yet Brougham never failed to do so—being a man whose sway was instinctively irresistible. Slightly tinged at all times with Scottish accent, his voice was broad, strong, flexible, vigorous and mentally healthful—the very opposite to that of his great ally, "silver-tongued Fenman," who, moreover, had the personal grace in which Brougham was so defective. . . . It was foreseen that Brougham the Lord would be the inferior of Brougham the Commoner. So it was undoubtedly. In the House of Peers he was never at home. I can only liken him there to a man who wears another man's clothes that do not fit him. His motions were uneasy at best, sometimes so much so that he appeared to be "seated on a hot griddle." He fidgeted from side to side, rose without dignity, and ungracefully resumed his seat—starting up

and flopping down.—HALL, SAMUEL CARTER, 1883, *Retrospect of a Long Life, p.* 105.

"Blundering Brougham," "D o m i n i e Hairy," "Foaming Fudge," "The God of Whiggish Idolatry," "Harry Twitcher," "Jupiter Placens."—FREY, ALBERT R., 1888, *Sobriquets and Nicknames, p.* 383.

Brougham was a man with whom nobody could get on. He had an over-bearing and even ferocious temper, and he had no idea of dignity, propriety, or prudence. He used to stump the country after the fashion of O'Connell, and deliver harangues such as, according to the etiquette of that time, an ex-Lord Chancellor was not supposed to deliver. He was always getting into quarrels, and always making compromising strokes off his own bat.—McCARTHY, JUSTIN, 1891, *Sir Robert Peel, p.* 131.

He didn't love to agree with anybody; one of those men it would seem who hardly wished his dinner to agree with him.—MITCHELL, DONALD G., 1897, *English Lands, Letters and Kings, the Later Georges to Victoria, p.* 88.

The boisterous force and ill-balanced energy of Brougham disturbed the serenity of the Court of Session for a few years before he carried them to a larger scene, where they failed to win for him the permanent respect of his countrymen.—CRAIK, SIR HENRY, 1901, *A Century of Scottish History, vol.* II, *p.* 251.

ORATORY

Mr. Brougham has one considerable advantage in debate: he is overcome by no false modesty, no deference to others. But then, by a natural consequence or parity of reasoning, he has little sympathy with other people and is liable to be mistaken in the effect his arguments will have upon them. He relies too much, among other things, on the patience of his hearers, and on his ability to turn everything to his own advantage. He accordingly goes to the full length of *his* tether (in vulgar phrase) and often overshoots the mark. . . . He is positive and abrupt, and is not in the habit of conciliating the feelings or soothing the follies of others. . . . Mr. Brougham speaks in a loud and unmitigated tone of voice, sometimes almost approaching to a scream. He is fluent, rapid, vehement, full of his subject, with evidently a great deal to say, and very regardless of the manner of saying it. As a lawyer, he has not hitherto been remarkably successful. He is not profound in cases and reports, nor does he take much interest in the peculiar features of a particular cause, or show much adroitness in the management of it. He carries too much weight of metal for ordinary and petty occasions: he must have a pretty large question to discuss and must make *thorough-stitch* work of it.— HAZLITT, WILLIAM, 1825, *The Spirit of the Age, pp.* 196, 197, 198.

Brougham's speech was four hours long: the greater part dull, cold, heavy, and tautologous to a *wonder*: insolent to intolerability in the placarding of *characters* on all persons he had or found occasion to mention, false to his party, and basely crawling to the Duke of Wellington—the whole a piece of treason under a splash of bravado. The impostor *knelt* at the end.—LOCKHART, JOHN GIBSON, 1831, *Letter to W. Blackwood, Oct.* 8; *William Blackwood and his Sons, ed. Oliphant, vol.* I, *p.* 250.

In *forensic eloquence* a comparison [with Lord Erskine] may be more correctly instituted. Both possessed POWER, the main engine of persuasion; both had a rapid, unhesitating utterance, and a fervid and beautiful fancy; but the latter, [Erskine] was more terrible and unsparing. The first won, the second commanded, the verdict. The former was the "Jupiter Placens" (but still *Jupiter*), the latter the "Jupiter Tonans." This *within* the courts of law; *out* of them, all comparison ceases.—DIBDIN, THOMAS FROGNALL, 1836, *Reminiscences of a Literary Life, vol.* I, *p.* 123, *note.*

Burke, to name two or three distinctions, was always a careful, while Brougham is often an extempore, thinker. Burke is a Cicero, and something far more; Brougham aspires to be a Demosthenes, and is something far less. Burke reasons philosophically—a mode of ratiocination which, as we have seen, can be employed with advantage on almost all subjects; Brougham reasons geometrically, and is one of those who, according to Aristotle, are sure to err when they turn their mathematical method to moral or mental themes. Burke's process of thought resembles the swift synthetic algebra; Brougham's, the slow, plodding, geometric analysis. Burke had prophetic insight, earnestness, and poetic fire; Brougham has marvellous acuteness, the earnestness of passion, and the fire of temperament. Burke had genuine imagination; Brougham has little or none.—GILFILLAN, GEORGE, 1855, *A Third Gallery of Portraits, p.* 320.

Lord Brougham is said to be hot and hasty, vehement, impetuous and offensively earnest in discussion. The great Lord Chatham has been taxed with similar defects; and, like him, Lord Brougham merges all minor imperfections in the countervailing merits of his vast powers of impulsive oratory and persuasive argument. His command of language, extent of information on every subject, in every science, embracing the whole circle of knowledge; his felicity in extracting arguments and illustrations from that vast store of varied information; his never-failing memory, marvelous ability of grappling with all the difficulties of a question, of seeing at a glance all its bearings, of sustaining a state of perpetual mental activity, of encountering opposition utterly fearless of all opponents, of bearing down on his enemies, of sending forth torrents of words of overwhelming eloquence on any occasion, however sudden the emergency— these peculiar talents and powers have seldom been equaled, never have been surpassed in parliament.—MADDEN, RICHARD ROBERT, 1855, *The Literary Life and Correspondence of the Countess of Blessington, vol.* II, *p.* 243.

Lord Brougham has wished to be known not only as an orator, but as a writer on oratory: he has written a "Discourse on Ancient Oratory," recommending, and very deservedly, its study to those who would now excel in the art. And there is no denying that he has rivaled the great Greek orator at least in one of his characteristic excellences: there is no more manly book in the world than Brougham's Speeches; he always "calls a spade a spade;" the rough energy strikes; we have none of the tawdry metaphor or half-real finery of the inferior orators; there is not a simile which a man of sense should not own. Nevertheless, we are inclined to question whether his studies on ancient oratory, especially on the great public oration of Demosthenes, have been entirely beneficial to him. — BAGEHOT, WALTER, 1857, *Lord Brougham, Works, ed. Morgan, vol.* III, *p.* 81.

We advise all who wish to qualify themselves as public speakers to study the orations of Lord Brougham. They will find them a store-house of manly thought, of vigorous argument, and lofty eloquence upon all the great questions of his time. Few may hope to rival the orator who defeated the bill of Pains and Penalties against Queen Caroline, and snapped asunder the chain of slavery; but none can fail to profit by the example.—FORSYTH, WILLIAM, 1858, *The Speeches of Lord Brougham, Edinburgh Review, vol.* 107, *p.* 463.

Brougham well earned a great reputation. With prodigious force of argument he struck down any common adversary, pouring fiery sarcasm, and unsparing, overwhelming refutation upon his head, and leaving him an object of ridicule or of pity, crushed beneath the weight of accumulated epithets and a burning mass of invective. . . . . Lord Brougham was a man of extraordinary powers of mind. It must be said also that, with many aberrations, those powers of mind were generally directed to great and worthy objects,—to the abolition of the Slave Trade and of slavery, to the improvement of law, to the promotion of education, to the furtherance of civil and religious liberty. His speech on the trial and condemnation of Missionary Smith combined the closest and most pressing logic with the most eloquent denunciations of oppression and the most powerful appeal to justice. It contributed, no doubt, in a very marked degree, to the extinction of slavery throughout the dominions of the Crown of England. . . . Lord Brougham's speeches at the bar of the House of Lords, on the Bill of Pains and Penalties against Queen Caroline, were striking specimens of a powerful understanding; and his great speech in opening the defense was the most wonderful effort of oratory I ever heard. Nor can any one who heard him remember with any other feelings than those of the highest admiration his speech on the second reading of the Reform Bill in the House of Lords. The speech which he made at the assizes, in defense of Ambrose Williams, in 1821, carries satire and sarcasm to a height that may be called sublime.—RUSSELL, JOHN EARL, 1874, *Recollections and Suggestions*, 1813–1873, *pp.* 46, 111, 112.

Brougham was one of the giants of the senate; but he wrote as if he were speaking from the woolsack, and the big words and labyrinthine sentences violated the first laws of literary composition. . . . Though Brougham has plenty of faults, they are the faults, not of weakness, but of power. He runs riot in the exuberance of his strength. His sentences are interminable in their length, stuffed with parentheses, and as full of folds as a sleeping boa-constrictor. He is

fond of repetition and exaggeration, clothes his ideas in almost endless forms of words; crowds qualifying clauses, explanatory statements, hints, insinuations, and even distinct thoughts, into a single sentence; piles Ossa upon Pelion; accumulates image upon image, metaphor upon metaphor, argument upon argument, till the hearer, perplexed by the multiplicity of ideas, almost loses the thread of the reasoning, and is lost in the labyrinth of his periods.— MATHEWS, WILLIAM, 1878, *Oratory and Orators, pp.* 188, 259.

He was beyond doubt a great parliamentary orator. His style was too diffuse and sometimes too uncouth to suit a day like our own, when form counts for more than substance, when passion seems out of place in debate, and not to exaggerate is far more the object than to try to be great. Brougham's action was wild, and sometimes even furious; his gestures were singularly ungraceful; his manners were grotesque; but of his power over his hearers there could be no doubt. That power remained with him until a far later date; and long after the years when men usually continue to take part in political debate, Lord Brougham could be impassioned, impressive, and even overwhelming. He was not an orator of the highest class; his speeches have not stood the test of time. Apart from the circumstances of the hour and the personal power of the speaker, they could hardly arouse any great delight, or even interest; for they are by no means models of English style, and they have little of that profound philosophical interest, that pregnancy of thought and meaning, and that splendor of eloquence which make the speeches of Burke always classic, and even in a certain sense always popular among us. In truth, no man could have done with abiding success all the things which Brougham did successfully for the hour. On law, on politics, on literature, on languages, on science, on art, on industrial and commercial enterprise, he professed to pronounce with the authority of a teacher. "If Brougham knew a little of law," said O'Connell when the former became Lord Chancellor, "he would know a little of everything." The anecdote is told in another way too, which perhaps makes it even more piquant. "The new Lord Chancellor knows a little of everything in the world—even the law."— McCARTHY, JUSTIN, 1879, *A History of Our Own Times from the Accession of Queen Victoria to the Berlin Congress, ch.* ii.

GENERAL

Beware lest blundering Brougham destroy the sale,
Turn beef to bannocks, cauliflower to kail.
—BYRON, LORD, 1809, *English Bards and Scotch Reviewers.*

His character has powerfully influenced the character of his age. His example of earnest, devoted, persevering labor to accomplish noble ends by noble means has been long before the world. If we were called upon to name the man, who, in our opinion has done more for the human race, we confess we should not know where to look. Franklin alone, in modern times may be compared to him as an instance of what one man, animated by a noble and enlarged philanthropy, may accomplish for his fellowmen; and, in his great efforts for the diffusion of knowledge, he seems constantly to have held the example of Franklin in full view.—CHASE, S. P., 1831, *Life and Character of Henry Brougham, North American Review, vol. 33, p.* 256.

As a writer, I have always thought him somewhat clumsy; more remarkable for rude force than refinement, and very deficient in the *ear.* Did he ever write a musical sentence? I began his first book on Natural Theology, but finding that I should gain little, I laid it aside. I hear good accounts of his second, and I certainly respect him for this use of his powers.—CHANNING, WILLIAM ELLERY, 1839, *To Miss Aikin, Sept.* 11; *Correspondence of William Ellery Channing and Lucy Aikin, ed. Le Breton, p.* 353.

He dazzles us by no lights of eloquence, he attracts us by not even a fictitious fluewarmth; but he perplexes and makes us stare and stumble by his angular intricacies and sudden glares. Not a sentence of his speeches or writings will be deposited in the memory as rich or rare; and even what is strange will be cast out of it for what is stranger, until this goes too. Is there a housewife who keeps a cupboardful of cups without handle or bottom; a selection of brokages and flaws?—LANDOR, WALTER SAVAGE, 1843, *Lord Brougham and the Examiner, Letters, ed. Wheeler, p.* 261.

His style is bold and manly, though sometimes strangely careless and lounging; but it is always expressive of his mind and heart and through the most labyrinthian sentence it is always easy to follow the sentiments and reasoning of the writer.—PEABODY, W. B. O., 1845, *Brougham's Lives of Men of Letters and Science, North American Review, vol.* 61, *p.* 421.

It is well known that no man has gone beyond Lord Brougham in the patient finish of particular passages of his speeches; he has himself recorded that the ultimate peroration on Queen Caroline's case was written ten times over before he thought it worthy of the occasion; and we have heard from his lips within these last few years several outpourings on the Whigs, which no doubt had been concocted with equal and more delightful elaboration. But with rare exceptions we cannot believe that he spends much time on the detail of any of his productions; nor do we suppose that his oral eloquence would be more effective than it is, if he took more pains in immediate preparation;—the preparation of lifelong study is a far better and here a quite sufficient thing. But it is somewhat different in the case of compositions avowedly and exclusively for the press. In these, we think, the public might reasonably expect more of care and deliberation than can usually be recognised in the authorship of Lord Brougham. Nothing like imbecility need be feared—but when there is such obvious strength, it is a pity that there should often be as obvious rashness.—CROKER, JOHN WILSON, 1845, *Lord Brougham's Lives of Men of Letters, Quarterly Review, vol.* 76, *p.* 62.

It was a bold—perhaps a rash—idea to collect the writings of Henry Brougham; they were written at such distant dates, their subjects are so various, they are often so wedged into the circumstances of an age, that they scarcely look natural in a series of volumes. Some men, doubtless, by a strong grasp of intellect, have compacted together subjects as various: the fingermarks of a few are on all human knowledge; others, by a rare illuminative power, have lit up as many with a light that seems peculiar to themselves; "Franciscus Baconus sic cogitavit" may well illustrate an "Opera Omnia." But Lord Brougham has neither power; his restless genius has no claim to the still, illuminating imagination; his many-handed, apprehensive intelligence is scarcely able to fuse and concentrate; variety is his taste, and versatility his power. His career has not been quiet; for many years rushing among the details of an age, he has written as he ran. There are not many undertakings bolder than to collect the works of such a life and such a man.—BAGEHOT, WALTER, 1857, *Lord Brougham, Works*, ed. *Morgan, vol.* III, *p.* 42.

He wrote *currente calamo*, and although probably no other man could have written so large and so good a book ["Colonial Policy of European Nations"] in so short a time, it was destined to a rather obscure career, and but for the fame subsequently acquired by the author, which reflects some interest upon it, long ere now it would have fallen into complete oblivion.—CAMPBELL, LORD JOHN, 1859–68, *Lives of Lord Lyndhurst and Lord Brougham, p.* 243.

One of the most *vital* of the sons of men. —CRAIK, GEORGE L., 1861, *A Compendious History of English Literature, vol.* II, *p.* 544.

"Discourse on the Objects, Advantages, and Pleasures of Science." The sale of this work has been as extraordinary as its merits were striking and almost unexampled. Some called it superficial, because it touched rapidly upon many departments of scientific knowledge; but the more just conclusion was that it was the work of "a full man," who had not laboriously elaborated this fascinating treatise out of books recently studied or hastily referred to, but had poured it forth out of the accumulated wealth of his rich treasury of knowledge. No reader to whom the subjects treated of were in any degree new could read this little book without feeling an ardent desire to know more—to know all. Such were my own feelings as I devoured this tract on the outside of an Aylesbury coach, and bitterly regretted that upon mere business considerations I had lost the chance of becoming intimate with the author of such a book, as his fellow-labourer in the work of popular enlightenment.—KNIGHT, CHARLES, 1863, *Passages of a Working Life During Half a Century, p.* 293.

Yet ambitious as he was of literary fame, and jealous of the success of other authors, he failed to obtain any lasting place in English literature. His style was slouching, involved, and incorrect. Like his handwriting, which was precipitate and almost illegible, except to the initiated, his composition bore marks of haste and carelessness, and nowhere shows any genuine originality of thought.—REEVE, HENRY, 1877, *Encyclopædia Britannica, Ninth Ed., vol.* IV.

He never quite achieved the distinction which his abilities thoroughly deserved. In one sense he had more brilliant powers than any of his contemporaries. There were men among them who could beat him on any given subject, but there was no one who had so extended an acquaintance with so many matters. He was ready to discuss a scientific problem with Playfair, to argue a point of law with Copley, or a question of policy with Canning. He could make a speech with the same facility with which he could write an article; and he could write an article as easily as another man could write a letter. His physical strength admirably assisted his extraordinary intellectual power. . . . Lord Brougham might have attained the eminence of Fox as a politician, of Erskine as an advocate, of Playfair as a mathematician, of Herschel as an astronomer, of Hallam as an historian. He tried to rival all these characters in their various stations; and, in consequence, though he ran a good second to them all, he did not win quite the first place in any race.—WALPOLE, SPENCER, 1878, *A History of England from the Conclusion of the Great War in* 1815, *vol.* I, *pp.* 310, 311.

The great ability and the prominence of this author entitle this volume ["British Constitution"] to consideration. The first eleven chapters are largely speculative, and to most students will be of less value than those which follow. From chapter xii. to the end, the volume is of considerable historical value. Especially able and discriminating is the discussion of the relations of monarch and parliament in the time of the Plantagenets and Tudors. Chapter xix., on judicial establishments in different countries and in England, is of especial value to the student of law.—ADAMS, CHARLES KENDALL, 1882, *A Manual of Historical Literature, p.* 481.

The "Edinburgh Review" had at that time among its chief contributors a young man of vast energy of brain and vast power of sarcasm, without the commensurate sense of responsibility which might have checked and guided his powers. His intellect was not for a moment to be measured with that of Young; but as a writer appealing to a large class of the public, he was, at that time, an athlete without a rival. He afterwards became Lord Chancellor of England. Young, it may be admitted, has given him some annoyance, but his retaliation,

GEORGE GROTE

*Engraving by H. Robinson. From a
Drawing by S. P. Denning.*

HENRY HART MILLMAN

*From a Water Color Drawing by
F. Cruikshank in 1839.*

if such it were, was out of all proportion to Young's offence. Besides, whatever his personal feelings were, it was not Young that he assailed so much as those sublime natural truths of which Young at the time was the foremost exponent. Through the undulatory theory he attacked Young without scruple or remorse.—TYNDALL, JOHN, 1886, *Thomas Young, New Fragments, p. 275.*

His literary labours can hardly be estimated highly. He attempted too much to be more than superficial. Yet, in the absence of more authoritative works, his "History of the House of Lancaster" is still useful, and his "Sketches of the Statesmen of the Time of George III." have a more permanent value as covering ground with which he was familiar. His "Speeches," collected in 1838, are powerful, though hardly of the highest rank. With energies less dissipated and temper more controlled, Brougham's place in history, and even in literature, must have been very high. As it was, his life was a splendid failure.—TOUT, T. F., 1887, *Celebrities of the Century, ed. Sanders, p. 177.*

As a man of letters, notwithstanding his literary industry and the fact that in the first twenty numbers of the *Edinburgh Review* he wrote eighty articles, he has left no work of lasting celebrity, and in science he made no real discovery. In the midst of all his triumphs, the friends who knew him best were aware that his extraordinary gifts and powers did not include all the important elements of true greatness. He lacked self-control, was too rash, arrogant,

and capricious for a successful leader, and although probably admired and feared more than any man in England, he drifted out of the main stream of national life, and his figure is already becoming indistinct.— LAMB, MARTHA J., 1889, *The Early Career of Lord Brougham, Magazine of American History, vol. 22, p. 453.*

Few eminent men have paid so heavily in posthumous reputation for any failing as Brougham for a jealous and insatiable vanity. His name—apart from the useful vehicle which bears it—conjures up almost no associations that are not ludicrous and grotesque; and as the fame of his achievements as a legislator—of his services to "liberty," education, and a variety of other "causes"—is tainted by the ever-present recollection of his feverish and overwhelming egotism, so his renown as a man of letters has suffered irretrievable damage from the versatility of his gifts. It were vain to look to this champion of progress for any substantial contribution to political philosophy, to physical science, or to literary criticism. Hasty and ill-considered judgments, rash and superficial generalisations, these, together with the commonplace and highsounding maxims dear to shallow and confident minds, are the chief legacy of one who, to borrow Rogers's enumeration, combined in his own person the characters of Solon, Lycurgus, Demosthenes, Archimedes, Sir Isaac Newton, Lord Chesterfield, and a great many more.—MILLAR, J. H., 1896, *English Prose, ed. Craik, vol. v, p. 213.*

Henry Hart Milman
1791–1868

Dean of St. Paul's. Born, in London, 10 Feb. 1791. At school at Greenwich and Eton. Matric. Brasenose Coll., Oxford, 25 May, 1810; Newdigate Prize Poem, 1812; Chancellor's Latin Verse Prize, 1813; B. A., 1814; Fellow of B. N. C., 1814–19; M. A., 1816; Chancellor's English Essay Prize, 1816; Chancellor's Latin Essay Prize, 1816. Ordained Deacon, 1816; Priest, 1816. Vicar of St. Mary's, Reading, 1817–35. Play "Fazio" (originally produced at Surrey Theatre under title of "The Italian Wife") performed at Covent Garden, 5 Feb. 1818. Frequent contributor to "Quarterly Rev." Prof. of Poetry, Oxford, 1821–31. Married Mary Ann Cockell, 11 March 1824. Bampton Lecturer, 1827. Canon of Westminister and Rector of St. Margaret's ,Westminster, 1835–49. Dean of St. Paul's, 1849. B. D. and D. D., Oxford, 1849. Died, near Ascot, 24 Sept. 1868. Buried in St. Paul's Cathedral. *Works:* "The Belvidere Apollo," 1812; "Alexander tumulum Achillis invisens," 1813; "Fazio," 1815; "A Comparative Estimate of Sculpture and Painting" (priv. ptd.), 1816; "In historia scribenda quænam præcipua inter auctores veteres et novos sit differentia?" (priv. ptd.), 1816; "Samor," 1818 (2nd edn. same year); "The Fall of Jerusalem," 1820 (2nd edn. same year); "The Martyr of Antioch," 1822; "Belshazzar," 1822; "Anne Boleyn," 1826; "The Character and Conduct of the Apostles" (Bampton Lectures), 1827; "History of the Jews" (anon.), 1829; "Life of Edward

Gibbon," 1839; "Poetical Works," 1839; "History of Christianity from the Birth of Christ to the Abolition of Paganism in the Roman Empire" (3 vols.), 1840; "History of Latin Christianity . . . to the Pontificate of Pope Nicholas V." (6 vols.), 1855; "A Memoir of Lord Macaulay," 1862 (2nd edn. same year); "Hebrew Prophecy," 1865. *Posthumous* "Annals of St. Paul's Cathedral," ed. by A. Milman, 1868; "Savonarola, Erasmus, and other essays," ed. by A. Milman, 1870. He *translated:* "Nala and Damayanti" (with H. H. Wilson), 1835; Horace's "Works," 1849; Sophocles' "Agamemnon," 1865; Euripidies' "Bacchæ," 1865; and *edited:* Gibbons' "Hist. of Decline and Fall of Roman Empire," 1838–39.—SHARP, R. FARQUHARSON, 1897, *A Dictionary of English Authors*, p. 198.

PERSONAL

I was agreeably disappointed in his appearance. He had been described to me as very much more bent, stooping to the ground; so he is, but the bend is so circular at his back that it has the appearance of a hump; while the face, with the coal-black eyes and raven eyebrows, surmounted by snow-white hair, is really in a true plumbline from his feet, and he appears to stand erect like a benignant Anthropophagus, with his head beneath his shoulders, at a height of three feet from the ground. He is a good deal more deaf, so that one must change the whole pitch of one's voice. But he is full of life, interested in all things political, scientific, literary; full of work and of plans. She [Mrs. Milman] is as sweet, stately, genial, and gentle as she always was—as silvery voiced; and also her sable hair has turned out its silver lining very completely upon the night. In the main I found them singularly unchanged, and as you know them so well, that is their best eulogy. It is most delightful to see that Time, which has been so effective upon his backbone and his tympanum, has had no effect on his splendid intellect and his genial disposition.—MOTLEY, JOHN LOTHROP, 1867, *Letter to his Wife, Aug. 12; Correspondence, ed. Curtis, vol.* II, p. 279.

You know how I loved the dear old Dean, and how much I valued his long, unvarying kindness. It has been a great pleasure to me that I saw him so lately; as always, with the sense that it might be for the last time; as always, with the hope that the extraordinary vitality which he showed might still battle with the advance of age, and keep him yet awhile amongst us. Bitterly, deeply as I mourn for his loss, publicly and privately, I cannot but feel that so to depart, with his eye not dimned nor his natural force abated, was a blessing such as one always in prospect and retrospect rejoices to think of for those we love. How very far back that closed chapter takes us! What a host of famous memories! What a defense and bulwark of all that was just and right! Dear, sacred old sage of other days—sacred with our own dearest recollections—there is no like of him left.—STANLEY, ARTHUR PENRHYN, 1868, *To Louisa Stanley, Sept. 28; Life and Correspondence, ed. Prothero and Bradley, vol.* II, p. 365.

There is one writer whom I must especially mention, for his name occurs continually in the following pages; and his memory has been more frequently and in these later months more sadly, present to my mind than any other. Brilliant and numerous as are the works of the late Dean Milman, it was those only who had the great privilege of his friendship who could fully realise the amazing extent and variety of his knowledge; the calm, luminous, and delicate judgment which he carried into so many spheres; the inimitable grace and tact of his conversation, coruscating with the happiest anecdotes and the brightest and yet the gentlest humour; and perhaps what was more remarkable than any single faculty, the admirable harmony and symmetry of his mind and character, so free from all the disproportion and eccentricity and exaggeration that sometimes make even genius assume the form of a splendid disease. They can never forget those yet higher attributes which rendered him so unspeakably reverent to all who knew him well,—his fervent love of truth; his wide tolerance; his large, generous, and masculine judgments of men and things; his almost instinctive perception of the good that is latent in each opposing party, his disdain for the noisy triumph and the flitting popularity of mere sectarian strife; the fond and touching affection with which he dwelt upon the images of the past, combining, even in extreme old age, with the keenest and most hopeful insight into the progressive movements of his time, and with a rare power of winning the confidence and reading the thoughts of the youngest about him.—LECKY, WILLIAM EDWARD HARTPOLE, 1869, *History of European Morals, Preface.*

In the full exercise of all his brilliant mental activities, in the midst of the peaceful country sights and sounds to which he was so sensitively alive, actually engaged in conversation with friends for whom he had the highest regard, the summons came. On the 29th day of August he was attacked by an illness, a paralytic stroke, which on the 24th of the following month had its fatal termination. Scholar, poet, critic, historian, but above and beyond all these a perfect Christian gentleman, the death of Dean Milman left a void which could not easily be filled. The concurrent testimony of all those who were numbered among his friends or bound by closer ties of nearer love bore witness to the charm and beauty, the kindliness and simplicity, of his character and disposition. He was absolutely guileless, a man of most transparent honesty, of undaunted moral courage. Bishop Stanley, of Norwich, used to say that "Milman, of all men whom he had known, had the greatest moral courage."—MILMAN, ARTHUR, 1900, *Henry Hart Milman, p.* 307.

HISTORY OF THE JEWS
1829

It was during his pastoral life at Reading that he published his "History of the Jews." Many are the waters of controversy, as the French say, that have rolled under the bridge since that time; many have been the storms which have rent the theological heavens. In our days the vehemence of conflict has been intensified by the increased rapidity of communication, by the multiplication of "religious journals," by the more compact organization of "religious parties." It may be doubted whether any subsequent tumult or obloquy has been more passionate than that which beset the first appearance of the "History of the Jews." It was the decisive inroad of German theology into England; the first palpable indication that the Bible "could be studied like another book;" that the characters and events of the sacred history could be treated at once critically and reverently. Those who were but children at the time can remember the horror created in remote rural districts by the rumour that a book had appeared in which Abraham was described as a "sheykh." In Oxford the book was denounced from the University pulpit.—STANLEY, ARTHUR PENRHYN, 1869, *The Late Dean of St. Paul's, Macmillan's Magazine, vol.* 19, *p.* 179.

If we pass from Egypt to Palestine, we have for the general reader the well-known and the well-written "History of the Jews," by the eloquent and scholarly H. H. Milman. This work is not as frequently and faithfully read as it deserves to be. It is written with the critical spirit of a thorough scholar, with the candor of an enlightened Biblical student, with the imagination of a poet, and the faith of a believing Christian. —PORTER, NOAH, 1870, *Books and Reading, p.* 168.

A popular presentation, making no pretence to equality with the great work of Ewald, but striving to bring together into readable form the results reached by the best scholarship of the day. It is written in the author's well-known style, which is remarkable for the smooth-flowing stream of its continuous narrative. The work is a civil and military, rather than a theological, history of the Jews. The author subjects Jewish history to the same canons of criticism as those to which all other histories should be subject. He plants himself on Paley's ground, and does not accept what is commonly known as plenary inspiration of the Old Testament. Beyond "the things necessary to salvation," he conceives that "all, not only in science, but also in history, is an open field." This position awakened much opposition among Milman's fellow-churchmen; but it was a position which, to the author's credit, he never abandoned.— ADAMS, CHARLES KENDALL, 1882, *A Manual of Historical Literature, p.* 77.

In truth, however, Milman, in the light of such Old Testament criticism as we are now familiar with, must be pronounced a highly conservative historian. Our modern schools would, I fear, judge him "unscientific." He repudiated in good faith any anti-supernatural bias, and deliberately separated himself from the extreme school of modern criticism. Its spirit of endless analysis and love of turning everything upside down was thoroughly uncongenial to his mind. He had too much imagination, as well as faith and sobriety of temper, for such work; and he remained to the end what he was plainly from the first, an historical genius who, while urged by his critical powers to sift everything to the bottom and to take nothing for granted merely because it was connected with traditional theology, was yet no less urged by his poetic and concrete tastes to paint a picture rather than give a

mere tableau of critical processes.—TUL-
LOCH, JOHN, 1885, *Movements of Religious
Thought in Britain During the Nineteenth
Century, p.* 57.

In point of composition and research,
the "History of the Jews," which appeared
in 1828, was quite worthy of the high reputation already achieved by the author; but
we can hardly be surprised that it created
alarm. There was an evident tendency to
reduce everything in the history of the
chosen people that could be so reduced to
the level of reason, and to explain away,
when it was at all possible to do so, the supernatural element in it. Men were shocked
to find Abraham treated as an ordinary
Arab sheik, and the appearance of the
manna and the quails attributed to natural
causes. The book came out as one of a
series called "The Family Library," and
caused such dismay that the series was
stopped. The learned writer was probably
a little misunderstood. In the interests of
truth and reality, it was desirable for some
one to bring out the human side of the history of the most remarkable people the
world has ever seen; and Dr. Milman's later
career, which was even more brilliant from
a literary point of view than his earlier,
seems to indicate that he had really no desire to depreciate the Bible. He lived quite
long enough to regain his character for orthodoxy, and perhaps also to show men
that his "History of the Jews" was not
quite what people thought it. But taking
the work simply by itself, there is certainly
some reason for regarding it as a precursor
of a class of works with which in our day
we are very familiar, but which were then
unknown—that is, works in derogation of
revelation from the Christian side.—OVER-
TON, JOHN HENRY, 1894, *The English
Church in the Nineteenth Century* (1800–
1833) *p.* 182.

In this work came a further evolution of
the truths and methods suggested by Bentley, Wolf, and Niebuhr, and their application to sacred history was made strikingly
evident. Milman, though a clergyman,
treated the history of the chosen people in
the light of modern knowledge of Oriental
and especially of Semitic peoples. He exhibited sundry great biblical personages of
the wandering days of Israel as sheiks or
emirs or Bedouin chieftains; and the tribes
of Israel as obedient then to the same general laws, customs, and ideas governing

wandering tribes in the same region now.
He dealt with conflicting sources somewhat
in the spirit of Bentley, and with the mythical, legendary, and miraculous somewhat
in the spirit of Niebuhr. This treatment of
the history of the Jews, simply as the development of an Oriental tribe, raised great
opposition. Such champions of orthodoxy
as Bishop Mant and Dr. Faussett straightway took the field, and with such effect that
the *Family Library*, a very valuable series
in which Milman's history appeared, was
put under the ban and its further publication stopped. For years Milman, though a
man of exquisite literary and lofty historical gifts, as well as of most honourable
character, was debarred from preferment
and outstripped by ecclesiastics vastly inferior to him in everything save worldly
wisdom; for years he was passed in the race
for honours by divines who were content
either to hold briefs for all the contemporary unreason which happened to be popular or to keep their mouths shut altogether.
This opposition to him extended to his
works. For many years they were sneered
at, decried, and kept from the public as
far as possible.—WHITE, ANDREW DICK-
SON, 1896, *A History of the Warfare of
Science with Theology in Christendom, vol.*
II, *p.* 340.

HISTORY OF CHRISTIANITY
1840.

The "History of Christianity" which Mr.
Milman has lately given to the world, is a
work of very considerable ability, and
bears upon it tokens of much thought and
varied research. No one could doubt that
such would be the character of any publication of the author's and the expectation
raised by his name has been increased by
the length of time during which reports
have been current of his having a work on
Christianity in hand. . . . It is indeed
most painful, independently of all personal
feelings which a scholar and poet so early
distinguished as Mr. Milman must excite in
the minds of his brethren, that a work so
elaborate and so important should be composed upon principles which are calculated
to turn all kindly feeling into mere antipathy
and disgust. Indeed there is so much to
shock people, that there is comparatively
little to injure. To one set of persons only is
he likely to do much mischief, those who just
at this moment are so ready to use his main
principle for the demolition of Catholic

views, without seeing that it applies to the New Testament history and teaching just as well. He will assist such persons in carrying out their principle. We observe that a publication, prominent in this warfare, cautions its readers against Mr. Milman's most *dangerous* and *insidious* work. We beg to join this publication and all other similar ones in its sage and seasonable warning. Let all who carp at the fathers and deny tradition, who argue against sacramental influence, who refer celibacy to gnosticism, and episcopal power to Judaism, who declaim against mysticism, and scoff at the miracles of the Church, while at the same time they uphold what is called orthodox Protestantism, steadily abstain from Mr. Milman's volumes. On their controversial principles his reasonings and conclusions are irresistible.—NEWMAN, JOHN HENRY, 1841, *Milman's View of Christianity, Essays Critical and Historical, vol.* II, *pp.* 186, 247.

Our high-churchmen are shocked at so free and fearless a book from a dignitary, and judiciously enough, instead of abusing, they try to smother it. Their Reviews do not choose to have heard of the work. It shows immense reading and a store-house of curious and interesting facts; but I cannot say that it makes upon my mind any single, strong, definite impression; nor perhaps could one well expect this from what may be called a *civil* history of the religion from its origin to the suppression of paganism in the Roman empire.—AIKIN, LUCY, 1841, *To Dr. Channing, Feb.* 7; *Correspondence of William Ellery Channing and Lucy Aikin, ed. Le Breton, p.* 380.

I had postponed the reading of Milman's "History of Christianity," as I do of many good books, but your favorable mention of it determined me to take it in hand; and as soon as I began to convalesce after my late illness, I applied myself to the pleasant task. Sometimes, indeed, my weak head was strained to take in his long, complicated sentences, and I wished that he had added the charm of a simple style to his other merits, but I was too much interested to be discouraged. I have been truly delighted as well as instructed by the work. What amazes me is, that it should have come from the hands of an Episcopalian clergyman. Am I wrong in seeing in it true moral courage? Are there many in that church who sympathize with such large, liberal views? —CHANNING, WILLIAM ELLERY, 1841, *To Miss Aikin, Dec.* 15; *Correspondence of William Ellery Channing and Lucy Aikin, ed. Le Breton, p.* 409.

Though it is written with an almost infidel coolness, it is the only English work that gives the distilled essence of the Germanic researches into out-of-the-way antiquities of our early mother church. — ALEXANDER, JAMES W., 1849, *Forty Years' Familiar Letters, vol.* II, *p.* 105.

HISTORY OF LATIN CHRISTIANITY
1855

Last night I finished your sixth volume. What can I say, except that you have written the finest historical work in the English language? The interest grows from, perhaps commences with, the four last volumes. The first two, covering a vast period comparatively little known, are less distinct, and fail so powerfully to hold the attention. But what a labour of intellect to have shifted so often your point of vision—to have looked at every event, at every character, on all sides, before you set yourself to draw it! Calmness, impartiality, a belief, fixed as the creed, that the history of man, judged as a whole, is the history of his better nature struggling against his lower, and struggling not altogether unsuccessfully; that in a divinely governed world no system of faith or policy have taken effective and enduring hold upon mankind unless the truth in them has been greater than the falsehood,— these are the essentials of a great writer; and these, more than any one who as yet has taken such subjects in hand, you possess. The "History of Christianity" did not prepare me for the "History of Latin Christianity." In the first I seemed to see chiefly the philosopher, in the second the man.— FROUDE, JAMES ANTHONY, 1855, *Letter to Milman; Henry Hart Milman, Dean of St. Paul's, ed. his Son, p.* 224.

One of the remarkable works of the present age, in which the author reviews, with curious erudition, and in a profoundly philosophical spirit, the various changes that have taken place in the Roman hierarchy; and while he fully exposes the manifold errors and corruptions of the system, he shows throughout that enlightened charity which is the most precious of Christian graces, as unhappily it is the rarest.—PRESCOTT, WILLIAM HICKLING, 1855, *The History of the Reign of Philip the Second, vol.* II, *p.* 580, *note.*

I began Milman's "Latin Christianity,"

and was more impressed than ever by the contrast between the substance and the style. The substance is excellent. The style very much otherwise.—MACAULAY, THOMAS BABINGTON, 1856, *Journal, Jan.; Life and Letters, ed. Trevelyan, ch.* xiv.

"The History of Christianity under the Empire," with its gorgeous style, its wide learning, its lucid argument, filled a gap which had been hitherto only supplied by the meagre narratives of Mosheim and Milner, or by the ill-adapted translations of Neander and Gieseler.—STANLEY, ARTHUR PENRHYN, 1869, *The Late Dean of St. Paul's, Macmillan's Magazine, vol.* 19, *p.* 180.

Milman's "History of Latin Christianity" is of the highest value, and is universally accepted as one of our best standard histories.—PORTER, NOAH, 1870, *Books and Reading, p.* 75.

Dean Milman's great and rare qualities were even perhaps more suited for the later history of the Church than for the earlier; and though we should be sorry to be without much of what he has done for the Middle Ages, we are not sure that we would not exchange it for the same amount of work on the time from the fifteenth to the eighteenth century. The English "History of the Reformation" has yet to be written. . . . Dean Milman's imagination and insight, his fearless courage, and his unusual combination of the strongest feelings about right and wrong with the largest equity, would have enabled him to handle this perplexed and difficult history in a manner in which no English writer has yet treated it. We do not say that he could be expected to be entirely successful. He wanted—what many of our most eminent teachers of the present day want—a due appreciation of the reality and depth of those eternal problems of religious thought and feeling which have made theology.—CHURCH, RICHARD WILLIAM, 1871, *Dean Milman's Essays, Occasional Papers, vol.* I, *p.* 156.

The "History of Latin Christianity" is the work on which Milman's fame rests. It does not display equal mastery of language with the "Decline and Fall;" nor was the author gifted with the same philosophical penetration, nor with equal power of combining complicated details into one harmonious and picturesque narrative, with the writer of that immortal work. But he had what Gibbon wanted, a sincere feeling of the vast importance of the subject; a

resolute candour which made him desirous to do justice to all whose views and differences of opinion his narrative led him to notice; and he added to these qualities a rich store of varied learning, which qualified him to form, and which gave weight to, the judgments which he calmly but resolutely expressed. The great merit of the work was promptly and universally acknowledged and is sufficiently attested by the fact that its bulk (it consists of six large volumes) did not prevent its rapidly going through four editions in a very few years.—YONGE, CHARLES DUKE, 1872, *Three Centuries of English Literature, p.* 169.

The public did not sustain his claims to the name of poet, and he has fallen into the limbo of poetical writers, like those who "senza speme vivono in disio." His more important work, however, held a different place, and the man who is recognised as the historian of Latin Christianity does not need to break his heart over the failure of poetic fame.—OLIPHANT, MARGARET O. W., 1882, *Literary History of England, XVIII–XIX Century, vol.* II, *p.* 320.

To the student of the Middle Ages this work is second in importance only to that of Gibbon. It covers substantially the same period, and, although its plan is much more limited, it is in its way scarcely less satisfactory.—ADAMS, CHARLES KENDALL, 1882, *A Manual of Historical Literature, p.* 173.

Just misses, it may be, being one of "the great books of history"—but will long hold its own as an almost necessary complement to Gibbon's "Decline and Fall." It was avowedly designed as its counterpart, its rival, and in one sense its antidote. And we cannot deny that this aim has been, to a great extent attained. It covers almost exactly the same epoch; it tells the same story; its chief characters are the same as in the work of Gibbon. But they are all viewed from another point of view and are judged by a different standard. Although the period is the same, the personages the same, and even the incidents are usually common to both histories, the subject is different, and the plot of the drama is abruptly contrasted. Gibbon recounts the dissolution of a vast system; Milman recounts the development of another vast system; first, the victim, then the rival, and ultimately the successor of the first. Gibbon tells us of the decline and fall of the Roman empire: Milman narrates the rise and constitution of the Catholic church—the religious and ecclesiastical, the moral and intellectual movements which sprang into full maturity as the political empire of Rome passed through its long transformation of a thousand years. The scheme and ground-plan of Milman are almost perfect. Had he the prodigious learning, the super-human accuracy of Gibbon, that infallible good-sense, that perennial humour, that sense of artistic proportion, the dean might have rivalled the portly ex-captain of yeomanry, the erudite recluse in his Swiss retreat. He may not be quite strong enough for his giant's task. But no one else has even essayed to bend the bow which Ulysses of Lausanne hung up on one memorable night in June, 1787, in his garden study; none has attempted to recount the marvellous tale of the consolidation of the Christianity of Rome over the whole face of western Europe during a clear period of a thousand years.—HARRISON, FREDERIC, 1894, *Some Great Books of History, The Meaning of History, p.* 107.

He lived to see his main ideas accepted, and his "History of Latin Christianity" received as certainly one of the most valuable and no less certainly the most attractive of all church histories ever written.—WHITE, ANDREW DICKSON, 1896, *A History of the Warfare of Science with Theology in Christendom, vol.* II, *p.* 340.

The "History of Latin Christianity" is a work of epic proportions, and, save in its style, approaches epic dignity. A subject hardly less majestic than that of Gibbon, it was less susceptible of historic treatment in the grand style because it lacked an inherent unity. Without Gibbon's marked distinction of manner, Milman possesses many of the virtues of a good writer, and sustains with fluent ease the weight of his great narrative. A notable man, one may say of him, in the best company, the company in which the highest names are those of Hooker, of Taylor, and of Berkeley; at his best comparable, if not superior, to any English historian after Gibbon, and one who in every page of his writing stands revealed as above all else a Christian, a scholar, and a gentleman,— DIXON, W. MACNEILE, 1896, *English Prose, ed. Craik, vol.* V, *p.* 346.

Is a great book, and will probably live. For Milman here really *knew*; he had (like most poets who write prose with fair prac-

tice) an excellent style; and he was able— as many men who have had knowledge have not been able, and as many who have had style have not tried or have failed to do—to rise to the height of a really great argument, and treat it with the grasp and ease which are the soul of history. That he owed much to Gibbon himself is certain; that he did not fail to use his pupilage to that greatest of historians so as to rank among the best of his followers is not less certain, and is high enough praise for any man.—SAINTSBURY, GEORGE, 1896, *A History of Nineteenth Century Literature, p.* 219.

Though errors have been detected in it, the tone and spirit are good, the method sound and the scholarship admirable.— WALKER, HUGH, 1897, *The Age of Tennyson, p.* 127.

The "History of Latin Christianity" has taken rank as one of the standard works of English literature; and I do not think that any one who is acquainted with the historical and ecclesiastical writings of the last forty years can fail to see the influence that it has exercised upon them, nor the vast mine of information which it has been to labourers in portions of the same field. In the schools of the Universities it is a recognized text-book; in the United States, among a kindred people, it has an equally established position.—MILMAN, ARTHUR, 1900, *Henry Hart Milman, Dean of St. Paul's, p.* 229.

POEMS

I have just finished Henry Milman's poem, a work of great power. But the story is ill-constructed, and the style has a vice analogous to that which prevailed in prose about one hundred and seventy years ago. . . With less poetry "Samor" would have been a better poem. . . . If Milman can perceive or be persuaded of his fault, he has powers enough for any thing; but it is a seductive manner. . . . He is a fine young man, and his powers are very great. They are, however, better fitted for the drama than for narration; the drama admits his favorite strain of composition, and is easier in its structure. Indeed, it is as much easier to plan a play than a poem of such magnitude as "Samor" as it is to build a gentleman's house than a cathedral.—SOUTHEY, ROBERT, 1812, *To C. H. Townshend, April* 12; *Life and Correspondence of Robert Southey, ed. C. C. Southey, ch.* XXIII.

"Fazio," the new tragedy, is in parts very

fine and in others as bad. It is written by a young Mr. Milman, son to the physician. It is well worth sending for. Some people think it beautiful. Lord Lansdowne brought it to Saltram and said it was one of the finest things he had ever read, so do get it. The woman's character is very interesting.—GRANVILLE, HARRIET COUNTESS, 1815, *To Lady G. Morpeth, Sept.* 29; *Letters, ed. Gower, vol.* I, *p.* 82.

The poem ["Samor"] opens with an eulogy on the author's country, and in the very first sentence we meet with that indistinctness which, from bad arrangement of words and the very worst punctuation we have ever met with, in almost every page, compels us to read some sentences two or three times in order to understand it. In the structure of the verse, there is a close imitation of Milton; it is, however, more involved, and crowded with vague epithets. . . . We are not willing to take this poem as a specimen of Mr. Milman's powers. The want of interest, arising from the unskilful direction of talent rather than from the want of it, is the great fault of "Samor." The subject does not admit of the exercise of those powers which Mr. Milman can exercise to most advantage. A humbler theme would suit him better. The description of natural scenery and domestic character would tame his soaring spirit and bring him to meet us on equal ground. He must meet us, for he has not the all-powerful energy of genius to transport us from the world of our own thoughts and feelings to one of his creation.—LORING, W., 1819, *Milman's Samor, North American Review, vol.* 9, *pp.* 28, 35.

He has now produced a poem ["Fall of Jerusalem"] in which the peculiar merits of his earlier efforts are heightened, and their besetting faults, even beyond expectation, corrected; a poem to which, without extravagant encomium, it is not unsafe to promise whatever immortality the English language can bestow, and which may, of itself, entitle its author to a conspicuous and honourable place in our poetical pantheon, among those who have drunk deep at the fountain-head of intellect and enriched themselves with the spoils without encumbering themselves with the trammels of antiquity.—HEBER, REGINALD, 1820, *Milman's Fall of Jerusalem, Quarterly Review, vol.* 23, *p.* 225.

I cannot conclude without expressing, however inadequately, the delight with which I have just risen from the perusal of the "Martyr of Antioch." It has added another noble proof to those you had already given the world of the power and dignity which genius derives from its consecration to high and sacred purposes. Never were the "gay religions full of pomp and gold" so beautifully contrasted with the deep and internal sublimity of Christianity. I could dwell upon many parts which have made a lasting impression upon my mind, did I not fear that it would appear almost presumptuous to offer a tribute of praise so insignificant as mine to that which must have already received the suffrage of all who are entitled to judge of excellence.—HEMANS, FELICIA DOROTHEA, 1822, *Letter to Milman, March* 7; *Henry Hart Milman, Dean of St. Paul's, ed. his Son, p.* 122.

Here's Milman, the Idol of Square-caps at
    Oxford,
Though his verses will scarce ever travel to
    Foxford;
His Pegasus broken, no longer is skittish,
Though he's puff'd in the Quarterly, puff'd in
    the British.

WILSON, JOHN, 1822, *Noctes Ambrosianæ, July.*

"The Fall of Jerusalem". . . quickly caught the public attention, and was crowned with the most general applause. The subject had strong hold upon our sympathies. . . . Mr. Milman has treated it with complete success.—DIBDIN, THOMAS FROGNALL, 1824, *The Library Companion, p.* 743.

We are always impressed with a conviction of his learning, his ability, and his cultivated taste, but are haunted at the same time with an unsatisfactory feeling, that his poetry is rather a clever recasting of fine things already familiar to us, than strikingly fresh and original. . . . With less leaning to authorities and greater reliance on his own powers and impressions, there can be no doubt that Milman would have written far finer poetry, and secured a more extended acceptibility; for his more simple strains are, after all, those best remembered and he could be at times alike natural and pathetic.—MOIR, D. M., 1851–52, *Sketches of the Poetical Literature of the Past Half-Century, Lecture* IV.

May be taken as representing a class of writers in whom the poetic fire is ever on the point, and only on the point, of breaking into a flame. His composition is admirable—refined, scholarly, sometimes rich and even gorgeous in expression—yet lacking that radiance of the unutterable to which the loftiest words owe their grandest power. Perhaps the best representative of his style is the hymn on the Incarnation, in his dramatic poem, "The Fall of Jerusalem."—MACDONALD, GEORGE, 1868, *England's Antiphon, p.* 312.

First came his brilliant poetical career. If some of its early splendour be overcast—if few of this generation turn with the same devouring eagerness as did their predecessors to the "Fall of Jerusalem" and the "Martyr of Antioch"—yet there are passages in that stage of his mental development which give no indication of losing their ground. The English visitor to the Apollo Belvedere will long recall the most perfect of all Oxford prize poems, every line of which catches some characteristic of the matchless statue—
" Too fair to worship—too divine to love."
The song of triumph, "For Thou art Born of Woman," will long keep its place, not unworthily, beside Milton's "Ode on the Nativity." The exquisite pathos of the funeral hymns, "Brother, Thou art Gone Before Us," and "When Our Heads are Bowed with Woe," will embalm the name of Milman in many a Christian household to which his more secular and his more theological works are alike unknown.—STANLEY, ARTHUR PENRHYN, 1869, *The Late Dean of St. Paul's, Macmillan's Magazine, vol.* 19, *p.* 178.

Although his poetry has failed to live, save in a few hymns, it remains an interesting monument of the early glow and splendor of his genius. "The Fall of Jerusalem" and "The Martyr of Antioch" contain passages of great power and beauty; but, like the poetic efforts of a great female genius of our times, they are lacking in creative art and movement. They are poetical essays, rather than poems springing spontaneously and irresistibly out of the heart and imagination of the writer.—TULLOCH, JOHN, 1885, *Movements of Religious Thought in Britain During the Nineteenth Century, p.* 55.

The "Latin Christianity" is still a valued book of reference, and gives its author a more lasting title to fame than many "Martyrs of Antioch" could do, even with the addition of Sir Arthur Sullivan's music.—

OLIPHANT, MARGARET O. W., 1892, *The Victorian Age of English Literature, p.* 191.

Milman's poetical works were received with enthusiasm, but they cannot be said to have retained a moiety of the interest they excited upon their appearance. Though he so frequently adopted the dramatic form he lacked dramatic instinct, and was wanting in passion and imagination. There are fine passages in all his works, passages in which elevated thought is clothed in ornate language, and adorned with picturesque imagery. . . . Some of his hymns, "Ride on, Ride on in Majesty," "When Our Heads are Bowed with Woe," and others are still in use, but his longer poems have ceased to attract attention or are only read in selections.—MILES, ALFRED H., *ed.* 1897, *The Poets and the Poetry of the Century, Sacred, Moral, and Religious Verse, p.* 110.

GENERAL

He was the unquestioned patriarch of English literature. He was the last of that brilliant galaxy which ushered in the beginning of this century—the intimate friend of some of them, the companion of all. In him the traditions of Byron and Scott, of Coleridge and Wordsworth, of Hallam and Macaulay, of Rogers and Sydney Smith, lived on into a younger generation. It was truly said of him that he belonged more to the English nation than to the English Church. His severe taste, his nicely-balanced judgment, his abundant knowledge, his keen appreciation of the varied forms of literary excellence, enabled him to keep always above, and at the same time almost always in sympathy with, the intellectual movements of the age.—STANLEY, ARTHUR PENRHYN, 1869, *The Late Dean of St. Paul's, Macmillan's Magazine, vol.* 19, *p.* 177.

A sort of measure of Dean Milman's qualifications for dealing with religious history is given in these "Essays." He writes of Savonarola, of Erasmus, and then of the Popes, from those of the Riario and Borgia type to those of the Lambertini and Ganganelli order. They are all vigorous and brilliant studies, full of knowledge, full of historical grasp and intelligence, full of noble sympathy and noble scorn, full of regulated humour of all the shades from amused and compassionate playfulness to indignant sarcasm; kindling, as Dean Milman's wont was, from a style of often careless roughness into passages of powerful and finished eloquence. But he had to deal in them with subjects which were in unequal degrees congenial to him, and for which he was, and probably felt himself, unequally adapted. Savonarola was a subject which, if the character was to be treated with sympathy at all, needed, it seems to us, a subtler and more delicate power of entering into the mysterious conditions and experiences of the spiritual side of human life than the historian ever gave evidence of possessing. . . . Turn from Savonarola to Erasmus, and there we find at once that the writer is far more at home. Dean Milman has given perhaps the best and truest portrait that has ever been presented of a man who was even a more important person in the history of his time than Savonarola.—CHURCH, RICHARD WILLIAM, 1871, *Dean Milman's Essays, Occasional Papers, vol.* I, *pp.* 158, 161.

The qualities of Dean Milman's mind, intellectual and moral, were such as to engage the affections of his friends even more than their admiration. Without noting his other and various works, the "History of Latin Christianity" would alone give him high and merited rank in English literature. As a writer he ever clung with masculine fidelity to what he believed to be truth.—HOLLAND, SIR HENRY, 1871, *Recollections of Past Life, p.* 220.

The name of Milman does not pale beside that of Thirlwall. There are those, indeed, who esteem it a still more brilliant name in sacred literature. So far both were alike. They never acquired the sort of popular distinction that waits on the leaders of great ecclesiastical parties—men of the stamp of the late Dr. Wilberforce or Dr. Pusey. . . . Milman is probably less known than even Thirlwall. I have met with people of education, and some degree of culture,

who were, if not ignorant of his name, ignorant of all he has done. They were astonished to hear him spoken of as a great historian. They had never read a word of his "History of Latin Christianity," nor even of his "History of the Jews." They had never heard of him as one of the greatest names that the Church of England has ever produced. In combination of pure genius with learning, of sweep of thought with picturesque and powerful variety of literary culture and expression, he has always seemed to me by far the first of modern English churchmen. — TULLOCH JOHN, 1885, *Movements of Religious Thought in Britain During the Nineteenth Century, p.* 54.

Without question one of the most accomplished men of letters of the present century, a distinguished editor and translator from the classics and from the Sanscrit, a poet of considerable imaginative range and lyrical sweetness, a far-sighted critic, an historian of ample learning and power, he seems to have his place on that border-line where rare and brilliant talent melts into genius. Test him by some searching touchstone of genius, and he may indeed fall short; measure him by any rule of talent, and he satisfies but transcends it with much to spare.—DIXON, W. MACNEILE, 1896, *English Prose, ed. Craik, vol.* V, *p.* 346.

Yet the "Halbheit" which characterizes Milman throughout his work prevented him from giving these fruitful ideas full scope; and in spite of his fine sympathetic insight, accomplished scholarship, and wide and deep learning, he belongs to the class, so frequent in the history of English culture, of those who but half apprehend the meaning and tendency of their own work.—HERFORD, CHARLES HAROLD, 1897, *The Age of Wordsworth, p.* 47.

Samuel Lover

1797–1868

Born, in Dublin, 24 Feb. 1797. Privately educated there. Early aptitude for music. In office of his father (a stockbroker), 1812–14. Began to study painting, 1814. Married (i.) Miss Berrel, 1827. Memb. of Royal Hibernian Acad., 1828; Secretary, 1830. Contrib. to "Dublin Literary Gaz." Exhibited at Royal Acad., London, 1833. One of the founders of "Dublin Univ. Mag.," 1833. To London, 1835; engaged in miniature painting. Play, "The Olympic Picnic," produced at Olympic Theatre, 1835; "The Beau Ideal," 1836; "Rory O'More" (dramatized from his novel), Adelphi Theatre, 1837; "The White Horse of the Peppers," Adelphi; "The Happy Man," Haymarket; "The Greek Boy," Covent Garden; " Il Paddy Whack in Italia," Lyceum. Helped to form "Bentley's

Miscellany," 1837. Gave up painting owing to failing eyesight, 1844. Produced entertainment, "Irish Evenings," performed by himself at Princess's Concert Rooms, March 1844; performed it in America, 1846–48; "Paddy's Portfolio," 1848. Wife died, 1847. Play "Sentinels of the Alma," produced, Haymarket; "Macarthy More," Lyceum. Married (ii.) Mary Wandby, Jan. 1852. Ill-health from 1864. Removed to St. Heliers, Jersey; died there, 6 July 1868. Buried at Kensal Green. *Works* [exclusive of various farces printed in Lacy's, Webster's, and Duncombe's "Acting Editions"]: "Rory O'More" (ballad), 1826; "Legends and Stories of Ireland" (2 series), 1831–34; "Rory O'More" (novel) 1837; "Songs and Ballads," 1839; "Handy Andy," 1842; "Treasure Trove," 1844; "Lyrics of Ireland," 1858; "Rival Rhymes in Honour of Burns" (under pseud. "Ben Trovato"), 1859; "Volunteer Songs," 1859; "Metrical Tales, and Other Poems," 1860 [1859]. *Life:* by W. Bayle Bernard, 1874. *Collected Works;* "Poetical Works" [1880].—SHARP, R. FARQUHARSON, 1897, *A Dictionary of English Authors, p.* 173.

PERSONAL

In his personal appearance Lover has no smack of superfine clay. He looks made out of the fresh turf of his country, sound, honest and natural. He is careless in his dress, a little absent in his gait and manner, just short and round enough to let his atmosphere of fun roll easily about him, and, if frayed at all in the thread of his nature, a little marked with an expression of care—the result of years of anxieties for the support of a very interesting family. His features seem to use his countenance as a hussar does his jacket—wearing it loosely till wanted—and a more mobile, nervous, changing set of lineaments never played photograph to a soul within. There is always about him the modest unconsciousness of a man who feels that he can always employ his thoughts better than upon himself, and he therefore easily slips himself off, and becomes the spirit of his song or story. He does nothing like an actor. If you had heard him singing the same song, by chance, at an Inn, you would have taken him to be a jewel of a good fellow, of a taste and talent deliciously peculiar and natural, but who would spoil at once with being found out by a connoisseur and told of his merits. He is the soul of pure, sweet, truthful Irish nature, though with the difference from others that, while he represents it truly and is a piece of it himself, he *has also the genius to create what inspires it.*—WILLIS, N. P., 1851, *Samuel Lover, Hurry-Graphs.*

A most good-natured, pleasant Irishman, with a shining and twinkling visage. . . . After supper, Mr. Lover sang some Irish songs, his own in music and words, with rich, humorous effect, to which the comicality of his face contributed almost as much as his voice and words.—HAWTHORNE, NATHANIEL, 1856, *English Note Books, vol.* II, *pp.* 96, 97.

Finally, he tried the stage—tempted, it is probable, by the great success of power in Irish characters; but I believe his first appearance was his last, a most vexatious but supremely ridiculous accident entirely destroyed his confidence, and damaged him fatally in the opinion of his audience. It was in a provincial theatre—I forget where—and I believe in his own drama of "Rory O'More." He had to make his entrance through a cottage-door in the center of the stage, which had a small bar of wood across it representing the threshold. Over this he unluckily tripped and fell flat on his face, to the great amusement of the gallery. Recovering himself from his confusion, and cheered by the general applause with which a good-natured audience generously endeavoured to drown the recollection of his misadventure, he proceeded with the part; but, of course, with less spirit than he might have done under more favourable circumstances, and at the conclusion of the scene, having to make his exit through the same door, as malicious fate would have it, caught his foot again in the same bar, and was precipitated out of the cottage exactly as he had been into it. This was too much for the audience; the whole house was convulsed with laughter, and I am not quite sure that poor Lover summoned up courage to face it again. At all events, he speedily abandoned histrionics, and I never knew him to allude in the slightest manner to his disheartening *coup d'essai* in them, nor, of course, was it ever mentioned by me or any of the few who heard of it.—PLANCHÉ, JAMES ROBINSON, 1872, *Recollections and Reflections, vol.* II, *p.* 292.

Not less notable, however, than the best of his endowments—and certainly not less important as a principal source of his success—was his unflagging application. He was not only one of the cleverest and most vivacious men of his time, but he was also one of the most laborious. The great moral of his life—next to that strong sense of self-reliance which led him, whilst still a boy, to exert his talents at all hazards—was his ready surrender of indulgence and patient submission to detail, as the only means which could convert a gift into either a gain or a distinction. It is true he was so happily constituted that he could make his various faculties serve as reliefs to one another. He could pass from the easel to the piano, and from the etching-stool to the pen, and renew his vigour with as much certainty as he could awaken his invention.—BERNARD, BAYLE, 1874, *The Life of Samuel Lover, Introduction, p.* xviii.

He was a rare humorist, had a bright Hibernian rollicking manner, a happy smile, and a rich brogue. He led the van of that noble army of British authors who have come here to show us their own heroes and heroines as they see them themselves,—to be the interpreters of their own works. His visit in every way was successful; he made hosts of friends in this country, and went back to his own with many of our dollars in his pocket, our good wishes and farewells ringing in his ears, and, as he always said, the happiest recollections of America and greatest affection for the Americans in his heart.—HUTTON, LAURENCE, 1875, *Plays and Players, p.* 115.

Such was the bright and happy career of one, who, from the time of his boyhood when he breathed health on the Wicklow mountains down to his peaceful end at St. Helier's, in his seventy-second year, was fortunate in all he undertook; because, along with a brilliant, versatile genius, he was honest, honourable and dowered with practical common sense; and he also possessed a force of character, with a rare capacity for persistent work, which enabled him successfully to carry through and master whatever he resolved to attempt. Warm-hearted and pure-minded, tender and true, joyous and brave,—Samuel Lover, humbly accepted the strengthening and comforting truths of Revelation, reverencing God, and sincerely loving his fellow-men. . . . His Irish peasant songs, —inimitable, piquant and unique, terse and musical, overflowing with tender affection and natural pathos, sparkling with wit and beaming with kindly humour, innocent fun, and cordial geniality,—are universally appreciated and sung "con amore," wherever the English language is known.— SMYINGTON, ANDREW JAMES, 1880, *Samuel Lover, pp.* 255, 256.

It was not uncommon to hear Lover described as "a Brummagem Tom Moore." That he certainly was not. Far from it. The one was as original as the other, but each in his own way. He was neither copyist nor imitator, and, if he had less of the inventive faculty than Moore, he had the art of making his own the thoughts for which there was no other owner. But it was as a teller of Irish stories Lover most delighted an audience. Few who heard him will forget the inimitable humor, the rich oily brogue, and the perfect ideal he conveyed into the character when relating "New Pettaties" and "Will ye lend me the loan of a gridiron?"—HALL, SAMUEL CARTER, 1883, *Retrospect of a Long Life.*

I saw a great deal of Samuel Lover when he was in America in 1848. He was advertised to appear at the Broadway Theatre, and when he attempted to play in his own piece, "The White Horse of the Peppers," he was certainly the most frightfully nervous man I ever saw in my life. There was a great house because of the natural curiosity to see the poet in his own play. He was a very intimate friend of my father's. I stood in the wings when he came down as *Gerald Pepper.* The costume was the military dress of a cavalier of the time of James II., the scene of the play being the Revolution,—William III. coming over and turning James II. out of the country,—and *Gerald Pepper* was one of the Irish who remained faithful to the Stuart king. His feathers on this occasion were stuck in the back of his hat, his sword-belt was over the wrong shoulder, one of his boots was pulled up over his knee and the other was down over his foot. He looked as if somebody had pitch-forked his clothes onto him, and he was trembling like a leaf. I induced him to put a little more color in his face, took his hat off and adjusted the feathers properly, put his sword on as it ought to go, fixed his boots right, and literally pushed him onto the stage. Of course there is no harm now in saying that it was one of the worst amateur performances I ever saw in my life, and I don't think Lover ever acted after that uncomfortable night.—WALLACK, LESTER, 1888, *Memories of Fifty Years, p.* 187.

He struck me only as a pleasant little man of society, of not much weight.— LINTON, WILLIAM JAMES, 1894, *Three-Score and Ten Years, p.* 174.

"Sam Lover," or "Little Lover," as his friends sometimes irreverently called him, was a great favorite in London society. Possessing an inexhaustible fund of high spirits, good humour and sparkling wit, no one could be better company. Nor was he one of those who, as the Irish neatly express it, "hang up their fiddles behind the door" when they come home. On the contrary, he was never more happy, delightful and entertaining than when he was at home with only his wife and daughters about him. His truly lovable character was not only shown in gaity: he was also deeply humane and kind, with the keenest sense of honor and the warmest heart in the world.—SCHMID, FANNY, 1897, *The Author of " Rory O'More," Century Magazine, vol.* 53, *p.* 581.

GENERAL

My children also read to me "Charles O'Malley," a book full of action and graphical power; the work of a fresh, ever-observant and inventive mind, not going far into human nature, but giving the surface of life very vividly; a book to intoxicate the adventurous, daring young men by sketches of war, in its strange mixture of gay conviviality, recklessness and bloodshed. — CHANNING, WILLIAM ELLERY, 1841, *To Miss Aikin, Dec.* 15; *Correspondence of William Ellery Channing and Lucy Aikin, ed. Le Breton, p.* 410.

Lover is a very forcibly effective, and truthful writer of Irish novels, and falls into the ranks after Banim. He has less passion, but more picturesque vivacity. As a writer and composer of songs (not to mention the charming expression with which he sings them) Mr. Lover is still more popular, and his ballads have a certain singable beauty in them, and a happy occasional fancifulness. His novels, however, are the stuff whereof his fame is made, and they are highly vital and of great value in the sense of commentary on the national character.—HORNE, RICHARD HENGIST, 1844, *A New Spirit of the Age.*

Lover is, as you know, the writer of songs equal (in popular effect) to any of Burns's. He is the author of Tales of humor

in a vein in which he has no equal. His songs are set to his own music, of a twin genius with the words it uses. His power of narration is peculiar and irresistible. His command of that fickle drawbridge between tears and laughter—that ticklish chasm across which touch Mirth and Pathos—is complete and wonderful. He is, besides, a most successful play-writer, and one of the best miniature painters living. He is a Crichton of the arts of joyance for eye and ear.—WILLIS, NATHANIEL PARKER, 1851, *Samuel Lover, Hurry-Graphs.*

Of Lover's merits as a critic, despite his own modest disclaimers, a fair acknowledgment is due. He was no antiquarian, as he confesses—no Celtic scholar who could compare the claims of ancient and modern Irish song—but he was familiar with its history, knew the causes, and could enlarge instructively on the distinctions of its various classes, and, well acquainted with their leading specimens, was not unqualified to weigh and authenticate them in the duty of selection. His biographical notices are always faithful and compact, and if, in his notes, he has chosen to adopt a rambling pleasantry of tone that is occasionally diffuse, this does not exclude exactness when any point of interest occurs.—BERNARD, BAYLE, 1874, *The Life of Samuel Lover, p.* 333.

His tastes were simple and his life pure. Thoroughly unselfish, hopeful himself and helpful to others, possessing a bright, happy disposition, and a noble nature which was the very soul of honour, he was respected and loved, by all who had the privilege of knowing him.—SYMINGTON, ANDREW JAMES, 1880, *Samuel Lover, p.* 256.

His "Handy Andy" is a formless book, and the fun of it grows tedious.—WALKER, HUGH, 1897, *The Age of Tennyson, p.* 99.

His "Rory O'More" took the general fancy. To its strains the Queen at her coronation was escorted to Buckingham Palace. To its strains the peasant baby in its box cradle fell asleep. To its strains Phelim O'Shea footed the reel at Limerick Fair, and the ladies at Dublin Castle trod their quadrille. — WARNER, CHARLES DUDLEY, ed. 1897, *Library of the World's Best Literature, vol.* XVI, *p.* 9217.

The versatility of Lover is one of the stock examples in Irish biography, and it is somewhat difficult to say in which of his various capacities he best succeeded. I am inclined to think that it is as a humorous poet that he ranks highest. He has many competitors in other branches of intellect-

ual activity, but there are very few indeed who can be placed on the same level as a humorist in verse.—O'DONOGHUE, D. J., 1900, *A Treasury of Irish Poetry, ed. Brooke and Rolleston, p. 64.*

Sir David Brewster
1781–1868

David Brewster, born at Jedburgh, Dec. 11, 1781, and educated for the Church of Scotland, undertook the editorship of the "Edinburgh Encyclopædia" in 1808. He received honorary degrees from various Universities in England and Scotland. In 1815 the Royal Society awarded him the Copley Medal for his discovery of the law of the polarization of light by reflexion; in 1816 the Institute of France adjudged him half of the prize of 3,000 francs given for the most important discoveries made in Europe in any branch of science during the two preceding years; and in 1819 the Royal Society awarded him the Rumford gold and silver medals. In 1825 he was elected a corresponding member of the Institute of France; in 1832 was knighted by William IV.; and in 1848 was elected one of the eight foreign associates of the Imperial Institute of France. He became principal of the united colleges of St. Salvator, St. Leonard and St. Andrews, in 1838, Principal of the University of Edinburgh in 1859, and died Feb. 10, 1868. Sir D. Brewster, who made many important inventions, amongst which lenses for light-houses and the kaleidoscope are best known, wrote "The Martyrs of Science," published in 1846; "More Worlds Than One," being an answer to Dr. Whewell's "Plurality of Worlds," in 1854; "Memoirs of the Life, Writings, and Discoveries of Sir Isaac Newton," in 1855; numerous scientific works, and contributed to the Quarterly Reviews, and to the Transactions of scientific societies.—TOWNSEND, GEORGE, 1870, *The Every-Day Book of Modern Literature, vol.* I, *p.* 457.

PERSONAL

As to Brewster, though he and I are as nearly opposite as two persons can well be, whom the world would class together, yet I found it a very tolerable and even not unpleasant thing to spend a week in his society, especially as I had the society of so many others at the same time. "All things are less dreadful than they seem," and a human interest and kindness can temper usefully the sense of philosophical difference. — HAMILTON, SIR WILLIAM ROWAN, 1832, *To Viscount Adare, July* 20; *Life by Graves, vol.* I, *p.* 573.

I thank God, with all my heart, for His departed servant that now, when the battle is over, he fought the good fight so well, and in days of doubt, and of darkness, and of declension, kept the faith—not only kept, but clung to it. He was one who was not ashamed in the highest assemblies of the land to stand up as a Christian, and avow himself a believer. . . . He knew the difference, which some seem not to see, between the sphere of revealed religion and that of arts and sciences. Theirs is the region for discoveries, and new truths, and novelties—for something the world never saw, or thought of, or

dreamed of before—for the progress that lies between the first log-hut which screened its tenants from the storm, and the proud palace of kings; that lies between the path man cut in the primeval forest, and the iron road along which he skims with fire and water yoked to his chariot wheels; that lies between those beacon fires that blazed far and near on your border hills, carrying the news of invasion across the land, and the wires by which I flash a message from the Old World to the New, through the bowels of the mountains and depths of the sea.— GUTHRIE, THOMAS, 1868, *Funeral Sermon, The Home Life of Sir David Brewster, ed. Mrs. Gordon, p.* 417.

Brewster's character was peculiarly liable to misconstruction from its distinctly dual nature; it was made up of opposites, and his peculiarly impulsive temperament and expressions laid him open to the charge of inconsistency, although he never recognised it in himself, conscious that he spoke what was consistent with the point of view whence he took his observations at the time. Accustomed to look at every subject with the critical investigation of the man of science, he yet united the feelings of the man of impulse, and he spoke as moved by either habit.—GORDON, MARGARET MARIA, 1869, *The Home Life of Sir David Brewster*, p. 294.

GENERAL

A philosopher who, while supreme in his own special walk, is perhaps of all living men the most extensively acquainted with the general domain of physical science.—MILLER, HUGH, 1854, *Geology versus Astronomy, Essays*, p. 372.

Since his own scientific sensibilities are keen, . . . we hope they will make him fully feel that he has linked his own name to that of his first object of human reverence ["Life of Newton"] for as long as our century shall retain a place in literary history. This will be conceded by all, how much soever they may differ from the author in opinions or conclusions; and though we shall proceed to attack several of Sir D. Brewster's positions, and though we have no hesitation in affirming that he is too much of a biographer, and too little of an historian, we admire his earnest enthusiasm, and feel as strongly as any one of his assentients the service he has rendered to our literature.—DE MORGAN, AUGUSTUS, 1855, *Brewster's Life of Newton*, *North British Review*, vol. 23, p. 309.

It is remarked of Brewster's style that while in his youth it was severe and almost cold, confining itself to rigid scientific statement, it became in his later days warm and glowing, giving free scope to the imagination and the fancy.—HART, JOHN S., 1872, *A Manual of English Literature*, p. 556.

The writings of Sir David Brewster present a remarkable union of the man of science with the man of letters. The experimental philosopher is seldom a master of rhetoric; but Sir David, far beyond the appointed period of threescore-and-ten,

was full of fancy and imagination, and had a copious and flowing style.—CHAMBERS, ROBERT, 1876, *Cyclopædia of English Literature*, ed. *Carruthers*.

We think of Brewster, the experimental philosopher, who combined in so extraordinary a degree the strictest severity of scientific argument and form with a freedom of fancy and imagination which lent picturesqueness to all his illustrations and invested his later writings especially with an indefinable charm.—MCCARTHY, JUSTIN, 1879, *A History of Our Own Times from the Accession of Queen Victoria to the Berlin Congress*, ch. XXIX.

A work ["Life of Newton"] of sterling merit, though not invariably accurate, and entering largely into details which, as unintelligible to general readers, have no business in an ordinary biography, and had better have been more thoroughly treated of apart in a monograph for students of science.—COPNER, JAMES, 1885, *Sketches of Celibate Worthies*, p. 208.

He may, therefore, be regarded, apart from his other claims to distinction, as one of those who did much to popularise physical science. But, as his successor in St. Andrews so justly remarked, if "his scientific glory is different in kind from that of Young and Fresnel, as the discoverer of the law of polarisation of biaxal crystals, of optical mineralogy, and of double refraction by compression, he will always occupy a foremost rank in the intellectual history of the age."—BROWN, ROBERT, 1887, *Celebrities of the Century*, ed. *Sanders*, p. 169.

Among the most prominent figures in the scientific world at the commencement of the reign was one also well known in wider fields of literature, David Brewster. —OLIPHANT, MARGARET O. W., 1892, *The Victorian Age of English Literature*, p. 358.

William Carleton

1794–1869

Born, at Prillisk, co. Tyrone, 20 Feb. 1794 (according to his autobiography; 4 March according to his tombstone). Educated at various small schools in neighbourhood. Intended for Church, but idea soon abandoned. Apprenticed to stone-cutter, 1814. Private tutor in farmer's family, co. Louth, 1814. To Dublin, 1818; engaged in tuition. Clerk to Sunday School Society. Married Jane Anderson, [1820?]. Began to contribute to various periodicals; to "Christian Examiner," 1828–30; to "National Magazine," 1830–31; Granted Crown pension of £200, 14 July 1848. Visit to London, Oct. to Nov., 1850. Died, at Sandford, co. Dublin, 30 Jan. 1869. *Works:* "Traits and Stories of the Irish

Peasantry" (anon.), 2 series, 1830–33; "Tales of Ireland" (anon.), 1834; "Fardorougha the Miser," 1839; "Father Butler," 1839; "The Fawn of Springvale, etc.," 1841 (2nd ed., entitled "Jane Sinclair," 1849); "Valentine McClutchy," 1845; "Rody the Rover," 1845; "Parra Sastha," 1845; "Art Maguire," 1847; "The Black Prophet," 1847; "The Emigrants of Ahadarra," 1847; "The Tithe Proctor," 1849; "The Clarionet, etc.," 1850; "Red Hall," 1852 (2nd edn., entitled "The Black Baronet," 1857); "The Squanders of Castle Squander," 1852; "Willy Reilly," 1855 (2nd edn., same year); "The Emigrants," 1857; "The Evil Eye," 1860; "The Double Prophecy," 1862; "Redmond, Count O'Hanlon," 1862; "The Silver Acre, etc.," 1862. *Posthumous:* "The Fair of Emyvale, etc.," 1870; "The Red-Haired Man's Wife," 1889. *Life:* (including Autobiography and Letters) by D. J. O'Donoghue, 1896. — SHARP, R. FARQUHARSON, 1897, *A Dictionary of English Authors,* p. 48.

PERSONAL

I have not much to say of Carleton, and very little that is good. Undoubtedly he was a powerful writer, a marvelous delineator of Irish character—seen, however, not from its best side. He was essentially of the people he describes, peasant-born and peasant-bred, and most at home in a mud cabin or shebeenshop. . . . He never obtained, never earned, the applause of his country or the respect of those whose respect was worth having in Dublin, the city where he dwelt. He was a Catholic today and a Protestant tomorrow, turning from one religion to the other as occasion served or invited. It is requisite to name him here, among the many Irish authors I have known; but I did not feel for him while he lived, nor can I feel for him now, any respect.—HALL, SAMUEL CARTER, 1883, *Retrospect of a Long Life,* p. 385.

For the right understanding of the whole of his character and his life, and for the full appraisement of his works, it is necessary always to bear in mind Carleton's peasant origin and all that it meant and comprised in the Ireland of his time, not only for the mere marvel of what the man achieved, but because, while he glorified his origin by interpreting his people to the world, he retained its salient characteristics and its distinctive limitations. This fact, while it was of disadvantage to him in the conduct of affairs, and the contacts of life, was of incalculable value to his work, and furnishes the true explanation of his pre-eminence over other national novelists whose endowments and sympathy equalled, while their skill and culture surpassed his own.—HOEY, FRANCES CASHEL, 1896, *The Life of William Carleton,* ed. O'Donoghue, Introduction, p. XIX.

Carleton had earned the reputation of being in every sense a "queer fish;" he had been accused of obvious and consistent insincerity; and charges of mercenary motives and of reckless partisanship were so often brought against him, with other more or less absurd accusations, that it is not surprising that the biographer has hitherto left him alone. That he has been too hardly judged, the present work, it is hoped, will make evident. It is, however, proven that he was somewhat reckless and inconsistent, and his more inexcusable actions cannot be condoned or explained satisfactorily. It would be manifestly impossible to conceal his patent defects, and equally so to explain them away or applaud them—the only way out of the difficulty is to tell the story of his life from the moment at which his own version breaks off, with impartiality, and, where it is possible, with the truest sympathy. That story reveals a great genius, an undisciplined temperament; a man of many moods and faults, but lovable withal; a man of whom his countrymen will always be justly proud, although he vexed them sorely. Carleton gave offense to every class of Irishmen in one or other of his books, and all that can be done by way of extenuation or excuse is to explain the incidents which seem to have occasioned his conduct.— O'DONOGHUE, DAVID J., 1896, *The Life of William Carleton, Preface, vol.* I, *p.* IX.

GENERAL

If Banim may be characterized as the dramatic historian of his countrymen, Carleton may with equal truth be styled their faithful portrait-painter. He draws from the life.—HORNE, RICHARD HENGIST, 1844, *A New Spirit of the Age.*

Carleton is the historian of the peasantry rather than a dramatist. The fiddler and piper, the *seanachie* and seer, the matchmaker and dancing-master, and a hundred characters beside, are here brought before you, moving, acting, playing, plotting and gossiping. You are never wearied by an inventory of wardrobes, as in short English descriptive fictions; yet you see how every one is dressed; you hear the honey brogue of the maiden, and the downy voice of the child, the managed accents of flattery or traffic, the shrill tones of woman's fretting, and the troubled gush of men's anger. The moory upland and the corn slopes, the glen where the rock juts through mantling heather, and bright brooks gurgle amid the scented banks of wild herbs, the shivering cabin and the rudely-lighted farmhouse, are as plain in Carleton's pages as if he used canvass and colours with a skill varying from Wilson and Poussin, to Teniers and Wilkie. . . . Endowed with the highest dramatic genius, he has represented their love and generosity, their wrath and negligence, their crimes and virtues, as a hearty peasant—not a note-taking critic.—DAVIS, THOMAS, 1845, *The Nation.*

He is not only Irish, but thoroughly Irish, intensely Irish, exclusively Irish. . . . It is in his pages, and in his alone, that future generations must look for the truest and fullest—though still far from complete—picture of those who will ere long have passed away from that troubled land, from the records of history, and from the memory of man forever.—MURRAY, PATRICK A., 1852, *Traits of the Irish Peasantry, Edinburgh Review, vol.* 96, *pp.* 388, 389.

The only three names which Ireland can point to with pride are Griffin's, Banim's, and—do not accuse me of vanity when I say—my own. Banim and Griffin are gone, and I will soon follow them—*ultimus Romanorum,* and after that will come a lull, an obscurity of perhaps half a century when a new condition of civil society and a new phase of manners and habits among the people—for this is a *transition* state—may introduce new fields and new tastes for other writers, for in this manner the cycles of literature and taste appear, hold their day, displace each other, and make room for others.—CARLETON, WILLIAM, 1869, *Autobiography.*

There is much in William Carleton's writings to instruct and delight us. There are some things which we might wish altered or forgotten; but if the best lines that he recorded, and these feeble words which have sprung from them, may lead any of us nearer to Him in whom he found

his peace, then his death will prove of more value than his life, and his last words more than all the rest.—WALSH, WILLIAM PAKENHAM, 1869, *Funeral Sermon.*

He seems to have formed a fair and just estimate of the character of his countrymen, and to have drawn it as it actually appeared to him at home and abroad—in feud and in festival—in the various scenes which passed before him in his native district and during his subsequent rambles.—CHAMBERS, ROBERT, 1876, *Cyclopædia of English Literature, ed. Carruthers.*

Those who are fond of studying the early stages of society will mark in these pages many primitive customs and ancient superstitions, while the narrative sparkles with quaint humor, and occasionally affords us glimpses of wild and romantic scenery. . . . As he moved more in town society, the tone of his writings altered: they lost their original simplicity, and became political. The famine years accelerated the change, and he now began to portray the tenant as an oppressed man, and to paint the landlord as a drunken profligate. . . . But it must be admitted that this was part of the strong coloring which the novelist generally adopted, and that, if he represented the landlord as often harsh and extravagant, he added that the tenant was often improvident and dishonest; if he depicted one nobleman as vicious, he contrasted him with another who was refined and honorable.—L'ES-TRANGE, A. G., 1882, *ed. The Friendships of Mary Russell Mitford.*

It is certain that under the often transparent guise of fiction Carleton is a faithful and a very sympathetic historian of the Irish people.—RUSSELL, PERCY, 1894, *A Guide to British and American Novels, p.* 85.

It is an easy task to define Carleton's position in Irish literature. He is unquestionably supreme so far as fiction is concerned. But his position in literature generally is not easy to define. Judging him by his best work only—by his wonderful knowledge of human nature, and not by his style—he should occupy one of the proudest places in the whole gallery of masters who have made a study of the human heart. It is imperative to consider for this purpose only the truest revelations of his genius. Judged otherwise, his average merit is not great. There is hardly another writer between whose best and worst writing there is so wide and deep a distinction. Any writer who has written so much must needs have produced something unworthy of his highest powers; but to be perfectly candid no writer has given to the world work more essentially unfit to live than are Carleton's weakest efforts.— O'DONOGHUE, DAVID J., 1896, *The Life of William Carleton, vol.* II, *p.* 350.

If fineness of literary quality alone were in question, the first place must be assigned to William Carleton, whose "Traits and Stories of the Irish Peasantry" are the most carefully executed of their class. Carleton had neither the verve nor the copiousness of Lover, who has been fixed upon by popular judgment as the leading Irish novelist of his time.— WALKER, HUGH, 1897, *The Age of Tennyson, p.* 98.

There was nothing classic in his writings, occasionally, indeed, there was an independence of grammar calculated to disturb the shade of Lindley Murray. But if his language was not always correct, it was *living* to a degree. There was nothing of the Dryasdust element about it. His sentences were warm, vivid, palpitating with energy and emotion. Although he might not be able to turn a period with men like Matthew Arnold or Sainte-Beuve, neither could such wielders of a model diction emulate his Titanic rendering of the passions, or his bursts of rugged and perfervid eloquence. . . . As a novelist, Carleton was superior in one respect to either Dickens or Thackeray. He could draw women better. So far as I remember there is not a weak creation among all his female characters. They are living, breathing, loving creatures—women capable of inspiring a deep affection, and at the same time worthy of it. Where is there a nobler being in fiction than Helen Folliard, the heroine of "Willy Reilly?" The way she cheers her lover in all his difficulties, remains true to him through unexampled trials, and finally testifies in his favour when he is tried for life, has something truly sublime in it. Similar praise is due for the way in which he draws many other heroines. I find in all Carleton's writings something of the forceful energy and dramatic intensity which characterize the novels of Charlotte and Emily Brontë. His people palpitate with life. From the moment they appear to the last glimpses we have of them we see real men and women, and not phantoms.—SMITH, GEORGE BARNETT, 1897, *A Brilliant Irish Novelist, Fortnightly Review, vol.* 67, *pp.* 104, 114.

Charles Dickens

1812–1870

Born, at Landport, Portsea, 7 Feb. 1812. (Christened "Charles John Huffham," but never used last two names). Family moved to Chatham, 1816. To school under Mr. Giles, Baptist minister. Family moved to Camden Town. Neglected education. Father arrested for debt, 1822 [?]. Dickens obtained situation as packer in a blacking warehouse. At Mr. Jones's school in Hampstead Road, 1824–26. Employed as solicitor's clerk, May 1827 to Nov. 1828. Taught himself shorthand. Parliamentary reporter to "The True Sun," 1831–32; for "The Mirror of Parliament;" for "The Morning Chronicle," from 1835. Contributed papers, afterwards pub. as "Sketches by 'Boz,' " to "Monthly Magazine," "Morning Chronicle," "Evening Chronicle," "Bell's Life," and "Library of Fiction," 1833–35. Married Catherine Hogarth, 2 April 1836. "The Strange Gentleman" produced at St. James's Theatre, 29 Sept. 1836; "Is she his Wife?" same theatre, 6 March 1837. Edited "Bentley's Miscellany," 1837–39. Growing popularity. Freedom of City of Edinburgh, summer of 1841. Severe illness, autumn of same year. Visit to America and Canada, Jan. to June 1842. Visits to Italy, July to Nov. 1844, and Jan. to June 1845. First editor of "Daily News," 21 Jan. to 9 Feb. 1846; subsequently an occasional contributor. Started General Theatrical Fund. Visit to Switzerland, June to Nov. 1846, in Paris, Nov. 1846 to Feb. 1847 (with visit to London, Dec. 1846). Active part in various amateur theatrical performances for charities, 1847–52. "Household Words" started 30 March 1849; edited it till 1859. Testimonial at Birmingham, 1853. At Boulogne, summers of 1853, 54, 56. In Switzerland and Italy, autumn of 1853; in Paris, Nov. 1855 to May 1856. Bought Gadshill Place, 1856; settled there, 1860. First public "Reading" from his works, 29 April 1858. Separation from his wife, May 1858. On cessation of "Household Words," started "All the Year Round," 30 April 1859. Four series of

CHARLES LEVER

From an Engraving by W. G. Jackman.

CHARLES DICKENS

Engraving by J. Greatbach. From a Photograph by J. & C. Watkins.

public Readings, 1858–59, 1861–63, 1866–67, 1868–70, in London, provinces and Scotland. Readings in Paris, 1863. Severe illness in 1865. Readings in America, Dec. 1867 to April 1868. Breakdown of health. Last Reading, in London, 1 March 1869. Died, at Gadshill, 9 June 1870. Buried in Westminster Abbey. *Works:* "Sketches by Boz," 1st series, 1835; 2nd, 1836; "Sunday under Three Heads . . . By Timothy Sparks," 1836; "The Strange Gentleman . . . By 'Boz'," 1837; "The Village Coquettes," 1836; "Posthumous Papers of the Pickwick Club," 1837 (in monthly nos., April 1836 to Nov. 1837); "Memoirs of Joseph Grimaldi, edited by 'Boz'," 1838; "Oliver Twist . . . By 'Boz'," (from "Bentley's Miscellany;" 2 vols.), 1838; "Sketches of Young Gentlemen" (anon.), 1838; "Life and Adventures of Nicholas Nickleby," 1839 (in monthly nos., April 1838 to Oct. 1839); "Sketches of Young Couples" (anon.), 1840; "Master Humphrey's Clock," vol. i., 1840; vols. ii. and iii., 1841 (in weekly nos., April 1840 to Nov. 1841); "Barnaby Rudge," 1841; "The Old Curiosity Shop," 1841; "American Notes," 1842; "A Christmas Carol," 1843; "The Life and Adventures of Martin Chuzzlewit," 1844 (in monthly nos., Jan. 1843 to July 1844); "The Chimes," 1844; "The Cricket on the Hearth," 1845; "Pictures from Italy" (from "Daily News"), 1846; "The Battle of Life," 1846; "Dealings with the firm of Dombey and Son," 1848 (in monthly nos., Oct. 1846 to April 1848); "The Haunted Man," 1848; "The Personal History of David Copperfield," 1850 (in monthly nos., May 1849 to Nov. 1850); "Bleak House," 1853 (in monthly nos., March 1852 to Sept. 1853); "A Child's History of England" (from "Household Words"), 1854; "Hard Times for these Times" (from "Household Words"), 1854; "Little Dorrit," 1857 (in monthly nos., Dec. 1855 to June 1857); "A Tale of Two Cities" (from "All the Year Round"), 1859; "The Uncommercial Traveler," 1861 [1860] (originally in weekly parts, Jan. to Oct., 1860; 2nd edn. enlarged, 1868; 3rd edn. enlarged, 1869); "Great Expectations" (from "All the Year Round"), 1861; "Our Mutual Friend," 1865 (in monthly nos., May 1864 to Nov. 1865); "The Mystery of Edwin Drood" (unfinished) six nos., April to Sept.,1870. *Posthumous:* "Speeches," 1870; "Mr. Nightingale's Diary," 1877; "Is she his Wife?" 1877; "The Lamplighter," 1879; "The Mudfog Papers" (from "Bentley's Miscellany"), 1880; "Letters" (3 vols.), 1880–82. He *edited:* "The Pic-Nic Papers," 1841: J. Overs' "Evenings of a Working Man," 1844; "Method of Employment," 1852; A. A. Procter's "Legends and Lyrics," 1866; "Religious Opinions of the late C. H. Townshend," 1869. *Collected Works* in 22 vols., 1858–59; in 21 vols., 1867–74. *Life:* by Forster, 1872; by Marzials, 1887.—SHARP, R. FARQUHARSON, 1897, *A Dictionary of English Authors, p.* 79.

PERSONAL

Who the *dickens* "Boz" could be
  Puzzled many a learned elf,
Till time revealed the mystery,
  And "Boz" appeared as *Dickens* self.
—DAVIDS, C. J., 1837, *Impromptu, Bentley's Miscellany, March.*

He is a fine little fellow—Boz, I think. Clear blue, intelligent eyes, eye-brows that he arches amazingly, large protrusive rather loose mouth, a face of most extreme *mobility*, which he shuttles about—eyebrows, eyes, mouth and all—in a very singular manner while speaking. Surmount this with a loose coil of common-coloured hair, and set it on a small compact figure, very small, and dressed à la D'Orsay rather than well—this is Pickwick. For the rest a quiet, shrewd-looking, little fellow, who seems to guess pretty well what he is and what others are.—CARLYLE, THOMAS, 1840, *Letter to John Carlyle, March* 17; *Thomas Carlyle, A History of His Life in London, ed. Froude, vol.* I, *p.* 152.

Mr. Dickens may be assured that there is felt for him all over Scotland a sentiment of kindness, affection, admiration, and love; and I know for certain that a knowledge of these sentiments must make him happy.— WILSON, JOHN, 1841, *Speech at a Public Dinner to Dickens in Edinburgh.*

Above all, of Charles Dickens, with whom I have struck up what I mean to be an eternal and intimate friendship. He lives very near us here, and I often run over and sit an hour *tête-à-tête,* or take a long walk in the park with him—the only way really to know or be known by either man or woman. Taken in this way, I think him very amiable and agreeable. In mixed company, where he is now much sought after as a lion, he is rather reserved, &c.—JEFFREY, FRANCIS LORD, 1841, *Letter to Lord Cockburn, May* 4; *Life of Lord Jeffrey, ed. Cockburn, vol.* II, *p.* 267.

I admire and love the man exceedingly, for he has a deep warm heart, a noble sympathy with and respect for human nature, and great intellectual gifts wherewith to make these fine moral ones fruitful for the delight and consolation and improvement of his fellow-beings.—KEMBLE, FRANCES ANN, 1842, *Letter, April 22; Records of Later Life, p.* 318.

Called on Dickens at 10.30 A. M. by appointment, as he leaves at one. He was at breakfast. Sat down with him. He was very agreeable and full of life. He is the *cleverest* man I ever met. I mean he impresses you more with the alertness of his various powers. His forces are all light infantry and light cavalry, and always in marching order. There are not many heavy pieces, but few *sappers and miners,* the scientific corps is deficient, and I fear there is no chaplain in the garrison.—DANA, RICHARD HENRY, 1842, *Journal, Feb.* 5; *Richard Henry Dana, ed. C. F. Adams, vol.* I, *p.* 33.

Among the passengers in the "Britannia" are Mr. Charles Dickens and his wife. This gentleman is the celebrated "Boz," whose name "rings through the world with loud applause,"—the fascinating writer whose fertile imagination and ready pen conceived and sketched the immortal Pickwick, his prince of valets, and his bodyguard of choice cronies; who has made us laugh with "Mantilini," and cry with poor "little Nell;" caused us to shrink with horror from the effects of lynch law, as administered by the misguided Lord George Gordon, and to listen with unmitigated delight to the ticking of "Master Humphrey's Clock." The visit of this popular writer has been heralded in advance. He was expected by this packet, and I signed, three or four days ago, with a number of other persons, a letter to be presented to him on his arrival in this city, giving him a hearty welcome and inviting him to a public dinner, which, from the spirit which appears to prevail on the subject, will be no common affair. . . . The great dinner to Dickens was given yesterday, at the City Hotel, and came off with flying colours. Two hundred and thirty persons sat down to dinner at seven o'clock. The large room was ornamented with two illuminated scenes from the works of "Boz," busts of celebrated persons and classical devices, all in good taste; and the eating and drinking part of the affair was excellent. The president was Washington Irving (I beg pardon,

"His Excellency"). "Non Nobis" was sung by Mr. Horn and his little band of vocalists, who gave several glees during the evening. After the unintellectual operation of eating and drinking was concluded, the president rose and began a prepared speech, in which he broke down flat (as he promised us beforehand he would), and concluded with this toast: "Charles Dickens, the literary guest of the nation." To this the guest made his acknowledgment in an excellent speech, delivered with great animation, and characterized by good taste and warm feeling.—HONE, PHILIP, 1842, *Diary, Jan.* 24, *Feb.* 19, *vol.* II, *pp.* 109, 118.

You ask about Mr. Boz. I am quite delighted with him. He is a thorough good fellow, with nothing of the author about him but the reputation, and goes through his task as Lion with exemplary grace, patience, and good-nature. He has the brilliant face of a man of genius, and a pretty Scottish lassie for a wife, with roses on her cheeks, and "een sae bonny blue." His writings you know. I wish you had listened to his eloquence at the dinner here. It was the only specimen of eloquence I have ever witnessed. Its charm was not in its words, but in the manner of saying them.—HALLECK, FITZ-GREENE, 1842, *To Mrs. Rush, March* 8; *Life and Letters, ed. Wilson, p.* 434.

At a dinner-party at Mr. Holland's last evening, a gentleman, in instance of Charles Dickens's unwearibilty, said that during some theatrical performances in Liverpool he acted in play and farce, spent the rest of the night making speeches, feasting, and drinking at table, and ended at seven o'clock in the morning by jumping leapfrog over the backs of the whole company.—HAWTHORNE, NATHANIEL, 1853, *English Note-Books, vol.* I, *p.* 59.

He is a virtuous and happy family man, in the first place. His glowing and generous heart is kept steady by the best domestic influences: and we may fairly hope now that he will fulfil the natural purpose of his life, and stand by literature to the last; and again, that he will be an honour to the high vocation by prudence as well as by power: so that the graces of genius and generosity may rest on the finest basis of probity and prudence; and that his old age may be honoured as heartily as his youth and manhood have been admired.—Nothing could exceed the frank kindness and consideration shown by him in the correspondence and personal intercourse we have had; and my cordial regard has grown with my knowledge of him.—MARTINEAU, HARRIET, 1855-77, *Autobiography, ed. Chapman, vol.* II, *p.* 63.

Dickens is forty-five years old, cheerful, amiable, noble, and good. However highly I may place him as an author, I must prize him just as highly as an actor in tragedy, as well as in comedy.—ANDERSEN, HANS CHRISTIAN, 1857, *To the Grand-Duke of Weimar, Aug.* 9; *Correspondence, ed. Crawford,* p. 358.

I heard Dickens last night; got a capital reserved seat by favour of the Director,—right opposite to him. It was a great treat, without any exaggeration. He has a voice of great compass and play of feeling, great dramatic gifts altogether, and he maintained unabated interest for upwards of two hours. It was all the better to me, I daresay, as I had pretty well forgot the "Christmas Carol." Scrooge, the hero, was his great *forte;* but he gives the Cratchetts also —both father and mother and the children —with great effect; and as his voice deepened into the sweetest pathetic tones in reading the death of Tiny Tim, nothing could have been finer. The only objection I could find to the whole was, that it was too *histrionic,* which, however, I daresay is a good deal owing to his appearance. The latter was in all respects a great disappointment. It is a sort of mixture of the *waiter* and the actor, Frenchified in his dress to a degree quite disagreeable. He has not a pleasant face, singular lines—I don't know whether of care—running under his eyes and from his mouth—in short, not very gentlemanly.—TULLOCH, JOHN, 1858, *Letter to his Wife, March; Memoir by Mrs. Oliphant,* p. 125.

He looks about the age of Longfellow. His hair is not much grizzled and is thick, although the crown of his head is getting bald. His features are good, and the nose rather high, the eyes largish, greyish and very expressive. He wears a moustache and beard, and dresses at dinner in exactly the same uniform which every man in London or the civilised world is bound to wear, as much as the inmates of a penitentiary are restricted to theirs. I mention this because I had heard that he was odd and extravagant in his costume. I liked him exceedingly. We sat next each other at table,

and I found him genial, sympathetic, agreeable, unaffected, with plenty of light easy talk and touch-and-go fun without any effort or humbug of any kind.—MOTLEY, JOHN LOTHROP, 1861, *To His Mother, March* 15; *Correspondence, ed. Curtis, vol.* I, *p.* 365.

My love to noble Dickens.—LANDOR, WALTER SAVAGE, 1864, *Letter to Forster, May* 9; *Life by Forster, p.* 674.

Dickens, at home, seems to be perpetually jolly, and enters into the interest of games with all the ardor of a boy. Physically (as well as mentally) he is immensely strong, having quite regained his wonted health and strength. He is an immense walker, and never seems to be fatigued. He breakfasts at eight o'clock; immediately afterward answers all the letters received that morning; writes until one o'clock; lunches, walks twelve miles (every day), dines at six, and passes the evening entertaining his numerous friends. — PHILP, FRANKLIN, 1869, *Diary, A Short Life of Charles Dickens by Jones, p.* 192.

I emphatically direct that I be buried in an inexpensive, unostentatious, and strictly private manner, that no public announcement be made of the time or place of my burial, that at the utmost not more than three plain mourning coaches be employed, and that those who attend my funeral wear no scarf, cloak, black bow, long hatband, or other such revolting absurdity. I direct that my name be inscribed in plain English letters on my tomb, without the addition of "Mr." or "Esquire." I conjure my friends on no account to make me the subject of any monument, memorial, or testimonial whatever. I rest my claims to the remembrance of my country upon my published works, and to the remembrance of my friends upon their experience of me; in addition thereto, I commit my soul to the mercy of God, through our Lord and Saviour Jesus Christ, and I exhort my dear children to try to guide themselves by the teaching of the New Testament in its broad spirit, and to put no faith in any man's narrow construction of its letter here or there.—DICKENS, CHARLES, 1869, *Will, May* 11.

No man ever kept himself more aloof than Dickens from the ordinary honours of life. No titles were written after his name. He was not C. B., or D. C. L., or F. R. S.; nor did he ever attempt to become M. P. What titles of honour may ever have been offered to him I cannot say; but that titles were offered I do not doubt. Lord Russell, a year or two ago, proposed a measure by which, if carried, certain men of high character and great capacity would have been selected as peers for life; but Charles Dickens would never have been made a lord. He probably fully appreciated his own position; and had a noble confidence in himself, which made him feel that nothing Queen, Parliament, or Minister, could do for him would make him greater than he was. No title to his ear could have been higher than that name which he made familiar to the ears of all reading men and women.—TROLLOPE, ANTHONY, 1870, *Charles Dickens, Saint Paul's Magazine, vol.* 6, *p.* 374.

A lithe, energetic man, of medium stature, crosses the platform at the brisk gait of five miles an hour, and takes his position behind the table. . . . Dickens has a broad, full brow, a fine head,—which, for a man of such power and energy, is singularly small at the base of the brain,—and a cleanly cut profile. There is a slight resemblance between him and Louis Napoleon in the latter respect, owing mainly to the nose; but it its unnecessary to add that the faces of the two men are totally different. Dickens's eyes are light-blue, and his mouth and jaw, without having any claim to beauty, possess a strength that is not concealed by the veil of iron-gray mustache and generous imperial. His head is but slightly graced with iron-gray hair, and his complexion is florid. If any one thinks to obtain an accurate idea of Dickens from the photographs that flood the country, he is mistaken. He will see Dickens's clothes, Dickens's features, as they appear when Nicholas Nickleby is in the art of knocking down Mr. Wackford Squeers; but he will not see what makes Dickens's face attractive, the geniality and expression that his heart and brain put into it.—FIELD, KATE, 1870, *Pen Photographs of Charles Dickens's Readings, p.* 20.

What portrait can do justice to the frankness, kindness, and power of his eyes? They seemed to look through you, and yet only to take notice of what was best in you and most worthy of notice. And then his smile, which was most charming! And then his laughter—not poor, thin, arid, ambiguous laughter, that is ashamed of itself, that moves one feature only of the face—but the largest and heartiest kind, irradiating his whole countenance, and compelling you to participate in his immense enjoyment of it.—HELPS, ARTHUR, 1870, *In Memoriam, Macmillan's Magazine, vol.* 22, *p.* 236.

Once when a bad man died, a savage wit, being apprised of the event, observed that the average value of mankind was sensibly raised. Who does not feel that, by the death of Charles Dickens, the average value of ourselves, as Englishmen of the nineteenth century, is incalculably lowered?—AUSTIN, ALFRED, 1870, *Charles Dickens, Temple Bar, vol.* 29, *p.* 554.

Dickens's personal taste in dress was always "loud." He loved gay vests, glittering jewelry, showy satin stocks, and everything rather *prononcé*, yet no man had a keener or more unsparing critical eye for these vulgarities in others. He once gave to a friend a vest of a most gorgeous shawl-pattern. Soon after, at a party, he quizzed his friend most unmercifully for his "stunning" vest, although he had on him at that very moment its twin-brother, or sister—whichever sex vests belong to —MACKENZIE, R. SHELTON, 1870, *Life of Charles Dickens, p.* 243.

How well I recall the bleak winter evening in 1842 when I first saw the handsome, glowing face of the young man who was even then famous over half the globe! He came bounding into the Tremont House, fresh from the steamer that had brought him to our shores, and his cheery voice rang through the hall, as he gave a quick glance at the new scenes opening upon him in a strange land on first arriving at a Transatlantic hotel. "Here we are!" he shouted, as the lights burst upon the merry party just entering the house, and several gentlemen came forward to greet him. . . . Young, handsome, almost worshipped for his genius, belted round by such troops of friends as rarely ever man had, coming to a new country to make new conquests of fame and honor. . . . From top to toe every fibre of his body was unrestrained and alert. What vigor, what keenness, what freshness of spirit, possessed him! He laughed all over, and did not care who heard him! He seemed like the Emperor of Cheerfulness on a cruise of pleasure, determined to conquer a realm or two of fun every hour of his overflowing existence. That night impressed itself on my memory for all time, so far as I am concerned with things sublunary. It was Dickens, the true "Boz," in flesh and blood, who stood before us at last, and with my companions, three or four lads of my own age, I determined to sit up late that night. None of us then, of course, had the honor of an acquaintance with the delightful stranger, and I little thought that I should afterwards come to know him in the beaten way of friendship, and live with him day after day in years far distant; that I should ever be so near to him that he would reveal to me his joys and his sorrows, and thus that I should learn the story of his life from his own lips.—FIELDS, JAMES T., 1871, *Yesterdays with Authors, pp.* 127, 128.

I had the honor of being Mr. Dickens's school-fellow for about two years (1824–1826), both being day-scholars at Mr. Jones's "Classical and Commercial Academy." . . . My recollection of Dickens whilst at school . . . is that of a healthy looking boy, small but well built, with a more than usual flow of spirits, inducing to harmless fun, seldom or never I think to mischief, to which so many lads at that age are prone. I cannot recall any thing that then indicated he would hereafter become a literary celebrity; but perhaps he was too young then. He usually held his head more erect than lads ordinarily do, and there was a general smartness about him. His week-day dress of jacket and trousers, I can clearly remember, was what is called pepper-and-salt; and, instead of the frill that most boys of his age wore then, he had a turn-down collar, so that he looked less youthful in consequence. He invented what he termed a "lingo," produced by the addition of a few letters of the same sound to every word; and it was our ambition, walking and talking thus along the street, to be considered foreigners.—THOMAS, OWEN P., 1871, *Letter to John Forster, Feb.; Forster's The Life of Charles Dickens, vol.* I, *ch.* III.

He helped men with a spontaneous grace and sweetness which are indescribable. The deep, rich, cheery voice; the brave and noble countenance; the hand that had the fire of friendship in its grip—all played their part in comforting in a moment the creature who had come to Charles Dickens for advice, for help, for sympathy. When he took a cause in hand, or a friend under his wing, people who knew him breathed in a placid sense of security. He had not only the cordial will to be of use wherever his services could be advantageously enlisted, but he could see at a glance the exact thing

he might do; and beyond the range of his conviction as to his own power, or the limit of proper asking or advancing, no power on earth could move him the breadth of a hair. —JERROLD, BLANCHARD, 1873, *Best of all Good Company.*

Of his attractive points in society and conversation I have particularized little, because in truth they were himself. Such as they were, they were never absent from him. His acute sense of enjoyment gave such relish to his social qualities that probably no man, not a great wit or a professed talker, ever left, in leaving any social gathering, a blank so impossible to fill up. In quick and varied sympathy, in ready adaptation to every whim or humour, in help to any mirth or game, he stood for a dozen men. If one may say such a thing, he seemed to he always the more himself for being somebody else, for continually putting off his personality. His versatility made him unique.—FORSTER, JOHN, 1874, *The Life of Charles Dickens, vol.* III, ch. xix.

Close under the bust of Thackeray lies Charles Dickens, not, it may be, his equal in humour, but more than his equal in his hold on the popular mind, as was shown in the intense and general enthusiasm evinced over his grave. The funeral, according to Dickens's urgent and express desire in his will, was strictly private. It took place at an early hour in the summer morning, the grave having been dug in secret the night before, and the vast solitary space of the Abbey was occupied only by the small band of mourners, and the Abbey Clergy, who, without any music except the occasional peal of the organ, read the funeral service. For days the spot was visited by thousands; many were the flowers strewn upon it by unknown hands; many tears shed by the poorer visitors. He rests beside Sheridan, Garrick, and Henderson.—STANLEY, ARTHUR PENRHYN, 1876–82, *Historical Memorials of Westminster Abbey, p.* 283.

In the midst of his own constant and arduous work, no household matter was considered too trivial to claim his care and attention. He would take as much pains about the hanging of a picture, the choosing of furniture, the superintending any little improvement in the house, as he would about the more serious business of his life; thus carrying out to the very letter his favourite motto of "What is worth doing at all is worth doing well."—DICKENS, MAMIE,

AND HOGARTH, GEORGINA, 1879, *The Letters of Charles Dickens, vol.* I, *Preface, p.* x.

It is idle to speculate whether he went into the state of matrimony from the heat and impulse of youth, or after long and sober reflection. He laid some store by his exact and practical wisdom, and probably in that he was superior to most authors. Nor was he one to plunge into the ocean of wedded possibility without retiring to some remote and tranquil inlet where he might adjust compasses before setting sail. Yet his incongruous incapability in erotic affairs in general must, we think, have given an oblique turn to any calculations he had formed on this subject; at all events, his romance, so far as his wife was concerned, does not seem to have extended much beyond the honeymoon. He never speaks of her with fondness; there was no ethereal mixing of souls, such as we find in the biographies of other equally gifted and ecstatic pairs. We are left in the dark as to the causes of the estrangement; there are only occasional murmurs of extravagant housekeeping on the one side and nervous irritability on the other. The former was of course a risk he faced, and a burden from which, however vexatious it might be, he should not have flinched. On the other hand, it does not say a great deal for the sympathy or patience of any wife, especially an intellectual one, that she did not understand or, failing to understand, that she did not bear with, a failing which many great thinkers and writers have found inseparable from the indulgence of fanciful or philosophic thought.—WATT, JAMES CRABB, 1880, *Great Novelists: Scott, Thackeray, Dickens, Lytton.*

Londoners were familiar with Dickens's personal appearance as well as with his writings, and certain London streets did not seem quite the same when his striking face and energetic movements could be seen there no more. It is likely that Dickens overworked his exuberant vital energy, his superb resources of physical health and animal spirits. In work and play, in writing and exercising, he was unsparing of his powers. Like the lavish youth with the full purse in "Gil Blas," he appeared to believe that his stock could never be spent. Men who were early companions of his, and who had not half his vital power, outlived him many years. He was buried in Westminster Abbey, although his own desire was to be laid quietly in Rochester churchyard. It was held that the national cemetery claimed him. We cannot help thinking it a pity the claim was made. All true admirers of Scott must be glad that he rests in his dear and congenial Dryburgh; most of the admirers of Dickens would have been better pleased to think that he lay beneath the green turf of the ancient churchyard, in venerable and storied Rochester, amid the scenes that he loved and taught so many others to love.—McCARTHY, JUSTIN, 1880, *A History of Our Own Times from the Accession of Queen Victoria to the General Election of* 1880, *vol.* IV, *p.* 287.

The blacking-warehouse at Old Hungerford Stairs, Strand, opposite Old Hungerford Market, in which he tied up the pots of blacking in company with Bob Fagin . . . has long since been torn down. That "crazy old house, with a wharf of its own, abutting on the water when the tide was in and on the mud when the tide was out, and literally overrun with rats," is now replaced by a row of stone buildings; the embankment has risen over the mud; and the vast Charing Cross Station stands opposite on the site of the old Hungerford Market and of "The Swan, or The Swan and something else"—the miserable old "public" where he used to get his bread and cheese and glass of beer. The very name of the street is gone, and Villiers street has sponged out the memory of Hungerford Stairs. . . . Indeed, it is no longer possible to find any of the places he makes mention of in his narrative to Forster. . . . Bayham street, where he lived, is entirely rebuilt.—MARTIN, B. E., 1881, *In London with Dickens, Scribner's Monthly, vol.* 21, *p.* 650.

There never was a man so unlike a professional writer: of tall, wiry, energetic figure; brisk in movement; a head well set on; a face rather bronzed or sunburnt; keen, bright, searching eyes, and a mouth which was full of expression, though hidden behind a wiry moustache and grizzled beard. Thus the French painter's remark that "he was more like one of the old Dutch admirals we see in the picture galleries, than a man of letters," conveyed an admirably true idea to his friends. He had, indeed, much of the quiet resolute manner of command of a captain of a ship. He strode along briskly as he walked; as he listened his searching eye rested on you, and the nerves in his face quivered, much like those in the delicately formed nostrils of a finely bred dog. There was a curl or two in his hair at each side which was characteristic; and the jaunty way he wore his little morning hat, rather on one side, added to the effect. But when there was anything droll suggested, a delightful sparkle of lurking humour began to kindle and spread to his mouth, so that, even before he uttered anything, you felt that something irresistibly droll was at hand. No one ever told a story so drolly, and, what is not so common, relished another man's story so heartily. A man of his great reputation and position might have chosen what company he pleased, and would have been welcome in the highest circles; but he never was so happy as with one or two intimate friends who understood him, who were in good spirits or in good humour. He was always grateful, as it were, to hear a good thing.—FITZGERALD, PERCY, 1882, *Recreations of a Literary Man, vol.* I, *p.* 97.

I knew the great novelist when he was a boy; again in the days of his early celebrity, while he was still a bachelor: and later, Mrs. Hall and I were present at the christening of his first-born. We had known Mrs. Dickens also while she was Miss Catherine Hogarth. Much has been said on the unhappy subject of their separation, and some of the most unfortunate utterances were those put in print by Dickens himself at the time. It is a theme that all will feel bound to treat with a reserve similar to that discreetly maintained by his biographer. Undoubtedly, sympathy was largely felt for Mrs. Dickens—and rightly so.—HALL, SAMUEL CARTER, 1883, *Retrospect of a Long Life, p.* 394.

I have heard Dickens described by those who knew him as aggressive, imperious, and intolerant, and I can comprehend the accusation; but to me his temper was always of the sweetest and·kindest. He would, I doubt not, have been easily bored, and would not have scrupled to show it; but he never ran the risk. He was imperious in the sense that his life was conducted in the *Sic volo sic jubeo* principle, and that everything gave way before him. The society in which he mixed, the hours which he kept, the opinions which he held, his likes and dislikes, his ideas of what should or should not be, were all settled by himself, not merely for himself, but for all those brought into connection with him, and it

was never imagined they could be called in question. Yet he was never regarded as a tyrant: he had immense power of will, absolute mesmeric force, as he proved beneficially more than once; and that he should lead and govern seemed perfectly natural to us. . . . Dickens was not only a genius, but he had the volcanic activity, the perturbed restlessness, the feverish excitability of genius. What he created, that he was. His personages were, as readers of his letters know, an integral part of his life. . . . In regard to the friendship which Dickens vouchsafed me, I have been frequently asked, "Did he come up to the expectations you had formed of him? Was Dickens the man as lovable as Dickens the author?" and I have always replied, "Yes; wholly."—YATES, EDMUND, 1884, *Recollections and Experiences.*

In bringing up his children, Charles Dickens was always most anxious to impress upon them that as long as they were honest and truthful, so would they always be sure of having justice done to them. . . . Notwithstanding his constant and arduous work, he was never too busy to be unmindful of the comfort and welfare of those about him, and there was not a corner in any of his homes, from kitchen to garret, which was not constantly inspected by him, and which did not boast of some of his neat and orderly contrivances. We used to laugh at him sometimes and say we believed that he was personally acquainted with every nail in the house. . . . He loved all flowers, but especially bright flowers, and scarlet geraniums were his favourite of all. . . . Charles Dickens was very fond of music, and not only of classical music. He loved national airs, old tunes, songs, and ballads, and was easily moved by anything pathetic in a song or tune, and was never tired of hearing his special favourites sung or played. He used to like to have music of an evening, and duets used to be played for hours together, while he would read or walk up and down the room. . . . Among his many attributes, that of a doctor must not be forgotten. He was invaluable in a sick room, or in any sudden emergency; always quiet, always cheerful, always useful, and skillful, always doing the right thing, so that his very presence seemed to bring comfort and help. From his children's earliest days his visits, during any time of sickness, were eagerly longed for and believed in, as doing more good than those even of the doctor himself. He had a curiously magnetic and sympathetic hand, and his touch was wonderfully soothing and quieting. As a mesmerist he possessed great power, which he used, most successfully, in many cases of great pain and distress.—DICKENS, MAMIE, 1885, *Charles Dickens at Home, Cornhill Magazine, vol.* 51, *pp.* 37, 39, 43, 47, 49.

It was at this time [1859] that John Forster called upon me to paint a portrait of his friend Dickens. I need scarcely say with what delight, mixed with fear, I heard of this commission—delight because of my veneration for the author and my love for the man; fear that I might fail, as so many had done already. Forster had hinted his wish to me a year or two before, when Dickens had adopted the moustache—a hirsute appendage of which Forster had a great horror; and with reason as regarded Dickens, for it partly covered, and certainly injured, a very handsome and characteristic mouth. "This is a whim—the fancy will pass. We will wait till the hideous disfigurement is removed," said Forster; but we waited in vain. Indeed, we waited till the beard was allowed to grow upon the chin as well as upon the upper lip; so, fearing that if we waited longer there would be little of the face to be painted, if whiskers were to be added to the rest, the order was given and the portrait begun.—FRITH, W. P., 1888, *My Autobiography and Reminiscences, vol.* I, *p.* 215.

We were at first disappointed, and disposed to imagine there must be some mistake. No! *that* is not the man who wrote "Pickwick!" What we saw was a dandified, pretty-boy-looking sort of figure; singularly young-looking, I thought, with a slight flavor of the whipper-snapper genius of humanity. . . . Dickens' eyes were not blue, but of a very distinct and brilliant hazel—the color traditionally assigned to Shakespeare's eyes. . . . Dickens was only thirty-three when I first saw him, being just two years my junior. I have said what he appeared to me then. As I knew him afterwards, and to the end of his days, he was a strikingly manly man, not only in appearance, but in bearing. The lustrous brilliancy of his eyes was very striking. And I do not think that I have ever seen it noticed that those wonderful eyes which saw so much and so keenly were appreciably,

though to a very slight degree, near-sighted eyes. Very few persons, even among those who knew him well, were aware of this, for Dickens never used a glass. But he continually exercised his vision by looking at distant objects, and making them out as well as he could without any artificial assistance. It was an instance of that force of will in him which compelled a naturally somewhat delicate frame to comport itself like that of an athlete. Mr. Forster somewhere says of him, "Dickens' habits were robust, but his health was not." This is entirely true as far as my observation extends.—TROLLOPE, THOMAS ADOLPHUS, 1888, *What I Remember, pp.* 315, 352, 353.

I have just returned from a pilgrimage (many a pilgrim has gone to a shrine with a far less reverent joy) to Gad's Hill Place. The present owner, Mr. Latham, has greatly improved, without altering the general appearance of, the home of Dickens. He has introduced more light and air both into the house and grounds, developing the capabilities of the place, after the example of those who preceded him; but there is no material change. The dear old study remains as it was, with the dummy books on the door and on part of the walls, bearing the quaint titles which Dickens invented for them.—HOLE, SAMUEL REYNOLDS, 1893, *Memories, p.* 83.

For all his genius as a novelist, I have always thought that his real vocation was as an actor of low comedy, much as the world might have lost by such a change. Warm-hearted and sentimental, but not unselfish, he was not the gentleman. There was no grace of manner, no soul of nobility in him.—LINTON, WILLIAM JAMES, 1894, *Threescore and Ten Years, p.* 160.

My first experience, I think, of my father's extraordinary energy and of the thoroughness—the even alarming thoroughness—with which he always threw himself into everything he had occasion to take up, was in connection with a toy theatre of which I was the proud possessor somewhere about the middle forties. Toy theatres with scenery and sheets of the characters only requiring painting and cutting out—one Skelt was the principal artist for such things—were very popular indeed in my very early youth, and it was the aim of every self-respecting boy to be the manager of one or more of them. . . . This extraordinary, eager, restless energy, which first showed itself to me in this small matter, was never absent from my father all through his life. Whatever he did he put his whole heart into, and did as well as ever he could. Whether it was for work or for play, he was always in earnest. Painting the scenes for a toy theatre, dancing Sir Roger de Coverley at a children's party, gravely learning the polka from his little daughters for a similar entertainment, walking, riding, picnicing, amateur acting, public reading, or the every-day hard work of his literary life—it was all one to him. Whatever lay nearest to his hand at the moment had to be done thoroughly.— DICKENS, CHARLES, JR., 1895, *Glimpses of Charles Dickens, North American Review, vol.* 160, *pp.* 526, 527.

I have mentioned the name of Charles Dickens, and done so with grateful affection. I know of no biography to compare with his, for I have not found a bitter word in it from first to last. All is sunshine—all is gentle humor. What patience he had with young authors! How he criticised, suggested, amended, and encouraged! I do not know of any minister who has taken equal pains with young preachers. Then, how Charles Dickens exerted himself to help poor artists and writers and widows! He was addicted to works of charity; he loved them, and therefore he found strength and time to do them. I shall be told that as an author he lived an idyllic life.— PARKER, JOSEPH, 1896, *Might Have Been, p.* 93.

Mr. Dickens's visit was measurably disappointing; we did too much for him and his lady; they did not appreciate the honor bestowed on them, and overrated their importance. When in Washington they were charged with a neglect of etiquette amounting to incivility. It must be added that on the subsequent visit of Mr. Dickens, at the Press Dinner given to him in April, 1868, just before his departure, he made a graceful and feeling statement in the nature of an apology, or even a recantation, which he engaged to have appended to every copy of the offending works so long as he or his representatives should retain control of their publication.— HASWELL, CHARLES H., 1896, *Reminiscences of an Octogenarian, p.* 384.

Suddenly there was a stir in the room, and all the ladies rose. A young Englishman, named Charles Dickens, entered the room. Then my heart stopped beating. I had read "Pickwick" and several of his

novels, and, like all the world, I admired and wondered how a genius looked. I can see him now, overdressed, with billows of green-satin necktie, long hair, a rather handsome face, and hanging on his arm a pretty little, fat, rosy-cheeked wife.— SHERWOOD, MARY E. W., 1897, *An Epistle to Posterity, p.* 23.

One fails to see that he ever thought for a moment about the title of gentleman. Commercial by instinct, he wished his genius to receive the material reward which was its due; he wanted to live largely, liberally, and generously. His tastes and his beneficence needed money, and the making of money by labour in his art probably tended to become, unconsciously, an end in itself. He never could bear to yield to age, to resign his endeavour, to leave his portentous energy unoccupied. Like Scott, he might have said, "No rest for me but in the woolen;" he could not withdraw, like Shakespeare, to country quiet. His native bent was as much towards the stage as to fiction, and he wore himself out untimely in working the theatrical side of his nature, in his Readings. The desire to be conspicuously before the world which idolised him, may have been as potent as the need of money in spurring the energy of Dickens to its fatal goal. It is to these circumstances, extraordinary energy, craving for employment, a half-suppressed genius for the stage, need of money, and need of publicity, that we trace these defects of Dickens's work which are due to surplusage. He did too much, with the inevitable consequences. He read too little. His nature was all for literary action; not for study, criticism, and reflection. The results were these blemishes with which he is reproached in that age of reaction which ever succeeds to a career of vast popular success. Criticism, indeed, was not lacking, even when he was best accepted. It is quite an error to think that Dickens's literary contemporaries did not see the motes where a younger generation is apt to see the beams.— LANG, ANDREW, 1898, *Charles Dickens, Fortnightly Review, vol.* 70, *p.* 945.

He was the second son (in a family of eight, six surviving infancy) of Mr. John Dickens, a clerk in the Navy Pay Office at the Dockyard. The name of his mother, previous to her marriage, was Elizabeth Barrow. The baptismal record at Portsea registers him as CHARLES JOHN HUFFHAM DICKENS, but he very seldom used any other signature than the one with which we are all familiar. On arrival at the Portsmouth town station, we leave the railway, turning to the right, and proceed onwards, in the main thoroughfare of Commercial Road. Thus we shortly reach, in due course, THE BIRTHPLACE OF DICKENS. The house (No. 387 Commercial Road, Landport,) stands about half a mile northward (to the right) from the railway station, with a neat fore court.—ALLBUT, ROBERT, 1899, *Rambles in Dickens' Land*, p. 145.

I have heard famous talkers,—Greeley when in vehement mood; Grant when among his friends, say at one in the morning; Conkling, with a grievance, Bismarck, Beaconsfield,—have been under the spell of perhaps the most exquisite of all, even the silvery spell of Wendell Phillips; have talked with *Tribune* Smalley and Gen. Sherman, Robert Ingersoll and Henry George, but the talk of Dickens was unique, an art in itself. The supreme dramatic power, dramatic expression in repose, as in Wendell Phillips; his way of setting himself in the chair as his narrative proceeded, head rather bent forward, the eye archly turned upon you, partly sidewise, glancing with its ascending look, as if studying the effect. This is as I recall him.—YOUNG, JOHN RUSSELL, 1901, *Men and Memories, ed. Young*, p. 130.

As regards the circumstances appertaining to his career—the start in life under harassing conditions, the brilliant success attending his initial efforts in authorship, the manner in which he took the world by storm and retained his grip of the public by the sheer force of genius—there is, I venture to believe, no parallel in the history of Literature. Born in a humble station of life, his early years spent in the midst of an uncongenial (not to say demoralising) environment, his natural gifts, combined with almost superhuman powers of perseverance, enabled him to overcome obstacles which would have deterred ordinary men, with the result that he rapidly attained the topmost rung of the ladder of fame, and remained there.—KITTON, F. G., 1901, *Charles Dickens, The Bookman, vol.* 13, *p.* 463.

READINGS AND THEATRICALS

I had to go yesterday to Dickens's Reading, 8 p. m., Hanover Rooms, to the complete upsetting of my evening habitudes and spiritual composure. Dickens does do it capitally, such as *it* is; acts better than

any Macready in the world; a whole tragic, comic, heroic *theatre* visible, performing under one *hat*, and keeping us laughing—in a sorry way, some of us thought, the whole night. He is a good creature, too, and makes fifty or sixty pounds by each of these readings.—CARLYLE, THOMAS, 1863, *Letter, Thomas Carlyle, A History of His Life in London, ed. Froude, vol.* II, *p.* 229.

To pronounce judgment on Mr. Dickens as a reader we are not in all respects competent. But we may say that as we listened to him it seemed to us that in the level passages he was not extraordinarily good: that his voice is not a particularly fine one; that many of his inflections and the spirit in which he reads many passages are not at all what we should have expected or what we liked, but that wherever his admirable histrionic abilities could supplement or almost take the place of his abilities as a reader merely—then all things were done at least well, many things excellently well, and some things done so well that we have not as yet conceived of their being done better.—DENNET, J. R., 1867, *Dickens in New York, The Nation, vol.* 5, *p.* 482.

Every character was individualized by the voice and by a slight change of expression. But the reader stood perfectly still, and the instant transition of the voice from the dramatic to the descriptive tone was unfailing and extraordinary. This was perfection of art. Nor was the evenness of the variety less striking. Every character was indicated with the same felicity. Of course the previous image in the hearer's mind must be considered in estimating the effect. The reader does not create the character, the writer has done that; and now he refreshes it into unwonted vividness, as when a wet sponge is passed over an old picture. Scrooge, and Tiny Tim, and Sam Weller and his wonderful father, and Sergeant Buzfuz, and Justice Stareleigh have an intenser reality and vitality than before. As the reading advances the spell becomes more entrancing. The mind and heart answer instantly to every tone and look of the reader. In a passionate outburst, as in Bob Cratchit's wail for his lost little boy, or in Scrooge's prayer to be allowed to repent, the whole scene lives and throbs before you. And when, in the great trial of Bardell against Pickwick, the thick, fat voice of the elder Weller wheezes from the gallery, "Put it down with a wee, me Lerd, put it down with a wee," you turn to look for the gallery and behold the benevolent parent.— CURTIS, GEORGE WILLIAM, 1867, *Dickens Reading, From the Easy Chair, p. 47.*

How it happened, in this instance, that a writer of celebrity like Charles Dickens became a reader of his own works before large public audiences may readily be explained. Before his first appearance in that character professionally—that is, as a public reader, on his own account —he had enjoyed more than twenty years of unexampled popularity as a novelist. During that period he had not only securely established his reputation in authorship, but had evidenced repeatedly, at intervals during the latter portion of it, histrionic powers hardly less remarkable in their way than those gifts which had previously won for him his wholly exceptional fame as a writer of imagination. Among his personal intimates, among all those who knew him best, it had long come to be recognised that his skill as an impersonator was only second to his genius as a creator of humorous and pathetic character. His success in each capacity sprang from his intense sympathy and his equally intense earnestness. Whatever with him was worth doing at all, was worth doing thoroughly. Anything he undertook, no matter what, he went at, according to the good old sea phrase, with a will. He always endeavoured to accomplish whatever had to be accomplished as well as it could possibly be effected within the reach of his capabilities.—KENT, CHARLES, 1872, *Charles Dickens as a Reader, p. 12.*

Unlike most professional rehearsals, where waiting about, dawdling, and losing time, seem to be the order of the day, the rehearsals under Charles Dickens' stage-managership were strictly devoted to work —serious, earnest work; the consequence was, that when the evening of performance came, the pieces went off with a smoothness and polish that belong only to finished stage-business and practised performers. He was always there among the first arrivers at rehearsals, and remained in a conspicuous position during their progress till the very last moment of conclusion. He had a small table placed rather to one side of the stage, at which he generally sat, as the scenes went on in which he himself took no part. On this table rested a moderate-sized box; its interior divided into con-

venient compartments for holding papers, letters, etc., and this interior was always the very pink of neatness and orderly arrangement. Occasionally he would leave his seat at the managerial table, and stand with his back to the foot-lights, in the very centre of the front of the stage, and view the whole effect of the rehearsed performance as it proceeded, observing the attitudes and positions of those engaged in the dialogue, their mode of entrance, exit, etc. He never seemed to overlook anything; but to note the very slightest point that conduced to the "going well" of the whole performance. With all this supervision, however, it was pleasant to remark the utter absence of dictatorialness or arrogation of superiority that distinguished his mode of ruling his troop; he exerted his authority firmly and perpetually; but in such a manner as to make it universally felt to be for no purpose of self-assertion or self-importance; on the contrary, to be for the sole purpose of ensuring general success to their united efforts.—CLARKE, MARY COWDEN, 1878, *Recollections of Writers, p. 300.*

The rendering of a piece by Dickens was composed as an oratorio is composed, and was then studied by heart as music is studied. And the piece was all given by memory, without any looking at the notes or words.—TROLLOPE, ANTHONY, 1879. *Thackeray (English Men of Letters), p. 45.*

He [Carlyle] had an admiration for Charles Dickens, especially after hearing that author read some of his own works. He could, he said, hardly recall any theatrical representation he had witnessed in which the whole company had exhibited more variety of effect than came from the play of Dickens's voice and features.—CONWAY, MONCURE DANIEL, 1881, *Thomas Carlyle, p. 85.*

In taking leave of Mr. Dickens in this capacity, it may be interesting to set down the total number of public Readings he gave. Putting aside those given for charitable or friendly purposes between the years 1854 and 1858, in which latter year, at St. Martin's Hall, April 29, 1858, he commenced reading for his own especial benefit, up to the time of his retirement from the platform, at St. James's Hall, March 15, 1870, the full number of Readings was 423. Of these 111 were given under the management of Mr. Arthur Smith; 70 under the management of Mr. Headland (who succeeded to the post of manager on the death of Mr. Smith), and 242 under my management. These latter were delivered in England, Ireland, Scotland, and America, between April 10, 1866, and March 15, 1870. Mr. Dickens kept no particular account of the amount of money he netted from the Readings under the management of Messrs. Arthur Smith and Headland, but he always computed it at about £12,000. Out of the 242 Readings given under my management (which included the three engagements of Messrs. Chappell and Co.), he cleared nearly £33,000. Handsome as these results were, and of course highly satisfactory to Mr. Dickens, they were purchased at the dear cost of the sacrifice of his health. But his career as a public reader was his own choice, and setting aside his pecuniary profits, the pleasure he derived from it is not to be told in words. For my part, at this distance of time, I think less of the dark than of the bright side of those never-to-be-forgotten days.—DOLBY, GEORGE, 1885, *Charles Dickens as I Knew Him,* p. 45.

PICKWICK PAPERS
1837

The most cursory reference to preceding English writers of the comic order will show, that, in his own peculiar walk, Mr. Dickens is not simply the most distinguished, but the first. Admirers and detractors will be equally ready to admit that he has little, if anything, in common with the novelists and essayists of the last century. Of Fielding's intuitive perception of the springs of action, and skill in the construction of the prose epic—or Smollett's dash, vivacity, wild spirit of adventure and rich poetic imagination—he has none: still less can he make pretensions to the exquisite delicacy, fine finish, and perfect keeping of Steele's and Addison's pet characters,—Sir Roger de Coverley, Will Wimble, Will Honeycombe, Sir Andrew Freeport, and the rest; though we know few things better in conception than Sam Weller, with his chivalrous attachment to his master, his gallantry to the fair sex, his imperturbable self-possession, and singularly acquired knowledge of the world.—CROKER, JOHN WILSON, 1837, *The Pickwick Papers, Quarterly Review, vol.* 59, *p.* 484.

But what praise can be sufficiently enthusiastic for the admirable conception of Sam Weller, that inimitable compound of wit, simplicity, quaint humour, and fidelity!

The "gamin de Paris" does not possess a more distinctive and attractive physiognomy than Dickens has here immortalised in this exquisite portrait of the Londoner; perhaps since Parson Adams literature cannot afford an instance of a personage so exquisitely true to nature, so intensely comic, so individual, and at the same time so perfect a type of a class, as this delightful creation.—SHAW, THOMAS B., 1847, *Outlines of English Literature,* p. 392.

In humour, he will hardly surpass "Pickwick," simply because "Pickwick" is scarcely surpassable in humour.—MARTINEAU, HARRIET, 1855–77, *Autobiography, ed. Chapman, vol.* II, *p.* 62.

It has been said that "The Pickwick Papers" was its author's best book; and, in certain respects, this judgment is sound. Humor was Mr. Dickens's great distinctive trait; and for humor, pure and simple, he produced in all his life nothing quite equal to "Pickwick"—nothing so sustained, so varied, so unstrained.—WHITE, RICHARD, GRANT, 1870, *The Styles of Disraeli and of Dickens, The Galaxy, vol.* 10, *p.* 258.

By most people "Pickwick" is accepted as Dickens's *Magnum Opus.* It certainly is a typical one, but while the whole book is farcical in the extreme, while character degenerates to caricature, and fun to pantomimic romp and "rally," there are now and then touches of very clever shrewd observation, most admirable sketches of character—Sergeant Buzfuz and the trial scene are evidently quite true to nature, and pathos of the genial easy and ordinary kind in which the author delighted. But as a novel of nature and of plot and character compared to Fielding, "Pickwick" is very small. Who ever met with man, woman, or child, who could sit down by a winter fire and tell the "plot" of "Pickwick?" Had it come out as a whole book, it would have failed to find readers, it would, like Hudibras, have palled on the taste; it is too full of incident, scene succeeds scene, and adventure adventure. The novel is crowded with persons, and each person is—how different from real life and Mr. Trollope—not cut to pattern, but a character.—FRISWELL, JAMES HAIN, 1870, *Modern Men of Letters Honestly Criticised, p.* 8.

There is perhaps no book more widely known in the English language, nor, strange enough, many which have been received with such favour on the Continent, though it is intensely national in character. It is, indeed, an almost perfect specimen of the strictly English quality of fun—using English in its very narrowest sense as applying only to that part of her Majesty's dominions called England—which differs as greatly from the humour of Scotland and Ireland as from French wit or American extravagance.—OLIPHANT, M. O.W., 1892, *The Victorian Age of English Literature, p.* 251.

The glory of Charles Dickens will always be in his "Pickwick," his first, his best, his inimitable triumph. It is true that it is a novel without a plot, without beginning, middle, or end, with much more of caricature than of character, with some extravagant tom-foolery, and plenty of vulgarity. But its originality, its irrepressible drolleries, its substantial human nature, and its intense vitality, place it quite in a class by itself.—HARRISON, FREDERIC, 1895, *Studies in Early Victorian Literature, p.* 143.

It would be vain to praise or to disparage the immortal "Pickwick." Everything about it is remarkable. No modern work of the century has engendered so many other books, commentaries, illustrations, &c., or been so Protean in its developments. Drama, opera, music, translations, pictures, topography, philology, almanacs, songsters, advertisements, pens, cigars, all exhibit this generative influence. There is a little library of writers on Pickwick. Grave professors, men of law, politicians, schoolmasters, all have been drawn to it. Neither Scott, nor Thackeray, nor Byron, nor Macaulay, nor Tennyson can show anything like it. The commentary on the Waverleys is quite meagre by comparison. The oddity, too, is that no other work of "Boz" has had this fruitfulness. The reason would seem to be the tone of perfect conviction and reality in which it is conceived and carried out. The characters are treated almost biographically, and move forward according to its dates.—FITZGERALD, PERCY, 1898, *Among My Books, Literature, vol.* 2, *p.* 384.

There are three official accounts variously explaining the veracious story, each materially differing in dates and details, and respectively emanating from the three principal personages most likely to be fully informed upon the actual facts of the case. The artist Seymour undoubtedly originated the initial scheme of illustrating various unconnected adventures of Cockney sportsmen, to be graphically portrayed under the convenient if trite expedient of a "Nimrod Club"—all three accounts are agreed to this extent. The vivacious author of "PICKWICK" from the first start, turned, twisted, shaped, and made the crude materials his very own by the absolute force of his genius, and fiery Pegasus-like, immediately dashing away with the lead, from ingredients, perhaps a trifle uncongenial to himself, produced the most popularly appreciated book of the century—possibly of any century; and, at one lucky bound, on the strength of his parts, became the most famous of novelists. The "third party" was the connecting link, the useful, necessary publishers, upon whose business-like conduct of the affair the commercial responsibilities depended.—GREGO, JOSEPH, 1899, *ed. Pictorial Pickwickiana, vol.* I, *p.* 6.

"Pickwick" has always been a fascinating book for the artist. At one time everybody who could draw attempted to illustrate it. Indeed, the number of artists who indulged in such attempts are legion, "Pickwick Papers" being more favored in this respect than the others. At the time of its issue in 1836 and 1837, more than one artist produced sets of etchings to be used as "extras" for the monthly parts as they appeared. The best of these were by Onwhyn, who used the pseudonym of "Sam Weller" on some of his engravings, William Heath, Alfred Crowquill (A. H. Forrester), and T. Gibson. We recall a characteristic one by Heath and also one by Sir John Gilbert, whose series on wood appeared later.—MATZ, B. W., 1902, *Dickens and his Illustrators, The Critic, vol.* 40, *p.* 44.

OLIVER TWIST
1838

Not only with the Author's happiest praise
Thy work should be rewarded;—it is kin
To theirs who, steeling finest nerves to win
Great blessings for mankind, explor'd the maze
Oppression's ages harden'd; trod the ways
Where fruitful Sorrow tracks and quickens Sin,
To draw forth strains of music from the din
Of passions; in the culprit soul to raise
Sweet thoughts of goodness; bid the fetters fall
And hail the slave immortal;—for within
Wan childhood's squalid haunts, where frightful
     needs
Make tyranny more bitter, at thy call
An angel face with patient sadness pleads
Undying kindred to the heart of all.
—TALFOURD, THOMAS NOON, 1838, *To Charles Dickens, on his "Oliver Twist."*

The work which is most full of crimes and atrocities and the lowest characters, of all its author's productions, in which these things are by no means scarce—there are some of the deepest touches of pathos, and of the purest tenderness, not exceeded by any author who ever lived—simply because they grow out of the very ground of our common humanity, and being Nature at her best, are in themselves perfect, by universal laws.—HORNE, RICHARD HEN-GIST, 1844, *A New Spirit of the Age, p.* 17.

Not Smollett, nor Fielding, nor perhaps all the romance-writers whose works we possess, could have produced anything equal, in terrific reality and vividness, to the murder of Nancy and the wanderings of the ruffian Sykes. Sykes and his dog alone are enough to establish Dickens's fame as a great original writer.—SHAW, THOMAS B., 1847, *Outlines of English Literature, p.* 393.

When Dickens wrote "Oliver Twist" he desired, as he says, to paint vice in its true characters, without the fascinations of highway adventure, or snug robbers' caves, or anything approaching the attractions that too often pervaded the literature of profligacy. He wished to answer those who
Proved, by cool discriminating sight,
Black's not so black, nor white so very white.
The dens and stews of London are painted from life, and the picture is not inviting. In the character of Nancy there is some redeeming quality—she might have been different under different circumstances; in the characters of Fagin or Bill Sikes there is none; they are simply bad, as bad as they can be, without one silver thread lining the edge of the cloud. Unfortunately for the artist, but fortunately for the rest of the world, the haunts of vice that were standing when this work was written are demolished; and whatever remains of the Bill Sikes or the Fagin element is left in the cold; but if we read the police summaries we are sadly reminded that they are hardly extinct.—RIMMER, ALFRED, 1883, *About England with Dickens, p.* 133.

Here and there appeared glimpses of the humor which had marked his earlier work, but, on the whole, the tale was cast in the mold of the horrible, and depended for its strength on the debased characters and the criminal life of which Fagin is the central figure. It was eighteen years since Ivanhoe had appeared, and what a contrast between its Jewish personage and the char-

acter in this, the next work of a great English writer, in which a Jew plays a prominent rôle! In the one the charm, in the other the disgrace of the work; in the one the possessor of all human virtues, in the other of all human vices; in the one fair in body and fairer in soul, in the other distorted in body and black in soul; the one a plea for kindness toward a community at that time still unrecognized as worthy of the rights of men and women, the other calculated to re-awaken all the old thoughts, if ever they had died out, of the baseness and wickedness of the Jews. . . . All that interests us here is the character of Fagin, who is continually intruded upon our notice as "the Jew." Were the miscreant, whenever introduced upon the scene, merely spoken of as Fagin, we would look upon him as an example of London's criminal class, and there would be nothing further to arrest our special attention. . . . The author presented this character as a Jew, and hence has laid himself open to the charge of gross wrong and injustice. The fact of Fagin being a Jew does not make him what he is; but when the novel was written such an idea was far from being deemed impossible. The Jew was still an unknown quantity; people thought him *sui generis;* it was not known, according to popular opinion, what he was likely to do. . . . Strange it is, at best, that Charles Dickens, who, of all fictionists, contributed the most toward reforming social abuses, should, in this one instance, have joined the vulgar cry, and marked his worst character as a Jew. Knowing what we do of his works, we should rather have looked for the opposite.—PHILIPSON, DAVID, 1889, *The Jew in English Fiction, pp.* 89, 90, 93.

It is a picaresque story humanized, and given a realistic setting in the London slums.—CROSS, WILBUR L., 1899, *The Development of the English Novel, p.* 182.

When we pass from the subjects of Dickens's stories to the mechanism of their plots we find little to admire and much to condemn. The most serious fault from the artistic stand-point is their lack of probability. In "Oliver Twist" the series of remarkable coincidences is perfectly absurd. When Oliver goes up to London and falls in with the pickpockets, the first person he comes across is the old gentleman whom he is suspected of robbing and who afterwards befriends him. This turns out to be his father's oldest friend. By a curious chance

Oliver is captured by the thieves again and forced to take part in the robbery of a house in the country. He is caught, and the young lady of the house, who befriends him, turns out to be his aunt! Really this is too childish. We allow a novelist a good deal of freedom in arranging his incidents to suit his purposes, but if he cannot manage them in a more convincing fashion than that, the whole illusion is gone.—OLIPHANT, JAMES, 1899, *Victorian Novelists, p. 38.*

NICHOLAS NICKLEBY
1839

Nickleby is very good. I stood out against Mr. Dickens as long as I could, but he has conquered me.—SMITH, SYDNEY, 1838, *To Sir George Philips, Sept.; Letters of Sydney Smith, ed. Mrs. Austin.*

The town of Barnard Castle is most picturesque, with a ruined castle of the Baliols. Dickens, in early life, used frequently to come down and stay there with some young artist friends of his. The idea of "Humphrey's Clock" first sprung from Humphrey, the watchmaker in the town, and the picture in the beginning of the book is of the clock over the door of his shop. While at Barnard Castle, Dickens heard of the school at Bowes which he afterwards worked up as Dotheboys Hall. Many of these schools, at £15 and £20 a year, existed at that time in the neighbourhood, and were principally used for the sons of London tradesmen, who, provided their sons got a moderate education, cared little or nothing what became of them in the meantime. Dickens went over to see the school at Bowes, and was carefully shown over it, for they mistook him for a parent coming to survey it, with a view of sending his son there. Afterwards the school was totally ruined. At one of Mr. Bowes's elections, the Nicholas Nickleby or former usher of the school, who was then in want of a place, wrote to him to say in what poverty he was. He "had formerly been living with Mr. Shawe at Bowes, and they had been happy and prosperous, when Mr. Dickens's misguided volume, sweeping like a whirlwind over the schools of the North, caused Mr. Shawe to become a victim to paralysis, and brought Mrs. Shawe to an untimely grave."—HARE, AUGUSTUS J. C., 1861, *The Story of My Life, Sept. 27, vol. II, p. 275.*

"Nicholas Nickleby" combined the comic and the sensational elements for the first time, and is still the type of Dickens's longer books, in which the strain of violent pathos or sinister mystery is incessantly relieved by farce, either of incident or description. In this novel, too, the easy-going, old-fashioned air of "Pickwick" is abandoned in favour of a humanitarian attitude more in keeping with the access of puritanism which the new reign had brought with it, and from this time forth a certain squeemishness in dealing with moral problems and a certain "gush" of unreal sentiment obscured the finer qualities of the novelist's genius.—GOSSE, EDMUND, 1897, *A Short History of Modern English Literature, p. 341.*

MASTER HUMPHREY'S CLOCK
1840–41

Read the two concluding numbers of "Humphrey's Clock," which ends very sadly and very sweetly. Wonderful Dickens!—MACREADY, W. C., 1841, *Diary, Nov. 26; Reminiscences, ed. Pollock, p. 507.*

Is somewhat diffuse and its characters are exaggerated.—SCHERR, J., 1874, *A History of English Literature, tr. M. V., p. 275.*

There is little except biographical interest in the half-forgotten history of "Master Humphrey's Clock."— WARD, ADOLPHUS WILLIAM, 1882, *Dickens (English Men of Letters), p. 40.*

BARNABY RUDGE
1841

That this fiction, or indeed that any fiction written by Mr. Dickens, should be based in the excitement and maintenance of curiosity, we look upon as a misconception, on the part of the writer, of his own very great yet very peculiar powers. He has done this thing well, to be sure—he would do anything well in comparison with the herd of his contemporaries; but he has not done it so thoroughly well as his high and just reputation would demand.—POE, EDGAR ALLAN, 1842, *Literary Criticism, Works, ed. Stedman and Woodberry, vol. VII, p. 64.*

In May, 1841, he [Poe] contributed to the Philadelphia "Saturday Evening Post"—a paper belonging to Mr. Graham—that *prospective* notice of the newly commenced story of "Barnaby Rudge," which drew from Dickens a letter of admiring acknowledgment. In this said notice the poet, with mathematical precision, explained and foretold the exact plot of the as yet unpublished story.—INGRAM, JOHN H., 1876, *A*

Biographical Sketch of Edgar Allan Poe, Poe Memorial, ed. Rice, p. 21.

This was Dickens's first attempt at what is called the historical novel, and it must be confessed that it contained slight promise of the conspicuous success which he afterwards achieved in this field with "The Tale of Two Cities." Though constructed with much care, and exceptionally well written, it seems to lack both reality and interest; and, though the management of the Raven is a masterpiece of humorous fancy, "Barnaby Rudge" has afforded fewer than any other of Dickens's novels of those types of character, and racy sayings, which fasten themselves upon the memory of the reader. —JONES, CHARLES H., 1880, *A Short Life of Charles Dickens, p.* 95.

What the author of "The Pupil of Pleasure" assayed to do in the last century, the author of "Barnaby Rudge" has essayed to do in our own time. On the unspeakable vulgarity and absurdity of Dickens's caricature and travesty—with pain do we say a disrespectful word of one to whom we in common with half the world are so much indebted—it would be superfluous to comment. But what is certain is that in the imagination of millions Chesterfield will exist, and exist only, in association with a character combining all that is worst, all that is most vile, most contemptible, most repulsive, in the traditionary portrait of him. —COLLINS, JOHN CHURTON, 1895, *Essays and Studies, p.* 200.

"Barnaby Rudge" is, by general consent, second-rate.—WALKER, HUGH, 1897, *The Age of Tennyson, p.* 87.

In any just sense there is no heroine in "Barnaby Rudge," which is a book of more skill and power than any that Dickens had yet written. We may dismiss without self-reproach such a ladylike lay-figure as Emma Haredale, and a goblin effigy like Miss Miggs, and come without delay to Dolly Varden, who, in turn, need hardly delay us longer. She is a cheap little coquette, imagined upon the commonest lines, with abundant assertion as to her good looks and graces, but without evidence of the charm that the silliest flirt has in reality. She is nothing and she does nothing; and she cannot be petted and patted by her inventor, with all his fondness, into any semblance or personality.— HOWELLS, WILLIAM DEAN, 1901, *Heroines of Fiction, vol.* I, *p.* 136.

OLD CURIOSITY SHOP
1841

Mr. Dickens's head must puzzle the phrenologists. The organs of ideality are small; and the conclusion of the "Old Curiosity Shop" is more truly ideal (in both phrenological senses) than any composition of equal length in the English language.—POE, EDGAR ALLAN, 1841, *Marginalia, Works, ed. Stedman and Woodberry, vol.* VII, *p.* 281.

Extravagance and want of fidelity to nature and the possibilities of life are what everywhere mar Dickens to me, and these faults are fatal, because the *modes* of life amongst which these extravagances intrude are always the absolute realities of vulgarized life as it exists in plebeian ranks amongst our countrymen at this moment. Were the mode of life one more idealized or removed from our own, I might be less sensible of the insupportable extravagances.— DEQUINCEY, THOMAS, 1847, *Letter to his Daughter, Life, ed. Japp, vol.* I, *p.* 349.

I admire Nell in the "Old Curiosity Shop" exceedingly. No doubt the whole thing is a good deal borrowed from Wilhelm Meister. But little Nell is a far purer, lovelier, more *English* conception than Mignon, treasonable as the saying would seem to some. No doubt it was suggested by Mignon.— COLERIDGE, SARA, 1849, *To Aubrey De Vere, Oct.* 2; *Memoir and Letters, ed. her Daughter, p.* 407.

We have buried warriors and poets, princes and queens, but no one of these was followed to the grave by sincerer mourners than was little Nell.—SMITH, ALEXANDER, 1863, *Dreamthorp, p.* 18.

Above the pines the moon was slowly drifting,
  The river sang below;
The dim Sierras, far beyond, uplifting
  Their minarets of snow:
The roaring camp-fire, with rude humour, painted
  The ruddy tints of health
On haggard face and form that drooped and fainted
  In the fierce race for wealth;
Till one arose, and from his pack's scant treasure
  A hoarded volume drew,
And cards were dropped from hands of listless leisure
  To hear the tale anew.
And then, while round them shadows gathered faster,
  And as the firelight fell,
He read aloud the book wherein the Master
  Had writ of "Little Nell."
—HARTE, FRANCIS BRET, 1870, *Dickens in Camp.*

In the "Old Curiosity Shop" was created the character of "Little Nell," the most famous of all the author's pathetic children, and perhaps as famous as any in literature—even as the Mignon of Goethe, a being as pure and good as Nell, though as impassioned as the little English girl is snow-cold.—PERKINS, F. B., 1870, *Charles Dickens, p.* 62.

Dear, sweet, loving little Nell! We doubt if any other creation of poet or novelist in any language has received the tribute of as many tears as thou. From high, from low, on land, on sea, wherever thy story has been read, there has been paid the spontaneous tribute of tears. Whether or not many of the fantastic creations of the great master's hand will live in the far future we cannot tell, but of thy immortality there is no more question than there is of that of Hamlet or Lear.—GRISWOLD, HATTIE TYNG, 1886, *Home Life of Great Authors, p.* 344.

A whole generation, on either side of the Atlantic, used to fall sobbing at the name of Little Nell, which will hardly bring tears to the eyes of any one now, though it is still apparent that the child was imagined with real feelings, and her sad little melodrama was staged with sympathetic skill. When all is said against the lapses of taste and truth, the notion of the young girl wandering up and down the country with her demented grandfather, and meeting good and evil fortune with the same devotion, till death overtakes her, is something that must always touch the heart. It is preposterously overdone, yes, and the author himself falls into pages of hysterical rhythm, which once moved people, when he ought to have been writing plain, straight prose; yet there is in all a sense of the divinity in common and humble lives, which is the most precious quality of literature, as it is almost the rarest, and it is this which moves and consoles. It is this quality in Dickens which Tolstoy prizes and accepts as proof of his great art, and which the true critic must always set above any effect of literary mastery.—HOWELLS, WILLIAM DEAN, 1901, *Heroines of Fiction, vol.* I, *p.* 131.

I believe that the first book—the first real, substantial book—I read through was "The Old Curiosity Shop." At all events, it was the first volume of Dickens which I made my own. . . . "The Old Curiosity Shop" makes strong appeal to a youthful imagination, and contains little that is be-

yond its scope. Dickens's sentiment, however it may distress the mature mind of our later day, is not unwholesome, and, at all events in this story, addresses itself naturally enough to feelings unsubdued by criticism. His quality of picturesqueness is here seen at its best, with little or nothing of that melodrama which makes the alloy of "Nicholas Nickleby" and "Oliver Twist" —to speak only of the early books. The opening scene, that dim-lighted storehouse of things old and grotesque, is the best approach to Dickens's world, where sights of every day are transfigured in the service of romance. The kindliness of the author's spirit, his overflowing sympathy with poor and humble folk, set one's mind to a sort of music which it is good to live with; and no writer of moralities ever showed triumphant virtue in so cheery a light as that which falls upon these honest people when rascality has got its deserts.—GISSING, GEORGE, 1902, *Dickens in Memory, The Critic, vol.* 40, *p.* 48.

AMERICAN NOTES
1842

I have read Dickens's book. It is jovial and good-natured, and at times very severe. You will read it with delight and, for the most part, approbation. He has a grand chapter on Slavery. *Spitting* and *politics at Washington* are the other topics of censure. Both you and I would censure them with equal severity, to say the least.—LONGFELLOW, HENRY WADSWORTH, 1842, *Letter to Charles Sumner, Oct.* 16; *Life, ed. Longfellow, vol.* I, *p.* 440.

His "Notes" upon America come out, I believe, immediately; and I shall be extremely curious to see them, and sorry if they are unfavorable, because his popularity as a writer is immense, and whatever he publishes will be sure of a wide circulation. Moreover, as it is very well known that, before going to America, he was strongly prepossessed in favor of its institutions, manners, and people, any disparaging remarks he may make upon them will naturally have proportionate weight, as the deliberate result of experience and observation. M— told me, after dining with Dickens immediately on his return, that one thing that had disgusted him was the almost universal want of conscience upon money matters in America; and the levity, occasionally approaching to something like self-satisfaction, for their "sharpness," which he had repeated occasions of observing, in your people when speaking of the present disgraceful condition of their finances and deservedly degraded state of their national credit. . . . But I do hope (because I have a friend's and not a "foe's" heart towards your country) that Dickens will not write unfavorably about it, for his opinion will influence public opinion in England, and deserves to do so.—KEMBLE, FRANCES ANN, 1842, *Letter Oct.* 2; *Records of Later Life,* p. 359.

A thousand thanks to you for your charming book! and for all the pleasure, profit, and relief it has afforded me. You have been very tender to our sensitive friends beyond sea, and really said nothing which should give any serious offence to any moderately rational patriot among them. The "Slavers," of course, will give you no quarter, and I suppose you did not expect they should. But I do not think you could have said less, and my whole heart goes along with every word you have written. Some people will be angry, too, that you have been so strict to observe their *spitting*, and neglect of ablutions, &c. And more, that you should have spoken with so little reverence of their courts of law and state legislature, and even of their grand Congress itself. But all this latter part is done in such a spirit of good-humoured playfulness, and so mixed up with clear intimations that you have quite as little veneration for things of the same sort at home, that it will not be easy to represent it as the fruit of English insolence and envy.—JEFFREY, FRANCIS LORD, 1842, *Letter to Dickens, Oct.* 16; *Life ed. Cockburn, vol.* II, p. 294.

Dear Napier,—This morning I received Dickens's book. I have now read it. It is impossible for me to review it; nor do I think that you would wish me to do so. I cannot praise it, and I will not cut it up. I cannot praise it, though it contains a few lively dialogues and descriptions; for it seems to me to be on the whole a failure. It is written like the worst part of "Humphrey's Clock." What is meant to be easy and sprightly is vulgar and flippant, as in the first two pages. What is meant to be fine is a great deal too fine for me, as the description of the Fall of Niagara. A reader who wants an amusing account of the United States had better go to Mrs. Trollope, coarse and malignant as she is. A reader who

wants information about American politics, manners, and literature, had better go even to so poor a creature as Buckingham. In short, I pronounce the book, in spite of some gleams of genius, at once frivolous and dull. Therefore I will not praise it. Neither will I attack it; first, because I have eaten salt with Dickens; secondly, because he is a good man, and a man of real talent; thirdly, because he hates slavery as heartily as I do; and, fourthly, because I wish to see him enrolled in our blue and yellow corps, where he may do excellent service as a skirmisher and sharp-shooter.—MACAULAY, THOMAS BABINGTON, 1842, *Letter, Oct.* 19; *Life and Letters, ed. Trevelyan, ch.* ix.

Since the voyage of Columbus in search of the New World, and of Raleigh in quest of El Dorado, no visit to America has excited so much interest and conjecture as that of the author of "Oliver Twist." . . . In the mean time the book, after long budding in advertisement has burst into full leaf, and however disconcerting to those persons who had looked for something quite different, will bring no disappointment to such as can be luxuriously content with good sense, good feeling, good fun, and good writing.—HOOD, THOMAS, 1842, *Boz in America, New Monthly Magazine, vol.* 66, pp. 396, 397.

The little information to be gleaned from these two volumes, with few exceptions, might be gained much more advantageously from the map and gazetteer. The perusal of them has served chiefly to lower our estimate of the man, and to fill us with contempt for such a compound of egotism, coxcombry, and cockneyism. . . . We have never read a book, professing to give an account of any country, which, in respect to its natural features, its towns and cities, its manners and customs, its social, civil, and religious institutions—in short, in respect to everything about which the reader wishes to receive information, or at least to ascertain the opinions of the author, is so profoundly silent as the book before us.—THOMPSON, J. P., 1843, *Dickens' Notes on America, The New Englander, vol.* I, pp. 67, 76.

Though the book is said to have given great offence on the other side of the Atlantic, we cannot see any sufficient reason for it. To us it appears that Mr. Dickens deserves great praise for the care with which he has avoided all offensive topics, and abstained from amusing his readers at the expense of his entertainers; and if we had an account of the temptations in this kind which he has resisted, we do not doubt that the reserve and self-control which he has exercised would appear scarcely less than heroical. But, on the other hand, we cannot say that his book throws any new light on his subject. He has done little more than confide to the public what should have been a series of letters for the entertainment of his private friends. Very agreeable and amusing letters they would have been; and as such, had they been posthumously published, would have been read with interest and pleasure. As it is, in the middle of our amusement at the graphic sketches of life and manners, the ludicrous incidents, the wayside conversations about nothing, so happily told, and the lively remarks, with which these "Notes" abound—in the middle of our respect for the tone of good sense and good humour which runs through them.—SPEDDING, JAMES, 1843, *Dickens's American Notes, Reviews and Discussions,* p. 247.

As shallow a book of travels as ever appeared.—TUCKERMAN, HENRY T., 1857, *Essays, Biographical and Critical,* p. 175.

The debt which America owed to this man was hardly less than that which England owed him. The insane fury with which his "American Notes" was received in our country was simply an outburst of the same rage that afterward was visited on Mrs. Stowe for her "Uncle Tom's Cabin." The outcries about "exaggerated and distorted statements" heard in England from poor-house authorities, when "Oliver Twist" was published, were counterparts of the angry denunciations of slavery when Dickens published the advertisements about negroes which he read daily. I remember that the Southerners were also furious at his description of the roads and the driver in Northern Virginia, declaring it all a caricature. But I happened to have been born and reared close to that old Acquis road, and have often seen the stage and the driver which figure in the "American Notes;" and it was known to me, as to others dwelling in the same region, that the descriptions were all not only graphic, but photographic in their accuracy.—CONWAY, MONCURE DANIEL, 1870, *Footprints of Charles Dickens, Harper's Magazine, vol. 41,* p. 612.

A CHRISTMAS CAROL
1843

It is the work of the master of all the English humourists now alive; the young man who came and took his place calmly at the head of the whole tribe, and who has kept it. . . . Who can listen to objections regarding such a book as this? It seems to me a national benefit, and to every man or woman who reads it a personal kindness. The last two people I heard speak of it were women; neither knew the other, or the author, and both said, by way of criticism, "God bless him!" . . . As for Tiny Tim, there is a certain passage in the book regarding that young gentleman about which a man should hardly venture to speak in print or in public, any more than he would of any other affections of his private heart. There is not a reader in England but that little creature will be a bond of union between the author and him; and he will say of Charles Dickens, as the woman just now, "God bless him!" What a feeling is this for a writer to be able to inspire, and what a reward to reap!—THACKERAY, WILLIAM MAKEPEACE, 1844, *Christmas Carols by Dickens, Fraser's Magazine, vol.* 29, *pp.* 167, 169.

There was indeed nobody that had not some interest in the message of the "Christmas Carol." It told the selfish man to rid himself of selfishness; the just man to make himself generous; and the good-natured man to enlarge the sphere of his good nature. Its cheery voice of faith and hope, ringing from one end of the island to the other, carried pleasant warning alike to all, that if the duties of Christmas were wanting no good could come out of its outward observances; that it must shine upon the cold hearth and warm it, and into the sorrowful heart and comfort it; that it must be kindness, benevolence, charity, mercy, and forbearance, or its plum pudding would turn to bile, and its roast beef be indigestible. Nor could any man have said it with the same appropriateness as Dickens.—FORSTER, JOHN, 1873, *The Life of Charles Dickens, vol.* II, *p.* 89.

Simple in its romantic design like one of Andersen's little tales, the "Christmas Carol" has never lost its hold upon a public in whom it has called forth Christmas thoughts which do not all center on "holly, mistletoe, red berries, ivy, turkeys, geese, game, poultry, brawn, meat, pigs, sausages, oysters, pies, puddings, fruit, and punch;" and the Cratchit household, with Tiny Tim, who did NOT die, are living realities even to those who have not seen Mr. Toole—an actor after Dickens's own heart—as the father of the family, shivering in his half-yard of comforter.—WARD, ADOLPHUS WILLIAM, 1882, *Dickens (English Men of Letters), p.* 60.

Another characteristic of Dickens's is benevolence, and here in his "Christmas Carol" we see it: peace, charity, good-will, does he not revel in it? does he not give way to joyous raptures, shout and sing? Yes; and even dances with delight at the happiness of others. Does he not get right to the heart, and enter into every little detail of joy; and does he not send bubbling up pleasures and delights, which are in themselves the best Christmas anthems ever sung?—O'DELL, STACKPOOL E.,1882, *Phrenology: Its Truthfulness and Usefulness.*

What a thrill ran through the whole English-speaking race when "A Christmas Carol in Prose" announced to it that Marley was dead, to begin with—as dead as a door-nail. No carol that ever was sung so stirred the deep heart of humanity. The world laughed and cried over it, and Scrooge and Scrooge's nephew, and old Fezziwig, and Bob Cratchit, and Tiny Tim, became household words in a million homes.—DORR, JULIA C. R., 1885, *Christmas and Its Literature, The Book Buyer, vol.* 2, *p.* 285.

MARTIN CHUZZLEWIT
1844

Dickens has just published, as one of the chapters of "Martin Chuzzlewit," an account of the arrival of his hero in New York, and what he saw, and heard, and did, and suffered, in this land of pagans, brutes, and infidels. I am sorry to see it. Thinking that Mr. Dickens has been ungenerously treated by my countrymen, I have taken his part on most occasions; but he has now written an exceedingly foolish libel upon us, from which he will not obtain credit as an author, nor as a man of wit, any more than as a man of good taste, good nature, or good manners. It is difficult to believe that such unmitigated trash should have flown from the same pen that drew the portrait of the immortal Pickwick and his expressive gaiters, the honest locksmith and his pretty Dolly of Clerkenwell, and poor little Nell, who has caused so many tears to flow. Shame, Mr. Dickens! Con-sidering all that we did for you, if, as some folks say, I and others made fools of ourselves to make much of you, you should not afford them the triumph of saying, "There! we told you so!" "It serves you right!" and other such consolatory phrases. If we were fools, you were the cause of it, and should have stood by us. "*Et tu, Brute!*"— HONE, PHILIP, 1843, *Diary, July* 29, *vol.* II, *p.* 189.

This novel is one of the finest of his compositions—not the American scenes, perhaps, for these have generally an air of exaggeration which injures them; but the adventures which occur before and after the hero makes his unfortunate and unsuccessful voyage across the Atlantic.—SHAW, THOMAS B., 1847, *Outlines of English Literature, p.* 394.

This last work contains, besides all the fun, some very marked and available morals. I scarce know any book in which the evil and odiousness of selfishness is more forcibly brought out, or in a greater variety of exhibitions. In the midst of the merry quotations, or at least on any fair opportunity, I draw the boys' attention to these points, bid them remark how *unmanly* is the selfishness of young Martin, and I insist upon it that Tom Pinch's character, if it could really exist, would be a very beautiful one.—COLERIDGE, SARA, 1848, *To Mrs. H. M. Jones, Aug.* 17; *Memoir and Letters, ed. her Daughter, p.* 346.

The novel "Martin Chuzzlewit" is a bitter but just satire on Yankeeism.—SCHERR, J., 1874, *A History of English Literature, tr. M. V., p.* 275.

I liked Martin Chuzzlewit, too, and the other day I read a great part of it again, and found it roughly true in the passages that referred to America, though it was surcharged in the serious moods, and caricatured in the comic. The English are always inadequate observers; they seem too full of themselves to have eyes and ears for any alien people; but as far as an Englishman could, Dickens had caught the look of our life in certain aspects. His report of it was clumsy and farcical; it wanted nicety of accent and movement, but in a large, loose way it was like enough; at least he had caught the note of our self-satisfied, intolerant and hypocritical provinciality, and this was not altogether lost in his mocking horse-play.—HOWELLS, WILLIAM DEAN, 1895, *My Literary Passions, p.* 100.

THE CRICKET ON THE HEARTH
1845

If the palm is to be granted to any one among them [Christmas books] above its fellows, few readers would hesitate, I think, to declare themselves in favour of "The Cricket on the Hearth," as tender and delicate a domestic idyl as any literature can boast.—WARD, ADOLPHUS WILLIAM, 1882, *Dickens (English Men of Letters), p.* 59.

It seems strange that Dickens's plots, though interesting, and his dialogue and characters apparently dramatic, should be unsatisfactory when arranged for the stage. The story of "The Cricket on the Hearth" is the one exception, for with trifling condensation it can be acted with effect from the book itself, having all the completeness and direct motives that go to make a play, together with a strong female interest which in a domestic drama seems to be an essential element. And though there are two distinct plots in the story, they are most adroitly woven together, and one wonders how the author could have missed detecting his own dramatic accident. For had Dickens known that his little Christmas story contained these qualities he would undoubtedly have given it to the stage.—JEFFERSON, JOE, 1898, *The Cricket on the Hearth, Introduction, p.* ix.

DOMBEY AND SON
1848

Oh, my dear, dear Dickens! what a No. 5 you have now given us! I have so cried and sobbed over it last night, and again this morning; and felt my heart purified by those tears, and blessed and loved you for making me shed them; and I never can bless and love you enough. Since the divine Nelly was found dead on her humble couch, beneath the snow and the ivy, there has been nothing like the actual dying of that sweet Paul, in the summer sunshine of that lofty room. And the long vista that leads us so gently and sadly, and yet so gracefully and winningly, to the plain consummation! Every trait so true and so touching—and yet lightened by the fearless innocence which goes playfully to the brink of the grave, and that pure affection which bears the unstained spirit, on its soft and lambent flash, at once to its source in eternity.—JEFFREY, FRANCIS LORD, 1847, *Letter to Dickens, Jan.* 31; *The Life of Charles Dickens, ed. Forster, vol.* II, *p.* 361.

It was Thackeray's delight to read each number of "Dombey and Son" with eagerness as it issued from the press. He had often been heard to speak of the work in terms of the highest praise, and when it had reached its fifth number, wherein Dickens describes the end of little Paul with a depth of pathos which produced a vibrating emotion in the hearts of all who read it, Thackeray seemed electrified at the thought that there was one man living who could exercise so complete a control over him. Putting No. 5 of "Dombey and Son" in his pocket, he hastened down to the printing-office of *Punch*, and entering the editor's room, he dashed it on the table with startling vehemence, and exclaimed, "There's no writing against such power as this—one has no chance! Read that chapter describing young Paul's death: it is unsurpassed—it is stupendous!"—HODDER, GEORGE, 1870, *Memories of My Time.*

Raymond's *Toots* was so thoroughly *Toots*, we had learned to know and to think of *Toots* so decidedly, as Raymond, and subsequently as Johnston had shown him to us, that the *Toots* of Dickens himself, when the novelist read "Dombey" to us here, was a woful disappointment. Neither in tone nor look was he our *Toots*, and *Toots* has never been *Toots* to us since. Dickens, who created *Toots*, ought to have known him, but we could not give up the friend of our youth for the *Toots* Dickens introduced to us that night at Steinway Hall, and between the two *Toots* we are *Tootsless*. Dickens's *Toots* may have been the real *Toots*, but we felt when we saw him that even "Diogenes" himself would not have recognized him.—HUTTON, LAURENCE, 1875, *Plays and Players, p.* 51.

It is, perhaps, not generally known that Dickens's pen-picture of Paul Dombey was inspired by the pathetic personality of a favourite nephew, Master Harry Burnett. This poor lad, who unfortunately became a cripple and died in his tenth year, resembled in many respects the little Paul of fiction; notwithstanding his affliction, he was one of the happiest and brightest of children, with a mind always marvellously active, and, especially during the last months of his short life, was full of religious sentiment, for he insisted upon having his much-thumbed Bible placed ready to his hand.—KITTON, FREDERIC G., 1897, *The Novels of Charles Dickens, p.* 106.

It is in the tragedy and the pathos that

the author oftenest falls down, as we now perceive, though the time was when Macaulay, the historian and critic, cried over Florence Dombey, as he has himself recorded, in inconsolable heart-break. This is the more wonderful because Macaulay, more than any other, had felt the incomparable fineness of Jane Austen's art. It must be that the critical fibre of the British public, never too sensitive, had been coarsened by a whole generation of romantistic fiction, until the bearing on and rubbing in of Dickens was not only not an affliction, but a positive delight.—HOWELLS, WILLIAM DEAN, 1901, *Heroines of Fiction, vol.* I, *p.* 144.

DAVID COPPERFIELD
1850

I hope you see Copperfield, it is delightful and useful.—ALEXANDER, JAMES W., 1849, *Forty Years' Familiar Letters, Sept.* 13, *vol.* II, *p.* 102.

I have read "David Copperfield;" it seems to me very good—admirable in some parts. You said it had affinity to "Jane Eyre." It has, now and then—only what an advantage has Dickens in his varied knowledge of men and things!—BRONTË, CHARLOTTE, 1849, *Letter to W. S. Williams, Sept.* 13; *Charlotte Brontë and her Circle, ed. Shorter, p.* 397.

I do not find it easy to get sufficiently far away from this Book, in the first sensations of having finished it, to refer to it with the composure which this formal heading would seem to require. My interest in it, is so recent and strong; and my mind is so divided between pleasure and regret—pleasure in the achievement of a long design, regret in the separation from many companions—that I am in danger of wearying the reader whom I love, with personal confidences, and private emotions. Besides which, all that I could say of the Story, to any purpose, I have endeavoured to say in it. It would concern the reader little, perhaps, to know, how sorrowfully the pen is laid down at the close of a two years' imaginative task; or how an Author feels as if he were dismissing some portion of himself into the shadowy world, when a crowd of the creatures of his brain are going from him for ever. Yet, I have nothing else to tell; unless, indeed, I were to confess (which might be of less moment still) that no one can ever believe this Narrative, in the reading, more than I have believed it in the writing. Instead of looking back, therefore, I will look forward. I cannot close this Volume more agreeably to myself, than with a hopeful glance towards the time when I shall again put forth my two green leaves once a month, and with a faithful remembrance of the genial sun and showers that have fallen on these leaves of David Copperfield, and made me happy.—DICKENS, CHARLES, 1850, *The Personal History and Experience of David Copperfield the Younger, Preface.*

Have you read "David Copperfield," by the way? How beautiful it is—how charmingly fresh and simple! In those admirable touches of tender humour—and I should call humour, Bob, a mixture of love and wit—who can equal this great genius? There are little words and phrases in his books which are like personal benefits to the reader. What a place it is to hold in the affections of man! What an awful responsibility hanging over a writer! What man holding such a place, and knowing that his words go forth to vast congregations of mankind,—to grown folks—to their children, and perhaps to their children's children,—but must think of his calling with a solemn and humble heart! May love and truth guide such a man always! It is an awful prayer; may heaven further its fulfilment! And then, . . . let the *Record* revile him.—THACKERAY, WILLIAM MAKEPEACE, 1856, *Brown the Younger at a Club, Sketches and Travels in London.*

It is a great pleasure to find in an author's innermost circle the types of those characters that have delighted one in his works. I had previously heard many people remark that Agnes in "David Copperfield" was like Dickens's own wife; and although he may not have chosen her deliberately as a model for Agnes, yet still I can think of no one else in his books so near akin to her in all that is graceful and amiable. Mrs. Dickens had a certain soft, womanly repose and reserve about her; but whenever she spoke there came such a light into her large eyes, and such a smile upon her lips, and there was such a charm in the tones of her voice, that henceforth I shall always connect her and Agnes together.—ANDERSEN, HANS CHRISTIAN, 1870, *A Visit to Charles Dickens, Temple Bar, vol.* 31, *p.* 29.

The imagination of Dickens's is like that of monomaniacs. To plunge oneself into an idea, to be absorbed by it, to see nothing else, to repeat it under a hundred forms, to enlarge it, to carry it thus enlarged to the eye of the spectator, to dazzle and overwhelm him with it, to stamp it upon him so tenacious and impressive that he can never again tear it from his memory,—these are the great features of this imagination and style. In this "David Copperfield" is a masterpiece. Never did objects remain more visible and present to the memory of a reader than those which he describes.— TAINE, H. A., 1871, *History of English Literature, tr. Van Laun. vol.* II, *bk.* v, *p.* 344.

In "David Copperfield" especially, Dickens's humour shows itself in the richest colours, recalling Smollett's power and Sterne's light-heartedness.—SCHERR, J., 1874, *A History of English Literature, tr. M. V., p.* 275.

There is a book familiar to us all, and the more familiar now, probably, to many of us, because Mr. Gladstone solaced himself with it after his illness, and so set all good Liberals (of whom I wish to be considered one) upon reading it over again. I mean "David Copperfield." Much as I have published, I do not think it has ever happened to me before to comment in print upon any production of Charles Dickens. What a pleasure to have the opportunity of praising a work so sound, a work so rich in merits, as "David Copperfield!" *Man lese nicht die mit-strebende, mit-wirkende,* says Goethe: do not read your fellow-strivers, your fellow-workers. Of the contemporary rubbish which is shot so plentifully all round us, we can, indeed, hardly read too little. But to contemporary work so good as "David Copperfield" we are in danger perhaps of not paying respect enough, of reading it (for who could help reading it?) too hastily, and then putting it aside for something else and forgetting it. What treasures of gaiety, invention, life, are in that book! what alertness and resource! what a soul of good-nature and kindness governing the whole! —ARNOLD, MATTHEW, 1881, *The Incompatibles, The Nineteenth Century, vol.* 9, *p.* 1034.

I have said that in "David Copperfield" Dickens is freer from defect than in any other of his works. It is rarely that public opinion has ratified an author's judgment so completely as it has here. As we all know, this was Dickens's favourite, and the reason we all know. It may be noted in passing how characteristic of the two men is their choice. To Dickens "David Cop-

perfield" was, to use his own words, his favourite child, because in its pages he saw the reflection of his own youth. . . . It is not only Dickens's most attractive work, but it is his best work. And it is his best for this reason, that whereas in all his others he is continually striving to realise the conception of his fancy, in this alone his business is to idealise the reality; in this alone, as it seems to me, his imagination prevails over his fancy. In this alone he is never grotesque, or for him so rarely that we hardly care to qualify the adverb. Nowhere else is his pathos so tender and so sure; nowhere else is his humour, though often more boisterous and more abundant, so easy and so fine; nowhere else is his observation so vivid and so deep; nowhere else has he held with so sure a hand the balance between the classes.—MORRIS, MOWBRAY, 1882, *Charles Dickens, The Fortnightly Review, vol.* 38, *p.* 776.

Copperfield's first meeting with Dora is Dickens's meeting (when little more than a boy) with a lady by no means so young as Dora is there represented. The courtship is derived from his youthful love for the original of Flora. The married life with Dora, so far as her household ways are concerned, presents Dickens's own experience, so that Dora there represents a third person, and that person his wife. And lastly the death of Dora, and Copperfield's sorrow during the following years, are drawn from the death of his wife's younger sister, Mary, and the sorrow Dickens felt for years thereafter. Yet, though the real Flora furnished only one of these four copies from which the Dora of fiction was combined, we find her forming part of two distinct and very unlike characters, the characteristics of her later years being in part reproduced in Flora—but only in part, for some of Dora's ways were derived from other sources. Nor can it be said that, after all, Dickens so artistically combines and distributes what he had observed that they become effective as if they were real creatiofis. For no one possessing any power of critical discrimination had failed to recognise the incongruity of many—one may almost say all—of Dickens's characters long before it became known that he had constructed them of heterogeneous materials and applied his materials to heterogeneous purposes.— PROCTOR, RICHARD A., 1885, *Dickens and Thackeray, Knowledge, vol.* 7, *p.* 537.

I am trying to get rested by reading Dickens, and am over "David Copperfield" now. I had never read it, I find, though Mr. Micawber has become so proverbial that, finding his name in it, I thought I had. Dickens says in his preface that David Copperfield was his "favorite child," and I don't wonder, for it is amazingly well done so far as I have got.—LOWELL, JAMES RUSSELL, 1887, To C. E. Norton, April 8; Letters, ed. Norton, vol. II, p. 334.

Here was a man and an artist, the most strenuous, one of the most endowed; and for how many years he laboured in vain to create a gentleman! With all his watchfulness of men and manners, with all his fiery industry, with his exquisite native gift of characterisation, with his clear knowledge of what he meant to do, there was yet something lacking. In part after part, novel after novel, a whole menagerie of characters, the good, the bad, the droll and the tragic, came at his beck like slaves about an oriental despot; there was only one who stayed away; the gentleman. If this ill fortune had persisted it might have shaken man's belief in art and industry. But years were given and courage was continued to the indefatigable artist; and at length, after so many and such lamentable failures, success began to attend upon his arms. David Copperfield scrambled through on hands and knees; it was at least a negative success; and Dickens, keenly alive to all he did, must have heaved a sigh of infinite relief.—STEVENSON, ROBERT LOUIS, 1888, Some Gentlemen in Fiction, Miscellaneous Papers, p. 368.

It is in the character of Agnes Wickfield that Charles Dickens has touched the height of his ideal of womanhood; of all his books, "David Copperfield," as he has told us himself, was the favourite "child of his fancy," and in its heroine we have the full realisation of that which he always conceived to be woman's mission—to lead men higher, to "point upward," to strengthen and to guide. In Agnes he has painted for us a perfectly unselfish character living day by day in the lives of others, but accustomed from childhood to a certain self-restraint, which enables her the better to conceal the one attachment of her life under the modest veil of true sisterly affection, to be for years as an adopted sister to the man whom in the secret shrine of her pure heart she worshipped as a lover. No description of Agnes in outward form or feature is given to us in any part of the book; we only see the soul shining through the face with a noble purity in keeping with her name.—TOWNSEND, M. E., 1893, Great Characters of Fiction, p. 75.

The popular instinct is not astray in selecting "David Copperfield" out of the long list of Dickens's stories and giving it the foremost place. It is not so powerful a story as "A Tale of Two Cities," the most dramatic and soundly constructed of all the stories that Dickens gave the world, but it is far more characteristic, sweeter in sentiment, and as fresh in feeling and touch. It is the personal note which gives this beautiful tale its victorious appeal for the suffrages of the greatest number of readers. It is significant of a sound taste, also, that "The Old Curiosity Shop" and "Dombey and Son," in which, to recall Mr. Lang's phrase, Dickens wallowed in a sea of sentimentalism, appear well down on the list, and that "Barnaby Rudge" does not appear.—MABIE, HAMILTON W., 1893, The Most Popular Novels in America, The Forum, vol. 16, p. 512.

I find, on examination, that my "David Copperfield" is more dilapidated than any other novel upon my shelves. As I turn its dog-eared pages, reading the familiar headlines: "Mr. Micawber in difficulties," "Mr. Micawber in prison," "I fall in love with Dora," "Mr. Barkis goes out with the tide," "My child wife," "Traddles in a nest of roses"—pages of my own life recur to me, so many of my sorrows, so many of my joys, are woven in my mind with this chapter or the other. That day—how well I remember it! I read of David's wooing, but Dora's death I was careful to skip. Poor, pretty little Mrs. Copperfield at the gate, holding up her baby in her arms, is always associated in my memory with a child's cry, long listened for. I found the book, face downwards on a chair, weeks afterwards, not moved from where I had hastily laid it. —JEROME, JEROME K., 1898, My Favorite Novelist and His best Book, Munsey's Magazine, vol. 19, p. 30.

That power, blowing where it listeth, came back in fullest measure with "David Copperfield," which, no doubt, is Dickens's masterpiece as a novel, "Pickwick," as has been said, being no novel, but simply an isolated phenomenon. . . . The entire charm of "Copperfield" was never recaptured by Dickens.—LANG, ANDREW,

1898, *Charles Dickens, Fortnightly Review, vol.* 70, *pp.* 954, 955.

In that unequal and irregular masterpiece his comic and his tragic genius rose now and then to the very highest pitch of all. — SWINBURNE, ALGERNON CHARLES, 1902, *Charles Dickens, Quarterly Review, vol.* 196, *p.* 23.

BLEAK HOUSE
1853

"Bleak House" is, even more than any of its predecessors, chargeable with not simply faults, but absolute want of construction. . . . In "Bleak House," the series of incidents which form the outward life of the actors and talkers has no close and necessary connexion; nor have they that higher interest that attaches to circumstances which powerfully aid in modifying and developing the original elements of human character. The great Chancery suit of Jarndyce and Jarndyce, which serves to introduce a crowd of persons as suitors, lawyers, law-writers, law-stationers, and general spectators of Chancery business, has positively not the smallest influence on the character of any one person concerned; nor has it any interest of itself.—BRIMLEY, GEORGE, 1853-58, *"Bleak House," Essays, ed. Clark, pp.* 282, 283.

In "Bleak House," Dickens exhibits his greatest defects, and his greatest excellencies, as a novelist; in none of his works are the characters more strongly marked, or the plot more loosely and inartistically constructed. One-half of the personages might be ruled out without their loss being perceived, for, although they are all introduced with a flourish, as though they had an important part to perform, yet there would be no halt in the story if they were dropped by the way, as some of them are.—BIGGS, CHARLES F., 1853, *Characters in "Bleak House," Putnam's Monthly Magazine, vol.* 2, *p.* 559.

His present romance, though as wonderfully rich as any of his former in observations on life and character, has some of his old faults in an aggravated form, and some which have not appeared before. His story is, as usual, inartificial; his mysteries perplex much more than they interest; his love of low life seems to grow upon him. We are detained too long in filthy corners, and surprised too unceremoniously at finding the delicacy of virtuous sentiment in the lowest depths of human degradation.—

DENMAN, THOMAS LORD, 1853, *Slavery and Slave Trade, p.* 51.

Whoever wishes to get a good look at Landor will not seek for it alone in John Forster's interesting life of the old man, admirable as it is, but will turn to Dickens's "Bleak House" for side-glances at the great author. In that vivid story Dickens has made his friend Landor sit for the portrait of Lawrence Boythorn. The very laugh that made the whole house vibrate, the roundness and fulness of voice, the fury of superlatives, are all given in Dickens's best manner, and no one who has ever seen Landor for half an hour could possibly mistake Boythorn for anybody else. Talking the matter over once with Dickens, he said, "Landor always took that presentation of himself in hearty good humor, and seemed rather proud of the picture."—FIELDS, JAMES F., 1875, *"Barry Cornwall" and some of his Friends, Harper's Magazine, vol.* 51, *p.* 785.

Those pages of Dickens which hold the story of Little Nell; a story in which all the elaborate accumulation of pathetic incident and interest, so tenderly and studiously built up, has never, to speak truth, given me one passing thrill—in the exquisitely fit and faithful phrase of a great living poet, one "sweet possessive pang"— of the tender delight and pity re-quickened well nigh to tears at every fresh reperusal or chance recollection of that one simpler page in "Bleak House" which describes the baby household tended by the little sister who leaves her lesser charges locked up while she goes out charing; a page which I can imagine that many a man unused to the melting mood would not undertake to read out aloud without a break.—SWINBURNE, ALGERNON CHARLES, 1877, *A Note on Charlotte Brontë, p.* 64.

"Bleak House" (1853) is constructed only too well. Here Dickens applied himself laboriously to the perfecting of that kind of story he had always had in view, and produced a fine example of theatrical plot. One cannot say, in this case, that the intrigue refuses to be remembered; it is a puzzle, yet ingeniously simple; the parts fitting together very neatly indeed. So neatly, that poor untidy Life disclaims all connection with these doings, however willingly she may recognize for her children a score or so of the actors. To be sure there are oversights. How could Dickens expect one to believe that Lady Dedlock recognized her lover's handwriting in a piece of work done by him *as law-writer*—she not even knowing that he was so employed? What fate pursued him that he could not, in all the resources of his brain, hit upon a device for such a simple end more convincing than this? Still, with an aim not worth pursuing, the author here wrought successfully. The story is child's play compared with many invented, for instance by Wilkie Collins; but in combination with Dickens's genuine powers, it produces its designed effect; we move in a world of choking fog and squalid pitfalls, amid plot and counterplot, cold self-interest and passion overwrought, and can never refuse attention to the magician who shows it all.—GISSING, GEORGE, 1898, *Charles Dickens*, p. 67.

In "Bleak House" the prominence accorded to the sensational is somewhat repellent, though this is artistically the best constructed of Dickens' novels, as it is also the most exciting.—ENGEL, EDWARD, 1902, *A History of English Literature, rev. Hamley Bent*, p. 452.

HARD TIMES
1854

I read Dickens' "Hard Times." One excessively touching, heart-breaking passage and the rest sullen socialism. The evils which he attacks he caricatures grossly, and with little humor. Another book of Pliny's letters. Read "Northanger Abbey;" worth all Dickens and Pliny together. Yet it was the work of a girl. She was certainly not more than twenty-six. Wonderful creature!—MACAULAY, THOMAS BABINGTON, 1854, *Journal, Aug.* 12; *Life and Letters, ed. Trevelyan, ch.* xiii.

The essential value and truth of Dickens' writings have been unwisely lost sight of by many thoughtful persons, merely because he presents his truths with some colour of caricature. Unwisely, because Dickens's caricature, though often gross, is never mistaken. Allowing for his manner of telling them, the things he tells us are always true. I wish that he could think it right to limit his brilliant exaggeration to works written only for public amusement; and when he takes up a subject of high national importance, such as that which he handled in "Hard Times," that he would use severer and more accurate analysis. The usefulness of that work (to my mind, in several respects, the greatest he has written) is with

many persons seriously diminished because Mr. Bounderby is a dramatic monster, instead of a characteristic example of a worldly master; and Stephen Blackpool a dramatic perfection, instead of a characteristic example of an honest workman. But let us not lose the use of Dickens's wit and insight, because he chooses to speak in a circle of stage fire. He is entirely right in his main drift and purpose in every book he has written; and all of them, but especially "Hard Times," should be studied with close and earnest care by persons interested in social questions. They will find much that is partial, and, because partial, apparently unjust; but if they examine all the evidence on the other side, which Dickens seems to overlook, it will appear, after all their trouble, that his view was the finally right one, grossly and sharply told.—RUSKIN, JOHN, 1862, *The Roots of Honour, "Unto this Last,"* note.

In comparison with most of Dickens's novels, "Hard Times" is contained within a narrow compass; and this, with the further necessity of securing to each successive small portion of the story a certain immediate degree of effectiveness, accounts, in some measure, for the peculiarity of the impression left by this story upon many of its readers. Short as the story relatively is, few of Dickens's fictions were elaborated with so much care.—WARD, ADOLPHUS WILLIAM, 1882, *Dickens (English Men of Letters)*, p. 126.

The novel of "Hard Times" is a satire on political economy, of which Dickens knew little, and the little he knew offended his benevolent feelings—as if the law of gravitation itself did not frequently offend benevolent feeling! Still, Mr. Gradgrind will for generations prevent a large number of amiable people from admitting the demonstrations of Adam Smith and Ricardo.—WHIPPLE, EDWIN PERCY, 1887, *In Dickens-Land, Scribner's Magazine, vol.* 2, *p.* 747.

Contains in the episode of Stephen and Rachel one of the best pieces of serious writing which Dickens ever did.—OLIPHANT, MARGARET O. W., 1892, *The Victorian Age of English Literature*, p. 260.

LITTLE DORRIT
1857

With the exception of the Circumlocution Office passages—adventitious as they are to the progress of the action—

"Little Dorrit" exhibits a palpable falling-off in inventive powers.—WARD, ADOLPHUS WILLIAM, 1882, *Dickens (English Men of Letters)*, p. 137.

About four months after Dickens's death, an incident happened that would have more than counteracted the effects upon the author's mind of the most unfavourable comments upon "Little Dorrit." The scene was the meeting of Bismarck and Jules Favre under the walls of Paris; as the Prussian was waiting to open fire on the city, the Frenchman was engaged in the arduous task of showing the wisdom of not doing it, and "while the two eminent statesmen were trying to find a basis of negotiation, Von Moltke was seated in a corner reading 'Little Dorrit.'" One is inclined to ask, with Mr. Forster, "Who will doubt that the chapter on 'How to do it' was then absorbing the old soldier's attention?"—KITTON, FREDERIC G., 1897, *The Novels of Charles Dickens*, p. 170.

Of "Little Dorritt," as of "Martin Chuzzlewit," who can pretend to bear the story in mind? There is again a moral theme; the evils of greed and vulgar ambition. As a rule, we find this book dismissed rather contemptuously; it is held to be tedious, and unlike Dickens in its prevalent air of gloom. For all that, I believe it to contain some of his finest work, some passages in which he attains an artistic finish hardly found elsewhere; and to these I shall return. . . . As a narrative, "Little Dorrit" is far from successful; it is cumbered with mysteries which prove futile, and has no proportion in its contrasting parts. Here and there the hand of the master is plainly weary.—GISSING, GEORGE, 1898, *Charles Dickens*, pp. 70, 71.

The conception of "Little Dorrit" was far happier and more promising than that of "Dombey and Son;" which indeed is not much to say for it. Mr. Dombey is a doll; Mr. Dorrit is an everlasting figure of comedy in its most tragic aspect and tragedy in its most comic phase. Little Dorrit herself might be less untruly than unkindly described as Little Nell grown big, or, in Milton's phrase, "writ large." But on that very account she is a more credible and therefore a more really and rationally pathetic figure.—SWINBURNE, ALGERNON CHARLES, 1902, *Charles Dickens, Quarterly Review*, vol. 196, p. 29.

87 E

A TALE OF TWO CITIES
1859

It is a story of human passions, of misery, crime, guilt, revenge, heroism, love, and happiness. And if the lack of the properly historical element does not so strongly appear in this novel as in "Barnaby Rudge," the reason is clear: it is, that the period was one that, beyond any other in history, boiled and burned with passion; so that in fact, the novelist who writes a romance of the French Revolution must, if his story is to seem truthful, write a story of psychology.—PERKINS, F. B., 1870, *Charles Dickens*, p. 63.

Mr. Dickens, however, wrote one book so noble in its spirit, so grand and graphic in its style, and filled with a pathos so profound and simple, that it deserves, and will surely take, a place among the great serious works of imagination. "The Tale of Two Cities," his shortest story, and the one least thought of by the public of his own day, is the work that will secure him an enduring fame. It has little humor, and that is not of its author's best; but its picture of the fierce passion of the first French Revolution, of the hideous oppression which provoked that outbreak of ruthless revenge on the part of a whole people, and above all its portrayal of the noble-natured castaway Sidney Carton, make it almost a peerless book in modern literature, and give it a place among the highest examples of all literary art.— WHITE, RICHARD GRANT, 1870, *The Styles of Disraeli and Dickens, The Galaxy*, vol. 10, p. 259.

It is a profitable experience for one who read Dickens forty years ago to try to read him now. Last winter I forced myself through the "Tale of Two Cities." It was a sheer dead pull from start to finish. It all seemed so insincere, such a transparent make-believe, a mere piece of acting. My sympathies were hardly once touched. I was not insensible to the marvelous genius displayed in the story, but it left me cold and unmoved. A feeling of unreality haunted me on every page.—BURROUGHS, JOHN, 1897, *On the Re-reading of Books, Century Magazine*, vol. 55, p. 149.

To Dickens as an historical novelist imperfect justice has been done. The "Tale of Two Cities" is said to be most admired by those who admire Dickens the least. A similar remark has been made of "Esmond."

The "Tale of Two Cities" is founded upon Carlyle's "French Revolution." It has no humour, or next to none. But it is a marvelous piece of writing; the plot, though simple, is excellent, and, whatever may be thought about the genuineness of the pathos in "Dombey and Son," or the "Old Curiosity Shop," the tragedy of Sidney Carton is a tragedy indeed.—PAUL, HERBERT, 1897, *The Apotheosis of the Novel, The Nineteenth Century, vol*, 41, *p.* 771.

"The Tale of Two Cities" is the best thing that could be expected of Dickens when this humour was veiled, and he was working at serious historical melodrama. It is hardly "the true Dickens," and is best liked by many who like the true Dickens least.—LANG, ANDREW, 1898, *Charles Dickens, Fortnightly Review, vol.* 70, *p.* 957

If no greatness can be claimed for a "Tale of Two Cities," either as an historical picture or as a well-constructed story, it cannot assuredly be praised for the excellence of its portraiture. There is not a single figure in the book that leaves any impression on the memory. The devotion of Sydney Carton, finding so dramatic a climax on the guillotine, is of course an outstanding feature, but its pathos gains little or nothing from any sympathetic grasp of the character of the devotee.—OLIPHANT, JAMES, 1899, *Victorian Novelists, p.* 42.

"A Tale of Two Cities" presents an interesting field for study of Dickens's varying literary style. From the first remarkably "balanced" paragraph to the supposed prophecies of Carton at the foot of the guillotine, are constant and conscious mannerisms. Of the use of balance, another passage may be instanced, where Madame Defarge seeks vengeance on Charles Darnay. . . . Dickens's narrative style appears at its best, not in the melodramatic scene at the guillotine, but in the flight from Paris and the thrilling narrative of Dr. Manette.—NETTLETON, GEORGE HENRY, 1901, *ed. Specimens of the Short Story, p.* 138.

GREAT EXPECTATIONS
1861

I am now reading "Great Expectations" and like it much. The characters, though, seem to me unreal somehow. Dickens appears to make his characters as the Chinese do those distorted wooden images. He picks out the crookedest and knottiest roots of temperament or accidental distortion and then cuts a figure to match. But this book is full of fine touches of nature, though I can't help dreading something melodramatic to come.—LOWELL, JAMES RUSSELL, 1861, *To C. E. Norton, Aug.* 7; *Letters, ed. Norton, vol.* I, *p.* 312.

Dickens is not a favourite of mine; I think it would go against the grain to applaud him highly in his present phase.—OLIPHANT, MARGARET O. W., 1862, *To Mr. Blackwood, Autobiography and Letters, ed. Mrs. Coghill, p.* 186.

Last night I made my Reader begin Dickens's wonderful "Great Expectations:" not considered one of his best, you know, but full of wonderful things, and even with a Plot which, I think, only needed less intricacy to be admirable. I had only just read the Book myself: but I wanted to see what my Reader would make of it; and he was so interested that he re-interested me too.—FITZGERALD, EDWARD, 1877, *Letter, May* 5; *Letters to Fanny Kemble, ed. Wright, p.* 122.

Notwithstanding the fact that the first edition of "Great Expectations" contains no illustrations, the price demanded for a clean copy is from £7 to £10. This high figure is accounted for by the great scarcity of the three consecutive volumes in their original form, purchasers having sometimes to be content with making up the set with volumes of varying editions. The book, when first issued, was sold out immediately, the greater part of the impression going to the libraries; it was therefore looked upon with comparative disrespect, and, being immensely popular, became popularly thumbed, torn, and marked; whereas the weekly instalments in "All the Year Round" were preferred by private purchasers and collectors, who preserved them for binding. Mr. Wilkie Collins's copy of "Great Expectations" realised £9, 5s in the auction-room, at the sale of his library in 1890.—KITTON, FREDERIC G., 1897, *The Novels of Charles Dickens, p.* 195.

OUR MUTUAL FRIEND
1865

We are justified in concluding that Dickens's opinion of the Jews underwent a complete change, as we may learn from this novel, which may be regarded in a manner as his literary last will and testament. . . . Riah is as little the picture of the Jew as Fagin is; he gives utterance to some words about the Jews which are true enough, but he can not stand as a representative of the Jews. If they are to be characters in fiction, they wish but justice, and no more. An advocate who gives a rose-colored account of his client will not be believed. The Jew has his faults as all men have. There is as much harm in overestimating as in undervaluing. A constant flow of praise loses all strength for an impartial mind, as does also a constant flow of abuse. We have in fiction demonically bad Jews, and ideally good ones. Barabbas and Fagin on the one hand, Sheva, Rebecca, and Riah on the other. In the works we have treated thus far, the true picture has not yet been given; it will only be drawn by such a one who has made a searching and psychological study of the religious and hereditary traits of the descendants of this most remarkable stock. —PHILIPSON, DAVID, 1889, *The Jew in English Fiction, pp.* 97, 101.

Consider "Our Mutual Friend," which he is stated to have regarded with peculiar satisfaction. I took it up, a few days ago, intending to read it carefully through. I was greatly tempted to lay it down at the second chapter. That chapter, as some of you will doubtless remember, gives an account of a dinner-party at the Veneerings. I wonder whether anything bearing a less appreciable relation to life was ever written. Twemlow is as unreal as Lord Dundreary, and much less amusing. Lady Tippins is as untrue as she is uninteresting. Was there ever a barrister bearing the remotest likeness to Eugene Wrayburn? or a solicitor possessing the smallest affinity with Mortimer Lightfoot?—LILLY, WILLIAM SAMUEL, 1895, *Four English Humourists of the Nineteenth Century, p.* 15.

It is very easy to select from the army of characters which Dickens has given us, those which were the truly beloved children of his brain. Sometimes he seemed to adopt a hero or a heroine, generally the latter, and to make himself believe that she was really his own offspring. Such a character occurs in one of Dickens' poorest novels, "Our Mutual Friend." This is *Bella,* and in regard to her, Dickens writes in the notes to the manuscript of "Our Mutual Friend," in which he frequently calls upon himself to do his duty by his characters,

these words: "Make *Bella* as attractive as I can." Now he would never have written, in relation to *Mr. Pickwick*: "Make him as jolly, as funny, and as good hearted as I can." It would not have been necessary. *Picwick,* in the mind of Dickens, was a real man; *Bella Wilfer* was not a real person, and, do his best, he could not make her the lovely woman he wanted her to be.—STOCKTON, FRANK R., 1897, *My Favorite Novelist and His Best Book, Munsey's Magazine, vol.* 17, *p.* 354.

We hear too much of the dragging of the river for dead bodies in "Our Mutual Friend." Dickens never could learn where to stop. His high pictorial imagination presented to him every detail of the scene; and, like a Pre-Raphaelite, he forgot that to the reader a general impression conveyed more truth than minute accuracy in every detail.—WALKER, HUGH, 1897, *The Age of Tennyson, p.* 90.

In "Our Mutual Friend" he relapsed into his outworn satire, the stage diction out of place, the needless and *voulu* phantastic.—LANG, ANDREW, 1898, *Charles Dickens, Fortnightly Review, vol.* 70, *p.* 957.

THE MYSTERY OF EDWIN DROOD
1870

Of Mr. Fildes's work for Charles Dickens's book, our own opinion is that it is the best illustrative interpretation which has ever been made of the author, albeit old and fine reputations belong to the former associations of artists' names with the great series of the Dickens novels.—MEYNELL, ALICE, 1884, *How Edwin Drood was Illustrated, The Century, vol.* 27, *p.* 527.

"Edwin Drood" would probably have been his best constructed book: as far as it goes, the story hangs well together, showing a care in the contrivance of detail which is more than commonly justified by the result. One cannot help wishing that Dickens had chosen another subject—one in which there was neither mystery nor murder, both so irresistibly attractive to him, yet so far from being the true material of his art. Surely it is unfortunate that the last work of a great writer should have for its theme nothing more human than a trivial mystery woven about a vulgar deed of blood. . . . His selection of scene was happy and promising—the old city of his childhood, Rochester. The tone, too, of his descriptive passages is much more appropriate than the subject. But Dickens had made his choice in life, and therefrom inevitably resulted his course in literature. —GISSING, GEORGE, 1898, *Charles Dickens*, pp. 76, 77.

LETTERS

Ten years are nearly enough to show that in Dickens himself the future admirers of his works will take almost no interest at all. In reading through these letters one's irresistible feeling is that it is at least well that their publication was not delayed longer, if, indeed, it has not been delayed too long already. They present the man very adequately, we imagine, and, in presenting him, inevitably betray how slight was the real foundation for the quick personal interest taken in him during the last thirty or forty years. . . But, though the lapse of time is slow, it is also certain, and, unless we are mistaken about the fact, popular interest in the man has already appreciably declined, if it has not subsided. There are probably few who will read these two volumes from cover to cover.—BROWNELL, W. C., 1879, *The Letters of Dickens*, *The Nation*, vol. 29, p. 388.

But after all, published collections of private letters are usually disappointing things, and these two large volumes, interesting as they are, constitute no exception to the general rule. We do, indeed, obtain glimpses of physical suffering and ill-health, for which the general public were quite unprepared; but the Dickens of these pages is the Dickens we already knew, and we have *not* the key to his interior life; while we are helped to discern inconsistencies of opinion and conduct of which there is no accessible explanation.—BROWNE, MATTHEW, 1880, *The Letters of the Late Mr. Dickens*, *The Contemporary Review*, vol. 37, p. 77.

Charles Dickens was an excellent correspondent—punctual, regular—and when he had said all that was necessary, he stopped. His letters are easy, simple, and unaffected, and show him to have been a frank, genial, vain, generous, egotistical fellow. His spirits were high, his enjoyment of life keen, and he was an industrious and indefatigable literary worker: in the latter respect he was like Scott. But he differed from the author of "Waverly" in being a very painstaking and laborious writer. These letters open to us glimpses of Dickens's domestic life which are calculated to increase our interest in their author. He was essentially a domestic man; his children ever occupied the first place in his thoughts; and, when absent from them, his letters were very frequent, and evinced the deepest interest in all that concerned them. —DIDIER, EUGENE L., 1880, *Recent Biography, etc.*, *North American Review*, vol. 130, p. 303.

GENERAL

A rhyme! a rhyme! from a distant clime,—
  From the gulph of the Genoese:
O'er the rugged scalps of the Julian Alps
  Dear Boz! I send you these,
To light the *Wick* your candlestick
  Holds up, or, should you list,
To usher in the yarn you spin
  Concerning Oliver Twist.
Immense applause you've gained, oh, Boz
  Through continental Europe;
You'll make Pickwick œcumenick;
  Of fame you have a sure hope:
For here your books are found, gadzooks!
  In greater *luxe* than any
That have issued yet, hotpress'd or wet,
  From the types of Galignani.

—MAHONY, FRANCIS, 1838, *Poetical Epistle from Father Prout to "Boz," on the Appearance of the First Portions of "Oliver Twist,"* *Bentley's Miscellany*, Jan.

That rare painter of human character.— HALLECK, FITZ-GREENE, 1842, *Letter to Louis Gaylord Clark, Life and Letters*, ed. *Wilson*, p. 439.

His more obvious excellences are of the kind which are easily understood by all classes—by the stable-boy as well as the statesman. His intimate knowledge of character, his familiarity with the language and experience of low life, his genuine humor, his narrative power, and the cheerfulness of his philosophy, are traits that impress themselves on minds of every description. But, besides these, he has many characteristics to interest the higher order of the mind. They are such as to recommend him peculiarly to Americans. His sympathies seek out that class with which American institutions and laws sympathize most strongly. He has found subjects of thrilling interest in the passions, sufferings, and virtues of the mass.—BRYANT, WILLIAM CULLEN, 1842, *New York Evening Post*, *A Biography of William Cullen Bryant*, ed. *Godwin*, vol. I, p. 396.

Not merely thine the tribute praise,
  Which greets an author's progress here;
Not merely thine the fabled bays,
  Whose verdure brightens his career.
Thine the pure triumph to have taught
  Thy brother man a gentle part;
In every line a fervent thought,
  Which gushes from thy generous heart.
For thine are words which rouse up all
  The dormant good among us found,
Like drops which from a fountain fall,
  To bless and fertilize the ground.
—NORTON, CAROLINE E. S., 1842, *A Tribute
to Charles Dickens, Bijou Almanac.*

Do you know that the royal Boz lives
close to us, three doors from Mr. Kenyon in
Harley Place? The new numbers appear to
me admirable, and full of life and blood—
whatever we may say to the thick rouging
and extravagance of gesture.   There is a
beauty, a tenderness, too, in the organ
scene, which is worthy of the gilliflowers.
But my admiration for "Boz" fell from its
"sticking place," I confess, a good furlong,
when I read Victor Hugo; and my creed is,
that, *not* in his tenderness, which is as much
his own as his humour, but in his serious
powerful Jew-trial scenes, he has followed
Hugo closely, and never scarcely looked
away from "Les Trois Jours d'un Con-
damné."—BROWNING, ELIZABETH BARRETT,
1843, *To James Martin*, Feb. 6; *Letters, ed.
Kenyon, vol.* I, *p.* 123.

Mentally he is indisputably below Fielding; but in tenderness, in pathos, in sweetness and purity of feeling, in that comprehensiveness of sympathy which springs
from a sense of brotherhood with mankind,
he is as indisputably above him. . . . He
has gleaned all his facts with observation
and sympathy, in a diligent scrutiny of
actual life, and no contemporary author is
less indebted to books. His style is all his
own, its quaint texture of fancy and humor
being spun altogether from his own mind,
with hardly a verbal felicity which bears
the mark of being stolen. . . . Had he been
an egotist, devoured by a ravenous vanity
for personal display, and eager to print the
image of himself on the popular imagination, his talents would hardly have made
him known beyond the street in which he
lived, and his mind by self-admiration
would soon have been self-consumed.   His
fellow-feeling with his race is his genius.—
WHIPPLE, EDWIN PERCY, 1844, *Novels and
Novelists, Literature and Life, pp.* 60, 62, 63.

Mr. Dickens' characters, numerous as
they are, have each the roundness of individual reality combined with generalization—most of them representing a class.
The method by which he accomplishes this,
is worth observing, and easily observed, as
the process is always the same.   He never
developes a character from within, but commences by showing how the nature of the
individual has *been* developed externally by
his whole life in the world.   To this effect,
he first paints his portrait at full-length;
sometimes his dress before his face, and
most commonly his dress and demeanor.
When he has done this to his satisfaction,
he *feels in* the man, and the first words that
man utters are the key-note of the character, and of all that he subsequently says
and does.   The author's hand never wavers,
never becomes untrue to his creations.
HORNE, RICHARD HENGIST, 1844, *A New
Spirit of the Age, p.* 21.

His writings are a continual preaching
from the text of Burns:
  "A man's a man for a' that!"
While they tend to call forth the best feelings of the wealthier classes, they tend
equally to elevate the self-respect and estimation of the people.   They make them
feel that humanity is paramount to all
artificial distinctions, and that, spite of the
harshest treatment of fortune, if we maintain our inward worth we never can become contemptible.—HOWITT, WILLIAM,
1846, *The People's Portrait Gallery, The
People's Journal, vol.* 1, *p.* 12.

Scott's higher characters possess massive
good sense, great shrewdness, much intelligence: they are always very superior, if
not always great men; and by a careful arrangement of drapery, and much study of
position and attitude, they play their parts
wonderfully well.   The higher characters of
Dickens do not stand by any means so
high; the fluid in the original tube rests at a
lower level: and no one seems better aware
of the fact than Dickens himself. He knows
his proper walk; and, content with expatiating in a comparatively humble province of human life and character, rarely
stands on tiptoe, in the vain attempt to
portray an intellect taller than his own.—
MILLER, HUGH, 1847, *First Impressions of
England and its People, p.* 280.

Dickens's Christmas story is paltry;
though one of its puns showed me how the

English pronounce "*Ma.*"—ALEXANDER, JAMES, 1849, *Forty Years' Familiar Letters, Jan.* 8, *vol.* II, *p.* 91.

> As when a friend (himself in music's list)
> Stands by some rare, full-handed organist,
> And glorying as he sees the master roll
> The surging sweets through all their depths
> of soul,
> Cannot, encouraged by his smile, forbear
> With his own hand to join them here and
> there;
> And so, if little, yet add something more
> To the sound's volume and the golden roar;
> So I, dear friend, Charles Dickens, though
> thy hand
> Needs but itself, to charm from land to land,
> Make bold to join in summoning men's ears
> To this thy new-found music of our spheres,
> In hopes that by thy *Household Words* and
> thee
> The world may haste to days of harmony.

—HUNT, LEIGH, 1849, *To Charles Dickens.*

Many of his portraits excite pity, and suggest the existence of crying social sins; but of almost all we are obliged to say that they border on and frequently reach caricature, of which the essence is to catch a striking likeness by exclusively selecting and exaggerating a peculiarity that marks the man but does not represent him. Dickens belongs in literature to the same class as his illustrator, Hablot Browne, in design, though he far surpasses the illustrator in range and power.—BRIMLEY, GEORGE, 1853-58, "*Bleak House,*" *Essays, ed. Clark, p.* 292.

The English novels of these days seem to me the more detestable the one than the other—Dickens all cant (Liberal cant, the worst sort) and caricature.—MITFORD, MARY RUSSELL, 1853, *To Mr. Starkey, Jan.* 31; *The Friendships of Mary Russell Mitford, ed. L'Estrange, ch.* xxvi.

There may be, and I believe there are, many who go beyond me in admiration of his works,—high and strong as is my delight in some of them. Many can more keenly enjoy his peculiar humour,—delightful as it is to me; and few seem to miss as I do the pure plain daylight in the atmosphere of his scenery. So many fine painters have been mannerists as to atmosphere and colour that it may be unreasonable to object to one more: but the very excellence and diversity of Mr. Dickens's powers makes one long that they should exercise their full force under the broad open sky of nature, instead of in the most brilliant place of art. While he tells us a world of things that are natural and even true, his personages are generally, as I suppose is undeniable, profoundly unreal. It is a curious speculation what effect his universally read works will have on the foreign conception of English character.—MARTINEAU, HARRIET, 1855-77, *Autobiography, ed. Chapman, vol.* II, *p.* 61.

We have one great novelist who is gifted with the utmost power of rendering the external traits of our town population; and if he could give us their psychological character— their conceptions of life, and their emotions—with the same truth as their idiom and manners, his books would be the greatest contribution Art has ever made to the awakening of social sympathies. But while he can copy Mrs. Plornish's colloquial style with the delicate accuracy of a sun-picture, while there is the same startling inspiration in his description of the gestures and phrases of "Boots," as in the speeches of Shakespeare's mobs or numskulls, he scarcely ever passes from the humorous and external to the emotional and tragic without becoming as transcendent in his unreality as he was a moment before in his artistic truthfulness. But for the precious salt of his humour, which compels him to reproduce external traits that serve in some degree as a corrective to his frequently false psychology, his preternaturally virtuous poor children and artisans, his melo-dramatic boatmen and courtesans, would be as obnoxious as Eugène Sue's idealized proletaires in encouraging the miserable fallacy that high morality and refined sentiment can grow out of harsh social relations, ignorance, and want; or that the working-classes are in a condition to enter at once into a millennial state of *altruism,* wherein everyone is caring for everyone else, and no one for himself.— ELIOT, GEORGE 1856, *The Natural History of German Life.*

Dickens, with preternatural apprehension of the language of manners and the varieties of street life; with pathos and laughter, with patriotic and still enlarging generosity writes London tracts. He is a painter of English details, like Hogarth; local and temporary in his tints and style, and local in his aims.—EMERSON, RALPH WALDO, 1856-84, *English Traits; Works, Riverside Ed., vol.* V, *p* 234.

If we glance over the wit and satire of the popular writers of the day, we shall find that the *manner* of it, so far as it is distinctive is always owing to Dickens; and that out of his first exquisite ironies branch innumerable other forms of wit, varying with the dispositions of the writers; original in the matter and substance of them, yet never to have been expressed as they now are, but for Dickens.—RUSKIN, JOHN, 1856, *Modern Painters, vol.* III, *Appendix.*

We do not know any instance of imaginative power on which we would more willingly rely, which we could more absolutely trust, than that of Dickens. Yet when he leaves the alleys of St. Giles and the office in Bow Street, which he has seen, and sets himself to depict what he merely imagines to exist, how strange is the work he produces! . . . His early works are all aglow with genius. The supreme potency with which he commands it, is shown in the total absence of effort, in the classic chasteness and limpid flow, of thought, fancy, and diction. You are in a meadow just after dawn; the flowers are fresh as if they had awakened from slumber, and the dew is on them all. A word, an idea, a glimpse of beauty, is always at hand; the writer never tarries a moment; yet there is no display, no profusion, of opulence. You do not see him waving the wand; the tear or the smile is on your cheek before you are aware.—BAYNE, PETER, 1857, *The Modern Novel: Dickens, Bulwer, Thackeray; Essays in Biography and Criticism, First Series,* pp. 370, 384.

His genius is essentially irregular and unsymmetrical,—hardly any English writer perhaps is much more so. His style is an example of it: it is descriptive, racy, and flowing; it is instinct with new imagery and singular illustration: but it does not indicate that due proportion of the faculties to one another which is a beauty in itself, and which cannot help diffusing beauty over every happy word and moulded clause. . . An artist once said of the best work of another artist. "Yes, it is a pretty patch:" if we might venture on the phrase, we should say that Mr. Dickens's pictures are graphic scraps, his best books are compilations of them. . . . The *bizarrerie* of Mr. Dickens's genius is rendered more remarkable by the inordinate measure of his special excellences.—BAGEHOT, WALTER, 1858, *Charles Dickens, Works, ed. Morgan, vol.* II.

Of Charles Dickens' fame a grand feature is its universality. His name is much a "Household Word" in every sequestered hamlet lying between the most extreme points of our *home* islands, as it is in the metropolis; and he is as well known in the United States, Canada, and Australia, as he is in the city round St. Paul's. Wherever there are men of English origin, speaking the English tongue, there the genius of Charles Dickens is one of the most important facts of life. It would be a long task to say all that Dickens has done for the English novel. It would be easier to state what he has not done for it. Indeed the novel of his generation is so completely a work of his *re*-creation, that it would be mere ingratitude, backed up by stupidity, not to hail him as the immediate parent of it.—JEAFFRESON, JOHN CORDY, 1858, *Novels and Novelists, vol.* II.

From the incessant repetition by Mr. Dickens of this inventive process openly and without variation, except in the results, the public have caught what is called his mannerism or trick; and hence a certain recoil from his later writings among the cultivated and fastidious. But let any one observe our current table-talk or our current literature, and, despite this profession of dissatisfaction, and in the very circles where it most abounds, let him note how gladly Dickens is used, and how frequently his phrases, his fancies and the names of his characters come in, as illustration, embellishment, proverb, and seasoning. Take any periodical in which there is a severe criticism of Dickens's last publication; and, ten to one, in the same periodical, and perhaps by the same hand, there will be a leading article, setting out with a quotation from Dickens that flashes on the mind of the reader the thought which the whole article is meant to convey, or containing some allusion to one of Dickens's characters which enriches the text in the middle and floods it an inch round with colour and humour.—MASSON, DAVID, 1859, *British Novelists and Their Styles,* p. 252.

Choosing some character of the most unpromising outward appearance—Smike, the starved, half-witted drudge of a Yorkshire school; Pinch, the awkward, shambling assistant of a rascally country architect; Ham, a rough, tar-splashed, weather-beaten fisherman of Yarmouth; Joe, the huge, stout blacksmith, whose dull brain can scarcely shape a thought clearly into words —he makes us love them all, for the truth, the honesty, the sweet, guileless, forgiving spirit that lives within the ungainly frame. If Dickens had done no more than create the Tom Pinch of "Chuzzlewit," and the blacksmith Joe of "Great Expectations," he deserves lasting gratitude and fame.— COLLIER, WILLIAM FRANCIS, 1861, *A History of English Literature, p.* 484.

> You ask me what I see in Dickens . . .
> A game-cock among bantam chickens.

—LANDOR, WALTER SAVAGE, 1863, *Heroic Idyls with Additional Poems; Works, vol.* VIII, *p.* 323.

If Mr. Dickens's characters were gathered together, they would constitute a town populous enough to send a representative to Parliament. Let us enter. The style of architecture is unparalleled. There is an individuality about the buildings. In some obscure way they remind one of human faces. There are houses sly-looking, houses wicked-looking, houses pompous-looking. Heaven bless us! what a rakish pump! what a self-important town-hall! what a hard-hearted prison! The dead walls are covered with advertisements of Mr. Slearey's circus. Newman Noggs comes shambling along. Mr. and the Misses Pecksniff come sailing down the sunny side of the street. Miss Mercy's parasol is gay; papa's neckcloth is white, and terribly starched. Dick Swiveller leans against a wall, his hands in his pockets, a primrose held between his teeth, contemplating the opera of Punch and Judy, which is being conducted under the management of Messrs. Codlings and Short. You turn a corner and you meet the coffin of little Paul Dombey borne along. Who would have thought of encountering a funeral in this place? In the afternoon you hear the rich tones of the organ from Miss LaCreevy's first floor, for Tom Pinch has gone to live there now; and as you know all the people as you know your own brothers and sisters, and consequently require no letters of introduction, you go up and talk with the dear old fellow about all his friends and your friends, and towards evening he takes your arm, and you walk out to see poor Nelly's grave—a place which he visits often, and which he dresses with flowers with his own hands.—SMITH, ALEXANDER, 1863, *Dreamthorp, p.* 283.

To give so much pleasure, to add so much to the happiness of the world, by his writings, as Mr. Dickens has succeeded in doing, is a felicity that has never been attained in such full measure by any other author. For the space of a generation he has done his beneficent work, and there are few English-speaking men or women who do not feel themselves under peculiar obligation to the great novelist, and bound to him, not by any mere cold literary tie, but by the warm and vital cords of personal sympathy. . . . No one thinks first of Mr. Dickens as a writer. He is at once, through his books, a friend. He belongs among the intimates of every pleasant-tempered and large-hearted person. He is not so much the guest as the inmate of our homes. He keeps holidays with us, he helps us to celebrate Christmas with heartier cheer, he shares at every New Year in our good wishes; for, indeed, it is not in his purely literary character that he has done most for us, it is as a man of the largest humanity, who has simply used literature as the means by which to bring himself into relation with his fellow-men, and to inspire them with something of his own sweetness, kindness, charity, and good-will. He is the great magician of our time. His wand is a book, but his power is in his own heart. It is a rare piece of good fortune for us that we are the contemporaries of this benevolent genius, and that he comes among us in bodily presence, brings in his company such old and valued friends as Mr. Pickwick, and Sam Weller, and Nicholas Nickleby, and David Copperfield, and Boots at the Swan, and Dr. Marigold.— NORTON, CHARLES ELIOT, 1868, *Charles Dickens, North American Review, vol.* 106, *p.* 671.

With a Thackeray, a Lytton, an Eliot, on the course, we cannot say that Dickens was first and the rest nowhere; but though, ever and anon, men might momentarily think that these would overtake and even outstrip him, they never did so. They made great spurts, and slackened; but he, though he sometimes amazed us by accelerating the pace, rarely diminished it, and never halted. If the meditation of novels may, in one sense, be said to be the meditation of trifles, of Dickens it may be affirmed that he was *totus in illis.* His whole heart, indeed his whole nature, was in them. And he is the only English novelist of real genius of whom this can truly be said.—AUSTIN, ALFRED, 1870, *Charles Dickens, Temple Bar, vol.* 29, *p.* 555.

The admiring and passionate devotee of Dickens is in danger of copying his broad caricature, his not very elevated or elevating slang, and the free and easy swing of the society in which Mr. Dickens delights.— PORTER, NOAH, 1870, *Books and Reading, p.* 230.

> The fierce debater's tongue grew mute,
> Wise men were silent for his sake;
> The poet threw aside his lute,
> And paused enraptured while he spake.
> The proudest lady in the land
> Forgot that praise and power were sweet;
> She dropped the jewels from her hand,
> And sat enchanted at his feet.
> . . . .
> Children, with locks of brown and gold,
> Gathered about like flocks of birds;
> The poor, whose story he had told,
> Drew near and loved him for his words.
> His eye burns bright, his voice is strong,
> A waiting people eager stands;
> Men on the outskirts of the throng
> Interpret him to distant lands.

—CARY, PHŒBE, 1870, *Dickens, The Last Poems of Alice and Phœbe Cary, ed. Ames, p.* 250.

The critics may lash and tie him as they will; one, we observe, queries if he is to be ranked as a great novelist at all; another, still more fearfully astute, questions if he could lay any claim to genius. Well, well; let them have their talk; the tormenting flies may buzz all through our August— they cannot steal away our sunshine. The English reading people everywhere have taken Charles Dickens to their hearts, and they will hold him there. God bless his memory! It shall be green for us always.— MITCHELL, DONALD G., 1870, *Hours at Home, August.*

He has the painter in him, and the English painter. Never surely did a mind figure to itself with more exact detail or greater energy all the parts and tints of a picture. . . . Dickens is a poet; he is as much at home in the imaginative world as in the actual. . . . His excessive imagination is like a string too tightly stretched; it produces of itself, without any violent shock, sounds not otherwise heard. . . . Dickens has drawn three or four portraits of madmen, very agreeable at first sight, but so **true that they are** in reality horrible. . . .

He never abandons his impassioned tone; he never rests in a natural style and in simple narrative; he only rails or weeps; he writes but satires or elegies. He has the feverish sensibility of a woman who laughs loudly, or melts into tears at the sudden shock of the slightest occurrence. This impassioned style is extremely potent, and to it may be attributed half the glory of Dickens. . . . At bottom, Dickens is gloomy, like Hogarth; but, like Hogarth, he makes us burst with laughter by the buffoonery of his inventions and the violence of his caricatures.—TAINE, H. A., 1871, *History of English Literature, tr. Van Laun, vol.* II, *bk. pp.* 340, 342, 343, 346, 349, 352.

Dickens knows nothing of science, and has, indeed, as little knowledge of any kind, save that which is derived from observation, as any respectable Englishman could well have.—McCARTHY, JUSTIN, 1872, *George Eliot and George Lewes, Modern Leaders, p.* 137.

The truest friend of humanity in the literary world. Neither Shakespeare, nor Byron, nor Walter Scott, nor Tom Moore, nor Alfred Tennyson, deigned to show so honest a devotion to the poor and the unfortunate as Charles Dickens.—FORNEY, JOHN W., 1872, *Anecdotes of Public Men, vol.* I, *p.* 400.

Dickens sees and feels, but the logic of feeling seems the only logic he can manage. Thought is strangely absent from his works. I do not suppose a single thoughtful remark on life or character could be found throughout the twenty volumes. Not only is there a marked absence of the reflective tendency, but one sees no indication of the past life of humanity having ever occupied him; keenly as he observes the objects before him, he never connects his observations into a general expression, never seems interested in general relations of things. Compared with that of Fielding or Thackeray, his was merely an *animal* intelligence, *i. e.*, restricted to perceptions. On this ground his early education was more fruitful and less injurious than it would have been to a nature constructed on a more reflective and intellectual type. It furnished him with rare and valuable experience, early developed his sympathies with the lowly and struggling, and did not starve any intellectual ambition. He never was and never would have been a student.—

LEWES, GEORGE HENRY, 1872, *Dickens in Relation to Criticism, Fortnightly Review,* vol. 17, p. 151.

To the praise of having written with invariable purity, of never having attempted to attract readers by the most distant suggestion of impropriety, he is fully entitled. It is probably rather overstraining his merits when he is further represented as having deliberately designed to bring about a reform of abuses by his writings: to make parish beadles humble and nurses abstemious by the moral drawn from Mr. Bumble and Mrs. Gamp. And even in respect to the quality of his abilities, as developed in his works, the novelty of his style led to his being greatly overpraised. . . . He never once attempted to delineate either man or woman the contemplation of whose character can refine or elevate the feelings of the reader: he does indeed on more than one occasion endeavor to be pathetic, but his talents were not formed to draw tears:

Si vis me flere dolendun est
Primum ipsi tibi.

His sense of fun is visible through his mask of dolefulness, and the effect he produces on the reader is certainly not that which he appears to desire.—YONGE, CHARLES DUKE, 1872, *Three Centuries of English Literature,* pp. 625, 626.

The number of names of characters included in the General Index, and more or less fully treated in the pages preceding the Index, is upwards of fifteen hundred and fifty. The number of names of imaginary places, societies, and literary works, and of familiar phrases or sayings, and the like,—also included in the Index,—is upwards of two hundred.—PIERCE, GILBERT A., 1872, *The Dickens Dictionary, Preface, p.* vii.

The mirror held up by him to Nature was certainly not provided with a properly even surface, and consequently all the images he saw in it, and drew from it, were apt to be distorted and out of proportion. . . . In this respect Dickens strikingly contrasts, to his disadvantage, with Chaucer, whose fidelity to nature is far too sincere to permit him to take such liberties with her fair works, or to select her monstrosities as her types. Both writers are pre-eminently realistic; no Englishmen, perhaps, exhibit more clearly that intense realism which it may be lies at the basis of the Low German mind, and which produced that school of painting amongst our own nearest kinsmen on the Continent which may compete with photography in the minute accuracy and exactness of its representations. Chaucer and Dickens are as precise in their delineations of external life and manners as are Hooge or Teniers. We know the outside look of the Miller and the Reeve just as we know that of Mr. Pickwick and Sam Weller. But even in wardrobe matters the modern is not seldom fantastic and grotesque, which Chaucer never is. To some extent the difference between these two great writers is one of culture. Chaucer was of the highest culture to be reached in his age, and all his works are fragrant with evidence of it. Dickens could have drawn certain of the Pilgrims with excellent success, but he could not have drawn the Knight or the Prioress. But the difference is not only of culture; it is also of soil.—HALES, JOHN W., 1873–84, *Notes and Essays on Shakespeare, p.* 73.

I have been sunning myself in Dickens—even in his later and very inferior "Mutual Friend," and "Great Expectations."—Very inferior to his best: but with things better than any one else's best, caricature as they may be. I really must go and worship at Gadshill, as I have worshipped a Abbotsford, though with less Reverence, to be sure. But I must look on Dickens as a mighty Benefactor of Mankind.—FITZGERALD, EDWARD, 1874, *Letter, Aug.* 24; *Letters to Fanny Kemble,* ed. Wright, p. 49.

Satirists have stormed against the abuses of the court, and governments, the intrigues of statesmen, and the intolerance of the pulpit. But Dickens was the first to employ fiction as an instrument to tell the dark history of those human beings who herd in the loathsome alleys of our great cities, to show that men are allowed to rot out of life into eternity because a duty was neglected which love ought to have dictated.—IRVING, WALTER, 1874, *Charles Dickens.*

Truth to life distinguishes nearly all the characters of Dickens, those at least which belong to the lower classes; but this truth is the obvious truth of caricature rather than of reality.—SMITH, GEORGE BARNETT, 1875, *William Makepeace Thackeray, Poets and Novelists, p.* 45.

He has an exuberance of animal spirits—a surplus vitality like that which makes him, after signing his name to a letter or note, give such a whirl of flourishing. . . . Sometimes his humour not only takes the show of mere animal spirits, but may be said to depend solely on them. . . . His boisterous fun and good-humour are like Smollett's, with this advantage, that to find his best things we have not to go to a dunghill and scratch them out.—DAVEY, SAMUEL, 1876, *Darwin, Carlyle and Dickens, and Other Essays.*

As one who flings large hospitable doors
Wide to a world of masquers whom he has bade
Sweep hurrying onward with their paces mad
And merrily flood his vacant chamber-floors,
Even so with him about whose form in scores
Humanity's eager passions, blithe or sad,
Rush reveling, and however strangely clad,
Are still the old rascals, bigots, fools and bores!
Ah, what a riotous witch-dance they prolong,
Of avarice, hatred, hope, revenge, despair!
How right flies timorous from the clutch of
    wrong!
How pleasure and ease take hands with toil and
    care!
While humor, that wild harlequin, here and
    there,
Dashes in spangled somersaults through the
    throng!
—FAWCETT, EDGAR, 1877, *Dickens, Fantasy and Passion, p.* 185.

Dickens's want of perfect sympathy with the cultured society of his time incapacitated him for that kind of novel which answers to comedy in dramatic composition, although it left him free for work of a greater and more enduring kind. What may be called the comedy novel, the novel of Thackeray in Dickens's generation, is much less sure of enduring fame, because the sentiments on which it rests, being the product of a particular knot of circumstances, are more fugitive, and pass sooner into the province of the historian. The novels of Dickens will live longer because they take hold of the permanent and universal sentiments of the race,—sentiments which pervade all classes, and which no culture can ever eradicate. His fun may be too boisterous for the refined tastes of his own time, or, for the matter of that, of posterity; his pathos may appear maudlin; but they carried everything before them when they first burst upon our literature, because, however much exaggerated, they were exaggerations of what our race feels in its inner heart; and unless culture in the future works a miracle, and carries its

changes beneath the surface, we may be certain that Dickens will keep his hold.— MINTO, WILLIAM, 1878, *Encyclopædia Britannica, Ninth Ed., vol.* VII, *p.* 154.

Dickens, alas! soon passed into a mannerism of artificial whimsicalities, alternating with shallow melodrama. — HARRISON, FREDERIC, 1879–86, *The Choice of Books and Other Literary Pieces, p.* 67.

It is very noticeable that Dickens seemed incapable of intellectual growth. The greatest expansion to which he ever attained he arrived at very early. Thereafter history, literature, even contemporaneous events, added little to his store of thought and knowledge. Endless fun, inimitable drollery, were the gifts which he had to bestow upon his fellow-men; these, indeed, he bestowed lavishly, gloriously, so that the English-reading world would doubtless much more readily part with any three of its profoundest thinkers than with this most witty and laughter-moving of all its writers. But this was all he had to give; and from the very nature of the gift it was nearer perfection in his earlier years than as he advanced in life. This is apparent enough in his letters. —MORSE, JOHN T., 1880, *Charles Dickens's Letters, The International Review, vol.* 8. *p.* 273.

Perhaps no one has succeeded better, or discovered a more effectual plan of drawing popular attention to public abuses, evils, and wrongs, than Dickens has done by mingling terrible descriptions of London misery and crime with the most amusing sketches of London life.—CANNING, ALBERT S. G., 1880, *Philosophy of Charles Dickens, p.* 335.

The primary object of a novelist is to please; and this man's novels have been found more pleasant than those of any other writer. It might, of course, be objected to this, that though the books have pleased, they have been injurious, that their tendency has been immoral and their teaching vicious; but it is almost needless to say that no such charge has ever been made against Dickens. His teaching has ever been good. From all which, there arises to the critic a question whether, with such evidence against him as to the excellence of this writer, he should not subordinate his own opinion to the collected opinion of the world of readers. To me it almost seems that I must be wrong to place Dickens after Thackeray and George Eliot, knowing as I do that so great a majority put him above those authors. . . . Of Dickens' style it is impossible to speak in praise. It is jerky, ungrammatical, and created by himself in defiance of rules—almost as completely as that created by Carlyle. To readers who have taught themselves to regard language, it must, therefore, be unpleasant. But the critic is driven to feel the weakness of his criticism, when he acknowledges to himself—as he is compelled in all honesty to do—that with the language, such as it is, the writer has satisfied the great mass of the readers of his country.— TROLLOPE, ANTHONY, 1882-83, *An Autobiography.*

Chief in thy generation born of men
Whom English praise acclaimed as English
    born,
With eyes that matched the world-wide eyes of
    morn
For gleam of tears or laughter, tenderest then
When thoughts of children warmed their light,
    or when
Reverence of age with love and labour worn,
Or godlike pity fired with godlike scorn,
Shot through them flame that winged thy swift
    live pen:
Where stars and suns that we behold not burn,
Higher even than here, though highest was
    here thy place,
Love sees thy spirit laugh and speak and shine
With Shakespeare, and the soft bright soul of
    Sterne,
And Fielding's kindliest might, and Goldsmith's
    grace;
Scarce one more loved or worthier love than
    thine.
—SWINBURNE, ALGERNON CHARLES, 1882, *Dickens.*

It would, of course, be against all experience to suppose that to future generations Dickens, as a writer, will be all that he was to his own. Much that constitutes the subject, or at least furnishes the background, of his pictures of English life, . . . has vanished, or is being improved off the face of the land. The form, again, of Dickens's principal works may become obsolete, as it was in a sense accidental. He was the most popular novelist of his day; but should prose fiction, or even the full and florid species of it which has enjoyed so long-lived a favour ever be out of season, the popularity of Dickens's books must experience an inevitable diminution. . . . Nature, when she

gifted Dickens with sensibility, observation, and imagination, had bestowed upon him yet another boon in the quality which seems more prominent than any other in his whole being. The vigour of Dickens—a mental and moral vigour supported by a splendid physical organism—was the parent of some of his foibles; amongst the rest, of his tendency to exaggeration. . . . But without this vigour he could not have been creative as he was; and in him there were accordingly united with rare completeness a swift responsiveness to the impulses of humour and pathos, an inexhaustible fertility in discovering and inventing materials for their exercise, and the constant creative desire to give to these newly-created materials a vivid, plastic form.—WARD, ADOLPHUS WILLIAM, 1882, *Dickens (English Men of Letters), pp.* 194, 202, 203.

If Dickens's taste did not incline strongly in the direction of the poetic drama—and so much perhaps is proved by his criticisms— his admiration for its chief interpreter and representative of those days, Macready, was without doubt very hearty and genuine. Into his criticisms, and especially his literary criticisms, the question of personal and private regard largely entered, and this man's tragedy or that man's book was all the better assured of approval if the man happened to occupy a place upon the critic's list of friends.—COOK, DUTTON, 1883, *Charles Dickens as a Dramatic Critic, Longman's Magazine, vol.* 2, *p.* 37.

"So we arraign her; but she," the Genius of Charles Dickens, "how brilliant, how kindly, how beneficent she is! dwelling by a fountain of laughter imperishable; though there is something of an alien salt in the neighbouring fountain of tears. How poor the world of fancy would be, how "dispeopled of her dreams," if, in some ruin of the social system, the books of Dickens were lost.—LANG, ANDREW, 1886, *Letters to Dead Authors, p.* 20.

Dickens was never happier than when he was writing a story with a moral as obvious and as sharply cut as the moral of one of Æsop's fables; indeed, after the "Pickwick Papers" he only wrote one or two works which had not some distinct purpose quite apart from any mere artistic end. He waged war against Yorkshire Schools, against the Court of Chancery, against popular political economy—against a score of real or supposed abuses; and he fought with such eagerness and persistency that more than half of his novels may be described as disguised pamphlets. He actually conceived the idea of writing a story to exhibit various manifestations of the vice of selfishness, and not only conceived it but carried it out in "Martin Chuzzlewit," which may therefore be read either as a novel or as a gigantic lay sermon. In any estimate of Dickens as a simple artist these facts might be used as evidence against him rather than in his favour.—NOBLE, JAMES ASHCROFT, 1886, *Morality in English Fiction, p.* 32.

Dickens is always a boy in his humour, and exaggerates his tragedy, as a man would who relies for his materials on imagination rather than experience; and, moreover, he seldom gives us any sense of intellectual resource.—DAWSON, W. J., 1886, *Quest and Vision.*

His style is easy, flowing, vigorous, picturesque, and humorous; his power of language is very great; and, when he is writing under the influence of strong passion, it rises into a pure and noble eloquence. The scenery—the external circumstances of his characters, are steeped in the same colors as the characters themselves; everything he touches seems to be filled with life and to speak—to look happy or sorrowful,—to reflect the feelings of the persons. His comic and humorous powers are very great; but his tragic power is also enormous—his power of depicting the fiercest passions that tear the human breast,—avarice, hate, fear, revenge, remorse. The great American statesman, Daniel Webster, said that Dickens had done more to better the condition of the English poor than all the statesmen Great Britian had ever sent into the English Parliament. — MEIKLEJOHN, J. M. D., 1887, *The English Language: Its Grammar, History and Literature, p.* 363.

I find it hard work to read Dickens, and, in fact, have but a very limited acquaintance with his novels, some of which I have begun, but laid aside. I dislike his literary method, which seems to proceed by repetitions of little peculiarities, and by describing traits and oddities of character rather than complete characters.—HAMERTON, PHILIP GILBERT, 1887, *Books which Have Influenced Me, p.* 59.

Cheerfulness was with him one of the Christian graces. Probably no character in English Letters more fully illustrates the influence on style of a happy, hopeful, hearty temperament. "He was so full of life," said our own Longfellow, "that it did not seem possible he could die." This often took the form, at home and elsewhere, of a good-natured expression of gladness of heart by which all others were made glad. Often, it took the form of innocent pleasantry, and, still again, often rose in its best expressions to the highest example of humor and satire combined. He could not but see the droll side of men and things. It was as natural for him to detect the eccentricities as the more regular features of character and one glance at an object was sufficient for him to make it the occasion of genuine English mirth.—HUNT, THEODORE W., 1887, *Representative English Prose and Prose Writers, p.* 457.

The only other writer of fiction who has had any enduring influence on my ways of thinking and feeling is Dickens, who moved me very strongly in the several directions in which his best stories were designed to move the English mind. I am sure that I derived from him a healthful stimulus to various sympathies and activities. I subsequently was disposed to think that I had overestimated him; but within the last two years I have reperused all his works, and the result has been the renewal and justification of my first impressions, though with a clear recognition of certain defects in conception, in plot, and in the drawing of the best, especially his female, characters, which had struck me less forcibly as I read the stories in monthly installments.—PEABODY, ANDREW P., 1888, *Books That Have Helped Me, p.* 45.

Such was my enthusiasm for Dickens, that when he visited Fredericksburg I sacrificed my reputation as an obedient pupil by jumping from our schoolroom window in order to get a glimpse of my hero on the stage-coach; my flogging was envied by some of my school-fellows when they heard I had seen the great man. Of all his works "Oliver Twist" moved me most deeply. An inland boy's first glimpse of the sea and its sails is a Copernican discovery; his homestead or village shrinks to an atom; but even more vast seemed that sea of humanity called London, and small indeed are remote affairs compared with the populations to which we were introduced by our magician. . . . Awakened the sentiment of humanity. From him, too, I learned how much the pen may achieve. We heard good stories of panics in Dotheboy's Halls and Bumbledom under these scathing exposures; and could well believe them, for even our old stage-road began to mend after its caricature in the "American Notes."—CONWAY, MONCURE D., 1888, *Books That Have Helped Me, p.* 92.

Dickens was of the middle class, thrown into work early, and at his best at twenty-three. His creations are imaginations as much as Puck or Ariel. In the which sense, certainly, Dickens was a poet, too. He knew nothing of Society, and cared less. Few things have been more unconsciously funny than his rather indignant rebuke of somebody who told him that he didn't know anything about lords, when he answered that Lord Chief Justice Cockburn was one of his greatest friends. Cockburn was of course "my lord" only in the legal sense, but one lord was as good to Dickens as another—in this case better. And perhaps he wasn't far wrong. Dickens's ladies and gentlemen were not the least like gentlemen and ladies—Thackeray's were the very thing. Dickens's characters are either black or white—Thackeray's are the grey mixture. Thackeray was the mighty master of that kind of humour whose brightest laughter has a touch of tears—Dickens was the master of its other side, which turns straight to the fun-god, and suffereth not its god to be eclipsed.—MERIVALE, HERMAN, 1888, *About Two Great Novelists, Temple Bar, vol.* 83, *p.* 202.

Although Dickens was endowed with quick perceptions and a ready sympathy with whatever he saw, his manner of working was too methodical, and his interest lay too much in England for him to be greatly affected by his surroundings when in the act of composition, or for his novels to show many traces of his life on the Continent. We all know the picture of his favourite writing-table at Gadshill, and he could do no work, either at Genoa or Lausanne, or Paris or Boulogne, unless his table were placed in the same way in front of the window, with the same orderly arrangement of paper and pens, knives and weights, and of the cheap and tasteless little ornaments, each of which had for him some particular meaning.—SCHUYLER, EUGENE, 1888-1901, *Italian Influences, p.* 73.

Dickens . . . gives caricatures instead of actual men and women. He does not suppress truth, but he enlarges and exaggerates it. Bumble, Tigg, Pecksniff, Dombey, Mrs. Gamp, Chadband, and Mark Tapley become standards of reference, not because such persons are known to us in the flesh, for they are not, but because the pictures, though exaggerated, are not perverted; they stand truly for character though not for persons.—LEWIN WALTER, 1889, *The Abuse of Fiction, The Forum, vol.* 7, *p.* 668.

His faults were many and grave. He wrote some nonsense; he sinned repeatedly against taste; he could be both noisy and vulgar; he was apt to be a caricaturist where he should have been a painter; he was often mawkish and often extravagant; and he was sometimes more inept than a great writer has ever been. But his work, whether bad or good, has in full measure the quality of sincerity. He meant what he did; and he meant it with his whole heart. He looked upon himself as representative and national —as indeed he was; he regarded his work as a universal possession; and he determined to do nothing that for lack of pains should prove unworthy of his function. If he sinned it was unadvisedly and unconsciously; if he failed it was because he knew no better. . . . I love to remember that I came into the world contemporaneously with some of his bravest work, and to reflect that even as he was the inspiration of my boyhood so is he a delight of my middle age. I love to think that while English literature endures he will be remembered as one that loved his fellow-men, and did more to make them happy and amiable than any other writer of his time.—HENLEY, WILLIAM ERNEST, 1890, *Views and Reviews, pp.* 5, 7.

The might of that great talent no one can gainsay, though in the light of the truer work which has since been done his literary principles seem almost as grotesque as his theories of political economy. In no one direction was his erring force more felt than in the creation of holiday literature as we have known it for the last half-century. Creation, of course, is the wrong word; it says too much; but in default of a better word, it may stand. He did not make something out of nothing; the material was there before him; the mood and even the need of his time contributed immensely to his success as the volition of the subject helps on the mesmerist; but it is within bounds to say that he was the chief agency in the development of holiday literature as we have known it, as he was the chief agency in universalizing the great Christian holiday as we now have it. Other agencies wrought with him and after him; but it was he who rescued Christmas from Puritan distrust, and humanized it and consecrated it to the hearts and homes of all.—HOWELLS, WILLIAM DEAN, 1891, *Criticism and Fiction, p.* 174.

The cheeriest of all humourists, Charles Dickens, whom the true Cockney is so fond of quoting and yet underrating, was awfully and hopelessly provincial, and was frequently reproached for the fact by the *Saturday Review.* An idealist and a dreamer he found in this great City, not Cockneydom, but Fairyland, and he was never tired of wondering at its piteous oddity and delightful quiddity.—BUCHANAN, ROBERT, 1891, *The Coming Terror, p.* 234.

His genius acted on the surface of English life as spilt water acts on the surface of unpolished marble. It suddenly made visible all its colors and veinings; and in this way he may be said to have revealed England to itself; and he still does so. It is true that this general statement must be made with one reservation. One part of English life was entirely beyond his grasp. He knew nothing of the highest class. He had no true knowledge even of the upper ranks of the middle class. His lords, his baronets, his majors, his ladies and gentlemen generally are not even like enough to reality to be called caricatures. But if we accept these classes and speak only of the bulk of the nation, no writer ever knew the English nation and represented the English nation so thoroughly and comprehensively as Dickens.—MALLOCK, WILLIAM HURREL, 1892, *Are Scott, Dickens, and Thackeray Obsolete? The Forum, vol.* 14, *p.* 510.

Why, if the public ceased to care for the books, they went on buying them, is a paradox which the critic did not explain. That the "increasing numbers" are a remarkable fact, even to this day, was proved beyond the possibility of doubt by the publication in a subsequent number of the

Standard of a letter from Mr. Frederick Chapman, which stated that the sale of Dickens's books by Messrs. Chapman and Hall during 1891 was four times greater than it had been in 1869, when the author was still living, and that in two and twenty years over five hundred and twenty thousand copies of "Pickwick" alone were sold. And these figures can only be properly appreciated when we remember that many of the books are out of copyright, and are being extensively sold by other publishers. If these books are not bought to be read what are they bought for? And if they are what becomes of the "waning popularity" of Dickens?—DICKENS, CHARLES, JR., 1892, *Pickwickian Topography, English Illustrated Magazine, vol.* 10, *p.* 186.

To tell the wealth of his imagination is beyond words, while no one has excelled him as a true painter of manners. . . . As a poet, little has been said of him, yet he wrote and published enough poems to fill a volume. The most important is "The Hymn of the Wiltshire Laborers." That song against oppression has found a loyal response in thousands of hearts. The "Ivy Green" and "A Word in Season" are also well known.—WARREN, INA RUSSELLE, 1893, *Charles Dickens, Magazine of Poetry, vol.* 5, *p.* 255.

A critical autocrat recently informed me that "Charles Dickens was going out of fashion;" whereupon I inquired as one profoundly impressed and gasping for more information, "whether he thought that Shakespeare would be *à la mode* this season, and what he considered the newest and sweetest thing in the *beau monde* of intellect?" "Pickwick," "Nicholas Nickleby," "Oliver Twist," "The Old Curiosity Shop," "David Copperfield," "A Tale of Two Cities," "A Christmas Carol," out of fashion! Not while the English language remains as now, and they who speak it have brains to appreciate humour, and hearts to sympathize with woe.—HOLE, SAMUEL REYNOLDS, 1893, *Memories, p.* 84.

Dickens has more than once been criticised for lack of powers of construction and arrangement. Such criticisms apply often to his large plans; but they are not just to his powers of analysis within the chapter. The unity of his narrative and descriptive paragraphs is organic and highly picturesque. There are slips at times, but again, there are whole chapters of the most subtle paragraph-unity—of a kind that none but the great novelists can secure, a kind that no essayist dreams of. His coherence is the coherence of oral style. There are very few connectives; their place is taken by explanatory clauses and sentences. Occasionally we feel that the style is diffuse, but obscure never—some bad grammar notwithstanding. Next to his coherence the best paragraphic quality of Dickens is his emphasis. This arises largely from his skilful ordering of words and a keen eye for the point where he should stop his sentence. He rambles when rambling is in order; but no man can make a shorter cut. The extent to which he uses the short sentence is not excessive for a novelist: in the "Old Curiosity Shop," with all the conversation included, the percentage of sentences of less than 15 words is 40 per cent. The melody of Dickens's prose is equable and flowing, with a tendency to metre now and then. He has no right feeling for the paragraph as a rhythmic whole.—LEWIS, EDWIN HERBERT, 1894, *The History of the English Paragraph, p.* 156.

Dickens was a humorist and nothing else; but Dickens took himself so seriously that he broke with *Punch* because that journal refused to publish his account of his quarrel with the wife he had promised to love, cherish, and protect. Probably, also, if the sense-of-humor had been more acutely developed in Dickens he would have spared us the blank-verse pathos of his dying children; he might even have refrained from out-heroding Herod in his massacre of the innocents.—MATTHEWS, BRANDER, 1894–1902, *Aspects of Fiction, p.* 47.

With the exception of William Cobbett, I doubt whether there has ever been, among modern English writers, a more thoroughly typical example of the plain, downright Englishman than Charles Dickens. One of the best characteristics of his simple, manly, ringing English prose is the entire absence of Gallicisms therefrom.—SALA, GEORGE AUGUSTUS, 1894, *Things I have Seen and People I have Known, vol.* I, *p.* 103.

I think he never again wrote so felicitously as in "David Copperfield." No doubt he did many fine things afterwards in the way of genre painting. We may regard him as a literary Teniers. But as years went on

his manner seems to me to grow more unnatural, more stilted, more intolerable. The higher art which he tried to grasp, ever eluded him. There is an absence of composition in his work; there is no play of light and shade; there is no proportion, no perspective. His books cannot be said to be composed, they are improvised. . . . The ethical sentiment breathes throughout the pages of Dickens, and it may well cover a multitude of sins of taste. Whatever the judgment of posterity may be upon him, we may to-day take leave of him with that judgment of Carlyle, "Every inch of him an honest man."—LILLY, WILLIAM SAMUEL, 1895, *Four English Humourists of the Nineteenth Century, pp.* 15, 33.

True to his general character of independence, Dickens owes hardly anything to any predecessor except Smollett, to whom his debts are rather large, and perhaps to Theodore Hook, to whom, although the fact has not been generally recognised, they exist.—SAINTSBURY, GEORGE, 1896, *A History of Nineteenth Century Literature, p.* 146.

The people who censure Dickens are those for whom he has served a purpose and is of no further use. They are a mere drop in the ocean of readers. It is not easy to-day to gauge his precise position. The exhaustion of many of his copyrights has given up his work to a host of rival publishers. There are probably thousands of men and women now, as there were in the fifties and sixties, who have been stimulated by him, and who have found in his writings the aid to a cheery optimism which has made life more tolerable amid adverse conditions.—SHORTER, CLEMENT, 1897, *Victorian Literature, Sixty Years of Books and Bookmen, p.* 43.

A man of wonderful talents, but of no deep seriousness; a matchless mimic through and through, and nothing else.—BURROUGHS, JOHN, 1897, *On the Re-reading of Books, Century Magazine, vol.* 55, *p.* 149.

The reading of the novels of Dickens suggests to my mind a walk through the Midway Plaisance of the Chicago Exposition. That was a little world filled with people, scenes, and things of all sorts and varieties and degrees of usefulness, beauty, rarity, and oddity. The people were all alive, real action was going on on every side, the roar of the lions in the animal house was as true to life as were the monotonous chants of the Javanese. Each separate building possessed its personages, its atmosphere, its peculiar characteristics, and its purpose, just as if it had been a novel distinct in itself, and yet owing its existence to the same originating brain.—STOCKTON, FRANK R., 1897, *My Favorite Novelist and His Best Book*, *Munsey's Magazine, vol.* 17, *p.* 354.

It is the language of a compliment and not of detraction to call him the Cockney's Shakespeare. In Shakespeare he was steeped. His favorite novelist was Smollett. But his art was all his own. He was the Hogarth of literature, painting with a broad brush, never ashamed of caricature, but always an artist, and not a dauber. There is little or no resemblance between Falstaff and Sam Weller. But they are the two comic figures which have most thoroughly seized upon the English mind. Touchstone and Mr. Micawber may be each a finer specimen of his creator's powers. They are not, however, quite so much to the taste of all readers. They require a little more fineness of palate.—PAUL, HERBERT, 1897, *The Apotheosis of the Novel*, *The Nineteenth Century, vol.* 41, *p.* 770.

Now, with the solitary exception of Sir Walter Scott, it is probable that no man ever inspired such a host of imitators as Charles Dickens. There is not a writer of fiction at this hour, in any land where fiction is a recognised trade or art, who is not, whether he knows it and owns it, or no, largely influenced by Dickens. . . . Dickens has a living part in the life of the whole wide world. He is on a hundred thousand magisterial benches every day. There is not a hospital patient in any country who has not at this minute a right to thank God that Dickens lived. What his blessed and bountiful hand has done for the poor and oppressed, and them that had no helper, no man knows. He made charity and good feeling a religion. Millions and millions of money have flowed from the coffers of the rich for the benefit of the poor because of his books. A great part of our daily life, and a good deal of the best of it, is of his making. No single man ever made such opportunities for himself. No single man was ever so widely and permanently useful. No single man ever sowed gentleness and mercy with so broad a sweep. . . .The new man says of Dickens that his sentiment rings false.

This is a mistake. It rings old-fashioned. No false note ever moved a world, and the world combined to love his very name. There were tears in thousands of households when he died, and they were as sincere and as real as if they had arisen at the loss of a personal friend.—MURRAY, DAVID CHRISTIE, 1897, *My Contemporaries in Fiction, pp.* 9, 10, 13.

It is immensely to the credit of the heart of the novelist, and will be a permanent addition to his fame, not only that he devoted fiction to the high end of exposing manifold social abuses, but even that, by the force of his genius, he contributed a material element to their correction. If cheap private schools are no longer what once they sometimes were, it is due in part to "Nicholas Nickleby." "Oliver Twist" helped to bring about the improvement of workhouses, and "Little Dorrit" of debtors' jails, and "Bleak House" of the Court of Chancery, and "David Copperfield" of Doctors' Commons. Fiction could have had no loftier aim than such an amelioration of social conditions.—FARRAR, FREDERICK W., 1897, *Men I have Known, p.* 265.

The characters of Dickens, then, are personified humours, his method is the method not of Shakespeare, but of Ben Jonson. Pecksniff is just another name for hypocrisy, Jonas Chuzzlewit for avarice, Quilp for cruelty. The result is excellent of its kind. The repetitions and catch-words are, within limits, highly effective. Sometimes they are genuinely illuminative; but sometimes, on the other hand, they reveal nothing and are used to weariness.—WALKER, HUGH, 1897, *The Age of Tennyson, p.* 87.

The greatest novelist since Scott, the earliest, and in some ways still the most typical of Victorian writers, was Charles Dickens.—GOSSE, EDMUND, 1897, *A Short History of Modern English Literature, p.* 341.

Realist as Dickens supposed himself to be, and in his descriptive method actually was, he is, dramatically speaking, an idealist pure and simple. He drew not individuals, but types; he dealt, not with concrete realities, but with abstract qualities; and strange as it may seem, the character of this prose humorist must be viewed as we view the purely ideal creations of the poet, if we would do justice either to him or to them. For it is only by studying these characters that we can fairly measure that inexhaustible wealth of comic imagination, that unflagging zest and dexterity of humorous portrayal, which carries captive the reader's judgment, and compels him for the time to share their creator's belief in their existence.—TRAILL, HENRY DUFF, 1897, *Social England, vol.* VI, *p.* 163.

Dickens was an artist; this gave his work vogue. Dickens lacked some of the artistic powers; this renders his future uncertain. Whether the balance between his powers and his weaknesses is such as to relegate him to obscurity after the generation who remembered him as the delight of their youthful days has passed away, no one would dare to decide. But if he does take his place among the temporary authors who have no message for future generations, we may be sure that his lack of a broad, sane view of human society is one of the reasons why he enters the great company of the unread.—JOHNSON, CHARLES, 1898, *Elements of Literary Criticism, p.* 136.

He knew the heart of man to the very core, and could draw a picture of human suffering with a more loving hand than any other English writer. He also possessed now and then the grand style, and even in his pictures of still life the hand of the master can always be perceived.—MÜLLER, F. MAX., 1898, *Auld Lang Syne, p.* 126.

Some of the critics would have us believe that Dickens has had his day, but here the booksellers have a word. So long as Dickens is a delightful companion at our firesides, in whose presence children leave their play and listen, he need not fear the critic, for love will keep its own.—GEORGE, ANDREW J., 1898, *From Chaucer to Arnold, Types of Literary Art, p.* 658.

Dickens was not a church member, or what is called an Orthodox Christian; but he preached many a good sermon for all that; and his text was the Golden Rule, in all its various readings. In many wholesome, reverent ways does the Bible figure throughout his pages. One of the earliest recollections of David Copperfield was the story of the raising of Lazarus, as it was read to him and Peggotty by his mother one Sunday evening. Little Nell used to take her Bible with her to read in the quiet, lovely retreat of the old church.—HUTTON, LAURENCE, 1898, *Charles Dickens, The Outlook, vol.* 60, *p.* 322.

With him I was not disappointed, for besides his humour, I found in him a style of phrase and epithet which gave me much satisfaction. When, for example, he describes an old-clothes shop as "one of those convenient emporiums where gentlemen's new and second-hand clothes are provided, and the troublesome and inconvenient formality of measurement dispensed with," or in speaking of Zephyr in the debtor's prison remarks that "Mr. Pickwick struck the Zephyr so smart a blow on the chest as to deprive him of a considerable portion of the commodity which sometimes bears his name," or in depicting the dispute at Bob Sawyer's party says that "one individual expressed his decided unwillingness to accept any 'sauce' on gratuitous terms either from the irascible young gentleman with the scorbutic countenance or any other person who was ornamented with a head," I was charmed, and thought it wonderfully clever, and the power of language it exhibited quite unique!—CROZIER, JOHN BEATTIE, 1898, *My Inner Life, p.* 216.

We have to go back to Shakspere to find a writer who, through fiction, has so enriched the thought of the people. Admit all Dickens' faults twice over, we still have one of the greatest writers of modern times. Such people as these creations of Dickens never lived, says your little critic. Nor was Prometheus, type of the spirit of man, nor was Niobe, mother of all mothers, a truthful picture of the citizen one could meet a thousand times during an hour's march through Athens. Nor grew there ever a wood like to the Forest of Arden, though every *Rosalind* and *Orlando* knows the path to glades having much resemblance to it.—JEROME, JEROME K., 1898, *My Favorite Novelist and His Best Book, Munsey's Magazine, vol.* 19, *p.* 32.

Into Dickens' Land, therefore, my masters, as you will and when you will! The high-roads thither are always open, the lanes and by-paths are free for us to tread. He that found out this rare world has made it fully ours. Let us visit our inheritance, or revisit it, if that be the better word. Let us make real the scenes we have read of and dreamt of—peopling them with the folk of Dickens, so that familiar faces shall look upon us from familiar windows, familiar voices greet us as we pass.—BRENAN, GERALD, 1899, *Rambles in Dickens' Land by Robert Allbut, Introduction, p.* xxi.

The following pages are sufficient to establish the claim of Mr. Hughes for Dickens as an educational reformer—the greatest that England has produced. It will be admitted that he has done more than any one else to secure for the child a considerate treatment of his tender age. "It is a crime against a child to rob it of its childhood." This principle was announced by Dickens, and it has come to be generally recognised and adopted. Gradually it is changing the methods of primary instruction and bringing into vogue a milder form of discipline and a more stimulative teaching—arousing the child's self-activity instead of repressing it. . . . He stands apart and alone as one of the most potent influences of social reform in the nineteenth century, and therefore deserves to be read and studied by all who have to do with schools and by all parents everywhere in our day and generation.— HARRIS, WILLIAM T., 1900, *Dickens as an Educator by Hughes, Editor's Preface, pp.* v, vii.

Dickens was England's greatest educational reformer. . . . Was Dickens consciously and intentionally an educator? The prefaces to his novels; the preface to his *Household Words;* the educational articles he wrote; the prominence given in his books to child training in homes, institutions, and schools; the statements of the highest educational philosophy found in his writings; and especially the clearness of his insight and the profoundness of his educational thought, as shown by his condemnation of the wrong and his appreciation of the right in teaching and training the child, prove beyond question that he was not only broad and true in his sympathy with childhood, but that he was a careful and progressive student of the fundamental principles of education.—HUGHES, JAMES L., 1900, *Dickens as an Educator, p.*1.

The first and the most widely popular of Victorian novelists was Dickens, whose work began less than five years after Scott's ended. The contrast between them is among the most instructive in literary history. Scott's ideal was always that of a gentleman: Dickens's, with equal instinctive honesty of feeling, was that of the small trading classes. Whatever merits Dickens had, and these were great and lasting, he fatally lacked one grace which up to his time the literature of his country had generally preserved,—that of distinction.— WENDELL, BARRETT, 1900, *A Literary History of America, p.* 147.

Probably no writer ever appealed so strongly or so universally to the feelings of his readers. His material was almost exclusively drawn from middle-class life, but his words came home the nearer to the heart like a true touch of human nature. It was this that made him a favourite above all recent novelists.—ENGLE, EDWARD, 1902, *A History of English Literature, rev. Hamley Bent, p.* 449.

Is there any other maker of story in modern English literature—after all allowances have been made, and not forgetting that some criticism of the man of Gadshill will have it that he is for a more careless age —who has begun to furnish such a portrait-gallery of worthies and adorable grotesques—a motley crowd whom we all know and enjoy and love? I wot not. The fact that Dickens is at times a trifle inchoate or careless in his English, or allows his exuberance to lead him into exaggeration, or fails to blend perfectly the discordant elements of comedy and tragedy, sinks into insignificance when set over against such a faculty as this. He was a veritable giant here. — BURTON, RICHARD, 1902, *Forces in Fiction and Other Essays, p.* 7.

It is only when such names as Shakespeare's or Hugo's rise and remain as the supreme witnesses of what was highest in any particular country at any particular time that there can be no question among any but irrational and impudent men as to the supremacy of their greatest. England under the reign of Dickens, had other great names to boast of which may well be allowed to challenge the sovereignty of his genius. But as there certainly was no Shakespeare and no Hugo to rival and eclipse his glory, he will probably and naturally always be accepted and acclaimed as the greatest Englishman of his generation. . . . . In "Oliver Twist" the quality of a great tragic and comic poet or dramatist in prose fiction was for the first time combined with the already famous qualities of a great humorist and a born master in the arts of narrative and dialogue. . . . These Christmas numbers are . . . gems as costly as any of the larger in his crown of fame. — SWINBURNE, A. C., 1902, *Charles Dickens, Quarterly Review, vol.* 196, *pp.* 20, 38.

William Gilmore Simms
1806-1870

American author, was born at Charleston, S. C., April 17, 1806, of Irish extraction. He made verses at the age of 7; and during the war of 1812, celebrated in rhyme the exploits of the American army and navy. Left in charge of his grandmother at Charleston, he was placed with a druggist; but at 18 began the study of law; was admitted to the bar at 22; published "Early Lays" and "Lyrical and Other Poems" (1827), and became (1828) editor of *The City Gazette*, and published "The Vision of Cortes, Cain and Other Poems" (1829), and "The Tri-Color," a poetical glorification of the French revolution (1830). In 1832, his paper, opposing nullification, failed; and he lost his wife, father, and grandmother, and took refuge in New England, where at Hingham, Mass., he wrote his best poem, "Atalantis, a Story of the Sea" (1833); and the same year "Martin Faber," the story of a criminal. From this time he poured out rather than wrote poems, novels, histories, and biographies in rapid succession, which may best be classed in groups. Of poems, he published "Southern Passages and Pictures" (1839); "Donna Anna" (1843); "Grouped Thoughts and Scattered Fancies" (1845); "Lays of the Palmetto"—ballads of southern heroism in the war with Mexico (1848); "Poems, Descriptive, Dramatic, and Legendary" (1854); "Areytos, or Songs and Ballads of the South" (1860). Of dramas—"Norman Maurin, or the Man of the People;" "Michael Bonham, or the Fall of the Alamo;" and a stage adaptation of "Timon of Athens." Of prose romances of the imagination—"The Book of My Lady" (1833); "Carl Werner" (1838); "Confession, or the Blind Heart" (1842); "Castle Dismal" (1845); "The Wigwam and the Cabin," two series (1845, 1846); "Marie de Bernière" (1853). Of historical romances— "The Yemassee" (1835); "Pelayo" (1838); "Count Julien" (1845); "The Damsel of Darien" (1845); "The Lily and the Totem, or the Huguenots in Florida" (1845); "The Maroon and Other Tales" (1855); "Vasconcelos" (1857); "Cassique of Kiawah" (1860). Of revolutionary stories—"The Partisan" (1835); "Mellichamp" (1851); "Katherine Walton" (1851); "The Scout" (1841); "The Kinsman, or the Black Riders of the Congaree" (1841); "Woodcraft" (1855); "The Foagers" (1855); "Eutaw" (1856); these five being stories of the war in the Carolinas. Of local tales—"Guy Rivers" (1834); "Richard Hurdis" (1838); "Border Beagles" (1840); "Beauchamps" (1842); "Helen Halsey" (1845); "The Golden Christmas" (1852); "Charlemont" (1856). His other works comprise a "History of South Carolina;" "South Carolina in the Revolution;" "Lives of General Marion, Captain John Smith, Chevalier Bayard, General Greene;" "Civil War in the South;" "American Loyalists of the Revolution;" "Views and Reviews of American Literature;" "The Morals of Slavery," etc. Residing in South Carolina during the war of secession, he sustained the southern cause in a weekly newspaper, and had his house and library wrecked by federal soldiers. Of his various and voluminous works, some are of high excellence. He died in 1870.—PECK, HARRY THURSTON, ed. 1898, *The International Cyclopædia, vol.* XIII, *p.* 511.

PERSONAL

For my part, and for the last six months I have been literally *hors de combat* from overwork of the brain,—brain sweat, as Ben Jonson called it,—and no body sweat, no physical exercise. In the extremity of my need, I took contracts . . . for no less than three romances, all to be worked at the same time. I got advances of money on each of these books, and the sense of obligation pressing upon me, I went rigidly to work, concentrating myself at the desk from 20th October, 1868, to the 1st of July, 1869, nearly nine months without walking a mile in a week, riding but twice, and absent from work but half a day on each of these occasions. The consequence

was that I finished two of the books and broke down on the third, having written during this period some three thousand pages of the measure of these which I now write to you.—SIMMS, WILLIAM GILMORE, 1869, *Letter to Paul Hamilton Hayne, Dec.* 22.

Behold, also, how our old circle of ancient friends and comrades is thinning! One by one they have quitted our sides, until at length old Simms himself, whom I had got into the habit of regarding as *immortal*, has finished his course, and said his final farewells! . . . Gallant old man! Whatever his faults, I, for one, loved him with all my heart! And there is no doubt that his time had *fully* come. He had fought a good fight and kept the faith, at least the faith he had plighted to his own genius and will. Yet, as Pierpont says of his deceased child, "I cannot *make* him *dead!*" So much *vitality* was there in the man, so vivid is his image before the "mind's eye," that all attempts at a *realization* of his death utterly fail!.. Simms's genius *never had fair play!* Circumstances hampered him! Thus, the *man* was greater than his *works.*—HAYNE, PAUL HAMILTON, 1870, *Letter to Dr. Porcher, July 9.*

No prim Precisian he! his fluent talk
Roved thro' all topics, vivifying all;
Now deftly ranging level plains of thought,
To sink, anon in metaphysical deeps;
Whence, by caprice of strange transition brought
Outward and upward, the free current sought
Ideal summits, gathering in its course,
Splendid momentum and imperious force,
Till, down it rushed as mighty cataracts fall,
Hurled from gaunt mountain steeps!
Sportive he could be as a gamesome boy!
By Heaven! as 'twere but yesterday, I see
His tall frame quake with throes of jollity;
Hear his rich voice that owned a jovial tone,
Jocund as Falstaff's own;
And catch moist glints of steel-blue eyes o'errun
Sideways, by tiny rivulets of fun!
—HAYNE, PAUL HAMILTON, 1877, *In Memoriam, W. Gilmore Simms.*

What a strong, earnest face [1840] and what a Byronic head.—MORFORD, HENRY, 1880, *John Keese, His Intimates, Morford's Magazine, June.*

I frequently met Mr. Simms at the houses of New York friends, and in my father's residence. He was a voluble talker and a good letter-writer. There was at the period of my first meeting with Mr. Simms, about 1850, something in his strong, earnest, clean-shaven face, blue eye, and stalwart figure singularly suggestive of Christopher North. When, some sixteen or seventeen years later, I met him for the last time under a friend's roof on the banks of the Hudson, he was much changed in appearance and in spirits—much embittered by his losses, and by the result of the war. Before it came, I had heard from his lips these extravagant words: "If it comes to blows between the North and the South, we will crush you [the North] as I would crush an egg," holding up his clenched hand as if in the act of performing that feat. It must be admitted that few men not in politics did more to bring on hostilities between the two sections than William Gilmore Simms, and few men suffered more from them.—WILSON, JAMES GRANT, 1886, *Bryant and his Friends, p. 260.*

From both his parents Simms inherited a sanguine, impulsive, and impressible temperament. It would seem that the father's traits were more strongly impressed upon the son than the mother's; for there was little in Simms' nature that was feminine. . . . A barbarian he could not be, since he was not an aristocrat by birth. Perhaps there has never been a man whose development was so sadly hampered by his environment; and that he succeeded as far as he did in escaping from the effects of his environment should move our admiration and respect. It is needless to dwell upon the native kindness of heart, the buoyant spirits, the superb physical and moral energy of the man, for these have been fully set forth already. Though at times seemingly eaten up with self-conceit, he was never either really conceited or selfish. He was never ashamed to acknowledge his own deficiencies; never so busy with his own affairs as to turn a deaf ear to a call for help or sympathy. The amount of good he did in his last feeble years cannot be calculated. Those who saw his eccentricities only, laughed at him; those who knew him well, loved him more and more until their love almost grew to reverence. If he often did a foolish action, he never did a mean one; and though not symmetrically great, he was essentially noble. He had virtues, too, not specially common in his time and section. While fond of stimulants and excitement, he refrained always from intoxication; while fond of the story that is told to men only, he was irreproachable in his private morals. . . . On the whole, one forms the impression that Simms was a vigorous, hearty man, with a versatile and talented mind, a very large heart, an indomitable will, and keen if not always delicate, sensibilities. His weaknesses and eccentricities were partly due to inherited tendencies, partly to environment, but, though they marred the symmetry of his character, they nevertheless could not efface the strength and lovableness of his personality.—TRENT, WILLIAM P., 1892, *William Gilmore Simms (American Men of Letters), pp. 324, 325, 326.*

GENERAL

His "Southern Passages and Pictures" appeared in New York, in 1839, and he has since published "Florida," in five cantos, and many shorter poems. They are on a great variety of subjects, and in almost every measure. Among them are several very spirited ballads, founded on Indian traditions and on incidents in the war for independence. His style is free and melodious, his fancy fertile and inventive, and his imagery generally well chosen, though its range is limited; but sometimes his rhymes are imperfect, and his meaning not easily understood. He is strongly attached to his country, but his sympathies seem to me to be too local. The rivers, forests, savannas, and institutions of the south, he regards with feelings similar to those with which Whittier looks upon the mountains, lakes, and social systems of New England.—Griswold, Rufus Wilmot, 1842, *The Poets and Poetry of America*, p. 303.

The author of these novels means to be understood as setting up for an original, patriotic, native American writer; but we are convinced that every judicious reader will set him down as uncommonly deficient in the first elements of originality. He has put on the cast-off garments of the British novelists, merely endeavoring to give them an American fit; and, like those fine gentlemen who make up their wardrobes from the second-hand clothing shops, or from the "unparalleled" establishment of Oak Hall, there is in his literary outfits a decided touch of the shabby genteel. The outward form of his novels is that of their English models; the current phrases of sentiment and description, worn threadbare in the circulating libraries, and out at the elbows, are the robes wherewith he covers imperfectly the nakedness of his invention. The *obligato* tone of sentimentality wearisomely drones through the soft passages of the thousand times repeated plot of love. . . . The style of Mr. Simms . . is deficient in grace, picturesqueness, and point. It shows a mind seldom able to seize the characteristic features of the object he undertakes to describe, and of course his descriptions generally fail of arresting the reader's attention by any beauty or felicity of touch. His characters are vaguely conceived, and either faintly or coarsely drawn. The dramatic parts are but bungling imitations of nature, with little sprightliness or wit, and laboring under a heavy load of words.—Felton, Cornelius C., 1846, *Simms's Stories and Reviews, North American Review, vol. 63, pp.* 357, 358.

Had he been even a Yankee, this genius would have been rendered immediately manifest to his countrymen, but unhappily (*perhaps*) he was a Southerner, and united the Southern pride, the Southern dislike to the making of bargains, with the Southern supineness and general want of tact in all matters relating to the making of money. His book, ["Martin Faber"] therefore, depended entirely upon its own intrinsic value and resources, but with these it made its way in the end.—Poe, Edgar Allan, 1846, *Simms's "The Wigwam and the Cabin," Works ed. Stedman and Woodberry, vol.* VII, *p.* 94.

Mr. Simms has a vivid imagination, and is by no means deficient in artistic skill. His language is frequently faulty, but that is undoubtedly owing to the fact he writes so much he does not take time to revise the productions of his pen. While he occupies a respectable rank among the poets of America, he stands at the head of that class of authors who entertain us with light literature.—Bungay, George W., 1854, *Off-Hand Takings, p.* 387.

In that wielding of events, that sacrificing of characters to situations, he stands unsurpassed—to a great extent unapproached. In America, neither Brown nor Cooper is his equal in this regard; though both surpass him far in certain other qualities. Here the contest for first place in general merit, or in the balance of merits (including quantity), lies between our author and Cooper. In characterization and in polish, Cooper has the advantage; while in the energy of action, variety of situations, and perhaps in literal truthfulness of delineation—I mean the absence of fanciful and impossible personages—Mr. Simms has clearly the advantage. In general results—take both for all in all, quantity, versatility, and quality—it may be reasonably questioned whether Mr. Simms has an equal in America. I believe he has not. In general value to his sphere of literature he is *facile princeps* both North and South.—Davidson, James Wood, 1869, *The Living Writers of the South, p.* 515.

A really *great author* (whether in *prose or verse*) *Simms emphatically was not,* and there is no use in maintaining so fulsome a proposition. But his *talents* were splendid, and his whole life seems to me *noble,* because of the "grit," the perseverance, the indomitable energy which it displayed. I've not the remotest idea that his *works* will endure. They were too carelessly written. They lack the "labor limæ'' to an extent which is distressing. Nevertheless Simms is worthy of *all honor.* "God rest his *soul.''*—HAYNE, PAUL HAMILTON, 1870, *Letter to Dr. Porcher, Aug.* 4.

No writer of modern times has excelled him in industry; but the rapidity with which his works were produced has had its usual effect. None of them show the matured and symmetrical design which marks a work of art, still less the hand of a master in their execution. There are passages of description in many of his novels that are vivid and picturesque, but the style is often redundant, lacking in repose, and sarcely ever free from provincialisms. The characters are like the lay figures of the studio, useful in exigencies and effective in tableaux, but devoid of interest in themselves. The best of his novels are of the historical kind, in which southern life in early times is painted, such as " The Yemassee" and "Guy Rivers." The most of them are irredeemably dull, at least for readers who value their time, and they must surely sink into neglect.—UNDERWOOD, FRANCIS H., 1872, *A Hand-Book of English Literature, American Authors, p.* 257.

What Cooper did for the pioneer life of the Middle States was done by Simms for that of the south, the characteristic features of whose colonial and revolutionary history he has preserved in a series of spirited and faithfully colored narratives. He is a picturesque and vigorous writer, evidently inspired by his subject (*i. e.* in his historical romances), cherishing a generous pride in the annals of his native section and the chivalrous character of her people. Although his books have, to a great extent, been superseded, as have Cooper's, by novels which deal with later times, they are still widely read and admired. Taking into account the variety and amount of Mr. Simms's literary work, its distinctively American character, and the positive merit possessed by much of it, his name deserves to be cherished among those of the most honored representatives of our literature.—CATHCART, GEORGE R., 1874, *The Literary Reader, p.* 190.

This work ["History of South Carolina''] has several distinctive merits above other histories of South Carolina. It covers the whole period down to our Civil War. It has all the beauties of the author's characteristic style. It shows an intense local patriotism, and, consequently, on all sectional questions it is ardently South Carolinian. From beginning to end the narration is spirited and graphic, but the sketch is too brief for details even on the most important points.—ADAMS, CHARLES KENDALL, 1882, *A Manual of Historical Literature, p.* 559.

Simms, with a downward proclivity toward the Newgate Calendar, began, in 1833, to flood the country with every style of fiction. There was no generation of Southern life which he did not touch upon, and no phase of romantic murder which he did not illustrate. With a feeling for reality, which was unknown to Cooper and Kennedy, a certain cleverness of invention and strong sense of subordination which kept him from the obvious artifices of both these writers, he was a superior student of human nature in the peculiar line which he took, and held his characters more rigidly to the sequence of cause and effect.—MORSE, JAMES HERBERT, 1883, *The Native Element in American Fiction, Century Magazine, vol.* 26, *p.* 293.

His brain and pen were never idle, and he essayed nearly every sort of writing. Though far removed in his South Carolina home, from the greater publishing centres, libraries, colleges, and author-coteries, Simms was poet, dramatist, Shakespearean editor, essayist, aphoristic philosopher, historian, biographer, lecturer, commemorative orator, legislator, pro-slavery apologist, journalist, magazinist, critic, and, above all, novelist. Authors have been hacks, helpers, or wage-earners since the art of writing was invented; but Simms' industry and fertility are remarkable in view of his environment, which was not favorable to such facile and miscellaneous productiveness. The novels, naturally, have survived the other writings, so that the "works" of Simms have come to mean, in publishers' parlance, merely the best of his romantic or historial fictions. The most attractive part of the novels, to tell the truth, is their titles.—RICHARDSON, CHARLES F., 1888, *American Literature, vol.* II, *p.* 398.

He was a versatile and diligent author, engaging in many branches of literary work. Of all that he did, his novels alone survive, and even they belong to a style of romance no longer in vogue. They are modelled upon the lines laid down by Sir Walter Scott, and are full of intrigue, incident and action, with a Southern historical background. Their faults are largely due to the time and conditions in which Simms wrote; he deserves credit for his vigorous effort to found a Southern literature.— HAWTHORNE, JULIAN, AND LEMMON, LEONARD, 1891, *American Literature, p.* 240.

Cooper today keeps his place close at the heels of Scott, while Simms is fading into oblivion as fast as G. P. R. James, with whose work his may fairly be compared, although Simms was probably far richer in native gifts.—MATTHEWS,BRANDER, 1892-1902, *Aspects of Fiction, p.* 38.

With regard to his prose, attention must be confined to his revolutionary and colonial romances. If the quality of permanence is to be found in his work, it is to be found there. . . . His place is not a high one; but it should never be forgotten that he was not only a pioneer, but *the* pioneer, of American literature, whose destiny forced him to labor in the least favorable section of all America for successful literary work. When his environment is considered, the work he did will be deemed worthy of admiration rather than of faultfinding.—TRENT, WILLIAM P., 1892, *William Gilmore Simms* (*American Men of Letters*), *pp.* 327, 332.

Simms was an inferior Cooper with a difference. His novels are good boys' books, but are crude and hasty in composition. . . . His poems have little value except as here and there illustrating local scenery and manners.—BEERS, HENRY A., 1895, *Initial Studies in American Letters, p.* 175.

Let it be remarked parenthetically, that while a few Carolinians never gave Simms due honor, his name will remain one of the brightest on their roll of great names, and will not stand far down the list of pioneer American writers. . . . The South cannot afford to ignore his work for, take him all in all, she has produced few greater men—

few men who have labored harder to give his section her true place in history and literature. . . . Hayne gives an account of how he sat and watched the pen glide over the paper while Simms wrote. Some marvelous accounts are given of the rapidity with which he turned off manuscript. Notwithstanding this, he studied his field so closely that, as Poe intimated, he did not depend enough upon his imagination, did not idealize enough. His narrative reads too much like history. His characters are people in whose history we can easily become interested, but his men and women ever remain on the outside, and do not come into our lives and become part of our spiritual furnishings.—LINK, SAMUEL ALBERT, 1896, *Pioneers of Southern Literature, vol.* I, *pp.* 93, 220.

The place of Simms, the veteran in Southern letters, is at once honorable and pathetic. Striving against wind and tide, he produed as many stories as Cooper, besides a goodly amount of poetry, biography and miscellany; but the bulk of his writing was too hasty for immortality.—BATES, KATHARINE LEE, 1897, *American Literature, p.* 277.

These romances have spirit and vigor of style, but show the defects of the author's lack of thorough literary training. They will always be of interest, however, as illustrations of the life of the time, and as the only important representative, in the Literature of the period, of the part of the country which was the author's home.— NOBLE, CHARLES, 1898, *Studies in American Literature, p.* 129.

The first Southern writer of distinction to follow literature as a profession. This circumstance, involving as it did a long and gallant struggle with adverse conditions, gives him an important place, aside from the intrinsic value of his writings, as the pioneer among the Southern men of letters. . . . Simms is distinctly inferior to Cooper, with whom he inevitably suggests comparison; yet his best stories form a kind of companion study to Cooper's work, depicting as they do the same period of our national growth under Southern instead of under Northern or Western conditions. In his portrayal of the Indian character Simms is probably more truthful than Cooper, whose Indian heroes, if more romantic, are, it is to be feared, more ideal.—PANCOAST, HENRY S., 1898, *An Introduction to American Literature*, pp. 254, 255.

He was full of strong self-assertion, and though a most friendly, hospitable man, carried in his step and speech a good deal of the combative spirit and the audacities which he put so cleverly into the pages of his tales of the Revolution. In the present revival of Colonial studies we may possibly look for a new cult of the author of "Melli-

champe."—MITCHELL, DONALD G., 1899, *American Lands and Letters, Leather-Stocking to Poe's "Raven," p. 122.

Though William Gilmore Simms published several volumes of verse, including some prosy dramas, they are, with the exception of a few descriptive passages, as completely ignored by the general reader as are the works of Crafts and Grayson.—ONDERDONK, JAMES L., 1899-1901, *History of American Verse, p. 208*

George Denison Prentice

1802–1870

Journalist; born at Preston, Conn., Dec. 18, 1802; graduated at Brown University 1823; was admitted to the bar in 1829; edited *The Weekly Review*, Hartford, Conn., 1828–30; from 1830 to his death was editor of the Louisville, Ky., *Journal*, which he made one of the leading Whig newspapers of the country; author of many fugitive poems and of a "Life" of Henry Clay (1831); "Prenticeana" (1859), a collection of his witticisms, has gone through several enlarged editions. Died at Louisville, Ky., Jan. 22, 1870. His "Life" has been written by G. W. Griffin, and a posthumous edition of his "Poems" was issued in 1876.—BEERS, HENRY A., 1897, *rev. Johnson's Universal Cyclopædia, vol. VI, p. 759.*

PERSONAL

In appearance Mr. Prentice is short and rather stout, but he has a splendid head. His forehead is massive and full, and his eyes are very black and of the medium size, although they are so over-shadowed by his shaggy eyebrows that at a glance they are supposed to be small and snaky. His nose is shapely, his cheeks are full, and the whole contour of his face is round. His hair retains a jetty blackness, but is thinly distributed over his head, although only a small space of the scalp is actually bald. He is careless about his clothes, and feels utterly desolate in full-dress, which he is sometimes compelled to undergo on state occasions. — SHANKS, CHARLES G., 1869, *George Denison Prentice, Lippincott's Magazine of Literature, Science and Education, vol. 4, p. 558.*

There are some names that have a mysterious charm in them — that go directly from the ear to the heart like echoes from a world of beauty and enchantment —that whisper to us somehow of song and blossom — whose very shadows are fragrant and seductive. Rupert and Voltaire, Richter and Chateaubriand, Sheridan and Tom Marshall, are of this nature, and represent in one sort and another, what might be called the knight errantry of civilization. Prentice belongs to the same class. What Rupert was in the saddle, and

Voltaire and Richter in the fight for free opinions; what the friend of Madame Recamier was in diplomacy; what Sheridan was in the commons; what Marshall was before the people — Prentice was to the press. . . . Prentice was a perfect interpreter of his own times; and when that is said we say of him what can only be said with truth of two or three men in an age. His personality was diffusive as well as ardent. He had a spirit vehement and daring. Now that he is gone there is no one to succeed him; and I doubt whether, if it were possible, it would be safe to trust to another the power which, as far as he himself was concerned, he used so unselfishly and so sparingly. There was a time when the splendor of his fame was very captivating to myself, as I dare say it was to thousands of other ambitious youths of the country. But you will believe me sincere when I tell you, paraphrasing the words of Tyndall upon Faraday, how lightly I hold the honor of being Prentice's successor compared with the honor of having been Prentice's friend. His friendship was energy and inspiration. His "mantle" is a burden I shall never pretend to carry.—WATTERSON, HENRY, 1870, *George Denison Prentice, A Memorial Address Delivered before the Legislature of Kentucky, pp. 8, 22.*

In person, Mr. Prentice was above the

medium height. His head was finely shaped; his figure was erect, but his exceedingly sloping shoulders gave him rather a drooping appearance. He was dignified and elegant in his bearing, and graceful and natural in all his movements and actions. His hands and feet were unusually small; his face was round and full; his features were irregular, but not homely. His forehead was broad and high, and awed the beholder by its expression of intellectual vigor. His eyes were his finest feature; they were of a dark brown color, rather small, but lustrous and full of strange intelligence—

"Deep searching seen, and seeing from afar."

His voice was low-toned and persuasive, but free as a fountain, it took the form of the conduit thought. He was one of the finest conversationalists I ever heard. It can be said of him, as was said of the little child in the fairy-story, that whenever he opened his mouth out came a pearl. He delivered no monologues. He never wearied his listeners, or insulted them by presuming upon their ignorance. He was as sparkling and brilliant at the table and in social circles as in the columns of his paper. The richness of his language was only equalled by the wit, humor, and philosophy of his thoughts and ideas.— GRIFFIN, G. W., 1871, *Studies in Literature, p.* 46.

Mr. Prentice was often much the worse for liquor. I once saw him at a party, sitting on a sofa, with a gentleman sitting on each side, keeping him from falling over. Afterwards he took the pledge, and joined a temperance society. How it was in the last years of his life I never knew, but it is certain that cloud rested over his latter days. He lost the commanding position which he once occupied. He tried to maintain slavery and yet oppose the rebellion, but his position was not logical, and was necessarily a failure. The man who once seemed to direct the destinies of Kentucky with his pen, the leading journalist of the west, was at last only retained as a subordinate in the office which had been the scene of his great triumphs. So passes away the influence of any mind, however brilliant, which clings to no convictions, and holds to no universal ideas.—CLARKE, JAMES FREEMAN, 1878, *Memorial and Biographical Sketches, p.* 258.

He was an excellent talker, and being a thorough Greek and Latin scholar, as well as French and German, he was at home among his favorite poets, Virgil, Byron and Shelley. His favorite German author was Jean Paul Richter; he always read everything the latter wrote, and his advice to young writers was to adopt Richter's style, if they must have a model.—DERBY, JAMES CEPHAS, 1884, *Fifty Years among Authors, Books and Publishers, p.* 423.

One of my teachers was George D. Prentice, the poet, who was born within a stone's throw of me. He is better known as the witty editor of the *Louisville Journal*, now the *Courier-Journal*, managed by Henry Watterson. Many were the literary favors I received from Prentice. He was a graduate of Brown, an admirable instructor, a ripe scholar, had a wonderful memory, and was a skillful wrestler. I have seen him, on a wager, read two large pages in a strange book twice through, and then repeat them without a miss.—STANTON, HENRY B., 1886, *Random Recollections, p.* 17

GENERAL

The poetical compositions of Mr. Prentice were written several years since, and many of them while he was a member of college. They were published in the "Review," and various other periodicals, but have never been collected. They have been very generally circulated, and have gained for their author, in its widest sense, a "newspaper reputation." They are characterized at times by great strength of thought and expression, and at others by tender feeling and delicate fancy. If their author would devote more of his time to such composition, he might win for himself a high name among the sons of song.—EVEREST, CHARLES W., 1843, *The Poets of Connecticut, p.* 321.

Whatever may be the sacrilege of giving utterance to such an opinion, I cannot forego saying, that in my estimation, George D. Prentice is one of the most perfect masters of blank verse in America, and that his writings in that style contain as much of the genuine element of genius in poetry as those of any of our countrymen. To such as question this decision, I can but refer to his two poems—one upon the "Flight of Years," and his lines upon the "Mammoth Cave." His "Dead

Mariner," and other rhymed pieces, evince how exquisite a master he is of versification. He has a fine musical ear, and the harmony of his numbers flows with the most mellifluous measure, while his verse is graced with diction as chaste as it is elegant. Every thing he preserves in the amber of his poesy is selected with unerring taste. What he has written as a poet only makes us wish for more.—FOSDICK, WILLIAM W., 1860, *The Poets and Poetry of the West, ed. Coggeshall, p. 121.*

His poetry is of the highest and sweetest order. His "Lines at My Mother's Grave" are among the most affecting, heartfelt expressions of love and sorrow ever uttered. They are the overflowings of a full heart which often throbs with fine and worthy sentiment. His poems are not very extensive, and of late years do not usually evince his old ardor. . . . His prose literary works are few. "A Life of Henry Clay" was written long ago, but never proved a success, and has now gone completely out of print. He lived with Clay at his home in Ashland for several months in order to complete the work, and became a bosom friend of the great statesman. He also published, about nine years ago, a book of witty paragraphs entitled, "Prenticeana," but it was a tasteless rehash of the short witticisms that had appeared from time to time in the *Journal,* and which, being clipped of their personal or political bearing, lost their prominent points. The book proved a complete failure. He regretted seriously that he had ever permitted its publication, and protested strongly against the title, "Prenticeana" which his publishers, had substituted for his own more modest designation. He also had two or three lectures which he was in the habit of delivering during the season, but they were not in his best style and none of them claimed to be witty. On the contrary, they were dull and didactic. His audiences, from his general reputation, had a right to expect a bright, humorous discussion, and were consequently seriously disappointed on being treated to a dry essay on the aspect of American politics.—SHANKS CHARLES, G., 1869, *George D. Prentice, Lippincott's Magazine, vol. 4, p. 558.*

I am disposed to think there is no other American poet, except Mr. Bryant, who has so finely handled blank verse as Mr. Prentice has done in several of his principal poems. His blank verse, indeed, occasionally suggests a resemblance to that of Mr. Bryant, although much more of emotional element and warmth of color—the visible life of human passion—are noticeable in it. He lacked that careful eye for the little half-secrets of Nature shown by Mr. Bryant, but his real love of Nature was no less true. . . If "Thanatopsis" is Mr. Bryant's representative poem in blank verse, "The Closing Year" may be said to be that of Mr. Prentice—it has long been so at least in popular regard. I do not know where there may be found a more stately and solemn meditation on the flight of Time, and the changes wrought thereby, than this poem presents; and I doubt if in English poetry there exists a more striking or loftier personification of Time, and allusion to his conquests, than its concluding lines afford.—PIATT, JOHN JAMES, 1875, *ed The Poems of George D. Prentice, Biographical Sketch, pp. xxvi, xxvii.*

All men have their weaknesses. Poetry, or what he was kind enough to believe such, was one of Prentice's weaknesses. In his youth, and later in life, he had done some very creditable versification, and on that account had been thrust before his time into the Southern Valhalla of song. He is entitled, perhaps, to a third rank among American poets; but, pushed into loftier company, the disharmony of his surroundings is unpleasantly apparent. He used to be greatly lauded for the incitement he had furnished to the wooers of the Muses. It is unfortunate that, with all their striving, not a single sister of the Nine was won. Prentice, from his amiability and overappreciation, is responsible for a vast deal of the quantitative fustian that still goes to the provincial press, and, missing its way to the waste-basket, gets to the composing room.—BROWNE, JUNIUS HENRI, 1875, *George D. Prentice, Harper's Magazine, vol. 50, p. 196.*

It is only six years since the author died; it is hardly sixteen since his "Closing Year" reappeared in many newspapers on every 31st of December. Yet, as we turn back to half-remembered poems and recall their former currency,—as we hear accents which are already beginning to sound strange to our ears, and scan with a sudden wonder forms of poetic expression once so welcome and familiar, the great gulf between free, self-asserting poetic genius, and poetic taste of even a very lofty and genuine character, is once more suggested. We do not know that Mr. Prentice ever claimed the title of poet; it was rather forced upon him by the many personal friends who heard in his verse the expression of the ardent, sincere, generous nature they loved. He never seemed to care especially—at least, not with the absorbing fondness and jealousy of the poets who feel their consecration—for the lyrics, in which the music of his emotions, rather than of his intellect or imagination, made itself heard. We can not judge him, therefore, according to the standard of artistic achievement; we must simply ask what he designed, and how far he has been successful therein.—TAYLOR, BAYARD, 1876, *Three Old and Three New Poets, The International Review, vol.* 3, *p.* 406.

His best work was in dashes of from two to ten lines, each with a "fist." The leaders were unrivaled as leaders, but they had not the keen sparkle of the inexhaustible Prentice paragraphs. His poems also had many fond readers, and he had a following of poets and poetesses whose efforts he carried with a few flattering and taking lines for each poetic gem; and it would have been unsafe to say that they were not all gems. There must have been at times a dozen ladies, each with the gift of song, contributing to the beautifully printed pages of the *Journal* of Louisville, and they never contributed lines, few or many, that they were not framed in words

of editorial praise, always pleasant and felicitous; and the poetry of the paper was held to be as valuable an attraction as its politics.—HALSTEAD, MURAT, 1892, *Early Editorial Experiences, Lippincott's Magazine, vol.* 49, *p.* 711.

I cannot say that I knew George D. Prentice, although I have had conversations with him. It would be hard under present press conditions to make intelligible his exact position in journalism. We looked at him as an erratic, ever-shining star,—a wonder in the Southwestern skies. There seemed no end to his genius,—that daily stream of wit, comment, verse, the saying of the oddest things in ten lines, a style with the freshness of spring, gayety, courtesy, snapping fire when provoked, but always marked with humanity and patriotism. Prentice was an American whose Americanism spread from sea to sea. He was neither insular, parochial, nor mountain-hemmed. There was as much in the granite of Massachusetts or the Louisiana loam as in the blue-grass of Kentucky. The soil to be sacred had simply to be American. That Kentucky remained true to the Union was due to George D. Prentice. I thought of this with reverent gratitude to his memory as I stood by his grave, not so many years ago.—YOUNG, JOHN RUSSELL, 1893, *Men who Reigned, Lippincott's Magazine, vol.* 51, *p.* 194.

Prentice delighted in giving pain with his caustic pen, and he used his great power of satire with reckless disregard of the feelings of his opponents.—PICKARD, SAMUEL T., 1894, *Life and Letters of John Greenleaf Whittier, vol.* I, *p.* 83.

John Pendleton Kennedy
1795–1870

Author and legislator; born in Baltimore, Md., Oct. 25, 1795; was educated at the University of Maryland; served for a short time in the war of 1812, after which he studied law, but devoted much of his time to literature, editing a new publication entitled *The Red Book*. He was elected to the State Legislature in 1820; was a member of Congress 1839–45, and in 1852 he was appointed by President Fillmore Secretary of the Navy. As the head of the Navy Department the Japanese expedition of Commodore Perry and the second Artic exploration of Dr. Kane were mainly due to him. In politics Kennedy had been an earnest Whig of the Henry Clay school, but early showed strong anti-slavery feelings, and during the civil war his sympathies were entirely on the Federal side. Died at Newport, R. I., Aug. 18, 1870. He is best known as the author of works of fiction, among which are "Swallow Barn" (1832); "Horseshoe Robinson" (1835), a tale of Revolutionary times; and "Rob of the Bowl" (1838), the scene of which is laid in Maryland in Colonial times.—ADAMS, CHARLES KENDALL, 1897, *rev. Johnson's Universal Cyclopædia, vol.* IV.

PERSONAL

From youth up he has had the good fortune to possess an ample competence, and a temperament that enabled him to take the world as he found it, without permitting himself to be annoyed by its trifles or its cares. He is, moreover, prudent in his style of living; and while not averse to a reasonable enjoyment of the gifts of Providence, is rigidly exact in his habits. This may account for the manner in which years have almost insensibly stolen upon him without leaving those tell-tale evidences that usually accompany their progress. But while thus placid in his domestic life, he has been an ardent politician, and in this capacity has filled several important positions, the last of which was Secretary of the Navy during the administration of Mr. Fillmore.—WYNNE, JAMES, 1862, *John P. Kennedy, Harper's Magazine, vol. 25, p.* 335.

Mr. Kennedy, as a man, was greater and better than all his books. One certainly looks in vain in all that he wrote or did for the full measure of those gifts and acquirements of mind and heart, that learning and wisdom, that wit and humor, that whole-souled cordiality and gayety and kindness, which shone out so conspicuously in the intimacies of daily intercourse. A truer friend or more charming companion has rarely been found or lost by those who have enjoyed the privilege of his companionship and friendship; and among those may be counted not a few of our most distinguished authors and statesmen.—WINTHROP, ROBERT C., 1870, *Addresses and Speeches, vol.* III, *p.* 77.

GENERAL

This ["Swallow Barn"] is a work of great merit and promise. It is attributed to a gentleman of Baltimore, already advantageously known to the public by several productions of less compass, and in various styles, but all excellent in their respective ways. The present attempt proves that he combines, with the talent and spirit which he had previously exhibited, the resource, perseverance and industry, that are necessary to the accomplishment of extensive works. We do not know that we can better evince our friendly feeling for him than by expressing the wish that the success which this production has met with may induce him to withdraw his attention from other objects, and devote himself entirely to the elegant pursuits of polite literature, for which his taste and talent are so well adapted, and in which the *demand for labor,*—to borrow an expression from a science, to which he is no stranger,—is still more pressing than in law, political economy, or politics.— EVERETT, ALEXANDER HILL, 1833, *Swallow Barn, North American Review, vol.* 36, *p.* 519.

Mr. Kennedy is altogether one of our most genial, lively, and agreeable writers. His style is airy, easy, and graceful, but various, and always in keeping with his subject. He excels both as a describer and as a raconteur. His delineations of nature are picturesque and truthful, and his sketches of character are marked by unusual freedom and delicacy. He studies the periods which he attempts to illustrate with the greatest care, becomes thoroughly imbued with their spirit, and writes of them with the enthusiasm and the apparent sincerity and earnestness of a contemporary and an actor. He pays an exemplary regard to the details of costume, manners, and opinion, and is scarce ever detected in any kind of anachronism. There are some inequalities in his works, arising perhaps from the interruptions to which a man in active public life is liable; there is occasional diffuseness and redundance of incident as well as of expression; but his faults are upon the surface, and could be easily removed.—GRISWOLD, RUFUS WILMOT, 1847-70, *The Prose Writers of America, p.* 343.

The position occupied by Kennedy as a writer is a prominent and highly respectable one. He is best known to the public as the author of "Swallow Barn" and "Horseshoe Robinson," two very popular and well written novels, whose scenes are laid in the Southern states, and whose incidents turn upon the peculiarities of Southern life as it presented itself nearly a century ago. . . . Although Kennedy has rendered good service to his country as a politician, yet, after all, it is to be regretted that he did not devote himself more exclusively to literature, for which he has certainly exhibited rare ability. Side by side with Scott's Meg Merrilies, of Cooper's Leather Stocking, of Dickens's Sam Weller, and of Irving's Rip Van Winkle, Horseshoe Robinson must be recognized as a real and veritable creation which occupies a permanent place in the minds of those who are familiar with the story.— WYNNE, JAMES, 1862, *John P. Kennedy, Harper's Magazine, vol. 25, pp. 335, 340.*

Mr. Kennedy wrote with delightful ease and freshness. His works are evidently the natural product of his thought and observation, and are pervaded by the happy genial temperament which characterized the man in his personal relations. We have a full reproduction in his volumes of the old Virginia life, with its old-time ideas of repose, content, and solid comfort; its hearty out-door existence, and the "humors" which are apt, in a fixed state of society, to develop quaint features in master and dependents. The author's books abound in delightful rural pictures and sketches of character, which, in easy style and quiet genial humor, recall the Sketch Book and Bracebridge Hall. The author has himself acknowledged the relationship in the graceful tribute to Irving which forms the dedication to the volume.—DUYCKINCK, EVERT A., AND GEORGE L., 1865–75, *Cyclopædia of American Literature, ed. Simons, vol. I, p. 950.*

When "Swallow Barn" first appeared few vivid and faithful pictures of American life had been executed. Paulding had described Dutch Colonial life in New York; Tudor had published letters from New England; Flint and Hall had given us graphic sketches from the West, toward which virgin domain the tide of emigration had set; but, with the exception of a few impressive and finished legendary tales from the then unappreciated pen of Hawthorne and the genuine American novels, the "Spy" and the "Pioneer," of Cooper, American authorship had scarcely surveyed, far less invaded, the rich fields of local tradition and native life. Accordingly "Swallow Barn" met with a prompt and cordial reception. Emanating from a man of leisure, it was hailed as the precursor of a series of works imbued with the spirit and devoted to the illustration of our history, scenery, and manners.—TUCKERMAN, HENRY T., 1870, *Life of John Pendleton Kennedy.*

Mr. Kennedy was a fluent and often elegant writer, and showed, in his descriptions, a love of the beautiful and a refined taste.— UNDERWOOD, FRANCIS H., 1872, *A Hand-Book of English Literature, American Authors, p. 162.*

This single creation ["Horseshoe Robinson"] lifts the work of Kennedy into national importance.—MORSE, JAMES HERBERT, 1883, *The Native Element in American Fiction, Century Magazine, vol. 26, p. 293.*

Mr. Kennedy's writings were very popular during his life-time and deserve to be so still, for his three novels give graphic and excellent pictures of their times, and are true in their historical details.—MANLY, LOUISE, 1895, *Southern Literature, p. 205.*

Among the most accomplished of the many brilliant men who adorned American public life during this period.—NOBLE, CHARLES, 1898, *Studies in American Literature, p. 130.*

George Grote

1794–1871

Born, at Clay Hill, Kent, 17 Nov. 1794. At school at Sevenoakes, June 1800 to 1804. At Charterhouse, 1804–10. Lived at home, 1810–20. Clerk in his father's bank, 1810–16; partner, 1816–43. Married Harriet Lewin, 5 March 1820. Active part in promotion of London University, opened 1828; Mem. of Council, 1828–71. Contrib. to "Westminster Rev.," 1826, 1843 and 1866; to "Spectator," 1839 and 1847; to "Classical Museum," 1844; to "Edinburgh Rev.," 1856. Travelled on Continent, 1830. M. P. for City of London, Dec. 1831, Jan. 1835, and July 1837. Travelled in Italy, Oct. 1841 to spring of 1842. Retired from banking, 1843. F. G. S., 1843. Resided partly in London, partly at Burnham Beeches. Visit to Paris, 1844; to Switzerland, 1847. Mem. of Council of University Coll., 1850; Treasurer, 1860; President, 1868–71. Elected on Governing body of new University of London, 1850; Vice-Chancellor, 1862. Trustee of British Museum, 1859. D. C. L., Oxford, 1853. F. R. S., 1857. Correspondent of French Acad. of Moral and Political Sciences, 1857; Foreign Associate, 1864. Prof. of Ancient History to Royal Academy, 1859. Foreign Mem. of Institute of France, Feb. 1864. Refused Peerage, Nov. 1869. Died, in London, 18 June 1871; buried in Westminster Abbey. *Works:* "Statement of the

Question of Parliamentary Reform," 1821; "Analysis of the Influence of Natural Religion" (under pseud. of Philip Beauchamp), 1822; "Essentials of Parliamentary Reform," 1831; "History of Greece," vols. i., ii., 1846; vols. iii., iv., 1847; vols. v., vi., 1848; vols. vii., viii., 1850; vols. ix., x., 1852; vol. xi., 1853; vol. xii., 1856; "Seven Letters on the Recent Politics of Switzerland" (from "Spectator"), 1847; "Plato's Doctrine respecting the Rotation of the Earth," 1860; "Plato and the other Companions of Sokrates," 1865; Review of J. S. Mill's "Examination of Hamilton" (from "Westminster Rev."), 1868 [1867]. *Posthumous:* "Aristotle," ed. by A. Bain and G. C. Robertson (2 vols.), 1872; "Poems" (priv. ptd.), 1872; "Minor Works," ed. by A. Bain, 1873; "Posthumous Papers" (priv. ptd.), 1874; "Fragments on Ethical Subjects," ed. by A. Bain, 1876.   He *edited:* G. Waddington's "History of the Reformation," 1841; J. Mill's "Analysis of the Phenomena of the Human Mind," 1869.   *Life:* by Mrs. Grote, 1873.—SHARP, R. FARQUHARSON, 1897, *A Dictionary of English Authors, p.* 120.

PERSONAL

You are right as to Mrs. Grote; she is, and will be for ever, jealous of everybody who puts Grote into the shade. She ought, in truth, to be jealous of Grote, for he himself causes his own eclipse. If he would *do* anything, his reward in praise and esteem would be boundless.—ROEBUCK, JOHN ARTHUR, 1837, *Letter to Mrs. Roebuck, Jan.* 6; *Life and Letters, ed. Leader, p.* 88.

Mr. and Mrs. Grote have been staying here some days. She is very clever and very odd. Grote is a reasonable and reasoning Radical, with manners a little formal but very polished.—SMITH, SYDNEY, 1843, *To Lady Holland, Oct.* 9; *Life and Times by Reid, p.* 377.

He is very kind-hearted, and with most genuine, childlike simplicity of manner, not always found in company with such exuberant and accurate erudition as he possesses. Mrs. Grote is a character, very firm, decided, clever, accomplished, strong-minded, tall, and robust, whom Sydney Smith called the most gentleman-like of women. She is very droll in her dress, despising crinoline and flounces, and attiring herself, when going out for a walk, in a shawl thrown over her shoulders and tied round her waist, with a poplin gown reaching to the tops of her boots, a tall, brown, man's hat, with a feather in it, and a stout walking-stick. She is the best company in the world, full of originality and humour, has seen and known every remarkable person in England and France, and is full of anecdotes about everybody and everything.—MOTLEY, JOHN LOTHROP, 1860, *To his Mother, Feb.* 13; *Correspondence, ed. Curtis, vol.* I, *p.* 333.

Similarity of literary taste, study, and knowledge gained for Sir George Lewis the intimate friendship of George Grote. He valued Mr. Grote's opinion and judgment so highly, that few, if any, of his pleasures exceeded that which he took in discussing with the learned historian of Greece, not only subjects connected with early history and philosophy, but likewise topics connected with politics and passing events. He had also great enjoyment in the society of Mrs. Grote, with whose varied and brilliant conversation he was always entertained.—LEWIS, SIR GILBERT FRANKLAND, 1870, *ed. Letters of the Right Hon. Sir George Cornewall Lewis, p.* 112.

Unlike most persons who have the prospect of being rich by inheritance, he had, though actively engaged in the business of banking, devoted a great portion of time to philosophic studies; and his intimacy with my father did much to decide the character of the next stage in his mental progress. Him I often visited, and my conversations with him on political, moral, and philosophical subjects gave me, in addition to much valuable instruction, all the pleasure and benefit of sympathetic communion with a man of the high intellectual and moral eminence which his life and writings have since manifested to the world. —MILL, JOHN STUART, 1873, *Autobiography, p.* 73.

The historian of Greece, one of the few serious English men of letters who has made his mark all the world over, within the past half century, was for many years indulgently kind to me. A more noble-hearted and accomplished gentleman than he who has departed full of years, and rich in honours, I have never seen. When the word "gentleman" is used, it is with express reference to that courtesy and consideration of manner which appears to me dying out of the world. Four men that I have known, the late Duc de Grâmont, the Duke of Ossuna, the late Duke of Beaufort, and Mr. Grote, in their high breeding and deference to women, in their instinctive avoidance of any topic or expression which could possibly give pain, recur to me as unparagoned.—CHORLEY, HENRY FOTHERGILL, 1873, *Autobiography, Memoir and Letters, vol.* I, *p.* 213.

In the depths of his character there was a fund of sympathy, generosity, and self-denial, rarely equalled among men; on the exterior, his courtesy, affability, and delicate consideration of the feelings of others were indelibly impressed upon every beholder; yet this amiability of demeanour was never used to mislead, and in no case relaxed his determination for what he thought right. Punctual and exact in his engagements, he inspired a degree of confidence and respect which acted most beneficially on all the institutions and trusts that he took a share in administering, and his loss to them was a positive calamity.—BAIN, ALEXANDER, 1873, *The Intellectual Character and Writings of George Grote.*

It was on the 7th of December, 1843, that I first met with George Grote, who, shaking off for the first time in thirty years the trammels of a banking house, had come to pass the winter in Italy. He was not yet known as a great historian, but as a strenuous advocate of parliamentary reform on the floor of St. Stephen's, and a student who might one day tread boldly in the footprints of Niebuhr. He came well provided with letters, and among them were two to me. . . . I held at that time the office of United States consul, and the day on which Grote presented his letters was my reception day, or rather my reception evening, and I sent him a card. Evening came; the rooms were filling fast; the broken ice of the first half-hour was well-nigh melted; acquaintances were gathering in groups, and strangers casting about them for a face that they might have seen before, when Grote was announced. I can see him now, —a man somewhat above the common height, with the air and bearing of one accustomed to act and be acted upon by his fellow-men, and mind written all over his spacious brow. You felt at once that you were in the presence of a remarkable man. . . . I have often regretted that, though I passed a month in daily intercourse with Grote, I kept no record of his conversation;

and I have regretted it all the more from the impression it made upon me at the time. He was not like Johnson, an over-whelming talker, nor like Macaulay, an eloquent talker, much less like Sydney Smith, a scintillating and brilliant talker; but he was an earnest and truth-loving talker, who made social intercourse a means of testing and elucidating his subject. . . . His manner corresponded with his matter,—calm, firm, and earnest; and though a frequent speaker in the House of Commons, he never put on the tone of a declaimer at the dinner table or an evening circle. His words were well chosen, neither elaborately Saxon, nor fastidiously Latin, but coming freely at his bidding from either source. The structure of his sentences was simple and direct, rising at times to eloquence under the inspiration of his deep convictions, but leaving something, perhaps, to desire in harmony and variety. He would seem, indeed, to have contented himself with a secondary place among pictorial historians, if he could but make for himself a sure place among the philosophers who have written history.—GREENE, GEORGE WASHINGTON, 1879, *Reminiscences of George Grote, The Atlantic Monthly, vol.* 44, *pp.* 770, 772.

After waiting two years in vain for his father's consent, Harriet Lewin met George Grote one March morning, 1820, at a neighboring church, where they were married early enough for her to take her usual place at the breakfast-table. . . . Mr. Grote shared his wife's tastes for poetry, painting and music, and even played the violoncello himself. They differed as to society, for he was both reserved and shy— she, as we have observed, neither, though awfully "stately," while little known. But her character in this respect overbore his; for society, especially of clever men, gravitated towards both of them as by a natural law. The way in which the young couple affected each other was very remarkable. Each gave and took an education. He endowed her mind with a more solid basis, she fashioned, mounted, framed and glazed him. People would not have missed the profounder instruction he imparted to her; she would always have been deep enough, and more than brilliant enough for society, but without her he would have remained, socially, and in a publicly literary sense, almost unknown.—EASTLAKE, ELIZABETH LADY, 1880, *Mrs. Grote, pp.* 42, 43.

Bishop Thirlwall was buried in Grote's grave 3 Aug., 1875.—STANLEY, ARTHUR PENRHYN, 1881, *ed. Letters to a Friend by Connop Thirlwall, p.* 270, *note.*

Direct successors of the Grotes were still doing business in 1885 on the site of the original banking-house, on Threadneedle Street, corner of Bartholomew Lane.——HUTTON, LAURENCE, 1885, *Literary Landmarks of London, p.* 130.

To courage and tenacity of intellectual purpose, with single-minded devotion to public ends, Grote joined an unfailing courtesy of nature and great dignity of demeanour. A certain shyness of manner was the outward token of an unaffected modesty that was beautiful to see in one whose work of its kind, for quantity and quality taken together, has never been surpassed. Consideration for others, on a full equality with self, was his guiding principle of action. It made him, as he was in private the most conscientious and methodical of workers, a man who could be absolutely relied upon in association, punctual and regular to a proverb in everything that he undertook with others, and scrupulously fairminded in all his judgments. At the same time, under the calm exterior there lay, as those who knew him best were aware, enthusiasms and fires of passion which took all his strength of reason and will to control.—ROBERTSON, G. CROOM, 1890, *Dictionary of National Biography, vol.* xxiii, *p.* 292.

The historian Grote and his wife also made our acquaintance. I especially remember her appearance because it was, and was allowed to be, somewhat *grotesque.* She was very tall and stout in proportion, and was dressed on this occasion [1843] in a dark-green or blue silk, with a necklace of pearls about her throat. I gathered from what I heard that hers was one of the marked personalities of that time in London society.— HOWE, JULIA WARD, 1899, *Reminiscences,* 1819–1899. *p.* 93.

HISTORY OF GREECE
1846–56

Endeavour to become acquainted with Mr. Grote, who is engaged on a Greek History; he, too, will receive you well if you take him my regards. If you become better acquainted with him, it is worth your while to obtain the proof-sheets of his work, in order to translate it. I expect a great deal from this production, and I will get you a publisher here.—NIEBUHR, BARTHOLD GEORG, 1827, *Letter to Professor Lieber.*

You have, no doubt, been enjoying, as I have, Grote's "History." High as my expectations were of it, it has very much surpassed them all, and affords an earnest of something which has never been done for the subject either in our own or any other literature. It has afforded me some gratification to find that in the flood of new light which he has poured upon it his views do not appear greatly to diverge from mine on more than a few important points, and those of a special nature not involving any general principles. For though I am not yet satisfied with the limits he prescribes in his first volume to the investigations which occupy a part of mine, I think it would be found on a further analysis that the difference between us is not very material.—THIRLWALL, CONNOP, 1846, *To Dr. Schmitz, April* 9; *Letters, ed. Perowne and Stokes, p.* 194.

I am reading Grote's "History." Wonderful it seems to me that a writer so fresh from the Attic, and particularly so conversant with Thucydides, should stand up to his chin among the greengrocery of Covent-garden! It would however be ungrateful to collect blemishes of language from an author to whom we are indebted for so much diligence and information, so much learning and wisdom.—LANDOR, WALTER SAVAGE, 1852, *Letter, Oct.; Walter Savage Landor, a Biography, by John Forster.*

A decided liberal, perhaps even a republican, in politics, Mr. Grote has laboured to counteract the influence of Milford in Grecian history, and construct a history of Greece from authentic materials, which should illustrate the animating influence of democratic freedom upon the exertions of the human mind. In the prosecution of this attempt he has displayed an extent of learning, a variety of research, a power of combination, which are worthy of the very highest praise, and have secured for him a lasting place among the historians of modern Europe.—ALISON, SIR ARCHIBALD, 1853, *History of Europe,* 1815-1852, *ch.* v.

Has penetrated more deeply than any writer of any country, into all the depths of the ancient philosophy. Others may have equalled him in descriptions of the heroism with which the Greeks, under Leonidas and Themistocles, repelled the invasion of the Persian monarch at Thermopylæ and Salamis, and retaliated it by the overthrow of his descendent at Issus and Arbela; or of the more painful contest when Athenians and Spartans turned their fratricidal arms against each other, and when the intestine strife of rival factions laid the greater nation prostrate at the mercy of its rival, and a way was thus prepared for the supremacy over both of a northern people who in the days of Xerxes were hardly acknowledged to be Greeks. But the teachings of philosophy are of wider and more enduring influence than the triumphs of the warrior; and in a judicious appreciation, in a clear and eloquent explanation, of the doctrines of Plato and Aristotle, of their diversity, and of their value, not only to the Athenians of their own day, but to the people of all other countries and of all subsequent generations, no one has approached Mr. Grote.—YONGE, CHARLES DUKE, 1872, *Three Centuries of English Literature*, p. 177.

Mr. Grote possessed that essential quality of a historian—the historical or narrative interest. In school days he devoured novels; in later life the place of these was taken by histories and biographies relating to every nation and time. He felt and avowed the still more peculiar interest in the process of growth or evolution, whether in political institutions, in literature, or in philosophy and science. The historical taste was thus with him a very wide and mixed susceptibility, and his narrative compositions became correspondingly varied in their interest. His earnest devotion to mental science, in all departments—psychology, ethics, metaphysics, and logic —had no small share in the characteristic excellencies of his historical compositions.— BAIN, ALEXANDER, 1873, *The Intellectual Character and Writings of George Grote*, p. 66.

I have understood that it was at the suggestion of Mr. James Mill, that Mr. Grote first thought of writing his History; and there seems to be no doubt that it was partly through the influence of Mr. James Mill, and of the other followers of Bentham (who is said to have called poetry "misrepresentation in verse"), that Mr. Grote laboured to repress his naturally strong imaginative faculty, and wrote in a style clear and forcible, but studiously unadorned. It was, perhaps, partly owing to this circumstance that he, as I have said, preferred the simple but rather unformed and diffuse style of Buckle to the style of Macaulay.—TOLLEMACHE, LIONEL A., 1873, *Recollections of Mr. Grote and Mr. Babbage, Macmillan's Magazine*, vol. 27, p. 493.

So much research and sound thinking had resulted in an achievement which set the author at once in the front rank of modern historians.—DAVIES, JAMES, 1873, *George Grote, Contemporary Review*, vol. 22, p. 401.

As a scholar, Thirlwall was Grote's superior. He equalled Grote in knowledge and probably surpassed him in judgment. The Bishop further possessed a greater command of style than his rival, who though a forcible is always an awkward and occasionally an incorrect writer. Grote, nevertheless, as the Bishop had the singular generosity both to see and admit, produced a work which has permanently thrown Dr. Thirlwall's meritorious labors into the shade. The cause of this is that Grote, with some defects, shows a force or grasp and above all an originality of mind and boldness of conception quite foreign to the somewhat episcopal caution of the Bishop's intellect. But this boldness in speculation is due, if in part to nature, in great measure also to the philosophy of James Mill, which taught his pupils not to be overawed by received opinions. . . . Grote's success at least is due above all things to the intellectual boldness which, while it did not lead him to waste his strength on the maintenance of unprofitable paradoxes, enabled him to look at the waste of the past with his own eyes unblinded by traditional phrases or prejudices sanctioned by a weight of high authority.—DICEY, A. V., 1874, *Grote's Character as an Historian, The Nation*, vol. 19, p. 91.

Grote was a man of extraordinary attainments, and an earnest lover of truth. His style is excellent, and his work on Greece ranks with Gibbon's classical work on Rome.—SCHERR, J., 1874, *A History of English Literature*, tr. M. V., p. 284.

Grote's learning, sagacity, candour, and perfect mastery over his materials give his work a place among the very few great histories which England has produced. But its literary execution is by no means firstrate; he never seems to have realised that prose composition is an art.—NICOLL,

HENRY J., 1882, *Landmarks of English Literature, p.* 429.

No one of the great historical works produced in the course of this century has received more general or more hearty commendation than has the work of Grote. It possesses nearly every quality of an historical work of the very highest order of merit. In extent of learning, in variety of research, in power of combination, in familiarity with the byways as well as the highways of Grecian literature, it leaves nothing whatever to be desired. Almost the only regret one feels in making use of this noble work is that the author never acquired a mastery of an easy, correct, and graceful English style. His sentences are often involved and awkward, and sometimes obscure and ungrammatical. This, to be sure, is a small drawback, when placed in comparison with the great merits of the work; but it is sufficient to drive many readers from its pages.—ADAMS, CHARLES KENDALL, 1882, *A Manual of Historical Literature, p.* 91.

Grote's "History of Greece" is undoubtedly a work of considerable value, though lacking the literary merit which is that of Thirlwall. It is an extraordinarily elaborate work, which contains perhaps all that can be said—or could be said then—on its subject, and enters at great length upon many matters, apparently of detail, which less careful historians are apt to slur over. Though we cannot say that it contains nothing but information, there can certainly be little complaint as to anything being left out, and to the student, whose interest in history is limited to facts, there is much to be learned from Grote. It may be said that he occasionally is too exact in following the ancient historians; his account of the Athenian expedition against Syracuse and the earlier years of the Peloponnesian war generally, being little more than a translation from Thucydides, including even the imaginary speeches put by that great historian into the mouths of the various statesmen and embassadors of his period. As a literary work, the prolix and tedious history can hardly be said to have any merit.—OLIPHANT, MARGARET O. W., 1892, *The Victorian Age of English Literature, p.* 195.

Grote's history displays immense painstaking and no inconsiderable scholarship, though it is very nearly as much a "party pamphlet" as Macaulay's own, the advocate's client being in this case not merely the Athenian democracy, but even the Athenian demagogue. Yet it to a great extent redeems this by the vivid way in which it makes the subject alive, and turns Herodotus and Thucydides, Demosthenes and Xenophon, from dead texts and school-books into theses of eager and stimulating interest. But it has absolutely no style; its scale is much too great; the endless discussions and arguments on quite minor points tend to throw the whole out of focus, and to disaccustom the student's eye and mind to impartial and judicial handling; and the reader constantly sighs for the placid Olympian grasp of Gibbon, nay, even for the confident dogmatism of Macaulay himself, instead of the perpetual singlestick of argument which clatters and flourishes away to the utter discomposure of the dignity of the Historic Muse.— SAINTSBURY, GEORGE, 1896, *A History of Nineteenth Century Literature, p.* 221.

Though wanting alike in the style and the scholarship of Thirlwall's history, and too often declining in its political disquisitions to the level of a mere Radical pamphlet, yet by the animation and graphic power of its narrative deserved at least some measure of the popularity which it obtained.—TRAILL, HENRY DUFF, 1897, *Social England, vol.* VI, *p.* 280.

Grote's history is a book of high educational value. In it we have all that is best in Herodotus, Thucydides, and the other ancient historians, added to the sound and weighty judgment of a clear-sighted modern critic, exceptionally free from the erroneous impressions which had so long prevailed as to the real character of the Athenian democracy, and we cannot find elsewhere a truer or juster picture of Athens at the height of her power.—SHORTER, CLEMENT, 1897, *Victorian Literature, Sixty Years of Books and Bookmen, p.* 101.

Grote's style is heavy and ungainly. He plods along, correct as a rule, but uninspiring and unattractive. He is similarly clumsy in the use of materials. Skillful selection might have appreciably shortened his history; but Grote rarely prunes with sufficient severity, and often he does not prune at all. His habit of pouring out the whole mass of his material in the shape of notes lightens the labour of his successors, but injures his own work as an artistic history. Nevertheless, though Grote had no genius, and nothing that deserves to be called a style, his "History of Greece" holds the field. It does so because of its solidity and conscientious thoroughness, because of its patient investigation of the origin and meaning of institutions, and because its very faults were, after all, faults which sprang from sympathy. Grote was the first who did full justice to the Athenian people; and he may be pardoned if he sometimes did them more than justice.— WALKER, HUGH, 1897, *The Age of Tennyson, p.* 126.

The language is unequal; passages of great beauty are closely followed by others that are dull and wearisome.—ENGEL, EDWARD, 1902, *A History of English Literature,* rev. Hamley Bent, p. 468.

PLATO AND THE OTHER COMPANIONS OF SOKRATES
1865

The most entertaining of all that he has written. And the subject is worthy of him. The history of no mere man that the world has seen is equal to that of the little stonemason figure-cutter of Athens who used to ask questions. The noble galaxy of great spirits who surrounded him—Plato, Xenophon, Critias, Crito, each a king of men—was only fitted to be crowned by the philosophical monarch, who died as he would have slept, the chief actor in a tragedy without the strut of the tragedian, the victim in a martyrdom without the song and crown of the martyr. We need not recommend Mr. Grote's work, but we will urge our readers to get it. If they want to get rid of contemporary nonsense, and to clear their minds of cant, while they fill them with great and sublime images, they should read of Plato and Socrates in the pages of Grote.—FRISWELL, JAMES HAIN, 1870, *Modern Men of Letters Honestly Criticised, p.* 189.

Grote's work is rich in suggestion and instruction; the author of the "History of Greece" maintains here his masterly superiority in historical presentation, but his acceptance as genuine of all the dialogues accredited by Thrasyllus has caused him to lose sight of the essential unity present in Plato's thought and works, and to admit in its stead a multifariousness abounding in change and contradiction.— —UEBERWEG, FRIEDRICH, 1871, *A History of Philosophy, tr. Morris, vol.* I, p. 110.

It is, necessarily, a less popular and less widely-known work than its predecessor; but has an equal if not a superior value, as a permanent addition to literature; for, while history teaches affairs by examples, the results of all profound philosophical thought. must, more or less, aid in the solution of the deepest and gravest problems which affect humanity. The felicities of Grote's style have done much to lighten the abstract tenor of the instruction conveyed by the "Plato"; he seems equally at home in the soberly-lighted porch of the Stoics, and among the revels of Olympus, and the shows at Corinth; and comprehends equally the value to all mankind of a Platonic aphorism, and the significance of Mercury's or Vulcan's godlike attributes. The intellectual activity and results of the Socratic age, the previous preparation in the Greek commonwealth for the advent of this remarkable school, and its influence upon that country at periods remotely subsequent, are clearly comprehended by Grote, who gives to his exposition a profoundly critical discrimination and analysis, which are of especial value to the reader who is not already familiar with the subject.—TOWLE, GEORGE M., 1871, *George Grote, Appleton's Journal, vol.* 6, p. 87.

GENERAL

The first of living historians.—MARTINEAU, JAMES, 1861, *Plato, Essays Philosophical and Theological, vol.* II, *p.* 356.

The accomplished historian of Greece, and the one-sided interpreter of Plato.— KNIGHT, WILLIAM, 1876-79, *Studies in Philosophy and Literature, p.* 5.

Mr. Grote's history of Greece is indeed a monumental piece of work. It has all that patience and exhaustive care which principally mark the German historians, and it has an earnestness which is not to be found generally in the representatives of what Carlyle has called the Dryasdust school. Grote threw himself completely into the life and the politics of Athens. It was said of him with some truth that he entered so thoroughly into all the political life of Greece as to become now and then the partisan of this or that public man. His own practical acquaintance with politics was undoubtedly of great service to him. We have all grown somewhat tired of hearing the words of Gibbon quoted in which he tells us that "the discipline and evolutions of a modern battalion gave me a clearer notion of the phalanx and the legion; and the captain of the Hampshire Grenadiers (the reader may smile) has not been useless to the historian of the Roman Empire." Assuredly the practical knowledge of politics which Grote acquired during the nine or ten years of his Parliamentary career was of much service to the historian of Greece. It has been said indeed of him that he never could quite keep from regarding the struggles of parties in Athens as exactly illustrating the principles disputed between the Liberals and the Tories in England. It does not seem to us, however, that his political career affected his historical studies in any way, but by throwing greater vitality and nervousness into his descriptions of Athenian controversies. The difference between a man who has mingled anywhere in the active life of politics, and one who only knows that life from books and the talk of others, is specially likely to show itself in such a study as Grote's history. His political training enabled Grote to see in the statesmen and soldiers of the Greek peoples men and not trees walking. It taught him how to make the dry bones live. Mr. Grote began life as what would have been called in later years a Philosophical Radical. He was a close friend of Stuart Mill, although he did not always agree with Mill in his opinions.—McCARTHY, JUSTIN, 1879, *A History of our Own Times from the Accession of Queen Victoria to the Berlin Congress, ch.* XXIX.

Mr. Grote must be pronounced, therefore, more of a Millite than John Stuart Mill himself. His attitude in the well-known controversy as to the Chair of Logic in University College in 1866, when Dr. James Martineau was a candidate, and was defeated almost entirely by his influence, is an unpleasant illustration of the same extreme tendency. The event is not one on which we are called to dwell; but it is highly significant, as showing how thoroughly so great an intellect can shut out all the influence of higher religious speculation, and intrench itself with undeviating complacency within the narrowest limits on so great a subject. This very intensity of negative dogmatism made Grote, to some extent, a power in his time even in relation to religion; it is the warrant of our touch-

ing his career at all in a manner in which we would rather have refrained from doing, seeing how great a figure he is otherwise. But the limits within which he confined his mind on this subject prove sufficiently that he was not, in any real sense, a teacher, and he can hardly be said to have exercised any definite influence on the development of religious thought.—TULLOCH, JOHN, 1885, *Movements of Religious Thought in Britain During the Nineteenth Century.*

Grote poured forth the precious contents of his portentous note-books with as little care for rhythm and as little sense of proportion as a German professor.—HARRISON, FREDERIC, 1895, *Studies in Early Victorian Literature, p.* 20.

In scope and conception all is admirable, but Grote's attitude is too confident, the very assurance of his knowledge in itself begets indefinable suspicions. The arguments are too good, the causes of things too abundantly evident, and despite the clearness of atmosphere we are not inclined to believe that the last secrets of the Hellenic temper and genius are presented to us in these pat conclusions of a disciple of Bentham. Were his reputation now in the balance, to part from so indefatigable a worker, and, despite his limitations, so strong a thinker and writer, with no word of praise, would be scant courtesy, and scanter appreciation. But we have passed in our intellectual development the point at which Grote, like his fellow-historian Macaulay, was an inspiring force, and no discriminating estimate could assign him the rank among Englishmen which he held among his contemporaries. Rhetoric has lost its ancient charm, we are no longer enamoured of logical vigour, unaccompanied by imaginative insight, or of style that lacks the light and shade everywhere present in nature. . . . . Indisputably, history was the field of Grote's best work, his equipment as historian embraced not a few of the essential qualities; a fresh and real interest in life, its colour, breadth, and variety, a true instinct for narrative, an impartial judgment, the patience of the student, and the knowledge of the man of affairs. A little more, and he might have been a great man; as it is, we can only say, that he is a commanding figure in the history of English scholarship.—DIXON, W. MACNEILE, 1896, *English Prose, ed. Craik, vol.* V, *pp.* 358, 359.

George Ticknor
1791–1871

Literary historian and biographer; born in Boston, Mass., Aug. 1, 1791; graduated at Dartmouth College in 1807; admitted to the bar in Boston in 1813; spent four years (1815–19) in study and travel in Europe, and during his absence was chosen (1817) to the Smith professorship of Modern Languages at Harvard; filled that post from 1820 to 1835, when he resigned; spent three years in Europe, chiefly engaged in preparatory researches for his principal work, to which he devoted several more years of assiduous labor; published in 1849 in London and New York his "History of Spanish Literature," which was translated into French, German, and Spanish, and accepted as the standard work on its subject even in Spain; printed some occasional essays, chiefly on educational topics, and several biographical sketches; wrote an elaborate "Life of William Hickling Prescott" (1864); contributed to various magazines and reviews; and was a munificent benefactor to the Boston Public Library, presenting it with 2,000 volumes in 1860. He was a member of the leading literary societies of Europe and the U. S. Died in Boston, Jan. 26, 1871. The 4th ed. of his "History of Spanish Literature" appeared shortly after his death under the editorship of George S. Hillard, who also published his "Life and Correspondence" (2 vols., Boston, 1876). See E. P. Whipple, "Recollections" (Boston, 1877), section on Ticknor.—BEERS, HENRY A., 1897, rev. *Johnson's Universal Cyclopædia, vol.* VIII, *p.* 149.

PERSONAL

In the evening I attended Ticknor's lecture, which was most beautiful and delightful, and on a subject as dry as possible. He explained to us on the map how languages progressed, and what was their origin. There is something very pleasing in his style and delivery, and he introduced figures very appropriately. But independently of this, there is a melody in his voice truly delightful.—QUINCY, JOSIAH, 1818, *Figures of the Past from the Leaves of Old Journals, p.* 22.

Mr. Ticknor has a great head, and his hair is gray or grayish. You recognize in him at once the man who knows the world, the scholar, too, which probably is his more distinctive character, though a little more under the surface. . . . Certainly, he is a fine example of a generous-principled scholar, anxious to assist the human intellect in its efforts and researches. Methinks he must have spent a happy life (as happiness goes among mortals), writing his great three-volumed book for twenty years; writing it, not for bread, nor with any uneasy desire of fame, but only with a purpose to achieve something true and enduring. He is, I apprehend, a man of great cultivation and refinement, and with quite substance enough to be polished and refined, without being worn too thin in the process,—a man of society.—HAWTHORNE, NATHANIEL, 1850. *American Note Books, May* 5, *vol.* II, *p.* 159.

It has been my happiness to know Mr. Ticknor long and well. I associate him with the pleasant memories of early life. I have accompanied him into the vale of declining age. I have known him youthful, social, genial, jovial. I have parted from him after more than sixty years' intercourse, infirm of limbs and of memory, but still courageous, still friendly, buoyant, and self-relying. Like many, even of the most gifted intellects of all times and ages, he has at last not always been able to complete the unfinished thought of the present hour; while at the same time the things, the persons, the readings of times long passed by, have remained, like the fern-prints and foot-tracks in ancient rocks, indelibly impressed on his remembrance.—BIGELOW, JACOB, 1871, *Letter to Robert C. Winthrop, Feb.* 8; *Proceedings of the Massachusetts Historical Society, vol.* XII, *p.* 23.

His qualities, his circumstances, and his opportunities were in some things unusual, in many things fortunate. He had the excellent gift of very decided tastes, in the good fortune of entire freedom. From the time when, a very young man, he took the then unusual step of going to study at Göttingen, to the last day of his life, he was singularly unhindered by circumstances. His two marked characteristics were a love of literature and a love of society, and they had full play for sixty years.—ADAMS, H., 1876, *Ticknor's Life, Letters, and Journals, North American Review, vol.* 123, *p.* 210.

Mr. Ticknor was the most marked type of the American man of letters and society of the first half of this century, as distinguished from the mere scholar or author.

GEORGE TICKNOR

Engraving by H. W. Smith. From a Photograph by Black, 1867.

EDWARD EVERETT

Engraving by J. C. Buttre. From a Photograph by Brady.

He combined traits not often found so happily mingled; his strong social tastes and his brilliant social gifts did not interfere with the steadiness of his literary industry or diminish the worth of its results. He had a fortunate temperament and an easy life. He was in fortunate relations to his times, and he succeeded in securing, together with such advantages as America could afford to a man of strong moral feeling, rational desires, and genial temper, the benefits of the best culture of Europe and the charms of its best society.—NORTON, CHARLES ELIOT, 1876, *The Nation, vol.* 22, *p.* 148.

No man, we imagine, was ever less troubled with self-dissatisfaction. He felt the limits of his faculties and qualities, if he felt them at all, only as useful and secure defences. Within them there was all the completeness that could be gained by persevering exercise and culture. There is not a page of his journals and letters that does not bear testimony to his earnest, careful and profitable study of men and books, while we doubt if a remark can be found in them that shows either sympathetic insight or subtle discrimination. His intellect had all its resources at command, but it had more of rigor than of vigor, more of formal precision in its methods than of well-directed force in its performances. Hence the semblence exceeded the reality, and it might have been said of him, as it was said of Guizot, "Il impose et il en impose."— PERRY, THOMAS SERGEANT, 1876, *The Life of George Ticknor, Lippincott's Magazine, vol.* 17, *p.* 634.

Were he living now, as a young man, he would probably be thought to be posing too much with reference to effect at magnificent distances. You hear him referred to by some as a literary autocrat. Cold he doubtless was, and conservative in the grain. One day when a young man was telling him of some new philosophical inquiries, he declared, with impatience, "John Locke settled all that for me, sir, years ago." Thackeray, however, made short work of his dignity when, as it is related. on the novelist's dining with him the historian of Spanish literature fell to musing of love. Ticknor resembled his guest in appearance, even to the latter's oddly shaped nose. "Yes, yes," assented Thackeray, listening to his rather sentimental monologue; "but, after all, what

have two broken-nosed old fellows like you and me got to do with love?" Another time, when a young Westerner, who was lecturing in Boston, was asked by Theodore Parker if he had seen Ticknor, "No," was the reply. "Well," Parker answered him, "you might as well go to hell without seeing the devil."—LATHROP, GEORGE PARSONS, 1881, *Literary and Social Boston, Harper's Magazine, vol.* 62, *p.* 385.

In Park Street, above the common, the ample mansion of George Ticknor—the chronicler of "Spanish Literature" and the autocrat of literary taste—was during many years a haunt of the best of Boston culture. We find its stately walls still standing, but the interior has been surrendered to the Philistines.—WOLFE, THEODORE F., 1895, *Literary Shrines, p.* 94.

As the first learned professor of modern languages in an American university, as the first exponent in our university life of continental scholarship, as the earliest of Americans to attempt the development of an American college into a modern university, and finally as the chief founder of the chief public library in the United States, Ticknor's claims upon popular memory are remarkable. What is more, those who knew him well felt for him a strong personal attachment; and it is probable that no scholar or man of letters was ever more generous in aiding and encouraging whomever he found eager in learning or letters. At least in his later years, however, Ticknor's manners did not impress the public as engaging. His dignity seemed forbidding; his tongue was certainly sharp; to people who did not attract him his address was hardly sympathetic; and his social habits, confirmed by almost lifelong intimacy with good European society, were a shade too exclusive for the growingly democratic taste about him. Yet it is hard to overestimate the difference which Ticknor's personal presence made in the intellectual history of New England, or the diffusion of knowledge which sprang from his generous impulse.—WENDELL, BARRETT, 1900, *A Literary History of America, p.* 266.

HISTORY OF SPANISH LITERATURE
1849

While reading it, one feels and recognizes the peculiar qualities of Spanish poetry and romance, which are so singularly in union with the chivalrous and romantic nation which produced them. You have given extracts enough from each prominent work to allow the reader to feel its character, and to produce upon his mind the agreeable illusion that he himself knows something of the literature to which you introduce him. You analyze enough to instruct, without wearying the reader with too elaborate details.—MOTLEY, JOHN LOTHROP, 1849, *Letter to Ticknor, Dec.* 29; *Life, Letters and Journals of George Ticknor, vol.* II, *p.* 257.

Your reach of knowledge is really marvellous in a foreigner; and I particularly admire the candor and good sense with which you have escaped the ordinary fault of exaggerating the writers whom you have occasion to bring before the public, while you have done ample justice to their real deserts. Your style is clear, firm, and well-sustained.—HALLAM, HENRY, 1850, *Letter to Ticknor, Jan.* 10; *Life, Letters and Journals of George Ticknor, vol.* II, *p.* 258

It is capital—capital! It takes me back into dear old Spain; into its libraries, its theatres; among its chronicles, its plays; among all those scenes and characters and customs that for years were my study and delight. No one that has not been in Spain can feel half the merit of your work; but to those who have, it is a perpetual banquet. I am glad you have brought it out during my lifetime, for it will be a *vade mecum* for the rest of my days. When I have once read it through, I shall keep it by me, like a Stilton cheese, to give a dig into whenever I want a relishing morsel. I began to fear it would never see the light in my day, or that it might fare with you as with that good lady who went thirteen years with child, and then brought forth a little old man, who died in the course of a month of extreme old age. But you have produced three strapping volumes, full of life and freshness and vigor, and that will live forever. You have laid the foundation of your work so deep that nothing can shake it; you have built it up with a care that renders it reliable in all its parts; and you have finished it off with a grace and beauty that leave nothing to be desired. It is well worth a lifetime to achieve such a work.—IRVING, WASHINGTON, 1850, *To George Ticknor, Feb.* 15; *Life and Letters, ed. Irving, vol.* IV, *p.* 69.

Much as I have read of Spanish, and though I counted myself among the connoisseurs in the province of poetry, your beautiful book has yet put me to shame, for I have gained an endless amount of new information from it. The chapters on the Romances seemed to me especially new and instructive, and I rejoice in the prospect of repeated readings, that I may study and learn more.—TIECK, LUDWIG, 1850, *Letter to Ticknor July* 28; *Life, Letters and Journals of George Ticknor, vol.* II, *p.* 260.

Mr. Ticknor, who has displayed the resources of a well-stored and accomplished mind in his recent work on the literature of Spain.— CARLISLE, EARL OF, 1851, *Travels in America, Lectures and Addresses, p.* 35.

The tone of criticism in these volumes is temperate and candid. . . . We cannot conclude without some notice of the style, so essential an element in a work of elegant literature. It is clear, classical, and correct, with a sustained moral dignity that not unfrequently rises to eloquence. But it is usually distinguished by a calm philosophical tenor that is well suited to the character of the subject. It is especially free from any tendency to mysticism,—from vagueness of expression,—a pretty sure indication of vague conceptions in the mind of the author, which he is apt to dignify with the name of philosophy. . . . We consider the work as one that does honour to English literature. It cannot fail to attract much attention from European critics who are at all instructed in the topics which it discusses. We predict with confidence that it will be speedily translated into Castilian and into German, and that it must become the standard work of Spanish literature, not only for those who speak our own tongue, but for the Spaniards themselves.—PRESCOTT, WILLIAM HICKLING, 1852-75, *Spanish Literature, Biographical and Critical Miscellanies, pp.* 680, 681.

That the best European critics have recognized it a permanent authority; it is both authentic and tasteful; the translations are excellent, the arrangement judicious, and the whole performance a work of genuine scholarship. It supplies a desideratum, and is an interesting and thorough exposition of a subject at once curious, attractive, and of general literary utility.—TUCKERMAN, HENRY T., 1852, *A Sketch of American Literature.*

Is of the highest authority, and is very readable.—PORTER, NOAH, 1870, *Books and Reading, p.* 177.

As far as solid and accurate reading is concerned, it is incomparably the best history of Spanish literature in existence, and is so acknowledged in Spain. . . . Erudition cannot confer insight, nor can genius be communicated by mere companionship with it. Mr. Ticknor's defect was a lack of sympathy and imagination, and to the historian of literature nothing can compensate for a deficiency in these. He could not mentally transform himself into a Spaniard, and therefore could not penetrate into the secret of the genius of Spain. He studied its great writers, but he did not look into and behold their souls. There was something cold, hard, resisting, and repellent in his mind. His criticism, therefore, externally judicious, had not for its basis mental facts vividly conceived and vitally interpreted. Had Mr. Ticknor possessed the realizing imagination of his friend Prescott,—who was never in Spain,—he would have made what is now a valuable work also a work of fascinating interest and extensive popularity.—WHIPPLE, EDWIN PERCY, 1876-86, *American Literature and Other Papers, ed. Whittier, pp.* 101, 102.

Is one of those laborious, careful works that never lose their value. It is allowed to be the best of its kind, the most complete treatment of its subject.—LAWRENCE, EUGENE, 1880, *A Primer of American Literature, p.* 127.

One of the most creditable contributions ever made to American letters. It is founded on the most extensive and critical studies; is written in a style that is a happy combination of force and grace, and it comprehends within its scope the whole period of Spanish literature down to the early part of the present century. It has been translated into the most important languages of Europe, and it is everywhere recognized as a work of great and permanent qualities. In no country have its merits received more hearty recognition than in Spain.—ADAMS, CHARLES KENDALL, 1882, *A Manual of Historical Literature.*

A careful and creditable performance. It is impartial, judicious and appreciative. —HAWTHORNE, JULIAN, AND LEMMON, LEONARD, 1891, *American Literature, p.* 89.

Spanish can scarcely be said to have shared, to an extent commensurate with its interest, in the benefit of recent study of the older forms of modern languages. There is, at any rate in English, and I think elsewhere, still nothing better than Ticknor's "History of Spanish Literature."— SAINTSBURY, GEORGE, 1897, *The Flourishing of Romance and the Rise of Allegory, p.* 393, *note.*

It was not until thirty years after he began the work of the Smith professorship that he published his history. Fifty years later, this deeply scholarly book, which involved untiring investigation of the best German type, remains authoritative; and it was perhaps the first American book to establish throughout the learned world the position of any American scholar. On the other hand, it is not interesting. Ticknor's mind was rather acquisitive and retentive than creative. His work is that of a thoroughly trained scholar; of a man, too, so sincerely devoted to literature that, as we have seen, his services to literary culture in America can hardly be overestimated; of a man, furthermore, whose letters and journals show him, though deficient in humour, to have had at command an agreeable and fluent everyday style. When all is said, however, the "History of Spanish Literature," taken by itself, is heavily respectable reading.— WENDELL, BARRETT, 1900, *A Literary History of America, p.* 266.

GENERAL

Ticknor is a thorough man,—armed at all points with information, and using it with great readiness.—DANA, RICHARD HENRY, 1842, *Journal, Feb.* 27; *Richard Henry Dana by C. F. Adams, vol.* I, *p.* 32.

We have in the work before us ["Life of Prescott"] a delightful edition to the class of literary biography, for which we venture to predict a wide and enduring popularity. It is the biography of one who was not only an eminent man of letters, but also, in his private character and personal relations, one of the most frank, amiable, warmhearted, and open-hearted of human beings. It is written by a man who from early youth was his intimate friend, and knew and understood him as well as one man can know and understand another,—whom all the common friends of the two would have pointed out as the most proper person to do the work which he has done.—HILLARD, GEORGE S., 1864, *Ticknor's Life of Prescott, North American Review, vol.* 98, *p.* 1

Mr. Ticknor's style was from the beginning simple and animated. He wrote with fluency and ease. His head was not turned by the flattering attentions he received at all hands, and his journals and letters are free from the conceit and egotism that too often mark productions of the sort. The freedom from extravagance of expression in the accounts of his experiences, was a characteristic sign of the even balance of his temper and of his fixed habit of self control. His sympathies, though quick, never betrayed him into enthusiasm, nor was his judgment overmastered by excitement of feeling.—NORTON, CHARLES ELIOT, 1876, *The Nation, vol.* 22, *p.* 148.

The "Life of Prescott" attained an immediate popularity, and it still holds its place among the most delightful of literary biographies. — WHIPPLE, EDWIN PERCY, 1886, *Recollections of Eminent Men, p.* 278.

There was perhaps no man of his time who was more widely read, or who used his reading with a steadier industry and a better judgment, than Mr. Ticknor.— SAINTSBURY, GEORGE, 1897, *The Flourishing of Romance and the Rise of Allegory, p.* XI.

Robert Chambers

1802–1871

Born, in Peebles, 10 July 1802. Educated at Burgh and Grammar schools there. Family removed to Edinburgh, Dec. 1813. He followed and went to school there, 1814–15. Taught in Portobello for a time, 1816. Two clerkships for short periods, 1817. Started bookshop in Leith Walk, 1818. Moved to India Place, 1823. Started "The Kaleidoscope" with his brother, 6 Oct. 1821. Edited it till 12 Jan. 1822. Made acquaintance of Scott, and engaged in literary work. Published various works. Married Anne Kirkwood, 7 Dec. 1829. Established "Chambers's Journal," with his brother William, 4 Feb. 1832. Started with him publishing firm of W. and R. Chambers, 1833. Fellow of Royal Soc. of Edinburgh, 1840. Received freedom of Peebles, 1841. Moved to St. Andrews, 1841. F. G. S., 1844. Returned to Edinburgh, 1844. Visit to Switzerland, 1848; to Norway, 1849; to Iceland, 1855; to U. S. A., 1860. Settled in London, March 1861. LL.D., St. Andrews, 1861. Elected member of Athenæum Club, 1860. Visit to France and Belgium, 1862. Wife and daughter died, Sept. 1863. Married Mrs. Frith, Jan. 1867; she died, 18 Jan. 1870. Hon. LL.D., St. Andrews, 1868. Died, at St. Andrews, 17 March 1871. *Works:* "Illustrations of the Author of Waverley," 1822; "Traditions of Edinburgh" (2 vols.), 1823; "Fires which have occurred in Edinburgh," 1824; "Walks in Edinburgh," 1825; "Popular Rhymes of Scotland," 1826; "Pictures of Scotland" (2 vols.), 1827; "History of the Rebellion in Scotland . . . 1638 till 1660" (2 vols.), 1828; "History of the Rebellion in Scotland in 1745–46" (2 vols.), 1828; "The Scottish Ballads," 1829; "The Scottish Songs," 1829; "History of the Rebellions in Scotland . . . in 1689 and 1715," 1829; "Scottish Jests and Anecdotes" [1830?]; "The Life of King James I." (2 vols.), 1830; "Biographical Dict. of Eminent Scotsmen" (4 vols.), 1832–35; "Gazetteer of Scotland" (with W. Chambers), 1832; "Poems" (privately printed), 1835; "Life of Sir Walter Scott" [1835?]; "History of the English Language and Literature," 1836; "The Land of Burns" (with Prof. Wilson), 1840; "Popular Rhymes . . . of Scotland" (anon.), 1842; "Vestiges of the Natural History of Creation" (anon.), 1844; "Cyclopædia of English Literature" (with R. Carruthers, 2 vols.), 1844; "Romantic Scotch Ballads," 1844; "Explanation; a sequel to 'Vestiges, etc.'," 1845; "Select Writings" (7 vols.), 1847; "Ancient Sea Margins," 1848; "The History of Scotland," 1849; "Life and Works of Robert Burns," 1851; "Tracings of the North of Europe," 1851; "Tracings in Iceland and the Faröe Islands," 1856; "Domestic Annals of Scotland from the Reformation to the Revolution" (2 vols.), 1858; "Domestic Annals of Scotland from the Revolution to the Rebellion of 1745," 1861; "Edinburgh Papers," pt. I–V., 1859–61; "Songs of Scotland prior to Burns," 1862; "Book of Days" (2 vols.), 1862–64; "Essays, Familiar and Humorous" (from "Chambers's Journal"), 1866; "Life of Smollett," 1867. *Posthumous:* "The Threiplands of Fingask," 1880. He *edited:* Bishop Forbes' "Jacobite Memoirs of the Rebellion of 1745," 1834; J. Currie's "Life of Burns," 1838; Burns' "Poetical Works," 1838, and "Prose Works," 1839; Sir William Forbes' "Memoirs of a Banking House," 1860; and published, with his brother, "Chambers's Information for the People," 1835; "Chambers's Miscellany," 1869, etc.; "Chambers's Encyclopædia" (10 vols.), 1859–68; and started "Chambers's Educational Course," 1835. *Life:* "Memoir," by W. Chambers, 13th edn. 1884.—SHARP, R. FARQUHARSON, 1897, *A Dictionary of English Authors, p.* 51.

PERSONAL

His genial and kindly disposition, to say nothing of his acquirements, gave him many friends. Never had children a more loving father. In public affairs, he was not qualified to take a prominent part. At one time, as has been seen, he edited a newspaper in the old Conservative interest, but his politics were of a mild type; and latterly he was numbered among the friends of social progress within sound constitutional limits. On few things was he more resolute than in upholding the principles of free trade, the opposition to which, particularly as regards the free importation of corn and other elements of food, he considered to be not only a prodigious economic blunder, but a great national crime. His generosity in extending aid to the needy and deserving was a marked trait in his character. His tastes led him to be elected a Fellow of several learned societies, and he was a member of the Athenæum Club. Diligent, accurate, and upright, he entertained clear views on all ordinary concerns; and no one could be more unscrupulous in his denunciation of whatever was narrow, mean, or dishonorable.—CHAMBERS, WILLIAM, 1872, *Memoir of Robert Chambers, p.* 309.

Of Robert Chambers's friendly, open-armed reception to those who went to Edinburgh and needed introduction to the beauties of this Queen City of North Britain, no terms can be too strong or too high. He placed himself at the disposal of such visitors with the utmost unreserve and the most unwearied kindness; and no man was better fitted to act cicerone by the most interesting among the numerous noteworthy objects there to be seen. He shone to great advantage himself while indicating them; for his talk was intelligent, clear, well-informed, and extremely pleasant. He seemed to enjoy afresh the things he was discussing and displaying for the thousandth time; and to be as much interested in them himself, as he made them doubly and trebly interesting to the person he was guiding.—CLARKE, CHARLES, AND MARY COWDEN, 1878, *Recollections of Writers, p.* 96.

Dr. Robert Chambers presented a curious

admixture of antiquarian and conservative instincts, and old nonjuring sympathies, with an extreme liberalism in thought on all educational or scientific questions of his own day, which often gave occasion for friendly banter in the lighter moods of social intercourse. But he was himself very tender in regard to the feelings of others; and had all the sensitiveness of a singularly gentle and loving nature, which made his friends careful not to push their banter to an extreme. With his keen Jacobite sentiment, and his no less ardent sympathy with all modern progress; his archaic veneration, and the bold scientific radicalism which won for him, rightly or not, the repute of author of the "Vestiges of Creation;" there was a rare compass in the genial sympathy of the man. Whatever interested his friends could not fail for the time being to command his interest.—WILSON, DANIEL, 1878, *Reminiscences of Old Edinburgh, vol.* II, *p.* 150.

His manner was dry, and though his eye twinkled with humor, I did not immediately recognize it as such. It was, in fact, the first acquaintance that I had made with a man of his type, and he puzzled me. . . . . Robert Chambers's humor was of the good-natured sort. His nature was essentially "good;" from the pleasure he took in the popularity of his friends, I used to call him "the Well-Wisher;" nor did he confine himself, as so many benevolent folks do, to wishing. I was intimately connected with him for twenty years, every one of which increased my regard for him, and when he died I lost one of the truest friends I ever had. His manner, however, on first acquaintance, was somewhat solid and unsympathetic. He had a very striking face and figure, as well known in Edinburgh as St. Giles' Cathedral, but a stranger would have taken him for a divine, possibly even for one of the "unco' guid." In London his white tie and grave demeanor caused him to be always taken for a clergyman—a very great mistake—which used to tickle him exceedingly. . . . He could appreciate a joke even upon a subject so sacred as the "Journal" itself.—PAYN, JAMES, 1884, *Some Literary Recollections, pp.* 109, 110.

VESTIGES OF THE NATURAL HISTORY OF CREATION
1844

A book which has been reprinted here, and read, perhaps, quite as much as it has in England. I read it through at once, in the beautiful copy you sent me, and enjoyed the transparent style in which it is written, and the boldness of its philosophical generalization, very much. But I have no faith in the conclusion to which it comes, because almost every step in the argument is set upon some not sure theory, and the whole consists of a series of nicely fitted links, in which "ten, or ten thousandth, breaks the chain alike." If the author fails in a single instance,—even in the poor matter of the Mac Lac speculations at the end,—the whole system explodes, just as a Prince Rupert's drop does when you break off its tail.—TICKNOR, GEORGE, 1845, *To John Kenyon, March* 30; *Life, Letters and Journals, vol.* II, *p.* 224.

I now know the "Vestiges" well, and I detest the book for its shallowness, for the intense vulgarity of its philosophy, for its gross, unblushing materialism, for its silly credulity in catering out of every fool's dish, for its utter ignorance of what is meant by induction, for its gross (and I dare to say filthy) views of physiology— most ingorant and most false—and for its shameful shuffling of the facts of geology so as to make them play a rogue's game. I believe some woman is the author, partly from the fair dress and agreeable exterior of the "Vestiges," and partly from the utter ignorance the book displays of all sound physical logic. A *man* who knew so much of the surface of physics must, at least on some one point or other, have taken a deeper plunge; but *all* parts of the book are shallow. . . . From the bottom of my soul I loathe and detest the "Vestiges." 'Tis a rank pill of asafœtida and arsenic covered with gold-leaf.— SEGDWICK, ADAM, 1845, *Letter to Macvey Napier, April* 10.

No notice of the works of Robert Chambers would be considered complete without some mention of a philosophical work, published anonymously, which created a great stir in the world of thought. This was the "Vestiges of Creation." The controversy which this remarkable book, the matrix of Darwin's, engendered, was most envenomed, and when in 1848 Mr.

Chambers was selected to be Lord Provost of Edinburgh, he thought it expedient to withdraw in the face of a storm raised against him as the supposed author. There were good reasons why he should not admit the authorship. Had he done so, the religious bodies of Scotland and England would have risen against the firm, and the numerous educational works of the Brothers Chambers would have been driven from the schools. For business reasons, rather than from any other cause, the author chose not to father a book which must certainly be regarded as one of the greatest speculative works of the nineteenth century. Should it be proved that Robert Chambers wrote it, his title to fame will be materially strengthened, for the writer of that book was the forerunner of Darwin. —WILSON, JAMES GRANT, 1871, *Robert Chambers, Lippincott's Magazine, vol.* 8, *p.* 23.

This work, which drew down upon its at first unknown author a perfect avalanche of ecclesiastical censure, was perhaps the boldest and most outspoken account of the origin of nature, as we know it, that had yet been published, but it substantially advanced little that was especially new. The most risky speculations of the author had been adventured already in each separate department of science. What Chambers was left to do was to make, as he himself says, "the first attempt to connect the natural sciences into a history of creation." The "Vestiges" dealt successively with the formation of the solar system, that of the earth itself with all its successive formations and the kinds of life to be found in each, the origin of all animated tribes and the early history of mankind. The book was undoubtedly conceived in a reverent spirit; it professed to give a wider and nobler view of the Creator's work than that which was ordinarily accepted. But the writer evidently knew, if only by the elaborate precautions that he took to conceal the authorship, that it would raise a storm of criticism. Indeed, to those who regarded the Mosaic account of the creation as the authoritative description revealed by God Himself of the various steps of the process, there was something peculiarly offensive in the manner in which the writer appeared to assume the part of one who was in the Creator's confidence.—OLIPHANT, MARGARET O. W.,

1892, *The Victorian Age of English Literature, p.* 372.

A remarkably advanced scientific book appeared in the year 1844, entitled "Vestiges of the Natural History of Creation." It was published anonymously, and for forty years the secret of its authorship was unknown. The book was variously ascribed to Thackeray, Lady Lovelace, Sir Charles Lyell, George Combe, Sir Richard Vyvyan, and even Prince Albert, but one of the depositories of the secret, Mr. Alexander Ireland, in a lecture delivered before the Manchester Literary Club in April 1884, stated that it was entirely from the pen of Robert Chambers. The most extraordinary precautions had been taken to preserve the anonymity of the author, who states in one of his letters: "To escape strife at the expense of losing any honour which may arise from my work is to me a most advantageous exchange."— OWEN, REV. RICHARD, 1894, *The Life of Richard Owen, vol.* I, *p.* 248.

Nothing he did was quite equal to the "Vestiges," a book rather literary than scientific, and treating the still crude evolution theory rather from the point of view of popular philosophy than from that of strict biological investigation; but curiously stimulating and enthusiastic, with a touch of poetry in it not often to be found in such books, and attractive as showing the way in which doctrines which are about to take a strong hold of the general mind not infrequently communicate themselves, in an unfinished but inspiring form, to persons who, except general literary culture and interest, do not seem to offer any specially favourable soil for their germination. Purely scientific men have usually rather pooh-poohed the "Vestiges," but there is the Platonic quality in it. — SAINTSBURY, GEORGE, 1896, *A History of Nineteenth Century Literature, p.* 414.

The "Vestiges of Creation" has been unduly appreciated since the time of Darwin. The gaps in the argument, and still more perhaps the untenable assumptions and mistaken assertions, are easy to detect now; but it is at least ungracious to insist upon them. Chambers was not an accomplished naturalist; on the contrary, Huxley charges him with "prodigious ignorance." He had not laboured as long, as patiently or as strenuously at the subject as Darwin; but at the same time his book is in an uncommon degree bold and suggestive. —WALKER, HUGH, 1897, *The Age of Tennyson, p.* 180.

CYCLOPÆDIA OF ENGLISH LITERATURE
1844

A publication of higher rank than any previous compilation of a similar character. Not less than a quarter of a million of copies of this excellent introduction to the British Classics have been sold in Great Britain and the United States.—WILSON, JAMES GRANT, 1871, *Robert Chambers, Lippincott's Magazine, vol.* 8, *p.* 22.

The work was a great success, and over 130,000 copies of it were sold in a few years. Careful revision of later editions has kept it abreast of the times, and though several works on English literature may be mentioned of greater brilliance of style and depth of criticism, it is, on the whole, the most useful companion the student can have.—NICOLL, HENRY J., 1881, *Great Movements and Those who Achieved Them, p.* 171.

GENERAL

Would be admirable ["Beauties of Scotland"] if they were accurate. He is a clever young fellow, but hurts himself by too much haste.—SCOTT, SIR WALTER, 1829, *Diary, Feb.* 24; *Life by Lockhart, ch.* lxxvii.

There are few literary men of the time who have exercised a more extensive or a more beneficial influence on their fellowmen, and who better deserve to be held in grateful remembrance by the people of Scotland and all other English-speaking portions of the globe, than Robert Chambers. He was not a writer of first-rate genius, but in the course of an industrious literary career of two-score and ten years he accomplished a vast amount of useful work. His name will occupy an honorable place in the royal guild of letters in connection with the introduction of cheap, instructive and unobjectionable popular literature.—WILSON, JAMES GRANT, 1871, *Robert Chambers, Lippincott's Magazine, vol.* 8, *p.* 17.

Altogether, as nearly as can be reckoned my brother produced upwards of seventy volumes, exclusive of detached papers which it would be impossible to enumerate. His whole writings had for their aim the good of society, the advancement in some shape or other of the true and beautiful. It will hardly be thought that I exceed the proper bounds of panegyric in stating, that in the long list of literary compositions of Robert Chambers, we see the zealous and successful student, the sagacious and benevolent citizen, and the devoted lover of his country.—CHAMBERS, WILLIAM, 1872, *Memoir of Robert Chambers, p.* 313.

Few men have worked so hard as Robert Chambers; his life, busy in its threefold capacity of author, editor, and publisher, can scarcely have known an unprofitable hour; few men have worked so well, for not a line that he has written, not a book that he has published, but has tended in some way to the education and social improvement of the people; and few men have reaped such an honourable and profitable reward for their labours.—CURWEN, HENRY, 1873, *A History of Booksellers, p.* 250.

Until the fourteenth number of the *Journal,* Robert Chambers was only in the position of a contributor. After that, he became associated with his brother as joint editor, and also became his partner in the business. There can be little doubt that it was to the numerous original contributions from his pen that the *Journal* owed a great part of its success. Though his essays cannot be said to display any great ability or originality, they are very fair specimens of a kind of writing where excellence is rarely even approached. "During fifteen years," he says in the preface to a collection of his essays, "I have laboured in this field, alternately gay, grave, sentimental, philosophical, until not much fewer than 400 separate papers have proceeded from my pen." The papers, he goes on to say, were written under some difficulties, particularly those of a provincial situation, and a life too studious and recluse to afford much opportunity for the observation of social characteristics. This, however, was partly compensated for by the fact that it made his treatment of subjects less local and less liable to accidents of fashion than it might otherwise have been.—NICOLL, HENRY J., 1881, *Great Movements and Those who Achieved Them, p.* 168.

His "Book of Days," a work upon which great labour was spent, was in course of issue from 1860 to 1867. Some help that was anticipated failed him, and the strain of labour was too great. While engaged in the work, he lost his wife, also a daughter.

"The Book of Days" was a success, but he himself spoke of it as his death blow. He went for health to St. Andrews, was made LL.D. by the University there, and known as "the Doctor;" but vigour of life was gone. In the course of his life he had produced, says his brother, upwards of seventy volumes, besides detached papers which could hardly be counted. So it is that our strong men now fight with the dragons.—MORLEY, HENRY, 1881, *Of English Literature in the Reign of Victoria, with a Glance at the Past, p.* 228.

I know no man who did so much literary work of such various kinds, and upon the whole so well, as Robert Chambers. There is now no doubt—indeed it was always an open secret—that he wrote the famous "Vestiges," though, until the late disclosure of Mr. Ireland, I had conjectured from the style that the book might have been written in collaboration. His scientific and antiquarian works were numerous; his essays of themselves fill many volumes, and admirably reflect his character— humor mixed with common-sense.—PAYN, JAMES, 1884, *Some Literary Recollections, p.* 111.

As a writer Chambers is vigorous, instructive, and interesting. He knew a great deal of men and books, and in communicating his knowledge he remembered his own precept, that dullness is "the last of literary sins." Thus he was well fitted to be a popular expounder of science and history. Occasional touches of humour give his writing additional interest. In treating, as he frequently did, of subjects illustrating Scottish character, he used the Scottish dialect with singular force and effect.—WATT, FRANCIS, 1887, *Dictionary of National Biography, vol.* x, *p.* 25.

Most industrious in the interviewing of everybody with even a remote acquaintance with the poet, and in the chronicling of tradition and report, he aimed, above all, at the production of a book which should do credit to his *Instructive and Entertaining Library.* His "Burns" has therefore the defects of its qualities. It contains much that was new, and is true; but it is overloaded with detail, in which hearsay too often does duty for fact. It is worth noting, too, that while Chambers—(who did not hesitate to suppress or even change, in the interests of decorum)—took credit for a faithfully zealous "attempt" to "place the writings of Burns before the world" with "fidelity as to text," he in the same breath declared that "here there is little room for amendment." The natural consequence of such fundamental nescience was that, instead of appreciably improving the text, he added to it his own peculiar quota of corruptions. Several new pieces were included by him, but little or no definite information was given as to how or where they were got.—HENLEY, WILLIAM ERNEST, AND HENDERSON, THOMAS F., 1896, *ed. The Poetry of Robert Burns, vol.* II, *p.* 289, *note.*

Robert Chambers stands by himself. He was of the best class of self-made men, and as a publisher perhaps even more than as a writer did service to literature.— WALKER, HUGH, 1897, *The Age of Tennyson, p.* 180.

Sir John Frederick William Herschel

1792–1871

The only son of Sir William, was born at Slough, 7th March 1792, and educated at Eton and St. John's, Cambridge, where in 1813 he was senior wrangler and first Smith's prizeman. His first publication was on the Calculus of finite differences (1820). In 1822 he applied himself especially to astronomy, and helped to re-examine the nebulæ and clusters of stars in his father's catalogues. The results were given in 1833 to the Royal Society along with observations on 525 nebulæ and clusters of stars not noticed by his father, and on a great number of double stars—in all between 3000 and 4000. His treatises on Sound and Light appeared in the "Encyclopædia Metropolitana" (1830–31); his Astronomy (1831) and Natural Philosophy in Lardner's "Cyclopædia." In 1834 he visited the Cape to examine the Southern hemisphere; the results published in 1847 completed a survey of the heavens begun in 1825. He was made a knight (1831), a baronet (1838), and a D. C. L of Oxford (1839), and was Master of the Mint (1850–55). His articles on Meteorology, Physical Geography, and Telescope, contributed to the "Encyclopædia Britannica," were published separately; and his "Popular Lectures" and "Collected Addresses" are well-known works. Herschel was a distinguished chemist, and attained important results in photography. His researches on the undulatory theory of light were very valuable. He had also a profound interest in poetry, and made translations from Schiller and from the "Iliad." He died at Collingwood near Hawkhurst, Kent, 12th May 1871, and was buried in Westminster Abbey. See Miss Clerke's "The Herschels." (1896).—PATRICK AND GROOME, *eds.*, 1897, *Chambers's Biographical Dictionary, p.* 487.

PERSONAL

At Captain Kater's breakfast yesterday we met Greenough, Captain Beaufort, Warburton, and young Herschel, a man of great abilities, to whom Sir Humphry Davy paid an elegant compliment the other day in a speech as President to the Royal Society. "His father must rejoice in such a son, who secures to him a double immortality."—EDGEWORTH, MARIA, 1822, *To Mrs. Edgeworth, May* 22; *Life and Letters ed. Hare, vol.* II, *p.* 82.

It has been said that distance of place confers the same privilege as distance of time, and I should gladly avail myself of the privilege which is thus afforded me by Sir John Herschel's separation from his country and friends, to express my admiration of his character in stronger terms than I should otherwise venture to use; for the language of panegyric however sincerely it may flow from the heart, might be mistaken for that of flattery, if it could not thus claim somewhat of an historical character; but his great attainments in almost every department of human knowledge, his fine powers as a philosophical writer, his great services and his distinguished devotion to science, the high principles which have regulated his conduct in every relation of life, and, above all, his engaging modesty, which is the crown of all his other virtues, presenting such a model of an accomplished philosopher as can rarely be found beyond the regions of fiction, demand abler pens than mine to describe them in adequate terms, however much inclined I might feel to undertake the task.—SUSSEX, DUKE OF, 1833, *Address before the Royal Society, Nov.* 30.

I dined with the Geological Club, and afterwards attended a meeting of the Geological Society. . . . . and especially Sir John Herschel, just returned from the Cape of Good Hope, and decidedly at this moment the lion of London. I sat between Sir John and Babbage, and had an excellent time. Sir John is a small man, and, I should think, a little more than fifty years old, and growing gray; very quiet and unpretending in his manner, and though at first seeming cold, getting easily interested in whatever is going forward.— TICKNOR, GEORGE, 1838, *Journal, May 22; Life, Letters and Journals, vol.* II, *p.* 176.

A very striking-looking man, with a face older than his age, but full of fire, and very intellectual. He asked me to pay him a visit in the country, and perhaps I shall, some day. Science is what I can least penetrate in the intellectual world, and I appreciate scientific greatness merely as a person who has no ear for music would appreciate the greatness of Handel, knowing it without understanding it. But it would still be interesting to me to see what a great philosopher is like.—TAYLOR, SIR HENRY, 1850, *Autobiography, vol.* II, *p.* 55.

He is womanly in his nature, not a tyrant like Whewell. Sir John is a better listener than any man I have met in England. He joins in all the chit-chat, is one of the domestic circle, and tells funny little anecdotes.—MITCHELL, MARIA, 1857, *To her Father, Nov.* 14; *Life, Letters and Journals, ed. Kendall, p.* 126.

Personally, the character of Sir John Herschel was extremely lovable. A fast friend, without jealousy, or self-seeking, or littleness, he neither disparaged the work of his rivals, nor neglected the labors of his juniors. As Master of the Mint, a member of nearly every scientific society in the world, and the greatest *savant* of his later years, he possessed an enormous amount of influence, which he exercised to the advantage of the nation. . . . In brief, what Humboldt was in Germany, Herschel was for many years in England, only Herschel was rather the larger-minded of the two men. Every opportunity of life was open to both of them, and it is not saying anything to the disparagement of the great German to affirm that the great Englishman accepted the position in which he found himself, with equal wisdom, patience, moderation, and high purpose.— BROWN, ROBERT, 1887, *Celebrities of the Century, ed. Sanders, p.* 563.

His return to England after five years of absence was naturally an occasion for much rejoicing among the lovers of astronomy. He was entertained at a memorable banquet, and the Queen, at her coronation, made him a baronet. His famous aunt Caroline, at the time aged eighty, was still in the enjoyment of her faculties, and was able to estimate at its true value the further lustre which was added to the name she bore. But there is reason to believe that her satisfaction was not quite unmixed with other feelings. With whatever favour she might regard her nephew, he was still not the brother to whom her life had been devoted. So jealous was this vigorous old lady of the fame of the great brother William, that she could hardly hear with patience of the achievements of any other astronomer, and this failing existed in some degree even when that other astronomer happened to be her illustrious nephew.—BALL, SIR ROBERT S., 1895, *Great Astronomers, p.* 265.

GENERAL

Mr. Herschel has contributed to "Lardner" a discourse on Natural Philosophy, the finest work of philosophical genius in our age, or perhaps (as I exclude the sciences) the finest since Bacon, who, though the greatest of philosophers, has properly no science. I firmly believe no other man in Europe could have written Herschel's discourse.— MACKINTOSH, SIR JAMES, 1831, *Letter to Miss Allen, March* 8; *Life, ed. Mackintosh, vol.* II, *p.* 481.

Without doing more than alluding to the delight with which this work—"Natural Philosophy"—has been several times perused by the writer of these pages, he can assure the reader that he has frequently heard the most eminent scientific men speak of it as a singularly beautiful, accurate, and masterly performance. Its author will be universally admitted to be consummately qualified for such an undertaking,—as far as the union of exact and profound science with elegant and varied accomplishments and refined taste can be considered as constituting such qualification. The style is severely chaste, and not obscured by technicalities.—WARREN, SAMUEL, 1836–45, *Popular and Practical Introduction to Law Studies, p.* 196.

Sir John Herschel, in his admirable "Discourse on Natural Philosophy," has added a greater number of illustrations from still more recent discoveries, and has also furnished such a luminous development of the difficulties of the "Novum Organum" as had been vainly hoped for in former times.—HALLAM, HENRY, 1837–39, *Introduction to the Literature of Europe, pt.* III, *ch.* III, *par.* 61.

Sir J. Herschel has done all that genius could do to rescue English hexameter verse from the reproach of Roger Ascham, that "it doth rather trot and hobble than run smoothly in our tongue." It may well be kept in mind in this case [translation of "The Iliad"] that it was the same genius which successfully accosted so many of the most profound problems in physical science. I have already mentioned Sir J. Herschel as one of the very few whom I have known, blending high literary attainments and a strong poetic feeling with these sterner pursuits.—HOLLAND, SIR HENRY, 1571, *Recollections of Past Life, p.* 293.

On Thursday, May 11, 1871, the greatest astronomer of our day passed from amongst us. In so characterizing Sir John Herschel we are not forgetting that others in our time have surpassed him in their mastery of special departments of astronomical science. But, as an astronomer in the true sense of the term, Sir John Herschel stood before all his contemporaries. Nay, he stood almost alone. Others in our day have worked right skilfully and well in advancing astronomy. By abstruse mathematical calculations, by laborious or by most delicate observations, by profound physical researches, or by the ingenious employment of various physical processes, they have added so much to our knowledge that the astronomy of the last generation seems altogether meagre by comparison with that of our own time. But how few have there been who have had, like Herschel, a real insight into the grandeur of astronomical truths, how few who, like him, could so touch the dry bones of fact that they become clothed at once with life and beauty! . . . Where, then, was the secret of Herschel's success—for successful he undoubtedly was—in attracting to the study of astronomy hundreds who but for him would have cared little for that science? There can be no question, we believe, that the answer must be sought in the considerations touched upon in the beginning of this paper. His soul was so

thoroughly imbued with the sense of the sublimity of the lessons taught by the celestial depths, that his descriptions, despite all faults of style, are irresistibly impressive. Here by a word, there by a happy turn of expression, now by some strikingly poetical conception, anon by a grand array of noble thoughts, he forces his readers to share his own enthusiasm. There are some passages in his writings which for grandeur and sublimity are surpassed by nothing that has been written in the English language, save, perhaps, some few portions of the "Paradise Lost."—PROCTOR, RICHARD A., 1871, *Essays on Astronomy, pp.* 1, 7.

Profoundly versed in almost every branch of physics, Sir John Herschel occasionally sported with the Muses, but in the garb of the ancients—in hexameter and pentameter verses. . . . The abstruse studies and triumphs of Sir John Herschel —his work on the Differential Calculus, his Catalogues of Stars and Nebulæ, and his Treatises on Sound and Light are well known; but perhaps the most striking instance of his pure devotion to science was his expedition to the Cape of Good Hope, and his sojourn there for four years, solely at his own expense, with the view of examining under the most favourable circumstances the southern hemisphere. This completed a telescopic survey of the whole surface of the visible heavens, commenced by Sir William Herschel above seventy years ago, assisted by his sister Caroline and his brother Alexander, and continued by him almost down to the close of a very long life.—CHAMBERS, ROBERT, 1876, *Cyclopædia of English Literature, ed. Carruthers.*

It is not likely that the name of Sir John Herschel, a gifted member of a gifted family, would be forgotten by any one taking even the hastiest glance at the science of our time—a family of whom it may truly be said, as the German prose-poet says of his dreaming hero, that their eyes were among the stars and their souls in the blue ether.—MCCARTHY, JUSTIN, 1879, *A History of Our Own Times from the Accession of Queen Victoria to the Berlin Congress, ch.* xxix.

It is no small virtue to have furnished the basis for the thoughts of the whole intelligent world. This, Sir John Herschel has done in more than one direction. His "Discourse on the Study of Natural Philosophy" and his "Outlines of Astronomy" will always remain as classic expositions of our certain knowledge and as eloquent suggestions for future progress. The chemical principles on which photography rests are his discovery, and it was undoubtedly only his intense occupation in other directions that prevented his anticipating the invention of Daguerre by many years. His public usefulness was very great. As a member of the Royal Society, as one of the founders of the Royal Astronomical Society, as a member of nearly every scientific society in the world, his authority was to England what Humboldt's authority was to Germany.—HOLDEN, EDWARD S., 1885, *The Three Herschels, Century Magazine, vol.* 30, *p.* 183.

Herschel was, however, not only a physicist and astronomer, he was also a man of letters, and possessed of none of the narrow intellectual prejudices of the specialist. His addresses to the Astronomical Society are models of elegant composition, and his "Discourse on the Study of Natural Philosophy," and "Outlines of Astronomy," must always remain classics, even after the data in their pages become more or less obsolete. Much of his time was spent in the useful work of simplifying his store of information. In this he was even more successful than his contem-

porary, Brewster, and was the forerunner of the eminent men who in later years displayed a laudable activity in the same direction. His "Familiar Lectures on Scientific Subjects" and his "Collected Addresses" are models at once of profound knowledge and of simple exposition, while his treatises on "Meteorology," "Physical Geography," and the "Telescope," are still among the best text-books.—BROWN, ROBERT, 1887, *Celebrities of the Century, ed. Sanders, p.* 563.

Herschel, without the soaring genius of his father, had a wider range and a more catholic mind. He was led to astronomy by filial piety, in opposition to a spontaneous preference for chemistry and optics. "Light," he used to say, "was his first love." Yet his position as a celestial explorer is unique. He was an unsurpassed observer, and his breadth of knowledge and power of vividly describing what he saw added incalculably to the value of his observations. His books hence take high rank among the elevating influences of this century. He . . . was in his element with children, loved gardening, and took interest in all techincal arts. His unpublished correspondence on scientific subjects is of historic interest; his letters to intimate friends are full of genial and tender sentiments.—CLERKE, MISS AGNES MARY, 1891, *Dictionary of National Biography, vol.* XXVI, *p.* 267.

Henry Longueville Mansel
1820–1871

Henry Longueville Mansel, Dean of St. Paul's, was born at Cosgrove rectory, Northamptonshire, October 6, 1820. Educated at Merchant Taylors' and St. John's College, Oxford, he became reader in Philosophy in 1855, Waynflete professor in 1859, professor of Ecclesiastical History and canon of Christ Church in 1867, and Dean of St. Paul's in 1869. He died at Cosgrove Hall, 31st July 1871. The pupil and part-editor of Hamilton, he went beyond his master in emphasising the relativity of knowledge—alleging, to the consternation of many, that we have no positive conception of the attributes of God. His works are Aldrich's "Logic" (1849), "Prolegomena Logica" (1851), article "Metaphysics" in 8th edition of the "Encyclopædia Britannica" (1857), "The Limits of Religious Thought" (Bampton Lectures, 1858), "The Philosophy of the Conditioned" (1866), and "The Gnostic Heresies" (with Life, 1874). See Dean Burgon's "Twelve Good Men" (1888).—PATRICK AND GROOME, *eds.*, 1897, *Chambers's Biographical Dictionary, p.* 627.

PERSONAL

My first acquaintance with Dean Mansel was made twenty years ago at the University, when he had everything to give, and I had everything to receive. As I think of him, his likeness seems to rise

before me. In one of those picturesque and old-world Colleges, in rooms which, if I remember rightly, on one side looked upon the collegiate quadrangle with its sober and meditative architecture, and on the other caught the play of light and shade cast by trees almost as venerable on the garden grass;—in one of those rooms, whose walls were built up to the ceilings with books, which, nevertheless, overflowed on the floor, and were piled in masses of disorderly order upon chairs and tables, might have been seen sitting day after day the late Dean, then my private tutor, and the most successful teacher of his time in the University. Young men are no bad judges of the capabilities of a teacher; and those who sought the highest honours of the University in the Class schools thought themselves fortunate to secure instruction such as he gave,—transparently lucid, accurate, and without stint, flowing on through the whole morning continuously making the most complicated questions clear.—CARNARVON, EARL, 1875, *Lectures on the Gnostic Heresies, Introduction, p.* 5.

Only incidentally hitherto has anything been said about Mansel's *wit.* So remarkable a feature may not be passed by with a passing allusion only. He stood alone among the men of his time for the brilliancy of his epigrams—repartees—puns—witty sayings. Wit in him was something all distinct from *humour,*—delightful, suppose, as Sydney Smith's. Further yet was it removed from that irresistible drollery which depends for its success on exuberant animal spirits—laughs immoderately at its own jokes—and at last sends you to bed with aching sides and eyes blinded with pleasant tears. Neither again was it as a *raconteur* that Mansel was famous: meaning thereby *that* delightful conversational faculty—(it must have been pre-eminently conspicuous in Sir Walter Scott)—which is ever illustrating the matter in hand by first-rate anecdotes, or by reproducing the brilliant sayings of famous men. Least of all was there in Mansel any of that sarcastic bitterness which makes certain utterers of *bons mots* the terror as much as the admiration of society. He was never known to say a cruel thing of anybody. Sarcasm was not one of his weapons. He was always good-natured, always good-tempered. His wit was purely intellectual; and its principal charm was that it was so spontaneous—so keen—so uncommon—above all, for the most part, so unpremeditated. . . . Let it be declared in conclusion concerning the Theologian, Metaphysician, and Phi-

losopher, whose life we have been tracing in outline,—that although he will be chiefly remembered by posterity for the profundity of his intellect,—as by his contemporaries he was chiefly noted for the brilliancy of his wit;—yet by those who knew him best, he will while memory lasts be held in reverence chiefly for his simple piety,—his unfeigned humility,—the unquenchable ardour of his childlike faith.—BURGON, J. W., 1885, *Henry Longueville Mansel, D. D., Dean of St. Paul's, Quarterly Review, vol.* 159, *pp.* 26, 39.

GENERAL

The general spirit of this book, "Limits of Religious Thought," is scholarly and liberal; and probably the deviations from this tone are involuntary and intellectual merely. But there are examples of controversial unfairness, which, though sanctioned by usage, we deeply lament to see.—MARTINEAU, JAMES, 1859, *Essays, Philosophical and Theological, vol.* I, *p.* 242.

It must be twenty years since, a boy, I read Hamilton's essay on the unconditioned, and from that time to this, ontological speculation has been a folly to me. When Mansel took up Hamilton's argument on the side of orthodoxy (!) I said he reminded me of nothing so much as the man who is sawing off the sign on which he is sitting, in Hogarth's picture.—HUXLEY, THOMAS HENRY, 1860, *To Charles Kingsley, Sept.* 23; *Life and Letters, ed. his Son, vol.* I, *p.* 234.

With regard to Mr. Mansel's book, "Limits of Religious Thought" itself, we must confess we find it a very difficult book on which to pass a judgment, favorable or unfavorable. The author is evidently a man of honest intentions, of ability, and varied and solid learning. He appears to be very well read in modern philosophical and theological literature, and, though not blessed with a true philosophical genius, he has much intellectual strength and logical acuteness. Whether we agree or disagree with him, we are obliged to respect him as a superior man, and, as a scholar who devotes himself honestly to serious studies. So much we willingly say of the author. But his Lectures themselves are very far from satisfying us. Though written by an Oxford scholar they are hardly English, at least are written in an English with which we are not, and hope we never shall be, familiar. Words are used in an unusual, frequently, it strikes us, in an un-English sense, and are unintelligible to one not familiar with the German schools of philosophy, either at first hand, or through the Scotsman Sir William Hamilton. His terminology is continually deceiving us, and we frequently find that we have understood his terms in a contrary sense from the one intended. His style has its merits, but is not our good old-fashioned English style; it wants the directness, clearness, and naturalness of the better class of English writers. His thought is not English, but Scoto-German, and is nearly as muddy as that of Schelling or Hegel. The reason of this is not in the original character of the author's mind, nor in the abstruse and difficult nature of the subjects treated, but in the false or defective system of philosophy which he has had the misfortune to adopt.—BROWNSON, ORESTES A., 1860, *Limits of Religious Thought, Works, ed. Brownson, vol.* III, *p.* 230.

Is ["Philosophy of the Conditioned"] nothing more than the doctrine of orthodox theology. But its essential feature is this: The faith which is ultimate and independent of knowledge is not in this philosophy a sentiment, the issue of the heart, or a conviction having its ground in aspiration, love, and devotion, but it subsists in the cold light of the intellect itself, where alone intellectual philosophy could profess to find it. It subsists as a logical necessity of thinking something to exist which is unthinkable—not merely something which we have not yet thought of—not the unknown simply, but the unknowable. Sir William Hamilton professes to demonstrate this necessity in the passage so often quoted from his review of Cousin.—WRIGHT, CHAUNCEY, 1867, *Mansel's Reply to Mill, Philosophical Discussions, p.* 351.

Mansel's Bampton Lecture on "The Limits of Religious Thought" was published some ten years ago. It was the application of Hamilton's "Philosophy of the Conditioned to Religious Thinking." Such application was not made to any great extent by the master himself. This was done most vigorously by the ablest disciple, doubtless, of the renowned philosopher. The work is carefully prepared,

and logically it is very able. It should also be said that in it valuable suggestions are made in respect to objections to some of the doctrines of religion. But that which gives to the work its special and permanent interest, as well as a temporary notoriety, is the main assumption of Mansel in regard to the possibilities of thought as wholly conditioned and relative.—HERRICK, J. R., 1869, *The Philosophy of Nescience, The Bibliotheca Sacra, vol.* 26, *p.* 442.

To my mind Mansel's "Bampton Lectures" and the reception they met with were a sign of the times. They seemed to me far more irreligious than Herbert Spencer. They left religion as a mere cry of despair.—MÜLLER, FRIEDRICH MAX, 1873, *To Canon Farrar, Jan.* 12; *Life and Letters, ed. his Wife, vol.* I, *p.* 472.

He stepped at once into the foremost rank of modern Theological writers; and the classical Tutor, the Professor of Moral Philosophy, however eminent locally, became at once a power beyond the walls of the University. From this time he wielded an influence which he never lost; and which, had he lived, he would, I believe, have largely increased. But those lectures were its origin. They passed through several editions; were repeatedly reviewed and canvassed; and became almost a text-book in the schools of the University.—CARNARVON, EARL, 1875, *Lectures on the Gnostic Heresies, Introduction.*

A writer whose works illustrate the literary beauty there may be in closeness, and with obvious repression or economy of a fine rhetorical gift.—PATER, WALTER, 1888, *Appreciations, with an Essay on Style, p.* 18.

Was rather a man of possibilities than of execution. In the wide range of his reading he cannot have fallen far short of his master, Hamilton. He was also a keen and able reasoner and the weight of his learning was relieved by flashes of a wit of the good old scholastic class. His works, however, have hardly been as successful as they perhaps deserved to be.—OLIPHANT, MARGARET O. W., 1892, *The Victorian Age of English Literature, p.* 400.

His style is essentially manly and straightforward, and he never beats the bush without starting a hare. But his prose, though devoid of ornament, was far from being colloquial. On the contrary, much of what he wrote is pitched in a high strain of rhetoric. It is rhetoric charged with unbending gravity; rhetoric in which the strokes of humour are severe and grim; rhetoric that often breaks into scathing rebuke and merciless denunciation; rhetoric withal that is never palpably forced, exaggerated, or insincere; but it is rhetoric the sombre tone of which is scarce once relieved by a touch of the gentler sentiments or kindlier feelings. In this respect Mansel presents a curious contrast to Butler. Butler is nothing if not persuasive and winning. Mansel would compel assent by sheer force of logic, nor does he condescend to disguise or keep in the background the consequences necessarily involved in the acceptance of his first proposition in a chain of reasoning. To persons of loose habits of thought he must be unsympathetic, if not actually repellent. But he will ever occupy a high place in the esteem of those who value consistency in argument, skill in controversy, and a powerful and impressive style of writing, which is often lofty and impassioned, though never animated by those tender and amiable emotions which are so popular with the mass of mankind.—MILLAR, J. H., 1896, *English Prose, ed. Craik, vol.* v, *p.* 686.

There are some who think that Henry Longueville Mansel was actually in more than one respect, and might, with some slight changes of accidental circumstance, have been indisputably, the greatest philosopher of Britain in the nineteenth century. Of the opinion entertained by contemporaries of great intellectual gifts, that of Mark Pattison, a bitter political and academical opponent, and the most acrimonious critic of his time, that Mansel was, though according to Pattison's view, an "archjobber," an "acute thinker, and a metaphysician" seems pretty conclusive. But Mansel died in middle age, he was much occupied in various kinds of University business, and he is said by those who knew him to have been personally rather indolent. . . . . It may be contended that Mansel was on the whole rather intended for a critic or historian of philosophy than for an independent philosophical teacher; and in this he would but have exhibited a tendency of his century. Yet he was very far from mere slavish following even of Hamilton, while the copying, with a little travesty and adjustment of German originals, on which so much philosophical repute has been founded in England, was entirely foreign to his nature and thought. . . . . His natural genius, moreover, assisted by his practice in miscellaneous writing, which though much less in amount of result than Mill's was even more various in kind, equipped him with a most admirable philosophical style, hitting the exact mean between the over-popular and the over-technical, endowing even the "Prolegomena Logica" with a perfect readableness, and in the "Metaphysics" and large parts of the editorial matter of the "Aldrich" showing capacities which make it deeply to be regretted that he never undertook a regular history of philosophy.—SAINTSBURY, GEORGE, 1896, *A History of Nineteenth Century Literature, pp.* 352, 353, 354.

Mansel's power of acute and lucid reasoning was shown in his "Prolegomena Logica" (1851), and afterwards in his "Philosophy of the Conditioned" (1866). Both were developments of Hamilton's principles, and they have suffered from the general discredit of the Hamiltonian school. Mansel is better known now, by name at least, on account of his "Limits of Religious Thought," . . . which was the occasion of a controversy between him and Maurice.—WALKER, HUGH, 1897, *The Age of Tennyson, p.* 168.

Sir Roderick Impey Murchison
1792–1871

Born at Tarradale, Ross-shire, 19th February 1792, was educated at Durham and the Military College, Great Marlow. He served in Spain and Portugal, and was present at Vimeiro and Corunna. Quitting the army in 1816, he devoted himself to geology, and travelled widely. His establishment of the Silurian system won him the Copley Medal and European fame, increased by his exposition of the Devonian, Permian, and Laurentian systems. He explored parts of Germany, Poland, and the Carpathians, and in 1840–45, with others, carried out a geological survey of the Russian empire. Struck with the resemblance between the Ural Mountains and Australian chains, Murchison in 1844 fore-shadowed the discovery of gold in Australia. He was president of the British Association in 1846, and for many years of the Royal Geographical Society. In 1855 he was made di-rector-general of the Geological Survey and director of the Royal School of Mines. His in-vestigations into the crystalline schists of the Highlands led him to a theory (not without error) of regional metamorphism on a large scale. A vice-president of the Royal Society and a foreign member of the French Academy, he was made K. C. B. in 1846, and a baronet in 1863. In 1870 he founded the Edinburgh chair of Geology. He died 22d October 1871. His principal works were "The Silurian System" (1839) and "The Geology of Russia in Europe and the Urals" (1845; 2d ed. 1853). See Life by Sir Archibald Geikie (1875).—PATRICK AND GROOME, *eds.*, 1897, *Chambers's Biographical Dictionary, p.* 681.

PERSONAL

Dined at Carclew; met Sir Roderick and Lady Murchison. He gave me a little lecture on geology, which he regards as an accomplished fact: all the principles of terrestrial arrangements clearly made out, only details to be looked after: mineral veins, however, a quite different case; infinite scope therein for papa and all mag-neticians. He is specially cautious about giving opinions on matter not immediately in his own province, and seems rather to enjoy the vague ignorance which keeps ob-servers in different branches of science forever guessing.—FOX, CAROLINE, 1846, *Memories of Old Friends, ed. Pym, Journal Oct.* 13, *p.* 231.

You will be glad to hear that yesterday, on our own spontaneous idea of Mr. Murchi-son's claims to a mark of favour from his own Sovereign, Sir James Graham, with my entire concurrence, wrote to the Queen, advising her Majesty to confer the honour of knighthood on Mr. Murchison at the first levée. The value of the distinction will be that it was unsolicited and un-prompted, and that it is intended as a recognition by the Queen of Mr. Murchi-son's services in the great cause of science and human knowledge.—PEEL, ROBERT, 1846, *Letter to Prof. Buckland, Feb.* 5; *Life of Murchison by Geikie, vol.* II, *p.* 54.

Murchison has returned ten years younger than he departed, belly gone, wig gone, and lo! a glossy dark chevelure of his own—how he triumphed at my greyness!—LOCK-HART, JOHN GIBSON, 1848, *To Milman, Oct.* 6; *Life and Letters, ed. Lang, vol.* II, *p.* 316.

Since these passages went to print Sir R. I. Murchison has passed away, full of years and of honours. · I had not the melancholy satisfaction of seeing for the last time our revered Chief, one of whose latest actions was to oppose my reading a paper about the so-called Victoria Nyanza before the Royal Geological Society; whilst another was to erase my name from the list of the Nile explorers when revising his own biography. But peace be to his manes! I respect the silence of a newly made grave.—BURTON, SIR RICHARD, 1871, *Journal, Life, ed. Burton, vol.* I, *p.* 594.

The picture which rises to the mind when one thinks of Murchison is that of a tall, wiry, muscular frame, which still kept its erectness even under the burden of almost fourscore years. It seemed the type of body for an active geologist who had to win his reputation by dint of hard climbing and walking almost as much as by mental power. It was moreover united in his case with a certain pomp or dignity of manner which at one time recalled the military training of the Peninsular days, at another the formal courtesy of the well-bred gentleman of a bygone generation. No learned body or business meeting or anniversary dinner could well be presided over by one who possessed in a greater degree the preliminary and often very useful advantage of a commanding pres-ence. The dignity, however, was blended with a courtesy and kindliness of manner which usually conciliated even those who might have been most disposed to object to any assumption, or appearance of as-sumption, of authority on his side. So he moved among his fellows as a leader under whom, in the conduct of affairs, his com-rades, even when confessedly his own superiors in mental power and scientific achievement, gladly, and indeed instinc-tively, ranged themselves. — GEIKIE, SIR ARCHIBALD, 1875, *Life of Sir Roderick I. Murchison, vol.* II, *p.* 347.

When Murchison was laid to rest at Brompton in 1871, the most conspicuous among those who walked bareheaded behind the bier was Mr. Gladstone, then First Minister of the Crown.—ROBBINS, ALFRED F., 1894, *The Early Public Life of William Ewart Gladstone, p.* 8.

In person Murchison was tall, wiry, muscular, of a commanding presence and dignified manner. A portrait was painted by Pickersgill, which has been engraved, and there are marble busts at the Geological Society and in the Museum of Economic Geology. Murchison was fortunate not only in the society of a wife who saved him from becoming a mere idler, but also in the possession of means which from the first placed him above want, and in later life were very ample. He was not insensible to the advantages of artistocratic friends and royal favour. His social influence was considerable, and it was exercised for the benefit of science and its workers. One of his last acts was to contribute half the endowment to a chair of geology at Edinburgh. He was a hospitable host, a firm and generous friend, though perhaps, especially in his later years, somewhat too self-appreciative and intolerant of opposition. He was a man of indomitable energy and great powers of work, blessed with an excellent constitution, very methodical and punctual in his habits.—BONNEY, T. G., 1894, *Dictionary of National Biography, vol.* XXXIX, *p.* 320.

THE SILURIAN SYSTEM
1839

His researches, now neglected, are embodied in "The Silurian System" (1839), in which he brought into notice for the first time a remarkable series of rock formations, each replete with distinctive organic remains, different from any other in England. . . . . Sir Roderick Murchison will always be remembered for his having added a new chapter to geological history, a chapter which contains the story of almost the earliest appearance of living things upon the earth.—SANDERS, LLOYD C., *ed.* 1887, *Celebrities of the Century, p.* 772.

A treatise of great value but somewhat difficult of perusal to any but the most earnest inquirer. Murchison displayed much skill as one of those "earthly godfathers" who roused the spleen of Byron, but who are regarded with gratitude by students of science—the Silurian, Laurentian and Permian series being all baptised

by him.—OLIPHANT, MARGARET O. W., 1892, *The Victorian Age of English Literature, p.* 367.

The publication of this splendid monograph forms a notable epoch in the history of modern geology, and well entitles its author to be enrolled among the founders of the science. For the first time, the succession of fossiliferous formations below the Old Red Sandstone was shown in detail. Their fossils were enumerated, described and figured. It was now possible to carry the vision across a vast series of ages, of which hitherto no definite knowledge existed, to mark the succession of their organisms, and thus to trace backward far farther than had ever before been possible, the history of organized existence on this globe.—GEIKIE, SIR ARCHIBALD, 1897, *The Founders of Geology, p.* 255.

GENERAL

Dear Murchison,—Many thanks for your yellow book, which is just come down to me. You have gained great fame, and I am very glad of it; had it been in theology, I should have been your rival, and probably have been jealous of you, but as it is in geology, my benevolence and real goodwill towards you have fair play. I shall read you out loud to-day. Heaven send I may understand you: not that I suspect your perspicuity, but that my knowledge of your science is too slender for that advantage—a knowledge which just enables me to distinguish between the Caseous and the Cretaceous formations, or, as the vulgar have it, to know chalk from cheese. —SMITH, SYDNEY, 1841, *Letter to Murchison, Dec.* 26; *Life of Murchison by Geikie, vol.* I, *p.* 361.

It is probably still too soon to attempt an estimate of the actual and lasting contributions made by Murchison to science. But as to the general nature and tendency of his work there can be little diversity of opinion. He was not gifted with the philosophic spirit which evolves broad laws and principles in science. He had hardly any imaginative power. He wanted therefore the genius for dealing with questions of theory, even when they had references to branches of science, the detailed facts of which were familiar to him. The kind of opposition he afforded to the views of the evolutionists, and to the doctrines of those who gainsaid his own favourite faith in former convulsions of nature, showing as it did a warmth of antagonism rather than an aptitude for coherent and logical argument, may be cited as evidence of this natural incapacity as well as of the want of early training in habits of accurate scientific reasoning. But though his name may never be inscribed among those of the recognised magnates in science who are both consummate observers and philosophic reasoners, and who mould the character of science for their own and future times, he will ever hold a high place among the pioneers by whose patient and sagacious power of gathering and marshalling facts new kingdoms of knowledge are added to the intellectual domain of man. He was not a profound thinker, but his contemporaries could hardly find a clearer, more keen-eyed, and careful observer. He had the shrewdness, too, to know wherein his strength lay. Hence he seldom ventured beyond the domain of fact where his first successes were won, and in which throughout his long life he worked so hard and so well. In that domain he had few equals.—GEIKIE, SIR ARCHIBALD, 1875, *Life of Sir Roderick I. Murchison, vol. II, p. 345.*

Murchison's name will live for ever as a clear, keen-eyed, careful observer of nature, and as a master of the facts relating to much of the ancient history of the earth. He was a great stimulator of men of science, assisted the weak, and helped the good worker. He had a great personal charac-ter, religious, honest, truthful, open and generous.— DUNCAN, P. MARTIN, 1882, *Heroes of Science, p. 305.*

Perhaps no man of the present century has done more to promote the progress of geographical science and kindle the spirit of adventure among those engaged in Arctic exploration on the one hand and of African discovery on the other. He traveled in various parts of the globe, and, struck with the resemblance in geological structure between the Ural mountains and the Australian chain, he was the first to predict the discovery of gold in Australia.—LAMB, MARTHA J., 1891, *Sir Roderick Impey Murchison, Magazine of American History, vol. 25, p. 97.*

Chiefly ["Geology of Russia"] remarkable for his argument deduced from structural resemblances of the gold districts of the Ural Mountains to the geological formations in Eastern Australia, that gold was to be found in the latter country. For some years Murchison continued to importune the Colonial authorities to put his assumption to the test, but without success. Gold was found later by unofficial searchers and Sir Roderick—he had been knighted on his return from Russia and was made K. C. B. in 1863 and a baronet three years later—had only the comfort of reflecting that he had been right when the public had forgotten all about his predictions.— OLIPHANT, MARGARET O. W., 1892, *The Victorian Age of English Literature, p. 366.*

Augustus De Morgan
1806–1871

The eminent English mathematician and logician, was born in Madura, in the Madras Presidency, but was educated under Airy at Trinity College, Cambridge, where he graduated as fourth wrangler in 1827. Next year he was appointed first professor of mathematics at University College, London, and the rest of his life was entirely devoted to his science. He became famous as the greatest teacher of mathematics then known, Todhunter and Routh being amongst his pupils. Of his numerous text-books and other treatises, we may here mention:—"The Elements of Arithmetic" (1830), the "Essay on Probabilities" (1838), still the best introduction to the science in our language; "The Elements of Trigonometry" (1837), his celebrated "Treatise on the Differential and Integral Calculus" (1842), "Formal Logic, or the Calculus of Inference," in which he expounds his and Sir W. Hamilton's principle of the quantified predicate; and four great treatises on the Syllogism (1850-60). He was also the author of innumerable popular essays and articles, and wrote biographies of Newton and Halley.—SANDERS, LLOYD C., *ed. 1887, Celebrities of the Century, p. 329.*

PERSONAL

First as to my eye. When I was in preparation, my mother attended much to a favourite native servant (in India) who had the ophthalmia, which they call the *country sore eyes.* When I was born it was found I had had it too, and one eye was not destroyed, but never completely formed: it is only a rudiment, with a discoloration in the centre, which shows that nature intended a pupil. The eyelid is of a different size from the other. . . . This is slightly exaggerated. I have been offered a binocular glass at the opera, &c., scores of times, by people who had known me for years, with recommendation to try if it were not better than my own. So that the thing does not show much, for which no doubt spectacles are partly answerable. Accordingly I have always been strictly unocular. I have seen as much with my right eye as with any one finger—no more, and no less. I am very short-sighted, and more so, I think, as I get older. Without spectacles my reading distance would be less than six inches for moderate type, or my own handwriting. Four inches would be agreeable and convenient. My eye bears any amount of work without fatigue. But on principle I have avoided anything like frequent use of a telescope, which is an insidious foe. Now I am not aware of any use of sight in which I differ from a short-sighted person with two eyes.—DE MORGAN, AUGUSTUS, 1864, *Letter to Sir W. R. Hamilton, July* 17; *Life of Hamilton by Graves, vol.* III, *p.* 612.

De Morgan's exposition combined excellences of the most varied kinds. It was clear, vivid, and succinct—rich, too, with abundance of illustration always at the command of enormously wide reading and an astonishingly retentive memory. A voice of sonorous sweetness, a grand forehead, and a profile of classic beauty, intensified the impression of commanding power which an almost equally complete mastery over mathematical truth, and over the forms of language in which he so attractively arrayed it, could not fail to make upon his auditors. Greater, however, than even these eminent qualities were the love of scientific truth for its own sake, and the utter contempt for all counterfeit knowledge, with which he was visibly possessed, and which he had an extraordinary power of arousing and sustaining in his pupils.— TAYLOR, SEDLEY, 1871, *Cambridge University Reporter.*

One thing which made his classes lively to men who were up to his mark, was the humorous horror he used to express at our blunders, especially when we took the conventional or book view instead of the logical view. The bland "hush!" with which he would suppress a suggestion which was simply stupid, and the almost grotesque surprise he would feign when a man betrayed that, instead of the classification by logical principles, he was thinking of the old unmeaning classification by rule in the common school-books, were exceedingly humorous, and gave a life to the classes beyond the mere scope of their intellectual interests. I think all my fellow-pupils would agree that never was there a more curious mixture of interests than the prepared discussions of principle in his lectures, and the Johnsonian force and sometimes fun of *his* part in the short dialogues with his pupils which occurred from time to time.—HUTTON, RICHARD HOLT, 1882, *Letter to Mrs. De Morgan, Memoir of Augustus De Morgan by his Wife, p.* 97.

Many as were our friends, we had but very little visiting, my husband's time being so fully filled with his work. The last was done with exceeding order and punctuality. . . . Not having the means to indulge in the luxuries enjoyed by richer and more affluent writers or experimentalists, he could not furnish his library with all the writing appliances and handsome bindings that ornament rich men's studies, and his old table and desk, and other cheap contrivances, looked shabby enough. Any one who went into his room would be struck at first by the homeliness of the whole, and the quantity of old and unbound books and packets of papers. But when it was seen how the books were arranged and the papers labelled and put into their proper places according to subjects, the adaptation of means to ends became as apparent as in the clearness and precision with which he laid down principles, and showed what was to be done before making a beginning on his work. His contrivances in the way of inkstand, penholder, and blotting-block, had none of them a new or unused look, but all showed that every contingency had been carefully provided for.—DE MORGAN, SOPHIA ELIZABETH, 1882, *Memoir of Augustus De Morgan, p.* 105.

De Morgan was a man of great simplicity and vivacity of character, of affectionate disposition, and entire freedom from all sordid self-interest. He had a love of puns, and all ingenious puzzles and paradoxes, which makes some of his books, especially his "Budget of Paradoxes" (1872, reprinted from the "Athenæum"), as amusing as they are learned. He held to his principles with a certain mathematical rigidity which excluded all possibility of compromise and gave ground for the charge of crotchetiness on some important occasions. But this was at worst the excess of a lofty sense of honour.—STEPHEN, LESLIE, 1888, *Dictionary of National Biography, vol.* XIV, *p.* 333.

GENERAL

The second of these is Sir William Hamilton's; the third is Mr. De Morgan's. The latter is the more ambitious of the two, and makes more formidable inroads upon the established boundaries of Logic. It is incumbent, therefore, on those who take an interest in the progress of the science, to scrutinize narrowly its pretensions; and if, in endeavouring to fulfil this duty, we find it necessary to express our dissent from the principles of the acute and learned author, we trust that we shall not be considered as feeling anything but the highest respect for the ability which he has in many ways displayed, and which indeed renders the task of opposing him more obligatory, as well as more difficult. Mr. De Morgan's great eminence as a mathematician makes it necessary for every student of Logic to see that he does not mar its doctrines by spurious importations from his favourite science; while the acuteness and ingenuity of many of his logical details render still more imperative the duty of detecting the unsoundness, if any exists, of his principles. It has been said that, next to him who forms the taste of a country, the greatest genius is he who corrupts. If Mr. De Morgan should rank with posterity as one who corrupted Logic with mathematics, he need not be ashamed of his partners in the offence; for he will find among them Bacon, who corrupted it with physics, and Hegel, who corrupted it with metaphysics.—MANSEL, HENRY LONGUEVILLE, 1851, *Letters, Lectures, and Reviews, ed. Chandler, p.* 46.

As a writer of mathematical text books, he took the highest rank, his books being more suitable, however, for teachers than for pupils. They were characterised by extreme clearness, exhaustiveness, and suggestiveness. Perhaps those best known are his "Elements of Arithmetic," published 1830; his "Elements of Algebra," published 1835; and his "Differential and Integral Calculus, with elementary illustrations," which is a perfect mine of original thought, and in which some of the most important extensions which the subject has since received, are distinctly indicated, and it was published by the Society for the Diffusion of Useful Knowledge. As an actuary he occupied the first place, though he was not directly associated with any particular office, but his opinion was sought for on all sides, by actuaries, on questions connected with the theory of probabilities as applied to life contingencies. In 1838 he wrote his "Essay on Probabilities," which still retains a high place among the literature of insurance offices.—RANYARD, ARTHUR C., 1871, *Augustus De Morgan, Nature, vol.* 3, *p.* 409.

He was not only the most successful teacher, but the most learned authority of his time upon the history of Mathematics, and in the practice of his science a most acute pleader for the union of Mathematics with Logic. He wrote books upon every department of Mathematics, and was conspicuous for union of shrewd critical wit with good sense and a wide erudition.—MORLEY, HENRY, 1881, *Of English Literature in the Reign of Victoria with a Glance at the Past, p.* 359.

Few men have ever possessed the scientific faculty more decisively, or have been more strictly bound both by temper and by destiny to the logical exercise of the wits; and few, at the same time, have escaped more completely from any narrow satisfaction with the things known, or have entertained more candidly the possibility of reaching some higher apprehension of realities.—HOWSE, EDWARD S., 1883, *Augustus De Morgan, The Modern Review, vol.* 4, *p.* 129.

As a teacher, De Morgan was particularly gifted. A voluminous writer on mathematics, he contributed essentially to those expansions of the fundamental conceptions which have rendered possible the new algebras, such as Quaternions and the Ausdehnungslehre, and have generalized the whole idea of a mathematical algorithm or calculus. But it is his logical work that will give De Morgan his most lasting fame. Here he stands alongside of his immortal contemporary, Boole.—HALSTED, GEORGE BRUCE, 1884, *De Morgan as Logician, The Journal of Speculative Philosophy, vol.* 18, *p.* 1.

The mathematical researches of men like Sir William Rowan Hamilton are far too technical, too difficult and too abstruse for popular apprehension. They remain a mere name, and not even their general import is understood. The same remark applies to the mathematical work of Augustus De Morgan, who, by the way, gave valuable hints for Hamilton's great work on quaternions. But DeMorgan was a logician as well, and the author of the "Budget of Parodoxes" is worthy of remembrance in literature.—WALKER, HUGH, 1897, *The Age of Tennyson, p.* 176.

Henry Alford

1810–1871

Born in London, and educated at Trinity College, Cambridge, where he took the Bell scholarship, and afterwards a fellowship. Shortly after his ordination he became curate of Ampton, and in 1835 he was presented with the living of Wymeswold. In 1841 he became Hulsean Lecturer at Cambridge, and was from 1835 to 1857 officiating minister of Quebec Street Chapel. In the latter year he succeeded Dean Lyall to the deanery of Canterbury, which he held till his death. He was the first editor of "The Contemporary Review," and is best known by his edition of the Greek Testament, which appeared in five volumes between 1841 and 1861. His poetical works are "Poems and Poetical Fragments," 1831; "The School of the Heart, and other Poems," 1835.—RANDOLPH, HENRY F., 1887, *ed. Fifty Years of English Song, vol.* IV, *p.* XV.

PERSONAL

If I might be permitted to point out a fault in the well-nigh perfect character of our departed friend, a fault, indeed, which was but a virtue carried to excess, I would say it consisted in his habitual forgetfulness of a precept contained in those very New Testament Scriptures which were so familiar to his mind—a precept, too, which fell from the lips of Christ Himself, whom he so endearingly loved and served, when He said to His disciples of old, and says to His disciples still, "Come ye yourselves apart, and rest awhile." So averse was the departed Dean to all idleness, either in spiritual or temporal things, that in very truth he seemed to be, and I believe really was, incapable of resting.—WARNER, G. B. LEE, 1871, *Funeral Sermon, Jan.* 15; *Life, Journals and Letters of Henry Alford, ed. Mrs. Alford, p.* 489, *note.*

Throughout his course at Cambridge many of the same qualities which marked his after-life were conspicuous: simplicity and purity of character; affection both warm and lasting; quick sensibility; unusual powers of acquiring and reproducing knowledge; much freshness of thought, combined with singular felicity of expression whether in speech or in writing; not a little of that undefinable something which distinguishes the man of genius from the merely clever or able man. His versatility was wonderful. Outdone by many of his competitors in each department, he could do more things very well than any of them, and succeeded accordingly. His father's early care and prayers had not been in vain. His inner life was always that of a truly religious man, and his outer life morally blameless.—VAUGHAN, EDWARD T., 1871, *Dean Alford, Contemporary Review, vol.* 16, *p.* 491.

Meeting you here to-day as the Cathedral body, can I forget the great loss which this church sustained scarcely two years ago? When I speak of Dean Alford, I remember that he was my friend, and therefore as his friend, I mourn his departure. But no feelings of mere personal regret need mingle on such an occasion with our regrets. Those who knew him in his public capacity, the crowds who heard him in London, the large numbers who came to this Cathedral, to hear him speak from the pulpit, the vast number of persons throughout the whole of England to whom his ample stores of learning opened an access to knowledge which they would not otherwise have attained, all attest his worth. The zeal with which he applied himself during the years when he was Dean of Canterbury to make this Cathedral in all respects what he desired it should be—a church to the glory of God, and the good of man; that peculiar position which he occupied, and which I may say almost he alone in the Church of England, in reference to the great non-conforming communities; — these things prevent us from forgetting this day the loss which the Church of England has sustained. —TAIT, ARCHIBALD CAMPBELL, 1872,

Charge in Canterbury Cathedral, Oct. 2; Life, Journals and Letters of Henry Alford, ed. Mrs. Alford, p. 486.

No one who lived with him could fail to be struck by his extreme quickness in *observation, thought,* and *action.* He was the first to notice any alteration, for instance, in the furniture of a room, or in the appearance of any person whom he met frequently, the first to read any inscription by the roadside. The gradual developments in the growth of plants in the garden, the changes of the sky seemed to chronicle themselves in his mind as soon as they occurred. Although on public occasions, as when he was in the pulpit, his utterance was measured and deliberate; yet, when he was quite at ease in his family circle, there was something unusual in the rapidity as well as vivacity with which he would follow up a train of thought to its conclusion, or would recall one after another recollections of his early days or travels.—ALFORD, MRS. HENRY, 1873, *ed. Life, Journals and Letters of Henry Alford, p.* 487.

He was a man of various accomplishments. He composed pieces for the piano and organ and vocal music; he both sang and played himself. He had considerable mechanical skill, and he carved in wood. He also was a water-colour painter. A book which he wrote about the Riviera with coloured lithographs from water-colour drawings of his own, was one of his last publications. His religious development was precocious. At ten years old he wrote a short sermon. At fifteen he wrote a long and serious letter to his cousin (afterwards his wife), who was then about to be confirmed. From his earliest days he had looked forward to ordination, and his letters and journals show that this purpose was always before him. When ordained he threw himself earnestly into the work of his parish, where he built schools and restored the church in a manner which at that time was quite uncommon. He had great facility in preaching, and adopted various styles, from the serious treatise to the extempore address, in all of which he was successful, his clear baritone voice aiding a good delivery. — FREMANTLE, WILLIAM HENRY, 1885, *Dictionary of National Biography, vol.* I, *p.* 283.

Henry Alford's habit was to rise at six, light his own fire in his study, and work there till one o'clock. One hour before breakfast was given to composing his sermons, and the rest of the morning to the Greek Testament. In the afternoon he visited amongst the poor inhabitants of his district, though the principal care of them devolved upon his curate. Evenings passed at home were spent in reading aloud to his family, and few read so well or effectively. His morning sermons were carefully written, and six volumes of these Quebec Sermons were published; but his afternoon sermons were extempore. Reading any of the sermons, however, is not what hearing them was. He had the manner and the voice which gave at once a solemnity and an interest to all he said; his hearers knew that he felt all he was saying to the uttermost, and his rich stores of knowledge of theology and literature of every kind made him especially acceptable to the cultivated classes who formed the main portion of his congregation. . . . He was enthusiastically fond of music, and looked upon it as the expression of poetic thought. Often hasty, he was always generous; and though often ruffled by slight annoyances, he could bear any great trial with more than patient—with happy resignation.—HARE, AUGUSTUS J. C., 1895, *Biographical Sketches, pp.* 115, 129.

GENERAL

His "School of the Heart" is an "Excursion" in a minor key. It is in a vein of high religious feeling and attachment to the English church, of which Mr. Alford is a clergyman. It is such poetry as Goldsmith's pure-hearted vicar would not have objected to.— GRISWOLD, RUFUS WILMOT, 1844, *The Poets and Poetry of England in the Nineteenth Century, p.* 447.

Of all the more intellectual ecclesiastics of our time, he was the most active and indefatigable *workman.* His study was literally an *officina librorum.* The handicraft which he possessed in so many other branches—mechanical, artistical, musical—reached its culminating point in his literary achievements. Others, no doubt, have written, in our time, more profoundly, more eloquently, more philosophically, but we doubt whether any of his ecclesiastical contemporaries rivalled Henry Alford in the amount of genuine labour undertaken. Many objections, both general and in detail, may be brought against his edition of the Greek Testament. But its great merit is, that it was done at all; and, being done, although far from reaching the ideal of such a work, and inferior in execution and conception to that which is displayed in particular portions of the Sacred Writings as edited by others, it remains, confessedly, the best that exists in English of the whole volume of the New Testament. To have done this, at once elevated its author to a high rank amongst the religious teachers of his country.—STANLEY, ARTHUR PENRHYN, 1871, *Dean Alford, Contemporary Review, vol.* 16, *p.* 486.

He has written a few sweet lyrics that may preserve his name.—STEDMAN, EDMUND CLARENCE, 1875–87, *Victorian Poets, p.* 242.

His Greek Testament and other biblical works constitute his chief claim to gratitude and fame. . . . The list of his works, with a short statement of their subjects, occupies an appendix to his "Life" of 15 pages 8vo. They comprise 48 volumes, some of which are slight, but others, like the Poems and the Greek Testament, exceedingly laborious; 104 articles in reviews, and 21 short separate pieces, hymns, sermons, or tracts.—FREMANTLE, WILLIAM HENRY, 1885, *Dictionary of National Biography, vol.* I, *pp.* 283, 284.

We may note, however, the valuable work of Dean Alford in his edition of the Greek New Testament in which the text has been carefully revised by the aid of all the new lights attainable. Dean Alford was a man of great accomplishments and culture, the author of several poetical and other works of a lighter description in his earlier years. His name, however, will be chiefly associated with this work, to which he dedicated a considerable portion of his life. Its publication was begun in 1841, and not completed till 1861. Much of what is called the new school of criticism did not exist when this work was begun, and even at the conclusion of his twenty years' labour, had been but little discussed in England, but there is no more careful edition of the text of the Gospels upon which all questions and discussions must be founded.—OLIPHANT, MARGARET O. W., 1892, *The Victorian Age of English Literature, p.* 348.

Dean Alford's general poems were never popular, nor do they possess the qualities which secure the "audience fit, though few," which is the consolation of so many who miss wider recognition. His translations show the scholar rather than the poet, and his other poems lack originality of thought and poetic felicity of diction.—MILES, ALFRED H., 1897, *The Poets and the Poetry of the Century, Sacred, Moral and Religious Verse, p.* 238.

Alice Cary

1820–1871

An American poet; born near Cincinnati, O., April 26, 1820; died in New York city, Feb. 12, 1871. When quite young she commenced writing sketches and poems for the press. In 1852 she, with her sister Phœbe, removed to New York city, where they lived during the rest of their lives. In 1850 the sisters published a volume entitled "Poems by Alice and Phœbe Cary." Alice soon after published "Clovernook, or Recollections of our Neighborhood in the West" (1851–53); "Hagar, a Story of To-Day" (1852); "Married not Mated" (1856); "The Lover's Diary" (1867); and "Snow-Berries: A Book for Young Folks" (1869).—WARNER, CHARLES DUDLEY, *ed.* 1897, *Library of the World's Best Literature, Biographical Dictionary, vol.* XXIX, *p.* 96.

PERSONAL

Miss Cary is simple in her tastes, unostentatious in her style of living, confiding in her disposition, hearty in her appreciation of goodness, charitable in her judgments to a remarkable degree, hopeful in faith, agreeable as a companion, disposed to constant deeds of charity, practicing self-denial as a privilege, and living the life of a pure, truly Christian woman.—VICTOR, ORVILLE J., 1860, *The Poets and Poetry of the West, ed.* Coggeshall, *p.* 346.

She was buried on Tuesday, amid one of the most violent storms of the winter. It seems sad to leave one we love in such desolation. But the storms cannot disturb her repose. There let her sleep, sweet, gentle spirit, child of nature and of song. The spring will come, and the grass grow green on her grave, and the flowers bloom, emblems of the resurrection unto life everlasting.— FIELD, HENRY MARTYN, 1871, *Alice Carg, Editorial Article, New York Evangelist.*

Timid and still, the elder had
Even then a smile too sweetly sad;
The crown of pain that all must wear
Too early pressed her midnight hair.
Yet ere the summer eve grew long,
Her modest lips were sweet with song;
A memory haunted all her words
Of clover-fields and singing birds.
Her dark, dilating eyes expressed
The broad horizons of the west;
Her speech dropped prairie flowers; the gold
Of harvest wheat about her rolled.
Fore-doomed to song she seemed to me;
I queried not with destiny;
I knew the trial and the need,
Yet, all the more, I said, God speed!
—WHITTIER, JOHN GREENLEAF, 1872, *The Singer*.

Business interests had brought into her western neighborhood a man at that time much her superior in years, culture, and fortune. Naturally he sought the society of a young, lovely woman so superior to her surroundings and associations. To Alice he was the man of men. It is doubtful if the most richly endowed man of the world whom she met afterwards in her larger sphere, ever wore to her the splendor of manhood which invested this king of her youth. Alice Cary loved this man, and in the profoundest sense she never loved another. A proud and prosperous family brought all their pride and power to bear on a son, to prevent his marrying a girl to them uneducated, rustic, and poor. "I waited for one who never came back," she said. "Yet I believed he would come, till I read in a paper his marriage to another. *Can* you think what life would be—loving one, waiting for one who would *never* come!" He did come at last. His wife had died. Alice was dying. The gray-haired man sat down beside the gray-haired woman. Life had dealt prosperously with him, as is its wont with men. Suffering and death had taken all from her save the lustre of her wondrous eyes. From her wan and wasted face they shone upon him full of tenderness and youth. Thus they met with life behind them—they who parted plighted lovers when life was young. He was the man whom she forgave for her blighted and weary life, with a smile of parting as divine as ever lit the face of woman.—AMES, MARY CLEMMER, 1873, *A Memorial of Alice and Phœbe Cary*, p. 29.

The sisters were in striking contrast, Phœbe, the younger, was a jocund, hearty, vivacious, witty, merry young woman, short and round; her older sister, Alice, was taller and more slender, with large, dark eyes; she was meditative, thoughtful, pensive, and rather grave in temperament; but the two were most heartily in sympathy in every opinion and in all their literary and social aims.—FROTHINGHAM, OCTAVIUS BROOKS, 1891, *Recollections and Impressions*, p. 225.

Sometimes the Whittiers had guests; and "Lizzie" delighted to tell how their mother was once met at the door by two plump maidens who announced that they had come from Ohio mainly to see her son. She explained that he was in Boston. No matter; they would come in and await his return. But he might be away a week. No matter; they would willingly wait that time for such a pleasure. So in they came. They proved to be Alice and Phœbe Cary, whose earlier poems, which had already preceded them, were filled with dirges and despair; but they were the merriest of housemates, and as the poet luckily returned next day, they stayed as long as they pleased, and were welcome.—HIGGINSON, THOMAS WENTWORTH, 1898, *Cheerful Yesterdays*, p. 134.

At No. 53 of the next block in Twentieth Street the sisters Cary dwelt many years and wrought the sweetness and purity of their natures into song and story. Their unpretentious little brick dwelling has been but slightly changed since it passed to strangers, and we may still see the pretty, bay-windowed parlor on the right, where for fifteen years were held the delightful Sunday night receptions which drew such spirits as Stoddard, Taylor, Whittier, Ripley, Aldrich, Whipple, Parton, Greeley, Fields, Ole Bull, Justin McCarthy, and others of similar gifts. Phœbe's study above the parlor, and the room at the left of the passage where Alice wrote her best books and carolled the songs for which she is remembered and loved; here her "Born Thrall" was begun, and here she breathed out her life, relinquishing her work only when, in the weariness of death, the pen literally fell from her hand.—WOLFE, THEODORE F., 1898, *Literary Haunts and Homes, American Authors*, p. 76.

GENERAL

Alice Cary evinces in many poems a genuine imagination and a creative energy that challenges peculiar praise. We have perhaps no other author, so young, in whom the poetical faculty is so largely developed.—GRISWOLD, RUFUS WILMOT, 1848, *The Female Poets of America, p.* 372.

Now conceded to be one of the most eminent writers, in prose and verse, which this country has produced.—VICTOR, ORVILLE J., 1860, *The Poets and Poetry of the West,* ed. *Coggeshall, p.* 343.

Few American women have written more than Miss Cary, and still fewer have written more successfully. Yet she does not write rapidly nor recklessly, and her works evince conscientious, painstaking effort, rather than transcendent genius or fitful inspiration.—GREELEY, HORACE, 1868, *Eminent Women of the Age, p.* 170.

> Years passed: through all the land her name
> A pleasant household word became:
> All felt behind the singer stood
> A sweet and gracious womanhood.
> Her life was earnest work, not play;
> Her tired feet climbed a weary way;
> And even through her lightest strain
> We heard an undertone of pain.

—WHITTIER, JOHN GREENLEAF, 1872, *The Singer.*

Her art is not so conspicuous as her poetic insight. Many of her most striking images are rather crudely wrought, and to read her lines smoothly requires such a variety of accents that the sensitive ear is constantly threatened with a shock. Some stanzas are padded to proper dimensions by phrases that we are accustomed to hear from young ladies with limited vocabularies, and which give us a sudden descent to the regions of the commonplace. But her poetic feeling is genuine; her cheerful temper kept her from morbid sentimentalism, the bane of modern poetry; she attempted no flights beyond her powers, and never sought to set out the plan of the universe in the cant words of metaphysics. For these solid excellences many faults of construction are forgiven. Hers poems can be read with hearty enjoyment, and ought to be remembered and esteemed as among the best utterances of American women.—UNDERWOOD, FRANCIS H., 1872, *A Hand-Book of English Literature, American Authors, p.* 465.

They were full of the freshness and fragrance of her native fields; full of simple, original, graphic pictures of the country life, and the men and women whom she knew best; full of the exquisite touches of a spontaneous, child-like genius, and they were gathered up as eagerly by the public as the children gather wild flowers. Their very simplicity and freshness won all hearts. . . . Nothing in her music touches one so nearly as its manifold variations of the hymns of human life—now tender, pathetic, and patient; now grand with resignation and faith, uttered always with a child-like simplicity; telling, most of all, how the human heart can love and suffer, how it can believe and find rest. It was her all-embracing pity, her yearning love for the entire race of Adam, which made her song a personal power, an ever present consolation to thousands of human souls who never measured her by any rule of poetic art.—AMES, MARY CLEMMER, 1873, *A Memorial of Alice and Phœbe Cary, pp.* 34, 116.

Whose individual strain of melancholy melody clings to remembrance, its charm stubbornly outliving our critical recognition of defects due, in great measure, to over-production. — CONE, HELEN GRAY, 1890, *Woman in American Literaure, The Century, vol.* 40, *p.* 929.

Much of Alice Cary's work has the true poetic method of indirectness, especially in "The Gray Swan." The details of this story are suggested rather than expressed; the gradual revealing of the sailor's identity, the emotions of the mother, and the character of the sailor are presented with art. In this respect the poem is one of the finest in American literature.—SIMONDS, ARTHUR B., 1894, *American Song, p.* 228.

In Alice's poems there is always an undertone of sadness, born of her own sorrows. For this she was often criticised, and yet she rose high above it in many of her works. So simple, forceful, direct is she as a ballad writer that she ranks first among those Americans who have produced ballads. Some of her poems, such as "Pictures from Memory" will last as long as the language in which they are written, for they speak to the *heart* of the people.—KEYSOR, JENNIE ELLIS, 1895, *Sketches of American Authors, vol.* II, *p.* 168.

Poe praised Alice Cary's "Pictures of Memory," and Phœbe's "Nearer Home" has become a favorite hymn. There is nothing peculiarly western about the verse of the Cary sisters. It is the poetry of sentiment, memory, and domestic affection, entirely feminine, rather tame and diffuse as a whole, but tender and sweet, cherished by many good women and dear to simple hearts.—BEERS, HENRY, A., 1895, *Initial Studies in American Letters*, p. 180.

Alice Cary's poems are colorless and passionless. They have little spontaneity or large creative power. Everywhere in them one finds the hackneyed epithets and phrases, the sing-song rhythm, and the sentimental pictures of the period in which they were written. Their charm consists in their sweet femininity and their rare delicacy and simplicity. With a certain large class of readers these poems have a perennial charm. Perhaps her best claim to remembrance is her "Clovernook," a series of prose studies of her early Ohio home.—PATTEE, FRED LEWIS, 1896, *A History of American Literature*, p. 403.

She lives chiefly by her poems of personal feeling, which at their best are sweetly lyrical, full of bright fancy, beautiful diction, and delicate observation of nature, resembling the verse of Keats and Tennyson. Her ballads and other verses for children, though often moral in intent, are playful. Her religious poems are at once devout and beautiful. Alice Cary's poetical vein was slender, but it was pure gold.—BRONSON, WALTER C., 1900, *A Short History of American Literature*, p. 149.

Phœbe Cary
1824–1871

An American poet and prose-writer, sister of Alice; born in Cincinnati, O., Sept. 4, 1824; died in Newport, R. I., July 31, 1871. She contributed numerous sketches to various periodicals; and with her sister published many books, among which are "Poems and Parodies" (1854), and "Poems of Faith, Hope, and Love."—WARNER, CHARLES DUDLEY, ed. 1897, *Library of the World's Best Literature, Biographical Dictionary, vol.* XXIX, p. 97.

PERSONAL

Years since (but names to me before),
Two sisters sought at eve my door;
Two song-birds wandering from their nest,
A gray old farm house in the West.
How fresh of life the younger one,
Half smiles, half tears, like rain in sun;
Her gravest mood could scarce displace
The dimples of her nut-brown face.
Wit sparkled on her lips not less
For quick and tremulous tenderness;
And, following close her merriest glance,
Dreamed through her eyes the heart's romance.
—WHITTIER, JOHN GREENLEAF, 1872, *The Singer*.

It breaks my heart to remember how hard Phœbe tried to be "brave" after Alice's death, as she thought her sister would wish to have her; how she opened the windows to let in the sunlight, filled her room with flowers, refused to put on mourning because Alice had requested her not to do so, and tried to interest herself in general schemes and plans for the advancement of women. But it was all of no use. She simply could not live after Alice was gone. "I do not know what is the matter with me," she said to me on one occasion; "I have lain down, and it seems, because Alice is not there, there is no reason why I should get up. For thirty years I have gone straight to her bedside as soon as I arose in the morning, and wherever she is, I am sure she wants me now." Could one think of these words without tears?—CROLY, JENNY C., 1873, *Letter to Mrs. Ames, A Memorial of Alice and Phœbe Cary by Mary Clemmer Ames*, p. 75.

During Elmina's decline it had been the custom of Alice and Phœbe to meet the first thing in the morning by her bed, to ask the dear one how she rested, and to begin the communion of the day. From her death it was the habit of Phœbe to go directly to Alice as soon as she arose. Sitting down on the edge of the bed, each would tell the story of her night, though it was Alice who, being very wakeful, really had a story of pains and thoughts and dreams to tell. I spent the summer, autumn, and a part of the winter of 1869 with them, and the memories of those days are as unique as they are precious. "We three" met each morning at the breakfast table, in that pleasant, pictured dining-room, which so many remember. The same dainty china which made Sunday evening teas so appetizing, made the breakfast table beautiful; often with the addition of a vase full of fresh flowers, brought by Phœbe from market. If Alice was able to be there at all, she had been able before coming down to deck her abundant locks with a dainty morning cap, brightened with pink ribbons, and, in her white robe and breakfast shawl, with its brilliant border, never looked lovelier than when pouring coffee for two ardent adorers of her own sex. She was always her brightest at this time. She had already done work enough to promise well for the rest of her day. She was glad to see us, glad to be able to be there, ready to tell us each our fortune anew, casting our horoscope afresh in her teacup each morning. Phœbe, in her street dress, just home from market, "had seen a sight," and had something funny to tell. More, she had any amount of funny things to tell. The wittiest Phœbe Cary that ever made delightful an evening drawing-room was tame, compared with this Phœbe Cary of the breakfast table, with only two women to listen to her, and to laugh till they cried and had strength to laugh no longer, over her irresistible remarks, which she made with the assumed solemnity of an owl.— AMES, MARY CLEMMER, 1873, *A Memorial of Alice and Phœbe Cary*, p. 43.

GENERAL

Writes with vigor, and a hopeful and genial spirit, and there are many felicities of expression, particularly in her later pieces. She refers more than Alice to the common experience, and has perhaps a deeper sympathy with that philosophy and those movements of the day, which look for a nearer approach to equality, in culture, fortune, and social relations.—GRISWOLD, RUFUS WILMOT, 1848, *The Female Poets of America*, p. 372.

Sister of the preceding [Alice], and usually named with her, though their poetical genius differs, as a double star, when viewed by a telescope, which makes the two distinctly visible, shows different colours of light. The elder sister is superior in genius to the younger, whose light seems to be rather a reflexion of the other's mental power, than an original gift of poetic fancy. The sympathies of the younger have made her a poet.—HALE, SARAH JOSEPHA, 1852, *Woman's Record*, p. 618.

Though she had been widely known as the author of good newspaper prose, as well as far more verse, I think the critical public was agreeably surprised by the quality of her "Poems of Faith, Hope, and Love," re-cently issued by Hurd & Houghton. There are one hundred pieces in all, covering two hundred and forty-nine pages; and hardly one of the hundred could well be spared, while there surely is no one of them which a friend would wish she had omitted from the collection. There are a buoyant faith, a sunny philosophy evinced throughout, with a hearty independence of thought and manner, which no one ever succeeded in affecting, and no one who possesses them could afford to barter for wealth or fame.—GREELEY, HORACE, 1868, *Eminent Women of the Age*, p. 170.

Perhaps the utterances of her soul which have most deeply impressed others, and by which she will be longest remembered, are her religious poems. They are among the rarest in the English tongue, as felicitous in utterance as they are devout and helpful in spirit. It is the soul of their melody, more than the melody itself, which makes us glad. It is the faith in the good, visible and invisible; the lark-like hope that soars and sings so high with such spontaneity of delight; the love brooding over the lowliest things, yet yearning out towards God's eternities, resting in his love at last, which make the inspiration of all these hymns.— AMES, MARY CLEMMER, 1873, *A Memorial of Alice and Phœbe Cary*, p. 172.

Both carolled as simply as the birds that gladdened their sweet-briar, but the verse of the younger has the keener edge.—BATES, KATHARINE LEE, 1897, *American Literature* p. 203.

No singer was ever more thoroughly identified with her own songs than was Phœbe Cary. She has been called the wittiest woman in America, but her wit left no sting behind the laughter which it evoked. —BAKER, ADALLA L., 1898, *Famous Authors of America*, p. 17.

Phœbe Cary's hymn, "One Sweetly Solemn Thought," has become one of the treasured possessions of religious spirits in all the English-speaking world.—NOBLE, CHARLES, 1898, *Studies in American Literature*, p. 281.

Henry Theodore Tuckerman

1813–1871

A writer once ranked among the first of American essayists, but whose criticisms, though delicate and discriminating, lack the force and originality of many later writers in the same field. Much of his life was spent abroad, largely in Italy, his intimate acquaintance with Italian affairs appearing in his earliest works, "The Italian Sketch Book;" "Isabel, or Sicily, a Pilgrimage" (1839), republished as "Sicily and Pilgrimage" (1852). His subsequent writings include, "Thoughts on the Poets;" "The Book of the Artists;" "Essays Biographical and Critical;" "Artist Life;" "Rambles and Reveries;" "Characteristics of Literature;" "The Criterion;" "Maga Papers about Paris;" "Leaves from the Diary of a Dreamer;" "Life of J. P. Kennedy;" "America and Her Commentators;" "The Optimist," a series of essays; "A Sheaf of Verse;" "Poems;" "Mental Portraits;" "The Collector," a volume of essays. See "Allibone's Dictionary;" "Foley's American Writers." —ADAMS, OSCAR FAY, 1897, *A Dictionary of American Authors*, p. 390.

PERSONAL

It would be impossible to fill his vacant niche in the social world; for not alone was the character of the man a rare one, but the conditions under which he was educated, the traditions of elegant breeding which existed in his youth, are now almost entirely obliterated and forgotten. The flippancy and irreverence of the present age are at war with that old-fashioned politeness which he loved and practised. Mr. Tuckerman belonged to the aristocratic class, if we have such a one, and he might well have been a useless, fine gentleman; but his goodness and greatness of heart, his interest in his fellows, his sympathy with all progressive ideas, saved him from sinking into the abyss of mere conventionalities. If ever a man deserved "the grand old name of gentleman" it was Henry T. Tuckerman. He loved beauty, talent, luxury, wealth, refinement; his home was the elegant *salon*, where all these graces meet. He considered his social duties as a part of the business of life, and was a famous diner-out; a payer of morning visits; and often seen in the evening at the gayest parties of the gayest city of this country. Yet the dignity and sweetness of his character kept him ever above the suspicion of being an idler, or mere man of pleasure. He was very fond of gossip. But what gossip—gossip which had been filtered through a golden medium, all the sparkle and wit remaining, all the malice and uncharitableness left out! He was the kindly ambassador of society, going from house to house, with the latest *mot*, the interesting anecdote, the friendly message. It was he who spread the news of the arrival of some intelligent foreigner, of the exhibition of some new picture, of the last readable book. His sympathy was so perfect, his wit so genial, his friendship so quiet and constant, that he was always gaining friends, and probably never lost one in his life.—SHERWOOD, MARY E. W., 1872, *Henry T. Tuckerman, Appletons' Journal*, vol. 8, p. 161.

One of the handsomest men of his day [1840], and one of the most accomplished gentlemen. . . . A figure of something more than medium height, with face slightly Roman in cast and Southern-European in suggestion; strong brows; pleasant dark eyes; close-cut, dark curling hair, and full beard and mustache, also dark and curling. Sweetly grave in manner, with flashes of absolute mischief in conversation.—MORFORD, HENRY, 1880, *John Keese, His Intimates; Morford's Magazine, June.*

GENERAL

He is a correct writer so far as mere English is concerned, but an insufferably tedious and dull one.—POE, EDGAR ALLAN, 1841, *A Chapter on Autography, Works ed. Stedman and Woodberry, vol. IX,* p. 220.

His principal poem, entitled "The Spirit of Poetry," was published in 1843. It is didactic and critical, carefully studied and highly finished. His minor pieces have more fancy and feeling. Some of them are passionate and tender, and they generally evince much delicacy, and a manly sincerity of disposition.—GRISWOLD, RUFUS WILMOT, 1847-70, *The Prose Writers of America* p. 531.

I do not know when I have read any work ["Essays"] more uniformly rich, full, and well sustained. The liberal, generous, catholic spirit in which it is written, is beyond all praise. The work is a model of its kind. I have no doubt that it will take a high stand in England, and will reflect great credit on our literature, of which it will remain a lasting ornament.—IRVING, WASHINGTON, 1857, *To Mr. H. T. Tuckerman, Jan. 26; Life and Letters, ed. Irving,* vol. IV, p. 229.

No more interesting and instructive books can be found in our literature than Tuckerman's "Thoughts on the Poets," "The Optimist," "Characteristics of Literature," and "Essays, Biographical and Critical." The two latter would be excellent books for the higher classes in schools; and the four

FREDERICK DENISON MAURICE

Engraving by F. Holl. After a Portrait
by Lowes Dickinson.

JOHN KEBLE

From an Engraving by Walker & Boutall.

should be in every district-school library in the land.—CLEVELAND, CHARLES D., 1859, *A Compendium of American Literature.*

H. T. Tuckerman is a genial and appreciative writer, combining extensive scholarship with elevated sentiment and feeling.— BOTTA, ANNE C. LYNCH, 1860, *Handbook of Universal Literature,* p. 528.

He published a volume of poems, which show a cultivated taste and considerable poetic feeling. He has also written several memoirs and biographies; but his chief employment was that of essayist, literary and art critic, and narrator of the lighter incidents of travel. His appreciative feeling, good taste, and long practice gave him the skill, and his pleasant habit of observation and retentive memory furnished the materials. He never probed a subject deeply, never developed principles, except very obvious ones, was never strongly graphic in description, nor keen in analysis; but the stream of his prose ran smoothly on until the salient points of his theme were pleasantly touched upon, and its associations were gracefully hinted at; and the reader, without fatigue, closed the book with the thought that he had spent an hour with more or less profit in the company of an amiable, well-informed, and well-bred man of the world.—UNDERWOOD, FRANCIS H.,

1872, *A Hand-book of English Literature, American Authors,* p. 393.

Before concluding, it may be well to mention some names without which even so limited a view of American literature as the present would be incomplete. And first, honor is due to Henry T. Tuckerman, who for nearly forty years was the associate of American authors, and who labored year after year to diffuse a taste for literature by his articles in reviews and magazines. He belonged to the class of appreciative critics, and was never more pleased than when he exercised the resources of a cultivated mind to analyze, explain, and celebrate the merits of others.—WHIPPLE, EDWIN PERCY, 1876–86, *American Literature and Other Papers, ed. Whittier,* p. 132.

He was a prolific, but never, in the commercial sense, a successful writer. . . . In poetry, he preferred the school of Pope, Cowper, and Burns to the modern style, so largely influenced by Tennyson, Browning, and their imitators. His principal poem, published in Boston in 1851, and entitled "The Spirit of Poetry," is an elaborate essay in heroic verse of some seven hundred lines. He was a close student of art, as his writings show.—SARGENT, EPES, 1880–81, *Harper's Cyclopædia of British and American Poetry,* p. 715.

John Frederick Denison Maurice

1805–1872

Theologian, the son of a Unitarian minister, was born at Normanston near Lowestoft, 29th August 1805, and studied at Trinity College and Trinity Hall, Cambridge, but as a dissenter, left in 1827 without a degree, and commenced a literary career in London. He wrote a novel, "Eustace Conway," and for a time edited the "Athenæum." Influenced by Coleridge, he resolved to take orders in the Church of England, at Oxford took his M. A., and was ordained a priest in 1834. He became chaplain to Guy's Hospital (1837), to Lincoln's Inn (1841–60); in 1840 professor of Literature at King's College, London, where he was professor of Theology 1846–53. In 1860 he accepted the incumbency of Vere Street Chapel, which he held until his election to the chair of Moral Philosophy at Cambridge in 1866. He died in London 1st April 1872. The publication in 1853 of his "Theological Essays," dealing with the atonement and eternal life, lost him the professorship of Theology in King's College. His principal books are "Moral and Metaphysical Philosophy," "Religions of the World," "Prophets and Kings of the Old Testament," "Patriarchs and Lawgivers of the Old Testament," "The Kingdom of Christ," "The Doctrine of Sacrifice," "Theological Essays," "Lectures on the Ecclesiastical History of the First and Second Centuries," "Gospel of St. John," "The Conscience," and "Social Morality."—PATRICK AND GROOME, eds., 1897, *Chambers's Biographical Dictionary,* p. 644.

PERSONAL

My decided opinion is, that Maurice is quite as able a man as Merivale, and infinitely a safer one than either Merivale or Twiss. He is a man who has always paid

particular attention to philosophy, and has always taken his philosophical premisses as much from the spiritual world revealed to us in the Bible, as from the sensible world by which our bodies are surrounded. He would, as I understand, if elected, endeavour to try the popular principles of political economy by the test of principles higher and more certain than themselves; and particularly to recall the attention of his hearers to that interference of moral considerations, which in practice will be sure to affect, if not materially to disturb, those results which modern economists have generally reasoned out by mere arithmetical calculation. All this seems to be very much needed in the present state of the science; and Oxford is just the place from which it ought to come.—PALMER, ROUNDELL, (EARL OF SELBORNE), 1836, *Letter to William Palmer; Memorials, Part I, Family and Personal, vol.* I, *p.* 215.

Mr. Maurice we rarely see, nor do I greatly regret his absence; for, to tell you the truth, I am never in his company without being attacked with a sort of paroxysm of mental cramp! He keeps one always, with his wire-drawings and paradoxes, as if one were dancing on the points of one's toes (spiritually speaking). And then he will help with the kettle, and never fails to pour it all over the milk-pot and sugar-basin!—CARLYLE, JANE WELSH, 1837, *To John Sterling, Feb.* 1; *Letters and Memorials, ed. Froude, vol.* I, *p.* 51.

The Maurices are wearisome and happily rare. All invitations "to meet the Maurices" I, when it is in any way possible, make a point of declining. One of the most entirely uninteresting men of genius that I can meet in society is poor Maurice to me; all twisted, screwed, wiredrawn, with such restless sensitiveness, the utmost unability to let nature have fair play with him. I do not remember that a word ever came from him betokening clear recognition or healthy free sympathy with anything. One must really let him alone till the prayers one does offer for him (pure-hearted, earnest creature as he is) begin to take effect.—CARLYLE, THOMAS, 1838, *Letter to Margaret Carlyle, Feb.* 15; *Thomas Carlyle, A History of his Life in London, ed. Froude, vol.* I, *p.* 108.

For, being of that honest few,
Who give the Fiend himself his due,
Should eighty thousand college-councils
Thunder "Anathema," friend, at you,
Should all our churchmen foam in spite
At you, so careful of the right,
Yet one lay-hearth would give you welcome—
Take it and come—to the Isle of Wight.
—TENNYSON, ALFRED LORD, 1854, *To The Rev. F. D. Maurice.*

I suppose I must have heard him, first and last, some thirty or forty times, and never carried away one clear idea, or even the impression that he had more than the faintest conception of what he himself meant. Aubrey De Vere was quite right when he said, that listening to him was like eating pea-soup with a fork, and Jowett's answer was not less to the purpose, when I asked him what a sermon, which Maurice had just preached before the University, was about, and he replied—"Well! all that I could make out was that to-day was yesterday, and this world the same as the next." John Stuart Mill, who had known him early in life, said to me about this time, "Frederick Maurice has philosophical powers of the highest order, but he spoils them all by torturing everything into Thirty-nine Articles." The fact that he should have exerted a distinctly stimulating and liberalising influence over many more or less remarkable people, is sufficiently strange; but it must be remembered that he was a noble fellow, with immense power of sympathy, and an ardent, passionate nature, which often led him to right conclusions in spite of his hopelessly confused reasoning. To listen to him was to drink spiritual champagne.—DUFF, SIR MOUNTSTUART E. GRANT, 1855, *Notes from a Diary, April* 22; *vol.* I, *p.* 78.

I thank you very much for the papers of Maurice's College. I was interested deeply and delighted with them; as for him, he is one of my *heroes.* I cannot too personally express how much I honour him—indeed envy him, I might almost say—but that there is no such alloy in the feeling with which he inspires me.—MACREADY, WILLIAM C., 1857, *Letter to Pollock, April* 20; *Reminiscences, ed. Pollock, p.* 710.

In more than five-and-twenty years, I have known no being so utterly unselfish, so utterly humble, so utterly careless of power or influence, for the mere enjoyment—and a terrible enjoyment it is—of using them. Staunch to his own opinion only when it seemed to involve some moral principle, he was almost too ready to yield it, in all practical matters, to anyone whom he supposed to possess more practical knowledge than he. To distrust himself, to accuse himself, to confess his proneness to hard judgments, while, to the eye of those who knew him and the facts, he was exercising a splendid charity and magnanimity; to hold himself up as a warning of "wasted time," while he was, but too literally, working himself to death,—this was the childlike temper which made some lower spirits now and then glad to escape from their consciousness of his superiority by patronizing and pitying him; causing in him—for he was, as all such great men are like to be, instinct with genial humour—a certain quiet good-natured amusement, but nothing more.—KINGSLEY, CHARLES, 1872, *Frederick Denison Maurice, Macmillan's Magazine, vol.* 26, *p.* 88.

Always in the same way he caught at every opportunity of pouring forth his gratitude for and appreciation of anything that was done for him by whomsoever it was done; as much for the thoughtfulness and affection with which all his servants waited on him, as for any other service. Quite to the last, if a cab was to be fetched, or some message outside the house to be delivered on a wet day, he was sure to slip out himself to get it done rather than let a maid-servant be exposed to bad weather. This was characteristic of his habit in all household matters. Some time before he left London evidence had been given that it was a great temptation to servants to be sent round to pay the tradesmen's bills. From that time he nearly always went round himself and paid the bills, both in London and in Cambridge, as a duty to the servants. One hardly can go into details because this kind of taking upon himself the rough and leaving to others the smooth, and if possible at the same time contriving to give some one else the credit of what had been done, extended to every little detail of life. If visitors called on him or were staying with him, who differed from him in points of opinion, his reticence in explaining, urging or enforcing any opinions of his own, unless he was almost forced to speak out, was always marked. No doubt his shyness was partly the cause, but much more than this the dread of trying merely to substitute his opinions for others, to proselytise in any way, was the reason for it.— MAURICE, FREDERICK, 1884, *ed. The Life of Frederick Denison Maurice, vol.* II, *p.* 630.

He was a good man, one of the best of men: incapable of a mean or self-seeking or dishonest action: with a tenderness of conscience which to the outer Philistine will appear Quixotic; and a self-depreciation which those who did not know him thought could not be sincere. He was also a great man, both in mind and heart: though one of the humblest. . . . To read through this biography is to rise into a purer atmosphere. So humble, so unselfish, was this great and saintly man, that mean souls commonly judged him an impostor: roughly concluding (through the necessity of their nature), that as no human being could be so wise as Thurlow looked, so no mortal could be as good as Maurice seemed.—BOYD, ANDREW K. H., 1884, *Maurice, Longman's Magazine, vol.* 4, *pp.* 286, 287.

It is hardly too much to say that the voice and manner of the preacher—his voice and manner in the reading-desk, at least as much as in the pulpit— have lived in my memory ever since, as no other voice and manner have ever lived in it. The half stern half pathetic emphasis with which he gave the words of the Confession, "And there is *no* health in *us*," throwing the weight of the meaning on to the last word, and the rising of his voice into a higher plane of hope as he passed away from the confession of weakness to the invocation of God's help, struck the one note of his life—the passionate trust in eternal help—as it had never been struck in my hearing before, though I never again saw or heard him without again hearing it. . . . A simpler and homelier man there never was in this world; indeed he was one who, though he could hardly speak without showing that his mind was occupied with invisible realities, had a quite pathetic sense of his own inadequacy to do what he desired to do, and the tenderest possible sympathy with the like incapacities of others.—HUTTON, RICHARD HOLT, 1884, *Frederick Denison Maurice, Good Words, vol.* 25, *p.* 381.

No man could be in a sense less self-asserting than he was. His shy humility was from early years a marked feature of his character. But along with an almost morbid self-depreciation there was also from the first—certainly from the time that he turned his thoughts to the Church—an intense spirit of religious confidence. Generalizing from his own family experiences, he was led to certain conclusions which he held as absolute truths. These conclusions were entirely unlike those to which his sisters and mother had come. But they were held with the same tenacity and disregard of consequences. If more enlightened, they were not the less downright. When his mother assured her astonished husband that "Calvinism *was true*," she said what her son would never have said—but the spirit of the saying may be traced in many of his utterances.—TULLOCH, JOHN, 1885, *Movements of Religious Thought in Britain During the Nineteenth Century, p.* 165.

He was one of the best men, and one of the greatest, whom I have ever known. His intellectual eminence never betrayed him into the slightest touch of scorn; and though he lived for years amid the roar and bray of religious obloquy, almost utterly neglected and unrewarded by those who dispense the patronage of the English Church, which he had so nobly served, he suffered neither neglect nor depreciation to weaken his high faith in human nature, and was incapable of an uncharitable thought. If ever there was a man who, living in the world, was not of it; if ever there was a man who, in the midst of religious virulence and vulgarity, was sustained by habitual intercourse with all that is high and noble in human thought; it was he.—FARRAR, FREDERIC WILLIAM, 1890, *Formative Influences, The Forum, vol.* 10, *p.* 378.

The most saintly personality of the nineteenth century, Newman, Pusey, and Keble not excepted. To me he made the phrase "*Virtue went out of him*" intelligible, for, as his life went on, the veil of the flesh seemed to wear so thin that the soul, almost ready for its emancipation, seemed to radiate goodness and to shine through. Yet was Maurice of all men most companionable, despite a certain shyness which made him seem to himself, and to himself only, to use his own words, "in most companies a bore." His greatness was never oppressive; his goodness was never obtrusive, but a light went wherever he passed. No one felt mean beside him; the cleverest and most self-conscious forgot themselves, and became simple and charming; whilst the stupidest discovered unsuspected worth and abilities in his presence.—HAWEIS, HUGH REGINALD, 1894, *Frederick Denison Maurice, The Contemporary Review, vol.* 65, *p.* 873.

Maurice was rather below middle height, but a singularly noble and expressive countenance gave dignity to his appearance. His voice and manner in conducting divine service were especially reverent and impressive. He suffered from severe illnesses, partly due to overwork, but behaved like a man in strong health. He rose early, often saw his friends at breakfast, and afterwards worked till his dinner-time, unless interrupted by business, dictating most of his writing. His manuscripts were elaborately corrected and rewritten. Maurice's character was most fascinating. Kingsley called him the "most beautiful human soul" he had known; and an early friend says that he was the "most saintlike," or, if he "dared to use the words," the most Christlike individual he had ever met. Those who knew him well would generally agree in the opinion. He was exceedingly gentle and courteous in personal intercourse, beloved by his servants, and an easy victim to begging impostors. He was absolutely unworldly, shrinking from preferment when it was within his reach, as in previous days he had frankly uttered the convictions which then made preferment impossible.—STEPHEN, LESLIE, 1894, *Dictionary of National Biography, vol.* XXXVII, *p.* 103.

He was the most hospitable of men, and yet his son tells us that he doubts if he ever gave an invitation without a certain shyness and hesitation, as though it was something of a liberty for him to take to ask any human being to come to his house. This shyness it was almost impossible for him to set aside. He had none of those qualities which make the bustling clergyman successful in his work. He lacked assurance. He lacked self-esteem. Though it is a peculiarity of his books that they are almost always autobiographical, that he speaks in the first person, and has much to say about himself, it is because he will not presume to speak for other people. He is never a critic unless he is forced to be so. It is his own duty with which he is most concerned. His books were composed in a hurry, and he did not regard them as likely to be of permanent reputation.—ROGERS, ARTHUR, 1898, *Men and Movements in the English Church, p.* 306.

GENERAL

There is something in Maurice, and his master Coleridge, which wakens thought in me more than any other writings almost: with all their imputed mysticism they seem to me to say plain things as often as most people. — CHURCH, RICHARD WILLIAM, 1838, *Note Book, Life and Letters of Dean Church, ed. Church, p.* 17.

I am reading Maurice's "Theological

Essays," and find them, notwithstanding a good deal of interest in parts, on the whole shadowy and unimpressive. I hardly think a man has any business to write till he has brought his thoughts into distincter shapes and better defined relations then I find in Maurice. He seems to me to have a mere presentiment of thinking, a tentative process in the direction that never fairly succeeds in getting home. But I have thus far read only some half-dozen of the Essays. —MARTINEAU, JAMES, 1853, *To R. H. Hutton, July 13; Life and Letters, ed. Drummond vol.* I, *p.* 257.

The most philosophical writer of the day. —GARBETT, EDWARD, 1867, *Bampton Lectures.*

He was not a great speaker or a great thinker; he was not a bold reformer; he had not a very subtle intellect; I doubt whether his writings will be much read in coming time. He was simply a great character, a grand influence. He sent a new life into the languid and decaying frame of the State Church of England. He quickened it with a fresh sense of duty.—MCCARTHY, JUSTIN, 1872, *The Reverend Charles Kingsley, Modern Leaders, p.* 213.

His writings always betray a certain indifference to form. They have often, hardly one would say a crude, but still an unformed character. It is not a lack of appreciation of art, for that appears in a very high degree, nor is it a disdain of the art of composition, but it is the characteristic of one who, having a word to utter and a message to give, is chiefly intent upon that. There is thus no regard for a formal rhetoric, and no cadence of tone nor balance of words, and no antithesis is allowed to divert him from the object of his thought. The expression is thus rarely obscure, although often involved. The style is simple and homely, while yet often interrupted by phrases and passages of singular beauty, and sometimes rising into great eloquence. It most frequently has the form of a direct address, as if of a person to a person, and there is a reluctance to use any other form. There is humour and strong irony, and sometimes a rare satirical power, but this always has a side of truth and is never unkindly.—MULFORD, ELISHA, 1872, *Frederick Denison Maurice, Scribner's Monthly vol.* 4, *p.* 532.

It was, after all, in this—in his personal influence—that Mr. Maurice was greatest. True, he was a great and rare thinker. Those who wish to satisfy themselves of this should measure the capaciousness of his intellect by studying—not by merely reading —his Boyle Lectures on the religions of the world; and that Kingdom of Christ, the ablest "Apology" for the Catholic Faith which England has seen for more than two hundred years. The ablest, and perhaps practically the most successful; for it has made the Catholic Faith look living, rational, practical, and practicable, to hundreds who could rest neither in modified Puritanism or modified Romanism, and still less in scepticism, however earnest. The fact that it is written from a Realist point of view, as all Mr. Maurice's books are, will make it obscure to many readers. . . . Much has been said of the obscurity of Mr. Maurice's style. It is a question whether any great thinker will be anything but obscure at times; simply because he is possessed by conceptions beyond his powers of expression.—KINGSLEY, CHARLES, 1872, *Frederick Denison Maurice, Macmillan's Magazine, vol.* 26, *p.* 85.

He, if any one, was an English citizen, even more than he was an English churchman. He, whilst clinging passionately, devotedly, to the ages of the past, yet was, if any one, full of all the thoughts and events of our own momentous century. Not a wave of speculation in Europe, not a public event of joy or sorrow in England, but called forth a sympathetic or indignant cry from that travailing soul. None of our time have in this respect so visibly been as the ancient prophets, reflecting all the movements of the age, yet themselves not led captive by them. For this was the contrast which makes his life so deeply instructive. In the midst of all this, he was in all those senses in which we have spoken of peace, the most peaceful, the most pacific, the most peace-making of men. Peace in himself; for, amidst the strife of tongues and the war of parties, he remained self-poised, independent, in a world above this world, in a land that was very far away, with utterances sometimes obscure, sometimes flashing with lightning splendour, yet always speaking from his own heart and conscience that which there he had truly found. . . . A true Pontiff of the English Church, a true paladin in the English State. He has built bridges that will not easily be broken across the widest chasms that separate class from class, and mind from mind. He has, with a more piercing sword than Roland's Durandel, made a breach in the mountain-wall of prejudice and ignorance that will never be entirely closed.—STANLEY, ARTHUR PENRHYN, 1872, *Frederick Denison Maurice, Good Words, vol.* 13, *p.* 319.

The two features which strike us at the moment as characteristic of Mr. Maurice as a writer and teacher, besides the vast range both of his reading and thought, and the singularly personal tone and language of all that he wrote, are, first, the combination in him of the most profound and intense religiousness with the most boundless claim and exercise of intellectual liberty; and next, the value which he set, exemplifying his estimate in his own long and laborious course, on processes and efforts, as compared with conclusions and definite results, in that pursuit of truth which was to him the most sacred of duties. . . . Mr. Maurice's desire to give the simplest and most real form to his thoughts as they arose in his own mind contributed more often than he supposed to prevent others from entering into his meaning. He asked them to put themselves in his place. He did not sufficiently put himself in theirs.—CHURCH, RICHARD WILLIAM, 1872, *Frederick Denison Maurice, Occasional Papers, vol.* II, *pp.* 321, 325.

I have so deep a respect for Maurice's character and purposes, as well as for his great mental gifts, that it is with some unwillingness I say anything which may seem to place him on a less high eminence than I would gladly be able to accord to him. But I have always thought that there was more intellectual power wasted in Maurice than in any other of my contemporaries. Few of them certainly have had so much to waste. Great powers of generalization, rare ingenuity and subtlety, and a wide perception of important and unobvious truths, served him not for putting something better into the place of the worthless heap of received opinions on the great subject of thought, but for proving to his own mind that the Church of England had known everything from the first, and that all the truths on the ground of which the Church and orthodoxy have been attacked (many of which he saw as clearly as anyone), are not only consistent with the Thirty-nine Articles, but are better understood and expressed in these Articles than by anyone who rejects them.—MILL, JOHN STUART, 1873, *Autobiography, p.* 153.

The general attitude of Mr. Maurice towards the speculation of his time may be easily defined. He was, it may be said, one product of the great reaction of the early part of this century. The fossilized theology of the preceding generation was to him unspeakably barren. The heresies which it encountered shared its faults. Paley and Horsley were as flat and unprofitable as Bentham and Priestley. Utilitarian moralists seemed to him to leave out of their calculations the animating principle of society; and their calculations were frigid and materialising. They made a machine out of a living organism, and reduced to a mere *caput mortuum* the body in which they should have recognised the inspiration of the divine spirit. On the other hand, Mr. Maurice's culture was too wide, his sympathies too keen and generous, to permit him to join the purely reactionary party. He sought therefore to escape from the prison-house under the congenial guidance of Coleridge, whose influence upon his mind is generously recognised in the preface to the "Kingdom of Christ."—STEPHEN, LESLIE, 1874, *Mr. Maurice's Theology, Fortnightly Review, vol.* 21, *p.* 596.

The first theologian of their time, who had done more than any other man to widen and deepen English thought.—HUGHES, THOMAS, 1874, *ed., The Friendship of Books, Preface, p.* v.

Mr. Maurice never erred, as a less practically devout nature might have erred, by theorizing away the facts of the inner life; conscious of a conflict between right and wrong within himself, God was for him not an impersonal force but a Righteous Will to which his loyalty was due, and from any pantheistic tendency to efface the distinction between good and evil Mr. Maurice was wholly free. A special gift of Mr. Maurice indeed lay in his power of lifting up into consciousness, without murdering or dissecting them, the things of the spiritual life; he saw them in the round, and contemplated rather than analyzed them.—DOWDEN, EDWARD, 1877–78, *Studies in Literature, p.* 72.

Maurice, in his volume "Learning and Working," has given four lectures on "The Religion of Rome" that show the author's

genius at its best.—ADAMS, CHARLES KEN-
DALL, 1882, *A Manual of Historical Literature, p.* 150.

The "Prophets and Kings," simple as its
pages seem in the stately rhythm of their
majestic thought, could never have been
written save by a Platonic scholar, and a
man of literary and dramatic genius; but
what shall we say of his great work, the
work of his life, which repeated editions and
ceaseless labour had wrought to the point
at which we have it in the last years of his
life—the "Moral and Metaphysical Philosophy?" He would be a bold man who would
undertake to criticise this book. Colonel
Maurice cites the testimony of specialists in any particular period, and of
teachers, who have used the book. They
testify, in the only way in which, in
the case of a book of such extent
(not less, indeed, than the entire history of human thought), it is possible for
anyone to testify, to its value. If I might
venture to add anything to what they have
said, I should wish to call attention to the
intellectual instinct which realised the later
Latin genius, and, with it, the situations of
absorbing interest, in which it was developed, amid the conflicts and alternating
vices and virtues of the old and new faiths.
No one, I imagine, can read the pages which
describe the Emperor Julian, Augustine,
Gregory the Great, and others, without being aware of the presence of this graphic
perception, to which only genius attains.—
SHORTHOUSE, J. HENRY, 1884, *Frederick
Denison Maurice, The Nineteenth Century,
vol.* 15, *p.* 863.

I have mentioned Professor Maurice, and
probably no man exerted a stronger impulse over my development. From his
lectures on literature and history, in which
I was his pupil for three years, I pass to his
writings. His was a mind with which no
one could be in contact without a sense of
elevation. He was absolutely removed
from everything that was mean, false, and
petty in the popular theology and religious
controversy of his day, and he always stood
before us as a living proof that a man could
be a prophet, a profound thinker, a man of
the deepest spirituality and the loftiest
moral nobleness, and yet be for all the party
"religious" newspapers of the day, as well
as for many of the secular journals—

"The very butt of slander, and the blot
For every dart that malice ever shot."

His little book on the Lord's Prayer, and
his "Prophets and Kings," and parts of his
"Moral and Metaphysical Philosophy,"
passed into the scanty store of my mental
possessions in early youth.—FARRAR, FRED-
ERIC WILLIAM, 1887, *Books Which Have
Influenced Me, p.* 84.

Mr. Maurice's literary works, all more or
less Sermons and Lectures reproduced, have
not attained any lasting celebrity. His
"Doctrine of Sacrifice" is an attempt to
show how vicarious suffering is really the
rule of life, but was supposed by many to
weaken while appearing to defend the
principle of the great Atonement. His
"Prophets and Kings of the Old Testament" has a clearness and picturesque force
of narrative which gives it a distinct and
attractive place among his many works,
since these were gifts by no means common
in his writings.—OLIPHANT, MARGARET O.
W., 1892, *The Victorian Age of English
Literature, p.* 338.

It is not too much to say that Maurice's
life and writings will be read chiefly by those
who knew him. I doubt whether, with the
exception of the thick volume "Moral
Philosophy," the "Kings and Prophets,"
and perhaps the sermons on the Lord's
Prayer and the "Theological Essays," any
of Maurice's books are read by the present
generation, and even the above named are
not much read. In his own lifetime, I was
told years ago by Macmillan, his devoted
publisher, that the sale of each new book
averaged about 800.   The same people
bought about the same number of copies,
and some were published at a loss. This
is not because they did not carry weight,
but because they were not generally intelligible, except to Mauricians. But the
men who read them were mostly accomplished writers and preachers themselves,
and through each one of such readers
Maurice practically addressed tens of thousands. . . . There were peculiarities about
Maurice's mind which those who were out
of sympathy with him—like Pusey, Mansel,
and to some extent Jowett, and even his
friend J. S. Mill—were apt to set down to
affectation or even insincerity.   The extreme subtlety of Maurice's intellect, which
led J. S. Mill to say that he was the greatest
metaphysical force at Oxford wasted upon
theological hairsplitting, was a distinct
hindrance to that clearness of statement
which carries conviction to the average

intellect. His readers sometimes felt they were being juggled with: each sentence was clear, but the whole page was misty, whilst the conclusions were jumped and the words, as it were, forced—difficulties were got done with, but somehow were not really solved.—HAWEIS, HUGH REGINALD, 1894, *Frederick Denison Maurice, The Contemporary Review, vol.* 65, *pp.* 874, 880.

A very generous and amiable person with a deficient sense of history, Maurice in his writing is a sort of elder, less gifted, and more exclusively theological Charles Kingsley, on whom he exercised great and rather unfortunate influence. But his looseness of thought, wayward eclecticism of system, and want of accurate learning, were not remedied by Kingsley's splendid pictorial faculty, his creative imagination, or his brilliant style.—SAINTSBURY, GEORGE,1896, *A History of Nineteenth Century Literature, p.* 376.

While the thought of Maurice does not lend itself easily to brief summaries, yet it is not difficult to trace in all his writings one common element which binds them together in a consistent whole. That "religious realism" which enabled him to grasp the fatherhood of God as an actual relationship which could not be broken may be discerned in every attitude of his mind. He looked upon religious institutions, not as identical with their divine idea, but as witnesses to a higher reality. Because the reality existed independently of its acknowledgment, he could be charitable while holding the strongest convictions, dogmatic while rejoicing in the largest freedom of thought. What to the popular mind seemed like divine indifference to human affairs was to his mind the visible token of His presence. The religious doubt from which others fled in alarm, he welcomed as an aid to the deeper knowledge of God.—ALLEN, ALEXANDER V. G., 1896, *The Prophets of the Christian Faith, p.* 210.

The want of clear outline is one of his chief defects. Though always suggestive, he is often somewhat elusive; and perhaps it is for this reason that his influence seems to dissipate itself without producing anything like the effect anticipated from it. The practical outcome of the school of Maurice is poor in comparison with that of the school of Pusey. This however was not wholly Maurice's fault. The Oxford school has drawn strength from what, nevertheless, may ultimately prove to be its weakness,— the appeal to authority, so tempting to many minds for the relief it promises. Maurice is not chargeable with this fault to the same degree. But neither is he entirely free from a kindred fault. He too, like Newman, argues to a foregone conclusion. In Mill's opinion, more intellectual power was wasted in Maurice than in any other of his contemporaries, and it was wasted because all Maurice's subtlety and power of generalisation served only "for proving to his own mind that the Church of England had known everything from the first."— WALKER, HUGH, 1897, *The Age of Tennyson, p.* 156.

It is hardly too much to say that it was the doctrine of Maurice, rather than that of Pusey or Newman, which for forty years— Maurice began his work in 1835; he died in 1872—"kept the whole of his forward movement in the social and political life of the English people in union with God and identified with religion," a doctrine which, idealized and transfigured in the two great poets of the century, Tennyson and Browning, . . . has, during this last decade of the century, turned so wisely the current of our English Christianity to the consideration of the great social problems of the age, and is at this moment so profoundly affecting, moulding, inspiring, transfusing the social ideals of the present.—STUBBS, CHARLES WILLIAM, 1899, *Charles Kingsley and the Christian Social Movement, p.* 16.

Charles James Lever

1806–1872

Born, in Dublin, 31 Aug. 1806. Educated at private schools. To Trinity College, Dublin, 14 Oct. 1822; B. A., 1827. Visit to Holland and Germany, 1828; to Canada, 1829. Returned to Dublin, 1830; studied medicine. M. D., Trinity College, Dublin, 1831. Held various Board of Health appointments, 1831–33. Married Catherine Baker, 1832 or 1833. Contrib. fiction to "Dublin Univ. Mag.," from May 1836. In Brussels, 1840–42; returned to Dublin, 1842. Editor of "Dublin Univ. Mag.," 1842–45. In Belgium and Germany, 1845–47. In Florence, 1847–57. British Consul at Spezzia, 1857–67; at Trieste, 1867–72.

Visit to Ireland, 1871. LL.D., Dublin, 1871. Died suddenly, at Trieste, 1 June 1872. *Works:* "The Confessions of Harry Lorrequer" (anon.), 1839; "Horace Templeton," 1840[?]; "Charles O'Malley" (anon.), 1841; "Our Mess" (vol. i., "Jack Hinton, the Guardsman;" vols. ii., iii., "Tom Burke of Ours"), 1843; "Arthur O'Leary" (anon.), 1844; "St. Patrick's Eve," 1845; "Tales of the Trains" (under pseud.: "Tilbury Tramp"), 1845; "The O'Donoghue," 1845; "The Knight of Gwynne," 1847; "Diary and Notes of Horace Templeton" (anon.), 1848; "Confessions of Con Cregan (anon.), 1849–50; "Roland Cashel," 1850; "The Daltons," 1852; "The Dodd Family Abroad," 1854; "Sir Jasper Carew" (anon.), [1855]; "The Fortunes of Glencore," 1857; "The Martins of Cro' Martin," 1856; "Davenport Dunn" [1857–59]; "One of Them," 1860; "Maurice Tiernay" (anon.), 1861; "Barrington" [1862]; "A Day's Ride," 1864; "Cornelius O'Dowd upon Men and Women" (anon.), 1864–65; "Luttrell of Arran," 1865; "Tony Butler" (anon.), 1865; Sir Brook Fossbrooke," 1866; "The Bramleighs of Bishop's Folly," 1868; "Paul Gosslett's Confessions," 1868; "That Boy of Norcott's," 1869; "A Rent in a Cloud, and St. Patrick's Eve," 1871; "Lord Kilgobbin," 1872. *Collected Novels:* ed. by his daughter, 1897, etc. *Life:* by W. F. Fitzpatrick, 1879.—SHARP, R. FARQUHARSON, 1897, *A Dictionary of English Authors, p.* 167.

PERSONAL

Besides the chestnut woods and you, your ownselves, I should be delighted to see Mr. Lever. You know I have always had a mannish sort of fancy for those "Charles O'Malley" and "Jack Hinton" books, which always put me in good spirits and good humor (I wish he wrote so now); and I remember hearing from his illustrator, Mr. Browne, that he was exactly the "Harry Lorrequer" he describes—that is to say, full of life and glee, and all that is animating and agreeable. I remember, too, most gratefully the pleasure his books gave to my father.—MITFORD, MARY RUSSELL, 1848, *To Mrs. Browning, Sep., Life, ed. L'Estrange, vol.* II, *p.* 296.

On our arrival here Mr. Lever called on us. A most cordial vivacious manner, a glowing countenance, with the animal spirits somewhat predominant over the intellect, yet the intellect by no means in default; you can't help being surprised into being pleased with him, whatever your previous inclination may be. Natural too, and a *gentleman* past mistake. His eldest daughter is nearly grown up, and his youngest six months old. He has children of every sort of intermediate age almost, but he himself is young enough still. Not the slightest Irish accent. He seems to have spent nearly his whole life on the Continent and by no means to be tired of it.—BROWNING, ELIZABETH BARRETT, 1849, *To Miss Mitford, July; Letters, ed. Kenyon, vol.* I, *p.* 413.

In his character were many different elements combined. He had the fearlessness of manhood, softened by woman's sensibility and purity, with the exuberance of life belonging to a boy. He possessed marvellous powers of fascination, attracting to him, and straightway converting into friends for a lifetime, men of different stations and moulds. The peer, the fellow of college, the judge, the country squire, the parson, the doctor, the statesman, the lawyer, the *littérateur,* the lowly peasant both in Italy and at home, alike appreciated him.—FITZPATRICK, W. J., 1879, *The Life of Charles Lever, vol.* II, *p.* 339.

With regard to the famous accusation of "lordolatry" which Thackeray is said to have brought against him, I think that the passage in the "Book of Snobs" has been somewhat misinterpreted. But nobody can read either his novels or his life without seeing that from the last infirmity of British minds he was not free. He gained plenty of money, but he got rid of it in all sorts of ways, to which it is difficult to apply any milder description than that which was applied to the extravagance of his greater countryman Goldsmith. If he did not exactly fling it away and hide it in holes and corners, like Lamb's eccentric friend, he did what amounted to nearly the same thing. He was an inveterate gambler. He kept absurd numbers of horses, and gave unreasonable prices for them. To his lavish hospitality one feels less inclined to object, were it not that "wax candles and some of the best wine in Europe" are not wholly indispensable to literary fellowship. Like many other men of letters in our country, he could not be satisfied without meddling with politics, and endeavouring, though with no great success, to mingle in political society. His wild oats were not of a very atrocious wildness, but he never ceased sowing them. The consequence was that his literary work was not only an indispensable *gagne-pain* to him, but was also never anything else than a *gagne-pain*. It was always written in hot haste, and with hardly any attention to style, to arrangement, or even to such ordinary matters as the avoidance of repetitions, anachronisms, and such-like slovenliness.—SAINTSBURY, GEORGE, 1879, *Two Men of Letters, Fortnightly Review, vol.* 32, *p.* 386.

How shall I speak of my dear old friend Charles Lever, and his rattling, jolly, joyous, swearing Irishman. Surely never did a sense of vitality come so constantly from a man's pen, nor from a man's voice, as from his! I knew him well for many years, and whether in sickness or in health I have never come across him without finding him to be running over with wit and fun. Of all the men I have encountered, he was the surest fund of drollery. I have known many witty men, many who could say good things, many who would sometimes be ready to say them when wanted, though they would sometimes fail—but he never failed. Rouse him in the middle of the night, and wit would come from him before he was half awake. And yet he never monopolized the talk, was never a bore. He would take no more than his own share of the words spoken, and would yet seem to brighten all that was said during the night. His earlier novels—the later I have not read—are just like his conversation. The fun never flags, and to me, when I read them, they were never tedious. As to character, he can hardly be said to have produced it. Corney Delaney, the old manservant, may perhaps be named as an exception.—TROLLOPE, ANTHONY, 1882–83, *An Autobiography, p.* 182.

Dr. Lever was at that time (1840) the only English physician in Brussels, and never perhaps was a physician less fitted for his calling. Although (possibly "pressed by hunger and request of friends") he "practised," he could not and did not inspire much confidence in his patients, for he made no secret of being a *médecin malgré lui,* loudly proclaiming, even among his *clientèle,* his hatred of the occupation, and taking every opportunity of practically proving his words. He used to come into his consulting-room in the most literary style of costume, wearing a black velvet dressing-gown, confined at the waist by a scarlet silk cord and tassels, and with the inevitable pen behind his ear, not for the convenience of inditing prescriptions, but to lose no time in getting back to his magazine articles as soon as he should have dispatched his patient.—BYRNE, MRS. WILLIAM PITT, 1898, *Social Hours with Celebrities, vol.* I, *p.* 204.

CHARLES O'MALLEY

1841

It would, indeed, be difficult to convey to one who has not examined this production for himself, any idea of the exceedingly rough, clumsy, and inartistical manner in which even this bald conception is carried out. The stories are absolutely dragged in by the ears. So far from finding them result naturally or plausibly from the conversation of the interlocutor, even the blindest reader may perceive the author's struggling and blundering effort to introduce them.—POE, EDGAR ALLAN, 1842, *Literary Criticism, Works ed.* Stedman and Woodberry, *vol.* VII, *p.* 72.

Modern English literature has not produced a more Shakespearian—I might say a more original—comic character than Lever's Major Monsoon in "Charles O'Malley." But Major Monsoon is well known to be a minutely accurate portrait of the character, a faithful chronicle of the sayings and doings, of a real living person.—MARSH, GEORGE P., 1862, *The Origin and History of the English Language and of the Early Literature it Embodies, p.* 567, *note.*

The charm of the book is complete; and for break-neck, dashing narrative, for wit, sparkle, and genuine Irish drollery, interspersed here and there with tender touches of pathos and soft gray tones of sorrow, "Charles O'Malley" stands unrivalled, and will hold its own when hundreds of so-called Irish romances shall have returned to the dust out of which they should never have emerged, even into a spasmodic vitality.—ROBINSON, N., 1877, *Charles Lever at Home, The Catholic World, vol.* 26, *p.* 206.

"O'Malley" is what you can recommend to a friend. Here is every species of diversion: duels and steeplechases, practical jokes at college (good practical jokes, not booby traps and apple-pie beds); here is fighting in the Peninsula. If any student is in doubt, let him turn chapter xiv.—the battle on the Douro. This is, indeed, excellent military writing, and need not fear comparison as art with Napier's famous history. Lever has warmed to his work; his heart is in it; he had the best information from an eye-witness; and the brief beginning, on the peace of nature before the strife of men, is admirably poetical. . . . The critics may praise Lever's thoughtful and careful later novels as they will, but "Charles O'Malley" will always be the pattern of a military romance. The anecdote of "a virtuous weakness" in O'Shaughnessy's father's character would alone make the fortune of many a story. The truth is, it is not easy to lay down "Charles O'Malley."—LANG, ANDREW, 1891, *Essays in Little, pp.* 165, 166.

High spirits and reckless adventure gave attractiveness to the early and most rollicking novels of Charles Lever; but even "Charles O'Malley," the best of them, needs to be read very light-heartedly to be convincing.—GOSSE, EDMUND, 1897, *A Short History of Modern English Literature, p.* 343.

GENERAL

He has a large circle of readers, and many of them would say they prefer him to anybody else; but if you tried to elicit from them one good reason, they would have no better answer to give than "Oh! he's a capital fellow!" What the French call *material life,* is the whole life he recognizes; and *that* life is a jest, and a very loud one, in his philosophy. The sense of beauty and love he does not recognize at all, except in our modern condition of social animals. To read him is like sitting in the next room to an orgie of gentlemen topers, with their noisy gentility and "hip! hip! hurras!" and the rattling din of plates and glasses. In his way, he is a very clever writer, nobody can deny; but he is contracted and conventional, and unrefined in his line of conventionality. His best descriptions are of military life. He is most at home in the mess-room. He has undoubted humour and a quick talent of invention of comic scenes, which generally end in broad farce. He does not represent fairly even the social and jovial side of men of much refinement, or, if he does he should not represent them as he does, on *all* sides thus social and jovial. —HORNE, RICHARD HENGIST, 1844, *A New Spirit of the Age.*

O'Dowd's anecdotes constitute his greatest charm; and his sketches of national character show minute and delicate portraiture.—SPALDING, WILLIAM, 1852, *A History of English Literature, p.* 417.

The "Prince of neck-or-nothing novelists," as he is called. . . . What Horace demanded has been permitted to Lever, who has not only told the truth with a smiling face, but has brought the tears into many eyes, and with all his fun and frolic has never brought a blush to any cheek. He has not attempted to preach; he has not been either a stoic or a cynic. His philosophy is rather of the garden of Epicurus, and the enjoyment he teaches is that of manliness and reason, and for good, clean, wholesome reading, which will leave no headache or heartache, and no dregs within the mind, commend us to Charles Lever.—FRISWELL, JAMES HAIN, 1870, *Modern Men of Letters Honestly Criticised, pp.* 171, 179.

As a delineator of the droll side of Irish life and character, and of army life in general, Lever is unequalled. The plot of his novels is usually weak, and the professed heroines are tame and conventional. But the other characters are all highly marked, and reveal a wealth of humor and fun that borders on the incredible. They are all excellent, and some of them, like Mickey Free and Major Monsoon, may be safely classed among the greatest literary creations. Lever's later works are not so good as his early ones, because they treat of the same general themes, and are consequently lacking in freshness. . . . Of all care-dispelling, mirth-provoking books, "Charles O'Malley" is the most genial. It is one carnival of wit, humor, and revelry from end to end, with just enough of the shady side of life to temper the merriment, and prevent it from becoming monotonous, as is the case in "Verdant Green."—HART, JOHN S., 1872, *A Manual of English Literature, pp.* 533, 534.

But a third name is wanting to complete the group of Irish novelists—that of the vivacious and delightful Lever. If judged by his later works, it is easy to think him superior to either of his predecessors [Maria Edgeworth and Lady Morgan], simply because he combines so much that is distinctive of them both. He partakes so largely the sagacious insight and practical purpose of the one, in union with the hearty buoyant, joyous temperament of the other. He traverses, in common with them, the higher and middle grades of life (he is less successful with the lower); but with an ampler knowledge of the world, and of the political history of his time. And if, as a Protestant and a Conservative, he seems less sensible of the national endurances and claims, he is alive to faults on all sides, can weigh excuses with offences, and, whatever his race's failings, can as warmly and proudly as any one acknowledge all their offsets. . . . And the style of these narrations is quite on a par with their details. It positively gallops across the pages. It is literature on horseback riding down a capital joke. And as the style, so is the knowledge. These stories are as authoritative on horse flesh, on field sports, on claret, or on cookery, as they are a perfect *vade mecum* on that higher indulgence—an affair of honour. From the insult and the uproar, up to the loading of the pistols and putting the parties in position, nothing is wanting to complete the picture of this grand climax to a festivity.—BERNARD, BAYLE, 1874, *The Life of Samuel Lover*, p. 173, 174.

Besides his strange adventures, his battle-scenes, and romantic exploits, Mr. Lever has a rich, racy, national humour. His heroes have all strong love of adventure, a national proneness to blundering, and a tendency to get into scrapes and questionable situations. The author's chief fault is his sometimes mistaking farce for comedy—mere animal spirits for wit or humour.—CHAMBERS, ROBERT, 1876, *Cyclopædia of English Literature, ed. Carruthers.*

It is with a pang of regret that we peruse the "Cornelius O'Dowd" papers. They are tinged with that abominable spirit which is sending Italy at the present hour to perdition, and we greatly fear that Mr. Lever wrote them for the London market. He was no bigot, however; on the contrary, his life was passed amongst Catholics, and his dearest and best friends were of the true church; consequently, the pain is intensified when we come to stand face to face with the fact that these papers were, if not the outcome of a pecuniary necessity, at least the result of a craving for money, and the hollow effusions of a hireling pen. His Italian sojourn led him gradually away from the more kindly tone towards Catholics which pervaded his earlier Irish novels.—ROBINSON, N., 1877, *Charles Lever at Home, The Catholic World*, vol. 26, p. 212.

The works of Charles Lever, while possessing considerable interest for most mature minds, are much more popular with the young. . . . The style is bold, dashing and careless. There is no attempt at close analysis of motives or balancing of probabilities. The hero relates his own adventures, and leaves his audience to guess at the motives which actuated those with whom he came in contact. Incidents follow each other in rapid succession. When one danger is escaped by the hero, he immediately gets into another scrape of some kind. We are kept in a state of constant concern for him. Either his liberty is threatened by the machinations of enemies, his life endangered by duels, or his hope of winning the one woman who can make him happy on the point of being changed to despair by his temporary yielding to the fascinations of pretty women, with whom he is brought into contact. He is no monster of perfection, like many heroes who are popular with the young, but endowed with a fair share of human weaknesses.—STEWART, J. L., 1878, *Lever's Military Tales, Canadian Monthly, vol. 1, p. 199.*

Perhaps a word ought to be said of the rattling romances of Irish electioneering, love-making, and fighting which set people reading "Charles O'Malley" and "Jack Hinton," even when "Pickwick" was still a novelty. Charles Lever had wonderful animal spirits and a broad, bright humor. He was quite genuine in his way. He afterwards changed his style completely, and with much success; and will be found in the later part of the period holding just the same relative place as in the earlier, just behind the foremost men, but in manner so different that he might be a new writer who had never read a line of the roystering adventures of Light Dragoons which were popular when Charles Lever first gave them to the world. There was nothing great about Lever, but the literature of the Victorian period would not be quite all that we know it without him.—McCARTHY, JUSTIN, 1879, *A History of Our Own Times from the Accession of Queen Victoria to the Berlin Congress, ch.* xxix.

Although it is only a few years since Lever died, his popularity as a novelist had been at the time so long waning that his death had not the effect, as in the case of Thackeray and Dickens, of bringing to an abrupt termination a brilliant career; but rather of reviving for a brief time a reputation already almost extinct. And yet there was a time when instalments of a new novel by the author of "Harry Lorrequer" were almost as eagerly awaited as those of the authors of "Vanity Fair" or "Oliver Twist," and there was never a period during his long literary activity when Lever's ready wit and fertile imagination were not equal to the task of producing fiction far more deserving of attention than nine-tenths of the successful novels of the present time.—SEDGWICK, A. G., 1879, *Charles Lever, The Nation, vol.* 29, *p.* 368.

In our opinion his best work was done in his latter years, when in a series of novels, wanting, indeed, the fire and dash of his early performances, but infinitely more accurate as delineations of life and character, he gave to the world the mellowed experience of an acute observer who had seen many phases of existence, and could comment on them with shrewdness and accuracy.—NICOLL, HENRY J., 1882, *Landmarks of English Literature, p.* 399.

Lever's novels will not live long, even if they may be said to be alive now. . . . What was his manner of working I do not know, but I should think it must have been very quick, and that he never troubled himself on the subject, except when he was seated with a pen in his hand. —TROLLOPE, ANTHONY, 1882–83, *An Autobiography, ch.* xiii.

The "first edition craze" shows no signs of abatement. Indeed, it is impossible to say where the extravagance of this latest form of bibliographical madness will end. At a recent sale at Sotheby's there were some good first editions of Thackeray, Dickens, and Charles Lever. The author of "Harry Lorrequer," however, seemed to be the favorite. A complete set of the first edition of Lever fetched the extraordinary price of £275.—ASHBY-STERRY, JOSEPH, 1889, *The Bookbuyer, vol.* 6, *p.* 140.

He never worked on a definite plan nor was at any pains to contrive a plot; he depended on the morning's impressions for the evening's task, and wrote "Con Cregan" under the immediate influence of a travelled Austrian, who used to talk to him every night ere he sat down to his story. But he was a wonderful improvisatore. He had imagination—(even romantic imagination: as the episode of Menelaus Crick in "Con Cregan" will show)—a keen, sure eye for character, incomparable facility in composition, an inexhaustible fund of shrewdness, whimsicality, high spirits, an

admirable knack of dialogue; and as consul at Spezzia and at Trieste, as a fashionable practitioner at Brussels, as dispensary doctor of the wild Ulster coast, he was excellently placed for the kind of literature it was in him to produce. Writing at random and always under the spur of necessity, he managed to inform his work with extraordinary vitality and charm. His books were only made to sell, but it is like enough that they will also live, for they are yet well nigh as readable as at first, and Nina and Kate O'Donoghue—(for instance)—seem destined to go down to posterity as typical and representative. — HENLEY, WILLIAM ERNEST, 1890; *Views and Reviews, p.* 175.

Had great ability as a story-teller, but little of the novelist's art. His stories are a collection of fragments. — EMERY, FRED PARKER, 1891, *Notes on English Literature, p.* 117.

It ["Harry Lorrequer"] is merely a string of Irish and other stories, good, bad, and indifferent—a picture gallery full of portraits of priests, soldiers, peasants and odd characters. The plot is of no importance; we are not interested in Harry's love affairs, but in his scrapes, adventures, duels at home and abroad. He fights people by mistake whom he does not know by sight, he appears on parade with his face blackened, he wins large piles at *trente et quarante*, he disposes of coopers of claret and bowls of punch, and the sheep on a thousand hills provide him with deviled kidneys. The critics and the authors thought little of the merry medley, but the public enjoyed it, and defied the reviewers. One paper preferred the book to a wilderness of "Pickwicks."—LANG, ANDREW, 1891, *Essays in Little, p.* 164.

The latter part of his life Lever spent chiefly on the continent as a consul at Spezza, Trieste, etc., and his later works were more elaborate, full of diplomacy and intrigue, full, too, of the speculations and devices of that special figure, the Irishman abroad, but failing considerably in the racy wit and fun of his earlier works. His plots become too intricate, and the various threads of his story so irretrievably mixed that the author himself often seemed to forget what his original intention had been, and merely sought the quickest way out of the labyrinth in which he had involved himself.—OLIPHANT, MARGARET O. W., 1892, *The Victorian Age of English Literature.*

An author without sufficient literary vocation. Had his circumstances been easy, he probably would not have written at all. His earliest and most popular writings can hardly rank as literature, though their vigour and gaiety, and the excellent anecdotes and spirited songs with which they are interspersed, will always render them attractive. He is almost destitute of invention or imagination, his personages are generally transcripts from the life, and his incidents stories told at second hand. At a later period in his career he awoke in some measure to the claims of art, and exhibited more proficiency as a writer, with less damage to his character as a humorist, than might have been expected.—GARNETT, RICHARD, 1893, *Dictionary of National Biography, vol.* XXXIII, *p.* 139.

The convivial spirit is one that, setting law and order at defiance, often shows too little respect for technique; and Lever's verse, like his prose, is popular more for its spirit than its form.— MILES, ALFRED H., 1894, *The Poets and the Poetry of the Century, Humour, Society, Parody, and Occasional Verse, p.* 310.

Although Lever died so recently as 1872, his biography contains much that is doubtful or obscure; many works are credited, or perhaps debited to him, which probably never issued from his pen, and for this reason the compilation of a correct, and at the same time a complete bibliography, which has never yet been attempted, would be an exceptionally difficult task. . . . In March 1889, Messrs. Sotheby disposed of the collection of Lever's works formed by Mr. John Mansfield Mackenzie of Edinburgh, and it is worthy of note that the catalogue contained the items mentioned below, and no others. The collection realised £275, an exceptional price, for the books were uniformly bound in Rivière's best manner, and were often extra illustrated with Browne's original drawings and many extra plates. So far as I know, no other collection can claim to approach this in point of perfection and beauty of appearance, the cardinal points that regulate the course of every advanced collector of early editions.—SLATER, J. H., 1894, *Early Editions, pp.* 167, 168.

Lever represents the world before the Revolution, before education, refinement, birth, respect for things old, were swamped in democracy. . . . We really cannot decorously request the Ibsenite to share our pleasure in Lever. An old fellow reading him again, remembers his early youth, when the Great Duke was his hero, when Charles O'Malley was his love, when, being a very idle little boy, he read Scott, Thackeray, Harry Lorrequer, Dickens, Marryat, Captain Mayne Reid, indiscriminately and assiduously, neglecting Cæsar's valuable commentaries "De Bello Gallico." We were not critical then, and we enjoyed a romance in the *London Journal*—a romance about the wicked Muscovites and the cruel Duke Constantine—almost as much as "Old Mortality." These uncritical days do not return, but time cannot shake our affection for Lever. As it was then, so it is yet with boys, one presumes. . . . It is undeniable that a more refined and self-conscious manner has arisen in fiction; and it is pretty certain that Lever is not at present widely read by men professionally engaged in literature. But the mere aspect of his books in a library shows that they have been well and duly thumbed by that large majority of readers who "read for human pleasure," and like a story for the story's sake. He aimed at no higher or more distant goal and what he aimed at he attained. He was sensitive, but he was not vain; and as to his achievements, he had not an atom of conceit or self-consciousness. To be the most popular romancer of his country, beyond all question the most widely read, sufficed for Charles Lever. In literature, as in life, he was an unsophisticated example of the natural man; and while we cannot place him among the six or seven great novelists of the world—with Cervantes, Lesage, Fielding, Scott, Dumas, Thackeray, Tolstoi—we owe him a great deal of gratitude and liking.—LANG, ANDREW, 1894, *Novels of Charles Lever, Introduction.*

Lever at different times of his life manifested almost all the gifts which the novelist requires, though unfortunately he never quite managed to exhibit them all together.—SAINTSBURY, GEORGE, 1896, *A History of Nineteenth Century Literature, p.* 158.

Lever's characters though lively are never subtle—the constant anecdotes interspersed in his stories were often second-hand—but he had a zest and spirit withal that carried him into popular favor.—NETTLETON, GEORGE HENRY, 1901, *ed. Specimens of the Short Story, p.* 112.

Mary Somerville
1780–1872

Mary Somerville, *née* Fairfax (born 1780, died 1872), well-known for her scientific researches, and for her popular and educational scientific works, was the daughter of Vice-Admiral Sir William George Fairfax, a Scottish naval officer. Mary was a great reader, learned Euclid surreptitiously while quite a girl, and at the same period got up a knowledge of Latin in order to be able to read Newton's "Principia," and was educated at a school at Musselburgh, a small town in Midlothian. Her first important contribution to science was made in 1826, when she presented to the Royal Society a paper on the magnetising powers of the more refrangible solar rays, the object of which was to prove that these rays of the solar spectrum have a strong magnetic influence. This paper led to much discussion, which only terminated many years later by the investigations of the German electricians, Riess and Moser, who showed that the action upon the magnetic needle was not caused by the violet rays. In 1831 Mrs. Somerville brought out her original treatise on the "Mechanism of the Heavens," and in 1834 published a work "On the Connection of the Physical Sciences," which has been referred to by Humboldt as "the generally exact and admirable treatise." In 1848 appeared the work by which, perhaps, she is most generally known, her "Physical Geography," and in 1869, at the age of eighty-nine, she published a volume "On Molecular and Microscopic Science," which contains a complete prospectus of some of the most recent and most abstruse researches of modern science. Mrs. Somerville was twice married, her first husband being Captain Greig, a naval officer, and her second being her cousin, Dr. William Somerville. In 1835 she received a literary pension of £300. Shortly after her death in December, 1872, a movement was started to commemorate her name, which culminated in the establishment of the Somerville Hall at Oxford, and the Mary Somerville scholarship in mathematics for women.—SANDERS, LLOYD C., ed., 1887, *Celebrities of the Century, p.* 938.

PERSONAL

Dined at Murray's: company, Dr. and Mrs. Somerville, Croker, and Sir David Wilkie and his sister; the first time of my meeting with Croker for many years. Mrs. Somerville, whom I had never before seen so much of, gained upon me exceedingly. So much unpretending womanliness of manner joined with such rare talent and knowledge is, indeed, a combination that cannot be too much admired.—MOORE, THOMAS, 1837, *Diary, April* 27; *Memoirs, Journal and Correspondence, ed. Russell, vol.* VII, *p.* 182.

Made a truly delightful visit to Mrs. Somerville at Chelsea, who is certainly among the most extraordinary women that have ever lived, both by the simplicity of her character and the singular variety, power, and brilliancy of her talents.—TICKNOR, GEORGE, 1838, *Journal, April* 13; *Life, Letters and Journals, vol.* II, *p.* 154.

It was delightful to see her always well-dressed and thoroughly womanly in her conversation and manners, while unconscious of any peculiarity in her pursuits. It was delightful to go to tea at her house at Chelsea, and find everything in order and beauty;—the walls hung with her fine drawings; her music in the corner, and her tea

table spread with good things. In the midst of these household elegances, Dr. Somerville one evening pulled open a series of drawers, to find something he wanted to show me. As he shut one after another, I ventured to ask what those strange things were which filled every drawer. "O! they are only Mrs. Somerville's diplomas," said he, with a droll look of pride and amusement.—MARTINEAU, HARRIET, 1855–77, *Autobiography, ed. Chapman, vol.* I, *p.* 269.

She was seventy-seven years old, but appeared twenty years younger. She was not handsome, but her face was pleasing; the forehead low and broad; the eyes blue; the features so regular, that in the marble bust by Chantrey, which I had seen, I had considered her handsome. . . . She spoke with a strong Scotch accent, and was slightly affected with deafness. . . . Mrs. Somerville's conversation was marked by great simplicity; it was rather of the familiar and chatty order, with no tendency to the essay style. . . . I could but admire Mrs. Somerville as a woman. The ascent of the steep and rugged path of science had not unfitted her for the drawing-room circle; the hours of devotion to close study have not been incompatible with the duties of wife and mother; the mind that has turned to rigid demonstration has not thereby lost its faith in those truths which figures will not prove. —MITCHELL, MARIA, 1858, *Journal, Life, Letters and Journals,* ed. *Kendall, pp.* 161, 162, 163.

So you have remembered me again, and I have the delight of receiving from you a new copy of that work which has so often instructed me; and I may well say, cheered me in my simple homely course through life in this house. It was most kind to think of me; but ah! how sweet it is to believe that I have your *approval* in matters where kindness would be nothing, where judgment alone must rule. I almost doubt myself when I think I have your approbation, to some degree at least, in what I may have thought or said about gravitation, the forces of nature, their conservation, &c.— FARADAY, MICHAEL, 1859, *Letter to Mrs. Somerville, Jan.* 17; *Personal Recollections of Mary Somerville,* ed. *Somerville, p.* 292.

I am now in my 92nd year, still able to drive out for several hours; I am extremely deaf, and my memory of ordinary events, and especially of the names of people, is failing, but not for mathematical and scientific subjects. I am still able to read books on the higher algebra for four or five hours in the morning, and even to solve the problems. Sometimes I find them difficult, but my old obstinacy remains, for if I do not succeed to-day, I attack them again on the morrow. I also enjoy reading about all the new discoveries and theories in the scientific world, and on all branches of science.—SOMERVILLE, MARY, 1872, *Personal Recollections,* ed. *Somerville, p.* 364.

It would be almost incredible were I to describe how much my mother contrived to do in the course of the day. When my sister and I were small children, although busily engaged in writing for the press, she used to teach us for three hours every morning, besides managing her house carefully, reading the newspapers (for she always was a keen, and, I must add, a liberal politician) and the most important new books on all subjects, grave and gay. In addition to all this, she freely visited and received her friends. She was, indeed, very fond of society, and did not look for transcendent talent in those with whom she associated, although no one appreciated it more when she found it. Gay and cheerful company was a pleasant relaxation after a hard day's work. My mother never introduced scientific or learned subjects into general conversation. When they were brought forward by others, she talked simply and naturally about them, without the slightest pretension to superior knowledge. Finally, to complete the list of her accomplishments, I must add that she was a remarkably neat and skilful needlewoman. We still possess some elaborate specimens of her embroidery and lace-work. — SOMERVILLE, MARTHA, 1874, ed. *Personal Recollections of Mary Somerville, p.* 5.

No one can read her autobiography, . . . without feeling that the woman was far greater than her works.— SMITH, C. C., 1874, *Mary Somerville, Old and New, vol.* 9, p. 340.

This brief outline of Mrs. Somerville's career cannot fail to convey some idea, however inadequate, of her high mental and moral qualities. The strength and activity of her intellect were early developed in her persevering efforts for the acquisition of knowledge; her firmness of purpose withstood the opposition of her friends and the cold indifference of her first husband; she would neither forsake nor suspend the studies which were as essential to her as her daily bread. Her firm grasp of all which she undertook is worthy of notice. She never seems to have known mistrust of her own powers; the only fear which ever arose in her mind was from the inherent impossibility of the task. The high place to which she attained in the most difficult branches of science shows that she did not misjudge her capabilities.—BAILEY, JOHN BURN, 1888, *Modern Methuselahs, p.* 323.

One of the most striking things about her was the many-sided character of her mind. Some people—men as well as women—who are scientific or mathematical seem to care for nothing but science or mathematics; but it may be truly said of her that "Everything was grist that came to her mill." There was hardly any branch of art or knowledge which she did not delight in. She studied painting under Mr. Nasmyth in Edinburgh, and he declared her to be the best pupil he had ever had. Almost to the day of her death she delighted in painting and drawing. She was also an excellent musician and botanist. The special study with which her name will always be associated was mathematics as applied to the study of the heavens, but she also wrote on physical geography and on microscopic science.—

FAWCETT, MILLICENT GARRETT, 1889, *Some Eminent Women of Our Times, p.* 38.

By far the best and dearest of my friends in Florence, however, was one who never came up our hill, and who was already then an aged woman—Mrs. Somerville. I had brought a letter of introduction to her, being anxious to see one who had been such an honor to womanhood; but I expected to find her an incarnation of science, having very little affinity with such a person as I. Instead of this, I found in her the dearest old lady in all the world, who took me to her heart as if I had been a newly-found daughter, and for whom I soon felt such tender affection that sitting beside her on her sofa, (as I mostly did on account of her deafness) I could hardly keep myself from caressing her. In a letter to Harriet St. Leger I wrote of her: "She is the very ideal of an old lady, so gentle, cordial and dignified, like my mother; and as fresh, eager, and intelligent *now*, as she can ever have been." Her religious ideas proved to be exactly like my own; and being no doubt somewhat athirst for sympathy on a subject on which she felt profoundly (her daughters differing from her), she opened her heart to me entirely.—COBBE, FRANCES POWER, 1894, *Life by Herself, vol.* II, *p.* 349.

Her grasp of scientific truth in all branches of knowledge, combined with an exceptional power of exposition, made her the most remarkable woman of her generation. Nor did her abstruse studies exclude the cultivation of lighter gifts, and she excelled in music, in painting, and in the use of the needle. Her endowments were enhanced by rare charm and geniality of manner, while the fair hair, delicate complexion, and small proportions which had obtained for her in her girlhood the sobriquet of "the rose of Jedburgh," formed a piquant contrast to her masculine breadth of intellect. Her contributions to science were recognised by various learned bodies. The Royal Astronomical Society elected her an honorary member, and the Victoria gold medal of the Royal Geographical Society was conferred on her in 1869. A similar distinction was awarded her by the Italian Royal Geographical Society, and her name was commemorated after her death in the foundation of Somerville Hall and in the Mary Somerville scholarship for women in mathematics at Oxford.—CLERKE, MISS E. M., 1898, *Dictionary of National Biography, vol.* LIII, *p.* 255.

GENERAL

Less ambitious in title ["Physical Geography"] and form than the "Cosmos" of Humboldt, the works of Mrs. Somerville embrace. really the whole scope of his design, and, as I think, with a more lucid definition and arrangement of the subjects it includes.—HOLLAND, SIR HENRY, 1871, *Recollections of Past Life, p.* 248.

It is a work ["Connexion of the Physical Sciences"] full of interest, not only to the student of advanced science, but to the general reader. In saying this we indicate its chief merit and its most marked defect. It is impossible to conceive that any reader, no matter how advanced or how limited his knowledge, could fail to find many most instructive pages in this work; but it is equally impossible to conceive that any one reader could find the *whole* work, or even any considerable portion, instructive or useful.—PROCTOR, RICHARD A., 1873, *Light Science for Leisure Hours, Second Series, p.* 10.

This ["Physical Geography"] was the fruit of much study and research; but, just as she was preparing to print, Humboldt began the publication of his "Cosmos." Her first impulse was to throw her own manuscript into the fire; and it was doubtless only the good sense of her husband which prevented her from doing so foolish a thing. "Don't be rash," said he: "consult some of our friends,—Herschel for instance." So the manuscript was sent to Sir John Herschel, who unhesitatingly advised its publication; and it was shortly afterward given to the world, and was everywhere welcomed as an important contribution to a very attractive department of knowledge. —SMITH, C. C., 1874, *Mary Somerville, Old and New, vol.* 9, *p.* 339.

This work at once achieved for its authoress a high place among the cultivators of physical science. The "Mechanism of the Heavens" commanded the hearty and kindly expressed approbation of Sir John Herschel, and Professor Whewell wrote a sonnet in its praise. It became a class-book at Cambridge. That Mrs. Somerville should have found time, in the midst of ordinary duties, to write a work requiring such depth of thought, is remarkable. One thing that helped her was a power of laying down and taking up a subject at pleasure;

she was also indebted to a singular capacity for abstracting the mind from what was going on before her eyes. She could hear a great deal of silly talk, or some ridiculous harangue, and be thinking all the time about mathematical problems.—CHAMBERS, WILLIAM, 1874, *Mary Somerville, Chambers's Journal, vol.* 51, *p.* 35.

Mary Somerville has probably no rival among women as a scientific scholar. . . . It is not exaggeration to say that Mrs. Somerville distinctly raised the world's estimate of woman's capacity for the severest and the loftiest scientific pursuits. She possessed the most extraordinary power of concentration, amounting to an entire absorption in the subject which she happened to be studying, to the exclusion of all disturbing sights and sounds. She had in a supreme degree that which Carlyle calls the first quality of genius, an immense capacity for taking trouble. She had also, happily for herself, an immense capacity for finding enjoyment in almost everything: in new places, people, and thoughts; in the old familiar scenes and friends and associations. Hers was a noble, calm, fully-rounded life.—MCCARTHY, JUSTIN, 1879, *A History of Our Own Times from the Accession of Queen Victoria to the Berlin Congress.*

It is possible that Mrs. Somerville profited somewhat in reputation by her coincidence with the period of "diffusion of useful knowledge." But she had real scientific knowledge and real literary gifts; and she made good use of both.—SAINTSBURY, GEORGE, 1896, *A History of Nineteenth Century Literature, p.* 411.

Norman Macleod

1812–1872

Was born a minister's son, at Campbeltown, Argyllshire, June 3, 1812. He attended Glasgow University, and was minister of London 1838–43, Dalkeith 1843–45, and the Barony Church, Glasgow, from 1851 till his death, June 16, 1872. He was made a Queen's Chaplain in 1857, and D. D. in 1858. An utterance of his on the Sabbath question in 1865 created much controversy. In 1869 he was moderator of the General Assembly. He visited Canada in 1845, Palestine in 1864–65, and India in 1867. From 1860 till 1872 he edited *Good Words*, contributing tales, essays, verses, sermons. In book-form he published "The Earnest Student" (1854), "Daily Meditations" (1861), "The Old Lieutenant" (1862), "Parish Papers" (1862), "Wee Davie" (1864), "Eastward" (1866), "Reminiscences of a Highland Parish" (his grandfather's parish of Morven, 1867), "The Starling" (1867), and "Peeps at the Far East" (1871). See "Memoir" by the Rev. Donald Macleod (1876).—PATRICK AND GROOME, *eds.*, 1897, *Chambers's Biographical Dictionary, p.* 618.

The Queen hardly knows how to begin a letter to Mr. Donald Macleod, so deep and strong are her feelings on this most sad and most painful occasion—for words are all too weak to say what she feels, and what all must feel who ever knew his beloved, excellent, and highly gifted brother, Dr. Norman Macleod! First of all, to his family—his venerable, loved, and honoured mother, his wife and large family of children—the loss of this good man is irreparable and overwhelming! But it is an irreparable public loss, and the Queen feels this deeply. To herself personally, the loss of dear Dr. Macleod is a very great one; he was so kind, and on all occasions showed her such warm sympathy, and in the early days of her great sorrow, gave the Queen so much comfort whenever she saw him, that she always looked forward eagerly to those occasions when she saw him here; and she can not realise the idea that in this world she is never to see his kind face, and listen to those admirable discourses which did every one good, and to his charming conversation again!—VICTORIA, QUEEN, 1872, *Letter to Donald Macleod, June* 17; *Memoir of Norman Macleod by Donald Macleod, vol.* II, *p.* 393.

The most manly man I ever knew, the most genial, the most many-sided, and yet the least angular. . . . Norman Macleod was no mere paper and pulpit and platform good man, putting all his goodness into books and sermons and speeches. Where he was best known—known as standing the crucial test of the "dreary intercourse of daily life"—there he was most respected and beloved.—STRAHAN, ALEXANDER, 1872, *Norman Macleod, Contemporary Review, vol.* 20, *pp.* 291, 292.

In every circle of society in which he had

ever moved—in every congregation which had crowded round his pulpit—in every public auditory which had hung on his spoken utterances or his written words— the same broad, vast, heart-stirring impression was produced, as of one who not only had within him an inexhaustible fund of pathos, of wit, of laughter, and of tears, but who feared not, nay, who loved to pour it forth for the benefit, for the enjoyment, for the instruction of his fellow-creatures. And this tender overflowing "compassion," to use the word in its largest sense, was tinged with no weak effeminacy, no unruly fanaticism. There was a force as of his own Highland clan, there was a shrewdness as of his own Scottish nation, which no one could mistake for feebleness or folly.— STANLEY, ARTHUR PENRHYN, 1872, *In Memoriam, Good Words, vol.* 13, *p.* 505.

In 1851, then, being called to the Barony Church of Glasgow, he finally took up his abode there, and substantially began the real work of his life. It was about this time I first saw him, and heard him address a public meeting. In the prime of life, tall, handsome, with a singularly winning expression, he was about as splendid a human creature as one could wish to look upon. Latterly, and especially when his health began to fail, he inclined to be too portly; but in those days his robust form showed immense power of work, and the Barony was the very sphere to put it to the proof. —SMITH, WALTER C., 1872, *Norman Macleod, D. D., Good Words, vol.* 13, *p.* 512.

His active nature did not survive its usefulness; and instead of being kept under what, to his vivid imagination, might have been the appalling consciousness of life slowly ebbing away, his spirit passed, without a struggle, into that Presence in which his thoughts and affections had long made themselves a beloved abode. The news of his death passed with extraordinary speed through the kingdom, and everywhere produced a profound impression. No man, since Chalmers, was so much mourned in Scotland. People who had never exchanged a word with him felt and spoke as if a personal friend had been taken away, and those who had deemed it their duty sometimes to oppose him even with bitterness, were the foremost to pay honour to the rich humanity and religious nobleness, which had raised him above the influence of all

party strife.—MACLEOD, DONALD, 1876, *Memoir of Norman Macleod, vol.* II, *p.* 393.

He was a wonderfully eloquent and impressive preacher: "the greatest and most convincing preacher I ever heard," was the estimate of Sir Arthur Helps, whose opinion was worth something. The solitary one among Scotch divines who was commonly placed before him was Dr. Caird, Principal of the University of Glasgow, who for thirty years has stood without question first among Scotch preachers. Guthrie and Macleod you would bracket as equal. Still more remarkable was his power as a platform speaker. When a great meeting of people was getting very tired, through many long-winded and remarkably sensible orations, he had but to rise, and instantly attention was keen, and there was life everywhere. Norman Macleod was never dull.— BOYD, ANDREW K. H., 1876, *Norman Macleod, Fraser's Magazine, vol.* 93, *p.* 498.

The name of Norman Macleod was a household word throughout Scotland for at least the last twenty years of his life. . . . His heart at sixty, while ripened by experience and grace, still retained all the natural characteristics of its boyhood. . . . There was no element of emotion lacking or defective in his nature; no hard, harsh, unsusceptible parts; and hence nothing was foreign to him which man could feel. A large and free joyousness was congenial to his whole constitution; yet there were fibres of feminine tenderness in his heart; and for so manly a man the tear was easily drawn to his eye. His ready sympathy with sorrow and suffering gave an immense value to his intercourse with the afflicted. It made him in many a house of mourning "Dr. M'Gavin" of his own "Wee Davie."— FLINT, ROBERT, 1883, *Scottish Divines, St. Giles' Lectures, Third Series, pp.* 425, 426, 444.

He was a great, full-rounded, whole-souled *man*, and his thorough humanness was the substratum of his power. Add to that his joyous love of nature, his Celtic temperament, with its poetic susceptibility and its occasional weird out-flashings of mystic might, his devotional fervor, which, to the surprise of so many—though Dr. Flint says it was no surprise to him—came out so fully in his diary, his deep well of tender sympathy with suffering, of which his "Wee Davie" may be taken as a specimen, and his intense desire to do good to all with whom he came into contact, and you have the qualities which were most distinctive in his character.—TAYLOR, WILLIAM M., 1887, *The Scottish Pulpit*, p. 262.

Macleod was one of the most notable ecclesiastics that Scotland has produced, an eloquent preacher, an earnest philanthropist, a highminded patriot, a man of broad and catholic spirit, a writer of no mean order, and a genial friend. Several monuments were raised to his memory. His Mission Church in Glasgow was made the "Macleod Parish Church." The Barony congregation built a "Macleod Memorial Missionary Institute" in a destitute part of the parish. A statue of him was set up in Glasgow, and the queen placed two beautiful memorial windows in Crathie Church, where he had often preached before her.—HAMILTON, THOMAS, 1893, *Dictionary of National Biography, vol.* XXXV, p. 218.

GENERAL

He felt that he never could give to what he wrote the finish which was needed. They must be taken for what they are, the mere coruscations of a mind preoccupied and pre-engaged. It was not that he did not appreciate—no one has read a page of his writings, but must perceive this — the grandeur, and relish the enjoyment of literary labour,—but like Mahomet, gazing down, according to the legend, on the world-famous view of Damascus, he felt, "Man has but one Paradise"—each man has but one great end in life—"and mine is fixed elsewhere." Yet, regarding his works as thus the secondary and accidental utterances of a full heart and full mind, they take no mean place in the Scottish literature of our day. The high glee of the "Song of the Curlers," the lofty strain of "Courage, Brother!" the delightful mixture of humour and pathos in the tales of the "Starling" and "Wee Davie," are not unworthy of the countryman of Scott and of Burns, of the Ettrick Shepherd and of Christopher North. — STANLEY, ARTHUR PENRHYN, 1872, *In Memoriam, Good Words, vol.* 13, p. 506.

In *Good Words* his chief contributions to literature appeared, all except his life of John Mackintosh, "The Earnest Student," which is perhaps the most artistically finished of them all. Our readers, therefore, must be familiar with those bright sketches of nature and human nature which

were among the first things the paper-cutter hurried to on the monthly apppearance of the welcome brown cover. "Wee Davie," it has been said, was his own favourite, and its exquisite pathos has, perhaps, made this the general verdict, though the humour of "Billy Buttons" shows a still finer touch, and is a fit rival to Bret Harte's "Luck of Roaring Camp." But I know that he reckoned "The Starling," of all his books, the one most likely to perpetuate his name, having cost him far more labour of thought than the others. Whether he was right in this estimate the future will tell. None of his other tales are so finished. . . . On the whole, my favourite is "The Recollections of a Highland Parish." It is fragmentary, but fresh, natural, and true; just the kind of work which could be best done under such conditions as were imposed upon him. But none of his books give anything like a full idea of the man's real greatness.— SMITH, WALTER C., 1872, *Norman Macleod, D. D., Good Words, vol.* 13, p. 514.

"Wee Davie" was his own favourite among his works. It was rattled off at a sitting. But he thought very little of his writings, and full of shrewd observation, lively description, and good humour, in two scenes, as they are, there can be no doubt that Norman Macleod was infinitely greater in his life than in his books.—STRAHAN, ALEXANDER, 1872, *Norman Macleod, Contemporary Review, vol.* 20, p. 298.

His writings, though lively and clever, give no idea of Norman Macleod. What he produced must be vivified by his personality. And he was so pushed and over-driven by excessive work, that he never had time to do his best with his pen.—BOYD, ANDREW K. H., 1876, *Norman Macleod, Fraser's Magazine, vol.* 93, p. 500.

"Eastward" and "Peeps at the Far East" are among the most enjoyable of books of travel. But probably Dr. Macleod's works of fiction are those of his writings which will live longest, and which even best deserve to do so. For he had in a rare degree every quality necessary to a great novelist, and in this line of literature there was no distinction which he might not have gained. The works of fiction which we have from him were rapidly composed, and were all written with a view to produce a moral and religious impression, because he thought himself entitled to write stories only if he could make them subservient and conducive to the same end as his ministry of the Gospel; and yet "Wee Davie" is an exquisite gem, "The Gold Thread," one of the most charming of children's books, and "The Starling" and "The Old Lieutenant and His Son" are in every way worthy of permanent fame. It is only in his works of fiction that we see fully displayed Norman Macleod's power of representing human characters and of touching the springs alike of laughter and of tears.—FLINT, ROBERT, 1883, *Scottish Divines, St. Giles' Lectures, Third Series, p. 458.*

These are what to the best of my ability I can recall as the most salient of the formative forces that acted on the important period of my youth and early manhood; but I cannot close this paper without expressing my obligations, though coming somewhat later, to two evangelists of this generation with whom it was my good fortune to be on terms of intimacy—Thomas Guthrie and Norman Macleod, two men the large human breadth, the sunny cheerfulness, the strong good sense, and the dignified grace of whose preaching will remain deeply graven in every Scottish heart so long as Scotland is Scotland. To this hour I remember the strong impression made on me by the Glasgow Doctor's "Annals of a Highland Parish," a book replete with more of the fresh breath, vivid colouring, and stirring action of a thoroughly manly style of life than any that I know outside of Homer. —BLACKIE, JOHN STUART, 1887, *Books which Have Influenced Me, p. 76.*

Norman Macleod wrote little verse, and except for one stirring song would have had no title to recognition here. This song, "Trust in God," first appeared in the *Edinburgh Christian Magazine* for January 1857 (a magazine edited by its author), and has since found its way into countless collections of verse.—MILES, ALFRED H., 1897, *The Poets and the Poetry of the Century, Sacred, Moral, and Religious Verse, p. 712.*

As a writer of fiction it is remarkable that Macleod should be forgotten, when work similar to his, only duller, is boomed over all the earth. His stories, it is true, have a set religious aim, but that should be no offence in days when the most belauded fiction is nothing if not didactic, nay, when the novel is made a pulpit for the promulgation of moral heresy. If art in fiction is to be strangled, religion may as well be the executioner as the last indecency. . . . Macleod purposed to write stories which should be religious, and yet do no violence to reality. And his characters are plainly genuine, except, perhaps, the hero of his first attempt—"The Old Lieutenant and his Son." . . . The most prevailing quality of Macleod's fiction is the pathos, and though one must be a Christian to feel it all, there is much that no humane reader will be able to resist. To be sure the occasion is always simple and ordinary, never such, for instance, as the elaborate decline of a consumptive scholar in his garden-chair; and the cause of these tears may be only a remark or a gesture. Under the restrictions of *Good Words* he could not do his best as a humorist, yet he permitted himself to be thoroughly Scottish and provoke hearty laughter. Within a modest range he displays real genius in the portrayal of character and the rendering of Scottish conversation.—WELLWOOD, JOHN, 1897, *Norman Macleod (Famous Scots Series), pp. 90, 91, 92.*

Sir John Bowring

1792–1872.

An English linguist, author, and noted diplomat; born in Exeter, Oct. 17, 1792; died there, Nov. 23, 1872. He was a great traveler and a close student; and boasted that he knew 200 languages and could speak 100. In 1825 he became editor of the Westminster Review, in which he advocated Free Trade by repeal of the Corn Laws in advance of Bright and Cobden. He was a member of Parliament in 1835-37 and 1841-47; was appointed on various commissions, to France, Switzerland, Italy, Syria, etc. In 1849 he was British consul at Hong-Kong, where he became governor in 1853. In 1855 he concluded a treaty with Siam; he was knighted in 1854. He rendered great service to English literature by translating the popular poems and folk-songs of various nations. Among his works are: "Specimens of the Russian Poets" (London, 1821-23); "Ancient Poetry and Romances of Spain" (1824); "Specimens of the Polish Poets" (1827); "Servian Popular Poetry" (1827); "Poetry of the Magyars" (1830) "Cheskian Anthology" (1832); "The Flowery Scroll, a Chinese Novel" (1868); "The Oak, Original

Tales and Sketches" (1869); and two important volumes of travel: "The Kingdom and People of Siam" (1857); and "A Visit to the Philippine Islands" (1859). He edited with a biography (22 vols., London, 1838) the works of Jeremy Bentham, of whom he was a disciple and admirer; and wrote a number of books on political and social topics, and also hymns and poems.—WARNER, CHARLES DUDLEY, ed. 1897, *Library of the World's Best Literature, Biographical Dictionary, vol.* XXIX, *p.* 70.

PERSONAL

Next morning (Tuesday) I went to Bowring's. Figure to yourself a thin man about my height and bent at the middle into an angle of 150°, the *back* quite straight, with large grey eyes, a huge turn-up nose with straight nostrils to the very point, and large projecting close-shut mouth: figure such a one walking restlessly about the room (for he had been thrown out of a gig, and was in pain), frank of speech, vivid, emphatic, and *verständig.* Such is the Radical Doctor.—CARLYLE, THOMAS, 1831, *To Mrs. Carlyle, Aug.* 17; *Thomas Carlyle, A History of the First Forty Years of His Life, vol.* II, *p.* 139.

I have never been able to understand the enormous unpopularity of this man, who appears civil, well-bred, intelligent, and agreeable (only rather a coxcomb), and has made a certain figure in the House of Commons, but it has been explained to me by a person who knows him well. He was originally a merchant, and had a quantity of counting-house knowledge. He became a member of a club of political economists, and a scholar of M'Culloch's. In this club there were some obscure but very able men, and by them he got crammed with the principles of commerce and political economy, and from his mercantile connections he got facts. He possessed great industry and sufficient ability to work up the materials he thus acquired into a very plausible exhibition of knowledge upon these subjects, and having opportunities of preparing himself for every particular question, and the advantage of addressing an audience the greater part of which is profoundly ignorant, he passed for a young gentleman of extraordinary ability and profound knowledge, and among the greatest of his admirers was Althorp, who, when the Whigs came in, promoted him to his present situation. Since he has been there he has not had the same opportunities of learning his lesson from others behind the curtain, and the envy which always attends success has delighted to pull down his reputation, so that he now appears something like the jackdaw stripped of the peacock's feathers.—GREVILLE, CHARLES C. F., 1831, *A Journal of the Reigns of King George IV and King William IV, ed.* Reeve, Nov. 28, *vol.* II, *p.* 29.

Dr. Bowring is a very striking-looking personage, with a most poetical, ardent, imaginative forehead, and a temperament all in keeping, as evidenced by his whole look and manner.—FOX, CAROLINE, 1838, *Memoirs of Old Friends, ed. Pym, Journal, Dec.* 28, *p.* 38.

The Doctor is a brisk person, with the address of a man of the world,—free, quick to smile, and of agreeable manners. He has a good face, rather American than English in aspect, and does not look much above fifty, though he says he is between sixty and seventy. I should take him rather for an active lawyer or a man of business than for a scholar and a literary man.—HAWTHORNE, NATHANIEL, 1853, *Passages from the English Note-Books, vol.* I, *p.* 13.

In his private life he was the most affectionate of husbands and fathers, and the firmest of friends. He never varied in his regard for his early associates, and in his own family his name was always mentioned with love and sympathy. In society, which he greatly relished, he was a most agreeable companion, having a fund of information and anecdote, while his genial and buoyant nature made him a general favourite. As an old man, his serene demeanour testified that, notwithstanding the assaults of time and the vicissitudes of a chequered life, in which there had been many and rapid alternations of joy and sorrow, his existence had been on the whole a happy one.—BOWRING, LEWIN B., 1877, *ed. Autobiographical Recollections of Sir John Bowring, Memoir, p.* 28.

Sir John Bowring was a man of considerable ability. At one time he seemed to be a candidate for something like fame. He was the political pupil and the literary executor of Jeremy Bentham, and for some years was editor of the "Westminster Review." He had a very large and varied, although not profound or scholarly, knowledge of European and Asiatic languages (there was not much scientific study of languages in his early days), he had traveled a great deal, and had sat in Parliament for some years. He understood political economy, and had a good knowledge of trade and commerce; and in those days a literary man who knew anything about trade and commerce was thought a person of almost miraculous versatility. Bowring had many friends and admirers, and set up early for a sort of great man. He was full of self-conceit, and without any very clear idea of political principles on the large scale.—McCARTHY, JUSTIN, 1880, *A History of our Own Time from the Accession of Queen Victoria to the Berlin Congress*, vol. iii, ch. xxx.

In politics he was a Benthamite, and in the House of Commons he made many enemies by his virulent attacks upon all who differed from him. He was a great scholar, and in literature and science a very learned man. He possessed a wonderful facility in acquiring foreign languages. At the age of sixteen he spoke and wrote French, Spanish, Italian, Portuguese, Dutch, and German, besides English. At a later period in life he could express himself with ease in thirty tongues and dialects. When he was governor of Hong Kong I have heard him converse at an official dinner with six foreigners who sat near him, addressing each in his own language. It was quite unnecessary to have done so, but Bowring was vain of his accomplishments, and not in the habit of hiding his light under a bushel. I first made his acquaintance when he was British consul at Canton. He must have been at the time about sixty, and, as a young man, I looked up to him with profound respect. — TUCKERMAN, CHARLES KEATING, 1890, *Sir John Bowring and American Slavery, Magazine of American History*, vol. 23, p. 232.

Dr. Bowring was another man to be depended on in any proceedings toward reform. I saw him often on public questions, once breakfasted with him at his house in Queen Square, Westminster, and had a pleasant meeting with him, after his return from China. There was a little of the Girondist, of the pedagogue about him, and I have no faith in his too facile translations; but he was a good citizen and a man to be respected.—LINTON, WILLIAM JAMES, 1894, *Threescore and Ten Years*, p. 160.

GENERAL

As an author, his reputation mainly rests on translations from languages with which few persons are acquainted, but his public services were considerable; as an advanced Liberal he largely aided his party, and was foremost as a promoter and advocate of many good and useful measures in Parliament; while as a man and a gentleman he was in all ways beyond reproach. He is one whom his native county may be proud to rank among the worthies of Devon. —HALL, SAMUEL CARTER, 1883, *Retrospect of a Long Life*, p. 408.

His poetry is quite unequal, and is mostly a reproduction of his literary readings. As sacred poetry, it is cold, and destitute of that glowing inspiration that characterizes so many of the productions of Trinitarian poets. Many who have so often sung with delight,—

"In the cross of Christ I glory," etc.,

may be surprised to learn that its author was then, and to the day of his death, a confirmed Unitarian.—HATFIELD, EDWIN F., 1884, *The Poets of the Church*, p. 93.

Among these renderings the magnificent "Oda Boy" of Derzhavin, the Russian poet, claims the foremost place for felicity and power in its English dress. But the acquirements of Bowring are little less than marvellous. To parody Praed's rhyme:

"You would have sworn as you looked at them
He had fished in the Flood with Ham and
    Shem."

He seems to have touched the very nerve centres of language, and to have comprehended by a supreme instinct, the essence of the poet's thought.—DUFFIELD, SAMUEL WILLOUGHBY, 1886, *English Hymns*, p. 261.

Bowring was an ardent reformer, and did good service, especially in the cause of free trade, on which subject he had gathered a great store of knowledge in the course of several commercial missions on which he was sent by the government to France, Belgium, Holland, Italy, Prussia, and Turkey.—OLIPHANT, MARGARET, O. W., 1892, *The Victorian Age of English Literature*, p. 74.

Sir John Bowring was a man of broad and open mind. He had a firm grip for fundamental principles, a clear eye for the intricacies of conflicting evidence, and a sound judgment for estimating subtle issues. His religious belief was an intelligent faith based upon reason and inquiry, of which the sonnet "Confidence" may be taken as a proof. Two of his hymns, "In the Cross of Christ I Glory," and "God is Love! His Mercy Brightens," have found world-wide acceptance among all classes of Christians. Such poems as "Matter and Mind" help to establish the reasonableness of faith.—MILES, ALFRED H., 1897, *The Poets and the Poetry of the Century, Moral and Religious Verse, p. 149.*

Horace Greeley
1811–1872.

Horace Greeley, American journalist, was born a small farmer's son at Amherst, N. H., February 3, 1811. He entered a printing-office as apprentice (1826) at East Poultney, Vermont, rose to assist in editorial work, and by-and-by worked as a journeyman printer. In 1834 he started the weekly *New Yorker,* for which he wrote essays, poetry, and other articles. His *Log Cabin,* a Whig campaign paper, contributed largely to the election of General Harrison as president in 1840. In April, 1841, he commenced the *New York Tribune,* of which he was the leading editor till his death. The *Tribune* was at first Whig, then anti-slavery Whig, and finally extreme Republican; it advocated to some extent the social theories of Fourier. In 1848 Greeley was elected to congress by a New York district, but lost popularity by agitating for a reform in the mileage payments to members. In 1851 he visited Europe, and was chairman of one of the committees of the Great Exhibition. Greeley at first upheld the constitutional right of the southern states to secede; but when the war began he became one of its most zealous advocates. He published in the *Tribune* the impressive "Prayer of Twenty Millions," and within a month the emancipation proclamation was issued. After Lee's surrender he warmly advocated a universal amnesty; and his going to Richmond and signing the bail-bond of Jefferson Davis awakened a storm of public indignation. In religious faith he was a Universalist. An unsuccessful candidate in 1872 for the presidency, he died in New York, 29th November of the same year. Greeley's works include "The American Conflict" (1864-66), "Recollections of a Busy Life" (1868), "Essays on Political Economy" (1870), and "What I Know of Farming" (1871). See Lives by Parton (new eds. 1882), Ingersoll (1873), Cornell (1882), and Sotheran (1892).—PATRICK AND GROOME,*eds.*1897, *Chambers's Biographical Dictionary, p. 432.*

PERSONAL

His manuscript is a remarkable one, having about it a peculiarity which we know not how better to designate than as a *converse* of the picturesque. His characters are scratchy and irregular, ending with an *abrupt taper*—if we may be allowed this contradiction in terms, where we have the fac-simile to prove that there is no contradiction in fact. All abrupt manuscripts save this, have square or *concise* terminations of the letters. The whole chirography puts us in mind of a *jig.* We can fancy the writer jerking up his hand from the paper at the end of each word, and, indeed, of each letter. What mental idiosyncrasy lies *perdu* beneath all this is more than we can say, but we will venture to assert that Mr. Greeley (whom we do not know personally) is, *personally,* a very remarkable man.—POE, EDGAR ALLAN, 1842, *A Chapter on Autography, Works ed. Stedman and Woodberry, vol.* IX, *p.* 249.

Was introduced to Greeley. Think him coarse and cunning.—DANA, RICHARD HENRY, 1851, *Journal, Jan.* 22; *Richard Henry Dana, A Biography, ed. C. F. Adams, vol.* I, *p.* 177.

My life has been busy and anxious, but not joyless. Whether it shall be prolonged few or more years, I am grateful that it has endured so long, and that it has abounded in opportunities for good not wholly unimproved, and in experiences of the nobler as well as the baser impulses of human nature. I have been spared to see the end of giant wrongs, which I once deemed invincible in this century, and to note the silent upspringing and growth of principles and influences which I hail as destined to root out some of the most flagrant and pervading evils that yet remain. . . . So, looking calmly, yet humbly, for that close of my mortal career which cannot be far distant, I reverently thank God for the blessings vouchsafed me in the past; and, with an awe that is not fear, and a consciousness of demerit which does not exclude hope, await the opening before my steps of the gates of the Eternal World.—

HORACE GREELEY

*From an **Engraving** by A. H. Ritchie.*

NATHANIEL PARKER WILLIS

*Engraving by Illman. From a
Portrait by Lawrence, 1837.*

GREELEY, HORACE, 1868, *Recollections of a Busy Life, p.* 429.

Horace learned to read before he had learned to talk; that is, before he could pronounce the longer words. No one regularly taught him. When he was little more than two years old, he began to pore over the Bible, opened for his entertainment on the floor, and examine with curiosity the newspaper given him to play with. He cannot remember a time when he could not read, nor can any one give an account of the process by which he learned, except that he asked questions incessantly, first about the pictures in the newspaper, then about the capital letters, then about the smaller ones, and finally about the words and sentences. At three years of age he could read easily and correctly any of the books prepared for children; and at four, any book whatever. But he was not satisfied with overcoming the ordinary difficulties of reading. Allowing that nature gives to every child a certain amount of mental force to be used in acquiring the art of reading, Horace had an overplus of that force, which he employed in learning to read with his book in positions which increased the difficulty of the feat. All the friends and neighbors of his early childhood, in reporting him a prodigy unexampled, adduce as the unanswerable and clinching proof of the fact, that, at the age of four years, he could read any book in whatever position it might be placed,—right-side up, up-side down, or sidewise.—PARTON, JAMES, 1868-96, *The Life of Horace Greeley, p.* 4.

He saw the goodness, not the taint,
In many a poor, do-nothing creature,
And gave to sinner and to saint,
But kept his faith in human nature;
Perchance he was not worldly-wise,
Yet we who noted, standing nearer,
The shrewd, kind twinkle in his eyes,
For every weakness held him dearer.
Alas that unto him who gave
So much, so little should be given!
Himself alone he might not save
Of all for whom his hands had striven.
Place, freedom, fame, his work bestowed;
Men took, and passed, and left him lonely;—
What marvel if, beneath his load,
At times he craved—for justice only!
—STEDMAN, EDMUND CLARENCE, 1872, *Horace Greeley.*

About the time—now over forty years ago—that Horace Greeley entered New York without money or friends, to seek employment in a printing office, another youth, as penniless and as friendless, was wandering about that city with the same object. Side by side they achieved their successes, visibly represented in the large neighbouring buildings whence issue each morning the two most powerful journals in America. But how different are the successes of James Gordon Bennett and Horace Greeley. The one is the triumphant demonstration that shrewdness, enterprise, and intelligence, when unimpeded by scruple of principle, and entirely concentrated on the task of adding cent to cent, may pile up a heap of gold and enshrine it in a palace. The other attests the power of Justice and Truth to endow those who have no other dower, and to reward self-sacrificing fidelity to them—not indeed with a pile of gold or marble, for Mr. Greeley has never been a rich man, but with character, which is sure to make for itself channels of influence.—CONWAY, MONCURE DANIEL, 1872, *Horace Greeley, Fraser's Magazine, vol.* 86, *p.* 474.

Mr. Greeley was neither cold nor tough. He was keenly sensitive both to praise and blame. The applause of even paltry men gladdened him, and their censure stung him. Moreover, he had that intense longing for reputation as a man of action by which men of the closet are so often torn. In spite of that his writing brought him in reputation, he writhed under the popular belief that he could do nothing but write, and he spent the flower of his years trying to convince the public that it was mistaken about him. It was to this we owed whatever was ostentatious in his devotion to farming and in his interest in the manufacturing industry of the country. It was to this, too, that we owed his keen and lifelong desire for office, and, in part at least, his activity in getting offices for other people. . . . Those who opposed him most earnestly must now regret sincerely that in his last hours he should have known the bitterness of believing, what was really not true, that the labors of his life, which were largely devoted to good causes, had not met with the appreciation they merited at the hands of his countrymen. It is for his own sake, as well as that of the public, greatly to be regretted that he should not have lived until the smoke of the late conflict had cleared away.—GODKIN, EDWIN LAURENCE,

1872, *The Death of Mr. Horace Greeley, The Nation, vol.* 15, *pp.* 362, 363.

Among my fellow-commissioners to the Exposition was my good old friend Horace Greeley. It was at that time in Mr. Greeley's career when he still affected very old white overcoats and equally old white hats. This peculiarity of summer attire caused him to attract more attention on the street in Paris than would have been attracted by a score of Japanese, Chinese, and South-Sea Islanders. Of this he appeared serenely unconscious. I remember one high-priced or gala day at the Exhibition, when all the fashion, elegance, and distinction of Paris were assembled there. While I was standing in our own part of the building, Horace entered in his usual costume. Telling me that he wanted to show me something, and seizing me by the arm, he started off, with his peculiar plowman's lope, dragging me along through space which the astonished visitors opened for us on either side. Wonder was expressed upon every face. All the way down the principal gallery we went, until we reached its farther extremity, a distance which I would be afraid to express in feet. What he desired to show me was well worth seeing. It was some specimens, in the Austrian department, of printing and book-binding, executed at the Imperial Press in Vienna, which excelled everything else of the same character to be found in the Exposition.— FIELD, MAUNSELL B., 1873, *Memoirs of Many Men and Some Women, p.* 116.

Mr. Greeley throughout life was twitted with his slovenliness of person, and many people were made to believe that he incurred the risk of being sold for a bag of ancient rags whenever he passed into Ann Street. The fit and quality of his clothes were not what Grammont or D'Orsay would have recommended; but he was always scrupulously neat—Beethoven himself having no greater passion for the bath. His linen was ever immaculate; his boots, though often coarse, well blacked; his face carefully shaven, and his hands as daintily kept as those of a fine woman. His cravat had a tendency, it is true, to assume the shape of a hangman's knot, and his trowsers were often suggestive of required continuance; but that he was really slovenly was palpably false. The idle tales that he disarranged his toilet before the looking-glass, and carefully squeezed his pantaloons

into the leg of his boot ere he appeared on the street, were purposely told to annoy him, and, strange to say, they had the effect intended. He was sensitive on the subject of his dress, and seldom received advice thereupon with becoming equanimity. Oddly enough, he believed himself a very well attired person, and that few men in his station went better clad.—BROWNE, JUNIUS HENRI, 1873, *Horace Greeley, Harper's Magazine, vol.* 46,*p.* 737.

No woman ever was his personal friend, trusting him, caring for him, who was not helped by the word and deed of his companionship toward the truest and noblest womanhood. No praise higher than this can woman offer to the memory of man. His friendships were Catholic, comprehensive, and abiding. They held within their steadfast range some of the most illustrious as well as some of the most purely and sweetly domestic women of his time.— AMES, MARY CLEMMER, 1873, *Outlines of Men, Women, and Things, p.* 118.

The high estimate I formed of Mr. Greeley's character at the outset of our acquaintance, was strengthened by all I saw and knew of him for the ensuing twelve years. I invested him with more good qualities than generally belong to the best of our public men. The great ability and greater industry displayed seemed designed to work out enlightened and beneficent purposes. He seemed also to work unselfishly, finding his reward in the consciousness of doing good. His happiness seemed to consist in laboring diligently for his country and his race. He had no vices great or small, no recreations, and few amusements. I do not remember in all our intercourse to have heard him speak of his boy-life, of ball-playing, of kites, of marbles, of tops, etc.; and I incline to the belief that he was a stranger to all or nearly all of these juvenile joys. Indeed, it is by no means certain that his case was not the exception to a rule which is supposed to be universal, of a grown-up man who had never played "High, low, Jack, and the game." . . . In looking back, therefore, through a vista of nearly forty years, I find myself seriously perplexed in endeavoring to understand Mr. Greeley's true character. While all I saw and knew of him in early life inspired feelings of confidence and admiration, there was very much in later years to occasion surprise and regret. I only can account for this change, if I am right in assuming that his character did so change, by attributing it to a cause which has worked men's downfall in all ages of the world. Ambition, while under the subjection of reason, is laudable; but when it breaks bounds and "o'erleaps itself," the consequences are disastrous.—WEED, THURLOW, 1873, *Recollections of Horace Greeley, The Galaxy, vol.* 15, *pp.* 381, 382.

I should like to speak of his tenderness and generosity. I should like to explain the awkward devices of his heart to hide itself, knowing that the exhibition of feeling is unconventional, and sensitive lest its earnest impulses should be misconstrued. But the veil which he wore during life must not be lifted by the privilege which follows death; enough of light shines through it to reveal all that the world need know. To me his nature seemed like a fertile tract of the soil of his native New Hampshire. It was cleared and cultivated and rich harvests clad its southern slopes; yet the rough primitive granite cropped out here and there, and there were dingles which defied the plough, where the sweet wild flowers blossomed in their season, and the wild birds built their nests unharmed. In a word, he was a man who kept his life as God fashioned it for him, neither assuming a grace which was not bestowed, nor disguising a quality which asserted its existence.—TAYLOR, BAYARD, 1876, *An Address on Unveiling the Bust of Horace Greeley in Greenwood Cemetery, Life and Letters of Bayard Taylor, ed. Taylor and Scudder, vol.* II, *p.* 605.

He had been assailed as the enemy of his country by the party which he had done more than any man in the Nation to organize. He had been hunted to his grave by political assassins whose calumnies broke his heart. He was scarcely less a martyr than Lincoln, or less honored after his death, and his graceless defamers now seemed to think they could atone for their crime by singing his praises. . . . What he had sorely needed and was religiously entitled to was the sympathy and succor of good men while he lived, and especially in his hereoic struggle for political reconciliation and reform. The circumstances of his death made it peculiarly touching and sacramental, and I was inexpressibly glad that I had fought his battle so unflinchingly and defended him everywhere against his conscienceless assailants.—JULIAN, GEORGE W., 1883, *Political Recollections, pp.* 351, 352.

I had never before seen Mr. Greeley, who was then beginning to attract notice as the editor of the New York "Tribune." At that time he was about thirty-five years old, round-faced and healthful, with blue eyes and very light hair. The restless eagerness of his interrogations denoted the character he afterwards established, which enabled him to change his convictions or ruling texts and hobbies as suddenly as a bird in a cage hops from one perch to another.—KEYES, GEN. E. D., 1884, *Fifty Years' Observation of Men and Events, p.* 103.

To the mind and the eyes of the whole country, there was no more familiar figure than that of Horace Greeley. The big round face, the spectacled blue eyes, the fringe of white whiskers, the slouching farmer-like figure, the pockets stuffed with newspapers—were known to every New-Yorker.—MERRIAM, GEORGE S., 1885, *The Life and Times of Samuel Bowles, vol.* II, *p.* 181.

Mr. Greeley was not an orator in any scholastic sense. He had a poor and somewhat squeaking voice; he knew nothing of gestures; and he could not take an orator's pose, which adds such emphasis sometimes to the matter and argument to be set forth. Not all his years of practice on the platform and on public occasions ever changed his habit and methods as a speaker, and he ended as poorly equipped for the vocation as he was when he began it. But he had one prime quality without which all the others are exploited in vain. He invariably had *something to say;* and he said it in such clear and wholesome English, with such utter sincerity, with such humane endeavor, and backed by such a character for probity and guilelessness, that he was an orator after all, in spite of all the rules. I have introduced Wendell Phillips, George William Curtis, and Anna Dickinson, and, in fact, all the most famous speakers of both sexes more than once and to various audiences, including P. T. Barnum, Mark Twain, and Josh Billings, but no one of them ever gave better satisfaction, different and notable as they were, than Horace Greeley. As a consequence he came to me oftenest, and wore the best.—BENTON, JOEL, 1887, *Reminiscences of Horace Greeley, The Cosmopolitan, vol.* 3, *p.* 312.

Mr. Greeley was one of those quaint men so surprisingly himself, so unlike everybody else, and the fact was so apparent not merely in face and figure and clothing, but in walk and voice and gesture, that there entered into one's affectionate regard a kindly sense of humor. Why, there is a way of winding up an umbrella and carrying it that is recognized as Greeley's fashion. I have seen him with his head tied up in a handkerchief, after he had been cruelly assaulted by a statesman from Arkansas, and so deliciously unconscious of anything comical in his aspect, that you did not dare laugh, and he had no more notion of animosity toward his assailant than if he had been attacked by a wild animal. The member of Congress who struck him with a stick was to him a stupid barbarian, it would have been at once criminal and ludicrous to kill. . . . Greeley was smooth, round-cheeked as a wholesome baby, with a delicate pallor, a brow white as alabaster, with just a suspicion of rosy tint, and his eyes were concealed by his glasses. . . . Mr. Greeley's earnings as editor, publisher, author, and lecturer were very large, but he was not a business manager who could grasp even his own. He sold half the *Tribune* for two thousand dollars after it was a success. In 1868 he owned but one-tenth of his paper, and in 1872 held but six shares out of a hundred. If he had been a fighter for the fractions of cents he might have joined the procession of the millionaires. But he enjoyed his own good opinion, and felt there was something tawdry in money-grabbing and hoarding.— HALSTEAD, MURAT, 1890, *Horace Greeley, The Cosmopolitan, vol. 8, pp. 461, 466.*

Greeley took a deep and practical interest in Brook Farm; several of his intimate and trusted friends were there, and he was glad to sustain them by kindly encouragement in the *Tribune*, and by an occasional visit. Miss Russell relates amusingly the coming of an apparition which proved to be Greeley, not in disguise, but simply his astonishing self. "His hair was so light that it was almost white; he wore a white hat; his face was entirely colorless, even the eyes not adding much to save it from its ghostly hue. His coat was a very light drab, almost white, and his nether garments the same." This Apostle of Light, however odd his personality, was welcome to the community to which he was never disloyal, though his heart was more with the North American Phalanx, a visit to which was easier for so busy a man. Little as they saw of him, Greeley's good will was valued by the Brook Farmers, none of whom is known to have held Emerson's opinion that he was both coarse and cunning. Through no fault of his own, Greeley was probably an injury to the West Roxbury community. It was his misfortune—a misfortune which followed him to his tragic end—to excite marked political antagonisms, and it was natural that such interests as he espoused should come also under the ban.—SWIFT, LINDSAY, 1900, *Brook Farm, p. 276.*

GENERAL

The prince of paragraphists—the Napolean of Essayists. For years he has employed his talents in winding and unwinding the "tangled yarn" of human affairs in Church and State—in Philosophy and Politics—in Art and Literature. He is the great recording secretary of this Continent, employed by the masses to take notes and print them. His business is to "hold the mirror up to Nature, and show the very age and body of the time its form and pressure." He has the pluck to say as an editor what he feels as a man—when he forgets that he is a politician. It is then that we find truth without concealment, and genuine open-heartedness without wire-working behind the curtain.— BUNGAY, GEORGE W., 1854, *Off-Hand Takings; or, Crayon Sketches, p. 237.*

With a shrewd, clear intellect, an astonishingly vigorous style, and a heart easily wrought up to that degree of passion necessary to the production of the best kind of writing, he fears not the quill of any man living.—BARTLETT, DAVID W., 1855, *Pen Portraits of Modern Agitators.*

Mr. Greeley's character and career as an editor and politician can be understood and appreciated by remembering his key note: *Benevolent ends by utilitarian means.* He desires the amelioration of all human conditions and the instrumentalities which he would propose are generally practical, common sense ones. Of magnificence, of formalities, of all the conventional part of life, whether in public or private, he is by nature as utterly neglectful as he is of the dandy element in costume, but he has a solid and real appreciation of many appreciable things, which go to make up the sum total of human advancement and happiness.—STOWE, HARRIET BEECHER, 1868, *Men of Our Times, p.* 310.

Mr. Greeley entered upon the career of journalism step by step, and became a writer without premeditation. He is a man of convictions, but the particular mode in which it has been his lot to express them has been plainly decided by destiny for him. The force with which his words have told upon the American mind has been due to the depth from which they have come in his own life and thought far more than to any natural literary ability.—CONWAY, MONCURE DANIEL, 1872, *Horace Greeley, Fraser's Magazine, vol.* 86, *p.* 487.

The best-known citizen of America, the foremost journalist of his time.—BROWNE, JUNIUS HENRI, 1873, *Horace Greeley, Harper's Magazine, vol.* 46, *p.* 734.

The greatest of American journalists, and eminent as a writer of pure and vigorous English. . . . Pure in mind, honest and upright to such an extent that he was called by many an eccentric man, he made his way, by his own unaided efforts, from poverty to well-deserved fame as a writer and philosopher. His style is better in certain respects than that of any of his contemporary writers. It is terse and masculine, so evenly balanced and nicely constructed, so simple and yet so graceful that it is equally admired by the uneducated farmer and the fastidious literary critic. Mr. Greeley will always be best known as the founder and first editor of the *New York Tribune*, but his collected writings will hold a place in standard *American literature.*—CATHCART, GEORGE R., 1874, *ed. The Literary Reader, p.* 251.

Distinctively a political rather than a military history ["American Conflict"] of the war. It is one of the most valuable, as it is quite the most interesting, of the numerous accounts of our great civil contest.—ADAMS, CHARLES KENDALL, 1882, *A Manual of Historical Literature, p.* 539.

No man of his generation talked to the common people so forcibly, so clearly, and with so much sense and benevolence as he. Other men made of the *Tribune* a great newspaper; to him it was the mouthpiece of his own personality,—a personality of the utmost energy and picturesqueness. His writing was as lucid and racy as Franklin's; as weighty with passion and hard sense as John Bright's; and copious be-

yond either, as the daily journalist exceeds in copiousness the essayist or parliamentarian. His sympathies were generous and humane; his religion was simple and genuine. His heart was with the common people; he had shared their experiences, he spoke their language. His culture was defective, and he had the fault incident to deficient culture,—ignorance of his own limitations. He was liable to be most dogmatic on subjects which he knew least about. In his beliefs, his instincts, his enthusiasms, his prejudices, he was as thoroughly a representative American as any man of his time.—MERRIAM, GEORGE S., 1885, *The Life and Times of Samuel Bowles, vol.* II, *p.* 181.

Intellectually, he was remarkable for technical memory, for mental activity, and for clear, racy, and forcible expression. His mind was stimulated to the neglect of the outer man's culture. He was as evidently marked by the stamp of the printing-press from his birth, as Plato is said to have drawn the Hybla bees to his budding lips, though, as is frequently the case with men of special genius, he imagined that his mission was to those agricultural pursuits from which he had been drawn away to the types, like a magnetized needle to iron filings. This is only an instance of the visionary and sentimental cast of his thought and theories, as contrasted with the practical and utilitarian tendency of his action. His was the unusual combination of a speculative mind and a realistic method. His opinions were formed amid a cloud-capped region of rarefied thought and lofty principle; his presentation of details was prosaic, plausible, and at least seemingly practical.—ZABRISKIE, FRANCIS NICOLL, 1890, *Horace Greeley, p.* 368.

Horace Greeley, a unique personality, simple, unaffected, earnest, an immense believer in American institutions, a staunch friend of the working-man, and a brave lover of impartial justice.—FROTHINGHAM, OCTAVIUS BROOKS, 1891, *Recollections and Impressions, p.* 227.

Our Later Franklin, as the poet John Greenleaf Whittier once designated Horace Greeley, was one of those noble souls associated with what has been styled the renaissance of New England literature, who earliest apprehended and taught the truths of Socialism to the people of the United States of America. He never wearied in the good work of propaganda by both pen and voice. The movement itself may have changed in its methods and assumed a wider scope in the four essentials of "agitation, education, organization and action," but its final objects and fundamental principles remain the same. And when the triumph of the Coöperative Commonwealth will be assured and the Emancipation of Labor accomplished, the work of Horace Greeley will be recognized by grateful generations, and will not be hidden out of sight and mind, as it has been, from the multitude, by those interested in keeping the American proletariat ignorant of economic truth and in the condition of wage-slaves.—SOTHERAN, CHARLES, 1892, *Horace Greeley and Other Pioneers of American Socialism, p.* 1.

During the years of his busy life, from the late thirties when he was in the *New Yorker* and the *Log Cabin*, until the sad unnecessary end in 1872, Greeley was ever in argument. . . . This was an atrocious world,— that he knew very well. It was permeated with Democrats and free-traders and idle folks given to drink. There were evil men and evil women; but that was no reason for giving it over to fire. It should be converted. There should be regeneration through the spirit of daily reproof and objurgation. Greeley labored with the world to better it, to give men moderate wages and honest food, and to teach women to earn their own living, and that it was better that they should learn how to make shoes than to play on the piano.— YOUNG, JOHN RUSSELL, 1893, *Men Who Reigned, Lippincott's Magazine, vol.* 51, *p.* 188.

The man who was second to no other citizen in establishing the intellectual ascendency of the metropolis.—BUEL, CLARENCE CLOUGH, 1897, *Library of the World's Best Literature, ed. Warner, vol.* XII, *p.* 6656.

William Henry Seward

1801–1872.

Born at Florida, Orange County, N. Y., May 16, 1801; died at Auburn, N. Y., Oct. 10, 1872. A noted American statesman. He graduated at Union College in 1820; was admitted to the bar in 1822; settled in Auburn in 1823; was elected in 1830 as anti-Masonic candidate to the New York State Senate, in which he served until 1834; was the unsuccessful Whig candidate for governor in 1834; was elected (Whig) governor of New York in 1838; was reëlected in 1840, and served till Jan. 1, 1843; was Whig and afterward Republican United States senator from New York 1849-61; made in 1858 a celebrated speech at Rochester, in which he declared that the antagonism between freedom and slavery was an "irrepressible conflict" between opposing forces; was a candidate for the Republican nomination for President in 1860; was secretary of state 1861-69; was severely wounded by an accomplice of John Wilkes Booth, April 14, 1865; made a journey to Europe 1859 (having made a similar journey in 1833); traveled in western United States and Mexico in 1869; and made a journey around the world 1870-71. During his incumbency of the secretaryship of state he averted serious complications with Great Britain by his prudence and skill in the negotiations over the "Trent affair;" prevailed on the French government to withdraw its troops from Mexico; and in 1867 concluded the negotiations with Russia for the cession of Alaska. He supported the reconstruction policy of President Johnson. His works were published by G. E. Baker in 5 vols. 1853-84.—SMITH, BENJAMIN E., *ed.* 1894-97, *The Century Cyclopedia of Names, p.* 921.

PERSONAL

He knew the mask of principle to wear,
And power accept while seeming to decline;
So cunningly he wrought, with tools so fine,
Setting his courses with so frank an air,
(Yet most secure when seeming most to dare,)
He did deceive us all: with mien benign
His malice smiled, his cowardice the sign
Of courage took, his selfishness grew fair,
So deftly could his foiled ambition show
As modest acquiescence. Now, 'tis clear
What man he is,—how false his high report;

Mean to the friend, caressing to the foe;
Plotting the mischief which he feigns to fear:
Chief Eunuch, were but ours the Sultan's court!
—TAYLOR, BAYARD, 1865, *A Statesman, Poetical Works, Household ed. p.* 143.

His wife and his children were constantly in his thoughts as in his heart, and his friendship was firm, warm, and lasting. There was in him a very high and delicate sense of honor, and he always held himself far above any position or office which he filled.—WHITE, RICHARD GRANT, 1877, *William Henry Seward, North American Review, vol.* 124, *p.* 228.

Seward in conversation was slow and methodical till warmed up, when he was one of the most voluminous and eloquent of talkers. No statesman in the country had a vaster range of reading, or wider experience in the management of public affairs. He had been almost continuously in public life since he was thirty, and was educated in a State where adroitness and audacity are needed to make a successful politician, who must sometimes pretend "to see the things he sees not."—SCOVEL, JAMES MATLACK, 1893, *Recollections of Seward and Lincoln, Lippincott's Magazine, vol.* 51, *p.* 239.

In all the relations of private life he was most admirable: a devoted husband, a kind and sympathetic father, a firm and loyal friend, an excellent neighbor and citizen. The bitter disappointment of the people of Auburn at his failure to receive the presidential nomination in 1860 shows the love they bore him. His optimism in politics and in life generally was not merely the result of a disposition naturally cheerful and buoyant, but of a firm faith in an overruling Providence. His industry was tireless, his capacity for work enormous. He often wrote far into the night, and during the years of his active practice as a lawyer the young men in his office would frequently find in the morning the floor of his room strewn with papers which he had written while they were asleep.—LOTHROP, THORNTON KIRKLAND, 1896, *William Henry Seward* (*American Statesmen*), *p.* 431.

STATESMAN

The most remarkable feature in his public career is his consistent adherence to principle. Guided not by a low worldly policy, or motives of secular expediency, but by the radiant light of ideal truth, his course has been like the path of a noble ship on the ocean, faithfully steering by celestial luminaries. His past history presents the best assurance of his future activity. Whatever the sphere in which he may be placed, it is certain that he will bring exalted talents to the performance of the humblest as well as the noblest duties, postponing all private interests to his love of humanity, and seeking as the highest boon of a manly life, the realization of truth, justice, and love, in the institutions

of society.—BAKER, GEORGE E., 1853, *ed. Works of William H. Seward, Preface, vol.* I.

The State of New York by a full delegation with complete unanimity of purpose at home, came to this convention and presented as its choice, one of its citizens who had served the State from boyhood up, who had labored for and loved it. We came from a great state with as we thought, a great statesman, and our love of the great republic from which we are all delegates, the great American Union, and our love of the great Republican party of the Union and our love of our statesman and candidate, made us think that we did our duty to the country and the whole country in expressing our preference for him. For it was from Gov. Seward that most of us learned to love Republican principles, and the Republican party. His fidelity to the country, the constitution and the laws, his fidelity to the party and the principle that the majority govern, his interest in the advancement of our party to its victory, that our country may rise to its true glory, induces me to assume to speak his sentiments as I do indeed the opinion of our whole delegation when I move you as I do now that the nomination of Abraham Lincoln, of Illinois, as the Republican candidate for the suffrages of the whole country for the office of Chief Magistrate of the American Union, be made unanimous.—EVARTS, WILLIAM M., 1859, *Speech at Chicago Republican Convention.*

Apart from politics, I liked the man, though not blind to his faults. His natural instincts were humane and progressive. . . . That his ends have ever been patriotic, I will not doubt; that his means have sometimes been mistaken, I think his warmest friends must admit. That he once aspired to the Presidency is a truth, but no reproach; able, wise, and good men have done so, without impeachment.—GREELEY, HORACE, 1868, *Recollections of a Busy Life, pp.* 311, 322.

It will be, however, as Secretary of State of the United States, during the whole period of the late Civil War, and for nearly four years after that war was closed, and while its results were in daily progress of development, that Mr. Seward will be longest remembered. To him is primarily and principally due the successful administration of our foreign affairs during that **eventful and critical period.** Volume after volume of official correspondence attests his unceasing labors. And if, in the vast mass of his written or spoken words, in a time of so much anxiety and agitation, there be some which even his best friends would willingly obliterate; or if, amid the many responsibilities he was compelled to assume, there were some acts to be regretted by any of us,—yet all such disparagements of his name and fame will be forgotten hereafter, in the grateful remembrance that through his leading intervention our peace with foreign nations was preserved, and our country left free to fight out the great battle of the Union to its final triumph.—WINTHROP, ROBERT C., 1872, *Addresses and Speeches, vol.* III, *p.* 191.

Mr. Lincoln could not fail soon to perceive the fact that, whatever estimate he might put on his own acute judgment, he had to deal with a superior in native intellectual power, in extent of acquirement, in breadth of philosophic experience, and in the force of moral discipline. On the other hand, Mr. Seward could not have been long blind to the deficiencies of the chief in these respects, however highly he might value his integrity of purpose, his shrewd capacity, and his generous and amiable disposition.—ADAMS, CHARLES FRANCIS, 1873, *Address on the Life, Character and Services of William Henry Seward, p.* 53.

A greater error could scarcely be committed than to represent that Mr. Lincoln "had to deal with a superior intellectual power" when he came in contact with Mr. Seward. The reverse was the fact. In mere scholastic acquirements "Mr. Seward, never a learned man," may have had the advantage, though in this respect there was less difference than is generally supposed; while "in breadth of philosophical experience and in the force of moral discipline" the almost self-taught and reflective mind of Mr. Lincoln, which surmounted difficulties and disadvantages that his Secretary never knew, conspicuously excelled. In the executive council and in measures of administration the Secretary had influence, not always happily exercised, but the President's was the master mind.—WELLES, GIDEON, 1873, *Mr. Lincoln and Mr. Seward, The Galaxy, vol.* 16, *p.* 518.

The conviction is almost universal that he knew less of law and cared less about it than any other man who has held high office in this country. If he had not abandoned the law, he might have been a sharp attorney; but he never could have risen to the upper walks of the profession. He would have been kept in the lowest rank, not by want of mental capacity or lack of diligent habits, but by the inherent defects of his moral nature. He did not *believe* in legal justice, and to assist in the honest administration of it was against the grain of all his inclinations. . . . When Mr. Seward went into the State Department he took a *Little Bell* to his office in place of the Statute Book, and this piece of sounding brass came to be a symbol of the Higher Law. When he desired to kidnap a free citizen, to banish him, to despoil him of his property, or to kill him after the mockery of a military trial, he rang his Little Bell and the deed was done. This man, to whom you would assign a place in history above all other American statesmen, took a childish delight in the perverted use of his power, and displayed it as ostentatiously as one of those half-witted boys who were sometimes raised to the purple in the evil days of the Roman empire.—BLACK, J. S., 1874, *Letter to Mr. Adams, Galaxy, vol.* 17, *pp.* 108, 119.

Seward was a favorite of fortune. He was fortunate in his gifts, his surroundings, his successes, his career, his temperament, his friendships. He was peculiarly blessed in the last respect by having as a lifelong friend Thurlow Weed, one of the most astute and powerful politicians we have ever produced, who relieved Seward of many of the burdens of politics, and left him free to work out the principles they both had at heart. It was a rare chance which gave Seward such a friend, and he made the most of it, as he did of all his opportunities, after the fashion of successful people. Very few men have made themselves count for more than Seward, in proportion to their ability. This arose from his wonderful capacity for dealing with his fellowmen, from his robust common sense, and from his cautious firmness.—LODGE, HENRY CABOT, 1884, *William H. Seward, Atlantic Monthly, vol.* 53, *p.* 699.

William H. Seward had all the higher qualities of statesmanship. Of a delicacy of temperament that indicated genius, he possessed a mind of rare power, which he filled with vast stores of information through patient and impartial study. His mind was singularly suggestive, and sustained by a courage and industry that moulded these suggestions into measures of legislation highly beneficial to the people he served. . . . How discouraging to the student of history to see men so great neglected, their services unrecognized, their work unknown, while epauletted creatures, upon whose imbecility rests the responsibility of uncalled for carnage that spread mourning and cruel desolation over all the land, are rewarded in life and honored to immortality in death. . . . In the heart of New York, a bronze statue of heroic size has been erected to the memory of New York's greatest statesman. It will darken into slow decay, as his memory fades into oblivion without pròbably one of the busy millions knowing that, for four years, nothing stood between that great commercial centre and the utter ruin of a bombardment but the subtle intellect and patriotic heart of that one man. Without a navy, possessed of no coast defences, our cities on the sea were at the mercy of the weakest naval power of Europe. In all this I detract nothing from the fame of Lincoln. Seward was a greater man in one thing, but not in all things, than Abraham Lincoln; and were we the enlightened people we claim to be, the great Secretary's name would live along the pages of our history as that of one whose cultured mind, indomitable will, high courage, and pure patriotism, made a debt we were proud to acknowledge, thus honoring ourselves in honoring him.—PIATT, DONN, 1887, *Memories of the Men Who Saved the Union, pp.* 139, 170.

Notwithstanding his limitations, Seward stands in the front rank of political leaders, both on account of the talents he displayed and the services he rendered to his country. And he holds the first place among all our Secretaries of State. Sumner had a more thorough knowledge of international law; Adams was by birth and education equipped for diplomacy; Chase had a genius for managing national finances in a critical time. Stanton was the broad and tireless organizer of the physical forces that saved the nation. Seward had dash, a knowledge of political conditions, and a versatility such as none of these men possessed, while his perfect tact and vigor of intellect, his enthusiasm and inspiring hope, made him the almost perfect supplement to Lin-

coln. The Secretary grew in diplomacy as the President grew in statesmanship.— BANCROFT, FREDERIC, 1900, *The Life of William H. Seward, vol.* II, *p.* 528.

He had many of the qualities of a diplomat—good temper, resolution, finesse and a high sense of national dignity. . . . Perhaps it will not be too much to say that the characteristic of Seward's whole public life was youth. He had the hopes, the ambitions, the convictions, the expectations of a young man; hence he easily reacted from the severe disappointments of 1856, 1860 and 1861. He was a man who loved to lead and who loved to be well thought of, but one who could nevertheless accept the leadership of another and who could even endure the pangs of unpopularity throughout all his later life. . . . His mind was quick, and he had the lawyer's habit of marking differences of conditions which might take away the force of cases cited against him; Seward so loved to be thought a frank, open, direct and candid man that in his own mind he always deserved that reputation. The greatest criticism upon Seward is his own remarkable suggestions sent to President Lincoln, April 1, 1861. Ever since the publication of that document by Nicolay and Hay, writers on the period have painted the moral. Bancroft is, however, the first to show a practical reason for Seward's attitude: he alone has discovered how much Seward had become involved by his own belief in a pacific settlement and by his own hope to bring about that settlement unaided. The fault was a great one; the atonement is equally great, for Lincoln's concise, considerate answer changed the chieftain into a loyal ancient. From the Sumter expedition to Lincoln's death, it does not appear that Seward hampered or disturbed the President by separate adventures, by carping criticism or by half-hearted service. In fact, Lincoln thoroughly liked and enjoyed him, and enjoyed those floating stories about Seward's forgetfulness which the biographer has left out of his book. In earnestness, in perception of the real nature of the slavery contest, in the moral indignation which nerved the nation to its great task, a lesser man than his great rival Chase, Seward was the better friend to Lincoln and the better aid. His international law might be faulty, his despatches might loose the eagle's screams, but he did direct his great abilities with a single heart toward his important task.—HART, ALBERT BUSHNELL, 1900, *New Light on Seward, Political Science Quarterly, vol.* 15, *pp.* 541, 545, 546.

GENERAL

There can be no doubt, however, of Governor Seward's talents, especially as a writer of pure English. His style is perspicuous and nervous, free from the tawdry and unmeaning embellishments of our modern public documents, and equally fitted for the good taste of the scholar and the comprehension of the plain man of sense.—HONE, PHILIP, 1842, *Diary, Oct.* 31, *ed. Tuckerman, vol.* II, *p.* 153.

Seward is a great man among great men. He is not so volcanic as Benton—not so logical as Webster—not so eloquent as Clay—not so brilliant as Foote—not so jovial as Hale; but he can write a better letter than any of them. A little from his pen will go a great distance and keep a long time. His classic style, his earnest air, his truthful manner,· his uncommon sense, his perfect self-control, his thorough knowledge of the leading questions of the day, compel the attention and admiration of the hearer. He is never timid, never tame, never squeam-

ish, never vulgar, never insulting. He is independent without egotism, modest without subserviency, dignified without pomposity, and sociable without affectation.— BUNGAY, GEORGE W., 1854, *Off-Hand Takings; or, Crayon Sketches, p.* 53.

Soon after the death of Mr. Adams, I proposed to Mr. Seward to write for publication, a life of John Quincy Adams. Although much engrossed in legal business he accepted my offer and undertook the work. He was greatly assisted in its production by the Rev. John M. Austin, a writer of several popular books, and in whom Mr. Seward had the utmost confidence. The work reached a sale of over 40,000 copies. This was one of my earlier successes as a publisher of that class of books.—DERBY, JAMES CEPHAS, 1884, *Fifty Years among Authors, Books and Publishers, p.* 60.

This work ["Diplomatic History of Civil War in America"] with its many documents by Mr. Seward, illustrates his mental, political, and literary powers. Not externally brilliant, they were of solid worth, and secured for the United States diplomatic triumphs as great and as essential as those of Gettysburg and Appomattox.—RICHARDSON, CHARLES F., 1886, *American Literature, vol.* I, p. 246.

Thomas Buchanan Read
1822–1872.

Born in Chester County, Pa., (1822-1872). In 1839 he entered the studio of a Cincinnati sculptor, intending to learn that branch of art. He quickly relinquished it for painting, however, and opened a studio of his own in New York, two years later. In 1846 he settled in Philadelphia, and in 1850 he went to Europe, working and studying in Florence and Rome. He made the latter city his home, with occasional visits to America, upon one of which, in 1872, he died in New York. Among the better known of his works are, "The Water-Sprite," "The Lost Pleiad," "The Star of Bethlehem," "Sheridan and His Horse." He began his career as a portrait painter with some success. His portrait of George Peabody is in the Peabody Institute, Baltimore. Mr. Claghorn, of Philadelphia, an early friend of Mr. Read's, purchased a number of his pictures, painted at different periods, illustrating his progress from time to time. He was a very versatile genius. He occasionally turned his attention to sculpture in his maturity, and executed a bust of General Sheridan, which proved how successful he might have been with his chisel, had he so decided in his youth. By his poems, perhaps, he will be best known in the future. His "Sheridan's Ride" is one of the most popular productions of the minor poets of America. His first book of "Poems" was published in 1847; his "Lays and Ballads" in 1848, "The New Pastoral" in 1855, "The Home by the Sea" in 1856. A collected edition of his works was published in 1860. —CLEMENT, CLARA ERSKINE, AND HUTTON, LAURENCE, 1879-84, *Artists of the Nineteenth Century, p.* 201.

PERSONAL

Next we went to the studio of Buchanan Read, the poet and painter, whose pictures, both in words and by the artist's

pencil and brush, are so enchanting. We had known each other in bright days "long ago," and imagine his amazement to meet me here, when he believed me quietly at home in the far-away South. He was earnestly glad to see me, and showed me many very bewitching ideal pictures.— LeVert, Octavia Walton, 1855, *Souvenirs of Travel, vol.* ii, *p.* 222.

He painted many portraits, and a number of pictures which, while they cannot be reckoned great works of art, were still full of imagaination and fancy and graceful thought. More could not have been expected of him as a painter with his divided ambition and want of early study and training. His pictures were poems, but without the mastery over the materials of expression which he possessed with his pen. His subjects were fine, but were rarely more finished than a cartoon or a vignette. They resembled the fantasies of Schwind and others of the German school, which were much more popular then than to-day. . . . While no one has described American scenery with more sympathy and truth in verse, Read's paintings were all figure-pictures, either allegorical or romantic genre. As far as I am aware, he never tried to paint landscape but once, and then the work remained unfinished. I remember it as a conglomeration rather than a composition of the features of a wide extent of scenery. There were a stream and a bridge, a fisherman, trees, a grain-field and the reapers, village spire on a hill, and distant mountains—not one *motif*, but several, sketched in just as they occurred to him, like memoranda for a pastoral. In a poem he would have taken many stanzas to portray the scene. He forgot, in painting, that a landscape painter would have required an equal number of canvases. . . . He rose early and went to bed late. He loved to be hospitable and to occupy a high social rank. He was at his easel with the earliest sunlight, and burned midnight oil over poetical and philosophic schemes. He dreamed of painting great historical pictures, writing new epics, even of creating a new theology, and of being at the same time an amphytrion, a club-man and a politician.—Tait, John R., 1877, *Reminiscences of a Poet-Painter, Lippincott's Magazine, vol.* 19, *pp.* 311, 320.

The next time Buchanan Read came to us [1850] we had perused his fresh, invigorating poems, and were delighted to see him again. And now the ice being broken, we found him to be a very generous, grateful young man, possessing much original power and fine discrimination of art. He

had been painting in Rossetti's studio, and in constant intercourse with his host, William Rossetti, Holman Hunt, and Woolner. As the day for his departure to Düsseldorf approached, a great gathering of all the P. R. B.'s took place, to commemorate his last evening in their midst. They read aloud his poetry, made much of him, and told such capital stories, that some of them rolled on the floor with laughter. But although they remained together until four or five in the morning, they could not part with him. He prolonged his stay, and as he absented himself in their company from his lodgings at Mr. Chapman's, in the Strand, it was reported that the pre-Raphaelites had carried off Read in a chariot of fire.—Howitt, Mary, 1888, *An Autobiography, vol.* ii, *p.* 74.

GENERAL

Mr. Read's shorter pieces have been collected and published in various forms, both in England and the United States, and have received the warmest commendations. They constitute indeed his highest claims to fame. His Lyrics are his greatest works. "Sheridan's Ride" is one of the few things written during the heat of the war that is likely to survive. Others of his short pieces, though not so widely known as this, are hardly inferior to it in merit. No writer of the present age, except Tennyson, has so delicate a fancy, or such wonderful nicety in the use of words. This exquisite delicacy in the use of words is the more remarkable in Mr. Read's case from the fact that his advantages of early education were very limited. It seems to grow out of the native poetical faculty of the man, which instinctively selects with infinitesimal precision exactly the right words to express its own airy fancies.—Hart, John S., 1872, *A Manual of American Literature, p.* 339.

Few poets have ever excelled him in "occasional verses," and many of his best poems were almost improvisations. "Sheridan's Ride" was written in a few hours, and was recited by Mr. Murdoch at Pike's Opera-House the same evening. The laying of the Atlantic Cable, the completion of a bridge, the celebration of a silver wedding, of a birthday or any anniversary was sufficient to inspire his Muse with fancies ever sympathetic and graceful. He once delivered a poem before the Mercantile Library Association in Cincinnati, the last lines of which were written while the carriage was waiting to convey him to the hall.—TAIT, JOHN R., 1877, *Reminiscenses of a Poet-Painter, Lippincott's Magazine, vol.* 19, *p.* 320.

That Read was a poet there can be no doubt, but his poetry was a gift, not an art, and he failed in accomplishing what was clearly within his limitations through his inaptitude for reflection, investigation, and study. That Poetry is something other and better than the language in which it is expressed, and that in this language there is a choice of words that express lights and shades of meaning, is a truth that he never learned. He wrote from instinct and impulse, not from knowledge, and he wrote easily and carelessly. That some things are more poetical than others, while others are not poetical at all, was another truth that he never learned, for from the beginning to the end of his career all was grist that came to his mill. Every theme that struck him as adaptable to a poetic handling was handled by him without regard to its intellectual or emotional value, for the consideration and determination of which he was unfitted. Attracted by the surface of things, he reproduced their surfaces, content with what they revealed, and careless of what they concealed. Moved by fancy rather than feeling, his verse was often smothered by the fancies with which it was bestrewn. — STODDARD, RICHARD HENRY, 1891, *Thomas Buchanan Read, Lippincott's Magazine, vol.* 47, *p.* 240.

He was distinctly a minor poet, but some of his Pennsylvania pastorals, like "The Deserted Road," have a natural sweetness; and his luxurious "Drifting," which combines the methods of painting and poetry, is justly popular. "Sheridan's Ride"— perhaps his most current piece—is a rather forced production, and has been overpraised.—BEERS, HENRY A., 1895, *Initial Studies in American Letters, p.* 180.

His "Sheridan's Ride" is among the most popular of our war-poems, but two lyrics, "Drifting" and "The Closing Scene" have a far higher poetic beauty. The last-named poem, with its subdued autumnal tone, has a grace and finish which remind us of the refined and delicate verse of Collins or of Gray.—PANCOAST, HENRY S., 1898, *An Introduction to American Literature, p.* 286.

A love of nature, patriotism, and chivalric respect for womanhood are the most obvious traits of Read's Americanism. "The Brave at Home," one of the lyrics interspersed throughout "The Wagoner of the Alleghanies," inspired countless imitations, none of which approached the original in its combination of beauty and simplicity. . . . The lyric, "Drifting," shows the work of both poet and artist, but in all the true essentials of lyric verse, "The Celestial Army" is easily first of all of Read's poems. —ONDERDONK, JAMES L., 1899-1901, *History of American Verse, p.* 257.

Sir Edward George Bulwer
Lord Lytton
1803-1873

Born [Edward George Earle Lytton Bulwer], in London, 25 May 1803. Educated privately. Matric. Trin. Coll., Camb., Easter, 1822; removed to Trin. Hall, Oct. 1822; Chancellor's Medal for Prize Poem, 1825; B. A., 1826; M. A., 1835. First visit to Paris, autum of 1825. Married Rosina Doyle Wheeler, 29 Aug. 1827. Settled near Pangbourne. Prolific contributor to periodicals. Removed to London, Sept. 1829. Active literary life. Edited "New Monthly Mag.," Nov. 1831 to Aug. 1833. M. P. for St. Ives, 1831–32. Legal separation from his wife, April 1836. Play, "The Duchess de la Vallière," produced at Drury Lane, 1836; "The Lady of Lyons," Drury Lane, 1838; "Richelieu," Drury Lane, 1839; "The Sea-Captain" (afterwards called "The Rightful Heir"), Haymarket, 1839; "Money," Haymarket, 1840. M. P. for Lincoln, 1833–41. Baronet, July 1838. Joint editor (with Brewster and Lardner) of "Monthly Chronicle," 1841. Play, "Not so Bad as we Seem," acted at Devonshire House, 1851. Succeeded to estate of Knebworth at his mother's death, Dec. 1843; assumed surname of Lytton, Feb. 1844. M. P. for Hertfordshire, 1852–66. Hon. D. C. L., Oxford, 9 June 1853. Lord Rector of Glasgow Univ., 1856 and 1858. Sec. of State for Colonies, 1858–59. Privy Councillor, June 1858. Hon. LL.D., Cambridge, 1864. Created Baron Lytton of Knebworth, 14 July 1866. G. C. M. G. 15 Jan. 1870. Died, at Torquay, 18 Jan. 1873. Buried in Westminster Abbey. *Works:* "Ismael," 1820; "Delmour" (anon.), 1823; "A Letter to a late

SIR EDWARD BULWER LYTTON

ELIZABETH BARRETT BROWNING

Cabinet Minister," 1824; "Sculpture" [1825]; "Weeds and Wild Flowers" (anon.; priv. ptd.), 1825; "O'Neill" (anon.), 1827; "Falkland" (anon.), 1827; "Pelham" (anon.), 1828; "The Disowned" (anon.), 1829; "Devereux" (anon.), 1829; "Paul Clifford" (under initials: E. B. L.), 1830; "The Siamese Twins," 1831; "Eugene Aram" (anon.), 1832; "Asmodeus at large" (anon.), 1833; "Godolphin" (anon.), 1833; "England and the English," 1833 (2nd edn. same year); "Pilgrims of the Rhine" (anon.), 1834; "The Last Days of Pompeii" (anon.), 1834; "Letter to a Cabinet Minister," 1834; "The Student" (from "New Monthly Mag."), 1835; "Rienzi," 1835; "The Duchesse de la Vallière" (under initials: E. B. L.), 1836; "Athens, its rise and fall" (2 vols.), 1837; "Ernest Maltravers" (anon.), 1837; "Alice" (anon.), 1838; "Leila," 1838; "Calderon the Courtier" (anon.), 1838; "The Lady of Lyons" (under initials: E. B. L.), 1838; "Richelieu" (anon.), 1838; "The Sea-Captain" (anon.), 1839; "Money" (anon.), 1840; "Works" (10 vols.), 1840; "Night and Morning" (anon.), 1841; "Dramatic Works," 1841; "Zanoni" (anon.), 1842; "Eva," 1842 (2nd edn. same year); "The Last of the Barons" (under initials: E. L. B.), 1843; "Confession of a Water Patient," 1845; "The Crisis" (anon.), 1845; "The New Timon" (anon.), 1846; "Lucretia" (anon.), 1846; "A Word to the Public" (anon.), 1847; "Harold" (anon.), 1848; "King Arthur," 1848–49 (2nd edn., 1849); "The Caxtons" (from "Blackwood's Mag."), 1849; "Night and Morning," 1851; "Letter to John Bull, Esq.", 1851 (11th edn. same year); "Not so Bad as we Seem," 1851; "Outlines of the early history of the East," 1852; "Poetical and Dramatic Works" (5 vols.), 1852–54; "My Novel" (from "Blackwood;" under pseud.: "Pisistratus Caxton"), 1853; "Address to the Associated Societies of the University of Edinburgh," 1854; "Clytemnestra" (anon.), 1855; "Speech at the Leeds Mechanics' Institution," 1854; "What will he do with it?" (under pseud.: Pisistratus Caxton), 1859; "Novels" (43 vols.), 1859–63; "St. Stephen's" (anon.), 1860; "A Strange Story" (anon.; from "All the Year Round"), 1862; "Caxtoniana," 1863; "The Boatman" (from "Blackwood;" under pseud.: Pisistratus Caxton), 1864; "The Lost Tales of Miletus," 1866; "The Rightful Heir" (anon.), 1868; "Miscellaneous Prose Works," 1868; "Walpole," 1869; "The Coming Race" (from "Blackwood;" anon.), 1871; "Kenelm Chillingly" (anon.), 1873; "The Parisians" (from "Blackwood"), 1873. *Posthumous:* "Speeches," and other political writings, ed. by his son, 1874; "Pausanias the Spartan," ed. by his son, 1876; "Life, Letters, and Literary Remains" (autobiog.), ed. by his son, 1883. He *translated:* "Poems and Ballads" from Schiller, 1844; Horace's "Odes and Epodes," 1869. *Collected Works:* in 37 vols., 1873–75. —SHARP, R. FARQUHARSON, 1897, *A Dictionary of English Authors*, p. 176.

PERSONAL

"Pelham" is writ by a Mr. Bulwer, a Norfolk squire, and horrid puppy. I have not read the book, from disliking the author, but shall do so since you approve it. —LOCKHART, JOHN GIBSON, 1828, *To Sir Walter Scott, Nov.; The Life and Letters, ed. Lang, vol.* II, p. 37.

Mr. Bulwer Lytton, a very young man and an enthusiast, wishes to be introduced to you. He is taking his degree at Cambridge; on his return pray let me make him acquainted with you.—LAMB, LADY CAROLINE, 1830, *Letter to Godwin, William Godwin by Paul, vol.* II, p. 302.

After the debate I walked about the streets with Bulwer till near three o'clock. I spoke to him about his novels with perfect sincerity, praising warmly, and criticising freely. He took the praise as a greedy boy takes apple pie, and the criticism as a good dutiful boy takes senna-tea. He has one eminent merit, that of being a most

enthusiastic admirer of mine; so that I may be the hero of a novel yet, under the name of Delamere or Mortimer. Only think what an honor!—MACAULAY, THOMAS BABINGTON, 1831, *To Hannah M. Macaulay; Life and Letters, ed. Trevelyan, ch.* IV.

Intrinsically a poor creature this Bulwer; has a bustling whisking agility and restlessness which may support him in a certain degree of significance with some, but which partakes much of the nature of *levity.* Nothing truly notable can come of him or of it.—CARLYLE, THOMAS, 1834, *Journal, Feb.* 13; *Early Life of Thomas Carlyle, ed. Froude, vol.* II, p. 327.

The author of "Pelham" is a younger son and depends on his writings for a livelihood, and truly, measuring works of fancy by what they will bring (not an unfair standard perhaps), a glance around his luxurious and elegant rooms is worth reams of puff in the quarterlies. He lives in the heart of the fashionable quarter of

London, where rents are ruinously extravagant, entertains a great deal, and is expensive in all his habits, and for this pay Messrs. Clifford, Pelham, and Aram—(it would seem) most excellent good bankers. As I looked at the beautiful woman [Mrs. Bulwer] seated on the costly ottoman before me, waiting to receive the rank and fashion of London, I thought that old close-fisted literature never had better reason for his partial largess. I half forgave the miser for starving a wilderness of poets.—WILLIS, NATHANIEL PARKER, 1835, *Pencillings by the Way, Letter* CXIX.

Yes, he is a thoroughly *satin* character; but then it is the *richest* satin. Whether it will wear as well as other less glossy materials remains to be seen. There was something inconceivably strange to me in his dwelling, with a sort of hankering, upon the Count d'Orsay's physical advantages; something beneath the dignity of an author, my fastidiousness fancied, in the manner in which he spoke of his own works, saying that the new ones only interested him as far as they were *experiments*. It is a fine, energetic, inquisitive, romantic mind, if I mistake not, that has been blighted and opened too soon. There wants the repose "the peace that passeth all understanding," which I must believe (and if it be a delusion, I hope I shall never cease to believe) is the accompaniment of the *highest* mind.—CHORLEY, HENRY FOTHERGILL, 1836. *Autobiography, Memoirs and Letters, ed. Hewlett, vol.* I, *p.* 194.

Bulwer was here a few moments ago in his flash *falsetto* dress, with high-heel boots, a white great coat, and a flaming blue cravat. How different from Rogers who is sitting near me, reading the "North American;" or Hallam who is lolling in an easy chair; or Milman,—both absorbed in some of the last Reviews or Magazines.—SUMNER, CHARLES, 1838, *To George S. Hillard, Dec.* 4; *Memoir and Letters of Sumner, ed. Pierce, vol.* II, *p.* 23.

> We know him, out of Shakespeare's art,
>   And those fine curses which he spoke;
> The old Timon, with his noble heart,
>   That, strongly loathing, greatly broke.
> So died the Old; here comes the New.
>   Regard him: a familiar face:
> I *thought* we knew him: what, it's you,
>   The padded man—that wears the stays—
> Who killed the girls and thrilled the boys
>   With dandy pathos when you wrote!
> A Lion, you, that made a noise,

> A shook a mane *en papillotes.*
> And once you tried the Muses too;
>   You failed, Sir; therefore now you turn,
> To fall on those who are to you
>   As Captain is to Subaltern.
> But men of long-enduring hopes,
>   And careless what this hour may bring,
> Can pardon little would-be POPES
>   And BRUMMELS, when they try to sing.
> . . . .
> What profits now to understand
>   The merits of a spotless shirt—
> A dapper boot—a little hand—
>   If half the little soul is dirt?

—TENNYSON, ALFRED LORD, 1846, *The New Timon and the Poets; Punch, vol.* 10, *p.* 103, signed "*Alcibiades.*"

A man with rather disagreeable manners, reminding me of some of the sub-heroes in his own books.—EASTLAKE, ELIZABETH LADY, 1846, *Journal, May* 22; *Journals and Correspondence, ed. Smith, vol.* I, *p.* 189.

In the adamantine chain of Mr. Ponsonby Ferrars' selfishness, to the links of which the complex miseries of OTHERS are ever appending, you develop the *apparently* contradictory, but perfectly compatible, vices of intense meanness and parsimony, with extreme ostentation and extravagance, which are the usual concomitants of the self-worshipping sensualist, and which is a true type of what our present social, or rather *anti-social*, system, with its intellectual *fiorettori*, can, and but too often *does*, produce, namely, a solid block of vice, gnarled with villainy but veneered with virtue! (?) and highly varnished with *hypocrisy*, which in these days of pretension and of SHAM, is a far more remarkable and popular commodity than the *rococo* genuine article of unvarnished excellence.—LYTTON, ROSINA LADY, 1854, *Behind the Scenes.*

His friendly temper, his generous heart, his excellent conversation (at his best) and his simple manners (when he forgot himself) have many a time "left me mourning" that such a being should allow himself to sport with perdition. Perhaps my interest in him was deepened by the evident growth of his deafness, and by seeing that he was not, as yet, equal to cope with the misfortune of personal infirmity. He could not bring himself practically to acknowledge it; and his ignoring of it occasioned scenes which, painful to others, must have been exquisitely so to a vain man like himself. I longed to speak, or get spoken, to him a word of warning and encouragement out of my own experience: but I never met with any who dared mention the subject to him; and I had no fair opportunity after the infirmity became conspicuous. From the time when, in contradicting in newspapers a report of his having lost his hearing altogether, he professed to think conversation not worth hearing, I had no hope for his fortitude: for it is the last resource of weakness to give out that grapes are sour.—MARTINEAU, HARRIET, 1855–77, *Autobiography, ed. Chapman, vol.* I, *p.* 266.

He is somewhat tall, and very spare, almost attenuated. He has a fine head and face, of which the portrait by Maclise gives a good representation. His nose is large, sharp, and prominent, fulfilling Napoleon's requirement of a man with a large nose for great enterprises. His action in speaking is good, though not perfect. Sometimes it is a little "wild," as when he draws back his head and slim body, and extends his arms, making one feel uncomfortable lest he should lose balance and upset. His voice is good,—strong, but not musical; and perhaps he is wanting in that delicate inflection of tone,—that variety, and light and shade, which the great orator is so careful to cultivate. Had Bulwer's practice been greater, doubtless he would have remedied such defects; for we must not forget that his life has been that of a student and a literary man, rather than of a man of action and public enterprise.—SMILES, SAMUEL, 1860, *Brief Biographies.*

He was in a better state at Knebworth than I have ever seen him in all these years, a little weird occasionally regarding magic and spirits, but perfectly fair and frank under opposition. He was talkative, anecdotical, and droll; looked young and well, laughed heartily, and enjoyed some games we played with great zest. In his artist character and talk he was full of interest and matter, but that he always is. Socially, he seemed to me almost a new man. I thoroughly enjoyed myself, and so did Georgina and Mary.—DICKENS, CHARLES, 1861, *To John Forster, July* 1; *Letters of Dickens, vol.* II, *p.* 167.

At the east end of the street, some five-and-twenty years since, lived Sir Edward Lytton Bulwer, in a house of moderate size on the north side, a few doors from Berkeley square. Sir Edward had the house em-bellished after his own taste: one of the drawing-rooms was a facsimile of a chamber which Bulwer had visited at Pompeii; vases, candelabra, chairs, tables, to correspond. James Smith humorously describes his hiding here: "Our host lighted a perfumed pastille modelled from Vesuvius. As soon as the cone of the mountain began to blaze, I found myself an inhabitant of the devoted city; and, as Pliny the elder, thus addressed Bulwer, my supposed nephew; 'Our fate is accomplished, nephew! Hand me yonder volume! I shall die as a student in my vocation. Do thou hasten to take refuge on board the fleet at Misenum; yonder cloud of hot ashes chides thy longer delay. Feel no alarm for me; I shall live in story; the author of "Pelham" will rescue my name from oblivion.' Pliny the younger made me a low bow," &c. Sir Edward's dining-room was furnished in the old English style, carved chairs, tables, and sideboard, which drew from a visitor the judicious remark that "such furniture is all right in old baronial halls, but to encounter it in a small house in a London street is too startling a transition." In his ancestral seat, Knebworth, Sir Bulwer Lytton is at home.—TIMBS, JOHN, 1865, *The Fair of May Fair, Walks and Talks about London, p.* 53.

The most pleasing thing about Lord Lytton is his humanity. He goes into the cottages of the poor people, and they seem to adore him. They have known him ever since he was a boy, and called him Sir and Mr. instead of My Lord, and when they correct themselves and beg pardon he says, "O never mind that."—ARNOLD, MATTHEW, 1869, *To his Mother, May* 12; *Letters, ed. Russell, vol.* II, *p.* 8.

He is not very strong, this gentleman, and has a scared kind of stare—that, indeed, of a student out in the world. In this living face, and in photographs from it, there is a suspicion that it is "got up" to what its owner thinks its best; that Pelham would be younger than he is. Vain struggle with Time; what gentle waggoner can put a "skid" on his wheel when he is going down hill, "or with a finger stay Ixion's wheel," as Keats has it? Look at the hair brushed forward and manipulated, the eyebrows, whiskers, and hair somewhat darkened, the moustache and imperial! The whole look of the man has just the clever *artistry*—not insincerity, for Lord Lytton is a true man—which is the little bit of bad taste which has prevented its master from being the very first in his rank. The little reft within the lute, and little rotten speck of garnered fruit—you know the rest.—FRISWELL, JAMES HAIN, 1870, *Modern Men of Letters Honestly Criticised,* p. 246.

Despite of physical defects which would have discouraged almost any other man from entering into public life at all, he had succeeded in winning a reputation as a great speaker in a debate where Palmerston, Gladstone, Bright, and Disraeli were champions. So deaf that he could not hear the arguments of his opponents, so defective in utterance as to become often almost unintelligible, he actually made the House of Commons doubt for a while whether a new great orator had not come among them.—MCCARTHY, JUSTIN, 1872, *Edward Bulwer Lord Lytton, Modern Leaders,* p. 157.

So Lytton is gone to Westminster Abbey. It was, on the whole, a noble life, for its untiring industry, energy, and many-sidedness both of genius and scholarship and practical business. He died pen in hand, and they say his novel soon to appear is among his best. His play of "Money," which I have read, is running hundreds of nights now at one of the chief theatres in London. He was a good Grecian, Latinist, German. He was a respectable Cabinet Minister. He achieved a peerage for his declining years, and a tomb in Westminster Abbey. I knew him very well, and once spent a few days with him at Knebworth, and always thought him delightful company.—MOTLEY, JOHN LOTHROP, 1873, *Letter to Oliver Wendell Holmes, Jan. 26; Correspondence, ed. Curtis, vol. II,* p. 360.

He played in his time many parts, some admirably, none discreditably. He was the most accomplished and industrious man of letters of his age, the most polished of novelists, and the only dramatist of his generation whose name can be mentioned in the same breath as Sheridan. As one reads the narrative of Bulwer's energy in the various *rôles* that he essayed, one is reminded of the Horatian ode, which paints the picture of the predestined votary of the Muses. Just as he whom Melpomene has marked for her own will neither win the laurels of the conqueror nor the glory of the statesman, nor vanquish his rivals in the palæstra, so, by a similar fatalism, was the heritage of distinction reserved for Bulwer purely and entirely literary.—ESCOTT, T. H. S., 1874, *Bulwer as Politician and Speaker, Fraser's Magazine, vol. 90,* p. 789.

Like almost every man, he was indebted to his mother for his greatness. Of his father, General Bulwer, we learn nothing; but his mother must have been a lady who possessed a large mind and natural ability of high order. She was an heiress of the Lyttons of Knebworth, and Bulwer, her favorite son, inherited her wealth, and at her death in 1843 assumed the name of which she was always proud—that of Lytton. Mrs. Bulwer was tall and slight, of a commanding presence: silent—it was thought from pride. She certainly conveyed to me the idea that she lived too much with her ancestors. That her celebrated son was devotedly attached to her is certain. . . . I believe Bulwer to have been a man made to be admired rather than loved. He achieved fame, but I am not sure that it brought him happiness. He seldom gave one the idea that he was in earnest: the good he did seemed rather the result of calculation than of impulse. I believe there would have been even among his friends and admirers a greater number to rejoice at his failure than triumph at his success. Had his earlier life been different from what it was, his prime and his decline might—I think would—have presented another picture. A married man must ask his wife if he is to be loved and respected, and if she says, "No," he will strive in vain to be either.—HALL, SAMUEL CARTER, 1883, *Retrospect of a Long Life, pp.* 152, 154.

He held strong opinions, and avowed them; he went into Parliament, and a literary career is even now with difficulty forgiven to a politician. Moreover, he was assuredly not orthodox in an age which had not forgiven Byron or Shelley, and an outward conformity at least was required to all the current religious acts and phrases in a degree which those can scarcely understand whose fate has fixed them in these latter days. Lord Lytton has a very interesting chapter on his father's religious opinions; but if closely examined, it all comes to the statement of him who maintained that his religion was that of all sensible men, and on being further pressed to say what that might be, rejoined that sensible men never tell. This was not enough for the days of the Reform Bill and of Catholic Emancipation. But with all these things against him, Bulwer won his way, and gained his place in the first rank of English novelists.—PAUL, C. KEGAN, 1884. *Edward Bulwer Lord Lytton, Harper's Magazine, vol.* 68, *p.* 730.

Next to Lord Lytton, the novelist, whose letters he [Charles Reade] religiously preserved, Charles Dickens occupied the highest place in his esteem.—READE, CHARLES L., AND COMPTON, 1887, *Memoir of Charles Reade, p.* 390.

Bulwig, a name originally given to Lord Bulwer in *Fraser's Magazine* in 1830. Thackeray, in *Fraser* and *Punch,* descended to personal sneers against Bulwer and his novel "Pelham," resorting even to such a miserable substitute for wit as calling the author *Bulwig.* Years after, when Thackeray collected his magazine articles, he announced that he did not know Bulwer when he sneered at him; still, he did not avoid perpetuating it, but reprinted the name in his collected works.—FREY, ALBERT R., 1888, *Sobriquets and Nicknames, p.* 55.

Lord Lytton had the very curious habit of making almost invisible hieroglyphics or crosses in his letters—at least I found them in those to me, as it were for luck. It was a very common practice from the most ancient Egyptian times to within two centuries. Lord Lytton's were evidently intended to escape observation. But there was indeed a great deal in his character which would escape most persons, and which has not been revealed by any writer on him. This I speedily divined, though, of course, I never discovered what it all was.—LELAND, CHARLES GODFREY, 1893, *Memoirs, p.* 400.

For Caryle the first Lord Lytton was "a poor fribble," and Mrs. Carlyle, who had espoused the cause of the novelist's wife, and championed her grievances, was still more plain-spoken, calling him "a lanthorn-jawed quack!" She told me that Carlyle had refused I know not how many invitations to dine with him.—ESPINASSE, FRANCIS, 1893, *Literary Recollections- and Sketches, p.* 215.

He was notoriously, and even self-consciously, penurious, and used to explain this by saying that he had the blood of Elwes the miser in his veins; but he was at the same time totally deficient in real sympathy with anyone. He was a word-painter and ideologist.—HAZLITT, W. CAREW, 1897, *Four Generations of a Literary Family, vol.* I, *p.* 226.

LADY LYTTON

I have now given, from the only authentic record of them, all the particulars relative to the circumstances of my father's marriage. Their multiplied evidence of his early affection for my mother is, I think, no unworthy tribute to her character and conduct at a time when, a young unmarried girl, she was placed in a very difficult and unhappy position. And on my father's side the history illustrates with great force that depth and strength of character which it is my object to portray with the utmost fidelity in my power. The facts which have here been related without reserve will, I trust, greatly abbreviate my task in dealing with the painful sequel of the story, into which it would be impossible for me to enter minutely without the appearance of sitting in judgment on my parents. I might have spared a part of what I have printed already if their ill-omened union had not produced a multiplicity of published extravagances which would not permit me to dismiss the subject with the simple statement that, at an early age, my father married for love, contrary to the wishes of his mother, and that his marriage was imprudent and unhappy. His own letters will now enable all candid persons to judge for themselves whether the writer of them could have been capable of the brutality, the cruelty, the meanness and selfishness, attributed to him in the numerous libels which he himself scorned to notice, and which cannot be repeated by his son, even for the purpose of refuting them.—LYTTON, EDWARD ROBERT BULWER EARL (OWEN MEREDITH), 1883, *The Life, Letters, and Literary Remains of Edward Bulwer Lord Lytton, vol.* II, *bk.* VII, *ch.* III.

His wife was beautiful, witty, and accomplished. Mr. Willis is entirely truthful when he speaks of her as the object of universal admiration in London. She was Irish by birth, and her maiden name was Rosina Wheeler. From early youth she had moved in a circle of some brilliancy in London, and had borne a distinguished place in it. In conjunction with Miss Elizabeth Spence she had written a novel called

"Dame Rebecca Berry," which had met with a certain measure of success. Miss Spence was a clever, kindly, and eccentric old maid, who affected literature and the society of eminent people. At her weekly reunions many of the rising celebrities were occasionally to be seen. It was here that Bulwer first met the lady who was to be his wife. Miss Wheeler was not then quite eighteen years of age, and Bulwer had only recently attained his majority. An attachment sprang up at once which soon developed into a passion, and when the young couple were married, it seemed as cordial a love-match as London society had ever known. And for a time perhaps it was. But a few years passed, and then it began to be known among Bulwer's intimate friends that he had caught a Tartar. Mrs. Bulwer had a furious temper, and she was insanely jealous of her husband. She quarrelled with all his female friends, without respect to their age. She accused Lady Blessington of alienating his affections, though Lady Blessington was almost old enough to be his mother. She had a fight with Lady Caroline Lamb, who was even older. She resented Bulwer's affection for Letitia Landon, the lively little woman who seemed so much his junior that his relations to her were almost paternal in their character. Nor did she vent her ill-humors on the ladies alone. She turned her husband's home into a small domestic hell.—WALSH, WILLIAM SHEPARD, 1884, *Pen Pictures of Earlier Victorian Authors, p.* 50.

Again, many years afterwards, he [my father] attempted to mediate between Lord and Lady Lytton (she was a cousin of ours), but in vain. Her temper was in such a state of inflammation, that she would listen to no moderate counsels, and my father had to sit still under her furious invectives whilst dying of heart disease. I have always thought that by her implacable egotism she shortened his life. Long after his death I put my resentment on one side, and tried to help her, but she soon became intractable. Lord Lytton, who always behaved with perfect courtesy both to my father and myself, offered to increase her allowance on certain conditions. I thought them reasonable enough, but the very mention of the word "conditions" drove her wild with rage, and a storm of abuse fell on my devoted head. Our inter-course ended with a letter, addressed to me thus:—

SIR FRANCIS HASTINGS DOYLE,
Bart., *Receiver-General of Customs*
(*However Infamous*),
Thames St.,
London.

The inside of the letter matched the outside, and I never saw or communicated with her again.—DOYLE, SIR FRANCIS HASTINGS, 1887, *Reminiscences and Opinions, p.* 379.

There are but a few more facts to narrate before I close this melancholy history. For the last seven years of her life Lady Lytton resided at a small house, "Glenómera," at Upper Sydenham, latterly with only one servant. She rarely left her room, and the house once only during the last five years. Naturally of a too generous disposition, wholly unselfish, and frequently left to the care of a servant who was equally unable to comprehend or to supply her requirements, she could hardly have lived so long had it not been for friends who commiserated her neglected and desolate condition, and tried to alleviate her sorrows and to supply what were really necessities by assisting her to the utmost extent of their ability. Although in her eightieth year, she possessed to the last the remains of a beauty that had been so noted in her youth. Neither her general tone nor manners had deteriorated through adversity, but remained to the last as distinguished as they were polished and winning. She was full of anecdote and wit, and though not reticent on the subject of her wrongs, she never failed to impress upon her hearers a feeling of sadness and regret that so much capacity for all that was loving and affectionate had been so ruthlessly destroyed by neglect, wrong, and persecution. No one can defend some of her published extravagances, but our blame should more justly be laid upon those who abused her highly sensitive nature, and induced those feelings of exasperation under the infliction of wrong which she had no other opportunity to express.—DEVEY, LOUISA, 1887, *Life of Rosina, Lady Lytton, p.* 388.

FALKLAND
1827

Published anonymously, a dreary and striking tale of crime and sorrow, containing the germ of many after-creations. This work cost its author more trouble than any of his novels, and is the least known among them.—CHORLEY, HENRY FOTHERGILL, 1838, *Authors of England, p. 37.*

PELHAM
1828

Pray who writes "Pelham?" I read it only yesterday and found it very interesting: the light is easy and gentleman-like, the dark very grand and sombrous. There are great improbabilities, but what can a poor devil do? There is, I am sorry to say, a *slang* tone of morality which is immoral, and of policy void of everything like sound wisdom. I am sorry if these should be the serious opinions of so powerful an author.— SCOTT, SIR WALTER, 1828, *Letter to Lockhart, Nov.* 20; *The Life and Letters of John Gibson Lockhart, ed. Lang, vol.* II, *p.* 35.

Read sections 6-10 of the eleventh "Philippic," and a very few chapters of "Pelham." The notes are changed to tragic. The chapter giving the account of the murder of Sir John Tyrrell is written with great powers of description, both of the scenes of nature and of the dark passions of the soul. Walter Scott is the founder of this school of writing, and the author of "Pelham" is an imitator not inferior to his original. There is more of nature in the characters, more of variety in the dialogue, less of pedantry in the discourses, and more frequent transitions in the narrative, than in Scott. There is also more invention, the basis of Scott's novels being historical, and this being altogether fictitious. All writing for the public should have some moral purpose. This indeed is the intended purpose of most, if not of all the novels of the present age. There is a refinement of delicacy in them which renders them more suitable for youth, but which takes from their merit as pictures of manners. Pelham goes to Paris, but he paints only Duchesses and gamblers, salons and boudoirs. In England it is the same —high life in London, and palaces in the country—Almacks or Newmarket. Notwithstanding this, he gives great interest to the story, and abounds with wit, though he has very little humor.—ADAMS, JOHN QUINCY, 1829, *Diary, April* 2; *Memoirs, ed. C. F. Adams, vol.* VIII, *p.* 126.

Were a good novel a more rare production, we should have much more to say of the excellencies and defects of this, which, liable as it is to the gravest exceptions on account of its moral lessons, is certainly one of very high character for striking portraits, richness of thought, strength and originality of conception, and vivacity and energy of style.—PHILLIPS, W., 1829, *Pelham, North American Review, vol.* 28, *p.* 433.

The publication of "Pelham" heralded a new intellectual dynasty of fops and puppies. Bulwer's original idea of a hero was the greatest satire ever written by a man of talent on his own lack of mental elevation. He attempted to realize in a fictitious character his notion of what a man should be, and accordingly produced an agglomeration of qualities, called Pelham, in which the dandy, the scholar, the sentimentalist, the statesman, the *roué*, and the blackguard, were all to be included in one "many-sided" man, whose merits would win equal applause from the hearty and the heartless, the lover and the libertine. Among these, however, the dandy stood preëminent; and scholarship, sentiment, politics, licentiousness, and ruffianism, were all bedizened in the frippery of Almacks.—WHIPPLE, EDWIN PERCY, 1844. *Literature and Life, Novels and Novelists, p.* 54.

Considered as a story, pure and simple, "Pelham" is full of power; and coming upon the world as it did in the period of Sir Walter Scott's decline, must have been a revelation. It was the Byronic school reduced to prose, and acclimatised to Berkeley-square. Read for the first time, or re-read after a lapse of years, it quickens the pulse and stirs the blood of the most *blasé* novel-reader.—BRADDON, MARY E., 1873, *Lord Lytton, Belgravia, vol.* 20, *p.* 77.

The book is brilliant with intellect. But no word is ever spoken as it would have been spoken—no detail is ever narrated as it would have occurred.—TROLLOPE, ANTHONY, 1879, *Thackeray (English Men of Letters), p.* 185.

Few books contain more absurdity or more affectation than "Pelham;" yet it was at once evident that it could only be the production of a writer of more than ordinary talent. For so young an author it was certainly a wonderful effort, showing considerable originality of thought, some humour, and a remarkable power of narrative, specially evinced in the sensational scenes of the end.—OLIPHANT, MARGARET, O. W., 1892, *The Victorian Age of English Literature, p.* 282.

"Falkland" was succeeded by "Pelham," which was published with his name, and which was the first, perhaps the most successful, and by far the most brilliant, of the novels in which authors have endeavoured to secure the rank of man of the world even more than that of man of letters, taking the method chiefly of fashionable, and therefore somewhat ephemeral, epigram.—SAINTSBURY, GEORGE, 1896, *A History of Nineteenth Century Literature, p.* 142.

"Pelham," written at twenty-five years of age, is a creditable boy's book; it aims to portray character as well as to develop incidents, and in spite of the dreadful silliness of its melodramatic passages it has merit. Conventionally it is more nearly a work of art than that other famous boy's book, Disraeli's "Vivian Grey."—HAWTHORNE, JULIAN, 1897, *Library of the World's Best Literature, ed. Warner, vol.* V, *p.* 2701.

The surprise that Bulwer operated in "Pelham" must have been much greater than we can imagine now when we look back and find the story so vulgarly and viciously commonplace under the glare of its worldly splendor. He called it "The Adventures of a Gentleman," and so it might have been, as gentlemen went in those days; but now it would rather be called "The Adventures of a Blackguard," so much have gentlemen or blackguards since improved. In abandoning the fanciful realm of the romancers, and returning to the world of actualities Bulwer did not return to the unsparing ideal of the first realists, and seek the good of his reader by pointing the moral of his tale; still less did he conceive of the principle which has vitalized the later realists, and leave a faithful study of life, in cause and effect, to enforce its own lesson. . . . The literary technique is so much better than Scott's; the story is so much shapelier, the style so much clearer and quicker, the diction so much more accurate, that one at first feels a certain joy in escaping to it. But this soon fades, and you find yourself longing for the foolishest page of romance, for the worst of Scott, of Cooper, of Brockden Brown, of Mrs. Radcliffe, as something truer and better, after all; for these authors, at their worst, were untrue only to the manifestations of human nature, and Bulwer, at his best, misrepresents the surface of life, and he is untrue to its essence. —HOWELLS, WILLIAM DEAN, 1901 *Heroines of Fiction, vol.* I, *pp.* 117, 118.

PAUL CLIFFORD
1830

I have this moment finished the perusal of "Paul Clifford." I know that you are not so wrapped up in self-confidence as not to feel a real pleasure in the approbation of others. And I regard it as a duty not to withhold my approbation when I am morally certain that it will be received as it is intended. There are parts of the book that I read with transport. There are many parts so divinely written that my first impulse was to throw my implements of writing in the fire, and to wish that I could consign all that I have published in the province of fiction to the same pyre. But this would be a useless sacrifice; and superior as I feel you to be in whatever kindles the finest emotions of the heart, I may yet preserve my peace, so far as relates to the mechanism of a story. This is but little, and does not satisfy my self-love, but I am capable of a sentiment that teaches me to rejoice in the triumph of others, without subjecting me to the mean and painful drawback of envy. I am bound to add that the penetration and acuteness you display are not inferior to the delicacy.— GODWIN, WILLIAM, 1830, *Letter to Bulwer, May* 13; *William Godwin, his Friends and Contemporaries by Paul, vol.* II, *p.* 306.

No one, we think, can read the work before us, without reprobation and disgust; no one, we mean, who is properly impressed with the importance of moral duty and religious obligation, or who feels sensible that the regulations of society, in regard to property, industry, and personal security, are entitled to any respect.— AUSTIN, J. T., 1830, *Paul Clifford, Christian Examiner, vol.* 9, *p.* 46.

You have ruined me by writing "Paul Clifford." I can think of nothing else. Adieu Jeremy Bentham! Adieu all my old teachers, more solemn, but not wiser, and less inspired! I thought that dramatic wit had died with Shakespeare. The meeting between Brandon and his wife is Dantesque. But there are others who can paint such scenes. The dramatic power of the book is wonderful, but it is in its wit that I find its wisdom. Wit I think your forte; and of all things it is what I envy most— perhaps because it never can be mine.

Your "Tomlinsoniana," by-the-way, seem to have excited some righteous indignation here.—ELLIOTT, EBENEZER, 1830, *Letter to Bulwer, May 25; Life, Letters, and Literary Remains of Edward Bulwer Lord Lytton, ed. Lytton, vol.* II, *bk.* VII, *ch.* XIII.

The publication of "Paul Clifford" did much to stimulate public opinion in favor of carrying Criminal Law Reform far beyond the point at which it had been left by the labors of Romilly: and the book itself was an incident in my father's constant course of endeavor to improve the condition of that large portion of the population which is most tempted to crime through poverty and ignorance—not by the proclamation of utopian promises, or recourse to violent constitutional changes, but through a better intellectual training facilitated by timely administrative reforms.—LYTTON, ROBERT BULWER EARL (OWEN MEREDITH), 1883, *The Life, Letters and Literary Remains of Edward Bulwer Lord Lytton, vol.* II, *bk.* VII, *ch.* XIII.

Just after "Paul Clifford" had appeared, under the *argot* of which was concealed, and very effectually, a serious attempt to draw public attention to our then vicious prison discipline and our sanguinary penal code. This moral has been forgotten by the world, but the book remains the special delight of foreigners, who will persist in looking on *Paul Clifford* as a real historic personage, so that even in distant Iceland a traveller who bore the honoured name of Clifford, and was nicknamed "Paul" by his friends, was hailed by one of the authorities as the descendant of the great English outlaw, whose deeds were worthy of comparison with those of the outlaws of that famous isle.—DASENT, G. W., 1884, *Two Biographies, Fortnightly Review, vol.* 41, *p.* 105.

EUGENE ARAM
1832

The offering which he had a right to lay at the feet of Scott.—CHORLEY, HENRY FOTHERGILL, 1838, *Authors of England p.* 37.

We consider that the revelations of genius here displayed may fairly be said to have recorded a consciousness that in the moral, as well as the physical frame, "we are fearfully and wonderfully made;" that when the instincts and the passions are over-mastered by the intellect, and man rests proudly on his boasted reason alone, he may work strange deeds before "high Heaven;" that he must beware of the casuistries of his brain no less than the wild workings of his heart, and that the affections and passions are the grand purifiers, the master movers, the voice of God in the soul, regulating the speculative, daring reason, and controlling as well as impelling action. This is to write greatly; to write philosophy and history, the physiology of sensation, and aggregate and individual truth.—HORNE, RICHARD HENGIST, 1844, *A New Spirit of the Age.*

It was in "Eugene Aram" that he first showed the mettle that was in him; it was the first distinct print of the lion's foot. Being early interested in the story of his hero, he set to work to collect the particulars of his life; and these he wove into a powerful and fascinating romance. In this story he has aimed to show what strange influences sometimes checker the web of life; how a mind essentially noble by deviating by an almost imperceptible angle from the path of virtue, may be gradually lured on till it is hopelessly entangled in the meshes of sin. *Obsta principiis,* "Resist beginnings," is the moral which he preaches. . . Some critics have objected to the psychological truthfulness of Eugene Aram's portrait. Is it possible, they have asked, for a man to be betrayed into a dreadful crime at the very moment when he is full of ardor for truth and virtue? Can a man harbor in his bosom a household devil in the shape of a consciousness of being a murderer without the whole mental atmosphere being made foul and poisonous? Those who ask these questions forget that Eugene Aram did not strike the blow which caused the death, and found, doubtless, in this a plausible reason for his own self-justification. They forget that, morally as well as physically, we are "fearfully and wonderfully made;" that when man trusts to his reason alone, and suffers his instincts to be overmastered by his intellect,—his better feelings to be cheated by the casuistries of the brain,—there is no inconsistency of which he may not be guilty, no deed of horror which he may not commit. The female characters in this work, especially Madeline and Ellinor, are regarded by Bulwer's admirers as masterpieces of portraiture.—MATHEWS, WILLIAM, 1887, *Men, Places, and Things, pp.* 56, 57.

THE LAST DAYS OF POMPEII
1834

We feel throughout his book all the inspiration of the poetic and sublime creations of ancient genius, and share in the scholar-like fervor which evidently swells the author's mind.—DEVEREUX, G. H., 1835, *The Last Days of Pompeii, North American Review, vol.* 40, *p.* 449.

"The Last Days of Pompeii," wove into a story of deep interest and beauty, the memories of the classic times; and the character of Nydia, the blind girl, will last as long as our language endures.—HORNE, RICHARD HENGIST, 1844, *A New Spirit of the Age.*

There is great talent, much learning, and vigorous conception, in the "Last Days of Pompeii," by Bulwer; and the catastrophe with which it concludes is drawn with his very highest powers; but still it is felt by every class of readers to be uninteresting. We have no acquaintance or association with Roman manners; we know little of their habits; scarce anything of their conversation in private; they stand forth to us in history in a sort of shadowy grandeur totally distinct from the interest of novelist composition. No amount of learning or talent can make the dialogues of Titus and Lucius, or Gallius and Vespasia, interesting to a modern reader.—ALISON, SIR ARCHIBALD, 1845, *The Historical Romance, Blackwood's Magazine, vol.* 58, *p.* 350.

"The Last Days of Pompeii" is also generally read with great interest; and though there is rather too much parade of not always very accurate antiquarian knowledge, it is written with great *verve* and brilliancy of imagination.—SHAW, THOMAS, B., 1847, *Outlines of English Literature, p.* 379.

Probably no historical romance has had more readers than "The Last Days of Pompeii."—CROSS, WILBUR L., 1899, *The Development of the English Novel, p.* 144.

I read all his books at that most impressionable time of life when but to name a woman's name is to conjure up a phantom of delight in the young fancy; but nothing remains to me now from the multitude of his inventions in the figure of women but the vague image of the blind girl Nydia in "The Last Days of Pompeii." I think this sort of general remembrance or oblivion no bad test in such matters, and I feel pretty sure that if Bulwer had imagined any other heroine of equal authenticity I should find some trace of her charm in my memory. But I find none from the books of an author whom I once thought so brilliant and profound, and whom I now think so solemnly empty, so imposingly unimportant. . . . Nydia fairly operates the whole action, in which the machinery creaks more audibly than it once did; but she is imagined upon old-fashioned lines of girlhood which have their charm. Like Milton's ideal of poetry, she is "simple, sensuous, passionate," and from her first meeting with Glaucus, the young Athenian swell who goes about snubbing the Latin civilization at Pompeii, she loves him. He saves her from the scourge of the savage virago who owns her, but when he has bought her he sends her to bear the declaration of his love to the beautiful Ione; and Nydia has to hear, if not to see, the tenderness of the lovers. . . . It may seem hard that a novelist whose fiction afterwards went so far and wide in the great English world of society and politics, should have lodged no other heroine so securely in the memory of his public as she of his early romance; but this appears to have been the fate of Bulwer. Yet, after all, it is no mean achievement. She was so well imagined, in a time when her type was fresher than now, that one's regret is rather for the heroine than the author; one wishes that she had been the creature of a talent able to do her full justice in the realization.—HOWELLS, WILLIAM DEAN, 1901, *Heroines of Fiction, vol.* I, *pp.* 118, 120, 124.

RIENZI
1835

All the richness of colouring, and fidelity in drawing, in Sir L. Bulwer's splendid historical romance of "Rienzi," cannot take away the painful impression produced by the long interval which elapses between the commencement of the story, where the characters first appear, its middle, where the real interest is developed, and its termination, where the catastrophe occurs.—ALISON, SIR ARCHIBALD, 1846, *The Romantic Drama, Blackwood's Magazine, vol.* 60, *p.* 171.

This novel, which is also better constructed than his works usually are in point of plot, was to a certain degree a labour of love, inasmuch as it served the author to embody many of his political convictions.—SHAW, THOMAS B., 1847, *Outlines of English Literature, p.* 379.

In style it is less pleasing than the "Last Days of Pompeii," and in vividness of description, as well as variety of incident, it is scarcely its equal. Yet it possesses many qualities of interest which will commend it to all lovers of romance.— BALDWIN, JAMES, 1883, *English Literature and Literary Criticism, Prose, p.* 185.

This work is not only delightful as a romance, as a fascinating tale of ambition and love placed amid scenes deeply stirring to the imagination; it is, besides, a contribution to history of uncommon value. Previously to the publication of "Rienzi," justice had never been done to the memory of the great Tribune, and even the Italians found in this romance the first correct view of their countryman. A legitimate criticism may be made concerning "Rienzi" to the effect that it contains too much historical material: that the fortunes of persons are deserted too often for the teachings and philosophy of history. But it is easy to forgive this artistic defect in view of the importance of the lessons to be learned from the Tribune's career and the wisdom with which the causes of great political events are traced.—TUCKERMAN, BAYARD, 1884, *Lord Lytton, Princeton Review, N. S., vol.* 14, *p.* 266.

THE LADY OF LYONS
1838

February 15*th*.—Went to an early rehearsal of the new play. Acted Claude Melnotte in Bulwer's play pretty well; the audience felt it very much, and were carried away by it; the play in the acting was completely successful. Was called for, and leading on Miss Faucit, was well received, gave out the play. Forster, Kenney, Bartley, &c., came into my room. *February* 17*th*.—Read over part of the play, being anxious to play well, as I knew Bulwer would be there. Acted pretty well; was called for, led on Miss Faucit, and was very cordially received. Bulwer came into my room, and expressed himself much pleased; offered to give his name whenever I might wish it.— MACREADY, WILLIAM C., 1838, *Diary, Reminiscences, ed. Pollock, p.* 440.

The charm of the "Lady of Lyons" results from the interest of the plot, the clear and often pathetic working of the story, the easy flow of the dialogue, the worldly morality, and the reality of the action, just sufficiently clothed in an atmosphere of poetry to take it out of the mere prose of existence, without calling upon the imagination for any effort to comprehend it. All this, united with every advantage that scenic effect and excellent acting could give, established the "Lady of Lyons" in a popularity which it has always retained. But this alone is not the mode of a great dramatist. The plot of the play in question will not bear examination by any high standard.— HORNE, RICHARD HENGIST, 1844, *A New Spirit of the Age.*

Probably the most successful acting drama produced in England since the days of Shakespeare.—McCARTHY, JUSTIN, 1872, *Edward Bulwer Lord Lytton, Modern Leaders, p.* 158.

He broke new ground and produced an acted play, "The Lady of Lyons," that in spite of artificial sentiment, and a plot turning upon an unmanly fraud, touched the old chord of revolutionary sentiment and, by help of clever dramatic construction, set it vibrating again. "The Lady of Lyons" has held the stage throughout the reign. — MORLEY, HENRY, 1881, *Of English Literature in the Reign of Victoria with a Glance at the Past, p.* 341.

It must be admitted that there is a certain "high-flown" strain in particular passages, certainly "bombastic," and which are almost impossible to deliver without provoking a smile. Such is the well-known description of the palace with which the suitor attempts to dazzle the imagination of his mistress. To the ordinary player this is, of course, inexpressibly dear, and perhaps the most precious morsel of "fat" in the whole. . . . The gracious, winsome part of Pauline has been essayed by all our most charming actresses, after being created by the once irresistible Miss Helen Faucit; and all, down to Miss Terry, Miss Anderson, and Mrs. Langtry, have increased their reputation by the performance. For over fifty years it has held its ground, and is always performed. Nay, it has been said that there is not a theatrical night in the year when it is not being played at some theatre of the kingdom. The young beginner, just stepping on the boards, turns fondly to the effective "gardener's son," and is certain he could deliver the passage ending, "Dost like the picture?"—a burst often laughed at, but never failing to tell. Every character is good and actable, and, though we may have seen it fifty times, as most playgoers have, there is always a reserve of novelty and attraction left which is certain to interest.—FITZGERALD, PERCY, 1889, *The Lady of Lyons, Gentleman's Magazine, vol. 267, pp. 136, 137.*

The most popular of his dramas, "The Lady of Lyons," has been a favourite work with the most distinguished players, and is still found to be a good acting piece. The plot may be improbable, and the hero's conduct by no means above reproach, but the dialogue, with all its tinsel, has at times the fine ring of passion, the situations are telling, and the action never flags.—WHYTE, WALTER, 1894, *The Poets and the Poetry of the Century, John Keats to Lord Lytton, ed. Miles, p. 624.*

It is the best specimen of Lytton's dramatic work.—WALKER, HUGH, 1897, *The Age of Tennyson, p. 74.*

RICHELIEU
1838

In one peculiarity, at least, Bulwer-Lytton the novelist surpassed all his rivals and contemporaries. His range was so wide as to take in all circles and classes of English readers. He wrote fashionable novels, historical novels, political novels, metaphysical novels, psychological novels, moral-purpose novels, immoral-purpose novels. "Wilhelm Meister" was not too heavy nor "Tristram Shandy" too light for him. He tried to rival Scott in the historical romance; he strove hard to be another Goethe in his "Ernest Maltravers;" he quite surpassed Ainsworth's "Jack Sheppard," and the general run of what we in England call "thieves' literature," in his "Paul Clifford;" he became a sort of pinch-beck Sterne in "The Caxtons," and was severely classical in "The Last Days of Pompeii." One might divide his novels into at least half a dozen classes, each class quite distinct and different from all the rest, and yet the one author, the one Bulwer-Lytton, showing and shining through them all. Bulwer is always there. He is masquerading now in the garb of a mediæval baron, and now in that of an old Roman dandy; anon he is disguised as a thief from St. Giles's, and again as a full-blooded aristocrat from the region of St. James's. But he is the same man always, and you can hardly fail to recognize him even in his cleverest disguise. It may be questioned whether there is one spark of true and original genius in Bulwer.—MCCARTHY, JUSTIN, 1872, *Edward Bulwer Lord Lytton, Modern Leaders, p. 160.*

In this drama the story is told by direct action, out of which the language naturally flows,—tinged, it is true, with the romantic sentimentalism that thoroughly saturated Bulwer's thought and style,—and to which, for the most part, it is a spontaneous necessity. It appears to have been Macready's impression that Bulwer had drawn, under the name of Richelieu, a character entirely different from the historic original; but he records that Bulwer at length satisfied him as to the justice of the portrayal, from the evidence of history. There is no doubt, however, that the poet has considerably—though neither unjustly nor inartistically—idealized the character of Richelieu.—WINTER, WILLIAM, 1878, *ed. The Miscellaneous Plays of Edwin Booth, Preface, vol. III, p. 3.*

Richelieu is a favourite character with all tragedians. We have seen in the earlier portion of this paper how much Mr. Macready admired the play; he had evidently an enjoyment, a positive pleasure in acting it. Mr. Phelps frequently acted Richelieu; he was admirably suited to the character, because he was a good comedian as well as a tragedian. There is an excellent likeness of him in this part at the Garrick Club; it is painted by Mr. Forbes Robertson, and was purchased by a subscription of some members of the club. It seems somewhat strange that Richelieu should not have been numbered amongst the characters of Mr. Charles Kean—surely it would have suited him; but I cannot find it on record that he ever acted it. He certainly did not in London. Cardinal Wolsey was a favourite character with him; Cardinal Richelieu might have proved a good companion-picture. Mr. Henry Irving has revived the play at the Lyceum. Mr. Barry Sullivan stars with it. Mr. Edwin Booth is now acting it at the Adelphi Theatre. Many of his admirers incline to place this personation foremost in his répertoire.—GORDON, WALTER, 1882, *Popular Plays, The Theatre, vol. 9, p. 78.*

This piece may be compared with the Cromwell of Victor Hugo. It was marked by the same mixture of tragedy and melodrama; the same display of historical documents and the same ignorance of what is essential in history; the same use of the lowest and the most eccentric expedients to raise a laugh or cause a shudder; the same superficial and crude psychology which in each character, male or female, great or small, reveals the personality of the author. Even when this author is a Victor Hugo it is bad enough! But when it is a Bulwer—!—FILON, AUGUSTIN, 1897, *The English Stage, tr. Whyte, p. 68.*

Booth's Richelieu was a great personality; Bulwer's, a mere suggestion, a skeleton of lath on which the fustian hung loosely.—JOHNSON, CHARLES F., 1898, *Elements of Literary Criticism, p. 59.*

THE NEW TIMON
1846

A perusal of "The New Timon" recalls another poet to the mind, however, much oftener than Crabbe. To us, it would rather seem as if the author had studied Byron with so intense an admiration, that not only in his style, but in the cast of his heroes, and even in some incidental passages of his verse, he has been unable to disengage his memory from the works of the object of his homage. Not that he is a mere imitator, and still less that he has intentionally borrowed anything from Byron; but that he has been unconsciously reflecting back impressions long ago received by him, and carefully treasured up until they seemed part and parcel of his native thoughts.—BELL, J. M., 1846, *The New Timon, North British Review, vol. 5, p. 401.*

The author of the "New Timon" avows himself a follower of Pope. We shall by-and-by have occasion to try him by his own standard. In the meantime, we shall barely remark, that his allusions to Wordsworth, Tennyson, and Keats are presumptuous and in bad taste. The fact that he misspells the name of one of these poets argues either a very petty affectation, or a shameful unfamiliarity with what he pretends to criticize. . . . The author is a professed disciple of Pope, but he is wanting in the vivid common-sense, the crystal terseness, and the epigrammatic point of his original. Moreover, he is something of a "snob." His foundling

Lucy must turn out to be an earl's daughter; his Hindoo Timon must be a nabob. It is clear that he reverences those very artificial distinctions which he professes to scorn. So much contempt could not be lavished on what was insignificant. Himself the child of a highly artificial state of society, there seems to be something unfilial and against nature in his assaults upon it. His "New Timon" is made a Timon by the very things which he affects to despise. Pope was quite superior to so subaltern a feeling. The plot of the story is not much to our taste. Morvale, the hero, is the son of a half-Hindoo father and an English mother.—LOWELL, JAMES RUSSELL, 1847, *The New Timon, North American Review, vol. 64, pp. 467, 473.*

Had, unfortunately, a romantic story interwoven with its satire; had it not *that*, had it been a satire *pur et simple*, it would have nearly equalled those of Pope, or, let us say, Gifford. In style, it was between the two.—FRISWELL, JAMES HAIN, 1870, *Modern Men of Letters Honestly Criticised, p. 249.*

KING ARTHUR
1848–49

The poet, bringing to his task powers in their full maturity, and long and variously exercised, has not contented himself either with telling a pathetic love-tale, or with weaving together effusions of lyric emotion. He has conceived the bold design of constructing, out of materials wonderfully varied, a symmetrical and powerful work of epic art: and, in the poem thus produced, he has proved himself to possess, not only the genuine feeling and imagination of the poet, but also that which is rarer and higher still, the deep thoughtfulness of the poetic artist.—SPALDING, WILLIAM, 1849, *Sir E. Bulwer Lytton; King Arthur, Edinburgh Review, vol. 90, p. 202.*

I should be willing to exchange a great mass of fiction—perhaps all Sir Edward's poem—for a few grains of unquestionable truth on the subject. Only, where this is not to be had, I think it wise to be content with the creature of the imagination, which after all is a fact, and a very precious fact, though of a different kind. The more I prize historical truth, the more jealous I am of all unauthenticated claims to its character. I do wish for leisure to read "Arthur," though I strongly suspect that the author is mistaken in his estimate of its comparative value. I know that everybody does not like it, which I believe could not be said of any of his greater novels.— THIRLWALL, CANNOP, 1865, *Letters to a Friend, March* 13, *ed. Stanley, p.* 22.

"King Arthur" may have been the best epic of its year, but it is now as dead as the Arthurian lays of Sir Richard Blackmore. Yet Lytton professed to regard it as the crowning work of all his days:—"I am unalterably convinced," he wrote, "that on this foundation I rest the least perishable monument of those thoughts and those labours which have made the life of my life." The epic is written in stanzas, consisting each of a quartrain followed by a couplet, a form which is unsuited for a long narrative poem, and which in Lytton's hands soon becomes intolerably monotonous. The allegory is dim, the story uninteresting, and the characters are puppets.—WHYTE, WALTER, 1894, *The Poets and the Poetry of the Century, John Keats to Lord Lytton, ed. Miles, p.* 625.

The epic of "King Arthur" is scarcely worthy of mention.—WALKER, HUGH, 1897, *The Age of Tennyson, p.* 74.

Not to be compared with Tennyson's "Idylls" in simplicity and beauty and spiritual power is Bulwer's "King Arthur." This has originality and epigrammatic smartness, and now and then some poetic power, but it lacks almost wholly a sympathetic feeling for the old romances, and serves mainly as a vehicle for the author's opinions on life and society.—MEAD, WILLIAM EDWARD, 1897, *Selections from Sir Thomas Malory's Morte Darthur, Introduction, p.* xlv.

THE CAXTONS
1849

It has well-drawn characters in it, but the style produces upon me the effect of a flashy waistcoat festooned with gold chains. —LONGFELLOW, HENRY WADSWORTH, 1849, *Journal, Nov.* 1, *Life by Longfellow, vol.* II, *p.* 161.

The "Caxtons" is Bulwer's *magnum opus*. The plot is simplicity itself, but there is, at least, one scene of rare dramatic power. The characters possess hardly the charm of perfect novelty, for they remind us of familiar figures, drawn by a master-hand, yet they surpass the older types, both in moral

beauty and intellectual variety, and are matchless among the creations of modern writers. . . . The author of the "Caxtons" never descends to puddles. The atmosphere of this book is pure as the ether of that new world to which its hero goes in quest of fortune. What a change since "Pelham!" Instead of the young man's knowledge of the world, we have the maturer mind, with its deep insight, its profound mastery of the human heart. Instead of the varnished graces of a Hervey or a Chesterfield, we have the soul of chivalry inspiring the modest acts and quiet words of English gentlemen—a life the most supremely Christian that fiction has ever embodied. If "Pelham" be a text-book for the worldling, a chart whereby the drawing-room navigator may avoid the rocks and shoals of society's shallow ocean, the "Caxtons" is assuredly a gospel for the mind which has holier aspirations than worldly success—a lantern to light the way to the stars.—BRADDON, MARY E., 1873, *Lord Lytton, Belgravia, vol.* 20, *p.* 82.

"The Caxtons," which practically retains its original simplicity throughout the three volumes. Austin and Roland Caxton are never thrust aside to make play for melodramatic schemers or conventional heroes, and the atmosphere in which they live is equally healthy from first to last. With these three novels, which rank so very much higher than any of his other works, the author's literary career came more or less to a standstill, though he continued writing up to his death in 1873.—OLIPHANT MARAGARET O. W., 1892, *The Victorian Age of English Literature, p.* 285.

As a straightforward and consecutive narrative of actual facts, duly set forth with appropriate comments, "Tristram Shandy" must be acknowledged, as Mr. Shandy said of the science of fortification, to have its weak points. Those who find it dull will probably find "The Caxtons" amusing, and I recommend them to try.— PAUL, HERBERT, 1896, *Sterne, The Nineteenth Century, vol.* 40, *p.* 996.

MY NOVEL
1853

I have read it with great pleasure, though Bulwer's nature is by no means a perfect one either, which makes itself felt in his book; but his gush, his better humour, his abundant materials, and his mellowed constructive skill—all these are great things.—ARNOLD, MATTHEW, 1853, *To Mrs. Forster, April* 14; *Letters, ed. Russell, vol.* I, *p.* 34.

He paints the froth of society; and very gay froth it is, and very pretty bubbles he can make of it: but this is not reconciling classes, or giving a philosophic representation in fiction of the great organic being we call the English nation; and so far as "My Novel" pretends to be anything more than anybody else's novel, anything more than a well-wrought story, constructed out of the old Bulwer-Lytton materials, the pretence is fabulous and the performance does not answer to it. We have a novel neither better nor worse than its predecessors; but we have not a great work of art reared on a basis so broad as a general survey of English life in the earlier half of the nineteenth century. . . . Dandy literature and superfine sensibilities are tokens and causes of a degenerate art and an emasculate morality; and among offenders in this way none has sinned more, or is of higher mark for a gibbet, than the author of "My Novel." Such books as his, when they appear in their true characters, are judged according to one standard; but when they come in the guise of profound meaning and lofty aims, and give themselves the airs of being grand concrete philosophies, the judge looks at them in quite another light, tries them by a higher code, and condemns them accordingly, as well-dressed impostors.—BRIMLEY, GEORGE, 1853-58, *"My Novel," Essays, ed. Clark, pp.* 278, 280.

A work which commences as a perfect idyl of country life, but wanders off later into complicated intrigues and melodramatic episodes in an unreal world peopled with impossible characters like Randal Leslie or Harley Lestrange. As long as we remain in the village of Hazledean with the Squire and the Parson, Dr. Riccabocca and Lenny Fairfield, we desire no wider horizon and no better company, and we think it most unfortunate that the writer was not of the same mind.—OLIPHANT, MARGARET O. W., 1892, *The Victorian Age of English Literature, p.* 284.

THE COMING RACE
1871

Many thanks for Bulwer. Only think I never knew him, never even saw him, and

learnt first after his death who had written "The Coming Race." One ought not to be proud of anything, but I was very much delighted. — MÜLLER, FRIEDRICH MAX, 1873, *To Dr. Althaus, Jan.* 1; *Life and Letters, ed. his Wife, vol.* I, *p.* 469.

The class of composition to which "The Coming Race" belongs is one peculiarly adapted to Bulwer's genius. Bulwer possessed in a high degree the rich fancy of the romancist and the keen perception of the satirist. If he had been less of a romancist he would have been more effective as a novelist. In "The Coming Race" he was free to let his imagination run romantic riot without weakening the effect of his satire.—ESCOTT, T. H. S., 1874, *Bulwer's Last Three Books, Fraser's Magazine, vol.* 89, *p.* 767.

The fact that in the fiftieth year of his authorship, after publishing at least fifty separate works, most of them popular, Lord Lytton had still vigor and freshness enough to make a new anonymous reputation with "The Coming Race" would seem to indicate that critics had not fairly gauged his versatility, and also that an erroneous fixed idea had been formed of his style.—MINTO, WILLIAM, 1883, *Encyclopædia Britannica, Ninth, Ed., vol.* XV.

My two favourite novels are Dickens's "Tale of Two Cities" and Lytton's "Coming Race." Both these books I can read again and again, and with an added pleasure. Only my delight in the last is always marred afresh by disgust at the behaviour of the hero, who, in order to return to this dull earth, put away the queenly Zoe's love.—HAGGARD, H. RIDER, 1887, *Books which Have Influenced Me, p.* 67.

"The Coming Race," published anonymously and never acknowledged during his life, was an unexpected product of his mind, but is useful to mark his limitations. It is a forecast of the future, and proves, as nothing else could so well do, the utter absence in Bulwer of the creative imagination. It is an invention, cleverly conceived, mechanically and rather tediously worked out, and written in a style astonishingly commonplace. The man who wrote that book (one would say) had no heaven in his soul, nor any pinions whereon to soar heavenward. Yet it is full of thought and ingenuity, and the central conception of "vril" has been much commended. But the whole concoction is tainted with the deadness of stark materialism.—HAWTHORNE, JULIAN, 1897, *Library of the World's Best Literature, ed. Warner, vol. v, p. 2703.*

KENELM CHILLINGLY
1873

There is one—perhaps only one—of the criticisms which have been passed on Lord Lytton as a novelist that a candid review of his works will prove to be undeserved. He never wrote himself out. "Kenelm Chillingly" is in all respects a characteristic performance, and will leave its author's reputation unaltered for better or worse. It may be that the characters are unreal, the thought shallow, and the feeling artificial; but from the days of "Pelham" onwards Lord Lytton's works have shown a singular capacity for living through such accusations without needing to live them down. And whatever merits there were in Pelham are just as conspicuous in Kenelm. The author has kept pace with the times, and unless his public has grown more critical or is *blasé* with the number of competitors for its favour there is no reason why his last success should be less than his first.—SIMCOX, EDITH, 1873, *Kenelm Chillingly, The Academy, vol. 4, p. 161.*

If he had been content to abandon his purpose in "Chillingly," and end with the first volume by some such commonplace contrivance as giving "motive power" to his hero in the love of Cecilia Travers, it would have been the most perfect of his works in unity of humorous sentiment.—MINTO, WILLIAM, 1883, *Encyclopædia Britannica, Ninth Ed., vol. xv.*

I can only once remember thoroughly breaking down and making a discreditable exhibition of feeling over a book, though I have before now been moved to tears of another sort by the music of some chant of battle. It happened when I was a lad of seventeen or eighteen, and the work was "Kenelm Chillingly." I read it till the small hours of the morning, and wept over the death of Lilly. It interested me much in after-years to learn from his biography that that episode was more or less real, taken from the life-experience of the writer and that he, too, broke down when he read it aloud. It had been written from the heart, and hence its hold upon the human sympathies.—HAGGARD, H. RIDER, 1887, *Books which Have Influenced Me, p. 66.*

The story of "Kenelm Chillingly; his Adventures and Opinions," by Lord Lytton is so simple, the plot so slight, that any one who takes up this novel hoping to find exciting adventures in it will be disappointed; but, on the other hand, we know of more than one habitual novel-reader who has cried before reaching the end, and no one can lay this book down without feeling the better for the pictures shown us of an upright country gentleman and his quaint, original son, of a noble woman who bears a secret sorrow bravely and patiently, and of one of the prettiest, most lovable heroines which an author of the male sex has ever drawn.—STUART, ESMÉ, 1893, *Great Characters of Fiction, ed. Townsend, p. 221.*

GENERAL

Tickler. "As for Mr. Bulwer, laying the most hackneyed common-places out of view, the majestic features, elegant mien, intense loves, and indomitable nerves which *his* heroes share with ten thousand Belvilles and Delvilles—these air-drawn personages are nothing, if not coxcombical. Who can think, with common patience of his endless chatter about their tapering fingers, their 'feet small to a fault,' their velvet robes-de-chambre, and the violet damask curtains of their dressing-rooms?"

North. "Horrid puppyism! — These books, however, all contain detached scenes of interest and power, both serious and comic—they are all written with ease and vigour, and abound in sentences and expressions which speak the man of observation and reflection—they convey the impressions of an ardent, ambitious, energetic mind, and of an elegant taste in letters."—WILSON, JOHN, 1831, *Noctes Ambrosianæ, September.*

Edward Lytton Bulwer has vigorous and varied powers; in all that he has touched on he has shown great mastery; his sense of the noble, the beautiful, or the ludicrous, is strong; he can move at will into the solemn or the sarcastic; he is equally excellent in describing a court or a cottage, and is familiar with gold spurs and with clouted shoon. — CUNNINGHAM, ALLAN, 1833, *Biographical and Critical History of the Literature of the Last Fifty Years.*

You speak of Bulwer's remarks on Englishwomen ["England and the English"] and their aristocratic tendencies. I doubt not they are true in the main. I have read only the first volume of his work as yet—a remarkable book, especially considering the haste in which it seems to have been thrown off. I felt that a man who could write so good a book ought to have written a better. He is generally superficial, and yet looks so often beneath the surface, that one wishes he had been more just to himself and his subject. His notions of religion are very crude. With all his egotism, he writes like a true friend of the people, of the mass of men. Is he not worthy this highest praise? — CHANNING, WILLIAM ELLERY, 1833, *To Miss Aikin, Dec.* 28; *Correspondence of William Ellery Channing and Lucy Aikin, ed. Le Breton, p.* 192.

In a vivid wit, in profundity and a Gothic massiveness of thought, in style, in a calm certainty and definiteness of purpose, in industry, and above all, in the power of controlling and regulating by volition his illimitable faculties of mind, he is unequalled, he is unapproached.— POE, EDGAR ALLAN, 1836, *Marginalia, Works, ed. Stedman and Woodberry, vol.* VII, p. 277.

If you care about the apinions, fur good or evil, of us poor suvvants, I tell you, in the most candied way, I like you, Barnet. I've had my fling at you in my day. . . . but I like you. One may objeck to an immence deal of your writings, which, betwigst you and me, contain more sham scentiment, sham morallaty, sham poatry, than you'd like to own; but, in spite of this, there's the *stuf* in you: you've a kind and loyal heart in you, Barnet—a trifle deboshed, perhaps; a kean i, igspecially for what's comic (as for your tradgady, it's mighty flatchulent), and a ready plesnt pen. The man who says you are an As is an As himself. Don't believe him, Barnet; not that I suppose you wil,—for, if I've formd a correck apinion of you from your wucks, you think your smallbeear as good as most men's: every man does,—and why not? We brew, and we love our own tap— amen; but the pint betwigst us, is this stewpid, absudd way of crying out, because the public don't like it too. Why shood they, my dear Barnet? You may vow that they are fools; or that the critix are your enemies; or that the wuld should judge your poams by your critticle rules, and not their own; you may beat your breast, and vow you are a marter, and you won't mend

the matter. Take heart, man! you're not so misrabble after all; your spirits need not be so *very* cast down; you are not so *very* badly paid. I'd lay a wager that you make, with one thing or another,—plays novvles, pamphlicks, and little odd jobbs here and there—your three thowsnd a-year. There's many a man, dear Bullwig, that works for less, and lives content. Why shouldn't you? Three thowsnd a-year is no such bad thing,—let alone the barnetcy: it must be a great comfort to have that bloody hand in your skitching.—THACKERAY, WILLIAM MAKEPEACE, 1840, *Yellowplush Papers, Fraser's Magazine, vol.* 21, p. 71.

Lord Lytton is, many believe, the greatest of English novelists, and it is probable that he will always be ranked among the classic writers of his country. . . . The general tendency of his works is immoral, and they are nearly all imbued with a sickly and shallow philosophy. He has no faith in humanity. He breaks down the barriers between right and wrong. By presenting vice divested of its grossness he renders it attractive. Instead of holding up virtue as the only source of felicity he makes his criminals happy men, and challenges for them in every condition our admiration.—GRISWOLD, RUFUS W., 1844, *The Poets and Poetry of England in the Nineteenth Century, p.* 401.

Bulwer is rather an eloquent and accomplished rhetorician than a delineator of life and character. His intellect and feelings are both narrowed by his personal character, and things which clash with his individual tastes he criticizes rather than delineates. Everything he touches is Bulwerized. A man of large acquirements, and ever ready to copy or pilfer from other authors, he discolors all that he borrows.— WHIPPLE, EDWIN P., 1844, *Literature and Life, Novels and Novelists, p.* 55.

Do you mean calmly, advisedly, and with your eyes open, to have a chapter on the novelists, and omit Bulwer? Or do you (which would be a satisfactory explanation) give him a room to himself? But if so, why not refer to him in this paper as a leader in the highest class of the art, to be mentioned hereafter? Think of "Ernest Maltravers," and "Alice," worth all the historical novels—I was near saying that ever were written! You, a poet and dramatist, to forget the passionate unity of that great work! for the two romances complete the single work. And then, even if you succeed in lifting the historical romance over the head of all other kinds of romance (a position which I protest solemnly and vociferously against—as untenable and unworthy of a poet's editorship), by that very sign, Sir Lytton Bulwer takes throne rank in his "Pompeii" and "Rienzi," while Mr. James lies under the footstool.— BROWNING, ELIZABETH BARRETT, 1844, *Letters of Elizabeth Barrett Browning Addressed to Richard Hengist Horne, Jan.* 5.

Burns' Songs are better than Bulwer's Epics.—BRONTË, CHARLOTTE, 1849, *Letter to W. S. Williams, April* 2; *Charlotte Brontë and her Circle, ed. Shorter, p.* 392.

The brilliant fame of Sir Edward Lytton Bulwer as a novelist, and as a dramatic writer, has tended much to eclipse and disparage his appearances as a poet. In the two former departments he ranks deservedly as a magnate; in the last, his status is more questionable, although, I confess, this is a thing rather to be felt than explained. He constantly touches the confines of success, and stands before the gate—but the "Open Sesame!" comes not to his lips. Perhaps it is that, in his themes, we have rather able and eloquent treatment than that colouring glow of imagination which has been termed an inspiration. With fine descriptive powers, and with boundless range of illustration, there is a want of reliance on simple nature —of that fusion of the poet in his subject, which can alone give that subject consecration—the poetic art, without the poetic vision; and this defect is apparent in all his verse, from his early "Weeds and Wildflowers," "O'Neil the Rebel," "Ismael," and "The Siamese Twins," down to his "Eva, or the Ill-omened Marriage," his "Modern Timon," and his more elaborate and ambitious "King Arthur." His translations of the poems and ballads of Schiller are, however, justly held in estimation among scholars for their spirit and fidelity. — MOIR, D. M., 1851–52, *Sketches of the Poetical Literature of the Past Half Century*,

Who that ever read that glorious romance ["Zanoni"], with its pictures of love, and life, and death, and the mysteries of the unseen world; the fine dance of the human and the preternatural elements which are in it, and keep time so admirably to the music of the genius which has

created both, and the melting sublimity of its close—will deny the author the name of poet?—GILFILLAN, GEORGE, 1855, *A Third Gallery of Portraits, p.* 341.

The author is an orator, and has tried to be a poet. Dickens' John the Carrier was perpetually on the verge of a joke, but never made one: Bulwer's relation to poetry is of the same provoking kind. The lips twitch, the face glows, the eyes light; but the joke is not there. An exquisite *savoir faire* has led him within sight of the intuitions of poetic instinct. Laborious calculation has almost stood for sight, but his maps and charts are not the earth and the heavens. His vision is not a dream, but a nightmare; you have Parnassus before you, but the light that never was on sea or shore is wanting. The whole reminds you of a lunar landscape, rocks and caves to spare, but *no atmosphere*. It is fairy-land travelled by dark. How you sigh even for the chaos, the *discordia semina* of genius, while toiling through the impotent waste of this sterile maturity.— DOBELL, SYDNEY, 1855, *Letter to George Gilfillan, A Third Gallery of Portraits, p.* 341.

Few English writers, whose compositions consist chiefly of works in imagination have attained such an eminence in literature as he has done. From "Pelham" to "My Novel," we have a series of works, extending to about fifty volumes, any one of which productions might suffice to make a reputation for an ordinary novelist.. . . . One of the most characteristic features of Bulwer's writings is the singular combination of worldly experience—perfect knowledge of life, and especially of life in the upper circles of society, a thorough acquaintance with its selfishness and specious fallacies—*ses misères et ses bassesses*, with the vast amount of genuine poetry that prevails in his prose writings.—MADDEN, RICHARD ROBERT, 1855, *The Literary Life and Correspondence of the Countess of Blessington, vol.* II, *p.* 171.

For Bulwer I always felt a cordial interest, amidst any amount of vexation and pity for his weakness. He seems to me to be a woman of genius enclosed by misadventure in a man's form. If the life of his affections had been a natural and fortunate one; and if (which would have been the consequence) he had not plunged over head and ears in the metaphysics of morals,

I believe he would have made himself a name which might have lasted as long as our literature. He has insight, experience, sympathy, letters, power and grace of expression, and an irrepressible impulse to utterance and industry which should have produced works of the noblest quality; and these have been intercepted by mischiefs which may be called misfortune rather than fault.—MARTINEAU, HARRIET, 1855–77, *Autobiography*, ed. *Chapman, vol.* I, *p.* 266.

Since seeing Captain Blackwood yesterday I have read over "Night and Morning," and put in a few words about it; but I really do not feel that I can do more in conscience. For my own part, I think a true partisan of Bulwer's ought to drop all his intermediate works. To say the best of them that one can, they are still only novels—more interesting than many, and perhaps rather more objectionable than most—freaks of his genius,—whereas his last works show all the nobler qualities of a great mind.—OLIPHANT, MARGARET O. W., 1855, *To Mr. Blackwood, Nov.* 24; *Autobiography and Letters, ed. Coghill, p.* 161.

Bulwer, an industrious writer, with occasional ability, is distinguished for his reverence of intellect as a temporality, and appeals to the worldly ambition of the student. His romances tend to fan these low flames.— EMERSON, RALPH WALDO, 1856–84, *Literature, English Traits, Works, Riverside Ed., vol.* V, *p.* 234.

The special ability of Bulwer appears to lie in the delineation of that passion with which the novel is so deeply concerned, the passion of love. All true and manly passions, let it be said, are honored and illustrated in his pages. But he stands alone among novelists of his sex in the portraiture of love, and specially of love in the female breast. The heroism, the perfect trust, the strength in death, are painted by him with a sympathetic truth for which we know not where to seek a parallel. The effect of Eugene Aram's speech at his trial, upon Madeline, his betrothed,—the calm, beautiful, satisfied smile, which lit up her wan features,—is a golden letter from the very handwriting of nature. Then, where, out of Shakspeare can we find such a series of female portraits as those in "Rienzi?" One scarce knows to which of the masterly delineations to accord the palm. There is the weak, womanly Adeline, strong only in love, able to die beautifully, but not to live well. In Irene, there is love's complete, ineradicable devotion, all-subduing, spontaneous, self-sacrificing. In Nina, proud love gazes, self-reliant, and self-satisfied, on all the world around, but sinks in womanly tenderness on the breast of the loved one. Adeline is the soft, flower-like woman, growing fair in the calm summer radiance, but withering in the wintry blast. Irene is the human angel, of whom poets have so long sung. Nina is the queen, ready to live with, or die for, her husband-king. Rienzi himself is nobly imagined, endeavoring to tread the surges and engulfed.— BAYNE, PETER, 1857, *Essays in Biography and Criticism, First Series, p.* 388.

He has written a History, which may take its place on the same shelves with Gibbon and Arnold and Grote. His "Athens, its Rise and Fall," has extorted praise from all quarters, and is a noble historical work, though but a fragment. In this department of literature Bulwer has succeeded where even Scott failed.— SMILES, SAMUEL, 1860, *Brief Biographies.*

Read not Milton, for he is dry; nor Shakespeare,
  for he wrote of common life:
Nor Scott, for his romances, though fascinating,
  are yet intelligible:
Nor Thackeray, for he is a Hogarth, a photog-
  rapher who flattereth not:
Nor Kingsley, for he shall teach thee that thou
  shouldst not dream, but do.
Read incessantly thy Burke; that Burke who,
  nobler than he of old,
Treateth of the Peer and Peeress, the truly
  Sublime and Beautiful:
Likewise study the "creations" of "the Prince
  of modern Romance";
Sigh over Leonard the Martyr, and smile on
  Pelham the puppy:
Learn how "love is the dram-drinking of
  existence";
And how we "invoke, in the Gadara of our still
  closets,
The beautiful ghost of the Ideal, with the simple
  wand of the pen."
Listen how Maltravers and the orphan "forgot
  all but love,"
And how Devereux's family chaplain "made
  and unmade kings":
How Eugene Aram, though a thief, a liar, and
  a murderer,
Yet, being intellectual, was amongst the noblest
  of mankind.
So shalt thou live in a world peopled with
  heroes and master-spirits;
And if thou canst not realize the Ideal, thou
  shalt at least idealize the Real.
—CALVERLEY, CHARLES STUART, 1862–84, *Of Reading, Verses and Translations, p.* 97.

Sir E. is a great master of language, and almost unequalled in the construction of fiction. But I think there is some ground for a remark which I have seen of a foreign critic, that he stands too visibly aloof from his own creations—like a deity of Epicurus—and that there is more of his mind than of his heart in his works. Their brilliance is too much like that of ice or marble.—THIRLWALL, CONNOP, 1865, *Letters to a Friend, Feb.* 27, *ed. Stanley, p.* 19.

Bulwer's "Lost Tales of Miletus" is a most noble book! He is an extraordinary fellow, and fills me with admiration and wonder.—DICKENS, CHARLES, 1866, *To William Charles Kent, Jan.* 18; *Letters, vol.* II, *p.* 288.

Whether as an author, standing apart from all literary cliques and coteries, or as a politician, never wholly subject to the exclusive dictation of any political party, he always thought and acted in sympathy with every popular aspiration for the political, social, and intellectual improvement of the whole national life.—LYTTON, EDWARD ROBERT BULWER EARL, 1874, *ed. Speeches of Edward Lord Lytton, Prefatory Memoir.*

Notwithstanding the eminence attained by the late Lord Lytton in so many different branches of literature, in poetry, in the drama, and in fiction, it is nevertheless strictly true that he was by no means a good English scholar. We have been struck in reading these volumes with the frequent occurrence of wrong words, clumsy constructions, and slipshod grammar; and we think that in some instances his editor would have done well to correct them.—KEBBEL, T. E., 1875, *Speeches of Lord Lytton, The Academy, vol.* 7, *p.* 27.

I am well aware of the modern tendency to belittle Bulwer, as a slight creature; but with the fresh recollection of his books as they fell upon my own boyhood, I cannot recall a single one which did not leave as a last residuum the picture in some sort of the chivalrous gentleman impressed upon my heart. I cheerfully admit that he sometimes came dangerously near snobbery, and that he was uncivil and undignified and many other bad things in the "New Timon" and the Tennyson quarrel; and I concede that it must be difficult for us—you and me, who are so superior and who have no faults of our own—to look upon these failings with patience; and yet I

cannot help remembering that every novel of Bulwer's is skillfully written and entertaining, and that there is not an ignoble thought or impure stimulus in the whole range of his works.—LANIER, SIDNEY, 1881, *The English Novel, p.* 195.

In one ambition only he altogether failed; but unfortunately that ambition was his most burning and unquenchable one. There was something almost pitiable about the way in which he went on publishing poem after poem without ever attaining such success as would place them high even in the second rank of writers of verse. Nature, bountiful to him in many respects, had denied him the poetical faculty; even his highest performances of this kind would have been better had they been written in prose.—NICOLL, HENRY J., 1882, *Landmarks of English Literature, p.* 393.

Among the most famous writers of fiction of the nineteenth century will always be mentioned the name of Sir Bulwer Lytton. More than any other writer, he studied and developed the novel as a form of literature. Almost every novelist has taken some special field and has confined himself to that. Dickens, George Eliot, Thackeray, made occasional incursions on historic ground, but still their chief work was expended upon the novel of life and manners. Lytton attempted, and successfully, every department of fiction.—TUCKERMAN, BAYARD, 1882, *A History of English Prose Fiction, p.* 293.

Much that he wrote sustains the testimony of his wife and neighbors, that his personal character was not admirable. Marvellous jewelry of thought and fancy, brilliant with many dyes, has he bequeathed us; but he needed the heart that should bring him into sympathy with the phases of humanity, and give him permanency in popular regard.—WELSH, ALFRED H., 1882, *Development of English Literature and Language, vol.* II, *p.* 415.

Invention and originality are matters of degree, and, though no one can deny that Lytton possessed great inventive powers, he did not put that individual stamp on his work without which no writer is entitled to a place in the foremost rank. He was not self-centred enough; he was too generally emulous to win the highest individual distinction. But his freshness of thought, brilliancy of invention, breadth and variety of portraiture, gave him a just title to his popularity, and, with all allowance for superficial affectations, his generous nobility of sentiment made his influence as wholesome as it was widespread.—MINTO, WILLIAM, 1883, *Encyclopædia Britannica*, Ninth Ed., vol. XV.

Was Bulwer a poet? His verse unquestionably has many poetical qualities,—grace, melody, striking imagery, picturesqueness,—but lacks that mysterious something, that divine afflatus, which we call poetry. The vigor, polish,. and terseness of "St. Stephen's" would not dishonor the masculine genius of Dryden; "The Lost Tales of Miletus" have charmed scholars with their playful fancy; and the translations from Schiller have been pronounced by Carlyle the ones from which an English reader will get the most vivid idea of the German poet.—MATHEWS, WILLIAM, 1887, *Men, Places, and Things*, p. 60.

Lytton is one of the authors upon whose merits the critics have never agreed with the public. He won immense popularity in the face of generally hostile criticism, and even his success failed to obtain a reversal of the judgment. Some of his qualities, however, are incontestable. No English author has displayed more industry, energy, versatility, or less disposition to lapse into slovenliness. His last works are among his best.—STEPHEN, LESLIE, 1893, *Dictionary of National Biography*, vol. XXXIV, p. 385.

Told the same romantic tales with a trifle less of skill and more of clatter than did Scott.—SIMONDS, WILLIAM EDWARD, 1894, *An Introduction to the Study of English Fiction*, p. 64.

Bulwer, who knew better, would quite revel in a stagey bombast.—HARRISON, FREDERIC, 1895, *Studies in Early Victorian Literature*, p. 18.

I read all the novels of Bulwer, for whom I had already a great liking from "The Caxtons" and "My Novel." I was dazzled by them, and I thought him a great writer, if not so great a one as he thought himself. Little or nothing of those romances, with their swelling prefaces about the poet and his function, their glittering criminals, and showy rakes and rogues of all kinds, and their patrician perfume and social splendor, remained with me; they may have been

better or worse; I will not attempt to say. If I may call my fascination with them a passion at all, I must say that it was but a fitful fever.—HOWELLS, WILLIAM DEAN, 1895, *My Literary Passions*, p. 161.

He had scholarship; he had indefatigable industry; he had abounding literary ambitions and enthusiasms, but he had no humor; I am afraid he had not a very sensitive conscience; and he had no such pervading refinement of literary taste as to make his work serve as the exemplar for other and honester workers.—MITCHELL, DONALD G., 1897, *English Lands Letters and Kings, The Later Georges to Victoria*, p. 179.

What Reade has in common with his greater brethren, and Lytton has not, is the light and shade of life. In Lytton all is polished glittering brilliance. The light is neither the sunlight of common day nor "the moonlight of romance," but the glare of innumerable gas lamps,—the rays from the footlights to which he was about to betake himself. All the softer shades disappear, and quiet effects are impossible.—WALKER, HUGH, 1897, *The Age of Tennyson*, p. 73.

Their popularity is not of the catchpenny sort; thoughtful people read them, as well as the great drove of the undiscriminating. For they are the product of thought: they show workmanship; they have quality; they are carefully made. If the literary critic never finds occasion to put off the shoes from his feet as in the sacred presence of genius, he is constantly moved to recognize with a friendly nod the presence of sterling talent. He is even inclined to think that nobody else ever had so much talent as this little red-haired, blue-eyed, high-nosed, dandified Edward Bulwer; the mere mass of it lifts him at times to the levels where genius dwells, though he never quite shares their nectar and ambrosia. He as it were catches echoes of the talk of the Immortals,—the turn of their phrase, the intonation of their utterance,—and straightway reproduces it with the fidelity of the phonograph. But, as in the phonograph, we find something lacking; our mind accepts the report as genuine, but our ear affirms an unreality; this is reproduction, indeed, but not creation. Bulwer, himself, when his fit is past, and his critical faculty re-awakens, probably knows as well as another that these labored and meritorious pages of his are not graven on the eternal adamant. But they are the best he can do, and perhaps there is none better of their kind. They have a right to be; for while genius may do harm as well as good, Bulwer never does harm, and in spite of sickly sentiment and sham philosophy, is uniformly instructive, amusing, and edifying.—HAWTHORNE, JULIAN, 1897, *Library of the World's Best Literature, ed. Warner, vol. v, p. 2699.*

Bulwer passed himself off as a *grand seigneur* and a genius; he was really but a clever man and a dandy, who exploited literature for his social advancement. He affected a lofty originality, but his talents were mostly imitative. His chief gift, almost entirely wanting in his books, but very notable in his life, was what we call *finesse.* He took from the Byronian Satanism as much as England would put up with in 1840. He copied Victor Hugo secretly and discreetly. A sort of Gothic democrat, he managed at the same time to charm romantic youths and flatter the proletariat by pretending to hurl down that society in whose front rank he aspired to take his place. His novels were terribly long-winded, but there are generations which find such a quality to their taste. When at last it was discovered that his sublimity was a spurious sublimity, that his history was false history, his "middle-ages" bric-a-brac, his poetry mere rhetoric, his democracy a farce, his human heart a heart that had never beat in a man's breast, his books mere windy bladders,—why, it was too late! The game had been played successfully and was over—the squireen of Knebworth, the self-styled descendant of the Vikings, had founded a family and hooked a peerage.—FILON, AUGUSTIN, 1897, *The English Stage, tr. Whyte, p.* 64.

Seemed a genius of the very highest order, but it was easily perceived that his dandiacal attitude was not perfectly sincere, that the graces of his style were too labored and prolix, and that the tone of his novels fostered national conceit and prejudice at the expense of truth. His sentiment was mawkish, his creations were unsubstantial and often preposterous. But the public liked the fastidious elaborateness of a gentleman who catered for their pleasures "with his fingers covered with dazzling rings, and his feet delightfully pinched in a pair of looking-glass boots;"

and Bulwer Lytton certainly possessed extraordinary gifts of activity, versatility, and sensitiveness to the requirements of his readers. What has shattered the once-glittering dome of his reputation is what early readers of "Zanoni" called his "fearfully beautiful word-painting," his hollow rhetoric, his puerile horrors. Towards the end of his glorious career Lord Lytton contrived to prune his literary extravagances, and his latest works are his best.—GOSSE, EDMUND, 1897, *A Short History of Modern English Literature, p.* 329.

For style he cared nothing: his own manner remained the same, explosive, and undisciplined, except in the very rare cases where he was interested in his own productions. But as for the matter, there is no subject capable of romantic treatment which this astonishingly versatile man did not make his own. So long as cheap cynicism, paltry witticisms, and little stories about "success in society" paid, Lytton wrote them, and wrote them as well as stories of this kind can be written. When taste grew ultra-Byronic—perhaps under the stimulus of Lytton's writing— Lytton followed it as far as was safe, and then commenced writing for the more domestic public. Thieves' patter was in the fashion for some time, and Lytton promptly showed his admiring public that he knew more about the patter than the thieves themselves. Then came the turn of the historical novel, and "Rienzi," "The Last of the Barons," and "Devereux" showed that Lytton could write about any country and any period, and could write quite well enough for his works to sell. His ghost stories scared his readers literally into fits. . . . His commercial instincts were admirable, but his works have very little relation to literature. Had he lived now, he would have written English, as he could very well have done in his own time if he had cared to take the trouble. He did not care to take the trouble because it did not pay.—LORD, WALTER FREWEN, 1901, *Lord Lytton's Novels, Nineteenth Century, vol.* 50, *p.* 457.

Bulwer's best quality is his inexhaustible invention; an exciting plot is the chief charm of his numerous stories. What makes him hardly endurable to the purified taste of educated readers of to-day is his inflated style. His narrative tone is foppish; he wants to make a show of his reading, of his worldly wisdom, even of his social position, the only result being that one looks upon him as a "snob." Hardly one of his novels is wholly uninteresting, not one of them is entirely artistic. If they were to appear to-day they would be devoured with avidity by the great masses of "educated" and tasteless readers, like numerous other novels, only to be almost at once forgotten. They are excellent examples of a large class; of clever mediocrity, which has always had a sufficient public.—ENGEL, EDWARD, 1902, *A History of English Literature, rev. Hamley Bent, p.* 458.

Altogether, with due deduction for the affected, the sensational, the sentimental in Bulwer's novels, the fact remains that his versatility and his long-continued energy make him a useful sign of the shifting literary currents during the middle years of the century.—MOODY, WILLIAM VAUGHN, AND LOVETT, ROBERT MORSS, 1902, *A History of English Literature, p.* 363.

John Stuart Mill
1806–1873

Born, in London, 20 May 1806. Educated by his father. In France, May 1820 to July 1821. On return studied for Bar for short time, till appointment as Junior Clerk in Examiner's Office, India House, May 1823; Assistant Examiner, 1828; First Assistant, 1836; Head of Office, 1856. Founded Utilitarian Soc., winter of 1822. Contrib. to "Traveller," 1822; to "Morning Chronicle," 1823; to "Westminster Rev.," 1824–28, 1835–38, 1864; to "Parliamentary Hist. and Rev.," 1826–28. Founded Speculative Soc., 1825. In Paris, 1830. Contrib. to "Examiner" and "Monthly Rev.," 1831–34; to "Tait's Mag.," 1832; to "Monthly Repository," 1834; and to "Jurist." Editor "London Rev.," afterwards "Westminster Rev.," 1834–40. Friendship with Mrs. Taylor begun, 1831; married her, April 1851. Proprietor of "Westminster Rev.," 1837–40. Severe illness, 1839. Correspondence with Comte, 1841–46. Contrib. to "Edinburgh Rev.," 1845–46, 1863. Severe illness, 1854. Retired from India House, 1858. In south of France, winter of 1858–59; wife died, at Avignon. For remainder of life spent half the year at Blackheath, half at Avignon. Contrib. articles on "Utilitarianism" to "Fraser's Mag.," 1861. M. P. for Westminster, 1865–68. Lord Rector of St. Andrews Univ., 1866. Died, at Avignon, 8 May 1873; buried there. *Works:* "A System of Logic" (2 vols.), 1843; "Essays on some unsettled Questions of Political-Economy," 1844; "Principles of Political Economy" (2 vols.), 1848; "Memorandum on the Improvements in the Administration of India during the last Thirty Years" (anon.), 1858; "On Liberty," 1859; "Thoughts on Parliamentary Reform," 1859 (2nd edn. same year); "Dissertations and Discussions" (4 vols.), 1859–75; "Considerations on Representative Government," 1861 (2nd edn. same year); "Utilitarianism" (from "Fraser's Mag."), 1863; "Examination of Sir William Hamilton's Philosophy," 1865 (2nd edn. same year); "Auguste Comte and Positivism" (from "Westminster Rev.,"), 1865; "Inaugural Address" at Univ. of St. Andrews, 1867; "Speech on the Admission of Women to the Electoral Franchise," 1867; "England and Ireland," 1868; "The Subjection of Women," 1869 (2nd edn. same year); "Chapters and Speeches on the Irish Land Question," 1870; "Speech in favour of Woman's Suffrage," 1871. *Posthumous:* "Autobiography," ed. by Miss Taylor, 1873–74; "Nature; the Utility of Religion; and Theism," ed. by Miss Taylor, 1874 (2nd edn. same year); "Views . . . on England's Danger through the Suppression of her Maritime Power," 1874; "Early Essays," ed. by J. W. M. Gibbs, 1897. He *edited:* Bentham's "Rationale of Judicial Evidence," 1827; and the 1869 edn. of James Mill's "Analysis of the Phenomena of the Human Mind." *Life:* "Autobiography," 1873; "Criticism, with Personal Recollections," by Prof. Bain, 1882; "Life," by W. L. Courtney, 1889.—SHARP, R. FARQUHARSON, 1897, *A Dictionary of English Authors, p.* 197.

PERSONAL

This young Mill, I fancy and hope, is "a *baying* you can love." A slender, rather tall and elegant youth, with small clear Roman-nosed face, two small earnestly-smiling eyes; modest, remarkably gifted with precision of utterance, enthusiastic, yet lucid, calm; not a great, yet distinctly a gifted and amiable youth.—CARLYLE, THOMAS, 1831, *Letter to Mrs. Carlyle, Sept.* 4; *Thomas Carlyle, A History of the First Forty Years of his Life, ed. Froude, vol.* II, *p.* 153.

John Mill is summoned to town, and goes to-night; the rest leave to-morrow. They feel leaving Falmouth deeply, and say that no place out of London will be so dear to them. Now for some glimpses at Truth through those wonderfully keen, quiet eyes. . . . His father made him study ecclesiastical history before he was ten. This method of early intense application he would not recommend to others; in most cases it would not answer, and where it does, the buoyancy of youth is entirely superseded by the maturity of manhood, and action is very likely to be merged in reflection. "I never was a boy," he said; "never played at cricket: it is better to let Nature have her own way." In his essays on French affairs he has infused more of himself than into any of his other writings, the whole subject of that country so deeply interests him.—Fox, Caroline, 1840, *Memories of Old Friends*, ed. *Pym, Journal, April* 10, p. 94.

His physical organization is of that fine and delicate sort which, with reference to the indwelling spirit, may be said to be almost transparent; and on this his first appearance his bearing was so diffident yet so sincere, so tremulous yet so intensely earnest, with so much of the reality of a great intellectual authority, yet so free from the slightest assumption of it, that the genuine English courtesy of the House was conciliated into a deferential and really applausive silence. . . . His voice, though tremulous and by no means loud, was perfectly distinct, and every syllable from his lips was audible in every part of the House. His manner was the perfection of dignified, scholarly, and sincere speaking; almost pathetic in its earnest tones; not facile with the glibness of practised oratory, yet fluent with the deliberation of one who is master alike of deep thought and of fitting words. It is strange, the magic there is in the slightest touch of genius upon an assemblage, however weary, however dull. The first real statesmanly thought born to us during all the long hours of that night seemed to open the heavens above our heads, and to let in light and the atmosphere of life. All felt the witchery of the spell; and the climax of admiration and of excitement was reached when, at the close of his compact and unanswerable demonstration, he uttered that exquisite peroration which one old member of Parliament told me was the most poetical and eloquent passage heard

there for many years.—Tyler, Moses Coit, 1866-98, *Glimpses of England, pp.* 57, 60.

Mr. Mill is of a light complexion—is long and thin; his clear blue eye is deep sunk, as if its gaze had been rather internal than external. He has a brisk, genial appearance, and is always neatly and scrupulously dressed in black. His appearance is different from that of any other member. His is not the horsey look of some, nor has he the business air of others, still less does he affect the style of a man of fashion. Altogether, he seems out of his element on his seat on the third row below the gangway on the Opposition side. The men around seem of a coarser and less refined nature. There is a *genus loci* connected with the House, of hard drinkers, mighty sportsmen, big blusterers, eager partisans. You would never expect to find a philosopher there, yet there is Mr. Mill; and there is not a more constant attendant, or one more able or willing to take his part in the debates when the opportunity occurs.— Ritchie, J. Ewing, 1869, *British Senators: or, Political Sketches Past and Present*, p. 300.

A gentleman, in manner like an old French count, full of courtesy, kindness, and small attentions, graceful and almost affectionate in his ways, his face beaming with sentiment, and his eyes lighting up when any heroic or chivalric feeling was called forth. From conversing with him, one would say his prominent characteristic was feeling and sympathy with all the nobler side of human nature.—Brace, Charles Loring, 1873, *Christian Union, May,* 31; *Life, ed. his Daughter,* p. 332.

It might, indeed, have been supposed that even those who never enjoyed the pleasure of personal acquaintance with Mr. Mill, would have been impressed with the nobility of his nature as indicated in his opinions and deeds. How entirely his public career has been determined by a pure and strong sympathy for his fellow-men— how entirely this sympathy has subordinated all desires for personal advantage— how little even the fear of being injured in reputation or position has deterred him from taking the course which he thought equitable or generous—ought to be manifest to every antagonist, however bitter. A generosity that might almost be called romantic was obviously the feeling prompting sundry of those courses of action which have been commented upon as errors. And nothing like a true conception of him can be formed unless, along with dissent from them, there goes recognition of the fact that they resulted from the eagerness of a noble nature, impatient to rectify injustice, and to further human welfare.—SPENCER, HERBERT, 1873, *John Stuart Mill, His Moral Character, London Examiner.*

His nature was, indeed, emotional, and even passionate. Considering what he wrote about his wife it is strange anybody should ever have doubted it. The conception of him which a political opponent vulgarly summed up in calling him a "book in breeches," was absurd. You could not hear him talk without seeing that he felt strongly, that he loved deeply, that the capacity of hating also was not wanting to him. It was, I suppose, his moderation in controversy as well as his addiction to philosophical pursuits which gave him with the general public the repute of coldness— especially with the public that had not read enough of him to discover the numerous passages that glow with enthusiasm or with indignation. As a talker he had a manner of his own. Talker in the common dinner-table sense he was not. He seldom told a story for the sake of telling it, nor kept a store of anecdotes to be produced for the mere amusement of listeners. Nor would he talk to everybody. On subjects that interested him and to people whom he thought interested, he would pour out in easy profusion his stores of information. Among the men whom I have known in England I remember but two who were comparable to him in the variety and fluent accuracy of his knowledge. These two were extremely unlike him and unlike each other, Mr. Carlyle and Mr. Gladstone.—SMALLEY, GEORGE W., 1873-91, *John Stuart Mill, May 10; London Letters and Some Others, vol.* I, *p.* 237.

He does not need our faint praise, and the perfect harmony of his intellect and character makes an interpreter unnecessary even could a fitting one be found. He laboured to promote the happiness of his fellow-men, and he has added to the number of their purest pleasures the spectacle of a blameless life. He wrote wisely of human liberty and necessary law, and silenced idle fears about a "blind fate," by living as the very clear-sighted agent of the noblest necessity which has ever been recognized in

human kind, the necessity of living well.— SIMCOX, EDITH, 1873, *Influence of J. S. Mill's Writings, Contemporary Review, vol.* 22, *p.* 317.

It is impossible to believe that Mrs. Mill was the woman her husband thought her to be; she was not such a woman to any one but him. At the same time she was the most powerful force that acted upon his later life. But how came he to form such an exaggerated opinion of her ability and character? How came the great dialectician to be so mistaken? She was, no doubt, an able and an accomplished woman; she opened up the long-pent emotional fountains of his soul; and his own thoughts and voice, which she echoed back to him, seemed to the devotee, as in many a similar case, a wisdom and a music that he had never heard. True to his training, Mill never calls this relation love; it is "the most valuable friendship of his life." But it was love,—rather, on his part, it was idolatry in what is perhaps its noblest form. It is strange that he was not led by the strength and fervor of his own devotion to see that religion is a genuine manifestation of the soul; strange that the grave at Avignon, covered by trees, the home of the nightingale, never taught him to see by faith, if not by analysis, an immortal life beyond.—HINSDALE, B. A., 1874-84, *Schools and Studies, p.* 144.

He was not apparently an amiable youth, but his history shows him capable of passionate personal attachment, and a nature capable of strong affections will always seek an object for them. He was also an egotist. He could hardly have been otherwise. An object of his father's unremitting attention, and debarred from the penetrating discipline of a boyish companionship, what could he think of but himself and his performances? . . . But egotist as he thus became, he was susceptible—highly susceptible—to the idea of disinterested devotion to an object. At the bottom of his nature the yearnings of affection and the sense of duty lay hidden in unsuspected strength.—BLACHFORD, LORD, 1876, *The Reality of Duty, Contemporary Review, vol.* 28, *p.* 522.

I found that Mill, although possessed of much learning, and thoroughly acquainted with the state of the political world, was, as might have been expected, the mere exponent of other men's ideas, those men being his father and Bentham; and that he was utterly ignorant of what is called society; that of the world, as it worked around him, he knew nothing; and, above all, of *woman*, he was as a child. He had never played with boys; in his life he had never known any, and we, in fact, who were now his associates, were the first companions he had ever mixed with. His father took occasion to remark to myself especially, that he had no great liking for his son's new friends. I, on the other hand, let him know that I had no fear of him who was looked upon as a sort of Jupiter Tonans. James Mill looked down upon us because we were poor, and not greatly allied, for while in words he was a severe democrat, in fact and in conduct he bowed down to wealth and position. To the young men of wealth and position who came to see him, he was gracious and instructive, while to us he was rude and curt, gave us no advice, but seemed pleased to hurt and offend us. This led to remonstrance and complaint on the part of John Mill, but the result was that we soon ceased to see John Mill at his home.—ROEBUCK, JOHN ARTHUR, 1879(?), 1897, *Autobiography, Life and Letters*, ed. *Leader*, p. 28.

As he mentioned his name to me, I recalled at once his portrait. It gave, however, as little idea of the expression of his countenance and the hue of his skin, as of the way in which he walked and stood. Although sixty-four years of age, his complexion was as pure and fresh as that of a child. He had the smooth, childlike skin and the rosy cheeks that are scarcely ever seen in elderly men of the continent, but that not seldom may be observed in the white-haired gentlemen who take their noonday horseback rides in Hyde Park. His eyes were bright, and of a deep, dark blue, his nose slender and curved, his brow high and arched, with a strongly marked protuberance over the left eye; he looked as though the labor of thought might have forced its organs to extend in order to make more room. The face, with its large and marked features, was full of simplicity, but was not calm; it was, indeed, continually distorted by a nervous twitching, which seemed to betray the restless, tremulous life of the soul. In conversation, he had difficulty in finding words, and sometimes stammered at the beginning of a sentence. Seated comfortably in my room, with his fresh, superb physiognomy, and his power-

ful brow, he looked like a younger and more vigorous man than he really was. When I accompanied him on the street later, however, I observed that his walk, in spite of its rapidity, was rather halting, and that, notwithstanding his slender form, age had left its impress on his bearing. His dress made him seem older than he was. The old-fashioned coat he wore proved how indifferent he was to his external appearance. He was clad in black, and a crape band was wound in many irregular folds about his hat. Although she had been long dead, he still wore mourning for his wife. No further signs of negligence were visible; a quiet nobility and a perfect self-control pervaded his presence. Even to one who had not read his works it would have been very evident that it was one of the kings of thought that had taken his seat in the red velvet armchair near the fireplace, whose mantel clock my unfounded suspicion led me to suppose he had come to wind up.—BRANDES, GEORGE, 1879, *Eminent Authors of the Nineteenth Century*, tr. *Anderson*, p. 124.

In the year 1851 occurred Mill's marriage to Mrs. Taylor, the "almost infallible counsellor," whose friendship and assistance he had previously enjoyed for many years, and whose memory, after their brief married life of seven and a half years, had been terminated by her death, remained to him a "religion." More remarkable and touching devotion to the memory of a woman has rarely been shown than that paid by Mill to the memory of his wife, in his Autobiography, and in the introductory page of his (or, as he says, their joint) work, "On Liberty." It is not only in most marked contrast with his father's unchivalrous, not to say brutally unkind, treatment of his own wife (J. S. Mill, too, has nothing to say, in his Autobiography, of his mother), but is also another passionate manifestation of that potentiality of essential human life which was wholly ignored in his training.—MORRIS, GEORGE S., 1880, *British Thought and Thinkers*, p. 326.

John Stuart Mill always seemed to me to grow suddenly aged when Carlyle was spoken of. The nearest to painful emotion in him which I ever saw was when he made that remark, "Carlyle turned against all his friends." I did not and do not think the remark correct. When Carlyle came out with his reactionary opinions, as they were deemed, his friends became afraid of him, and nearly all stopped going to see him at the very time when they should have insisted on coming to a right understanding.—CONWAY, MONCURE DANIEL, 1881, *Thomas Carlyle*, p. 90.

With the same indomitable perseverance and patience which were necessary to enable him [James Mill] in ten years' time, besides the constant necessities of pot-boiling for a large family, to write the "History of India," this extraordinary Scotsman set himself to re-create a human soul, and did it triumphantly, making of a susceptible and sensitive nature, full of attractive weakness, credulity, and sentiment, an infant freethinker, a baby philosopher, a scholar in petticoats—a man, when he grew up, who knew almost everything except himself, and whose rigidity of second nature, the art and influence of his father, never ceased to jar against, yet never overcame, the docility and softness of the first. In the strange household thus revealed to us, there is no shadow of any woman, no sound of domestic chat, no genial companionship of brothers and sisters, but only a prolonged encounter of two wits, the one teaching, the other listening and obeying; the man without ruth or thought for the flesh and blood he is straining, the other with innocent child's eyes fixed upon that prominent figure, ready to follow till he dies. The only thing it reminds us of is the painful training of a young acrobat, where the child obeying a lifted figure goes sheer on to risk any fall or mutilation, or death itself, nothing being worse to its scared faculties than the beating or vituperation which a mistake would occasion. Mill did not either whip or vituperate so far as appears, but his son, we can see even in the record, has his eye nervously, constantly, upon him from beginning to end: and a more extraordinary exhibition of the mental force which one nature can exercise upon another never was.—OLIPHANT, MARGARET O. W., 1882, *Literary History of England*, XVIII-XIX *Century*, vol. III, p. 287.

Mill's voice was agreeable, although not specially melodious; it was thin and weak. His articulation was not very clear. His elocution was good, without being particularly showy or impressive; he had a mastery of emphasis; his modulation was sufficiently removed from monotone, so that there was nothing wearying in his

manner. He had not much gesture, but it was all in keeping; his features were expressive without his aiming at strong effects. Everything about him had the cast of sobriety and reserve; he did no more than the end required. There was so little of marked peculiarity in his speaking, that I never knew anyone that could mimic him successfully in the enunciation of a sentence. Very few people could assume his voice, to begin with; and his modulation was simply correct colourless elocution. I can account for his seeming hesitation of manner. Although he did not study grand and imposing talk, he always aimed at saying the right things clearly and shortly. He was perfectly fluent, but yet would pause for an instant to get the best word, or the neatest collocation: and he also liked to finish with an epigrammatic turn.—BAIN, ALEXANDER, 1882, *John Stuart Mill, A Criticism: with Personal Recollections*, p. 188.

John Mill was the most severely single-minded of the set. He was of an impassioned nature, but I should conjecture, though I do not *know*, that in his earliest youth the passion of his nature had not found a free and unobstructed course through the affections and had got a good deal pent up in his intellect; in which, however large (and among the *scientific* intellects of his time I hardly know where to look for a larger), it was but as an eagle in an aviary. The result was that his political philosophy, cold as was the creed and hard the forms and discipline, caught fire; and while working, as in duty bound, through dry and rigorous processes of induction, was at heart something in the nature of political fanaticism. He was pure-hearted—I was going to say conscientious—but at that time he seemed so naturally and necessarily good, and so inflexible, that one hardly thought of him as having occasion for a conscience, or as a man with whom any question could arise for reference to that tribunal. But his absorption in abstract operations of the intellect, his latent ardors, and his absolute simplicity of heart were hardly, perhaps, compatible with knowledge of men and women, and with wisdom in living his life. His manners were plain, neither graceful nor awkward; his features refined and regular; the eyes small, relatively to the scale of the face, the jaw large, the nose straight and finely shaped, the lips thin and compressed, the forehead and head capacious; and both face and body seemed to represent outwardly the inflexibility of the inner man. He shook hands with you from the shoulder.—TAYLOR, SIR HENRY, 1885, *Autobiography, vol.* I, *p.* 65.

We well knew Mr. Mill's intellectual eminence before he entered Parliament. What his conduct there principally disclosed, at least to me, was his singular moral elevation. I remember now that at the time, more than twenty years back, I used familiarly to call him the Saint of Rationalism, a phrase roughly and partially expressing what I now mean. Of all the motives, stings, and stimulants that reach men through their egoism in Parliament, no part could move or even touch him. His conduct and his language were, in this respect, a sermon. Again, though he was a philosopher, he was not, I think, a man of crotchets. He had, I think, the good sense and practical tact of politics, together with the high independent thought of a recluse. I need not tell you, that, for the sake of the House of Commons at large, I rejoiced in his advent, and deplored his disappearance. He did us all good. In whatever party, whatever form of opinion, I sorrowfully confess that such men are rare.—GLADSTONE, WILLIAM EWART, 1888, *Letter to W. L. Courtney, Life of John Stuart Mill (Great Writers), p.* 141.

He was the natural leader of Liberal thought; not in the House, but out of it. "Saint of Rationalism," however, in Mr. Gladstone's happy phrase, he remained. He had been declared to be Adam Smith and Petrarch rolled into one; and if he thus combined sentimentalism with the doctrines of political economy, he equally exhibited the cold clearness of the Rationalistic thinker, tempered by the emotional warmth of high moral ideas.—COURTNEY, WILLIAM L., 1888, *Life of John Stuart Mill (Great Writers), p.* 142.

On the publication of John Stuart Mill's "Elements of Political Economy," he sent a presentation-copy of it to Carlyle, his intimacy with whom, though there was no actual breach between them, had ceased for some years. Contemptuous though he was of the "dismal science," Carlyle called Mill's a "very clever book," while comparing its complex treatment of his subject to the operation of "extracting the cube root in Roman numerals." "It could be done, but was not worth doing," a rather striking Carlylian comment; whether it was a just one is another matter. Carlyle, in those days at least, always spoke of Mill with a certain regard, his expression of which seemed to indicate a regret that their active friendship had come to an end. His chief criticism on Mill as a companion was that he insisted on "having everything demonstrated." Mill might have replied that demonstration was sometimes more trustworthy and practically useful than Carlyle's favourite intuition, which experience proved to be by no means an infallible guide either to himself or to others. Mill, he said, used at one time to come to him every Sunday for a walk. On one point, he added, they were agreed. It was that if the Bible could be buried for a generation and then dug up again, it would in that case be rightly enjoyed.—ESPINASSE, FRANCIS, 1893, *Literary Recollections and Sketches, p.* 218.

Poles asunder in premiss and conclusion, Ward and Mill, in their purely intellectual intercourse, as completely understood each other as two mathematicians who are engaged in proving a proposition in geometry. Given the relevant hypotheses, there can be no dispute as to the proof. They may differ as to facts, if they apply their geometry or trigonometry to practical measurements. The initial understanding as to distances, which may determine whether an angle be of 90° or of 60°, or whether a triangle be equilateral or scalene, may involve points of dispute. Such things may have been ascertained by authorities which seem to one trustworthy, to another not so; but once the facts are agreed upon, the reasoning is clear to both alike. So, too, Ward and Mill,—utterly as they differed on the primary truths which were the *data* from which to reason,—in their method, and in the conclusions resting on a given hypothesis, reached an agreement which was very remarkable.—WARD, WILFRID, 1893, *William George Ward and the Catholic Revival, p.* 17.

When Mill made her [Mrs. Taylor] acquaintance, his father remonstrated, but he replied that he had no other feeling towards her than he would have towards an equally able man. The equivocal friendship, which was the talk of all Mill's circle of acquaintances, lasted for twenty years, when Mr. Taylor died, and Mill married his widow. It is impossible to regard the enthusiasm of Mill for this lady without feeling how much there was in it of the humorous, how much also of the pathetic. That Mill had a most exaggerated opinion of her intellectual attainments there can be no doubt. . . . His language with regard to her was always extravagant, and Grote said that "only John Mill's reputation could survive such displays." Mill's brother George declared that she was "nothing like what John thought her," and there is much evidence to show that she was but a weak reflection of her husband. Still, it is impossible not to sympathize with such an illusion. . . . It was at Avignon that the Crown Princess of Prussia and the Princess Alice of Hesse proposed to visit him, when he, with due courtesy, declined to see them. — SHORTER, CLEMENT, 1897, *Victorian Literature, p.* 139.

His countenance, in its final conviction of a thinker whose mind upon weighty subjects was irrevocably made up, from whose ethic verdicts there was no appeal, had something awful, even sublime, in its rigidity and marble-like implacableness. You felt . . . that here were the immovable purpose, iron will, and unflinching self-oblivion of which, for good or for evil, the world's umpires and leaders are made.—EDWARDS, MATILDA BETHAM, 1898, *Reminiscences.*

To a generation who know him only by his work there is a danger of losing sight of Mill's humanity. The student of the "Logic" finds himself, in spite of his pride —his proper pride as a reasoning animal— in the presence of the infallible. It is a feeling he cannot get rid of; the "Autobiography" and Bain's gossip have no connection with this godlike majesty delivering divine truths. Has the master who was but half-an-hour ago in cricketing flannels, a comrade, anything in common with the being, gowned and awful, in the schoolroom?—PRINGLE, G. O. S., 1898, *Mill's Humanity, Westminster Review, vol.* 150, *p.* 159.

My friend Mr. John Morley, in a speech which he made not very long after Mill's death, paid a noble tribute to the memory of his lost teacher and friend. "A wiser and more virtuous man," he said, "I have never known and never hope to know." I venture to adopt Mr. Morley's words as the best representation I could possibly find of my own judgment and my own feelings with regard to John Stuart Mill—a wiser and more virtuous man I have never known and do not expect to know; and yet I have had the good fortune to know many wise and virtuous men. I never knew any man of really great intellect who carried less of the ordinary ways of greatness about him. There was an added charm in the very shyness of his manner when one remembered how strong he could be and how fearless he could be, if the occasion called for a display of fortitude and courage.—McCARTHY, JUSTIN, 1899, *Reminiscences, vol.* I, *p.* 100.

No more just, patient, and generous soul ever adorned our public life. One had to be admitted to his intimacy and to association with him in the public movements, to which the whole of his later life was devoted, to know how warm a heart, what fire of enthusiasm lay covered up, like a volcano under snow, beneath the dry, formal, antiquated official which the world saw as Stuart Mill. I spent with him the last night I think he passed in England, but a week or two before his sudden death at Avignon. I have visited his grave in the most romantic of cemeteries beside the rushing Rhone and in sight of the huge palace of the mediæval Popes. And as I meditated on the strange vicissitudes of his career and the historic associations of his last resting-place, I was filled with regret that I could not have worked with him and under him in the new organ of Reform which in leaving England he had contemplated to found.—HARRISON, FREDERIC, 1901, *George Washington and other American Addresses, p.* 205.

A SYSTEM OF LOGIC
1843

The effect of the "Logic" has been enormous, — half the minds of the younger generation of Englishmen have been greatly colored by it, and would have been sensibly different if they had not been influenced by it; and there is no other book of English philosophy of which the same can be said, even with a pretext of truth.—BAGEHOT, WALTER, 1873, *The Late Mr. Mill, Works, ed. Morgan, vol.* V, *p.* 416.

When his "System of Logic" was published, he stood almost alone in his opinions. The work was not written in exposition or defence of this philosophy, but in accordance with its tenets, which were thus reduced to a proximate application, or to a more determinate or concrete form. A qualified nominalism, thoroughly English, and descended from the English schoolman William of Ockham, was its philosophical basis. He welcomed and introduced to English readers the revival of this philosophy in France, by Auguste Comte, with whom he agreed in many positions,—more especially in those which were not original with Comte. His accordance with Comte can hardly be regarded as one of discipleship, since in most important practical matters Mill dissented from the views of the French philosopher. His real allegiance was to the once prevalent teachings of Locke, and to those of Berkeley, Hume, Brown, Hartley, and his father James Mill. No modern thinker has striven more faithfully to restore and build upon those speculations of the past, which appeared to him just and true, or more modestly to exhibit and acknowledge his indebtedness to previous thinkers; yet, by the excellence of his works, this past has fallen to the inheritance of his name and fame. To give scientific form or systematic coherency to views put forth unsystematically by others, was to give soul and life to doctrines which were thus made especially his own.— WRIGHT, CHAUNCEY, 1873–74, *John Stuart Mill, Philosophical Discussions, p.* 422.

If, however, we ask whether the "System of Logic" is destined to live as a classic on the subject, we open a question of wider issue. Clearly, it is a work which no student of the subject can possibly forego; it has been extensively used as an instrument of education both at the Universities and elsewhere, though at Oxford, at all events, a reaction on the lines of German thought has for some time been in progress. . . . If we regard the work as a whole, we are forced to distinguish its scientific character from its metaphysical ground work. Probably no other work on Logic can give the reader so clear an idea of what Science is and what it is doing; and its merits in this respect have received emphatic testimony from scientists themselves. On the other hand, it might be urged that Logic somewhat unduly extends its boundaries when it covers all that Mill makes it cover; and especially that it ought to rest on sounder metaphysical foundations than can be discovered in the work of Mill. If it be true that these foundations include irreconcilable dogmas, then the shiftiness of the groundwork must in time make itself felt in

every department of the superstructure.— COURTNEY, WILLIAM L., 1888, *Life of John Stuart Mill (Great Writers), pp.* 79, 81.

Has in all countries a high reputation, and must take its rank among the great treatises on logic of all times. He is frequently called the founder of the inductive logic, so great was the contribution which he made in his treatment of induction.—ELY, RICHARD T., 1897, *Library of the World's Best Literature, ed.Warner,vol.* XVII, *p.* 10011.

PRINCIPLES OF POLITICAL
ECONOMY
1848

Five years after his "Logic," Mr. Mill published a not less monumental work on Political Economy, in which he attacked every question, and showed on all points at once a profound knowledge of all theories, and that independence of mind which enslaves itself to none. Yet this work, which in England has ranked the author by the side of Adam Smith and of Ricardo, had less originality than thoroughness. The author showed more sense and information than freshness: and gave us an encyclopædia of the science rather than a system of his own.—SCHERER, EDMUND, 1862–91, *John Stuart Mill, Essays on English Literature, tr. Saintsbury, p.* 18.

Through his "Principles of Political Economy" he has exercised a remarkable influence upon men in all lands; not so much because of great originality, since, in truth, he only put Ricardo's principles in better and more attractive form, but chiefly by a method of systematic treatment more lucid and practical than had been hitherto reached, by improving vastly beyond the dry treatises of his predecessors (including Ricardo, who was concise and dull), by infusing a human element into his aims, and by illustrations and practical applications. Even yet, however, some parts of his book show the tendency to too great a fondness for abstract statement, induced probably by a dislike to slighting reasons (due to his early training), and by the limits of his book, which obliged him to omit many possible illustrations. With deep sympathy for the laboring-classes, he was tempted into the field of sociology in this book, although he saw distinctly that political economy was but one of the sciences, a knowledge of which was necessary to a legislator in reaching a decision upon social questions. Mill shows an advance beyond

Ricardo in this treatise, by giving the study a more practical direction.—LAUGHLIN, J. LAURENCE, 1884, *ed. Principles of Political Economy by John Stuart Mill, A Sketch of the History of Political Economy, p.* 22.

Before saying a few words on what is called the "vulgar" economy, we must not forget to mention John Stuart Mill, who, although in no sense an original thinker, is one of the most popular writers on political economy. His "Principles of Political Economy," published in 1848, though in substance little more than a manual of the classical system, is distinguished by breadth of sympathy, and by the consciousness that the so-called economic laws, that is the deductions of political economy based on the present conditions of society, have not the absolute character other exponents of the science were apt to assign to them. At the same time it must be remembered that J. S. Mill was totally deficient in what has been sometimes called the "historical sense," and had little conception of the historical method. His heart rebelled against the hard and fast conclusions and pretended laws of the orthodox economy, but his intellect saw no effectual means of escaping them. In consequence, his book is an alteration of clear statements of the current views and confused attempts to evade their consequences.—BAX, ERNEST BELFORT, 1887, *ed. The Wealth of Nations, Introduction, vol.* I, *p.* xxxiv.

Mill was not the founder of a school in Political Economy; scarcely the originator of a single new economic conception. His economics are those of Ricardo, plus Malthusianism, and several new practical measures proposed by various thinkers between Ricardo and himself. The main significance and the main value of Mill's work is that, in fluent style and in popular method, he has with scientific reasoning discussed the principles of Political Economy in constant reference to their practical application. This, Mill says in his introduction to his "Political Economy," was his aim, and in this he, to a large extent, succeeded. Hence his hold and his influence upon the economic and practical thinking of his day, and of succeeding days down to the very present.—BLISS, W. D. P., 1891, *ed. Socialism, Introduction, p.* v.

Mill mastered and expressed with great lucidity and force of style all that he considered best in his predecessors, and if he

was not very original himself, he has been the cause or occasion of originality in others. In England at any rate many of the recent changes in economic theory may be traced to the criticism or development of Mill's teaching. At the same time the abundance of these commentaries—to say nothing of the work of both foreign and English writers on independent lines—has rendered Mill's treatment year by year less satisfactory as a survey of the whole subject, though it is still excellent for students who have time to trace the growth of economic thought.— NICHOLSON, J. SHIELD, 1893, *Principles of Political Economy, Preface, vol.* I, *p.* v.

Mill's "Political Economy" is, like his general philosophy, lucid, full and thorough. Though cautious here, as always, in the admission of new principles, Mill made considerable contributions to economics. The theory of international exchanges is almost wholly his, and many particular turns and details of economic doctrine are due to him. In a still greater number of cases he has been, not the originator, but the best exponent of economic theory. The caution and judiciousness of his reasoning were qualities peculiarly valuable in this sphere; and where the views of "orthodox" political economy are accepted at all, Mill's opinions are treated with respect.—WALKER, HUGH, 1897, *The Age of Tennyson, p.* 164.

Mill's "Political Economy" is a transitional work; and indeed, it may not be too much to say of all his work that it was transitional. He brought to a close a line of development in economics proceeding from Adam Smith through Ricardo, Malthus, and James Mill, and opened a new era. He added on to the superstructure large humanitarian and social considerations which were hardly consistent with the foundations upon which he built; and this he himself recognized late in life. Yet the very imperfections of his book on political economy render it interesting and also instructive. It must be read carefully and in connection with his other writings to be fully understood; but its mastery has been called in itself a liberal education.—ELY, RICHARD T., 1897, *Library of the World's Best Literature, ed. Warner, vol.* XVII, *p.* 10013.

Mill's contributions to political economy are not mere reasoned products, but are the creation of certain social ideals so blended with the older economic reasoning as to become indistinguishable. Political economy, thus raised above the level of a mere study of environmental facts, has become a concrete form of idealism. The forcible books since Mill's time have followed his example, and strengthened the idealistic tendencies he stimulated. Such books unite reasoning and ideals as he did. Their initial chapters are drills in close reasoning, followed by a clear presentation of the ideals the writer wishes to attain. Henry George's "Progress and Poverty," and Karl Marx's "Capital," use Mill's plan, and a host of other books are written in the same fashion. The reasoning is not always of the same character, but it serves the same purpose by creating a state of mind in which ideals can be appreciated.—PATTEN, SIMON N., 1899, *The Development of English Thought, p.* 339.

ON LIBERTY
1859

To the beloved and deplored memory of her who was the inspirer, and in part the author, of all that is best in my writings—the friend and wife whose exalted sense of truth and right was my strongest incitement, and whose approbation was my chief reward—I dedicate this volume. Like all that I have written for many years, it belongs as much to her as to me; but the work as it stands has had, in a very insufficient degree, the inestimable advantage of her revision; some of the most important portions having been reserved for a more careful re-examination, which they are now never destined to receive. Were I but capable of interpreting to the world one half the great thoughts and noble feelings which are buried in her grave, I should be the medium of a greater benefit to it than is ever likely to arise from anything that I can write, unprompted and unassisted by her all but unrivalled wisdom.—MILL, JOHN STUART, 1859, *On Liberty, Dedication.*

I am reading that terrible book of John Mill's on "Liberty," so clear and calm and cold; he lays it on one as a tremendous duty to get oneself well contradicted, and admit always a devil's advocate into the presence of your dearest, most sacred truths, as they are apt to grow windy and worthless without such tests, if, indeed, they can stand the shock of argument at all. He looks you through like a basilisk, relentless as Fate. We knew him well at one time, and owe him very much. I fear his remorseless logic has led him far since then. No, my dear, I

don't agree with Mill, though I, too, should be very glad to have some of my "ugly opinions" corrected, however painful the process; but Mill makes me shiver, his blade is so keen and so unhesitating.—FOX, CAROLINE, 1859, *Letter to E. T. Carne, Life of John Stuart Mill by Courtney, p.* 125.

Nowhere is there to be read a more eloquent defence of the rights of individualism, a more generous protest against the tyranny of governments, and still more against that of custom and opinion. It is still in this religious respect for the liberty of all, this tolerance for every idea, this confidence in the final results of the struggle, that we recognize true Liberalism. The author's notions have not always equal solidity, but his instincts are always lofty. We see on every page the man whose own independence has set him at odds with prejudice.—SCHERER, EDMUND, 1862–91, *John Stuart Mill, Essays on English Literature, tr. Saintsbury, p.* 22.

"On Liberty" was probably the most popular of all his books, as it is the most charming to read. There are few minds of a liberal turn who can have perused it for the first time without a thrill of delight, even if the continued advance of liberal thought has now made some of its eloquence comparatively commonplace.—TULLOCH, JOHN, 1885, *Movements of Religious Thought in Britain During the Nineteenth Century, p.* 143.

So far as it confuses character with eccentricity, so far as it belongs to the combative, negative spirit of revolt, rather than to the positive, constructive spirit of organised reform; so far it shares the fate of the old *laisser-faire* doctrine of political economy, and is out of harmony with the tendencies and the ideas of the modern age. We have advanced fast and far in the last thirty years, and organism and synthesis are our mottoes rather than atomism and individuality. Herbert Spencer is indeed an exception, but in times of change the best men are found on both sides of the dividing line.—COURTNEY, WILLIAM L., 1888, *Life of John Stuart Mill (Great Writers), p.* 126.

Mill's contribution to the movement which he represented seems to have been twofold, lying partly in the moral force and concentration of the man himself, partly in his protest against existing authority in those cases in which it appeared to him to embody injustice. His "Essay on Liberty," published in 1859, is a masterly exposition of his principles. It is a noble protest against the tyranny of society and legislation, but, as it stands, will seem incomplete to minds which require the statement of some positive principle which, whatever its embodiment, is to take the place of society and legislation.—NETTLESHIP, HENRY, 1892–95, *Authority in the Sphere of Conduct and Intellect, Lectures and Essays, Second Series, ed. Haverfield, p.* 221.

The book on "Liberty," from beginning to end, is an invaluable text-book for the legislator, for the politician, for the social reformer; and its powerful protest against all forms of over-legislation, intolerance, and the tyranny of majorities, is rich with perennial wisdom and noble manliness. But as a piece of social philosophy it is based upon a sophism as radical as that of Rousseau himself, with his assumption of a primordial Contract. And, if these absolute dogmas as to "the sovereignity of the individual" against even the moral coercion of his fellow-citizens were literally enforced, there would be a bar put to the moral and religious development of civilised communities.—HARRISON, FREDERIC, 1896, *John Stuart Mill, Nineteenth Century, vol.* 40, *p.* 496.

THE SUBJECTION OF WOMEN
1869

The highest encomium which John Stuart Mill now receives—that which he would most value—is that every noble woman's heart in Europe is this day comfortless beside his grave. I remember to have been present once in a company composed chiefly of ladies of the higher class in Moscow, when a friend, introducing me, said, "He is a friend of John Stuart Mill," when instantly I was surrounded by all of that sex in the room, begging to be told of his look, his manner, and every word I had ever heard him speak. Each declared that she kept his work on "The Subjection of Woman" by her side, and read it as her gospel. Throughout Russia I found it the same, and heard the sentiments of that work quoted on the stage amidst applause in which every woman made her hands attest the homage of her heart. In France the best women proudly claimed him as their adopted fellow-citizen, and the tribute he had written on his wife's grave made them forget the romances of Hugo and About.— CONWAY, MONCURE DANIEL, 1873, *John Stuart Mill, Harper's Magazine, vol.* 47, *p.* 529.

He did not hesitate, either in his written or in his spoken words, to use the strongest expression in order to place in the right light his conception of the unnaturalness of women's state of dependence. Indeed, he had not been afraid to challenge universal laughter through his vehement assertion, that, as we had never seen woman in freedom, we did know nothing whatever until now of her nature; as though Raphael's Sistine Madonna, Shakespeare's young maidens, all the literature about women, in fact, had taught us nothing of the feminine character. On this point he was almost fanatical. He, who in all the relations between man and woman was refinement and delicacy itself, allowed himself to be positively insulting in his expressions when an opinion differing from his own on his favorite topic was uttered in his presence. One day I chanced to be visiting a celebrated French *savant* when the mail brought him a letter from Stuart Mill. It was an answer to a communication in which the Frenchman had expressed the opinion that the change in the social status of women, demanded in Mill's essay on "The Subjection of Women," might turn out well in England, where it would harmonize with the character of the race, but that in France, where the talents and tastes of the women were so contrary to it, there could be no possibility of success. Mill's pithy reply, which was handed to me with a smile, read as follows: "I see in your remarks that contempt for women which is so prevalent in France. All that I can say on the subject is, that the French women pay this contempt back with interest to the men of France."—BRANDES, GEORGE, 1879, *Eminent Authors of the Nineteenth Century, tr. Anderson, p.* 131.

In many ways the most eloquent of his works, the most characteristic, and perhaps that which has had the most direct and immediate effect. Like the "Liberty," it was written many years before it was published, and was to a great degree a joint production. His biographer, Professor Bain, very justly calls it "the most sustained exposition of Mill's life-long theme— the abuses of power." And Mr. John Morley calls it "the best illustration of the best and richest qualities of its author's mind." "It is fortunate," he adds, "that a subject of such incomparable importance should have been first effectively presented for discussion in so worthy and pregnant a form."—HARRISON, FREDERIC, 1896, *John Stuart Mill, Nineteenth Century, vol.* 40, *p.* 500.

None of his writings is more emphatically marked by generosity and love of justice. A certain shrillness of tone marks the recluse too little able to appreciate the animal nature of mankind. Yet in any case, he made a most effective protest against the prejudices which stunted the development and limited the careers of women.—STEPHEN, LESLIE, 1900, *The English Utilitarians, vol.* III, *p.* 281.

AUTOBIOGRAPHY
1873-74

You have lost nothing by missing the autobiography of Mill. I have never read a more uninteresting book, nor should I say a sillier, by a man of sense, integrity, and seriousness of mind. The penny-a-liners were very busy with it, I believe, for a week or two, but were evidently pausing in doubt and difficulty by the time the second edition came out. It is wholly the life of a logic-chopping engine, little more of human in it than if it had been done by a thing of mechanized iron. Autobiography of a steam-engine, perhaps, you may sometimes read it. As a mournful psychical curiosity, but in no other point of view, can it interest anybody. I suppose it will deliver us henceforth from the cock-a-leerie crow about "the Great Thinker of his Age." Welcome, though inconsiderable! The thought of poor Mill altogether, and of his life and history in this poor muddy world, gives me real pain and sorrow.—CARLYLE, THOMAS, 1873, *To John Carlyle, Nov.* 5; *Thomas Carlyle, History of his Life in London, ed. Froude, vol.* II, *p.* 358.

I have read Mill's "Autobiography," and was much surprised when I came to the passage concerning myself. I do not think it biasses my judgment of the work, though I find that I think better of it than most of his critics. But I had always considered him as a noble spirit, who had the misfortune of being educated by a narrow-minded pedant, who cultivated his intellectual faculties at the expense of all the rest, yet did not succeed in stifling them.—THIRLWALL, CONNOP, 1873, *Lettters to a Friend, Dec.* 1, *ed. Stanley, p.* 295.

As an autobiography, the book has but little merit; though this should not be insisted on, since success in writing of this kind is extremely rare. . . . Mill seems to have been incapable of a healthful sentiment of any kind. The same quality in his stunted and warped moral nature which caused him to have a false and exaggerated sense of the evil that is in the world, leading him to atheism, made him a blind and superstitious worshipper of the imaginary endowments of his wife. . . . We have never read a sadder book, nor one which to our mind contains stronger proof that the soul longs with an infinite craving for God, and, not finding him, will worship anything—a woman, a stone, a memory.—SPAULDING, J. L., 1874, *John Stuart Mill, Catholic World, vol.* 18, *pp.* 721, 733.

Mill's life is an autobiography with a vengeance! It is his life of himself, and of nobody else! Account for this as you please. He seems to have regarded his father's life and his own as one; that it was his duty and work to continue his father's work and duty with such added light as time gave. His wife's life and his own he seems to consider as one life. There are no more profound and interesting passages in the book than those which describe their perfect communion. These two lives, therefore, are alluded to in the autobiography. Miss Taylor gets mentioned in a postscript, as if for the same reason. But, for the rest, people are mentioned as Westminster Bridge might be mentioned, or the penny-post, if they served to carry out Mill's wishes and plans, and only so. You would not know that he had a mother, or brothers, or sisters. There are associates spoken of sometimes; but the same plan of the book, or the temperament of the author, or both, hinder him from pausing one moment to give us any view of them. This book is simply and wholly given to the life of John Stuart Mill. . . . A fascinating book it is from beginning to end.—HALE, EDWARD EVERETT, 1874, *John Stuart Mill, Old and New, vol.* 9, *p.* 128.

Perhaps it is his best composition from the point of view of literature; and certainly it is the most valuable document for a study of the growth of his school.—WALKER, HUGH, 1897, *The Age of Tennyson, p.* 162.

The life of John Stuart Mill is in several particulars one of the most remarkable of which we have any record; and it can scarcely be an exaggeration to call his autobiography—in which we find presented in simple, straightforward style the main features of his life—a wonderful book.—ELY, RICHARD T., 1897, *Library of the World's Best Literature, ed. Warner, vol.* XVII, *p.* 10007.

GENERAL

No writer, it is probable, was ever more read between the lines: his authoritative force of intellect, his perfect mastery of his materials, his singular neatness of exposition, marked him as a great power in the speculative world: but, as usual, the real interest felt was not less scientific than moral, —as to the direction in which that power would work. A certain air of suppression occasionally assumed by Mr. Mill himself, with hints for a revision of the existing narrow-minded morals, has increased this tendency. This suppressive air is the greatest fault we find in him; it is his only illegitimate instrument of power, for it weighs chiefly on the weak: and the shade which it passes across his face is sometimes so strong as almost to darken the philosopher into the mystagogue.—MARTINEAU, JAMES, 1859, *Essays, Philosophical and Theological, vol.* I, *p.* 118.

The acknowledged chief of English thinkers, John Stuart Mill!—MOTLEY, JOHN LOTHROP, 1862, *Letter to Dr. O. W. Holmes, Feb.* 26; *Correspondence, ed. Curtis, vol.* II, *p.* 64.

British speculation, to which, notwithstanding adverse Continental opinion, the chief initial ideas and established truths of Modern Philosophy are due, is no longer dormant. By his "System of Logic," Mr. Mill probably did more than any other writer to reawaken it. And to the great service he thus rendered some twenty years ago, he now adds by his "Examination of Sir William Hamilton's Philosophy,"—a work which, taking the views of Sir William Hamilton as texts, reconsiders sundry ultimate questions that still remain unsettled.—SPENCER, HERBERT, 1865, *Mill versus Hamilton—The Test of Truth, Fortnightly Review, vol.* 1, *p.* 531.

Now, if there is any man among us who has pre-eminently helped to keep Britain from that danger of intellectual death to many which would arise from her being of one religion in Philosophy, it is Mr. Mill. *He* has never forgotten his true love, the principle of Empiricism, nor in any way denied its name—though the name "Empiricism" is one which he would not himself choose, and

for which he would probably substitute *Experientialism.*—MASSON, DAVID, 1865–77, *Recent British Philosophy, p.* 70.

In all matters of Political Economy, the present generation of Englishmen pins its faith to the sleeve of Mr. Mill. Any utterance of his, therefore, is an event, not only in the history of the science but in the history of the nation.—STIRLING, JAMES, 1869, *Mr. Mill on Trade Unions, Recess Studies, ed. Grant, p.* 309.

Rarely, I grant you, has a thinker better summed up in his teaching the practice of his country; seldom has a man better represented by his negations and his discoveries the limits and scope of his race.—TAINE, H. A., 1871, *History of English Literature, tr. Van Laun, vol.* II, *bk.* v, *ch.* v, *p.* 506.

Himself pervadingly an intellectual machine, Mr. Mill seems to have interest in his countrymen only to the extent that they can be made intellectual machines too. His faith appears to be boundless in the omnipotence of the alphabet: his test of merit and of fitness is wholly mental. . . . Mr. Mill, by the inexorable directness and the faultless limpidity of his speech, forces back to reality the brain which has been bewildered by a vapoury, chaotic pictorialism. He is the Priessnitz of Literature, and much is a Priessnitz of Literature needed when there has been a reckless revel in furibond and fantastic phrases. If, then, you know any one who has been ensnared of the Carlyle apes—for whom, however, the great and good man they outrageously imitate should not be held responsible—send him to the physician Mill. . . . The physician Mill, though he gives us water in abundance, furnishes us with rather scanty fare; and those of us who have a good appetite are obliged to go elsewhither. . . . The works of Mr. Mill, masterpieces under more than one aspect, reveal to us a mind cultivated, disciplined to excess; a mind trained like the body of a boxer, *sweated* like the body of a jockey. Never was a more perfect thinking and calculating machine. And by thinking and calculating machines alone has Mr. Mill in his studies been attracted. If ever Mr. Mill deserts for a moment his own province, it is from an artificial taste.—MACCALL, WILLIAM, 1873, *The Newest Materialism.*

I should find it hard to say why I dislike John Stuart Mill, but I have an instinct that he has done lots of harm.—LOWELL, JAMES RUSSELL, 1873, *To Leslie Stephen, April* 29; *Letters, ed. Norton, vol.* II, *p.* 97.

Except Darwin, no philosopher has left a deeper impression on the thought of his age. The Utilitarian school, of which he was one of the teachers, we trust is to have but a passing influence. But Mr. Mill himself, in his personal character and his political writings, belongs to that higher school of intuitional moralists, who, in all ages, have shown the utmost attainments of the human soul, in utter and unselfish devotion to the principles of truth and justice and humanity.—BRACE, CHARLES LORING, 1873, *Christian Union, May* 31; *Life, ed. his Daughter, p.* 332.

We have lost in John Stuart Mill the best philosophical writer—if not the greatest philosopher—whom England has produced since Hume: and perhaps the most influential teacher of thought, if we consider the variety as well as the intensity of his influence, that this country has ever seen. Originality of the highest kind he only showed in one department—the theory of method and evidence; but the unequalled mastery of method which his logical speculations developed, his patient tenacity and comprehensiveness of study, his rare gifts of exposition and discussion, and the controlled fervour of his intellectual and social enthusiasm enabled him to do in other departments work equally important in forming the minds of his contemporaries.— SIDGWICK, HENRY, 1873, *John Stuart Mill, The Academy, vol.* 4, *p.* 193.

To treatises such as Mr. Mill's "Logic" and his "Political Economy," it is not usually easy to give important praise which no one will deny: the subjects with which they deal, the "Logic" particularly, are too full of doubts and too fertile in animosities. But no one, we think, will deny that hardly ever, perhaps never, in the history of philosophy, have two books so finished and so ample been written by a man who had only his leisure moments to give to them, and who had a day's work to do besides. The quantity of writing in these four thick volumes is not small: but many men, in detached essays and on varied points, equal or surpass that quantity,—even a daily occupation in laborious business is easily compatible with much desultory labor. But Mr. Mill's "Logic" and his "Political Economy" are not collections of desultory re-

marks; they are orderly, systematic works, in which the beginning has reference to the end, and almost every part has some relation, often a very close relation, to most other parts. To compose such books requires an incessant reminiscence of the past and an equally incessant foresight of the future; and both these, more almost than anything else, strain and fatigue the brain. Only men with their whole time and whole strength can usually accomplish such tasks; but Mr. Mill wrote both these books when a laborious man of business, who had daily difficult and exhausting duties to perform as well. Instead of wondering at occasional faults in such books, we should rather wonder that they exist at all.—BAGEHOT, WALTER, 1873, *The Late Mr. Mill, Works, ed. Morgan, vol.* V, *p.* 412.

Mr. Mill's works, partly from their natural clearness, partly from their appropriateness to the intellectual demands of the day, are already so familiar that they have been threatened with promotion to the shelf of classic commonplace; but we should ask, before accepting this fate for them, whether his followers or his opponents have quite exhausted the problems he raised, either by carrying his method to its last legitimate consequences, or by disproving his particular conclusions seriatim. Till this has been done, indifference to his writings can only be accounted for by the unreasoning fickleness to which the principle—not yet become a commonplace and nowhere better illustrated than by himself—affords the best antidote, that the only security against the periodical rediscovery of error lies in recognizing (as he did) the substantial continuity of all right thinking, so that to abandon a legitimate inference is constructively to abandon all the grounds upon which it rested. . . . Mr. Mill's influence has been much greater on the manner or processes of contemporary thought than on its substance and results, and if his estimate of the comparative importance of the two elements is correct, the fact will not injure his reputation with posterity.—SIMCOX, EDITH, 1873, *Influence of J. S. Mill's Writings, Contemporary Review, vol.* 22, *pp.* 298, 299.

The character of his intellectual, no less than of his moral nature, led him to strive to connect his thoughts, whatever was the branch of knowledge at which he labored, with the previously existing body of speculation, to fit them into the same framework, and exhibit them as parts of the same scheme; so that it might be truly said of him that he was at more pains to conceal the originality and independent value of his contributions to the stock of knowledge than most writers are to set forth those qualities in their compositions. As a consequence of this, hasty readers of his works, while recognizing the comprehensiveness of his mind, have sometimes denied its originality; and in political economy in particular he has been frequently represented as little more than an expositor and popularizer of Ricardo. It cannot be denied that there is a show of truth in this representation; about as much as there would be in asserting that Laplace and Herschel were the expositors and popularizers of Newton, or that Faraday performed a like office for Sir Humphry Davy. — CAIRNES, J. E., 1873, *John Stuart Mill, His Work in Political Economy, London Examiner.*

If it is asked why Mr. Mill, with all his width of knowledge and sympathy, has achieved so little of a reputation as a miscellaneous writer, part of the reason no doubt is, that he sternly repressed his desultory tendencies and devoted his powers to special branches of knowledge, attaining in them a distinction that obscured his other writings. Another reason is, that, although his style is extremely clear, he was for popular purposes dangerously familiar with terms belonging more or less to the schools.—MINTO, WILLIAM, 1873, *John Stuart Mill, His Place as a Critic, London Examiner.*

He weighed his arguments as dispassionately as if his aim had been pure science. Rarely have strength of emotion and purpose and strength of intellect been combined in a thinker with such balance and harmony. The strength of his moral emotions gave him insights or premises which had been overlooked by the previous thinkers whose views he expounded or defended. This advantage over his predecessors was conspicuous in the form he gave to the utilitarian theory of moral principles, and in what was strictly original in his "Principles of Political Economy."—WRIGHT, CHAUNCEY, 1873-74, *John Stuart Mill, Philosophical Discussions, p. 415.*

A man so good and great, that even his mistakes and deficiencies (as I needs must deem them) are more instructive to us than a million platitudes and truisms of teachers

whom his transcendent intellectual honesty should put to the blush, and whose souls never kindled with a spark of the generous ardor for the welfare of his race which flamed in his noble heart and animated his entire career.—COBBE, FRANCES POWER, 1874, *The Hopes of the Human Race Hereafter and Here, Preface.*

I rather think that Mr. Mill himself is scarcely aware of the extent of the resemblance between his doctrines and those of the Scottish sceptic; as he seems to have wrought out his conclusions from data supplied him by his own father, Mr. James Mill, who, however, has evidently drawn much from Hume. The circumstance that Mr. Mill's work was welcomed by such acclamations by the chief literary organs in London is a proof, either that the would-be leaders of opinion are so ignorant of philosophy that they do not see the consequences; or that the writers, being chiefly young men bred at Oxford or Cambridge, are fully prepared to accept them in the reaction against the revived mediævalism which was sought to be imposed upon them.—McCOSH, JAMES, 1874, *The Scottish Philosophy, p. 133.*

Mr. John Stuart Mill was well known in France. His reputation as an economist; his works on politics and social questions; his various translations; an analysis of his Logic, which the author M. Taine in his "Etude sur Stuart Mill" pronounces "masterly;" the attacks of his numerous adversaries;—all these have contributed to spread abroad his fame. No name has been more frequently quoted among us in contemporary polemics.—RIBOT, THÉODULE, 1874, *English Psychology, p. 78.*

It is also observable, that, in Mill's analysis of the conception of an external world, he makes no mention at all of space-relations; and yet the absence of this most important element of the objective world is scarcely missed by writer or reader, forasmuch as the terms of common life so readily supply and suggest them. We contend that it is not unfair to say, that, by this interchange of common and technical terminology, Mr. Mill contrives to muddle almost every subject which he essays to treat with philosophical exactness. It is no paradox to say, that when he seems to be the most clear and convincing, and because his terms are familiar and his illustrations are easily followed, he is the most emphatically confusing and disappointing. We need only contrast him with Berkeley to be sensible of these marked defects.—PORTER, NOAH, 1874–82, *Science and Sentiment, p.* 145.

For my part, I will no longer consent to live silently under the incubus of bad logic and bad philosophy which Mill's Works have laid upon us. On almost every subject of social importance—religion, morals, political philosophy, political economy, metaphysics, logic—he has expressed unhesitating opinions, and his sayings are quoted by his admirers as if they were the oracles of a perfectly wise and logical mind. Nobody questions, or at least ought to question, the force of Mill's style, the persuasive power of his words, the candour of his discussions, and the perfect goodness of his motives. If to all his other great qualities had been happily added logical accurateness, his writings would indeed have been a source of light for generations to come. But in one way or another Mill's intellect was wrecked. The cause of injury may have been the ruthless training which his father imposed upon him in tender years; it may have been Mill's own life-long attempt to reconcile a false empirical philosophy with conflicting truth. But however it arose, Mill's mind was essentially illogical.— JEVONS, WILLIAM STANLEY, 1877, *John Stuart Mill's Philosophy Tested, Contemporary Review, vol.* 31, *p.* 168.

I conclude that J. S. Mill's greatest personal misfortune was that he was born the son of James Mill, and not of Johann Gottlieb Fichte. He presents the appearance of a noble nature confined in intellectual fetters, which, forged for him, he himself did his best to rivet upon himself, without wholly succeeding. He attracts a sympathy at once regretful and affectionate. Perhaps his speculative failures, engraved already so conspicuously upon the tablets of the intellectual history of his race, may contribute more for the world's final instruction than the inconspicuous successes of many another less renowned.—MORRIS, GEORGE S., 1880, *British Thought and Thinkers, p.* 336.

These approximations of Mr. Mill to Christianity are also the more remarkable, that they come from one who had not, like Strauss and Rénan, any Christian training; and while Mr. Mill has not, any more than they, solved the problem of the origin of Christianity, his willingness to accept a supernatural theory, if it could be found, is also to be noted as what, after so long a period, shows a gleam of Butler more than a reflection of English Deism.—CAIRNS, JOHN, 1881, *Unbelief in the Eighteenth Century.*

He is allowed to be not only a great thinker, but a good writer. His lucidity, in particular, is regarded as pre-eminent. Exceptions are taken by the more fastidious critics; he is said by Mr. Pattison to be wanting in classical grace and literary polish. . . . He was greatly inferior to Bentham in the copiousness, the variety of his primary stock of language elements. He was surpassed, if I mistake not, by both the Austins, by Grote and by Roebuck. Had he been required to express the same idea in ten different forms, all good, he would have come to a standstill sooner than any of those. His grammar is often more defective than we should expect in any one so carefully disciplined as he was from the first. . . . Critically examined, his style is wanting in delicate attention to the placing of qualifying words generally. He had apparently never thought of this matter farther than to satisfy himself that his sentences were intelligible. Another peculiarity of grammar tending to make his style not unfrequently heavy, and sometimes a little obscure, was the excess of relatives, and especially of the heavy relatives "which" and "who." . . . Of arts of the rhetorical kind in the structure of his sentences, he was by no means wanting. He could be sharp and pithy, which goes a great way. He had likewise caught up, probably in a good measure from the French writers, his peculiar epigrammatic smartness, which he practised also in conversation. . . . As a whole, I should say that Mill was wanting in strength, energy, or momentum. His happiest strokes were of the nature of a corruscation—a lightning flash, rather than effects of impetus or mass of motion. His sentences and paragraphs are apt to diffuse; not because of unnecessary circumstances, but from a want of steady endeavour after emphasis by good collocation and condensation. Every now and then, one of his pithy sentences comes across us, with inexpressible welcome. He is himself conscious when he is becoming too involved, and usually endeavours to relieve us by a terse summary at the close of the paragraph.—BAIN, ALEXANDER, 1882, *John Stuart Mill, A Criticism; with Personal Recollections, pp.* 174, 175, 176, 177.

The style of J. S. Mill is a style which expresses thought, and even feeling, in a very abstract manner; and, consequently, there are few writers who gain more by being studied concretely in connexion with life and circumstances.—STEWART, J. A., 1882, *Literature, The Academy, vol.* 21, *p.* 167.

Exercised, without doubt, a greater influence in the field of English economics than any other writer since Ricardo. His systematic treatise has been, either directly or through manuals founded on it, especially that of Fawcett, the source from which most of our contemporaries in these countries have derived their knowledge of the science.—INGRAM, JOHN KELLS, 1888, *A History of Political Economy, p.* 146.

Of all this new generation, the most precocious was certainly John Stuart Mill. He began his contributions to the *Westminster Review* in 1824, when he was only some eighteen years of age. Two years subsequently there fell on his spirit that darkness, which, as we have seen, the study of Wordsworth dispersed or reduced; and very shortly afterwards, ever bent on some good service for his day and generation, he became one of the noblest and best influences of his time. About the year 1837, stimulated by the perusal of Whewell's "History of the Inductive Sciences," he was devoting his attention to those studies of *Logic* which resulted in his two memorable volumes in 1843.—HALES, JOHN W., 1888–93, *Folia Litteraria, p.* 329.

When a man lives much in the country he is likely, if he reads, to be chiefly influenced by books. In this way I have been strongly influenced by John Mill, whom I once met, but did not know personally. Mill had a power over all my thinking.—HAMERTON, PHILIP GILBERT, 1894, *The Chief Influences on My Career, The Forum, vol.* 18, *p.* 423.

What, then, is it in Mill's philosophical writings that has given him this eminence as a thinker? Two qualities, we think, very rarely combined: a philosophical style which for clearness and cogency has, perhaps, never been surpassed, and a conscientious painstaking, with a seriousness of conviction, and an earnestness of purpose which did not in general characterize the thinkers whose views he adopted. It was by bringing to the support of doctrines previously regarded as irreligious a truly religious spirit

that Mill acquired in part the influence and respect which have given him his eminence as a thinker. He thus redeemed the word "utility" and the utilitarian doctrine of morals from the ill repute they had, for "the greatest happiness principle" was with him a religious principle. An equally important part of his influence is doubtless due to the thoroughness of his early training — the education — received from his father's instruction—which, as we have said, has made him truly regarded as the most accomplished of modern dialecticians. —GODKIN, EDWIN LAURENCE, 1895, *Reflections and Comments, p.* 76.

Mill must be accounted on the whole by good judges, even if they are utterly opposed to his whole system of philosophy, the chief philosophical *writer* of England in this century; and the enormous though not permanent influence which he attained about its middle was deserved, partly by qualities purely literary, but partly also by some purely philosophical. . . . Even those, however, who, as the present writer acknowledges in his own case, are totally opposed to the whole Millian conception of logic and politics, of metaphysics and morality, must, unless prejudiced, admit his great merits of method and treatment. He not only very seldom smuggles in sophistry into the middle of his arguments, but even paralogisms are not common with him; it is with his premises, not with his conclusions, that you must deal if you wish to upset him. Unlike most contemners of formal logic, he is not in much danger, as far as his merely dialectic processes go, from formal logic itself; and it is in the arbitrary and partial character of his preliminary admissions, assumptions, and exclusions that the weak points of his system are to to be found. His style has also very considerable merits. It is not brilliant or charming; it has neither great strength nor great stateliness. But it is perfectly clear, it is impossible to mistake its meaning, and its simplicity is unattended by any of the down-at-heel neglect of neatness and elegance which is to be found, for instance, in Locke.— SAINTSBURY, GEORGE, 1896, *A History of Nineteenth Century Literature, pp.* 347, 348.

He strives laboriously, and with success, to make his meaning quite plain. His chain of reasoning may be confused, but it is never more confused to the reader than to himself. Though he does not avoid technical language when that is necessary, his drift may be caught by any man of average intelligence who will take the trouble to study his books. On the other hand, he is never for a single moment familiar or colloquial. The man of average intelligence, whom we have figured as applying to his works, will not be tempted into the belief that speculation is all plain-sailing. Rather will he have an agreeable and flattering consciousness that he is grappling with problems of no ordinary magnitude and solemnity. And this pleasing impression all Mr. Mill's artifices—his long sentences, his long words of which he is extremely fond, even his turns and tricks of phrase, such as the habitual use of "needs" for "need" in the third person—will only deepen and confirm. It is in his political enquiries that this combination of qualities—this admixture of the popular with the severe—is most effective; but in all he wrote, it was this which, combined with his moral fervour, raised him so high in the esteem of his own generation, and it is this which is destined, possibly, to atone for the want of many more solid and more brilliant literary excellencies in the judgment of generations yet to come.—MILLAR, J. H., 1896, *English Prose, ed. Craik, vol.* v. *p.* 511.

In all his writings he is clear in expression and abundant in illustration. This abundance, in truth, appears to the reader not wholly ignorant of the subject to be cognate to verbosity. It was however part of the secret of Mill's great influence. He forced people to understand him. He talked round and round the subject, looked at it from every point of view and piled example upon example, until it was impossible to miss his meaning. When we add wide knowledge, patient study, keen intelligence and a considerable, if not exactly a great talent for original speculation, Mill's influence as a philosopher is explained. He wielded, from the publication of his "Logic" till his death, a greater power than any other English thinker, unless Sir William Hamilton is to be excepted for the earlier part of the period.—WALKER, HUGH, 1897, *The Age of Tennyson, p.* 163.

In the seventies his philosophy dominated Oxford. It is of no account to-day. On the philosophical side Mill's position is weakened by his ignorance of the more simple sciences, which we now know to be of the greatest moment in the study of intellectual problems. Mill knew little of physics, and of biology still less. His education in this respect belonged to the old-fashioned type. His work in logic is all but unshaken, although his book has been superseded for school and college use. His psychology, however, his ethics, much of his economics, and above all, his metaphysics, must be corrected by later ideas. Doubtless Mill's readjustments in mental science are most valuable, especially his rehandling of the old doctrines; but fundamentally these are Hume's. Mill's chief philosopical work was destructive. He utterly routed the remnants of a still earlier philosophy, furbished up with all the knowledge and all the acuteness of Sir William Hamilton.— SHORTER, CLEMENT, 1897, *Victorian Literature, p.* 141.

Mill's writings are useful, not only because they mark a period of change in English Philosophy, but also because they possess qualities of thought and expression which give permanent weight to their speculative freedom and precision. To study them is an education in ethics, both because they treat the chief topics of the science in a broad and vigorous way, and because they evoke the mood of mind which is appropriate to the whole subject. It is very important that the student should approach the problems of moral experience in a treatment of them which maintains the human interest of the subject, rather than in purely technical discussions, in which this interest may not appear to those who have not learned their importance; and Mill's simplicity, his seriousness, the fervour of his appreciation of morality, and his largeness of outlook, help to make his work a real introduction to ethical studies. That his errors are not the least instructive part of his writings is one of the many good results of his singular and unfailing candour. — DOUGLAS, CHARLES, 1897, *ed. The Ethics of John Stuart Mill, Preface, p.* v.

He was in an eminent degree compassionate and just, and, to use a happy phrase which Condorcet applied to Turgot, he resembled a volcano clothed in ice. It was indeed the altruistic element in his character that informed and coloured his political philosophy; and he might perhaps without impropriety be described as a Benthamite purified, sublimated and refined.— KENT, C. B. ROYLANCE, 1899, *The English Radicals, p.* 326.

Jean Louis Rodolphe Agassiz

1807–1873

Naturalist, was born at Motier, in the Swiss canton of Fribourg, 28th May 1807, and studied at Bienne, Lausanne, Zurich, Heidelberg, and Munich. He graduated in medicine in 1830, his Latin description of the "Fishes of Brazil" having the year before elicited a warm encomium from Cuvier. In 1831–32 he worked in Paris, and in 1832 accepted a professorship at Neuchâtel. In 1833 he commenced the publication of his "Researches on the Fossil Fishes," and in 1836 undertook those studies on the glacial phenomena of the Alps whose fruit was his "Études sur les Glaciers" (1840) and his "Système Glaciaire" (1847). In 1839 he published a "Natural History of the Fresh-water Fishes of Central Europe." In 1840–44 he and his assistants spent the summers at a station on the Alps, and in the following autumn he visited the Scottish Highlands. In 1846–48 he lectured with success in the principal cities of the United States, and in 1848 was elected to the chair of Natural History at Harvard. He spent the winter of 1850–51 in an expedition to the Florida Reefs. In 1851–52 he taught at Charleston, S. C., and lectured at Washington, before the Smithsonian Institution. In 1855–63 he and his daughters conducted a young ladies' school at Cambridge; he declined chairs at Zurich and Paris, and received the Order of the Legion of Honour. Of his "Contributions to the Natural History of the United States," he lived to issue only four of ten 4to vols. To a Museum of Comparative Zoology, established at Harvard in 1858, Agassiz gave all of his collections; and four years of incessant work here so undermined his health that he decided upon a trip to Brazil, ultimately transformed into an important scientific expedition, described in "A Journey in Brazil." He died at Cambridge, 14th Dec. 1873. See "Life and Correspondence," edited by Mrs. Agassiz (1886), the monograph by C. F. Holder (1892), and "Life, Letters, and Works," by Jules Marcou (1896).—PATRICK AND GROOME *eds.*, 1897, *Chambers's Biographical Dictionary, p. 13.*

PERSONAL

It was fifty years ago
  In the pleasant month of May,
  In the beautiful Pays de Vaud,
    A child in its cradle lay.
And Nature, the old nurse, took
    The child upon her knee,
Saying: "Here is a story-book
    Thy Father has written for thee."
"Come wander with me," she said,
    "Into regions yet untrod;
And read what is still unread
    In the manuscripts of God."
And he wandered away and away
    With Nature, the dear old nurse,
Who sang to him night and day
    The rhymes of the universe.

—LONGFELLOW, HENRY WADSWORTH, 1857,
The Fiftieth Birthday of Agassiz.

God bless the great Professor!
And Madam, too, God bless her!
Bless him and all his band,
On the sea and on the land,
Bless them head and heart and hand,
Till their glorious raid is o'er,
And they touch our ransomed shore!
Then the welcome of a nation,
  With its shout of exultation,
Shall awake the dumb creation,
  And the shapes of buried æons
Join the living creature's pæans,
  Till the fossil echoes roar;
While the mighty megalosaurus

Leads the palæozoic chorus,—
God bless the great Professor,
  And the land his proud possessor,—
  Bless them now and evermore!

—HOLMES, OLIVER WENDELL, 1865, *A Farewell to Agassiz.*

Agassiz is very ill—probably dying. What a different world it will be to us without him. Such a rich, expansive, loving nature.—FIELDS, JAMES T., 1873, *Diary, Nov.; Biographical Notes and Personal Sketches, p. 122.*

He was not of that type of scholars whose shrivelled faces and whose withered forms declare the neglect of exercise, and the misuse of food; nor was he one who gained by stimulants extraordinary force. He possessed what might be called a commanding presence, a favorable personal equation, a magnetic influence, a manly beauty, or an easy dignity—a quality not to be defined, but everywhere appreciated, which may be in-bred, yet must be first in-born. He came of good descent, having a mother of rare intellectual qualities, and on his father's side an ancestry of six generations of Protestant ministers, going back to the Huguenot refugees. But his was not the parentage of wealth or fashion, and the narrow circumstances of his early life quickened his industry, his patience, and fitted him forever after to sympathise with and encourage those who have high aims and shallow purses.—GILMAN, DANIEL COIT, 1873, *Address before the California Academy of Science; Louis Agassiz by C. F. Holder, p.* 232.

His magic was not far to seek,—
He was so human! Whether strong or weak,
Far from his kind he neither sank nor soared,
But sate an equal guest at every board;
No beggar ever felt him condescend,
No prince presume; for still himself he bare
At manhood's simple level, and where'er
He met a stranger, there he left a friend.
How large an aspect! nobly unsevere,
With freshness round him of Olympian cheer,
Like visits of those earthly gods he came;
His look, wherever its good-fortune fell,
Doubled the feast without a miracle,
And on the hearthstone danced a happier flame;
Philemon's crabbed vintage grew benign;
Amphitryon's gold-juice humanized to wine.
—LOWELL, JAMES RUSSELL, 1874, *Agassiz, Heartsease and Rue.*

To Agassiz applies the familiar saying that he was winning in his ways; nay, more than this, the ways were often irresistible. He was a French Swiss, and in him was developed in its highest degree the Gallic power of pleasing. No man was more set in his aims; no man more determined and courageous in their pursuit; but he had not the Saxon style of riding rough-shod over people who were in the path. He worked his way through the crowd of the world deftly; and, when he arrived, as he always did, at the wished-for place, it was with a kindly smile on his face, and accompanied by the good-will even of his opponents. His kindliness was inseparable from his nature, and was a force in itself. It was shown by his love of children and his inexhaustible patience with them, and by his toleration of dull or ignorant people. Behind this came his enthusiasm, like the line after its skirmishers; his kindliness charmed, his enthusiasm overwhelmed and carried off captive. These qualities gave an extraordinary play to a face which would otherwise have been massive, and a boyish twinkle to an eye which had not been a boy's for half a century. His powers were all mobilized; none were reserved, or shut up, or in places of difficult access; therefore he was the most brilliant of talkers. Although cheerful and fond of laughter, he was not exactly humorous; and, singularly enough, was incapable of comprehending the ludicrous mixture of exaggeration and contradiction which we call a *joke.*—LYMAN, THEODORE, 1874, *Recollections of Agassiz, Atlantic Monthly, vol.* 33, *p.* 227.

Great keeper of the magic keys
   That could unlock the guarded gates,
Where Science like a Monarch stands,
   And sacred Knowledge waits—
Thine ashes rest on Charles's banks,
   Thy memory all the world contains,
For thou could'st bind in human love
   All hearts in golden chains!
Thine was the heaven-born spell that sets
   Our warm and deep affections free,—
Who knew thee best must love thee best,
   And longest mourn for thee!
—FIELDS, JAMES T., 1874, *Agassiz, Scribner's Monthly, vol.* 7, *p.* 570.

Agassiz was one of the most brilliant men of his time. Young, handsome, of an athletic constitution, gifted with a captivating eloquence, his spirit was animated with an insatiable curiosity, his memory excellent, his perspicacity rare and very keen, and his way of judging and coördinating facts highly philosophical in its tendency.—LEBERT, HERMANN, 1877, *Actes de la Société helvétique des sciences naturelles réunies à Bex.*

On his modest tomb, in Cambridge, under the hallowed shades of Mount Auburn Cemetery, a huge boulder of solid granite, transported from the glacier of the Aar, the theatre of his glorious investigations, fitly marks the resting place of his mortal remains; but Agassiz's memory will live in the hearts of all those who have known him well, and his name will shine forever in a high place in the Temple of Science.—GUYOT, ARNOLD, 1878, *Memoir of Louis Agassiz Read before the National Academy, April; Biographical Memoirs, vol.* II, *p.* 73.

With his large, generous, and sensitive countenance, suggesting that of an intellectualized god Pan.—LATHROP, GEORGE PARSONS, 1881, *Literary and Social Boston, Harper's Magazine, vol.* 62, *p.* 388.

Teaching was a passion with him, and his power over his pupils might be measured by his own enthusiasm. He was, intellectually as well as socially, a democrat in the best sense. He delighted to scatter broadcast the highest results of thought and research, and to adapt them even to the youngest and most uninformed minds.

In his later American travels he would talk of glacial phenomena to the driver of a country stage-coach among the mountains, or to some workman, splitting rock at the roadside, with as much earnestness as if he had been discussing problems with a brother geologist; he would take the common fisherman into his scientific confidence, telling him the intimate secrets of fish-structure or fish-embryology, till the man in his turn grew enthusiastic and began to pour out information from the stores of his own rough and untaught habits of observation. Agassiz's general faith in the susceptibility of the popular intelligence, however untrained, to the highest truths of nature, was contagious, and he created or developed that in which he believed.— AGASSIZ, ELIZABETH CARY, 1885, *Louis Agassiz, His Life and Correspondence, vol.* I, *p.* 207.

Among the chief scientific names of the middle decades of the nineteenth century the name of Agassiz will always stand forth in full prominence with a certain brilliant and melancholy glory all its own. To few men does science owe more; from few men did its main achievement in the present age receive more steadfast, sturdy, and unreasoning opposition. . . . It was his fate to leave the Word of God and serve tables; but, in truth, his life's work was already finished. He had fairly reached the end of his tether. With the publication of Darwin's theory, he declined from the position of an accepted and respected scientific leader to that of a recalcitrant and reactionary scientific heresiarch. He could not digest the new doctrines. "I detest them," Sedgwick had written to him long before, "because I think them untrue." A strange perversion of the genuine fact: they thought them untrue because they detested them. In all Agassiz's violent denunciations on this cardinal point we nowhere come across one single reason, one definite argument, one gleam of the dry light of logic. Mere prejudice governed his conviction. Unhappily too—and see here how error in belief necessarily leads up to error in action —Agassiz was induced by his theoretic views on specific fixity into that pestilent heresy of asserting the total distinctness of the negro from the white man, thus directly playing into the hands of the unspeakable and doomed pro-slavery party. Such an error was the more unpardonable, because he had been in the south, and knew the negro; and the man who, knowing the negro, denies his essential community with ourselves, proves himself thereby a bad systematist, a worse psychologist, and a worse humanitarian. Of evolutionism he said cheerily "I trust to outlive this mania also."—ALLEN, GRANT, 1885, *Science, The Academy, vol.* 28, *pp.* 309, 310.

The marvel of Agassiz, and a never-ceasing source of wonder and delight to his friends and companions, was the union in his individuality of this solidity, breadth, and depth of mind with a joyousness of spirit, and immense overwhelming geniality of disposition, which flooded every company he entered with the wealth of his own opulent nature. Placed at the head of a table, with a shoulder of mutton before him, he so carved the meat that every guest was flattered into the belief that the host had given him the best piece. His social power exceeded that of the most brilliant conversationalists and of the most delicate epicures; for he was not only fertile in thoughts, but wise in wines and infallible in matters of fish and game. It was impossible to place him in any company where he was out of place. The human nature *in* him fell into instinctive relations with every kind and variety of human nature outside of him.—WHIPPLE, EDWIN PERCY, 1886, *Recollections of Eminent Men, p.* 83.

Agassiz was a little above the average height, although not tall. He was squarely built, with broad shoulders and a powerful and well-proportioned body, and with remarkably large, and at the same time well-formed hands, which he always used most skilfully. They were the hands of an artist or of a naturalist, ready to use the pencil, the hammer, the scalpel, or the microscope, and his manner of shaking hands was very cordial and friendly. He stood firmly, though his feet were rather small in comparison with his herculean structure, and seemed formed for walking; indeed, he was all his life a capital pedestrian, both on level ground and among the Alpine mountains. His head was simply magnificent, his forehead large and well developed; and his brilliant, intelligent, and searching eyes can be best described by the word fascinating, while his mouth and somewhat voluptuous lips were expressive, and in perfect harmony with an aquiline nose and well-shaped chin. His hair was chestnut color and rather thin, especially on the top of his head; indeed, after he was thirty-six years old he showed signs of baldness, which greatly increased after his fiftieth year. The only part of Agassiz's body which was not in harmony with the rest was his short neck, which gave him the appearance of carrying his head on his shoulders,—a defect which he possessed in common with Napoleon Bonaparte. It was his weak point, and the part which failed first. He was easily moved to tears and at times cried like a child. He had spells of laughing, which sometimes seemed forced, but which were perfectly spontaneous. It was almost impossible for him to conceal his emotions. This remark applies more especially to the first forty years of his life; later, he was less apt to show his feelings.—MARCOU, JULES, 1895, *Life, Letters, and Works of Louis Agassiz, vol.* II, *p.* 217.

If ever a man made nature give up her secrets, that man was Agassiz. He was large, hearty, and most agreeable. His sympathy amounted to enthusiasm. He had polite French manners, and left you with the impression that you had contributed very largely to his stock of information. . . . The nation was listening with hand behind her ear, and Nature threw her sea-urchins and starfish and every fish suspected of any eccentricity at his feet. He gave lectures all over the country, and told me that he could invoke sleep when he needed it, even to sleeping when standing up. His health seemed to be perfect. He gave one the idea of an immense and very agreeable boy who somehow had come to know everything, not by the usual hard penance of learning it at a school, but by intuition.—SHERWOOD, MARY E. W., 1897, *An Epistle to Posterity, pp.* 121, 122.

He was the largest in personality and in universality of knowledge of all the men I have ever known. No one who did not know him personally can conceive the hold he had on those who came into relations with him. His vast knowledge of scientific facts, and his ready command of them for all educational purposes, his enthusiasm for science and the diffusion of it, even his fascinating way of imparting it to others, had even less to do with his popularity than the magnetism of his presence, and the sympathetic faculty which enabled him to find at once the plane on which he should meet every one with whom he had to deal.

—STILLMAN, WILLIAM JAMES, 1900, *Autobiography, Atlantic Monthly, vol.* 85, *p.* 623.

The Goethean face and figure of Louis Agassiz were in those days to be seen in the shady walks of Cambridge, to which for me they lent a Weimarish quality, in the degree that in Weimar itself, a few years ago, I felt a quality of Cambridge. Agassiz, of course, was Swiss and Latin, and not Teutonic, but he was of the Continental European civilization, and was widely different from the other Cambridge men in everything but love of the place.—HOWELLS, WILLIAM DEAN, 1900, *Some Literary Memories of Cambridge, Harper's Magazine, vol.* 101, *p.* 829.

GENERAL

It is delightful to hear all that he says on Agassiz: how very singular it is that so *eminently* clever a man, with such *immense* knowledge on many branches of Natural History, should write as he does. Lyell told me that he was so delighted with one of his (Agassiz) lectures on progressive development, &c., &c., that he went to him afterwards and told him, "that it was so delightful, that he could not help all the time wishing it was true." I seldom see a Zoological paper from North America, without observing the impress of Agassiz's doctrines — another proof, by the way, of how great a man he is.—DARWIN, CHARLES, 1854, *To J. D. Hooker, March* 26; *Life and Letters of Charles Darwin, ed. Darwin, vol.* I. *p.* 403.

He possesses not merely the talent of observation, but its genius; and hence his ability to perform the enormous tasks which he imposes on his industry. His mind is eminently large, sound, fertile, conscientious, and sagacious, quick and deep in its insight, wide in the range of its argumentation, capable equally of the minutest microscopic scrutiny and the broadest generalizations, independent of schools and systems, and inspired by that grand and ennobling love of truth which is serenely superior to fear, interest, vanity, ambition, or the desire of display.—WHIPPLE, EDWIN PERCY, 1864, *Agassiz, Character and Characteristic Men, p.* 271.

Prof. Agassiz is a naturalist who is justly world-renowned for his achievements. His contributions to geology, to paleontology, and to systematic zoology, have been such as to place him in a very high rank among contemporary naturalists. Not quite in the highest place, I should say; for, apart from all questions of theory, it is probable that Mr. Darwin's gigantic industry, his wonderful thoroughness and accuracy as an observer, and his unrivalled fertility of suggestion, will cause him in the future to be ranked along with Aristotle, Linnæus, and Cuvier; and upon this high level we cannot place Prof. Agassiz. Leaving Mr. Darwin out of the account, we may say that Prof. Agassiz stands in the first rank of contemporary naturalists. But any exceptional supremacy in this first rank can by no means be claimed for him. Both for learning and for sagacity, the names of Gray, Wyman, Huxley, Hooker, Wallace, Lubbock, Lyell, Vogt, Haeckel, and Gegenbaur, are quite as illustrious as the name of Agassiz; and we may note, in passing, that these are the names of men who openly indorse and defend the Darwinian theory. . . . There is, to the popular eye, a halo about the name of Agassiz which there is not about the name of Gray; though, if there is any man now living in America, of whom America might justly boast as her chief ornament and pride, so far as science is concerned, that man is unquestionably Prof. Asa Gray. . . Agassiz has long been accustomed to making profoundly dark metaphysical phrase do the work which properly belongs to observation and deduction—FISKE, JOHN, 1873, *Agassiz and Darwinism, Popular Science Monthly, vol. 3, pp.* 693, 705.

He became a master of English composition, and spoke the language not only with fluency, but with a voluble eloquence which was peculiarly his own. He studied the modes of thought among the people, and learned to know in what they differed from the European. His family ties, his household, his associates were of the country; and yet, after all, he was unchanged. A genius like his could put itself in communication with many and different people; it could grow also, but it could not change.—LYMAN, THEODORE, 1874, *Recollections of Agassiz, Atlantic Monthly, vol.* 33.

The history of his work in the twenty-five years of his life in this country is too familiar to require a detailed statement; it is sufficient to say that for many years he was esteemed by universal consent the foremost *savant* in the United States and the peer of the greatest of the brotherhood in Europe. It should be added that the recent rapid

growth of popular interest in science and the establishment and gratifying progress of many scientific institutions in this country are fairly attributable to his example and influence. Long before his emigration to America Agassiz had become a famous author, and had won an enviable fame in connection with the Glacial Theory, which he promulgated in 1837.—CATHCART, GEORGE R., 1874, *ed. The Literary Reader, p.* 199.

Said the master to the youth:
"We have come in search of truth,
Trying with uncertain key
Door by door of mystery;
We are reaching, through His laws,
To the garment-hem of Cause,
Him, the endless, unbegun,
The Unnamable, the One
Light of all our light the Source,
Life of life, and Force of force.
As with fingers of the blind,
We are groping here to find
What the hieroglyphics mean
Of the Unseen in the seen,
What the Thought which underlies
Nature's masking and disguise,
What it is that hides beneath
Blight and bloom and birth and death.
By past efforts unavailing,
Doubt and error, loss and failing,
Of our weakness made aware,
On the threshold of our task
Let us light and guidance ask,
Let us pause in silent prayer."

—WHITTIER, JOHN GREENLEAF, 1874, *The Prayer of Agassiz.*

The name of Agassiz, for twenty years intimately connected with the history of science in America, has nevertheless retained its popularity in Switzerland, where his works have a great celebrity. It is in our country that he was born, in our country he acquired renown, and Switzerland can never forget that he is among the number of her children. Without other resource than his intelligence and his energy, he rose to the first rank among the eminent men of science of our country. . . . The work he executed in the field of zoology and of paleontology is of very high importance. He possessed the double merit of accomplishing great things himself, and of knowing how to make science popular without diminishing its prestige. . . . In Switzerland, in Germany, in England, in America, in every country where he took up his abode he made himself the center of the scientific movement and succeeded in interesting the public.—FAVRE, ERNEST, 1877–78, *Louis Agassiz, tr. Henry, Smithsonian Institution Report*, pp. 236, 261.

Agassiz was born a naturalist as Raphael was born a painter. Nature was his first and last love; to live with her and study her was his life. His allegiance to her was unreserved. To be false to nature, or to belittle her—to warp her teachings, or to set them aside—was an offense which he resented almost as a personal one to himself. One of his last sayings (in the Atlantic Monthly) was that "philosophers and theologians have still to learn that a physical fact is as sacred as a moral principle." Nature was his main teacher. From her he knew God as a personal mind; all wise, all powerful. Each specific form of plant or animal was to him a thought of God. The life system was God's connected system of thought, realized by His power in time and space. These forms were not the result of blind physical forces. To these he conceded no power to produce any change in their permanent specific types. New species were new creations. Hence his constant and resolute opposition to Darwinism and to all evolution hypotheses. This zoölogical view he applied equally to mankind. Though a believer in the psychological unity of mankind, he maintained the doctrine of an original variety in the different types of man.—GUYOT, ARNOLD, 1878, *Memoir of Louis Agassiz Read before the National Academy, April, Biographical Memoirs, vol. II, p. 72.*

In a small circle of naturalists, almost the first that was assembled to greet him on his coming to this country, and of which the writer is the sole survivor, when Agassiz was inquired of as to his conception of "species," he sententiously replied: "A species is a thought of the Creator." To this thoroughly theistic conception he joined the scientific deduction which he had already been led to draw, that the animal species of each geological age, or even stratum, were different from those preceding and following, and also unconnected by natural derivation. And his very last published words reiterated his steadfast conviction that "there is no evidence of a direct descent of later from earlier species in the geological succession of animals." Indeed, so far as we know, he would not even admit that such "thoughts of the Creator" as these might have been actualized in the natural course of events. If he had accepted such a view, and if he had himself apprehended and developed in his own way the now well-nigh assured significance of some of his early and pregnant generalizations, the history of the doctrine of development would have been different from what it is, a different spirit and another name would have been prominent in it, and Agassiz would not have passed away while fighting what he felt to be—at least for the present—a losing battle. It is possible that the "whirligig of time" may still "bring in his revenges," but not very probable.—GRAY, ASA, 1886, *Louis Agassiz, Andover Review, vol. 5, p. 38.*

There can be no doubt that the vessel which brought Louis Agassiz to our shores brought a scientific intelligence and scientific force which outvalued not only all the rest of the cargo, but of a thousand ordinary cargoes. In getting thorough possession of him, in making him an American citizen, and in resolutely refusing, with his hearty concurrence, to deliver him up to the country which afterward claimed his services, the United States must be considered to have made a good bargain. He was too poor when he arrived here to pay any "duties" into the Treasury; but the impulse he gave to science in this country enriched us in a degree that cannot be measured by any money standard. . . . It was my good fortune to meet him often during the last twenty-five years of his life; but my first impression—the impression of the comprehensiveness of his mind—was more and more confirmed as I came to know him more intimately. All the facts and principles of his special science were systematized in his vast and joyous memory, so that he was ever ready to reply to any unexpected question concerning the most obscure nooks and corners of natural history; but in replying, he ever indicated that his immense grasp of the details of his science was free from any disposition to exaggerate any detail out of its connections. No isolated fact could exist in his mind. The moment it was apprehended, it fell easily into relationship to the throng of other facts quietly stored in his broad intelligence, and became one of a group which illustrated a principle. His knowledge of particulars was extensive, minute, and accurate.—WHIPPLE, EDWIN PERCY, 1886, *Recollections of Eminent Men*, pp. 78, 81.

It is the picture of a sweet, strong nature turning in its first young simplicity to noble things, and keeping its simplicity through a long life by its perpetual association with them. It is a human creature loving the earth almost as we can imagine that a beast loves it, and yet at the same time studying it like a wise man. The sea and the glacier tell him their secrets. In his very dreams the extinct fishes build again for him their lost construction.— BROOKS, PHILLIPS, 1886, *Biography, Essays and Addresses, p.* 442.

The title of any scientist to greatness must be determined, not so much by the multitude of new facts he has discovered as by the new laws he has established, and especially by the new methods he has inaugurated or perfected. Now, I think it can be shown that to Agassiz, more than to any other man, is due the credit of having *established the laws of succession of living forms* in the geological history of the earth —laws upon which must rest any true theory of evolution. Also, that to him, more than to any other man, is due the credit of having *perfected the method* (method of comparison) by the use of which alone biological science has advanced so rapidly in modern times. . . . It is evident that Agassiz laid the whole foundation of evolution, solid and broad, but refused to build any scientific structure on it; he refused to recognize the legitimate, the scientifically necessary outcome of his own work. Nevertheless without his work a scientific theory of evolution would have been impossible. Without Agassiz (or his equivalent), there would have been no Darwin. There is something to us supremely grand in this refusal of Agassiz to accept the theory of evolution. The opportunity to become the leader of modern thought, the foremost man of the century, was in his hands, and he refused, because his religious, or, perhaps better, his philosophic intuitions, forbade. To Agassiz, and, indeed, to all men of that time, to many, alas! even now, evolution is materialism. But materialism is Atheism.—LE CONTE, JOSEPH, 1888, *Evolution and its Relation to Religious Thought, pp.* 37, 44.

And what of Agassiz?   No more he leads
His pupils to the sea-girt Penikese,
That there, alone with nature, they may seek
To know her better, and from her may learn
The hidden thoughts of God.   The dashing waves

That beat against that rocky island, chant,
In ceaseless monotone, no requiem sad
O'er him departed.   Their far-sounding roar
Rings out the glorious anthem, "Victory."
His work is finished here.   For seventy years
He toiled in patience, and rejoiced to find
In nature ever some new voice that told
Of skill creative. While he found no time
To coin his rarest gifts of heart and brain
For gold, to those who eagerly desired
To know the truth, he freely gave his best.
O'er such a one, gone from us, sorrow not
Nor wish him back.   He did full well the work
Committed to his trust, and laid it down
With joy when came the summons to depart.
He is not dead.   His influence lives with us
To-day.   We hear his voice, and well for us,
If hearing, we shall heed and understand.
He lives with God.   With eyes undimmed by scales
Of flesh and sense, creation's mighty plan
Is clearer seen, and well he knows, ere now,
How much was true of all he tried to teach.
Like him may we, with meek humility,
Endeavor Nature's sacred truths to know;
Like him, find God revealed in every stone,
And bow in reverence at his mighty power.
   —COOLEY, JAMES A., 1892, *Agassiz.*

He was above all else a teacher. His work in America was that of a teacher of science,—of science in the broadest sense as the orderly arrangement of the results of all human experience. He would teach men to know, not simply to remember or to guess. He believed that men in all walks of life would be more useful and more successful through the thorough development of the powers of observation and judgment. He believed that the sense of reality should be the central axis of human life. He would have the student trained through contact with real things, not merely exercised in the recollection of the book descriptions of things. "If you study Nature in books," he said, "when you go out of doors you cannot find her."—JORDAN, DAVID STARR, 1892-96, *Science Sketches, p.* 134.

In a single chapter it is impossible to give more than a suggestion of the works of Louis Agassiz, but a study of his bibliography shows him to have been one of the most exhaustive and comprehensive thinkers in the field of science that any age has produced. — HOLDER, CHARLES FREDERICK, 1893, *Louis Agassiz (Leaders in Science), p.* 217.

A man of transcendent genius for scientific discovery, with intense earnestness and enthusiasm for the pursuit of truth, and rare eloquence and literary skill. If any man was devoted to the cause of truth and determined to accept it whatever it might prove to be, that man was Agassiz; for while his impulses were notably devout and reverential, he proved, on many occasions, that he was fearless and independent in the search for truth. It is no disparagement to Buckland, and Bell, and Chalmers, and the other authors of the Bridgewater Treatises to assert that Agassiz far surpassed them all in acquaintance with the methods which lead to success in the interpretation of nature, and in ability to treat the problems of natural theology from the standpoint of the zoölogist.—BROOKS, WILLIAM KEITH, 1899, *The Foundations of Zoölogy*, p. 318.

Agassiz is studying not the human but the divine mind, and the result is doubly startling. We are not apt to think of mysticism and anthropomorphism together, but with Agassiz we find them inextricably mixed. It is easy to put what we may choose to call Agassiz's real meaning into terms which his opponents would accept. But it is not easy to convince ourselves that he would have accepted any such interpretation, nor is it easy to juggle his distinct and repeated statements into any shape which shall avoid his plain acceptance of a Deity as frankly anthropomorphic as ever child addressed in prayer or painter throned on clouds.—GOULD, ALICE BACHE, 1900, *Louis Agassiz (Beacon Biographies)*, p. 125.

David Livingstone
1813–1873

Born, at Blantyre, 19 March 1813. Worked in cotton factory in Glasgow, 1823–38. Attended classes at Anderson College and Glasgow University, 1836–38. Training for Missionary, under auspices of London Missionary Soc., Sept. 1838 to Nov. 1840. Licentitate of Faculty of Physicians, Glasgow Univ., Nov. 1840. Ordained Missionary, 20 Nov. 1840. Sailed for Cape of Good Hope, 8 Dec. 1840. Missionary and Exploring labours in South and Central Africa, 1841–56. Married Mary Moffat, 1844. Hon. LL.D., Glasgow, Dec. 1854. In England, 1856–57. Gold Medal, Royal Geog. Soc., 15 Dec. 1856. Freedom of City of London, 21 May 1857; of Cities of Glasgow, Edinburgh, and Dundee, 1857. Hon. D. C. L., Oxford, 1857. F. R. S., 1857. Exploring in Africa, 1858–64. In England, July 1864 to Aug. 1865. In India, Sept. 1865 to Jan. 1866. Resumed exploration in Africa, April 1866. Relieved by H. M. Stanley, Oct. 1871. Died, in Africa, 1 May 1873. Buried in Westminster Abbey, 18 April 1874. *Works:* "Missionary Travels and Researches in South Africa," 1857; "Cambridge Lectures," 1858; "Narrative on an Expedition to the Zambesi" (with C. Livingstone), 1865. *Posthumous:* "Last Journals," ed. by H. Waller (2 vols.), 1874. *Life:* by J. Marrat, 1877; by W. G. B. Blaikie, 1888; by Thomas Hughes, 1891.—SHARP, R. FARQUHARSON, 1897, *A Dictionary of English Authors*, p. 170.

PERSONAL

Dr. Livingstone tall, thin, earnest-looking, and business-like; far more given, I should say, to do his work than to talk about it.—FOX, CAROLINE, 1857, *Memories of Old Friends*, ed. Pym, *Journal*, Aug. 28, p. 337.

A figure of medium height, the tough wiry frame denoting great powers of endurance, the left arm, slightly shortened, recalling the perilous encounter with the lion; firmset features, weather-beaten and browned though not roughened by exposure, passive and thoughtful rather than demonstrative, the eyes' keen glance, and a rapidly changing expression, betraying furtive enthusiasm: a low voice, winning address, manners quiet, frank, and un-

affected, even reserved; such was David Livingstone as he is remembered in his favourite dress of rough blue naval cloth, the jacket short, and the low cap of the same material, surrounded by a broad silver band. Nor is it easy to forget the kindliness of disposition, and the readiness to give sympathy wherever there was zeal, though hesitation, or a self-sparing timidity was derided as much as it was despised. Full of courage and self-reliant, he expects to find something of a like spirit in others; and he gives them credit for it, never assuming backwardness or incapacity, but sternly meeting and dealing with it when its existence is perceived. With a fund of quiet humour—and sarcasm, too, if he pleased—Livingstone possessed a keen sense of the ridiculous, and entered thoroughly into a joke. He might often be seen talking to the Makololo he had brought down from the country of Sekeletu, and their attention and respect as they listened or replied to him plainly showed the influence he had with them. Indeed, one of Livingstone's strongest points, and one that has conduced, no doubt, as much to his safety as his success, is his power of understanding and dealing with the natives, and of winning their confidence while he overawes their truculence.—PROCTER, L. J., 1872, *Dr. Livingstone, Fraser's Magazine, vol.* 86, *p.* 621.

Dr. Livingstone is about sixty years old, though after he was restored to health he appeared more like a man who had not passed his fiftieth year. His hair has a brownish colour yet, but is here and there streaked with grey lines over the temples; his whiskers and moustache are very grey. He shaves his chin daily. His eyes, which are hazel, are remarkably bright; he has a sight keen as a hawk's. His teeth alone indicate the weakness of age; the hard fare of Lunda has made havoc in their lines. His form, which soon assumed a stoutish appearance, is a little over the ordinary height with the slightest possible bow in the shoulders. When walking he has a firm but heavy tread, like that of an overworked or fatigued man. . . . There is a good-natured *abandon* about Livingstone which was not lost on me. Whenever he began to laugh, there was a contagion about it, that compelled me to imitate him. It was such a laugh as Herr Teufelsdröckh's —a laugh of the whole man from head to heel. . . . The wan features which had shocked me at first meeting, the heavy step which told of age and hard travel, the grey beard and bowed shoulders, belied the man. Underneath that well-worn exterior lay an endless fund of high spirits and inexhaustible humor; that rugged frame of his enclosed a young and most exuberant soul. . . . The study of Dr. Livingstone would not be complete if we did not take the religious side of his character into consideration. His religion is not of the theoretical kind, but it is a constant, earnest, sincere practice. It is neither demonstrative nor loud, but manifests itself in a quiet, practical way, and is always at work. It is not aggressive, which sometimes is troublesome, if not impertinent. In him,

religion exhibits its loveliest features; it governs his conduct not only towards his servants, but towards the natives, the bigoted Mohammedans, and all who came in contact with him. Without it, Livingstone, with his ardent temperament, his enthusiasm, his high spirit and courage, must have become uncompanionable, and a hard master. Religion has tamed him, and made him a Christian gentleman: the crude and wilful have been refined and subdued; religion has made him the most companionable of men and indulgent of masters—a man whose society is pleasureable. In Livingstone I have seen many amiable traits. His gentleness never forsakes him; his hopefulness never deserts him. No harassing anxieties, distraction of mind, long separation from home and kindred, can make him complain. He thinks "all will come out right at last;" he has such faith in the goodness of Providence.—STANLEY, HENRY MORTON, 1872, *How I Found Livingstone, pp.* 348, 349, 350, 351.

𝔅𝔯𝔬𝔲𝔤𝔥𝔱 𝔟𝔶 𝔣𝔞𝔦𝔱𝔥𝔣𝔲𝔩 𝔥𝔞𝔫𝔡𝔰
𝔬𝔟𝔢𝔯 𝔩𝔞𝔫𝔡 𝔞𝔫𝔡 𝔰𝔢𝔞,
𝔥𝔢𝔯𝔢 𝔯𝔢𝔰𝔱𝔰
𝔇𝔞𝔟𝔦𝔡 𝔏𝔦𝔟𝔦𝔫𝔤𝔰𝔱𝔬𝔫𝔢,
𝔪𝔦𝔰𝔰𝔦𝔬𝔫𝔞𝔯𝔶, 𝔱𝔯𝔞𝔟𝔢𝔩𝔩𝔢𝔯, 𝔭𝔥𝔦𝔩𝔞𝔫𝔱𝔥𝔯𝔬𝔭𝔦𝔰𝔱,
𝔟𝔬𝔯𝔫 𝔐𝔞𝔯𝔠𝔥 19, 1813,
𝔞𝔱 𝔅𝔩𝔞𝔫𝔱𝔶𝔯𝔢, 𝔏𝔞𝔫𝔞𝔢𝔨𝔰𝔥𝔦𝔯𝔢,
𝔇𝔦𝔢𝔡 𝔐𝔞𝔶 4, 1873.
𝔄𝔱 𝔒𝔨𝔦𝔱𝔞𝔪𝔟𝔬'𝔰 𝔟𝔦𝔩𝔩𝔞𝔤𝔢, 𝔍𝔩𝔞𝔩𝔞,

For thirty years his life was spent in an unwearied effort to evangelise the native races, to explore the undiscovered secrets, and abolish the desolating slave-trade of Central Africa, where, with his last words, he wrote: "All I can say in my solitude is, may Heaven's rich blessing come down on every one— American, English, Turk—who will help to heal this open sore of the world."
—INSCRIPTION ON TOMB, 1873, *Westminster Abbey.*

The greatest man of his generation, for Dr. Livingstone stood alone. There are few enough, but a few statesmen. There are few enough, but a few great in medicine, or in art, or in poetry. There are a few great travellers. But Dr. Livingstone stood alone as the great Missionary Traveller, the bringer-in of civilisation; or rather the pioneer of civilisation—he that cometh before — to races lying in darkness. I always think of him as what John the Baptist, had he been living in the nineteenth century, would have been.—NIGHTINGALE, FLORENCE, 1874, *Letter to Miss*

Livingstone, Feb. 18; *The Personal Life of David Livingstone by W. G. Blaikie, p.* 458.

The traveller being completely successful, it appeared to the Royal Geographical Society that their alliance with him would be mutually advantageous. Both sought notoriety, which might be best attained by a joint effort. The one could address the public, play the patron's part, and play it well. The other, as a novice about to appear before the public, and as a Scot, much desired a patron. To rouse the public a moving speech was necessary. The traveller was, therefore, introduced as an extraordinary man, who had done wonders, and had marvellous escapes. . . . Attention was never fixed on any one point in the history of his achievements. Not a word was said about truth or authenticity. The spirit of enquiry was kept at a distance. As sensation and pathos usually go hand in hand, the President (Sir R. Murchison) immediately conceived the warmest friendship for the inimitable traveller; and whenever the merits of the latter were discussed in a tone which showed a tendency to become actually critical, a soothing silence was soon brought about by the outpouring of heartfelt affection from the chair. To exaltation of this kind; to the incessant puffing of the good, the great, the noble-minded Livingstone, continued for twenty years, and to nothing else, is due the traveller's unparalleled celebrity. — COOLEY, WILLIAM DESBOR-OUGH, 1874, *Dr. Livingstone and the Royal Geographical Society, p.* 26.

Of Livingstone's character it is difficult for those who knew him intimately to speak without appearance of exaggeration. Of his intellectual force and energy he has given such proof as few men can afford. Any five years of his life might, in any other occupation, have established a character, and raised for him a fortune, such as none but the most energetic of our race can realise. His powers of observation and practical sagacity I have never seen exceeded. Both, possibly, were rendered more acute by the life he led; but he had the quickness of eye and the power of judging of forces and results which belong only to the great organizer. politician, or general. Equally remarkable was his knowledge of character and penetration. No flattery could blind him, no allurements could lead him aside; his estimate of men was unfail-

ing. But his great characteristic was his perfect simplicity and single-mindedness.— FRERE, SIR BARTLE, 1874, *Dr. Livingstone, Good Words, vol.* 15, p. 285.

The heart of David Livingstone was laid under the mvula tree in Ilala, and his bones in Westminster Abbey; but his spirit marched on. The history of his life is not completed with the record of his death. The continual cry of his heart to be permitted to finish his work was answered, answered thoroughly, though not in the way he thought of. The thrill that went through the civilised world when his death and all its touching circumstances became known, did more for Africa than he could have done had he completed his task and spent years in this country following it up. From the worn-out figure kneeling at the bedside in the hut in Ilala, an electric spark seemed to fly, quickening hearts on every side. The statesman felt it; it put new vigour into the dispatches he wrote and the measures he devised with regard to the slave-trade. The merchant felt it, and began to plan in earnest how to traverse the continent with roads and railways, and open it to commerce from shore to centre. The explorer felt it, and started with high purpose on new scenes of unknown danger. The missionary felt it,—felt it a reproof of past languor and unbelief, and found himself lifted up to a higher level of faith and devotion. No parliament of philanthropy was held; but the verdict was as unanimous and as hearty as if the Christian world had met and passed the resolution—"Livingstone's work shall not die:—AFRICA SHALL LIVE."—BLAIKIE, WILLIAM GARDEN, 1880, *The Personal Life of David Livingstone, p.* 461.

Between Blantyre Spinning Mill and Westminster Abbey Livingstone had just half a century of working life. Did any of his illustrious fellow-slumberers in the silent congregation leave a better record for the fifty years? None have better earned their fame than he, and few, if any, have as well earned their repose.—SMILES, ROBERT, 1885, *David Livingstone* (*The World's Workers*), p. 128.

Has not the experience of every martyr been the same? The more perfect the self-sacrifice in life, the more surely would this shadow seem to have hung over the last **hours of the world's best and bravest, the** only perfect life being not only no exception, but the great exemplar of the law. It is written "Except a grain of wheat die it beareth no fruit." Never were those mighty words illustrated more perfectly than in the death of David Livingstone. The first-fruits ripened within a few hours of the master's death. Susi and Chumah called the men together outside the hut. Not a man of the fifty-six faltered for a moment: they had learned much in those nine months. "You are old men," they said, "in travelling and hardships. You must be our chiefs. We will do whatever you order." — HUGHES, THOMAS, 1889, *David Livingstone, p.* 193.

Almost in the centre of this newest addition to the Queen's vast Empire, near the southern shores of Lake Bangweolo, the heart and entrails of Livingstone were buried. To this shrine, it may be—unless all sentiment is repressed by a bran-new civilisation—tribes of Africans will come to pay a pilgrimage of respect to the memory of their great advocate. Possibly over this spot we may raise a temple or place a statue; or it may be—and more likely—that in the gold-rush, in the land-grabbing, in the coffee-planting, sugar-baking, and the prosaic prosperity that will undoubtedly some day fill this land, the local inhabitants will be too material-minded, too busy, too mean, to spend their money or thought on sentiment or statues or monuments; but, to quote the last stanza of the fine memorial verses which *Punch* offered up to the dead Livingstone—

"He needs no epitaph to guard a name
　Which men shall praise while worthy work
　　is done;
He lived and died for good—be that his fame:
　Let marble crumble; this is LIVING-STONE."
—JOHNSTON, H. H., 1891, *Livingstone and the Exploration of Central Africa, p.* 367.

To our pleasure-loving generation comes the career of David Livingstone, telling us that the age of heroism has not ended and must not end. If for the countless millions of the Dark Continent Livingstone's legend has become a "pillar of cloud by day and a pillar of fire by night," leading them out of the bondage and the wilderness, his influence upon civilized nations has been scarcely less, rebuking our ease and smiting self-indulgence. For courage in Livingstone was as high and fine as in Sir Galahad of old. Heroism was in his blood like iron,

in his eye like fire, in his voice like the trumpet call. This man, who flung himself upon the African slave traffic, and single-handed determined to give a continent to commerce and Christianity—this scarred hero differs from our perfumed effeminates as an ironclad differs from a pleasure yacht, as a piece of iron from a painted lath, as Cromwell differs from some Beau Brummell. History holds no career so strangely marked by heroic adventure and hairbreadth escapes, perils in jungle and perils in swamp, perils of the lion's stroke and the serpent's bite, perils of war-clubs and poisoned arrows, perils of dwarfs in forests and strong men in the hill country. —HILLIS, NEWELL DWIGHT, 1899, *Great Books as Life-Teachers, p.* 281.

This was on 20th November, 1840. On 8th December he set sail for South Africa. The Rev. Dr. David Livingstone was then in his twenty-eighth year. He was a strongly built man of middle height; broad shouldered, deep chested, sound in every fibre. He had a plain, frank countenance. His eyes were hazel coloured, and of remarkable power and keenness. His most noticeable feature they were; and their frequent flashes of kindliness and quiet humour relieved the sternness which firmly defined brows, a massive jaw, and a rounded chin gave to his face. He was direct and simple in speecch, in manner, and in all his ways. There was not a shred of formalism in his nature. He cared nothing for mere outward appearance, so be it that his work was thoroughly done. He had not the faintest trace of professionalism about him, and was rather averse to wearing the distinctive clerical garb. When he was mauled by the lion at Mabotsa he wore a tartan coat. When he went out on his last expedition, and had given to him the post of honorary consul, he was attired in a blue surtout with gilt buttons, shepherd-tartan trousers, and a peaked cap with a gold band. And when Stanley found him on the shores of Lake Tanganyika, the worn old veteran was dressed in grey tweed trousers, a red-sleeved waistcoat, and a faded, weather beaten, blue gold-banded cap.—MAC-LACHLAN, T. BANKS, 1901, *David Livingstone (Famous Scots Series), p.* 15.

GENERAL

Poor Livingstone, he little thought what it was to write a book when he began!—

OWEN, RICHARD, 1857, *Letter, July; Life, by Rev. Richard Owen, vol.* II, *p.* 62.

It has been said of him, with much truth, that as an explorer he stands in the highest rank, and as a geographer in the very lowest. His chief defect is a total want, and apparently a strong dislike, of preliminary information. He knows nothing of what has been already effected, by travel or study, in the field of his labours, and seems determined to remain ignorant. Regardless of all preceding authorities, he speaks in the character of a great discoverer who addresses a totally ignorant public. Had his volumes of Missionary Travels been prepared for the press with the utmost critical rigour, it would not have thereby suffered from abridgement, nor would any amount of correction have diminished the brilliancy of his achievements. His remarks on natural history gained in copiousness as well as correctness from the conscientious revision of a sincere friend. But his geographical advisers, on whom he probably placed implicit reliance, gave him flattery without stint, but not a particle of literary assistance. Hence the volume in question was, in all that relates to geography, an unparalleled collection of mistakes and misstatements.—COOLEY, WILLIAM DESBOROUGH. 1866, *Dr. Livingstone's Errors, Fortnightly Review, vol.* 4, *p.* 96.

His style as a writer is simple and unpretending, but the matter itself is sufficiently thrilling to gratify the most eager imagination. So many reports of his death have been recently published and then contradicted, that his actual existence begins to assume somewhat of a mythical character.—HART, JOHN S., 1872, *A Manual of English Literature, p.* 613.

If the letters and journals of his last journeyings contain no more than minor details of what we already know, what a vast amount of work has this one man achieved! In geography it is no exaggeration to say that to him, and to the example he set, may be fairly attributed the filling up of the blank which the maps of the interior of Africa presented to our grandfathers. It derogates nothing from Livingstone's claim to this honour that we are now aware how much was known to Portuguese travellers of a former generation. Their memories must often pay the penal-

ties imposed on them by the reticence of their government and countrymen regarding all that the Portuguese have discovered during the last century in Africa. They wished to exclude all other nations from that continent, and to keep their knowledge of the interior to themselves, and they succeeded but too well. It would be idle to estimate to what extent the misery which Africa has suffered since is due to this policy of concealment; but we may fairly credit those who have done their best to pour light into the darkness, with all the good results which are likely to follow our better acquaintance with the great central home of the negro races.—FRERE, SIR BARTLE, 1874, *Dr. Livingstone, Good Words, vol.* 15, *p.* 283.

These "Journals" are the best work that we have ever had from Livingstone's pen, but it is impossible to condemn too severely the careless, vulgar, and ignorant way in which Mr. Waller has edited them. . . . It is in the exposition of the scientific results of Livingstone's expedition that Mr. Waller most conspicuously fails. . . . He has virtually left Livingstone's notes just as he found them,—a jungle without signpost or tracks, more bewildering to the general reader than the wilds and desolate wastes through which Livingstone himself passed. . . . The narrative of Livingstone's last sufferings and death, and of the transport of his body to Zanzibar, . . . has been admirably elaborated by Mr. Waller.— BIRDWOOD, GEORGE, 1875, *The Academy, vol.* 7, *pp.* 159, 160, 161.

It is an enormous mass of raw material, ["Last Journals"] which the author alone could have put into coherent and presentable form. But the author died at his work, in the African forests; and, under the circumstances, it is matter of surprise and gratitude that the record of his labors, imperfect as it is, should have survived him and found its way back to civilization. . . . The journal is largely interspersed with religious reflections and ejaculations intended solely for Dr. Livingstone's own use. They are interesting to students of character, for they help to explain the sources of the great explorer's indomitable resolution and patience. He was an ardently sincere missionary, and he believed that he was doing his work with the eye of God constantly upon him. . . . The story of his death is compiled very successfully from the statements of those two faithful servants who made their weary pilgrimage back to Zanzibar with his remains. They found him on his knees in the attitude of prayer, beside his bed, with life extinct. This was extremely characteristic. Half the interest of this volume will be found in the reflection it offers of his devotion (when we feel we have a right to observe it), his candor, his singleness of purpose and simplicity. The combination of these qualities, with his unshrinking pluck, his extraordinary endurance, his faculty of universal observation, and of what we may call geographical constructiveness, made him of all great travellers one of the very greatest.—JAMES, HENRY, 1875, *Livingstone's Last Journals, The Nation, vol. 20, pp.* 175, 176.

Of his primary work the "record is on high," and its imperishable fruits remain on earth. The seeds of the Word of Life, implanted lovingly, with pains and labour, and above all, with faith;— the out-door scenes of the simple Sabbath service;—the testimony of HIM, to whom the worship was paid, given in words of such simplicity as were fitting to the comprehension of the dark-skinned listeners;—these seeds will not have been scattered by him in vain. Nor have they been sown in words alone, but in deeds, of which some part of the honour will redound to his successors. The teaching by forgiveness of injuries,— by trust, however unworthy the trusted,— by that confidence which imputed his own noble nature to those whom he would win, —by the practical enforcement of the fact, that a man might promise and perform, might say the thing he meant;—of this teaching by good deeds, as well as by the words of truth and love, the successor who treads in the steps of LIVINGSTONE, and accomplishes the discovery he aimed at and pointed the way to, will assuredly reap the benefit. The records of his labours for progress towards that discovery were of a more perishable kind, and their possession

is a gain beyond our expectation, or perhaps our deserts.—OWEN, SIR RICHARD, 1875, *Last Journals of David Livingstone, Quarterly Review, vol.* 138, *p.* 498.

No one would dream of accusing Livingstone of exaggeration, and the great value of his journals consists in the absolute certainty of their integrity; but the whole story of seven years' travel is a repetition of barbarity such as should dispel for ever the idea that the African race is naturally docile and ready to welcome the pioneers of civilization. . . . In closing the journals after reading his last unfinished entry, the painful impression is felt that we have just parted for ever with a loved and respected friend, and it seems hard to believe that Livingstone, whose name has been a household word for so many years, is actually gone from among us. Having carefully read every word of his long diary, we feel that we have been his companion throughout his seven years of difficulty; we have shared his emotions, his troubles, disappointments, and the short joys that so seldom came, until we almost see him die. Closing the book in sorrow, it becomes impossible to criticize now that he is dead. His geographical opinions may or may not be accepted upon all points, but there can be only one opinion concerning the man: he was the greatest of all explorers of this century; he was one of a noble army of martyrs who have devoted their lives to the holy cause of freedom; and he has laid down his life as a sacrifice upon a wild and unknown path, upon which he has printed the first footsteps of civilization.—BAKER, SAMUEL W., 1875, *The Last Journals of David Livingstone, Macmillan's Magazine, vol.* 31, *pp.* 288, 291.

No one has done more than Dr. Livingstone to acquaint us with the boundless resources of the African Continent, with the character of its inhabitants, or with the evils of the hateful slave-trade, which forms the great barrier to its civilization. —SPALDING, WILLIAM, 1882, *A History of English Literature,* 14th *Ed., p.* 436.

Samuel Wilberforce

1805–1873

Was born at Clapham, Sept. 7, 1805. In 1826 he graduated from Oriel, Oxford, with first-class honours in mathematics and second-class in classics. In December he was ordained curate of Checkendon near Henley, and in 1830 became rector of Brightsone, Isle of Wight; in 1836 was a rural dean there, and in 1839 archdeacon of Surrey. In 1840 he was appointed rector of Alberstoke and canon of Winchester, in 1841 chaplain to the Prince-Consort, in March 1845 Dean of Westminster, and in October Bishop of Oxford. He shared in the troubles of the Hampden, Gorham, "Essays and Reviews," and Colenso cases, and suffered many domestic trials, yet so governed the diocese for twenty-four years as to earn the title of "Remodeller of the Episcopate." He instituted Cuddesdon theological college (1854), and was mainly instrumental in reviving Convocation (1852). The charm of his many-sided personality, his administrative capacity, his extraordinary faculty of work, his social gifts, and his gifts as an orator were too much forgotten in the versatile ecclesiastic, nicknamed "Soapy Sam." He suffered keenly from the secession to Rome of his brother-in-law, his two brothers, his only daughter, and his son-in-law. He edited "Letters and Journals of Henry Martyn" (1837), wrote along with his brother the Life of his father (1838), and himself wrote "Agathos" (1839), "Rocky Island" (1840), and "History of the American Church" (1844), and contributed to the *Quarterly*. In 1869 he was transferred to the see of Winchester, and on 19th July 1873 was killed by falling from his horse near Dorking. He is buried at Lavington, Sussex, which he inherited through his marriage in 1828 to Emily Sargent, Cardinal Manning's sister-in-law. See "Life" by Ashwell and his eldest son (1879–82), shorter Lives by that son (1888) and Daniell (1891), and the sketch by Dean Burgon in his "Twelve Good Men" (1888).—PATRICK AND GROOME, *eds.*, 1897, *Chamber's Biographical Dictionary*, p. 970.

PERSONAL

Compounded of many simples—full of fire and impulse, yet perfect in social tact; full of drollery, but governed by a competent measure of discretion; bright, sharp and subtile, ready and graceful and full of resource in conversation; with a cordiality of manner which is very true to his nature, I dare say, though it might lead to a mistake if it were understood as expressing more than mere *sociable* cordiality. I can easily suppose, however, that there are depths in his nature, and that there may be some genuine and powerful feelings and affections dwelling in them.— TAYLOR, SIR HENRY, 1855, *Autobiography, vol.* II, *p.* 110.

On the Sunday we had a sermon from the Bishop of Oxford, and I was immensely struck by his consummate style of pulpit eloquence—familiar without approaching the verge of vulgarity, didactic without the slightest boredom, fervid and touching without bombast, altogether a *maître accompli*, and one could not help lamenting that he should not have been at the Bar, or in the House of Commons, for he certainly would have been Prime Minister or Lord Chancellor by this time. He is a capital story-teller, too, inimitable at the breakfast table or when the dinner cloth is removed. Altogether too strenuous, too good and too bad for the feeble *rôle* of an Anglican bishop. As a cardinal in the days when Rome had power, or a prize fighter in the great political ring, he would have had scope for his energies.— MOTLEY, JOHN LOTHROP, 1867, *Letter to his Wife, Aug.* 20; *Correspondence, ed. Curtis, vol.* II, *p.* 285.

He was a man of great mark, and now that he is gone, people admit this more freely than they did. He took such a leading part, that of course he came into violent collision with great numbers; and he was so abounding in resources of all kinds, that it was easy to say that he was too clever in all ways. But the truth is that he was a statesman, and a statesman's ways in great religious divisions are liable to offend people of strong, simple, perhaps one-sided, religious ideas. He was, I believe, a thoroughly sincere man, with a very lofty and large idea of the religious aims to which he devoted his life. He was a man of very large sympathies, of untiring interest in all that interested mankind—too extensive, perhaps, in his interests for any deep and accurate knowledge—a very strong, bold, and earnest man. Of all men of his time he comes next to Gladstone as a man of inexhaustible powers of work.—CHURCH, RICHARD WILLIAM, 1873, *To Dr. Asa Gray, July* 25; *Life and Letters of Dean Church, ed. his Daughter, p.* 284.

I altogether sympathize in what you say of poor Sam of Winchester. The event is pitiful, tragical and altogether sadder to me than I could have expected. He was far from being a bad man, and was a most dexterous, stout, and clever one, and I have often exchanged pleasant dialogues with him for the last thirty years—finished now—silent for all eternity! I find he was really of religious nature, and thought in secret, in spite of his bishophood, very much in regard to religion as we do.— CARLYLE, THOMAS, 1873, *Letter to Froude*,

July 29; *Thomas Carlyle, History of his Life in London, ed. Froude, vol.* II, *p.* 358.

Those who witnessed the Bishop's power and prowess in debate might think that he was nothing more than a Parliamentary debater; those who knew nothing but the brilliancy of his social qualities—exceeded by none, if equalled by any, in his generation—might fail to appreciate the loftiness of his aims, and the true purpose and constant employment of his life. In these things he was great; but those who formed their judgment of him from these things alone, or from these things mainly, would misunderstand the man. . . . Were I asked to name the most remarkable of all the characteristics of Bishop Wilberforce, I think I should state it to be this—that while, to a degree surpassing every other man, his time and his mind were apparently absorbed in the great concerns of his diocese and of the Church at large; he, more than any other person I have ever known, seemed to retain a close, intimate, and detailed knowledge of all that was happening in the circles of private life to every one whom he knew. These things never faded from his memory, and he entered into them from day to day with a strength of sympathy and a minutely clear recollection that would have been astonishing even in an unoccupied man. . . . Who can count the numbers—they are not in hundreds, they are not in thousands, they are in hundreds of thousands—who in every part of this country listened from time to time to the tones of that silver voice now stilled among us, sometimes like a murmuring brook, sometimes like a trumpet-call? No spot in this land, I may say, can be found—certainly none where there is any considerable concentration of the people—in which that extraordinary influence of his has not been brought to bear, and there was not one in which, when he visited it, he did not seem to spend his entire self on the purpose which he had before him, as though nothing had come before it in his life, and nothing was to come after it.
—GLADSTONE, WILLIAM EWART, 1873, *Speech on the Inauguration of the Wilberforce Memorial Fund, Dec.* 3.

Of a temperament peculiarly mobile and sympathetic, his nature answered to every touch from without as instantaneously as the æolian harp answers to each breath of air. Each character with which he came in contact drew forth its own response, so that there were almost as many estimates formed of him as there were persons with whom he had to do. Intensely affectionate, and with a passionate craving for the sympathy which he gave so readily, he was capable also of the sternest severity and of a tenacity of purpose which no desire for the approbation even of his dearest friends could divert for a moment. Singularly honest in his own purposes, he was not unfrequently mistaken in placing confidence in others, although usually a keen judge of character; and he was capable of the most vehement indignation when face to face with meanness or duplicity. Similar traits marked his intellectual character. Great power of concentration was combined with an incessant readiness to turn aside to fasten upon any new object which came before him. He took an interest in everything. His observation was sleepless, and made him an excellent naturalist. If you were driving with him across a country that was new to him, the conversation would be again and again interrupted by some remark upon its geology or its vegetation. His inquisitiveness of mind was extreme, and habit had developed the natural faculty of extracting from every one whom he met whatever special information could be derived from him. In his earlier days he may have been somewhat over-bold in action, but from the first he was cautious in counsel, and his balance of judgment would have made him an admirable casuist.
—ASHWELL, A. R., 1879, *Life of the Right Reverend Samuel Wilberforce, D.D., Introduction, vol.* I, *p.* xiv.

Wilberforce had quite a royal memory of persons and trivial associations which was essentially useful to him in his episcopal intercourse, and not without its advantage in the general London world where small people were flattered by his immediate recognition of themselves and their concerns.—MILNES, RICHARD MONCKTON (LORD HOUGHTON), 1880, *Samuel Wilberforce, Bishop of Oxford and Winchester, Fortnightly Review, vol.* 33, *p.* 355.

In his own generation—the generation which is now just disappearing—he was one of the most conspicuous and remarkable figures—remarkable not more for the quantity of his powers than for their surprising variety. He was a good preacher and a still better platform speaker, who drew immense audiences wherever he went; moving men, and still more women, not so much by his argument as by his skill in touching the emotions. He was an unwearied ecclesiastical politician, always involved in discussions and controversies, sometimes, it was thought, in intrigues; without whom nothing was done in Convocation, nor, where Church interests were involved, in the House of Lords. In literature he was not idle, for besides producing a Life of his father, the famous philanthropist and abolitionist, he wrote religious tales, and not seldom contributed articles, whose anonymous character was soon stripped off, to the *Quarterly Review*. However, it was as a man of society that his fame was perhaps greatest. He was not merely a brilliant talker, full of anecdotes and ideas, admirably quick in repartee, but also, what many good talkers are not, a most agreeable companion, whose charm of manner could hardly be resisted even by those who came inclined to distrust him. There was a brightness and flow about his conversation, together with a sympathetic way of putting things, which made him more sought after for dinner parties, or as a guest at country houses, than any one else in England. There was probably no other public man, and certainly no other ecclesiastic, who was so constantly in the public eye, whose doings were watched with so much curiosity and excited so much controversy. In spite of his winning ways, he had many enemies; for he was a strong partisan, dealt hard blows, and was deemed, not only by his opponents, but by some of his friends, to be neither straightforward nor trustworthy. His abilities no one could deny. But was he sincere? Was he truthful? Was his ecclesiastical zeal the outcome of real religious feeling or only an engine of personal ambition? Could a man externally so worldly, and at least as welcome among worldlings as to the good, be really pious? These were the questions which the mention of his name never failed to raise, and which were debated with that zest which specially belongs to personal questions.— BRYCE, JAMES, 1883, *Two Biographies, The Nation, vol.* 36, *p.* 250.

He was neither a great reader nor a mere student nor a profound thinker, but he was a man of action, and public questions were his delight. If he had any relaxations he found them in botany, and especially in ornithology. Then, as all his life through, his love of birds as well as his knowledge of their notes and habits were most remarkable. Once indeed he was known to have forgiven a little boy for the heinous offence of breaking through a hedge because he did it to show the bishop a rare bird. . . . Our view is that Samuel Wilberforce, after his adversaries have said their worst of him, was a very great man, an honour to the Church, and, what is better still, an ornament and even a glory to England in his generation.— DASENT, SIR G. W., 1883, *Samuel Wilberforce, Fortnightly Review, vol.* 39, *pp.* 184, 195.

I do not think that any of the numerous photographs of Bishop Wilberforce ever did him justice. How should they? You may photograph a man's features, but you cannot convey much conception of his expression. And this was his special characteristic, that his countenance changed with every emotion as his thoughts passed rapidly from the grave to the gay and from the gay to the grave. Then, no one who had not seen and heard him could have an idea of the music of his voice, the charm of his conversation, or the fascination of his manners. . . . As an orator, in spite of some mannerisms, Bishop Wilberforce was, to my thinking, never surpassed certainly by any prelate of the Church of England. Yet I never thought that his printed sermons conveyed the same impressions.—HUNTINGTON, GEORGE, 1888, *Some Recollections of Bishop Wilberforce, Temple Bar, vol.* 83, *pp.* 246, 248.

Soapy Sam. A nickname given to Bishop Samuel Wilberforce while at Oxford, and which clung to him throughout his life.— FREY, ALBERT R., 1888, *Sobriquets and Nicknames, p.* 326.

GENERAL

If Wilberforce judged himself severely he judged others no less so. He was never satisfied with the effect of his first speeches, either at public meetings or in the House of Lords, perhaps because he prepared for his first appearance more elaborately, and in the preparation excited himself with expectations which it was impossible to satisfy. And in his diary he repeatedly accuses himself, not only of worldliness and ambition, but of indolence and covetousness, faults which no one else, however malicious, would have thought of detecting. He was from the first one of the busiest and most generous of men. He believed that the clergy of a rich country ought to be richly endowed, and that any sacrifices they made should be purely voluntary. He certainly practised what he preached: during the five years that he held the rich living of Alverstoke he gave away more than two-thirds of the income, so that he might with a very good conscience obey his bishop, who thought it a plain duty to retain the living with the Deanery of Westminster.—SIMCOX, GEORGE AUGUSTUS, 1880, *Bishop Wilberforce, Macmillan's Magazine, vol.* 41, *p.* 403.

He was a very admirable preacher, though his sermons do not read as well as they "heard;" some of his devotional manuals are of great excellence; and in the heyday of High Church allegory (an interesting bywalk of literature which can only be glanced at here, but which was trodden by some estimable and even some eminent writers) he produced the well hit-off tale of "Agathos" (1839). But it may be that he will, as a writer, chiefly survive in the remarkable letters and diaries in his "Life," which are not only most valuable for the political and ecclesiastical history of the time, but precious always as human documents and sometimes as literary compositions.—SAINTSBURY, GEORGE, 1896, *A History of Nineteenth Century Literature, p.* 372.

His wit and power of expression find their best outlet in the letters which give to his "Life" a zest rare in ecclesiastical biography.—WALKER, HUGH, 1897, *The Age of Tennyson, p.* 155.

Wilberforce was at once too energetic and too resourceful a man to have justice done him till after his death. In spite of the accusation of ambition often brought against him, it is plain that the interest of the church of England alone occupied his best thoughts. He was, as he said, "no party man," but a churchman of the type of Hooker and Cosin, and had no sympathy with those whose love for ceremonial led them to favour ritualistic innovations on the suggestion of Roman doctrines. "I hate and abhor the attempt to Romanize the Church of England," were almost the last words spoken by him in the House of Lords four days before his death, and the words formed a fitting summary of the policy which he had unfalteringly pursued throughout his life. At the same time, he was quick to see in the Anglo-catholic movement a means of infusing life into a church which had not yet shaken off the apathy of Georgian times. Hence he was long hated by the evangelical party, who saw their hitherto dominant position every day slipping from them, while the firm though kindly hand with which he ruled his diocese stirred up against him many jealousies. Yet he lived down the feeling against him, and came to be recognised as in a peculiar way the representative of the English episcopate, and the prelate to whom Scottish, colonial, and American bishops naturally resorted for advice and counsel.—LEGGE, FRANCIS, 1900, *Dictionary of National Biography.*

Thomas Guthrie

1803–1873

Pulpit orator and philanthropist; son of a banker; born at Brechin, Forfarshire, Scotland, July 12, 1803; graduated at the University of Edinburgh; studied medicine in Paris; was settled at Arbirlot, in his native county, in 1830; in 1837 removed to Old Grey Friars church in Edinburgh, and in 1840 to St. John's, a new church built for him in the same city; in 1843 took a prominent part in the establishment of the Free Church; encouraged the building of manses; became in 1847 the "Apostle" of the Ragged School system; was moderator of the General Assembly in 1862; was compelled to give up public speaking in 1864, when he began to edit *The Sunday Magazine* (Edinburgh and London). He was an earnest philanthropist and social reformer, and a very brilliant orator. Among his humanitarian publications may be named "A Plea for Ragged Schools" (Edinburgh, 1847); "A Plea on Behalf of Drunkards" (1850); "The City, its Sins and Sorrows" (1857). He published also "The Gospel in Ezekiel" (1855); "Christ and the Inheritance of the Saints" (1858); and "The Way to Life" (1862). Died at St. Leonard's, Fifeshire, Feb. 24, 1873. His sons issued his "Autobiography and Memoir" in 1874 and 1875 (2 vols., London).— JACKSON, S. M., 1897, *rev. Johnson's Universal Cyclopædia, vol.* IV, *p.* 85.

PERSONAL

Practical and natural; passionate without vehemence; with perfect self-possession, and always generous and devoted, he is a very powerful preacher. His language and accent are very Scotch, but nothing can be less vulgar; and his gesture (which seems as unthought-about as a child's) is the most graceful I have ever seen in any public speaker. He deals in the broad expository Ovidian page, and is comprehended and felt by the poor woman on the steps of the pulpit as thoroughly as by the strangers who are attracted solely by his eloquence. Everything he does glows with a frank, gallant warm-heartedness, rendered more delightful by a boyish simplicity of air and style.—COCKBURN, HENRY THOMAS LORD, 1854, *Journals: Being a Continuation of the Memorials of his Time.*

At 2 [P. M.] I went to Free St. John's. Strangers (how truly I comprehend the term!) are admitted only after the first singing. I found myself waiting in a basement with about five hundred others. At length I was dragged through a narrow passage, and found myself in a very hot overcrowded house, near the pulpit. Dr. Guthrie was praying. He preached from Isaiah xliv. 22—"Return unto Me, for I have redeemed thee." It was fifty minutes, but they passed like nothing. I was instantly struck with his strong likeness to Dr. John H. Rice. If you remember him you have perfectly the type of man he is; but then it is Dr. Rice with an impetuous freedom of motion, a play of ductile and speaking features, and an overflowing unction of passion and compassion which would carry home even one of my sermons; conceive what it is with his exuberant diction and poetic imagery. The best of all is, it was honey from the comb, dropping, dropping, in effusive gospel beseeching. I cannot think Whitefield surpassed him in *this.* You know while you listen to his mighty voice, broken with sorrow, that he is overwhelmed with the "love of the Spirit." He has a colleague, and preaches only in the afternoon. As to manner, it is his own, but in general like Duff's, with as much motion, but more significant, and less grotesque, though still ungraceful. His English, moreover, is not spoiled so much. The audience was rapt and melting. It was just like his book, all application, and he rose to his height in the first

sentence. . . . Dr. Guthrie is the link between Evangelical religion and the aristocracy. People of all sects go. Nobility coming down from London and stopping here, cannot pass without hearing him. They are willing to pay any sum for pews, in order to secure an occasional hearing. Dr. G. called on me, and was very cordial. — ALEXANDER, JAMES W., 1857, *Forty Years' Familiar Letters.*

Perhaps it is not too much to say, that Dr. Guthrie is the greatest living preacher in Scotland. And yet, until recently, he was comparatively unknown in America. At the present time, however, it is quite the reverse. . . . His popularity is very great, the poor, to a great extent, flocking to his ministry, and the congregations often reaching fifteen hundred hearers. A frequent hearer describes his appearance on entering the pulpit as calm and dignified. On the street, careless in his personal appearance, and apparently uninteresting, the dull look is now gone; the dark eye is gleaming, speakingly, from under an ample forehead, and the countenance kindles with animation and earnest affection. Though possessing a voice of varied modulations there is nothing in his gesture, nothing in his speech, at all attractive. His hand at first often grasps the collar of his coat; he moves slowly backward and forward, and leans at times over the pulpit, speaking in a mellow north-country accent, with great ease and fluency, but in the plainest and most idiomatic Saxon. In the *matter* the attraction lies; his preaching resembling more a conversation than a sermon, each hearer feeling as if it were directed to him.—FISH, HENRY C., 1857, *Pulpit Eloquence of the Nineteenth Century, p.* 623.

His preaching had already (1835) the characteristics which afterwards made him so marked a man, and made him what I was accustomed to call him, "the pictorial preacher of the age." . . . His preparation for the pulpit was conscientiously careful. Possessed of a ready power of speech, he could have extemporised a sermon at any time, and thus saved himself much labour. But during all the seven years he was in Arbirlot, I believe he never entered the pulpit without having his discourse written and committed. . . . He was already the most popular minister by far in the district, though as yet scarcely known beyond it. In all the surrounding country parishes, when he preached at the week-day service in connection with the dispensation of the sacrament of the Lord's Supper, the whole people rushed to hear him; and, in Arbroath, where he often preached on the Sabbath evenings after officiating at home during the day, the churches were crowded to excess. Some hard men thought that his discourses were not very logical; some finical men and women regarded his Forfarshire pronunciation as very broad and his illustrations rather vivid; but they all went to hear him, because they got their hearts warmed.—McCOSH, JAMES, 1873, *Letter, Autobiography and Memoir of Thomas Guthrie, ed. Guthrie, vol.* I, *p.* 321.

The city weeps: with slow and solemn show
The dark-plumed pomp sails through the crowded way,
And walls and roofs are topped with thick display
Of waiting eyes that watch the wending woe.
What man was here, to whose last fateful march,
The marshalled throng its long-drawn convoy brings,
Like some great conqueror's when victory swings
Her vans o'er flower-spread path and wreathèd arch?
No conqueror's kind was here, nor conqueror's kin,
But a strong-breasted, fervid-hearted man,
Who from dark dens redeemed, and haunts of sin,
The city waifs, the loose unfathered clan
With prouder triumph than when wondering Rome
Went forth, all eyes, to bring great Cæsar home.
—BLACKIE, JOHN STUART, 1873, *On the Burial of Thomas Guthrie.*

The remains were conveyed from St. Leonards to Edinburgh, on Wednesday morning, and interred on Friday, the 28th of February. Unless when Dr. Chalmers and Sir James Simpson were carried to the grave, Edinburgh had seen no such funeral in this generation. The magistrates in their robes of office, and various other public bodies, clergymen of every Protestant denomination in Scotland, representatives of the Wesleyan Methodists from England, and of the Waldensian Church from Italy, passed to the Grange Cemetery through a living vista of 30,000 spectators. But the most touching feature in all the procession was the presence of 230 children from the Original Ragged Schools, many of whom

might truly have said, as one little girl of their number was overheard to tell, "He was all the father I ever knew."—GUTHRIE, DAVID K., AND CHARLES J., 1875, *eds. Autobiography and Memoir of Thomas Guthrie, vol.* II, *p.* 492.

I knew him well by sight,—a man over six feet two inches, with genial face, the favorite of the working-men, and much more catholic in his sympathies than the men who were associated with him in the ministry.—GREEN, J. B., 1875, *Rev. Thomas Guthrie, D.D., The Unitarian Review, vol.* 4, *p.* 588.

Of Dr. Guthrie in private, those who, like the present writer, were honoured with his friendship and had much intercourse with him, cannot speak too highly. The high-toned Christian always was seen, the delightful companion, and the faithful friend. His friendship was very remarkable. His genuine interest in those whom he loved, and in all their concerns; the pains he took to advance their interests; the care he showed not to hurt their feelings; his forbearance, his generosity, his warmth and tenderness, must always live in the remembrance of those that were much about him.—BLAIKIE, WILLIAM GARDEN, 1884, *Leaders in Modern Philanthropy, p.* 196.

On Monday February 24, Dr. Guthrie died. He had for a while been laid aside from preaching: but everybody remembered what he had been; and one felt it was a light put out, and a link to the old times broken. When he published his sermons, he could not publish the charm of his presence and manner: and they are disappointing, like those of Chalmers and Caird. But it was not the pathos of a common "popular preacher" that made the tears run down Mr. Thackeray's cheeks. And Guthrie had the gift of so saying a thing with not much in it, that it brought the tears to your eyes, straight. He was as great in humour as in pathos. — BOYD, ANDREW K. H., 1892, *Twenty-five Years of St. Andrews, vol.* I, *p.* 218.

The Professor [Blackie] had chosen Dr. Guthrie to be his pastor in ordinary, and sat Sunday after Sunday in a corner of the big square pew sacred to the elders and to distinguished worshippers—just under the pulpit, where the tall Doctor spake rousing words that moved and swayed the crowd beneath him. For his eloquence,—full of emotion, of simile, of elevation, of conviction, vibrating with love of nature and of man,—Professor Blackie chose him, and because his large sympathy refused all channels dug by sect, and flowed out into the broad stream whose waters God has designed for the refreshing of all mankind. The plaid, the thick stick, the low-crowned hat, the brown wig worn for some years, the finely cut profile, the devout attitude in prayer, the close attention, were all familiar to the congregation of Free St. John's during the latter half of Dr. Guthrie's ministry.—STODDART, ANNA M., 1895, *John Stuart Blackie, vol.* I, *p.* 305.

Guthrie influenced his age and his fellow-men as much by his life as by his works. "Guthrie the Man" was found to practise in life what "Guthrie the Preacher" inculcated in precept. Had he been less sympathetic, had his broad humanity touched the sorrow-seamed existence of his fellow-men at fewer points of contact, he might have felt less call to spend and be spent so completely in the cause of ameliorating the lot of destitute and despairing *brethren*. But in that case he would have graven his name less deeply on the hearts of his countrymen. The intensity of his devotion to their cause was manifested by the fact that he was shattered in health at the comparatively early age of fifty-nine. To act otherwise than he did, however, would have been foreign to his nature. Besides, he would have fallen short of his own ideal of right. His lofty enthusiasm in the cause of the friendless and downtrodden prevented him from feeling aught but delight in suffering for those whom he sought to save. Literally with the price of his own life did he pay for the souls and bodies of those pariahs whom he succeeded in snatching from moral and spiritual ruin.—SMEATON, OLIPHANT, 1900, *Thomas Guthrie (Famous Scots Series)*, *p.* 156

GENERAL

His "Gospel in Ezekiel"—consisting of twenty sermons on texts from this old prophet, lately published and now widely circulated in this country—breathes with life and animation from beginning to end. Open sometimes to criticism in matters of interpretation, and with too little contact, or evident connection between the several parts of the discourse, each sermon is never-

theless a thing of exquisite beauty. You seem to be walking in a picture gallery; or rather in a garden of sweets, with meandering streams, and every form of animate and inanimate life surrounding you. Now you weep under the depths of the preacher's pathos; now you are startled with some dazzling luminous sentence rolling out suddenly before you; now you are captivated with the freshness and originality of some thought, the aptness and vividness of some illustrations, or the ease and effectiveness with which some error is exploded, or some glorious doctrine unfolded; but you always arise from the perusal feeling that you have been led beside the waters of salvation, amid the flowers and fruits of paradise, and now return both delighted and enriched. — FISH, HENRY C., 1857, *Pulpit Eloquence of the Nineteenth Century, p.* 624.

The variety of his illustrations was immense, but he delighted most, and was most successful, in those of a nautical character. A storm at sea and a shipwreck from Guthrie were paintings never to be forgotten.—CHAMBERS, ROBERT, 1876, *Cyclopædia of English Literature, ed. Carruthers*.

One of the most eloquent preachers of the day was the late Dr. Guthrie, of Edinburgh; yet the reader of his sermons hardly discovers in them adequate proofs of this fact. Much of his charm lay in his illustrations, which were apt and striking as they came from his lips, but lose much of their impressiveness on paper. In listening to his vivid appeals, a metaphor dazzled you and was gone; in his printed page, you examine it coolly and carefully; it is pinned down for you like a butterfly on a card, and you can critically finger it and pick holes in it. Hence a reviewer of his published sermons, who would probably have been captivated by their delivery, complains that there is in them a great deal of illustration, and very little to illustrate; a very small army, but a most valorous noise of drums.—MATHEWS, WILLIAM, 1878, *Oratory, p.* 199.

Thomas Guthrie was not, like Candlish, a great debater and ecclesiastical statesman, but he was the popular orator, carrying all before him, not so much by the power of logic as by the appositeness of his illustrations, the force of his humor, and the depth of his pathos. . . . As a preacher, he did not so much belong to any class as he constituted a whole class by himself. Since his appearance he has had many imitators, but when he rose to fame he was, in Great Britain at least, the only one of his kind. He was not an expository preacher, neither could he be called dogmatic or doctrinal. He did not deal very liberally either in what has been termed the hortatory method. But he was what Dr. McCosh has called him, "the pictorial preacher of his age."— TAYLOR, WILLIAM M., 1887, *The Scottish Pulpit, pp.* 268, 269.

His style was florid and fluent in the highest degree, and the effect he produced upon the large audiences he gathered round him was often of the most powerful kind; but the metaphors, in which he indulged freely, and which, even in the height of his public oratory, were seen to be of the most highly differing qualities, some full of simple natural poetry, while the others were forced, extravagant and turbid, became sadly like pinchbeck and tinsel when preserved in a book. It is not an unusual effect

with a popular preacher.—OLIPHANT, MARGARET O. W., 1892, *The Victorian Age of English Literature, p.* 332.

These sixteen volumes, beginning with the "Gospel in Ezekiel" and ending with "Sundays Abroad," form a valuable library in themselves of popular evangelical teaching. Of the professed, or professional, theologian there is, as I have said, no trace. The writer is simply talking face to face with his reader, even as formerly he had been face to face with his congregation— for most of the papers were originally delivered as sermons—and the result achieved is, a depth of impression rarely experienced outside the walls of a church. Space will not permit me to deal with these books in any detail. I can only add that those who have yet to read them for the first time have a rich spiritual as well as intellectual treat in store.—SMEATON, OLIPHANT, 1900, *Thomas Guthrie (Famous Scots Series), p.* 150.

Caroline Clive

1801–1873

Born in London, was the daughter of Edmund Mersey-Wigley, of Shakenhurst, Worcestershire, and in 1840 was married to Rev. Archer Clive. Mrs. Clive was a confirmed invalid for some years previous to her death, which was the result of an accident, her dress having caught fire while she was writing in her boudoir at Whitfield, Herefordshire. Her works were all published anonymously. 1. IX Poems. By V. Lon., 1840, p.8vo; 2d ed., 1841. (This volume attracted much notice, and was very favorably reviewed in the Quarterly. The second edition includes nine additional poems). 2. I Watched the Heavens: a Poem. By V. Lon., 1842, p.8vo. (The first canto of an unfinished poem.) 3. The Queen's Ball: a Poem By V. Lon., 1847, p.8vo. 4. The Valley of the Rea: a Poem By V. Lon., 1851, p.8vo. 5. The Morlas: a Poem. By V. Lon., 1853, p.8vo. 6. Paul Ferroll: a Tale. By the Author of "IX Poems," by V. Lon., 1855, p.8vo. (The fourth edition contains a concluding chapter, bringing the story down to the death of Paul Ferroil.) . . 7. Poems. By the Author of "Paul Ferroll." Including a New Edition of "IX Poems," by V.: with Former and Recent Editions. Lon., 1856, 8vo. (Some of the earlier poems are omitted in this edition). 8. Year after Year. By the Author of "Paul Ferroll" and "IX Poems." Lon., 1858, 12mo. 9. Why Paul Ferroll Killed his Wife, Lon., 1860, 12mo.; new ed., 1864. (The preface contains a defence of "Paul Ferroll" against some strictures in the Edinburgh Review). . . . 10. John Greswold. By the Author of "Paul Ferroll." Lon., 1864, 2 vols. p.8vo. . . . 11. Poems. By V., Author of "Paul Ferroll." Including the "IX Poems." Lon., 1872, 8vo. (This contains twelve new poems, but is not a complete edition).—KIRK, JOHN FOSTER, 1891, *A Supplement to Allibone's Critical Dictionary of English Literature, vol.* I. *p.* 348.

PERSONAL

There never was a more remarkable contrast between the temperament of the poetess and the temperament of the woman, than that which exists between the thoughtful gravity, the almost gloomy melancholy that characterizes the writings of that celebrated initial letter, the "V." of "Blackwood's Magazine," and the charm-

ing, cheerful, light-hearted lady, known as Mrs. Clive. . . . I have never known any creature half so cheerful. Happy sister, happy mother, happy wife, she even bears the burden of a large fortune and a great house without the slightest diminution of the delightful animal spirits, which always seem to me to be of her many gifts the choicest. Moreover, enjoyment seems to be her mode of thankfulness; as, not content with being happy herself, she has a trick of making every body happy that comes near her. I do not know how she contrives it, but such is the effect. There is no resisting the contagious laughter of those dancing eyes.—MITFORD, MARY RUSSELL, 1851, *Recollections of a Literary Life, p.* 274.

We have reclaimed from "Paul Ferroll" a hitherto inedited poem that bears pathetic evidence of the unlifted shadow her lameness cast over her entire after life. All the more, however, her natively powerful intellect was strengthened by her being thrown upon her inward resources. By surely an unhappy misjudgment and reticence the family has given no memoir of her beyond the meagre Note prefixed to her collected poems by her daughter (Mrs. Alice Greathed) of 1890 (Longmans). This is the more to be regretted, because she wrote all her life, was a brilliant conversationalist, was held in highest regard within an exceptionally notable intellectual circle, and carried on a large correspondence. —GROSART, ALEXANDER B., 1897, *The Poets and the Poetry of the Century, Sacred, Moral, and Religious Verse,* ed. *Miles, p.* 201.

GENERAL

Of "IX Poems by V." we emphatically say in old Greek—βαιὰ μὲν, ἀλλὰ 'ΡΟΔΑ. It is an Ennead to which every Muse may have contributed her ninth. We suppose V. stands for Victoria, and really she queens it among our fair friends. Perhaps V. will think it is a questionable compliment, if we say, like the late Baron Graham to Lady —— in the assize court at Exeter, "We beg your ladyship's pardon, but we really took you for a *man*." Indeed these few pages are distinguished by a sad Lucretian tone, which very seldom comes from a woman's lyre. But V. is a woman, and no ordinary woman, certainly:—though whether spinster, wife, or widow, we have not been informed. Her poems are of such equal merit, that it matters little to her reputation or our readers' pleasure which we quote.—COLERIDGE, HARTLEY, 1840, *Modern English Poetesses, Quarterly Review,* vol. 66, *p.* 408.

Of "IX. Poems by V.," we would say with the *Quarterly,* βαιὰ μὲν, ἀλλὰ 'ΡΟΔΑ. They combine rare excellences; the strength, the finish, the gravity of a man's thoughts, with the tenderness, the insight, the constitutional sorrowfulness of a woman's—

her purity, her passionateness, her delicate and just sense and expression. We confess we would rather have been the author of any one of the nine poems in this little volume, than of the very tremedous, very absurd, very raw, loud, and fuliginous "Festus," with his many thousands of lines and his amazing reputation, his bad English, bad religion, bad philosophy, and very bad jokes— his "buttered thunder" (this is his own phrase), and his poor devil of a Lucifer—we would, we repeat (having in this our *subita ac sæva indignatio* run ourselves a little out of breath), as much rather keep company with "V." than with Mr. Bailey, as we would prefer going to sea for *pleasure,* in a trim little yacht, with its free motions, its quiet, its cleanliness, and its gliding at its own sweet will, to taking a state berth in some Fire-King steamer of 1000 horse-power, with his mighty and troublous throb, his smoke, his exasperated steam, his langour and fire and fury, his oils and smells.—BROWN, JOHN, 1849, *Vaughan's Poems, etc., North British Review, vol.* 11., *p.* 59.

As every body that thinks deeply, as she does, must have some moments of sadness, she is content to put them into her writings: sometimes in prose, for her "Story of the Great Drought" has an intensity of tragic power, a realization of impossible horrors, such as give their fascination to the best works of Godwin; sometimes in verse, where the depth of thought and fearless originality of treatment, frequently redeem the commonest subject from any thing like commonplace.—MITFORD, MARY RUSSELL, 1851, *Recollections of a Literary Life, p.* 274.

The title-page of the volume of poems by the author of "Paul Ferroll" reminds us that the *Quarterly Review* in 1840 committed itself to the belief that the nine poems, which were all Mrs. Archer Clive had yet published, contained stanzas "worthy of any one of our greatest poets in his happiest moments." Certainly we are more struck with the quality of the writer's talent than with its quantity, and yet this quality is too abstract, not to say too ghostly, to be really individual. The originality of the poems lies wholly in their intensity. There is nothing uncommon about the style, which never emancipates itself from the conventional range of the better class of album verses. There is nothing uncommon about the topics. . . . This is V.'s peculiar distinction to be so powerful as to be strange without ceasing to be obvious; she sees nothing which other people do not see, but she cares with all the strength of a proud, passionate nature about things that other people seldom care about. . . . It is curious, perhaps, that so abnormal a nature should be so eagerly submissive to traditional beliefs; the only approach to a cry of revolt is the feverish prayer for death at once sudden and triumphant, which forms the substance of the lines written in health. Perhaps it may explain this submission if we remember that mental intensity does not always imply mental activity, and that the author of "Paul Ferroll" has certainly written very little. Perhaps, too, this submission is one condition of the sustained quietness to which so much of the power and the horror of that singular tale is due.— SIMCOX, GEORGE AUGUSTUS, 1872, *Poems by V., The Academy, vol.* 3, *p.* 362.

This novel ["Paul Ferroll"] has passed through a number of editions, and has been translated into French by Madame H. Loreau. In the fourth edition a concluding chapter was added, bringing the story down to the death of Paul Ferroll. . . . "Why Paul Ferroll killed his Wife, by the author of 'Paul Ferroll'," London, 1860, 12mo. Though the names of the characters are different, the object of this novel is to explain the opening chapter of "Paul Ferroll." It is not, however, at all equal in power to its predecessor.—BARKER, G. F. RUSSELL, 1887, *Dictionary of National Biography, vol.* XI, *p.* 104.

The author of the remarkable novel of "Paul Ferroll," whose "IX. Poems by V." attracted much attention from competent critics in the doubtful time of poetry about the middle of the century, and are really good.—SAINTSBURY, GEORGE, 1896, *A His-*

tory of Nineteenth Century Literature, p. 302.

Mrs. Clive's reputation chiefly rests upon her story of "Paul Ferroll," published in 1855, and its sequel, "Why Paul Ferroll Killed his Wife." The second story was, however, in no way equal to the first; and a subsequent novel, "John Greswold," which appeared in 1864, was decidedly inferior to its predecessors, although containing passages of considerable literary merit. "Paul Ferroll" has passed through several editions, and has been translated into French. It was not until the fourth edition that the concluding chapter, which brings the story down to the death of Paul Ferroll, was added. . . . "Paul Ferroll" may be considered as the precursor of the purely sensational novel, or of what may be called the novel mystery. Miss Brontë in "Jane Eyre" uses to some extent the same kind of material, but her work is far more a study of character than the story of "Paul Ferroll" can claim to be. In "Paul Ferroll," indeed, the analysis of motive is entirely absent. The motives that actuated Paul Ferroll are to be gathered simply from chance expressions or his actions. No description of the human heart has been attempted. The picture of the violent, revengeful, strongly passionate nature of the man is forcible enough, but it is displayed by action and not by introspection. It is for this reason that Mrs. Clive may be placed in the forefront of the sensational novelists of the century. She anticipated the work of Wilkie Collins, of Charles Reade, of Miss Braddon, and many others of their school, in showing human nature as expressed by its energies, neither diagnosing it like a physician, nor analysing it like a priest.—SERGEANT, ADELINE, 1897, *Women Novelists of Queen Victoria's Reign.*

Charles Knight

1791–1873

Author and publisher, was born in 1791, the son of a Windsor bookseller. In 1811 with his father he established the *Windsor and Eton Express*, and edited it until 1821, at the same time printing the *Etonian*. The *Plain Englishman* (1820–22), a first attempt to produce good cheap literature, was jointly edited by Charles Knight and Commissioner Locker of Greenwich Hospital. Removing to London in 1822, Knight began general publishing and founded *Knight's Quarterly Magazine*. For the Society for the Diffusion of Useful Knowledge he published many works and serials, including the *Penny Magazine* (1832–45). The "Penny Cyclopædia" was begun in 1838, followed by the "English Cyclopædia" (1854–61), the "British Almanac," and its "Companion." He edited the "Pictorial Shakespeare," and was the author of "William Shakespeare: a Biography" (1843). Other works were "The Land We Live In" (1848), "Once Upon a Time" (1853), and "Knowledge is Power" (1855). In 1862 he completed his "Popular History of England." "Half-hours with the Best Authors," "Half-hours of English History," and "Half-hours with the Best Letter-writers" were compilations by him. Appointed in 1860 publisher of the *London Gazette*, he secured an income of £1,200. He died at Addlestone, Surrey, 9th March, 1873. *See* his "Passage of a Working Life" (1863–65), and "Life" by Alice Clowes (1892).—PATRICK AND GROOME, *eds.*, 1897, *Chambers' Biographical Dictionary, p.* 557.

PERSONAL

Looking back upon the August of 1812, at which time my working time really commenced, it occurred to me that there were passages of that working life of fifty years which might have an interest for a wider circle than that of my family and my immediate friends, if presented without the tedious egotism of a formal Auto-Biography. During that period my social position has not materially altered, and I have not had the advantage of seeing "life in many lands." I have therefore no startling incidents to relate, and no great variety of scenes to describe. My occupation has been that of a publisher and a writer. But, in the course of my long connection with the Press (I use this word in its most extended meaning), I have been brought into communication with many eminent persons, and have been somewhat extensively mixed up with vast changes in the social condition of the people, in the progress of which elementary education and popular literature have been amongst the most efficient instruments of amelioration. — KNIGHT, CHARLES, 1863, *Passages from a Working Life During Half a Century, p.* v.

But although our purpose is to paint Charles Knight the publisher, yet it is impossible to look upon him as a publisher merely. He is emphatically a social reformer. He has always ends beyond those of literature itself. He walks in a patriotic sphere; and it is from this that his highest impulses are derived. His mind, as we have seen, was first directed to cheap literature of a sound and healthy nature in seeking a panacea to the discontent and disorganization which in his youth prevailed among the working classes, issuing in riots and sedition, and direct assaults upon the throne itself. And this patriotic idea did not lose, but gained force from being viewed in relation to religious wants. Importing into every subject an immediate human interest, he softens political differences, and almost unconsciously unites in the most permanent and effective manner the dif-

ferent classes of society, by awakening ideas round which common activities may center. . . . For himself, the writer is free to say that he is proud of being a follower in the footsteps of Charles Knight, and that he will be well pleased if he can help to carry on the work of his master, by supplying such literature as will not ignobly interest nor frivolously amuse, but convey the wisest instruction in the pleasantest manner, and supply it in such a form that it will find its way to tens of thousands of British homes, to be well thumbed and dog-eared by the children and the grown people, on the journey and at the fireside—STRAHAN, ALEXANDER, 1867, *Charles Knight, Publisher, Good Words, vol.* 8, *p.* 621.

Full of years and of honours, Mr. Knight died at Addlestone, in Surrey, on the 9th of March, 1873, aged eighty-one; and five days afterwards was buried in the family vault at Windsor. The funeral was very large, from the number of literary men attending, who wished to show their feeling of affection and respect for the deceased. In the newspaper notices, too, the tribute of praise was unanimous and hearty; and it was resolved that the gratitude of writers and readers should not stop here. A committee has been formed to erect some kind of memorial, and many of the leading men of letters, as well as some of the leading publishers, are taking part in it. It has been hoped that this memorial may assume the shape of a free public library for London, and thus initiate a movement that, to our shame, has made such successful way in our great provincial towns. Nothing else could so appropriately perpetuate the memory of a life so earnest in its purpose of spreading cheap literature far and wide, so brave in difficulty, so utterly unmindful of self-gain in the work planned out and done; that none who knew its story can gainsay Douglas Jerrold's most happy epitaph, "Good Knight."—CURWEN, HENRY, 1873, *A History of Booksellers, p.* 266.

His singularly amiable character, which had amply merited for him Douglas Jerrold's surname of "Good Knight," endeared him to all with whom he was acquainted, and when he was laid in the grave it was felt that many years might come and go ere the publishing trade would be adorned by one so generous, so appreciative of merit, and so ready to sacrifice his private interest to the public weal.—NICOLL, HENRY J., 1881, *Great Movements and Those Who Achieved Them, p.* 184.

Knight was a man of middle stature, with finely cut features, and a countenance indicative of his character, in which a sanguine temperament somewhat preponderated over accurate judgment. His schemes, though often sound in themselves, were apt to be carried into effect somewhat prematurely, and without sufficient regard to probable obstacles. Consequently after all his great publishing operations he remained a poor man. He was thoroughly honourable in business and considerate to his fellow-workers. His temper was quick, and when moved he could speak and write strongly; but he bore no ill-will, and seems never to have made an enemy. The often-quoted jest with which Jerrold took leave of him one evening after a social meeting—"Good Knight"—gives the measure of the estimate formed of him by his friends. In politics he was a liberal, and was one of the earliest members of the Reform Club. When M. D. Hill was candidate for Hull in the first reformed parliament, Knight worked for him. "Tell Mrs. Knight," wrote Hill to his wife, "that her husband is one of the best speakers I ever heard."—BUTLER, ARTHUR JOHN, 1892, *Dictionary of National Biography, vol.* XXXI, *p.* 248.

GENERAL

Having long ardently desired the appearance of a complete History of England, *and the English*—of the people as well as their kings—of the customs of the fire-side, as well as the intrigues of the court—we acknowledge with gratitude the accomplishment of our wish in the "Pictorial History of England" published by Charles Knight, one of the first literary benefactors of the age. This excellent work is arranged upon Henry's plan, with advantages which neither Henry nor any one man could have secured.—ALLIBONE, S. A., 1854–58, *Critical Dictionary of English Literature, vol.* I, *p.* 60.

Nothing has ever appeared superior, if anything has been published equal, to the account of the state of commerce, government, and society, at different periods.—BROUGHAM, HENRY LORD, 1858, *Address, Oct.* 12.

The appearance of the "Penny Magazine" distinctly marks an era in our social history. Together with the "Penny Cyclopædia" to which it directly gave rise, it forms the first instalment of the Poor Man's Library, to complete which so much has since been accomplished. Though this last was the least successful of Mr. Knight's adventures in a pecuniary point of view, there can be no doubt that these two penny issues were by far the most fruitful of his works with regard to intellectual and moral results. The enterprises he had previously engaged in were to a considerable extent preliminary experiments to guide him, or buttresses to afford leverage in effectively applying this, his great idea.—STRAHAN, ALEXANDER, 1867, *Charles Knight, Publisher, Good Words, vol.* 8, *p.* 619.

While the work ["History"] is not profound, it is thoroughly healthful in tone; and, with the exception of Green, for the purposes of the general reader, is probably the best history of England yet completed. — ADAMS, CHARLES KENDALL, 1882, *A Manual of Historical Literature, p.* 438.

He devoted himself to the spread of literature with an unselfish enterprise which merits the highest praise.—KIRKLAND, E. S., 1892, *A Short History of English Literature, p.* 337.

Charles Knight will ever be remembered with honour as the great pioneer in the cheapening of good literature. The excellence of his shilling volumes was a marvel when they were first published, and even now it would be difficult to find their equal. Knight had a great belief in the adequacy of the penny as a price for a number of a book. He published large quantities of books at a penny a number—as one of the first cheap periodicals—the "Penny Magazine," and the first of cheap cyclopædias— the "Penny Cyclopædia." How much good has been done by the large issues of such excellent books as Knight's weekly and monthly volumes, the Libraries of Useful and Entertaining Knowledge, Constable's Miscellany, Murray's Family Library, Home and Colonial Library, and Bohn's Libraries!—WHEATLEY, HENRY B., 1898, *Prices of Books, p.* 28.

Bryan Waller Procter

1787-1874

1787, Born, November 21st, in London.—1800, *circa*, A scholar at Harrow.—1815, Contributes poems to the *London Literary Gazette.*—1816, Comes into possession of property, upon the death of his father.—1819, Publishes "Dramatic Scenes."—1820, Publishes "A Sicilian Story," and "Marcian Colonna."—1821, His tragedy of "Mirandola," performed at Covent Garden Theatre.—1823, Publishes "The Flood of Thessaly," and other poems.—1824, Marries Miss Skepper.—1831, Called to the bar. Publishes "English Songs."—1832, Appointed Commissioner of Lunacy. Publishes second edition of "English Songs."—1835, Publishes the "Life of Edmund Kean."—1861, Resigns his office of Commissioner.—1866, Publishes "Charles Lamb, a Biography."—1874, Dies, October 4th.— MASON, EDWARD T., 1885, *ed. Personal Traits of British Authors, Wordsworth—Procter, p.* 262.

PERSONAL

Well, Byron is gone, and ———— is now the best poet in England. Fill up the gap to your fancy. Barry Cornwall has at last carried the pretty A. S. They are just in the treacle moon. Hope it won't clog his wings—gaum we used to say at school.— LAMB, CHARLES, 1823, *Correspondence of Leigh Hunt, vol.* I, *p.* 249.

He is a slender, rough-faced, palish, gentle, languid-looking man, of three or four and thirty. There is a dreamy mildness in his eye; he is kind and good in his manners, and I understand in his conduct. He is a poet by the ear and the fancy, but his heart and intellect are not strong. He is a small poet.—CARLYLE, THOMAS, 1824, *Letter to Miss Welsh, Thomas Carlyle, The First Forty Years of His Life, Froude, vol.* I, *p.* 177.

I left Procter writing, more for the Edinburgh, New Monthly, & retrospective, I fear, than for the drama; he is locked up every morning from 10 till ½ p. 1 by his wife with ½ a quire of foolscap & a quill.— BEDDOES, THOMAS LOVELL, 1825, *To Thomas Forbes Kelsall, Apr.* 14; *Letters, ed. Gosse, p.* 65.

Mr. Procter—for you know that is the real name of Barry Cornwall—is about forty-two or forty-five, and is a conveyancer by profession. His days are spent in the toilsome study of abstracts of titles; and when I saw him last Sunday, at his house, he was poring over one which press of business had compelled him to take home. He is a small, thin man, with a very dull countenance, in which, nevertheless,— knowing what he has written,—I can detect the "poetical frenzy." His manner is gentle and quiet, and his voice low. He thought if he could live life over again he would be a gardener.—SUMNER, CHARLES, 1839, *To George S. Hillard, Jan.* 23; *Mem-*

oir and Letters of Sumner, ed. Pierce, vol. II, *p.* 44.

There are three or four individuals who used to form part of those pleasant *symposii,* to whom the nature of these Recollections calls upon me to refer more particularly than in a passing paragraph. The most distinguished of these was the amiable and gifted poet, so universally known to the reading world under the name of Barry Cornwall. This gentleman used but seldom to grace our simple feasts ("of reason," or of folly, as the case might be); but when he did look in by accident, or was induced by Hazlitt's request to come, everything went off the better for his presence; for, besides the fact of Hazlitt's being fond of his society, and, at the same time, thinking so highly of his talents as always to talk his best when he (P———r) was a partaker in the talk, there is an endearing something in the personal manner of that exquisite writer, an appearance of gentle and genial sympathy with the feelings of those with whom he talks, which has the effect of exciting towards him that *personal* interest from which it seems itself to spring, and in the absence of which the better feelings and mental characteristics incident to social converse are seldom if ever called forth. In P———r Hazlitt always found a man of fine and delicate intellectual pretensions, who was nevertheless eager and pleased to listen, with attention and interest, to all the little insignificant details of his daily life.—PATMORE, PETER GEORGE, 1854, *My Friends and Acquaintance, vol.* III, *p.* 86.

Barry Cornwall, Mr. Procter, called on me a week or more ago, but I happened not to be in the office. Saturday last he called again, and as I had crossed to Rock Park he followed me thither. A plain, middle-sized, English-looking gentleman, elderly, with short white hair, and particularly quiet in his manners. He talks in a somewhat low tone without emphasis, scarcely distinct. . . . His head has a good outline, and would look well in marble. I liked him very well. He talked unaffectedly, showing an author's regard to his reputation, and was evidently pleased to hear of his American celebrity. He said that in his younger days he was a scientific pugilist, and once took a journey to have a sparring encounter with the Game-Chicken. Certainly, no one would have looked for a pugilist in this subdued old gentleman. He is now Commissioner of Lunacy, and makes periodical circuits through the country, attending to the business of his office. He is slightly deaf, and this may be the cause of his unaccented utterance,—owing to his not being able to regulate his voice exactly by his own ear. . . . He is a good man, and much better expressed by his real name, Procter, than by his poetical one, Barry Cornwall. . . . He took my hand in both of his at parting.—HAWTHORNE, NATHANIEL, 1854, *English Note-Books, vol.* I, *p.* 92.

I breakfasted with Barry Cornwall and Browning. Dear old Barry! I loved him from the first minute. He is reputed silent, but he opened his heart to me like an uncle. He showed me all his MSS., lots of unpublished poems, etc., and talked out of the abundance of his golden nature.—TAYLOR, BAYARD, 1856, *To Mr. and Mrs. R. H. Stoddard, Aug.* 4; *Life and Letters, ed. Taylor and Scudder, vol.* I, *p.* 321.

A decidedly rather pretty little fellow Procter, bodily and spiritually; manners prepossessing, slightly London-elegant, not unpleasant; clear judgment in him, though of narrow field; a sound honourable morality, and airy friendly ways; of slight, neat figure, vigorous for his size; fine genially rugged little face, fine head; something curiously dreamy in the eyes of him, lids drooping at the *outer* ends into a cordially meditative and drooping expression.—CARLYLE, THOMAS, 1867, *Edward Irving, Reminiscences, ed. Morton.*

It is impossible for those who did not know him personally to have any adequate idea of the charm of the man. "Everybody loves him," wrote Crabb Robinson in 1866, and having, as he told me, "no politics," he throughout life was on good terms with men of all parties. One of his most conspicuous characteristics to the last was

his chivalrous courtesy to women, reminding one of the unparagoned high breeding of the late Duke of Beaufort, George Grote, Samuel Rogers (when he liked the lady!), and the late John Stuart Mill. The nearest living approach to them in this respect is Robert Browning. It was the half-playful, protecting deference of the old school, almost unknown to this generation.—MAYER, S. R. TOWNSHEND, 1874, *Barry Cornwall, Gentleman's Magazine, N. S. vol.* 13, *p.* 567.

Who that ever came habitually into his presence can forget the tones of his voice, the tenderness in his gray retrospective eyes, or the touch of his sympathic hand laid on the shoulder of a friend! The elements were indeed so kindly mixed in him that no bitterness, or rancor, or jealousy had part or lot in his composition. No distinguished person was ever more ready to help forward the rising and as yet nameless literary man or woman who asked his counsel and warmhearted suffrage. His mere presence was sunshine and courage to a new-comer into the growing world of letters and criticism. Indeed, to be *human* only entitled any one who came near him to receive the gracious bounty of his goodness and courtesy. He made it the happiness of his life never to miss, whenever opportunity occurred, the chance of conferring pleasure and gladness on those who needed kind words and substantial aid. . . . The poet's figure was short and full, and his voice had a low, veiled tone habitually in it, which made it sometimes difficult to hear distinctly what he was saying. When he spoke in conversation, he liked to be very near his listener, and thus stand, as it were, on confidential ground with him. His turn of thought was apt to be cheerful among his friends, and he proceeded readily into a vein of wit and nimble expression. Verbal felicity seemed natural to him, and his epithets, evidently unprepared, were always perfect. He disliked cant and hard ways of judging character. He praised easily. He had no wish to stand in any body's shoes but his own, and he said there is no literary vice of a darker shade than envy. . . . He impressed every one who came near him as a born gentleman, chivalrous and generous in a marked degree, and it was a habit of all who knew him to have an affection for him.—FIELDS, JAMES F., 1875, *"Barry Cornwall" and Some of his Friends, Harper's Magazine, vol.* 51, *p.* 777, *vol.* 52, *p.* 65.

No one who has passed an hour in the company of Charles Lamb's "dear boy" can ever lose the impression made upon him by that simple, sincere, shy, and delicate soul. His small figure, his head, not remarkable for much besides its expression of intelligent and warm good-will, and its singular likeness to that of Sir Walter Scott; his conversation, which had little decision or "point" in the ordinary sense, and often dwelt on truths which a novelty-loving society banishes from its repertory as truisms, never disturbed the effect, in any assemblage, of his real distinction. His silence seemed wiser, his simplicity subtler, his shyness more courageous than the wit, philosophy, and assurance of others. When such a man expressed himself more or less faithfully in a series of gracious poems, of which he alone, of all his circle, did not seem proud, it naturally followed that all who knew him were eager to declare and extend the credit and honor to which he had aspired with so much simplicity, and which he bore with so entire an absence of self-assertion.—PATMORE, COVENTRY, 1877, *ed. Bryan Waller Procter, an Autobiographical Fragment and Biographical Notes, p. 5.*

He had a modest—nay, shy—manner in company (1821); heightened by a singular nervous affection, a kind of sudden twitch or contraction, that spasmodically flitted athwart his face as he conversed upon any lofty theme, or argued on some high-thoughted topic.—CLARKE, CHARLES COWDEN, 1878, *Recollections of Writers, p. 36.*

He was short of stature with little evidence of energy, but with a peculiarly gentle and contemplative countenance, such as usually begets liking rather than the loftier tributes poets receive from those who venerate the vocation of the bard.—HALL, SAMUEL CARTER, 1883, *Retrospect of a Long Life, p. 318.*

Mrs. Procter was for the larger part of a century one of the most brilliant women in London society. Dickens said of her that, no matter how brilliant the men were who surrounded her—and they were all that London had of the best—she always gave the last and wittiest rejoinder. Her social powers of endurance were wonderful. The last time I had the pleasure of seeing her she had long passed her eightieth birthday. She has "assisted" in the morning at a marriage in the family of Lord Houghton;

she had lunched in company; she was holding a reception at her own house, and, in speaking with a young lady who was taking leave, I heard her say: "But I shall see you this evening!" "No," said the young lady; "I am rather tired after our day, and I shall not go out again." "Nonsense, my child," answered the old soldier. "Why, I am going to dine out first, and go to the reception afterward. What is the matter with you young people?" When she passed away, a few years ago, the world lost almost the last person acquainted nearly and socially with the brilliant group of poets who made the first quarter of the century an epoch in English literature.—FIELD, ANNIE, 1894, *A Third Shelf of Old Books, Scribner's Magazine, vol. 16, p. 354.*

GENERAL

Let hate, or grosser hearts, their foulness mask
Under the vizor of a borrow'd name;
Let things eschew the light deserving blame:
No cause hast thou to blush for thy sweet task.
"Marcian Colonna" is a dainty book;
And thy "Sicilian Tale" may boldly pass;
Thy "Dream" hath all, in which, as in a glass,
On the great world's antique glories we may
  look.
No longer then, as "lowly substitute,
Factor, or PROCTOR, for another's gains,"
Suffer the admiring world to be deceived;
Lest thou thyself, by self of fame bereaved,
Lament too late the lost prize of thy pains,
And heavenly tunes piped through an alien
  flute.
—LAMB, CHARLES, 1820, *To the Author of Poems, Published under the Name of Barry Cornwall.*

If it be the peculiar province of poetry to give delight, this author should rank very high among our poets: and, in spite of his neglect of the terrible passions, he *does* rank very high in our estimation. He has a beautiful fancy and a beautiful diction—and a fine ear for the music of verse, and great tenderness and delicacy of feeling. He seems, moreover, to be altogether free from any tincture of bitterness, rancour or jealousy; and never shocks us with atrocity, or stiffens us with horror, or confounds us with the dreadful sublimities of demoniacal energy. His soul, on the contrary, seems filled to overflowing with images of love and beauty, and gentle sorrows, and tender pity, and mild and holy resignation. The character of his poetry is to soothe and melt and delight: to make us kind and thoughtful and imaginative—to purge away the dregs of our earthly passions, by the refining fires of a pure imagination, and to lap us up from the eating cares of life, in visions so soft and bright, as to sink like morning dreams on our senses, and at the same time so distinct and truly fashioned upon the eternal patterns of nature, as to hold them before our eyes long after they have again been opened on the dimmer scenes of the world. — JEFFREY, FRANCIS LORD, 1820, *Cornwall's Marcian Colonna, Edinburgh Review, vol. 34, p. 449.*

A gentleman of the name of Cornwall, who has lately published a volume of "Dramatic Scenes," has met with a very different reception, but I cannot say that he has *deserved* it. He has made no sacrifice at the shrine of fashionable affectation or false glitter. There is nothing common-place in his style to soothe the complacency of dullness, nothing extravagant to startle the grossness of ignorance. He writes with simplicity, delicacy, and fervour; continues a scene from Shakspeare, or works out a hint from Boccacio, in the spirit of his originals, and though he bows with reverence at the altar of those great masters, he keeps an eye curiously intent on nature, and a mind awake to the admonitions of his own heart. As he has begun, so let him proceed. Any one who will turn to the glowing and richly-coloured conclusion of "The Falcon," will, I think, agree with me in this wish!—HAZLITT, WILLIAM, 1820, *Lectures on the Dramatic Literature of the Age of Elizabeth, Lecture* VIII.

I just see, by the papers of Galignani, that there is a new tragedy of great expectation, by Barry Cornwall. Of what I have read of his works I liked the "Dramatic Sketches," but thought his "Sicilian Story" and "Marcian Colonna," in rhyme, quite spoilt, by I know not what affectation of Wordsworth, and Moore, and myself, all mixed up into a kind of chaos. I think him very likely to produce a good tragedy, if he keep to a natural style, and not play tricks to form harlequinades for an audience. — BYRON, LORD, 1821, *Letter to Mr. Murray, Jan.* 4.

I saw Barry Cornwall's tragedy the first night. It succeeded well, and has some exceedingly deep things, but he has not experienced enough to compose his materials for the best effect. . . . The subject of Procter's tragedy is dreadful. A father marries a young creature his son loved,

without knowing it, and the girl marries him under the belief that the son is dead. His letters informing her that he was alive were intercepted by under characters, and when he returns he finds her married to his father! His interview with her is very fine and torturing; and with his father also, but then comes a third regular set interview which weakens the effect of the others and of all. . . . This is the most striking thing I have seen on the stage. I do not like such subjects. . . . But Procter is a man of exquisite and tender genius, and will yet do more beautiful things.—HAYDON, BENJAMIN ROBERT, 1821, *Letter to Miss Mitford, Jan,* 12; *Life, Letters and Table-Talk of Haydon, ed. Stoddard, p.* 204.

And here's to the lady-like, lisping, sweet fellow
Who thinks he can write in the vein of Othello,
Without plot or passion—Alas! Peter Proctor—
But it scandals the muse that makes him need
   a Doctor.
But still he has written some stanzas of merit,
And caught a fine spark of the delicate spirit
Of the rich Bards of old—and might be an
   apology
For a Minstrel—wer't not for Cockaigne and
   Mythology.
  —WILSON, JOHN, 1822, *Noctes Ambrosianæ, July.*

Your Muse is younger in her soul than mine:
O feed her still on woman's smiles and wine,
And give the world a tender song once more;
For all the good can love and can adore
What's human, fair, and gentle. Few, I know,
Can bear to sit at my board, when I show
The wretchedness and folly of man's all,
And laugh myself right heartily. Your call
Is higher and more human: I will do
Unsociably my part, and still be true
To my own soul; but e'er admire you,
And own that you have nature's kindest trust,
Her weak and dear to nourish,—that I must.
Then fare, as you deserve it, well, and live
In the calm feelings you to others give.
  —BEDDOES, THOMAS LOVELL, 1836, *Letter to B. W. Procter, Esq.*

Feeling—strong, vehement, rushing feeling—which clutches at illustrations speaking to the ear and sensibility rather than the imagination, is the inspiration of much of his poetry. Occasionally his verse splits on the racks of obscurity and rant. But there is a breadth of passion in some of his poems, which, whether it is expressed in vast and vague metaphors, or simmers and gleams in radiant fancies, or is poured out on his page in one hot gush, or leaps delirously down the "dark deep thundering river" of his style, has ever a kindling effect on sensibility. There never was a poet more honest in the expression of his nature. His songs are the reflections of all moods of his mind, and he cares not if the sentiment of one contradicts that of another. In grief, or love, or fear, or despair, at the festive board, or the bed of sickness, wherever and whenever the spirit of song comes to him, it takes the color of the emotion which animates or saddens the moment. He is a large-hearted and most loveable man; and his poetry is admired because it is the expression of his character.—WHIPPLE, EDWIN P., 1845, *Essays and Reviews, vol.* I, *p.* 330.

> Barry Cornwall! by what right
> Wring you my breast and dim my sight,
> And make me wish at every touch
> My poor old hand could do as much?
> No other in these later times
> Has bound me in so potent rhymes.
> I have observed the curious dress
> And jewelry of brave Queen Bess,
> But always found some o'ercharged thing,
> Some flaw in even the brightest ring,
> Admiring in her men of war,
> A rich but too argute guitar.
> Our foremost now are more prolix,
> And scrape with three-fell fiddlesticks,
> And whether bound for griefs or smiles,
> Are slow to turn as crocodiles.

—LANDOR, WALTER SAVAGE, 1846, *To Barry Cornwall, Miscellaneous Poems.*

There is a healthy, active vigor about all the latter writings of Barry Cornwall, that show that he has never yet fairly and fully developed his whole power. His reputation is of the first class, but every one feels, in reading one of his lyrics, that he would not surprise us now to come forth with some high and stirring drama of real life, that would stamp him as a true tragic poet. The elements of this lie everywhere in his poems. There is a clear and decided dramatic tact and cast of thought. Pathos and indignation against wrong live equally and vividly in him. His thoughts and feelings are put forth with a genuineness and a perspicuous life, that tell at once on the reader, making him feel how real and how earnest is his spirit.—HOWITT, WILLIAM, 1847, *Homes and Haunts of the Most Eminent British Poets, vol.* II, *p.* 512.

The "Dramatic Scenes," his earliest, is in several respects still his best work; for they were evident overflowings from his feelings and fancy, and are written *con amore.* Besides this, they had the charm of novelty, and bewitched all finer sensibilities by their being so thoroughly tinctured with "Elysian beauty, melancholy grace."—MOIR, D. M., 1851–52, *Sketches of the Poetical Literature of the Past Half-Century.*

They are almost the only real *songs* in the language; that is, lyrics that have the pulsation of music in them. The Germans and the Spaniards have so many, and we so few, particularly of late.—LONGFELLOW, HENRY WADSWORTH, 1852, *Letter to Bryan Waller Procter, Nov.* 29; *An Autobiographical Fragment and Biographical Notes, ed.* Patmore, *p.* 298.

> To
> BRYAN WALLER PROCTER,
> THIS SELECTION
> FROM THE WORKS OF THE ILLUSTRIOUS POETS,
> TO WHOSE GENIUS HIS OWN IS IN MANY RESPECTS AKIN,
> WITHOUT HAVING TO REGRET A PARTICLE OF WHAT STAINED IT,
> IS INSCRIBED,
> BY HIS EVER OBLIGED AND AFFECTIONATE FRIEND.

—HUNT, LEIGH, 1855, *Correspondence, ed. His Eldest Son, vol.* II, *p.* 177.

A variety of detached poems, of various merit, and many of them of the highest, constitute the claims of this most amiable and accomplished man to literary reputation.—MADDEN, RICHARD ROBERT, 1855, *The Literary Life and Correspondence of the Countess of Blessington, vol.* II, *p.* 275.

An elegant poet, and a reproducer, in the form of fragments, of many of the excellencies of the Elizabethan dramatists. Graceful, tender, finished, and with the true spirit of a high-class gentleman in all he writes and does, there are few pleasanter books than Barry Cornwall's "Songs and Dramatic Scenes." — FRISWELL, JAMES HAIN, 1869, *Essays on English Writers, p.* 347.

> Beloved of men, whose words on our lips were honey,
> Whose name in our ears and our fathers' ears was sweet,
> Like summer gone forth of the land his song made sunny,
> To the beautiful veiled bright world where the glad ghosts meet,
> Child with father, and bridegroom with bride, and anguish with rest,
> No soul shall pass of a singer than this more blest.

—SWINBURNE, ALGERNON CHARLES, 1874, *In Memory of Barry Cornwall, Fortnightly Review, vol.* 22, *p.* 659.

Among the last agreeable visits I made to the old poet was one with reference to a proposition of his own to omit several songs and other short poems from a new issue of his works then in press. I stoutly opposed the ignoring of certain old favorites of mine, and the poet's wife joined with me in deciding against the author in his proposal to cast aside so many beautiful songs—songs as well worth saving as any in the volume. Procter argued that, being past seventy, he had now reached to years of discretion, and that his judgment ought to be followed without a murmur. I held out firm to the end of our discussion, and we settled the matter with this compromise: he was to expunge whatever he chose from the English edition, but I was to have my own way with the American one. So to this day the American reprint is the only complete collection of Barry Cornwall's earliest pieces, for I held on to all the old lyrics, without discarding a single line.—FIELDS, JAMES T., 1875, *"Barry Cornwall" and Some of His Friends, Harper's Magazine, vol. 52, p.* 65.

To freedom and melody he adds more refinement than any song-writer of his time. . . . His stanzaic poems have, in fact, the rare merit of uniting the grace and imagery of the lyric to the music and fashion of song. . . . The Songs of Barry Cornwall, beyond those of any other modern, have an excellence of "mode" which renders them akin to the melodies of Shakespeare, Marlowe, Jonson, Heywood, Fletcher, and to the choicer treasures of Davison, and of the composers, Byrd, Wilbye, and Weelkes. They are, at once, delightful to poets and dear to the singing commonalty. I refer, of course, to their pervading character. It may be that none are so absolutely flawless as the "Bugle-Song" of Tennyson. The melody and dying fall of that lyric are almost without comparison this side of Amiens' ditties in "As You Like It" and Ariel's in "The Tempest." But how few there are of Procter's numerous songs which stand lower than the nearest place beneath it! . . . The fact that Procter's genius was essentially dramatic finally gave him a position independent of Keats, and, against external restrictions, drew him in advance of Hunt, who—whatever he may have been as critic and essayist—was in some respects the lesser poet. Nevertheless, those restrictions compelled Procter, as

Landor was compelled, to forego the work at which he would have been greatest, and to exercise his gift only in a fragmentary or lyrical manner.—STEDMAN, EDMUND CLARENCE, 1875–87, *Victorian Poets, pp.* 101, 102, 104.

We remember that in our young days Barry Cornwall's songs were commonly to be found in school-boys' desks, and many a man of middle-age may trace his first feeling for lyric verse to the charm of those sweet strains. That they are now greatly neglected and forgotten seems owing to the fact that we are a less musical people than the Germans, and that our weakness is chiefly on the side of simple song.—PAUL, C. KEGAN, 1877, *Bryan Waller Procter, The Academy, vol.* 11, *p.* 503.

The poetry of Barry Cornwall is the record of the extravagances of one who was habitually sober, the audacities of one who was habitually cautious, the eloquence of one who was habitually reserved. And yet there is no inconsistency, the contrasted elements heighten and sustain each other. —SIMCOX, GEORGE AUGUSTUS, 1877, *Barry Cornwall, Fortnightly Review, vol.* 27, *p.* 709.

One cannot fail to trace in it ["Autobiography"] the tenderness and gentleness of heart, the tolerant temper, generous impulses, and simple sincerity that endeared him to his family and friends; the clear, well-balanced intellect which, having been formed by a long course of legal and official experience, gave weight to all his estimates of men and things; the dainty fancy and refined taste for all that is beautiful in nature, art, and life, that are his chief credentials as a poet; and the old-fashioned grace and courtesy of manner, partly native and partly acquired from his fortunate associations, which are the uniform note of his style whether in verse or prose.—HEWLETT, HENRY G., 1878, *Barry Cornwall, Nineteenth Century, vol.* 4, *p.* 643.

A poet never attaining the first rank, yet reaching a gentle eminence on which his name, more than his work, perhaps, is still fully known. . . . His shorter lyrics, many of them very melodious and graceful, are what has lasted longest.—OLIPHANT, MARGARET O. W., 1882, *Literary History of England, XVIII-XIX Century, vol.* II, *pp.* 264, 266.

His dramatic scenes, his songs, and his

narrative and descriptive poems form a body of verse of no inconsiderable bulk and variety,—in bulk exceeding that of the poetic works of Collins, Gray, and Campbell combined. It cannot be said that any portions of his writings can claim to elude criticism on the ground that they were youthful productions. In 1815, when the name of "Barry Cornwall" first became known by his occasional contributions to the "Literary Gazette," he was three years older than Keats was when he died. . . . Taking his works as a whole, the one criticism to be made upon them is that their apparent substance, estimated by the number of printed pages they occupy, is disproportioned to their real substance, estimated by the amount of thought, imagination, knowledge, experience, and passion they convey. We have to pick and cull, sift and reject, when we come to distinguish between the faculties which the poet displays and the matter on which they are exercised. . . . After making all proper deductions, however, from the mass of Procter's poetry, we find that what remains is a solid addition to the poetical literature of the century.—WHIPPLE, EDWIN PERCY, 1886, *Recollections of Eminent Men*, pp. 338, 339, 340.

He was the author of two or three poetical works, of no particular merit, but especially of a volume of English songs, which had been received with a chorus of jubilation by all the critics of the day, though it has long since passed into the limbo that is the ultimate destination of all mediocre books, especially of mediocrities in rhyme. — MACKAY, CHARLES, 1887, *Through the Long Day, vol.* I, *p.* 271.

He was, under the pseudonym of "Barry Cornwall," a fluent verse writer of the so-called cockney school, and had not a little reputation, especially for songs about the sea and things in general. They still, occasionally from critics who are not generally under the bondage of traditional opinion, receive high praise, which the present writer is totally unable to echo.—SAINTSBURY, GEORGE, 1896, *A History of Nineteenth Century Literature, p.* 109.

Procter wrote some spirited songs, but his poetry, notwithstanding the laudations which his friends were pleased to lavish on it as a matter of compliment, is of the thinnest and poorest quality. Lamb characterized it as redundant, like the wen which once appeared on the author's neck.—HAZLITT, W. CAREW. 1897, *Four Generations of a Literary Family, vol.* I, *p.* 238.

Two things distinguish him as a poet: his fine ear for melody, for a tone which must touch the heart, and his deep sense of the miseries of life. As a writer of songs, he takes an honourable place by the side of Tennyson and Moore.—ENGEL, EDWARD, 1902, *A History of English Literature, rev. Hamley Bent, p.* 420.

Charles Sumner
1811–1874

Born at Boston, Jan. 6, 1811: died at Washington, D. C., March 11, 1874. A noted American statesman. He was educated at the Boston Latin School and at Harvard, graduating in 1830; studied law at Harvard; and was admitted to the bar in 1834. He travelled in Europe 1837–40; became noted as an advocate of anti-slavery ideas; took an active part in politics as a Whig, and from 1848 as a Free-soiler; was an unsuccessful Free-soil candidate for Congress in 1848; was elected United States senator from Massachusetts by Free-soil and Democratic votes 1851; became a leading opponent of slavery in Congress; was assaulted in the senate-chamber by Preston Brooks May 22, 1856; was reëlected senator as a Republican in 1857, 1863, and 1869; was absent from his seat 1856–59; became chairman of the committee on foreign affairs in 1861; and was removed from it in 1871 for his opposition to Grant's policy regarding the annexation of Santo Domingo. He was a champion of the Civil Rights Bill for the negroes, and opposed the reëlection of Grant in 1872. His works, in 15 vols., were published 1870–83.—SMITH, BENJAMIN E., *ed.* 1894–97, *The Century Cyclopedia of Names, p.* 966.

PERSONAL

My friend Charles Sumner will be with you in the spring. You will not fail to make much of him, as nature has done before you; for he stands six feet two in his stockings,—a *colossus* holding his burning heart in his hand, to light up the sea of life: I am in earnest. He is a very lovely character, as you will find,— full of talent; with a most keen enjoyment of life; simple, energetic, hearty, good; with a great deal of poetry and no nonsense about him. You will take infinite delight in his society, and in walking old Rome with him.—LONG-FELLOW, HENRY WADSWORTH, 1838, *Letter to George W. Greene, Aug. 6; Life, ed. Long-fellow, vol.* I, *p. 204.*

Popular Sumner is off to Italy, the most popular of men,— inoffensive, like a worn sixpence that has no physiognomy left. We preferred Coolidge to him in this circle.—CARLYLE, THOMAS, 1839, *To Emerson, Apr.* 13; *Correspondence of Carlyle and Emerson, ed. Norton, vol.* I, *p. 232.*

Mr. Charles Sumner dined with me, and spent the evening with my son. He returned yesterday from Europe, having been absent two years from last December. He talked incessantly; is inflated with exaggerated egotism; has been familiar with Bench and Bar of Westminster; has ridden an English Circuit, and been familiar with the gentry and nobility; has seen the best literary characters in France and Germany, Vienna, Berlin, Brussels, Heidelberg, and Italy. Mr. Sumner showed me one of the original exchequer tallies, he also gave me the address of M. Mittermaier.—KENT, JAMES, 1840, *Diary, March 5; Memoirs and Letters, ed. Kent, p. 261.*

> Garlands upon his grave,
> And flowers upon his hearse,
> And to the tender heart and brave
> The tribute of this verse.
> His was the troubled life,
> The conflict and the pain,
> The grief, the bitterness of strife,
> The honor without stain.
> Like Winkelried, he took
> Into his manly breast
> The sheaf of hostile spears, and broke
> A path for the oppressed.
> Then from the fatal field
> Upon a nation's heart
> Borne like a warrior on his shield!—
> So should the brave depart.

—LONGFELLOW, HENRY WADSWORTH, 1873, *Charles Sumner, Birds of Passage.*

> For there was nothing base or small
> Or craven in his soul's broad plan;
> Forgiving all things personal,
> He hated only wrong to man.
> The old traditions of his State,
> The memories of her great and good,
> Took from his life a fresher date,
> And in himself embodied stood.

> How felt the greed of gold and place,
> The venal crew that schemed and planned,
> The fine scorn of that haughty face,
> The spurning of that bribeless hand!

—WHITTIER, JOHN GREENLEAF, 1874, *Sumner, Hazel Blossoms.*

> At least your noble thoughts can never die—
> They live to stir and lift humanity—
> They live to sweeten life and cheer us on:
> If they are with us, surely you are nigh.
> Yes, in our memory, long as sense remains,
> That stalwart frame shall live, that voice whose strains
> To lofty purpose pitched, struck like a fire
> Into our blood, and thrilled through all our veins.
> That full sonorous voice, whose high-strung key
> Was tuned to Justice and to Liberty—
> That sounded like a charge to rouse the world
> From the deep slumber of its apathy.
> Nor these alone;—we shall remember too
> The kind familiar tones of love we knew,
> The genial converse and the storied lore,
> The cultured charm that every listener drew.
> The gladsome smile, the gleam of quick surprise,
> That thrilled the face and lightened through the eyes;
> The uplifting brow, the utterance frank and clear,
> And all that sullen death to sight denies.

—STORY, WILLIAM WETMORE, 1874, *To Charles Sumner, Blackwood's Magazine, vol.* 116, *p. 345.*

Sumner's social success at this early period, before his reputation was established, was most remarkable. He was a welcome guest at most of the best houses both in town and country, and the impression he uniformly left was that of an amiable, sensible, high-minded, well-informed gentleman. But his powers of conversation were not striking; and when you ask me to recall the qualities which account for his success, I most frankly own that it was and is to me as much a puzzle as the eminent and widespread success of your countryman and townsman, George Ticknor. At the same time, I feel satisfied that, in each instance, the success was indisputable and well deserved.—HAYWARD, ABRAHAM, 1877, *Letter to Edward L. Pierce; Memoir and Letters of Charles Sumner, ed. Pierce, vol.* I, *p. 306.*

He was neither Sybarite nor ascetic. To excess of any kind he had the aversion which comes of good breeding as well as good morals; but he did not accept the rule of ethics on which many good people now insist,—that, for example and self-discipline, one ought to abstain from what is very liable to abuse. He seasoned his food with hock and claret, always however with moderation; but these he never took except at meals, and rigidly abstained from the violent drinks. From the political controversy involving legislation for the suppression of intemperance, which beginning as early as 1837 has continued ever since, he kept entirely aloof.—PIERCE, EDWARD L., 1877, ed. *Memoir and Letters of Charles Sumner, vol.* II, *p.* 156.

Mr. Sumner was never successfully attacked when living, except with bludgeon, —and his friends have more than sufficiently vindicated him since his death.— HOLMES, OLIVER WENDELL, 1878, *John Lothrop Motley, A Memoir, p.* 174.

About 1828, I became acquainted with Charles Sumner. He was then a tall, bony, and not graceful youth, with a great deal of brown, waving hair. He was natural, ingenuous, enthusiastic, had a way of blushing frequently when interested in his subject. He was full of ideas, and fond of expressing them.—OAKEY, S. W., 1881, *Recollections of American Society, Scribner's Monthly, vol.* 21, *p.* 783.

It was the misfortune of Sumner that, more than any other public man of his time, he was subjected to the extremes of adulation and obloquy. His real character can hardly be discerned amid the tumult of puffs and scoffs, of exultations and execrations, which the mere mention of his name excited during his public career. Sumner himself was inclined to take the compliments at more than their real worth, while he experienced another though different satisfaction in reading the calumnies. . . . He never swore as an individual; nobody ever heard an oath slip from his lips even in his ecstasies of philanthropic rage; but he was the best swearer by proxy and quotation that I ever listened to. The oaths launched at him by his Southern enemies, the oaths which some Republican Senators would occasionally hurl at him when they were vexed by his obstinacy in clinging to his own view of a party question that had been decided against him by a majority of Republican statesmen,—these, in narrating his experiences in political life to a friend, he would roll over on his tongue in quite an unsanctified but still innocent fashion, and laugh at the profanity as something exquisitely comical. The more people swore at him, the more delighted he was; and it is a pity that he did not have the same sense of humour in estimating the hyperboles of panegyric addressed to him by his admirers, which he unquestionably had in estimating the hyperboles of execration shot at him by his assailants.— WHIPPLE, EDWIN PERCY, 1886, *Recollections of Eminent Men, pp.* 205, 206.

Mr. Sumner stood six feet two inches high without his shoes, and he was so well built that his height was only noticeable when he was near a person of ordinary size. But there was a manner about him, a free swing of the arm, a stride, a pose of his shaggy head, a sway of his broad shoulders, that gave to those who knew him best the idea that he was of heroic size. Then, too, there was something in the intent look of his deep-set eye, his corrugated brow, the frown born of intense thought, and his large head, made to seem yet larger by its crown of thick, heavy, longish gray hair, all of which gave the idea of physical greatness; but with his frequent smile the set frown passed, his whole appearance changed, and his face beamed like a dark lantern suddenly lighted. His smile effected a wonderful transformation in his whole appearance, and it set up a peculiar sympathy between himself and its recipient.—JOHNSON, ARNOLD BURGES, 1887, *Charles Sumner, The Cosmopolitan, vol.* 3, *p.* 406.

Mr. Sumner was interesting by both his merits and his faults. He was a ripe scholar, an elegant and instructive writer. As an orator, he had few if any superiors. His style was ornate, his delivery impressive. His speeches in the Senate were carefully prepared, and were worthy of the close attention which they received from most of the senators, although they were better fitted for the platform than the halls of legislation. His face was handsome and highly intellectual. He was tall, well formed and of commanding presence, a "man of mark" in the street or in an assembly. He was also a pure man, a man of unsullied and unassailable integrity. All this can be justly said of him. On the other hand, his prejudices were hastily formed and violent. His self-esteem was limitless. Impatient of contradiction, his manner to those who differed with him was arrogant and offensive. His ears were ever open to flattery, of which he was omnivorous. His friendship was confined to the very few whom he acknowledged to be his equals, or to the many who looked up to him as a superior. His sympathies were for races—too lofty to descend to persons. For the freedom of the slaves he was an earnest worker; of their claims to all the privileges of freedom, after their emancipation, he was an able and eloquent advocate and defender; but to appeals of needy colored people to his charity, or even his sympathy, he was seemingly indifferent. These constitutional defects in his character did not greatly impair his usefulness, nor lessen the estimation in which he was held by those who knew him well and properly appreciated his excellent qualities and the value of his public services. He was one of the most distinguished of that gallant band whom the slavery question made prominent in the United States, and his name will be at all times and everywhere honored by the lovers of freedom.— McCulloch, Hugh, 1888, *Men and Measures of Half a Century, p. 233.*

He was a light-haired, light-complexioned man, of agreeable presence and kindly manner.—Guild, Curtis, 1896, *A Chat about Celebrities, p. 245.*

Few public men whom I have seen had as commanding a presence as Charles Sumner. He had all the stature and the bulk of Bismarck; but he had a very handsome, finely cut face, which Bismarck certainly had not. —McCarthy, Justin, 1899, *Reminiscences, vol. 1, p. 214.*

STATESMAN

After a long trial and much anxiety, our grand object in Massachusetts has been attained. We have sent Charles Sumner into the United States Senate,—a man physically and spiritually head and shoulders above the old hackneyed politicians of that body. The plan for this was worked out last summer at Phillips Beach, and I sounded Sumner upon it the evening we left you at that place. He really did not want the office, but we forced it upon him. I am proud of old Massachusetts, and thankful that I have had an humble share in securing her so true and worthy a representative of her honor, her freedom, and intellect, as Charles Sumner. He is a noble and gifted man, earnest and truthful. I hope great

things of him, and I do not fear for his integrity and fidelity, under any trial.—Whittier, John Greenleaf, 1851, *Letter to Grace Greenwood, May 18; Life and Letters, by Pickard, vol. 1, p. 355.*

First, he was the most accomplished man in public life in America; second, the ablest orator in Congress; third, of unblemished private character; fourth, of unblemished public character, which no breath of calumny had ever reached, and whom no one had ever dared approach with a dishonorable proposition; fifth, a man whose zeal and talents had been expended, not upon selfish schemes, but upon measures and policies looking to the improvement of the condition of society,—such ends as, whatever difference of opinion may prevail as to the adaptation of his means to secure them, must possess the sympathy and respect of all good citizens; sixth, he is very amiable; and seventh, a man whose decorum of character and whose talents have done and are doing more than those of any other man in the Senate to arrest the gradual decline of that body in the estimation of the country, in itself a service which those who feel the important rôle the Senate ought to play in our constitutional system know how to appreciate.—Bigelow, John, 1861, *Journal, Feb.; Memoir and Letters of Charles Sumner, ed. Pierce, vol. IV, p. 87.*

Strange as, in looking back upon the past, the assertion may seem impossible, it would have been ten years ago to make it, it is not the less true that to-day Mississippi regrets the death of Charles Sumner, and sincerely unites in paying honors to his memory. Not because of the splendor of his intellect, though in him was extinguished one of the brightest of the lights which have illuminated the councils of the government for nearly a quarter of a century; not because of the high culture, the elegant scholarship, and the varied learning which revealed themselves so clearly in all his public efforts, as to justify the application to him of Johnson's felicitous expression, "He touched nothing which he did not adorn;" not this, though these are qualities by no means, it is to be feared, so common in public places as to make their disappearance, in even a single instance, a matter of indifference; but because of those peculiar and strongly marked moral traits of his character, which gave the coloring to the whole tenor of his singularly dramatic public career; traits which made him for a long period, to a large portion of his countrymen, the object of as deep and passionate a hostility, as to another he was one of enthusiastic admiration, and which are not the less the cause that now unites all these parties, once so widely differing, in a common sorrow to-day over his lifeless remains.—LAMAR, LUCIUS Q. C., 1874, *Eulogy on Sumner delivered in the House of Representatives, April* 27.

We are commanded by the Senate to render back to you your illustrious dead. Nearly a quarter of a century ago, you dedicated to the public service a man who was even then greatly distinguished. He remained in it, quickening its patriotism, informing its councils, and leading in its deliberations, until, having survived in continuous service all his original associates, he has closed his earthly career. With reverent hands we bring to you his mortal part, that it may be committed to the soil of the renowned Commonwealth that gave him birth. Take it; it is yours. The part which we do not return to you is not wholly yours to receive, nor altogether ours to give. It belongs to the country, to freedom, to civilization, to humanity. We come to you with the emblems of mourning, which faintly typify the sorrow which dwells in the breast they cover. So much we must concede to the infirmity of human nature; but in the view of reason and philosophy, is it not rather a matter of high exultation that a life so pure in its personal qualities, so lofty in its public aims, so fortunate in the fruition of noble effort, has closed safely without a stain, before age had impaired its intellectual vigour, before time had dimmed the lustre of its genius? Our mission is completed. We commit to you the body of Charles Sumner. His undying fame the Muse of History has already taken into her keeping.—ANTHONY, HENRY B., 1874, *Eulogy, State House, Boston.*

That a man should go through the fiery furnace of Washington politics, nay, live in it half a lifetime, and be found at his death like an ingot of finest gold, is something for a country to be proud of. I do not think we ever had exactly such a public man, and it will be most difficult to replace him. What was remarkable about him, it always seemed to me, was his progressiveness. As a scholar he was always improving, always a hard student. As a statesman he had always an ideal goal far ahead of present possibilities, and yet he lived to see the nation come up to the mark which had seemed so long in the cloudland of fanaticism, while he had again moved far in advance of those original aims. The great gift of keeping his eyes fixed on something far away which was to benefit the nation and the world, of stopping his ears against the chatterings and howlings which made so many others turn back and so be changed to stone, was never more marked in a public man in any country, while the utter absence of self-seeking and vulgar commonplace ambition was equally remarkable. His loss is irreparable to the country and to his personal friends.—MOTLEY, JOHN LOTHROP, 1874, *Letter to Oliver Wendell Holmes, April* 17; *Correspondence, ed. Curtis, vol.* II, *p.* 377.

Among Americans the distinctive Puritan statesman of our time, the worthy political descendant of John Winthrop and Samuel Adams, whose name can never be mentioned at this New England table without affection and honor, who added to that indomitable conviction of the Roundhead the cultivated graces of the Cavalier, and whose lofty character and unstained life was a perpetual rebuke of mercenary politics and mean ambitions, was Charles Sumner.—CURTIS, GEORGE WILLIAM, 1883, *Puritan Principle and Puritan Pluck, Orations and Addresses, vol.* I, *p.* 256.

Sixty-three years this man had lived upon earth. For more than a score of them he had been counted among her great men, with what reason his life has shown. A child of New England, and the product of her institutions, he was a citizen of the world; a scholar, he neglected learning that he might act nobly; a statesman, he taught his country that greatness was only greatness when it was founded upon justice; loving the praise of men, he cast it aside as a thing of no worth that he might serve the lowest of his brethren; very human, he made of his faults an offering, and hesitated not before suffering, and welcomed scorn, if so be these were the fiery tokens of duty; a man of eloquent speech, he trained his lips to speak no word that did not express a purpose of his soul, till men taunted him with his constancy. Strong for the right, he was fierce against wrong; loving liberty, he looked neither to the right hand nor to the left, but pursued her with a single eye, and forgot the lions in the way that he might the sooner bring his people to her pleasant paths; the sworn knight of righteousness and freedom, he dallied not with pleasure nor hesitated for danger: all things were his, that he might use them for mankind,—and mankind crowned him with great glory, and laid in his right hand the gift of fame. —DAWES, ANNA LAURENS, 1892, *Charles Sumner (Makers of America)*, p. 324.

There is no statesman of his time whom we can compare with Charles Sumner for unerring instinct, save Lincoln alone,—and Lincoln owed much to his counsels. . . . He was a leader and not a follower. He never studied the direction of the popular breeze. He did not gather other men's opinions before he formed or uttered his own. He was courageous, and absolutely without regard to personal consequences when great principles were involved. . . . If we judge him by the soundness of his principles, by the wisdom of his measures, by his power to command the support of the people, by the great public results he accomplished, there is no statesman of his time to be named in the same breadth with him, save Abraham Lincoln.—HOAR, GEORGE F., 1894, *Sumner, The Forum*, vol. 16, p. 553.

He brought, first, a magnificent physical organization, just in its prime. There is an Arabian proverb that no man is called of God till the age of forty; and Sumner was just that age when he entered the Senate. He had a grand, imposing presence, strong health, and athletic habits. He was, if I mistake not, one of the few persons who have ever swum across the Niagara River just below the Falls. Niagara River; slavery afterward. He felt fully the importance of bodily vigor, and I remember that once, in looking at a fine engraving of Charles Fourier, in my study, after I had remarked "What a head!" he answered: "Yes; and what a body! A head is almost worthless without an adequate body to sustain it." His whole physique marked him as a leader and ruler among men; and I remember well that when I first visited the English Parliament, I looked in vain among Lords and Commons for the bodily peer of Charles Sumner.—HIGGINSON, THOMAS WENTWORTH, 1899, *Contemporaries*, p. 284.

The field of his success is to be found in the argumentative power that he possessed and in its use for the overthrow of slavery. Of the anti-slavery advocates who entered the Senate previous to the opening of the war, he was the best equipped in learning, and his influence in the country was not surpassed by the influence of any one of his associates. In his knowledge of diplomacy, he had the first rank in the Senate for the larger part of his career. His influence in the Senate was measured, however, by his influence in the country. His speeches, especially in the period of national controversy, were addressed *to* the country. He relied upon authorities and precedents. His powers as a debater were limited, and it followed inevitably that in purely parliamentary contests he was not a match for such masters as Fessenden and Conkling, who in learning were his inferiors.—BOUTWELL, GEORGE S., 1900, *Reminiscences of Charles Sumner, McClure's Magazine*, vol. 14. p. 362.

Charles Sumner was an idealist and a politico-moral revolutionist. He acted with enthusiasm and intense feeling, and was the representative of the anti-slavery extremists. In regard to all the phases of the question of slavery, he was as unyielding as cast iron. . . . Few persons conscious of their political power have been less selfishly ambitious than Sumner. Although egotistical, vain, and overbearing, he never sought control and glory chiefly for his own advancement. To him public life was not a personal affair. If there ever was a brutal, cowardly act, it was Brooks's assault. It made Sumner an invalid for years, and permanently injured his health; yet the victim bore the bully no grudge. . . . He was preëminently a man of principles and strong personality. Sumner also possessed some of the best attributes of statesmanship; he was a great student, and always commanded a vast fund of information. By far his best work was done as chairman of the Senate Committee on Foreign Affairs.— BANCROFT, FREDERIC, 1900, *Some Radicals as Statesmen, Atlantic Monthly*, vol. 86, p. 281.

ORATORY

Mr. Sumner is distinguished for his learning, especially in history and public law. In his efforts on great occasions his citations of authorities are absolutely bewildering. His mind is comprehensive and logical, his methods direct and forcible, his spirit vehement and indomitable. As he moves on he leaves no point untouched, no matter how trite or familiar it may be. There are no gaps in his sentences, and no ellipses in his thought. He leaves nothing for the imagination. Proposition is riveted to proposition until the whole statement is like a piece of plate armor. But this scrupulous gathering up of details, and the copiousness of illustration by historical parallels, though effective with audiences and useful for popular instruction, often render portions of his speeches, when printed, tedious to cultivated readers, who are oppressed by the amplifications, the repetitions, and the profusion of learned quotations with which the argument is loaded. The field he has passed over is sure to be thoroughly swept. The audiences who listen, whether friendly or otherwise, are always profoundly impressed with his power and sincerity. The antagonist who follows him has always a task demanding his best efforts. His style has unconsciously acquired a certain professional or state-paper tone. We see by the formal and stately manner that it is the statesman and the author of didactic treaties that is writing. The elevation of his thought is a moral elevation. As we read we seem to be on high ground, and breathe pure mountain air. There is no compromise with wrong, no paltering with worldly policy. Political discussions conducted in such a spirit rise to the dignity of pure ethics, and are as inspiring as they are impressive. Much of the effect of Mr. Sumner's speeches is due to this pervading moral element. He is not greatly imaginative, and his ample utterances, unlike the copious and glowing diction of Burke, appear to be the results of painstaking industry.— UNDERWOOD, FRANCIS H., 1872, *A Hand-Book of English Literature, American Authors, p.* 362.

An accomplished, careful speaker, trained under Everett and Webster, Charles Sumner approached and retained much of their peculiar grace; but he never equalled them. His voice wanted Everett's sweetness, although fine, sonorous, deep; his action was less graceful; he had little of Webster's mental clearness and strength. Yet animated by the great cause in which he was engaged, filled with the ardor of truth, Sumner wielded an instrument of offence sharper and more powerful than Webster or Everett had ever ventured to use. He lived in stormier, sadder days. His eloquence aroused nations and aided freedom.—LAWRENCE, EUGENE, 1880, *A Primer of American Literature, p.* 76.

His speeches, elaborate, logical, clear, and eloquent, needed no adventitious aid to fasten them in the public mind. Twelve compact volumes contain his chief speeches in Congress and elsewhere. They are virtually a history of the anti-slavery movement, in and out of Congress, and of the legislation which secured to the freed negroes their civil rights. . . . Lacking the quick fire of Garrison's or Phillips' words, their lofty scorn of wrong, their intense enthusiasm, and their loyal devotion to the "genius of universal emancipation" make them seem, even now, like words from the heights. Sumner's speeches mirror the character of the man: ever devoted to principle, free from sordid aim or mercenary ambition, intolerant of subterfuge or disloyal compromise, eager to lay at the feet of freedom the spoils of learning and of time. . . . He lacked those important equipments of a great orator: wit, and the power to see and to make visible all sides of a subject. His speeches, even the great argument for peace, called "The True Grandeur of Nations," sometimes seem heavy and dull, save when he spoke in anger. But his words would last in the literature of oratory, if only because, with all their faults, they expressed and vindicated the right of free speech at a time when too many were timid.—RICHARDSON, CHARLES F., 1886, *American Literature, vol.* I, *pp.* 253, 254.

There have been greater orators than Sumner in the direction of native ability and of acquired art, but they have been few. Some have been devoted to their respective causes with a similar earnestness, but they have been fewer still. If, however, one be sought for in all the illustrious succession who has combined surpassing talent for public speech with wide learning, profound convictions, and uncompromising surrender of self to a righteous purpose, none will be so able to stand the test as this man, who was deaf to every solicitation to swerve from the single aim of his public life. This is the secret of his oratorical power—the whole heart was in it, the entire life was given to it. His opportunity was great, and his strength was equal to his opportunity. Equally great was the moral power, the ethical force, the strongest element of all, buttressing and fortifying every other.— SEARS, LORENZO, 1895, *The History of Oratory, p.* 388.

As an orator Sumner was logical and convincing. While he had not the tact and fire of Phillips, his orations were, nevertheless, impetuous and overwhelming. They forced conviction, point by point, by a culmination of arguments seemingly unanswerable. The power of his orations has not departed with the occasions that called them forth. They are still full of life and beauty. The reader is surprised at the wealth of scholarly allusions, and the brilliancy, at times, of the rhetoric. The style is stately and finished. Many of the orations, strongly in contrast with those of Phillips, rise at times almost to sublimity. On the whole, the orations of Sumner are an addition to American literature only less important than the work of Webster, Choate, and Everett.—PATTEE, FRED LEWIS, 1896, *A History of American Literature, p.* 329.

Came nearer to Webster as an orator than any one I remember.—SHERWOOD, MARY E. W., 1897, *An Epistle to Posterity, p.* 126.

He was a man of great ability but not of the highest intellectual power, nor was he a master of style. He was not incisive in thought or speech. His orations were overloaded, his rhetoric was often turgid, he was easily led into irrelevance and undue stress upon undisputed points. His untiring industry as a reader had filled his memory with associations which perhaps he valued unduly. Originally modest and not self-confident, the result of his long contest was to make him egotistical and dogmatic.—STOREY, MOORFIELD, 1900, *Charles Sumner* (*American Statesmen*), *p.* 431.

GENERAL

Charles Sumner is a stockholder in the bank of original thought. We may know he has considerable bullion there, for his drafts are honored at sight, and our first men are his endorsers. He has great power of condensation, without the wearisome monotony which often accompanies the writings and sayings of close thinkers and rigid reasoners. There is a vigorous and graceful stateliness, an easy felicity, a fastidious accuracy, and an imperial dignity in his style, which is both commanding and fascinating. There is a vast breadth of comprehension and a vast depth of meaning in his matter. There is also a luminous beauty, a Gothic grandeur, a sublime gorgeousness, in his labored and polished essays, which entitle them to the appellation of prose poems.—BUNGAY, GEORGE W., 1854, *Off-Hand Takings; or, Crayon Sketches, p.* 274.

As a writer, a lecturer, a debater, and an orator, he had acquired the strongest hold on public attention everywhere, both at home and abroad; and few scholars have brought to the illustration of their topics, whether political or literary, the fruits of greater research. His orations and speeches, of which a new edition, revised by his own hand, is understood to be approaching a completion, cannot fail to be a rich storehouse of classical and historical lore, and will certainly furnish a most valuable series of pictures, from his own point of view, of the stirring scenes to which they relate.— WINTHROP, ROBERT C., 1874, *Fillmore and Sumner, Addresses and Speeches, vol.* III, *p.* 310.

Mr. Sumner is known widely as a student and scholar. His speeches were invariably injured by his too faithful memory. Indeed, he was not unfrequently carried away by the aptness of some analogy which he recollected in some bit of recondite history; and you had the contrast, fairly droll, of the work of an extreme idealist and that of a dry antiquarian. The Senate detested his historical and classical allusions. Men said they were dragged in by way of presumptuous boast of his superior attainments; while, in truth, he could as easily have spoken without vowels as without quotations. His memory was too good for the balance of his other intellectual qualities; and his citations, whether apt or not, only weakened the positions for which he introduced them.—HALE, EDWARD EVERETT, 1874, *Charles Sumner, Old and New, vol.* 9, *p.* 521.

Mr. Sumner's efforts in literature were almost exclusively in the department of oratory, and the many volumes of his published works are mainly filled with speeches. Many of these have a place among the masterpieces of American eloquence. Unlike most American public men, he was not a politician; he held himself aloof from the petty obligations and entanglements of party, and maintained a lofty and unswerving independence. His integrity and purity of purpose were never questioned by those to whom his political doctrines were most abhorrent. By his profound intellectual ability, his thorough and elegant scholarship, and above all by his high-mindedness and unimpeachable probity, he commanded the respect of the whole country. His speeches were rather scholarly than statesmanlike. Though his mastery of whatever subjects he grappled with was thorough, and his presentation of them vigorous and effective, there is an excess of elaboration, an ultra-classicism in all his writings that never, or very rarely, accompanies the highest spontaneous oratory. As specimens of careful, finished composition, his speeches are hardly surpassed in the annals of American eloquence.—CATHCART, GEORGE R., 1874, *ed. The Literary Reader,* p. 266.

Throughout his career Sumner was felt as a force as well as an intelligence, and probably the future historian will rank him high among the select class of American public men who have the right to be called creative statesmen. He always courted obloquy, not only when his party was depressed, but when it was triumphant. "Forward!" was ever his motto. When his political friends thought they had at last found a resting-place, his voice was heard crying loudly for a new advance. Many of his addresses belong to that class of speeches which are events. His collected works, carefully revised by himself, have now become a portion of American literature. They quicken the conscience of the reader, but they also teach him the lesson that moral sentiment is of comparatively small account unless it hardens into moral character, and is also accompanied by that thirst for knowledge by which intellect is broadened and enriched, and is trained to the task of supporting by facts and arguments what the insight of moral manliness intuitively discerns.—WHIPPLE, EDWIN PERCY, 1876–86, *American Literature and Other Papers, ed. Whittier,* p. 109.

No Fourth of July oration ever attracted so much attention as the one to which this chapter is devoted. For a considerable time it was the frequent topic of society, as well as of the public journals. No American tract or address has probably ever had so wide a circulation in Great Britain. Its questionable proposition so startled the public, that they commanded the more attention for its unmistakable truths. It touched the hearts of Christian people, whether accepting or holding back from its logical statements. Its style, less academic than Everett's, less weighty than Webster's, glowed as theirs never glowed with moral enthusiasm. . . . The oration on "The True Grandeur of Nations" was the most important epoch in Sumner's life. All he had written before was in the style of the essay,—ornate and vigorous in expression, but wanting the declamatory force and glow of passion by which the masses of men are swayed.—PIERCE, EDWARD L., 1877, *ed. Memoir and Letters of Charles Sumner, vol.* II, p. 383.

A somewhat heavy person, with little sense of humor.—BEERS, HENRY A., 1895, *Initial Studies in American Letters,* p. 147.

His addresses are learned, logical, elegant, impressive. They do not, however, have the spontaneity, the flash and fire, of the true orator. Probably the most effective speech he ever made was an oration before a popular audience, on "The True Grandeur of Nations."—NOBLE, CHARLES, 1898, *Studies in American Literature,* p. 346.

Of cold and egotistic personality but of high principles and stainless integrity, in his somewhat labored orations also fought a courageous fight for freedom and national honor.—BRONSON, WALTER C., 1900, *A Short History of American Literature,* p. 277.

Sydney Thompson Dobell

1824–1874

Born, at Cranbrook, Kent, 5 April 1824. Family removed to Cheltenham, 1836. Educated privately. Married Emily Fordham, 18 July 1844. Literary activity, and enthusiasm in patriotic causes of various countries. Visit to Switzerland, Aug. 1850. Lived in Edinburgh, 1854–57. Wintered in Isle of Wight, 1858-61. Increasing ill-health. Wintered near Cannes, 1862; in Spain, 1863; in Italy, 1864. Lived in Gloucestershire from 1866 till death. Died, at Barton-End House, Gloucestershire, 22 Aug. 1874. Buried in Painswick Cemetery. *Works:* "The Roman" (under pseud. "Sydney Yendys"),

1850; "Balder" (anon.), 1854 [1853]; "Sonnets on the War" (with A. Smith; anon.), 1855; "England in Time of War," 1856; "The Nature of Poetry," 1857; " Of Parliamentary Reform," 1865. *Collected Works:* Poems (2 vols.), 1875; Prose, 1876; "Thoughts on Art, Philosophy and Religion," ed. by G. Nichol, 1876; "Life and Letters" (2 vols.), 1878.— SHARP, R. FARQUHARSON, 1897, *A Dictionary of English Authors, p.* 82.

PERSONAL

And thou, too, gone! One more bright soul away
To swell the mighty sleepers 'neath the sod.
One less to honour and to love, and say,
Who lives with thee doth live half-way to God.
My chaste-souled Sydney! Thou wert carved too fine
For coarse observance of the general eye:
But who might look into thy soul's fair shrine
Saw bright gods there, and felt their presence nigh.
Oh, if we owe warm thanks to Heaven, 'tis when
In the slow progress of the struggling years
Our touch is blest to feel the pulse of men
Who walk in light and love above their peers
White-robed, and forward point with guiding hand,
Breathing a heaven around them where they stand.
—BLACKIE, JOHN STUART, 1874, *To the Memory of Sydney Dobell, Messis Vitæ.*

Pure without pedantry, he had the "scorn of scorn" for every form of falsehood; but the range of his charity was limited only by his love of truth. The sense of humour, comparatively absent from his writings, showed itself in the delicate irony of his rare rebukes. His loyalty to friendship—that half-forgotten virtue of an earlier age—has never been surpassed. He was chivalrous to an extreme, and this sometimes led his judgment astray on behalf of fallen causes, with a touch of lofty yet gracious manner- ism which recalled the ideal of a Castilian knight. A radical reformer in some direc- tions, he had little sympathy with the ex- treme phases of democracy, and held the tyranny of mobs and autocrats in equal aversion. Like those of most poets, his theoretical politics had a visionary side: but he was far from being a mere dreamer. Of practical well-doing towards the poor, of encouragement to the young and all who were struggling for a recognition of their merits, he was never weary: for of the jealousy which is one of the main blots of our literature, he had not a tinge. He could afford to be generous: and to almost all with whom he came in contact, grateful or ungrateful, he had done some kindnesses.—

NICHOL, JOHN, 1875, *ed. The Poetical Works of Sydney Dobell, Memoir, vol.* I, *p.* 35.

A life lived, as it were, in the Divine Presence chamber, in unremitting endeav- our to keep the Divine attributes constantly before the mental vision, and to bring its own being more and more into harmony with the glorified humanity of Christ, is not likely to hide ugly things in dark places; nor was Sydney Dobell's character, spite of his in- tellectual subtlety, difficult for any ordi- narily intelligent love to read. The child's open heart was as signally his as the poet's open eye. He was most a hero for those most familiarly associating with him. His whole later life was heroic with that surely most difficult heroism—of submission. No disappointment and no suffering ever soured or embittered one moment of his manhood; no murmur ever passed his lips. Yet his was never a stunned submission. The very breath of his life was sweet; his gracious pleasantness made all who served him, in things great or things small, find such service self-rewarding. His simplest words and deeds were dignified by the noble- ness of his nature.—JOLLY, EMILY, 1878, *ed. The Life and Letters of Sydney Dobell, vol.* II, *p.* 422.

His own letters and the testimony of all his friends concerning him go to prove that, full of trial as his life was, there was in him little or none of that morbidness or even melancholy to which men of genius are supposed to be prone. "Spasmodic" as his poetry was considered, he himself was of a cheerful and healthy mind, and there re- mained in him and with him to the very last a most touching enjoyment of all that was left him to enjoy, which must have been one of its greatest charms in the eyes of those who loved him. And these were not few. For if he exacted much, he gave much, especially to women, with whom his friendships were many and sincere, and whom he treated, high and low, near or dis- tant, with the chivalrous tenderness of a stainless heart, as seeing in all womanhood the reflection of his own ideal of it—his wife. —CRAIK, DINAH MARIA MULOCK. 1879,

Sydney Dobell, International Review, vol. 6, p. 490.

No one who knew Sydney Dobell, no one who had ever so brief a glimpse of him, can read without tears the simple and beautiful Memorials, now just published, of his gracious, quiet, and uneventful life. Predestined to physical martyrdom, he walked the earth for fifty years, at the bidding of what to our imperfect vision seems a pitiless and inscrutable Destiny. Why this divinely gifted being, whose soul seemed all goodness, and whose highest song would have been an inestimable gain to humanity, should have been struck down again and again by blows so cruel, is a question which pricks the very core of that tormenting conscience which is in us all. Ill-luck dogged his footsteps; sickness encamped wherever he found a home. His very goodness and gentleness seemed at times his bane. At an age when other men are revelling in mere existence he was being taught that mere existence is torture. We have read of Christian martyrs, of all the fires through which they passed; but surely not one of them ever fought with such tormenting flames as did this patient poet, whose hourly cry was of the kindness and goodness of God. From first to last, no word of anger, no utterance of fierce arraignment, passed his lips.—BUCHANAN, ROBERT, 1879-86, *A Look Round Literature,* p. 187.

The poet's mother was a very religious woman, and with fond enthusiasm she devoted her first-born, when she was only nineteen years old, to the Church. This was the primitive Christian Church founded by her father, Mr. Samuel Thompson. His mother pondered all the boy's sayings, like the mother of Jesus, and his father kept memoranda of the son's doings, and his plans for the boy. His mind and his emotions were thus unduly stimulated. At ten, his biographers say, he had read all Miss Martineau's books on political economy, besides having ventured on the Trinitarian controversy. He was educated by his father at home, and at twelve he entered his father's counting-house. While there, he studied the languages, and wrote poetry, and also interested himself in religious and scientific subjects. He joined the Church and was married at twenty. His mind was eminently religious. His courtship . . . was carried on over the Bible. He refused

in his early married life to associate with any families of the neighborhood who did not belong to his own sect. He smiles in his after life at his own narrowness; but in spite of it all, he says he looks back at this period with "a kind of self-reverence," because "he never thought a thought or said a word but under the very eyes of God."— LOWE, MARTHA P., 1879, *Things at Home and Abroad, Unitarian Review, vol.* 11, *p.* 557.

Of the resources of the intellect so mysteriously held back from what seemed its fitting work, perhaps only a few, even of those who knew him best, can judge; but his life evidenced, as no words or work could have done, the vitality of his faith, at once enlightened and deeply reverent — faith that was never shaken by the temptations of the intellect, nor weakened by years of disappointment and deprivation. No pressure of suffering was able to exhaust his cheerfulness, nor to wear out the sweetness of his patience. In him innate brightness and elasticity had been strengthened and elevated by spiritual culture into something beyond and above the result of mere temperament. To the last moment of his conscious life he remained bravely submissive, "trusting not God the less for an unanswered prayer."—SHARP, WILLIAM, 1887, ed. *The Poems of Sydney Dobell, (selected) Introductory Memoir, p.* xviii.

In our rambles [1860] under the clematis-festooned cliff, on the rocky, broken meadow-ground, and by the sea-driven woods, we were occasionally accompanied by Sydney Dobell, who, suffering from rheumatism of the heart, had passed the winter in the island. He idolised Nature after a microscopic fashion; hunted amid a million primroses for one flower that combined in the hue and shape of petals and stem the perfection of seven; rapturously studied the tints of the sparrows' backs, assuring us no two sparrows were alike; and descanted on the varied shades of grey in the stone walls. Yet even this fatiguing minuteness of observation trained the eye to perceive the marvellous perfection, beauty, grace, and diversity of colour and form in the tiny handiworks of the Almighty Creator.— HOWITT, MARY, 1888?-89, *Autobiography ed. Her Daughter, vol.* II, *p.* 132.

His character as a man, far from reproducing the inequalities of his poetry, was one of uniform elevation: he was chivalrous, transparently candid, lofty in all his aims, and capable of the most disinterested and self-sacrificing kindness.—GARNETT, RICHARD, 1892, *The Poets and the Poetry of the Century, Charles Kingsley to James Thomson, ed. Miles, p.* 180.

THE ROMAN
1850

There is a hearty purpose and a solemn earnestness in "The Roman" which we think is calculated to teach an admirable lesson to, and produce a powerful effect upon, the minds of the present age. . . . Our poet shows us the dignity of man—the power he can exercise, the active power of kindling great thoughts in his fellow-men— rousing them up from their lethargic sleep— snapping the fetters which cramp their spiritual freedom, and bidding them pursue the path which God has placed before them, and along which duty guides them— peradventure to a grave. He shows us also Man's passive power—the nobler of the two, and by far the more difficult to practise —the power which can impel the soul right onward, like an arrow to its mark; which yields not to the sun-smile of fortune nor to the pitiless peltings of the tempest-cloud: the power from which the shafts of scorn fall off with deadened point; which walks unscathed through the fiery furnace of a nation's mockery; and gazes with an unblenched eye upon the ghastliest insignia of death. He shows us Pity bending with unutterable tenderness; Love sacrificing self at the altar of its divinity; Resolution stern as fate, sheathing the spirit as in a panoply of steel; Hope, baffled, bleeding, but like the dolphin, beautiful in death; Faith lifting its flashing eyes to Heaven, and speaking forth the words of inspiration. He takes us by the hand and conducts us reverently among the ruins of the past—he leads us within the circle of its magic presence, and bids us look and wonder.—LESTER, JOHN W., 1854, *Cambridge Criticisms.*

"The Roman," with its noble fervour of tone and wealth of illustration, proved that we had amongst us a new poet, whose genius was dedicated, not chiefly to the expression of personal feeling, or to the treatment of domestic themes, but to the worship of liberty and the defence of a glorious but enslaved country. The sympathy which, in the first poem, he showed with the larger interests of human life, is indeed discernible in all the more important works that subsequently proceeded from his pen. —MARSTON, WESTLAND, 1878, *Letter, Life and Letters of Sydney Dobell, p.* 20.

The success of his first considerable work, "The Roman," was rapid and unmistakable. The theme and its treatment, in accord with popular sentiment, in no less degree the flow of the lyrics, the strong sweep of the graver verse, the frequent richness of the imagery, enlisted the favour alike of the general public and of discerning critics. With defects readily condoned to the writer's youth, and many minor merits, its main charm lay in the novelty of its aim. It was hailed as the product of a man of refined culture, whose sympathies went beyond the mere love of "harmony in tones and numbers' lisp," and crossed the "silver streak" to welcome the wider movements of his age. "The Roman" was continental in a sense that the work of none of our poets, since Byron, had been.—NICHOL, JOHN, 1880, *The English Poets, ed. Ward, vol.* IV, *p.* 615.

This is not merely a vigorous, but a thoroughly sane performance, but the orator is more evident than the poet.—GARNETT, RICHARD, 1892, *The Poets and the Poetry of the Century, Charles Kingsley to James Thomson, ed. Miles, p.* 179.

BALDER
1854

I find that many reviewers have mistaken the moral purpose and import of "Balder," and I therefore prefix to my Second Edition these few explanatory lines. The present book is the first part of a work, which I hope to complete in three Parts. I intend as the principal subject of that work the Progress of a Human Being from Doubt to Faith, from Chaos to Order. Not of Doubt incarnate to Faith incarnate, but of a doubtful mind to a faithful mind. In selecting the type and conditions of humanity to be represented, I chose, for several important reasons, the poetic type and the conditions of modern civilization. And in treating the first and sadder portion of my subject I felt that justice to Nature required me to avoid all conventional portraits of the doubter, and—since in these days his malady is more often negative than positive—to indicate the absence of

faith rather by the states and proportions
of the other qualities than by a more distinct and formal statement of the differential defect. . . . I have reason, however, to
blame some of these powerful witnesses for
the indecorous haste and uncharitable dogmatism with which, as I have seen and am informed, they have taken for granted that I
must personally admire the character I
think fit to delineate, and that I present as
a model what, in truth, I expose as a warning. That I, in common with many of my
critics, am not altogether free from some of
the sins of my hero is probable on the general principal that "Balderism" in one form
or another is a predominant intellectual
misfortune of our day. But that I have no
theoretical approbation of such errors, may,
I think, be naturally inferred from the history of failure and sorrow which I have
herein attached to them.—DOBELL, SYDNEY,
1854, *Balder, Prefatory Note, Second Ed.,*
pp. 3, 4.

"Balder" arrived safely. I looked at
him, before cutting his leaves, with singular pleasure. Remembering well his elder
brother—the potent "Roman," it was
natural to give a cordial welcome to a fresh
scion of the same house and race. I have
read him. He impressed me thus. He
teems with power. I found in him even a
wild wealth of life; but I thought this favourite and favoured child would bring his
sire trouble; would make his heart ache. It
seemed to me that his strength and beauty
were not so much those of Joseph—the pillar of Jacob's age, as of the Prodigal Son
who troubled his father, though he always kept his love. How is it that—while
the first-born of genius often brings honour—the second, almost as often, proves a
source rather of depression and care? I
could almost prophesy that your third will
atone for any anxiety inflicted by this his
immediate predecessor. There is power in
that character of "Balder" and, to me, a
certain horror. Did you mean it to embody, along with force, many of the special
defects of the artistic character? It seems
to me that those defects were never thrown
out in stronger lines. I did not and could
not think you meant to offer him as your
cherished ideal of the true great poet. I regarded him as a vividly coloured picture of
inflated self-esteem, almost fanatic aspiration—of a nature that has made a Moloch
of the intellect—offered up in pagan fires

the natural affections, sacrificed the heart
to the brain.—BRONTË, CHARLOTTE, 1854,
To Sydney Dobell, Feb. 3; *Life and Letters*
of Sydney Dobell, ed. Jolly, vol. I, *p.* 328.

We think that the two main objections to
"Balder" will be monotony and obscurity.
We will not say of the hero, what an admirer
of Yendys said of the Monk in "The
Roman," that he is a great bore and humbug; but we will say that he talks too much,
and does too little. The poem is little
else than one long soliloquy.—GILFILLAN,
GEORGE, 1855, *A Third Gallery of Portraits,*
p. 126.

"Balder" is the longest poem of our time,
with the exception perhaps of "Festus;"
and apart from the exquisite songs of Amy,
which if extracted would of themselves
make a mournful anthology, there are not
in its entire length a dozen pages of purely
human interest. It contains wonderful
things, it has passages of marvellous
subtlety and music, but these fail to make
pleasing the stupendous egotism. Now it is
evident that if you wish to cure a sick man
you must give him a medicine which it is
possible for him to take, and if you wish by
means of a poem to make the world better,
you must needs write a poem which it will
be possible for the world to read. "Balder"
is to the large majority of persons simply
unreadable, and this not from any defect of
genius, but because it is based upon an
erroneous theory. In "Balder" too, one is
perpetually conscious of a certain compulsion, of effort; there is a lack of spontaneity, of easy, unconscious, unsolicitous
result, as of an Æolian harp sighing to the
caprices of intermittent wind. At times the
writer almost ceases to be a poet, and becomes a pamphleteer. . . . Altogether,
"Balder" is one of the most painful of
books. There is in it an atmosphere of
stagnant formless woe, a crude misty misery,
a selfishness that might be felt; in reading
it you grope, as it were, through some solid
breathless gloom. And yet if any one would
form a just estimate of the power and originality of Mr. Dobell's genius, of the
swift-cleaving character of his intellect, to
this book he must come and endure its pain.
With all its gloom and horror I do not know
where else you will meet such sudden, unexpected, exquisite sweetness; such radiant
sunniness of nature; such lovely lyrical
trills, like the carol of a bird from the
blossomed apple-tree in the orchard heard

through the silence of a house in which a dead man is lying; such strokes of sharp pathos at which the printed page disappears to slowly glimmer back.—SMITH, ALEX-ANDER, 1866, *Sydney Dobell, The Argosy, vol. 2, pp.* 317, 324.

The incomplete and painful plot was felt to be unnatural, and many of the details were disagreeable. The luxuriance of its imagery was like cloth of gold thrown over the limbs of a Frankenstein. But few contemporary English poets had scaled the heights of its finest passages. Every chapter bore witness to the author's analytic subtlety and passionate power. Few descriptions of external nature surpass the master sketches of "Balder:" they are drawn by the eye and pencil of one who, from a watch-tower on the hills, outgazed the stars and paid homage, like the Persian, to a hundred dawns.—NICHOL, JOHN, 1880, *The English Poets, ed. Ward, vol.* IV, *p.* 615.

It would be no exaggeration to affirm that it contains beauties beyond the reach of any contemporary poet: but the plan is so preposterous, and the general effect so chaotic, that the character "arena sine calce" would be fatally applicable were not the sand so often dust of diamond. What the second and third parts would have been like is difficult to conjecture, though we know that the second part was to have been eked out by the inclusion of a drama to have been entitled "The Cardinal." Dobell probably discovered that he was on a wrong track, for he never attempted to continue the poem, and the self-confessed failure may have co-operated with aggravated ill-health in producing the paralysis of intellectual activity which befell his later years.—GARNETT, RICHARD, 1892, *The Poets and the Poetry of the Century, Charles Kingsley to James Thomson, ed. Miles, p.* 180.

If we regard the poem in the light most favourable to it, as a collection of passages in verse, we have to admit the most amazing inequalities. Few passages in literature are more hideous than the description of the monster on which Tryanny rides; but, on the other hand, the best passages may challenge comparison with all but the greatest poetry. Even this comparison has been sometimes made. The description of Chamouni has been said to rival the great hymn of Coleridge, and that of the Coliseum

the celebrated stanzas of Byron on the same subject. The comparison, especially with Coleridge, is unkind to Dobell. At his best he cannot rival one of the most poetic minds in all literature in one of its highest flights. Nevertheless, both passages are exceedingly good. The subjects moreover are characteristic. Magnitude and massiveness are congenial to Dobell, and almost necessary to draw out his best. "Alone among our modern poets," says Dr. Garnett, "he finds the sublime a congenial element." It is in such passages as those named, and in Balder's magnificent vision of war, that Dobell shows the grand material of poetry that was in him.—WALKER, HUGH, 1897, *The Age of Tennyson, p.* 248.

GENERAL

Smith's females are houris in a Mahometan heaven; those of Yendys are angels in the Paradise of our God. Smith's emblem of woman is a rich and luscious rose, bending to every breath of wind, and wooing every eye; that of Yendys is a star looking across gulfs of space and galaxies of splendor, to one chosen earthly lover, whose eyes alone respond to the mystic messages of the celestial bride. Smith's idea of love, though not impure, is passionate; that of Yendys is more Platonic than Plato's own. —GILFILLAN, GEORGE, 1855, *A Third Gallery of Portraits, p.* 129.

In the sense of having something personal and peculiar, some new thing to supplement and enrich modern culture, Sydney Dobell is fairly entitled to be considered an original poet. I have remarked elsewhere that Chaucer and Spenser are the fountain-heads of all succeeding English poetry. Chaucer is the father of the humorous, kindly, dramatic, genially-lyrical men; Spenser of the intense, allegorical, didactic, remote, and, by comparison, unsocial men. Shakespeare, Dryden, Burns, Byron, Browning, draw descent from Chaucer, Milton, Young, Wordsworth, Shelley, and Tennyson from Spenser. Sydney Dobell too is of the line and stock of Spenser. His mental constitution is high, solitary, disdainful. His genius is of an ascetic and fakir kind. He stands apart from his fellows, and wraps himself up in the mantle of his own thoughts. He is terribly self-conscious; he is the slave of ideas; he writes for a purpose, and as if under a certain compulsion. There is nothing he hates so

intensely as commonplace; nothing he loves
so intensely as beauty—the more ideal the
better; and in his fine music a quick ear will
not unfrequently detect a stridulous tone,
as if the string from which it is drawn were
a trifle too tightly strung.   In whatever he
writes, whether he is purely and simply
beautiful, or haughty as Apollo conscious
of glowing limbs, or grotesque or extravagant, you will find nothing done at haphazard; he knows precisely the why and the
wherefore, and will be able to render you a
sufficient reason for everything.   If it be at
all admissible, now that the word has been
so foully fingered and misused, to call a
man *earnest* that man is Sydney Dobell. He
is essentially a missionary.   He has neither
written for the mere enjoyment of writing
nor for money, nor for fame, but mainly because he has a doctrine to preach, a cause
to plead; and his doctrine he has preached
in ears too long accustomed to sounding
brasses and tinkling cymbals to give heed
to high discourse.—SMITH, ALEXANDER,
1866, *Sydney Dobell, The Argosy, vol. 2, p.*
315.

I was equally delighted with what you
say about Dobell's "Keith of Ravelston"—
not only because you have so flatteringly
lugged in my name in connexion with it,
but because I have always regarded that
poem as being one of the finest, of its length,
in any modern poet—ranking with Keats's
"La Belle Dame, sans Merci," and the
other masterpieces of the condensed and
hinted order so dear to imaginative minds.
What a pity it is that Dobell generally insists on being so long-winded, when he can
write like that!   There is a snatch of sea-
song (about the *Betsy Jane*) in "Balder"
which is fifty times as good as anything in
Dibdin, who is nevertheless not contemptible.— ROSSETTI, DANTE GABRIEL, 1868,
*Letter to James Smetham; Dante Gabriel,
Rossetti, his Family-Letters, ed. Rossetti, vol.*
I, *p.* 420.

A singularly original and lofty-natured,
as well as subtly-intellectual man.—NOEL,
RODEN, 1876, *The Academy, vol. 9, p.* 478.

A man of cultivated intellectual tastes
and benevolence of character, Mr. Dobell
seems to have taken up some false or exaggerated theories of poetry and philosophy,
and to have wasted fine thoughts and conceptions on uncongenial themes.   The
great error of some of our recent poets is
the want of simplicity and nature. They

heap up images and sentiments, the ornaments of poetry, without aiming at order,
consistency, and the natural development
of passion or feeling.   We have thus many
beautiful and fanciful ideas, but few complete or correct poems.   Part of this defect is no doubt to be attributed to the
youth of the poets, for taste and judgment
come slowly even where genius is abundant,
but part also is due to neglect of the old
masters of song.   In Mr. Dobell's first poem,
however, are some passages of finished
blank verse.—CHAMBERS, ROBERT, 1876,
*Cyclopædia of English Literature, ed. Car-
ruthers.*

Probably there never was a better
loved or better hated—at any rate better
abused man, during his lifetime, than
Sydney Dobell.   Bursting into sudden
notoriety by his remarkable drama "The
Roman;" watched hopefully by all the
critics as the new poet of the age, then
disappointing the expectations of most
by his incomprehensible next work, "Balder—the First Part" (the second part,
which might have elucidated it, being, alas!
never written); afterwards dwindling down
through "England in Time of War" and
other lyrics of fragmentary kind to a style
of writing, poetry or prose, of which the
few published specimens were, to the ordinary mind, almost wholly incomprehensible; until, after a long, sad silence, during
which he was almost forgotten, came the
news of his death in the prime of his days.
. . . Whether or not Sydney Dobel was a
man of genius—whether his writings, which
have been pronounced by some to contain
passages as grand as Milton, and to evince
a knowledge of humanity not unworthy of
Shakspeare, and been condemned by others
as hopelessly obscure, long-winded, and
puerile, will live for posterity, this paper
does not attempt to decide. The poems are
open to all—every one can read and judge
for himself. "The Roman" was written
and published when he was but twenty-
five.   "Balder" followed soon after. These
are his only complete poems; though they
were followed by a good many sonnets and
lyrics, especially "England in Time of War,"
which contains passages of unparalleled
beauty.   And at thirty-five the poet—
"spasmodic," eccentric, unintelligible as his
writings may be called, few will deny to
him that title—the poet published his last
work. This single decade, then, is all that

posterity has to judge him by. . . . Dobell's correspondence must have been very voluminous, and it is much to be regretted that the book contains so little of it. His is an exquisitely polished epistolary style, perhaps even too perfect, as in its striving after originality it sacrifices that frank simplicity which must be given up if people write their commonest letters " with an eye to posterity."—CRAIK, DINAH MARIA MULOCK, 1879, *De Mortuis, Good Words, vol.* 20, *pp.* 313, 314.

Such warping and blighting influences made Sydney Dobell's public service fall so far short of his extraordinary capacities as to amount practically to failure. His senses were abnormally acute, like those of a savage, and this made his appreciation of natural loveliness remarkably keen; his powers of imagination and sympathy and his super-subtle reflective faculty completed his poetic endowment. The bent of his mind, the surcharging of his soul with religious emotion and mystical feeling, led him sometimes into that region of dreamy poetic conjecture with which readers of the transcendentalists are familiar, where the object, too vague for thought, is grasped at through symbols, and the qualities of the symbol extended fancifully to the unknown object. . . . His poetry is unwrought ore, his published prose stray leaves of thought, but in himself it is not too much to say he came near to his own conception of the poet's ideal life.—WOODBERRY, GEORGE EDWARD, 1879, *Dobell's Life and Letters, The Nation, vol.* 28, *pp.* 289, 290.

"Portions of Dobell's 'The Roman' have greatly impressed me, particularly its songs and descriptive and recitative passages; and I have inferred from the melody of their versification and the unwavering unity of their design and treatment that his sonnets must be of a high order. Have you any specimens of his style?" "Yes; but I fear they will disappoint your expectations. Dobell's sonnets are forcible and coherent enough, but are seldom poetical. Their coherence is that of statement and assertion merely, far different from the poetic unity whose office it is, as a poet yet to be cited tells us, to fuse many modes of light in one bright thought. His forcibleness, too, is more in the manner of the utterance than in its matter. The language of his sonnets is bold, resonant, stilted—the sentiments literal and prosaic, inspired by the will rather than by the fancy or imagination."—DESHLER, CHARLES D., 1879, *Afternoons With the Poets, p.* 306.

Although only a short period has elapsed since Dobell's death, though it seems only yesterday that the poet lay forgotten in some dark limbo of poetic failures, the public is already aware of him as one of the strong men of his generation, strong, too, in the sublimest sense of goodness, courage, and all the old-fashioned Christian virtues. He would have been recognised, perhaps, sooner or later, though I have my doubts; but that he has been recognised so soon is due to such love and duty as are the crown and glory of a good man's life. The public gratitude is due to those who have vindicated him, and made impossible all mistakes as to the strength of his genius and the beauty of his character. His music was not for this generation, his dreams were not of this earth, his final consecration was not to be given here below.

Vex not his ghost; oh, let him pass ! He hates
        him much
That would upon the rack of this rough world
Stretch him out longer.

But henceforth his immortality is secure. He sits by Shelley's side, in the loneliest and least accessible heaven of Mystic Song.—BUCHANAN, ROBERT, 1879-86, *A Look Round Literature, p.* 203.

Dobell's character was above criticism. The nature of his work has been indicated, its quality will be variously estimated, Original and independent of formulæ to the verge of aggressiveness, he shared by nature, by no means through imitation, in some of the defects, occasional obscurity, involved conceits, and remoteness, of the seventeenth-century school which Dr. Johnson called metaphysical; but in loftiness of thought and richness of imagery his best pages have been surpassed by few, if any, of his contemporaries. His form is often faulty, but his life and writings together were in healthy protest against the subordination of form to matter that characterises much of the effeminate æstheticism of our age. Manliness in its highest attributes of courage and courtesy pervaded his career; his poetry is steeped in that keen atmosphere to which it is the aim of all enduring literature to raise our spirits.—NICHOL, JOHN, 1888, *Dictionary of National Biography, vol.* XV, *p.* 134.

His really poetical works (the "Roman" is merely fine rhetoric) are a succession of these contrasts,—splendid diction alternating with dull verbiage, true sublimity with outrageous extravagance or mere inanity. To Dobell it was all one. He was utterly incapable of discriminating between his good work and his bad. He depreciated his own "Keith of Ravelston," a ballad unsurpassed in our literature for its weird suggestiveness, and in his later productions, fortunately few and far between, he exaggerated the obscurity and pretentiousness of the worst passages of "Balder." In his "England in time of War," more provokingly because more inexcusably unequal than "Balder," he never seems to know when he is writing from the heart and when he is condescending to sentimental and sonorous claptrap. He saw no reason why he should not be the Shakespeare or the Dante of his age, and had no glimmering of the mental angularities and the external disadvantages which made such a pretence preposterous. In a word, scarcely any poet equally inspired has been equally insane. The redeeming feature in the man and the poet is magnanimity. By a native instinct he seeks the highest things. He works on a large scale: indeed, it may be almost said that the greater his theme the better he succeeds with it.—GARNETT, RICHARD, 1892, *The Poets and the Poetry of the Century, Kingsley to Thomson, ed. Miles*, p. 181.

Nor do this charm, this grandeur, fail to reappear (always more or less closely accompanied by the faults just mentioned, and also by a kind of flatulent rant which is worse than any of them) both in Dobell's war-songs, which may be said in a way to hand the torch on from Campbell to Mr. Kipling, and in his marvellously unequal blank verse, where the most excellent thought and phrase alternate with sheer balderdash—a pun which (it need hardly be said) was not spared by contemporary critics to the author of "Balder."—SAINTSBURY, GEORGE, 1896, *A History of Nineteenth Century Literature*, p. 306.

Few poets are so uneven, perhaps hardly any poet capable of rising so high has ever sunk so low. Many passages are mere fustian, some are outrages against all taste; but others have a sublimity not often surpassed.— WALKER, HUGH, 1897, *The Age of Tennyson*, p. 247.

Notwithstanding Dobell's glaring faults, it may be questioned if he had not a more genuine faculty than Bailey. Granting all that may be said about the thinness of the thought, and the triviality of the passion underlying so much inflated language, there remain passages of true lyrical power in which the writer approves himself an undoubted poet.—GRAHAM, RICHARD D., 1897, *The Masters of Victorian Literature*, p. 340.

Agnes Strickland

1796–1874

Was the daughter of Mr. Thomas Strickland, of Roydon Hall, Suffolk. Her earlier literary efforts are collected in a volume entitled "Historic Scenes, and other Poetic Fancies." She wrote popular books for the young, among which may be mentioned "The Pilgrims of Walsingham" (1835). In 1840 appeared the first volume of "Lives of the Queens of England from the Norman Conquest," the last in 1849; in this work she was assisted by her sister Elizabeth. In conjunction the two sisters next produced, in 1850, "Lives of the Queens of Scotland and English Princesses connected with the Royal Succession of Great Britain." Agnes's next work was "The Bachelor Kings of England" (1862). Other of her books are "How Will It End?" (1865), and "Lives of the Seven Bishops" (1866). In recognition of her literary labors Mr. Gladstone in 1871 placed her on the Civil List, and she received a pension of £100. As an historical biographer Miss Strickland was more remarkable for the thoroughness with which she collected her materials than for her critical penetration.—SANDERS, LLOYD C., 1887, *ed. Celebrities of the Century*, p. 961.

PERSONAL

March 9.—. . . Talked to Miss Strickland about Professor Wilson. She is a very sweet-looking person, with a lovely throat and bust, and a gown fitting as well as all well-made women's gowns do. . . . *March* 13.—Called on Miss Strickland—the perfection of blues: she seems to think the most fortunate thing in life is to "get a name;" nevertheless, very interesting both to herself and me upon the queens. She showed me letters from Guizot, &c., and evidently thought herself the historian of the age.— EASTLAKE, ELIZABETH LADY, 1844, *Journals and Correspondence, ed. Smith, vol.* I, *pp.* 121, 122.

Is tall, formal, and stately, but with an earnest and kind manner.—LEVERT, OCTAVIA WALTON, 1853, *Souvenirs of Travel, vol.* I, *p.* 79.

With the exception of some early trials, the life of Agnes Strickland had been a long and happy one. Few female authors have realised such a brilliant and successful career. Of her it might be truly said, she made many friends and lost none. She was indeed much beloved in life and deeply lamented in death. In person she was attractive, though not to be called beautiful. In stature she was tall, and remarkably upright. Her bust and arms were very fine; her hair black as ebony, glossy and silky in texture, as well as abundant; her complexion somewhat pale, unless brightened by exercise or excitement, when it became roseate. If she were seen writing, working, or sitting, it would have been difficult to find a more graceful figure. In short, take her for all in all, "the like of Agnes Strickland may never be seen again." Her peculiar position carried her more frequently into society and exposed her to more temptations than fall to the lot of most women. She was made a complete idol of—surrounded by the great and gay, and overwhelmed with adulation or praise, in whatever circles she appeared. The heavy affliction of the last years of her life, by detaching her from the world, led her to look beyond it, and to realise that peace which only the believer can experience in the closing scenes of life.—STRICKLAND, JANE MARGARET, 1887, *Life of Agnes Strickland, p.* 380.

She was a welcome guest in the houses of many distinguished persons, and her warm heart and conversational powers won for her many friends. With the exception of Jane Porter, whom she visited at Bristol, and with whom she carried on a frequent correspondence, and a casual meeting with Macaulay, whom she found uncongenial, she came little in contact with the authors of her day.— LEE, ELIZABETH, 1898, *The Dictionary of National Biography, vol.* LV, *p.* 50.

LIVES OF THE QUEENS OF ENGLAND
1840–49

The "Lives of the Queens of England," by Miss Strickland, is a work of great diligence and merit, full of new facts from authentic records, which throw strong light on the manners of our Plantagenet times, full both of interest and amusement. There are indeed some mistakes, and the writer labours under the usual female misfortune, a want of sound and solid literature; but she merits great commendation for doing so much and so well as she has.—AIKIN, LUCY, 1841, *To Dr. Channing, Feb.* 7; *Correspondence of William Ellery Channing and Lucy Aikin, ed. LeBreton, p.* 381.

Miss Mitford reminds me of Miss Strickland. Craik, whom I saw yesterday, told me that the book which is the most decided success at present is "The Queens of England!" Colburn has made some twenty thousand pounds by it! And the authoress too is enriched. She goes to the Duke of Cleveland's, &c., &c. (Lady Clara told John), and is treated there like a high-priestess! everybody defering to her opinions.—CARLYLE, JANE WELSH, 1847, *To Thomas Carlyle, Oct.* 9; *Letters and Memorials, ed. Froude, vol.* I. *p.* 306.

I can safely say that I have acquired a much clearer idea of English history from your own than I ever did from general history—and so I never fail to say, both at home and abroad; and the reason is, that the history of each queen forms a separate cell in the memory in which to deposit the events of the past, and that your genius has given an interest to the narrative which renders the storing no longer a labour but a most agreeable occupation.— ALISON, SIR ARCHIBALD, 1851, *Letter to Miss Strickland, Aug.* 7; *Life of Agnes Strickland by her Sister, p.* 201.

Picturesque, clear, and always interesting. She has not much mental grasp, and always writes like a woman, which is no more than was to be expected; but she has this merit, that she realizes the home feelings, the costume, and the domestic life of the period. To draw a simile from the stage, she dresses her characters extremely well; and the reader does grasp a certain amount of suggestive information from her pages. FRISWELL, JAMES HAIN, 1869, *Essays on English Writers, p.* 28.

Accurate, philosophic, anecdotal, and

entertaining, this work ranks among the most valuable histories in English. If the style is not so nervous as that of masculine writers, there is a ready intuition as to the rights and the motives of the queens, and a great delicacy combined with entire lack of prudery in her treatment of their crimes. The library of English history would be singularly incomplete without Miss Strickland's work.—COPPÉE, HENRY, 1872, *English Literature*, p. 447.

The author has produced a spirited and interesting series of biographical sketches. It cannot be claimed, however, that they possess very great historical value. The writer studied carefully and thoroughly, and she has given her readers the advantage of a large number of valuable extracts from original and somewhat obscure sources. But she was moved by strong partialities and prejudices, and her pages constantly show that her judgment was not above being warped by her sympathies. This characteristic is most obvious in her partiality for the Stuarts and in her antipathy to the supporters of the Revolution.—ADAMS, CHARLES KENDALL, 1882, *A Manual of Historical Literature*, p. 441.

GENERAL

She posses all the zealous industry and indefatigable research which characterize Macaulay, and, like him, she has her prepossessions and dislikes. A vail is sometimes drawn over the weak points of the favorite Princesses or Houses who form the subject of her narrative. But it is all done in a noble spirit: the foundation of her judgment is always admiration of the gallant in conduct, the chivalrous in disposition; and though the intensity of this feeling has often biased her judgment, it does not diminish the respect due to her motives. The reader may sometimes be misled in the estimate of individual character by her captivating pen, but he is sure never to be so on the side, whether of virtue or vice, which is the fit subject of praise or condemnation.— ALISON, SIR ARCHIBALD, 1853, *History of Europe, 1815–1852*, ch. v.

Miss Strickland's interesting volumes are particularly valuable to the historian for the copious extracts which they contain from curious unpublished documents, which had escaped the notice of writers too exclusively occupied with political events to give much heed to details of a domestic and personal nature.—PRESCOTT, WILLIAM, HICKLING, 1855, *History of the Reign of Philip the Second, vol.* I, *p.* 125, *note.*

She has proved herself a very useful writer. Her "Queens of England" have induced many, to whom stronger diet would have been unpalatable, to gain a respectable knowledge of the leading facts of English history. For her own sex, her work is not only of deep interest, but must prove, in many ways, highly beneficial. Her own unwearied industry is an example of much importance; the devotion of her talents to a great subject is another commendable trait in her character; and the success attending her labors has a wide influence for good. Miss Strickland has incurred considerable censure from some of the British critics on account of her High Church and Tory principles, which she never attempts to conceal; but she seems so thoroughly convinced of the truth of her own opinions, that we must believe she is honestly sure her statements are correct. In short, she is a sincere queen-worshipper; and certainly, if there be a "divinity" to hedge kings who have usually been very poor specimens of humanity, queens may well be exalted. Since she commenced her work, other biographies of some of these ladies have appeared, but none have equaled Miss Strickland's in the interest of the narrative or in the originality of materials.—BIDWELL, W. H., 1857, *Eclectic Magazine, vol.* 42, *p.* 428.

Miss Strickland's power of writing is far from equalling her industry in research. The style is rather poor and thin, and the statements sometimes inaccurate.— HART, JOHN S., 1872, *A Manual of English Literature*, p. 569.

Miss Strickland was laborious and painstaking, but she lacked the judicial temper and critical mind necessary for dealing in the right spirit with original authorities. This, in conjunction with her extraordinary devotion to Mary Queen of Scots and her strong tory prejudices, detract from the value of her conclusions. Her literary style is weak, and the popularity of her books is in great measure due to their trivial gossip and domestic details. Yet in her extracts from contemporary authorities she amassed much valuable material, and her works contain pictures of the court, of society, and of domestic life not to be found elsewhere.— LEE, ELIZABETH, 1898, *Dictionary of National Biography, vol.* LV, *p.* 49.

DATE DUE

7-15	9620	c5	